((Collins *Gem*

Italian
Dictionary

Italian ▶ English   English ▶ Italian

MONDADORI

Collins Gem

An Imprint of HarperCollinsPublishers

first published in this edition 1982
fifth edition 2001

© William Collins Sons & Co. Ltd. 1982, 1989
© HarperCollins Publishers 1993, 1998, 2001

ISBN 0-00-472411-9

The Collins Gem website address is
www.collins-gem.com

Collins Gem® and Bank of English® are registered
trademarks of HarperCollins Publishers Limited

ISBN 88-04-37179-X

http://www.mondadori.com/libri

first edition prepared by/edizione originale a cura di

LEXUS
Catherine E. Love
P.L.Rossi, D.M. Chaplin,
F. Villa, E. Bilucaglia

---

based on revised edition by/basato sull'edizione a cura di
C.E. Love and M. Clari

A catalogue record for this book is available from the British Library

Typeset by Morton Word Processing Ltd, Scarborough

Printed and bound in Great Britain by
Omnia Books Ltd, Glasgow, G64

INDICE

CONTENTS

Introduzione italiana	iv	Italian introduction
Introduzione inglese	vi	English introduction
abbreviazioni	viii	abbreviations
simboli fonetici	xi	phonetic symbols
la pronuncia dell'italiano	xii	Italian pronunciation
ITALIANO-INGLESE	1	ITALIAN-ENGLISH
INGLESE-ITALIANO	309	ENGLISH-ITALIAN
verbi	617	verb tables
i numeri e l'ora	623	numbers and time
la data	626	dates
pesi e misure	628	conversion charts

contributors to fourth edition
hanno collaborato alla quarta edizione
M. Clari, G. Bacchelli
L. Riu, B. Grossmith

editorial staff/segreteria di redazione
J. Littlejohn

I marchi registrati

I termini che a nostro parere
costituiscono un marchio
registrato sono stati designati
come tali. In ogni caso, né la
presenza né l'assenza di tale
designazione implicano alcuna
valutazione del loro reale stato
giuridico.

Note on trademarks

Words which we have reason to
believe constitute trademarks
have been designated as such.
However, neither the presence
nor the absence of such
designation should be regarded
as affecting the legal status of any
trademark.

INTRODUZIONE

Vi ringraziamo di aver scelto il Dizionario inglese Collins Gem e ci auguriamo che esso si riveli uno strumento utile e piacevole da usare nello studio, in vacanza e sul lavoro.

In questa introduzione troverete alcuni suggerimenti per aiutarvi a trarre il massimo beneficio dal vostro nuovo dizionario, ricco non solo per il suo ampio lemmario ma anche per il gran numero di informazioni contenute in ciascuna voce. Ciò vi consentirà di imparare a capire ed esprimervi correttamente in un inglese attuale.

All'inizio del dizionario troverete l'elenco delle abbreviazioni usate nel testo e l'illustrazione della pronuncia espressa con i simboli fonetici. In fondo troverete un utile elenco delle forme dei verbi irregolari italiani e inglesi, seguito da una sezione finale con i numeri e le ore.

COME USARE IL DIZIONARIO COLLINS GEM

Per imparare ad usare in modo efficace il dizionario è importante comprendere la funzione delle differenziazioni tipografiche, dei simboli e delle abbreviazioni usati nel testo. Vi forniamo pertanto qui di seguito alcuni chiarimenti in merito a tali convenzioni.

I lemmi

Sono le parole in **neretto** elencate in ordine alfabetico. Il primo e l'ultimo lemma di ciascuna pagina appaiono al margine superiore.

Dove opportuno, informazioni sull'ambito d'uso o il livello di formalità di certe parole vengono fornite tra parentesi in corsivo e spesso in forma abbreviata dopo la trascrizione fonetica (es. (COMM), (inf)).

In certi casi più parole con radice comune sono raggruppate sotto lo stesso lemma. Tali parole appaiono in neretto ma in un carattere leggermente ridotto (es. **acceptance**).

Esempi d'uso del lemma sono a loro volta in neretto ma in un carattere diverso dal lemma (es. **to be cold**).

La trascrizione fonetica

La trascrizione fonetica che illustra la corretta pronuncia del lemma è in parentesi quadra e segue immediatamente il lemma (es. **knead** [ni:d]). L'elenco dei simboli fonetici è alle pagine xi-xii.

Le traduzioni

Le traduzioni sono in carattere tondo e se si riferiscono a diversi significati del lemma sono separate da un punto e virgola. Spesso diverse traduzioni di un lemma sono introdotte da una o più parole in corsivo in parentesi tonda: la loro funzione è di chiarire a quale significato del lemma si riferisce la traduzione. Possono essere sinonimi, indicazioni di ambito d'uso o di registro del lemma (es. **party** (*POL*) (*team*) (*celebration*), **laid back** (*inf*) etc.).

Le "parole chiave"

Un trattamento particolare è stato riservato a quelle parole che, per frequenza d'uso o complessità, necessitano una strutturazione più chiara ed esauriente (es. **da, di, avere** in italiano, **at, to, be, this** in inglese). Il simbolo ♦ e dei numeri sono usati per guidarvi attraverso le varie distinzioni grammaticali e di significato e, dove necessario, ulteriori informazioni sono fornite in corsivo tra parentesi.

Informazioni grammaticali

Le parti del discorso (noun, adjective ecc.) sono espresse da abbreviazioni convenzionali in corsivo (*n*, *adj* ecc) e seguono la trascrizione fonetica del lemma.

Eventuali ulteriori informazioni grammaticali, come ad esempio le forme di un verbo irregolare o il plurale irregolare di un sostantivo, precedono tra la parentesi la parte del discorso (es. **fall** (*pt* **fell**, *pp* **fallen**) *n*; **man** (*pl* **men**) *n*).

INTRODUCTION

We are delighted you have decided to buy the Collins Gem Italian Dictionary and hope you will enjoy and benefit from using it at school, at home, on holiday or at work.

This introduction gives you a few tips on how to get the most out of your dictionary — not simply from its comprehensive wordlist but also from the information provided in each entry. This will help you to read and understand modern Italian, as well as communicate and express yourself in the language.

The Collins Gem Italian Dictionary begins by listing the abbreviations used in the text and illustrating the sounds shown by the phonetic symbols. You will find Italian verb tables and English irregular verbs at the back, followed by a final section on numbers and time expressions.

USING YOUR COLLINS GEM DICTIONARY

A wealth of information is presented in the dictionary, using various typefaces, sizes of type, symbols, abbreviations and brackets. The conventions and symbols used are explained in the following sections.

Headwords
The words you look up in a dictionary — "headwords" — are listed alphabetically. They are printed in **bold type** for rapid identification. The two headwords appearing at the top of each page indicate the first and last word dealt with on the page in question.

Information about the usage or form of certain headwords is given in brackets after the phonetic spelling. This usually appears in abbreviated form and in italics (e.g. (*fam*), (*COMM*)).

Where appropriate, words related to headwords are grouped in the same entry (**illustrare, illustrazione**) in a slightly smaller bold type than the headword.

Common expressions in which the headword appears are shown

in a different bold roman type (e.g. **aver freddo**).

Phonetic spellings

Where the phonetic spelling of headwords (indicating their pronunciation) is given, it will appear in square brackets immediately after the headword (e.g. **calza** ['kaltsa]). A list of these symbols is given on pages xi-xii.

Translations

Headword translations are given in ordinary type and, where more than one meaning or usage exists, these are separated by a semi-colon. You will often find other words in italics in brackets before the translations. These offer suggested contexts in which the headword might appear (e.g. **duro** (*pietra*) or (*lavoro*)) or provide synonyms (e.g. **duro** (*ostinato*)).

"Key" words

Special status is given to certain Italian and English words which are considered as "key" words in each language. They may, for example, occur very frequently or have several types of usage (e.g. **da, di, avere**). A combination of lozenges ♦ and numbers helps you to distinguish different parts of speech and different meanings. Further helpful information is provided in brackets and in italics.

Grammatical information

Parts of speech are given in abbreviated form in italics after the phonetic spellings of headwords (e.g. *vt, av, cong*).

Genders of Italian nouns are indicated as follows: *sm* for a masculine and *sf* for a feminine noun. Feminine and irregular plural forms of nouns are also shown (**dottore, essa; droga, ghe**).

Feminine adjective endings are given as are plural forms (**opaco, a, chi, che**).

ABBREVIAZIONI

ABBREVIATIONS

abbreviazione	**abbr**	abbreviation
aggettivo	**adj**	adjective
amministrazione	**ADMIN**	administration
avverbio	**adv**	adverb
aeronautica, viaggi aerei	**AER**	flying, air travel
aggettivo	**ag**	adjective
agricoltura	**AGR**	agriculture
amministrazione	**AMM**	administration
anatomia	**ANAT**	anatomy
architettura	**ARCHIT**	architecture
articolo determinativo	**art def**	definite article
articolo indeterminativo	**art indef**	indefinite article
attributivo	**attrib**	attributive
ausiliare	**aus, aux**	auxiliary
l'automobile	**AUT**	the motor car and motoring
avverbio	**av**	adverb
aeronautica, viaggi aerei	**AVIAT**	flying, air travel
biologia	**BIOL**	biology
botanica	**BOT**	botany
inglese della Gran Bretagna	**BRIT**	British English
consonante	**C**	consonant
chimica	**CHIM, CHEM**	chemistry
commercio, finanza, banca	**COMM**	commerce, finance, banking
comparativo	**compar**	comparative
informatica	**COMPUT**	computers
congiunzione	**cong, conj**	conjunction
edilizia	**CONSTR**	building
sostantivo usato come aggettivo, non può essere usato né come attributo, né dopo il sostantivo qualificato	**cpd**	compound element: noun used as adjective and which cannot follow the noun it qualifies
cucina	**CUC, CULIN**	cookery
davanti a	**dav**	before
articolo determinativo	**def art**	definite article
determinativo: articolo, aggettivo dimostrativo o indefinito etc	**det**	determiner: article, demonstrative etc
diminutivo	**dimin**	diminutive
diritto	**DIR**	law

ABBREVIAZIONI

ABBREVIATIONS

economia	ECON	economics
edilizia	EDIL	building
elettricità, elettronica	ELETTR, ELEC	electricity, electronics
esclamazione	escl, excl	exclamation
femminile	f	feminine
familiare (! da evitare)	fam(!)	colloquial usage (! particularly offensive)
ferrovia	FERR	railways
figurato	fig	figurative use
fisiologia	FISIOL	physiology
fotografia	FOT	photography
verbo inglese la cui particella è inseparabile dal verbo	fus	(phrasal verb) where the particle cannot be separated from main verb
nella maggior parte dei sensi; generalmente	gen	in most or all senses; generally
geografia, geologia	GEO	geography, geology
geometria	GEOM	geometry
impersonale	impers	impersonal
articolo indeterminativo	indef art	indefinite article
familiare (!da evitare)	inf(!)	colloquial usage (!particularly offensive)
infinitivo	infin	infinitive
informatica	INFORM	computers
insegnamento, sistema scolastico e universitario	INS	schooling, schools and universities
invariabile	inv	invariable
irregolare	irreg	irregular
grammatica, linguistica	LING	grammar, linguistics
maschile	m	masculine
matematica	MAT(H)	mathematics
termine medico, medicina	MED	medical term, medicine
il tempo, meteorologia	METEOR	the weather, meteorology
maschile o femminile	m/f	either masculine or feminine depending on sex
esercito, linguaggio militare	MIL	military matters
musica	MUS	music
sostantivo	n	noun
nautica	NAUT	sailing, navigation
numerale (aggettivo, sostantivo)	num	numeral adjective or noun
	o.s.	oneself

ABBREVIAZIONI		ABBREVIATIONS
peggiorativo	**peg, pej**	derogatory, pejorative
fotografia	**PHOT**	photography
fisiologia	**PHYSIOL**	physiology
plurale	**pl**	plural
politica	**POL**	politics
participio passato	**pp**	past participle
preposizione	**prep**	preposition
pronome	**pron**	pronoun
psicologia, psichiatria	**PSIC, PSYCH**	psychology, psychiatry
tempo passato	**pt**	past tense
qualcosa	**qc**	
qualcuno	**qn**	
religione, liturgia	**REL**	religions, church service
sostantivo	**s**	noun
		somebody
insegnamento, sistema scolastico e universitario	**SCOL**	schooling, schools and universities
singolare	**sg**	singular
soggetto (grammaticale)	**sog**	(grammatical) subject
		something
congiuntivo	**sub**	subjunctive
soggetto (grammaticale)	**subj**	(grammatical) subject
superlativo	**superl**	superlative
termine tecnico, tecnologia	**TECN, TECH**	technical term, technology
telecomunicazioni	**TEL**	telecommunications
tipografia	**TIP**	typography, printing
televisione	**TV**	television
tipografia	**TYP**	typography, printing
inglese degli Stati Uniti	**US**	American English
vocale	**V**	vowel
verbo	**vb**	verb
verbo o gruppo verbale con funzione intransitiva	**vi**	verb or phrasal verb used intransitively
verbo riflessivo	**vr**	reflexive verb
verbo o gruppo verbale con funzione transitiva	**vt**	verb or phrasal verb used transitively
zoologia	**ZOOL**	zoology
marchio registrato	**®**	registered trademark
introduce un'equivalenza culturale	**≈**	introduces a cultural equivalent

TRASCRIZIONE FONETICA

PHONETIC TRANSCRIPTION

CONSONANTS CONSONANTI

NB The pairing of some vowel sounds only indicates approximate equivalence/La messa in equivalenza di certi suoni indica solo una rassomiglianza approssimativa.

puppy	p	*padre*	
baby	b	*bambino*	
tent	t	*tutto*	
daddy	d	*dado*	
cork kiss	k	*cane che*	
chord			
gag guess	g	*gola ghiro*	
so rice kiss	s	*sano*	
cousin buzz	z	*svago esame*	
sheep sugar	ʃ	*scena*	
pleasure beige	ʒ		
church	tʃ	*pece lanciare*	
judge general	dʒ	*giro gioco*	
farm raffle	f	*afa faro*	
very rev	v	*vero bravo*	
thin maths	θ		
that other	ð		
little ball	l	*letto ala*	
	ʎ	*gli*	
rat brat	r	*rete arco*	
mummy comb	m	*ramo madre*	
no ran	n	*no fumante*	
	ɲ	*gnomo*	
singing bank	ŋ		
hat reheat	h		
yet	j	*buio piacere*	
wall bewail	w	*uomo guaio*	
loch	x		

VOWELS VOCALI

NB **p, b, t, d, k, g** are not aspirated in Italian/sono seguiti da un'aspirazione in inglese.

heel bead	iː i	*vino idea*	
hit pity	ɪ		
set tent	e	*stella edera*	
apple bat	ɛ æ a	*epoca eccetto*	
		mamma	
after car calm	ɑː	*amore*	
fun cousin	ʌ		
over above	ə		
urn fern work	ɜː		
wash pot	ɔ	*rosa occhio*	
born cork	ɔː		
	o	*ponte ognuno*	
full soot	ø	*föhn*	
boon lewd	u	*utile zucca*	

DIPHTHONGS DITTONGHI

ɪə	*beer tier*	
ɛə	*tear fair there*	
eɪ	*date plaice*	
	day	
aɪ	*life buy cry*	
au	*owl foul now*	
əu	*low no*	
ɔɪ	*boil boy oily*	
uə	*poor tour*	

MISCELLANEOUS

VARIE

* per l'inglese: la "r" finale viene pronunciata se seguita da una vocale.

' precede the stressed syllable/precede la sillaba accentata.

ITALIAN PRONUNCIATION

VOWELS

Where the vowel **e** or the vowel **o** appears in a stressed syllable it can be either open [e], [ɔ] or closed [e], [o]. As the open or closed pronunciation of these vowels is subject to regional variation, the distinction is of little importance to the user of this dictionary. Phonetic transcription for headwords containing these vowels will therefore only appear where other pronunciation difficulties are present.

CONSONANTS

c before "e" or "i" is pronounced *tch*.

ch is pronounced like the "*k*" in "kit".

g before "e" or "i" is pronounced like the "*j*" in "jet".

gh is pronounced like the "*g*" in "get".

gl before "e" or "i" is normally pronounced like the "*lli*" in "million", and in a few cases only like the "*gl*" in "glove".

gn is pronounced like the "*ny*" in "canyon".

sc before "e" or "i" is pronounced *sh*.

z is pronounced like the "*ts*" in "stetson", or like the "*d's*" in "bird'seye".

Headwords containing the above consonants and consonantal groups have been given full phonetic transcription in this dictionary.

NB All double written consonants in Italian are fully sounded: eg. the *tt* in "tutto" is pronounced as in "ha*t t*rick".

ITALIANO - INGLESE
ITALIAN - ENGLISH

A, a

A *abbr* (= *autostrada*) ≈ M (= *motorway*)

PAROLA CHIAVE

a (*a+il* = **al**, *a+lo* = **allo**, *a+l'* = **all'**, *a+la* = **alla**, *a+i* = **ai**, *a+gli* = **agli**, *a+le* = **alle**) *prep* **1** (*stato in luogo*) at; (: *in*) in; **essere alla stazione** to be at the station; **essere ~ casa/~ scuola/~ Roma** to be at home/at school/in Rome; **è ~ 10 km da qui** it's 10 km from here, it's 10 km away

2 (*moto a luogo*); **andare ~ casa/~ scuola** to go home/to school

3 (*tempo*) at; (*epoca, stagione*) in; **alle cinque** at five (o'clock); **~ mezzanotte/Natale** at midnight/Christmas; **al mattino** in the morning; **~ maggio/primavera** in May/spring; **~ cinquant'anni** at fifty (years of age); **~ domani** see you tomorrow!

4 (*complemento di termine*) to; **dare qc ~ qn** to give sth to sb

5 (*mezzo, modo*) with, by; **~ piedi/cavallo** on foot/horseback; **fatto ~ mano** made by hand, handmade; **una barca ~ motore** a motorboat; **~ uno ~ uno** one by one; **all'italiana** the Italian way, in the Italian fashion

6 (*rapporto*) a, per; (: *con prezzi*) at; **prendo 500.000 lire al mese** I get 500,000 lire a o per month; **pagato ~ ore** paid by the hour; **vendere qc ~ 2500 lire il chilo** to sell sth at 2,500 lire a o per kilo

abbacchi'ato, a [abbak'kjato] *ag* downhearted, in low spirits

abbagli'ante [abbaʎ'ʎante] *ag* dazzling; **~i** *smpl* (*AUT*): **accendere gli ~i** to put one's headlights on full (*BRIT*) o high (*US*) beam

abbagli'are [abbaʎ'ʎare] *vt* to dazzle; (*illudere*) to delude; **ab'baglio** *sm* blunder; **prendere un abbaglio** to blunder, make a blunder

abbai'are *vi* to bark

abba'ino *sm* dormer window; (*soffitta*) attic room

abbando'nare *vt* to leave, abandon, desert; (*trascurare*) to neglect; (*rinunciare a*) to abandon, give up; **~rsi** *vr* to let o.s. go; **~rsi a** (*ricordi, vizio*) to give o.s. up to; **abban'dono** *sm* abandonment; neglect; (*SPORT*) withdrawal; (*fig*) abandon; **in abbandono** (*edificio, giardino*) neglected

abbas'sare *vt* to lower; (*radio*) to turn down; **~rsi** *vr* (*chinarsi*) to stoop; (*livello, sole*) to go down; (*fig: umiliarsi*) to demean o.s.; **~ i fari** (*AUT*) to dip o dim (*US*) one's lights

ab'basso *escl*: **~ il re!** down with the king!

abbas'tanza [abbas'tantsa] *av* (*a sufficienza*) enough; (*alquanto*) quite, rather, fairly; **non è ~ furbo** he's not shrewd enough; **un vino ~ dolce** quite a sweet wine; **averne ~ di qn/qc** to have had enough of sb/sth

ab'battere *vt* (*muro, casa*) to pull down; (*ostacolo*) to knock down; (*albero*) to fell; (: *sog: vento*) to bring down; (*bestia da macello*) to slaughter; (*cane, cavallo*) to destroy, put down;

(*selvaggina, aereo*) to shoot down; (*fig: sog: malattia, disgrazia*) to lay low; **~rsi** *vr* (*avvilirsi*) to lose heart; **abbat'tuto, a** *ag* (*fig*) depressed

abba'zia [abbat'tsia] *sf* abbey

abbece'dario [abbetʃe'darjo] *sm* primer

abbel'lire *vt* (*ornare*) to embellish

abbeve'rare *vt* to water; **~rsi** *vr* to drink

'abbia *etc vb vedi* **avere**

abbicci [abbit'tʃi] *sm inv* alphabet; (*sillabario*) primer; (*fig*) rudiments *pl*

abbi'enti *smpl*: **gli ~** the well-to-do

abbiglia'mento [abbiʎʎa'mento] *sm* dress *no pl*; (*indumenti*) clothes *pl*; (*industria*) clothing industry

abbi'gliare [abbiʎ'ʎare] *vt* to dress up

abbi'nare *vt*: **~ (a)** to combine (with)

abbin'dolare *vt* (*fig*) to cheat, trick

abbocca'mento *sm* talks *pl*, meeting

abboc'care *vi* (*pesce*) to bite; (*tubi*) to join; **~ (all'amo)** (*fig*) to swallow the bait

abboc'cato, a *ag* (*vino*) sweetish

abbona'mento *sm* subscription; (*alle ferrovie etc*) season ticket; **fare l'~** to take out a subscription (*o* season ticket)

abbo'narsi *vr*: **~ a un giornale** to take out a subscription to a newspaper; **~ al teatro/alle ferrovie** to take out a season ticket for the theatre/the train; **abbo'nato, a** *sm/f* subscriber; season-ticket holder

abbon'dante *ag* abundant, plentiful; (*giacca*) roomy

abbon'danza [abbon'dantsa] *sf* abundance; plenty

abbon'dare *vi* to abound, be plentiful; **~ in** *o* **di** to be full of, abound in

abbor'dabile *ag* (*persona*) approachable; (*prezzo*) reasonable

abbor'dare *vt* (*nave*) to board; (*persona*) to approach; (*argomento*) to tackle

abbotto'nare *vt* to button up, do up

abboz'zare [abbot'tsare] *vt* to sketch,

outline; (*SCULTURA*) to rough-hew; **~ un sorriso** to give a hint of a smile; **ab'bozzo** *sm* sketch, outline; (*DIR*) draft

abbracci'are [abbrat'tʃare] *vt* to embrace; (*persona*) to hug, embrace; (*professione*) to take up; (*contenere*) to include; **~rsi** *vr* to hug *o* embrace (one another); **ab'braccio** *sm* hug, embrace

abbrevi'are *vt* to shorten; (*parola*) to abbreviate

abbreviazi'one [abbrevjat'tsjone] *sf* abbreviation

abbron'zante [abbron'dzante] *ag* tanning, sun *cpd*

abbron'zare [abbron'dzare] *vt* (*pelle*) to tan; (*metalli*) to bronze; **~rsi** *vr* to tan, get a tan; **abbronza'tura** *sf* suntan

abbrusto'lire *vt* (*pane*) to toast; (*caffè*) to roast

abbru'tire *vt* to exhaust; to degrade

abbu'ono *sm* (*COMM*) allowance, discount; (*SPORT*) handicap

abdi'care *vi* to abdicate; **~ a** to give up, renounce

aberrazi'one [aberrat'tsjone] *sf* aberration

a'bete *sm* fir (tree); **~ rosso** spruce

a'bietto, a *ag* despicable, abject

'abile *ag* (*idoneo*): **~ (a qc/a fare qc)** fit (for sth/to do sth); (*capace*) able; (*astuto*) clever; (*accorto*) skilful; **~ al servizio militare** fit for military service; **abilità** *sf inv* ability; cleverness; skill

abili'tato, a *ag* qualified; (*TEL*) which has an outside line; **abilitazi'one** *sf* qualification

a'bisso *sm* abyss, gulf

abi'tacolo *sm* (*AER*) cockpit; (*AUT*) inside; (*: di camion*) cab

abi'tante *sm/f* inhabitant

abi'tare *vt* to live in, dwell in ♦ *vi*: **~ in campagna/a Roma** to live in the country/in Rome; **abi'tato, a** *ag* inhabited; lived in ♦ sm (anche: centro abitato) built-up area; **abitazi'one** sf residence; house

'**abito** sm dress no pl; (da uomo) suit; (da donna) dress; (abitudine, disposizione, REL) habit; **~i** smpl (vestiti) clothes; **in ~ da sera** in evening dress

abitu'ale ag usual, habitual; (cliente) regular

abitu'are vt: **~ qn a** to get sb used o accustomed to; **~rsi a** to get used to, accustom o.s. to

abitudi'nario, a ag of fixed habits ♦ sm/f regular customer

abi'tudine sf habit; **aver l'~ di fare qc** to be in the habit of doing sth; **d'~** usually; **per ~** from o out of habit

abo'lire vt to abolish; (DIR) to repeal

abomi'nevole ag abominable

abo'rigeno [abo'ridʒeno] sm aborigine

abor'rire vt to abhor, detest

abor'tire vi (MED) to miscarry, have a miscarriage; (: deliberatamente) to have an abortion; (fig) to miscarry, fail; **a'borto** sm miscarriage; abortion

abrasi'one sf abrasion; **abra'sivo, a** ag, sm abrasive

abro'gare vt to repeal, abrogate

A'bruzzo sm: **l'~, gli ~i** the Abruzzi

'**abside** sf apse

a'bulico, a, ci, che ag lacking in will power

abu'sare vi: **~ di** to abuse, misuse; (alcool) to take to excess; (approfittare, violare) to take advantage of; **a'buso** sm abuse, misuse; excessive use

a.C. av abbr (= avanti Cristo) B.C.

a'cacia, cie [a'katʃa] sf (BOT) acacia

'**acca** sf letter H; **non capire un'~** not to understand a thing

acca'demia sf (società) learned society; (scuola: d'arte, militare) academy; **acca'demico, a, ci, che** ag academic ♦ sm academician

acca'dere vb impers to happen; **acca'duto** sm: **raccontare**

l'accaduto to describe what has happened

accalappi'are vt to catch

accal'carsi vr: **~ (in)** to crowd (into)

accal'darsi vr to grow hot

accalo'rarsi vr (fig) to get excited

accampa'mento sm camp

accam'pare vt to encamp; (fig) to put forward, advance; **~rsi** vr to camp

accani'mento sm fury; (tenacia) tenacity, perseverance

acca'nirsi vr (infierire) to rage; (ostinarsi) to persist; **acca'nito, a** ag (odio, gelosia) fierce, bitter; (lavoratore) assiduous, dogged; (fumatore) inveterate

ac'canto av near, nearby; **~ a** prep near, beside, close to

accanto'nare vt (problema) to shelve; (somma) to set aside

accapar'rare vt (COMM) to corner, buy up; **~rsi qc** (fig: simpatia, voti) to secure sth (for o.s.)

accapigli'arsi [akkapiʎ'ʎarsi] vr to come to blows; (fig) to quarrel

accap'patoio sm bathrobe

accappo'nare vt: **far ~ la pelle a qn** to bring sb out in goose pimples

accarez'zare [akkaret'tsare] vt to caress, stroke, fondle; (fig) to toy with

acca'sarsi vr to set up house; to get married

accasci'arsi [akkaʃ'ʃarsi] vr to collapse; (fig) to lose heart

accat'tone, a sm/f beggar

accaval'lare vt (gambe) to cross; **~rsi** vr (sovrapporsi) to overlap; (addensarsi) to gather

acce'care [attʃe'kare] vt to blind ♦ vi to go blind

ac'cedere [at'tʃedere] vi: **~ a** to enter; (richiesta) to grant, accede to

accele'rare [attʃele'rare] vt to speed up ♦ vi (AUT) to accelerate; **~ il passo** to quicken one's pace; **accele'rato, a** ag quick, rapid; sm (FERR) slow train; **accelera'tore** sm (AUT) accelerator; **accelerazi'one** sf acceleration

ac'cendere [at'tʃɛndere] vt (fuoco, sigaretta) to light; (luce, televisione) to put on, switch on, turn on; (AUT: motore) to switch on; (COMM: conto) to open; (fig: suscitare) to inflame, stir up; **~rsi** vr (luce) to come o go on; (legna) to catch fire, ignite; **accen'dino** sm, **accendi'sigaro** sm (cigarette) lighter

accen'nare [attʃen'nare] vt (MUS) to pick out the notes of; to hum ♦ vi: **~ a** (fig: alludere a) to hint at; (: far atto di) to make as if; **~ un saluto** (con la mano) to make as if to wave; (col capo) to half nod; **accenna a piovere** it looks as if it's going to rain

ac'cenno [at'tʃɛnno] sm (cenno) sign; nod; (allusione) hint

accensi'one [attʃen'sjone] sf (vedi accendere) lighting; switching on; opening; (AUT) ignition

accen'tare [attʃen'tare] vt (parlando) to stress; (scrivendo) to accent

ac'cento [at'tʃɛnto] sm accent; (FONETICA, fig) stress; (inflessione) tone (of voice)

accen'trare [attʃen'trare] vt to centralize

accentu'are [attʃentu'are] vt to stress, emphasize; **~rsi** vr to become more noticeable

accerchi'are [attʃer'kjare] vt to surround, encircle

accerta'mento [attʃerta'mento] sm check; assessment

accer'tare [attʃer'tare] vt to ascertain; (verificare) to check; (reddito) to assess; **~rsi** vr: **~rsi (di)** to make sure (of)

ac'ceso, a [at'tʃeso] pp di **accendere** ♦ ag lit; on; open; (colore) bright

acces'sibile [attʃes'sibile] ag (luogo) accessible; (persona) approachable; (prezzo) reasonable

ac'cesso [at'tʃɛsso] sm (anche INFORM) access; (MED) attack, fit; (impulso violento) fit, outburst

acces'sorio, a [attʃes'sɔrjo] ag

secondary, of secondary importance; **~i** smpl accessories

ac'cetta [at'tʃetta] sf hatchet

accet'tabile [attʃet'tabile] ag acceptable

accet'tare [attʃet'tare] vt to accept; **~ di fare qc** to agree to do sth; **accettazi'one** sf acceptance; (locale di servizio pubblico) reception; **accettazione bagagli** (AER) check-in (desk)

ac'cetto, a [at'tʃɛtto] ag: **(ben) ~** welcome; (persona) well-liked

accezi'one [attʃet'tsjone] sf meaning

acchiap'pare [akkjap'pare] vt to catch

acci'acco, chi [at'tʃakko] sm ailment

acciaie'ria [attʃaje'ria] sf steelworks sg

acci'aio [at'tʃajo] sm steel

acciden'tale [attʃiden'tale] ag accidental

acciden'tato, a [attʃiden'tato] ag (terreno etc) uneven

acci'dente [attʃi'dɛnte] sm (caso imprevisto) accident; (disgrazia) mishap; **non si capisce un ~** it's as clear as mud; **~!** (fam: per rabbia) damn (it)!; (: per meraviglia) good heavens!

accigli'ato, a [attʃiλ'λato] ag frowning

ac'cingersi [at'tʃindʒersi] vr: **~ a fare qc** to be about to do sth

acciuf'fare [attʃuf'fare] vt to seize, catch

acci'uga, ghe [at'tʃuga] sf anchovy

accla'mare vt (applaudire) to applaud; (eleggere) to acclaim; **acclamazi'one** sf applause; acclamation

acclima'tare vt to acclimatize; **~rsi** vr to become acclimatized

ac'cludere vt to enclose; **ac'cluso, a** pp di **accludere** ♦ ag enclosed

accocco'larsi vr to crouch

accogli'ente [akkoλ'λɛnte] ag welcoming, friendly; **accogli'enza** sf reception; welcome

ac'cogliere [ak'kɔλλere] vt (ricevere) to receive; (dare il benvenuto) to welcome; (approvare) to agree to, accept; (*contenere*) to hold, accommodate

accol'lato, a *ag* (*vestito*) high-necked

accol'lare *vt* to knife, stab

ac'colto, a *pp di* **accogliere**

accoman'dita *sf* (*DIR*) limited partnership

accomia'tare *vt* to dismiss; **~rsi** *vr*: **~rsi (da)** to take one's leave (of)

accomoda'mento *sm* agreement, settlement

accomo'dante *ag* accommodating

accomo'dare *vt* (*aggiustare*) to repair, mend; (*riordinare*) to tidy; (*conciliare*) to settle; **~rsi** *vr* (*sedersi*) to sit down; **s'accomodi!** (*venga avanti*) come in!; (*si sieda*) take a seat!

accompagna'mento [akkompaɲɲa'mento] *sm* (*MUS*) accompaniment

accompa'gnare [akkompaɲ'ɲare] *vt* to accompany, come o go with; (*MUS*) to accompany; (*unire*) to couple; **~ la porta** to close the door gently

accompagna'tore, trice *sm/f* companion; **~ turistico** courier

accomu'nare *vt* to pool, share; (*avvicinare*) to unite

acconcia'tura [akkontʃa'tura] *sf* hairstyle

accondi'scendere [akkondiʃ'ʃendere] *vi*: **~ a** to agree o consent to; **accondi'sceso, a** *pp di* **accondiscendere**

acconsen'tire *vi*: **~ (a)** to agree o consent (to)

acconten'tare *vt* to satisfy; **~rsi di** to be satisfied with, content o.s. with

ac'conto *sm* part payment; **pagare una somma in ~** to pay a sum of money as a deposit

accoppi'are *vt* to couple, pair off; (*BIOL*) to mate; **~rsi** *vr* to pair off; to mate

acco'rato, a *ag* heartfelt

accorci'are [akkor'tʃare] *vt* to shorten; **~rsi** *vr* to become shorter

accor'dare *vt* to reconcile; (*colori*) to match; (*MUS*) to tune; (*LING*): **~ qc con qc** to make sth agree with sth; (*DIR*) to grant; **~rsi** *vr* to agree, come to an agreement; (*colori*) to match

ac'cordo *sm* agreement; (*armonia*) harmony; (*MUS*) chord; **essere d'~** to agree; **andare d'~** to get on well together; **d'~!** all right!, agreed!

ac'corgersi [ak'kordʒersi] *vr*: **~ di** to notice; (*fig*) to realize; **accorgi'mento** *sm* shrewdness *no pl*; (*espediente*) trick, device

ac'correre *vi* to run up

ac'corso, a *pp di* **accorrere**

ac'corto, a *pp di* **accorgersi ♦** *ag* shrewd; **stare ~** to be on one's guard

accos'tare *vt* (*avvicinare*): **~ qc a** to bring sth near to, put sth near to; (*avvicinarsi a*) to approach; (*socchiudere: imposte*) to half-close; (: *porta*) to leave ajar ♦ *vi* (*NAUT*) to come alongside; **~rsi a** to draw near, approach; (*fig*) to support

accovacci'arsi [akkovat'tʃarsi] *vr* to crouch

accoz'zaglia [akkot'tsaʎʎa] (*peg*) *sf* (*di idee, oggetti*) jumble, hotchpotch

accredi'tare *vt* (*notizia*) to confirm the truth of; (*COMM*) to credit; (*diplomatico*) to accredit; **~rsi** *vr* (*fig*) to gain credit

ac'crescere [ak'kreʃʃere] *vt* to increase; **~rsi** *vr* to increase, grow; **accresci'tivo, a** *ag, sm* (*LING*) augmentative; **accresci'uto, a** *pp di* **accrescere**

accucci'arsi [akkut'tʃarsi] *vr* (*cane*) to lie down

accu'dire *vt* (*anche: vi*: **~ a**) to attend to

accumu'lare *vt* to accumulate

accumula'tore *sm* (*ELETTR*) accumulator

accura'tezza [akkura'tettsa] *sf* care; accuracy

accu'rato, a *ag* (*diligente*) careful; (*preciso*) accurate

ac'cusa *sf* accusation; (*DIR*) charge; **la pubblica ~** the prosecution

accu'sare *vt*: **~ qn di qc** to accuse sb of sth; (*DIR*) to charge sb with sth; **~ ricevuta di** (*COMM*) to acknowledge receipt of

accu'sato, a *sm/f* accused; defendant

accusa'tore, 'trice *sm/f* accuser ♦ *sm* (*DIR*) prosecutor

a'cerbo, a [a'tʃerbo] *ag* bitter; (*frutta*) sour, unripe; (*persona*) immature

acero [a'tʃero] *sm* maple

a'cerrimo, a [a'tʃerrimo] *ag* very fierce

a'ceto [a'tʃeto] *sm* vinegar

ace'tone [atʃe'tone] *sm* nail varnish remover

A.C.I. [a'tʃi] *sigla m* = Automobile Club d'Italia

'acido, a ['atʃido] *ag* (*sapore*) acid, sour; (*CHIM*) acid ♦ *sm* (*CHIM*) acid

'acino ['atʃino] *sm* berry; **~ d'uva** grape

acne *sf* acne

'acqua *sf* water; (*pioggia*) rain; **~e** *sfpl* (*di mare, fiume etc*) waters; **fare ~** (*NAUT*) to leak, take in water; **~ in bocca!** mum's the word!; **~ corrente** running water; **~ dolce** fresh water; **~ minerale** mineral water; **~ potabile** drinking water; **~ salata** salt water; **~ tonica** tonic water

acqua'forte (*pl* **acque'forti**) *sf* etching

a'cquaio *sm* sink

acqua'ragia [akkwa'radʒa] *sf* turpentine

a'cquario *sm* aquarium; (*dello zodiaco*) **A~** Aquarius

acqua'santa *sf* holy water

ac'quatico, a, ci, che *ag* aquatic; (*SPORT, SCIENZA*) water *cpd*

acqua'vite *sf* brandy

acquaz'zone [akkwat'tsone] *sm* cloudburst, heavy shower

acque'dotto *sm* aqueduct; waterworks *pl*, water system

'acqueo, a *ag*: **vapore ~** water vapour

acque'rello *sm* watercolour

acqui'rente *sm/f* purchaser, buyer

acqui'sire *vt* to acquire

acqui'stare *vt* to purchase, buy; (*fig*) to gain; **a'cquisto** *sm* purchase; **fare acquisti** to go shopping

acqui'trino *sm* bog, marsh

acquo'lina *sf*: **far venire l'~ in bocca a qn** to make sb's mouth water

a'cquoso, a *ag* watery

'acre *ag* acrid, pungent; (*fig*) harsh, biting

a'crobata, i, e *sm/f* acrobat

acu'ire *vt* to sharpen

a'culeo (*ZOOL*) sting; (*BOT*) prickle

a'cume *sm* acumen, perspicacity

a'custica (*scienza*) acoustics *sg*; (*di una sala*) acoustics *pl*

a'cuto, a *ag* (*appuntito*) sharp, pointed; (*suono, voce*) shrill, piercing; (*MAT, LING, MED*) acute; (*MUS*) high-pitched; (*fig: dolore, desiderio*) intense; (*: perspicace*) acute, keen

ad (*before V*) *prep* = **a**

adagi'are [ada'dʒare] *vt* to lay o set down carefully; **~rsi** *vr* to lie down, stretch out

a'dagio [a'dadʒo] *av* slowly ♦ *sm* (*MUS*) adagio; (*proverbio*) adage, saying

adatta'mento *sm* adaptation

adat'tare *vt* to adapt; (*sistemare*) to fit; **~rsi (a)** (*ambiente, tempi*) to adapt (to); (*essere adatto*) to be suitable (for); **a'datto, a** *ag*: **~ (a)** suitable (for), right (for)

addebi'tare *vt*: **~ qc a qn** to debit sb with sth

ad'debito *sm* (*COMM*) debit

adden'sare *vt* to thicken; **~rsi** *vr* to thicken; (*nuvole*) to gather

adden'tare *vt* to bite into

adden'trarsi *vr*: **~ in** to penetrate, go into

ad'dentro *av*: **essere molto ~ in qc** to be well-versed in sth

addestra'mento *sm* training

addes'trare *vt* to train; **~rsi** *vr* to train; **~rsi in qc** to practise (*BRIT*) o practice

(US) sth

ad'detto, a *ag*: ~ **a** (*persona*) assigned to; (*oggetto*) intended for ♦ *sm* employee; (*funzionario*) attaché; ~ **commerciale/stampa** commercial/press attaché; **gli ~i ai lavori** authorized personnel; (*fig*) those in the know

addì *av* (AMM): ~ **3 luglio 1998** on the 3rd of July 1998 (BRIT), on July 3rd 1998 (US)

addi'accio [ad'djattʃo] *sm* (MIL) bivouac; **dormire all'~** to sleep in the open

addi'etro *av* (*indietro*) behind; (*nel passato, prima*) before, ago

ad'dio *sm, escl* goodbye, farewell

addirit'tura *av* (*veramente*) really, absolutely; (*perfino*) even; (*direttamente*) directly, right away

ad'dirsi *vr*: ~ **a** to suit, be suitable for

addi'tare *vt* to point out; (*fig*) to expose

addi'tivo *sm* additive

addizio'nare [addittsjo'nare] *vt* (MAT) to add (up); **addizi'one** *sf* addition

addob'bare *vt* to decorate; **ad'dobbo** *sm* decoration

addol'cire [addol'tʃire] *vt* (*caffè etc*) to sweeten; (*acqua, fig: carattere*) to soften; **~rsi** *vr* (*fig*) to mellow, soften

addolo'rare *vt* to pain, grieve; **~rsi** (**per**) to be distressed (at)

ad'dome *sm* abdomen

addomesti'care *vt* to tame

addormen'tare *vt* to put to sleep; **~rsi** *vr* to fall asleep, go to sleep

addos'sare *vt* (*appoggiare*): ~ **qc a qc** to lean sth against sth; (*fig*): ~ **la colpa a qn** to lay the blame on sb; **~rsi qc** (*responsabilità etc*) to shoulder sth

ad'dosso *av* on; **mettersi ~ il cappotto** to put one's coat on; ~ **a** (*sopra*) on; (*molto vicino*) right next to; **stare ~ a qn** (*fig*) to breathe down sb's neck; **dare ~ a qn** (*fig*) to attack

sb

ad'dotto, a *pp di* **addurre**

ad'durre *vt* (DIR) to produce; (*citare*) to cite

adegu'are *vt*: ~ **qc a** to adjust o relate sth to; **~rsi** *vr* to adapt; **adegu'ato, a** *ag* adequate; (*conveniente*) suitable; (*equo*) fair

a'dempiere *vt* to fulfil, carry out

adem'pire *vt* = **adempiere**

ade'rente *ag* adhesive; (*vestito*) close-fitting ♦ *sm/f* follower; **ade'renza** *sf* adhesion; **aderenze** *sfpl* connections, contacts

ade'rire *vi* (*stare attaccato*) to adhere, stick; ~ **a** to adhere to, stick to; (*fig: società, partito*) to join; (: *opinione*) to support; (*richiesta*) to agree to

ades'care *vt* to lure, entice

adesi'one *sf* adhesion; (*fig*) agreement, acceptance; **ade'sivo, a** *ag, sm* adhesive

a'desso *av* (*ora*) now; (*or ora, poco fa*) just now; (*tra poco*) any moment now

adia'cente [adja'tʃɛnte] *ag* adjacent

adi'bire *vt* (*usare*): ~ **qc a** to turn sth into

adi'rarsi *vr*: ~ (**con** o **contro qn per qc**) to get angry (with sb over sth)

a'dire *vt* (DIR): ~ **le vie legali** to take legal proceedings

'adito *sm*: **dare ~ a** to give rise to

adocchi'are [adok'kjare] *vt* (*scorgere*) to catch sight of; (*occhieggiare*) to eye

adole'scente [adoleʃ'ʃɛnte] *ag, sm/f* adolescent; **adole'scenza** *sf* adolescence

adope'rare *vt* to use; **~rsi** *vr* to strive; **~rsi per qn/qc** to do one's best for sb/sth

ado'rare *vt* to adore; (REL) to worship

adot'tare *vt* to adopt; (*decisione, provvedimenti*) to pass; **adot'tivo, a** *ag* (*genitori*) adoptive; (*figlio, patria*) adopted; **adozi'one** *sf* adoption

adri'atico, a, ci, che *ag* Adriatic ♦ *sm*:

l'A~, il mare A~ the Adriatic, the Adriatic Sea

adu'lare vt to adulate, flatter

adulte'rare vt to adulterate

adul'terio sm adultery

a'dulto, a ag adult; (fig) mature ♦ sm adult, grown-up

adu'nanza [adu'nantsa] sf assembly, meeting

adu'nare vt to assemble, gather; ~rsi vr to assemble, gather; adu'nata sf (MIL) parade, muster

a'dunco, a, chi, che ag hooked

a'ereo, a, a air cpd; (radice) aerial ♦ sm aerial; (aeroplano) plane; ~ a reazione jet (plane); ~ di linea airliner; ae'robica sf aerobics sg; aerodi'namica a aerodynamics sg; aerodi'namico, a, ci, che ag aerodynamic; (affusolato) streamlined; aero'nautica sf (scienza) aeronautics sg; aeronautica militare air force; aero'plano sm (aero)plane (BRIT), (air)plane (US)

aero'porto sm airport

aero'sol sm inv aerosol

'afa sf sultriness

af'fabile ag affable

affacen'dato, a [affatt∫en'dato] ag (persona) busy

affacci'arsi [affatt'∫arsi] vr: ~ (a) to appear (at)

affa'mato, a ag starving; (fig): ~ (di) eager (for)

affan'nare vt to leave breathless; (fig) to worry; ~rsi vr: ~rsi per qn/qc to worry about sb/sth; af'fanno sm breathlessness; (fig) anxiety, worry; affan'noso, a ag (respiro) difficult; (fig) troubled, anxious

af'fare sm (faccenda) matter, affair; (COMM) piece of business, (business) deal; (occasione) bargain; (DIR) case; (fam: cosa) thing; ~i smpl (COMM) business sg; Ministro degli A~i esteri Foreign Secretary (BRIT), Secretary of State (US); affa'rista, i sm

profiteer, unscrupulous businessman

affasci'nante [affa∫∫i'nante] ag fascinating

affasci'nare [affa∫∫i'nare] vt to bewitch; (fig) to charm, fascinate

affati'care vt to tire; ~rsi vr (durar fatica) to tire o.s. out

af'fatto av completely; non ... ~ not ... at all; niente ~ not at all

affer'mare vt (dichiarare) to maintain, affirm; ~rsi vr to assert o.s., make one's name known; affermazi'one sf affirmation, assertion; (successo) achievement

affer'rare vt to seize, grasp; (fig: idea) to grasp; ~rsi vr: ~rsi a to cling to

affet'tare vt (tagliare a fette) to slice; (ostentare) to affect; affet'tato, a ag sliced; affected ♦ sm sliced cold meat

affet'tivo, a ag emotional, affective

af'fetto sm affection; affettu'oso, a ag affectionate

affezio'narsi [affettsjo'narsi] vr: ~ a to grow fond of

affian'care vt to place side by side; (MIL) to flank; (fig) to support; ~ qc a qc to place sth next to o beside sth; ~rsi a qn to stand beside sb

affia'tato, a ag: essere molto ~i to get on very well

affibbi'are vt (fig: dare) to give

affi'dabile ag reliable

affida'mento sm (DIR: di bambino) custody; (fiducia): fare ~ su qn to rely on sb; non dà nessun ~ he's not to be trusted

affi'dare vt: ~ qc o qn a qn to entrust sth o sb to sb; ~rsi vr: ~rsi a to place one's trust in

affievo'lirsi vr to grow weak

af'figgere [af'fidd3ere] vt to stick up, post up

affi'lare vt to sharpen

affili'arsi vr: ~ a to become affiliated to

affi'nare vt to sharpen

affin'ché [affin'ke] cong in order that, so that

af'fine *ag* similar; **affinità** *sf inv* affinity

affio'rare *vi* to emerge

affissi'one *sf* billposting

af'fisso, a *pp di* **affiggere** ♦ *sm* bill, poster; (*LING*) affix

affit'tare *vt* (*dare in affitto*) to let, rent (out); (*prendere in affitto*) to rent; **af'fitto** *sm* rent; (*contratto*) lease

af'fliggere [af'flidd3ere] *vt* to torment; **~rsi** *vr* to grieve; **af'flitto, a** *pp di* **affliggere**; **afflizi'one** *sf* distress, torment

afflosci'arsi [afflof'farsi] *vr* to go limp

afflu'ente *sm* tributary; **afflu'enza** *sf* flow; (*di persone*) crowd

afflu'ire *vi* to flow; (*fig: merci, persone*) to pour in; **af'flusso** *sm* influx

affo'gare *vt, vi* to drown; **~rsi** *vr* to drown; (*deliberatamente*) to drown o.s.

affol'lare *vt* to crowd; **~rsi** *vr* to crowd; **affol'lato, a** *ag* crowded

affon'dare *vt* to sink

affran'care *vt* to free, liberate; (*AMM*) to redeem; (*lettera*) to stamp; (:
meccanicamente) to frank (*BRIT*), meter (*US*); **~rsi** *vr* to free o.s.; **affranca'tura** *sf* (*di francobollo*) stamping; franking (*BRIT*), metering (*US*); (*tassa di spedizione*) postage

af'franto, a *ag* (*esausto*) worn out; (*abbattuto*) overcome

af'fresco, schi *sm* fresco

affret'tare *vt* to quicken, speed up; **~rsi** *vr* to hurry; **~rsi a fare qc** to hurry o hasten to do sth

affron'tare *vt* (*pericolo etc*) to face; (*nemico*) to confront; **~rsi** *vr (reciproco*) to come to blows

af'fronto *sm* affront, insult

affumi'care *vt* to fill with smoke; to blacken with smoke; (*alimenti*) to smoke

affuso'lato, a *ag* tapering

a'foso, a *ag* sultry, close

'Africa [a'frika] *sf* l'~ Africa; **afri'cano, a** *ag, sm/f* African

afrodi'siaco, a, ci, che *ag, sm* aphrodisiac

a'genda [a'dzɛnda] *sf* diary

a'gente [a'dzɛnte] *sm* agent; **~ di cambio** stockbroker; **~ di polizia** police officer; **agen'zia** *sf* agency; (*succursale*) branch; **agenzia di collocamento** employment agency; **agenzia immobiliare** estate agent's (office) (*BRIT*), real estate office (*US*); **agenzia pubblicitaria/viaggi** advertising/travel agency

agevo'lare [adzevo'lare] *vt* to facilitate, make easy

a'gevole [a'dzevole] *ag* easy; (*strada*) smooth

aggan'ciare [aggan'tfare] *vt* to hook up; (*FERR*) to couple

ag'geggio [ad'dzeddzo] *sm* gadget, contraption

agget'tivo [addzet'tivo] *sm* adjective

agghiacci'ante [aggjat'fante] *ag* chilling

agghin'darsi [aggin'darsi] *vr* to deck o.s. out

aggior'nare [addzor'nare] *vt* (*opera, manuale*) to bring up-to-date; (*seduta etc*) to postpone; **~rsi** *vr* to bring (o keep) o.s. up-to-date; **aggior'nato, a** *ag* up-to-date

aggi'rare [addzi'rare] *vt* to go round; (*fig: ingannare*) to trick; **~rsi** *vr* to wander about; **il prezzo s'aggira sul milione** the price is around the million mark

aggiudi'care [addzudi'kare] *vt* to award; (*all'asta*) to knock down; **~rsi qc** to win sth

aggi'ungere [ad'dzundzere] *vt* to add; **aggi'unta** *sf* addition; **aggi'unto, a** *pp di* **aggiungere** ♦ *ag* assistant *cpd* ♦ *sm* assistant

aggius'tare [addzus'tare] *vt* (*accomodare*) to mend, repair; (*riassettare*) to adjust; (*fig: lite*) to settle; **~rsi** *vr* (*arrangiarsi*) to make do; (*con senso reciproco*) to come to an agreement

agglome'rato *sm* (*di rocce*) conglomerate; (*per la fabbricazione*) chipboard; ~ **urbano** built-up area

aggrap'parsi *vr*: ~ **a** to cling to

aggra'vare *vt* (*aumentare*) to increase; (*appesantire: anche fig*) to weigh down, make heavy; (*pena*) to make worse; **~rsi** *vr* to worsen, become worse

aggrazi'ato, a [aggrat'tsjato] *ag* graceful

aggre'dire *vt* to attack, assault

aggre'gare *vt*: ~ **qn a qc** to admit sb to sth; **~rsi** *vr* to join; **~rsi a** to join, become a member of

aggressi'one *sf* aggression; (*atto*) attack, assault

aggres'sivo, a *ag* aggressive

aggrot'tare *vt*: ~ **le sopracciglia** to frown

aggrovigli'are [aggroviʎ'ʎare] *vt* to tangle; **~rsi** *vr* (*fig*) to become complicated

agguan'tare *vt* to catch, seize

aggu'ato *sm* trap; (*imboscata*) ambush; **tendere un ~ a qn** to set a trap for sb

agguer'rito, a *ag* fierce

agi'ato, a [a'dʒato] *ag* (*vita*) easy; (*persona*) well-off, well-to-do

'agile ['adʒile] *ag* agile, nimble; **agilità** *sf* agility, nimbleness

'agio ['adʒo] *sm* ease, comfort; **mettersi a proprio ~** to make o.s. at home o comfortable

a'gire [a'dʒire] *vi* to act; (*esercitare un'azione*) to take effect; (*TECN*) to work, function; ~ **contro qn** (*DIR*) to take action against sb

agi'tare [adʒi'tare] *vt* (*bottiglia*) to shake; (*mano, fazzoletto*) to wave; (*fig: turbare*) to disturb; (*: incitare*) to stir (up); (*: dibattere*) to discuss; **~rsi** *vr* (*mare*) to be rough; (*malato, dormitore*) to toss and turn; (*bambino*) to fidget; (*emozionarsi*) to get upset; (*POL*) to agitate; **agi'tato, a** *ag* rough; restless; fidgety; upset, perturbed; **agitazi'one**

sf agitation; (*POL*) unrest, agitation; **mettere in agitazione qn** to upset o distress sb

'agli ['aʎʎi] *prep* + *det vedi* **a**

'aglio ['aʎʎo] *sm* garlic

a'gnello [aɲ'ɲɛllo] *sm* lamb

'ago (*pl* **'aghi**) *sm* needle

ago'nia *sf* agony

ago'nistico, a, ci, che *ag* athletic; (*fig*) competitive

agoniz'zare [agonid'dzare] *vi* to be dying

agopun'tura *sf* acupuncture

a'gosto *sm* August

a'graria *sf* agriculture

a'grario, a *ag* agrarian, agricultural; (*riforma*) land *cpd*

a'gricolo, a *ag* agricultural, farm *cpd*; **agricol'tore** *sm* farmer; **agricol'tura** *sf* agriculture, farming

agri'foglio [agri'fɔʎʎo] *sm* holly

agrimen'sore *sm* land surveyor

agritu'rismo *sm* farm holidays *pl*

'agro, a *ag* sour, sharp; **~dolce** *ag* bittersweet; (*salsa*) sweet and sour

a'grume *sm* (*spesso al pl: pianta*) citrus; (*: frutto*) citrus fruit

aguz'zare [agut'tsare] *vt* to sharpen; ~ **gli orecchi** to prick up one's ears

a'guzzo, a [a'guttso] *ag* sharp

'ai *prep* + *det vedi* **a**

'Aia *sf*: **l'~** the Hague

'aia *sf* threshing floor

AIDS *sigla f* o *m* AIDS

ai'rone *sm* heron

aiu'ola *sf* flower bed

aiu'tante *sm/f* assistant ♦ *sm* (*MIL*) adjutant; (*NAUT*) master-at-arms; ~ **di campo** aide-de-camp

aiu'tare *vt* to help; ~ **qn (a fare)** to help sb (to do)

ai'uto *sm* help, assistance, aid; (*aiutante*) assistant; **venire in ~ di qn** to come to sb's aid; ~ **chirurgo** assistant surgeon

aiz'zare [ait'tsare] *vt* to incite; ~ **i cani contro qn** to set the dogs on sb

al prep + det vedi **a**

'ala (pl **'ali**) sf wing; **fare ~** to fall back, make way; **~ destra/sinistra** (SPORT) right/left wing

'alacre ag quick, brisk

'alano sm Great Dane

a'lare ag wing cpd

'alba sf dawn

Alba'nia sf: **l'~** Albania

'albatro sm albatross

albeggi'are [albed'dʒare] vi, vb impers to dawn

alberghi'ero, a [alber'gjero] ag hotel cpd

al'bergo, ghi sm hotel; **~ della gioventù** youth hostel

'albero sm tree; (NAUT) mast; (TECN) shaft; **~ genealogico** family tree; **~ a gomiti** crankshaft; **~ di Natale** Christmas tree; **~ maestro** mainmast; **~ di trasmissione** transmission shaft

albi'cocca, che sf apricot; **albi'cocco, chi** sm apricot tree

'albo sm (registro) register, roll; (AMM) notice board

'album sm album; **~ da disegno** sketch book

al'bume sm albumen

'alce [altʃe] sm elk

al'colico, a, ci, che ag alcoholic ♦ sm alcoholic drink

alcoliz'zato, a [alcolid'dzato] sm/f alcoholic

'alcool sm alcohol; **alco'olico** etc = **alcolico** etc

al'cuno, a (a: det: dav sm: **alcun** +C, V, **alcuno** +s impura, gn, pn, ps, x, z; dav sf: **alcuna** +C, **alcun'** +V) det (nessuno): **non ... ~** no, not any; **~i, e** det pl some, a few; **non c'è ~a fretta** there's no hurry, there isn't any hurry; **senza alcun riguardo** without any consideration ♦ pron pl: **~i, e** some, a few

aldilà sm: **l'~** the after-life

alfa'beto sm alphabet

alfi'ere sm standard-bearer; (MIL)

ensign; (SCACCHI) bishop

'alga, ghe sf seaweed no pl, alga

'algebra ['aldʒebra] sf algebra

Alge'ria [aldʒe'ria] sf: **l'~** Algeria

ali'ante sm (AER) glider

'alibi sm inv alibi

a'lice [a'litʃe] sf anchovy

alie'nare vt (DIR) to alienate; transfer; (rendere ostile) to alienate; **~rsi qn** to alienate sb; **alie'nato, a** ag alienated; transferred; (fuor di senno) insane ♦ sm lunatic, insane person; **alienazi'one** sf alienation; transfer; insanity

ali'eno, a (avverso): **~ (da)** opposed (to), averse (to) ♦ sm/f alien

alimen'tare vt to feed; (TECN) to feed; to supply; (fig) to sustain ♦ ag food cpd; **~i** smpl foodstuffs; (anche: negozio di **~i**) grocer's shop; **alimentazi'one** sf feeding; supplying; (gli alimenti) diet

ali'mento sm food; **~i** smpl (cibo) food sg; (DIR) alimony

a'liquota sf share; (d'imposta) rate

alis'cafo sm hydrofoil

'alito sm breath

all. abbr (= allegato) encl.

'alla prep + det vedi **a**

allacci'are [allat'tʃare] vt (scarpe) to tie, lace (up); (cintura) to do up, fasten; (luce, gas) to connect; (amicizia) to form

alla'gare vt to flood; **~rsi** vr to flood

allar'gare vt to widen; (vestito) to let out; (aprire) to open; (fig: dilatare) to extend

allar'mare vt to alarm

al'larme sm alarm; **~ aereo** air-raid warning

allar'mismo sm scaremongering

allat'tare vt to feed

'alle prep + det vedi **a**

alle'anza [alle'antsa] sf alliance

alle'arsi vr to form an alliance; **alle'ato, a** ag allied ♦ sm/f ally

alle'gare vt (accludere) to enclose; (DIR: citare) to cite, adduce; (denti) to set on edge; **alle'gato, a** ag enclosed ♦ sm enclosure; **in allegato** enclosed

allegge'rire [alleddʒe'rire] vt to lighten, make lighter; (fig: lavoro, tasse) to reduce

alle'gria sf gaiety, cheerfulness

al'legro, a ag cheerful, merry; (un po' brillo) merry, tipsy; (vivace: colore) bright ♦ sm (MUS) allegro

allena'mento sm training

alle'nare vt to train; **~rsi** vr to train; **allena'tore** sm (SPORT) trainer, coach

allen'tare vt to slacken; (disciplina) to relax; **~rsi** vr to become slack; (ingranaggio) to work loose

aller'gia, 'gie [aller'dʒia] sf allergy; **al'lergico, a, ci, che** ag allergic

alles'tire vt (cena) to prepare; (esercito, nave) to equip, fit out; (spettacolo) to stage

allet'tare vt to lure, entice

alleva'mento sm breeding, rearing; (luogo) stock farm

alle'vare vt (animale) to breed, rear; (bambino) to bring up

allevi'are vt to alleviate

alli'bito, a ag astounded

allibra'tore sm bookmaker

allie'tare vt to cheer up, gladden

alli'evo sm pupil; (apprendista) apprentice; (MIL) cadet

alliga'tore sm alligator

alline'are vt (persone, cose) to line up; (TIP) to align; (fig: economia, salari) to adjust, align; **~rsi** vr to line up; (fig: a idee): **~rsi a** to come into line with

'allo prep + det vedi **a**

al'locco, a, chi, che sm tawny owl ♦ sm/f oaf

allocuzi'one [allokut'tsjone] sf address, solemn speech

al'lodola sf (sky)lark

alloggi'are [allod'dʒare] vt to accommodate ♦ vi to live; **al'loggio** sm lodging, accommodation (BRIT), accommodations (US)

allontana'mento sm removal;

dismissal

allonta'nare vt to send away, send off; (impiegato) to dismiss; (pericolo) to avert, remove; (estraniare) to alienate; **~si vr: ~rsi (da)** to go away (from); (estraniarsi) to become estranged (from)

al'lora av (in quel momento) then ♦ cong (in questo caso) well then; (dunque) well then, so; **la gente d'~** people then o in those days; **da ~ in poi** from then on

allor'ché [allor'ke] cong (formale) when, as soon as

al'loro sm laurel

'alluce ['allutʃe] sm big toe

alluci'nante [allutʃi'nante] ag awful; (fam) amazing

allucinazi'one [allutʃinat'tsjone] sf hallucination

al'ludere vi: **~ a** to allude to, hint at

allu'minio sm aluminium (BRIT), aluminum (US)

allun'gare vt to lengthen; (distendere) to prolong, extend; (diluire) to water down; **~rsi** vr to lengthen; (ragazzo) to stretch, grow taller; (sdraiarsi) to lie down, stretch out

allusi'one sf hint, allusion

al'luso, a pp di **alludere**

alluvi'one sf flood

al'meno av at least ♦ cong: **(se) ~ if** only; **(se) ~ piovesse!** if only it would rain!

a'logeno, a [a'lɔdʒeno] ag: **lampada ~a** halogen lamp

a'lone sm halo

'Alpi sfpl: **le ~** the Alps

alpi'nismo sm mountaineering, climbing; **alpi'nista, i, e** sm/f mountaineer, climber

al'pino, a ag Alpine; mountain cpd

al'quanto av rather, a little; **~, a** det a certain amount of, some ♦ pron a certain amount; some; **~i, e** det pl, pron pl several, quite a few

alt escl halt!, stop!

alta'lena sf (a funi) swing; (in bilico, anche fig) seesaw

al'tare sm altar

alte'rare vt to alter, change; (cibo) to adulterate; (registro) to falsify; (persona) to irritate; **~rsi** vr to alter; (cibo) to go bad; (persona) to lose one's temper

al'terco, chi sm altercation, wrangle

alter'nare vt to alternate; **~rsi** vr to alternate; **alterna'tiva** sf alternative; **alterna'tivo, a** ag alternative; **alter'nato, a** ag alternate; (ELETTR) alternating; **alterna'tore** sm alternator

al'terno, a ag alternate; **a giorni ~i** on alternate days, every other day

al'tezza [al'tettsa] sf height; width, breadth; depth; pitch; (GEO) latitude; (titolo) highness; (fig: nobiltà) greatness; **essere all'~ di** to be on a level with; (fig) to be up to o equal to; **altez'zoso, a** ag haughty

al'ticcio, a, ci, ce [al'tittʃo] ag tipsy

altipi'ano sm = **altopiano**

alti'tudine sf altitude

'alto, a ag high; (persona) tall; (tessuto) wide, broad; (sonno, acque) deep; (suono) high(-pitched); (GEO) upper; (: settentrionale) northern ♦ sm top (part) ♦ av high; (parlare) aloud, loudly; **il palazzo è ~ 20 metri** the building is 20 metres high; **ad ~a voce** aloud; **a notte ~a** in the dead of night; **in ~** up, upwards; at the top; **dall'~ in basso** up and down; **degli ~i e bassi** (fig) ups and downs; **~a fedeltà** high fidelity, hi-fi; **~a finanza** high finance; **~a moda** haute couture; **~a società** high society

alto'forno sm blast furnace

altolo'cato, a ag of high rank

altopar'lante sm loudspeaker

altopi'ano (pl altipi'ani) sm plateau, upland plain

altret'tanto, a ag, pron as much; (pl) as many ♦ av equally; **tanti auguri! — grazie, ~** all the best! — thank you, the same to you

'altri pron inv (qualcuno) somebody; (: in espressioni negative) anybody; (un'altra persona) another (person)

altri'menti av otherwise

'altro, a det **1** (diverso) other, different; **questa è un'~a cosa** that's another o a different thing

2 (supplementare) other; **prendi un ~ cioccolatino** have another chocolate; **hai avuto ~e notizie?** have you had any more o any other news?

3 (nel tempo): **l'~ giorno** the other day; **l'altr'anno** last year; **l'~ ieri** the day before yesterday; **domani l'~** the day after tomorrow; **quest'~ mese** next month

4: d'~a parte on the other hand ♦ pron **1** (persona, cosa diversa o supplementare): **un ~, un'~a** another (one); **lo farà un ~** someone else will do it; **~i, e** others; **gli ~i** (la gente) others, other people; **l'uno e l'~** both (of them); **aiutarsi l'un l'~** to help one another; **da un giorno all'~** from day to day; (nel giro di 24 ore) from one day to the next; (da un momento all'altro) any day now

2 (sostantivato: solo maschile) something else; (: in espressioni interrogative) anything else; **non ho ~ da dire** I have nothing else o I don't have anything else to say; **più che ~** above all; **se non ~** at least; **tra l'~** among other things; **ci mancherebbe ~!** that's all we need!; **non faccio ~ che lavorare** I do nothing but work; **contento? — e come!** are you pleased? — and how!; vedi **senza; noialtri; voialtri; tutto**

al'tronde av: **d'~** on the other hand

al'trove av elsewhere, somewhere else

al'trui ag inv other people's ♦ sm: **l'~** other people's belongings pl

altru'ista, i, e *ag* altruistic

al'tura *sf (rialto)* height, high ground; *(alto mare)* open sea; **pesca d'~** deep-sea fishing

a'lunno, a *sm/f* pupil

alve'are *sm* hive

'alveo *sm* riverbed

al'zare [al'tsare] *vt* to raise, lift; *(issare)* to hoist; *(costruire)* to build, erect; **~rsi** *vr* to rise; *(dal letto)* to get up; *(crescere)* to grow tall (*o* taller); **~ le spalle** to shrug one's shoulders; **~rsi in piedi** to stand up, get to one's feet; **al'zata di** lifting, raising; **un'alzata di spalle** a shrug

a'mabile *ag* lovable; *(vino)* sweet

a'maca, che *sf* hammock

amalga'mare *vt* to amalgamate

a'mante *ag:* **~ di** *(musica etc)* fond of ♦ *sm/f* lover/mistress

a'mare *vt* to love; *(amico, musica, sport)* to like

amareggi'ato, a [amared'dʒato] *ag* upset, saddened

ama'rena *sf* sour black cherry

ama'rezza [ama'rettsa] *sf* bitterness

a'maro, a *ag* bitter ♦ *sm* bitterness; *(liquore)* bitters *pl*

ambasci'ata [ambaʃ'ʃata] *sf* embassy; *(messaggio)* message; **ambascia'tore, 'trice** *sm/f* ambassador/ambassadress

ambe'due *ag inv:* **~ i ragazzi** both boys ♦ *pron inv* both

ambien'tare *vt* to acclimatize; *(romanzo, film)* to set; **~rsi** *vr* to get used to one's surroundings

ambi'ente *sm* environment; *(fig: insieme di persone)* milieu; *(stanza)* room

am'biguo, a *ag* ambiguous

am'bire *vt (anche: vi:* **~ a)** to aspire to

'ambito *sm* sphere, field

ambizi'one [ambit'tsjone] *sf* ambition; **ambizi'oso, a** *ag* ambitious

'ambo *ag inv* both ♦ *(al gioco)* double

'ambra *sf* amber; **~ 'grigia** ambergris

ambu'lante *ag* itinerant ♦ *sm* peddler

ambu'lanza [ambu'lantsa] *sf* ambulance

ambula'torio *sm (studio medico)* surgery

a'meno, a *ag* pleasant; *(strano)* funny

A'merica *sf:* **l'~** America; **l'~ latina** Latin America; **ameri'cano, a** *ag, sm/f* American

ami'anto *sm* asbestos

a'mica *sf vedi* **amico**

ami'chevole [ami'kevole] *ag* friendly

ami'cizia [ami'tʃittsja] *sf* friendship; **~e** *sfpl (amici)* friends

a'mico, a, ci, che *sm/f* friend; *(fidanzato)* boyfriend/girlfriend; **~ del cuore** *o* **intimo** bosom friend

'amido *sm* starch

ammac'care *vt (pentola)* to dent; *(persona)* to bruise; **~rsi** *vr* to bruise

ammaes'trare *vt (animale)* to train

ammai'nare *vt* to lower, haul down

amma'larsi *vr* to fall ill; **amma'lato, a** *ag* ill, sick ♦ *sm/f* sick person; *(paziente)* patient

ammali'are *vt (fig)* to enchant, charm

am'manco, chi *sm* deficit

ammanet'tare *vt* to handcuff

ammas'sare *vt (ammucchiare)* to amass; *(raccogliere)* to gather together; **~rsi** *vr* to pile up; to gather; **am'masso** *sm* mass; *(mucchio)* pile, heap; *(ECON)* stockpile

ammat'tire *vi* to go mad

ammaz'zare [ammat'tsare] *vt* to kill; **~rsi** *vr (uccidersi)* to kill o.s.; *(rimanere ucciso)* to be killed; **~rsi di lavoro** to work o.s. to death

am'menda *sf* amends *pl*; *(DIR, SPORT)* fine

am'messo, a *pp di* **ammettere** ♦ *cong:* **~ che** supposing that

am'mettere *vt* to admit; *(riconoscere: fatto)* to acknowledge, admit; *(permettere)* to allow, accept; *(supporre)* to suppose

ammez'zato [ammed'dzato] *sm (anche: piano ~)* mezzanine, entresol

ammic'care vi: ~ **(a)** to wink (at)

amminis'trare vt to run, manage; (REL, DIR) to administer; **amministra'tivo, a** ag administrative; **amministra'tore** sm administrator; (di condominio) flats manager; **amministratore delegato** managing director; **amministrazi'one** sf management; administration

ammiragli'ato [ammiraʎ'ʎato] sm admiralty

ammi'raglio [ammi'raʎʎo] sm admiral

ammi'rare vt to admire; **ammira'tore, 'trice** sm/f admirer; **ammirazi'one** sf admiration

ammissi'one sf admission

ammobili'ato, a ag furnished

am'modo av properly ♦ ag inv respectable, nice

am'mollo sm: **lasciare in ~** to leave to soak

ammo'niaca sf ammonia

ammoni'mento sm warning; admonishment

ammo'nire vt (avvertire) to warn; (rimproverare) to admonish; (DIR) to caution

ammon'tare vi: ~ **a** to amount to ♦ sm (total) amount

ammorbi'dente sm fabric conditioner

ammorbi'dire vt to soften

ammortiz'zare [ammortid'dzare] vt (ECON) to pay off, amortize; (: spese d'impianto) to write off; (AUT, TECN) to absorb, deaden; **ammortizza'tore** sm (AUT, TECN) shock-absorber

ammucchi'are [ammuk'kjare] vt to pile up, accumulate

ammuf'fire vi to go mouldy (BRIT) o moldy (US)

ammuti'namento sm mutiny

ammuto'lire vi to be struck dumb

amnis'tia sf amnesty

'amo sm (PESCA) hook; (fig) bait

a'modo av = **ammodo**

a'more sm love; ~**i** smpl love affairs; **il tuo bambino è un ~** your baby's a

darling; **fare l'~ o all'~** to make love; **per ~ o per forza** by hook or by crook; **amor proprio** self-esteem, pride; **amo'revole** ag loving, affectionate

a'morfo, a ag amorphous; (fig: persona) lifeless

amo'roso, a ag (affettuoso) loving, affectionate; (d'amore: sguardo) amorous; (: poesia, relazione) love cpd

ampi'ezza [am'pjettsa] sf width, breadth; spaciousness; (fig: importanza) scale, size

'ampio, a ag wide, broad; (spazioso) spacious; (abbondante: vestito) loose; (: gonna) full; (: spiegazione) ample, full

am'plesso sm intercourse

ampli'are vt (ingrandire) to enlarge; (allargare) to widen

amplifi'care vt to amplify; **amplifica'tore** sm (TECN, MUS) amplifier

am'polla sf (vasetto) cruet

ampu'tare vt (MED) to amputate

amu'leto sm lucky charm

anabbagli'ante [anabbaʎ'ʎante] ag (AUT) dipped (BRIT), dimmed (US); ~**i** smpl dipped (BRIT) o dimmed (US) headlights

a'nagrafe sf (registro) register of births, marriages and deaths; (ufficio) registry office (BRIT), office of vital statistics (US)

anal'colico, a, ci, che ag non-alcoholic ♦ sm soft drink

analfa'beta, i, e ag, sm/f illiterate

anal'gesico, a, ci, che [anal'dʒɛziko] ag, sm analgesic

a'nalisi sf inv analysis; (MED: esame) test; ~ **grammaticale** parsing; **ana'lista, i, e** sm/f analyst; (PSIC) (psycho)analyst

analiz'zare [analid'dzare] vt to analyse; (MED) to test

analo'gia, 'gie [analo'dʒia] sf analogy

a'nalogo, a, ghi, ghe ag analogous

'ananas sm inv pineapple

anar'chia [anar'kia] sf anarchy;

a'narchico, a, ci, che *ag* anarchic(al)
♦ *sm/f* anarchist

'ANAS *sigla f* (= *Azienda Nazionale Autonoma delle Strade*) national roads department

anato'mia *sf* anatomy; **ana'tomico, a, ci, che** *ag* anatomical; (*sedile*) contoured

'anatra *sf* duck

'anca, che *sf* (ANAT) hip

'anche ['anke] *cong* (*inoltre, pure*) also, too; (*perfino*) even; **vengo anch'io** I'm coming too; **~ se** even if

an'cora¹ *av* still; (*di nuovo*) again; (*di più*) some more; (*persino*): **~ più forte** even stronger; **non ~** not yet; **una volta** once more, once again; **~ un po'** a little more; (*di tempo*) a little longer

an'cora² *sf* anchor; **gettare/levare l'~** to cast/weigh anchor; **anco'raggio** *sm* anchorage; **anco'rare** *vt* to anchor; **ancorarsi** *vr* to anchor

anda'mento *sm* progress, movement; course; state

an'dante *ag* (*corrente*) current; (*di poco pregio*) cheap, second-rate ♦ *sm* (MUS) andante

an'dare *sm*: **a lungo ~** in the long run ♦ *vi* to go; (*essere adatto*): **~ a** to suit; (*piacere*): **il suo comportamento non mi va** I don't like the way he behaves; **ti va di andare al cinema?** do you feel like going to the cinema?; **andarsene** to go away; **questa camicia va lavata** this shirt needs a wash o should be washed; **~ a cavallo** to ride; **~ in macchina/aereo** to go by car/plane; **~ a fare qc** to go and do sth; **~ a pescare/sciare** to go fishing/skiing; **~ a male** to go bad; **come va?** (*lavoro, progetto*) how are things?; **come va? — bene, grazie!** how are you? — fine, thanks!; **va fatto entro oggi** it's got to be done today; **ne va della nostra vita** our lives are at stake; **an'data** *sf* going; (*viaggio*) outward journey; **biglietto di sola andata** single (BRIT) o one-way ticket; **biglietto di andata e ritorno** return (BRIT) o round-trip (US) ticket; **anda'tura** *sf* (*modo di andare*) walk, gait; (SPORT) pace; (NAUT) tack

an'dazzo [an'dattso] (*peg*) *sm*: **prendere un brutto ~** to take a turn for the worse

andirivi'eni *sm inv* coming and going

'andito *sm* corridor, passage

an'drone *sm* entrance hall

a'neddoto *sm* anecdote

ane'lare *vi*: **~ a** to long for, yearn for

a'nelito *sm* (*fig*): **~ di** longing o yearning for

a'nello *sm* ring; (*di catena*) link

a'nemico, a, ci, che *ag* anaemic

a'nemone *sm* anemone

aneste'sia *sf* anaesthesia; **anes'tetico, a, ci, che** *ag, sm* anaesthetic

anfite'atro *sm* amphitheatre

an'fratto *sm* ravine

an'gelico, a, ci, che [an'dʒeliko] *ag* angelic(al)

'angelo ['andʒelo] *sm* angel; **~ custode** guardian angel

anghe'ria [ange'ria] *sf* vexation

an'gina [an'dʒina] *sf* tonsillitis; **~ pectoris** angina

angli'cano, a *ag* Anglican

angli'cismo [angli'tʃizmo] *sm* anglicism

anglo'sassone *ag* Anglo-Saxon

ango'lare *ag* angular

angolazi'one [angolat'tsjone] *sf* (FOT etc, fig) angle

'angolo *sm* corner; (MAT) angle

an'goscia, sce [an'goʃʃa] *sf* deep anxiety, anguish *no pl*; **angosci'oso, a** *ag* (*d'angoscia*) anguished; (*che dà angoscia*) distressing, painful

angu'illa *sf* eel

an'guria *sf* watermelon

an'gustia *sf* (*ansia*) anguish, distress; (*povertà*) poverty, want

angusti'are vt to distress; **~rsi** vr: **~rsi (per)** to worry (about)

an'gusto, a ag (stretto) narrow

'anice ['anitʃe] sm (CUC) aniseed; (BOT) anise

a'nidride sf (CHIM): **~ carbonica/solforosa** carbon/sulphur dioxide

'anima sf soul; (abitante) inhabitant; **non c'era ~ viva** there wasn't a living soul

ani'male sm, ag animal; **~ domestico** pet

ani'mare vt to give life to, liven up; (incoraggiare) to encourage; **~rsi** vr to become animated, come to life; **ani'mato, a** ag animate; (vivace) lively, animated; (: strada) busy; **anima'tore, 'trice** sm/f guiding spirit; (CINEMA) animator; (di festa) life and soul; **animazi'one** sf liveliness; (di strada) bustle; (CINEMA) animation; **animazione teatrale** amateur dramatics

'animo sm (mente) mind; (cuore) heart; (coraggio) courage; (disposizione) character, disposition; **avere in ~ di fare qc** to intend o have a mind to do sth; **perdersi d'~** to lose heart

'anitra sf = **anatra**

anna'cquare vt to water down, dilute

annaffi'are vt to water; **annaffia'toio** sm watering can

an'nali smpl annals

annas'pare vi to flounder

an'nata sf year; (importo annuo) annual amount; **vino d'~** vintage wine

annebbi'are vt (fig) to cloud; **~rsi** vr to become foggy; (vista) to become dim

annega'mento sm drowning

anne'gare vt, vi to drown; **~rsi** vr (accidentalmente) to drown; (deliberatamente) to drown o.s.

anne'rire vt to blacken ♦ vi to become black

an'nesso, a pp di **annettere** ♦ ag attached; (POL) annexed; ... **e tutti gli ~i e connessi** and so on and so forth

an'nettere vt (POL) to annex; (accludere) to attach

annichi'lire [anniki'lire] vt = **annichilire**

an'nidarsi vr to nest

annien'tare vt to annihilate, destroy

anniver'sario sm anniversary

'anno sm year; **ha 8 ~i** he's 8 (years old)

anno'dare vt to knot, tie; (fig: rapporto) to form

annoi'are vt to bore; (seccare) to annoy; **~rsi** vr to be bored; to be annoyed

an'noso, a ag (problema etc) age-old

anno'tare vt (registrare) to note, note down; (commentare) to annotate; **annotazi'one** sf note; annotation

annove'rare vt to number

annu'ale ag annual

annu'ario sm yearbook

annu'ire vi to nod; (acconsentire) to agree

annul'lare vt to annihilate, destroy; (contratto, francobollo) to cancel; (matrimonio) to annul; (sentenza) to quash; (risultati) to declare void

annunci'are [annun'tʃare] vt to announce; (dar segni rivelatori) to herald; **annuncia'tore, 'trice** sm/f (RADIO, TV) announcer; **l'Annunciazi'one** sf the Annunciation

an'nuncio [an'nuntʃo] sm announcement; (fig) sign; **~ pubblicitario** advertisement; **~i economici** classified advertisements, small ads

'annuo, a ag annual, yearly

annu'sare vt to sniff, smell; **~ tabacco** to take snuff

'ano sm anus

anoma'lia sf anomaly

a'nomalo, a ag anomalous

a'nonimo, a ag anonymous ♦ sm (autore) anonymous writer (o painter etc); **società ~a** (COMM) joint stock company

anores'sia sf anorexia

anor'male ag abnormal ♦ sm/f subnormal person

ANSA sigla f (= Agenzia Nazionale Stampa Associata) press agency

'ansa sf (manico) handle; (di fiume) bend, loop

'ansia sf anxiety

ansietà sf = ansia

ansi'mare vi to pant

ansi'oso, a ag anxious

'anta sf (di finestra) shutter; (di armadio) door

antago'nismo sm antagonism

an'tartico, a, ci, che ag Antarctic ♦ sm: **l'A~** the Antarctic

An'tartide sf: **l'~** Antarctica

antece'dente [antetʃeˈdɛnte] ag preceding, previous

ante'fatto sm previous events pl; previous history

antegu'erra sm pre-war period

ante'nato sm ancestor, forefather

an'tenna sf (RADIO, TV) aerial; (ZOOL) antenna, feeler; (NAUT) yard; **~ parabolica** satellite dish

ante'prima sf TV preview

anteri'ore ag (ruota, zampa) front; (fatti) previous, preceding

antia'ereo, a ag anti-aircraft

antia'tomico, a ag anti-nuclear; **rifugio ~** fallout shelter

antibi'otico, a, ci, che ag, sm antibiotic

anti'camera sf anteroom; **fare ~** to wait (for an audience)

antichità [antikiˈta] sf inv antiquity; (oggetto) antique

antici'pare [antitʃiˈpare] vt (consegna, visita) to bring forward, anticipate; (somma di denaro) to pay in advance; (notizia) to disclose ♦ vi to be ahead of time; **anticipaz'one** sf anticipation; (di notizia) advance information; (somma di denaro) advance; **an'ticipo** sm anticipation; (di denaro) advance; **in**

anticipo early, in advance

an'tico, a, chi, che ag (quadro, mobili) antique; (dell'antichità) ancient; **all'~** old-fashioned

anticoncezio'nale [antikontʃettsjo-'nale] sm contraceptive

anticonfor'mista, i, e ag, sm/f nonconformist

anti'corpo sm antibody

antidepres'sivo sm antidepressant

an'tidoto sm antidote

anti'furto sm anti-theft device

anti'gelo [antiˈdʒɛlo] ag inv: **(liquido)** **~** (per motore) antifreeze; (per cristalli) de-icer

An'tille sfpl: **le ~** the West Indies

antin'cendio [antinˈtʃɛndjo] ag inv fire cpd

antio'rario [antioˈrarjo] ag: **in senso** **~** anticlockwise

anti'pasto sm hors d'œuvre

antipa'tia sf antipathy, dislike; **anti'patico, a, ci, che** ag unpleasant, disagreeable

antiquari'ato sm antique trade; **un oggetto d'~** an antique

anti'quario sm antique dealer

anti'quato, a ag antiquated, old-fashioned

antise'mita, i, e ag anti-Semitic

anti'settico, a, ci, che ag, sm antiseptic

antista'minico, a, ci, che ag, sm antihistamine

antolo'gia, 'gie [antoloˈdʒia] sf anthology

anu'lare ag ring cpd ♦ sm third finger

'anzi [ˈantsi] av (invece) on the contrary; (o meglio) or rather, or more still

anziani'tà [antsjaniˈta] sf old age; (AMM) seniority

anzi'ano, a [anˈtsjano] ag old; (AMM) senior ♦ sm/f old person; senior member

anziché [antsiˈke] cong rather than

anzi'tutto [antsiˈtutto] av first of all

apa'tia sf apathy, indifference

a'patico, a, ci, che ag apathetic

'ape sf bee

aperi'tivo sm apéritif

a'perto, a pp di **aprire** ♦ ag open; **all'** ~ in the open (air)

aper'tura sf opening; (*ampiezza*) width; (*FOT*) aperture; ~ **alare** wing span

'apice ['apitfe] sm apex; (*fig*) height

ap'nea sf: **immergersi in** ~ to dive without breathing apparatus

a'postolo sm apostle

a'postrofo sm apostrophe

appa'gare vt to satisfy

ap'palto (*COMM*) contract; **dare/prendere in** ~ **un lavoro** to let out/undertake a job on contract

appan'nare vt (*vetro*) to mist; (*vista*) to dim; ~**rsi** vr to mist over; to grow dim

appa'rato sm equipment, machinery; (*ANAT*) apparatus; ~ **scenico** (*TEATRO*) props pl

apparecchi'are [apparek'kjare] vt to prepare; (*tavola*) to set ♦ vi to set the table; **apparecchia'tura** sf equipment; (*macchina*) machine, device

appa'recchio [appa'rekkjo] sm piece of apparatus, device; (*aeroplano*) aircraft inv; ~ **televisivo/telefonico** television set/telephone

appa'rente ag apparent; **appa'renza** sf appearance; **in** o **all'apparenza** apparently

appa'rire vi to appear; (*sembrare*) to seem, appear; **appari'scente** ag (*colore*) garish, gaudy; (*bellezza*) striking

ap'parso, a pp di **apparire**

apparta'mento sm flat (*BRIT*), apartment (*US*)

appar'tarsi vr to withdraw; **appar'tato, a** ag (*luogo*) secluded

apparte'nere vi: ~ **a** to belong to

appassio'nare vt to thrill; (*commuovere*) to move; ~**rsi a qc** to

take a great interest in sth;

appassio'narsi vr (*ricorrere*): ~ **a** to be passionate; (*entusiasta*): **appassionato (di)** keen (on)

appas'sire vi to wither

appel'larsi vr (*ricorrere*): ~ **a** to appeal to; (*DIR*): ~ **contro** to appeal against; **ap'pello** sm roll-call; (*implorazione, DIR*) appeal; **fare appello a** to appeal to

ap'pena av (*a stento*) hardly, scarcely; (*solamente, da poco*) just ♦ cong as soon as; (**non**) ~ **furono arrivati** ... as soon as they had arrived ...; ~ ... **che** o **quando** no sooner ... than

ap'pendere vt to hang (up)

appen'dice [appen'ditfe] sf appendix; **romanzo d'**~ popular serial

appendi'cite [appendi'tfite] sf appendicitis

Appen'nini smpl: **gli** ~ the Apennines

appesan'tire vt to make heavy; ~**rsi** vr to grow stout

ap'peso, a pp di **appendere**

appe'tito sm appetite; **appeti'toso, a** ag appetising; (*fig*) attractive, desirable

appia'nare vt to level; (*fig*) to smooth away, iron out

appiat'tire vt to flatten; ~**rsi** vr to become flatter; (*farsi piatto*) to flatten o.s.; ~**rsi al suolo** to lie flat on the ground

appic'care vt: ~ **il fuoco a** to set fire to, set on fire

appicci'care [appittʃi'kare] vt to stick; ~**rsi** vr to stick; (*fig: persona*) to cling

appi'eno av fully

appigli'arsi [appiʎ'ʎarsi] vr: ~ **a** (*afferrarsi*) to take hold of; (*fig*) to cling to; **ap'piglio** sm hold; (*fig*) pretext

appiso'larsi vr to doze off

applau'dire vt, vi to applaud; **ap'plauso** sm applause

appli'care vt to apply; (*regolamento*) to enforce; ~**rsi** vr to apply o.s.; **applicazi'one** sf application; enforcement

appoggi'are [appod'dʒare] vt (mettere contro): ~ **qc a qc** to lean o rest sth against sth; (fig: sostenere) to support; **~rsi** vr: **~rsi a** to lean against; (fig) to rely upon; **ap'poggio** sm support

appollai'arsi vr (anche fig) to perch

ap'porre vt to affix

appor'tare vt to bring

apposita'mente av specially; (apposta) on purpose

ap'posito, a ag appropriate

ap'posta av on purpose, deliberately

appos'tarsi vr to lie in wait

ap'prendere vt (imparare) to learn

appren'dista, i, e sm/f apprentice

apprensi'one sf apprehension; **appren'sivo, a** ag apprehensive

ap'presso av (accanto, vicino) by, near; (dietro) behind; (dopo, più tardi) after, later ♦ ag inv (dopo): **il giorno ~** the next day; **~ a** (vicino a) near, close to

appres'tare vt to prepare, get ready; **~rsi** vr: **~rsi a fare qc** to prepare o get ready to do sth

ap'pretto sm starch

apprezza'mento [apprettsa'mento] sm appreciation; (giudizio) opinion

apprez'zare [appret'tsare] vt to appreciate

ap'proccio [ap'prɔttʃo] sm approach

appro'dare vi (NAUT) to land; (fig): **non ~ a nulla** to come to nothing; **ap'prodo** sm landing; (luogo) landing-place

approfit'tare vi: **~ di** to make the most of; (peg) to take advantage of

approfon'dire vt to deepen; (fig) to study in depth

appropri'ato, a ag appropriate

approssi'marsi vr: **~ a** to approach

approssima'tivo, a ag approximate, rough; (impreciso) inexact, imprecise

appro'vare vt (condotta, azione) to approve of; (candidato) to pass; (progetto di legge) to approve; **approvazi'one** sf approval

approvvigio'nare [approvvidʒo'nare] vt to supply

appunta'mento sm appointment; (amoroso) date; **darsi ~** to arrange to meet (one another)

appun'tato sm (CARABINIERI) corporal

ap'punto sm note; (rimprovero) reproach ♦ av (proprio) exactly, just; **per l'~!, ~!** exactly!

appu'rare vt to check, verify

apribot'tiglie [apribot'tiʎʎe] sm inv bottle opener

a'prile sm April

a'prire vt to open; (via, cadavere) to open up; (gas, luce, acqua) to turn on ♦ vi to open; **~rsi** vr to open; **~rsi a qn** to confide in sb, open one's heart to sb

apris'catole sm inv tin (BRIT) o can opener

a'quario sm = **acquario**

'aquila sf (ZOOL) eagle; (fig) genius

aqui'lone sm (giocattolo) kite; (vento) North wind

A'rabia Sau'dita sf: **l'~** Saudi Arabia

'arabo, a ag, sm/f Arab ♦ sm (LING) Arabic

a'rachide [a'rakide] sf peanut

ara'gosta sf crayfish; lobster

a'rancia, ce [a'rantʃa] sf orange; **aranci'ata** sf orangeade; **a'rancio** sm (BOT) orange tree; (colore) orange ♦ ag inv (colore) orange; **aranci'one** ag inv: **(color) arancione** bright orange

a'rare vt to plough (BRIT), plow (US)

a'ratro sm plough (BRIT), plow (US)

a'razzo [a'rattso] sm tapestry

arbi'trare vt (SPORT) to referee; to umpire; (DIR) to arbitrate

arbi'trario, a ag arbitrary

ar'bitrio sm will; (abuso, sopruso) arbitrary act

'arbitro sm arbiter, judge; (DIR) arbitrator; (SPORT) referee; (: TENNIS, CRICKET) umpire

ar'busto sm shrub

'arca, che sf (sarcofago) sarcophagus;

l'~ di Noè Noah's ark

ar'cangelo [ar'kandʒelo] *sm* archangel

ar'cata *sf* (ARCHIT, ANAT) arch; (*ordine di archi*) arcade

archeolo'gia [arkeolo'dʒia] *sf* arch(a)eology; **arche'ologo, a, gi, ghe** *sm/f* arch(a)eologist

ar'chetto [ar'ketto] *sm* (MUS) bow

architet'tare [arkitet'tare] *vt* (*fig: ideare*) to devise; (*: macchinare*) to plan, concoct

archi'tetto [arki'tetto] *sm* architect; **architet'tura** *sf* architecture

ar'chivio [ar'kivjo] *sm* archives *pl*; (INFORM) file

arci'ere [ar'tʃere] *sm* archer

ar'cigno, a [ar'tʃiɲɲo] *ag* grim, severe

arci'vescovo [artʃi'veskovo] *sm* archbishop

'arco (*arma*, MUS) bow; (ARCHIT) arch; (MAT) arch

arcoba'leno *sm* rainbow

arcu'ato, a *ag* curved, bent

ar'dente *ag* burning; (*fig*) burning, ardent

'ardere *vt, vi* to burn

ar'desia *sf* slate

ar'dire *vi* to dare ♦ *sm* daring; **ar'dito, a** *ag* brave, daring, bold; (*sfacciato*) bold

ar'dore *sm* blazing heat; (*fig*) ardour, fervour

'arduo, a *ag* arduous, difficult

'area *sf* area; (EDIL) land, ground

a'rena *sf* arena; (*per corride*) bullring; (*sabbia*) sand

are'narsi *vr* to run aground

areo'plano *sm* = **aeroplano**

'argano *sm* winch

argente'ria [ardʒente'ria] *sf* silverware, silver

Argen'tina [ardʒen'tina] *sf:* **l'~** Argentina; **argen'tino, a** *ag, sm/f* Argentinian

ar'gento [ar'dʒento] *sm* silver; **~ vivo** quicksilver

ar'gilla [ar'dʒilla] *sf* clay

'argine ['ardʒine] *sm* embankment, bank; (*diga*) dyke, dike

argo'mento *sm* argument; (*motivo*) motive; (*materia, tema*) subject

argu'ire *vt* to deduce

ar'guto, a *ag* sharp, quick-witted; **ar'guzia** *sf* wit; (*battuta*) witty remark

'aria *sf* air; (*espressione, aspetto*) air, look; (MUS: *melodia*) tune; (*: di opera*) aria; **mandare all'~** **qc** to ruin o upset sth; **all'~ aperta** in the open (air)

'arido, a *ag* arid

arieggi'are [arjed'dʒare] *vt* (*cambiare aria*) to air; (*imitare*) to imitate

ari'ete *sm* ram; (MIL) battering ram; (*dello zodiaco*): **A~** Aries

a'ringa, ghe *sf* herring *inv*

a'rista *sf* (CUC) chine of pork

aristo'cratico, a, ci, che *ag* aristocratic

arit'metica *sf* arithmetic

arlec'chino [arlek'kino] *sm* harlequin

'arma, i *sf* weapon, arm; (*parte dell'esercito*) arm; **chiamare alle ~i** to call up (BRIT), draft (US); **sotto le ~i** in the army (o forces); **alle ~i!** to arms!; **~ da fuoco** firearm

ar'madio *sm* cupboard; (*per abiti*) wardrobe; **~ a muro** built-in cupboard

armamen'tario *sm* equipment

arma'mento *sm* (MIL) armament; (*: materiale*) arms *pl*, weapons *pl*; (NAUT) fitting out; manning

ar'mare *vt* to arm; (*arma da fuoco*) to cock; (NAUT: *nave*) to rig, fit out; to man; (EDIL: *volta*, *galleria*) to prop up, shore up; **~rsi** *vr* to arm o.s.; (MIL) to take up arms; **ar'mata** *sf* (MIL) army; (NAUT) fleet; **arma'tore** *sm* shipowner

arma'tura *sf* (*struttura di sostegno*) framework; (*impalcatura*) scaffolding; (STORIA) armour *no pl*, suit of armour

armeggi'are [armed'dʒare] *vi*: **~ (intorno a** **qc)** to mess about (with sth)

armis'tizio [armis'tittsjo] *sm* armistice

armo'nia *sf* harmony; **ar'monica, che**

sf (MUS) harmonica; ~ **a bocca** mouth organ; **ar'monico, a, ci, che** *ag* harmonic; (*fig*) harmonious; **armoni'oso, a** *ag* harmonious

armoniz'zare [armonid'dzare] *vt* to harmonize; (*colori, abiti*) to match ♦ *vi* to be in harmony; to match

ar'nese *sm* tool, implement; (*oggetto indeterminato*) thing, contraption; **male in ~** (*malvestito*) badly dressed; (*di salute malferma*) in poor health; (*di condizioni economiche*) down-at-heel

'arnia *sf* hive

a'roma, i *sm* aroma; fragrance; **~i** *smpl* (CUC) herbs and spices;
aromatera'pia *sf* aromatherapy;
aro'matico, a, ci, che *ag* aromatic; (*cibo*) spicy

'arpa *sf* (MUS) harp

ar'peggio [ar'pedd30] *sm* (MUS) arpeggio

ar'pia *sf* (*anche fig*) harpy

arpi'one *sm* (*gancio*) hook; (*cardine*) hinge; (PESCA) harpoon

arrabat'tarsi *vr* to do all one can, strive

arrabbi'are *vi* (*cane*) to be affected with rabies; **~rsi** *vr* (*essere preso dall'ira*) to get angry, fly into a rage; **arrabbi'ato, a** *ag* rabid, with rabies; furious, angry

arraf'fare *vt* to snatch, seize; (*sottrarre*) to pinch

arrampi'carsi *vr* to climb (up)

arran'care *vi* to limp, hobble

arran'giare [arran'dʒare] *vt* to arrange; **~rsi** *vr* to manage, do the best one can

arre'care *vt* to bring; (*causare*) to cause

arreda'mento *sm* (*studio*) interior design; (*mobili etc*) furnishings *pl*

arre'dare *vt* to furnish; **arreda'tore, 'trice** *sm/f* interior designer; **ar'redo** *sm* fittings *pl*, furnishings *pl*

ar'rendersi *vr* to surrender

arres'tare *vt* (*fermare*) to stop, halt;

(*catturare*) to arrest; **~rsi** *vr* (*fermarsi*) to stop; **ar'resto** *sm* (*cessazione*) stopping; (*fermata*) stop; (*cattura*, MED) arrest; **subire un arresto** to come to a stop o standstill; **mettere agli arresti** to place under arrest; **arresti domiciliari** house arrest *sg*

arre'trare *vt, vi* to withdraw;
arre'trato, a *ag* (*lavoro*) behind schedule; (*paese, bambino*) backward; (*numero di giornale*) back *cpd*;
arretrati *smpl* arrears

arric'chire [arrik'kire] *vt* to enrich;
~rsi *vr* to become rich

arricci'are [arrit'tʃare] *vt* to curl

ar'ringa, ghe *sf* harangue; (DIR) address by counsel

arrischi'are [arris'kjare] *vt* to risk; **~rsi** *vr* to venture, dare; **arrischi'ato, a** *ag* risky; (*temerario*) reckless, rash

arri'vare *vi* to arrive; (*accadere*) to happen, occur; **~ a** (*livello, grado etc*) to reach; **lui arriva a Roma alle 7** he gets to o arrives at Rome at 7; **non ci arrivo** I can't reach it; (*fig: non capisco*) I can't understand it

arrive'derci [arrive'dertʃi] *escl* goodbye!

arrive'derla *escl* (*forma di cortesia*) goodbye!

arri'vista, i, e *sm/f* go-getter

ar'rivo *sm* arrival; (SPORT) finish, finishing line

arro'gante *ag* arrogant

arro'lare *vb* = **arruolare**

arros'sire *vi* (*per vergogna, timidezza*) to blush, flush; (*per gioia, rabbia*) to flush

arros'tire *vt* to roast; (*pane*) to toast; (*ai ferri*) to grill

ar'rosto *sm, ag inv* roast

arro'tare *vt* to sharpen; (*investire con un veicolo*) to run over

arroto'lare *vt* to roll up

arroton'dare *vt* (*forma, oggetto*) to round; (*stipendio*) to add to; (*somma*) to round off

arrovel'larsi vr to rack one's brains

arruf'fare vt to ruffle; (fili) to tangle; (fig: questione) to confuse

arrugi'nire vt to rust; (fig) to become rusty; ~**rsi** vr to rust; (fig) to become rusty

arruo'lare vt (MIL) to enlist; ~**rsi** vr to enlist, join up

arse'nale sm (MIL) arsenal; (cantiere navale) dockyard

'arso, a pp di **ardere** ♦ ag (bruciato) burnt; (arido) dry; **ar'sura** sf (calore opprimente) burning heat; (siccità) drought

'arte sf art; (abilità) skill

arte'fatto, a ag (cibo) adulterated; (fig: modi) artificial

ar'tefice sm/f craftsman/woman; (autore) author

ar'teria sf artery

'artico, a, ci, che ag Arctic

artico'lare ag (ANAT) of the joints, articular ♦ vt to articulate; (suddividere) to divide, split up; **articolazi'one** sf articulation; (ANAT, TECN) joint

ar'ticolo sm article; ~ **di fondo** (STAMPA) leader, leading article

'Artide sm: l'~ the Arctic

artifici'ale [artifi'tʃale] ag artificial

arti'ficio [arti'fitʃo] sm (espediente) trick, artifice; (ricerca di effetto) artificiality

artigia'nato [artidʒa'nato] sm craftsmanship; craftsmen pl

artigi'ano, a [arti'dʒano] sm/f craftsman/woman

artiglie'ria [artiʎʎe'ria] sf artillery

ar'tiglio [ar'tiʎʎo] sm claw; (di rapaci) talon

ar'tista, i, e sm/f artist; **ar'tistico, a, ci, che** ag artistic

'arto sm (ANAT) limb

ar'trite sf (MED) arthritis

ar'trosi sf osteoarthritis

ar'zillo, a [ar'dzillo] ag lively, sprightly

a'scella [aʃ'ʃella] sf (ANAT) armpit

ascen'dente [aʃʃen'dɛnte] sm ancestor; (fig) ascendancy; (ASTR) ascendant

ascensi'one [aʃʃen'sjone] sf (ALPINISMO) ascent; (REL): l'A~ the Ascension

ascen'sore [aʃʃen'sore] sm lift

a'scesa [aʃ'ʃesa] sf ascent; (al trono) accession

a'scesso [aʃ'ʃesso] sm (MED) abscess

'ascia [aʃʃa] (pl **'asce**) sf axe

asciugaca'pelli [aʃʃugaka'pelli] sf hair-drier

asciuga'mano [aʃʃuga'mano] sm towel

asciu'gare [aʃʃu'gare] vt to dry; ~**rsi** vr to dry o.s.; (diventare asciutto) to dry

asci'utto, a [aʃ'ʃutto] ag dry; (fig: magro) lean; (: burbero) curt; **restare a bocca ~a** (fig) to be disappointed

ascol'tare vt to listen to; **ascolta'tore, 'trice** sm/f listener; **as'colto** sm: **essere o stare in ascolto** to be listening; **dare o prestare ascolto (a)** to pay attention (to)

as'falto sm asphalt

asfissi'are vt to suffocate

'Asia sf: l'~ Asia; **asi'atico, a, ci, che** ag, sm/f Asiatic, Asian

a'silo sm refuge, sanctuary; ~ **(d'infanzia)** nursery(-school); ~ **nido** crèche; ~ **politico** political asylum

'asino sm donkey, ass

'asma sf asthma

'asola sf buttonhole

as'parago, gi sm asparagus no pl

aspet'tare vt to wait for; (anche COMM) to await; (aspettarsi) to expect ♦ vi to wait; ~**rsi** vr to expect; ~ **un bambino** to be expecting (a baby); **questo non me l'aspettavo** I wasn't expecting this; **aspetta'tiva** sf wait; expectation; **inferiore all'aspettativa** worse than expected; **essere in aspettativa** (AMM) to be on leave of absence

as'petto sm (apparenza) aspect, appearance, look; (punto di vista) point of view; **di bell'~** good-looking

aspi'rante *ag* (*attore etc*) aspiring
♦ *sm/f* candidate, applicant

aspira'polvere *sm inv* vacuum cleaner

aspi'rare *vt* (*respirare*) to breathe in,
inhale; (*sog: apparecchio*) to suck (up)
♦ *vi*: **~ a** to aspire to; **aspira'tore** *sm*
extractor fan

aspi'rina *sf* aspirin

aspor'tare *vt* (*anche* MED) to remove,
take away

'aspro, a *ag* (*sapore*) sour, tart; (*odore*)
acrid, pungent; (*voce, clima, fig*) harsh;
(*superficie*) rough; (*paesaggio*) rugged

assaggi'are [assad'dʒare] *vt* to taste

assag'gini [assad'dʒini] *smpl* (CUC)
selection of first courses

as'sai *av* (*molto*) a lot, much; (: *con ag*)
very; (*a sufficienza*) enough ♦ *ag inv*
(*quantità*) a lot of, much; (*numero*) a
lot of, many; **~ contento** very pleased

assa'lire *vt* to attack, assail

as'salto *sm* attack, assault

assapo'rare *vt* to savour

assassi'nare *vt* to murder; to
assassinate; (*fig*) to ruin; **assas'sinio**
sm murder; assassination; **assas'sino,
a** *ag* murderous ♦ *sm/f* murderer;
assassin

'asse *sm* (TECN) axle; (MAT) axis ♦ *sf*
board; **~ da stiro** ironing board

assedi'are *vt* to besiege; **as'sedio** *sm*
siege

asse'gnare [assen'ɲare] *vt* to assign,
allot; (*premio*) to award

as'segno [as'seɲɲo] *sm* allowance;
(*anche*: **~ bancario**) cheque (BRIT),
check (US); **contro ~** cash on delivery;
~ circolare bank draft; **~ sbarrato**
crossed cheque; **~ di viaggio**
traveller's cheque; **~ a vuoto** dud
cheque; **~i familiari** ≈ child benefit *no
pl*

assem'blea *sf* assembly

assen'nato, a *ag* sensible

as'senso *sm* assent, consent

as'sente *ag* absent; (*fig*) faraway;

vacant; **as'senza** *sf* absence

asses'sore *sm* (POL) councillor

asses'tare *vt* (*mettere in ordine*) to put
in order, arrange; **~si** *vr* to settle in;
~ un colpo a qn to deal sb a blow

asse'tato, a *ag* thirsty, parched

as'setto *sm* order, arrangement; (NAUT,
AER) trim; **in ~ di guerra** on a war
footing

assicu'rare *vt* (*accertare*) to ensure;
(*infondere certezza*) to assure; (*fermare,
legare*) to make fast, secure; (*fare un
contratto di assicurazione*) to insure;
~si *vr* (*accertarsi*): **~si (di)** to make
sure (of); (*contro il furto etc*): **~si
(contro)** to insure o.s. (against);
assicu'rata *sf* (*anche*: *lettera
assicurata*) registered letter;
assicu'rato, a *ag* insured;
assicurazi'one *sf* assurance; insurance

assidera'mento *sm* exposure

as'siduo, a *ag* (*costante*) assiduous;
(*frequentatore etc*) regular

assi'eme *av* (*insieme*) together; **~ a**
(*together*) with

assil'lare *vt* to pester, torment

as'sillo *sm* (*fig*) worrying thought

as'sise *sfpl* (DIR) assizes; **Corte d'A~**
Court of Assizes; ≈ Crown Court (BRIT)

assis'tente *sm/f* assistant; **~ sociale**
social worker; **~ di volo** (AER) steward/
stewardess

assis'tenza [assis'tɛntsa] *sf* assistance;
~ ospedaliera free hospital treatment;
~ sanitaria health service; **~ sociale**
welfare services *pl*

as'sistere *vt* (*aiutare*) to assist, help;
(*curare*) to treat ♦ *vi*: **~ (a qc)** (*essere
presente*) to be present (at sth), to
attend (sth)

'asso *sm* ace; **piantare qn in ~** to
leave sb in the lurch

associ'are [asso'tʃare] *vt* to associate;
~si *vr* to enter into partnership; **~si
a** to become a member of, join; (*dolori,
gioie*) to share in; **~ qn alle carceri** to
take sb to prison

associazi'one [assotʃat'tsjone] *sf* association; (*COMM*) association, society; **~ a delinquere** (*DIR*) criminal association

asso'dato, a *ag* well-founded

assogget'tare [assoddʒet'tare] *vt* to subject, subjugate

asso'lato, a *ag* sunny

assol'dare *vt* to recruit

asso'lto, a *pp di* **assolvere**

assoluta'mente *av* absolutely

asso'luto, a *ag* absolute

assoluzi'one [assolut'tsjone] *sf* (*DIR*) acquittal; (*REL*) absolution

as'solvere *vt* (*DIR*) to acquit; (*REL*) to absolve; (*adempiere*) to carry out, perform

assomigli'are [assomiʎ'ʎare] *vi*: **~ a** to resemble, look like

asson'nato, a *ag* sleepy

asso'pirsi *vr* to doze off

assor'bente *ag* absorbent ♦ *sm*: **~ igienico** sanitary towel; **~ interno** tampon

assor'bire *vt* to absorb

assor'dare *vt* to deafen

assorti'mento *sm* assortment

assor'tito, a *ag* assorted; matched, matching

as'sorto, a *ag* absorbed, engrossed

assottigli'are [assottiʎ'ʎare] *vt* to make thin, to thin; (*aguzzare*) to sharpen; (*ridurre*) to reduce; **~rsi** *vr* to grow thin; (*fig*: *ridursi*) to be reduced

assue'fare *vt* to accustom; **~rsi a** to get used to, accustom o.s. to

as'sumere *vt* (*impiegato*) to take on, engage; (*responsabilità*) to assume, take upon o.s.; (*contegno*, *espressione*) to assume, put on; (*droga*) to consume; **as'sunto, a** *pp di* **assumere** ♦ *sm* (*tesi*) proposition

assur'dità *sf inv* absurdity; **dire delle ~** to talk nonsense

as'surdo, a *ag* absurd

'asta *sf* pole; (*vendita*) auction

astan'te'ria *sf* casualty department

as'temio, a *ag* teetotal ♦ *sm/f* teetotaller

aste'nersi *vr*: **~ (da)** to abstain (from), refrain (from); (*POL*) to abstain (from)

aste'risco, schi *sm* asterisk

'astice ['astitʃe] *sm* lobster

asti'nenza [asti'nɛntsa] *sf* abstinence; **essere in crisi di ~** to suffer from withdrawal symptoms

'astio *sm* rancour, resentment

as'tratto, a *ag* abstract

'astro *sm* star

astro... *prefisso*: **astro'logia** [astrolo'dʒia] *sf* astrology; **as'trologo, a, ghi, ghe** *sm/f* astrologer; **astro'nauta, i, e** *sm/f* astronaut; **astro'nave** *sf* space ship; **astrono'mia** *sf* astronomy; **astro'nomico, a, ci, che** *ag* astronomic(al)

as'tuccio [as'tuttʃo] *sm* case, box, holder

as'tuto, a *ag* astute, cunning, shrewd; **as'tuzia** *sf* astuteness, shrewdness; (*azione*) trick

A'tene *sf* Athens

ate'neo *sm* university

'ateo, a *ag, sm/f* atheist

at'lante *sm* atlas

at'lantico, a, ci, che *ag* Atlantic ♦ *sm*: **l'A~, l'Oceano A~** the Atlantic, the Atlantic Ocean

at'leta, i, e *sm/f* athlete; **at'letica** *sf* athletics *sg*; **atletica leggera** track and field events *pl*; **atletica pesante** weightlifting and wrestling

atmos'fera *sf* atmosphere

a'tomico, a, ci, che *ag* atomic; (*nucleare*) atomic, atom *cpd*, nuclear

'atomo *sm* atom

'atrio *sm* entrance hall, lobby

a'troce [a'trotʃe] *ag* (*che provoca orrore*) dreadful; (*terribile*) atrocious

attacca'mento *sm* (*fig*) attachment, affection

attacca'panni *sm* hook, peg; (*mobile*) hall stand

attac'care vt (unire) to attach; (cucendo) to sew on; (far aderire) to stick (on); (appendere) to hang (up); (assalire: anche fig) to attack; (iniziare) to begin, start; (fig: contagiare) to pass on ♦ vi to stick, adhere; **~rsi** vi to stick, adhere; (trasmettersi per contagio) to be contagious; (afferrarsi): **~rsi (a)** to cling (to); (fig: affezionarsi): **~rsi (a)** to become attached (to); **~ discorso** to start a conversation; **at'tacco, chi** sm (azione offensiva: anche fig) attack; (MED) attack, fit; (SCI) binding; (ELETTR) socket

atteggia'mento [atteddʒa'mento] sm attitude

atteggi'arsi [atted'dʒarsi] vr: **~ a** to pose as

attem'pato, a ag elderly

at'tendere vt to wait for, await ♦ vi: **~ a** to attend to

atten'dibile ag (storia) credible; (testimone) reliable

atte'nersi vr: **~ a** to keep o stick to

atten'tare vi: **~ a** to make an attempt on; **atten'tato** sm attack; **attentato alla vita di qn** attempt on sb's life

at'tento, a ag attentive; (accurato) careful, thorough; **stare ~ a qc** to pay attention to sth; **~!** be careful!

attenu'ante sf (DIR) extenuating circumstance

attenu'are vt to attenuate; (dolore, rumore) to lessen, deaden; (pena, tasse) to alleviate; **~rsi** vi to ease, abate

attenzi'one [atten'tsjone] sf attention; **~!** watch out!, be careful!

atter'raggio [atter'raddʒo] sm landing

atter'rare vt to bring down ♦ vi to land

atter'rire vt to terrify

at'tesa sf waiting; (tempo trascorso aspettando) wait; **essere in attesa di qc** to be waiting for sth

at'teso, a pp di **attendere**

attes'tato sm certificate

'attico, ci sm attic

at'tiguo, a ag adjacent, adjoining

attil'lato, a ag (vestito) close-fitting

'attimo sm moment; **in un ~** in a moment

atti'nente ag: **~ a** relating to, concerning

atti'rare vt to attract

atti'tudine sf (disposizione) aptitude; (atteggiamento) attitude

atti'vare vt to activate; (far funzionare) to set going, start

attivi'tà sf inv activity; (COMM) assets pl

at'tivo, a ag active; (COMM) profit-making, credit cpd ♦ sm (COMM) assets pl; **in ~** in credit

attiz'zare [attit'tsare] vt (fuoco) to poke

'atto sm act; (azione, gesto) action, act, deed; (DIR: documento) deed, document; **~i** smpl (di congressi etc) proceedings; **mettere in ~** to put into action; **fare ~ di fare qc** to make as if to do sth

at'tonito, a ag dumbfounded, astonished

attorcigli'are [attortʃiʎ'ʎare] vt to twist; **~rsi** vr to twist

at'tore, 'trice sm/f actor/actress

at'torno av round, around, about; **~ a** round, around, about

at'tracco, chi sm (NAUT) docking no pl; berth

attra'ente ag attractive

at'trarre vt to attract; **attrat'tiva** sf (fig: fascino) attraction, charm; **at'tratto, a** pp di **attrarre**

attraversa'mento sm: **~ pedonale** pedestrian crossing

attraver'sare vt to cross; (città, bosco, fig: periodo) to go through; (sog: fiume) to run through

attra'verso prep through; (da una parte all'altra) across

attrazi'one [attrat'tsjone] sf attraction

attrez'zare [attret'tsare] vt to equip; (NAUT) to rig; **attrezza'tura** sf equipment no pl; rigging; **at'trezzo**

sm tool, instrument; (*SPORT*) piece of equipment

attribu'ire *vt*: ~ **qc a qn** (*assegnare*) to give o award sth to sb; (*quadro etc*) to attribute sth to sb; **attri'buto** *sm* attribute

at'trice [at'tritʃe] *sf vedi* **attore**

at'trito *sm* (*anche fig*) friction

attu'ale *ag* (*presente*) present; (*di attualità*) topical; (*che è in atto*) actual; **attualità** *sf inv* topicality; (*avvenimento*) current event; **attual'mente** *av* at the moment, at present

attu'are *vt* to carry out; ~**rsi** *vr* to be realized

attu'tire *vt* to deaden, reduce

au'dace [au'datʃe] *ag* audacious, daring, bold; (*provocante*) provocative; (*sfacciato*) impudent, bold; **au'dacia** *sf* audacity, daring, boldness; provocativeness; impudence

audiovi'sivo, a *ag* audiovisual

audizi'one [audit'tsjone] *sf* hearing; (*MUS*) audition

'auge ['audʒe] *sf*: **in ~** popular

augu'rare *vt* to wish; ~**rsi qc** to hope for sth

au'gurio *sm* (*presagio*) omen; (*voto di benessere etc*) (good) wish; **essere di buon/cattivo ~** to be of good omen/ be ominous; **fare gli ~i a qn** to give sb one's best wishes; **tanti ~i!** all the best!

'aula *sf* (*scolastica*) classroom; (*universitaria*) lecture theatre; (*di edificio pubblico*) hall

aumen'tare *vt, vi* to increase; **au'mento** *sm* increase

au'reola *sf* halo

au'rora *sf* dawn

ausili'are *ag, sm, sm/f* auxiliary

aus'picio [aus'pitʃo] *sm* omen; (*protezione*) patronage; **sotto gli ~i di** under the auspices of

aus'tero, a *ag* austere

Aus'tralia *sf*: **l'~** Australia;

australi'ano, a *ag, sm/f* Australian

'Austria *sf*: **l'~** Austria; **aus'triaco, a, ci, che** *ag, sm/f* Austrian

au'tentico, a, ci, che *ag* authentic, genuine

au'tista, i *sm* driver

'auto *sm inv* car

autoade'sivo, a *ag* self-adhesive ♦ *sm* sticker

autobiogra'fia *sf* autobiography

auto'botte *sf* tanker

'autobus *sm inv* bus

auto'carro *sm* lorry (*BRIT*), truck

autocorri'era *sf* coach, bus

au'tografo, a *ag, sm* autograph

auto'grill ® *sm inv* motorway restaurant

autogrù *sf inv* breakdown van

auto'linea *sf* bus company

au'toma, i *sm* automaton

auto'matico, a, ci, che *ag* automatic ♦ *sm* (*bottone*) snap fastener; (*fucile*) automatic

automazi'one [automat'tsjone] *sf* automation

auto'mezzo [auto'meddzo] *sm* motor vehicle

automo'bile *sf* (motor) car

automobi'lista, i, e *sm/f* motorist

autono'leggio *sm* car hire

autono'mia *sf* autonomy; (*di volo*) range

au'tonomo, a *ag* autonomous, independent

autop'sia *sf* post-mortem, autopsy

auto'radio *sf inv* (*apparecchio*) car radio; (*autoveicolo*) radio car

au'tore, 'trice *sm/f* author

auto'revole *ag* authoritative; (*persona*) influential

autori'messa *sf* garage

autorità *sf inv* authority

autoriz'zare [autorid'dzare] *vt* (*permettere*) to authorize; (*giustificare*) to allow, sanction; **autorizzazi'one** *sf* authorization

autoscu'ola *sf* driving school

autos'top sm hitchhiking;
autostop'pista, i, e smf hitchhiker

autos'trada sf motorway (BRIT), highway (US)

auto'treno sm articulated lorry (BRIT), semi (trailer) (US)

autove'icolo sm motor vehicle

auto'velox ® sm inv (police) speed camera

autovet'tura sf (motor) car

au'tunno sm autumn

avam'braccio [avam'brattʃo] (pl (f) -cia) sm forearm

avangu'ardia sf vanguard

a'vanti av (stato in luogo) in front; (moto: andare, venire) forward; (tempo: prima) before ♦ prep (luogo): **~ a** before, in front of; (tempo): **~ Cristo** before Christ ♦ escl (entrate) come (o go) in!; (MIL) forward!; (coraggio) come on! ♦ sm inv (SPORT) forward; **~ e indietro** backwards and forwards; **andare ~** to go forward; (continuare) to go on; (precedere) to go (on) ahead; (orologio) to be fast; **essere ~ negli studi** to be well advanced with one's studies

avanza'mento [avantsa'mento] sm progress; promotion

avan'zare [avan'tsare] vt (spostare in avanti) to move forward, advance; (domanda) to put forward; (promuovere) to promote; (essere creditore): **~ qc da qn** to be owed sth by sb ♦ vi (andare avanti) to move forward, advance; (progredire) to make progress; (essere d'avanzo) to be left, remain; **avan'zata** sf (MIL) advance;
a'vanzo sm (residuo) remains pl, leftovers pl; (MAT) remainder, (COMM) surplus; **averne d'avanzo di qc** to have more than enough of sth; **avanzo di galera** jailbird

ava'ria sf (guasto) damage; (: meccanico) breakdown

a'varo, a ag avaricious, miserly ♦ sm miser

a'vena sf oats pl

a'vere sm (COMM) credit; **gli ~i** (ricchezze) wealth sg
♦ vt **1** (possedere) to have; **ha due bambini/una bella casa** she has (got) two children/a lovely house; **ha i capelli lunghi** he has (got) long hair; **non ho da mangiare/bere** I've (got) nothing to eat/drink, I don't have anything to eat/drink

2 (indossare) to wear, have on; **aveva una maglietta rossa** he was wearing o he had on a red tee-shirt; **ha gli occhiali** he wears o has glasses

3 (ricevere) to get; **hai avuto l'assegno?** did you get o have you had the cheque?

4 (età, dimensione) to be; **ha 9 anni** he is 9 (years old); **la stanza ha 3 metri di lunghezza** the room is 3 metres in length; **vedi fame; paura** etc

5 (tempo): **quanti ne abbiamo oggi?** what's the date today?; **ne hai per molto?** will you be long?

6 (fraseologia): **avercela con qn** to be angry with sb; **cos'hai?** what's wrong o what's the matter (with you)?; **non ha niente a che vedere o fare con me** it's got nothing to do with me
♦ vb aus **1** to have; **aver bevuto/mangiato** to have drunk/eaten

2 (+da +infinito): **~ da fare qc** to have to do sth; **non hai che da chiederlo** you only have to ask him

'avi smpl ancestors, forefathers

aviazi'one [avjat'tsjone] sf aviation; (MIL) air force

avidità sf eagerness; greed

'avido, a ag eager; (peg) greedy

avo'cado sm avocado

a'vorio sm ivory

Avv. abbr = **avvocato**

avvalla'mento sm sinking no pl; (effetto) depression

avvalo'rare vt to confirm

avvam'pare vi (incendio) to flare up

avvantaggi'are [avvantad'dʒare] vt to favour; **~rsi** vr: **~rsi negli affari/sui concorrenti** to get ahead in business/of one's competitors

avvele'nare vt to poison

avve'nente ag attractive, charming

avveni'mento sm event

avve'nire vi, vb impers to happen, occur ♦ sm future

avven'tarsi vr: **~ su** o **contro qn/qc** to hurl o.s. o rush at sb/sth

avven'tato, a ag rash, reckless

avven'tizio, a [avven'tittsjo] ag (impiegato) temporary; (guadagno) casual

av'vento sm advent, coming; (REL): **l'A~** Advent

avven'tore sm (regular) customer

avven'tura sf adventure; (amorosa) affair

avventu'rarsi vr to venture

avventu'roso, a ag adventurous

avve'rarsi vr to come true

av'verbio sm adverb

avver'sario, a ag opposing ♦ sm opponent, adversary

av'verso, a ag (contrario) contrary; (sfavorevole) unfavourable

avver'tenza [avver'tentsa] sf (ammonimento) warning; (cautela) care; (premessa) foreword; **~e** sfpl (istruzioni per l'uso) instructions

avverti'mento sm warning

avver'tire vt (avvisare) to warn; (rendere consapevole) to inform, notify; (percepire) to feel

av'vezzo, a [av'vettso] ag: **~ a** used to

avvi'are vt (mettere sul cammino) to direct; (impresa, trattative) to begin, start; (motore) to start; **~rsi** vr to set off, set out

avvicen'darsi [avvitʃen'darsi] vr to alternate

avvici'nare [avvitʃi'nare] vt to bring near; (trattare con: persona) to approach; **~rsi** vr: **~rsi (a qn/qc)** to approach (sb/sth), draw near (to sb/sth)

avvi'lire vt (umiliare) to humiliate; (degradare) to disgrace; (scoraggiare) to dishearten, discourage; **~rsi** vr (abbattersi) to lose heart

avvilup'pare vt (avvolgere) to wrap up

avvinaz'zato, a [avvinat'tsato] ag drunk

avvin'cente [avvin'tʃente] ag captivating

av'vincere [av'vintʃere] vt to charm, enthral

avvinghi'are [avvin'gjare] vt to clasp; **~rsi** vr: **~rsi a** to cling to

avvi'sare vt (far sapere) to inform; (mettere in guardia) to warn; **av'viso** sm warning; (annuncio) announcement; (: affisso) notice; (inserzione pubblicitaria) advertisement; **a mio avviso** in my opinion; **avviso di chiamata** (TEL) call waiting service

avvis'tare vt to sight

avvi'tare vt to screw down (o in)

avviz'zire [avvit'tsire] vi to wither

avvo'cato, 'essa sm/f (DIR) barrister (BRIT), lawyer; (fig) defender, advocate

av'volgere [av'voldʒere] vt to roll up; (avviluppare) to wrap up; **~rsi** vr (avvilupparsi) to wrap o.s. up; **avvol'gibile** sm roller blind (BRIT), blind

avvol'toio sm vulture

azi'enda [ad'dzjenda] sf business, firm, concern; **~ agricola** farm

azio'nare [attsjo'nare] vt to activate

azi'one [at'tsjone] sf action; (COMM) share; **azio'nista, i, e** sm/f (COMM) shareholder

a'zoto [ad'dzoto] sm nitrogen

azzan'nare [attsan'nare] vt to sink one's teeth into

azzar'darsi [addzar'darsi] vr: **~ a fare** to dare (to) do; **azzar'dato, a** ag (*impresa*) risky; (*risposta*) rash

az'zardo [ad'dzardo] *sm* risk

azzec'care |attsek'kare| *vt* (*risposta etc*) to get right

azzuf'farsi |attsuf'farsi| *vr* to come to blows

az'zurro, a [ad'dzurro] *ag* blue ♦ *sm* (*colore*) blue; **gli ~i** (SPORT) the Italian national team

B, b

bab'beo *sm* simpleton

'babbo *sm* (*fam*) dad, daddy; **B~ Natale** Father Christmas

bab'buccia, ce |bab'buttʃa| *sf* slipper; (*per neonati*) bootee

ba'bordo *sm* (NAUT) port side

ba'cato, a *ag* worm-eaten, rotten

'bacca, che *sf* berry

baccalà *sm* dried salted cod; (*fig: peg*) dummy

bac'cano *sm* din, clamour

bac'cello |bat'tʃɛllo| *sm* pod

bac'chetta |bak'ketta| *sf* (*verga*) stick, rod; (*di direttore d'orchestra*) baton; (*di tamburo*) drumstick; **~ magica** magic wand

baci'are |ba'tʃare| *vt* to kiss; **~rsi** *vr* to kiss (one another)

baci'nella |batʃi'nɛlla| *sf* basin

ba'cino |ba'tʃino| *sm* basin; (MINERALOGIA) field, bed; (ANAT) pelvis; (NAUT) dock

'bacio |'batʃo| *sm* kiss

'baco, chi *sm* worm; **~ da seta** silkworm

ba'dare *vi* (*fare attenzione*) to take care, be careful; (*occuparsi di*): **~ a** to look after, take care of; (*dar ascolto*): **~ a** to pay attention to; **bada ai fatti tuoi!** mind your own business!

ba'dia *sf* abbey

ba'dile *sm* shovel

'baffi *smpl* moustache *sg*; (*di animale*) whiskers; **ridere sotto i ~** to laugh up

one's sleeve; **leccarsi i ~** to lick one's lips

ba'gagli [ba'gaʎʎi] *smpl* luggage *sg*; **fare i ~** to pack

bagagli'aio [bagaʎ'ʎajo] *sm* luggage van (BRIT) o car (US); (AUT) boot (BRIT), trunk (US)

bagli'ore |baʎ'ʎore| *sm* flash, dazzling light; **un ~ di speranza** a ray of hope

ba'gnante |baɲ'ɲante| *sm/f* bather

ba'gnare |baɲ'ɲare| *vt* to wet; (*inzuppare*) to soak; (*innaffiare*) to water; (*sog: fiume*) to wash, bathe; **~rsi** *vr* to get wet; (*al mare*) to go swimming o bathing; (*in vasca*) to have a bath

ba'gnato, a |baɲ'ɲato| *ag* wet

ba'gnino |baɲ'ɲino| *sm* lifeguard

'bagno ['baɲɲo] *sm* bath; (*locale*) bathroom; **~i** *smpl* (*stabilimento*) baths; **fare il ~** to have a bath; (*nel mare*) to go swimming o bathing; **fare il ~ a qn** to give sb a bath; **mettere a ~** to soak; **~ schiuma** bubble bath

bagnoma'ria |baɲɲoma'ria| *sm*: **cuocere a ~** to cook in a double saucepan

'baia *sf* bay

baio'netta *sf* bayonet

balbet'tare *vi* to stutter, stammer; (*bimbo*) to babble ♦ *vt* to stammer out

balbuzi'ente |balbut'tsjɛnte| *ag* stuttering, stammering

bal'cone *sm* balcony

baldac'chino |baldak'kino| *sm* canopy

bal'danza |bal'dantsa| *sf* self-confidence

'baldo, a *ag* bold, daring

bal'doria *sf*: **fare ~** to have a riotous time

ba'lena *sf* whale

bale'nare *vb impers*: **balena** there's lightning ♦ *vi* to flash; **mi balenò un'idea** an idea flashed through my mind; **ba'leno** *sm* flash of lightning; **in un baleno** in a flash

ba'lestra sf crossbow

ba'lia sf: **in ~ di** at the mercy of

'balla sf (di merci) bale; (fandonia) (tall) story

bal'lare vt, vi to dance; **bal'lata** sf ballad

balle'rina sf dancer; ballet dancer; (scarpa) ballet shoe

balle'rino sm dancer; ballet dancer

bal'letto sm ballet

'ballo sm dance; (azione) dancing no pl; **essere in ~** (fig: persona) to be involved; (: cosa) to be at stake

ballot'taggio [ballot'taddʒo] sm (POL) second ballot

balne'are ag seaside cpd; (stagione) bathing

balneazi'one sf bathing; **è vietata la ~** bathing strictly prohibited

ba'locco, chi sm toy

ba'lordo, a ag stupid, senseless

'balsamo sm (aroma) balsam; (lenimento, fig) balm

balu'ardo sm bulwark

'balza ['baltsa] sf (dirupo) crag; (di stoffa) frill

bal'zare [bal'tsare] vi to bounce; (lanciarsi) to jump, leap; **'balzo** sm bounce; jump, leap; (del terreno) crag

bam'bagia [bam'badʒa] sf (ovatta) cotton wool (BRIT), absorbent cotton (US); (cascame) cotton waste

bam'bina ag, sf vedi **bambino**

bambi'naia sf nanny, nurse(maid)

bam'bino, a sm/f child

bam'boccio [bam'bottʃo] sm plump child; (pupazzo) rag doll

'bambola sf doll

bambù sm bamboo

ba'nale ag banal, commonplace

ba'nana sf banana; **ba'nano** sm banana tree

'banca, che sf bank; **~ dei dati** data bank

banca'rella sf stall

ban'cario, a ag banking, bank cpd ♦ sm bank clerk

banca'rotta sf bankruptcy; **fare ~** to go bankrupt

ban'chetto [ban'ketto] sm banquet

banchi'ere [ban'kjere] sm banker

ban'china [ban'kina] sf (di porto) quay; (per pedoni, ciclisti) path; (di stazione) platform; **~ cedevole** (AUT) soft verge (BRIT) o shoulder (US)

'banco, chi sm bench; (di negozio) counter; (di mercato) stall; (di officina) (work-)bench; (GEO, banca) bank; **~ di corallo** coral reef; **~ degli imputati** dock; **~ dei pegni** pawnshop; **~ di nebbia** bank of fog; **~ di prova** (fig) testing ground; **~ dei testimoni** witness box

'Bancomat ® sm inv automated banking; (tessera) cash card

banco'nota sf banknote

'banda sf band; (di stoffa) band, stripe; (lato, parte) side; **~ perforata** punch tape

banderu'ola sf (METEOR) weathercock

bandi'era sf flag, banner

ban'dire vt to proclaim; (esiliare) to exile; (fig) to dispense with

ban'dito sm outlaw, bandit

bandi'tore sm (di aste) auctioneer

'bando sm proclamation; (esilio) exile, banishment; **~ alle chiacchiere!** that's enough talk!

'bandolo sm: **il ~ della matassa** (fig) the key to the problem

bar sm inv bar

'bara sf coffin

ba'racca, che sf shed, hut; (peg) hovel; **mandare avanti la ~** to keep things going

bara'onda sf hubbub, bustle

ba'rare vi to cheat

'baratro sm abyss

barat'tare vt: **~ qc con** to barter sth for, swap sth for; **ba'ratto** sm barter

ba'rattolo sm (di latta) tin; (di vetro) jar; (di coccio) pot

'barba sf beard; **farsi la ~** to shave; **farla in ~ a qn** (fig) to do sth to sb's

face; **che ~!** what a bore!
barbi'etola sf beetroot (BRIT), beet (US); **~ da zucchero** sugar beet
bar'barico, a, ci, che ag barbarian; barbaric
'**barbaro, a** ag barbarous; **~i** smpl barbarians
barbi'ere sm barber
bar'bone sm (cane) poodle; (vagabondo) tramp
bar'buto, a ag bearded
'**barca, che** sf boat; **~ a remi** rowing boat; **~ a vela** sail(ing) boat; **barcai'olo** sm boatman
barcol'lare vi to stagger
bar'cone sm (per ponti di barche) pontoon
ba'rella sf (lettiga) stretcher
ba'rile sm barrel, cask
ba'rista, i, e sm/f barman/maid; (proprietario) bar owner
ba'ritono sm baritone
bar'lume sm glimmer, gleam
ba'rocco, a, chi, che ag, sm baroque
ba'rometro sm barometer
ba'rone sm baron; **baro'nessa** sf baroness
'**barra** sf bar; (NAUT) helm; (linea grafica) line, stroke
barri'care vt to barricade; **barri'cata** sf barricade
barri'era sf barrier; (GEO) reef
ba'ruffa sf scuffle
barzel'letta [bardzel'letta] sf joke, funny story
ba'sare vt to base, found; **~rsi** vi: **~rsi su** (sog: fatti, prove) to be based o founded on; (: persona) to base one's arguments on
'**basco, a, schi, sche** ag Basque ♦ sm (copricapo) beret
'**base** sf base; (fig: fondamento) basis; (POL) rank and file; **di ~** basic; **in ~ a** on the basis of, according to; **a ~ di caffè** coffee-based
ba'setta sf sideburn
ba'silica, che sf basilica

ba'silico sm basil
bassi'fondi smpl: **i ~** the slums
'**basso, a** ag low; (di statura) short; (meridionale) southern ♦ sm bottom, lower part; (MUS) bass; **la ~a Italia** southern Italy
bassorili'evo sm bas-relief
'**basta** escl (that's) enough!, that will do!
bas'tardo, a ag (animale, pianta) hybrid, crossbreed; (persona) illegitimate, bastard (peg) ♦ sm/f illegitimate child, bastard (peg)
bas'tare vi, vb impers to be enough, be sufficient; **~ a qn** to be enough for sb; **basta chiedere** o **che chieda a un vigile** you have only to o need only ask a policeman
basti'mento sm ship, vessel
basto'nare vt to beat, thrash
baston'cino [baston'tʃino] sm (SCI) ski pole; **~i di pesce** fish fingers
bas'tone sm stick; **~ da passeggio** walking stick
bat'taglia [bat'taʎʎa] sf battle; fight
bat'taglio [bat'taʎʎo] sm (di campana) clapper; (di porta) knocker
battagli'one [battaʎ'ʎone] sm battalion
bat'tello sm boat
bat'tente sm (imposta: di porta) wing, flap; (: di finestra) shutter; (batacchio: di porta) knocker; (: di orologio) hammer; **chiudere i ~i** (fig) to shut up shop
'**battere** vt to beat; (grano) to thresh; (percorrere) to scour ♦ vi (bussare) to knock; (urtare): **~ contro** to hit o strike against; (pioggia, sole) to beat down; (cuore) to beat; (TENNIS) to serve; **~rsi** vr to fight; **~ le mani** to clap; **~ i piedi** to stamp one's feet; **~ a macchina** to type; **~ bandiera italiana** to fly the Italian flag; **~ in testa** (AUT) to knock; **in un batter d'occhio** in the twinkling of an eye
bat'teri smpl bacteria
batte'ria sf battery; (MUS) drums pl

bat'tesimo sm (rito) baptism; christening

battez'zare [batted'dzare] vt to baptize; to christen

batti'cuore sm palpitations pl

batti'mano sm applause

batti'panni sm inv carpet-beater

batti'stero sm baptistry

battis'trada sm inv (di pneumatico) tread; (di gara) pacemaker

battitap'peto sm vacuum cleaner

'battito sm beat, throb; ~ **cardiaco** heartbeat

bat'tuta sf blow; (di macchina da scrivere) stroke; (MUS) bar; beat; (TEATRO) cue; (frase spiritosa) witty remark; (di caccia) beating; (POLIZIA) combing, scouring; (TENNIS) service

ba'ule sm trunk; (AUT) boot (BRIT), trunk (US)

'bava sf (di animale) slaver, slobber; (di lumaca) slime; (di vento) breath

bava'glino [bavaʎ'ʎino] sm bib

ba'vaglio [ba'vaʎʎo] sm gag

'bavero sm collar

Bavi'era sf Bavaria

ba'zar [bad'dzar] sm inv bazaar

baz'zecola [bad'dzekola] sf trifle

bazzi'care [battsi'kare] vt to frequent
♦ vi: ~ **in/con** to frequent

be'ato, a ag blessed; (fig) happy; ~ **te!** lucky you!

bebè sm inv baby

bec'caccia, ce [bek'kattʃa] sf woodcock

bec'care vt to peck; (fig: raffreddore) to catch; **~rsi qc** to catch sth

bec'cata sf peck

beccheggi'are [bekked'dʒare] vi to pitch

bec'chino [bek'kino] sm gravedigger

'becco, chi sm beak, bill; (di caffettiera etc) spout; lip

Be'fana sf old woman who, according to legend, brings children their presents at the Epiphany; (Epifania) Epiphany; (donna brutta): **b~** hag, witch

'beffa sf practical joke; **farsi ~e di qn** to make a fool of sb; **bef'fardo, a** ag scornful, mocking; **bef'fare** vt (anche: **beffarsi di**) to make a fool of, mock

'bega, ghe sf quarrel

begli ['beʎʎi] ag vedi **bello**

'bei ag vedi **bello**

bel ag vedi **bello**

be'lare vi to bleat

'belga, gi, ghe ag, sm/f Belgian

'Belgio ['beldʒo] sm: **il ~** Belgium

bel'lezza [bel'lettsa] sf beauty

'bella sf (SPORT) decider; vedi anche **bello**

PAROLA CHIAVE

'bello, a (ag: dav sm **bel** +C, **bell'** +V, **bello** +s impura, gn, pn, ps, x, z, pl **bei** +C, **begli** +s impura etc o V) ag **1** (oggetto, donna, paesaggio) beautiful, lovely; (uomo) handsome; (tempo) beautiful, fine, lovely; **le belle arti** fine arts

2 (quantità): **una ~a cifra** a considerable sum of money; **un bel niente** absolutely nothing

3 (rafforzativo): **è una truffa ~a e buona!** it's a real fraud!; **è bell'e finito** it's already finished

♦ sm **1** (bellezza) beauty; (tempo) fine weather

2: **adesso viene il ~** now comes the best bit; **sul più ~** at the crucial point; **cosa fai di ~?** are you doing anything interesting?

♦ av: **fa ~** the weather is fine, it's fine

'belva sf wild animal

belve'dere sm inv panoramic viewpoint

benché [ben'ke] cong although

'benda sf bandage; (per gli occhi) blindfold; **ben'dare** vt to bandage; to blindfold

'bene av well; (completamente, affatto): **è ben difficile** it's very difficult ♦ ag inv: **gente ~** well-to-do people ♦ sm good; **~i** smpl (averi) property sg, estate sg; **io sto ~/poco ~** I'm well/ not very well; **va ~** all right; **volere un ~ dell'anima a qn** to love sb very much; **un uomo per ~** a respectable man; **fare ~ a** to do the right thing; **fare ~ a** (salute) to be good for; **fare del ~ a qn** to do sb a good turn; **~i di consumo** consumer goods

bene'detto, a pp di **benedire** ♦ ag blessed, holy

bene'dire vt to bless; to consecrate; **benedizi'one** sf blessing

benedu'cato, a ag well-mannered

benefi'cenza [benefi'tʃɛntsa] sf charity

bene'ficio [bene'fitʃo] sm benefit; **con ~ d'inventario** (fig) with reservations

be'nefico, a, ci, che ag beneficial; charitable

beneme'renza [beneme'rɛntsa] sf merit

bene'merito, a ag meritorious

be'nessere sm well-being

benes'tante ag well-to-do

benes'tare sm consent, approval

be'nevolo, a ag benevolent

be'nigno, a [be'niɲɲo] ag kind, kindly; (critica etc) favourable; (MED) benign

benin'teso av of course

bensì cong but (rather)

benve'nuto, a ag, sm welcome; **dare il ~ a qn** to welcome sb

ben'zina [ben'dzina] sf petrol (BRIT), gas (US); **fare ~** to get petrol (BRIT) or gas (US); **~ verde** unleaded (petrol);

benzi'naio sm petrol o gas (US) pump attendant

'bere vt to drink; **darla a ~ a qn** (fig) to fool sb

ber'lina sf (AUT) saloon (car) (BRIT), sedan (US)

Ber'lino sm Berlin

ber'noccolo sm bump; (inclinazione) flair

ber'retto sm cap

bersagli'are [bersaʎ'ʎare] vt to shoot at (colpire ripetutamente, fig) to bombard

ber'saglio [ber'saʎʎo] sm target

bes'temmia sf curse; (REL) blasphemy

bestemmi'are vi to curse, swear; to blaspheme ♦ vt to curse, swear at; to blaspheme

'bestia sf animal; **andare in ~** (fig) to fly into a rage; **besti'ale** ag beastly; animal cpd; (fam): **fa un freddo bestiale** it's bitterly cold; **besti'ame** sm livestock; (bovino) cattle pl

'bettola (peg) sf dive

be'tulla sf birch

be'vanda sf drink, beverage

bevi'tore, 'trice sm/f drinker

be'vuta sf drink

be'vuto, a pp di **bere**

bi'ada sf fodder

bianche'ria [bjanke'ria] sf linen; **~ intima** underwear; **~ da donna** ladies' underwear, lingerie

bi'anco, a, chi, che ag white; (non scritto) blank ♦ sm white; (intonaco) whitewash ♦ sm/f white, white man/ woman; in **~** (foglio, assegno) blank; (notte) sleepless; in **~ e nero** (TV, FOT) black and white; **mangiare in ~** to follow a bland diet; **pesce in ~** boiled fish; **andare in ~** (non riuscire) to fail; **~ dell'uovo** egg-white

biasi'mare vt to disapprove of, censure; **bi'asimo** sm disapproval, censure

'bibbia sf (anche fig) bible

bibe'ron sm inv feeding bottle

'bibita sf (soft) drink

biblio'teca, che sf library; (mobile)

bookcase; **bibliote'cario, a** *sm/f* librarian

bicarbo'nato *sm*: ~ **(di sodio)** bicarbonate (of soda)

bicchi'ere [bik'kjɛre] *sm* glass

bici'cletta [bitʃi'kletta] *sf* bicycle; **andare in** ~ to cycle

bidé *sm inv* bidet

bi'dello, a *sm/f* (INS) janitor

bi'done *sm* drum, can; (*anche*: ~ *dell'immondizia*) (dust)bin; (*fam*: *truffa*) swindle; **fare un ~ a qn** (*fam*) to let sb down; **to cheat sb**

bien'nale *ag* biennial

<table><tr><td>Biennale di Venezia</td></tr></table>

The Biennale di Venezia is an international contemporary art festival, which takes place every two years at Giardini. In its current form, it includes exhibits from the countries taking part, a thematic exhibition and a section for young artists.

bi'ennio *sm* period of two years

bi'etola *sf* beet

bifor'carsi *vr* to fork; **biforcazi'one** *sf* fork

bighello'nare [bigelo'nare] *vi* to loaf (about)

bigiotte'ria [bidʒotte'ria] *sf* costume jewellery; (*negozio*) jeweller's (*selling only costume jewellery*)

bigli'ardo [biʎ'ʎardo] *sm* = **biliardo**

bigliet'taio, a *sm/f* (*in treno*) ticket inspector; (*in autobus*) conductor

bigliette'ria [biʎʎette'ria] *sf* (*di stazione*) ticket office; booking office; (*di teatro*) box office

bigli'etto [biʎ'ʎetto] *sm* (*per viaggi, spettacoli etc*) ticket; (*cartoncino*) card; (*anche*: ~ *di banca*) (bank)note; ~ **d'auguri/da visita** greetings/ visiting card; ~ **d'andata e ritorno** return (ticket), round-trip ticket (US)

bignè [biɲ'ɲe] *sm inv* cream puff

bigo'dino *sm* roller, curler

bi'gotto, a *ag* over-pious ♦ *sm/f* church fiend

bi'lancia, ce [bi'lantʃa] *sf* (*pesa*) scales *pl*; (: *di precisione*) balance; (*dello zodiaco*): **B~** Libra; ~ **commerciale/ dei pagamenti** balance of trade/ payments; **bilanci'are** *vt* (*pesare*) to weigh; (: *fig*) to weigh up; (*pareggiare*) to balance

bi'lancio [bi'lantʃo] *sm* (COMM) balance (-sheet); (*statale*) budget; **fare il ~ di** (*fig*) to assess; ~ **consuntivo** (final) balance; ~ **preventivo** budget

'bile *sf* bile; (*fig*) rage, anger

bili'ardo *sm* billiards *sg*; billiard table

'bilico, chi *sm*: **essere in** ~ to be balanced; **tenere qn in** ~ (*fig*) to keep sb in suspense

bi'lingue *ag* bilingual

bili'one *sm* (*mille milioni*) thousand million; (*milione di milioni*) billion (BRIT), trillion (US)

'bimbo, a *sm/f* little boy/girl

bimen'sile *ag* fortnightly

bimes'trale *ag* two-monthly, bimonthly

bi'nario, a *ag* (*sistema*) binary ♦ *sm* (*railway*) track o line; (*piattaforma*) platform; ~ **morto** dead-end track

bi'nocolo *sm* binoculars *pl*

bio... *prefisso*: **bio'chimica** [bio'kimika] *sf* biochemistry; **biodegra'dabile** *ag* biodegradable; **biogra'fia** *sf* biography; **biolo'gia** *sf* biology; **bio'logico, a, ci, che** *ag* biological

bi'ondo, a *ag* blond, fair

bir'bante *sm* rogue, rascal

biri'chino, a [biri'kino] *ag* mischievous ♦ *sf* scamp, little rascal

bi'rillo *sm* skittle (BRIT), pin (US); ~i *smpl* (*gioco*) skittles *sg* (BRIT), bowling (US)

'biro ® *sf inv* biro ®

'birra *sf* beer; **a tutta** ~ (*fig*) at top speed; **birra chiara** ≈ lager; **birra scura** ≈ stout; **birre'ria** *sf* ≈ bierkeller

bis escl, sm inv encore

bis'betico, a, ci, che ag ill-tempered, crabby

bisbigli'are [bizbiʎ'ʎare] vt, vi to whisper

'bisca, sche sf gambling-house

'biscia, sce ['biʃʃa] sf snake; **~ d'acqua** grass snake

bis'cotto sm biscuit

bises'tile ag: **anno ~** leap year

bis'lungo, a, ghi, ghe ag oblong

bis'nonno, a sm/f great grandfather/ grandmother

biso'gnare [bizoɲ'ɲare] vb impers: **bisogna che tu parta/lo faccia** you'll have to go/do it; **bisogna parlargli** we'll (o I'll) have to talk to him

bi'sogno [bi'zoɲɲo] sm need; ~ i smpl: **fare i propri ~i** to relieve o.s.; **avere ~ di qc/di fare qc** to need sth/to do sth; **al ~, in caso di ~** if need be; **biso'gnoso, a** ag needy, poor; **bisognoso di** in need of, needing

bis'tecca, che sf steak, beefsteak

bisticci'are [bistit'tʃare] vi to quarrel, bicker; **~rsi** vr to quarrel, bicker; **bis'ticcio** sm quarrel, squabble; (gioco di parole) pun

'bisturi sm scalpel

bi'sunto, a ag very greasy

'bitter sm inv bitters pl

bi'vacco, chi sm bivouac

'bivio sm fork; (fig) dilemma

'bizza ['biddza] sf tantrum; **fare le ~e** (bambino) to be naughty

biz'zarro, a [bid'dzarro] ag bizarre, strange

biz'zeffe [bid'dzeffe]: **a ~** av in plenty, galore

blan'dire vt to soothe; to flatter

'blando, a ag mild, gentle

bla'sone sm coat of arms

blate'rare vi to chatter

blin'dato, a ag armoured

bloc'care vt to block; (isolare) to isolate, cut off; (porto) to blockade; (prezzi, beni) to freeze; (meccanismo) to jam; **~rsi** vr (motore) to stall; (freni, porta) to jam, stick; (ascensore) to stop, get stuck

bloc'chetto [blok'ketto] sm notebook; (di biglietti) book

'blocco, chi sm block; (MIL) blockade; (dei fitti) restriction; (quadernetto) pad; (fig: unione) coalition; (il bloccare) blocking; isolating, cutting-off; blockading; freezing; jamming; **in ~** (nell'insieme) as a whole; (COMM) in bulk; **~ cardiaco** cardiac arrest

blu ag inv, sm dark blue

'blusa sf (camiciotto) smock; (camicetta) blouse

'boa sm inv (ZOOL) boa constrictor; (sciarpa) feather boa ♦ sf buoy

bo'ato sm rumble, roar

bo'bina sf reel, spool; (di pellicola) spool; (di film) reel; (ELETTR) coil

'bocca, che sf mouth; **in ~ al lupo!** good luck!

boc'caccia, ce [bok'kattʃa] sf (malalingua) gossip; **fare le ~ce** to pull faces

boc'cale sm jug; **~ da birra** tankard

boc'cetta [bot'tʃetta] sf small bottle

boccheggi'are [bokked'dʒare] vi to gasp

boc'chino [bok'kino] sm (di sigaretta, sigaro: cannella) cigarette-holder; cigar-holder; (di pipa, strumenti musicali) mouthpiece

'boccia, ce ['bottʃa] sf bottle; (da vino) decanter, carafe; (palla) bowl; **gioco delle ~ce** bowls sg

bocci'are [bot'tʃare] vt (proposta, progetto) to reject; (INS) to fail; (BOCCE) to hit; **boccia'tura** sf failure

bocci'olo [bot'tʃolo] sm bud

boc'cone sm mouthful, morsel

boc'coni av face downwards

'boia sm inv executioner; hangman

boi'ata sf botch

boicot'tare vt to boycott

'bolide sm meteor; **come un ~** like a

flash, at top speed

'bolla sf bubble; (MED) blister; **~ papale** papal bull; **~ di consegna** (COMM) delivery note

bol'lare vt to stamp; (fig) to brand

bol'lente ag boiling; boiling hot

bol'letta sf bill; (ricevuta) receipt; **essere in ~** to be hard up

bol'lettino sm bulletin; (COMM) note; **~ meteorologico** weather report; **~ di spedizione** consignment note

bol'lire vt, vi to boil; **bol'lito** sm (CUC) boiled meat

bolli'tore sm (CUC) kettle; (per riscaldamento) boiler

'bollo sm stamp; **~ per patente** driving licence tax

'bomba sf bomb; **~ atomica** atom bomb

bombarda'mento sm bombardment; bombing

bombar'dare vt to bombard; (da aereo) to bomb

bombardi'ere sm bomber

bom'betta sf bowler (hat)

'bombola sf cylinder

bo'naccia, ce [bo'nattʃa] sf dead calm

bo'nario, a ag good-natured, kind

bo'nifica, che sf reclamation; reclaimed land

bo'nifico, ci sm (riduzione, abbuono) discount; (versamento a terzi) credit transfer

bontà sf goodness; (cortesia) kindness; **aver la ~ di fare qc** to be good o kind enough to do sth

borbot'tare vi to mumble

'borchia ['borkja] sf stud

borda'tura (SARTORIA) border, trim

bor'deaux [bor'do] ag inv, sm inv maroon

'bordo sm (NAUT) ship's side; (orlo) edge; (striscia di guarnizione) border, trim; **a ~ di** (nave, aereo) aboard, on board; (macchina) in

bor'gata sf (in campagna) hamlet

bor'ghese [bor'geze] ag (spesso peg)

middle-class; bourgeois; **abito ~** civilian dress; **borghe'sia** sf middle classes pl; bourgeoisie

'borgo, ghi sm (paesino) village; (quartiere) district; (sobborgo) suburb

'boria sf self-conceit, arrogance

boro'talco sm talcum powder

bor'raccia, ce [bor'rattʃa] sf canteen, water-bottle

'borsa sf bag; (anche: **~ da signora**) handbag; (ECON): **la B~ (valori)** the Stock Exchange; **~ nera** black market; **~ della spesa** shopping bag; **~ di studio** grant; **borsai'olo** sm purse; pickpocket; **borsel'lino** sm purse; **bor'setta** sf handbag; **bor'sista, i, e** sm/f (ECON) speculator; (INS) grant-holder

bos'caglia [bos'kaʎʎa] sf woodlands pl

boscai'olo sm woodcutter; forester

'bosco, schi sm wood; **bos'coso, a** ag wooded

'bossolo sm cartridge-case

bo'tanica sf botany

bo'tanico, a, ci, che ag botanical
♦ sm botanist

'botola sf trap door

'botta sf blow; (rumore) bang

'botte sf barrel, cask

bot'tega, ghe sf shop; (officina) workshop; **botte'gaio, a** sm/f shopkeeper; **botte'ghino** sm ticket office; (del lotto) public lottery office

bot'tiglia [bot'tiʎʎa] sf bottle; **bottiglie'ria** sf wine shop

bot'tino sm (di guerra) booty; (di rapina, furto) loot

'botto sm bang; crash; **di ~** suddenly

bot'tone sm button; **attaccare ~ a qn** (fig) to buttonhole sb

bo'vino, a ag bovine; **~i** smpl cattle

boxe [bɔks] sf boxing

'bozza ['bɔttsa] sf draft; sketch; (TIP) proof; **boz'zetto** sm sketch

'bozzolo ['bɔttsolo] sm cocoon

BR sigla fpl = **Brigate Rosse**

brac'care vt to hunt

brac'cetto [brat'tʃetto] *sm*: **a ~** arm in arm

bracci'ale [brat'tʃale] *sm* bracelet; (*distintivo*) armband; **braccia'letto** *sm* bracelet, bangle

bracci'ante [brat'tʃante] *sm* (AGR) day labourer

bracci'ata [brat'tʃata] *sf* (*nel nuoto*) stroke

'braccio ['brattʃo] (*pl(f)* **braccia**) *sm* (ANAT) arm; (*pl(m)* **bracci**: *di gru, fiume*) arm; (: *di edificio*) wing; **~ di mare** sound; **bracci'olo** *sm* (*appoggio*) arm

'bracco, chi *sm* hound

bracconi'ere *sm* poacher

'brace ['bratʃe] *sf* embers *pl*; **braci'ere** *sm* brazier

braci'ola [bra'tʃola] *sf* (CUC) chop

bra'mare *vt*: **~ qc/di fare** to long for sth/to do

'branca, che *sf* branch

'branchia ['brankja] *sf* (ZOOL) gill

'branco, chi *sm* (*di cani, lupi*) pack; (*di pecore*) flock; (*peg: di persone*) gang, pack

branco'lare *vi* to grope, feel one's way

'branda *sf* camp bed

bran'dello *sm* scrap, shred; **a ~i** in tatters, in rags

bran'dire *vt* to brandish

'brano *sm* piece; (*di libro*) passage

bra'sato *sm* braised beef

Bra'sile *sm*: **il ~** Brazil; **brasili'ano, a** *ag*, *sm/f* Brazilian

'bravo, a *ag* (*abile*) clever, capable, skilful; (*buono*) good, honest; (: *bambino*) good; (*coraggioso*) brave; **~!** well done!; (*a teatro*) bravo!

bra'vura *sf* cleverness, skill

'breccia, ce ['brettʃa] *sf* breach

bre'tella [bre'tɛlla] *sf* (AUT) link; **~e** *sfpl* (*di calzoni*) braces

'breve *ag* brief, short; **in ~** in short

brevet'tare *vt* to patent

bre'vetto *sm* patent; **~ di pilotaggio** pilot's licence (BRIT) o license (US)

'brezza ['breddza] *sf* breeze

'bricco, chi *sm* jug; **~ del caffè** coffeepot

bric'cone, a *sm/f* rogue, rascal

'briciola ['britʃola] *sf* crumb

'briciolo ['britʃolo] *sm* (*specie fig*) bit

'briga, ghe *sf* (*fastidio*) trouble, bother; **pigliarsi la ~ di fare qc** to take the trouble to do sth

brigadi'ere (*dei carabinieri etc*) ≈ sergeant

bri'gante *sm* bandit

bri'gata *sf* (MIL) brigade; (*gruppo*) group, party; **B~e Rosse** (POL) Red Brigades

'briglia ['briʎʎa] *sf* rein; **a ~ sciolta** at full gallop; (*fig*) at full speed

bril'lante *ag* bright; (*anche fig*) brilliant; (*che luccica*) shining ♦ *sm* diamond

bril'lare *vi* to shine; (*mina*) to blow up ♦ *vt* (*mina*) to set off

'brillo, a *ag* merry, tipsy

'brina *sf* hoarfrost

brin'dare *vi*: **~ a qn/qc** to drink to o toast sb/sth

'brindisi *sm inv* toast

'brio *sm* liveliness, go

bri'oche [bri'ɔʃ] *sf inv* brioche

'brioso, a *ag* lively

bri'tannico, i, che *ag* British

'brivido *sm* shiver; (*di ribrezzo*) shudder; (*fig*) thrill

brizzo'lato, a [brittso'lato] *ag* (*persona*) going grey; (*barba, capelli*) greying

'brocca, che *sf* jug

broc'cato *sm* brocade

'broccolo *sm* broccoli *sg*

'brodo *sm* broth; (*per cucinare*) stock; **~ ristretto** consommé

brogli'accio [broʎ'ʎattʃo] *sm* scribbling pad

'broglio ['brɔʎʎo] *sm*: **~ elettorale** gerrymandering

bron'chite [bron'kite] *sf* (MED) bronchitis

'broncio ['brontʃo] *sm* sulky

expression; **tenere il ~** to sulk
'**bronco, chi** sm bronchial tube
bronto'lare vi to grumble; (tuono, stomaco) to rumble
'**bronzo** ['brondzo] sm bronze
'**browser** ['brauzer] sm inv (INFORM) browser
brucia'pelo [brutʃa'pelo]: **a ~** av point-blank
bruci'are [bru'tʃare] vt to burn; (scottare) to scald ♦ vi to burn; **brucia'tore** sm burner; **brucia'tura** sf (atto) burning no pl; (segno) burn; (scottatura) scald; **bruci'ore** sm burning o smarting sensation; **bruciore di stomaco** heartburn
'**bruco, chi** sm caterpillar; grub
brughi'era [bru'gjɛra] sf heath, moor
bruli'care vi to swarm
'**brullo, a** ag bare, bleak
'**bruma** sf mist
'**bruno, a** ag brown, dark; (persona) dark(-haired)
'**brusco, a, schi, sche** ag (sapore) sharp; (modi, persona) brusque, abrupt; (movimento) abrupt, sudden
bru'sio sm buzz, buzzing
bru'tale ag brutal
'**bruto, a** ag (forza) brute cpd ♦ sm brute
brut'tezza [brut'tettsa] sf ugliness
'**brutto, a** ag ugly; (cattivo) bad; (malattia, strada, affare) nasty, bad; **~ tempo** bad weather; **brut'tura** sf (cosa brutta) ugly thing; (sudiciume) filth; (azione meschina) mean action
Bru'xelles [bry'sɛl] sf Brussels
bub'bone sm swelling
'**buca, che** sf hole; (avvallamento) hollow; **~ delle lettere** letterbox
buca'neve sm inv snowdrop
bu'care vt (forare) to make a hole (o holes) in; (pungere) to pierce; (biglietto) to punch; **~rsi** vr (di eroina) to mainline; **~ una gomma** to have a

puncture
bu'cato sm (operazione) washing; (panni) wash, washing
'**buccia, ce** ['buttʃa] sf skin, peel
bucherel'lare [bukerel'lare] vt to riddle with holes
'**buco, chi** sm hole
bu'dello sm (ANAT: pl(f) ~a) bowel, gut; (fig: tubo) tube; (vicolo) alley
bu'dino sm pudding
'**bue** sm ox; **carne di ~** beef
'**bufalo** sm buffalo
bu'fera sf storm
'**buffo, a** ag funny; (TEATRO) comic
buf'fone sm buffoon; (peg) clown
bu'gia, 'gie [bu'dʒia] sf lie; **dire una ~** to tell a lie; **bugi'ardo, a** ag lying, deceitful ♦ sm/f liar
bugi'gattolo [budʒi'gattolo] sm poky little room
'**buio, a** ag dark ♦ sm dark, darkness
'**bulbo** sm (BOT) bulb; **~ oculare** eyeball
Bulga'ria sf: **la ~** Bulgaria
bul'lone sm bolt
buona'notte escl good night! ♦ sf: **dare la ~ a** to say good night to
buona'sera escl good evening!
buongi'orno [bwon'dʒorno] escl good morning (o afternoon)!
buongus'taio, a sm/f gourmet
buon'gusto sm good taste

PAROLA CHIAVE

---

bu'ono, a (ag: dav sm buon +C o V, buono +s impura, gn, pn, ps, x, z; dav sf buon' +V) ag **1** (gen) good; **un buon pranzo/ristorante** a good lunch/restaurant; **(stai) ~!** behave!
2 (benevolo): **~ (con)** good (to), kind (to)
3 (giusto, valido) right; **al momento ~** at the right moment
4 (adatto): **~ a/da** fit for/to; **essere ~ a nulla** to be no good o use at anything
5 (auguri): **buon anno!** happy New

Year!; **buon appetito!** enjoy your
meal!; **buon compleanno!** happy
birthday!; **buon divertimento!** have
a nice time!; **~a fortuna!** good luck!;
buon riposo! sleep well!; **buon
viaggio!** bon voyage!, have a good
trip!
6: a buon mercato cheap; **di
buon'ora** early; **buon senso**
common sense; **alla ~a ag** simple ♦ **av**
in a simple way, without any fuss
♦ **sm 1** (*bontà*) goodness, good
2 (*COMM*) voucher, coupon; **~ di cassa**
cash voucher; **~ di consegna** delivery
note; **~ del Tesoro** Treasury bill

buontem'pone, a *sm/f* jovial person
burat'tino *sm* puppet
'burbero, a *ag* surly, gruff
'burla *sf* prank, trick; **bur'lare** *vt*:
burlare qc/qn, burlarsi di qc/qn to
make fun of sth/sb
burocra'zia [burokrat'tsia] *sf*
bureaucracy
bur'rasca, sche *sf* storm
'burro *sm* butter
bur'rone *sm* ravine
bus'care *vt* (*anche*: ~**si: raffreddore**) to
get, catch; **buscarle** (*fam*) to get a
hiding
bus'sare *vi* to knock
'bussola *sf* compass
'busta *sf* (*da lettera*) envelope;
(*astuccio*) case; **in ~ aperta/chiusa** in
an unsealed/sealed envelope; **~ paga**
pay packet
busta'rella *sf* bribe, backhander
'busto *sm* bust; (*indumento*) corset,
girdle; **a mezzo ~** (*foto*) half-length
buttafu'ori *sm inv* bouncer
but'tare *vt* to throw; (*anche*: ~ *via*) to
throw away; **~ giù** (*scritto*) to scribble
down; (*cibo*) to gulp down; (*edificio*) to
pull down, demolish; (*pasta, verdura*)
to put into boiling water

C, c

ca'bina *sf* (*di nave*) cabin; (*da spiaggia*)
beach hut; (*di autocarro, treno*) cab; (*di
aereo*) cockpit; (*di ascensore*) cage;
~ telefonica call o (tele)phone box;
cabi'nato *sm* cabin cruiser
ca'cao *sm* cocoa
'caccia ['kattʃa] *sf* hunting; (*con fucile*)
shooting; (*inseguimento*) chase;
(*cacciagione*) game ♦ *sm inv* (*aereo*)
fighter; (*nave*) destroyer; **~ grossa**
big-game hunting; **~ all'uomo**
manhunt
cacciabombardi'ere
[kattʃabombar'djere] *sm* fighter-
bomber
cacciagi'one [kattʃa'dʒone] *sf* game
cacci'are [kat'tʃare] *vt* to hunt;
(*mandar via*) to chase away; (*ficcare*) to
shove, stick ♦ *vi* to hunt; ~**rsi** *vr*: **dove
s'è cacciata la mia borsa?** where
has my bag got to?; ~**rsi nei guai** to
get into trouble; **~ fuori qc** to whip o
pull sth out; **~ un urlo** to let out a
yell; **caccia'tore** *sm* hunter;
cacciatore di frodo poacher
caccia'vite [kattʃa'vite] *sm inv*
screwdriver
'cactus *sm inv* cactus
ca'davere *sm* (dead) body, corpse
ca'dente *ag* falling; (*casa*) tumbledown
ca'denza [ka'dentsa] *sf* cadence;
(*ritmo*) rhythm; (*MUS*) cadenza
ca'dere *vi* to fall; (*denti, capelli*) to fall
out; (*tetto*) to fall in; **questa gonna
cade bene** this skirt hangs well;
lasciar ~ (*anche fig*) to drop; **~ dal
sonno** to be falling asleep on one's
feet; **~ dalle nuvole** (*fig*) to be taken
aback
ca'detto, a *ag* younger; (*squadra*)
junior ♦ *sm* cadet
ca'duta *sf* fall; **la ~ dei capelli** hair
loss

caffè sm inv coffee; (locale) café; ~ **macchiato** coffee with a dash of milk; ~ **macinato** ground coffee

caffel'latte sm inv white coffee

caffetti'era sf coffeepot

cagio'nare [kadʒo'nare] vt to cause

cagio'nevole [kadʒo'nevole] ag delicate, weak

cagli'are [kaʎ'ʎare] vi to curdle

cagna ['kanɲa] sf (ZOOL, peg) bitch

ca'gnesco, a, schi, sche [kan'nesko] ag (fig): **guardare qn in ~** to scowl at sb

cala'brone sm hornet

cala'maio sm inkpot; inkwell

cala'maro sm squid

cala'mita sf magnet

calamità sf inv calamity, disaster

ca'lare vt (far discendere) to lower; (MAGLIA) to decrease ♦ vi (discendere) to go (o come) down; (tramontare) to set, go down; ~ **di peso** to lose weight

calca sf throng, press

cal'cagno [kal'kanɲo] sm heel

cal'care limestone ♦ vt (premere coi piedi) to tread, press down; (premere con forza) to press down; (mettere in rilievo) to stress; ~ **la mano** to overdo it, exaggerate

calce ['kaltʃe] sm: **in ~** at the foot of the page ♦ sf lime; ~ **viva** quicklime

calces'truzzo [kaltʃes'truttso] sm concrete

calci'are [kal'tʃare] vt, vi to kick; **calcia'tore** sm footballer

'calcio ['kaltʃo] sm (pedata) kick; (sport) football, soccer; (di pistola, fucile) butt; (CHIM) calcium; ~ **d'angolo** (SPORT) corner (kick); ~ **di punizione** (SPORT) free kick

'calco, chi sm (ARTE) casting, moulding; cast, mould

calco'lare vt to calculate, work out, reckon; (ponderare) to weigh (up); **calcola'tore, 'trice** ag calculating ♦ sm calculator; (fig) calculating person; **calcolatore elettronico**

computer; **calcola'trice** sf calculator

'calcolo sm (anche MAT) calculation; (infinitesimale etc) calculus; (MED) stone; **fare i propri ~i** (fig) to weigh the pros and cons; **per ~** out of self-interest

cal'daia sf boiler

caldeggi'are [kalded'dʒare] vt to support

'caldo, a ag warm; (molto ~) hot; (fig: appassionato) keen; hearty ♦ sm heat; **ho ~** I'm warm; I'm hot; **fa ~** it's warm; it's hot

calen'dario sm calendar

'calibro sm (di arma) calibre, bore; (TECN) callipers pl; (fig) calibre; **di grosso ~** prominent

'calice ['kalitʃe] sm goblet; (REL) chalice

ca'ligine [ka'lidʒine] sf fog; (mista con fumo) smog

'callo sm callus; (ai piedi) corn

'calma sf calm

cal'mante sm tranquillizer

cal'mare vt to calm; (lenire) to soothe; ~**rsi** vr to grow calm, calm down; (vento) to abate; (dolori) to ease

calmi'ere sm controlled price

'calmo, a ag calm, quiet

'calo sm (COMM: di prezzi) fall; (: di volume) shrinkage; (: di peso) loss

ca'lore sm warmth; heat; **in ~** (ZOOL) on heat

calo'ria sf calorie

calo'roso, a ag warm

calpes'tare vt to tread on, trample on; **"è vietato ~ l'erba"** "keep off the grass"

ca'lunnia sf slander; (scritta) libel

cal'vario sm (fig) affliction, cross

cal'vizie [kal'vittsje] sf baldness

'calvo, a ag bald

'calza ['kaltsa] sf (da donna) stocking; (da uomo) sock; **fare la ~** to knit; ~**e di nylon** nylons, (nylon) stockings

cal'zare [kal'tsare] vt (scarpe, guanti: mettersi) to put on; (: portare) to wear ♦ vi to fit; **calza'tura** sf footwear

calzet'tone [kaltset'tone] sm heavy

knee-length sock

cal'zino [kal'tsino] *sm* sock

calzo'laio [kaltso'lajo] *sm* shoemaker; (*che ripara scarpe*) cobbler; **calzole'ria** *sf* (*negozio*) shoe shop

calzon'cini [kaltson'tʃini] *smpl* shorts

cal'zone [kal'tsone] *sm* trouser leg; (*CUC*) savoury turnover made with pizza dough; **~i** *smpl* (*pantaloni*) trousers (*BRIT*), pants (*US*)

cambi'ale *sf* bill (of exchange); (*pagherò cambiario*) promissory note

cambia'mento *sm* change

cambi'are *vt* to change; (*modificare*) to alter, change; (*barattare*): **~ qc con qn/qc** to exchange (sth with sb/for sth) ♦ *vi* to change, alter; **~rsi** *vr* (*d'abito*) to change; **~ casa** to move (house); **~ idea** to change one's mind; **~ treno** to change trains

'cambio *sm* change; (*modifica*) alteration, change; (*scambio*, *COMM*) exchange; (*corso dei cambi*) rate of exchange; (*TECN*, *AUT*) gears *pl*; **in ~ di** in exchange for; **dare il ~ a qn** to take over from sb

'camera *sf* room; (*anche: ~ da letto*) bedroom; (*POL*) chamber, house; **~ ardente** mortuary chapel; **~ d'aria** inner tube; (*di pallone*) bladder; **C~ di Commercio** Chamber of Commerce; **C~ dei Deputati** Chamber of Deputies, ≈ House of Commons (*BRIT*), ≈ House of Representatives (*US*); **~ a gas** gas chamber; **~ a un letto/a due letti/matrimoniale** single/twin-bedded/double room; **~ oscura** (*FOT*) dark room

came'rata, i, e *sm/f* companion, mate ♦ *sf* dormitory

cameri'era *sf* (*domestica*) maid; (*che serve a tavola*) waitress; (*che fa le camere*) chambermaid

cameri'ere *sm* (man)servant; (*di ristorante*) waiter

came'rino *sm* (*TEATRO*) dressing room

'camice ['kamitʃe] *sm* (*REL*) alb; (*per*

medici etc) white coat

cami'cetta [kami'tʃetta] *sf* blouse

ca'micia, cie [ka'mitʃa] *sf* (*da uomo*) shirt; (*da donna*) blouse; **~ di forza** straitjacket

cami'netto *sm* hearth, fireplace

ca'mino *sm* chimney; (*focolare*) fireplace, hearth

'camion *sm inv* lorry (*BRIT*), truck (*US*); **camion'cino** *sm* van

cam'mello *sm* (*ZOOL*) camel; (*tessuto*) camel hair

cammi'nare *vi* to walk; (*funzionare*) to work, go; **cammi'nata** *sf* walk

cam'mino *sm* walk; (*sentiero*) path; (*itinerario, direzione, tragitto*) way; **mettersi in ~** to set o start off

camo'milla *sf* camomile; (*infuso*) camomile tea

ca'morra *sf* camorra; racket

ca'moscio [ka'moʃʃo] *sm* chamois; **di ~** (*scarpe, borsa*) suede *cpd*

cam'pagna [kam'paɲɲa] *sf* country, countryside; (*POL, COMM, MIL*) campaign; **in ~** in the country; **andare in ~** to go to the country; **fare una ~** to campaign; **campa'gnola** *sf* (*AUT*) cross-country vehicle; **campa'gnolo, a** *ag* country *cpd*

cam'pale *ag* field *cpd*; (*fig*): **una giornata ~** a hard day

cam'pana *sf* bell; (*anche: ~ di vetro*) bell jar; **campa'nella** *sf* small bell; (*di tenda*) curtain ring; **campa'nello** *sm* (*all'uscio, da tavola*) bell

campa'nile *sm* bell tower, belfry; **campani'lismo** *sm* parochialism

cam'pare *vi* to live; (*tirare avanti*) to get by, manage

cam'pato, a *ag*: **~ in aria** unfounded

campeggi'are [kampeddʒare] *vi* to camp; (*risaltare*) to stand out; **campeggia'tore, 'trice** *sm/f* camper; **cam'peggio** *sm* camping; (*terreno*) camp site; **fare (del) campeggio** to go camping

cam'pestre *ag* country *cpd*, rural

Campidoglio

*The **Campidoglio**, one of the Seven Hills of Rome, is the site of the Comune di Roma.*

campio'nario, a *ag*: fiera ~a trade fair ♦ *sm* collection of samples

campio'nato *sm* championship

campi'one, 'essa *sm/f* (SPORT) champion ♦ *sm* (COMM) sample

'campo *sm* field; (MIL) field; (: accampamento) camp; (spazio delimitato: sportivo etc) ground; field; (di quadro) background; **i ~i** (campagna) the countryside; ~ **da aviazione** airfield; ~ **di battaglia** (MIL, fig) battlefield; ~ **di golf** golf course; ~ **da tennis** tennis court; ~ **visivo** field of vision

campo'santo (*pl* campisanti) *sm* cemetery

camuf'fare *vt* to disguise

'Canada *sm*: il ~ Canada; cana'dese *ag*, *sm/f* Canadian ♦ *sf* (anche: tenda canadese) ridge tent

ca'naglia [ka'naʎʎa] *sf* rabble, mob; (persona) scoundrel, rogue

ca'nale *sm* (anche fig) channel; (artificiale) canal

'canapa *sf* hemp; ~ **indiana** (droga) cannabis

cana'rino *sm* canary

cancel'lare [kantʃel'lare] *vt* (con la gomma) to rub out, erase; (con la penna) to strike out; (annullare) to annul, cancel; (disdire) to cancel

cancelle'ria [kantʃelle'ria] *sf* chancery; (materiale per scrivere) stationery

cancelli'ere [kantʃel'ljere] *sm* chancellor; (di tribunale) clerk of the court

can'cello [kan'tʃello] *sm* gate

can'crena [kan'krena] *sf* gangrene

'cancro *sm* (MED) cancer; (dello zodiaco) C~ Cancer

cande'gina [kandeʹdʒina] *sf* bleach

can'dela *sf* candle; ~ **(di accensione)** (AUT) spark(ing) plug

cande'labro *sm* candelabra

candeli'ere *sm* candlestick

candi'dato, a *sm/f* candidate; (aspirante a una carica) applicant

'candido, a *ag* white as snow; (puro) pure; (sincero) sincere, candid

can'dito, a *ag* candied

can'dore *sm* brilliant white; purity; sincerity, candour

'cane *sm* dog; (di pistola, fucile) cock; **fa un freddo** ~ it's bitterly cold; **non c'era un** ~ there wasn't a soul; ~ **da caccia/guardia** hunting/guard dog; ~ **lupo** alsatian

ca'nestro *sm* basket

'canfora *sf* camphor

cangi'ante [kan'dʒante] *ag* iridescent

can'guro *sm* kangaroo

ca'nile *sm* kennel; (di allevamento) kennels *pl*; ~ **municipale** dog pound

ca'nino, a *ag*, *sm* canine

'canna *sf* (pianta) reed; (: indica, da zucchero) cane; (bastone) stick, cane; (di fucile) barrel; (di organo) pipe; (fam: droga) joint; ~ **da pesca** (fishing) rod; ~ **da zucchero** sugar cane

can'nella *sf* (CUC) cinnamon

cannel'loni *smpl* pasta tubes stuffed with sauce and baked

cannocchi'ale [kannok'kjale] *sm* telescope

can'none *sm* (MIL) gun; (: STORIA) cannon; (tubo) pipe, tube; (piega) box pleat; (fig) ace

can'nuccia, ce [kan'nuttʃa] *sf* (drinking) straw

ca'noa *sf* canoe

ca'none *sm* canon, criterion; (mensile, annuo) rent; fee

ca'nonico, ci (REL) canon

ca'noro, a *ag* (uccello) singing, song *cpd*

canot'taggio [kanot'taddʒo] *sm* rowing

canotti'era *sf* vest

ca'notto *sm* small boat, dinghy; canoe

cano'vaccio [kano'vattʃo] *sm* (tela) canvas; (strofinaccio) duster; (trama) plot

can'tante *sm/f* singer

can'tare *vt, vi* to sing; **cantau'tore, 'trice** *sm/f* singer-composer

canti'ere *sm (EDIL)* (building) site; (*anche: ~ navale*) shipyard

canti'lena *sf (filastrocca)* lullaby; (*fig*) sing-song voice

can'tina *sf* cellar; (*bottega*) wine shop

'canto *sm* song; (*arte*) singing; (*REL*) chant; chanting; (*poesia*) poem, lyric; (*parte di una poesia*) canto; (*parte, lato*): **da un ~** on the one hand; **d'altro ~** on the other hand

canto'nata *sf* corner; **prendere una ~** (*fig*) to blunder

can'tone *sm (in Svizzera)* canton

can'tuccio [kan'tuttʃo] *sm* corner, nook

canzo'nare [kantso'nare] *vt* to tease

can'zone [kan'tsone] *sf* song; (*POESIA*) canzone; **canzoni'ere** *sm (MUS)* songbook; (*LETTERATURA*) collection of poems

'caos *sm inv* chaos; **ca'otico, a, ci, che** *ag* chaotic

C.A.P. *sigla m* = **codice di avviamento postale**

ca'pace [ka'patʃe] *ag* able, capable; (*ampio, vasto*) large, capacious; **sei ~ di farlo?** can you o are you able to do it?; **capacità** *sf inv* ability; (*DIR, di recipiente*) capacity; **capaci'tarsi** *vr* to understand

ca'panna *sf* hut

capan'none *sm (AGR)* barn; (*fabbricato industriale*) (factory) shed

ca'parbio, a *ag* stubborn

ca'parra *sf* deposit, down payment

ca'pello *sm* hair; **~i** *smpl (capigliatura)* hair *sg*

capez'zale [kapet'tsale] *sm* bolster; (*fig*) bedside

ca'pezzolo [ka'pettsolo] *sm* nipple

capi'enza [ka'pjɛntsa] *sf* capacity

capiglia'tura [kapiʎʎa'tura] *sf* hair

ca'pire *vt* to understand

capi'tale *ag (mortale)* capital; (*fondamentale*) main, chief ♦ *sf (città)* capital ♦ *sm (ECON)* capital

capita'lismo *sm* capitalism

capita'lista, i, e *ag, sm/f* capitalist

capitane'ria *sf*: **~ di porto** port authorities *pl*

capi'tano *sm* captain

capi'tare *vi (giungere casualmente)* to happen to go, find o.s.; (*accadere*) to happen; (*presentarsi: cosa*) to turn up, present itself ♦ *vb impers* to happen; **mi è capitato un guaio** I've had a spot of trouble

capi'tello *sm (ARCHIT)* capital

ca'pitolo *sm* chapter

capi'tombolo *sm* headlong fall, tumble

'capo *sm* head; (*persona*) head, leader; (: *in ufficio*) head, boss; (: *in tribù*) chief; (*di oggetti*) head; top; end; (*GEO*) cape; **andare a ~** to start a new paragraph; **da ~** over again; **~ di bestiame** head *inv* of cattle; **~ di vestiario** item of clothing

'capo... prefisso: capocu'oco, chi *sm* head cook; **Capo'danno** *sm* New Year; **capo'fitto** *av* a capofitto *av* headfirst, headlong; **capo'giro** *sm* dizziness *no pl*; **capola'voro, i** *sm* masterpiece; **capo'linea** (*pl* **capi'linea**) *sm* terminus; **capo'lino** *sm*: **fare capolino** to peep out (*o in etc*); **capolu'ogo** (*pl* -**ghi** *o* -**ghi**) *sm* chief town, administrative centre

capo'rale *sm (MIL)* lance corporal (*BRIT*), private first class (*US*)

'capo... prefisso: capostazi'one (*pl* **capistazi'one**) *sm* station master; **capo'treno** (*pl* **capi'treno** *o* **capo'treni**) *sm* guard

capo'volgere [kapo'vɔldʒere] *vt* to overturn; (*fig*) to reverse; **~rsi** *vr* to overturn; (*barca*) to capsize; (*fig*) to be reversed; **capo'volto, a** *pp di* **capovolgere**

'**cappa** *sf* (*mantello*) cape, cloak; (*del camino*) hood

cap'**pella** *sf* (*REL*) chapel; **cappel'lano** *sm* chaplain

cap'**pello** *sm* hat

'**cappero** *sm* caper

cap'**pone** *sm* capon

cap'**potto** *sm* (over)coat

cappuc'**cino** [kapput'tʃino] *sm* (*frate*) Capuchin monk; (*bevanda*) cappuccino, frothy white coffee

cap'**puccio** [kap'puttʃo] *sm* (*copricapo*) hood; (*della biro*) cap

'**capra** *sf* (she-)goat; **ca'pretto** *sm* kid

ca'**priccio** [ka'prittʃo] *sm* caprice, whim; (*bizza*) tantrum; **fare i ~i** to be very naughty; **capricci'oso, a** *ag* capricious, whimsical; naughty

Capri'**corno** *sm* Capricorn

capri'**ola** *sf* somersault

capri'**olo** *sm* roe deer

'**capro** *sm*: **~ espiatorio** scapegoat

'**capsula** *sf* capsule; (*di arma, per bottiglie*) cap

cap'**tare** *vt* (*RADIO, TV*) to pick up; (*cattivarsi*) to gain, win

cara'**bina** *sf* rifle

carabini'**ere** *sm* member of Italian military police force

---

carabinieri

Originally part of the armed forces, the **carabinieri** are police who now perform both military and civil duties and include paratroop units and mounted divisions.

---

ca'**raffa** *sf* carafe

cara'**mella** *sf* sweet

ca'**rattere** *sm* character; (*caratteristica*) characteristic, trait; **avere un buon ~** to be good-natured; **caratte'ristica, che** *sf* characteristic, trait, peculiarity; **caratte'ristico, a, ci, che** *ag* characteristic; **caratteriz'zare** *vt* to characterize

car'**bone** *sm* coal

carbu'**rante** *sm* (motor) fuel

carbura'**tore** *sm* carburettor

car'**cassa** *sf* carcass; (*fig: peg: macchina etc*) (old) wreck

carce'**rato, a** [kartʃe'rato] *sm/f* prisoner

'**carcere** ['kartʃere] *sm* prison; (*pena*) imprisonment

carci'**ofo** [kar'tʃɔfo] *sm* artichoke

car'**diaco, a, ci, che** *ag* cardiac, heart *cpd*

cardi'**nale** *ag, sm* cardinal

'**cardine** *sm* hinge

'**cardo** *sm* thistle

ca'**renza** [ka'rɛntsa] *sf* lack, scarcity; (*vitaminica*) deficiency

cares'**tia** *sf* famine; (*penuria*) scarcity, dearth

ca'**rezza** [ka'rettsa] *sf* caress; **carez'zare** *vt* to caress, stroke

'**carica, che** *sf* (*mansione ufficiale*) office, position; (*MIL, TECN, ELETTR*) charge; **ha una forte ~ di simpatia** he's very likeable; *vedi anche* **carico**

cari'**care** *vt* to load; (*orologio*) to wind up; (*batteria, MIL*) to charge

'**carico, a, chi, che** *ag* (*che porta un peso*): **~ di** loaded o laden with; (*fucile*) loaded; (*orologio*) wound up; (*batteria*) charged; (*colore*) deep; (*caffè, tè*) strong ♦ *sm* (*il caricare*) loading; (*ciò che si carica*) load; (*fig: peso*) burden, weight; **persona a ~** dependent; **essere a ~ di qn** (*spese etc*) to be charged to sb

'**carie** *sf* (*dentaria*) decay

ca'**rino, a** *ag* (*grazioso*) lovely, pretty, nice; (*riferito a uomo, anche simpatico*) nice

cari'**tà** *sf* charity; **per ~!** (*escl di rifiuto*) good heavens, no!

carnagi'**one** [karna'dʒone] *sf* complexion

car'**nale** *ag* (*amore*) carnal

'**carne** *sf* flesh; (*bovina, ovina etc*) meat; **~ di manzo/maiale/pecora** beef/

pork/mutton; **~ tritata** mince (*BRIT*), hamburger meat (*US*), minced (*BRIT*) or ground (*US*) meat

car'nefice [kar'nefitʃe] *sm* executioner; (*alla forca*) hangman

carne'vale *sm* carnival

---
carnevale

Carnevale *is the period between Epiphany (Jan. 6th) and the beginning of Lent. People wear fancy dress, and there are parties, processions of floats and bonfires. It culminates immediately before Lent in the festivities of* **martedì grasso** *(Shrove Tuesday).*

---

car'noso, a *ag* fleshy

'caro, a *ag* (*amato*) dear; (*costoso*) dear, expensive

ca'rogna [ka'roɲɲa] *sf* carrion; (*fig: fam*) swine

ca'rota *sf* carrot

caro'vana *sf* caravan

caro'vita *sm* high cost of living

carpenti'ere *sm* carpenter

car'pire *vt:* **~ qc a qn** (*segreto etc*) to get sth out of sb

car'poni *av* on all fours

car'rabile *ag* suitable for vehicles; **"passo ~"** "keep clear"

car'raio, a *ag: passo* ~ driveway

carreggi'ata [karred'dʒata] *sf* carriageway (*BRIT*), (road)way

car'rello *sm* trolley; (*AER*) undercarriage; (*CINEMA*) dolly; (*di macchina da scrivere*) carriage

carri'era *sf* career; **fare ~** to get on; **a gran ~** at full speed

carri'ola *sf* wheelbarrow

'carro *sm* cart, wagon; **~ armato** (*MIL*) tank; **~ attrezzi** breakdown van

car'rozza [kar'rɔttsa] *sf* carriage, coach

carrozze'ria [karrottse'ria] *sf* body, coachwork (*BRIT*); (*officina*) coachbuilder's workshop (*BRIT*), body shop

carroz'zina [karrot'tsina] *sf* pram (*BRIT*), baby carriage (*US*)

'carta *sf* paper; (*al ristorante*) menu; (*GEO*) map; plan; (*documento, da gioco*) card; (*costituzione*) charter; **~e** *sfpl* (*documenti*) papers, documents; **alla ~** (*al ristorante*) à la carte; **~ assegni** bank card; **~ assorbente** blotting paper; **~ bollata** o **da bollo** official stamped paper; **~ di credito** credit card; **~ (geografica)** map; **~ d'identità** identity card; **~ igienica** toilet paper; **~ d'imbarco** (*AER*, *NAUT*) boarding card; **~ da lettere** writing paper; **~ libera** (*AMM*) unstamped paper; **~ da parati** wallpaper; **~ stradale** road map; **~ verde** (*AUT*) green card; **~ vetrata** sandpaper; **~ da visita** visiting card

cartacar'bone (*pl* **cartecar'bone**) *sf* carbon paper

car'taccia, ce [kar'tattʃa] *sf* waste paper

carta'pecora *sf* parchment

carta'pesta *sf* papier-mâché

car'teggio [kar'teddʒo] *sm* correspondence

car'tella (*scheda*) card; (*custodia: di cartone*) folder; (*: di uomo d'affari etc*) briefcase; (*: di scolaro*) schoolbag, satchel; **~ clinica** (*MED*) case sheet

car'tello *sm* sign; (*pubblicitario*) poster; (*stradale*) sign, signpost; (*ECON*) cartel; (*in dimostrazioni*) placard; **cartel'lone** *sm* (*pubblicitario*) advertising poster; (*della tombola*) scoring frame; (*TEATRO*) playbill; **tenere il cartellone** (*spettacolo*) to have a long run

carti'era *sf* paper mill

car'tina *sf* (*AUT*, *GEO*) map

car'toccio [kar'tɔttʃo] *sm* paper bag

cartole'ria *sf* stationer's (shop)

carto'lina *sf* postcard; **~ postale** ready-stamped postcard

car'tone *sm* cardboard; (*ARTE*) cartoon; **~i animati** *smpl* (*CINEMA*) cartoons

car'tuccia, ce [kar'tuttʃa] *sf* cartridge

'casa *sf* house; (*in senso astratto*) home; (*COMM*) firm, house; **essere a ~** to be at home; **vado a ~ mia/tua** I'm going home/to your house; **~ di cura** nursing home; **~ dello studente** student hostel; **~e popolari** ≈ council houses (o flats) (*BRIT*), ≈ public housing units (*US*); **vino della ~** house wine

ca'sacca, che *sf* military coat; (*di fantino*) blouse

casa'linga, ghe *sf* housewife

casa'lingo, a, ghi, ghe *ag* household, domestic; (*fatto a casa*) home-made; (*semplice*) homely; (*amante della casa*) home-loving; **~ghi** *smpl* household articles; **cucina ~a** plain home cooking

cas'care *vi* to fall; **cas'cata** *sf* fall; (*d'acqua*) cascade, waterfall

ca'scina [kaʃ'ʃina] *sf* farmstead

'casco, schi *sm* helmet; (*del parrucchiere*) hair-drier; (*di banane*) bunch

casei'ficio [kazei'fitʃo] *sm* creamery

ca'sella *sf* pigeon-hole; **~ postale** post office box

casel'lario *sm* filing cabinet; **~ giudiziale** court records *pl*

ca'sello *sm* (*di autostrada*) toll-house

ca'serma *sf* barracks *pl*

ca'sino (*fam*) *sm* brothel; (*confusione*) row, racket

casinò *sm inv* casino

'caso *sm* chance; (*fatto, vicenda*) event, incident; (*possibilità*) possibility; (*MED, LING*) case; **a ~** at random; **per ~** by chance, by accident; **in ogni ~, in tutti i ~i** in any case, at any rate; **al ~** should the opportunity arise; **nel ~ che** in case; **~ mai** if by chance; **~ limite** borderline case

caso'lare *sm* cottage

'cassa *sf* case, crate, box; (*bara*) coffin; (*mobile*) chest; (*involucro: di orologio etc*) case; (*macchina*) cash register, till; (*luogo di pagamento*) checkout (*counter*); (*fondo*) fund; (*istituto*

bancario) bank; **~ automatica prelievi** cash dispenser; **~ continua** night safe; **~ integrazione: mettere in ~ integrazione** ≈ to lay off; **~ mutua** o **malattia** health insurance scheme; **~ di risparmio** savings bank; **~ toracica** (*ANAT*) chest

cassa'forte (*pl* **casse'forti**) *sf* safe

cassa'panca (*pl* **casse'panche** o **casse'panche**) *sf* settle

casse'rola *sf* = **casseruola**

casseru'ola *sf* saucepan

cas'setta *sf* box; (*per registratore*) cassette; (*CINEMA, TEATRO*) box-office takings *pl*; **film di ~** box-office draw; **~ di sicurezza** strongbox; **~ delle lettere** letterbox

cas'setto *sm* drawer; **casset'tone** *sm* chest of drawers

cassi'ere, a *sm/f* cashier; (*di banca*) teller

casso'netto *sm* wheelie-bin

'casta *sf* caste

cas'tagna [kas'taɲɲa] *sf* chestnut

cas'tagno [kas'taɲɲo] *sm* chestnut (tree)

cas'tano, a *ag* chestnut (brown)

cas'tello *sm* castle; (*TECN*) scaffolding

casti'gare *vt* to punish; **cas'tigo, ghi** *sm* punishment

castità *sf* chastity

cas'toro *sm* beaver

cas'trare *vt* to castrate; to geld; to doctor (*BRIT*), fix (*US*)

casu'ale *ag* chance *cpd*; (*INFORM*) random *cpd*

cata'comba *sf* catacomb

ca'talogo, ghi *sm* catalogue

catarifran'gente [katarifran'dʒɛnte] *sm* (*AUT*) reflector

ca'tarro *sm* catarrh

ca'tasta *sf* stack, pile

ca'tasto *sm* land register; land registry office

ca'tastrofe *sf* catastrophe, disaster

catego'ria *sf* category

ca'tena *sf* chain; **~ di montaggio**

assembly line; **~e da neve** (AUT) snow chains; **cate'naccio** sm bolt

cate'ratta sf cataract; (chiusa) sluice-gate

cati'nella sf: **piovere a ~e** to pour

ca'tino sm basin

ca'trame sm tar

'cattedra sf teacher's desk; (di docente) chair

catte'drale sf cathedral

catti'veria sf malice, spite; naughtiness; (atto) spiteful act; (parole) malicious o spiteful remark

cattività sf captivity

cat'tivo, a ag bad; (malvagio) bad, wicked; (turbolento: bambino) bad, naughty; (: mare) rough; (odore, sapore) nasty, bad

cat'tolico, a, ci, che ag, sm/f (Roman) Catholic

cat'tura sf capture

cattu'rare vt to capture

caucciù [kaut'tʃu] sm rubber

'causa sf cause; (DIR) lawsuit, case, action; **a ~ di, per ~ di** because of; **fare o muovere ~ a qn** to take legal action against sb

cau'sare vt to cause

cau'tela sf caution, prudence

caute'lare vt to protect; **~rsi** vr: **~rsi (da)** to take precautions (against)

'cauto, a ag cautious, prudent

cauzi'one [kaut'tsjone] sf security; (DIR) bail

cav. abbr = **cavaliere**

'cava sf quarry

caval'care vt (cavallo) to ride; (muro) to sit astride; (sog: ponte) to span; **caval'cata** sf ride; (gruppo di persone) riding party

cavalca'via sm inv flyover

cavalci'oni [kaval'tʃoni]: **a ~ di** prep astride

cavali'ere sm rider; (feudale, titolo) knight; (soldato) cavalryman; (al ballo) partner; **cavalle'resco, a, schi, sche** ag chivalrous; **cavalle'ria** sf (di persona) chivalry; (milizia a cavallo) cavalry

cavalle'rizzo, a [kavalle'rittso] sm/f riding instructor; circus rider

caval'letta sf grasshopper

caval'letto sm (FOT) tripod; (da pittore) easel

ca'vallo sm horse; (SCACCHI) knight; (AUT: anche: **~ vapore**) horsepower; (dei pantaloni) crotch; **a ~** on horseback; **a ~ di** astride, straddling; **~ di battaglia** (fig) hobby-horse; **~ da corsa** racehorse

ca'vare vt (togliere) to draw out, extract, take out; (: giacca, scarpe) to take off; (: fame, sete, voglia) to satisfy; **cavarsela** to manage, get on all right; (scamparla) to get away with it

cava'tappi sm inv corkscrew

ca'verna sf cave

'cavia sf guinea pig

cavi'ale sm caviar

ca'viglia [ka'viʎʎa] sf ankle

ca'villo sm quibble

'cavo, a ag hollow ♦ sm (ANAT) cavity; (corda, ELETTR, TEL) cable

cavol'fiore sm cauliflower

'cavolo sm cabbage; (fam): **non m'importa un ~** I don't give a damn; **~ di Bruxelles** Brussels sprout

cazzu'ola [kat'tswɔla] sf trowel

c/c abbr = **conto corrente**

CD sm inv CD

CD-ROM [tʃidi'rɔm] sm inv CD-ROM

C.E. [tʃe] sigla f (= Comunità Europea) EC

ce [tʃe] pron, av vedi **ci**

'cece ['tʃetʃe] sm chickpea

cecità [tʃetʃi'ta] sf blindness

'ceco, a ['tʃɛko] ag, sm/f Czech; **la Repubblica ~a** the Czech Republic

Cecoslo'vacchia [tʃekoslo'vakkja] sf: **la ~** Czechoslovakia

'cedere ['tʃɛdere] vt (concedere: posto) to give up; (DIR) to transfer, make over ♦ vi (cadere) to give way, subside; **~ (a)** to surrender (to), yield (to), give in (to); **ce'devole** ag (terreno) soft; (fig) yielding

cedola ['tʃedola] sf (COMM) coupon; voucher

cedro ['tʃedro] sm cedar; (albero da frutto, frutto) citron

ceffo ['tʃeffo] (peg) sm ugly mug

cef'fone [tʃef'fone] sm slap, smack

ce'lare [tʃe'lare] vt to conceal; **~rsi** to hide

cele'brare [tʃele'brare] vt to celebrate; **celebrazi'one** sf celebration

celebre ['tʃelebre] ag famous, celebrated; **celebrità** sf inv fame; (persona) celebrity

celere ['tʃelere] ag fast, swift; (corso) crash cpd

ce'leste [tʃe'leste] ag celestial; heavenly; (colore) sky-blue

celibe ['tʃelibe] ag single, unmarried

cella ['tʃella] sf cell

cellula ['tʃellula] sf (BIOL, ELETTR, POL) cell; **cellu'lare** sm cellphone

cellu'lite [tʃellu'lite] sf cellulite

cemen'tare [tʃemen'tare] vt (anche fig) to cement

ce'mento [tʃe'mento] sm cement; **~ armato** reinforced concrete

cena ['tʃena] sf dinner; (leggera) supper

ce'nare [tʃe'nare] vi to dine, have dinner

cencio ['tʃentʃo] sm piece of cloth, rag; (per spolverare) duster

cenere ['tʃenere] sf ash

cenno ['tʃenno] sm (segno) sign, signal; (gesto) gesture; (col capo) nod; (con la mano) wave; (allusione) hint, mention; (breve esposizione) short account; **far ~ di si/no** to nod (one's head)/shake one's head

censi'mento [tʃensi'mento] sm census

cen'sura [tʃen'sura] sf censorship; censor's office; (fig) censure

cente'nario, a [tʃente'narjo] ag (che ha cento anni) hundred-year-old; (che ricorre ogni cento anni) centennial, centenary cpd ♦ sm/f centenarian ♦ sm centenary

cen'tesimo, a [tʃen'tezimo] ag, sm hundredth

cen'tigrado, a [tʃen'tigrado] ag centigrade; **20 gradi ~i** 20 degrees centigrade

cen'timetro [tʃen'timetro] sm centimetre

centi'naio [tʃenti'najo] (pl(f) **-aia**) sm: **un ~ (di)** a hundred; about a hundred

cento ['tʃento] num a hundred, one hundred

cen'trale [tʃen'trale] ag central ♦ sf: **~ telefonica** (telephone) exchange; **~ elettrica** electric power station; **centra'lista** sm/f operator; **centra'lino** sm (telephone) exchange; (di albergo etc) switchboard

cen'trare [tʃen'trare] vt to hit the centre of; (TECN) to centre

cen'trifuga [tʃen'trifuga] sf spin-drier

centro ['tʃentro] sm centre; **~ civico** civic centre; **~ commerciale** shopping centre; (città) commercial centre

ceppo ['tʃeppo] sm (di albero) stump; (pezzo di legno) log

cera ['tʃera] sf wax; (aspetto) appearance

ce'ramica, che [tʃe'ramika] sf ceramic; (ARTE) ceramics sg

cerbi'atto [tʃer'bjatto] sm (ZOOL) fawn

cerca ['tʃerka] sf: **in o alla ~ di** in search of

cer'care [tʃer'kare] vt to look for, search for ♦ vi: **~ di fare qc** to try to do sth

cerchia ['tʃerkja] sf circle

cerchio ['tʃerkjo] sm circle; (giocattolo, di botte) hoop

cere'ale [tʃere'ale] sm cereal

ceri'monia [tʃeri'mɔnja] sf ceremony

ce'rino [tʃe'rino] sm wax match

cernia ['tʃernja] sf (ZOOL) stone bass

cerniera [tʃer'njɛra] sf hinge; **~ lampo** zip (fastener) (BRIT), zipper (US) '**cernita** [ˈtʃernita] *sf* selection

'**cero** [ˈtʃero] *sm* (church) candle

ce'**rotto** [tʃeˈrɔtto] *sm* sticking plaster

certa'**mente** [tʃertaˈmente] *av* certainly

cer'**tezza** [tʃerˈtettsa] *sf* certainty

certifi'**cato** *sm* certificate; ~ **medico/ di nascita** medical/birth certificate

---

PAROLA CHIAVE

'**certo, a** [ˈtʃerto] *ag* (*sicuro*): ~ (**di/ che**) certain o sure (of/that)
♦ *det* 1 (*tale*) certain; **un** ~ **signor Smith** a (certain) Mr Smith
2 (*qualche; con valore intensivo*) some; **dopo un** ~ **tempo** after some time; **un fatto di una ~a importanza** a matter of some importance; **di una ~a età** past one's prime, not so young
♦ *pron*: ~**i, e** pl some
♦ *av* (*certamente*) certainly; (*senz'altro*) of course; **di** ~ certainly; **no (di)** ~!, ~ **che no!** certainly not!; **sì** ~ yes indeed, certainly

cer'**vello, i** [tʃerˈvɛllo] (ANAT: pl(f) -**a**) *sm* brain

'**cervo, a** [ˈtʃervo] *sm/f* stag/doe ♦ *sm* deer; ~ **volante** stag beetle

ce'**sello** [tʃeˈzɛllo] *sm* chisel

ce'**soie** [tʃeˈzoje] *sfpl* shears

ces'**puglio** [tʃesˈpuʎʎo] *sm* bush

ces'**sare** [tʃesˈsare] *vi, vt* to stop, cease; ~ **di fare qc** to stop doing sth

'**cesso** [ˈtʃɛsso] (*fam*) *sm* (*gabinetto*) bog

'**cesta** [ˈtʃesta] *sf* (large) basket

ces'**tino** [tʃesˈtino] *sm* basket; (*per la carta straccia*) wastepaper basket; ~ **da viaggio** (FERR) packed lunch (o dinner)

'**cesto** [ˈtʃesto] *sm* basket

'**ceto** [ˈtʃeto] *sm* (*social*) class

cetrio'**lino** [tʃetrioˈlino] *sm* gherkin

cetri'**olo** [tʃetriˈɔlo] *sm* cucumber

CFC *sm inv* (= clorofluorocarburo) CFC

cfr. *abbr* (= confronta) cf

CGIL *sigla f* (= Confederazione Generale Italiana del Lavoro) trades union organization

---

PAROLA CHIAVE

che [ke] *pron* 1 (*relativo: persona: soggetto*) who; (: *oggetto*) whom, that; (: *cosa, animale*) which, that; **il ragazzo** ~ **è venuto** the boy who came; **l'uomo** ~ **io vedo** the man (whom) I see; **il libro** ~ **è sul tavolo** the book which o that is on the table; **il libro** ~ **vedi** the book (which o that) you see; **la sera** ~ **ti ho visto** the evening I saw you
2 (*interrogativo, esclamativo*) what; ~ (**cosa**) **fai?** what are you doing?; **a** ~ (**cosa**) **pensi?** what are you thinking about?; **non sa** ~ (**cosa**) **fare** he doesn't know what to do; **ma** ~ **dici!** what are you saying!
3 (*indefinito*): **quell'uomo ha un** ~ **di losco** there's something suspicious about that man; **un certo non so** ~ an indefinable something
♦ *det* 1 (*interrogativo: tra tanti*) what; (: *tra pochi*) which; ~ **tipo di film preferisci?** what sort of film do you prefer?; ~ **vestito ti vuoi mettere?** what (o which) dress do you want to put on?
2 (*esclamativo: seguito da aggettivo*) how; (: *seguito da sostantivo*) what; ~ **buono!** how delicious!; ~ **bel vestito!** what a lovely dress!
♦ *cong* 1 (*con proposizioni subordinate*) that; **credo** ~ **verrà** I think he'll come; **voglio** ~ **tu studi** I want you to study; **so** ~ **tu c'eri** I know (that) you were there; **non** ~: **non** ~ **sia sbagliato, ma ...** not that it's wrong, but ...
2 (*finale*) so that; **vieni qua,** ~ **ti veda** come here, so (that) I can see you
3 (*temporale*): **arrivai** ~ **eri già partito** you had already left when I arrived; **sono anni** ~ **non lo vedo** I

haven't seen him for years

4 (in frasi imperative, concessive):
~ **venga pure!** let him come by all means!; ~ **tu sia benedetto!** may God bless you!

5 (comparativo: con più, meno) than; vedi anche **più**; **meno**; **così** etc

cheti'chella [keti'kɛlla]: **alla** ~ av stealthily, unobtrusively

---

PAROLA CHIAVE

chi [ki] pron **1** (interrogativo: soggetto) who; (: oggetto) who, whom; ~ **è?** who is it?; **di** ~ **è questo libro?** whose book is this?; **con** ~ **parli?** who are you talking to?; **a** ~ **pensi?** who are you thinking about?; ~ **di voi?** which of you?; **non so a** ~ **rivolgermi** I don't know who to ask

2 (relativo) whoever, anyone who; **dillo a** ~ **vuoi** tell whoever you like

3 (indefinito): ~ ... ~ ... some ... others ...; ~ **dice una cosa,** ~ **dice un'altra** some say one thing, others say another

---

chiacchie'rare [kjakkje'rare] vi to chat; (discorrere futilmente) to chatter; (far pettegolezzi) to gossip; **chiacchie'rata** sf chat; **chi'acchiere** sfpl: **fare due o quattro chiacchiere** to have a chat; **chiacchie'rone, a** ag talkative, chatty; gossipy ♦ sm/f chatterbox; gossip

chia'mare [kja'mare] vt to call; (rivolgersi a qn) to call (in), send for; ~**rsi** vr (aver nome) to be called; **mi chiamo Paolo** my name is Paolo, I'm called Paolo; ~ **alle armi** to call up; ~ **in giudizio** to summon; **chia'mata** sf (TEL) call; (MIL) call-up

chia'rezza [kja'rettsa] sf clearness, clarity

chia'rire [kja'rire] vt to make clear; (fig: spiegare) to clear up, explain; ~**rsi** vr to become clear

chi'aro, a ['kjaro] ag clear; (luminoso) clear, bright; (colore) pale, light

chiaroveg'gente [kjaroved'dʒɛnte] sm/f clairvoyant

chi'asso ['kjasso] sm uproar, row; **chias'soso, a** ag noisy, rowdy; (vistoso) showy, gaudy

chi'ave ['kjave] sf key ♦ ag inv key cpd: ~ **d'accensione** (AUT) ignition key; ~ **inglese** monkey wrench; ~ **di volta** keystone; **chiavis'tello** sm bolt

chi'azza ['kjattsa] sf stain; splash

chicco, chi ['kikko] sm grain; (di caffè) bean; ~ **d'uva** grape

chi'edere ['kjɛdere] vt (per sapere) to ask; (per avere) to ask for ♦ vi: ~ **di qn** to ask after sb; (al telefono) to ask for o want sb; ~ **qc a qn** to ask sb sth; to ask sb for sth

chi'erico, ci ['kjɛriko] sm cleric; altar boy

chi'esa ['kjɛza] sf church

chi'esto, a pp di **chiedere**

'chiglia ['kiʎʎa] sf keel

'chilo ['kilo] sm kilo; **chilo'grammo** sm kilogram(me); **chilome'traggio** sm ≈ mileage; ~**metraggio illimitato** unlimited mileage; **chi'lometro** sm kilometre

'chimica ['kimika] sf chemistry

'chimico, ci, che ['kimiko] ag chemical ♦ sm chemist

'china ['kina] sf (pendio) slope, descent; (inchiostro) Indian ink

chi'nare [ki'nare] vt to lower, bend; ~**rsi** vr to stoop, bend

chi'nino [ki'nino] sm quinine

chi'occiola ['kjɔttʃola] sf snail; **scala a** ~ spiral staircase

chi'odo ['kjɔdo] sm nail; (fig) obsession

chi'oma ['kjɔma] sf (capelli) head of hair

chi'osco, schi ['kjɔsko] sm kiosk, stall

chi'ostro ['kjɔstro] sm cloister

chiro'mante [kiro'mante] sm/f palmist

chirur'gia [kirur'dʒia] sf surgery;

~ **estetica** cosmetic surgery; **chi'rurgo, ghi o gi** *sm* surgeon

chissà [kis'sa] *av* who knows, I wonder

chi'tarra [ki'tarra] *sf* guitar

chi'udere ['kjudere] *vt* to close, shut; *(luce, acqua)* to put off, turn off; *(definitivamente: fabbrica)* to close down, shut down; *(strada)* to close; *(recingere)* to enclose; *(porre termine a)* to end ♦ *vi* to close, shut; to close down, shut down; to end; **~rsi** *vr* to shut, close; *(ritirarsi: anche fig)* to shut o.s. away; *(ferita)* to close up

chi'unque [ki'unkwe] *pron (relativo)* whoever; *(indefinito)* anyone, anybody; ~ **sia** whoever it is

chi'uso, a ['kjuso] *pp di* **chiudere** ♦ *sf (di corso d'acqua)* sluice, lock; *(recinto)* enclosure; *(di discorso etc)* conclusion, ending; **chiu'sura** *(vedi* **chiudere**) closing; shutting; closing o shutting down; enclosing; putting o turning off; ending; *(dispositivo)* catch; fastening; fastener

─────────────────
PAROLA CHIAVE
─────────────────

ci [tʃi] *(dav lo, la, li, le, ne diventa* **ce**) *pron* **1** *(personale: complemento oggetto)* us; *(: a noi: complemento di termine)* (to) us; *(: riflessivo)* ourselves; *(: reciproco)* each other, one another; *(impersonale):* ~ **si veste** we get dressed; ~ **ha visti** he's seen us; **non** ~ **ha dato niente** he gave us nothing; ~ **vestiamo** we get dressed; ~ **amiamo** we love one another o each other

2 *(dimostrativo: di ciò, su ciò, in ciò etc)* about (o on o of) it; **non so cosa far**~ I don't know what to do about it; **che c'entro io?** what have I got to do with it?

♦ *av (qui)* here; *(lì)* there; *(moto attraverso luogo):* ~ **passa sopra un ponte** a bridge passes over it; **non** ~ **passa più nessuno** nobody comes

this way any more; **esser**~ *vedi* **essere**

─────────────────
L
─────────────────

cia'batta [tʃa'batta] *sf* slipper; *(pane)* ciabatta

ci'alda [tʃalda] *sf (cuc)* wafer

ciam'bella [tʃam'bɛlla] *sf (cuc)* ring-shaped cake; *(salvagente)* rubber ring

ci'ao ['tʃao] *escl (all'arrivo)* hello!; *(alla partenza)* cheerio! *(BRIT)*, bye!

cias'cuno, a [tʃas'kuno] *(det: dav sm:* **ciascun** +*C, V,* **ciascuno** +*s impura, gn, pn, ps, x, z; dav sf:* **ciascuna** +*C,* **ciascun'** +*V) det* every, each; *(ogni)* every ♦ *pron* each (one); *(tutti)* everyone, everybody

ci'barie [tʃi'barje] *sfpl* foodstuffs

'cibo ['tʃibo] *sm* food

ci'cala [tʃi'kala] *sf* cicada

cica'trice [tʃika'tritʃe] *sf* scar

'cicca ['tʃikka] *sf* cigarette end

'ciccia ['tʃittʃa] *(fam) sf* fat

cice'rone [tʃitʃe'rone] *sm* guide

ci'clismo [tʃi'klizmo] *sm* cycling; **ci'clista, i, e** *sm/f* cyclist

'ciclo ['tʃiklo] *sm* cycle; *(di malattia)* course

ciclomo'tore [tʃiklomo'tore] *sm* moped

ci'clone [tʃi'klone] *sm* cyclone

ci'cogna [tʃi'konna] *sf* stork

ci'coria [tʃi'kɔrja] *sf* chicory

ci'eco, a, chi, che ['tʃɛko] *ag* blind ♦ *sm/f* blind man/woman

ci'elo ['tʃɛlo] *sm* sky; *(REL)* heaven

'cifra ['tʃifra] *sf (numero)* figure; numeral; *(somma di denaro)* sum, figure; *(monogramma)* monogram, initials *pl; (codice)* code, cipher

'ciglio, i ['tʃiʎʎo] *(delle palpebre: pl(f)* **ciglia**) *sm (margine)* edge, verge; *(eye)lash; (eye)lid; (sopracciglio)* eyebrow

'cigno ['tʃiɲɲo] *sm* swan

cigo'lare [tʃigo'lare] *vi* to squeak, creak

'Cile ['tʃile] *sm:* **il** ~ Chile

ci'lecca [tʃi'lekka] *sf:* far ~ to fail

cili'egia, gie o **ge** [tʃi'ljedʒa] *sf* cherry; **cili'egio** *sm* cherry tree

cilin'drata [tʃilin'drata] *sf* (AUT) (cubic) capacity; **una macchina di grossa** ~ a big-engined car

ci'lindro [tʃi'lindro] *sm* cylinder; (*cappello*) top hat

'cima ['tʃima] *sf* (*sommità*) top; (*di monte*) top, summit; (*estremità*) end; **in** ~ **a** at the top of; **da** ~ **a fondo** from top to bottom; (*fig*) from beginning to end

'cimice ['tʃimitʃe] *sf* (ZOOL) bug; (*puntina*) drawing pin (BRIT), thumbtack (US)

cimini'era [tʃimi'njɛra] *sf* chimney; (*di nave*) funnel

cimi'tero [tʃimi'tɛro] *sm* cemetery

'Cina ['tʃina] *sf:* **la** ~ China

cin'cin [tʃin'tʃin] *escl* cheers!

cin cin [tʃin'tʃin] *escl* = **cincin**

ci'nema ['tʃinema] *sm inv* cinema; **cine'presa** *sf* cine-camera

ci'nese [tʃi'nese] *ag, sm/f, sm* Chinese *inv*

'cingere ['tʃindʒere] *vt* (*attorniare*) to surround, encircle

'cinghia ['tʃingja] *sf* strap; (*cintura, TECN*) belt

cinghi'ale [tʃin'gjale] *sm* wild boar

cinguet'tare [tʃingwet'tare] *vi* to twitter

'cinico, a, ci, che ['tʃiniko] *ag* cynical ♦ *sm/f* cynic; **ci'nismo** *sm* cynicism

cin'quanta [tʃin'kwanta] *num* fifty; **cinquan'tesimo, a** *num* fiftieth

cinquan'tina [tʃinkwan'tina] *sf* (*serie*): **una** ~ (**di**) about fifty; (*età*): **essere sulla** ~ to be about fifty

'cinque ['tʃinkwe] *num* five; **avere** ~ **anni** to be five (years old); **il** ~ **dicembre 1998** the fifth of December 1998; **alle** ~ (*ora*) at five (o'clock)

cinque'cento [tʃinkwe'tʃento] *num* five hundred ♦ *sm:* **il C~** the sixteenth century

'cinto, a ['tʃinto] *pp di* **cingere**

cin'tura [tʃin'tura] *sf* belt; ~ **di salvataggio** lifebelt (BRIT), life preserver (US); ~ **di sicurezza** (AUT, AER) safety o seat belt

ciò [tʃɔ] *pron* this; that; ~ **che** what; ~ **nonostante** o **nondimeno** nevertheless, in spite of that

ci'occa, che ['tʃɔkka] *sf* (*di capelli*) lock

ciocco'lata [tʃokko'lata] *sf* chocolate; (*bevanda*) (hot) chocolate; **cioccola'tino** *sm* chocolate; **ciocco'lato** *sm* chocolate

cioè [tʃo'ɛ] *av* that is (to say)

ciondo'lare [tʃondo'lare] *vi* to dangle; (*fig*) to loaf (about); **ci'ondolo** *sm* pendant

ci'otola ['tʃotola] *sf* bowl

ci'ottolo ['tʃɔttolo] *sm* pebble; (*di strada*) cobble(stone)

ci'polla [tʃi'polla] *sf* onion; (*di tulipano etc*) bulb

ci'presso [tʃi'presso] *sm* cypress (tree)

'cipria ['tʃiprja] *sf* (*face*) powder

'Cipro ['tʃipro] *sm* Cyprus

'circa ['tʃirka] *av* about, roughly ♦ *prep* about, concerning; **a mezzogiorno** ~ about midday

'circo, chi ['tʃirko] *sm* circus

circo'lare [tʃirko'lare] *vi* to circulate; (AUT) to drive (along), move (along) ♦ *ag* circular ♦ *sf* (AMM) circular; (*di autobus*) circle (line); **circolazi'one** *sf* circulation; (AUT): **la circolazione** (the) traffic

'circolo ['tʃirkolo] *sm* circle

circon'dare [tʃirkon'dare] *vt* to surround

circonfe'renza [tʃirkonfe'rentsa] *sf* circumference

circonvallazi'one [tʃirkonvallat'tsjone] *sf* ring road (BRIT), beltway (US); (*per evitare una città*) by-pass

circos'critto, a [tʃirkos'kritto] *pp di* **circoscrivere**

circos'crivere [tʃirkos'krivere] *vt* to

circumscribe; *(fig)* to limit, restrict;
circoscrizi'one *sf (AMM)* district, area;
circoscrizione elettorale
constituency

circos'petto, a [tʃirkos'petto] *ag*
circumspect, cautious

circos'tante [tʃirkos'tante] *ag*
surrounding, neighbouring

circos'tanza [tʃirkos'tantsa] *sf*
circumstance; *(occasione)* occasion

cir'cuito [tʃir'kuito] *sm* circuit

CISL *sigla f (= Confederazione Italiana Sindacati Lavoratori)* trades union
organization

'ciste ['tʃiste] *sf* = **cisti**

cis'terna [tʃis'terna] *sf* tank, cistern

'cisti ['tʃisti] *sf* cyst

C.I.T. [tʃit] *sigla f* = **Compagnia
Italiana Turismo**

ci'tare [tʃi'tare] *vt (DIR)* to summon;
(autore) to quote; *(a esempio, modello)*
to cite; **citazi'one** *sf* summons *sg*;
quotation; *(di persona)* mention

ci'tofono [tʃi'tɔfono] *sm* entry phone;
(in uffici) intercom

città [tʃit'ta] *sf inv* town; *(importante)*
city; ~ **universitaria** university
campus

cittadi'nanza [tʃittadi'nantsa] *sf*
citizens *pl*; *(DIR)* citizenship

citta'dino, a [tʃitta'dino] *ag* town *cpd*;
city *cpd* ♦ *sm/f (di uno Stato)* citizen;
(abitante di città) townsman, city
dweller

ci'uco, a, chi, che ['tʃuko] *sm/f ass*

ci'uffo ['tʃuffo] *sm* tuft

ci'vetta [tʃi'vetta] *sf (ZOOL)* owl; *(fig: donna)* coquette, flirt ♦ *ag inv*: **auto/
nave** ~ decoy car/ship

'civico, a, ci, che ['tʃiviko] *ag (scienza)*
civic; *(museo)* municipal, town *cpd*; city *cpd*

ci'vile [tʃi'vile] *ag* civil; *(non militare)*
civilian; *(nazione)* civilized ♦ *sm* civilian

civilizzazi'one [tʃiviliddzat'tsjone] *sf*
civilization

civiltà [tʃivil'ta] *sf* civilization; *(cortesia)*
civility

'clacson *sm inv (AUT)* horn

cla'more *sm (frastuono)* din, uproar,
clamour; *(fig)* outcry; **clamo'roso, a**
ag noisy; *(fig)* sensational

clandes'tino, a *ag* clandestine; *(POL)*
underground, clandestine ♦ *sm/f*
stowaway

clari'netto *sm* clarinet

'classe *sf* class; **di** ~ *(fig)* with class; of
excellent quality

'classico, a, ci, che *ag* classical;
(tradizionale: moda) classic(al) ♦ *sm*
classic; classical author

clas'sifica *sf* classification; *(SPORT)*
placings *pl*

classifi'care *vt* to classify; *(candidato,
compito)* to grade; **~rsi** *vr* to be placed

'clausola *sf (DIR)* clause

'clava *sf* club

clavi'cembalo [klavi'tʃembalo] *sm*
harpsichord

cla'vicola *sf (ANAT)* collar bone

cle'mente *ag* merciful; *(clima)* mild;
cle'menza *sf* mercy, clemency;
mildness

'clero *sm* clergy

clic'care *vi (INFORM)*: ~ **su** to click on

cli'ente *sm/f* customer, client;
clien'tela *sf* customers *pl*, clientèle

'clima, i *sm* climate; **cli'matico, a, ci,
che** *ag* climatic; **stazione climatica**
health resort; **climatizzatore** *sm* air
conditioning system;
climatizzazi'one *sf (TECN)* air
conditioning

'clinica, che *sf (scienza)* clinical
medicine; *(casa di cura)* clinic, nursing
home; *(settore d'ospedale)* clinic

'clinico, a, ci, che *ag* clinical ♦ *sm
(medico)* clinician

clo'aca, che *sf* sewer

'cloro *sm* chlorine

cloro'formio *sm* chloroform

club *sm inv* club

c.m. *abbr* = **corrente mese**

coabi'tare *vi* to live together

coagu'lare *vt* to coagulate ♦ *vi* to

coagulate; (*latte*) to curdle; **~rsi** vr to coagulate; to curdle

coalizi'one [koalit'tsjone] sf coalition

co'atto, a ag (*DIR*) compulsory, forced

'COBAS sigla mpl (= *Comitati di base*) independent trades unions

Coca-Cola ® sf Coca-Cola ®

coca'ina sf cocaine

cocci'nella [kottʃi'nɛlla] sf ladybird (*BRIT*), ladybug (*US*)

'coccio ['kɔttʃo] sm earthenware; (*vaso*) earthenware pot; **~i** smpl (*frammenti*) fragments of pottery

cocci'uto, a [kot'tʃuto] ag stubborn, pigheaded

'cocco, chi sm (*pianta*) coconut palm; (*frutto*): **noce di ~** coconut ♦ sm/f (*fam*) darling

cocco'drillo sm crocodile

cocco'lare vt to cuddle, fondle

co'cente [ko'tʃɛnte] ag (*anche fig*) burning

co'comero sm watermelon

co'cuzzolo [ko'kuttsolo] sm top; (*di capo, cappello*) crown

'coda sf tail; (*fila di persone, auto*) queue (*BRIT*), line (*US*); (*di abiti*) train; **con la ~ dell'occhio** out of the corner of one's eye; **mettersi in ~** to queue (up) (*BRIT*), line up (*US*); to join the queue (*BRIT*) o line (*US*); **~ di cavallo** (*acconciatura*) ponytail

co'dardo, a ag cowardly ♦ sm/f coward

'codice ['koditʃe] sm code; **~ di avviamento postale** postcode (*BRIT*), zip code (*US*); **~ fiscale** tax code; **~ della strada** highway code

coe'rente ag coherent; **coe'renza** sf coherence

coe'taneo, a ag, sm/f contemporary

'cofano sm (*AUT*) bonnet (*BRIT*), hood (*US*); (*forziere*) chest

'cogli ['kɔʎʎi] prep + det = **con + gli**; vedi **con**

'cogliere ['kɔʎʎere] vt (*fiore, frutto*) to pick, gather; (*sorprendere*) to catch,

surprise; (*bersaglio*) to hit; (*fig: momento opportuno etc*) to grasp, seize, take; (: *capire*) to grasp; **~ qn in flagrante** o **in fallo** to catch sb red-handed

co'gnato, a [kon'nato] sm/f brother-/sister-in-law

co'gnome [kon'nome] sm surname

'coi prep + det = **con + i**; vedi **con**

coinci'denza [kointʃi'dɛntsa] sf coincidence; (*FERR, AER, di autobus*) connection

coin'cidere [koin'tʃidere] vi to coincide; **coin'ciso, a** pp di **coincidere**

coin'volgere [koin'vɔldʒere] vt: **~ in** to involve in; **coin'volto, a** pp di **coinvolgere**

col prep + det = **con + il**; vedi **con**

cola'brodo sm inv strainer

cola'pasta sm inv colander

co'lare vt (*liquido*) to strain; (*pasta*) to drain; (*oro fuso*) to pour ♦ vi (*sudore*) to drip; (*botte*) to leak; (*cera*) to melt; **~ a picco** vt, vi (*nave*) to sink

co'lata sf (*di lava*) flow; (*FONDERIA*) casting

colazi'one [kolat'tsjone] sf (*anche*: *prima ~*) breakfast; (*anche*: *seconda ~*) lunch; **fare ~** to have breakfast (o lunch)

co'lei pron vedi **colui**

co'lera sm (*MED*) cholera

'colica sf (*MED*) colic

'colla sf glue; (*di farina*) paste

collabo'rare vi to collaborate; **~ a** to collaborate in; (*giornale*) to contribute to; **collabora'tore, 'trice** sm/f collaborator; contributor

col'lana sf necklace; (*collezione*) collection, series

col'lant [kɔ'lã] sm inv tights pl

col'lare sm collar

col'lasso sm (*MED*) collapse

collau'dare vt to test, try out; **col'laudo** sm testing no pl; test

'colle sm hill

col'lega, ghi, ghe *sm/f* colleague

collega'mento *sm* connection; (*MIL*) liaison

colle'gare *vt* to connect, join, link; **~rsi** *vr* (*RADIO, TV*) to link up; **~rsi con** (*TEL*) to get through to

col'legio [kol'lɛdʒo] *sm* college; (*convitto*) boarding school; **~ elettorale** (*POL*) constituency

'collera *sf* anger

col'lerico, a, ci, che *ag* quick-tempered, irascible

col'letta *sf* collection

collettività *sf* community

collet'tivo, a *ag* collective; (*interesse*) general, everybody's; (*biglietto, visita etc*) group *cpd* ♦ *sm* (*POL*) (political) group

col'letto *sm* collar

collezio'nare [kollettsjo'nare] *vt* to collect

collezi'one [kollet'tsjone] *sf* collection

colli'mare *vi* to correspond, coincide

col'lina *sf* hill

col'lirio *sm* eyewash

collisi'one *sf* collision

'collo *sm* neck; (*di abito*) neck, collar; (*pacco*) parcel; **~ del piede** instep

colloca'mento *sm* (*impiego*) employment; (*disposizione*) placing, arrangement

collo'care *vt* (*libri, mobili*) to place; (*COMM: merce*) to find a market for

col'loquio *sm* conversation, talk; (*ufficiale, per un lavoro*) interview; (*INS*) preliminary oral exam

col'mare *vt*: **~ di** (*anche fig*) to fill with; (*dare in abbondanza*) to load o overwhelm with; **'colmo, a** *ag*: **colmo (di)** full (of) ♦ *sm* summit, top; (*fig*) height; **al colmo della disperazione** in the depths of despair; **è il colmo!** it's the last straw!

co'lombo, a *sm/f* dove; pigeon

co'lonia *sf* colony; (*per bambini*) holiday camp; (**acqua di**) **~** (eau de) cologne; **coloni'ale** *ag* colonial ♦ *sm/f* colonist, settler

co'lonna *sf* column; **~ vertebrale** spine, spinal column

colon'nello *sm* colonel

co'lono *sm* (*coltivatore*) tenant farmer

colo'rante *sm* colouring

colo'rare *vt* to colour; (*disegno*) to colour in

co'lore *sm* colour; **a ~i** in colour, colour *cpd*; **farne di tutti i ~i** to get up to all sorts of mischief

colo'rito, a *ag* coloured; (*viso*) rosy, pink; (*linguaggio*) colourful ♦ *sm* (*tinta*) colour; (*carnagione*) complexion

co'loro *pron pl vedi* **colui**

co'losso *sm* colossus

'colpa *sf* fault; (*biasimo*) blame; (*colpevolezza*) guilt; (*azione colpevole*) offence; (*peccato*) sin; **di chi è la ~?** whose fault is it?; **è ~ sua** it's his fault; **per ~ di** through, owing to; **col'pevole** *ag* guilty

col'pire *vt* to hit, strike; (*fig*) to strike; **rimanere colpito da qc** to be amazed o struck by sth

'colpo *sm* (*urto*) knock; (*: affettivo*) blow, shock; (*: aggressivo*) blow; (*di pistola*) shot; (*MED*) stroke; (*rapina*) raid; **di ~** suddenly; **fare ~** to make a strong impression; **~ di grazia** coup de grâce; **~ di scena** (*TEATRO*) coup de théâtre; (*fig*) dramatic turn of events; **~ di sole** sunstroke; **~ di Stato** coup d'état; **~ di telefono** phone call; **~ di testa** (sudden) impulse o whim; **~ di vento** gust (of wind)

coltel'lata *sf* stab

col'tello *sm* knife; **~ a serramanico** clasp knife

colti'vare *vt* to cultivate; (*verdura*) to grow, cultivate; **coltiva'tore** *sm* farmer; **coltivazi'one** *sf* cultivation; growing

'colto, a *pp di* **cogliere** ♦ *ag* (*istruito*) cultured, educated

'coltre *sf* blanket

col'tura *sf* cultivation

co'lui (f **co'lei**, pl **co'loro**) pron the one; **~ che parla** the one o the man o the person who is speaking; **colei che amo** the one o the woman o the person (whom) I love

'coma sm inv coma

comanda'mento sm (REL) commandment

coman'dante sm (MIL) commander, commandant; (di reggimento) commanding officer; (NAUT, AER) captain

coman'dare vi to be in command ♦ vt to command; (imporre) to order, command; **~ a qn di fare** to order sb to do; **co'mando** sm (ingiunzione) order, command; (autorità) command; (TECN) control

co'mare sf (madrina) godmother

combaci'are [komba'tʃare] vi to meet; (fig: coincidere) to coincide

com'battere vt, vi to fight; **combatti'mento** sm fight; fighting no pl; (di pugilato) match

combi'nare vt to combine; (organizzare) to arrange; (fam: fare) to make, cause; **combinazi'one** sf combination; (caso fortuito) coincidence; **per combinazione** by chance

combus'tibile ag combustible ♦ sm fuel

com'butta (peg) sf: **in ~** in league

PAROLA CHIAVE

'come av **1** (alla maniera di) like; **ti comporti ~ lui** you behave like him o like he does; **bianco ~ la neve** (as) white as snow; **~ se** as if, as though

2 (in qualità di) as a; **lavora ~ autista** he works as a driver

3 (interrogativo) how; **~ ti chiami?** what's your name?; **~? (prego?)** pardon?, sorry?; **~ mai?** how come?; **~ mai non ci hai avvertiti?** why on earth

didn't you warn us?

4 (esclamativo): **~ sei bravo!** how clever you are!; **~ mi dispiace!** I'm terribly sorry!

♦ cong **1** (in che modo) how; **mi ha spiegato ~ l'ha conosciuto** he told me how he met him

2 (correlativo) as; (con comparativi di maggioranza) than; **non è bravo ~ pensavo** he isn't as clever as I thought; **è meglio di ~ pensassi** it's better than I thought

3 (appena che, quando) as soon as; **~ arrivò, iniziò a lavorare** as soon as he arrived, he set to work; vedi **così; tanto**

'comico, a, ci, che ag (TEATRO) comic; (buffo) comical ♦ sm (attore) comedian, comic actor

co'mignolo [ko'miɲɲolo] sm chimney top

cominci'are [komin'tʃare] vt, vi to begin, start; **~ a fare/col fare** to begin to do/by doing

comi'tato sm committee

comi'tiva sf party, group

co'mizio [ko'mittsjo] sm (POL) meeting, assembly

com'mando sm inv commando (squad)

com'media sf comedy; (opera teatrale) play; (: che fa ridere) comedy; (fig) playacting no pl; **commedi'ante** (peg) sm/f third-rate actor/actress; (fig) sham

commemo'rare vt to commemorate

commenda'tore sm official title awarded for services to one's country

commen'tare vt to comment on; (testo) to annotate; (RADIO, TV) to give a commentary on; **commenta'tore, 'trice** sm/f commentator; **com'mento** sm comment; (a un testo, RADIO, TV) commentary

commerci'ale [kommer'tʃale] ag commercial, trading; (peg) commercial

commerci'ante [kommer'tʃante] sm/f

trader, dealer; (*negoziante*) shopkeeper

commerci'are [kommer'tʃare] *vt, vi*: ~ **in** to deal *o* trade in

com'mercio [kom'mertʃo] *sm* trade, commerce; **essere in ~** (*prodotto*) to be on the market *o* in trade; **essere nel ~** (*persona*) to be in business; **~ elettronico** e-commerce

com'messa *sf* (*COMM*) order

com'messo, a *pp di* **commettere** ♦ *sm/f* shop assistant (*BRIT*), sales clerk (*US*) ♦ *sm* (*impiegato*) clerk; **~ viaggiatore** commercial traveller

commes'tibile *ag* edible; **~i** *smpl* foodstuffs

com'mettere *vt* to commit

com'miato *sm* leave-taking

commi'nare *vt* (*DIR*) to threaten; to inflict

commissari'ato *sm* (*AMM*) commissionership; (*: sede*) commissioner's office; (*: di polizia*) police station

commis'sario *sm* commissioner; (*di pubblica sicurezza*) ≈ (police) superintendent (*BRIT*), (police) captain (*US*); (*SPORT*) steward; (*membro di commissione*) member of a committee *o* board

commissio'nario *sm* (*COMM*) agent, broker

commissi'one *sf* (*incarico*) errand; (*comitato, percentuale*) commission; (*COMM: ordinazione*) order

commit'tente *sm/f* (*COMM*) purchaser, customer

com'mosso, a *pp di* **commuovere**

commo'vente *ag* moving

commozi'one [kommot'tsjone] *sf* emotion, deep feeling; **~ cerebrale** (*MED*) concussion

commu'overe *vt* to move, affect; **~rsi** *vr* to be moved

commu'tare *vt* (*pena*) to commute; (*ELETTR*) to change *o* switch over

comò *sm inv* chest of drawers

como'dino *sm* bedside table

comodità *sf inv* comfort; convenience

'comodo, a *ag* comfortable; (*facile*) easy; (*conveniente*) convenient; (*utile*) useful, handy ♦ *sm* comfort; convenience; **con ~** at one's convenience *o* leisure; **fare il proprio ~** to do as one pleases; **far ~** to be useful *o* handy

compae'sano, a *sm/f* fellow countryman; person from the same town

com'pagine [kom'padʒine] *sf* (*squadra*) team

compa'gnia [kompaɲ'nia] *sf* company; (*gruppo*) gathering

com'pagno, a [kom'paɲno] *sm/f* (*di classe, gioco*) companion; (*POL*) comrade

compa'rare *vt* to compare

compara'tivo, a *ag, sm* comparative

compa'rire *vi* to appear; **com'parsa** *sf* appearance; (*TEATRO*) walk-on; (*CINEMA*) extra; **comparso, a** *pp di* **comparire**

compartecipazi'one [kompartetʃipat'tsjone] *sf* sharing; (*quota*) share; **~ agli utili** profit-sharing

comparti'mento *sm* compartment; (*AMM*) district

compas'sato, a *ag* (*persona*) composed

compassi'one *sf* compassion, pity; **avere ~ di qn** to feel sorry for sb, to pity sb

com'passo *sm* (pair of) compasses *pl*; callipers *pl*

compa'tibile *ag* (*scusabile*) excusable; (*conciliabile, INFORM*) compatible

compa'tire *vt* (*aver compassione di*) to sympathize with, feel sorry for; (*scusare*) to make allowances for

com'patto, a *ag* compact; (*roccia*) solid; (*folla*) dense; (*fig: gruppo, partito*) united

com'pendio *sm* summary; (*libro*) compendium

compen'sare *vt* (*equilibrare*) to

compensate for, make up for; **~ qn** di (*rimunerare*) to pay o remunerate sb for; (*risarcire*) to pay compensation to sb for; (*fig: fatiche, dolori*) to reward sb for; **com'penso** sm compensation; payment, remuneration; reward; **in compenso** (*d'altra parte*) on the other hand

'**compera** sf (*acquisto*) purchase; **fare le ~e** to do the shopping

compe'rare vt = comprare

compe'tente ag competent; (*mancia*) apt, suitable; **compe'tenza** sf competence; **competenze** sfpl (*onorari*) fees

com'petere vi to compete, vie; (*DIR: spettare*): **~ a** to lie within the competence of; **competizi'one** sf competition

compia'cente [kompja'tʃɛnte] ag courteous, obliging; **compia'cenza** sf courtesy

compia'cere [kompja'tʃere] vi: **~ a** to gratify, please ♦ vt to please; **~rsi** vr (*provare soddisfazione*): **~rsi di** o **per qc** to be delighted at sth; (*rallegrarsi*): **~rsi con qn** to congratulate sb; (*degnarsi*): **~rsi di fare** to be so good as to do; **compiaci'uto, a** pp di **compiacere**

compi'angere [kom'pjandʒere] vt to sympathize with, feel sorry for; **compi'anto, a** pp di **compiangere**

'**compiere** (*concludere*) to finish, complete; (*adempiere*) to carry out, fulfil; **~rsi** vr (*avverarsi*) to be fulfilled, come true; **~ gli anni** to have one's birthday

compi'lare vt (*modulo*) to fill in; (*dizionario, elenco*) to compile

com'pire vt = compiere

compi'tare vt to spell out

'**compito** sm (*incarico*) task, duty; (*dovere*) duty; (*INS*) exercise; (*: a casa*) piece of homework; **fare i ~i** to do one's homework

com'pito, a ag well-mannered, polite

comple'anno sm birthday

complemen'tare ag complementary; (*INS: materia*) subsidiary

comple'mento sm complement; (*MIL*) reserve (troops); **~ oggetto** (*LING*) direct object

comples'sità sf complexity

comples'sivo, a ag (*globale*) comprehensive, overall; (*totale: cifra*) total

com'plesso, a ag complex ♦ sm (*PSIC, EDIL*) complex; (*MUS: corale*) ensemble; (*: orchestrina*) band; (*: di musica pop*) group; **in** o **nel ~** on the whole

comple'tare vt to complete

com'pleto, a ag complete; (*teatro, autobus*) full ♦ sm suit; **al ~** full; (*tutti presenti*) all present

compli'care vt to complicate; **~rsi** vr to become complicated; **complicazi'one** sf complication

'**complice** ['komplitʃe] sm/f accomplice

complimen'tarsi vr: **~ con** to congratulate

compli'mento sm compliment; **~i** smpl (*cortesia eccessiva*) ceremony sg; (*ossequi*) regards, compliments; **~i!** congratulations!; **senza ~i!** don't stand on ceremony!; make yourself at home!; help yourself!

complot'tare vi to plot, conspire

com'plotto sm plot, conspiracy

compo'nente sm/f member ♦ sm component

componi'mento sm (*INS*) composition; (*poetico, teatrale*) work

com'porre vt (*musica, testo*) to compose; (*mettere in ordine*) to arrange; (*DIR: lite*) to settle; (*TIP*) to set; (*TEL*) to dial

comporta'mento sm behaviour

compor'tare vt (*implicare*) to involve; **~rsi** vr to behave

composi'tore, 'trice sm/f composer; (*TIP*) compositor, typesetter

composizi'one [kompozit'tsjone] *sf* composition; (*DIR*) settlement

com'posta *sf* (*CUC*) stewed fruit *no pl*; (*AGR*) compost; *vedi anche* **composto**

compos'tezza [kompos'tettsa] *sf* composure; decorum

com'posto, a *pp di* **comporre ♦** *ag* (*persona*) composed, self-possessed; (: *decoroso*) dignified; (*formato da più elementi*) compound *cpd* ♦ *sm* compound

com'prare *vt* to buy; **compra'tore, 'trice** *sm/f* buyer, purchaser

com'prendere *vt* (*contenere*) to comprise, consist of; (*capire*) to understand

comprensi'one *sf* understanding

compren'sivo, a *ag* (*prezzo*): **~ di** inclusive of; (*indulgente*) understanding

com'preso, a *pp di* **comprendere ♦** *ag* (*incluso*) included

com'pressa *sf* (*MED: garza*) compress; (: *pastiglia*) tablet; *vedi anche* **compresso**

compressi'one *sf* compression

com'presso, a *pp di* **comprimere ♦** *ag* (*vedi comprimere*) pressed; compressed; repressed

com'primere *vt* (*premere*) to press; (*FISICA*) to compress; (*fig*) to repress

compro'messo, a *pp di* **compromettere ♦** *sm* compromise

compro'mettere *vt* to compromise

compro'vare *vt* to confirm

com'punto, a *ag* contrite

compu'tare *vt* to calculate

com'puter *sm inv* computer

computiste'ria *sf* accounting, book-keeping

'computo *sm* calculation

comu'nale *ag* municipal, town *cpd*, ≈ borough *cpd*

co'mune *ag* common; (*consueto*) common, everyday; (*di livello medio*) average; (*ordinario*) ordinary ♦ *sm* (*AMM*) town council; (: *sede*) town hall ♦ *sf* (*di persone*) commune; **fuori del ~**

out of the ordinary; **avere in ~** to have in common, share; **mettere in ~** to share

comuni'care *vt* (*notizia*) to pass on, convey; (*malattia*) to pass on; (*ansia etc*) to communicate; (*trasmettere: calore etc*) to transmit, communicate; (*REL*) to administer communion to ♦ *vi* to communicate; **~rsi** *vr* (*propagarsi*): **~rsi a** to spread to; (*REL*) to receive communion

comuni'cato *sm* communiqué; **~ stampa** press release

comunicazi'one [komunikat'tsjone] *sf* communication; (*annuncio*) announcement; (*TEL*): **~ (telefonica)** (telephone) call; **dare la ~ a qn** to put sb through; **ottenere la ~** to get through

comuni'one *sf* communion; **~ di beni** (*DIR*) joint ownership of property

comu'nismo *sm* communism; **comu'nista, i, e** *ag, sm/f* communist

comunità *sf inv* community; **C~ Europea** European Community

co'munque *cong* however, no matter how ♦ *av* (*in ogni modo*) in any case; (*tuttavia*) however, nevertheless

con *prep* with; **partire col treno** to leave by train; **~ mio grande stupore** to my great astonishment; **~ tutto ciò** for all that

co'nato *sm*: **~ di vomito** retching

'conca, che *sf* (*GEO*) valley

con'cedere [kon'tʃedere] *vt* (*accordare*) to grant; (*ammettere*) to admit, concede; **~rsi qc** to treat o.s. to sth, to allow o.s. sth

concentra'mento [kontʃentra'mento] *sm* concentration

concen'trare [kontʃen'trare] *vt* to concentrate; **~rsi** *vr* to concentrate; **concentrazi'one** *sf* concentration

conce'pire [kontʃe'pire] *vt* (*bambino*) to conceive; (*progetto, idea*) to conceive (of); (*metodo, piano*) to devise

con'cernere [kon'tʃernere] *vt* to

concern

concer'tare [kontʃer'tare] vt (MUS) to harmonize; (ordire) to devise, plan; **~rsi** vr to agree

con'certo [kon'tʃerto] sm (MUS) concert; (: componimento) concerto

concessio'nario [kontʃessjo'narjo] sm (COMM) agent, dealer

con'cesso, a [kon'tʃesso] pp di **concedere**

con'cetto [kon'tʃetto] sm (pensiero, idea) concept; (opinione) opinion

concezi'one [kontʃet'tsjone] sf conception

con'chiglia [kon'kiʎʎa] sf shell

'concia ['kontʃa] sf (di pelle) tanning; (di tabacco) curing; (sostanza) tannin

conci'are [kon'tʃare] vt (pelli) to tan; (tabacco) to cure; (fig: ridurre in cattivo stato) to beat up; **~rsi** vr (sporcarsi) to get in a mess; (vestirsi male) to dress badly

concili'are [kontʃi'ljare] vt to reconcile; (contravvenzione) to pay on the spot; (sonno) to be conducive to, induce; **~rsi qc** to gain o win sth (for o.s.); **~rsi qn** to win sb over; **~rsi con** to be reconciled with; **conciliazi'one** sf reconciliation; (DIR) settlement

con'cilio [kon'tʃiljo] sm (REL) council

con'cime [kon'tʃime] sm manure; (chimico) fertilizer

con'ciso, a [kon'tʃizo] ag concise, succinct

conci'tato, a [kontʃi'tato] ag excited, emotional

concitta'dino, a [kontʃitta'dino] sm/f fellow citizen

con'cludere vt to conclude; (portare a compimento) to conclude, finish, bring to an end; (operare positivamente) to achieve ♦ vi (essere convincente) to be conclusive; **~rsi** vr to come to an end, close; **conclusi'one** sf conclusion; (risultato) result; **conclu'sivo, a** ag conclusive; (finale) final; **con'cluso, a** pp di **concludere**

concor'danza [konkor'dantsa] sf (anche LING) agreement

concor'dare vt (tregua, prezzo) to agree on; (LING) to make agree ♦ vi to agree; **concor'dato** sm agreement; (REL) concordat

con'corde ag (d'accordo) in agreement; (simultaneo) simultaneous

concor'rente sm/f competitor; (INS) candidate; **concor'renza** sf competition

con'correre vi: ~ (in) (MAT) to converge o meet (in); ~ (a) (competere) to compete (for); (: INS: a una cattedra) to apply (for); (partecipare: a un'impresa) to take part (in), contribute (to); **con'corso, a** pp di **concorrere** ♦ sm competition; (INS) competitive examination; **concorso di colpa** (DIR) contributory negligence

con'creto, a ag concrete

concussi'one sf (DIR) extortion

con'danna sf sentence; conviction; condemnation

condan'nare vt (DIR): ~ **a** to sentence to; ~ **per** to convict of; (disapprovare) to condemn; **condan'nato, a** sm/f convict

conden'sare vt to condense; **~rsi** vr to condense; **condensazi'one** sf condensation

condi'mento sm seasoning; dressing

con'dire vt to season; (insalata) to dress

condi'videre vt to share; **condi'viso, a** pp di **condividere**

condizio'nale [kondittsjo'nale] ag conditional ♦ sm (LING) conditional ♦ sf (DIR) suspended sentence

condizio'nare [kondittsjo'nare] vt to condition; **ad aria condizionata** air-conditioned; **condiziona'tore** sm air conditioner

condizi'one [kondit'tsjone] sf condition; **~i** sfpl (di pagamento etc) terms, conditions; **a ~ che** on condition that, provided that

condogli'anze [kondoʎ'ʎantse] *sfpl* condolences

condo'minio *sm* joint ownership; (*edificio*) jointly-owned building

condo'nare *vt* (DIR) to remit; **con'dono** *sm* remission; **condono fiscale** conditional amnesty for people evading tax

con'dotta *sf* (*modo di comportarsi*) conduct, behaviour; (*di un affare etc*) handling; (*di acqua*) piping; (*incarico sanitario*) country medical practice controlled by a local authority

con'dotto, a *pp di* **condurre** ♦ *ag*: **medico** ~ local authority doctor (*in country district*) ♦ *sm* (*canale, tubo*) pipe, conduit; (ANAT) duct

condu'cente [kondu't∫ɛnte] *sm* driver

con'durre *vt* to conduct; (*azienda*) to manage; (*accompagnare: bambino*) to take; (*automobile*) to drive; (*trasportare: acqua, gas*) to convey, conduct; (*fig*) to lead ♦ *vi* to lead; **condursi** *vr* to behave, conduct o.s.

condut'tore *ag*: **filo** ~ (*fig*) thread ♦ *sm* (*di mezzi pubblici*) driver; (FISICA) conductor

con'farsi *vr*: ~ **a** to suit, agree with

confederazi'one [konfederat'tsjone] *sf* confederation

confe'renza [konfe'rɛntsa] *sf* (*discorso*) lecture; (*riunione*) conference; ~ **stampa** press conference; **conferenzi'ere, a** *sm/f* lecturer

confe'rire *vt*: ~ **qc a qn** to give sth to sb, bestow sth on sb ♦ *vi* to confer

con'ferma *sf* confirmation

confer'mare *vt* to confirm

confes'sare *vt* to confess; ~**rsi** *vr* to confess; **andare a ~rsi** (REL) to go to confession; **confessio'nale** *ag, sm* confessional; **confessi'one** *sf* confession; (*setta religiosa*) denomination; **confes'sore** *sm* confessor

con'fetto *sm* sugared almond; (MED) pill

confezio'nare [konfettsjo'nare] *vt* (*vestito*) to make (up); (*merci, pacchi*) to package

confezi'one [konfet'tsjone] *sf* (*di abiti: da uomo*) tailoring; (: *da donna*) dressmaking; (*imballaggio*) packaging; ~ **regalo** gift pack; ~**i per signora** ladies' wear; ~**i da uomo** menswear

confic'care *vt*: ~ **qc in** to hammer o drive sth into; ~**rsi** *vr* to stick

confi'dare *vi*: ~ **in** to confide in, rely on ♦ *vt* to confide; ~**rsi con qn** to confide in sb; **confi'dente** *sm/f* confidant/confidante; (*informatore*) informer; **confi'denza** *sf* (*familiarità*) intimacy, familiarity; (*fiducia*) trust, confidence; (*rivelazione*) confidence; **confidenzi'ale** *ag* confidential

configu'rarsi *vr*: ~ **a** to assume the shape o form of

confi'nare *vi*: ~ **con** to border on ♦ *vt* (POL) to intern; (*fig*) to confine; ~**rsi in** (*isolarsi*): ~**rsi in** to shut o.s. up in

Confin'dustria *sigla f* (= Confederazione Generale dell'Industria Italiana) employers' association, ≈ CBI (BRIT)

con'fine *sm* boundary; (*di paese*) border, frontier

con'fino *sm* internment

confis'care *vt* to confiscate

con'flitto *sm* conflict

conflu'enza [konflu'ɛntsa] *sf* (*di fiumi*) confluence; (*di strade*) junction

conflu'ire *vi* (*fiumi*) to flow into each other, meet; (*strade*) to meet

con'fondere *vt* to mix up, confuse; (*imbarazzare*) to embarrass; ~**rsi** *vr* (*mescolarsi*) to mingle; (*turbarsi*) to be confused; (*sbagliare*) to get mixed up

confor'mare *vt* (*adeguare*): ~ **a** to adapt o conform to; ~**rsi** *vr*: ~**rsi (a)** to conform (to)

confor'tare *vt* to comfort, console; **confor'tevole** *ag* (*consolante*) comforting; (*comodo*) comfortable;

con'forto sm comfort, consolation

confron'tare vt to compare

con'fronto sm comparison; **in o a ~ di** in comparison with, compared to; **nei miei** (o **tuoi** etc) **~i** towards me (o you etc)

confusi'one sf confusion; (chiasso) racket, noise; (imbarazzo) embarrassment

con'fuso, a pp di **confondere** ♦ ag (vedi confondere) confused; embarrassed

confu'tare vt to refute

conge'dare [kondʒe'dare] vt to dismiss; (MIL) to demobilize; **~rsi** vr to take one's leave; **con'gedo** sm (anche MIL) leave; **prendere congedo da qn** to take one's leave of sb; **congedo assoluto** (MIL) discharge

conge'gnare [kondʒeɲ'ɲare] vt to construct, put together; **con'gegno** sm device, mechanism

conge'lare [kondʒe'lare] vt to freeze; **~rsi** vr to freeze; **congela'tore** sm freezer

congestio'nare [kondʒestjo'nare] vt to congest

congesti'one [kondʒes'tjone] sf congestion

conget'tura [kondʒet'tura] sf conjecture

con'giungere [kon'dʒundʒere] vt to join (together); **~rsi** vr to join (together)

congiunti'vite [kondʒunti'vite] sf conjunctivitis

congiun'tivo [kondʒun'tivo] sm (LING) subjunctive

congi'unto, a [kon'dʒunto] pp di **congiungere** ♦ ag (unito) joined ♦ sm/f relative

congiun'tura [kondʒun'tura] sf (giuntura) junction, join; (ANAT) joint; (circostanza) juncture; (ECON) economic situation

congiunzi'one [kondʒun'tsjone] sf (LING) conjunction

congi'ura [kon'dʒura] sf conspiracy; **congiu'rare** vi to conspire

conglome'rato sm (GEO) conglomerate; (fig) conglomeration; (EDIL) concrete

congratu'larsi vr: **~ con qn per qc** to congratulate sb on sth

congratulazi'oni [kongratulat'tsjoni] sfpl congratulations

con'grega, ghe sf band, bunch

con'gresso sm congress

congu'aglio [kon'gwaʎʎo] sm balancing, adjusting; (somma di denaro) balance

coni'are vt to mint, coin; (fig) to coin

co'niglio [ko'niʎʎo] sm rabbit

coniu'gare vt (LING) to conjugate; **~rsi** vr to get married; **coniu'gato, a** ag (sposato) married; **coniugazi'one** sf (LING) conjugation

'coniuge ['konjudʒe] sm/f spouse

connazio'nale [konnattsjo'nale] sm/f fellow-countryman/woman

connessi'one sf connection

con'nesso, a pp di **connettere**

con'nettere vt to connect, join ♦ vi (fig) to think straight

conni'vente ag conniving

conno'tati smpl distinguishing marks

'cono sm cone; **~ gelato** ice-cream cone

cono'scente [konoʃ'ʃente] sm/f acquaintance

cono'scenza [konoʃ'ʃentsa] sf (il sapere) knowledge no pl; (persona) acquaintance; (facoltà sensoriale) consciousness no pl; **perdere ~** to lose consciousness

co'noscere [ko'noʃʃere] vt to know; **ci siamo conosciuti a Firenze** we (first) met in Florence; **conosci'tore, 'trice** sm/f connoisseur; **conosci'uto, a** pp di **conoscere** ♦ ag well-known

con'quista sf conquest

conqui'stare vt to conquer; (fig) to gain, win

consa'crare vt (REL) to consecrate;

(: *sacerdote*) to ordain; (*dedicare*) to dedicate; (*fig: uso etc*) to sanction; **~rsi a** to dedicate o.s. to

consangu'ineo, a *sm/f* blood relation

consa'pevole *ag*: **~ di** aware o conscious of; **consapevo'lezza** *sf* awareness, consciousness

'conscio, a, sci, sce ['kɔnʃo] *ag*: **~ di** aware o conscious of

consecu'tivo, a *ag* consecutive; (*successivo: giorno*) following, next

con'segna [kon'seɲɲa] *sf* delivery; (*merce consegnata*) consignment; (*custodia*) care, custody; (*MIL: ordine*) orders *pl*; (: *punizione*) confinement to barracks; **pagamento alla ~** cash on delivery; **dare qc in ~ a qn** to entrust sth to sb

conse'gnare [konseɲ'ɲare] *vt* to deliver; (*affidare*) to entrust, hand over; (*MIL*) to confine to barracks

consegu'enza [konse'gwentsa] *sf* consequence; **per o di ~** consequently

consegu'ire *vt* to achieve ♦ *vi* to follow

con'senso *sm* approval, consent

consen'tire *vi*: **~ a** to consent o agree to ♦ *vt* to allow, permit

con'serva *sf* (*cuc*) preserve; **~ di frutta** jam; **~ di pomodoro** tomato purée

conser'vare *vt* (*cuc*) to preserve; (*custodire*) to keep; (: *dalla distruzione etc*) to preserve, conserve; **~rsi** *vr* to keep

conserva'tore, 'trice *sm/f* (*POL*) conservative

conservazi'one [konservat'tsjone] *sf* preservation; conservation

conside'rare *vt* to consider; (*reputare*) to consider, regard; **consideraz'one** *sf* consideration; (*stima*) regard, esteem; **prendere in considerazione** to take into consideration

conside'revole *ag* considerable

consigli'are [konsiʎ'ʎare] *vt* (*persona*) to advise; (*metodo, azione*) to

recommend, advise, suggest; **~rsi** *vr*: **~rsi con qn** to ask sb for advice; **consigli'ere, a** *sm/f* adviser ♦ *sm*: **consigliere d'amministrazione** board member; **consigliere comunale** town councillor; **con'siglio** *sm* (*suggerimento*) advice *no pl*, piece of advice; (*assemblea*) council; **consiglio d'amministrazione** board; **il Consiglio dei Ministri** (*POL*) ≈ the Cabinet; **Consiglio d'Europa** Council of Europe

consis'tente *ag* thick; solid; (*fig*) sound, valid; **consis'tenza** *sf* consistency, thickness; solidity; validity

con'sistere *vi*: **~ in** to consist of; **consis'tito, a** *pp di* **consistere**

conso'lare *ag* consular ♦ *vt* (*confortare*) to console, comfort; (*rallegrare*) to cheer up; **~rsi** *vr* to be comforted; to cheer up

conso'lato *sm* consulate

consolazi'one [konsolat'tsjone] *sf* consolation, comfort

'console¹ *sm* consul

con'sole² [kon'sɔl] *sf* (*quadro di comando*) console

conso'nante *sf* consonant

'consono, a *ag*: **~ a** consistent with, consonant with

con'sorte *sm/f* consort

con'sorzio [kon'sɔrtsjo] *sm* consortium

con'stare *vi*: **~ di** to consist of ♦ *vb impers*: **mi consta che** it has come to my knowledge that, it appears that

cons'tare *vt* to establish, verify; **constatazi'one** *sf* observation; **constatazione amichevole** jointly-agreed statement for insurance purposes

consu'eto, a *ag* habitual, usual; **consue'tudine** *sf* habit, custom; (*usanza*) custom

consu'lente *sm/f* consultant; **consu'lenza** *sf* consultancy

consul'tare *vt* to consult; **~rsi** *vr*: **~rsi**

con qn to seek the advice of sb;
consultazi'one sf consultation;
consultazioni sfpl (POL) talks,
consultations

consul'torio sm: **~ familiare** family
planning clinic

consu'mare vt (logorare: abiti, scarpe)
to wear out; (usare) to consume, use
up; (mangiare, bere) to consume; (DIR)
to consummate; **~rsi** vr to wear out; to
be used up; (anche fig) to be
consumed; (combustibile) to burn out;
consuma'tore sm consumer;
consumazi'one sf (bibita) drink,
(spuntino) snack; (DIR) consummation;
consu'mismo sm consumerism;
con'sumo sm consumption; wear; use

consun'tivo sm (ECON) final balance

con'tabile ag accounts cpd,
accounting ♦ sm/f accountant;
contabilità sf (attività, tecnica)
accounting, accountancy; (insieme dei
libri etc) books pl, accounts pl; (ufficio)
accounts department

contachi'lometri [kontaki'lɔmetri]
sm inv ≈ mileometer

conta'dino, a sm/f countryman/
woman; farm worker; (peg) peasant

contagi'are [konta'dʒare] vt to infect

con'tagio [kon'tadʒo] sm infection;
(per contatto diretto) contagion;
(epidemia) epidemic; **contagi'oso, a**
ag infectious; contagious

conta'gocce [konta'gottʃe] sm inv
(MED) dropper

contami'nare vt to contaminate

con'tante sm cash; **pagare in ~i** to
pay cash

con'tare vt to count; (considerare) to
consider ♦ vi to count, be of
importance; **~ su qn** to count o rely
on sb; **~ di fare qc** to intend to do
sth; **conta'tore** sm meter

contat'tare vt to contact

con'tatto sm contact

'**conte** sm count

conteggi'are [konted'dʒare] vt to

charge, put on the bill; **con'teggio** sm
calculation

con'tegno [kon'teɲɲo] sm
(comportamento) behaviour;
(atteggiamento) attitude; **darsi un ~** to
act nonchalant; to pull o.s. together

contem'plare vt to contemplate, gaze
at; (DIR) to make provision for

contempora'nea'mente av
simultaneously; at the same time

contempo'raneo, a ag, sm/f
contemporary

conten'dente sm/f opponent,
adversary

con'tendere vi (competere) to
compete; (litigare) to quarrel ♦ vt: **~ qc
a qn** to contend with o be in
competition with sb for sth

conte'nere vt to contain;
conteni'tore sm container

conten'tare vt to please, satisfy; **~rsi
di** to be satisfied with, content o.s.
with

conten'tezza [konten'tettsa] sf
contentment

con'tento, a ag pleased, glad; **~ di**
pleased with

conte'nuto sm contents pl;
(argomento) content

con'tesa sf dispute, argument

con'teso, a pp di **contendere**

con'tessa sf countess

contes'tare vt (DIR) to notify; (fig) to
dispute; **contestazi'one** sf (DIR)
notification; dispute; (protesta) protest

con'testo sm context

con'tiguo, a ag: **~ (a)** adjacent (to)

continen'tale ag, sm/f continental

conti'nente ag continent ♦ sm (GEO)
continent; (: terra ferma) mainland

contin'gente [kontin'dʒente] ag
contingent ♦ sm (COMM) quota; (MIL)
contingent; **contin'genza** sf
circumstance; (ECON): **(indennità di)
contingenza** cost-of-living allowance

continu'are vt to continue (with), go
on with ♦ vi to continue, go on; **~ a**

fare qc to go on o continue doing sth; **continuaz'one** sf continuation

continuità sf continuity

con'tinuo, a ag (numerazione) continuous; (pioggia) continual, constant; (ELETTR): **corrente ~a** direct current; (fig: stima) consideration, esteem; **fare i ~i con qn** to count o rely on sb; **rendere ~ a qn di qc** to be accountable to sb for sth; **tener ~ di qn/qc** to take sb/sth into account; **per ~ mio** as far as I'm concerned; **a ~i fatti, in fin dei ~i** all things considered; **~ corrente** current account; **~ alla rovescia** countdown

con'torcere [kon'tortʃere] vt to twist; **~rsi** vr to twist, writhe

contor'nare vt to surround

con'torno sm (linea) outline, contour; (ornamento) border; (CUC) vegetables pl

con'torto, a pp di contorcere

contrabbandi'ere, a sm/f smuggler

contrab'bando sm smuggling; contraband; **merce di ~** contraband, smuggled goods pl

contrab'basso sm (MUS) (double) bass

contraccambi'are vt (favore etc) to return

contraccet'tivo, a [kontratʃet'tivo] ag, sm contraceptive

contrac'colpo sm rebound; (di arma da fuoco) recoil; (fig) repercussion

con'trada sf street; district

contrad'detto, a pp di contraddire

contrad'dire vt to contradict; **contraddit'torio, a** ag contradictory; (sentimenti) conflicting ♦ sm (DIR) cross-examination; **contraddizi'one** sf contradiction

contraf'fare vt (persona) to mimic; (alterare: voce) to disguise; (firma) to forge, counterfeit; **contraf'fatto, a** pp

di contraffare ♦ ag counterfeit; **contraffazi'one** sf mimicking no pl; disguising no pl; forging no pl; (cosa contraffatta) forgery

contrap'mente av: **~ a** contrary to, counterbalance, counterweight

contrap'porre vt: **~ qc a qc** to counter sth with sth; (paragonare) to compare sth with sth; **contrap'posto, a** pp di contrapporre

contraria'mente av: **~ a** contrary to

contrari'are vt (contrastare) to thwart, oppose; (irritare) to annoy, bother; **~rsi** vr to get annoyed

contrarietà sf adversity; (fig) aversion

con'trario, a ag opposite; (sfavorevole) unfavourable ♦ sm opposite; **essere ~ a qc** (persona) to be against sth; **in caso ~** otherwise; **avere qc in ~** to have some objection; **al ~** on the contrary

con'trarre vt to contract; **contrarsi** vr to contract

contrasse'gnare [kontrassen'ɲare] vt to mark; **contras'segno** sm (distintivo) distinguishing mark; **spedire in contrassegno** to send C.O.D.

contras'tare vt (avversare) to oppose; (impedire) to bar; (negare: diritto) to contest, dispute ♦ vi: **~ (con)** (essere in disaccordo) to contrast (with); (lottare) to struggle (with); **con'trasto** sm contrast; (conflitto) conflict; (litigio) dispute

contrat'tacco sm counterattack

contrat'tare vt, vi to negotiate

contrat'tempo sm hitch

con'tratto, a pp di contrarre ♦ sm contract; **contrattu'ale** ag contractual

contravvenzi'one [kontravven'tsjone] sf contravention; (ammenda) fine

contrazi'one [kontrat'tsjone] sf contraction; (di prezzi etc) reduction

contribu'ente sm/f taxpayer; ratepayer (BRIT), property tax payer (US)

contribu'ire vi to contribute; **contri'buto** sm contribution; (tassa) tax

'contro prep against; **~ di me/lui** against me/him; **pastiglie ~ la tosse** throat lozenges; **~ pagamento** (COMM) on payment ♦ prefisso: **contro'battere** vt (fig: a parole) to answer back; (: confutare) to refute; **controfi'gura** sf (CINEMA) double; **controfir'mare** vt to countersign **control'lare** vt (accertare) to check; (sorvegliare) to watch, control; (tenere nel proprio potere, fig: dominare) to control; **con'trollo** sm check; watch; control; **controllo delle nascite** birth control; **control'lore** sm (FERR, AUTOBUS) (ticket) inspector

controprodu'cente [kontroprodu'tʃɛnte] ag counterproductive

contro'senso sm (contraddizione) contradiction in terms; (assurdità) nonsense

controspio'naggio [kontrospio'naddʒo] sm counterespionage

contro'versia sf controversy; (DIR) dispute

contro'verso, a ag controversial

contro'voglia [kontro'vɔʎʎa] av unwillingly

contu'macia [kontu'matʃa] sf (DIR) default

contusi'one sf (MED) bruise

convale'scente [konvale'ʃɛnte] ag, sm/f convalescent; **convale'scenza** sf convalescence

convali'dare vt (AMM) to validate; (fig: sospetto, dubbio) to confirm

con'vegno [kon'veɲɲo] sm (incontro) meeting; (congresso) convention, congress; (luogo) meeting place

conve'nevoli smpl civilities

conveni'ente ag suitable; (vantaggioso) profitable; (: prezzo) cheap; **conveni'enza** sf suitability;

advantage; cheapness; **le convenienze** sfpl social conventions

conve'nire vi (riunirsi) to gather, assemble; (concordare) to agree; (tornare utile) to be worthwhile ♦ vb impers: **conviene fare questo** it is advisable to do this; **conviene andarsene** we should go; **ne convengo** I agree

con'vento sm (di frati) monastery; (di suore) convent

convenzio'nale [konventsjo'nale] ag conventional

convenzi'one [konven'tsjone] sf (DIR) agreement; (nella società) convention; **le ~i** sfpl social conventions

conver'sare vi to have a conversation, converse

conversazi'one [konversat'tsjone] sf conversation; **fare ~** to chat, have a chat

conversi'one sf conversion; **~ ad U** (AUT) U-turn

conver'tire vt (trasformare) to change; (POL, REL) to convert; **~rsi** vr: **~rsi (a)** to be converted (to)

con'vesso, a ag convex

con'vincere [kon'vintʃere] vt to convince; **~ qn di qc** to convince sb of sth; **~ qn a fare qc** to persuade sb to do sth; **con'vinto, a** pp di **convincere; convinzi'one** sf conviction, firm belief

convis'suto, a pp di **convivere**

con'vivere vi to live together

convo'care vt to call, convene; (DIR) to summon; **convocazi'one** sf meeting; summons sg

convogli'are [konvoʎ'ʎare] vt to convey; (dirigere) to direct, send; **con'voglio** sm (di veicoli) convoy; (FERR) train

convulsi'one sf convulsion

con'vulso, a ag (pianto) violent, convulsive; (attività) feverish

coope'rare vi: **~ (a)** to cooperate (in); **coopera'tiva** sf cooperative;

cooperazi'one sf cooperation

coordi'nare vt to coordinate;
coordi'nate sfpl (MAT, GEO)
coordinates; **coordi'nati** smpl (MODA)
coordinates

co'perchio [ko'perkjo] sm cover; (di
pentola) lid

co'perta sf cover; (di lana) blanket; (da
viaggio) rug; (NAUT) deck

coper'tina sf (STAMPA) cover, jacket

co'perto, a pp di **coprire ♦** ag
covered; (cielo) overcast **♦** sm place
setting; (posto a tavola) place; (al
ristorante) cover charge; **al ~** di covered
in o with

coper'tone sm (AUT) rubber tyre

coper'tura sf (anche ECON, MIL) cover;
(di edificio) roofing

'copia sf copy; **brutta/bella ~** rough/
final copy

copi'are vt to copy; **copia'trice** sf
copier, copying machine

copi'one sm (CINEMA, TEATRO) script

'coppa sf (bicchiere) goblet; (per frutta,
gelato) dish; (trofeo) cup, trophy;
~ dell'olio oil sump (BRIT) o pan (US)

'coppia sf (di persone) couple; (di
animali, SPORT) pair

coprifu'oco, chi sm curfew

copri'letto sm bedspread

co'prire vt to cover; (occupare: carica,
posto) to hold; **~rsi** vr (cielo) to cloud
over; (vestirsi) to wrap up, cover up;
(ECON) to cover o.s.; **~rsi di** (macchie,
muffa) to become covered in

co'raggio [ko'raddʒo] sm courage,
bravery; **~!** (forza!) come on!; (animo!)
cheer up!; **coraggi'oso, a** ag
courageous, brave

co'rallo sm coral

co'rano sm (REL) Koran

co'razza [ko'rattsa] sf armour; (di
animali) carapace, shell; (MIL)
armour(-plating); **coraz'zata** sf
battleship

corbelle'ria sf stupid remark; **~e** sfpl
nonsense no pl

'corda sf cord; (fune) rope; (spago, MUS)
string; **dare ~ a qn** to let sb have his
(o her) way; **tenere sulla ~ qn** to
keep sb on tenterhooks; **tagliare la ~**
to slip away, sneak off; **~e vocali** vocal
cords

cordi'ale ag cordial, warm **♦** sm
(bevanda) cordial

cor'doglio [kor'dɔʎʎo] sm grief; (lutto)
mourning

cor'done sm cord, string; (linea: di
polizia) cordon; **~ ombelicale**
umbilical cord

Co'rea sf: **la ~** Korea

coreogra'fia sf choreography

cori'andolo [kori'andolo] sm (BOT) coriander; **~i**
smpl confetti sg

cori'carsi vr to go to bed

'corna sfpl vedi **corno**

cor'nacchia [kor'nakkja] sf crow

corna'musa sf bagpipes pl

cor'netta sf (MUS) cornet; (TEL) receiver

cor'netto sm (CUC) croissant; (gelato)
cone

cor'nice [kor'nitʃe] sf frame; (fig)
setting, background

cornici'one [korni'tʃone] sm (di
edificio) ledge; (ARCHIT) cornice

'corno (pl(f) **-a**) sm (ZOOL) horn; (pl(m)
-i: MUS) horn; **fare le ~a a qn** to be
unfaithful to sb

Corno'vaglia [korno'vaʎʎa] sf: **la ~**
Cornwall

cor'nuto, a ag (con corna) horned;
(fam!: marito) cuckolded **♦** sm (fam!:
cuckold; (: insulto) bastard (!)

'coro sm chorus; (REL) choir

co'rona sf crown; (di fiori) wreath;
coro'nare vt to crown

'corpo sm body; (militare, diplomatico)
corps inv; **prendere ~** to take shape; **a
~ a ~** hand-to-hand; **~ di ballo** corps
de ballet; **~ insegnante** teaching
staff

corpo'rale ag bodily; (punizione)
corporal

corpora'tura sf build, physique

corporazi'one [korporat'tsjone] *sf* corporation

corpu'lento, a *ag* stout

corre'dare *vt*: ~ **di** to provide o furnish with; **cor'redo** *sm* equipment; (*di sposa*) trousseau

cor'reggere [kor'reddʒere] *vt* to correct; (*compiti*) to correct, mark

cor'rente *ag* (*acqua: di fiume*) flowing; (*: di rubinetto*) running; (*moneta, prezzo*) current; (*comune*) everyday ♦ *sm*: **essere al ~ (di)** to be well-informed (about); **mettere al ~ (di)** to inform (of) ♦ *sf* (*d'acqua*) current, stream; (*spiffero*) draught; (*ELETTR, METEOR*) current; (*fig*) trend, tendency; **la vostra lettera del 5 ~ mese** (*COMM*) your letter of the 5th of this month; **corrente'mente** *av* commonly; **parlare una lingua correntemente** to speak a language fluently

'correre *vi* to run; (*precipitarsi*) to rush; (*partecipare a una gara*) to race, run; (*fig: diffondersi*) to go round ♦ *vt* (*SPORT: gara*) to compete in; (*rischio*) to run; (*pericolo*) to face; **~ dietro a qn** to run after sb; **corre voce che ...** it is rumoured that ...

cor'retto, a *pp di* **correggere** ♦ *ag* (*comportamento*) correct, proper; **caffè ~ al cognac** coffee laced with brandy

correzi'one [korret'tsjone] *sf* correction; marking; **~ di bozze** proofreading

corri'doio *sm* corridor

corri'dore *sm* (*SPORT*) runner; (*: su veicolo*) racer

corri'era *sf* coach (*BRIT*), bus

corri'ere *sm* (*diplomatico, di guerra, postale*) courier; (*COMM*) carrier

corrispet'tivo (*somma*) amount due

corrispon'dente *ag* corresponding ♦ *sm/f* correspondent

corrispon'denza [korrispon'dentsa] *sf* correspondence

corris'pondere *vi* (*equivalere*): ~ **(a)** to correspond (to) ♦ *vt* (*stipendio*) to pay; (*fig: amore*) to return; **corris'posto, a** *pp di* **corrispondere**

corrobo'rare *vt* to strengthen, fortify; (*fig*) to corroborate, bear out

cor'rodere *vt* to corrode; ~**rsi** *vr* to corrode

cor'rompere *vt* to corrupt; (*comprare*) to bribe

corrosi'one *sf* corrosion

cor'roso, a *pp di* **corrodere**

cor'rotto, a *pp di* **corrompere** ♦ *ag* corrupt

corruc'ciarsi [korrut'tʃarsi] *vr* to grow angry o vexed

corru'gare *vt* to wrinkle; **~ la fronte** to knit one's brows

corruzi'one [korrut'tsjone] *sf* corruption; bribery

'corsa *sf* running *no pl*; (*gara*) race; (*di autobus, taxi*) journey, trip; **fare una ~** to run, dash; (*SPORT*) to run a race

cor'sia *sf* (*AUT, SPORT*) lane; (*di ospedale*) ward

cor'sivo *sm* cursive (writing); (*TIP*) italics *pl*

'corso, a *pp di* **correre** ♦ *sm* course; (*strada cittadina*) main street; (*di unità monetaria*) circulation; (*di titoli, valori*) rate, price; **in ~** in progress, under way; (*annata*) current; **~ d'acqua** river, stream; (*artificiale*) waterway; **~ d'aggiornamento** refresher course; **~ serale** evening class

'corte *sf* (court)yard; (*DIR, regale*) court; **fare la ~ a qn** to court sb; **~ marziale** court-martial

cor'teccia, ce [kor'tettʃa] *sf* bark

corteggi'are [korted'dʒare] *vt* to court

cor'teo *sm* procession

cor'tese *ag* courteous; **corte'sia** *sf* courtesy; **per cortesia ...** excuse me, please ...

cortigi'ana [korti'dʒana] *sf* courtesan

cortigi'ano, a [korti'dʒano] *sm/f* courtier

cor'tile *sm* (court)yard

cor'tina *sf* curtain; (*anche fig*) screen

'corto, a *ag* short; **essere a ~ di qc** to be short of sth; **~ circuito** short-circuit

'corvo *sm* raven

'cosa *sf* thing; (*faccenda*) affair, matter, business *no pl*; (*che*) **(che)** what?; **(che) cos'è?** what is it?; **a ~ pensi?** what are you thinking about?

'coscia, sce ['kɔʃʃa] *sf* thigh; **~ di pollo** (*CUC*) chicken leg

cosci'ente [koʃʃɛnte] *ag* conscious; **~ di** conscious *o* aware of; **cosci'enza** *sf* conscience; (*consapevolezza*) consciousness; **coscienzi'oso, a** *ag* conscientious

cosci'otto [koʃʃɔtto] *sm* (*CUC*) leg

cos'critto *sm* (*MIL*) conscript

PAROLA CHIAVE
---

così *av* **1** (*in questo modo*) like this, (in) this way; (*in tal modo*) so; **le cose stanno ~** this is the way things stand; **non ho detto ~!** I didn't say that!; **come stai? — (e) ~ ~** how are you? — so-so; **e ~ via** and so on; **per ~ dire** so to speak

2 (*tanto*) so; **~ lontano** so far away; **un ragazzo ~ intelligente** such an intelligent boy

♦ *ag inv* (*tale*): **non ho mai visto un film ~** I've never seen such a film

♦ *cong* **1** (*perciò*) so, therefore

2: **~ ... come** as ... as; **non è ~ bravo come te** he's not as good as you; **~ ... che** so ... that

---

cosid'detto, a *ag* so-called

cos'metico, a, ci, che *ag, sm* cosmetic

cos'pargere [kosˈpardʒere] *vt*: **~ di** to sprinkle with; **cos'parso, a** *pp di* **cospargere**

cos'petto *sm*: **al ~ di** in front of; in the presence of

cos'picuo, a *ag* considerable, large

cospi'rare *vi* to conspire; **cospirazi'one** *sf* conspiracy

'costa *sf* (*tra terra e mare*) coast(line); (*litorale*) shore; (*ANAT*) rib; **la C~ Azzurra** the French Riviera

cos'tante *ag* constant; (*persona*) steadfast ♦ *sf* constant

cos'tare *vi, vt* to cost; **~ caro** to be expensive, cost a lot

cos'tata *sf* (*CUC*) large chop

cos'tato *sm* (*ANAT*) ribs *pl*

costeggi'are [kostedˈdʒare] *vt* to be close to; to run alongside

cos'tei *pron vedi* **costui**

costi'era *sf* stretch of coast

costi'ero, a *ag* coastal, coast *cpd*

costitu'ire *vt* (*comitato, gruppo*) to set up, form; (*sog: elementi, parti: comporre*) to make up, constitute; (*rappresentare*) to constitute; (*DIR*) to appoint; **~rsi alla polizia** to give o.s. up to the police

costituzio'nale [kostituttsjoˈnale] *ag* constitutional

costituzi'one [kostitutˈtsjone] *sf* setting up; building up; constitution

'costo *sm* cost; **a ogni** *o* **qualunque ~, a tutti i ~i** at all costs

'costola *sf* (*ANAT*) rib

cos'toro *pron pl vedi* **costui**

cos'toso, a *ag* expensive, costly

cos'tretto, a *pp di* **costringere**

cos'tringere [kosˈtrindʒere] *vt*: **~ qn a fare qc** to force sb to do sth; **costrizi'one** *sf* coercion

costru'ire *vt* to construct, build; **costruzi'one** *sf* construction, building

cos'tui (*f* **cos'tei**, *pl* **cos'toro**) *pron* (*soggetto*) he/she; *pl* they; (*complemento*) him/her; *pl* them; **si può sapere chi è ~?** (*peg*) just who is that fellow?

cos'tume *sm* (*uso*) custom; (*foggia di vestire, indumento*) costume; **~i** *smpl* (*condotta morale*) morals, morality *sg*; **~ da bagno** bathing *o* swimming costume (*BRIT*), swimsuit; (*da uomo*) bathing *o* swimming trunks *pl*

co'tenna sf bacon rind

co'togna [ko'toɲɲa] sf quince

coto'letta sf (di maiale, montone) chop; (di vitello, agnello) cutlet

co'tone sm cotton; ~ **idrofilo** cotton wool (BRIT), absorbent cotton (US)

'cotta sf (fam: innamoramento) crush

'cottimo sm: **lavorare a ~** to do piecework

'cotto, a pp di **cuocere** ♦ ag cooked; (fam: innamorato) head-over-heels in love; **ben ~** (carne) well done

cot'tura sf cooking; (in forno) baking; (in umido) stewing

co'vare vt to hatch; (fig: malattia) to be sickening for; (: odio, rancore) to nurse ♦ vi (fuoco, fig) to smoulder

'covo sm den

co'vone sm sheaf

'cozza ['kɔttsa] sf mussel

coz'zare [kot'tsare] vi: ~ **contro** to bang into, collide with

C.P. abbr (= casella postale) P.O. Box

crack [kræk] sm inv (droga) crack

'crampo sm cramp

'cranio sm skull

cra'tere sm crater

cra'vatta sf tie

cre'anza [kre'antsa] sf manners pl

cre'are vt to create; **cre'ato** sm creation; **crea'tore, 'trice** ag creative ♦ sm creator; **crea'tura** sf creature; (bimbo) baby, infant; **creazi'one** sf creation; (fondazione) foundation, establishment

cre'dente sm/f (REL) believer

cre'denza [kre'dentsa] sf belief; (armadio) sideboard

credenzi'ali [kreden'tsjali] sfpl credentials

'credere vt to believe ♦ vi: ~ **in, ~ a** to believe in; ~ **qn onesto** to believe sb (to be) honest; ~ **che** to believe o think that; **~rsi furbo** to think one is clever

'credito sm (anche COMM) credit; (reputazione) esteem, repute;

comprare a ~ to buy on credit

'credo sm inv creed

'crema sf cream; (con uova, zucchero etc) custard; **~ solare** sun cream

cre'mare vt to cremate

Crem'lino sm: **il ~** the Kremlin

'crepa sf crack

cre'paccio [kre'pattʃo] sm large crack, fissure; (di ghiacciaio) crevasse

crepacu'ore sm broken heart

cre'pare vi (fam: morire) to snuff it, kick the bucket; ~ **dalle risa** to split one's sides laughing

crepi'tare vi (fuoco) to crackle; (pioggia) to patter

cre'puscolo sm twilight, dusk

'crescere ['kreʃʃere] vi to grow ♦ vt (figli) to raise; **'crescita** sf growth; **cresci'uto, a** pp di **crescere**

cresima sf (REL) confirmation

'crespo, a ag (capelli) frizzy; (tessuto) puckered ♦ sm crêpe

'cresta sf crest; (di polli, uccelli) crest, comb

'creta sf chalk; clay

cre'tino, a ag stupid ♦ sm/f idiot, fool

cric sm inv (TECN) jack

'cricca, che sf clique

cri'ceto [kri'tʃeto] sm hamster

crimi'nale ag, sm/f criminal

'crimine sm (DIR) crime

'crine sm horsehair; **crini'era** sf mane

crisan'temo sm chrysanthemum

'crisi sf inv crisis; (MED) attack, fit; ~ **di nervi** attack o fit of nerves

cristalliz'zare [kristalid'dzare] vi to crystallize; (fig) to become fossilized; **~rsi** vr to crystallize; to become fossilized

cris'tallo sm crystal

cristia'nesimo sm Christianity

cristi'ano, a ag, sm/f Christian

'Cristo sm Christ

cri'terio sm criterion; (buon senso) (common) sense

'critica, che sf criticism; **la ~** (attività) criticism; (persone) the critics pl; vedi *anche* **critico**

criti'care *vt* to criticize

'critico, a, ci, che *ag* critical ♦ *sm* critic

Croa'zia [kroa'ttsja] *sf* Croatia

croc'cante *ag* crisp, crunchy

'croce ['krotʃe] *sf* cross; **in ~** (*di traverso*) crosswise; (*fig*) on tenterhooks; **la C~ Rossa** the Red Cross

croce'figgere *etc* = **crocifiggere** *etc*

croce'via *sm inv* crossroads *sg*

croci'ata [kro'tʃata] *sf* crusade

cro'cicchio [kro'tʃikkjo] *sm* crossroads *sg*

croci'era [kro'tʃɛra] *sf* (*viaggio*) cruise; (*ARCHIT*) transept

croci'figgere [krotʃi'fiddʒere] *vt* to crucify; **crocifissi'one** *sf* crucifixion; **croci'fisso, a** *pp di* **crocifiggere**

crogi'olo [kro'dʒɔlo] *sm* (*fig*) melting pot

crol'lare *vi* to collapse; **'crollo** *sm* collapse; (*di prezzi*) slump, sudden fall

cro'mato, a *ag* chromium-plated

'cromo *sm* chrome, chromium

'cronaca, che (*STAMPA*) news *sg*; (*: rubrica*) column; (*TV, RADIO*) commentary; **fatto o episodio di ~** news item; **~ nera** crime news *sg*; crime column

'cronico, a, ci, che *ag* chronic

cro'nista, i *sm* (*STAMPA*) reporter

cronolo'gia [kronolo'dʒia] *sf* chronology

cro'nometro *sm* chronometer; (*a scatto*) stopwatch

'crosta *sf* crust

cros'tacei [kros'tatʃei] *smpl* shellfish

cros'tata *sf* (*CUC*) tart

cros'tino *sm* (*CUC*) croûton; (*: da antipasto*) canapé

'cruccio ['kruttʃo] *sm* worry, torment

cruci'verba *sm inv* crossword (puzzle)

cru'dele *ag* cruel; **crudeltà** *sf* cruelty

'crudo, a *ag* (*non cotto*) raw; (*aspro*) harsh, severe

cru'miro (*peg*) *sm* blackleg (*BRIT*), scab (*US*)

'crusca *sf* bran

crus'cotto *sm* (*AUT*) dashboard

CSI *sigla f inv* (= *Comunità Stati Indipendenti*) CIS

'Cuba *sf* Cuba

cu'betto *sm*: **~ di ghiaccio** ice cube

'cubico, a, ci, che *ag* cubic

'cubo, a *ag* cubic ♦ *sm* cube; **elevare al ~** (*MAT*) to cube

cuc'cagna [kuk'kaɲɲa] *sf*: **paese della ~** land of plenty; **albero della ~** greasy pole (*fig*)

cuc'cetta [kut'tʃetta] *sf* (*FERR*) couchette; (*NAUT*) berth

cucchiai'ata [kukkja'jata] *sf* spoonful

cucchia'ino [kukkja'ino] *sm* teaspoon; coffee spoon

cucchi'aio [kuk'kjajo] *sm* spoon

'cuccia, ce ['kuttʃa] *sf* dog's bed; **a ~!** down!

'cucciolo ['kuttʃolo] *sm* cub; (*di cane*) puppy

cu'cina [ku'tʃina] *sf* (*locale*) kitchen; (*arte culinaria*) cooking, cookery; (*le vivande*) food, cooking; (*apparecchio*) cooker; **~ componibile** fitted kitchen; **cuci'nare** *vt* to cook

cu'cire [ku'tʃire] *vt* to sew, stitch; **cuci'trice** *sf* stapler; **cuci'tura** *sf* sewing, stitching; (*costura*) seam

cucù *sm inv* = **cuculo**

cu'culo *sm* cuckoo

'cuffia *sf* bonnet, cap; (*da infermiera*) cap; (*da bagno*) (bathing) cap; (*per ascoltare*) headphones *fpl*, headset

cu'gino, a [ku'dʒino] *sm/f* cousin

PAROLA CHIAVE

'cui *pron* **1** (*nei complementi indiretti: persona*) whom; (*: oggetto, animale*) which; **la persona/le persone a ~ accennavi** the person/people you were referring to o to whom you were referring; **i libri di ~ parlavo** the books I was talking about o about which I was talking; **il quartiere in ~ abito** the district where I live; **la ragione per ~** the reason why **2** (*inserito tra articolo e sostantivo*) whose; **la donna i ~ figli sono scomparsi** the woman whose children have disappeared; **il signore, dal ~ figlio ho avuto il libro** the man from whom son I got the book

culi'naria sf cookery

'culla sf cradle

cul'lare vt to rock

culmi'nare vi: **~ con** to culminate in

'culmine sm top, summit

'culo (fam!) sm arse (Brit!), ass (US!); (fig: fortuna): **aver ~** to have the luck of the devil

'culto sm (religione) religion; (adorazione) worship, adoration; (venerazione: anche fig) cult

cul'tura sf culture; education, learning; **cultu'rale** ag cultural

cumula'tivo, a ag cumulative; (prezzo) inclusive; (biglietto) group cpd

'cumulo sm (mucchio) pile, heap; (METEOR) cumulus

'cuneo sm wedge

cu'netta sf (avvallamento) dip; (di scolo) gutter

cu'oca sf vedi cuoco

cu'ocere ['kwɔtʃere] vt (alimenti) to cook; (mattoni etc) to fire ♦ vi to cook; **~ al forno** (pane) to bake; (arrosto) to roast; **cu'oco, a, chi, che** sm/f cook; (di ristorante) chef

cu'oio sm leather; **~ capelluto** scalp

cu'ore sm heart; **~i** smpl (CARTE) hearts; **avere buon ~** to be kind-hearted; **stare a ~ a qn** to be important to sb

cupi'digia [kupi'didʒa] sf greed, covetousness

'cupo, a ag dark; (suono) dull; (fig) gloomy, dismal

'cupola sf dome; cupola

'cura sf care; (MED: trattamento) (course of) treatment; **aver ~ di** (occuparsi di)

to look after; **a ~ di** (libro) edited by; **~ dimagrante** diet

cu'rare vt (malato, malattia) to treat; (: guarire) to cure; (aver cura di) to take care of; (testo) to edit; **~rsi** vr to take care of o.s.; (MED) to follow a course of treatment; **~rsi di** to pay attention to

cu'rato sm parish priest; (protestante) vicar, minister

cura'tore, 'trice sm/f (DIR) trustee; (di antologia ecc) editor

curio'sare vi to look round, wander round; (tra libri) to browse; **~ nei negozi** to look o wander round the shops

curiosità sf inv curiosity; (cosa rara) curio, curiosity

curi'oso, a ag curious; **essere ~ di** to be curious about

cur'sore sm (INFORM) cursor

'curva sf curve; (stradale) bend, curve

cur'vare vt to bend ♦ vi (veicolo) to take a bend; (strada) to bend, curve; **~rsi** vr to bend; (legno) to warp

'curvo, a ag curved; (piegato) bent

cusci'netto [kuʃʃi'netto] sm pad; (TECN) bearing ♦ ag inv: **stato ~** buffer state; **~ a sfere** ball bearing

cu'scino [kuʃʃino] sm cushion; (guanciale) pillow

'cuspide sf (ARCHIT) spire

cus'tode sm/f keeper, custodian

cus'todia sf care; (DIR) custody; (astuccio) case, holder

custo'dire vt (conservare) to keep; (assistere) to look after, take care of; (fare la guardia) to guard

'cute sf (ANAT) skin

C.V. abbr (= cavallo vapore) h.p.

D, d

da (da+il = **dal**, da+lo = **dallo**, da+l' = **dall'**, da+la = **dalla**, da+i = **dai**,

da+gli = **dagli**, *da+le* = **dalle** *prep* **1**
(*agente*) by; **dipinto ~ un grande
artista** painted by a great artist
2 (*causa*) with; **tremare dalla paura**
to tremble with fear
3 (*stato in luogo*) at; **abito ~ lui** I'm
living at his house o with him; **sono
dal giornalaio/~ Francesco** I'm
at the newsagent's/Francesco's
(house)
4 (*moto a luogo*) to; (*moto per luogo*)
through; **vado ~ Pietro/dal
giornalaio** I'm going to Pietro's
(house)/to the newsagent's; **sono
passati dalla finestra** they came in
through the window
5 (*provenienza, allontanamento*) from;
arrivare/partire ~ Milano to arrive/
depart from Milan; **scendere dal
treno/dalla macchina** to get off the
train/out of the car; **si trova a 5 km
~ qui** it's 5 km from here
6 (*tempo: durata*) for; (*: a partire da:
nel passato*) since; (*: nel futuro*) from;
vivo qui ~ un anno I've been living
here for a year; **è dalle 3 che ti
aspetto** I've been waiting for you
since 3 (o'clock); **~ oggi in poi** from
today onwards; **~ bambino** as a child,
when I (o he *etc*) was a child
7 (*modo, maniera*) like; **comportarsi
~ uomo** to behave like a man; **l'ho
fatto ~ me** I did it (by) myself
8 (*descrittivo*) with; **comportarsi
~ uomo** a racing car; **una macchina ~ corsa**
a racing car; **una ragazza dai capelli
biondi** a girl with blonde hair; **un
vestito ~ 100.000 lire** a 100,000 lire
dress

da 'capo *av* = **daccapo**
dac'capo *av* (*di nuovo*) (once) again;
(*dal principio*) all over again, from the
beginning
'dado *sm* (*da gioco*) dice o die; (*CUC*)
stock (*BRIT*) o bouillon (*US*) cube;
(*TECN*) (screw)nut; **giocare a ~i** to play
dice

daf'fare *sm* work, toil
'dagli ['daʎʎi] *prep* + *det vedi* **da**
'dai *prep* + *det vedi* **da**
'daino *sm* (*fallow*) deer *inv*; (*pelle*)
buckskin
dal *prep* + *det vedi* **da**
dall' *prep* + *det vedi* **da**
'dalla *prep* + *det vedi* **da**
'dalle *prep* + *det vedi* **da**
'dallo *prep* + *det vedi* **da**
dal'tonico, a, ci, che *ag* colour-blind
'dama *sf* lady; (*nei balli*) partner; (*gioco*)
draughts *sg* (*BRIT*), checkers *sg* (*US*)
dami'giana [dami'dʒana] *sf* demijohn
da'naro *sm* = **denaro**
da'nese *ag* Danish ♦ *sm/f* Dane ♦ *sm*
(*LING*) Danish
Dani'marca *sf*: **la ~** Denmark
dan'nare *vt* (*REL*) to damn; **~rsi** *vr* (*fig:
tormentarsi*) to be worried to death; **far
~ qn** to drive sb mad; **dannazi'one** *sf*
damnation
danneggi'are [danned'dʒare] *vt* to
damage; (*rovinare*) to spoil; (*nuocere*)
to harm
'danno *sm* damage; (*a persona*) harm,
injury; **~i** *smpl* (*DIR*) damages;
dan'noso, a *ag*: **dannoso (a, per)**
harmful (to), bad (for)
Da'nubio *sm*: **il ~** the Danube
'danza ['dantsa] *sf*: **la ~** dancing; **una
~ a** dance
dan'zare [dan'tsare] *vt, vi* to dance
dapper'tutto *av* everywhere
dap'poco *ag inv* inept, worthless
dap'prima *av* at first
'dare *sm* (*COMM*) debit ♦ *vt* to give;
(*produrre: frutti, suono*) to produce ♦ *vi
(guardare*): **~ su** to look (out) onto;
~rsi *vr*: **~rsi a** to dedicate o.s. to; **~rsi
al commercio** to go into business;
~rsi al bere to take to drink; **~ da
mangiare a qn** to give sb sth to eat;
~ per certo qc to consider sth certain;
~ per morto qn to give sb up for
dead; **~rsi per vinto** to give in
'darsena *sf* dock; dockyard

'**data** sf date; **~ di nascita** date of birth; **~ limite d'utilizzo o di consumo** best-before date

da'**tare** vt to date ♦ vi: **~ da** to date from

'**dato, a** ag (stabilito) given ♦ sm datum; **~i** smpl data pl; **~ che** given that; **un ~ di fatto** a fact

da'**tore, trice** sm/f: **~ di lavoro** employer

'**dattero** sm date

dattilogra'**fare** vt to type; **dattilografi'a** sf typing; **datti'lografo, a** sm/f typist

da'**vanti** av in front; (dirimpetto) opposite ♦ ag in front ♦ sm front; **~ a** in front of; facing, opposite; (in presenza di) before, in front of

davan'**zale** [davan'tsale] sm windowsill

d'a'**vanzo** [da'vantso] av more than enough

dav'**vero** av really, indeed

'**dazio** ['dattsjo] sm (somma) duty; (luogo) customs pl

DC sigla f = Democrazia Cristiana

d. C. abbr (= dopo Cristo) A.D.

'**dea** sf goddess

'**debito, a** ag due, proper ♦ sm (COMM: dare) debit; **a tempo ~** at the right time; **debi'tore, 'trice** sm/f debtor

'**debole** ag weak, feeble; (suono) faint; (luce) dim ♦ sm weakness; **debo'lezza** sf weakness

debut'**tare** vi to make one's début; **de'butto** sm début

deca'**denza** [deka'dentsa] sf decline; (DIR) loss, forfeiture

decaffei'**nato, a** ag decaffeinated

decan'**tare** vt to praise, sing the praises of

decappot'**tabile** ag, sf convertible

dece'**duto, a** [detfe'duto] ag deceased

de'**cennio** [de'tfɛnnjo] sm decade

de'**cente** [de'tfɛnte] ag decent,

respectable, proper; (accettabile) satisfactory, decent

de'**cesso** [de'tfɛsso] sm death

de'**cidere** [de'tfidere] vt: **~ qc** to decide on sth; (questione, lite) to settle sth; **~ di fare/che** to decide to do/ that; **~ di qc** (sog: cosa) to determine sth; **~rsi (a fare)** to decide (to do), make up one's mind (to do)

deci'**frare** [detfi'frare] vt to decode; (fig) to decipher, make out

deci'**male** [detfi'male] ag decimal

'**decimo, a** ['detfimo] num tenth

de'**cina** [de'tfina] sf ten; (circa dieci): **una ~ (di)** about ten

decisi'**one** [detfi'zjone] sf decision; **prendere una ~** to make a decision

de'**ciso, a** [de'tfizo] pp di **decidere**

declas'**sare** vt to downgrade; to lower in status

decli'**nare** vi (pendio) to slope down; (fig: diminuire) to decline ♦ vt to decline

declinazi'**one** [LING] sf declension

de'**clino** sm decline

decodifica'**tore** sm (TEL) decoder

decol'**lare** vi (AER) to take off; **de'collo** sm take-off

decolo'**rare** vt to bleach

decom'**porre** vt to decompose; **decomporsi** vr to decompose; **decom'posto, a** pp di **decomporre**

deconge'**lare** [dekondʒe'lare] vt to defrost

deco'**rare** vt to decorate; **decora'tore, 'trice** sm/f (interior) decorator; **decorazi'one** sf decoration

de'**coro** sm decorum; **deco'roso, a** ag decorous, dignified

de'**correre** vi to pass, elapse; (avere effetto) to run, have effect; **de'corso, a** pp di **decorrere** ♦ sm (evoluzione: anche MED) course

de'**crepito, a** ag decrepit

de'**crescere** [de'kreʃʃere] vi (diminuire) to decrease, diminish; (acque) to subside, go down; (prezzi) to go down;

decresci'uto, a pp di **decrescere**

de'creto sm decree; **~ legge** decree with the force of law

'dedalo sm maze, labyrinth

'dedica, che sf dedication

dedi'care vt to dedicate

'dedito, a ag: **~ a** (studio etc) dedicated o devoted to; (vizio) addicted to

de'dotto, a pp di **dedurre**

de'durre vt (concludere) to deduce; (defalcare) to deduct; **deduzi'one** sf deduction

defal'care vt to deduct

defe'rente ag respectful, deferential

defe'rire vt: **~ a** (DIR) to refer to

defezi'one [defet'tsjone] sf defection, desertion

defici'ente [defit'ʃɛnte] ag (mancante): **~ di** deficient in; (insufficiente) insufficient ♦ sm/f mental defective; (peg: cretino) idiot

'deficit ['dɛfitʃit] sm inv (ECON) deficit

defi'nire vt to define; (risolvere) to settle; **defini'tivo, a** ag definitive, final; **definizi'one** sf definition, settlement

deflet'tore sm (AUT) quarter-light

de'flusso (della marea) ebb

defor'mare vt (alterare) to put out of shape; (corpo) to deform; (pensiero, fatto) to distort; **~rsi** vr to lose its shape

de'forme ag deformed; disfigured; **deformità** sf inv deformity

defrau'dare vt: **~ qn di qc** to defraud sb of sth, cheat sb out of sth

de'funto, a ag late cpd ♦ sm/f deceased

degene'rare [dedʒene'rare] vi to degenerate; **de'genere** ag degenerate; **de'gente** [de'dʒɛnte] sm/f (in ospedale) in-patient

'degli ['deʎʎi] prep + det vedi **di**

de'gnarsi [deɲ'narsi] vr: **~ di fare** to deign o condescend to do

'degno, a ag dignified; **~ di** worthy of;

~ di lode praiseworthy

degra'dare vt (MIL) to demote; (privare della dignità) to degrade; **~rsi** vr to demean o.s.

degustazi'one [degustat'tsjone] sf sampling, tasting

'dei prep + det vedi **di**

del prep + det vedi **di**

dela'tore, 'trice sm/f police informer

'delega, ghe sf (procura) proxy

dele'gare vt to delegate; **dele'gato** sm delegate

dele'terio, a ag damaging; (per salute etc) harmful

del'fino sm (ZOOL) dolphin; (STORIA) dauphin; (fig) probable successor

delibe'rare vt to come to a decision on ♦ vi (DIR): **~ (su qc)** to rule (on sth)

delica'tezza [delika'tettsa] sf delicacy; frailty; thoughtfulness; tactfulness

deli'cato, a ag delicate; (salute) delicate, frail; (fig: gentile) thoughtful, considerate; (: che dimostra tatto) tactful

deline'are vt to outline; **~rsi** vr to be outlined; (fig) to emerge

delin'quente sm/f criminal, delinquent; **~ abituale** regular offender, habitual offender; **delin'quenza** sf criminality, delinquency; **delinquenza minorile** juvenile delinquency

deli'rare vi to be delirious, rave; (fig) to rave

de'lirio sm delirium; (ragionamento insensato) raving; (fig): **andare/mandare in ~** to go/send into a frenzy

de'litto sm crime

de'lizia [de'littsja] sf delight; **delizi'oso, a** ag delightful; (cibi) delicious

dell' prep + det vedi **di**

'della prep + det vedi **di**

'delle prep + det vedi **di**

'dello prep + det vedi **di**

delta'plano sm hang-glider; **volo col**

~ hang-gliding

de'ludere vt to disappoint; **delusi'one** sf disappointment; **de'luso, a** pp di **deludere**

de'manio sm state property

de'menza [de'mɛntsa] sf dementia; (stupidità) foolishness

demo'cratico, a, ci, che ag democratic

democra'zia [demokrat'tsia] sf democracy

democristi'ano, a ag, sm/f Christian Democrat

demo'lire vt to demolish

'demone sm demon

de'monio sm demon, devil; **il D~** the Devil

de'naro sm money

denomi'nare vt to name; **denominazi'one** sf name; denomination; **denominazione d'origine controllata** label guaranteeing the quality and origin of a wine

densità sf inv density

'denso, a ag thick, dense

den'tale ag dental

'dente sm tooth; (di forchetta) prong; **al ~** (CUC: pasta) al dente; **~i del giudizio** wisdom teeth; **denti'era** sf (set of) false teeth pl

denti'fricio [denti'fritʃo] sm toothpaste

den'tista, i, e sm/f dentist

'dentro av inside; (in casa) indoors; (fig: nell'intimo) inwardly ♦ prep: ~ a) in; **piegato in** ~ folded over; **qui/là** ~ in here/there; **~ di sé** (pensare, brontolare) to oneself

de'nuncia, ce o **cie** [de'nuntʃa] sf denunciation; declaration; **~ dei redditi** (income) tax return

denunci'are [denun'tʃare] vt to denounce; (dichiarare) to declare

de'nunzia etc [de'nuntsja] = **denuncia** etc

denutrizi'one [denutrit'tsjone] sf

malnutrition

deodo'rante sm deodorant

depe'rire vi to waste away

depila'torio, a ag hair-removing cpd, depilatory

dépli'ant [depli'ã] sm inv leaflet; (opuscolo) brochure

deplo'revole ag deplorable

de'porre vt (depositare) to put down; (rimuovere: da una carica) to remove; (: re) to depose; (DIR) to testify

depor'tare vt to deport

deposi'tare vt (gen, GEO, ECON) to deposit; (lasciare) to leave; (merci) to store

de'posito sm deposit; (luogo) warehouse; depot; (: MIL) depot; **~ bagagli** left-luggage office

deposizi'one [depozit'tsjone] sf deposition; (da una carica) removal

de'posto, a pp di **deporre**

depra'vato, a ag depraved ♦ sm/f degenerate

depre'dare vt to rob, plunder

depressi'one sf depression

de'presso, a pp di **deprimere** ♦ ag depressed

deprez'zare [depret'tsare] vt (ECON) to depreciate

de'primere vt to depress

depu'rare vt to purify

depu'tato sm (POL) deputy, ≈ Member of Parliament (BRIT), ≈ Member of Congress (US)

deragli'are [deraʎ'ʎare] vi to be derailed; **far ~** to derail

de'ritto, a ag derelict

dere'tano (fam) sm bottom, buttocks pl

de'ridere vt to mock, deride; **de'riso, a** pp di **deridere**

de'riva sf (NAUT, AER) drift; **andare alla ~** (anche fig) to drift

deri'vare vi: **~ da** to derive from ♦ vt to derive; (corso d'acqua) to divert; **derivazi'one** sf derivation; diversion

derma'tologo, a, gi, ghe sm/f

dermatologist

der'rate sfpl: ~ **alimentari** foodstuffs

deru'bare vt to rob

des'critto, a pp di **descrivere**

des'crivere vt to describe;
descrizi'one sf description

de'serto, a ag deserted ♦ sm (GEO)
desert; **isola ~a** desert island

deside'rare vt to want, wish for;
(sessualmente) to desire; ~ **fare/che**
qn faccia to want o wish to do/sb to
do; **desidera fare una passeggiata?**
would you like to go for a walk?

desi'derio sm wish; (più intenso,
carnale) desire

deside'roso, a ag: ~ **di** longing o
eager for

desi'nenza [dezi'nentsa] sf (LING)
ending, inflexion

de'sistere vi: ~ **da** to give up, desist
from; **desis'tito, a** pp di **desistere**

deso'lato, a ag (paesaggio) desolate;
(persona: spiacente) sorry

des'tare vt to wake (up); (fig) to
awaken, arouse; ~**rsi** vr to wake up

desti'nare vt to destine; (assegnare) to
appoint, assign; (indirizzare) to address;
~ **qc a qn** to intend to give sth to sb,
intend sb to have sth; **destina'tario,**
a sm/f (di lettera) addressee

destinazi'one [destinat'tsjone] sf
destination; (uso) purpose

des'tino sm destiny, fate

destitu'ire vt to dismiss, remove

'desto, a ag (wide) awake

'destra sf (mano) right hand; (parte)
right (side); (POL): **la ~ the** Right; **a ~**
(essere) on the right; (andare) to the
right

destreggi'arsi [destred'dʒarsi] vr to
manoeuvre (BRIT), maneuver (US)

des'trezza [des'trettsa] sf skill,
dexterity

'destro, a ag right, right-hand

dete'nere vt (incarico, primato) to hold;
(proprietà) to have, possess; (in
prigione) to detain, hold; **dete'nuto, a**

sm/f prisoner; **detenzi'one** sf holding;
possession; detention

deter'gente [deter'dʒɛnte] ag
detergent; (crema, latte) cleansing ♦ sm
detergent

deterio'rare vt to damage; ~**rsi** vr to
deteriorate

determi'nare vt to determine;
determinazi'one sf determination;
(decisione) decision

deter'sivo sm detergent

detes'tare vt to detest, hate

de'trarre vt: ~ **(da)** to deduct (from),
take away (from); **de'tratto, a** pp
di **detrarre**; **detrazi'one** sf
deduction; **detrazione d'imposta** tax
allowance

de'trito sm (GEO) detritus

'detta sf: **a ~ di** according to

dettagli'are [dettaʎ'ʎare] vt to detail,
give full details of

det'taglio [det'taʎʎo] sm detail;
(COMM): **il ~** retail; **al ~** (COMM) retail;
separately

det'tare vt to dictate; ~ **legge** (fig) to
lay down the law; **det'tato** sm
dictation; **detta'tura** sf dictation

'detto, a pp di **dire** ♦ ag
(soprannominato) called, known as; (già
nominato) above-mentioned ♦ sm
saying; ~ **fatto** no sooner said than
done

detur'pare vt to disfigure;
(moralmente) to sully

devas'tare vt to devastate; (fig) to
ravage

devi'are vi: ~ **(da)** to turn off (from)
♦ vt to divert; **deviazi'one** sf (anche
AUT) diversion

devo'luto, a pp di **devolvere**

devoluzi'one [devolut'tsjone] sf (DIR)
devolution, transfer

de'volvere vt (DIR) to transfer, devolve

de'voto, a ag (REL) devout, pious;
(affezionato) devoted

devozi'one [devot'tsjone] sf
devoutness; (anche REL) devotion

---PAROLA CHIAVE---

di (di+il = **del**, di+lo = **dello**, di+l' = **dell'**, di+la = **della**, di+i = **dei**, di+gli = **degli**, di+le = **delle**) prep **1** (possesso, specificazione) of; (composto da, scritto da) by; **la macchina ~ Paolo/mio fratello** Paolo's/my brother's car; **un amico ~ mio fratello** a friend of my brother's, one of my brother's friends; **un quadro ~ Botticelli** a painting by Botticelli **2** (caratterizzazione, misura) of; **una casa ~ mattoni** a brick house, a house made of bricks; **un orologio d'oro** a gold watch; **un bimbo ~ 3 anni** a child of 3, a 3-year-old child **3** (causa, mezzo, modo) with; **tremare ~ paura** to tremble with fear; **morire ~ cancro** to die of cancer; **spalmare ~ burro** to spread with butter **4** (argomento) about, of; **discutere ~ sport** to talk about sport **5** (luogo: provenienza) from; out of; **essere ~ Roma** to be from Rome; **uscire ~ casa** to come out o leave the house **6** (tempo) in; **d'estate/d'inverno** in (the) summer/winter; **~ notte** by night, at night; **~ mattina/sera** in the morning/evening; **~ lunedì** on Mondays
♦ det (una certa quantità di) some; (: negativo) any; (: interrogativo) any, some; **del pane** (some) bread; **delle caramelle** (some) sweets; **degli amici miei** some friends of mine; **vuoi del vino?** do you want o any some wine?

dia'bete sm diabetes sg
di'acono sm (REL) deacon
dia'dema, i sm diadem; (di donna) tiara
dia'framma, i sm (divisione) screen; (ANAT, FOT, contraccettivo) diaphragm
di'agnosi [di'aɲɲozi] sf diagnosis sg
diago'nale ag, sf diagonal

dia'gramma, i sm diagram
dia'letto sm dialect
di'alisi sf dialysis sg
di'alogo, ghi sm dialogue
dia'mante sm diamond
di'ametro sm diameter
di'amine escl: **che ~ ...?** what on earth ...?
diaposi'tiva sf transparency, slide
di'ario sm diary
diar'rea sf diarrhoea
di'avolo sm devil
di'battere vt to debate, discuss; **~rsi** vr to struggle; **di'battito** sm debate, discussion
dicas'tero sm ministry
di'cembre [di'tʃembre] sm December
dice'ria [ditʃe'ria] sf rumour, piece of gossip
dichia'rare [dikja'rare] vt to declare; **dichiarazi'one** sf declaration
dician'nove [ditʃan'nɔve] num nineteen
dicias'sette [ditʃas'sette] num seventeen
dici'otto [di'tʃɔtto] num eighteen
dici'tura [ditʃi'tura] sf words pl, wording
di'eci ['djetʃi] num ten; **die'cina** sf = **decina**
'diesel ['dizal] sm inv diesel engine
di'eta sf diet; **essere a ~** to be on a diet
di'etro av behind; (in fondo) at the back ♦ prep behind; (tempo: dopo) after ♦ sm back, rear ♦ ag inv back cpd; **le zampe di ~** the hind legs; **~ richiesta** on demand; (scritta) on application
di'fatti cong in fact, as a matter of fact
di'fendere vt to defend; **difen'sivo, a** ag defensive ♦ sf: **stare sulla difensiva** (anche fig) to be on the defensive; **difen'sore, a** sm/f defender; **avvocato difensore** counsel for the defence; defending counsel; **di'fesa** sf defence; **di'feso, a** pp di **difendere**
difet'tare vi to be defective; **~ di** to be

lacking in, lack; **difet'tivo, a** *ag* defective

di'fetto *sm* (*mancanza*): ~ **di** lack of; shortage of; (*di fabbricazione*) fault, flaw, defect; (*morale*) fault, failing, defect; (*fisico*) defect; **far ~** to be lacking; **in ~** at fault; in the wrong; **difet'toso, a** *ag* defective, faulty

diffa'mare *vt* to slander; to libel

diffe'rente *ag* different

diffe'renza [diffe'rentsa] *sf* difference; **a ~ di** unlike

differenzi'are [differen'tsjare] *vt* to differentiate; **~rsi da** to differentiate o.s. from; to differ from

diffe'rire *vt* to postpone, defer ♦ *vi* to be different

dif'ficile [dif'fitʃile] *ag* difficult; (*persona*) hard to please, difficult (to please); (*poco probabile*): **è ~ che sia libero** it is unlikely that he'll be free ♦ *sm* difficult part; difficulty; **difficoltà** *sf inv* difficulty

dif'fida *sf* (*DIR*) warning, notice

diffi'dare *vi*: **~ di** to be suspicious o distrustful of ♦ *vt* (*DIR*) to warn; **~ qn dal fare qc** to warn sb not to do sth, caution sb against doing sth; **diffi'dente** *ag* suspicious, distrustful; **diffi'denza** *sf* suspicion, distrust

dif'fondere *vt* (*luce, calore*) to diffuse; (*notizie*) to spread, circulate; **~rsi** *vr* to spread; **diffusi'one** *sf* diffusion; spread; (*anche di giornale*) circulation; (*FISICA*) scattering; **dif'fuso, a** *pp di* **diffondere ♦** *ag* (*malattia, fenomeno*) widespread

difi'lato *av* (*direttamente*) straight, directly; (*subito*) straight away

difte'rite *sf* (*MED*) diphtheria

'diga, ghe *sf* dam; (*portuale*) breakwater

dige'rente [didʒe'rɛnte] *ag* (*apparato*) digestive

dige'rire [didʒe'rire] *vt* to digest; **digesti'one** *sf* digestion; **diges'tivo, a** *ag* digestive ♦ *sm* (*after-dinner*)

liqueur

digi'tale [didʒi'tale] *ag* digital; (*delle dita*) finger *cpd*, digital ♦ *sf* (*BOT*) foxglove

digi'tare [didʒi'tare] *vt, vi* (*INFORM*) to key (in)

digiu'nare [didʒu'nare] *vi* to starve o.s.; (*REL*) to fast; **digi'uno, a** *ag*: **essere digiuno** not to have eaten ♦ *sm* fast; **a digiuno** on an empty stomach

dignità [diɲɲi'ta] *sf inv* dignity; **digni'toso, a** *ag* dignified

'DIGOS ['digɔs] *sigla f* (= *Divisione Investigazioni Generali e Operazioni Speciali*) *police department dealing with political security*

digri'gnare [digriɲ'ɲare] *vt*: **~ i denti** to grind one's teeth

dila'gare *vi* to flood; (*fig*) to spread

dilani'are *vt* (*preda*) to tear to pieces

dilapi'dare *vt* to squander, waste

dila'tare *vt* to dilate; (*gas*) to cause to expand; (*passaggio, cavità*) to open (up); **~rsi** *vr* to dilate; (*FISICA*) to expand

dilazio'nare [dilattsjo'nare] *vt* to delay, defer; **dilazi'one** *sf* delay; (*COMM: di pagamento etc*) extension; (*rinvio*) postponement

dilegu'are *vi* to vanish, disappear; **~rsi** *vr* to vanish, disappear

di'lemma, i *sm* dilemma

dilet'tante *sm/f* dilettante; (*anche SPORT*) amateur

dilet'tare *vt* to give pleasure to, delight; **~rsi** *vr*: **~rsi di** to take pleasure in, enjoy

di'letto, a *ag* dear, beloved ♦ *sm* pleasure, delight

dili'gente [dili'dʒɛnte] *ag* (*scrupoloso*) diligent; (*accurato*) careful, accurate; **dili'genza** *sf* diligence; care; (*carrozza*) stagecoach

dilu'ire *vt* to dilute

dilun'garsi *vr* (*fig*): **~ su** to talk at length on o about

diluvi'are vb impers to pour (down)

di'luvio sm downpour; (inondazione, fig) flood

dima'grire vi to get thinner, lose weight

dime'nare vt to wave, shake; ~**rsi** vr to toss and turn; (fig) to struggle; ~ **la coda** (sog: cane) to wag its tail

dimensi'one sf dimension; (grandezza) size

dimenti'canza [dimenti'kantsa] sf forgetfulness; (errore) oversight, slip; **per** ~ inadvertently

dimenti'care vt to forget; ~**rsi di qc** to forget sth

di'messo, a pp di **dimettere** ♦ ag (voce) subdued; (uomo, abito) modest, humble

dimesti'chezza [dimesti'kettsa] sf familiarity

di'mettere vt: ~ **qn da** to dismiss sb from; (dall'ospedale) to discharge sb from; ~**rsi (da)** to resign (from)

dimez'zare [dimed'dzare] vt to halve

diminu'ire vt to reduce, diminish; (prezzi) to bring down, reduce ♦ vi to decrease, diminish; (rumore) to die down, die away; (prezzi) to fall, go down; **diminuzi'one** sf decreasing, diminishing

dimissi'oni sfpl resignation sg; **dare o presentare le** ~ to resign, hand in one's resignation

di'mora sf residence

dimo'rare vi to reside

dimos'trare vt to demonstrate, show; (provare) to prove, demonstrate; ~**rsi** vr: ~**rsi molto abile** to show o.s. o prove to be very clever; **dimostra 30 anni** he looks about 30 (years old); **dimostrazi'one** sf demonstration; proof

di'namica sf dynamics sg

di'namico, a, ci, che ag dynamic

dina'mite sf dynamite

'dinamo sf inv dynamo

di'nanzi [di'nantsi]: ~ **a** prep in front

of

dini'ego, ghi sm refusal; denial

dinocco'lato, a ag lanky

din'torno av round, (round) about; ~**i** smpl outskirts; **nei ~i di** in the vicinity o neighbourhood of

'dio (pl **'dei**) sm god; **D~** God; **gli dei** the gods; **D~ mio!** my goodness!, my God!

di'ocesi [di'ɔtʃezi] sf inv diocese

dipa'nare (lana) to wind into a ball; (fig) to disentangle, sort out

diparti'mento sm department

dipen'dente ag dependent ♦ sm/f employee; **dipen'denza** sf dependence; **essere alle dipendenze di qn** to be employed by sb o in sb's employ

di'pendere vi: ~ **da** to depend on; (finanziariamente) to be dependent on; (derivare) to come from, be due to; **di'peso, a** pp di **dipendere**

di'pingere [di'pindʒere] vt to paint; **di'pinto, a** pp di **dipingere** ♦ sm painting

di'ploma, i sm diploma

diplo'mare vt to award a diploma to, graduate (us); ~**rsi** vr to obtain a diploma, graduate (us)

diplo'matico, a, ci, che ag diplomatic ♦ sm diplomat

diploma'zia [diplomat'tsia] sf diplomacy

di'porto: imbarcazione da ~ sf pleasure craft

dira'dare vt to thin (out); (visite) to reduce, make less frequent; ~**rsi** vr to disperse; (nebbia) to clear (up)

dira'mare vt to issue ♦ vi (strade) to branch; ~**rsi** vr to branch

'dire vt to say; (segreto, fatto) to tell; ~ **qc a qn** to tell sb sth; ~ **a qn di fare qc** to tell sb to do sth; ~ **di si/no** to say yes/no; **si dice che ...** they say that ...; **si direbbe che ...** it looks (o sounds) as though ...; **dica, signora?** (in un negozio) yes, Madam, can I help you?

di'retto, a pp di **dirigere ♦** ag direct **♦** sm (FERR) through train

diret'tore, 'trice sm/f (di azienda) director; manager/ess; (di scuola elementare) head (teacher) (BRIT), principal (US); ~ **d'orchestra** conductor; ~ **vendite** sales director o manager

direzi'one [diret'tsjone] sf board of directors; management; (senso di movimento) direction; **in ~ di** in the direction of, towards

diri'gente [diri'dʒɛnte] sm/f executive; (POL) leader ♦ ag: **classe ~** ruling class

di'rigere [di'ridʒere] vt to direct; (impresa) to run, manage; (MUS) to conduct; **~rsi** vr: **~rsi verso** o **a** to make o head for

dirim'petto av opposite; ~ **a** opposite, facing

di'ritto, a ag straight; (onesto) straight, upright ♦ av straight, directly; **andare ~** to go straight on ♦ sm right side; (TENNIS) forehand; (MAGLIA) plain stitch; (prerogativa) right; (leggi, scienza): **il ~** law; **~i** smpl (tasse) duty sg; **stare ~** to stand up straight; **aver ~ a qc** to be entitled to sth; **~i d'autore** royalties

dirit'tura sf (SPORT) straight; (fig) rectitude

diroc'cato, a ag tumbledown, in ruins

dirot'tare vt (nave, aereo) to change the course of; (aereo: sotto minaccia) to hijack; (traffico) to divert ♦ vi (nave, aereo) to change course; **dirotta'tore, 'trice** sm/f hijacker

di'rotto, a ag (pioggia) torrential; (pianto) unrestrained; **piovere a ~** to pour; **piangere a ~** to cry one's heart out

di'rupo sm crag, precipice

disabi'tato, a ag uninhabited

disabitu'arsi vr: **~ a** to get out of the habit of

disac'cordo sm disagreement

disadat'tato, a ag (PSIC) maladjusted

disa'dorno, a ag plain, unadorned

disagi'ato, a [diza'dʒato] ag poor, needy; (vita) hard

di'sagio [di'zadʒo] sm discomfort; (disturbo) inconvenience; (fig: imbarazzo) embarrassment; **essere a ~** to be ill at ease

disappro'vare vt to disapprove of; **disapprovazi'one** sf disapproval

disap'punto sm disappointment

disar'mare vt, vi to disarm; **di'sarmo** sm (MIL) disarmament

di'sastro sm disaster

disat'tento, a ag inattentive; **disattenzi'one** sf carelessness, lack of attention

disa'vanzo [diza'vantso] sm (ECON) deficit

disavven'tura sf misadventure, mishap

dis'brigo, ghi sm (prompt) clearing up o settlement

dis'capito sm: **a ~ di** to the detriment of

dis'carica, che sf (di rifiuti) rubbish tip o dump

discen'dente [diʃʃen'dɛnte] ag descending ♦ sm/f descendant

di'scendere [diʃ'ʃendere] vt to go (o come) down ♦ vi to go (o come) down; (strada) to go down; (smontare) to get off; ~ **da** (famiglia) to be descended from; ~ **dalla macchina/ dal treno** to get out of the car/out of o off the train; ~ **da cavallo** to dismount, get off one's horse

di'scepolo, a [diʃ'ʃepolo] sm/f disciple

di'scernere [diʃ'ʃernere] vt to discern

di'scesa [diʃ'ʃesa] sf descent; (pendio) slope; **in ~** (strada) downhill cpd, sloping; **~ libera** (SCI) downhill (race)

di'sceso, a [diʃ'ʃeso] pp di **discendere**

disci'ogliere [diʃʃ'ʎʎere] vt to dissolve; (fondere) to melt; **~rsi** vr to dissolve; to melt; **disci'olto, a** pp di **disciogliere**

disci'plina [diʃʃi'plina] sf discipline; **discipli'nare** ag disciplinary ♦ vt to discipline

'disco, schi sm disc; (SPORT) discus; (fonografico) record; (INFORM) disk; **~ orario** (AUT) parking disc; **~ rigido** (INFORM) hard disk; **~ volante** flying saucer

discol'pare vt to clear of blame

disco'noscere [disko'noʃʃere] vt (figlio) to disown; (meriti) to ignore, disregard; **disconosci'uto, a** pp di **disconoscere**

dis'corde ag conflicting, clashing; **dis'cordia** sf discord; (dissidio) disagreement, clash

dis'correre vi: **~ (di)** to talk (about)

dis'corso, a pp di **discorrere** ♦ sm speech; (conversazione) conversation, talk

dis'costo, a ag faraway, distant ♦ av far away; **~ da** far from

disco'teca, che sf (raccolta) record library; (locale) disco

discre'panza [diskre'pantsa] sf disagreement

dis'creto, a ag discreet; (abbastanza buono) reasonable, fair; **discrezi'one** sf discretion; (giudizio) judgment, discernment; **a discrezione di** at the discretion of

discriminazi'one [diskriminat'tsjone] sf discrimination

discussi'one sf discussion; (litigio) argument; **fuori ~** out of the question

dis'cusso, a pp di **discutere**

dis'cutere vt to discuss, debate; (contestare) to question ♦ vi (conversare): **~ (di)** to discuss; (litigare) to argue

disde'gnare [disde'ɲare] vt to scorn

dis'detta sf (di prenotazione etc) cancellation; (sfortuna) bad luck

dis'detto, a pp di **disdire**

dis'dire vt (prenotazione) to cancel; (DIR): **~ un contratto d'affitto** to give notice (to quit)

dise'gnare [disen'ɲare] vt to draw; (progettare) to design; (fig) to outline

disegna'tore, 'trice sm/f designer

di'segno [di'seɲɲo] sm drawing; design; outline; **~ di legge** (DIR) bill

diser'bante sm weed-killer

diser'tare vt, vi to desert; **diser'tore** sm (MIL) deserter

dis'fare vt to undo; (valigie) to unpack; (meccanismo) to take to pieces; (neve) to melt; **~rsi** vr to come undone; (neve) to melt; **~ il letto** to strip the bed; **~rsi di qn** (liberarsi) to get rid of sb; **dis'fatta** sf (sconfitta) rout; **dis'fatto, a** pp di **disfare**

dis'gelo [diz'dʒɛlo] sm thaw

dis'grazia [diz'grattsja] sf (sventura) misfortune; (incidente) accident, mishap; **disgrazi'ato, a** ag unfortunate ♦ sm/f wretch

disgre'gare vt to break up; **~rsi** vr to break up

disgu'ido sm hitch; **~ postale** error in postal delivery

disgus'tare vt to disgust; **~rsi** vr: **~rsi di** to be disgusted by

dis'gusto sm disgust; **disgus'toso, a** ag disgusting

disidra'tare vt to dehydrate

disil'ludere vt to disillusion, disenchant

disimpa'rare vt to forget

disinfet'tante ag, sm disinfectant

disinfet'tare vt to disinfect

disini'bito, a ag uninhibited

disinte'grare vt, vi to disintegrate

disinte'ressarsi vr: **~ di** to take no interest in

disinte'resse sm indifference; (generosità) unselfishness

disintossi'care vt (alcolizzato, drogato) to treat for alcoholism (o drug addiction); **~ l'organismo** to clear out one's system

disin'volto, a ag casual, free and easy; **disinvol'tura** sf casualness, ease

disles'sia sf dyslexia

dislo'care *vt* to station, position

dismi'sura *sf* excess; **a ~** to excess, excessively

disobbe'dire *etc* = **disubbidire** *etc*

disoccu'pato, a *ag* unemployed ♦ *sm/f* unemployed person; **disoccupazi'one** *sf* unemployment

diso'nesto, a *ag* dishonest

diso'nore *sm* dishonour, disgrace

di'sopra *av* (*con contatto*) on top; (*senza contatto*) above; (*al piano superiore*) upstairs ♦ *ag inv* (*superiore*) upper ♦ *sm inv* top, upper part

disordi'nato, a *ag* untidy; (*privo di misura*) irregular, wild

di'sordine *sm* (*confusione*) disorder, confusion; (*sregolatezza*) debauchery

disorien'tare *vt* to disorientate; **~rsi** *vr* (*fig*) to get confused, lose one's bearings

di'sotto *av* below, underneath; (*in fondo*) at the bottom; (*al piano inferiore*) downstairs ♦ *ag inv* (*inferiore*) lower; bottom *cpd* ♦ *sm inv* (*parte inferiore*) lower part; bottom

dis'paccio [dis'pattʃo] *sm* dispatch

'dispari *ag inv* odd, uneven

dis'parte: in ~ *av* (*da lato*) aside, apart; **tenersi** o **starsene in ~** to keep to o.s., hold o.s. aloof

dispen'dioso, a *ag* expensive

dis'pensa *sf* pantry, larder; (*mobile*) sideboard; (*DIR*) exemption; (*REL*) dispensation; (*fascicolo*) number, issue

dispen'sare *vt* (*elemosine, favori*) to distribute; (*esonerare*) to exempt

dispe'rare *vi*: **~ (di)** to despair (of); **~rsi** *vr* to despair; **dispe'rato, a** *ag* (*persona*) in despair; (*caso, tentativo*) desperate; **disperazi'one** *sf* despair

dis'perdere *vt* (*disseminare*) to disperse; (*MIL*) to scatter, rout; (*fig: consumare*) to waste, squander; **~rsi** *vr* to disperse; to scatter; **dis'perso, a** *pp di* **disperdere** ♦ *sm/f* missing person

dis'petto *sm* spite *no pl*, spitefulness *no pl*; **fare un ~ a qn** to play a (nasty)

trick on sb; **a ~ di** in spite of; **dispet'toso, a** *ag* spiteful

dispia'cere [dispja'tʃere] *sm* (*rammarico*) regret, sorrow; (*dolore*) grief; **~i** *smpl* (*preoccupazioni*) troubles, worries ♦ *vi*: **~ a** to displease ♦ *vb impers*: **mi dispiace (che)** I am sorry (that); **se non le dispiace, me ne vado adesso** if you don't mind, I'll go now; **dispiaci'uto, a** *pp di* **dispiacere** ♦ *ag* sorry

dispo'nibile *ag* available; **disponibilità** *sf inv* (*di biglietti, camere*) availability; (*gentilezza*) helpfulness; (*spec pl: FIN*) liquid assets *pl*

dis'porre *vt* (*sistemare*) to arrange; (*preparare*) to prepare; (*DIR*) to order; (*persuadere*): **~ qn a** to incline o dispose sb towards ♦ *vi* (*decidere*) to decide; (*usufruire*): **~ di** to use, have at one's disposal; (*essere dotato*): **~ di** to have; **disporsi** *vr* (*ordinarsi*) to place o.s., arrange o.s.

dis'posto, a *pp di* **disporre**

dispprez'zare [dispprez'tsare] *vt* to despise

dis'prezzo [dis'prettso] *sm* contempt

'disputa *sf* dispute, quarrel

dispu'tare *vt* (*contendere*) to dispute, contest; (*gara*) to take part in ♦ *vi* to quarrel; **~ di** to discuss; **~rsi qc** to fight for sth

dissan'guare *vt* (*fig: persona*) to bleed white; (*: patrimonio*) to suck dry; **~rsi** *vr* (*MED*) to lose blood; (*fig: rovinarsi*) to ruin o.s.

dissec'care *vt* to dry up; **~rsi** *vr* to dry up

dissemi'nare *vt* to scatter; (*fig: notizie*) to spread

dis'senso *sm* dissent; (*disapprovazione*)

disapproval

dissente'ria sf dysentery

dissen'tire vi: ~ (da) to disagree (with)

dissertazi'one [dissertat'tsjone] sf dissertation

disser'vizio [disser'vittsjo] sm inefficiency

disses'tare vt (ECON) to ruin; **dis'sesto** sm (financial) ruin

disse'tante ag refreshing

dis'sidio sm disagreement

dis'simile ag different, dissimilar

dissimu'lare vt (fingere) to dissemble; (nascondere) to conceal

dissi'pare vt to dissipate; (scialacquare) to squander, waste

dis'solto, a pp di **dissolvere**

disso'luto, a pp di **dissolvere** ♦ ag dissolute, licentious

dis'solvere vt to dissolve; (neve) to melt; (fumo) to disperse; **~rsi** vr to dissolve; to melt; to disperse

dissu'adere vt: ~ qn da to dissuade sb from; **dissu'aso, a** pp di **dissuadere**

distac'care vt to detach, separate; (SPORT) to leave behind; **~rsi** vr to be detached; (fig) to stand out; **~rsi da** (fig: allontanarsi) to grow away from

dis'tacco, chi sm (separazione) separation; (fig: indifferenza) detachment; (SPORT): **vincere con un ~ di** ... to win by a distance of ...

dis'tante av far away ♦ ag: ~ (da) distant (from), far away (from)

dis'tanza [dis'tantsa] sf distance

distanzi'are [distan'tsjare] vt to space out, place at intervals; (SPORT) to outdistance; (fig: superare) to outstrip, surpass

dis'tare vi: **distiamo pochi chilometri da Roma** we are only a few kilometres (away) from Rome

dis'tendere vt (coperta) to spread out; (gambe) to stretch (out); (mettere a giacere) to lay; (rilassare: muscoli, nervi)

to relax; **~rsi** vr (rilassarsi) to relax; (sdraiarsi) to lie down; **disten'sione** sf stretching; relaxation; (POL) détente

dis'tesa sf expanse, stretch

dis'teso, a pp di **distendere**

distil'lare vt to distil

distille'ria sf distillery

dis'tinguere vt to distinguish

dis'tinta sf (nota) note; (elenco) list

distin'tivo, a ag distinctive; distinguishing ♦ sm badge

dis'tinto, a pp di **distinguere** ♦ ag (dignitoso ed elegante) distinguished; **~i saluti** (in lettera) yours faithfully

distinzi'one [distin'tsjone] sf distinction

dis'togliere [dis'tɔʎʎere] vt: ~ **da** to take away from; (fig) to dissuade from; **dis'tolto, a** pp di **distogliere**

distorsi'one sf (MED) sprain; (FISICA, OTTICA) distortion

dis'trarre vt to distract; (divertire) to entertain, amuse; **distrarsi** vr (non fare attenzione) to be distracted, let one's mind wander; (svagarsi) to amuse o enjoy o.s.; **dis'tratto, a** pp di **distrarre** ♦ ag absent-minded; (disattento) inattentive; **distrazi'one** sf absent-mindedness; inattention; (svago) distraction, entertainment

dis'tretto sm district

distribu'ire vt to distribute; (CARTE) to deal (out); (posta) to deliver; (lavoro) to allocate, assign; (ripartire) to share out; **distribu'tore** sm (di benzina) petrol (BRIT) o gas (US) pump; (AUT, ELETTR) distributor; (automatico) vending machine; **distribuzi'one** sf distribution; delivery

distri'care vt to disentangle, unravel

dis'truggere [dis'truddʒere] vt to destroy; **dis'trutto, a** pp di **distruggere**; **distruzi'one** sf destruction

distur'bare vt to disturb, trouble; (sonno, lezioni) to disturb, interrupt; **~rsi** vr to put o.s. out

dis'turbo sm trouble, bother, inconvenience; (*indisposizione*) (slight) disorder, ailment; **~i** smpl (RADIO, TV) static sg

disubbidi'ente ag disobedient; **disubbidi'enza** sf disobedience

disubbi'dire vi: **~ (a qn)** to disobey (sb)

disugu'ale ag unequal; (*diverso*) different; (*irregolare*) uneven

disu'mano, a ag inhuman

di'suso sm: andare o cadere in ~ to fall into disuse

'dita fpl di dito

di'tale sm thimble

'dito (pl(f) **'dita**) sm finger; (*misura*) finger, finger's breadth; ~ **(del piede)** toe

'ditta sf firm, business

ditta'tore sm dictator

ditta'tura sf dictatorship

dit'tongo, ghi sm diphthong

di'urno, a ag day cpd, daytime cpd

'diva sf vedi divo

diva'gare vi to digress

divam'pare vi to flare up, blaze up

di'vano sm sofa; divan

divari'care vt to open wide

di'vario sm difference

dive'nire vi = **diventare**

diven'tare vi to become; ~ **famoso/professore** to become famous/a teacher

dive'nuto, a pp di **divenire**

di'verbio sm altercation

di'vergere [di'vɛrdʒere] vi to diverge

diversifi'care vt to diversify, vary; to differentiate

diversi'one sf diversion

diversità sf inv difference, diversity; (*varietà*) variety

diver'sivo sm diversion, distraction

di'verso, a ag (*differente*): ~ **(da)** different (from); ~**i, e** det pl several, various; (COMM) sundry ♦ pron pl several (people), many (people)

diver'tente ag amusing

diverti'mento sm amusement, pleasure; (*passatempo*) pastime, recreation

diver'tire vt to amuse, entertain; **~rsi** vr to amuse o enjoy o.s.

divi'dendo sm dividend

di'videre vt (*anche* MAT) to divide; (*distribuire, ripartire*) to divide (up), split (up); (*separare*) to separate; (*strade*) to fork

divi'eto sm prohibition; "~ **di sosta**" (AUT) "no parking"

divin'colarsi vr to wriggle, writhe

divinità sf inv divinity

di'vino, a ag divine

di'visa sf (MIL etc) uniform; (COMM) foreign currency

divisi'one sf division

di'viso, a pp di **dividere**

'divo, a sm/f star

divo'rare vt to devour

divorzi'are [divor'tsjare] vi: ~ **(da qn)** to divorce (sb); **divorzi'ato, a** sm/f divorcee

di'vorzio [di'vɔrtsjo] sm divorce

divul'gare vt to divulge, disclose; (*rendere comprensibile*) to popularize; **~rsi** vr to spread

dizio'nario [dittsjo'narjo] sm dictionary

dizi'one [dit'tsjone] sf diction; pronunciation

do sm (MUS) C; (: solfeggiando) do(h)

DOC [dɔk] abbr (= denominazione di origine controllata) label guaranteeing the quality of wine

'doccia, ce ['dottʃa] sf (bagno) shower; fare la ~ to have a shower

do'cente [do'tʃɛnte] ag teaching ♦ sm/f teacher; (di università) lecturer

'docile ['dɔtʃile] ag docile

documen'tare vt to document; **~rsi** vr: **~rsi (su)** to gather information o material (about)

documen'tario sm documentary

docu'mento sm document; **~i** smpl (d'identità etc) papers

'dodici ['dodittʃi] num twelve

do'gana sf (ufficio) customs pl; (tassa) (customs) duty; **passare la ~** to go through customs; **doga'nale** ag customs cpd; **dogani'ere** sm customs officer

'doglie ['dɔʎʎe] sfpl (MED) labour sg, labour pains

'dolce ['doltʃe] ag sweet; (carattere, persona) gentle, mild; (fig: mite: clima) mild; (non ripido: pendio) gentle ♦ sm (sapore dolce) sweetness, sweet taste; (CUC: portata) sweet, dessert; (: torta) cake; **dol'cezza** sf sweetness; softness; mildness; gentleness; **dolci'cante** sm sweetener; **dolci'umi** smpl sweets

do'lente ag sorrowful, sad

do'lere vi to be sore, hurt, ache; **~rsi** vr to complain; (essere spiacente) **~rsi di** to be sorry for; **mi duole la testa** my head aches, I've got a headache

'dollaro sm dollar

'dolo sm (DIR) malice

Dolo'miti sfpl: **le ~** the Dolomites

do'lore sm (fisico) pain; (morale) sorrow, grief; **dolo'roso, a** ag painful; sorrowful, sad

do'loso, a ag (DIR) malicious

do'manda sf (interrogazione) question; (richiesta) demand; (: cortese) request; (DIR: richiesta scritta) application; (ECON): **la ~** demand; **fare una ~ a qn** to ask sb a question; **fare ~ (per un lavoro)** to apply (for a job)

doman'dare vt (per avere) to ask for; (per sapere) to ask; (esigere) to demand; **~rsi** vr to wonder; to ask o.s.; **~ qc a qn** to ask sb for sth; to ask sb sth

do'mani av tomorrow ♦ sm: **il ~** (il futuro) the future; (il giorno successivo) the next day; **~ l'altro** the day after tomorrow

do'mare vt to tame

domat'tina av tomorrow morning

do'menica, che sf Sunday; **di o la ~** on Sundays; **domeni'cale** ag Sunday cpd

do'mestica, che sf vedi **domestico**

do'mestico, a, ci, che ag domestic ♦ sm/f servant, domestic

domi'cilio [domi'tʃiljo] sm (DIR) domicile, place of residence

domi'nare vt to dominate; (fig: sentimenti) to control, master ♦ vi to be in the dominant position; **~rsi** vr (controllarsi) to control o.s.; **~ su** (fig) to surpass, outclass; **dominazi'one** sf domination

do'minio sm dominion; (fig: campo) field, domain

do'nare vt to give, present; (per beneficenza etc) to donate ♦ vi (fig): **~ a** to suit, become; **~ sangue** to give blood; **dona'tore, 'trice** sm/f donor; **donatore di sangue/di organi** blood/organ donor

dondo'lare vt (cullare) to rock; **~rsi** vr to swing, sway; **dondolo** sm: **sedia/ cavallo a dondolo** rocking chair/horse

'donna sf woman; **~ di casa** housewife; home-loving woman; **~ di servizio** maid

donnai'olo sm ladykiller

'donnola sf weasel

'dono sm gift

'dopo av (tempo) afterwards; (: più tardi) later; (luogo) after, next ♦ prep after ♦ cong (temporale): **~ aver studiato** after having studied; **~ mangiato va a dormire** after having eaten o after a meal he goes for a sleep ♦ ag inv: **il giorno ~** the following day; **un anno ~** a year later; **~ di me/lui** after me/him

dopo'barba sm inv after-shave

dopodo'mani av the day after tomorrow

dopogu'erra sm postwar years pl

dopo'pranzo [dopo'prandzo] av after lunch (o dinner)

doposci [dopoʃ'ʃi] sm inv après-ski outfit

doposcu'ola sm inv school club offering

extra tuition and recreational facilities

dopo'sole *sm inv* aftersun (lotion)

dopo'tutto *av* (*tutto considerato*) after all

doppi'aggio [dop'pjaddʒo] *sm* (*CINEMA*) dubbing

doppi'are *vt* (*NAUT*) to round; (*SPORT*) to lap; (*CINEMA*) to dub

'doppio, a *ag* double; (*fig: falso*) double-dealing, deceitful ♦ *sm* (*quantità*): **il ~ (di)** twice as much (o many), double the amount (o number) of; (*SPORT*) doubles *pl* ♦ *av* double

doppi'one *sm* duplicate (copy)

doppio'petto *sm* double-breasted jacket

do'rare *vt* to gild; (*CUC*) to brown; **do'rato, a** *ag* golden; (*ricoperto d'oro*) gilt, gilded; **dora'tura** *sf* gilding

dormicchi'are [dormik'kjare] *vi* to doze

dormigli'one, a [dormiʎ'ʎone] *sm/f* sleepyhead

dor'mire *vt, vi* to sleep; **andare a ~** to go to bed; **dor'mita** *sf*: **farsi una dormita** to have a good sleep

dormi'torio *sm* dormitory

dormi'veglia [dormi'veʎʎa] *sm* drowsiness

'dorso *sm* back; (*di montagna*) ridge, crest; (*di libro*) spine; **a ~ di cavallo** on horseback

do'sare *vt* to measure out; (*MED*) to dose

'dose *sf* quantity, amount; (*MED*) dose

'dosso *sm* (*rilievo*) rise; (*di strada*) bump; (*dorso*): **levarsi di ~ i vestiti** to take one's clothes off

do'tare *vt*: **~ di** to provide o supply with; **dotazi'one** *sf* (*insieme di beni*) endowment; (*di macchine etc*) equipment

'dote *sf* (*di sposa*) dowry; (*assegnata a un ente*) endowment; (*fig*) gift, talent

Dott. *abbr* (= *dottore*) Dr.

'dotto, a *ag* (*colto*) learned ♦ *sm* (*sapiente*) scholar; (*ANAT*) duct

dotto'rato *sm* degree; **~ di ricerca** doctorate, doctor's degree

dot'tore, essa *sm/f* doctor

dot'trina *sf* doctrine

Dott.ssa *abbr* (= *dottoressa*) Dr.

'dove *av* (*gen*) where; (*in cui*) where, in which; (*dovunque*) wherever ♦ *cong* (*mentre, laddove*) whereas; **~ sei?/vai?** where are you?/are you going?; **dimmi dov'è** tell me where it is; **di ~ sei?** where are you from?; **per ~ si passa?** which way should we go?; **la città ~ abito** the town where o in which I live; **siediti ~ vuoi** sit wherever you like

do'vere *sm* (*obbligo*) duty ♦ *vt* (*essere debitore*): **~ qc (a qn)** to owe (sb) sth ♦ *vi* (*seguito dall'infinito: obbligo*) to have to; **rivolgersi a chi di ~** to apply to the appropriate authority o person; **lui deve farlo** he has to do it, he must do it; **è dovuto partire** he had to leave; **ha dovuto pagare** he had to pay; (: *intenzione*): **devo partire domani** I'm (due) to leave tomorrow; (: *probabilità*): **dev'essere tardi** it must be late; **come si deve** (*lavorare, comportarsi*) properly; **una persona come si deve** a respectable person

dove'roso, a *ag* (right and) proper

do'vunque *av* (*in qualunque luogo*) wherever; (*dappertutto*) everywhere; **~ io vada** wherever I go

do'vuto, a *ag* (*causato*): **~ a** due to

doz'zina [dod'dzina] *sf* dozen; **una ~ di uova** a dozen eggs

dozzi'nale [doddzi'nale] *ag* cheap, second-rate

dra'gare *vt* to dredge

'drago, ghi *sm* dragon

'dramma, i *sm* drama; **dram'matico, a, ci, che** *ag* dramatic; **drammatiz'zare** *vt* to dramatize; **dramma'turgo, ghi** *sm* playwright, dramatist

drappeggi'are [draped'dʒare] *vt* to drape

drap'pello sm (MIL) squad; (gruppo) band, group

'drastico, a, ci, che ag drastic

dre'naggio [dre'naddʒo] sm drainage

dre'nare vt to drain

'dritto, a ag, av = **diritto**

driz'zare [drit'tsare] vt (far tornare dritto) to straighten; (innalzare: antenna, muro) to erect; **~rsi** vr: **~rsi (in piedi)** to stand up; **~ le orecchie** to prick up one's ears

'droga, ghe sf (sostanza aromatica) spice; (stupefacente) drug; **dro'gare** vt to season, spice; to drug; dope; **drogarsi** vr to take drugs; **dro'gato, a** sm/f drug addict

droghe'ria [droge'ria] sf grocer's shop (BRIT), grocery (store) (US)

'dubbio, a ag (incerto) doubtful, dubious; (ambiguo) dubious ♦ sm (incertezza) doubt; **avere il ~ che** to be afraid that, suspect that; **mettere in ~ qc** to question sth; **dubbi'oso, a** ag doubtful, dubious

dubi'tare vi: **~ di** to doubt; (risultato) to be doubtful of

Dub'lino sf Dublin

'duca, chi sm duke

du'chessa [du'kessa] sf duchess

'due num two

due'cento [due'tʃento] num two hundred ♦ sm: **il D~** the thirteenth century

due'pezzi [due'pettsi] sm (costume da bagno) two-piece swimsuit; (abito femminile) two-piece suit

du'etto sm duet

'dunque cong (perciò) so, therefore; (riprendendo il discorso) well (then) ♦ sm inv: **venire al ~** to come to the point

du'omo sm cathedral

'duplex sm inv (TEL) party line

dupli'cato sm duplicate

'duplice ['duplitʃe] ag double, twofold; **in ~ copia** in duplicate

du'rante prep during

du'rare vi to last; **~ fatica a** to have difficulty in; **du'rata** sf length (of time); duration; **dura'turo, a** ag lasting

du'rezza [du'rettsa] sf hardness; stubbornness; harshness; toughness

'duro, a ag (pietra, lavoro, materasso, problema) hard; (persona: ostinato) stubborn, obstinate; (: severo) harsh, hard; (voce) harsh; (carne) tough ♦ sm hardness; (difficoltà) hard part; (persona) tough guy; **tener ~** to stand firm, hold out; **~ d'orecchi** hard of hearing

du'rone sm hard skin

E, e

e (dav V spesso **ed**) cong and; **~ lui?** what about him?; **~ compralo!** well buy it then!

E. abbr (= est) E

è vb vedi **essere**

'ebano sm ebony

eb'bene cong well (then)

eb'brezza [eb'brettsa] sf intoxication

'ebbro, a ag drunk; **~ di** (gioia etc) beside o.s. with; wild with

'ebete ag stupid, idiotic

ebolli'zione [ebolli'tsjone] sf boiling; **punto di ~** boiling point

e'braico, a, ci, che ag Hebrew, Hebraic ♦ sm (LING) Hebrew

e'breo, a ag Jewish ♦ sm/f Jew/Jewess

'Ebridi sfpl: **le (isole)** ~ the Hebrides

ecc av abbr (= eccetera) etc

ecce'denza [ettʃe'dentsa] sf excess, surplus

ec'cedere [et'tʃedere] vt to exceed ♦ vi to go too far; **~ nel bere/mangiare** to indulge in drink/food to excess

eccel'lente [ettʃel'lente] ag excellent; **eccel'lenza** sf excellence; (titolo) Excellency

ec'cellere [et'tʃellere] vi: **~ (in)** to excel (at); **ec'celso, a** pp di **eccellere**

ec'centrico, a, ci, che [ett'ʃɛntriko] *ag* eccentric

ecces'sivo, a [ettʃes'sivo] *ag* excessive

ec'cesso [ett'ʃɛsso] *sm* excess; **all'~** (*gentile, generoso*) to excess, excessively; **~ di velocità** (*AUT*) speeding

ec'cetera [ett'ʃɛtera] *av* et cetera, and so on

ec'cetto [ett'ʃɛtto] *prep* except, with the exception of; **~ che** except, other than; **~ che (non)** unless

eccet'tuare [ettʃettu'are] *vt* to except

eccezio'nale [ettʃetsjo'nale] *ag* exceptional

eccezi'one [ettʃet'tsjone] *sf* exception; (*DIR*) objection; **a ~ di** with the exception of, except for; **d'~** exceptional

ec'cidio [ett'ʃidjo] *sm* massacre

ecci'tare [ettʃi'tare] *vt* (*curiosità, interesse*) to excite, arouse; (*folla*) to incite; **~rsi** *vr* to get excited; (*sessualmente*) to become aroused; **eccitazi'one** *sf* excitement

'ecco *av* (*per dimostrare*): **~ il treno!** here's o here comes the train!; (*dav pron*): **~mi!** here I am!; **~ne uno!** here's one (of them)!; (*dav pp*): **~ fatto!** there, that's it done!

echeggi'are [eked'dʒare] *vi* to echo

e'clissi *sf* eclipse

'eco (*pl*(*m*) **'echi**) *sm* o *f* echo

ecogra'fia *sf* (*MED*) scan

ecolo'gia [ekolo'dʒia] *sf* ecology

econo'mia [ekono'mia] *sf* (*scienza*) economics *sg*; (*risparmio: azione*) saving; **fare ~** to economize, make economies; **eco'nomico, a, ci, che** *ag* economic; (*poco costoso*) economical; **econo'mista, i** *sm* economist; **economiz'zare** *vt, vi* to save; **e'conomo, a** *ag* thrifty ♦ *sm/f* (*INS*) bursar

E'CU [e'ku] *sm inv* (= *Unità monetaria europea*) ECU *n*

ed *cong vedi* **e**

'edera *sf* ivy

e'dicola *sf* newspaper kiosk o stand (*US*)

edifi'care *vt* to build; (*fig: teoria, azienda*) to establish; (*indurre al bene*) to edify

edi'ficio [edi'fitʃo] *sm* building

e'dile *ag* building *cpd*; **edi'lizia** *sf* building, building trade; **edi'lizio, a** *ag* building *cpd*

Edim'burgo *sf* Edinburgh

edi'tore, 'trice *ag* publishing *cpd* ♦ *sm/f* publisher; (*curatore*) editor; **edito'ria** *sf* publishing; **editori'ale** *ag* publishing *cpd* ♦ *sm* editorial, leader

edizi'one [edit'tsjone] *sf* edition; (*tiratura*) printing

edu'care *vt* to educate; (*gusto, mente*) to train; **~ qn a fare** to train sb to do; **edu'cato, a** *ag* polite, well-mannered; **educazi'one** *sf* education; (*familiare*) upbringing; (*comportamento*) (good) manners *pl*; **educazione fisica** (*INS*) physical training o education

effemi'nato, a *ag* effeminate

effet'tivo, a *ag* (*reale*) real, actual; (*impiegato, professore*) permanent; (*MIL*) regular ♦ *sm* (*MIL*) strength; (*di patrimonio etc*) sum total

ef'fetto *sm* effect; (*COMM: cambiale*) bill; (*fig: impressione*) impression; **in ~i** in fact, actually; **~ serra** greenhouse effect; **effettu'are** *vt* to effect, carry out

effi'cace [effi'katʃe] *ag* effective

effici'ente [effi'tʃɛnte] *ag* efficient; **effici'enza** *sf* efficiency

ef'fimero, a *ag* ephemeral

E'geo [e'dʒɛo] *sm*: **l'~, il mare ~** the Aegean (Sea)

E'gitto [e'dʒitto] *sm*: **l'~** Egypt

egizi'ano, a [edʒit'tsjano] *ag, sm/f* Egyptian

'egli [ˈeʎʎi] *pron* he; **~ stesso** he himself

ego'ismo *sm* selfishness, egoism; **ego'ista, i, e** *ag* selfish, egoistic

♦ *sm/f* egoist

egr. *abbr* = **egregio**

e'gregio, a, gi, gie [e'gredʒo] *ag* (*nelle lettere*): **E~ Signore** Dear Sir

eguagli'anza *etc* [egwaʎ'ʎantsa] = **uguaglianza** *etc*

E.I. *abbr* = **Esercito Italiano**

elabo'rare *vt* (*progetto*) to work out, elaborate; (*dati*) to process; **elabora-'tore** *sm* (*INFORM*): **elaboratore elettronico** computer; **elaborazi'one** *sf* elaboration; **elaborazione dei dati** data processing

elasticiz'zato, a [elastitʃid'dzato] *ag* stretch *cpd*

e'lastico, a, ci, che *ag* elastic; (*fig: andatura*) springy; (: *decisione, vedute*) flexible ♦ *sm* (*di gomma*) rubber band; (*per il cucito*) elastic *no pl*

ele'fante *sm* elephant

ele'gante *ag* elegant

e'leggere [e'leddʒere] *vt* to elect

elemen'tare *ag* elementary; **le (scuole) ~i** *sfpl* primary (*BRIT*) o grade (*US*) school

ele'mento *sm* element; (*parte componente*) element, component, part; **~i** *smpl* (*della scienza etc*) elements, rudiments

ele'mosina *sf* charity, alms *pl*; **chiedere l'~** to beg

elen'care *vt* to list

e'lenco, chi *sm* list; **~ telefonico** telephone directory

e'letto, a *pp di* **eleggere** ♦ *sm/f* (*nominato*) elected member; **elet'torale** *ag* electoral, election *cpd*; **eletto'rato** *sm* electorate; **elet'tore, 'trice** *sm/f* voter, elector

elet'trauto *sm inv* workshop for car electrical repairs; (*tecnico*) car electrician

elettri'cista, i [elettri'tʃista] *sm* electrician

elettricità [elettritʃi'ta] *sf* electricity

e'lettrico, a, ci, che *ag* electric(al)

elettriz'zare [elettrid'dzare] *vt* to

electrify

e'lettro... prefisso: elettrocar-dio'gramma, i *sm* electrocardiogram; **elettrodo'mestico, a, ci, che** *ag*: **apparecchi elettrodomestici** domestic (electrical) appliances; **elet'trone** *sm* electron; **elet'tronica** *sf* electronics *sg*; **elet'tronico, a, ci, che** *ag* electronic

ele'vare *vt* to raise; (*edificio*) to erect; (*multa*) to impose

elezi'one [elet'tsjone] *sf* election; **~i** *sfpl* (*POL*) election(s)

'elica, che *sf* propeller

eli'cottero *sm* helicopter

elimi'nare *vt* to eliminate; **elimina-'toria** *sf* eliminating round

'elio *sm* helium

elisoc'corso *sm* helicopter ambulance

'ella *pron she*; (*forma di cortesia*) you; **~ stessa** she herself; you yourself

el'metto *sm* helmet

e'logio [e'lɔdʒo] *sm* (*discorso, scritto*) eulogy; (*lode*) praise (*di solito no pl*)

elo'quente *ag* eloquent

e'ludere *vt* to evade; **elu'sivo, a** *ag* evasive

ema'nare *vt* to send out, give off; (*fig: leggi, decreti*) to issue ♦ *vi*: **~ da** to come from

emanci'pare [emantʃi'pare] *vt* to emancipate; **~rsi** *vr* (*fig*) to become liberated o emancipated

embri'one *sm* embryo

emenda'mento *sm* amendment

emen'dare *vt* to amend

emer'genza [emer'dʒentsa] *sf* emergency; **in caso di ~** in an emergency

e'mergere [e'mɛrdʒere] *vi* to emerge; (*sommergibile*) to surface; (*fig: distinguersi*) to stand out; **e'merso, a** *pp di* **emergere**

e'messo, a *pp di* **emettere**

e'mettere *vt* (*suono, luce*) to give out, emit; (*onde radio*) to send out; (*assegno, francobollo, ordine*) to issue

emi'crania sf migraine

emi'grare vi to emigrate;
  emigrazi'one sf emigration

emi'nente ag eminent, distinguished

emis'fero sm hemisphere; **~ boreale/
australe** northern/southern
hemisphere

emissi'one sf (vedi emettere) emission;
sending out; issue; (RADIO) broadcast

emit'tente ag (banca) issuing; (RADIO)
broadcasting, transmitting ♦ sf (RADIO)
transmitter

emorra'gia, 'gie [emorra'dʒia] sf
haemorrhage

emor'roidi sfpl haemorrhoids pl (BRIT),
hemorrhoids pl (US)

emo'tivo, a ag emotional

emozio'nante [emottsjo'nante] ag
exciting, thrilling

emozio'nare [emottsjo'nare] vt
(appassionare) to thrill, excite;
(commuovere) to move; (innervosire) to
upset; **~rsi** vr to be excited; to be
moved; to be upset

emozi'one [emot'tsjone] sf emotion;
(agitazione) excitement

'empio, a ag (sacrilego) impious;
(spietato) cruel, pitiless; (malvagio)
wicked, evil

emulsi'one sf emulsion

enciclope'dia [entʃiklope'dia] sf
encyclopaedia

endove'noso, a ag (MED) intravenous

'ENEL ['enel] sigla m (= Ente Nazionale
per l'Energia Elettrica) national electricity
company

ener'gia, 'gie [ener'dʒia] sf (FISICA)
energy; (fig) energy, strength, vigour;
~ eolica wind power; **~ solare** solar
energy, solar power; **e'nergico, a, ci,
che** ag energetic, vigorous

'enfasi sf emphasis; (peg) bombast,
pomposity; **en'fatico, a, ci, che** ag
emphatic; pompous

en'nesimo, a ag (MAT, fig) nth; **per
l'~a volta** for the umpteenth time

e'norme ag enormous, huge;

enormità sf inv enormity, huge size;
(assurdità) absurdity; **non dire
enormità!** don't talk nonsense!

'ente sm (istituzione) body, board,
corporation; (FILOSOFIA) being

en'trambi, e pron pl both (of them)
♦ ag pl: **~ i ragazzi** both boys, both of
the boys

en'trare vi to go (o come) in; **~ in**
(luogo) to enter, go (o come) into;
(trovar posto, poter stare) to fit into;
(essere ammesso a: club etc) to join,
become a member of; **~ in
automobile** to get into the car; **far
~ qn** (visitatore etc) to show sb in;
questo non c'entra (fig) that's got
nothing to do with it; **en'trata**
entrance, entry; **entrate** sfpl (COMM)
receipts, takings; (ECON) income sg

'entro prep (temporale) within

entusias'mare vt to excite, fill with
enthusiasm; **~rsi (per qc/qn)** to
become enthusiastic (about sth/sb);
entusi'asmo sm enthusiasm;
entusi'asta, i, e ag enthusiastic
♦ sm/f enthusiast; **entusi'astico, a,
ci, che** ag enthusiastic

enunci'are [enun'tʃare] vt (teoria) to
set out

epa'tite sf hepatitis

'epico, a, ci, che ag epic

epide'mia sf epidemic

epi'dermide sf skin, epidermis

Epifa'nia sf Epiphany

epiles'sia sf epilepsy

e'pilogo, ghi sm conclusion

epi'sodio sm episode

e'piteto sm epithet

'epoca, che sf (periodo storico) age,
era; (tempo) time; (GEO) age

ep'pure cong and yet, nevertheless

equa'tore sm equator

equazi'one [ekwat'tsjone] sf (MAT)
equation

e'questre ag equestrian

equi'latero, a ag equilateral

equili'brare vt to balance; **equi'librio**

sm balance, equilibrium; **perdere l'~** to lose one's balance

e'**quino, a** *ag* horse *cpd*, equine

equipaggi'are [ekwipad'dʒare] *vt* (*di persone*) to man; (*di mezzi*) to equip; **equi'paggio** *sm* crew

equipa'rare *vt* to make equal

equità *sf* equity, fairness

equitazi'one [ekwitat'tsjone] *sf* (horse-)riding

equiva'lente *ag, sm* equivalent; **equiva'lenza** *sf* equivalence

equivo'care *vi* to misunderstand; **e'quivoco, a, ci, che** *ag* equivocal, ambiguous; (*sospetto*) dubious ♦ *sm* misunderstanding; **a scanso di equivoci** to avoid any misunderstanding; **giocare sull'equivoco** to equivocate

'**equo, a** *ag* fair, just

'**era** *sf* era

'**erba** *sf* grass; (*aromatica, medicinale*) herb; **in ~** (*fig*) budding; **er'baccia, ce** *sf* weed

e'**rede** *sm/f* heir; **eredità** *sf* (*DIR*) inheritance; (*BIOL*) heredity; **lasciare qc in eredità a qn** to leave o bequeath sth to sb; **eredi'tare** *vt* to inherit; **eredi'tario, a** *ag* hereditary

ere'**mita, i** *sm* hermit

ere'**sia** *sf* heresy; **e'retico, a, ci, che** *ag* heretical ♦ *sm/f* heretic

e'**retto, a** *pp di* **erigere** ♦ *ag* erect, upright; **erezi'one** *sf* (*FISIOL*) erection

er'**gastolo** *sm* (*DIR: pena*) life imprisonment

'**erica** *sf* heather

e'**rigere** [e'ridʒere] *vt* to erect, raise; (*fig: fondare*) to found

ERM *sigla* (= *Meccanismo dei tassi di cambio*) ERM *n*

ermel'**lino** *sm* ermine

er'**metico, a, ci, che** *ag* hermetic

'**ernia** *sf* (*MED*) hernia

e'**roe** *sm* hero

ero'**gare** *vt* (*somme*) to distribute; (*gas, servizi*) to supply

e'**roico, a, ci, che** *ag* heroic

ero'**ina** *sf* heroine; (*droga*) heroin

ero'**ismo** *sm* heroism

erosi'**one** *sf* erosion

e'**rotico, a, ci, che** *ag* erotic

er'**rare** *vi* (*vagare*) to wander, roam; (*sbagliare*) to be mistaken

er'**rore** *sm* error, mistake; (*morale*) error; **per ~** by mistake

'**erta** *sf* steep slope; **stare all'~** to be on the alert

erut'**tare** (*sog: vulcano*) to throw out, belch

eruzi'**one** [erut'tsjone] *sf* eruption

esacer'**bare** [ezatʃer'bare] *vt* to exacerbate

esage'**rare** [ezadʒe'rare] *vt* to exaggerate ♦ *vi* to exaggerate; (*eccedere*) to go too far; **esagerazi'one** *sf* exaggeration

e'**sagono** *sm* hexagon

esal'**tare** *vt* to exalt; (*entusiasmare*) to excite, stir; **esal'tato, a** *sm/f* fanatic

e'**same** *sm* examination; (*INS*) exam, examination; **fare** o **dare un ~** to sit o take an exam; **~ del sangue** blood test

esami'**nare** *vt* to examine

e'**sanime** *ag* lifeless

esaspe'**rare** *vt* to exasperate; to exacerbate; **~rsi** *vr* to become annoyed o exasperated; **esasperazi'one** *sf* exasperation

esatta'**mente** *av* exactly; accurately, precisely

esat'**tezza** [ezat'tettsa] *sf* exactitude, accuracy; precision

e'**satto, a** *pp di* **esigere** ♦ *ag* (*calcolo, ora*) correct, right, exact; (*preciso*) accurate, precise; (*puntuale*) punctual

esat'**tore** *sm* (*di imposte etc*) collector

esau'**dire** *vt* to grant, fulfil

esau'**riente** *ag* exhaustive

esauri'**mento** *sm* exhaustion; **~ nervoso** nervous breakdown

esau'**rire** (*stancare*) *vt* to exhaust, wear out; (*provviste, miniera*) to exhaust;

~rsi vr to exhaust o.s., wear o.s. out; (*proviste*) to run out; **esau'rito, a** ag exhausted; (*merci*) sold out; **registrare il tutto esaurito** (TEATRO) to have a full house; **e'sausto, a** ag exhausted

'esca (*pl* **'esche**) *sf* bait

escande'scenza [eskandeʃ'ʃɛntsa] *sf*: **dare in ~e** to lose one's temper, fly into a rage

'esce *etc* ['eʃe] *vb vedi* **uscire**

eschi'mese [eski'mese] *ag, sm/f* Eskimo

escla'mare *vi* to exclaim, cry out; **esclamazi'one** *sf* exclamation

es'cludere *vt* to exclude

esclu'siva *sf* (DIR, COMM) exclusive o sole rights *pl*

esclu'sivo, a *ag* exclusive

es'cluso, a *pp di* **escludere**

'esco *etc* *vb vedi* **uscire**

escogi'tare [eskodʒi'tare] *vt* to devise, think up

escursi'one *sf* (*gita*) excursion, trip; (*: a piedi*) hike, walk; (METEOR) range

ese'crare *vt* to loathe, abhor

esecu'tivo, a *ag, sm* executive

esecu'tore, 'trice *sm/f* (MUS) performer; (DIR) executor

esecuzi'one [ezekut'tsjone] *sf* execution, carrying out; (MUS) performance; **~ capitale** execution

esegu'ire *vt* to carry out, execute; (MUS) to perform, execute

e'sempio *sm* example; **per ~** for example, for instance; **fare un ~** to give an example; **esem'plare** *ag* exemplary ♦ *sm* example; (*copia*) copy; **esemplifi'care** *vb* to exemplify

esen'tare *vt*: **~ qn/qc da** to exempt sb/sth from

e'sente *ag*: **~ da** (*dispensato da*) exempt from; (*privo di*) free from; **esenzi'one** *sf* exemption

e'sequie *sfpl* funeral rites; funeral service *sg*

eser'cente [ezer'tʃɛnte] *sm/f* trader, dealer; shopkeeper

eserci'tare [ezertʃi'tare] *vt* (*professione*) to practise (BRIT), practice (US); (*allenare: corpo, mente*) to exercise, train; (*diritto*) to exercise; (*influenza, pressione*) to exert; **~rsi** *vr* to practise; **~rsi alla lotta** to practise fighting; **esercitazi'one** *sf* (*scolastica, militare*) exercise

e'sercito [e'zertʃito] *sm* army

eser'cizio [ezer'tʃittsjo] *sm* practice; exercising; (*fisico, di matematica*) exercise; (ECON) financial year; (*azienda*) business, concern; **in ~** (*medico etc*) practising

esi'bire *vt* to exhibit, display; (*documenti*) to produce, present; **~rsi** *vr* (*attore*) to perform; (*fig*) to show off; **esibizi'one** *sf* exhibition; (*di documento*) presentation; (*spettacolo*) show, performance

esi'gente [ezi'dʒɛnte] *ag* demanding; **esi'genza** *sf* demand, requirement

e'sigere [e'zidʒere] *vt* (*pretendere*) to demand; (*richiedere*) to demand, require; (*imposte*) to collect

e'siguo, a *ag* small, slight

'esile *ag* (*persona*) slender, slim; (*stelo*) thin; (*voce*) faint

esili'are *vt* to exile; **e'silio** *sm* exile

e'simere *vt*: **~ qn/qc da** to exempt sb/sth from; **~rsi** *vr*: **~rsi da** to get out of

esis'tenza [ezis'tɛntsa] *sf* existence

e'sistere *vi* to exist

esis'tito, a *pp di* **esistere**

esi'tare *vi* to hesitate; **esitazi'one** *sf* hesitation

'esito *sm* result, outcome

'esodo *sm* exodus

esone'rare *vt* to exempt

e'sordio *sm* début

esor'tare *vt*: **~ qn a fare** to urge sb to do

e'sotico, a, ci, che *ag* exotic

es'pandere *vt* to expand; (*confini*) to extend; (*influenza*) to extend, spread; **~rsi** *vr* to expand; **espansi'one** *sf*

expansion; **espan'sivo, a** ag
expansive, communicative

espatri'are vt to leave one's country

espedi'ente sm expedient

es'pellere vt to expel

esperi'enza [espe'rjɛntsa] sf
experience

esperi'mento sm experiment

es'perto, a ag, sm expert

espi'are vt to atone for

espi'rare vt, vi to breathe out

espli'care vt (attività) to carry out,
perform

es'plicito, a [es'plitʃito] ag explicit

es'plodere vi (anche fig) to explode
♦ vt to fire

esplo'rare vt to explore; **explora'tore**
sm explorer; **giovane esploratore**
(boy) scout

esplosi'one sf explosion; **esplo'sivo,
a** ag, sm explosive; **es'ploso, a** pp di
esplodere

espo'nente sm/f (rappresentante)
representative

es'porre vt (merci) to display; (quadro)
to exhibit, show; (fatti, idee) to explain,
set out; (porre in pericolo, FOT) to
expose

espor'tare vt to export;
esportazi'one sf exportation; export

esposizi'one [espozit'tsjone] sf
displaying; exhibiting; setting out;
(anche FOT) exposure; (mostra)
exhibition; (narrazione) explanation,
exposition

es'posto, a pp di **esporre** ♦ ag: ~ a
nord facing north ♦ sm (AMM)
statement, account; (: petizione)
petition

espressi'one sf expression

espres'sivo, a ag expressive

es'presso, a pp di **esprimere** ♦ ag
express ♦ sm (lettera) express letter;
(anche: treno ~) express train; (anche:
caffè ~) espresso

es'primere vt to express

espulsi'one sf expulsion; **es'pulso, a**

pp di **espellere**

'essa (pl **'esse**) pron f vedi **esso**

es'senza [es'sɛntsa] sf essence;
essenzi'ale ag essential; **l'essenziale**
the main o most important thing

PAROLA CHIAVE

'essere sm being; ~ **umano** human
being

♦ vb copulativo **1** (con attributo,
sostantivo) to be; **sei giovane/
simpatico** you are o you're young/
nice; **è medico** he is o he's a doctor
2 (+di: appartenere) to be; **di chi è la
penna?** whose pen is it?; **è di Carla** it
is o it's Carla's, it belongs to Carla
3 (+di: provenire) to be; **è di Venezia**
he is o he's from Venice
4 (data, ora): **è il 15 agosto/lunedì** it
is o it's the 15th of August/Monday;
che ora è, che ore sono? what
time is it?; **è l'una** it is o it's one
o'clock; **sono le due** it is o it's two
o'clock
5 (costare): **quant'è?** how much is it?;
sono 20.000 lire it's 20,000 lire

♦ vb aus **1** (attivo): ~ **arrivato/venuto**
to have arrived/come; **è gia partita**
she has already left
2 (passivo) to be; ~ **fatto da** to be
made by; **è stata uccisa** she has been
killed
3 (riflessivo): **si sono lavati** they
washed, they got washed
4 (+da +infinito): **è da farsi subito** it
must be o is to be done immediately

♦ vi **1** (esistere, trovarsi) to be; **sono a
casa** I'm at home; ~ **in piedi/seduto**
to be standing/sitting
2: **esserci**: **c'è** there is; **ci sono** there
are; **che c'è?** what's the matter?; **what
is it?**; **ci sono!** (fig: ho capito) I get it!;
vedi anche ci

♦ vb impers: **è tardi/Pasqua** it's late/
Easter; **è possibile che venga** he
may come; **è così** that's the way it is

'esso, a *pron* it; *(riferito a persona: soggetto)* he/she; *(: complemento)* him/her; **~i, e** *pron pl* they; *(complemento)* them

est *sm* east

'estasi *sf* ecstasy

es'tate *sf* summer

es'tendere *vt* to extend; **~rsi** *vr (diffondersi)* to spread; *(territorio, confini)* to extend; **estensi'one** *sf* extension; *(di superficie)* expanse; *(di voce)* range

esteri'ore *ag* outward, external

ester'nare *vt* to express

es'terno, a *ag (porta, muro)* outer, outside; *(scala)* outside; *(alunno, impressione)* external ♦ *sm* outside, exterior ♦ *sm/f (allievo)* day pupil; **per uso ~** for external use only

'estero, a *ag* foreign ♦ *sm*: **all'~** abroad

es'teso, a *pp di* **estendere** ♦ *ag* extensive, large; **scrivere per ~** to write in full

es'tetico, a, ci, che *ag* aesthetic ♦ *sf (disciplina)* aesthetics *sg*; *(bellezza)* attractiveness; **este'tista, i, e** *sm/f* beautician

'estimo *sm* valuation; *(disciplina)* surveying

es'tinguere *vt* to extinguish, put out; *(debito)* to pay off; **~rsi** *vr* to go out; *(specie)* to become extinct; **es'tinto, a** *pp di* **estinguere**; **estin'tore** *sm (fire)* extinguisher; **estinzi'one** *sf* putting out; *(di specie)* extinction

estir'pare *vt (pianta)* to uproot, pull up; *(fig: vizio)* to eradicate

es'tivo, a *ag* summer *cpd*

es'torcere [es'tortʃere] *vt*: **~ qc (a qn)** to extort sth (from sb); **es'torto, a** *pp di* **estorcere**

estradizi'one [estradit'tsjone] *sf* extradition

es'traneo, a *ag* foreign ♦ *sm/f* stranger; **rimanere ~ a qc** to take no part in sth

es'trarre *vt* to extract; *(minerali)* to mine; *(sorteggiare)* to draw; **es'tratto, a** *pp di* **estrarre** ♦ *sm* extract; *(di documento)* abstract; **estratto conto** statement of account; **estratto di carne** *(CUC)* meat extract; **estratto di nascita** birth certificate; **estrazi'one** *sf* extraction; mining; drawing *no pl*; draw

estremità *sf inv* extremity, end ♦ *sfpl (ANAT)* extremities

es'tremo, a *ag* extreme; *(ultimo: ora, tentativo)* final, last ♦ *sm* extreme; *(di pazienza, forze)* limit, end; **~i** *smpl (AMM: dati essenziali)* details, particulars; **l'~ Oriente** the Far East

'estro *sm (capriccio)* whim, fancy; *(ispirazione creativa)* inspiration;

es'troso, a *ag* whimsical, capricious; inspired

estro'verso, a *ag, sm* extrovert

'esule *sm/f* exile

età *sf inv* age; **all'~ di 8 anni** at the age of 8, 7 years of age; **ha la mia ~** he (o she) is the same age as me o as I am; **raggiungere la maggiore ~** to come of age; **essere in ~ minore** to be under age

'etere *sm* ether; **e'tereo, a** *ag* ethereal

eternità *sf* eternity

e'terno, a *ag* eternal

etero'geneo, a [etero'dʒεneo] *ag* heterogeneous

'etica *sf* ethics *sg*; *vedi anche* **etico**

eti'chetta [eti'ketta] *sf* label; *(cerimoniale)*: **l'~** etiquette

'etico, a, ci, che *ag* ethical

etimolo'gia, 'gie [etimolo'dʒia] *sf* etymology

Eti'opia *sf*: **l'~** Ethiopia

'Etna *sm*: **l'~** Etna

'etnico, a, ci, che *ag* ethnic

e'trusco, a, schi, sche *ag, sm/f* Etruscan

'ettaro *sm* hectare (= 10,000 m^2)

'etto *sm abbr* = **ettogrammo**

etto'grammo *sm* hectogram(me) (=

100 grams)

Eucaris'tia *sf:* **l'~** the Eucharist

'euro *sm inv (divisa)* euro

eurocity [euro'siti] *sm* international express train

Euro'landia *sf* Euroland

Eu'ropa *sf:* **l'~** Europe; **euro'peo, a** *ag, sm/f* European

evacu'are *vt* to evacuate

e'vadere *vi (fuggire):* **~ da** to escape from ♦ *vt (sbrigare)* to deal with, dispatch; *(tasse)* to evade

evan'gelico, a, ci, che [evan'dʒɛliko] *ag* evangelical

evapo'rare *vi* to evaporate; **evaporazi'one** *sf* evaporation

evasi'one *sf (vedi evadere)* escape; dispatch; **~ fiscale** tax evasion

eva'sivo, a *ag* evasive

e'vaso, a *pp di* **evadere** ♦ *sm* escapee

eveni'enza [eve'njentsa] *sf:* **pronto(a) per ogni ~** ready for any eventuality

e'vento *sm* event

eventu'ale *ag* possible

eventual'mente *av* if necessary

evi'dente *ag* evident, obvious; **evi'denza** *sf* obviousness; **mettere in evidenza** to point out, highlight; **evidenzi'are** *vt* to emphasize; *(con evidenziatore)* to highlight; **evidenzia'tore** *sm* highlighter

evi'tare *vt* to avoid; **~ di fare** to avoid doing; **~ qc a qn** to spare sb sth

'evo *sm* age, epoch

evo'care *vt* to evoke

evo'luto, a *pp di* **evolvere** ♦ *ag (civiltà)* (highly) developed, advanced; *(persona)* independent

evoluzi'one [evolut'tsjone] *sf* evolution

e'volversi *vr* to evolve

ev'viva *escl* hurrah!; **~ il re!** long live the king!, hurrah for the king!

ex *prefisso* ex, former

'extra *ag inv* first-rate; top-quality ♦ *sm inv* extra; **extracomuni'tario, a** *ag* from outside the EC ♦ *sm/f* non-EC

citizen; **extraconiu'gale** *ag* extramarital

F, f

fa *vb vedi* **fare** ♦ *sm inv (MUS)* F; *(: solfeggiando la scala)* fa ♦ *av:* **10 anni ~** 10 years ago

fabbi'sogno [fabbi'zoɲɲo] *sm* needs *pl*, requirements *pl*

'fabbrica *sf* factory; **fabbri'cante** *sm* manufacturer, maker; **fabbri'care** *vt* to build; *(produrre)* to manufacture, make; *(fig)* to fabricate, invent

'fabbro *sm* (black)smith

fac'cenda [fat'tʃɛnda] *sf* matter, affair; *(cosa da fare)* task, chore

fac'chino [fak'kino] *sm* porter

'faccia, ce [fattʃa] *sf* face; *(di moneta, medaglia)* side; **~ a ~** face to face

facci'ata [fat'tʃata] *sf* façade; *(di pagina)* side

'faccio ['fattʃo] *vb vedi* **fare**

'facile ['fatʃile] *ag* easy; *(disposto):* **~ a** inclined to, prone to; *(probabile):* **è ~ che piova** it's likely to rain; **facilità** *sf* easiness; *(disposizione, dono)* aptitude; **facili'tare** *vt* to make easier

facoltà *sf inv* faculty; *(autorità)* power

facolta'tivo, a *ag* optional; *(fermata d'autobus)* request *cpd*

fac'simile *sm* facsimile

'faggio ['faddʒo] *sm* beech

fagi'ano [fa'dʒano] *sm* pheasant

fagio'lino [fadʒo'lino] *sm* French *(BRIT)* o string bean

fagi'olo [fa'dʒɔlo] *sm* bean

fa'gotto *sm* bundle; *(MUS)* bassoon; **far ~** *(fig)* to pack up and go

'fai *vb vedi* **fare**

'falce ['faltʃe] *sf* scythe; **falci'are** *vt* to cut; *(fig)* to mow down

'falco, chi *sm* hawk

fal'cone *sm* falcon

'falda *sf* layer, stratum; *(di cappello)* brim; *(di cappotto)* tails *pl*; *(di monte)* lower slope; *(di tetto)* pitch

fale'gname [faleɲ'ɲame] *sm* joiner

fal'lace [fal'latʃe] *ag* misleading

falli'mento *sm* bankruptcy

fal'lire *vi (non riuscire):* ~ **(in)** to fail (in); *(DIR)* to go bankrupt ♦ *vt (colpo, bersaglio)* to miss; **fal'lito, a** *ag* unsuccessful; bankrupt ♦ *sm/f* bankrupt

'fallo *sm* error, mistake; *(imperfezione)* defect, flaw; *(SPORT)* foul; fault; **senza ~** without fail

falò *sm inv* bonfire

fal'sare *vt* to distort, misrepresent; **fal'sario** *sm* forger; counterfeiter; **falsifi'care** *vt* to forge; *(monete)* to forge, counterfeit

'falso, a *ag* false; *(errato)* wrong; *(falsificato)* forged; fake; (: *oro, gioielli*) imitation *cpd* ♦ *sm* forgery; **giurare il ~** to commit perjury

'fama *sf* fame; *(reputazione)* reputation, name

'fame *sf* hunger; **aver ~** to be hungry; **fa'melico, a, ci, che** *ag* ravenous

fa'miglia [fa'miʎʎa] *sf* family

famili'are *ag (della famiglia)* family *cpd*; *(ben noto)* familiar; *(rapporti, atmosfera)* friendly; *(LING)* informal, colloquial ♦ *sm/f* relative, relation; **familiarità** *sf* familiarity; friendliness; informality

fa'moso, a *ag* famous, well-known

fa'nale *sm (AUT)* light, lamp *(BRIT)*; *(luce stradale, NAUT)* light; *(di faro)* beacon

fa'natico, a, ci, che *ag* fanatical; *(del teatro, calcio etc):* ~ **di** *o* **per** mad *o* crazy about ♦ *sm/f* fanatic; *(tifoso)* fan

fanci'ullo, a [fan'tʃullo] *sm/f* child

fan'donia *sf* tall story; **~e** *sfpl (assurdità)* nonsense *sg*

fan'fara *sf (musica)* fanfare

'fango, ghi *sm* mud; **fan'goso, a** *ag* muddy

'fanno *vb vedi* **fare**

fannul'lone, a *sm/f* idler, loafer

fantasci'enza [fantaʃ'ʃɛntsa] *sf* science fiction

fanta'sia *sf* fantasy, imagination;

(capriccio) whim, caprice ♦ *ag inv:* **vestito ~** patterned dress

fan'tasma, i *sm* ghost, phantom

fan'tastico, a, ci, che *ag* fantastic; *(potenza, ingegno)* imaginative

'fante *sm* infantryman; *(CARTE)* jack, knave *(BRIT)*; **fante'ria** *sf* infantry

fan'toccio [fan'tɔttʃo] *sm* puppet

fara'butto *sm* crook

fard *sm inv* blusher

far'dello *sm* bundle; *(fig)* burden

PAROLA CHIAVE

'fare *sm* 1 *(modo di fare):* **con ~ distratto** absent-mindedly; **ha un ~ simpatico** he has a pleasant manner

2: **sul far del giorno/della notte** at daybreak/nightfall

♦ *vt* 1 *(fabbricare, creare)* to make; (: *casa*) to build; (: *assegno*) to make out; ~ **un pasto/una promessa/un film** to make a meal/a promise/a film; ~ **rumore** to make a noise

2 *(effettuare: lavoro, attività, studi)* to do; (: *sport*) to play; **cosa fa?** *(adesso)* what are you doing?; *(di professione)* what do you do?; ~ **psicologia/italiano** *(INS)* to do psychology/Italian; ~ **un viaggio** to go on a trip *o* journey; ~ **una passeggiata** to go for a walk; ~ **la spesa** to do the shopping

3 *(funzione)* to be; *(TEATRO)* to play, be; ~ **il medico** to be a doctor; ~ **il malato** *(fingere)* to act the invalid

4 *(suscitare: sentimenti)*: ~ **paura a qn** to frighten sb; **(non) fa niente** *(non importa)* it doesn't matter

5 *(ammontare)*: **3 più 3 fa 6** 3 and 3 are *o* make 6; **fanno 6.000 lire** that's 6,000 lire; **Roma fa 2.000.000 di abitanti** Rome has 2,000,000 inhabitants; **che ora fai?** what time do you make it?

6 (+ *infinito*): **far** ~ **qc a qn** *(obbligare)* to make sb do sth; *(permettere)* to let sb do sth; **fammi vedere** let me see;

far partire il motore to start (up) the engine; **far riparare la macchina/ costruire una casa** to get o have the car repaired/a house built

7: **~rsi: ~rsi una gonna** to make o.s. a skirt; **~rsi un nome** to make a name for o.s.; **~rsi la permanente** to get a perm; **~rsi tagliare i capelli** to get one's hair cut; **~rsi operare** to have an operation

8 (*fraseologia*): **farcela** to succeed, manage; **non ce la faccio più** I can't go on; **ce la faremo** we'll make it; **me l'hanno fatta!** (*imbrogliare*) I've been done!; **lo facevo più giovane** I thought he was younger; **fare sì/no con la testa** to nod/shake one's head
♦ vi 1 (*agire*) to act, do; **fate come volete** do as you like; **~ presto** to be quick; **~ da** to act as; **non c'è niente da ~** it's no use; **saperci ~ con qn/ qc** to know how to deal with sb/sth; **faccia pure!** go ahead!
2 (*dire*) to say; **"davvero?" fece** "really?" he said
3: **~ per** (*essere adatto*) to be suitable for; **~ per ~ qc** to be about to do sth; **fece per andarsene** he made as if to leave
4: **~rsi: si fa così** you do it like this, this is the way it's done; **non si fa così!** (*rimprovero*) that's no way to behave!; **la festa non si fa** the party is off
5: **~ a gara con qn** to compete o vie with sb; **~ a pugni** to come to blows; **~ in tempo a** to be in time to do
♦ vb impers: **fa bel tempo** the weather is fine; **fa caldo/freddo** it's hot/cold; **fa notte** it's getting dark
♦ vr: **~rsi 1** (*diventare*) to become; **~rsi prete** to become a priest; **~rsi grande/vecchio** to grow tall/old
2 (*spostarsi*) **~rsi avanti/indietro** to move forward/back
3 (*fam: drogarsi*) to be a junkie

far'falla sf butterfly

fa'rina sf flour

farma'cia, 'cie [farma'tʃia] sf pharmacy; (*negozio*) chemist's (shop) (*BRIT*), pharmacy; **farma'cista, i, e** sm/f chemist (*BRIT*), pharmacist

'farmaco, ci o **chi** sm drug, medicine

'faro sm (*NAUT*) lighthouse; (*AER*) beacon; (*AUT*) headlight

farsa sf farce

fascia, sce ['faʃʃa] sf band, strip; (*MED*) bandage; (*di sindaco, ufficiale*) sash; (*parte di territorio*) strip, belt; (*di contribuenti etc*) group, band; **essere in ~sce** (*anche fig*) to be in one's infancy; **~ oraria** time band

fasci'are [faʃ'ʃare] vt to bind; (*MED*) to bandage

fa'scicolo [faʃ'ʃikolo] sm (*di documenti*) file, dossier; (*di rivista*) issue, number; (*opuscolo*) booklet, pamphlet

'fascino ['faʃʃino] sm charm, fascination

'fascio ['faʃʃo] sm bundle, sheaf; (*di fiori*) bunch; (*di luce*) beam; (*POL*): **il F~** the Fascist Party

fa'scismo [faʃ'ʃizmo] sm fascism

'fase sf phase; (*TECN*) stroke; **fuori ~** (*motore*) rough

fa'stidio sm bother, trouble; **dare ~ a qn** to bother o annoy sb; **sento ~ allo stomaco** my stomach's upset; **avere ~i con la polizia** to have trouble o bother with the police; **fastidi'oso, a** ag annoying, tiresome

'fasto sm pomp, splendour

'fata sf fairy

fa'tale ag fatal; (*inevitabile*) inevitable; (*fig*) irresistible; **fatalità** sf inv inevitability; (*avversità*) misfortune; (*fato*) fate, destiny

fa'tica, che sf hard work, toil; (*sforzo*) effort; (*di metalli*) fatigue; **a ~** with difficulty; **a fare qc** to have difficulty doing sth; **fati'care** vi to toil; **faticare a fare qc** to have difficulty doing sth; **fati'coso, a** ag tiring, exhausting; (*lavoro*) laborious

'fato *sm* fate, destiny

'fatto, a *pp di* **fare** ♦ *ag:* **un uomo ~** a grown man; **~ a mano/in casa** hand-/home-made ♦ *sm* fact; (*azione*) deed; (*avvenimento*) event, occurrence; (*di romanzo, film*) action, story; **cogliere qn sul ~** to catch sb red-handed; **il ~ sta o è che** the fact remains o is that; **in ~ di** as for, as far as ... is concerned

fat'tore *sm* (AGR) farm manager; (MAT, *elemento costitutivo*) factor

fatto'ria *sf* farm; farmhouse

fatto'rino *sm* errand-boy; (*di ufficio*) office-boy; (*d'albergo*) porter

fat'tura *sf* (COMM) invoice; (*di abito*) tailoring; (*malia*) spell

fattu'rare *vt* (COMM) to invoice

fattu'rato *sm* (COMM) turnover

'fatuo, a *ag* vain, fatuous

'fauna *sf* fauna

fau'tore, trice *sm/f* advocate, supporter

fa'villa *sf* spark

'favola *sf* (*fiaba*) fairy tale; (*d'intento morale*) fable; (*fandonia*) yarn; **favo'loso, a** *ag* fabulous; (*incredibile*) incredible

fa'vore *sm* favour; **per ~** please; **fare un ~ a qn** to do sb a favour; **favo'revole** *ag* favourable

favo'rire *vt* to favour; (*il commercio, l'industria, le arti*) to promote, encourage; **vuole ~?** won't you help yourself?; **favorisca in salotto** please come into the sitting room; **favo'rito, a** *ag, sm/f* favourite

fazzo'letto [fattso'letto] *sm* handkerchief; (*per la testa*) (head)scarf; **~ di carta** tissue

feb'braio *sm* February

'febbre *sf* fever; **aver la ~** to have a high temperature; **~ da fieno** hay fever; **feb'brile** *ag* (*anche fig*) feverish

'feccia, ce ['fettʃa] *sf* dregs *pl*

'fecola *sf* potato flour

fecondazi'one [fekondat'tsjone] *sf* fertilization; **~ artificiale** artificial insemination

fe'condo, a *ag* fertile

'fede *sf* (*credenza*) belief, faith; (REL) faith; (*fiducia*) faith, trust; (*fedeltà*) loyalty; (*anello*) wedding ring; (*attestato*) certificate; **aver ~ in qn** to have faith in sb; **in buona/cattiva ~** in good/bad faith; **"in ~"** (DIR) "in witness whereof"; **fe'dele** *ag:* **fedele (a)** faithful (to) ♦ *sm/f* follower; **i fedeli** (REL) the faithful; **fedeltà** *sf* faithfulness; (*coniugale*) fidelity; **alta fedeltà** (RADIO) high fidelity

'federa *sf* pillowslip, pillowcase

fede'rale *ag* federal

'fegato *sm* liver; (*fig*) guts *pl*, nerve

'felce ['feltʃe] *sf* fern

fe'lice [fe'litʃe] *ag* happy; (*fortunato*) lucky; **felicità** *sf* happiness

felici'tarsi [felitʃi'tarsi] *vr* (*congratularsi*): **~ con qn per qc** to congratulate sb on sth

fe'lino, a *ag* feline

'felpa *sf* sweatshirt

'feltro *sm* felt

'femmina *sf* (ZOOL, TECN) female; (*figlia*) girl, daughter; (*spesso peg*) woman; **femmi'nile** *ag* feminine; (*sesso*) female; (*lavoro, giornale, moda*) woman's ♦ *sm* (LING) feminine; **femmi'nismo** *sm* feminism

'fendere *vt* to cut through; **fendi'nebbia** *sm inv* (AUT) fog lamp

fe'nomeno *sm* phenomenon

'feretro *sm* coffin

feri'ale *ag:* **giorno ~** weekday

'ferie *sfpl* holidays (BRIT), vacation *sg* (US); **andare in ~** to go on holiday o vacation

fe'rire *vt* to injure; (*deliberatamente:* MIL *etc*) to wound; (*colpire*) to hurt; **fe'rita** *sf* injury, wound; **fe'rito, a** *sm/f* wounded o injured man/woman

'ferma *sf* (MIL) (period of) service; (CACCIA): **cane da ~** pointer

fer'maglio [fer'maʎʎo] *sm* clasp; (*per documenti*) clip

fer'mare *vt* to stop, halt; (*POLIZIA*) to detain, hold ♦ *vi* to stop; **~rsi** *vr* to stop, halt; **~rsi a fare qc** to stop to do sth

fer'mata *sf* stop; **~ dell'autobus** bus stop

fer'mento *sm* (*anche fig*) ferment; (*lievito*) yeast

fer'mezza [fer'mettsa] *sf* (*fig*) firmness, steadfastness

'fermo, a *ag* still, motionless; (*veicolo*) stationary; (*orologio*) not working; (*saldo: anche fig*) firm; (*voce, mano*) steady ♦ *escl* stop!; keep still! ♦ *sm* (*chiusura*) catch, lock; (*DIR*): **~ di polizia** police detention

'fermo 'posta *av, sm inv* poste restante (*BRIT*), general delivery (*US*)

fe'roce [fe'rɔtʃe] *ag* (*animale*) fierce, ferocious; (*persona*) cruel, fierce; (*fame, dolore*) raging; **le bestie ~i** wild animals

ferra'gosto *sm* (*festa*) feast of the Assumption; (*periodo*) August holidays *pl*

ferra'menta *sfpl*: **negozio di ~** ironmonger's (*BRIT*), hardware shop *o* store (*US*)

fer'rato, a *ag* (*FERR*): **strada ~** (*BRIT*) *o* railroad (*US*) line; (*fig*): **essere ~ in** to be well up in

'ferro *sm* iron; **una bistecca ai ~i** a grilled steak; **~ battuto** wrought iron;

~ da calza knitting needle; **~ di cavallo** horseshoe; **~ da stiro** iron

ferro'via *sf* railway (*BRIT*), railroad (*US*); **ferrovi'ario, a** *ag* railway *cpd* (*BRIT*), railroad *cpd* (*US*); **ferrovi'ere** *sm* railwayman (*BRIT*), railroad man (*US*)

'fertile *ag* fertile; **fertiliz'zante** *sm* fertilizer

'fervido, a *ag* fervent

fer'vore *sm* fervour, ardour

'fesso, a *pp di* **fendere** ♦ *ag* (*fam: sciocco*) crazy, cracked

fes'sura *sf* crack, split; (*per gettone, moneta*) slot

'festa *sf* (*religiosa*) feast; (*pubblica*) holiday; (*compleanno*) birthday; (*onomastico*) name day; (*ricevimento*) celebration, party; **far ~** to have a holiday; to live it up; **far ~ a qn** to give sb a warm welcome

festeggi'are [fested'dʒare] *vt* to celebrate; (*persona*) to have a celebration for

fes'tino *sm* party; (*con balli*) ball

fes'tivo, a *ag* (*atmosfera*) festive; **giorno ~** holiday

fes'toso, a *ag* merry, joyful

fe'ticcio [fe'tittʃo] *sm* fetish

'feto *sm* foetus (*BRIT*), fetus (*US*)

'fetta *sf* slice

fettuc'cine [fettut'tʃine] *sfpl* (*CUC*) ribbon-shaped pasta

FF.SS. *abbr* = **Ferrovie dello Stato**

fi'aba *sf* fairy tale

fiac'ca *sf* weariness; (*svogliatezza*) listlessness

fiac'care *vt* to weaken

fi'acco, a, chi, che ag (stanco) tired, weary; (svogliato) listless; (debole) weak; (mercato) slack

fi'accola sf torch

fi'ala sf phial

fi'amma sf flame

fiam'mante ag (colore) flaming; **nuovo ~** brand new

fiam'mifero sm match

fiam'mingo, a, ghi, ghe ag Flemish ♦ sm/f Fleming ♦ sm (LING) Flemish; **i F~ghi** the Flemish

fiancheggi'are [fjankeddʒare] vt to border; (fig) to support, back (up); (MIL) to flank

fi'anco, chi sm side; (MIL) flank; **di ~** sideways, from the side; **a ~ a ~** side by side

fi'asco, schi sm flask; (fig) fiasco; **fare ~** to fail

fi'ato sm breath; (resistenza) stamina; **avere il ~ grosso** to be out of breath; **prendere ~** to catch one's breath; **~i** smpl (MUS) wind instruments; **strumento a ~** wind instrument

'fibbia sf buckle

'fibra sf fibre; (fig) constitution

fic'care vt to push, thrust, drive; **~rsi** vr (andare a finire) to get to

'fico, chi sm (pianta) fig tree; (frutto) fig; **~ d'India** prickly pear; **~ secco** dried fig

fidanza'mento [fidantsa'mento] sm engagement

fidan'zarsi [fidan'tsarsi] vr to get engaged; **fidan'zato, a** sm/f fiancé/fiancée

fi'darsi vr: **~ di** to trust; **fi'dato, a** ag reliable, trustworthy

'fido, a ag faithful, loyal ♦ sm (COMM) credit

fi'ducia [fi'dutʃa] sf confidence, trust; **incarico di ~** position of trust, responsible position; **persona di ~** reliable person

fi'ele sm (fig) bitterness

fie'nile sm barn; hayloft

fi'eno sm hay

fi'era sf fair

fie'rezza [fje'rettsa] sf pride

fi'ero, a ag proud; (audace) bold

'fifa (fam) sf: **aver ~** to have the jitters

'figlia ['fiʎʎa] sf daughter

figli'astro, a [fiʎ'ʎastro] sm/f stepson/daughter

'figlio ['fiʎʎo] sm son; (senza distinzione di sesso) child; **~ di papà** spoilt, wealthy young man; **~** only child; **figli'occio, a, ci, ce** sm/f godchild, godson/daughter

fi'gura sf figure; (forma, aspetto esterno) form, shape; (illustrazione) picture, illustration; **far ~** to look important; **fare una brutta ~** to make a bad impression

figu'rare vi to appear ♦ vt: **~rsi qc** to imagine sth; **~rsi** vr: **figurati!** imagine that!; **ti do noia? — ma figurati!** am I disturbing you? — not at all!

figura'tivo, a ag figurative

figu'rina sf figurine; (cartoncino) picture card

'fila sf row, line; (coda) queue; (serie) series, string; **di ~** in succession; **fare la ~** to queue; **in ~ indiana** in single file

filantro'pia sf philanthropy

fi'lare vt to spin ♦ vi (baco, ragno) to spin; (formaggio fuso) to go stringy; (discorso) to hang together; (fam: amoreggiare) to go steady; (muoversi a forte velocità) to go at full speed; **~ diritto** (fig) to toe the line; **~ via** to dash off

filas'trocca, che sf nursery rhyme

fila'telia sf philately, stamp collecting

fi'lato, a ag spun ♦ sm yarn; **3 giorni ~i** 3 days running o on end

fi'letto sm (di vite) thread; (di carne) fillet

fili'ale ag filial ♦ sf (di impresa) branch

fili'grana sf (in oreficeria) filigree; (su carta) watermark

film sm inv film; **fil'mare** vt to film

filo 103 **fisarmonica**

'**filo** sm (anche fig) thread; (filato) yarn; (metallico) wire; (di lama, rasoio) edge; **per ~ e per segno** in detail; **~ d'erba** blade of grass; **~ interdentale** dental floss; **~ di perle** string of pearls; **~ spinato** barbed wire; **con un ~ di voce** in a whisper

'**filobus** sm inv trolley bus

filon'cino [filon'tʃino] sm ≈ French stick

fi'lone sm (di minerali) seam, vein; (pane) ≈ Vienna loaf; (fig) trend

filoso'fia sf philosophy; **fi'losofo, a** sm/f philosopher

fil'trare vt, vi to filter

'**filtro** sm filter; **~ dell'olio** (AUT) oil filter

fin av, prep = **fino**

fi'nale ag final ♦ sm (di opera) end, ending; (: MUS) finale ♦ sf (SPORT) final; **finalità** sf (scopo) aim, purpose; **final'mente** av finally, at last

fi'nanza [fi'nantsa] sf finance; **~e** sfpl (di individuo, Stato) finances; **finanzi'ario, a** ag financial; **finanzi'ere** sm financier; (doganale) customs officer; (della tributaria) inland revenue official

finché [fin'ke] cong (per tutto il tempo che) as long as; (fino al momento in cui) until; **aspetta ~ io (non) sia ritornato** wait until I get back

'**fine** ag (lamina, carta) thin; (capelli, polvere) fine; (vista, udito) keen, sharp; (persona: raffinata) refined, distinguished; (osservazione) subtle ♦ sf end ♦ sm aim, purpose; (esito) result, outcome; **secondo ~** ulterior motive; **in o alla ~** in the end, finally; **~ settimana** sm o f inv weekend

fi'nestra sf window; **fines'trino** sm (di treno, auto) window

'fingere ['findʒere] vt to feign; (supporre) to imagine, suppose; **~rsi** vr: **~rsi ubriaco/pazzo** to pretend to be drunk/mad; **~ di fare** to pretend to do

fini'mondo sm pandemonium

fi'nire vt to finish ♦ vi to finish, end; **~ di fare** (compiere) to finish doing; (smettere) to stop doing; **~ in galera** to end up o finish up in prison; **fini'tura** sf finish

finlan'dese ag, sm (LING) Finnish ♦ sm/f Finn

Fin'landia sf: **la ~** Finland

'**fino, a** ag (capelli, seta) fine; (oro) pure; (fig: acuto) shrewd ♦ av (spesso troncato in **fin**: pure, anche) even ♦ prep (spesso troncato in **fin**: tempo): **fin quando?** till when?; (: luogo): **fin qui** as far as here; **~ a** (tempo) until, till; (luogo) as far as, (up) to; **fin da domani** from tomorrow onwards; **fin da ieri** since yesterday; **fin dalla nascita** from o since birth

fi'nocchio [fi'nɔkkjo] sm fennel; (fam: peg: omosessuale) queer

fi'nora av until now

'finta sf pretence, sham; (SPORT) feint; **far ~a (di fare)** to pretend (to do)

'**finto, a** pp di **fingere** ♦ ag false; artificial

finzi'one [fin'tsjone] sf pretence, sham

fi'occo, chi sm (di nastro, seta) bow; (di stoffa, lana) flock; (di neve) flake; (di granoturco) cornflakes

fi'ocina ['fjɔtʃina] sf harpoon

fi'oco, a, chi, che ag faint, dim

fio'raio, a sm/f florist

fi'onda sf catapult

fio'retto sm (SCHERMA) foil

fio'rire vi (rosa) to flower; (albero) to blossom; (fig) to flourish

Fi'renze [fi'rentse] sf Florence

'**firma** sf signature

fir'mare vt to sign; **un abito firmato** a designer suit

fisar'monica, che sf accordion

fis'cale *ag* fiscal, tax *cpd*; **medico ~** doctor employed by Social Security to verify cases of sick leave

fischi'are [fis'kjare] *vi* to whistle ♦ *vt* to whistle; (*attore*) to boo, hiss

'fischio ['fiskjo] *sm* whistle

'fisco *sm* tax authorities *pl*, ≈ Inland Revenue (BRIT), ≈ Internal Revenue Service (US)

'fisica *sf* physics *sg*

'fisico, a, ci, che *ag* physical ♦ *sm/f* physicist ♦ *sm* physique

fisiolo'gia [fizjolo'dʒia] *sf* physiology

fisiono'mia *sf* face, physiognomy

fisiotera'pia *sf* physiotherapy

fis'sare *vt* to fix, fasten; (*guardare intensamente*) to stare at; (*data, condizioni*) to fix, establish, set; (*prenotare*) to book; **~rsi su** (*sog: sguardo, attenzione*) to focus on; (*fig: idea*) to become obsessed with; **fissazi'one** *sf* (PSIC) fixation

'fisso, a *ag* fixed; (*stipendio, impiego*) regular ♦ *av:* **guardare ~ qc/qn** to stare at sth/sb

'fitta *sf* sharp pain; *vedi anche* **fitto**

fit'tizio, a *ag* fictitious, imaginary

'fitto, a *ag* thick, dense; (*pioggia*) heavy ♦ *sm* depths *pl*, middle; (*affitto, pigione*) rent

fi'ume *sm* river

fiu'tare *vt* to smell, sniff; (*sog: animale*) to scent; (*fig: inganno*) to get wind of, smell; **~ tabacco/cocaina** to take snuff/cocaine; **fi'uto** *sm* (sense of) smell; (*fig*) nose

fla'gello [fla'dʒɛllo] *sm* scourge

fla'grante *ag:* **cogliere qn in ~** to catch sb red-handed

fla'nella *sf* flannel

flash [flaʃ] *sm inv* (FOT) flash; (*giornalistico*) newsflash

'flauto *sm* flute

'flebile *ag* faint, feeble

'flemma *sf* (*calma*) coolness, phlegm

fles'sibile *ag* pliable; (*fig: che si adatta*) flexible

'flesso, a *pp di* **flettere**

flessu'oso, a *ag* supple, lithe

'flettere *vt* to bend

'flipper *sm inv* pinball machine

F.lli *abbr* (= *fratelli*) Bros.

'flora *sf* flora

'florido, a *ag* flourishing; (*fig*) glowing with health

'floscio, a, sci, sce ['flɔʃʃo] *ag* (*cappello*) floppy, soft; (*muscoli*) flabby

'flotta *sf* fleet

'fluido, a *ag, sm* fluid

flu'ire *vi* to flow

flu'oro *sm* fluorine

fluo'ruro *sm* fluoride

'flusso *sm* flow; (FISICA, MED) flux; **~ e riflusso** ebb and flow

flut'tuare *vi* (*mare*) to rise and fall; (ECON) to fluctuate

fluvi'ale *ag* river *cpd*, fluvial

'foca, che *sf* (ZOOL) seal

fo'caccia, ce [fo'katt∫a] *sf* kind of pizza; (*dolce*) bun

'foce ['fot∫e] *sf* (GEO) mouth

foco'laio *sm* (MED) centre of infection; (*fig*) hotbed

foco'lare *sm* hearth, fireside; (TECN) furnace

'fodera *sf* (*di vestito*) lining; (*di libro, poltrona*) cover; **fode'rare** *vt* to line; to cover

'fodero *sm* (*di spada*) scabbard; (*di pugnale*) sheath; (*di pistola*) holster

'foga *sf* enthusiasm, ardour

'foggia, ge ['fɔddʒa] *sf* (*maniera*) style; (*aspetto*) form, shape

'foglia ['fɔʎʎa] *sf* leaf; **~ d'argento/ d'oro** silver/gold leaf; **fogli'ame** *sm* foliage, leaves *pl*

'foglio ['fɔʎʎo] *sm* (*di carta*) sheet (of paper); (*di metallo*) sheet; **~ rosa** (AUT) provisional licence; **~ di via** (DIR) expulsion order; **~ volante** pamphlet

'fogna ['foɲɲa] *sf* drain, sewer; **fogna'tura** *sf* drainage, sewerage

föhn [fø:n] *sm inv* hair dryer

folgo'rare *vt* (*sog: fulmine*) to strike

down; (: *alta tensione*) to electrocute

'folla *sf* crowd, throng

'folle *ag* mad, insane; (*TECN*) idle; **in ~** (*AUT*) in neutral

fol'lia *sf* folly, foolishness; foolish act; (*pazzia*) madness, lunacy

'folto, a *ag* thick

fomen'tare *vt* to stir up, foment

fon *sm inv* hair dryer

fondamen'tale *ag* fundamental, basic

fonda'mento *sm* foundation; **~a** *sfpl* (*EDIL*) foundations

fon'dare *vt* to found; (*fig: dar base*): **~ qc su** to base sth on; **fondazi'one** *sf* foundation

'fondere *vt* (*neve*) to melt; (*metallo*) to fuse, melt; (*fig: colori*) to merge, blend; (: *imprese, gruppi*) to merge ♦ *vi* to melt; **~rsi** *vr* to melt; (*fig: partiti, correnti*) to unite, merge; **fonde'ria** *sf* foundry

'fondo, a *ag* deep ♦ *sm* (*di recipiente, pozzo*) bottom; (*di stanza*) back; (*quantità di liquido che resta, deposito*) dregs *pl*; (*sfondo*) background; (*unità immobiliare*) property, estate; (*somma di denaro*) fund; (*SPORT*) long-distance race; **~i** *smpl* (*denaro*) funds; **a notte ~a** at dead of night; **in ~ a** at the bottom of; at the back of; (*strada*) at the end of; **andare a ~** (*nave*) to sink; **conoscere a ~** to know inside out; **dar ~ a** (*fig: provviste, soldi*) to use up; **in ~** (*fig*) after all, all things considered; **andare fino in ~ a** (*fig*) to examine thoroughly; **a ~ perduto** (*COMM*) without security; **~i di caffè** coffee grounds; **~i di magazzino** old o unsold stock *sg*

fo'netica *sf* phonetics *sg*

fon'tana *sf* fountain

'fonte *sf* spring, source; (*fig*) source ♦ *sm*: **~ battesimale** (*REL*) font

fon'tina *sf* sweet full-fat hard cheese from Val d'Aosta

fo'raggio [fo'raddʒo] *sm* fodder, forage

fo'rare *vt* to pierce, make a hole in; (*pallone*) to burst; (*biglietto*) to punch; **~ una gomma** to burst a tyre (*BRIT*) o tire (*US*)

'forbici ['fɔrbitʃi] *sfpl* scissors

'forca, che (*AGR*) fork, pitchfork; (*patibolo*) gallows *sg*

for'cella [for'tʃella] *sf* (*TECN*) fork; (*di monte*) pass

for'chetta [for'ketta] *sf* fork

for'cina [for'tʃina] *sf* hairpin

'forcipe ['fɔrtʃipe] *sm* forceps *pl*

fo'resta *sf* forest

foresti'ero, a *ag* foreign ♦ *sm/f* foreigner

'forfora *sf* dandruff

forgi'are *vt* to forge

'forma *sf* form; (*aspetto esteriore*) form, shape; (*DIR: procedura*) procedure; (*per calzature*) last; (*stampo da cucina*) mould; **~e** *sfpl* (*del corpo*) figure, shape; **le ~e** (*convenzioni*) appearances; **essere in ~** to be in good shape

formag'gino [formad'dʒino] *sm* processed cheese

for'maggio [for'maddʒo] *sm* cheese

for'male *ag* formal; **formalità** *sf inv* formality

for'mare *vt* to form, shape, make; (*numero di telefono*) to dial; (*fig: carattere*) to form, mould; **~rsi** *vr* to form, take shape; **for'mato** *sm* format, size; **formazi'one** *sf* formation; (*fig: educazione*) training

for'mica, che o' *ant*; **formi'caio** *sm* anthill

formico'lare *vi* (*anche fig*): **~ di** to be swarming with; **mi formicola la gamba** I've got pins and needles in my leg; **formico'lio** *sm* pins and needles *pl*; swarming

formi'dabile *ag* powerful, formidable; (*straordinario*) remarkable

'formula *sf* formula; **~ di cortesia** courtesy form

formu'lare *vt* to formulate; to express

for'nace [for'natʃe] *sf (per laterizi etc)* kiln; *(per metalli)* furnace; **~ a microonde** microwave oven

for'naio *sm* baker

for'nello *sm (elettrico, a gas)* ring; *(di pipa)* bowl

for'nire *vt*: **~ qn di qc**, **~ qc a qn** to provide *o* supply sb with sth, to supply sth to sb

'forno *sm (di cucina)* oven; *(panetteria)* bakery; *(TECN: per calce etc)* kiln; *(: per metalli)* furnace; **~ a microonde** microwave oven

'foro *sm (buco)* hole; *(STORIA)* forum; *(tribunale)* (law) court

'forse *av* perhaps, maybe; *(circa)* about; **essere in ~** to be in doubt

forsen'nato, a *ag* mad, insane

'forte *ag* strong; *(suono)* loud; *(spesa)* considerable, great; *(passione, dolore)* great, deep ♦ *av* strongly; *(velocemente)* fast; *(a voce alta)* loud(ly); *(violentemente)* hard ♦ *sm (edificio)* fort; *(specialità)* forte, strong point; **essere ~ in qc** to be good at sth

for'tezza [for'tettsa] *sf (morale)* strength; *(luogo fortificato)* fortress

for'tuito, a *ag* fortuitous, chance

for'tuna *sf (destino)* fortune, luck; *(buona sorte)* success, fortune; *(eredità, averi)* fortune; **per ~** luckily, fortunately; **di ~** makeshift, improvised; **atterraggio di ~** emergency landing; **fortu'nato, a** *ag* lucky, fortunate; *(coronato da successo)* successful

'forza [ˈfɔrtsa] *sf* strength; *(potere)* power; *(FISICA)* force; **~e** *sfpl (fisiche)* strength *sg*; *(MIL)* forces ♦ *escl* come on!; **per ~** against one's will; *(naturalmente)* of course; **a viva ~** by force; **a ~ di** by dint of; **~ maggiore** circumstances beyond one's control; **la ~ pubblica** the police *pl*; **le ~e armate** the armed forces; **~e dell'ordine** the forces of law and order

for'zare [for'tsare] *vt* to force; **~ qn a fare** to force sb to do; **for'zato, a** *ag*

forced ♦ *sm (DIR)* prisoner sentenced to hard labour

fos'chia [fos'kia] *sf* mist, haze

'fosco, a, schi, sche *ag* dark, gloomy

'fosforo *sm* phosphorous

'fossa *sf (buca)* pit; *(di cimitero)* grave; **~ biologica** septic tank

fos'sato *sm* ditch; *(di fortezza)* moat

fos'setta *sf* dimple

'fossile *ag, sm* fossil

'fosso *sm* ditch; *(MIL)* trench

'foto *sf* photo ♦ *prefisso*: **foto'copia** *sf* photocopy; **fotocopi'are** *vt* to photocopy; **fotocopia'trice** *sf* photocopier; **fotografare** *vt* to photograph; **fotogra'fia** *sf (procedimento)* photography; *(immagine)* photograph; **fare una fotografia** to take a photograph; **una fotografia a colori/in bianco e nero** a colour/black and white photograph; **fo'tografo, a** *sm/f* photographer; **fotoro'manzo** *sm* romantic picture story; **foto'tessera** *sf* passport-size photo

fra *prep* = **tra**

fracas'sare *vt* to shatter, smash; **~rsi** *vr* to shatter, smash; *(veicolo)* to crash; **fra'casso** *sm* smash; crash; *(baccano)* din, racket

'fradicio, a, ci, ce [ˈfraditʃo] *ag (molto bagnato)* soaking (wet); **ubriaco ~** blind drunk

'fragile [ˈfradʒile] *ag* fragile; *(fig: salute)* delicate

'fragola *sf* strawberry

fra'gore *sm* roar; *(di tuono)* rumble

frago'roso, a *ag* deafening

fra'grante *ag* fragrant

frain'tendere *vt* to misunderstand; **frain'teso, a** *pp di* **fraintendere**

fram'mento *sm* fragment

'frana *sf* landslide; *(fig: persona)*: **essere una ~** to be useless; **fra'nare** *vi* to slip, slide down

fran'cese [fran'tʃeze] *ag* French ♦ *sm/f* Frenchman/woman ♦ *sm (LING)* French; **i F~i** the French

fran'chezza [fran'kettsa] *sf* frankness, openness

'Francia ['frantʃa] *sf*: **la ~** France

'franco, a, chi, che *ag* (*COMM*) free; (*sincero*) frank, open, sincere ♦ *sm* (*moneta*) franc; **farla ~a** (*fig*) to get off scot-free; **~ di dogana** duty-free; **prezzo ~ fabbrica** ex-works price; **~ tiratore** sniper

franco'bollo *sm* (postage) stamp

fran'gente [fran'dʒɛnte] *sm* (*onda*) breaker; (*scoglio emergente*) reef; (*circostanza*) situation, circumstance

'frangia, ge ['frandʒa] *sf* fringe

frantu'mare *vt* to break into pieces, shatter; **~rsi** *vr* to break into pieces, shatter

frap'pé *sm* milk shake

'frasca, sche *sf* (leafy) branch

'frase *sf* (*LING*) sentence; (*locuzione, espressione, MUS*) phrase; **~ fatta** set phrase

'frassino *sm* ash (tree)

frastagli'ato, a [frasta'ʎʎato] *ag* (*costa*) indented, jagged

frastor'nare *vt* to daze; to befuddle

frastu'ono *sm* hubbub, din

'frate *sm* friar, monk

fratel'lanza [fratel'lantsa] *sf* brotherhood; (*associazione*) fraternity

fratel'lastro *sm* stepbrother

fra'tello *sm* brother; **~i** *smpl* brothers; (*nel senso di fratelli e sorelle*) brothers and sisters

fra'terno, a *ag* fraternal, brotherly

frat'tanto *av* in the meantime, meanwhile

frat'tempo *sm*: **nel ~** in the meantime, meanwhile

frat'tura *sf* fracture; (*fig*) split, break

frazi'one [frat'tsjone] *sf* fraction; (*di comune*) small town

'freccia, ce ['frettʃa] *sf* arrow; **~ di direzione** (*AUT*) indicator

fred'dare *vt* to shoot dead

fred'dezza [fred'dettsa] *sf* coldness

'freddo, a *ag, sm* cold; **fa ~** it's cold;

aver ~ to be cold; **a ~** (*fig*) deliberately; **freddo'loso, a** *ag* sensitive to the cold

fred'dura *sf* pun

fre'gare *vt* to rub; (*fam: truffare*) to take in, cheat; (: *rubare*) to swipe, pinch; **fregarsene** (*fam!*): **chi se ne frega?** who gives a damn (about it)?

fre'gata *sf* rub; (*fam*) swindle; (*NAUT*) frigate

'fregio ['fregdʒo] *sm* (*ARCHIT*) frieze; (*ornamento*) decoration

'fremere *vi*: **~ di** to tremble o quiver with; **'fremito** *sm* tremor, quiver

fre'nare *vt* (*veicolo*) to slow down; (*cavallo*) to rein in; (*lacrime*) to restrain, hold back ♦ *vi* to brake; **~rsi** *vr* (*fig*) to restrain o.s., control o.s.; **fre'nata** *sf*: **fare una frenata** to brake

frene'sia *sf* frenzy

'freno *sm* brake; (*morso*) bit; **~ a disco** disc brake; **~ a mano** handbrake; **tenere a ~** to restrain

frequen'tare *vt* (*scuola, corso*) to attend; (*locale, bar*) to go to, frequent; (*persone*) to see (often)

fre'quente *ag* frequent; **di ~** frequently; **fre'quenza** *sf* frequency; (*INS*) attendance

fres'chezza [fres'kettsa] *sf* freshness

'fresco, a, schi, sche *ag* fresh; (*temperatura*) cool; (*notizia*) recent, fresh ♦ *sm*: **godere il ~** to enjoy the cool air; **stare ~** (*fig*) to be in for it; **mettere al ~** to put in a cool place

'fretta *sf* hurry, haste; **in ~** in a hurry; **in ~ e furia** in a mad rush; **aver ~** to be in a hurry; **fretto'loso, a** *ag* (*persona*) in a hurry; (*lavoro etc*) hurried, rushed

fri'abile *ag* (*terreno*) friable; (*pasta*) crumbly

'friggere ['friddʒere] *vt* to fry ♦ *vi* (*olio etc*) to sizzle

'frigido, a ['fridʒido] *ag* (*MED*) frigid

'frigo *sm* fridge

frigo'rifero, a *ag* refrigerating ♦ *sm*

refrigerator

fringu'ello *sm* chaffinch

frit'tata *sf* omelette; **fare una ~** *(fig)* to make a mess of things

frit'tella *sf (cuc)* fritter

'fritto, a *pp di* **friggere ♦** *ag* fried **♦** *sm* fried food; **~ misto** mixed fry

frit'tura *sf (cuc):* **~ di pesce** mixed fried fish

'frivolo, a *ag* frivolous

frizi'one [frit'tsjone] *sf* friction; *(di pelle)* rub, rub-down; *(AUT)* clutch

friz'zante [frid'dzante] *ag (anche fig)* sparkling

fro'dare *vt* to defraud, cheat

'frode *sf* fraud; **~ fiscale** tax evasion

'frollo, a *ag (carne)* tender; (: *di selvaggina)* high; **pasta ~a** short(crust) pastry

'fronda *sf (leafy)* branch; *(di partito politico)* internal opposition

fron'tale *ag* frontal; *(scontro)* head-on

'fronte *sf (ANAT)* forehead; *(di edificio)* front, façade **♦** *sm (MIL, POL, METEOR)* front; **a ~, di ~** facing, opposite; **di ~ a** *(posizione)* opposite, facing, in front of; *(a paragone di)* compared with

fronteggi'are [fronted'dʒare] *vt (avversari, difficoltà)* to face, stand up to; *(spese)* to cope with

fronti'era *sf* border, frontier

'fronzolo ['frondzolo] *sm* frill

'frottola *sf* fib; **~e** *sfpl (assurdità)* nonsense *sg*

fru'gare *vi* to rummage **♦** *vt* to search

frul'lare *vt (cuc)* to whisk **♦** *vi (uccelli)* to flutter; **frul'lato** *sm* milk shake; fruit drink; **frulla'tore** *sm* electric mixer; **frul'lino** *sm* whisk

fru'mento *sm* wheat

fru'scio [fruʃʃio] *sm* rustle; rustling; *(di acque)* murmur

'frusta *sf* whip; *(cuc)* whisk

frus'tare *vt* to whip

frus'tino *sm* riding crop

frus'trare *vt* to frustrate

'frutta *sf* fruit; *(portata)* dessert; **~ candita/secca** candied/dried fruit

frut'tare *vi* to bear dividends, give a return

frut'teto *sm* orchard

frutti'vendolo, a *sm/f* greengrocer *(BRIT)*, produce dealer *(US)*

'frutto *sm* fruit; *(fig: risultato)* result(s); *(ECON: interesse)* interest; (: *reddito)* income; **~i di mare** seafood *sg*

FS *abbr* = **Ferrovie dello Stato**

fu *vb vedi* **essere ♦** *ag inv:* **il ~ Paolo Bianchi** the late Paolo Bianchi

fuci'lare [futʃi'lare] *vt* to shoot; **fuci'lata** *sf* rifle shot

fu'cile [fu'tʃile] *sm* rifle, gun; *(da caccia)* shotgun, gun

fu'cina [fu'tʃina] *sf* forge

'fuga *sf* escape, flight; *(di gas, liquidi)* leak; *(MUS)* fugue; **~ di cervelli** brain drain

fu'gace [fu'gatʃe] *ag* fleeting, transient

fug'gevole [fud'dʒevole] *ag* fleeting

fuggi'asco, a, schi, sche [fud'dʒasko] *ag, sm/f* fugitive

fuggi'fuggi [fuddʒi'fuddʒi] *sm* scramble, stampede

fug'gire [fud'dʒire] *vi* to flee, run away; *(fig: passar veloce)* to fly **♦** *vt* to avoid; **fuggi'tivo, a** *sm/f* fugitive, runaway

ful'gore *sm* brilliance, splendour

fu'liggine [fu'liddʒine] *sf* soot

fulmi'nare *vt (sog: fulmine)* to strike; (: *elettricità)* to electrocute; *(con arma da fuoco)* to shoot dead; *(fig: con lo sguardo)* to look daggers at

'fulmine *sm* thunderbolt; lightning *no pl*

fu'mare *vi* to smoke; *(emettere vapore)* to steam **♦** *vt* to smoke; **fu'mata** *sf (segnale)* smoke signal; **farsi una fumata** to have a smoke; **fuma'tore, 'trice** *sm/f* smoker

fu'metto *sm* comic strip; **giornale** *sm* **a ~i** comic

'fumo *sm* smoke; *(vapore)* steam; *(il*

fumare tabacco) smoking; **~i** smpl (industriali etc) fumes; **i ~i dell'alcool** the after-effects of drink; **vendere ~** to deceive, cheat; **~ passivo** passive smoking; **fu'moso, a** ag smoky; (fig) muddled

fu'nambolo, a sm/f tightrope walker

'fune sf rope, cord; (più grossa) cable

'funebre ag (rito) funeral; (aspetto) gloomy, funereal

fune'rale sm funeral

'fungere ['fundʒere] vi: **~ da** to act as

'fungo, ghi sm fungus; (commestibile) mushroom; **~ velenoso** toadstool

funico'lare sf funicular railway

funi'via sf cable railway

funzio'nare [funtsjo'nare] vi to work, function; (fungere): **~ da** to act as

funzio'nario [funtsjo'narjo] sm official

funzi'one [funtsjone] sf function; (carica) post, position; (REL) service; **in ~** (meccanismo) in operation; **in ~ di** (come) as; **fare la ~ di qn** (farne le veci) to take sb's place

fu'oco, chi sm fire; (fornello) ring; (FOT, FISICA) focus; **dare ~ a qc** to set fire to sth; **far ~** (sparare) to fire; **~ d'artificio** firework

fuorché [fwor'ke] cong, prep except

fu'ori av outside; (all'aperto) outdoors, outside; (fuori di casa, SPORT) out; (esclamativo) get out! ♦ prep: **~ (di)** out of, outside ♦ sm outside; **lasciar ~ qc/qn** to leave sth/sb out; **far ~ qn** (fam) to kill sb, do sb in; **essere ~ di sé** to be beside o.s.; **~ luogo** (inopportuno) out of place, uncalled for; **~ mano** out of the way, remote; **~ pericolo** out of danger; **~ uso** old-fashioned; obsolete

fu'ori... prefisso fuori'bordo sm inv speedboat (with outboard motor); outboard motor; **fuori'classe** sm/f inv (undisputed) champion; **fuorigi'oco** sm offside; **fuori'legge** sm/f inv outlaw; **fuori'serie** ag inv (auto etc) custom-built ♦ sf custom-built car;

fuori'strada sm (AUT) cross-country vehicle; fuor(i)u'scito, a sm/f exile; **fuorvi'are** vt to mislead; (fig) to lead astray ♦ vi to go astray

'furbo, a ag clever, smart; (peg) cunning

fu'rente ag: **~ (contro)** furious (with)

fur'fante sm rascal, scoundrel

fur'gone sm van

'furia sf (ira) fury, rage; (fig: impeto) fury, violence; (fretta) rush; **a ~ di** by dint of; **andare su tutte le ~e** to get into a towering rage; **furi'bondo, a** ag furious

furi'oso, a ag furious

fu'rore sm fury; (esaltazione) frenzy; **far ~** to be all the rage

fur'tivo, a ag furtive

'furto sm theft; **~ con scasso** burglary

'fusa sfpl: **fare le ~** to purr

fu'sibile sm (ELETTR) fuse

fusi'one sf (di metalli) fusion, melting; (colata) casting; (COMM) merger; (fig) merging

'fuso, a pp di fondere ♦ sm (FILATURA) spindle; **~ orario** time zone

fus'tagno [fus'taɲɲo] sm corduroy

fus'tino sm (di detersivo) tub

'fusto sm stem; (ANAT, di albero) trunk; (recipiente) drum, can

fu'turo, a ag, sm future

G, g

gab'bare vt to take in, dupe; **~rsi** vr: **~rsi di qn** to make fun of sb

'gabbia sf cage; (da imballaggio) crate; **~ dell'ascensore** lift (BRIT) o elevator (US) shaft; **~ toracica** (ANAT) rib cage

gabbi'ano sm (sea)gull

gabi'netto sm (MED etc) consulting room; (POL) ministry; (WC) toilet, lavatory; (INS: di fisica etc) laboratory

'gaffe [gaf] sf inv blunder

gagli'ardo, a [ga'ʎʎardo] ag strong, vigorous

'gaio, a *ag* cheerful, gay

'gala *sf* (*sfarzo*) pomp; (*festa*) gala

ga'lante *ag* gallant, courteous; (*avventura*) amorous; **galante'ria** *sf* gallantry

galantu'omo (*pl* galantu'omini) *sm* gentleman

ga'lassia *sf* galaxy

gala'teo *sm* (good) manners *pl*

gale'otto *sm* (*rematore*) galley slave; (*carcerato*) convict

ga'lera *sf* (NAUT) galley; (*prigione*) prison

'galla *sf*: **a ~** afloat; **venire a ~** to surface, come to the surface; (*fig: verità*) to come out

galleggi'ante [galled'dʒante] *ag* floating ♦ *sm* (*di pescatore, lenza*, TECN) float

galleggi'are [galled'dʒare] *vi* to float

galle'ria *sf* (*traforo*) tunnel; (ARCHIT, d'arte) gallery; (TEATRO) circle; (*strada coperta con negozi*) arcade

'Galles *sm*: **il ~** Wales; **gal'lese** *ag, sm* (LING) Welsh ♦ *sm/f* Welshman/woman

gal'letta *sf* cracker

gall'lina *sf* hen

'gallo *sm* cock

gal'lone *sm* piece of braid; (MIL) stripe; (*unità di misura*) gallon

galop'pare *vi* to gallop

ga'loppo *sm* gallop; **al o di ~ a** gallop

'gamba *sf* leg; (*asta: di lettera*) stem; **in ~** (*in buona salute*) well; (*bravo, sveglio*) bright, smart; **prendere qc sotto ~** (*fig*) to treat sth too lightly

gambe'retto *sm* shrimp

'gambero *sm* (*di acqua dolce*) crayfish; (*di mare*) prawn

'gambo *sm* stem; (*di frutta*) stalk

'gamma *sf* (MUS) scale; (*di colori, fig*) range

ga'nascia, sce [ga'naʃʃa] *sf* jaw; **~sce del freno** (AUT) brake shoes

'gancio [gantʃo] *sm* hook

'gan.gheri ['gangeri] *smpl*: **uscire dai**

~ (*fig*) to fly into a temper

'gara *sf* competition; (SPORT) competition; contest; match; (: *corsa*) race; **fare a ~** to compete, vie

ga'rage [ga'raʒ] *sm inv* garage

garan'tire *vt* to guarantee; (*debito*) to stand surety for; (*dare per certo*) to assure

garan'zia [garan'tsia] *sf* guarantee; (*pegno*) security

gar'bato, a *ag* courteous, polite

'garbo *sm* (*buone maniere*) politeness, courtesy; (*di vestito etc*) grace, style

gareggi'are [gared'dʒare] *vi* to compete

garga'rismo *sm* gargle; **fare i ~i** to gargle

ga'rofano *sm* carnation; **chiodo di ~** clove

'garza ['gardza] *sf* (*per bende*) gauze

gar'zone [gar'dzone] *sm* (*di negozio*) boy

gas *sm inv* gas; **a tutto ~** at full speed; **dare ~** (AUT) to accelerate

ga'solio *sm* diesel (oil)

ga's(s)ato, a *ag* (*di bibita*) aerated, fizzy

gas'sosa *sf* fizzy drink

gas'soso, a *ag* gaseous; gassy

gastrono'mia *sf* gastronomy

gat'tino *sm* kitten

'gatto, a *sm/f* cat, tomcat/she-cat; **~ selvatico** wildcat; **~ delle nevi** (AUT, SCI) snowcat

gatto'pardo *sm*: **~ africano** serval; **~ americano** ocelot

'gaudio *sm* joy, happiness

ga'vetta *sf* (MIL) mess tin; **venire dalla ~** (MIL, fig) to rise from the ranks

'gazza ['gaddza] *sf* magpie

gaz'zetta [gad'dzetta] *sf* news sheet; **G~ Ufficiale** official publication containing details of new laws

gel [dʒel] *sm inv* gel

ge'lare [dʒe'lare] *vt, vi, vb impers* to freeze; **ge'lata** *sf* frost

gelate'ria [dʒelate'ria] *sf* ice-cream

shop

gela'tina [dʒelaˈtina] sf gelatine; **~ esplosiva** dynamite; **~ di frutta** fruit jelly

ge'lato, a [dʒeˈlato] ag frozen ♦ sm ice cream

'gelido, a [ˈdʒɛlido] ag icy, ice-cold

'gelo [ˈdʒɛlo] sm (temperatura) intense cold; (brina) frost; (fig) chill; **ge'lone** sm chilblain

gelo'sia [dʒeloˈsia] sf jealousy

ge'loso, a [dʒeˈloso] ag jealous

'gelso [ˈdʒɛlso] sm mulberry (tree)

gelso'mino [dʒelsoˈmino] sm jasmine

ge'mello, a [dʒeˈmɛllo] ag, sm/f twin; **~i** smpl (di camicia) cufflinks; (dello zodiaco): **G~i** Gemini sg

'gemere [ˈdʒɛmere] vi to moan, groan; (cigolare) to creak; **'gemito** sm moan, groan

'gemma [ˈdʒɛmma] sf (BOT) bud; (pietra preziosa) gem

gene'rale [dʒeneˈrale] ag, sm general; **in ~** (per sommi capi) in general terms; (di solito) usually, in general; **generalità** sfpl (dati d'identità) particulars; **generaliz'zare** vt, vi to generalize; **general'mente** av generally

gene'rare [dʒeneˈrare] vt (dar vita) to give birth to; (produrre) to produce; (causare) to arouse; (TECN) to produce, generate; **genera'tore** sm (TECN) generator; **generazi'one** sf generation

'genere [ˈdʒɛnere] sm kind, type, sort; (BIOL) genus; (merce) article, product; (LING) gender; (ARTE, LETTERATURA) genre; **in ~** generally, as a rule; **il ~ umano** mankind; **~i alimentari** foodstuffs

ge'nerico, a, ci, che [dʒeˈnɛriko] ag generic; (vago) vague, imprecise

'genero [ˈdʒɛnero] sm son-in-law

generosità [dʒenerosiˈta] sf generosity

gene'roso, a [dʒeneˈroso] ag generous

ge'netica [dʒeˈnɛtika] sf genetics

ge'netico, a, ci, che [dʒeˈnɛtiko] ag genetic

gen'giva [dʒenˈdʒiva] sf (ANAT) gum

geni'ale [dʒenˈjale] ag (persona) of genius; (idea) ingenious, brilliant

'genio [ˈdʒɛnjo] sm genius; **andare a ~ a qn** to be to sb's liking, appeal to sb

geni'tale [dʒeniˈtale] ag genital; **~i** smpl genitals

geni'tore [dʒeniˈtore] sm parent, father o mother; **i miei ~i** my parents, my father and mother

gen'naio [dʒenˈnajo] sm January

'Genova [ˈdʒɛnova] sf Genoa

gen'taglia [dʒenˈtaʎʎa] sf (peg) rabble

'gente [ˈdʒɛnte] sf people pl

gen'tile [dʒenˈtile] ag (persona, atto) kind; (: garbato) courteous, polite; (nelle lettere): **G~ Signore** Dear Sir; (: sulla busta): **G~ Signor Fernando Villa** Mr Fernando Villa; **genti'lezza** sf kindness; courtesy, politeness; **per gentilezza** (per favore) please

gentilu'omo [dʒentiˈlwɔmo] (pl **gentilu'omini**) sm gentleman

genu'ino, a [dʒenuˈino] ag (prodotto) natural; (persona, sentimento) genuine, sincere

geogra'fia [dʒeograˈfia] sf geography

geolo'gia [dʒeoloˈdʒia] sf geology

ge'ometra, i, e [dʒeˈɔmetra] sm/f (professionista) surveyor

geome'tria [dʒeomeˈtria] sf geometry; **geo'metrico, a, ci, che** ag geometric(al)

gerar'chia [dʒerarˈkia] sf hierarchy

ge'rente [dʒeˈrɛnte] sm/f manager/ manageress

'gergo, ghi [ˈdʒɛrgo] sm jargon; slang

geria'tria [dʒerjaˈtria] sf geriatrics

Ger'mania [dʒerˈmanja] sf: **la ~** Germany; **la ~ occidentale/orientale** West/East Germany

'germe [ˈdʒɛrme] sm germ; (fig) seed

germogli'are [dʒermoʎˈʎare] vi to sprout; to germinate; **ger'moglio** sm shoot; bud

gero'glifico, ci [dʒero'glifiko] sm hieroglyphic

'gesso ['dʒɛsso] sm chalk; (SCULTURA, MED, EDIL) plaster; (statua) plaster figure; (minerale) gypsum

gesti'one [dʒes'tjone] sf management

ges'tire [dʒes'tire] vt to run, manage

'gesto ['dʒɛsto] sm gesture

ges'tore [dʒes'tore] sm manager

Gesù [dʒe'zu] sm Jesus

gesu'ita, i [dʒezu'ita] sm Jesuit

get'tare [dʒet'tare] vt to throw; (anche: ~ via) to throw away o out; (SCULTURA) to cast; (EDIL) to lay; (acqua) to spout; (grido) to utter; **~rsi** vr: **~rsi in** (sog: fiume) to flow into; **~ uno sguardo su** to take a quick look at; **get'tata** sf (di cemento, gesso, metalli) cast; (diga) jetty

'getto ['dʒɛtto] sm (di gas, liquido, AER) jet; **a ~ continuo** uninterruptedly; **di ~** (fig) straight off, in one go

get'tone [dʒet'tone] sm token; (per giochi) counter; (: roulette etc) chip; **~ telefonico** telephone token

ghiacci'aio [gjat'tʃajo] sm glacier

ghiacci'are [gjat'tʃare] vt to freeze; (fig): **~ qn** to make sb's blood run cold ♦ vi to freeze, ice over; **ghiacci'ato, a** ag frozen; (bevanda) ice-cold

ghi'accio ['gjattʃo] sm ice

ghiacci'olo ['gjad'dʒɔlo] sm icicle; (tipo di gelato) ice lolly (BRIT), popsicle (US)

ghi'aia ['gjaja] sf gravel

ghi'anda ['gjanda] sf (BOT) acorn

ghi'andola ['gjandola] sf gland

ghigliot'tina [giʎʎot'tina] sf guillotine

ghi'gnare [giɲ'ɲare] vi to sneer

ghi'otto, a ['gjotto] ag greedy; (cibo) delicious, appetizing; **ghiot'tone, a** sm/f glutton

ghiri'goro [giri'gɔro] sm scribble, squiggle

ghir'landa [gir'landa] sf garland, wreath

'ghiro ['giro] sm dormouse

'ghisa ['giza] sf cast iron

già [dʒa] av already; (ex, in precedenza) formerly ♦ escl of course!, yes indeed!

gi'acca, che [dʒakka] sf jacket; **~ a vento** windcheater (BRIT), windbreaker (US)

giacché [dʒak'ke] cong since, as

giac'chetta [dʒak'ketta] sf (light) jacket

gia'cenza [dʒa'tʃɛntsa] sf: **merce in ~** goods in stock; **~e di magazzino** unsold stock

gia'cere [dʒa'tʃere] vi to lie; **giaci'mento** sm deposit

gia'cinto [dʒa'tʃinto] sm hyacinth

gi'ada [dʒada] sf jade

giaggi'olo [dʒad'dʒɔlo] sm iris

giagu'aro [dʒa'gwaro] sm jaguar

gi'allo ['dʒallo] ag yellow; (carnagione) sallow ♦ sm yellow; (anche: romanzo ~) detective novel; (anche: film ~) detective film; **~ dell'uovo** yolk

giam'mai [dʒam'mai] av never

Giap'pone [dʒap'pone] sm Japan; **giappo'nese** ag, sm/f, sm Japanese inv

gi'ara [dʒara] sf jar

giardi'naggio [dʒardi'naddʒo] sm gardening

giardini'era [dʒardi'njera] sf (misto di sottaceti) mixed pickles pl

giardini'ere, a [dʒardi'njere] sm/f gardener

giar'dino [dʒar'dino] sm garden; **~ d'infanzia** nursery school; **~ pubblico** public gardens pl, (public) park; **~ zoologico** zoo

giarretti'era [dʒarret'tjera] sf garter

giavel'lotto [dʒavel'lɔtto] sm javelin

gi'gante, essa [dʒi'gante] sm/f giant ♦ ag giant, gigantic; (COMM) giant-size; **gigan'tesco, a, schi, sche** ag gigantic

giglio ['dʒiʎʎo] sm lily

gilè [dʒi'le] sm inv waistcoat

gin [dʒin] sm inv gin

gine'cologo, a, gi, ghe [dʒine'kɔlogo] sm/f gynaecologist

gi'nepro [dʒi'nepro] *sm* juniper

gi'nestra [dʒi'nestra] *sf (BOT)* broom

Gi'nevra [dʒi'nevra] *sf* Geneva

gingil'larsi [dʒindʒil'larsi] *vr* to fritter away one's time; *(giocare)*: ~ **con** to fiddle with

gin'gillo [dʒin'dʒillo] *sm* plaything

gin'nasio [dʒin'nazjo] *sm* the 4th and 5th year of secondary school in Italy

gin'nasta, i, e [dʒin'nasta] *sm/f* gymnast; **gin'nastica** *sf* gymnastics *sg*; *(esercizio fisico)* keep-fit exercises; *(INS)* physical education

gi'nocchio [dʒi'nɔkkjo] *(pl(m)* **gi'nocchi** *o pl(f)* **gi'nocchia)** *sm* knee; **stare in ~** to kneel, be on one's knees; **mettersi in ~** to kneel (down); **ginocchi'oni** *av* on one's knees

gio'care [dʒo'kare] *vt* to play; *(scommettere)* to stake, bet; *(ingannare)* to take in ♦ *vi* to play; *(a roulette etc)* to gamble; *(fig)* to play a part, be important; **~ a** *(gioco, sport)* to play; *(cavalli)* to bet on; **~rsi la carriera** to put one's career at risk; **gioca'tore, 'trice** *sm/f* player; gambler

gio'cattolo [dʒo'kattolo] *sm* toy

gio'chetto [dʒo'ketto] *sm (tranello)* trick; *(fig)*: **è un ~** it's child's play

gi'oco, chi [dʒɔko] *sm (anche: divertimento, TECN)* play; *(al casinò)* gambling; *(CARTE)* hand; *(insieme di pezzi che necessari per un gioco)* set; **per ~** for fun; **fare il doppio ~ con qn** to double-cross sb; **~ d'azzardo** game of chance; **~ degli scacchi** chess set; **i Giochi Olimpici** the Olympic Games

giocoli'ere [dʒoko'ljere] *sm* juggler

gio'coso, a [dʒo'koso] *ag* playful, jesting

gi'ogo, ghi [dʒɔgo] *sm* yoke

gi'oia [dʒɔja] *sf* joy, delight; *(pietra preziosa)* jewel, precious stone

gioiel'leria [dʒojel'leria] *sf* jeweller's craft; jeweller's (shop)

gioielli'ere, a [dʒojel'ljere] *sm/f* jeweller

gioi'ello [dʒo'jello] *sm* jewel, piece of jewellery; **i miei ~i** my jewels *o* jewellery

gioi'oso, a [dʒo'joso] *ag* joyful

Gior'dania [dʒor'danja] *sf*: **la ~** Jordan

gior'naio, a [dʒor'najo] *sm/f* newsagent *(BRIT)*, newsdealer *(us)*

gior'nale [dʒor'nale] *sm (news)* paper; *(diario)* journal, diary; *(COMM)* journal; **~ di bordo** log; **~ radio** radio news *sg*

giornali'ero, a [dʒorna'ljero] *ag* daily; *(che varia: umore)* changeable ♦ *sm* day labourer

giorna'lismo [dʒorna'lizmo] *sm* journalism

giorna'lista, i, e [dʒorna'lista] *sm/f* journalist

gior'nata [dʒor'nata] *sf* day; **~ lavorativa** working day

gi'orno [dʒorno] *sm* day; *(opposto alla notte)* day, daytime; *(luce del ~)* daylight; **al ~** per day; **di ~** by day; **al ~ d'oggi** nowadays

---

giorno dei morti

Il **giorno dei Morti**, All Souls' Day, falls on 2 November. On that day, relatives make a special visit to the graves of loved ones, to lay flowers.

---

gi'ostra [dʒɔstra] *sf (per bimbi)* merry-go-round; *(torneo storico)* joust

gi'ovane [dʒovane] *ag* young; *(aspetto)* youthful ♦ *sm/f* youth/girl, young man/woman; **i ~i** young people; **giova'nile** *ag* youthful; *(scritti)* early; *(errore)* of youth; **giova'notto** *sm* young man

gio'vare [dʒo'vare] *vi*: **~ a** *(essere utile)* to be useful to; *(far bene)* to be good for ♦ *vb impers (essere bene, utile)* to be useful; **~rsi di qc** to make use of sth

giovedì [dʒove'di] *sm inv* Thursday; **di** *o* **il ~** on Thursdays

gioventù [dʒoven'tu] *sf (periodo)*

youth; (*i giovani*) young people *pl*, youth

giovi'ale [dʒo'vjale] *ag* jovial, jolly

giovi'nezza [dʒovi'nettsa] *sf* youth

gira'dischi [dʒira'diski] *sm inv* record player

gi'raffa [dʒi'raffa] *sf* giraffe

gi'randola [dʒi'randola] *sf (fuoco d'artificio)* Catherine wheel; *(giocattolo)* toy windmill; *(banderuola)* weather vane, weathercock

gi'rare [dʒi'rare] *vt (far ruotare)* to turn; *(percorrere, visitare)* to go round; *(CINEMA)* to shoot; to make; *(COMM)* to endorse ♦ *vi* to turn; *(più veloce)* to spin; *(andare in giro)* to wander, go around; ~**rsi** *vr* to turn; ~ **attorno a** to go round; to revolve round; ~ **la testa a qn** to make sb dizzy; *(fig)* to turn sb's head

girar'rosto [dʒirar'rosto] *sm (CUC)* spit

gira'sole [dʒira'sole] *sm* sunflower

gi'rata [dʒi'rata] *sf (passeggiata)* stroll; *(con veicolo)* drive; *(COMM)* endorsement

gira'volta [dʒira'volta] *sf* twirl, turn; *(curva)* sharp bend; *(fig)* about-turn

gi'revole [dʒi'revole] *ag* revolving, turning

gi'rino [dʒi'rino] *sm* tadpole

'giro ['dʒiro] *sm (circuito, cerchio)* circle; *(di chiave, manovella)* turn; *(viaggio)* tour, excursion; *(passeggiata)* stroll, walk; *(in macchina)* drive; *(in bicicletta)* ride; *(SPORT: della pista)* lap; *(di denaro)* circulation; *(CARTE)* hand; *(TECN)* revolution; **prendere in ~ qn** *(fig)* to pull sb's leg; **fare un ~** to go for a walk *(o* a drive *o* a ride); **andare in ~** to go about, walk around; **a stretto ~ di posta** by return of post; **nel ~ di un mese** in a month's time; **essere nel ~** *(fig)* to belong to a circle of friends); ~ **d'affari** *(COMM)* turnover; ~ **di parole** circumlocution; ~ **di prova** *(AUT)* test drive; ~ **turistico** sightseeing tour; **giro'collo** *sm*: **a**

girocollo crew-neck *cpd*

gironzo'lare [dʒirondzo'lare] *vi* to stroll about

'gita ['dʒita] *sf* excursion, trip; **fare una** ~ to go for a trip, go on an outing

gi'tano, a [dʒi'tano] *sm/f* gipsy

giù [dʒu] *av* down; *(dabbasso)* downstairs; **in** ~ downwards, down; ~ **di lì** *(pressappoco)* thereabouts; **bambini dai 6 anni in** ~ children aged 6 and under; ~ **per: cadere** ~ **per le scale** to fall down the stairs; **essere** ~ *(fig: di salute)* to be run down; *(: di spirito)* to be depressed

giub'botto [dʒub'botto] *sm* jerkin; ~ **antiproiettile** bulletproof vest

giu'bilo [dʒu'bilo] *sm* rejoicing

giudi'care [dʒudi'kare] *vt* to judge; *(accusato)* to try; *(lite)* to arbitrate in; ~ **qn/qc bello** to consider sb/sth (to be) beautiful

gi'udice [dʒu'ditʃe] *sm* judge; ~ **conciliatore** justice of the peace; ~ **istruttore** examining *(BRIT)* o committing *(US)* magistrate; ~ **popolare** member of a jury

giu'dizio [dʒu'dittsjo] *sm* judgment; *(opinione)* opinion; *(DIR)* judgment, sentence; *(: processo)* trial; *(: verdetto)* verdict; **aver** ~ to be wise o prudent; **citare in** ~ to summons; **giudizi'oso, a** *ag* prudent, judicious

gi'ugno ['dʒuɲo] *sm* June

giul'lare [dʒul'lare] *sm* jester

giu'menta [dʒu'menta] *sf* mare

gi'unco, chi [ˈdʒunko] *sm* rush

giu'ngere [ˈdʒundʒere] *vi* to arrive ♦ *vt (mani etc)* to join; ~ **a** to arrive at, reach

gi'ungla [ˈdʒungla] *sf* jungle

gi'unta [ˈdʒunta] *sf* addition; *(organo esecutivo, amministrativo)* council, board; **per ~a** into the bargain, in addition; ~**a militare** military junta

gi'unto, a [ˈdʒunto] *pp di* giungere ♦ *sm (TECN)* coupling, joint; **giun'tura**

sf joint

giuo'care [dʒwo'kare] *etc* = **giocare** *etc*

giura'mento [dʒura'mento] *sm* oath; ~ **falso** perjury

giu'rare [dʒu'rare] *vt* to swear ♦ *vi* to swear, take an oath; **giu'rato, a** *ag*: **nemico giurato** sworn enemy ♦ *sm/f* juror, juryman/woman

giu'ria [dʒu'ria] *sf* jury

giu'ridico, a, ci, che [dʒu'ridiko] *ag* legal

giustifi'care [dʒustifi'kare] *vt* to justify; **giustificazi'one** *sf* justification; (INS) (note of) excuse

gius'tizia [dʒus'tittsja] *sf* justice; **giustizi'are** *vt* to execute, put to death; **giustizi'ere** *sm* executioner

gi'usto, a ['dʒusto] *ag* (*equo*) fair, just; (*vero*) correct; (*adatto*) right, suitable; (*preciso*) exact, correct ♦ *av* (*esattamente*) exactly, precisely; (*per l'appunto, appena*) just; **arrivare ~** to arrive just in time; **ho ~ bisogno di te** you're just the person I need

glaci'ale [gla'tʃale] *ag* glacial

gli [ʎi] (*dav V, s impura, gn, pn, ps, x, z*) *det mpl* the ♦ *pron* (*a lui*) to him; (*a esso*) to it; (*in coppia con lo, la, li, le, ne: a lui, a lei, a loro etc*): **gliele do** I'm giving them to him (*o her o them*); *vedi anche* **il**

gli'ela ['ʎela] *etc vedi* **gli**

glo'bale *ag* overall

'globo *sm* globe

'globulo *sm* (ANAT): ~ **rosso/bianco** red/white corpuscle

'gloria *sf* glory; **glori'oso, a** *ag* glorious

glos'sario *sm* glossary

'gnocchi ['ɲɔkki] *smpl* (CUC) small dumplings made of semolina pasta or potato

'gobba *sf* (ANAT) hump; (*protuberanza*) bump

'gobbo, a *ag* hunchbacked; (*ricurvo*) round-shouldered ♦ *sm/f* hunchback

'goccia, ce ['gottʃa] *sf* drop; **goccio'lare** *vi, vt* to drip

go'dere *vi* (*compiacersi*): ~ **(di)** to be delighted (at), rejoice (at); (*trarre vantaggio*): ~ **di** to enjoy, benefit from ♦ *vt* to enjoy; ~**rsi la vita** to enjoy life; ~**sela** to have a good time, enjoy o.s.; **godi'mento** *sm* enjoyment

'goffo, a *ag* clumsy, awkward

'gola *sf* (ANAT) throat; (*golosità*) gluttony, greed; (*di camino*) flue; (*di monte*) gorge; **fare** ~ (*anche fig*) to tempt

golf *sm inv* (SPORT) golf; (*maglia*) cardigan

'golfo *sm* gulf

go'loso, a *ag* greedy

'gomito *sm* elbow; (*di strada etc*) sharp bend

go'mitolo *sm* ball

'gomma *sf* rubber; (*per cancellare*) rubber, eraser; (*di veicolo*) tyre (BRIT), tire (US); ~ **americana** *o* **da masticare** chewing gum; ~ **a terra** flat tyre (BRIT) *o* tire (US); **gommapi'uma** ® *sf* foam rubber; **gom'mone** *sm* rubber dinghy

'gondola *sf* gondola; **gondoli'ere** *sm* gondolier

gonfa'lone *sm* banner

gonfi'are *vt* (*pallone*) to blow up, inflate; (*dilatare, ingrossare*) to swell; (*fig: notizia*) to exaggerate; ~**rsi** *vr* to swell; (*fiume*) to rise; **'gonfio, a** *ag* swollen; (*stomaco*) bloated; (*vela*) full; **gonfi'ore** *sm* swelling

gongo'lare *vi* to look pleased with o.s.; ~ **di gioia** to be overjoyed

'gonna *sf* skirt; ~ **pantalone** culottes *pl*

'gonzo ['gondzo] *sm* simpleton, fool

gorgheggi'are [gorged'dʒare] *vi o* to warble; to trill

'gorgo, ghi *sm* whirlpool

gorgogli'are [gorgoʎ'ʎare] *vi* to gurgle

go'rilla *sm inv* gorilla; (*guardia del*

corpo) bodyguard

'gotta *sf* gout

gover'nante *sm/f* ruler ♦ *sf (di bambini)* governess; *(donna di servizio)* housekeeper

gover'nare *vt (stato)* to govern, rule; *(pilotare, guidare)* to steer; *(bestiame)* to tend, look after; **governa'tivo, a** *ag* government *cpd*; **governa'tore** *sm* governor

go'verno *sm* government

gozzovigli'are [gottsoviʎˈʎare] *vi* to make merry, carouse

gracchi'are [grakˈkjare] *vi* to caw

graci'dare [gratʃiˈdare] *vi* to croak

'gracile [ˈgratʃile] *ag* frail, delicate

gra'dasso *sm* boaster

gradazi'one [gradatˈtsjone] *sf (sfumatura)* gradation; **~ alcolica** alcoholic content, strength

gra'devole *ag* pleasant, agreeable

gradi'mento *sm* pleasure, satisfaction; **è di suo ~?** is it to your liking?

gradi'nata *sf* flight of steps; *(in teatro, stadio)* tiers *pl*

gra'dino *sm* step; *(ALPINISMO)* foothold

gra'dire *vt (accettare con piacere)* to accept; *(desiderare)* to wish, like; **gradisce una tazza di tè?** would you like a cup of tea?; **gra'dito, a** *ag* pleasing; welcome

'grado *sm (MAT, FISICA etc)* degree; *(stadio)* degree, level; *(MIL, sociale)* rank; **essere in ~ di fare** to be in a position to do

gradu'ale *ag* gradual

gradu'are *vt* to grade; **gradu'ato, a** *ag (esercizi)* graded; *(scala, termometro)* graduated ♦ *sm (MIL)* non-commissioned officer

'graffa *sf (gancio)* clip; *(segno grafico)* brace

graffi'are *vt* to scratch

'graffio *sm* scratch

gra'fia *sf* spelling; *(scrittura)* handwriting

'grafica *sf* graphic arts *pl*

'grafico, a, ci, che *ag* graphic ♦ *sm* graph; *(persona)* graphic designer

gra'migna [graˈminɲa] *sf* weed; couch grass

gram'matica, che *sf* grammar; **grammati'cale** *ag* grammatical

'grammo *sm* gram(me)

gran *ag vedi* **grande**

'grana *sf (granello, di minerali, corpi spezzati)* grain; *(fam: seccatura)* trouble; (: *soldi)* cash ♦ *sm inv* Parmesan (cheese)

gra'naio *sm* granary, barn

gra'nata *sf (proiettile)* grenade

Gran Bre'tagna [-breˈtaɲɲa] *sf*: **la ~** Great Britain

'granchio [ˈgrankjo] *sm* crab; *(fig)* blunder; **prendere un ~** *(fig)* to blunder

grandango'lare *sm* wide-angle lens *sg*

'grande *(qualche volta* **gran** *+C,* **grand'** *+V) ag (grosso, largo, vasto)* big, large; *(alto)* tall; *(lungo)* long; *(in sensi astratti)* great ♦ *sm/f (persona adulta)* adult, grown-up; *(chi ha ingegno e potenza)* great man/woman; **fare le cose in ~** to do things in style; **una gran bella donna** a very beautiful woman; **non è una gran cosa** *o* **un gran che** it's nothing special; **non ne so gran che** I don't know very much about it

grandeggi'are [grandedˈdʒare] *vi (emergere per grandezza)*: **~ su** to tower over; *(darsi arie)* to put on airs

gran'dezza [granˈdettsa] *sf (dimensione)* size; magnitude; *(fig)* greatness; **in ~ naturale** lifesize

grandi'nare *vb impers* to hail

'grandine *sf* hail

gran'duca, chi *sm* grand duke

gra'nello *sm (di cereali, uva)* seed; *(di frutta)* pip; *(di sabbia, sale etc)* grain

gra'nita *sf* kind of water ice

gra'nito *sm* granite

'grano *sm (in quasi tutti i sensi)* grain; *(frumento)* wheat; *(di rosario, collana)*

bead; **~ di pepe** peppercorn
gran'turco sm maize
'grappa sf rough, strong brandy
'grappolo sm bunch, cluster
gras'setto sm (TIP) bold (type)
'grasso, a ag fat; (cibo) fatty; (pelle)
greasy; (terreno) rich; (fig: guadagno,
annata) plentiful ♦ sm (di persona,
animale) fat; (sostanza che unge)
grease; **gras'soccio, a, ci, ce** ag
plump
'grata sf grating
gra'ticola sf grill
gra'tifica, che sf bonus
'gratis av free, for nothing
grati'tudine sf gratitude
'grato, a ag grateful; (gradito) pleasant,
agreeable
gratta'capo sm worry, headache
grattaci'elo [gratta'tʃɛlo] sm
skyscraper
grat'tare vt (pelle) to scratch;
(raschiare) to scrape; (pane, formaggio,
carote) to grate; (fam: rubare) to pinch
♦ vi (stridere) to grate; (AUT) to grind;
~rsi vr to scratch o.s.; **gratta e vinci**
≈ scratch card
grat'tugia, gie [grat'tudʒa] sf grater;
grattugi'are vt to grate; **pane
grattugiato** breadcrumbs pl
gra'tuito, a ag free; (fig) gratuitous
gra'vare vt to burden ♦ vi: **~ su** to
weigh on
'grave ag (danno, pericolo, peccato etc)
grave, serious; (responsabilità) heavy,
grave; (contegno) grave, solemn; (voce,
suono) deep, low-pitched; (LING):
accento ~ grave accent; **un malato ~**
a person who is seriously ill
gravi'danza [gravi'dantsa] sf
pregnancy
'gravido, a ag pregnant
gravità sf seriousness; (anche FISICA)
gravity
gra'voso, a ag heavy, onerous
'grazia ['grattsja] sf grace; (favore)
favour; (DIR) pardon; **grazi'are** vt (DIR)

to pardon
'grazie ['grattsje] escl thank you!;
~ mille! o **tante!** o **infinite!** thank
you very much!; **~ a** thanks to
grazi'oso, a [grat'tsjoso] ag charming,
delightful; (gentile) gracious
'Grecia ['grɛtʃa] sf: **la ~** Greece;
'greco, a, ci, che ag, sm/f, sm Greek
'gregge ['grɛddʒe] sf(pl(f) -i) sm flock
'greggio, gi ['grɛddʒo] sm (anche:
petrolio ~) crude (oil)
grem'biule sm apron; (sopravveste)
overall
'grembo sm lap; (ventre della madre)
womb
gre'mito, a ag: **~ (di)** packed o
crowded (with)
'gretto, a ag mean, stingy; (fig)
narrow-minded
'greve ag heavy
'grezzo, a ['grɛddzo] ag raw,
unrefined; (diamante) rough, uncut;
(tessuto) unbleached
gri'dare vi (per chiamare) to shout, cry
(out); (strillare) to scream, yell ♦ vt to
shout (out), yell (out); **~ aiuto** to cry o
shout for help
'grido (pl(m) -i o pl(f) -a) sm shout, cry;
scream, yell; (di animale) cry; **di ~**
famous
'grigio, a, gi, gie ['gridʒo] ag, sm
grey
'griglia ['griʎʎa] sf (per arrostire) grill;
(ELETTR) grid; (inferriata) grating; **alla ~**
(CUC) grilled; **grigli'ata** sf (CUC) grill
gril'letto sm trigger
'grillo sm (ZOOL) cricket; (fig) whim
grimal'dello sm picklock
'grinta sf grim expression; (SPORT)
fighting spirit
'grinza ['grintsa] sf crease, wrinkle;
(ruga) wrinkle; **non fare una ~** (fig:
ragionamento) to be faultless;
grin'zoso, a ag creased; wrinkled
gris'sino sm bread-stick
'gronda sf eaves pl
gron'daia sf gutter

gron'dare vi to pour; (essere bagnato): ~ **di** to be dripping with ♦ vt to drip with

'groppa sf (di animale) back, rump; (fam: dell'uomo) back, shoulders pl

'groppo sm tangle; **avere un ~ alla gola** (fig) to have a lump in one's throat

gros'sezza sf [gros'settsa] sf size; thickness

gros'sista, i, e sm/f (COMM) wholesaler

'grosso, a ag big, large; (di spessore) thick; (grossolano: anche fig) coarse; (grave, insopportabile) serious, great; (tempo, mare) rough ♦ sm: **il ~ di** the bulk of; **un pezzo ~** (fig) a VIP, a bigwig; **farla ~a** to do something very stupid; **dirle ~e** to tell tall stories; **sbagliarsi di ~** to be completely wrong

grosso'lano, a ag rough, coarse; (fig) coarse, crude; (: errore) stupid

grosso'modo av roughly

'grotta sf cave; grotto

grot'tesco, a, schi, sche ag grotesque

grovi'era sm o f gruyère (cheese)

gro'viglio [gro'viʎʎo] sm tangle; (fig) muddle

gru sf inv crane

'gruccia, ce ['gruttʃa] sf (per camminare) crutch; (per abiti) coathanger

gru'gnire [gruɲ'ɲire] vi to grunt; **gru'gnito** sm grunt

'grugno ['gruɲɲo] sm snout; (fam: faccia) mug

'grullo a ag silly, stupid

'grumo sm (di sangue) clot; (di farina etc) lump

'gruppo sm group; ~ **sanguigno** blood group

gruvi'era sm o f = **groviera**

guada'gnare [gwadaɲ'ɲare] vt (ottenere) to gain; (soldi, stipendio) to earn; (vincere) to win; (raggiungere) to reach

gua'dagno [gwa'daɲɲo] sm earnings pl; (COMM) profit; (vantaggio, utile) advantage, gain; ~ **lordo/netto** gross/net earnings pl

gu'ado sm ford; **passare a ~** to ford

gu'ai escl: ~ **a lui (o lui etc)!** woe betide you (o him etc)!

gua'ina sf (fodero) sheath; (indumento per donna) girdle

gu'aio sm trouble, mishap; (inconveniente) trouble, snag

gua'ire vi to whine, yelp

gu'ancia, ce ['gwantʃa] sf cheek

guanci'ale [gwan'tʃale] sm pillow

gu'anto sm glove

gu'arda... prefisso: ~**'boschi** sm inv forester; ~**'caccia** sm inv gamekeeper; ~**'coste** sm inv coastguard; (nave) coastguard patrol vessel; ~**'linee** sm inv (SPORT) linesman

guar'dare vt (con lo sguardo: osservare) to look at; (film, televisione) to watch; (custodire) to look after, take care of ♦ vi to look; (badare): ~ **a** to pay attention to; (luoghi: esser orientato): ~ **a** to face; ~**rsi** vr to look at o.s.; ~**rsi da** (astenersi) to refrain from; (stare in guardia) to beware of; ~**rsi dal fare** to take care not to do; **guarda di non sbagliare** try not to make a mistake; ~ **a vista qn** to keep a close watch on sb

guarda'roba sm inv wardrobe; (locale) cloakroom; **guardarobi'ere, a** sm/f cloakroom attendant

gu'ardia sf (individuo, corpo) guard; (sorveglianza) watch; **fare la ~ a qc/qn** to guard sth/sb; **stare in ~** (fig) to be on one's guard; **di ~** (medico) on call; ~ **carceraria** (prison) warder; ~ **del corpo** bodyguard; ~ **di finanza** (corpo) customs pl; (persona) customs officer; ~ **medica** emergency doctor service

---

Guardia di finanza

The **Guardia di finanza** is a

military body which deals with infringements of the laws relating to income tax and monopolies. It reports to the Ministers of Finance, Justice or Agriculture.

guardi'ano, a sm/f (di carcere) warder; (di villa etc) caretaker; (di museo) custodian; (di zoo) keeper; ~ **notturno** night watchman

guar'dingo, a, ghi, ghe ag wary, cautious

guardi'ola sf porter's lodge; (MIL) look-out tower

guard'rail ['ga:dreil] sm inv crash barrier

guarigi'one [gwari'dʒone] sf recovery

gua'rire vt (persona, malattia) to cure; (ferita) to heal ♦ vi to recover, be cured; (to heal (up)

guarnigi'one [gwarni'dʒone] sf garrison

guar'nire vt (ornare: abiti) to trim; (CUC) to garnish; **guarnizi'one** sf trimming; garnish; (TECN) gasket

guasta'feste sm/f inv spoilsport

guas'tare vt to spoil, ruin; ~**rsi** vr (cibo) to go bad; (meccanismo) to break down; (tempo) to change for the worse

gu'asto, a ag (non funzionante) broken; (: telefono etc) out of order; (andato a male) bad, rotten; (: dente) decayed, bad; (fig: corrotto) depraved ♦ sm breakdown; (avaria) failure; ~ **al motore** engine failure

gu'ercio, a, ci, ce ['gwertʃo] ag cross-eyed

gu'erra sf war; (tecnica: atomica, chimica etc) warfare; **fare la ~ (a)** to wage war (against); ~ **mondiale** world war; **guerri'ero, a** ag warlike ♦ sm warrior; **guer'riglia** sf guerrilla warfare; **guerrigli'ero** sm guerrilla

gufo sm owl

gu'ida sf guidebook; (comando, direzione) guidance, direction; (AUT)

driving; (tappeto, di tenda, cassetto) runner; ~ **a destra/sinistra** (AUT) right-/left-hand drive; ~ **telefonica** telephone directory; ~ **turistica** tourist guide

gui'dare vt to guide; (squadra, rivolta) to lead; (auto) to drive; (aereo, nave) to pilot; **sai ~?** can you drive?; **guida'tore, trice** sm/f (conducente) driver

guin'zaglio [gwin'tsaʎʎo] sm leash, lead

gu'isa sf: **a ~ di** like, in the manner of

guiz'zare [gwit'tsare] vi to dart; to flicker; to leap

'guscio ['guʃʃo] sm shell

gus'tare vt (cibi) to taste; (: assaporare con piacere) to enjoy, savour; (fig) to enjoy, appreciate ♦ vi: ~ **a** to please; **non mi gusta affatto** I don't like it at all

'gusto sm taste (sapore) flavour; (godimento) enjoyment; **al ~ di fragola** strawberry-flavoured; **mangiare di ~** to eat heartily; **prenderci ~:** **ci ha preso ~** he's acquired a taste for it, he's got to like it; **gus'toso, a** ag tasty; (fig) agreeable

H, h

h abbr = **ora; altezza**

ha etc |a| vb vedi **avere**

ha'cker [ˈhæˈkəˈ] sm inv hacker

hall [hɔl] sf inv hall, foyer

'handicap ['handikap] sm inv handicap; **handicap'pato, a** ag handicapped ♦ sm/f handicapped person, disabled person

'hanno ['anno] vb vedi **avere**

hascisc ['haʃiʃ] sm hashish

herpes ['ɛrpes] sm (MED) herpes sg; ~ **zoster** shingles sg

ho |ɔ| vb vedi **avere**

'hobby ['hɔbi] sm inv hobby

'hockey ['hɔki] sm hockey; ~ su
 ghiaccio ice hockey
'hostess ['houstis] sf inv air hostess
 (BRIT) o stewardess
ho'tel sm inv hotel

I, i

i det mpl the
i'ato sm hiatus
ibernazi'one [ibernat'tsjone] sf
 hibernation
'ibrido, a ag, sm hybrid
Id'dio sm God
i'dea sf idea; (opinione) opinion, view;
 (ideale) ideal; dare l'~ di to seem, look
 like; ~ fissa obsession; neanche o
 neppure per ~! certainly not!
ide'ale ag, sm ideal
ide'are vt (immaginare) to think up,
 conceive; (progettare) to plan
i'dentico, a, ci, che ag identical
identifi'care vt to identify;
 identificazi'one sf identification
identità sf inv identity
ideolo'gia, 'gie [ideolo'dʒia] sf
 ideology
idi'oma, i sm idiom, language;
 idio'matico, a, ci, che ag idiomatic;
 frase idiomatica idiom
idi'ota, i, e ag idiotic ♦ sm/f idiot
idola'trare vt to worship; (fig) to
 idolize
'idolo sm idol
idoneità sf suitability
i'doneo, a ag: ~ a suitable for, fit for;
 (MIL) fit for; (qualificato) qualified for
i'drante sm hydrant
idra'tante ag moisturizing ♦ sm
 moisturizer
i'draulica sf hydraulics sg
i'draulico, a, ci, che ag hydraulic
 ♦ sm plumber
idroe'lettrico, a, ci, che ag
 hydroelectric
i'drofilo, a ag vedi cotone

i'drogeno [i'drɔdʒeno] sm hydrogen
idros'calo sm seaplane base
idrovo'lante sm seaplane
i'ena sf hyena
i'eri av, sm yesterday; il giornale di ~
 yesterday's paper; l'altro ~ the day
 before yesterday; ~ sera yesterday
 evening
igi'ene [i'dʒene] sf hygiene;
 ~ pubblica public health; igi'enico,
 a, ci, che ag hygienic; (salubre)
 healthy
i'gnaro, a [iɲ'ɲaro] ag: ~ di unaware
 of, ignorant of
i'gnobile [iɲ'ɲɔbile] ag despicable, vile
igno'rante [iɲɲo'rante] ag ignorant
igno'rare [iɲɲo'rare] vt (non sapere,
 conoscere) to be ignorant o unaware of,
 not to know; (fingere di non vedere,
 sentire) to ignore
i'gnoto, a [iɲ'ɲɔto] ag unknown

┌─────────────────────────────┐
│ PAROLA CHIAVE   │
└─────────────────────────────┘

il (pl (m) i; diventa lo (pl gli) davanti a
 s impura, gn, pn, ps, x, z; f la (pl le)) det
 m 1 the; ~ libro/lo studente/l'acqua
 the book/the student/the water; gli
 scolari the pupils
2 (astrazione): ~ coraggio/l'amore/la
 giovinezza courage/love/youth
3 (tempo): ~ mattino/la sera in the
 morning/evening; ~ venerdì etc
 (abitualmente) on Fridays etc; (quel
 giorno) on (the) Friday etc; la
 settimana prossima next week
4 (distributivo) a, an; 2.500 lire
 ~ chilo/paio 2,500 lire a o per kilo/
 pair
5 (partitivo) some, any; hai messo lo
 zucchero? have you added sugar?;
 hai comprato ~ latte? did you buy
 (some o any) milk?
6 (possesso): aprire gli occhi to open
 one's eyes; rompersi la gamba to
 break one's leg; avere i capelli neri/
 ~ naso rosso to have dark hair/a red
 nose

7 (con nomi propri): **~ Petrarca** Petrarch; **~ Presidente Clinton** President Clinton; **dov'è la Francesca?** where's Francesca?

8 (con nomi geografici): **~ Tevere** the Tiber; **l'Italia** Italy; **il Regno Unito** the United Kingdom; **l'Everest** Everest

---

'ilare ag cheerful; **ilarità** sf hilarity, mirth

illazi'one [illat'tsjone] sf inference, deduction

ille'gale ag illegal

illeg'gibile [illed'dʒibile] ag illegible

ille'gittimo, a [ille'dʒittimo] ag illegitimate

il'leso, a ag unhurt, unharmed

illi'bato, a ag: **donna ~a** virgin

illimi'tato, a ag boundless; unlimited

il.mo abbr = **illustrissimo**

il'ludere vt to deceive, delude; **~rsi** vr to deceive o.s., delude o.s.

illumi'nare vt to light up, illuminate; (fig) to enlighten; **~rsi** vr to light up; **~ a giorno** to floodlight;

illuminazi'one sf lighting; illumination; floodlighting; (fig) flash of inspiration

illusi'one sf illusion; **farsi delle ~i** to delude o.s.

illusio'nismo sm conjuring

il'luso, a pp di **illudere**

illus'trare vt to illustrate; **illustra'tivo, a** ag illustrative; **illustrazi'one** sf illustration

il'lustre ag eminent, renowned; **illus'trissimo, a** ag (negli indirizzi) very revered

imbacuc'care vt to wrap up; **~rsi** vr to wrap up

imbal'laggio [imbal'laddʒo] sm packing no pl

imbal'lare vt to pack; (AUT) to race; **~rsi** vr (AUT) to race

imbalsa'mare vt to embalm

imbambo'lato, a ag (sguardo) vacant, blank

imban'dire vt: **~ un pranzo** to prepare a lavish meal

imbaraz'zare [imbarat'tsare] vt (mettere a disagio) to embarrass; (ostacolare: movimenti) to hamper

imba'razzo [imba'rattso] sm (disagio) embarrassment; (perplessità) puzzlement, bewilderment; **~ di stomaco** indigestion

imbarca'dero sm landing stage

imbar'care vt (passeggeri) to embark; (merci) to load; **~rsi** vr: **~rsi su** board; **~rsi per l'America** to sail for America; **~rsi in** (fig: affare etc) to embark on

imbarcazi'one [imbarkat'tsjone] sf (small) boat, (small) craft inv; **~ di salvataggio** lifeboat

im'barco, chi sm embarkation; loading; boarding; (banchina) landing stage

imbas'tire vt (cucire) to tack; (fig: abbozzare) to sketch, outline

im'battersi vr: **~ in** (incontrare) to bump o run into

imbat'tibile ag unbeatable, invincible

imbavagli'are [imbavaʎ'ʎare] vt to gag

imbec'cata sf (TEATRO) prompt

imbe'cille [imbe'tʃille] ag idiotic ♦ sm/f idiot; (MED) imbecile

imbel'lire vt to adorn, embellish ♦ vi to grow more beautiful

im'berbe ag beardless

im'bevere vt to soak; **~rsi** vr: **~rsi di** to soak up, absorb

imbian'care vt to whiten; (muro) to whitewash ♦ vi to become o turn white

imbian'chino [imbjan'kino] sm (house) painter, painter and decorator

imboc'care vt (bambino) to feed; (entrare: strada) to enter, turn into

imbocca'tura sf mouth; (di strada, porto) entrance; (MUS, del morso) mouthpiece

im'bocco, chi sm entrance

imbos'care vt to hide; **~rsi** vr (MIL) to

evade military service

imbos'cata sf ambush

imbottigli'are [imbottiʎ'ʎare] vt to bottle; (NAUT) to blockade; (MIL) to hem in; **~rsi** vr to be stuck in a traffic jam

imbot'tire vt to stuff; (giacca) to pad; **imbot'tita** sf quilt; **imbot'tito, a** ag stuffed; (giacca) padded; **panino imbottito** filled roll; **imbot'titura** sf stuffing; padding

imbrat'tare vt to dirty, smear, daub

imbrigli'are [imbriʎ'ʎare] vt to bridle

imbroc'care vt (fig) to guess correctly

imbrogli'are [imbroʎ'ʎare] vt to mix up; (fig: raggirare) to deceive, cheat; (: confondere) to confuse, mix up; **~rsi** vr to get tangled; (fig) to become confused; **im'broglio** sm (groviglio) tangle; (situazione confusa) mess; (truffa) swindle, trick; **imbrogli'one, a** sm/f cheat, swindler

imbronci'ato, a ag sulky

imbru'nire vi, vb impers to grow dark; **all'~** at dusk

imbrut'tire vt to make ugly ♦ vi to become ugly

imbu'care vt to post

imbur'rare vt to butter

im'buto sm funnel

imi'tare vt to imitate; (riprodurre) to copy; (assomigliare) to look like; **imitazi'one** sf imitation

immaco'lato, a ag spotless; immaculate

immagazzi'nare [immagaddzi'nare] vt to store

immagi'nare [immadʒi'nare] vt to imagine; (supporre) to suppose; (inventare) to invent; **s'immagini!** don't mention it!, not at all!; **immagi'nario, a** ag imaginary; **immaginazi'one** sf imagination; (cosa immaginata) fancy

im'magine [im'madʒine] sf image; (rappresentazione grafica, mentale) picture

imman'cabile ag certain; unfailing

im'mane ag (smisurato) enormous; (spaventoso) terrible

immangi'abile [imman'dʒabile] ag inedible

immatrico'lare vt to register; **~rsi** vr (INS) to matriculate, enrol; **immatricolazi'one** sf registration; matriculation, enrolment

imma'turo, a ag (frutto) unripe; (persona) immature; (prematuro) premature

immedesi'marsi vr: **~ in** to identify with

immediata'mente av immediately, at once

immedi'ato, a ag immediate

im'memore ag: **~ di** forgetful of

im'menso, a ag immense

im'mergere [im'mɛrdʒere] vt to immerse, plunge; **~rsi** vr to plunge; (sommergibile) to dive, submerge; (dedicarsi a): **~rsi in** to immerse o.s. in

immeri'tato, a ag undeserved

immeri'tevole ag undeserving, unworthy

immersi'one sf immersion; (di sommergibile) submersion, dive; (di palombaro) dive

im'merso, a pp di **immergere**

im'mettere vt: **~ (in)** to introduce (into); **~ dati in un computer** to enter data on a computer

immi'grato, a sm/f immigrant; **immigrazi'one** sf immigration

immi'nente ag imminent

immischi'are [immis'kjare] vt: **~ qn in** to involve sb in; **~rsi in** to interfere o meddle in

immissi'one sf (di aria, gas) intake; **~ di dati** (INFORM) data entry

im'mobile ag motionless, still; **~i** smpl (anche: beni **~i**) real estate sg; **immobili'are** ag (DIR) property cpd; **immobilità** sf stillness; immobility

immo'desto, a ag immodest

immo'lare vt to sacrifice, immolate

immon'dizia [immon'dittsja] sf dirt,

immondo 123 imperativo

filth; (*spesso al pl: spazzatura, rifiuti*) rubbish *no pl*, refuse *no pl*

im'mondo, a *ag* filthy, foul

immo'rale *ag* immoral

immor'tale *ag* immortal

im'mune *ag* (*esente*) exempt; (MED, DIR) immune; **immunità** *sf* immunity; **immunità parlamentare** parliamentary privilege

immu'tabile *ag* immutable; unchanging

impacchet'tare [impakket'tare] *vt* to pack up

impacci'are [impat'tʃare] *vt* to hinder, hamper; **impacci'ato, a** *ag* awkward, clumsy; (*imbarazzato*) embarrassed; im'paccio *sm* obstacle; (*imbarazzo*) embarrassment; (*situazione imbarazzante*) awkward situation

im'pacco, chi *sm* (MED) compress

impadro'nirsi *vr*: ~ di to seize, take possession of; (*fig: apprendere a fondo*) to master

impa'gabile *ag* priceless

impagi'nare [impadʒi'nare] *vt* (TIP) to paginate, page (up)

impagli'are [impaʎ'ʎare] *vt* to stuff (with straw)

impa'lato, a *ag* (*fig*) stiff as a board

impalca'tura *sf* scaffolding

impal'lidire *vi* to turn pale; (*fig*) to fade

impa'nare *vt* (CUC) to dip in breadcrumbs

impanta'narsi *vr* to sink (in the mud); (*fig*) to get bogged down

impappi'narsi *vr* to stammer, falter

impa'rare *vt* to learn

imparen'tarsi *vr*: ~ con to marry into

'impari *ag inv* (*disuguale*) unequal; (*dispari*) odd

impar'tire *vt* to bestow, give

imparzi'ale [impar'tsjale] *ag* impartial, unbiased

impas'sibile *ag* impassive

impas'tare *vt* (*pasta*) to knead

im'pasto *sm* (*l'impastare: di pane*)

kneading; (: *di cemento*) mixing; (*pasta*) dough; (*anche fig*) mixture

im'patto *sm* impact

impau'rire *vt* to scare, frighten ♦ *vi* (*anche: ~rsi*) to become scared *o* frightened

im'pavido, a *ag* intrepid, fearless

impazi'ente [impat'tsjɛnte] *ag* impatient; **impazi'enza** *sf* impatience; impaz'zata [impat'tsata] *sf*: all'~ (*precipitosamente*) at breakneck speed

impaz'zire [impat'tsire] *vi* to go mad; ~ per qn/qc to be crazy about sth/sb

impec'cabile *ag* impeccable

impe'dire *vt* (*vietare*): ~ a qn di fare to prevent sb from doing; (*ostruire*) to obstruct; (*impacciare*) to hamper, hinder

impedi'mento *sm* obstacle, hindrance

impe'gnare [impeɲ'ɲare] *vt* (*dare in pegno*) to pawn; (*onore etc*) to pledge; (*prenotare*) to book, reserve; (*obbligare*) to oblige; (*occupare*) to keep busy; (MIL: *nemico*) to engage; **~rsi** *vr* (*vincolarsi*): ~rsi a fare to undertake to do; (*mettersi risolutamente*): ~rsi in qc to devote o.s. to sth; **~rsi con qn** (*accordarsi*) to come to an agreement with sb; **impegna'tivo, a** *ag* binding; (*lavoro*) demanding, exacting; impe'gnato, a *ag* (*occupato*) busy; (*fig: romanzo, autore*) committed, engagé

im'pegno [im'peɲɲo] *sm* (*obbligo*) obligation; (*promessa*) promise, pledge; (*zelo*) diligence, zeal; (*compito, d'autore*) commitment

impel'lente *ag* pressing, urgent

impene'trabile *ag* impenetrable

impen'narsi *vr* (*cavallo*) to rear up; (AER) to nose up; (*fig*) to bridle

impen'sato, a *ag* unforeseen, unexpected

impensie'rire *vt* to worry; **~rsi** *vr* to worry

impe'rare *vi* (*anche fig*) to reign, rule

impera'tivo, a *ag, sm* imperative

impera'tore, 'trice sm/f emperor/empress

imperdo'nabile ag unforgivable, unpardonable

imper'fetto, a ag imperfect ♦ sm (LING) imperfect (tense);
imperfezi'one sf imperfection

imperi'ale ag imperial

imperi'oso, a ag (persona) imperious; (motivo, esigenza) urgent, pressing

impe'rizia [impe'rittsja] sf lack of experience

imperma'lirsi vr to take offence

imperme'abile ag waterproof ♦ sm raincoat

imperni'are vt: ~ qc su to hinge sth on; (fig) to base sth on; ~rsi su (fig): ~rsi su to be based on

im'pero sm empire; (forza, autorità) rule, control

imperscru'tabile ag inscrutable

imperso'nale ag impersonal

imperso'nare vt to personify; (TEATRO) to play, act (the part of)

imperter'rito, a ag fearless, undaunted; impassive

imperti'nente ag impertinent

imperver'sare vi to rage

'impeto sm (moto, forza) force, impetus; (assalto) onslaught; (fig: impulso) impulse; (: slancio) transport; **con** ~ energetically; vehemently

impet'tito, a ag stiff, erect

impetu'oso, a ag (vento) strong, raging; (persona) impetuous

impian'tare vt (motore) to install; (azienda, discussione) to establish, start

impi'anto sm (installazione) installation; (apparecchiature) plant; (sistema) system; ~ **elettrico** wiring; ~ **sportivo** sports complex; ~i **di risalita** (SCI) ski lifts

impiastricci'are [impjastrit'tʃare] vt = **impiastrare**

impi'astro sm poultice

impic'care vt to hang; ~rsi vr to hang o.s.

impicci'are [impit'tʃare] vt to hinder, hamper; ~rsi vr to meddle, interfere;

im'piccio sm (ostacolo) hindrance; (seccatura) trouble, bother; (affare imbrogliato) mess; **essere d'impiccio** to be in the way

impie'gare vt (usare) to use, employ; (spendere: denaro, tempo) to spend; (investire) to invest; **impie'gato, a** sm/f employee

impi'ego, ghi sm (uso) use; (occupazione) employment; (posto di lavoro) (regular) job, post; (ECON) investment

impieto'sire vt to move to pity; ~rsi vr to be moved to pity

impie'trire vt (fig) to petrify

impigli'are [impiʎ'ʎare] vt to catch, entangle; ~rsi vr to get caught up o entangled

impi'grire vt to make lazy ♦ vi (anche: ~rsi) to grow lazy

impli'care vt to imply; (coinvolgere) to involve; **implicazi'one** sf implication

im'plicito, a [im'plitʃito] ag implicit

implo'rare vt to implore; (pietà etc) to beg for

impolve'rare vt to cover with dust; ~rsi vr to get dusty

impo'nente ag imposing, impressive

impo'nibile ag taxable ♦ sm taxable income

impopo'lare ag unpopular

im'porre vt to impose; (costringere) to force, make; (far valere) to impose, enforce; **imporsi** vr (persona) to assert o.s.; (cosa: rendersi necessario) to become necessary; (aver successo: moda, attore) to become popular; ~ **a qn di fare** to force sb to do, make sb do

impor'tante ag important;
impor'tanza sf importance; **dare importanza a qc** to attach importance to sth; **darsi importanza** to give o.s. airs

impor'tare vt (introdurre dall'estero) to

import ♦ vi to matter, be important ♦ vb impers (essere necessario) to be necessary; (interessare) to matter; **non importa!** it doesn't matter!; **non me ne importa!** I don't care!; **importazi'one** sf importation; (merci importate) imports pl

im'**porto** sm (total) amount

importu'**nare** vt to bother

impor'**tuno, a** ag irksome, annoying

imposizi'**one** [impozit'tsjone] sf imposition; order, command; (onere, imposta) tax

imposses'**sarsi** vr: ~ **di** to seize, take possession of

impos'**sibile** ag impossible; **fare l'~** to do one's utmost, do all one can; **impossibilità** sf impossibility; **essere nell'impossibilità di fare qc** to be unable to do sth

im'**posta** sf (di finestra) shutter; (tassa) tax; ~ **sul reddito** income tax; ~ **sul valore aggiunto** value added tax (BRIT), sales tax (US)

impos'**tare** vt (imbucare) to post; (preparare) to plan, set out; (avviare) to begin, start off; (voce) to pitch

im'**posto, a** pp di imporre

impo'**tente** ag weak, powerless; (anche MED) impotent

impove'**rire** vt to impoverish ♦ vi (anche: ~rsi) to become poor

imprati'**cabile** ag (strada) impassable; (campo da gioco) unplayable

imprati'**chirsi** [imprati'kirsi] vr: ~**rsi in qc** to practise (BRIT) o practice (US) sth

impre'**gnare** [impreɲ'ɲare] vt: ~ **(di)** (imbevere) to soak o impregnate (with); (riempire: anche fig) to fill (with)

imprendi'**tore** sm (industriale) entrepreneur; (appaltatore) contractor; **piccolo ~** small businessman

im'**presa** sf (iniziativa) enterprise; (azione) exploit; (azienda) firm, concern

impre'**sario** sm (TEATRO) manager,

impresario; ~ **di pompe funebri** funeral director

imprescin'**dibile** [impreʃʃin'dibile] ag not to be ignored

impressio'**nante** ag impressive; upsetting

impressio'**nare** vt to impress; (turbare) to upset; (FOT) to expose; ~**rsi** vr to be easily upset

impressi'**one** sf impression; (fig: sensazione) sensation, feeling; (stampa) printing; **fare ~** (colpire) to impress; (turbare) to frighten, upset; **fare buona/cattiva ~** to make a good/ bad impression on

im'**presso, a** pp di imprimere

impres'**tare** vt: ~ **qc a qn** to lend sth to sb

impreve'**dibile** ag unforeseeable; (persona) unpredictable

imprevi'**dente** ag lacking in foresight

impre'**visto, a** ag unexpected, unforeseen ♦ sm unforeseen event; **salvo ~i** unless anything unexpected happens

imprigio'**nare** [impridʒo'nare] vt to imprison

im'**primere** vt (anche fig) to impress, stamp; (comunicare: movimento) to transmit, give

impro'**babile** ag improbable, unlikely

im'**pronta** sf imprint, impression, sign; (di piede, mano) print; (fig) mark, stamp; ~ **digitale** fingerprint

impro'**perio** sm insult

impro'**prio, a** ag improper; **arma ~a** offensive weapon

improvvisa'**mente** av suddenly; unexpectedly

improvvi'**sare** vt to improvise; ~**rsi** vr: ~**rsi cuoco** to (decide to) act as cook; **improvvi'sata** sf (pleasant) surprise

improv'**viso, a** ag unexpected; (subitaneo) sudden; **all'~** unexpectedly; suddenly

impru'**dente** ag unwise, rash

impu'**dente** ag impudent

impu'dico, a, chi, che ag immodest

impu'gnare [impun'ɲare] vt to grasp, grip; (DIR) to contest

impul'sivo, a ag impulsive

im'pulso sm impulse

impun'tarsi vr to stop dead, refuse to budge; (fig) to be obstinate

impu'tare vt (ascrivere): ~ qc a to attribute sth to; (DIR: accusare): ~ qn di to charge sb with, accuse sb of; **impu'tato, a** sm/f (DIR) accused, defendant; **imputazi'one** sf (DIR) charge

imputri'dire vi to rot

PAROLA CHIAVE

---

in (in+il = **nel**, in+lo = **nello**, in+l' = **nell'**, in+la = **nella**, in+i = **nei**, in+gli = **negli**, in+le = **nelle**) prep **1** (stato in luogo) in; **vivere ~ Italia/città** to live in Italy/town; **essere ~ casa/ufficio** to be at home/the office; **se fossi ~ te** if I were you

2 (moto a luogo) to; (: dentro) into; **andare ~ Germania/città** to go to Germany/town; **andare ~ ufficio** to go to the office; **entrare ~ macchina/casa** to get into the car/go into the house

3 (tempo): **nel 1989** in 1989; **~ giugno/estate** in June/summer

4 (modo, maniera) in; **~ silenzio** in silence; **~ abito da sera** in evening dress; **~ guerra** at war; **~ vacanza** on holiday; **Maria Bianchi ~ Rossi** Maria Rossi née Bianchi

5 (mezzo) by; **viaggiare ~ autobus/treno** to travel by bus/train

6 (materia) made of; **~ marmo** made of marble, marble cpd; **una collana ~ oro** a gold necklace

7 (misura): **siamo ~ quattro** there are four of us; **~ tutto** in all

8 (fine): **dare ~ dono** to give as a gift; **spende tutto ~ alcool** he spends all his money on drink; **~ onore di** in honour of

---

inabi'tabile ag uninhabitable

inacces'sibile [inattʃes'sibile] ag (luogo) inaccessible; (persona) unapproachable

inaccet'tabile [inattʃet'tabile] ag unacceptable

ina'datto, a ag: ~ **(a)** unsuitable o unfit (for)

inadegu'ato, a ag inadequate

inadempi'enza [inadem'pjɛntsa] sf: ~ **a** non-fulfilment (of)

inaffer'rabile ag elusive; (concetto, senso) difficult to grasp

inalbe'rarsi vr (fig) to flare up, fly off the handle

inalte'rabile ag unchangeable; (colore) fast, permanent; (affetto) constant

inalte'rato, a ag unchanged

inami'dato, a ag starched

inani'mato, a ag inanimate; (senza vita: corpo) lifeless

inap'pagabile ag insatiable

inappel'labile ag (decisione) final, irrevocable; (DIR) final, not open to appeal

inappe'tenza [inappe'tɛntsa] sf (MED) lack of appetite

inappun'tabile ag irreproachable

inar'care vt (schiena) to arch; (sopracciglia) to raise; **~rsi** vr to arch

inari'dire vt to make arid, dry up ♦ vi (anche: **~rsi**) to dry up, become arid

inaspet'tato, a ag unexpected

inas'prire vt (disciplina) to tighten up, make harsher; (carattere) to embitter; **~rsi** vr to become harsher; to become bitter; to become angry

inattac'cabile ag (anche fig) unassailable; (alibi) cast-iron

inatten'dibile ag unreliable

inat'teso, a ag unexpected

inattu'abile ag impracticable

inau'dito, a ag unheard of

inaugu'rare vt to inaugurate, open; (monumento) to unveil

inavver'tenza [inavver'tɛntsa] sf

carelessness, inadvertence

incagli'are [inkaʎ'ʎare] vi (NAUT: anche: ~rsi) to run aground

incal'lito, a ag calloused; (fig) hardened, inveterate; (: insensibile) hard

incal'zare [inkal'tsare] vt to follow o pursue closely; (fig) to press ♦ vi (urgere) to be pressing; (essere imminente) to be imminent

incammi'nare vt (fig: avviare) to start up; ~**rsi** vr to set off

incande'scente [inkandeʃ'ʃɛnte] ag incandescent, white-hot

incan'tare vt to enchant, bewitch; ~**rsi** vr (rimanere intontito) to be spellbound; to be in a daze; (meccanismo: bloccarsi) to jam; **incanta'tore, 'trice** ag enchanting, bewitching ♦ sm/f enchanter/enchantress; **incan'tesimo** sm spell, charm; **incan'tevole** ag charming, enchanting

in'canto sm spell, charm, enchantment; (asta) auction; **come per ~** as if by magic; **mettere all'~** to put up for auction

inca'pace [inka'patʃe] ag incapable; **incapacità** sf inability; (DIR) incapacity

incapo'nirsi vr to be stubborn, be determined

incap'pare vi: ~ **in qc/qn** (anche fig) to run into sth/sb

incapricci'arsi [inkaprit'tʃarsi] vr: ~ **di** to take a fancy to o for

incapsu'lare vt (dente) to crown

incarce'rare [inkartʃe'rare] vt to imprison

incari'care vt: ~ **qn di fare** to give sb the responsibility of doing; ~**rsi di** to take care o charge of; **incari'cato, a** ag: **incaricato (di)** in charge (of), responsible (for) ♦ sm/f delegate, representative; **professore incaricato** teacher with a temporary appointment

in'carico, chi sm task, job

incar'nare vt to embody; ~**rsi** vr to be embodied; (REL) to become incarnate

incarta'mento sm dossier, file

incar'tare vt to wrap (in paper)

incas'sare vt (merce) to pack (in cases); (gemma: incastonare) to set; (ECON: riscuotere) to collect; (PUGILATO: colpi) to take, stand up to; **in'casso** sm cashing, encashment; (introito) takings pl

incasto'nare vt to set; **incasto'natura** sf setting

incas'trare vt to fit in, insert; (fig: intrappolare) to catch; ~**rsi** vr (combaciare) to fit together; (restare bloccato) to become stuck; **in'castro** sm slot, groove; (punto di unione) joint

incate'nare vt to chain up

incatra'mare vt to tar

incatti'vire vt to make wicked; ~**rsi** vr to turn nasty

in'cauto, a ag imprudent, rash

inca'vare vt to hollow out; **in'cavo** sm hollow; (solco) groove

incendi'are [intʃen'djare] vt to set fire to; ~**rsi** vr to catch fire, burst into flames

incendi'ario, a [intʃen'djarjo] ag incendiary ♦ sm/f arsonist

in'cendio [in'tʃɛndjo] sm fire

incene'rire [intʃene'rire] vt to burn to ashes, incinerate; (cadavere) to cremate; ~**rsi** vr to be burnt to ashes

in'censo [in'tʃɛnso] sm incense

incensu'rato, a [intʃensu'rato, a] ag (DIR): **essere ~** to have a clean record

incen'tivo [intʃen'tivo] sm incentive

incep'pare [intʃep'pare] vt to obstruct, hamper; ~**rsi** vr to jam

ince'rata [intʃe'rata] sf (tela) tarpaulin; (impermeabile) oilskins pl

incer'tezza [intʃer'tettsa] sf uncertainty

in'certo, a [in'tʃɛrto] ag uncertain; (irresoluto) undecided, hesitating ♦ sm uncertainty

in'cetta [in'tʃetta] sf buying up; **fare ~ di qc** to buy up sth

inchi'esta [in'kjɛsta] sf investigation,

inquiry

inchi'nare [inki'nare] vt to bow; **~rsi** vr to bend down; (per riverenza) to bow; (: donna) to curtsy; **in'chino** sm bow; curtsy

inchio'dare [inkjo'dare] vt to nail (down); **~ la macchina** (AUT) to jam on the brakes

inchi'ostro [in'kjɔstro] sm ink; **~ simpatico** invisible ink

inciam'pare [intʃam'pare] vi to trip, stumble

inci'ampo [in'tʃampo] sm obstacle; **essere d'~ a qn** (fig) to be in sb's way

inci'dente [intʃi'dɛnte] sm accident; **~ d'auto** car accident

inci'denza [intʃi'dɛntsa] sf incidence; **avere una forte ~ su qc** to affect sth greatly

in'cidere [in'tʃidere] vi: **~ su** to bear upon, affect ♦ vt (tagliare incavando) to cut into; (ARTE) to engrave; to etch; (canzone) to record

in'cinta [in'tʃinta] ag f pregnant

incipri'are [intʃi'prjare] vt to powder

in'circa [in'tʃirka] av: **all'~** more or less, very nearly

incisi'one [intʃi'zjone] sf cut; (disegno) engraving; etching; (registrazione) recording; (MED) incision

in'ciso, a [in'tʃizo] pp di **incidere** ♦ sm: **per ~** incidentally, by the way

inci'tare [intʃi'tare] vt to incite

inci'vile [intʃi'vile] ag uncivilized; (villano) impolite

incl. abbr (= incluso) encl.

incli'nare vt to tilt; **~rsi** vr (barca) to list; (aereo) to bank; **incli'nato, a** ag sloping; **inclinazi'one** sf slope; (fig) inclination, tendency; **in'cline** ag: **incline a** inclined to

in'cludere vt to include; (accludere) to enclose; **in'cluso, a** pp di **includere** ♦ ag included; enclosed

incoe'rente ag incoherent; (contraddittorio) inconsistent

in'cognita [in'kɔɲɲita] sf (MAT, fig) unknown quantity

in'cognito, a [in'kɔɲɲito] ag unknown ♦ sm: **in ~** incognito

incol'lare vt to glue, gum; (unire con colla) to stick together

incolon'nare vt to draw up in columns

inco'lore ag colourless

incol'pare vt: **~ qn di** to charge sb with

in'colto, a ag (terreno) uncultivated; (trascurato: capelli) neglected; (persona) uneducated

in'colume ag safe and sound, unhurt

incom'benza [inkom'bɛntsa] sf duty, task

in'combere vi (sovrastare minacciando): **~ su** to threaten, hang over

incominci'are [inkomin'tʃare] vi, vt to begin, start

in'comodo sm inconvenience

incompe'tente ag incompetent

incompi'uto, a ag unfinished, incomplete

incom'pleto, a ag incomplete

incompren'sibile ag incomprehensible

incom'preso, a ag not understood; misunderstood

inconce'pibile [inkontʃe'pibile] ag inconceivable

inconcili'abile [inkontʃi'ljabile] ag irreconcilable

inconclu'dente ag inconclusive; (persona) ineffectual

incondizio'nato, a [inkondittsjo'nato] ag unconditional

inconfu'tabile ag irrefutable

incongru'ente ag inconsistent

inconsa'pevole ag: **~ di** unaware of, ignorant of

in'conscio, a, sci, sce [in'kɔnʃo] ag unconscious ♦ sm (PSIC): **l'~** the unconscious

inconsis'tente ag insubstantial; unfounded

inconsu'eto, a *ag* unusual

incon'sulto, a *ag* rash

incon'trare *vt* to meet; *(difficoltà)* to meet with; **~rsi** *vr* to meet

incontras'tabile *ag* incontrovertible, indisputable

in'contro *av:* **~ a** *(verso)* towards ♦ *sm* meeting; *(SPORT)* match; meeting; **~ di calcio** football match

inconveni'ente *sm* drawback, snag

incoraggia'mento [inkoraddʒa'mento] *sm* encouragement

incoraggi'are [inkorad'dʒare] *vt* to encourage

incornici'are [inkorni'tʃare] *vt* to frame

incoro'nare *vt* to crown; **incoronazi'one** *sf* coronation

incorpo'rare *vt* to incorporate; *(fig: annettere)* to annex

in'correre *vi:* **~ in** to meet with, run into

incosci'ente [inkoʃ'ʃɛnte] *ag* *(inconscio)* unconscious; *(irresponsabile)* reckless, thoughtless; **incosci'enza** *sf* unconsciousness; recklessness, thoughtlessness

incre'dibile *ag* incredible, unbelievable

in'credulo, a *ag* incredulous, disbelieving

incremen'tare *vt* to increase; *(dar sviluppo a)* to promote

incre'mento *sm* *(sviluppo)* development; *(aumento numerico)* increase, growth

incresci'oso, a [inkreʃ'ʃoso] *ag* *(incidente etc)* regrettable

incres'parsi *vr* *(acqua)* to ripple; *(capelli)* to go frizzy; *(pelle, tessuto)* to wrinkle

incrimi'nare *vt* (DIR) to charge

incri'nare *vt* to crack; *(fig: rapporti, amicizia)* to cause to deteriorate; **~rsi** *vr* to crack; to deteriorate; **incrina'tura** *sf* crack; *(fig)* rift

incroci'are [inkro'tʃare] *vt* to cross;

(incontrare) to meet ♦ *vi* (NAUT, AER) to cruise; **~rsi** *vr* *(strade)* to cross, intersect; *(persone, veicoli)* to pass each other; **~ le braccia/le gambe** to fold one's arms/cross one's legs;

incrocia'tore *sm* cruiser

in'crocio [in'krotʃo] *sm* *(anche FERR)* crossing; *(di strade)* crossroads

incros'tare *vt* to encrust

incuba'trice [inkuba'tritʃe] *sf* incubator

'incubo *sm* nightmare

in'cudine *sf* anvil

incu'rante *ag:* **~ (di)** heedless (of), careless (of)

incurio'sire *vt* to make curious; **~rsi** *vr* to become curious

incursi'one *sf* raid

incur'vare *vt* to bend, curve; **~rsi** *vr* to bend, curve

in'cusso, a *pp di* **incutere**

incus'todito, a *ag* unguarded, unattended

in'cutere *vt:* **~ timore/rispetto a qn** to strike fear into sb/command sb's respect

'indaco *sm* indigo

indaffa'rato, a *ag* busy

inda'gare *vt* to investigate

in'dagine [in'dadʒine] *sf* investigation, inquiry; *(ricerca)* research, study

indebi'tarsi *vr* to run o get into debt

in'debito, a *ag* undue; undeserved

indebo'lire *vt, vi* *(anche: ~rsi)* to weaken

inde'cente [inde'tʃɛnte] *ag* indecent; **inde'cenza** *sf* indecency

inde'ciso, a [inde'tʃizo] *ag* indecisive; *(irresoluto)* undecided

inde'fesso, a *ag* untiring, indefatigable

indefi'nito, a *ag* *(anche LING)* indefinite; *(impreciso, non determinato)* undefined

in'degno, a [in'deɲɲo] *ag* *(atto)* shameful; *(persona)* unworthy

indelica'tezza [indelika'tettsa] *sf*

tactlessness

indemoni'ato, a *ag* possessed (by the devil)

in'denne *ag* unhurt, uninjured;
indennità *sf inv* (*rimborso: di spese*) allowance; (*: di perdita*) compensation, indemnity; **indennità di contingenza** cost-of-living allowance; **indennità di trasferta** travel expenses *pl*

indenniz'zare [indennid'dzare] *vt* to compensate; **inden'nizzo** *sm* (*somma*) compensation, indemnity

indero'gabile *ag* binding

'India *sf*: **l'~** India; **indi'ano, a** *ag* Indian ♦ *sm/f* (*d'India*) Indian; (*d'America*) Native American, (American) Indian

indiavo'lato, a *ag* possessed (by the devil); (*vivace, violento*) wild

indi'care *vt* (*mostrare*) to show, indicate; (*: col dito*) to point to, point out; (*consigliare*) to suggest, recommend; **indica'tivo, a** *ag* indicative ♦ *sm* (*LING*) indicative (mood); **indica'tore** *sm* (*elenco*) guide; directory; (*TECN*) gauge; indicator; **indicatore di velocità** (*AUT*) speedometer; **indicatore della benzina** fuel gauge; **indicazi'one** *sf* indication; (*informazione*) piece of information

'indice ['inditʃe] *sm* index; (*fig*) sign; (*dito*) index finger, forefinger; **~ di gradimento** (*RADIO, TV*) popularity rating

indi'cibile [indi'tʃibile] *ag* inexpressible

indietreggi'are [indietred'dzare] *vi* to draw back, retreat

indi'etro *av* back; (*guardare*) behind, back; (*andare, cadere: anche: all'~*) backwards; **rimanere ~** to be left behind; **essere ~** (*col lavoro*) to be behind; (*orologio*) to be slow; **rimandare qc ~** to send sth back

indi'feso, a *ag* (*città etc*) undefended; (*persona*) defenceless

indiffe'rente *ag* indifferent;
indiffe'renza *sf* indifference

in'digeno, a [in'didʒeno] *ag* indigenous, native ♦ *sm/f* native

indi'gente [indi'dʒɛnte] *ag* poverty-stricken, destitute; **indi'genza** *sf* extreme poverty

indigesti'one [indidʒes'tjone] *sf* indigestion

indi'gesto, a [indi'dʒesto] *ag* indigestible

indi'gnare [indin'ɲare] *vt* to fill with indignation; **~rsi** *vr* to get indignant

indimenti'cabile *ag* unforgettable

indipen'dente *ag* independent;
indipen'denza *sf* independence

in'dire *vt* (*concorso*) to announce; (*elezioni*) to call

indi'retto, a *ag* indirect

indiriz'zare [indirit'tsare] *vt* (*dirigere*) to direct; (*mandare*) to send; (*lettera*) to address

indi'rizzo [indi'rittso] *sm* address; (*direzione*) direction; (*avvio*) trend, course

indis'creto, a *ag* indiscreet

indis'cusso, a *ag* unquestioned

indispen'sabile *ag* indispensable, essential

indispet'tire *vt* to irritate, annoy ♦ *vi* (*anche: ~rsi*) to get irritated *o* annoyed

in'divia *sf* endive

individu'ale *ag* individual;
individualità *sf* individuality

individu'are *vt* (*dar forma distinta a*) to characterize; (*determinare*) to locate; (*riconoscere*) to single out

indi'viduo *sm* individual

indizi'ato, a *ag* suspected ♦ *sm/f* suspect

in'dizio [in'dittsjo] *sm* (*segno*) sign, indication; (*POLIZIA*) clue; (*DIR*) piece of evidence

'indole *sf* nature, character

indolen'zito, a [indolen'tsito] *ag* stiff, aching; (*intorpidito*) numb

indo'lore *ag* painless

indo'mani sm: l'~ the next day, the following day

Indo'nesia sf: l'~ Indonesia

indos'sare vt (mettere indosso) to put on; (avere indosso) to have on; **indossa'tore, 'trice** sm/f model

in'dotto, a pp di **indurre**

indottri'nare vt to indoctrinate

indovi'nare vt (scoprire) to guess; (immaginare) to imagine, guess; (il futuro) to foretell; **indovi'nato, a** ag successful; (scelta) inspired; **indovi'nello, a** sm riddle; **indo'vino, a** sm/f fortuneteller

indubbia'mente av undoubtedly

in'dubbio, a ag certain, undoubted

indugi'are [indu'dʒare] vi to take one's time, delay

in'dugio [in'dudʒo] sm (ritardo) delay; **senza ~** without delay

indul'gente [indul'dʒente] ag indulgent; (giudice) lenient; **indul'genza** sf indulgence; leniency

in'dulgere [in'duldʒere] vi: **~ a** (accondiscendere) to comply with; (abbandonarsi) to indulge in; **in'dulto, a** pp di **indulgere** ♦ sm (DIR) pardon

indu'mento sm article of clothing, garment; **~i** smpl (vestiti) clothes

indu'rire vt to harden ♦ vi (anche: ~rsi) to harden, become hard

in'durre vt: **~ qn a fare qc** to induce o persuade sb to do sth; **~ qn in errore** to mislead sb

in'dustria sf industry; **industri'ale** ag industrial ♦ sm industrialist

industri'arsi vr to do one's best, try hard

industri'oso, a ag industrious, hard-working

induzi'one [indut'tsjone] sf induction

inebe'tito, a ag dazed, stunned

inebri'are vt (anche fig) to intoxicate; **~rsi** vr to become intoxicated

inecce'pibile [inettʃe'pibile] ag unexceptionable

i'nedia sf starvation

i'nedito, a ag unpublished

ineffi'cace [ineffi'katʃe] ag ineffective

ineffici'ente [ineffi'tʃɛnte] ag inefficient

inegu'ale ag unequal; (irregolare) uneven

ine'rente ag: **~ a** concerning, regarding

i'nerme ag unarmed; defenceless

inerpi'carsi vr: **~ (su)** to clamber (up)

i'nerte ag inert, (inattivo) indolent, sluggish; **i'nerzia** sf inertia; indolence, sluggishness

ine'satto, a ag (impreciso) inexact; (erroneo) incorrect; (AMM: non riscosso) uncollected

inesis'tente ag non-existent

inesperi'enza [inespe'rjentsa] sf inexperience

ines'perto, a ag inexperienced

i'netto, a ag (incapace) inept; (che non ha attitudine): **~ (a)** unsuited (to)

ine'vaso, a ag (ordine, corrispondenza) outstanding

inevi'tabile ag inevitable

i'nezia [i'nettsja] sf trifle, thing of no importance

infagot'tare vt to bundle up, wrap up; **~rsi** vr to wrap up

infal'libile ag infallible

infa'mante ag defamatory

in'fame ag infamous; (fig: cosa, compito) awful, dreadful

infan'gare vt to cover with mud; (fig: reputazione) to sully

infan'tile ag child cpd; childlike; (adulto, azione) childish; **letteratura ~** children's books pl

in'fanzia [in'fantsja] sf childhood; (bambini) children pl; **prima ~** babyhood, infancy

infari'nare vt to cover with (o sprinkle with o dip in) flour; **infarina'tura** sf (fig) smattering

in'farto sm (MED) heart attack

infasti'dire vt to annoy, irritate; **~rsi** vr to get annoyed o irritated

infati'cabile ag tireless, untiring

in'fatti cong as a matter of fact, in fact, actually

infatu'arsi vr: ~ **di** to become infatuated with, fall for; **infatuazi'one** sf infatuation

in'fausto, a ag unpropitious, unfavourable

infe'condo, a ag infertile

infe'dele ag unfaithful; **infedeltà** sf infidelity

infe'lice [infe'litʃe] ag unhappy; (sfortunato) unlucky, unfortunate; (inopportuno) inopportune, ill-timed; (mal riuscito: lavoro) bad, poor; **infelicità** sf unhappiness

inferi'ore ag lower; (per intelligenza, qualità) inferior ♦ sm/f inferior; ~ **a** (numero, quantità) less o smaller than; (meno buono) inferior to; ~ **alla media** below average; **inferiorità** sf inferiority

inferme'ria sf infirmary; (di scuola, nave) sick bay

infermi'ere, a sm/f nurse

infermità sf inv illness; infirmity

in'fermo, a ag (ammalato) ill; (debole) infirm

infer'nale ag infernal; (proposito, complotto) diabolical

in'ferno sm hell

inferri'ata sf grating

infervo'rarsi vr to get excited, get carried away

infes'tare vt to infest

infet'tare vt to infect; **~rsi** vr to become infected; **infet'tivo, a** ag infectious; **in'fetto, a** ag infected; (acque) polluted, contaminated; **infezi'one** sf infection

infiac'chire [infjak'kire] vt to weaken ♦ vi (anche: **~rsi**) to grow weak

infiam'mabile ag inflammable

infiam'mare vt to set alight; (fig, MED) to inflame; **~rsi** vr to catch fire; (MED) to become inflamed; **infiammazi'one** sf (MED) inflammation

in'fido, a ag unreliable, treacherous

infie'rire vi: ~ **su** (fisicamente) to attack furiously; (verbalmente) to rage at

in'figgere [in'fiddʒere] vt: ~ **qc in** to thrust o drive sth into

infi'lare vt (ago) to thread; (mettere: chiave) to insert; (: anello, vestito) to slip o put on; (strada) to turn into, take; **~rsi** vr: ~ **in** to slip into; (indossare) to slip on; ~ **l'uscio** to slip in; to slip out

infil'trarsi vr to penetrate, seep through; (MIL) to infiltrate; **infiltrazi'one** sf infiltration

infil'zare [infil'tsare] vt (infilare) to string together; (trafiggere) to pierce

in'fimo, a ag lowest

in'fine av finally; (insomma) in short

infinità sf infinity; (in quantità): **un'~ di** an infinite number of

infi'nito, a ag infinite; (LING) infinitive ♦ sm infinity; (LING) infinitive; **all'~** (senza fine) endlessly

infinocchi'are [infinok'kjare] (fam) vt to hoodwink

infischi'arsi [infis'kjarsi] vr: ~ **di** not to care about

in'fisso, a pp di **infiggere** ♦ sm fixture; (di porta, finestra) frame

infit'tire vt, vi (anche: **~rsi**) to thicken

inflazi'one [inflat'tsjone] sf inflation

in'fliggere [in'fliddʒere] vt to inflict; **in'flitto, a** pp di **infliggere**

influ'ente ag influential; **influ'enza** sf influence; (MED) influenza, flu

influ'ire vi: ~ **su** to influence

in'flusso sm influence

infol'tire vt, vi to thicken

infon'dato, a ag unfounded, groundless

in'fondere vt: ~ **qc in qn** to instill sth in sb

infor'care vt to fork (up); (bicicletta, cavallo) to get on; (occhiali) to put on

infor'mare vt to inform, tell; **~rsi** vr: **~rsi (di o su)** to inquire (about)

infor'matica sf computer science

informa'tivo, a ag informative

informa'tore *sm* informer

informazi'one *sf* piece of information; **prendere ~i sul conto di qn** to get information about sb; **chiedere un'~** to ask for (some) information

in'forme *ag* shapeless

informico'larsi *vr* = **informicolirsi**

informico'lirsi *vr* to have pins and needles

infor'tunio *sm* accident; **~ sul lavoro** industrial accident, accident at work

infos'sarsi *vr* (*terreno*) to sink; (*guance*) to become hollow; **infos'sato, a** *ag* hollow; (*occhi*) deep-set; (: *per malattia*) sunken

in'frangere [in'frandʒere] *vt* to smash; (*fig: legge, patti*) to break; **~rsi** *vr* to smash, break; **infran'gibile** *ag* unbreakable; **in'franto, a** *pp di* **infrangere** ♦ *ag* broken

infrazi'one [infrat'tsjone] *sf*: **~ a** breaking of, violation of

infredda'tura *sf* slight cold

infred'dolito, a *ag* cold, chilled

infruttu'oso, a *ag* fruitless

infu'ori *av* out; **all'~ outwards; all'~ di** (*eccetto*) except, with the exception of

infuri'are *vi* to rage; **~rsi** *vr* to fly into a rage

infusi'one *sf* infusion

in'fuso, a *pp di* **infondere** ♦ *sm* infusion

Ing. *abbr* = **ingegnere**

ingabbi'are *vt* to cage

ingaggi'are [ingad'dʒare] *vt* (*assumere con compenso*) to take on, hire; (*SPORT*) to sign on; (*MIL*) to engage; **in'gaggio** *sm* hiring; signing on

ingan'nare *vt* to deceive; (*fisco*) to cheat; (*eludere*) to dodge, elude; (*fig: tempo*) to while away ♦ *vi* (*apparenza*) to be deceptive; **~rsi** *vr* to be mistaken, be wrong; **ingan'nevole** *ag* deceptive

in'ganno *sm* deceit, deception; (*azione*) trick; (*menzogna, frode*) cheat,

swindle; (*illusione*) illusion

ingarbugli'are [ingarbuʎ'ʎare] *vt* to tangle; (*fig*) to confuse, muddle; **~rsi** *vr* to become confused o muddled

inge'gnarsi [indʒe'ɲarsi] *vr* to do one's best, try hard; **~ per vivere** to live by one's wits

inge'gnere [indʒe'ɲere] *sm* engineer; **~ civile/navale** civil/naval engineer; **ingegne'ria** *sf* engineering; **~ genetica** genetic engineering

in'gegno [in'dʒeɲo] *sm* (*intelligenza*) intelligence, brains *pl*; (*capacità creativa*) ingenuity; (*disposizione*) talent; **inge'gnoso, a** *ag* ingenious, clever

ingelo'sire [indʒelo'zire] *vt* to make jealous ♦ *vi* (*anche: ~rsi*) to become jealous

in'gente [in'dʒɛnte] *ag* huge, enormous

ingenuità [indʒenui'ta] *sf* ingenuousness

in'genuo, a [in'dʒɛnuo] *ag* ingenuous, naïve

inge'rire [indʒe'rire] *vt* to ingest

inges'sare [indʒes'sare] *vt* (*MED*) to put in plaster; **ingessa'tura** *sf* plaster

Inghil'terra [ingil'terra] *sf*: **l'~** England

inghiot'tire [ingjot'tire] *vt* to swallow

ingial'lire [indʒal'lire] *vi* to go yellow

ingigan'tire [indʒigan'tire] *vt* to enlarge, magnify ♦ *vi* to become gigantic o enormous

inginocchi'arsi [indʒinok'kjarsi] *vr* to kneel (down)

ingiù [in'dʒu] *av* down, downwards

ingiunzi'one [indʒun'tsjone] *sf* injunction

ingi'uria [in'dʒurja] *sf* insult; (*fig: danno*) damage; **ingiuri'are** *vt* to insult, abuse; **ingiuri'oso, a** *ag* insulting, abusive

ingius'tizia [indʒus'tittsja] *sf* injustice

ingi'usto, a [in'dʒusto] *ag* unjust, unfair

in'glese *ag* English ♦ *sm/f* Englishman/woman ♦ *sm* (*LING*)

English; **gli l~i** the English; **andarsene** *o* **filare all'~** to take French leave

ingoi'are *vt* to gulp (down); (*fig*) to swallow (up)

ingol'fare *vt* (*motore*) to flood; **~rsi** *vr* to flood

ingom'brante *ag* cumbersome

ingom'brare *vt* (*strada*) to block; (*stanza*) to clutter up; **in'gombro, a** *ag* (*strada, passaggio*) blocked ♦ *sm* obstacle; **essere d'ingombro** to be in the way

in'gordo, a *ag*: **~ di** greedy for; (*fig*) greedy *o* avid for

in'gorgo, ghi *sm* blockage, obstruction; (*anche*: **~ stradale**) traffic jam

ingoz'zare [ingot'tsare] *vt* (*animali*) to fatten; (*fig: persona*) to stuff; **~rsi** *vr*: **~rsi (di)** to stuff o.s. (with)

ingra'naggio [ingra'naddʒo] *sm* (*TECN*) gear; (*di orologio*) mechanism; **gli ~i della burocrazia** the bureaucratic machinery

ingra'nare *vi* to mesh, engage ♦ *vt* to engage; **~ la marcia** to get into gear

ingrandi'mento *sm* enlargement, extension

ingran'dire *vt* (*anche FOT*) to enlarge; (*estendere*) to extend; (*OTTICA, fig*) to magnify ♦ *vi* (*anche: ~rsi*) to become larger *o* bigger; (*aumentare*) to grow, increase; (*espandersi*) to expand

ingras'sare *vt* to make fat; (*animali*) to fatten; (*lubrificare*) to oil, lubricate ♦ *vi* (*anche: ~rsi*) to get fat, put on weight

in'grato, a *ag* ungrateful; (*lavoro*) thankless, unrewarding

ingredi'ente *sm* ingredient

in'gresso *sm* (*porta*) entrance; (*atrio*) hall; (*l'entrare*) entrance, entry; (*facoltà di entrare*) admission; **"~ libero"** "admission free"

ingros'sare *vt* to increase; (*folla, livello*) to swell ♦ *vi* (*anche: ~rsi*) to increase; to swell

in'grosso *av*: **all'~** (*COMM*) wholesale;

(*all'incirca*) roughly, about

ingua'ribile *ag* incurable

'inguine *sm* (*ANAT*) groin

ini'bire *vt* to forbid, prohibit; (*PSIC*) to inhibit; **inibizi'one** *sf* prohibition; inhibition

iniet'tare *vt* to inject; **~rsi** *vr*: **~rsi di sangue** (*occhi*) to become bloodshot; **iniezi'one** *sf* injection

inimi'carsi *vr*: **~ con qn** to fall out with sb

ininter'rotto, a *ag* unbroken; uninterrupted

iniquità *sf inv* iniquity; (*atto*) wicked action

inizi'ale [init'tsjale] *ag, sf* initial

inizi'are [init'tsjare] *vi, vt* to begin, start; **~ qn a** to initiate sb into; (*pittura etc*) to introduce sb to; **~ a fare qc** to start doing sth

inizia'tiva [inittsja'tiva] *sf* initiative; **~ privata** private enterprise

i'nizio [i'nittsjo] *sm* beginning; **all'~** at the beginning, at the start; **dare ~ a qc** to start sth, get sth going

innaffi'are *etc* = **annaffiare**

innal'zare [innal'tsare] *vt* (*sollevare, alzare*) to raise; (*rizzare*) to erect; **~rsi** *vr* to rise

innamo'rarsi *vr*: **~ (di qn)** to fall in love (with sb); **innamo'rato, a** *ag* (*che nutre amore*): **innamorato (di)** in love (with); (*appassionato*): **innamorato di** very fond of ♦ *sm/f* lover; sweetheart

in'nanzi [in'nantsi] *av* (*stato in luogo*) in front, ahead; (*moto a luogo*) forward, on; (*tempo: prima*) before ♦ *prep* (*prima*) before; **~ a** in front of; **innanzi'tutto** *av* first of all

in'nato, a *ag* innate

innatu'rale *ag* unnatural

inne'gabile *ag* undeniable

innervo'sire *vt*: **~ qn** to get on sb's nerves; **~rsi** *vr* to get irritated *o* upset

innes'care *vt* to prime

innes'tare *vt* (*BOT, MED*) to graft; (*TECN*)

to engage; (*inserire: presa*) to insert; **in'nesto** *sm* graft; grafting *no pl*; (*TECN*) clutch; (*ELETTR*) connection

'**inno** *sm* hymn; **~ nazionale** national anthem

inno'cente [inno'tʃɛnte] *ag* innocent; inno'cenza *sf* innocence

in'nocuo, a *ag* innocuous, harmless

innova'tivo, a *ag* innovative

innume'revole *ag* innumerable

ino'doro, a *ag* odourless

inol'trare *vt* (*AMM*) to pass on, forward; **~rsi** *vr* (*addentrarsi*) to advance, go forward

i'noltre *av* besides, moreover

inon'dare *vt* to flood; inondazi'one *sf* flooding *no pl*; flood

inope'roso, a *ag* inactive, idle

inoppor'tuno, a *ag* untimely, ill-timed; (*inappropriate*); (*momento*) inopportune

inorgo'glire [inorgoʎ'ʎire] *vt* to make proud ♦ *vi* (*anche: ~rsi*) to become proud; **~rsi di qc** to pride o.s. on sth

inorri'dire *vt* to horrify ♦ *vi* to be horrified

inospi'tale *ag* inhospitable

inosser'vato, a *ag* (*non notato*) unobserved; (*non rispettato*) not observed, not kept

inossi'dabile *ag* stainless

inqua'drare *vt* (*foto, immagine*) to frame; (*fig*) to situate, set

inquie'tare *vt* (*turbare*) to disturb, worry; **~rsi** *vr* to worry, become anxious; (*impazientirsi*) to get upset

inqui'eto, a *ag* restless; (*preoccupato*) worried, anxious; **inquie'tudine** *sf* anxiety, worry

inqui'lino, a *sm/f* tenant

inquina'mento *sm* pollution

inqui'nare *vt* to pollute

inqui'sire *vt, vi* to investigate; inquisi'tore, 'trice *ag* (*sguardo*) inquiring; inquisizi'one *sf* (*STORIA*) inquisition

insab'biare *vt* (*fig: pratica*) to shelve;

~rsi *vr* (*arenarsi: barca*) to run aground; (*fig: pratica*) to be shelved

insac'cati *smpl* (*CUC*) sausages

insa'lata *sf* salad; **~ mista** mixed salad; insalati'era *sf* salad bowl

insa'lubre *ag* unhealthy

insa'nabile *ag* (*piaga*) which cannot be healed; (*situazione*) irremediable; (*odio*) implacable

insangui'nare *vt* to stain with blood

insa'puta *sf*: **all'~ di qn** without sb knowing

insce'nare [inʃe'nare] *vt* (*TEATRO*) to stage, put on; (*fig*) to stage

insedi'are *vt* to install; **~rsi** *vr* to take up office; (*popolo, colonia*) to settle

in'segna [in'seɲɲa] *sf* sign; (*emblema*) sign, emblem; (*bandiera*) flag, banner; **~e** *sfpl* (*decorazioni*) insignia *pl*

insegna'mento [inseɲɲa'mento] *sm* teaching

inse'gnante [inseɲ'ɲante] *ag* teaching ♦ *sm/f* teacher

inse'gnare [inseɲ'ɲare] *vt, vi* to teach; **~ a qn qc** to teach sb sth; **~ a qn a fare qc** to teach sb (how) to do sth

insegui'mento *sm* pursuit, chase

insegu'ire *vt* to pursue, chase

inselvati'chire [inselvati'kire] *vi* (*anche: ~rsi*) to grow wild

insena'tura *sf* inlet, creek

insen'sato, a *ag* senseless, stupid

insen'sibile *ag* (*nervo*) insensible; (*persona*) indifferent

inse'rire *vt* to insert; (*ELETTR*) to connect; (*allegare*) to enclose; (*annuncio*) to put in, place; **~rsi** *vr* (*fig*): **~rsi in** to become part of; in'serto *sm* (*pubblicazione*) insert

inservi'ente *sm/f* attendant

inserzi'one [inser'tsjone] *sf* insertion; (*avviso*) advertisement; **fare un'~ sul giornale** to put an advertisement in the paper

insetti'cida, i [insetti'tʃida] *sm* insecticide

in'setto *sm* insect

insi'curo, a *ag* insecure

in'sidia *sf* snare, trap; (*pericolo*) hidden danger; **insidie** *vt*: ~ **la vita di qn** to make an attempt on sb's life

insi'eme *av* together ♦ *prep*: ~ **a o con** together with ♦ *sm* whole; (*MAT, servizio, assortimento*) set; (*MODA*) ensemble, outfit; **tutti** ~ all together; **tutto** ~ all together; (*in una volta*) at one go; **nell'~** on the whole; **d'~** (*veduta etc*) overall

in'segne [in'seɲɲe] *ag* (*persona*) famous, distinguished; (*città, monumento*) notable

insignifi'cante [insiɲɲifi'kante] *ag* insignificant

insi'gnire [insiɲ'ɲire] *vt*: ~ **qn di** to honour o decorate sb with

insin'cero, a [insin'tʃero] *ag* insincere

insinda'cabile *ag* unquestionable

insinu'are *vt* (*introdurre*): ~ **qc in** to slip o slide sth into; (*fig*) to insinuate, imply; **~rsi** *vr*: **~rsi in** to seep into; (*fig*) to creep into; to worm one's way into

in'sipido, a *ag* insipid

insis'tente *ag* insistent; persistent

in'sistere *vi*: ~ **su qc** to insist on sth; ~ **in qc/a fare** (*perseverare*) to persist in sth/in doing; **insis'tito, a** *pp di* **insistere**

insoddis'fatto, a *ag* dissatisfied

insoffe'rente *ag* intolerant

insolazi'one [insolat'tsjone] *sf* (*MED*) sunstroke

inso'lente *ag* insolent; **insolen'tire** *vi* to grow insolent ♦ *vt* to insult, be rude to

in'solito, a *ag* unusual, out of the ordinary

inso'luto, a *ag* (*non risolto*) unsolved

in'somma *av* (*in conclusione*) in short; (*dunque*) well ♦ *escl* for heaven's sake!

in'sonne *ag* sleepless; **in'sonnia** *sf* insomnia, sleeplessness

inson'no'lito, a *ag* sleepy, drowsy

insoppor'tabile *ag* unbearable

in'sorgere [in'sordʒere] *vi* (*ribellarsi*) to rise up, rebel; (*apparire*) to come up, arise

in'sorto, a *pp di* **insorgere** ♦ *sm/f* rebel, insurgent

insospet'tire *vt* to make suspicious ♦ *vi* (*anche*: **~rsi**) to become suspicious

inspi'rare *vt* to breathe in, inhale

in'stabile *ag* (*carico, indole*) unstable; (*tempo*) unsettled; (*equilibrio*) unsteady

instal'lare *vt* to install; **~rsi** *vr* (*sistemarsi*): **~rsi in** to settle in; **installazi'one** *sf* installation

instan'cabile *ag* untiring, indefatigable

instau'rare *vt* to introduce, institute

instra'dare *vt*: ~ (*verso*) to direct (towards)

insuc'cesso [insut'tʃesso] *sm* failure, flop

insudici'are [insudi'tʃare] *vt* to dirty; **~rsi** *vr* to get dirty

insuffici'ente [insuffi'tʃente] *ag* insufficient; (*compito, allievo*) inadequate; **insuffici'enza** *sf* insufficiency; inadequacy; (*INS*) fail

insu'lare *ag* insular

insu'lina *sf* insulin

in'sulso, a *ag* (*sciocco*) inane, silly; (*persona*) dull, insipid

insul'tare *vt* to insult, affront

in'sulto *sm* insult, affront

insussis'tente *ag* non-existent

intac'care *vt* (*fare tacche*) to cut into; (*corrodere*) to corrode; (*fig: cominciare a usare: risparmi*) to break into; (: *ledere*) to damage

intagli'are [intaʎ'ʎare] *vt* to carve; **in'taglio** *sm* carving

intan'gibile [intan'dʒibile] *ag* untouchable; inviolable

in'tanto *av* (*nel frattempo*) meanwhile, in the meantime; (*per cominciare*) just to begin with; ~ **che** while

in'tarsio *sm* inlaying *no pl*, marquetry *no pl*; inlay

inta'sare *vt* to choke (up), block (up);

(AUT) to obstruct, block; **~rsi** *vr* to become choked o blocked

intas'care *vt* to pocket

in'tatto, a *ag* intact; *(puro)* unsullied

intavo'lare *vt* to start, enter into

inte'grale *ag* complete; *(pane, farina)* wholemeal *(BRIT)*, whole-wheat *(US)*; *(MAT)*: **calcolo ~** integral calculus

inte'grante *ag*: **parte ~** integral part

inte'grare *vt* to complete; *(MAT)* to integrate; **~rsi** *vr (persona)* to become integrated

integrità *sf* integrity

'integro, a *ag (intatto, intero)* complete, whole; *(retto)* upright

intelaia'tura *sf* frame; *(fig)* structure, framework

intel'letto *sm* intellect; **intellettu'ale** *ag, sm/f* intellectual

intelli'gente [intelli'dʒɛnte] *ag* intelligent; **intelli'genza** *sf* intelligence

intem'perie *sfpl* bad weather *sg*

intempes'tivo, a *ag* untimely

inten'dente *sm*: **~ di Finanza** inland *(BRIT)* o internal *(US)* revenue officer; **inten'denza** *sf*: **intendenza di Finanza** inland *(BRIT)* o internal *(US)* revenue office

in'tendere *vt (avere intenzione)*: **~ fare qc** to intend o mean to do sth; *(comprendere)* to understand; *(udire)* to hear; *(significare)* to mean; **~rsi** *vr (conoscere)*: **~rsi di** to know a lot about, be a connoisseur of; *(accordarsi)* to get on (well); **intendersela con qn** *(avere una relazione amorosa)* to have an affair with sb; **intendi'mento** *sm (intelligenza)* understanding; *(proposito)* intention; **intendi'tore, 'trice** *sm/f* connoisseur, expert

intene'rire *vt (fig)* to move (to pity); **~rsi** *vr (fig)* to be moved

inten'sivo, a *ag* intensive

in'tenso, a *ag* intense

in'tento, a *ag (teso, assorto)*: **~ (a)** intent (on), absorbed (in) ♦ *sm* aim, purpose

intenzio'nale [intentsjo'nale] *ag* intentional

intenzi'one [inten'tsjone] *sf* intention; *(DIR)* intent; **avere ~ di fare qc** to intend to do sth, have the intention of doing sth

interat'tivo, a *ag* interactive

interca'lare *sm* pet phrase, stock phrase ♦ *vt* to insert

interca'pedine *sf* gap, cavity

intercet'tare [intertʃet'tare] *vt* to intercept

intercity [intasi'ti] *sm inv (FERR)* ≈ intercity (train)

inter'detto, a *pp di* **interdire** ♦ *ag* forbidden, prohibited; *(sconcertato)* dumbfounded ♦ *sm (REL)* interdict

inter'dire *vt* to forbid, prohibit, ban; *(REL)* to interdict; *(DIR)* to deprive of civil rights; **interdizi'one** *sf* prohibition, ban

interessa'mento *sm* interest

interes'sante *ag* interesting; **essere in stato ~** to be expecting (a baby)

interes'sare *vt* to interest; *(concernere)* to concern, be of interest to; *(far intervenire)*: **~ qn a** to draw sb's attention to ♦ *vi*: **~ a** to interest, matter to; *(mostrare interesse)*: **~rsi a** to take an interest in, be interested in; *(occuparsi)*: **~rsi di** to take care of

inte'resse *sm (anche COMM)* interest

inter'faccia, ce [inter'fattʃa] *sf (INFORM)* interface

interfe'renza [interfe'rentsa] *sf* interference

interfe'rire *vi* to interfere

interiezi'one [interjet'tsjone] *sf* exclamation, interjection

interi'ora *sfpl* entrails

interi'ore *ag* interior, inner, inside, internal; *(fig)* inner

inter'ludio *sm (MUS)* interlude

inter'medio, a *ag* intermediate

inter'mezzo [inter'mɛddzo] *sm (intervallo)* interval; *(breve spettacolo)* intermezzo

inter'nare vt (arrestare) to intern; (MED) to commit (to a mental institution)

'Internet ['internet] sf Internet; **in ~** on the Internet

internazio'nale [internattsjo'nale] ag international

in'terno, a ag (di dentro) internal, interior, inner; (: mare) inland; (nazionale) domestic; (allievo) boarding ♦ sm inside, interior; (di paese) interior; (fodera) lining; (di appartamento) flat (number); (TEL) extension ♦ sm/f (INS) boarder; **~i** smpl (CINEMA) interior shots; **all'~** inside; **Ministero degli I~i** Ministry of the Interior, ≈ Home Office (BRIT), Department of the Interior (US)

in'tero, a ag (integro, intatto) whole, entire; (completo, totale) complete; (numero) whole; (non ridotto: biglietto) full; (latte) full-cream

interpel'lare vt to consult

inter'porre vt (ostacolo): **~ qc a qc** to put sth in the way of sth; (influenza) to use; **interporsi** vr to intervene; **interporsi fra** (mettersi in mezzo) to come between; **inter'posto, a** pp di **interporre**

interpre'tare vt to interpret; **in'terprete** sm/f interpreter; (TEATRO) actor/actress, performer; (MUS) performer

interregio'nale [interredʒo'nale] sm long distance train (stopping frequently)

interro'gare vt to question; (INS) to test; **interroga'tivo, a** ag (occhi, sguardo) questioning, inquiring; (LING) interrogative ♦ sm (fig) mystery; **interroga'torio, a** ag interrogatory, questioning ♦ sm (DIR) questioning no pl; **interrogazi'one** sf questioning no pl; (INS) oral test

inter'rompere vt (studi, trattative) to break off, interrupt; **~rsi** vr to break off, stop; **inter'rotto, a** pp di **interrompere**

interrut'tore sm switch

interruzi'one [interrut'tsjone] sf interruption; break

interse'care vt to intersect; **~rsi** vr to intersect

inter'stizio [inter'stittsjo] sm interstice, crack

interur'bana sf trunk o long-distance call

interur'bano, a ag inter-city; (TEL: chiamata) trunk cpd, long-distance; (: telefono) long-distance

inter'vallo sm interval; (spazio) space, gap

interve'nire vi (partecipare): **~ a** to take part in; (intromettersi: anche POL) to intervene; (MED: operare) to operate; **inter'vento** sm participation; (intromissione) intervention; (MED) operation; **fare un intervento nel corso di** (dibattito, programma) to take part in

inter'vista sf interview; **intervis'tare** vt to interview

in'tesa sf understanding; (accordo) agreement, understanding

in'teso, a pp di **intendere** ♦ ag agreed; **siamo ~i?** OK?

intes'tare vt (lettera) to address; (proprietà): **~ a** to register in the name of; **~ un assegno a qn** to make out a cheque to sb; **intestazi'one** sf heading; (su carta da lettere) letterhead

intes'tino sm (ANAT) intestine

inti'mare vt to order, command

intimidazi'one [intimidat'tsjone] sf intimidation

intimi'dire vt to intimidate ♦ vi (anche: **~rsi**) to grow shy

intimità sf intimacy; privacy; (familiarità) familiarity

'intimo, a ag intimate; (affetti, vita) private; (fig: profondo) inmost ♦ sm (persona) intimate o close friend; (dell'animo) bottom, depths pl; **parti ~e** (ANAT) private parts

intimo'rire vt to frighten; **~rsi** vr to become frightened

in'tingolo sm sauce; (pietanza) stew

intiriz'zire [intirid'dzire] vt to numb
♦ vi (anche: ~rsi) to go numb

intito'lare vt to give a title to; (dedicare) to dedicate

intolle'rabile ag intolerable

intolle'rante ag intolerant

in'tonaco, ci o **chi** sm plaster

into'nare vt (canto) to start to sing; (armonizzare) to match; **~rsi** vr (colori) to go together; **~rsi a** (carnagione) to suit; (abito) to go with, match

inton'tire vt to stun, daze ♦ vi (anche: ~rsi) to be stunned o dazed

in'toppo sm stumbling block, obstacle

in'torno av around; **~ a** (attorno a) around; (riguardo, circa) about

intorpi'dire vt to numb; (fig) to make sluggish ♦ vi (anche: ~rsi) to grow numb; (fig) to become sluggish

intossi'care vt to poison; **intossicazi'one** sf poisoning

intralci'are [intral'tʃare] vt to hamper, hold up

'intranet ['intranet] sf intranet

intransi'tivo, a ag, sm intransitive

intrapren'dente ag enterprising, go-ahead

intra'prendere vt to undertake

intrat'tabile ag intractable

intrat'tenere vt to entertain; to engage in conversation; **~rsi** vr to linger; **~rsi su qc** to dwell on sth

intrave'dere vt to catch a glimpse of; (fig) to foresee

intrecci'are [intret'tʃare] vt (capelli) to plait, braid; (intessere: anche fig) to weave, interweave, intertwine; **~rsi** vr to intertwine, become interwoven; **~ le mani** to clasp one's hands; **in'treccio** sm (fig: trama) plot, story

intri'gare vi to manoeuvre (BRIT), maneuver (US); **in'trigo, ghi** sm plot, intrigue

in'trinseco, a, ci, che ag intrinsic

in'triso, a ag: **~ (di)** soaked with

intro'durre vt to introduce; (chiave

etc): **~ qc in** to insert sth into; (persone: far entrare) to show in; **introdursi** vr (moda, tecniche) to be introduced; **introdursi in** (persona: penetrare) to enter; (: entrare furtivamente) to steal o slip into; **introduzi'one** sf introduction

in'troito sm income, revenue

intro'mettersi vr to interfere, meddle; (interporsi) to intervene

in'truglio [in'truʎʎo] sm concoction

in'truso, a sm/f intruder

intu'ire vt to perceive by intuition; (rendersi conto) to realize; **in'tuito** sm intuition; (perspicacia) perspicacity; **intuizi'one** sf intuition

inu'mano, a ag inhuman

inumi'dire vt to dampen, moisten; **~rsi** vr to become damp o wet

i'nutile ag useless; (superfluo) pointless, unnecessary; **inutilità** sf uselessness; pointlessness

inutil'mente av unnecessarily; (senza risultato) in vain

inva'dente ag (fig) interfering, nosey

in'vadere vt to invade; (affollare) to swarm into, overrun; (sog: acque) to flood

inva'ghirsi [inva'girsi] vr: **~ di** to take a fancy to

invalidità sf infirmity; disability; (DIR) invalidity

in'valido, a ag (infermo) infirm, invalid; (al lavoro) disabled; (DIR: nullo) invalid ♦ sm/f invalid; disabled person

in'vano av in vain

invasi'one sf invasion

in'vaso, a pp di **invadere**

inva'sore, invadi'trice [invadi'tritʃe] ag invading ♦ sm invader

invecchi'are [invek'kjare] vi (persona) to grow old; (vino, popolazione) to age; (moda) to become dated ♦ vt to age; (far apparire più vecchio) to make look older

in'vece [in'vetʃe] av instead; (al contrario) on the contrary; **~ di** instead of

inve'ire vi: ~ **contro** to rail against

inven'tare vt to invent; (pericoli, pettegolezzi) to make up, invent

inven'tario sm inventory; (COMM) stocktaking no pl

inven'tivo, a ag inventive ♦ sf inventiveness

inven'tore sm inventor

invenzi'one [inven'tsjone] sf invention; (bugia) lie, story

inver'nale ag winter cpd; (simile all'inverno) wintry

in'verno sm winter

invero'simile ag unlikely

inversi'one sf inversion; reversal; "divieto d'~" "no U-turns"

in'verso, a ag opposite; (MAT) inverse ♦ sm contrary, opposite; **in senso** ~ in the opposite direction; **in ordine** ~ in reverse order

inver'tire vt to invert, reverse; ~ **la marcia** (AUT) to do a U-turn; **inver'tito, a** sm/f homosexual

investi'gare vt, vi to investigate; **investiga'tore, trice** sm/f investigator, detective; **investigazi'one** sf investigation, inquiry

investi'mento sm (ECON) investment

inves'tire vt (denaro) to invest; (sog: veicolo: pedone) to knock down; (: altro veicolo) to crash into; (apostrofare) to assail; (incaricare): ~ **qn di** to invest sb with

invi'are vt to send; **invi'ato, a** sm/f envoy; (STAMPA) correspondent

in'vidia sf envy; **invidi'are** vt: **invidiare qn** (**per qc**) to envy sb for sth; **invidiare qc a qn** to envy sb sth; **invidi'oso, a** ag envious

in'vio, 'vii sm sending; (insieme di merci) consignment

invipe'rito, a ag furious

invischi'are [invis'kjare] vt (fig): ~ **qn in** to involve sb in; ~**rsi** vr: ~**rsi (con qn/in qc)** to get mixed up o involved (with sb/in sth)

invi'sibile ag invisible

invi'tare vt to invite; ~ **qn a fare** to invite sb to do; **invi'tato, a** sm/f guest; **in'vito** sm invitation

invo'care vt (chiedere: aiuto, pace) to cry out for; (appellarsi: la legge, Dio) to appeal to, invoke

invogli'are [invoʎ'ʎare] vt: ~ **qn a fare** to tempt sb to do, induce sb to do

involon'tario, a ag (errore) unintentional; (gesto) involuntary

invol'tino sm (CUC) roulade

in'volto sm (pacco) parcel; (fagotto) bundle

invo'lucro sm cover, wrapping

involuzi'one [involut'tsjone] sf (di stile) convolutedness; (regresso): **subire un'~** to regress

inzacche'rare [intsakke'rare] vt to spatter with mud

inzup'pare [intsup'pare] vt to soak; ~**rsi** vr to get soaked

'io pron I ♦ sm inv: **l'~** the ego, the self; ~ **stesso(a)** I myself

i'odio sm iodine

l'onio sm: **lo ~, il mar** ~ the Ionian (Sea)

iperme'rcato sm hypermarket

ipertensi'one sf high blood pressure, hypertension

iper'testo sm hypertext

ip'nosi sf hypnosis; **ipno'tismo** sm hypnotism; **ipnotiz'zare** vt to hypnotize

ipocri'sia sf hypocrisy

i'pocrita, i, e ag hypocritical ♦ sm/f hypocrite

ipo'teca, che sf mortgage; **ipote'care** vt to mortgage

i'potesi sf inv hypothesis; **ipo'tetico, a, ci, che** ag hypothetical

ip'potesi sf horseracing

'ippico, a, ci, che ag horse cpd

ippocas'tano sm horse chestnut

ip'podromo sm racecourse

ippo'potamo sm hippopotamus

'ira *sf* anger, wrath

'ran *sm*: **l'~** Iran

l'raq *sm*: **l'~** Iraq

'iride *sf* (*arcobaleno*) rainbow; (*ANAT, BOT*) iris

lr'landa *sf*: **l'~** Ireland; **l'~ del Nord** Northern Ireland, Ulster; **la Repubblica d'~** Eire, the Republic of Ireland; **irlan'dese** *ag* Irish ♦ *sm/f* Irishman/woman; **gli Irlandesi** the Irish

iro'nia *sf* irony; **i'ronico, a, ci, che** *ag* ironic(al)

irradi'are *vt* to radiate; (*sog: raggi di luce: illuminare*) to shine on ♦ *vi* (*diffondersi: anche: ~si*) to radiate

irragio'nevole [irrad͡ʒo'nevole] *ag* irrational; unreasonable

irrazio'nale [irrattsjo'nale] *ag* irrational

irre'ale *ag* unreal

irrecupe'rabile *ag* irretrievable; (*fig: persona*) irredeemable

irrecu'sabile *ag* (*offerta*) not to be refused; (*prova*) irrefutable

irrego'lare *ag* irregular; (*terreno*) uneven

irremo'vibile *ag* (*fig*) unshakeable, unyielding

irrepa'rabile *ag* irreparable; (*fig*) inevitable

irrepe'ribile *ag* nowhere to be found

irrequi'eto, a *ag* restless

irresis'tibile *ag* irresistible

irrespon'sabile *ag* irresponsible

irridu'cibile [irridu'tʃibile] *ag* irreducible; (*fig*) indomitable

irri'gare *vt* (*annaffiare*) to irrigate; (*sog: fiume etc*) to flow through;

irrigazi'one *sf* irrigation

irrigi'dire [irrid͡ʒi'dire] *vt* to stiffen; **~si** *vr* to stiffen

irri'sorio, a *ag* derisory

irri'tare *vt* (*mettere di malumore*) to irritate, annoy; (*MED*) to inflame; **~si** *vr* (*stizzirsi*) to become irritated o annoyed; (*MED*) to become irritated;

irritazi'one *sf* irritation; annoyance

ir'rompere *vi*: **~ in** to burst into

irro'rare *vt* to sprinkle; (*AGR*) to spray

irru'ente *ag* (*fig*) impetuous, violent

irruzi'one [irrut'tsjone] *sf*: **fare ~ in** to burst into; (*sog: polizia*) to raid

'irto, a *ag* bristly; **~ di** bristling with

is'critto, a *pp di* **iscrivere** ♦ *sm/f* member; **per o in ~** in writing

is'crivere *vt* to register, enter; (*persona*): **~ (a)** to register (in), enrol (in); **~si** *vr*: **~si (a)** (*club, partito*) to join; (*università*) to register o enrol (at); (*esame, concorso*) to register o enter (for); **iscrizi'one** *sf* (*epigrafe etc*) inscription; (*a scuola, società*) enrolment, registration; (*registrazione*) registration

ls'lam *sm*: **l'~** Islam

ls'landa *sf*: **l'~** Iceland

'isola *sf* island; **~ pedonale** (*AUT*) pedestrian precinct

isola'mento *sm* isolation; (*TECN*) insulation

iso'lante *ag* insulating ♦ *sm* insulator

iso'lare *vt* to isolate; (*TECN*) to insulate; (: *acusticamente*) to soundproof; **iso'lato, a** *ag* isolated; insulated ♦ *sm* (*gruppo di edifici*) block

ispetto'rato *sm* inspectorate

ispet'tore *sm* inspector

ispezio'nare [ispettsjo'nare] *vt* to inspect; **ispezi'one** *sf* inspection

'ispido, a *ag* bristly, shaggy

ispi'rare *vt* to inspire; **~si** *vr*: **~si a** to draw one's inspiration from

lsra'ele *sm*: **l'~** Israel; **israeli'ano, a** *ag, sm/f* Israeli

is'sare *vt* to hoist

istan'taneo, a *ag* instantaneous ♦ *sf* (*FOT*) snapshot

is'tante *sm* instant, moment; **all'~, sull'~** instantly, immediately

is'tanza [is'tantsa] *sf* petition, request

is'terico, a, ci, che *ag* hysterical

iste'rismo *sm* hysteria

isti'gare *vt* to incite; **istigazi'one** *sf*

incitement; **istigazione a delinquere**
(DIR) incitement to crime

is'tinto sm instinct

istitu'ire vt (fondare) to institute,
found; (porre: confronto) to establish;
(intraprendere: inchiesta) to set up

isti'tuto sm institute; (di università)
department; (ente, DIR) institution; ~ **di
bellezza** beauty salon

istituzi'one [istitut'tsjone] sf
institution

'istmo sm (GEO) isthmus

'istrice ['istritfe] sm porcupine

istri'one (peg) sm ham actor

istru'ire vt (insegnare) to teach;
(ammaestrare) to train; (informare) to
instruct, inform; (DIR) to prepare;
istrut'tore, 'trice sm/f instructor
♦ ag: **giudice istruttore** vedi **giudice**;
istrut'toria sf (DIR) (preliminary)
investigation and hearing; **istruzi'one**
sf education; training; (direttiva)
instruction

l'talia sf: **l'~** Italy

itali'ano, a ag Italian ♦ sm/f Italian
♦ sm (LING) Italian; **gli l~i** the Italians

itine'rario sm itinerary

itte'rizia [itte'rittsja] sf (MED) jaundice

'ittico, a, ci, che ag fish cpd; fishing
cpd

lugos'lavia etc = **Jugoslavia** etc

i'uta sf jute

I.V.A. ['iva] sigla f (= imposta sul valore
aggiunto) VAT

J, j

jazz [dʒaz] sm jazz

jeans [dʒinz] smpl jeans

Jugos'lavia [jugoz'lavja] sf: **la ~**
Yugoslavia; **la ex-~** former Yugoslavia;
jugos'lavo, a ag, sm/f Yugoslav(ian)

'juta ['juta] sf = **iuta**

K, k

K abbr (INFORM) K

k abbr (= kilo) k

karatè sm karate

Kg abbr (= chilogrammo) kg

'killer sm inv gunman, hired gun

'kiwi ['kiwi] sm inv kiwi fruit

km abbr (= chilometro) km

'krapfen sm inv (CUC) doughnut

L, l

l' vedi **la**; **lo**; **il**

la¹ (dav V **l'**) det f the ♦ pron (oggetto:
persona) her; (: cosa) it; (: forma di
cortesia) you; vedi anche **il**

la² sm inv (MUS) A; (: solfeggiando) la

là av there; **di ~** (da quel luogo) from
there; (in quel luogo) in there; (dall'altra
parte) over there; **di ~ di** beyond; **per
di ~** that way; **più in ~** further on;
(tempo) later on; **fatti in ~** move up;
~ dentro/sopra/sotto in (o on)
there/up (o on) there/under there; vedi anche **quello**

'labbro (pl(f): **labbra**: solo nel senso
ANAT) sm lip

labi'rinto sm labyrinth, maze

labora'torio (di ricerca) laboratory;
(di arti, mestieri) workshop;
~ linguistico language laboratory

labori'oso, a ag (faticoso) laborious;
(attivo) hard-working

labu'rista, i, e ag Labour (BRIT) cpd
♦ sm/f Labour Party member (BRIT)

'lacca, che sf lacquer

'laccio ['lattʃo] sm noose; (legaccio,
tirante) lasso; (di scarpa) lace;
~ emostatico tourniquet

lace'rare [latʃe'rare] vt to tear to
shreds, lacerate; **~rsi** vr to tear;
'lacero, a ag (logoro) torn, tattered;
(MED) lacerated

'lacrima sf tear; **in ~e** in tears;

lacri'mare vi to water; **lacri'mogeno, a** ag: **gas lacrimogeno** tear gas

la'cuna sf (fig) gap

'ladro sm thief; **ladro'cinio** sm theft, larceny

laggiù [lad'dʒu] av down there; (di là) over there

la'gnarsi [laɲ'ɲarsi] vr: ~ (di) to complain (about)

'lago, ghi sm lake

la'guna sf lagoon

'laico, a, ci, che ag (apostolato) lay; (vita) secular; (scuola) non-denominational ♦ sm/f layman/woman

'lama sm inv (ZOOL) llama; (REL) lama ♦ sf blade

lam'bire vt to lick; to lap

lamen'tare vt to lament; **~rsi** vr (emettere lamenti) to moan, groan; (rammaricarsi): **~rsi (di)** to complain (about); **lamen'tela** sf complaining no pl; **lamen'tevole** ag (voce) complaining, plaintive; (destino) pitiful; **la'mento** sm moan, groan; wail; **lamen'toso, a** ag plaintive

la'metta sf razor blade

lami'era sf sheet metal

'lamina sf (lastra sottile) thin sheet (o layer o plate); ~ **d'oro** gold leaf; gold foil; **lami'nare** vt to laminate; (tessuto) **lami'nato, a** ag laminated; lamé ♦ sm laminate

'lampada sf lamp; ~ **a gas** gas lamp; ~ **da tavolo** table lamp

lampa'dario sm chandelier

lampa'dina sf light bulb; ~ **tascabile** pocket torch (BRIT) o flashlight (US)

lam'pante ag (fig: evidente) crystal clear, evident

lampeggi'are [lamped'dʒare] vi (luce, fari) to flash ♦ vb impers: **lampeggia** there's lightning; **lampeggia'tore** sm (AUT) indicator

lampi'one sm street light o lamp (BRIT)

'lampo sm (METEOR) flash of lightning; (di luce, fig) flash; **~i** smpl lightning no

pl ♦ ag inv: **cerniera ~** zip (fastener) (BRIT), zipper (US); **guerra ~** blitzkrieg

lam'pone sm raspberry

'lana sf wool; ~ **d'acciaio** steel wool; **pura ~ vergine** pure new wool; ~ **di vetro** glass wool

lan'cetta [lan'tʃetta] sf (indice) pointer, needle; (di orologio) hand

'lancia ['lantʃa] sf (arma) lance; (: picca) spear; (di pompa antincendio) nozzle; (imbarcazione) launch

lanciafi'amme [lantʃa'fjamme] sm inv flamethrower

lanci'are [lan'tʃare] vt to throw, hurl, fling; (SPORT) to throw; (far partire: automobile) to get up to full speed; (bombe) to drop; (razzo, prodotto, moda) to launch; **~rsi** vr: **~rsi contro/su** to throw o hurl o fling o.s. against/on; **~rsi in** (fig) to embark on

lanci'nante [lantʃi'nante] ag (dolore) shooting, throbbing; (grido) piercing

'lancio ['lantʃo] sm throwing no pl; throw; dropping no pl; drop; launching no pl; launch; ~ **del peso** putting the shot

'landa sf (GEO) moor

'languido, a ag (fiacco) languid, weak; (tenero, malinconico) languishing

langu'ore sm weakness, languor

lani'ficio [lani'fitʃo] sm woollen mill

la'noso, a ag woolly

lan'terna sf lantern; (faro) lighthouse

la'nugine [la'nudʒine] sf down

lapi'dario, a ag (fig) terse

'lapide sf (di sepolcro) tombstone; (commemorativa) plaque

'lapis sm inv pencil

Lap'ponia sf Lapland

'lapsus sm inv slip

laptop ['læptɔp] sm inv laptop (computer)

'lardo sm bacon fat, lard

lar'ghezza [lar'gettsa] sf width; breadth; looseness; generosity; ~ **di vedute** broad-mindedness

'largo, a, ghi, ghe ag wide; broad;

(maniche) wide; *(abito: troppo ampio)*
loose; *(fig)* generous ♦ *sm* width;
breadth; *(mare aperto)*: **il ~** the open
sea ♦ *sf*: **stare** o **tenersi alla ~ (da
qn/qc)** to keep one's distance (from
sb/sth), keep away (from sb/sth);
~ due metri two metres wide; **~ di
spalle** broad-shouldered; **di ~ghe
vedute** broad-minded; **su ~a scala**
on a large scale; **di manica ~a**
generous, open-handed; **al ~ di
Genova** off (the coast of) Genoa;
farsi ~ tra la folla to push one's way
through the crowd

larice ['laritʃe] *sm (BOT)* larch

larin'gite [larin'dʒite] *sf* laryngitis

larva *sf* larva; *(fig)* shadow

la'sagne [la'zaɲɲe] *sfpl* lasagna *sg*

lasci'are [laʃʃare] *vt* to leave;
(abbandonare) to leave, abandon, give
up; *(cessare di tenere)* to let go of ♦ *vb
aus*: **~ qn** to let sb do; **~ andare**
o **correre** o **perdere** to let things go
their own way; **~ stare qc/qn** to leave
sth/sb alone; **~rsi** *vr (persone)* to part;
(coppia) to split up; **~rsi andare** to let
o.s. go

lascito ['laʃʃito] *sm (DIR)* legacy

laser ['lazer] *ag, sm inv*: **(raggio) ~**
laser (beam)

lassa'tivo, a *ag, sm* laxative

lasso *sm*: **~ di tempo** interval, lapse
of time

lassù *av* up there

lastra *sf (di pietra)* slab; *(di metallo,
FOT)* plate; *(di ghiaccio, vetro)* sheet;
(radiografica) X-ray (plate)

lastri'cato *sm* paving

late'rale *ag* lateral, side *cpd*; *(uscita,
ingresso ecc)* side *cpd* ♦ *sm (CALCIO)*
half-back

late'rizio [late'rittsjo] *sm* (perforated)
brick

lati'fondo *sm* large estate

la'tino, a *ag, sm* Latin; **~-ameri'cano,
a** *ag* Latin-American

lati'tante *sm/f* fugitive (from justice)

lati'tudine *sf* latitude

'lato, a *ag (fig)* wide, broad ♦ *sm* side;
(fig) aspect, point of view; **in senso ~**
broadly speaking

la'trare *vi* to bark

la'trina *sf* public lavatory

'latta *sf* tin (plate); *(recipiente)* tin, can

lat'taio, a *sm/f* milkman/woman;
dairyman/woman

lat'tante *ag* unweaned

'latte *sm* milk; **~ detergente** cleansing
milk o lotion; **~ in polvere** dried o
powdered milk; **~ scremato** skimmed
milk; **latte'ria** *sf* dairy; **latti'cini** *smpl*
dairy products

lat'tina *sf (di birra etc)* can

lat'tuga, ghe *sf* lettuce

'laurea *sf* degree; **laure'arsi** *vr* to
graduate; **laure'ato, a** *ag, sm/f*
graduate

'lauro *sm* laurel

'lauto, a *ag (pranzo, mancia)* lavish

lava *sf* lava

la'vabo *sm* washbasin

la'vaggio [la'vaddʒo] *sm* washing *no
pl*; **~ del cervello** brainwashing *no pl*

la'vagna [la'vaɲɲa] *sf (GEO)* slate; *(di
scuola)* blackboard

la'vanda *sf (anche MED)* wash; *(BOT)*
lavender; **lavan'daia** *sf* washerwoman;
lavande'ria *sf* laundry; **lavanderia
automatica** launderette; **lavan'dino** *sm*
sink

lavapi'atti *sm/f* dishwasher

la'vare *vt* to wash; **~rsi** *vr* to wash,
have a wash; **~ a secco** to dry-clean;
~rsi le mani/i denti to wash one's
hands/clean one's teeth

lava'secco *sm* o *f inv* drycleaner's

lavasto'viglie [lavasto'viʎʎe] *sm* o *f
inv (macchina)* dishwasher

lava'trice [lava'tritʃe] *sf* washing
machine

lava'tura *sf* washing *no pl*; **~ di piatti**
dishwater

lavo'rante *sm/f* worker

lavo'rare vi to work; (fig: bar, studio etc) to do good business ♦ vt to work; **~rsi qn** (persuaderlo) to work on sb; **~ a** to work on; **~ a maglia** to knit; **lavora'tivo, a** ag working; **lavora'tore, 'trice** sm/f worker ♦ ag working; **lavorazi'one** sf (gen) working; (di legno, pietra) carving; (di film) making; (di prodotto) manufacture; (modo di esecuzione) workmanship; **lavo'rio** sm intense activity

la'voro sm work; (occupazione) job, work no pl; (opera) piece of work, job; (ECON) labour; **~i pubblici** public works

le det fpl the ♦ pron (oggetto) them; (: a lei, a essa) to her; (: forma di cortesia) (to) you; vedi anche **il**

le'ale ag loyal; (sincero) sincere; (onesto) fair; **lealtà** sf loyalty; sincerity; fairness

'lebbra sf leprosy

'lecca 'lecca sm inv lollipop

leccapi'edi (peg) sm/f inv toady, bootlicker

lec'care vt to lick; (sog: gatto: latte etc) to lick o lap up; (fig) to flatter; **~rsi i baffi** to lick one's lips

'leccio ['lɛttʃo] sm holm oak, ilex

leccor'nia sf titbit, delicacy

'lecito, a ['lɛtʃito] ag permitted, allowed

'ledere vt to damage, injure

'lega, ghe sf league; (di metalli) alloy

le'gaccio [le'gattʃo] sm string, lace

le'gale ag legal ♦ sm lawyer; **legaliz'zare** vt to authenticate; (regolarizzare) to legalize

le'game sm (corda, fig: affettivo) tie, bond; (nesso logico) link, connection

le'gare vt (prigioniero, capelli, cane) to tie (up); (libro) to bind; (CHIM) to alloy; (fig: collegare) to bind, join ♦ vi (far lega) to unite; (fig) to get on well

le'gato sm (REL) legate; (DIR) legacy, bequest

lega'tura sf (di libro) binding; (MUS) ligature

le'genda [le'dʒɛnda] sf (di carta geografica etc) = **leggenda**

legge ['lɛddʒe] sf law

leg'genda [led'dʒɛnda] sf (narrazione) legend; (di carta geografica etc) key, legend

'leggere ['lɛddʒere] vt, vi to read

legge'rezza [leddʒe'rettsa] sf lightness; thoughtlessness; fickleness

leg'gero, a [led'dʒɛro] ag light; (agile, snello) nimble, agile, light; (tè, caffè) weak; (fig: non grave, piccolo) slight; (: spensierato) thoughtless; (: incostante) fickle; free and easy; **alla ~a** thoughtlessly

leggi'adro, a [led'dʒadro] ag pretty, lovely; (movimenti) graceful

leg'gio, 'gii [led'dʒio] sm lectern; (MUS) music stand

legisla'tura [ledʒizla'tura] sf legislature

legislazi'one [ledʒizlat'tsjone] sf legislation

le'gittimo, a [le'dʒittimo] ag legitimate; (fig: giustificato, lecito) justified, legitimate; **~a difesa** (DIR) self-defence

'legna ['leɲɲa] sf firewood; **le'gname** sm wood, timber

'legno ['leɲɲo] sm wood; (pezzo di ~) piece of wood; **di ~** wooden; **~ compensato** plywood; **le'gnoso, a** ag wooden; woody; (carne) tough

le'gumi smpl (BOT) pulses

'lei pron (soggetto) she; (oggetto: per dare rilievo, con preposizione) her; (forma di cortesia: anche: L~) you ♦ sm: **dare del ~ a qn** to address sb as "lei"; **~ stessa** she herself; you yourself

'lembo sm (di abito, strada) edge; (striscia sottile: di terra) strip

'lemma, i sm headword

'lemme 'lemme av (very) very slowly

'lena sf (fig) energy, stamina

le'nire vt to soothe

lenta'mente av slowly

lente sf (OTTICA) lens sg;
~ **d'ingrandimento** magnifying glass;
~**i a contatto** o **corneali** contact lenses

len'tezza [len'tettsa] sf slowness

len'ticchia [len'tikkja] sf (BOT) lentil

len'tiggine [len'tiddʒine] sf freckle

lento, a ag slow; (molle: fune) slack; (non stretto: vite, abito) loose ♦ sm (ballo) slow dance

lenza ['lentsa] sf fishing-line

lenzu'olo [len'tswɔlo] sm sheet; ~**a** sfpl pair of sheets

le'one sm lion; (dello zodiaco): **L~** Leo

lepo'rino, a ag: **labbro ~** harelip

lepre sf hare

'lercio, a, ci, cie ['lɛrtʃo] ag filthy

'lesbica, che sf lesbian

lesi'nare vt to be stingy with ♦ vi: ~ **(su)** to skimp (on), be stingy (with)

lesi'one sf (MED) lesion; (DIR) injury, damage; (EDIL) crack

'leso, a pp di **ledere** ♦ ag (offeso) injured; **parte ~a** (DIR) injured party

les'sare vt (CUC) to boil

'lessico, ci sm vocabulary; lexicon

'lesso, a ag boiled ♦ sm boiled meat

'lesto, a ag quick; (agile) nimble; ~ **di mano** (per rubare) light-fingered; (per picchiare) free with one's fists

le'tale ag lethal; fatal

leta'maio sm dunghill

le'tame sm manure, dung

le'targo, ghi sm lethargy; (ZOOL) hibernation

le'tizia [le'tittsja] sf joy, happiness

'lettera sf letter; ~**e** sfpl (letteratura) literature sg; (studi umanistici) arts (subjects); **alla ~** literally; **in ~e** in words, in full; **lette'rale** ag literal

lette'rario, a ag literary

lette'rato, a ag well-read, scholarly

lettera'tura sf literature

let'tiga, ghe sf (barella) stretcher

let'tino sm cot (BRIT), crib (US)

'letto, a pp di **leggere** ♦ sm bed; **andare a ~** to go to bed; ~ **a castello** bunk beds pl; ~ **a una piazza/a due piazze** o **matrimoniale** single/double bed

let'tore, 'trice sm/f reader; (INS) (foreign language) assistant (BRIT), (foreign) teaching assistant (US) ♦ sm (TECN): ~ **ottico** optical character reader

let'tura sf reading

leuce'mia [leutʃe'mia] sf leukaemia

'leva sf lever; (MIL) conscription; **far ~ su qn** to work on sb; ~ **del cambio** (AUT) gear lever

le'vante sm east; (vento) East wind; **il L~** the Levant

le'vare vt (occhi, braccio) to raise; (sollevare, togliere: tassa, divieto) to lift; (indumenti) to take off, remove; (rimuovere) to take away; (: dal di sopra) to take off; (: dal di dentro) to take out; ~**rsi** vr to get up; (sole) to rise; **le'vata** sf (di posta) collection

leva'toio, a ag: **ponte ~** drawbridge

leva'tura sf intelligence, mental capacity

levi'gare vt to smooth; (con carta vetrata) to sand

levri'ere sm greyhound

lezi'one [let'tsjone] sf lesson; (UNIV) lecture; **fare ~** to teach; to lecture; **dare una ~ a qn** to teach sb a lesson

lezi'oso, a [let'tsjoso] ag affected; simpering

'lezzo ['leddzo] sm stench, stink

li pron pl (oggetto) them

lì av there; **di** o **da ~** from there; **per di ~** that way; **di ~ a pochi giorni** a few days later; ~ **per ~** there and then; **di** ~ **a poco** in a while, shortly afterwards; **essere ~ (~) per fare** to be on the point of doing, to be about to do; ~ **dentro** in there; ~ **sotto** under there; ~ **sopra** on there; up there; vedi **anche quello**

liba'nese ag, sm/f Lebanese inv

Li'bano sm: **il ~** the Lebanon

'libbra sf (peso) pound
li'beccio [li'bettʃo] sm south-west wind
li'bello sm libel
li'bellula sf dragonfly
libe'rale ag, sm/f liberal
liberaliz'zare [liberalid'dzare] vt to liberalize
libe'rare vt (rendere libero: prigioniero) to release; (: popolo) to free, liberate; (sgombrare: passaggio) to clear; (: stanza) to vacate; (produrre: energia) to release; **~rsi** vr: **~rsi di qc/qn** to get rid of sth/sb; **libera'tore, 'trice** ag liberating ♦ sm/f liberator; **liberazi'one** sf liberation, freeing; release; rescuing

---
Liberazione

The **Liberazione** is a national holiday which falls on 25 April. It commemorates the liberation of Italy at the end of the Second World War.

'libero, a ag free; (strada) clear; (non occupato: posto etc) vacant; not taken; empty; not engaged; **~ di fare qc** free to do sth; **~ da** free from; **~ arbitrio** free will; **~ professionista** self-employed professional person; **~ scambio** free trade; **libertà** sf inv freedom; (tempo disponibile) free time ♦ sfpl (licenza) liberties; **in libertà provvisoria/vigilata** released without bail/on probation
'Libia sf: **la ~** Libya; **'libico, a, ci, che** ag, sm/f Libyan
li'bidine sf lust
li'braio sm bookseller
li'brarsi vr to hover
libre'ria sf (bottega) bookshop; (stanza) library; (mobile) bookcase
li'bretto sm booklet; (taccuino) notebook; (MUS) libretto; **~ degli assegni** cheque book; **~ di circolazione** (AUT) logbook; **~ di risparmio** (savings) bank-book, passbook; **~ universitario** student's

report book
'libro sm book; **~ di cassa** cash book; **~ mastro** ledger; **~ paga** payroll; **~ di testo** textbook
li'cenza [li'tʃentsa] sf (permesso) permission, leave; (di pesca, caccia, circolazione) permit, licence; (MIL) leave; (INS) school leaving certificate; (libertà) liberty; licence; licentiousness; **andare in ~** (MIL) to go on leave
licenzia'mento [litʃentsja'mento] sm dismissal
licenzi'are [litʃentsja're] vt (impiegato) to dismiss; (COMM: per eccesso di personale) to make redundant; (INS) to award a certificate to; **~rsi** vr (impiegato) to resign, hand in one's notice; (INS) to obtain one's school-leaving certificate
li'ceo [li'tʃeo] sm (INS) secondary (BRIT) o high (US) school (for 14- to 19-year-olds)
'lido sm beach, shore
li'eto, a ag happy, glad; **"molto ~"** (nelle presentazioni) "pleased to meet you"
li'eve ag light; (di poco conto) slight; (sommesso: voce) faint, soft
lievi'tare vi (anche fig) to rise ♦ vt to leaven
li'evito sm yeast; **~ di birra** brewer's yeast
'ligio, a, gi, gie ['lidʒo] ag faithful, loyal
'lilla sm inv lilac
'lillà sm inv lilac
'lima sf file
limac'cioso, a [limat'tʃoso] ag slimy; muddy
li'mare vt to file (down); (fig) to polish
'limbo sm (REL) limbo
li'metta sf nail file
limi'tare vt to limit, restrict; (circoscrivere) to bound, surround; **limita'tivo, a** ag limiting, restricting; **limi'tato, a** ag limited, restricted
'limite sm limit; (confine) border,

boundary; **~ di velocità** speed limit

li'mitrofo, a *ag* neighbouring

limo'nata *sf* lemonade (*BRIT*), (lemon) soda (*US*); (lemon) squash (*BRIT*), lemonade (*US*)

li'mone *sm* (*pianta*) lemon tree; (*frutto*) lemon

'limpido, a *ag* clear; (*acqua*) limpid, clear

'lince ['lintʃe] *sf* lynx

linci'are *vt* to lynch

'lindo, a *ag* tidy, spick and span; (*biancheria*) clean

'linea *sf* line; (*di mezzi pubblici di trasporto: itinerario*) route; (*: servizio*) service; **a grandi ~e** in outline; **mantenere la ~** to look after one's figure; **aereo di ~** airliner; **nave di ~** liner; **volo di ~** scheduled flight; **~ aerea** airline; **~ di partenza/d'arrivo** (*SPORT*) starting/finishing line; **~ di tiro** line of fire

linea'menti *smpl* features; (*fig*) outlines

line'are *ag* linear; (*fig*) coherent, logical

line'etta *sf* (*trattino*) dash; (*d'unione*) hyphen

lin'gotto *sm* ingot, bar

'lingua *sf* (*ANAT*, *CUC*) tongue; (*idioma*) language; **mostrare la ~** to stick out one's tongue; **di ~ italiana** Italian-speaking; **~ madre** mother tongue; **una ~ di terra** a spit of land

lingu'aggio [lin'gwaddʒo] *sm* language

lingu'etta *sf* (*di strumento*) reed; (*di scarpa*, *TECN*) tongue; (*di busta*) flap

lingu'istica *sf* linguistics *sg*

'lino *sm* (*pianta*) flax; (*tessuto*) linen

li'noleum *sm inv* linoleum, lino

liposuzi'one [liposut'tsjone] *sf* liposuction

lique'fare *vt* (*render liquido*) to liquefy; (*fondere*) to melt; **~rsi** *vr* to liquefy; to melt

liqui'dare *vt* (*società*, *persona*: *uccidere*) to liquidate; (*persona*: *sbarazzarsene*) to get rid of; (*conto*,

problema) to settle; (*COMM*: *merce*) to sell off, clear; **liquidazi'one** *sf* liquidation; settlement; clearance sale

liquidità *sf* liquidity

'liquido, a *ag*, *sm* liquid; **~ per freni** brake fluid

liqui'rizia [likwi'rittsja] *sf* liquorice

li'quore *sm* liqueur

'lira *sf* (*unità monetaria*) lira; (*MUS*) lyre; **~ sterlina** pound sterling

'lirica, che *sf* (*poesia*) lyric poetry; (*componimento poetico*) lyric; (*MUS*) opera

'lirico, a, ci, che *ag* lyric(al); (*MUS*) lyric; **cantante/teatro ~** opera singer/house

'lisca, sche *sf* (*di pesce*) fishbone

lisci'are [liʃ'ʃare] *vt* to smooth; (*fig*) to flatter

'liscio, a, sci, sce *ag* smooth; (*capelli*) straight; (*mobile*) plain; (*bevanda alcolica*) neat; (*fig*) straightforward, simple **♦** *av*: **andare ~** to go smoothly; **passarla ~a** to get away with it

'liso, a *ag* worn out, threadbare

'lista *sf* (*elenco*) list; **~ elettorale** electoral roll; **~ delle vivande** menu; **~ delle spese** shopping list

lis'tino *sm* list; **~ dei cambi** (foreign) exchange rate; **~ dei prezzi** price list

Lit. *abbr* = **lire italiane**

'lite *sf* quarrel, argument; (*DIR*) lawsuit

liti'gare *vi* to quarrel; (*DIR*) to litigate

li'tigio [li'tidʒo] *sm* quarrel; **litigi'oso, a** *ag* quarrelsome; (*DIR*) litigious

litogra'fia *sf* (*sistema*) lithography; (*stampa*) lithograph

lito'rale *ag* coastal, coast *cpd* **♦** *sm* coast

'litro *sm* litre

livel'lare *vt* to level, make level; **~rsi** *vr* to become level; (*fig*) to level out, balance out

li'vello *sm* level; (*fig*) level, standard; **ad alto ~** (*fig*) high-level; **~ del mare** sea level

'livido, a *ag* livid; (*per percosse*) bruised, black and blue; (*cielo*) leaden ♦ *sm* bruise

li'vore *sm* malice, spite

Li'vorno *sf* Livorno, Leghorn

li'vrea *sf* livery

'lizza ['littsa] *sf* lists *pl*; **scendere in ~** (*anche fig*) to enter the lists

lo (*dav s impura, gn, pn, ps, x, z; dav V* **l'**) *det m* ♦ *pron* (*oggetto: persona*) him; (: *cosa*) it; **~ sapevo** I knew it; **~ so** I know; **sii buono, anche se lui non ~ è** be good, even if he isn't; *vedi anche* **il**

lo'cale *ag* local ♦ *sm* room; (*luogo pubblico*) premises *pl*; **~ notturno** nightclub; **località** *sf inv* locality; **localiz'zare** *vt* (*circoscrivere*) to confine, localize; (*accertare*) to locate, place

lo'canda *sf* inn; **locandi'ere, a** *sm/f* innkeeper

loca'tario, a *sm/f* tenant

loca'tore, 'trice *sm/f* landlord/lady

locazi'one [lokat'tsjone] *sf* (*da parte del locatario*) renting *no pl*; (*da parte del locatore*) renting out *no pl*, letting *no pl*; (*contratto di*) ~ lease; (*canone di*) ~ rent; **dare in ~** to rent out, let

locomo'tiva *sf* locomotive

locomo'tore *sm* electric locomotive

locomozi'one [lokomot'tsjone] *sf* locomotion; **mezzi di ~** vehicles, means of transport

lo'custa *sf* locust

locuzi'one [lokut'tsjone] *sf* phrase, expression

lo'dare *vt* to praise

'lode *sf* praise; (*INS*): **laurearsi con 110 e ~ ≈** to graduate with a first-class honours degree (*BRIT*), graduate summa cum laude (*US*)

'loden *sm inv* (*stoffa*) loden; (*cappotto*) loden overcoat

lo'devole *ag* praiseworthy

loga'ritmo *sm* logarithm

'loggia, ge ['lɔddʒa] *sf* (*ARCHIT*) loggia;

(*circolo massonico*) lodge; **loggi'one** *sm* (*di teatro*): **il loggione** the Gods *sg*

'logica *sf* logic

'logico, a, ci, che ['lɔdʒiko] *ag* logical

logo'rare *vt* to wear out; (*sciupare*) to waste; **~rsi** *vr* to wear out; (*fig*) to wear o.s. out

logo'rio *sm* wear and tear; (*fig*) strain

'logoro, a *ag* (*stoffa*) worn out, threadbare; (*persona*) worn out

lom'baggine [lom'baddʒine] *sf* lumbago

Lombar'dia *sf*: **la ~** Lombardy

lom'bata *sf* (*taglio di carne*) loin

'lombo *sm* (*ANAT*) loin

lom'brico, chi *sm* earthworm

londi'nese *ag* London *cpd* ♦ *sm/f* Londoner

'Londra *sf* London

lon'gevo, a [lon'dʒɛvo] *ag* long-lived

longi'tudine [londʒi'tudine] *sf* longitude

lonta'nanza [lonta'nantsa] *sf* distance; absence

lon'tano, a *ag* (*distante*) distant, faraway; (*assente*) absent; (*vago: sospetto*) slight, remote; (*tempo: remoto*) far-off, distant; (*parente*) distant, remote ♦ *av* far; **è ~ la casa?** is it far to the house?, is the house far from here?; **è ~ un chilometro** it's a kilometre away o a kilometre from here; **più ~** farther; **da o di ~** from a distance; **~ da** a long way from; **alla ~a** slightly, vaguely

'lontra *sf* otter

lo'quace [lo'kwatʃe] *ag* talkative, loquacious; (*fig: gesto etc*) eloquent

'lordo, a *ag* dirty, filthy; (*peso, stipendio*) gross

'loro *pron pl* (*oggetto, con preposizione*) them; (*complemento di termine*) to them; (*soggetto*) they; (*forma di cortesia: anche: L~*) you; to you; **il(la) ~, i(le) ~** *det* their; (*forma di cortesia: anche: L~*) your ♦ *pron* theirs; (*forma di cortesia: anche: L~*) yours; **~ stessi(e)**

they themselves; you yourselves
'losco, a, schi, sche ag (fig) shady, suspicious
'lotta sf struggle, fight; (SPORT) wrestling; **~ libera** all-in wrestling; **lot'tare** vi to fight, struggle; (fig) to wrestle; **lotta'tore, trice** sm/f wrestler
lotte'ria sf lottery; (di gara ippica) sweepstake
'lotto sm (gioco) (state) lottery; (parte) lot; (EDIL) site
lozi'one [lot'tsjone] sf lotion
lubrifi'cante sm lubricant
lubrifi'care vt to lubricate
luc'chetto [luk'ketto] sm padlock
lucci'care [luttʃi'kare] vi to sparkle, glitter, twinkle
'luccio ['luttʃo] sm (ZOOL) pike
'lucciola ['luttʃola] sf (ZOOL) firefly; glowworm
'luce ['lutʃe] sf light; (finestra) window; **alla ~ di** by the light of; **fare ~ su qc** (fig) to shed o throw light on sth; **~ del sole/della luna** sun/moonlight; **lu'cente** ag shining
lucer'nario [lutʃer'narjo] sm skylight
lu'certola [lu'tʃertola] sf lizard
luci'dare [lutʃi'dare] vt to polish
lucida'trice [lutʃida'tritʃe] sf floor polisher
'lucido, a ['lutʃido] ag shining, bright; (lucidato) polished; (fig) lucid ♦ sm shine, lustre; (per scarpe etc) polish; (disegno) tracing
'lucro sm profit, gain; **lu'croso, a** ag lucrative, profitable
'luglio ['luʎʎo] sm July
'lugubre ag gloomy
'lui pronome (soggetto) he; (oggetto: per dare rilievo, con preposizione) him; **~ stesso** he himself
lu'maca, che sf slug; (chiocciola) snail
'lume sm light; (lampada) lamp; (fig): **chiedere ~i a qn** to ask sb for advice; **a ~ di naso** (fig) by rule of thumb
lumi'naria sf (per feste) illuminations pl
lumi'noso, a ag (che emette luce)

luminous; (cielo, colore, stanza) bright; (sorgente) of light, light cpd; (fig: sorriso) bright, radiant
'luna sf moon; **~ nuova/piena** new/full moon; **~ di miele** honeymoon
luna park sm inv amusement park, funfair
lu'nare ag lunar, moon cpd
lu'nario sm almanac; **sbarcare il ~** to make ends meet
lu'natico, a, ci, che ag whimsical, temperamental
lunedì sm inv Monday; **di o il ~** on Mondays
lun'gaggine [lun'gaddʒine] sf slowness; **~i della burocrazia** red tape
lun'ghezza [lun'gettsa] sf length; **~ d'onda** (FISICA) wavelength
'lungi ['lundʒi]: **~ da** prep far from
'lungo, a, ghi, ghe ag long; (lento: persona) slow; (diluito: caffè, brodo) weak, watery, thin ♦ sm length ♦ prep along; **~ 3 metri** 3 metres long; **a ~** for a long time; **a ~ andare** in the long run; **di gran ~a** (molto) by far; **andare in ~ o per le lunghe** to drag on; **saperla ~a** to know what's what; **in ~ e in largo** far and wide, all over; **~ il corso dei secoli** throughout the centuries
lungo'mare sm promenade
lu'notto sm (AUT) rear o back window; **~ termico** heated rear window
lu'ogo, ghi sm place; (posto: di incidente etc) scene, site; (punto, passo di libro) passage; **in ~ di** instead of; **in primo ~** in the first place; **aver ~** to take place; **dar ~ a** to give rise to; **~ comune** commonplace; **~ di nascita** birthplace; (AMM) place of birth; **~ di provenienza** place of origin
luogote'nente sm (MIL) lieutenant
lu'para sf sawn-off shotgun
'lupo, a sm/f wolf
'luppolo sm (BOT) hop

'**lurido, a** *ag* filthy

lu'**singa, ghe** *sf* (*spesso al pl*) flattery *no pl*

lusin'**gare** *vt* to flatter; **lusinghi'ero, a** *ag* flattering, gratifying

lus'**sare** *vt* (*MED*) to dislocate

Lussem'burgo *sm* (*stato*): **il ~** Luxembourg ♦ *sf* (*città*) Luxembourg

'**lusso** *sm* luxury; **di ~** luxury *cpd*; **lussu'oso, a** *ag* luxurious

lussureggi'**ante** [lussured'dʒante] *ag* luxuriant

lus'**suria** *sf* lust

lus'**trare** *vt* to polish, shine

lustras'**carpe** *sm/f inv* shoeshine

lus'**trino** *sm* sequin

'**lustro, a** *ag* shiny; (*pelo*) glossy ♦ *sm* shine, gloss; (*fig*) prestige, glory; (*quinquennio*) five-year period

'**lutto** *sm* mourning; **essere in/ portare il ~** to be in/wear mourning; **luttu'oso, a** *ag* mournful, sad

M, m

ma *cong* but; **~ insomma!** for goodness sake!; **~ no!** of course not!

'**macabro, a** *ag* gruesome, macabre

macché [mak'ke] *escl* not at all!, certainly not!

macche'**roni** [makke'roni] *smpl* macaroni *sg*

'**macchia** ['makkja] *sf* stain, spot; (*chiazza di diverso colore*) spot; splash, patch; (*tipo di boscaglia*) scrub; **alla ~** (*fig*) in hiding; **macchi'are** *vt* (*sporcare*) to stain, mark; **macchiarsi** *vr* (*persona*) to get o.s. dirty; (*stoffa*) to stain; (*fig*) to get stained o marked

'**macchina** ['makkina] *sf* machine; (*motore, locomotiva*) engine; (*automobile*) car; (*fig: meccanismo*) machinery; **andare in ~** (*AUT*) to go by car; (*STAMPA*) to go to press; **~ da cucire** sewing machine; **~ fotografica** camera; **~ da presa** cine o movie

camera; **~ da scrivere** typewriter; **~ a vapore** steam engine

macchi'**nare** [makki'nare] *vt* to plot

macchi'**nario** [makki'narjo] *sm* machinery

macchi'**netta** [makki'netta] *sf* (*fam*) (*caffettiera*) percolator; (*accendino*) lighter

macchi'**nista, i** [makki'nista] *sm* (*di treno*) engine-driver; (*di nave*) engineer

macchi'**noso, a** [makki'noso] *ag* complex, complicated

mace'**donia** [matʃe'dɔnja] *sf* fruit salad

macel'**laio** [matʃel'lajo] *sm* butcher

macel'**lare** [matʃel'lare] *vt* to slaughter, butcher; **macelle'ria** *sf* butcher's (shop); **ma'cello** *sm* (*mattatoio*) slaughterhouse, abattoir (*BRIT*); (*fig*) slaughter, massacre; (*: disastro*) shambles *sg*

mace'**rare** [matʃe'rare] *vt* to macerate; (*CUC*) to marinate; **~rsi** *vr* (*fig*): **~rsi in** to be consumed with

ma'**cerie** [ma'tʃerje] *sfpl* rubble *sg*, debris *sg*

ma'**cigno** [ma'tʃiɲɲo] *sm* (*masso*) rock, boulder

macina ['matʃina] *sf* (*pietra*) millstone; (*macchina*) grinder; **macinacaffè** *sm inv* coffee grinder; **macinapepe** *sm inv* peppermill

maci'**nare** [matʃi'nare] *vt* to grind; (*carne*) to mince (*BRIT*), grind (*US*); **maci'nato** *sm* meal, flour; (*carne*) minced (*BRIT*) o ground (*US*) meat

maci'**nino** [matʃi'nino] *sm* coffee grinder; peppermill

'**madido, a** *ag*: **~ (di)** wet o moist (with)

Ma'donna *sf* (*REL*) Our Lady

mador'**nale** *ag* enormous, huge

'**madre** *sf* mother; (*matrice di bolletta*) counterfoil ♦ *ag inv* mother *cpd*; **ragazza ~** unmarried mother; **scena ~** (*TEATRO*) principal scene; (*fig*) terrible scene

madre'lingua sf mother tongue, native language

madre'perla sf mother-of-pearl

ma'drina sf godmother

maestà sf inv majesty; **maes'toso, a** ag majestic

ma'estra sf vedi **maestro**

maes'trale sm north-west wind, mistral

maes'tranze [maes'trantse] sfpl workforce sg

maes'tria sf mastery, skill

ma'estro, a sm/f (INS: anche: ~ di scuola o elementare) primary (BRIT) o grade school (US) teacher; (esperto) expert ♦ sm (artigiano, fig: guida) master; (MUS) maestro ♦ ag (principale) main; (di grande abilità) masterly, skilful; **~a d'asilo** nursery teacher; **~ di cerimonie** master of ceremonies

'mafia sf Mafia; **mafi'oso** sm member of the Mafia

'maga sf sorceress

ma'gagna [ma'gaɲɲa] sf defect, flaw, blemish; (noia, guaio) problem

ma'gari escl (esprime desiderio): **~ fosse vero!** if only it were true!; **ti piacerebbe andare in Scozia? — ~!** would you like to go to Scotland? — and how! ♦ av (anche) even; (forse) perhaps

magaz'zino [magad'dzino] sm warehouse; **grande ~** department store

'maggio ['maddʒo] sm May

maggio'rana [maddʒo'rana] sf (BOT) (sweet) marjoram

maggio'ranza [maddʒo'rantsa] sf majority

maggio'rare [maddʒo'rare] vt to increase, raise

maggior'domo [maddʒor'dɔmo] sm butler

maggi'ore [mad'dʒore] ag (comparativo: più grande) bigger, larger; taller; greater; (: più vecchio: sorella, fratello) older, elder; (: di grado:

superiore) senior; (: più importante, MIL, MUS) major; (superlativo) biggest, largest; tallest; greatest; oldest, eldest ♦ sm/f (di grado) superior; (: di età) elder; (MIL) major; (: AER) squadron leader; **la maggior parte** the majority; **andare per la ~** (cantante etc) to be very popular; **maggio'renne** ag of age ♦ sm/f person who has come of age; **maggior'mente** av much more; (con senso superlativo) most

ma'gia [ma'dʒia] sf magic; **'magico, a, ci, che** ag magic; (fig) fascinating, charming, magical

'magio [madʒo] sm (REL): **i re Magi** the Magi, the Three Wise Men

magis'tero [madʒis'tero] sm: **facoltà di M~** = teachers' training college; **magis'trale** ag primary (BRIT) o grade school (US) teachers', primary (BRIT) o grade school (US) teaching cpd; skilful

magis'trato [madʒis'trato] sm magistrate; **magistra'tura** sf magistrature; (magistrati): **la magistratura** the Bench

'maglia ['maʎʎa] sf stitch; (lavoro ai ferri) knitting no pl; (tessuto, SPORT) jersey; (maglione) jersey, sweater; (di catena) link; (di rete) mesh; **~ diritta/rovescia** plain/purl; **maglie'ria** sf knitwear; (negozio) knitwear shop; **magli'etta** sf (canottiera) vest; (tipo camicia) T-shirt; **magli'ficio** sm knitwear factory

magli'one sm sweater, jumper

ma'gnanimo, a [maɲ'ɲanimo, a] ag magnanimous

ma'gnete [maɲ'ɲete] sm magnet; **ma'gnetico, a, ci, che** ag magnetic; **magne'tofono** [maɲɲe'tɔfono] sm tape recorder

ma'gnifico, a, ci, che [maɲ'ɲifiko] ag magnificent, splendid; (ospite) generous

'magno, a ['maɲɲo] *ag*: **aula ~a** main hall

ma'gnolia [maɲˈnɔlja] *sf* magnolia

'mago, ghi *sm* (*stregone*) magician, wizard; (*illusionista*) magician

ma'grezza [maˈɡrettsa] *sf* thinness

'magro, a *ag* (very) thin, skinny; (*carne*) lean; (*formaggio*) low-fat; (*fig: scarso, misero*) meagre, (*: meschino: scusa*) poor, lame; **mangiare di ~** not to eat meat

'mai *av* (*nessuna volta*) never; (*talvolta*) ever; **non ... ~** never; **~ più** never again; **come ~?** why (o how) on earth?; **chi/dove/quando ~?** whoever/wherever/whenever?

mai'ale *sm* (ZOOL) pig; (*carne*) pork

maio'nese *sf* mayonnaise

'mais *sm inv* maize

mai'uscola *sf* capital letter

mai'uscolo, a *ag* (*lettera*) capital; (*fig*) enormous, huge

mal *av*, *sm vedi* **male**

malac'corto, a *ag* rash, careless

mala'fede *sf* bad faith

mala'lingua (*pl* **male'lingue**) *sf* gossip(monger)

mala'mente *av* badly; dangerously

malan'dato, a *ag* (*persona: di salute*) in poor health; (*: di condizioni finanziarie*) badly off; (*trascurato*) shabby

ma'lanno *sm* (*disgrazia*) misfortune; (*malattia*) ailment

mala'pena *sf*: **a ~** hardly, scarcely

ma'laria *sf* (MED) malaria

mala'sorte *sf* bad luck

mala'ticcio, a [malaˈtittʃo] *ag* sickly

ma'lato, a *ag* ill, sick; (*gamba*) bad; (*pianta*) diseased ♦ *sm/f* sick person; (*in ospedale*) patient; **malat'tia** (*infettiva etc*) illness, disease; (*cattiva salute*) illness, sickness; (*di pianta*) disease

malau'gurio *sm* bad o ill omen

mala'vita *sf* underworld

mala'voglia [malaˈvɔʎʎa] *sf*: **di ~**

unwillingly, reluctantly

mal'concio, a, ci, ce [malˈkontʃo] *ag* in a sorry state

malcon'tento *sm* discontent

malcos'tume *sm* immorality

mal'destro, a *ag* (*inabile*) inexpert, inexperienced; (*goffo*) awkward

maldi'cenza [maldiˈtʃentsa] *sf* malicious gossip

maldis'posto, a *ag*: **~ (verso)** ill-disposed (towards)

'male *av* badly ♦ *sm* (*ciò che è ingiusto, disonesto*) evil; (*danno, svantaggio*) harm; (*sventura*) misfortune; (*dolore fisico, morale*) pain, ache; **di ~ in peggio** from bad to worse; **sentirsi ~** to feel ill; **far ~** (*dolere*) to hurt; **far ~ alla salute** to be bad for one's health; **far del ~ a qn** to hurt o harm sb; **restare o rimanere ~** to be sorry; to be disappointed; to be hurt; **andare a ~** to go bad; **come va? — non c'è ~** how are you? — not bad; **mal di cuore** heart trouble; **~ di dente** toothache; **mal di mare** seasickness; **avere mal di gola/testa** to have a sore throat/a headache; **aver ~ ai piedi** to have sore feet

male'detto, a *pp di* **maledire** ♦ *ag* cursed, damned; (*fig: fam*) damned, blasted

male'dire *vt* to curse; **maledizi'one** *sf* curse; **maledizione!** damn it!

maledu'cato, a *ag* rude, ill-mannered

male'fatta *sf* misdeed

male'ficio [maleˈfitʃo] *sm* witchcraft

ma'lefico, a, ci, che *ag* (*influsso, azione*) evil

ma'lessere *sm* indisposition, slight illness; (*fig*) uneasiness

ma'levolo, a *ag* malevolent

malfa'mato, a *ag* notorious

mal'fatto, a *ag* (*persona*) deformed; (*oggetto*) badly made; (*lavoro*) badly done

malfat'tore, 'trice *sm/f* wrongdoer

mal'fermo, a *ag* unsteady, shaky;

(*salute*) poor, delicate

malformazi'one [malformat'tsjone] *sf* malformation

malgo'verno *sm* maladministration

mal'grado *prep* in spite of, despite ♦ *cong* although; **mio** (*o* **tuo** *etc*) ~ against my (*o* your *etc*) will

mali'gnare [malin'ɲare] *vi*: ~ **su** to malign, speak ill of

ma'ligno, a [ma'liɲɲo] *ag* (*malvagio*) malicious, malignant; (*MED*) malignant

malinco'nia *sf* melancholy, gloom; **malin'conico, a, ci, che** *ag* melancholy

malincu'ore: a ~ *av* reluctantly, unwillingly

malintenzio'nato, a [malinten-tsjo'nato] *ag* ill-intentioned

malin'teso, a *ag* misunderstood; (*riguardo, senso del dovere*) mistaken, wrong ♦ *sm* misunderstanding

ma'lizia [ma'littsja] *sf* (*malignità*) malice; (*furbizia*) cunning; (*espediente*) trick; **malizi'oso, a** *ag* malicious, cunning; (*vivace, birichino*) mischievous

mal'loppo *sm* (*involto*) bundle; (*fam: refurtiva*) loot

malme'nare *vt* to beat up

mal'messo, a *ag* shabby

malnu'trito, a *ag* undernourished

ma'locchio [ma'lɔkkjo] *sm* evil eye

ma'lora *sf*: **andare in ~** to go to the dogs

ma'lore *sm* (*sudden*) illness

mal'sano, a *ag* unhealthy

malsi'curo, a *ag* unsafe

'Malta *sf* Malta

'malta *sf* (*EDIL*) mortar

mal'tempo *sm* bad weather

'malto *sm* malt

maltrat'tare *vt* to ill-treat

malu'more *sm* bad mood; (*irritabilità*) bad temper; (*discordia*) ill feeling; **di ~** in a bad mood

mal'vagio, a, gi, gie [mal'vadʒo] *ag* wicked, evil

malversazi'one [malversat'tsjone] *sf*

(*DIR*) embezzlement

mal'visto, a *ag*: ~ **(da)** disliked (by), unpopular (with)

malvi'vente *sm* criminal

malvolenti'eri *av* unwillingly, reluctantly

'mamma *sf* mummy, mum; ~ **mia!** my goodness!

mam'mella *sf* (*ANAT*) breast; (*di vacca, capra etc*) udder

mam'mifero *sm* mammal

mam'mola *sf* (*BOT*) violet

ma'nata *sf* (*colpo*) slap; (*quantità*) handful

'manca *sf* left (hand); **a destra e a ~** left, right and centre, on all sides

man'canza [man'kantsa] *sf* lack; (*carenza*) shortage, scarcity; (*fallo*) fault; (*imperfezione*) failing, shortcoming; **per ~ di tempo** through lack of time; **in ~ di meglio** for lack of anything better

man'care *vi* (*essere insufficiente*) to be lacking; (*venir meno*) to fail; (*sbagliare*) to be wrong, make a mistake; (*non esserci*) to be missing, not to be there; (*essere lontano*): ~ **(da)** to be away (from) ♦ *vt* to miss; ~ **di** to lack; (*promessa*) to fail to keep; **tu mi manchi** I miss you; **mancò poco che morisse** he very nearly died; **mancano ancora 10 sterline** we're still £10 short; **manca un quarto alle 6** it's a quarter to 6; **man'cato, a** *ag* (*tentativo*) unsuccessful; (*artista*) failed

'mancia, ce ['mantʃa] *sf* tip; ~ **competente** reward

manci'ata [man'tʃata] *sf* handful

man'cino, a [man'tʃino] *ag* (*braccio*) left; (*persona*) left-handed; (*fig*) underhand

'manco *av* (*nemmeno*): ~ **per sogno** *o* **per idea!** not on your life!

man'dante *sm/f* (*di delitto*) instigator

manda'rancio [manda'rantʃo] *sm* clementine

man'dare *vt* to send; (*far funzionare:*

macchina) to drive; (emettere) to send out; (: grido) to give, utter, let out; ~ a chiamare qn to send for sb; ~ avanti (fig: famiglia) to provide for; (: fabbrica) to run, look after; ~ giù to send down; (anche fig) to swallow; ~ via to send away; (licenziare) to fire

manda'rino sm mandarin (orange); (cinese) mandarin

man'data sf (quantità) lot, batch; (di chiave) turn; chiudere a doppia ~ to double-lock

man'dato sm (incarico) commission; (DIR: provvedimento) warrant; (di deputato etc) mandate; (ordine di pagamento) postal o money order; ~ d'arresto warrant for arrest

man'dibola sf mandible, jaw

'mandorla sf almond; 'mandorlo sm almond tree

'mandria sf herd

maneggi'are [maned'dʒare] vt (creta, cera) to mould, work, fashion; (arnesi, utensili) to handle; (: adoperare) to use; (fig: persone, denaro) to handle, deal with; ma'neggio sm moulding; handling; (intrigo) plot, scheme; (per cavalli) riding school

ma'nesco, a, schi, sche ag free with one's fists

ma'nette sfpl handcuffs

manga'nello sm club

manga'nese sm manganese

mange'reccio, a, ci, ce [mandʒe'rettʃo] ag edible

mangi'are [man'dʒare] vt to eat; (intaccare) to eat into o away; (CARTE, SCACCHI etc) to take ♦ vi to eat ♦ sm eating; (cibo) food; (cucina) cooking; ~rsi le parole to mumble; ~rsi le unghie to bite one's nails; mangia'toia sf feeding-trough

man'gime [man'dʒime] sm fodder

'mango, ghi sm mango

ma'nia sf (PSIC) mania; (fig) obsession, craze; ma'niaco, a, ci, che ag suffering from a mania; maniaco (di)

obsessed (by), crazy (about)

'manica sf sleeve; (fig: gruppo) gang, bunch; (GEO): la M~, il Canale della M~ the (English) Channel; essere di ~ larga/stretta to be easy-going/strict; ~ a vento (AER) wind sock

mani'chino [mani'kino] sm (di sarto, vetrina) dummy

'manico, ci sm handle; (MUS) neck

mani'comio sm mental hospital; (fig) madhouse

mani'cotto sm muff; (TECN) coupling; sleeve

mani'cure sm o f inv manicure ♦ sf inv manicurist

mani'era sf way, manner; (stile) style, manner; ~e sfpl (comportamento) manners; in ~ che so that; in ~ da so as to; in tutte le ~e at all costs

manie'rato, a ag affected

manifat'tura sf (lavorazione) manufacture; (stabilimento) factory

manifes'tare vt to show, display; (esprimere) to express; (rivelare) to reveal, disclose ♦ vi to demonstrate; ~rsi vr to show o.s.; ~rsi amico to prove o.s. (to be) a friend; manifestazi'one sf show, display; expression; (sintomo) sign, symptom; (dimostrazione pubblica) demonstration; (cerimonia) event

mani'festo, a ag obvious, evident ♦ sm poster, bill; (scritto ideologico) manifesto

ma'niglia [ma'niʎʎa] sf handle; (sostegno: negli autobus etc) strap

manipo'lare vt to manipulate; (alterare: vino) to adulterate; manipolazi'one sf manipulation; adulteration

---

mani pulite

Mani pulite is a term used to describe the judicial operation which identified, gathered evidence against, and brought to trial a number of politicians and industrialists *implicated in bribery and corruption scandals. See also* **Tangentopoli.**

'manna *sf* (REL) manna; (*fig*) godsend

man'naia *sf* (*del boia*) (executioner's) axe; (*per carni*) cleaver

man'naro: lupo ~ *sm* werewolf

'mano, i *sf* hand; (*strato: di vernice etc*) coat; **di prima ~** (*notizia*) first-hand; **di seconda ~** second-hand; **man ~** little by little, gradually; **man ~ che** as; **darsi** *o* **stringersi la ~** to shake hands; **mettere le ~i avanti** (*fig*) to safeguard o.s.; **restare a ~i vuote** to be left empty-handed; **venire alle ~i** to come to blows; **a ~ by hand; ~i in alto!** hands up!

mano'dopera *sf* labour

mano'messo, a *pp di* **manomette-re**

ma'nometro *sm* gauge, manometer

mano'mettere *vt* (*alterare*) to tamper with; (*aprire indebitamente*) to break open illegally

ma'nopola *sf* (*dell'armatura*) gauntlet; (*guanto*) mitt; (*di impugnatura*) hand-grip; (*pomello*) knob

manos'critto, a *ag* handwritten ♦ *sm* manuscript

mano'vale *sm* labourer

mano'vella *sf* handle; (TECN) crank

ma'novra *sf* manoeuvre (BRIT), maneuver (US); (FERR) shunting; **mano'vrare** *vt* (*veicolo*) to manoeuvre (BRIT), maneuver (US); (*macchina, congegno*) to operate; (*fig: persona*) to manipulate ♦ *vi* to manoeuvre

manro'vescio [manro'veʃʃo] *sm* slap (*with back of hand*)

man'sarda *sf* attic

mansi'one *sf* task, duty, job

mansu'eto, a *ag* gentle, docile

man'tello *sm* cloak; (*fig: di neve etc*) blanket, mantle; (ZOOL) coat

mante'nere *vt* to maintain; (*adempiere: promesse*) to keep, abide by; (*provvedere a*) to support, maintain;

~rsi *vr*: **~rsi calmo/giovane** to stay calm/young; **manteni'mento** *sm* maintenance

'mantice ['mantitʃe] *sm* bellows *pl*

'manto *sm* cloak; **~ stradale** road surface

manu'ale *ag* manual ♦ *sm* (*testo*) manual, handbook

ma'nubrio *sm* handle; (*di bicicletta etc*) handlebars *pl*; (SPORT) dumbbell

manu'fatto *sm* manufactured article

manutenzi'one [manuten'tsjone] *sf* maintenance, upkeep; (*d'impianti*) maintenance, servicing

'manzo ['mandzo] *sm* (ZOOL) steer; (*carne*) beef

'mappa *sf* (GEO) map; **mappa'mondo** *sm* map of the world; (*globo girevole*) globe

mara'tona *sf* marathon

'marca, che *sf* (COMM: *di prodotti*) brand; (*contrassegno, scontrino*) ticket, check; **prodotto di ~** (*di buona qualità*) high-class product; **~ da bollo** official stamp

mar'care *vt* (*munire di contrassegno*) to mark; (*a fuoco*) to brand; (SPORT: *gol*) to score; (*: avversario*) to mark; (*accentuare*) to stress; **~ visita** (MIL) to report sick

'Marche ['marke] *sfpl*: **le ~** the Marches (*region of central Italy*)

mar'chese, a [mar'keze] *sm/f* marquis *o* marquess/marchioness

marchi'are [mar'kjare] *vt* to brand; **'marchio** *sm* (*di bestiame*, COMM, *fig*) brand; **marchio depositato** registered trademark; **marchio di fabbrica** trademark

'marcia, ce ['martʃa] *sf* (*anche* MUS, MIL) march; (*funzionamento*) running; (*il camminare*) walking; (AUT) gear; **mettere in ~** to start; **mettersi in ~** to get moving; **far ~ indietro** (AUT) to reverse; (*fig*) to back-pedal

marciapi'ede [martʃa'pjɛde] *sm* (*di strada*) pavement (BRIT), sidewalk (US);

(FERR) platform

marci'are [mar'tʃare] vi to march; (andare: treno, macchina) to go; (funzionare) to run, work

'marcio, a, ci, ce ['martʃo] ag (frutta, legno) rotten, bad; (MED) festering; (fig) corrupt, rotten

mar'cire [mar'tʃire] vi (andare a male) to go bad, rot; (suppurare) to fester; (fig) to rot, waste away

'marco, chi sm (unità monetaria) mark

'mare sm sea; **in ~** at sea; **andare al ~** (in vacanza etc) to go to the seaside; **il M~ del Nord** the North Sea

ma'rea sf tide; **alta/bassa ~** high/low tide

mareggi'ata [mared'dʒata] sf heavy sea

mare'moto sm seaquake

maresci'allo [mareʃ'ʃallo] sm (MIL) marshal; (: sottufficiale) warrant officer

marga'rina sf margarine

marghe'rita [marge'rita] sf (ox-eye) daisy, marguerite; (di stampante) daisy wheel

'margine ['mardʒine] sm margin; (di bosco, via) edge, border

ma'rina sf navy; (costa) coast; (quadro) seascape; **~ mercantile/militare** navy/merchant navy (BRIT) o marine (US)

mari'naio sm sailor

mari'nare vt (CUC) to marinate; **~ la scuola** to play truant; **mari'nata** sf marinade

ma'rino, a ag sea cpd, marine

mario'netta sf puppet

mari'tare vt to marry; **~rsi** vr: **~rsi a o con qn** to marry sb, get married to sb

ma'rito sm husband

ma'rittimo, a ag maritime, sea cpd

mar'maglia [mar'maʎʎa] sf mob, riff-raff

marmel'lata sf jam; (di agrumi) marmalade

mar'mitta sf (recipiente) pot; (AUT) silencer; **~ catalitica** catalytic

converter

'marmo sm marble

mar'mocchio [mar'mɔkkjo] (fam) sm tot, kid

mar'motta sf (ZOOL) marmot

Ma'rocco sm: **il ~** Morocco

mar'rone ag inv brown ♦ sm (BOT) chestnut

mar'sala sm inv (vino) Marsala

mar'sina sf tails pl, tail coat

mar'supio sm pouch; (per denaro) bum bag; (per neonato) sling

martedì sm inv Tuesday; **di o il ~** on Tuesdays; **~ grasso** Shrove Tuesday

martel'lare vt to hammer ♦ vi (pulsare) to throb; (: cuore) to thump

mar'tello sm hammer; (di uscio) knocker

marti'netto sm (TECN) jack

'martire sm/f martyr; **mar'tirio** sm martyrdom; (fig) agony, torture

'martora sf marten

martori'are vt to torment, torture

mar'xista, i, e ag, sm/f Marxist

marza'pane [martsa'pane] sm marzipan

'marzo ['martso] sm March

mascal'zone [maskal'tsone] sm rascal, scoundrel

ma'scella [maʃ'ʃella] sf (ANAT) jaw

'maschera ['maskera] sf mask; (travestimento) disguise; (: per un ballo etc) fancy dress; (TEATRO, CINEMA) usher/usherette; (personaggio del teatro) stock character; **masche'rare** vt to mask; (travestire) to disguise; to dress up; (fig: celare) to hide, conceal; (MIL) to camouflage; **~rsi da** to disguise o.s. as; to dress up as; (fig) to masquerade as

mas'chile [mas'kile] ag masculine; (sesso, popolazione) male; (abiti) men's; (per ragazzi: scuola) boys'

'maschio, a ['maskjo] ag (BIOL) male; (virile) manly ♦ sm (anche ZOOL, TECN) male; (uomo) man; (ragazzo) boy; (figlio) son

masco'lino, a ag masculine

'massa sf mass; (di errori etc): **una ~ di** heaps of, masses of; (di gente) mass, multitude; (di tutti insieme) en masse; **adunata in ~** mass meeting; **di ~** (cultura, manifestazione) mass cpd

mas'sacro sm massacre, slaughter; (fig) mess, disaster

mas'saggio [mas'saddʒo] sm massage

mas'saia sf housewife

masse'rizie [masse'rittsje] sfpl (household) furnishings

mas'siccio, a, ci, ce [mas'sittʃo] ag (oro, legno) solid; (palazzo) massive; (corporatura) stout ♦ sm (GEO) massif

'massima sf (sentenza, regola) maxim; (METEOR) maximum temperature; **in linea di ~** generally speaking; vedi anche **massimo**

massi'male sm maximum

'massimo, a ag, sm maximum; **al ~** at (the) most

'masso sm rock, boulder

mas'sone sm freemason; **masso'neria** sf freemasonry

mas'tello sm tub

masti'care vt to chew

'mastice ['mastitʃe] sm mastic; (per vetri) putty

mas'tino sm mastiff

ma'tassa sf skein

mate'matica sf mathematics sg

mate'matico, a, ci, che ag mathematical ♦ sm/f mathematician

materas'sino sm mat; (gonfiabile) air bed

mate'rasso sm mattress; **~ a molle** spring o interior-sprung mattress

ma'teria sf (FISICA) matter; (TECN, COMM) material, matter no pl; (disciplina) subject; (argomento) subject matter, material; **~e prime** raw materials; **in ~ di** (per quanto concerne) on the subject of

materi'ale ag material; (fig: grossolano) rough, rude ♦ sm material; (insieme di strumenti etc) equipment no pl, materials pl

mater'nità sf motherhood, maternity; (reparto) maternity ward

ma'terno, a ag (amore, cura etc) maternal, motherly; (nonno) maternal; (lingua, terra) mother cpd

ma'tita sf pencil

ma'trice [ma'tritʃe] sf matrix; (COMM) counterfoil; (fig: origine) background

ma'tricola sf (registro) register; (numero) registration number; (nell'università) freshman, fresher

ma'trigna [ma'triɲɲa] sf stepmother

matrimoni'ale ag matrimonial, marriage cpd

matri'monio sm marriage, matrimony; (durata) marriage, married life; (cerimonia) wedding

ma'trona sf (fig) matronly woman

mat'tina sf morning; **matti'nata** sf morning; (spettacolo) matinée; afternoon performance; **matti'niero, a** ag: **essere mattiniero** to be an early riser

mat'tino sm morning

'matto, a ag mad, crazy; (fig: falso) false, imitation ♦ sm/f madman/ woman; **avere una voglia ~a di qc** to be dying for sth

mat'tone sm brick; (fig): **questo libro/film è un ~** this book/film is heavy going

matto'nella sf tile

matu'rare vi (anche: ~rsi) (frutta, grano) to ripen; (ascesso) to come to a head; (fig: persona, idea, ECON) to mature ♦ vt to ripen; to (make) mature

maturità sf maturity; (di frutta) ripeness, maturity; (INS) school-leaving examination; ≈ GCE A-levels (BRIT)

ma'turo, a ag mature; (frutto) ripe, mature

maxiprocesso n criminal trial involving large numbers of co-accused

'mazza ['mattsa] sf (bastone) club; (martello) sledge-hammer; (SPORT: da *golf*) club; (: *da baseball, cricket*) bat

maz'zata [mat'tsata] *sf* (*anche fig*) heavy blow

'mazzo ['mattso] *sm* (*di fiori, chiavi etc*) bunch; (*di carte da gioco*) pack

me *pron me*; ~ **stesso(a)** myself; **sei bravo quanto ~** you are as clever as I (am) o as me

me'andro *sm* meander

mec'canica, che *sf* mechanics *sg*; (*attività tecnologica*) mechanical engineering; (*meccanismo*) mechanism

mec'canico, a, ci, che *ag* mechanical ♦ *sm* mechanic

mecca'nismo *sm* mechanism

me'daglia [me'daʎʎa] *sf* medal; **medagli'one** *sm* (*ARCHIT*) medallion; (*gioiello*) locket

me'desimo, a *ag* same; (*in persona*): **io ~ I** myself

'media *sf* average; (*MAT*) mean; (*INS: voto*) end-of-term average; **in ~** on average; *vedi anche* **medio**

medi'ano, a *ag* median; (*valore*) mean ♦ *sm* (*CALCIO*) half-back

medi'ante *prep* by means of

medi'are *vt* (*fare da mediatore*) to act as mediator in; (*MAT*) to average

media'tore, 'trice *sm/f* mediator; (*COMM*) middle man, agent

medica'mento *sm* medicine, drug

medi'care *vt* to treat; (*ferita*) to dress; **medicazi'one** *sf* treatment, medication; dressing

medi'cina [medi'tʃina] *sf* medicine; ~ **legale** forensic medicine; **medici'nale** *ag* medicinal ♦ *sm* drug, medicine

'medico, a, ci, che *ag* medical ♦ *sm* doctor; ~ **generico** general practitioner, GP

medie'vale *ag* medieval

'medio, a *ag* average; (*punto, ceto*) middle; (*altezza, statura*) medium ♦ *sm* (*dito*) middle finger; **licenza ~a** *leaving certificate awarded at the end of 3 years of secondary education;* **scuola ~a** first

3 years of secondary school

medi'ocre *ag* mediocre, poor

medioe'vale *ag* = **medievale**

medio'evo *sm* Middle Ages *pl*

medi'tare *vt* to ponder over, meditate on; (*progettare*) to plan, think out ♦ *vi* to meditate

mediter'raneo, a *ag* Mediterranean; **il (mare) M~** the Mediterranean (Sea)

me'dusa *sf* (*ZOOL*) jellyfish

me'gafono *sm* megaphone

'meglio ['meʎʎo] *av, ag inv* better; (*con senso superlativo*) best ♦ *sm* (*la cosa migliore*): **il ~** the best (thing); **faresti ~ ad andartene** you had better leave; **alla ~** as best one can; **andar di bene in ~** to get better and better; **fare del proprio ~** to do one's best; **per il ~** for the best; **aver la ~ su qn** to get the better of sb

'mela *sf* apple; ~ **cotogna** quince

mela'grana *sf* pomegranate

melan'zana [melan'dzana] *sf* aubergine (*BRIT*), eggplant (*US*)

mel'lenso, a *ag* dull, stupid

mel'lifluo, a (*peg*) *ag* sugary, honeyed

'melma *sf* mud, mire

'melo *sm* apple tree

melo'dia *sf* melody

me'lone *sm* (musk)melon

'membro *sm* member; (*pl(f) ~a: arto*) limb

memo'randum *sm inv* memorandum

me'moria *sf* memory; ~**e** *sfpl* (*opera autobiografica*) memoirs; **a ~** (*imparare, sapere*) by heart; **a ~ d'uomo** within living memory; **memori'ale** *sm* (*raccolta di memorie*) memoirs *pl*; (*DIR*) memorial

mena'dito: a ~ *av* perfectly, thoroughly; **sapere qc a ~** to have sth at one's fingertips

me'nare *vt* to lead; (*picchiare*) to hit, beat; (*dare: colpi*) to deal; ~ **la coda** (*cane*) to wag its tail

mendi'cante *sm/f* beggar

mendi'care *vt* to beg for ♦ *vi* to beg

PAROLA CHIAVE

'**meno** av 1 (in minore misura) less;
dovresti mangiare ~ you should eat
less, you shouldn't eat so much
2 (comparativo): **~ ... di** not as ... as,
less ... than; **sono ~ alto di te** I'm not
as tall as you (are), I'm less tall than
you (are); **~ ... che** not as ... as, less ...
than; **~ che mai** less than ever; **è
~ intelligente che ricco** he's more
rich than intelligent; **~ fumo più
mangio** the less I smoke the more I
eat
3 (superlativo) least; **il ~ dotato degli
studenti** the least gifted of the
students; **è quello che compro
~ spesso** it's the one I buy least often
4 (MAT) minus; **8 ~ 5** 8 minus 5, 8 take
away 5; **sono le 8 ~ un quarto** it's a
quarter to 8; **~ 5 gradi** 5 degrees
below zero, minus 5 degrees; **mille
lire in ~** a thousand lire less
5 (fraseologia): **quanto ~ poteva
telefonare** he could at least have
phoned; **non so se accettare o ~** I
don't know whether to accept or not;
fare a ~ di qc/qn to do without sth/
sb; **non potevo fare a ~ di ridere** I
couldn't help laughing; **~ male!** thank
goodness!; **~ male che sei arrivato**
it's a good job that you've come
♦ ag inv (tempo, denaro) less; (errori,
persone) fewer; **ha fatto ~ errori di
tutti** he made fewer mistakes than
anyone, he made the fewest mistakes
of all
♦ sm inv 1: **il ~** (il minimo) the least;
parlare del più e del ~ to talk about
this and that
2 (MAT) minus
♦ prep (eccetto) except (for), apart
from; **a ~ che, a ~ di** unless; **a ~ che
non piova** unless it rains; **non posso,
a ~ di prendere ferie** I can't, unless I
take some leave

meno'mare vt (danneggiare) to maim,
disable
meno'pausa sf menopause
'mensa sf (locale) canteen; (: MIL) mess;
(: nelle università) refectory
men'sile ag monthly ♦ sm (periodico)
monthly (magazine); (stipendio)
monthly salary
'mensola sf bracket; (ripiano) shelf;
(ARCHIT) corbel
'menta sf mint; (anche: ~ piperita)
peppermint; (bibita) peppermint
cordial; (caramella) mint, peppermint
men'tale ag mental; mentalità sf inv
mentality
'mente sf mind; imparare/sapere qc
a ~ to learn/know sth by heart; avere
in ~ qc to have sth in mind; passare
di ~ a qn to slip sb's mind
men'tire vi to lie
'mento sm chin
men'tolo sm menthol
'mentre cong (temporale) while;
(avversativo) whereas
menù sm inv menu; ~ turistico set
menu
menzio'nare [mentsjo'nare] vt to
mention
menzi'one [men'tsjone] sf mention;
fare ~ di to mention
men'zogna [men'tsɔɲɲa] sf lie
mera'viglia [mera'viʎʎa] sf
amazement, wonder; (persona, cosa)
marvel, wonder; a ~ perfectly,
wonderfully; meravigli'are vt to
amaze, astonish; meravigliarsi (di)
to marvel (at); (stupirsi) to be amazed
(at), be astonished (at);
meravigli'oso, a ag wonderful,
marvellous
mer'cante sm merchant; ~ d'arte art
dealer; mercanteggi'are vt (onore,
voto) to sell ♦ vi to bargain, haggle;
mercan'tile ag commercial; (: nave, marina) merchant
cpd ♦ sm (nave) merchantman;
mercan'zia sf merchandise, goods pl

mer'cato sm market; ~ **dei cambi** exchange market; ~ **nero** black market

'merce ['mertʃe] sf goods pl, merchandise; ~ **deperibile** perishable goods pl

mercé [mer'tʃe] sf mercy

merce'nario, a [mertʃe'narjo] ag, sm mercenary

merce'ria [mertʃe'ria] sf (articoli) haberdashery (BRIT); notions pl (US); (bottega) haberdasher's shop (BRIT), notions store (US)

mercoledì sm inv Wednesday; **di** o **il ~** on Wednesdays; ~ **delle Ceneri** Ash Wednesday

---
| mercoledì delle ceneri |

Mercoledì delle ceneri, in the Catholic Church, marks the beginning of Lent. On that day, people go to church and are marked on the forehead with ash from the burning of the blessed olive branch. Ash Wednesday is a day of fasting, abstinence and penitence.

---

mer'curio sm mercury

'merda (fam!) sf shit (!)

me'renda sf afternoon snack

meridi'ana sf (orologio) sundial

meridi'ano, a ag meridian; midday cpd, noonday ♦ sm meridian

meridio'nale ag southern ♦ sm/f southerner

meridi'one sm south

me'ringa, ghe [-ʃe] (CUC) meringue

meri'tare vt to deserve, merit ♦ vb impers: **merita andare** it's worth going

meri'tevole ag worthy

'merito sm merit; (valore) worth; **in ~ a** as regards, with regard to; **dare ~ a qn di** to give sb credit for; **finire a pari ~** to finish joint first (o second etc); to tie; **meri'torio, a** ag praiseworthy

mer'letto sm lace

'merlo sm (ZOOL) blackbird; (ARCHIT) battlement

mer'luzzo [mer'luttso] sm (ZOOL) cod

mes'chino, a [mes'kino] ag wretched; (scarso) scanty, poor; (persona: gretta) mean; (: limitata) narrow-minded, petty

mesco'lanza [mesko'lantsa] sf mixture

mesco'lare vt to mix; (vini, colori) to blend; (mettere in disordine) to mix up, muddle up; (carte) to shuffle; **~rsi** vr to mix; to blend; to get mixed up; (fig): **~rsi in** to get mixed up in, meddle in

'mese sm month

'messa sf (REL) mass; (il mettere): ~ **in moto** starting; ~ **in piega** set; ~ **a punto** (TECN) adjustment; (AUT) tuning; (fig) clarification; ~ **in scena** = **messinscena**

messag'gero [messad'dʒero] sm messenger

mes'saggio [mes'saddʒo] sm message

mes'sale sm (REL) missal

'messe sf harvest

Mes'sia sm inv (REL): **il ~** the Messiah

'Messico sm: **il ~** Mexico

messin'scena [messin'ʃena] sf (TEATRO) production

'messo, a pp di **mettere** ♦ sm messenger

mesti'ere sm (professione) job; (: manuale) trade; (: artigianale) craft; (fig: abilità nel lavoro) skill, technique; **essere del ~** to know the tricks of the trade

'mesto, a ag sad, melancholy

'mestolo sm (CUC) ladle

mestruazi'one [mestruat'tsjone] sf menstruation

'meta sf destination; (fig) aim, goal

metà sf inv half; (punto di mezzo) middle; **dividere qc a** o **per ~** to divide sth in half, halve sth; **fare a ~ (di qc con qn)** to go halves (with sb in sth); **a ~ prezzo** at half price; **a**

~ strada halfway
me'tafora sf metaphor
me'tallico, a, ci, che ag (di metallo)
metal cpd; (splendore, rumore etc)
metallic
me'tallo sm metal
metalmec'canico, a, ci, che ag
engineering cpd ♦ sm engineering
worker
me'tano sm methane
meteorolo'gia [meteorolo'dʒia] sf
meteorology; **meteoro'logico, a, ci,
che** ag meteorological, weather cpd
me'ticcio, a, ci, che [me'tittʃo] sm/f
half-caste, half-breed
me'todico, a, ci, che ag methodical
'metodo sm method
'metrica sf metrics sg; **'metrico, a, ci,
che** ag metric; (POESIA) metrical
'metro sm metre; (nastro) tape
measure; (asta) (metre) rule
metropoli'tana sf underground,
subway
metropoli'tano, a ag metropolitan
'mettere vt to put; (abito) to put on;
(: portare) to wear; (installare: telefono)
to put in; (fig: provocare): **~ fame/
allegria a qn** to make sb hungry/
happy; (supporre): **mettiamo che ...**
let's suppose o say that ... ; **~rsi** vr
(persona) to put o.s.; (oggetto) to go;
(disporsi: faccenda) to turn out; **~rsi a
sedere** to sit down; **~rsi a letto** to
get into bed; (per malattia) to take to
one's bed; **~rsi il cappello** to put on
one's hat; **~rsi a (cominciare)** to begin
to, start to; **~rsi al lavoro** to set to
work; **~rsi con qn (in società)** to team
up with sb; (in coppia) to start going
out with sb; **~rci: ~rci molta cura/
molto tempo** to take a lot of care/a
lot of time; **ci ho messo 3 ore per
venire** it's taken me 3 hours to get
here; **~rcela tutta** to do one's best;
~ a tacere qn/qc to keep sb/sth
quiet; **~ su casa** to set up house; **~ su
un negozio** to start a shop; **~ via** to
put away
'mezza ['meddza] sf: **la ~** half-past
twelve (in the afternoon); vedi anche
mezzo
mez'zadro [med'dzadro] sm (AGR)
sharecropper
mezza'luna [meddza'luna] sf half-
moon; (dell'islamismo) crescent;
(coltello) (semicircular) chopping knife
mezza'nino [meddza'nino] sm
mezzanine (floor)
mez'zano, a [med'dzano] ag (medio)
average, medium; (figlio) middle cpd
♦ sm/f (ruffiano) pimp
mezza'notte [meddza'nɔtte] sf
midnight
'mezzo, a ['meddzo] ag half; **un
~ litro/panino** half a litre/roll ♦ av
half; **~ morto** half-dead ♦ sm (metà)
half; (parte centrale: di strada etc)
middle; (per raggiungere un fine) means
sg; (veicolo) vehicle; (nell'indicare l'ora):
le nove e ~ half past nine;
mezzogiorno e ~ half past twelve; **~i**
smpl (possibilità economiche) means; **di
~a età** middle-aged; **un soprabito di
~a stagione** a spring (o autumn)
coat; **di ~** in the middle, in the middle;
andarci di ~ (patir danno) to suffer;
levarsi o togliersi di ~ to get out of
the way; **in ~ a** in the middle of; **per o
a ~ di** by means of; **~i di
comunicazione di massa** mass
media pl; **~i pubblici** public transport
sg; **~i di trasporto** means of transport
mezzogi'orno [meddzo'dʒorno] sm
midday, noon; **a ~** at 12 (o'clock) o
midday o noon; **il ~ d'Italia** southern
Italy
mez'z'ora [med'dzora] sf half-hour,
half an hour
mi (dav lo, la, li, le, ne diventa **me**) pron
(oggetto) me; (complemento di termine)
to me; (riflessivo) myself ♦ sm (MUS) E;
(: solfeggiando la scala) mi
'mia vedi mio
miago'lare vi to miaow, mew

'mica *av* (*fam*): **non ... ~ not ... a bit;
non sono ~ stanco** I'm not a bit
tired; **non sarà ~ partito?** he
wouldn't have left, would he?; **~ male**
not bad

'miccia, ce ['mittʃa] *sf* fuse

micidi'ale [mitʃi'djale] *ag* fatal;
(*dannosissimo*) deadly

mi'crofono *sm* microphone

micros'copio *sm* microscope

mi'dollo (*pl(f)* ~a) *sm* (ANAT) marrow;
~ osseo bone marrow

'mie *vedi* **mio**

mi'ei *vedi* **mio**

'miele *sm* honey

mi'etere *vt* (AGR) to reap, harvest; (*fig:
vite*) to take, claim

'miglia ['miʎʎa] *sfpl di* **miglio**

migli'aio [miʎ'ʎajo] (*pl(f)* ~a) *sm*
thousand; **un ~ (di)** about a thousand;
a ~a by the thousand, in thousands

'miglio ['miʎʎo] *sm* (BOT) millet; (*pl(f)*
~a: *unità di misura*) mile; **~ marino** o
nautico nautical mile

migliora'mento [miʎʎora'mento] *sm*
improvement

miglio'rare [miʎʎo'rare] *vt, vi* to
improve

migli'ore [miʎ'ʎore] *ag* (*comparativo*)
better; (*superlativo*) best ♦ *sm*: **il ~** the
best (thing) ♦ *sm/f*: **il(la) ~** the best
(person); **il miglior vino di questa
regione** the best wine in this area

'mignolo ['minɲolo] *sm* (ANAT) little
finger, pinkie; (: *dito del piede*) little toe

mi'grare *vi* to migrate

Mi'lano *sf* Milan

miliar'dario, a *sm/f* millionaire

mili'ardo *sm* thousand million, billion
(US)

mili'are *ag*: **pietra ~** milestone

mili'one *sm* million; **due ~i di lire** two
million lire

mili'tante *ag, sm/f* militant

mili'tare *vi* (MIL) to be a soldier, serve;
(*fig: in un partito*) to be a militant ♦ *ag*

military ♦ *sm* serviceman; **fare il ~** to
do one's military service

'milite *sm* soldier

millanta'tore, 'trice *sm/f* boaster

'mille (*pl* **mila**) *num* a o one thousand;
dieci mila ten thousand

mille'foglie [mille'fɔʎʎe] *sm inv* (CUC)
cream o vanilla slice

mil'lennio *sm* millennium

millepi'edi *sm inv* centipede

mil'lesimo, a *ag, sm* thousandth

milli'grammo *sm* milligram(me)

milli'metro *sm* millimetre

'milza ['miltsa] *sf* (ANAT) spleen

mi'mosa *sf* mimosa

mimetiz'zare [mimetid'dzare] *vt* to
camouflage; **~rsi** *vr* to camouflage o.s.

'mimica *sf* (*arte*) mime

'mimo *sm* (*attore, componimento*)
mime

'mina *sf* (*esplosiva*) mine; (*di matita*)
lead

mi'naccia, ce [mi'nattʃa] *sf* threat;
minacci'are *vt* to threaten;
minacciare qn di morte to threaten
to kill sb; **minacciare di fare qc** to
threaten to do sth; **minacci'oso, a** *ag*
threatening

mi'nare *vt* (MIL) to mine; (*fig*) to
undermine

mina'tore *sm* miner

mina'torio, a *ag* threatening

mine'rale *ag, sm* mineral

mine'rario, a *ag* (*delle miniere*)
mining; (*dei minerali*) ore *cpd*

mi'nestra *sf* soup; **~ in brodo/di
verdure** noodle/vegetable soup;
mines'trone *sm* thick vegetable and
pasta soup

mingher'lino, a [minger'lino] *ag*
thin, slender

'mini *ag inv* mini ♦ *sf inv* miniskirt

minia'tura *sf* miniature

mini'era *sf* mine

mini'gonna *sf* miniskirt

'minimo, a *ag* minimum, least,
slightest; (*piccolissimo*) very small,

slight; (il più basso) lowest, minimum ♦ sm minimum; al ~ at least; girare al ~ (AUT) to idle

mini'stero sm (POL, REL) ministry; (governo) government; M~ delle Finanze Ministry of Finance, ≈ Treasury

mi'nistro sm (POL, REL) minister

mino'ranza [mino'rantsa] sf minority

mino'rato, a ag handicapped ♦ sm/f physically (o mentally) handicapped person

mi'nore (comparativo) less; (più piccolo) smaller; (numero) lower; (inferiore) lower, inferior; (meno importante) minor; (più giovane) younger; (superlativo) least; smallest; lowest; youngest ♦ sm/f = minorenne

mino'renne ag under age ♦ sm/f minor, person under age

mi'nuscolo, a ag (scrittura, carattere) small; (piccolissimo) tiny ♦ sf small letter

mi'nuta sf rough copy, draft

mi'nuto, a ag tiny, minute; (pioggia) fine; (corporatura) delicate, fine ♦ sm (unità di misura) minute; al ~ (COMM) retail

'mio (f 'mia, pl mi'ei, 'mie) det: il ~, la mia etc my ♦ pron: il ~, la mia etc mine; i miei my family; un ~ amico a friend of mine

'miope ag short-sighted

'mira sf (anche fig) aim; prendere la ~ to take aim; prendere di ~ qn (fig) to pick on sb

mi'rabile ag admirable, wonderful

mi'racolo sm miracle

mi'raggio [mi'raddʒo] sm mirage

mi'rare vi: ~ a to aim at

mi'rino sm (TECN) sight; (FOT) viewer, viewfinder

mir'tillo sm bilberry (BRIT), blueberry (US), whortleberry

mi'scela [miʃ'ʃela] sf mixture; (di caffè) blend

miscel'lanea [miʃʃel'lanea] sf miscellany

'mischia ['miskja] sf scuffle; (RUGBY) scrum, scrummage

mischi'are [mis'kjare] vt to mix, blend; ~rsi vr to mix, blend

mis'cuglio [mis'kuʎʎo] sm mixture, hotchpotch, jumble

mise'rabile ag (infelice) miserable, wretched; (povero) poverty-stricken; (di scarso valore) miserable

mi'seria sf extreme poverty; (infelicità) misery; ~e sfpl (del mondo etc) misfortunes, troubles; porca ~! (fam) blast!, damn!

miseri'cordia sf mercy, pity

'misero, a ag miserable, wretched; (povero) poverty-stricken; (insufficiente) miserable

mis'fatto sm misdeed, crime

mi'sogino [mi'zɔdʒino] sm misogynist

'missile sm missile

missio'nario, a ag, sm/f missionary

missi'one sf mission

misteri'oso, a ag mysterious

mis'tero sm mystery

'misto, a ag mixed; (scuola) mixed, coeducational ♦ sm mixture

mis'tura sf mixture

mi'sura sf measure; (misurazione, dimensione) measurement; (taglia) size; (provvedimento) measure, step; (moderazione) moderation; (MUS) time; (: divisione) bar; (fig: limite) bounds pl, limit; nella ~ in cui inasmuch as, insofar as; (fatto) su ~ made to measure

misu'rare vt (ambiente, stoffa) to measure; (terreno) to survey; (abito) to try on; (pesare) to weigh; (fig: parole etc) to weigh up; (: spese, cibo) to limit ♦ vi to measure; ~rsi vr: ~rsi con qn to have a confrontation with sb; to compete with sb; misu'rato, a ag (ponderato) measured; (moderato) moderate

'mite ag mild

miti'gare vt to mitigate, lessen; (lenire) to soothe, relieve; ~rsi vr (odio) to subside; (*tempo*) to become milder

'**mito** *sm* myth; **mitolo'gia, 'gie** *sf* mythology

'**mitra** *sf* (REL) mitre ♦ *sm inv* (*arma*) sub-machine gun

mitra'glia'trice [mitraʎʎa'tritʃe] *sf* machine gun

mit'tente *sm/f* sender

'**mobile** *ag* mobile; (*parte di macchina*) moving; (DIR: *bene*) movable, personal ♦ *sm* (*arredamento*) piece of furniture; **~i** *smpl* (*mobilia*) furniture *sg*

mo'bilia *sf* furniture

mobili'are *ag* (DIR) personal, movable

mo'bilio *sm* = **mobilia**

mobili'tare *vt* to mobilize

mocas'sino *sm* moccasin

mocci'oso, a [mot'tʃoso, a] *sm/f* (*peg*) snotty(-nosed) kid

'**moccolo** *sm* (*di candela*) candle-end; (*fam: bestemmia*) oath; (: *moccio*) snot; **reggere il ~** to play gooseberry (BRIT), act as chaperon

'**moda** *sf* fashion; **alla ~, di ~** fashionable, in fashion

modalità *sf inv* formality

mo'della *sf* model

model'lare *vt* (*creta*) to model, shape; **~rsi** *vr*: **~rsi su** to model o.s. on

mo'dello *sm* model; (*stampo*) mould ♦ *ag inv* model *cpd*

'**modem** *sm inv* modem

mode'rare *vt* to moderate; **~rsi** *vr* to restrain o.s.; **mode'rato, a** *ag* moderate

modera'tore, 'trice *sm/f* moderator

mo'derno, a *ag* modern

mo'destia *sf* modesty

mo'desto, a *ag* modest

'**modico, a, ci, che** *ag* reasonable, moderate

mo'difica, che *sf* modification

modifi'care *vt* to modify, alter; **~rsi** *vr* to alter, change

mo'dista *sf* milliner

'**modo** *sm* way, manner; (*mezzo*) means, way; (*occasione*) opportunity;

(LING) mood; (MUS) mode; **~i** *smpl* (*comportamento*) manners; **a suo ~, a ~ suo** in his own way; **ad** *o* **in ogni ~** anyway; **di** *o* **in ~ che** so that; **in ~ da** so as to; **in tutti i ~i** at all costs; (*comunque sia*) anyway; (*in ogni caso*) in any case; **in qualche ~** somehow or other; **~ di dire** turn of phrase; **per ~ di dire** so to speak

modu'lare *vt* to modulate; **modulazi'one** *sf* modulation; **modulazione di frequenza** frequency modulation

'**modulo** *sm* (*modello*) form; (ARCHIT, *lunare, di comando*) module

mo'gano *sm* mahogany

'**mogio, a, gi, gie** ['mɔdʒo] *ag* down in the dumps, dejected

'**moglie** ['moʎʎe] *sf* wife

mo'ine *sfpl* cajolery *sg*; (*leziosità*) affectation *sg*

'**mola** *sf* millstone; (*utensile abrasivo*) grindstone

mo'lare *sm* (*dente*) molar

'**mole** *sf* mass; (*dimensioni*) size; (*edificio grandioso*) massive structure

moles'tare *vt* to bother, annoy; **mo'lestia** *sf* annoyance, bother; **recar molestia a qn** to bother sb; **mo'lesto, a** *ag* annoying

'**molla** *sf* spring; **~e** *sfpl* (*per camino*) tongs

mol'lare *vt* to release, let go; (NAUT) to ease; (*fig: ceffone*) to give ♦ *vi* (*cedere*) to give in

'**molle** *ag* soft; (*muscoli*) flabby

mol'letta *sf* (*per capelli*) hairgrip; (*per panni stesi*) clothes peg

'**mollica, che** *sf* crumb, soft part

mol'lusco, schi *sm* mollusc

'**molo** *sm* mole, breakwater; jetty

mol'teplice [mol'teplitʃe] *ag* (*formato di più elementi*) complex; **~i** *pl* (*svariati: interessi, attività*) numerous, various

moltipli'care *vt* to multiply; **~rsi** *vr* to multiply; to increase in number; **moltiplicazi'one** *sf* multiplication

PAROLA CHIAVE

'molto, a det (quantità) a lot of, much; (numero) a lot of, many; **~ pane/ carbone** a lot of bread/coal; **~a gente** a lot of people, many people; **~i libri** a lot of books, many books; **non ho ~ tempo** I haven't got much time; **per ~ (tempo)** for a long time
♦ av **1** a lot, (very) much; **viaggia ~** he travels a lot; **non viaggia ~** he doesn't travel much o a lot
2 (intensivo: con aggettivi, avverbi) very; (: con participio passato) (very) much; **~ buono/ragazzo** o **~ migliore, ~ meglio** much o a lot better
♦ pron (molta cosa) a lot; **~a, e** pron pl many, a lot; **~i pensano che ...** many (people) think ...

momen'taneo, a ag momentary, fleeting

mo'mento sm moment; **da un ~ all'altro** at any moment; (all'improvviso) suddenly; **al ~ di fare** just as I was (o you were o he was etc) doing; **per il ~** for the time being; **dal ~ che** ever since; (dato che) since; **a ~i** (da un ~ all'altro) any time o moment now; (quasi) nearly

'monaca, che sf nun

'Monaco sf Monaco; **~ (di Baviera)** Munich

'monaco, ci sm monk

mo'narca, chi sm monarch; **monar'chia** sf monarchy

monas'tero sm (di monaci) monastery; (di monache) convent; **mo'nastico, a, ci, che** ag monastic

'monco, a, chi, che ag maimed; (fig) incomplete

mon'dano, a ag (anche fig) worldly; (dell'alta società) society cpd; fashionable

mon'dare vt (frutta, patate) to peel; (piselli) to shell; (pulire) to clean

mondi'ale ag (campionato, popolazione) world cpd; (influenza) world-wide

'mondo sm world; (grande quantità): **un ~ di** lots of, a host of; **il bel ~** high society

mo'nello, a sm/f street urchin; (ragazzo vivace) scamp, imp

mo'neta sf coin; (ECON: valuta) currency; (denaro spicciolo) (small) change; **~ estera** foreign currency; **~ legale** legal tender; **mone'tario, a** ag monetary

mongo'loide ag, sm/f (MED) mongol

'monito sm warning

'monitor sm inv (TECN, TV) monitor

monolo'cale sm studio flat

mono'polio sm monopoly

mo'notono, a ag monotonous

monsi'gnore [monsiɲˈɲore] sm (REL: titolo) Your (o His) Grace

mon'sone sm monsoon

monta'carichi [montaˈkariki] sm inv hoist, goods lift

mon'taggio [monˈtaddʒo] sm (TECN) assembly; (CINEMA) editing

mon'tagna [monˈtaɲɲa] sf mountain; (zona montuosa): **la ~** the mountains pl; **andare in ~** to go to the mountains; **~e russe** roller coaster sg, big dipper sg (BRIT); **monta'gnoso, a** ag mountainous

monta'naro, a ag mountain cpd
♦ sm/f mountain dweller

mon'tano, a ag mountain cpd; alpine

mon'tare vt to go (o come) up; (cavallo) to ride; (apparecchiatura) to set up, assemble; (CUC) to whip; (ZOOL) to cover; (incastonare) to mount, set; (CINEMA) to edit; (FOT) to mount ♦ vi to go (o come) up; (a cavallo): **~ bene/ male** to ride well/badly; (aumentare di livello, volume) to rise; **~rsi** vr to become big-headed; **~ qc** to exaggerate sth; **~ qn** o **la testa a qn** to turn sb's head; **~ in bicicletta/ macchina/treno** to get on a bicycle/ into a car/on a train; **~ a cavallo** to get on o mount a horse

monta'tura sf assembling no pl; (di occhiali) frames pl; (di gioiello) mounting, setting; (fig): ~ **pubblicitaria** publicity stunt

'monte sm mountain; **a ~ upstream; mandare a ~ qc** to upset sth, cause sth to fail; **il M~ Bianco** Mont Blanc; **~ di pietà** pawnshop

mon'tone sm (ZOOL) ram; **carne di ~** mutton

montu'oso, a ag mountainous

monu'mento sm monument

mo'quette [mɔ'kɛt] sf inv fitted carpet

'mora sf (del rovo) blackberry; (del gelso) mulberry; (DIR) delay; (: somma) arrears pl

mo'rale ag moral ♦ sf (scienza) ethics sg, moral philosophy; (complesso di norme) moral standards pl, morality; (condotta) morals pl; (insegnamento morale) ~ sm morale; **essere giù di ~** to be feeling down; **moralità** sf morality; (condotta) morals pl

'morbido, a ag soft; (pelle) soft, smooth

mor'billo sm (MED) measles sg

'morbo sm disease

mor'boso, a ag (fig) morbid

mor'dace [mor'datʃe] ag biting, cutting

mor'dente sm (fig: di satira, critica) bite; (: di persona) drive

'mordere vt to bite; (addentare) to bite into

mori'bondo, a ag dying, moribund

morige'rato, a [moridʒe'rato] ag of good morals

mo'rire vi to die; (abitudine, civiltà) to die out; **~ di fame** to die of hunger; (fig) to be starving; **~ di noia/paura** to be bored/scared to death; **fa un caldo da ~** it's terribly hot

mormo'rare vi to murmur; (brontolare) to grumble

'moro, a ag dark(-haired); dark(-complexioned); **i M~i** smpl

(STORIA) the Moors

mo'roso, a ag in arrears ♦ sm/f (fam: innamorato) sweetheart

'morsa sf (TECN) vice; (fig: stretta) grip

morsi'care vt to nibble (at), gnaw (at); (sog: insetto) to bite

'morso, a pp di **mordere** ♦ sm bite; (di insetto) sting; (parte della briglia) bit; **~i della fame** pangs of hunger

mor'taio sm mortar

mor'tale ag, sm mortal; **mortalità** sf mortality, death rate

'morte sf death

mortifi'care vt to mortify

'morto, a pp di **morire** ♦ ag dead ♦ sm/f dead man/woman; **i ~i** the dead; **fare il ~** (nell'acqua) to float on one's back; **il Mar M~** the Dead Sea

mor'torio sm (anche fig) funeral

mo'saico, ci sm mosaic

'Mosca sf Moscow

'mosca, sche [e] sf fly; **~ cieca** blind-man's-buff

mos'cato sm muscatel (wine)

mosce'rino [moʃʃe'rino] sm midge, gnat

mos'chea [mos'kea] sf mosque

mos'chetto [mos'ketto] sm musket

'moscio, a, sci, sce ['mɔʃʃo] ag (fig) lifeless

mos'cone sm (ZOOL) bluebottle; (barca) pedalo; (: a remi) kind of pedalo with oars

'mossa sf movement; (nel gioco) move

'mosso, a pp di **muovere** ♦ ag (mare) rough; (capelli) wavy; (FOT) blurred

mos'tarda sf mustard

'mostra sf exhibition, show; (ostentazione) show; **in ~** on show; **far ~ di** (fingere) to pretend; **far ~ di sé** to show off

mos'trare vt to show; **~rsi** vr to appear

'mostro sm monster; **mostru'oso, a** ag monstrous

mo'tel sm inv motel

moti'vare vt (causare) to cause;

(*giustificare*) to justify, account for; **motivazi'one** sf justification; motive; (*PSIC*) motivation

mo'tivo sm (*causa*) reason, cause; (*movente*) motive; (*letterario*) (central) theme; (*disegno*) motif, design, pattern; (*MUS*) motif; **per quale ~?** why?, for what reason?

'moto sm (*anche FISICA*) motion; (*movimento, gesto*) movement; (*esercizio fisico*) exercise; (*sommossa*) rising, revolt; (*commozione*) feeling, impulse ♦ sf inv (*motocicletta*) motorbike; **mettere in ~** to set in motion; (*AUT*) to start up

motoci'cletta sf motorcycle; **motoci'clismo** sm motorcycling, motorcycle racing; **motoci'clista, i, e** sm/f motorcyclist

mo'tore, 'trice ag motor; (*TECN*) driving ♦ sm engine, motor; **a ~** motor cpd, power-driven; **~ a combustione interna/a reazione** internal combustion/jet engine; **moto'rino** sm moped; **motorino di avviamento** (*AUT*) starter; **motoriz'zato, a** ag (*truppe*) motorized; (*persona*) having a car o transport

motos'cafo sm motorboat

'motto sm (*battuta scherzosa*) witty remark; (*frase emblematica*) motto, maxim

'mouse ['maus] sm inv (*INFORM*) mouse

mo'vente sm motive

movimen'tare vt to liven up

movi'mento sm movement; (*fig*) activity, hustle and bustle; (*MUS*) tempo, movement

mozi'one [mot'tsjone] sf (*POL*) motion

moz'zare [mot'tsare] vt to cut off; (*coda*) to dock; **~ il fiato** o **il respiro a qn** (*fig*) to take sb's breath away

mozza'rella [mottsa'rɛlla] sf mozzarella

mozzi'cone [mottsi'kone] sm stub, butt, end; (*anche*: **~ di sigaretta**) cigarette end

'mozzo ['mottso] sm (*NAUT*) ship's boy

'mucca, che sf cow

'mucchio ['mukkjo] sm pile, heap; (*fig*): **un ~ di** lots of, heaps of

'muco, chi sm mucus

'muffa sf mould, mildew

mug'gire [mud'dʒire] vi (*vacca*) to low, moo; (*toro*) to bellow; (*fig*) to roar; **mug'gito** sm low, moo; bellow; roar

mu'ghetto [mu'getto] sm lily of the valley

mu'gnaio, a [muɲ'najo] sm/f miller

mugo'lare vi (*cane*) to whimper, whine; (*fig: persona*) to moan

muli'nare vi to whirl, spin (round and round)

muli'nello sm (*moto vorticoso*) eddy, whirl; (*di canna da pesca*) reel

mu'lino sm mill; **~ a vento** windmill

'mulo sm mule

'multa sf fine; **mul'tare** vt to fine

'multiplo, a ag, sm multiple

multiproprietà sf inv time-share

'mummia sf mummy

'mungere ['mundʒere] vt (*anche fig*) to milk

munici'pale [munitʃi'pale] ag municipal; town cpd

muni'cipio [muni'tʃipjo] sm town council, corporation; (*edificio*) town hall

mu'nire vt: **~ qc/qn di** to equip sth/sb with

munizi'oni [munit'tsjoni] sfpl (*MIL*) ammunition sg

'munto, a pp di **mungere**

mu'overe, vt to move; (*ruota, macchina*) to drive; (*sollevare: questione, obiezione*) to raise, bring up; (: *accusa*) to make, bring forward; **~rsi** vr to move; **muoviti!** hurry up!, get a move on!

'mura sfpl vedi **muro**

mu'raglia [mu'raʎʎa] sf (high) wall

mu'rale ag wall cpd; mural

mu'rare vt (*persona, porta*) to wall up

mura'tore sm mason; bricklayer

'**muro** *sm* wall; **~a** *sfpl* (*cinta cittadina*) walls; **a ~** wall *cpd*; (*armadio etc*) built-in; **~ del suono** sound barrier; **mettere al ~** (*fucilare*) to shoot o execute (by firing squad)

'**muschio** ['muskjo] *sm* (*ZOOL*) musk; (*BOT*) moss

musco'lare *ag* muscular, muscle *cpd*

'**muscolo** *sm* (*ANAT*) muscle

mu'seo *sm* museum

museru'ola *sf* muzzle

'**musica** *sf* music; **~ da ballo/camera** dance/chamber music; **musi'cale** *ag* musical; **musi'cista, i, e** *sm/f* musician

'**muso** *sm* muzzle; (*di auto, aereo*) nose; **tenere il ~** to sulk; **mu'sone, a** *sm/f* sulky person

'**muta** *sf* (*di animali*) moulting; (*di serpenti*) sloughing; (*per immersioni subacquee*) diving suit; (*gruppo di cani*) pack

muta'mento *sm* change

mu'tande *sfpl* (*di uomo*) (under)pants; **mutan'dine** *sfpl* (*da donna, bambino*) pants (*BRIT*), briefs

mu'tare *vt, vi* to change, alter; **mutazi'one** *sf* change, alteration; (*BIOL*) mutation; **mu'tevole** *ag* changeable

muti'lare *vt* to mutilate, maim; (*fig*) to mutilate, deface; **muti'lato, a** *sm/f* disabled person (*through loss of limbs*)

mu'tismo *sm* (*MED*) mutism; (*atteggiamento*) (stubborn) silence

'**muto, a** *ag* (*MED*) dumb; (*emozione, dolore, CINEMA*) silent; (*LING*) silent, mute; (*carta geografica*) blank; **~ per lo stupore** *etc* speechless with amazement *etc*

'**mutua** *sf* (*anche: cassa ~*) health insurance scheme

mutu'are *vt* (*fig*) to borrow

mutu'ato, a *sm/f* member of a health insurance scheme

'**mutuo, a** *ag* (*reciproco*) mutual ♦ *sm* (*ECON*) (long-term) loan

N, n

N. *abbr* (= *nord*) N

'nacchere ['nakkere] *sfpl* castanets

'**nafta** *sf* naphtha; (*per motori diesel*) diesel oil

nafta'lina *sf* (*CHIM*) naphthalene; (*tarmicida*) mothballs *pl*

'**naia** *sf* (*MIL*) slang term for national service

'**nailon** *sm* nylon

'**nanna** *sf* (*linguaggio infantile*): **andare a ~** to go to beddy-byes

'**nano, a** *ag, sm/f* dwarf

napole'tano, a *ag, sm/f* Neapolitan

'**Napoli** *sf* Naples

'**nappa** *sf* tassel

nar'ciso [nar'tʃizo] *sm* narcissus

nar'cosi *sf* narcosis

nar'cotico, ci *sm* narcotic

na'rice [na'ritʃe] *sf* nostril

nar'rare *vt* to tell the story of, recount; **narra'tiva** *sf* (*branca letteraria*) fiction; **narra'tivo, a** *ag* narrative; **narra'tore, 'trice** *sm/f* narrator; **narrazi'one** *sf* narration; (*racconto*) story, tale

na'sale *ag* nasal

'**nascere** ['naʃʃere] *vi* (*bambino*) to be born; (*pianta*) to come o spring up; (*fiume*) to rise, have its source; (*sole*) to rise; (*dente*) to come through; (*fig: derivare, conseguire*): **~ da** to arise from, be born out of; **è nata nel 1952** she was born in 1952; '**nascita** *sf* birth

nas'condere *vt* to hide, conceal; **~rsi** *vr* to hide; **nascon'diglio** *sm* hiding place; **nascon'dino** *sm* (*gioco*) hide-and-seek; **nas'costo, a** *pp di* **nascondere** ♦ *ag* hidden; *di* **nascosto** secretly

na'sello *sm* (*ZOOL*) hake

'**naso** *sm* nose

'**nastro** *sm* ribbon; (*magnetico, isolante,*

SPORT) tape; **~ adesivo** adhesive tape; **~ trasportatore** conveyor belt

nas'turzio [nas'turtsjo] *sm* nasturtium

na'tale *ag* of one's birth ♦ *sm (REL)*: **N~** Christmas; *(giorno della nascita)* birthday; **natalità** *sf* birth rate; **nata'lizio, a** *ag (del Natale)* Christmas *cpd*

na'tante *sm* craft *inv*, boat

'natica, che *sf (ANAT)* buttock

na'tio, a, 'tii, 'tie *ag* native

Nativita *sf (REL)* Nativity

na'tivo, a *ag, sm/f* native

'nato, a *pp di* nascere ♦ *ag*: **un attore ~** a born actor; **~a Pieri** née Pieri

na'tura *sf* nature; **pagare in ~** to pay in kind; **~ morta** still life

natu'rale *ag* natural; **natura'lezza** *sf* naturalness; **natura'lista, i, e** *sm/f* naturalist

naturaliz'zare [naturalid'dzare] *vt* to naturalize

natural'mente *av* naturally; *(certamente, sì)* of course

naufra'gare *vi (nave)* to be wrecked; *(persona)* to be shipwrecked; *(fig)* to fall through; **nau'fragio** *sm* shipwreck; *(fig)* ruin, failure; **'naufrago, ghi** *sm* castaway, shipwreck victim

'nausea *sf* nausea; **nausea'bondo, a** *ag* nauseating, sickening; **nause'are** *vt* to nauseate, make (feel) sick

'nautica *sf (art of)* navigation

'nautico, a, ci, che *ag* nautical

na'vale *ag* naval

na'vata *sf (anche: ~ centrale)* nave; *(anche: ~ laterale)* aisle

'nave *sf* ship, vessel; **~ cisterna** tanker; **~ da guerra** warship; **~ passeggeri** passenger ship

na'vetta *sf* shuttle; *(servizio di collegamento)* shuttle (service)

navi'cella [navi'tʃɛlla] *sf (di aerostato)* gondola; **~ spaziale** spaceship

navi'gare *vi* to sail; **~ in Internet** to surf the Net; **navigazi'one** *sf*

navigation

na'viglio [na'viʎʎo] *sm (canale artificiale)* canal; **~ da pesca** fishing fleet

nazio'nale [nattsjo'nale] *ag* national ♦ *sf (SPORT)* national team; **naziona'lismo** *sm* nationalism; **nazionalità** *sf inv* nationality

nazi'one [nat'tsjone] *sf* nation

PAROLA CHIAVE

ne *pron* **1** *(di lui, lei, loro)* of him/her/ them; about him/her/them; **~ riconosco la voce** I recognize his (o her) voice

2 *(di questa, quella cosa)* of it; about it; **~ voglio ancora** I want some more (of it o them); **non parliamone più!** let's not talk about it any more!

3 *(con valore partitivo)*: **hai dei libri? — sì, ~ ho** have you any books? — yes, I have (some); **hai del pane? — no, non ~ ho** have you any bread? — no, I haven't any; **quanti anni hai? — ~ ho 17** how old are you? — I'm 17

♦ *av (moto da luogo: da lì)* from there; **~ vengo ora** I've just come from there

---

né *cong*: **~ ... ~** neither ... nor; **l'uno ~ l'altro lo vuole** neither of them wants it; **non parla ~ l'italiano ~ il tedesco** he speaks neither Italian nor German, he doesn't speak either Italian or German; **non piove ~ nevica** it isn't raining or snowing

ne'anche [ne'anke] *av, cong* not even; **non ... ~** not even; **~ se volesse potrebbe venire** he couldn't come even if he wanted to; **non l'ho visto — ~ io** I didn't see him — neither did I o I didn't either; **~ per idea o sogno!** not on your life!

'nebbia *sf* fog; *(foschia)* mist; **nebbi'oso, a** *ag* foggy; misty

nebu'loso, a *ag (atmosfera)* hazy; *(fig)* hazy, vague

necessaria'mente [netʃessarja'mente] av necessarily

neces'sario, a [netʃes'sarjo] ag necessary

necessità [netʃessi'ta] sf inv necessity; (povertà) need, poverty; **necessi'tare** vt to require ♦ vi (aver bisogno): **necessitare di** to need

necro'logio [nekro'lɔdʒo] sm obituary notice

ne'fando, a ag infamous, wicked

ne'fasto, a ag inauspicious, ill-omened

ne'gare vt to deny; (rifiutare) to deny, refuse; ~ **di aver fatto/che** to deny having done/that; **nega'tivo, a** ag, sf, sm negative; **negazi'one** sf negation

ne'gletto, a ag (trascurato) neglected

ne'gli ['neʎʎi] prep +det vedi **in**

negli'gente [negli'dʒɛnte] ag negligent, careless; **negli'genza** sf negligence, carelessness

negozi'ante [negot'tsjante] sm/f trader, dealer; (bottegaio) shopkeeper (BRIT), storekeeper (US)

negozi'are [negot'tsjare] vt to negotiate ♦ vi: ~ **in** to trade o deal in; **negozi'ato** sm negotiation

ne'gozio [ne'gɔttsjo] sm (locale) shop (BRIT), store (US)

'negro, a ag, sm/f Negro

'nei prep +det vedi **in**

nel prep +det vedi **in**

nell' prep +det vedi **in**

'nella prep +det vedi **in**

'nelle prep +det vedi **in**

'nello prep +det vedi **in**

'nembo sm (METEOR) nimbus

ne'mico, a, ci, che ag hostile; (MIL) enemy cpd ♦ sm/f enemy; **essere ~ di** to be strongly averse o opposed to

nem'meno av, cong = **neanche**

'nenia sf dirge; (motivo monotono) monotonous tune

neo sm mole; (fig) (slight) flaw

neo... prefisso neo...

neon sm (CHIM) neon

neo'nato, a ag newborn ♦ sm/f

newborn baby

neozelan'dese [neoddzelan'dese] ag New Zealand cpd ♦ sm/f New Zealander

nep'pure av, cong = **neanche**

'nerbo sm lash; (fig) strength, backbone; **nerbo'ruto, a** ag muscular; robust

ne'retto sm (TIP) bold type

'nero, a ag black; (scuro) dark ♦ sm black; **il Mar N~** the Black Sea

nerva'tura sf (ANAT) nervous system; (BOT) veining; (ARCHIT, TECN) rib

'nervo sm (ANAT) nerve; (BOT) vein; **avere i ~i** to be on edge; **dare sui ~i a qn** to get on sb's nerves; **ner'voso, a** ag nervous; (irritabile) irritable ♦ sm (fam): **far venire il nervoso a qn** to get on sb's nerves

'nespola sf (BOT) medlar; (fig) blow, punch; **'nespolo** sm medlar tree

'nesso sm connection, link

nes'suno, a (det: dav sm **nessun** +C, V, **nessuno** +s impura, gn, pn, ps, x, z; dav sf **nessuna** +C, **nessun'** +V) det 1 (non uno) no, espressione negativa +any; **non c'è nessun libro** there isn't any book, there is no book; **nessun altro** no one else, nobody else; **nessun'altra cosa** nothing else; **in nessun luogo** nowhere

2 (qualche) any; **hai ~a obiezione?** do you have any objections?

♦ pron 1 (non uno) no one, nobody, espressione negativa +any(one); (: cosa) none, espressione negativa +any; ~ **è venuto, non è venuto** nobody came

2 (qualcuno) anyone, anybody; **ha telefonato ~?** did anyone phone?

net'tare¹ vt to clean

'nettare² sm nectar

net'tezza [net'tettsa] sf cleanness, cleanliness; ~ **urbana** cleansing department

'netto, a ag (pulito) clean; (chiaro) clear, clear-cut; (deciso) definite; (ECON) net

nettur'bino sm dustman (BRIT), garbage collector (US)

neu'rosi sf = nevrosi

neu'trale ag neutral; **neutralità** sf neutrality; **neutraliz'zare** vt to neutralize

'neutro, a ag neutral; (LING) neuter ♦ sm (LING) neuter

ne'vaio sm snowfield

'neve sf snow; **nevi'care** vb impers to snow; **nevi'cata** sf snowfall

ne'vischio [ne'viskjo] sm sleet

ne'voso, a ag snowy; snow-covered

nevral'gia [nevral'dʒia] sf neuralgia

nevras'tenico, a, ci, che ag (MED) neurasthenic; (fig) hot-tempered

ne'vrosi sf neurosis

'nibbio sm (ZOOL) kite

'nicchia ['nikkja] sf niche; (naturale) cavity, hollow

nicchi'are [nik'kjare] vi to shilly-shally, hesitate

'nichel ['nikel] sm nickel

nico'tina sf nicotine

'nido sm nest; **a ~ d'ape** (tessuto etc) honeycomb cpd

PAROLA CHIAVE

ni'ente pron 1 (nessuna cosa) nothing; **~ può fermarlo** nothing can stop him; **~ di** absolutely nothing; **nient'altro** nothing else; **nient'altro che** nothing but, just, only; **~ affatto** not at all, not in the least; **come se ~ fosse** as if nothing had happened; **cose da ~** trivial matters; **per ~** (gratis, invano) for nothing

2 (qualcosa): **hai bisogno di ~?** do you need anything?

3: **non ... ~** nothing, espressione negativa + anything; **non ho visto ~** I saw nothing, I didn't see anything; **non ho ~ da dire** I have nothing o

haven't anything to say

♦ av nothing; **un bel ~** absolutely nothing; **basta un ~ per farla piangere** the slightest thing is enough to make her cry

♦ av (in nessuna misura): **non ... ~** not ... at all; **non è (per) ~ buono** it isn't good at all

nientedi'meno av actually, even ♦ escl really!, I say!

niente'meno av, escl = nientedimeno

'Nilo sm: **il ~** the Nile

'ninfa sf nymph

nin'fea sf water lily

ninna-'nanna sf lullaby

'ninnolo sm (gingillo) knick-knack

ni'pote sm/f (di zii) nephew/niece; (di nonni) grandson/daughter, grandchild

'nitido, a ag clear; (specchio) bright

ni'trato sm nitrate

'nitrico, a, ci, che ag nitric

ni'trire vi to neigh

ni'trito sm (di cavallo) neighing no pl; neigh; (CHIM) nitrite

nitroglice'rina [nitroglitʃe'rina] sf nitroglycerine

no av (risposta) no; **vieni o ~?** are you coming or not?; **perché ~?** why not?; **lo conosciamo? — tu ~ ma io sì** do we know him? — you don't but I do; **verrai, ~?** you'll come, won't you?

'nobile ag noble ♦ sm/f noble, nobleman/woman; **nobili'are** ag noble; **nobiltà** sf nobility; (di azione) nobleness

'nocca, che sf (ANAT) knuckle

nocci'ola [not'tʃɔla] ag inv (colore) hazel, light brown ♦ sf hazelnut

noccio'lina [nottʃo'lina] sf: **~ americana** peanut

'nocciolo¹ ['nɔttʃolo] sm (di frutto) stone; (fig) heart, core

noc'ciolo² [not'tʃɔlo] sm (albero) hazel

'noce ['nɔtʃe] sm (albero) walnut tree ♦ sf (frutto) walnut; **~ moscata**

nutmeg

no'civo, a [no'tʃivo] ag harmful, noxious

'nodo sm (di cravatta, legname, NAUT) knot; (AUT, FERR) junction; (MED, ASTR, BOT) node; (fig: legame) bond, tie; (: punto centrale) heart, crux; **avere un ~ alla gola** to have a lump in one's throat; **no'doso, a** ag (tronco) gnarled

'noi pron (soggetto) we; (oggetto: per dare rilievo, con preposizione) us; **~ stessi(e)** we ourselves; (oggetto) ourselves

'noia sf boredom; (disturbo, impaccio) bother no pl, trouble no pl; **avere qn/qc a ~** not to like sb/sth; **mi è venuto a ~** I'm tired of it; **dare ~ a** to annoy; **avere delle ~e con qn** to have trouble with sb

noi'altri pron we

noi'oso, a ag boring; (fastidioso) annoying, troublesome

noleggi'are [noled'dʒare] vt (prendere a noleggio) to hire (BRIT), rent; (dare a noleggio) to hire out (BRIT), rent (out); (aereo, nave) to charter; **no'leggio** sm hire (BRIT), rental; charter

'nolo sm hire (BRIT), rental; charter; (per trasporto merci) freight; **prendere/dare a ~ qc** to hire/hire out sth

'nomade ag nomadic ♦ sm/f nomad

'nome sm name; (LING) noun; **in/a ~ di** in the name of; **di o per ~** (chiamato) called, named; **conoscere qn di ~** to know sb by name; **~ d'arte** stage name; **~ di battesimo** Christian name; **~ di famiglia** surname

no'mea sf notoriety

no'mignolo [no'miɲɲolo] sm nickname

'nomina sf appointment

nomi'nale ag nominal; (LING) noun cpd

nomi'nare vt to name; (eleggere) to appoint; (citare) to mention

nomina'tivo, a ag (LING) nominative; (ECON) registered ♦ sm (LING: anche: **caso ~**) nominative (case); (AMM) name

non av not ♦ prefisso non-; vedi **affatto; appena** etc

nonché [non'ke] cong (tanto più, tanto meno) let alone; (e inoltre) as well as

noncu'rante ag: **~ (di)** careless (of), indifferent (to); **noncu'ranza** sf carelessness, indifference

nondi'meno cong (tuttavia) however; (nonostante) nevertheless

'nonno, a sm/f grandfather/mother; (in senso più familiare) grandma/grandpa; **~i** smpl grandparents

non'nulla sm inv: **un ~** nothing, a trifle

'nono, a ag, sm ninth

nonos'tante prep in spite of, notwithstanding ♦ cong although, even though

nontiscordardimé sm inv (BOT) forget-me-not

nord sm North ♦ ag inv north; northern; **il Mare del N~** the North Sea; **nor'dest** sm north-east; **'nordico, a, ci, che** ag nordic, northern European; **nor'dovest** sm north-west

'norma sf (principio) norm; (regola) regulation, rule; (consuetudine) custom, rule; **a ~ di legge** according to law, as laid down by law

nor'male ag normal; standard cpd; **normalità** sf normality; **normaliz'zare** vt to normalize, bring back to normal

normal'mente av normally

norve'gese [norve'dʒese] ag, sm/f, sm Norwegian

Nor'vegia [nor'vedʒa] sf: **la ~** Norway

nostal'gia [nostal'dʒia] sf (di casa, paese) homesickness; (del passato) nostalgia; **nos'talgico, a, ci, che** ag homesick; nostalgic

nos'trano, a ag local; national; home-produced

'nostro, a det: **il(la) ~(a)** etc our ♦ pron: **il(la) ~(a)** etc ours ♦ sm: **il ~** our money; our belongings; **i ~i** our family; our own people; **è dei ~i** he's one of us

'**nota** *sf* (*segno*) mark; (*comunicazione scritta, MUS*) note; (*fattura*) bill; (*elenco*) list; **degno di ~** noteworthy, worthy of note

no'**tabile** *ag* notable ♦ *sm* prominent citizen

no'**taio** *sm* notary

no'**tare** *vt* (*segnare: errori*) to mark; (*registrare*) to note (down), write down; (*rilevare, osservare*) to note, notice; **farsi ~** to get o.s. noticed

no'**tevole** *ag* (*talento*) notable, remarkable; (*peso*) considerable

no'**tifica, che** *sf* notification

notifi'**care** *vt* (*DIR*): **~ qc a qn** to notify sb of sth, give sb notice of sth

no'**tizia** [no'tittsja] *sf* (*piece of*) news *sg*; (*informazione*) piece of information; **~e** *sfpl* (*informazioni*) news *sg*; information *sg*; **notiz**'**iario** *sm* (*RADIO, TV, STAMPA*) news *sg*

'**noto, a** *ag* (well-)known

notorie'**tà** *sf* fame; notoriety

no'**torio, a** *ag* well-known; (*peg*) notorious

not'**tambulo, a** *sm/f* night-bird (*fig*)

not'**tata** *sf* night

'**notte** *sf* night; **di ~** at night; (*durante la notte*) in the night, during the night; **~ bianca** sleepless night; **notte-**'**tempo** *av* at night; during the night

not'**turno, a** *ag* nocturnal; (*servizio, guardiano*) night *cpd*

no'**vanta** *num* ninety; **novan**'**tesimo, a** *num* ninetieth; **novan**'**tina** *sf*: **una novantina (di)** about ninety

'**nove** *num* nine

nove'**cento** [nove'tʃento] *num* nine hundred ♦ *sm*: **il N~** the twentieth century

no'**vella** *sf* (*LETTERATURA*) short story

novel'**lino, a** *ag* (*pivello*) green, inexperienced

no'**vello, a** *ag* (*piante, patate*) new; (*insalata, verdura*) early; (*sposo*) newly-married

no'**vembre** *sm* November

novi'**lunio** *sm* (*ASTR*) new moon

novi'**tà** *sf inv* novelty; (*innovazione*) innovation; (*cosa originale, insolita*) something new; (*notizia*) (piece of) news *sg*; **le ~ della moda** the latest fashions

no'**vizio, a** [no'vittsjo] *sm/f* (*REL*) novice; (*tirocinante*) beginner, apprentice

nozi'**one** [not'tsjone] *sf* notion, idea; **~i** *sfpl* (*rudimenti*) basic knowledge *sg*, rudiments

'**nozze** ['nɔttse] *sfpl* wedding *sg*, marriage *sg*; **~ d'argento/d'oro** silver/golden wedding *sg*

ns. *abbr* (*COMM*) = **nostro**

'**nube** *sf* cloud; **nubi**'**fragio** *sm* cloudburst

'**nubile** *ag* (*donna*) unmarried, single

'**nuca** *sf* nape of the neck

nucle'**are** *ag* nuclear

'**nucleo** *sm* nucleus; (*gruppo*) team, unit, group; (*MIL, POLIZIA*) squad; **il ~ familiare** the family unit

nu'**dista, i, e** *sm/f* nudist

'**nudo, a** *ag* (*persona*) bare, naked, nude; (*membra*) bare, naked; (*montagna*) bare ♦ *sm* (*ARTE*) nude

'**nugolo** *sm*: **un ~ di** a whole host of

'**nulla** *pron, av* = **niente** ♦ *sm*: **il ~** nothing

nulla'**osta** *sm inv* authorization

nulli'**tà** *sf inv* nullity; (*persona*) nonentity

'**nullo, a** *ag* useless, worthless; (*DIR*) null (and void); (*SPORT*): **incontro ~** draw

nume'**rale** *ag, sm* numeral

nume'**rare** *vt* to number; **numerazi**'**one** *sf* numbering; (*araba, decimale*) notation

nu'**merico, a, ci, che** *ag* numerical

'**numero** *sm* number; (*romano, arabo*) numeral; (*di spettacolo*) act, turn; **~ civico** house number; **~ di telefono** telephone number; **nume**'**roso, a** *ag* numerous, many; (*con sostantivo sg*) large

'nunzio ['nuntsjo] *sm* (REL) nuncio

nu'ocere ['nwɔtʃere] *vi*: ~ **a** to harm, damage; **nuoci'uto, a** *pp di* **nuocere**

nu'ora *sf* daughter-in-law

nuo'tare *vi* to swim; (galleggiare: oggetti) to float; **nuota'tore, 'trice** *sm/f* swimmer; **nu'oto** *sm* swimming

nu'ova *sf* (notizia) (piece of) news *sg*; *vedi anche* **nuovo**

nuova'mente *av* again

Nu'ova Ze'landa [-dze'landa] *sf*: **la ~** New Zealand

nu'ovo, a *ag* new; **di ~** again; **~ fiammante** o **di zecca** brand-new

nutri'ente *ag* nutritious, nourishing

nutri'mento *sm* food, nourishment

nu'trire *vt* to feed; (fig: sentimenti) to harbour, nurse; **nutri'tivo, a** *ag* nutritional; (alimento) nutritious; **nutrizi'one** *sf* nutrition

'nuvola *sf* cloud; **nuvo'loso, a** *ag* cloudy

nuzi'ale [nut'tsjale] *ag* nuptial; wedding *cpd*

O, o

o (dav V spesso **od**) *cong* or; **~ ... ~** either ... or; **~ l'uno ~ l'altro** either (of them)

O. *abbr* (= ovest) W

'oasi *sf inv* oasis

obbedi'ente *etc* = **ubbidiente** *etc*

obbli'gare *vt* (costringere): **~ qn a fare** to force o oblige sb to do; (DIR) to bind; **~rsi** *vr*: **~rsi a fare** to undertake to do; **obbli'gato, a** *ag* (costretto, grato) obliged; (percorso, tappa) set, fixed; **obbliga'torio, a** *ag* compulsory, obligatory; **obbligazi'one** *sf* (COMM) bond, debenture; **'obbligo, ghi** *sm* obligation; (dovere) duty; **avere l'obbligo di fare** to be obliged to do; **essere d'obbligo** (discorso, applauso)

to be called for

ob'brobrio *sm* disgrace; (fig) eyesore

o'beso, a *ag* obese

obiet'tare *vt*: **~ che** to object that; **~ su qc** to object to sth, raise objections concerning sth

obiet'tivo, a *ag* objective ♦ *sm* (OTTICA, FOT) lens *sg*, objective; (MIL, fig) objective

obiet'tore *sm* objector; **~ di coscienza** conscientious objector

obiezi'one [objet'tsjone] *sf* objection

obi'torio *sm* morgue, mortuary

o'bliquo, a *ag* oblique; (inclinato) slanting; (fig) devious, underhand

oblite'rare *vt* (biglietto) to stamp; (francobollo) to cancel

oblò *sm inv* porthole

o'blungo, a, ghi, ghe *ag* oblong

'oboe *sm* (MUS) oboe

'oca (pl **'oche**) *sf* goose

occasi'one *sf* (caso favorevole) opportunity; (causa, motivo, circostanza) occasion; (COMM) bargain; **d'~** (a buon prezzo) bargain *cpd*; (usato) secondhand

occhi'aia [ok'kjaja] *sf* eye socket; **avere le ~e** to have shadows under one's eyes

occhi'ali [ok'kjali] *smpl* glasses, spectacles; **~ da sole** sunglasses; **~ da vista** (prescription) glasses

occhi'ata [ok'kjata] *sf* look, glance; **dare un'~ a** to have a look at

occhi'ello [ok'kjɛllo] *sm* buttonhole; (asola) eyelet

'occhio ['ɔkkjo] *sm* eye; **~!** careful!, watch out!; **a ~ nudo** with the naked eye; **a quattr'~i** privately, tête-à-tête; **dare all'~ o nell'~ a qn** to catch sb's eye; **fare l'~ a qc** to get used to sth; **tenere d'~ qn** to keep an eye on sb; **vedere di buon/mal ~ qc** to look favourably/unfavourably on sth

occhio'lino [okkjo'lino] *sm*: **fare l'~ a qn** to wink at sb

occiden'tale [ottʃiden'tale] *ag*

western ♦ *sm/f* Westerner

occi'dente [ottʃiˈdɛnte] *sm* west; (POL): **l'O~** the West; **a ~** in the west

oc'cipite [otˈtʃipite] *sm* back of the head, occiput

oc'cludere *vt* to block; **occlusi'one** *sf* blockage, obstruction; **oc'cluso, a** *pp di* **occludere**

occor'rente *ag* necessary ♦ *sm* all that is necessary

occor'renza [okkorˈrɛntsa] *sf* necessity, need; **all'~** in case of need

oc'correre *vi* to be needed, be required ♦ *vb impers*: **occorre farlo** it must be done; **occorre che tu parta** you must leave, you'll have to leave; **mi occorrono i soldi** I need the money; **oc'corso, a** *pp di* **occorrere**

occul'tare *vt* to hide, conceal

oc'culto, a *ag* hidden, concealed; (*scienze, forze*) occult

occu'pare *vt* to occupy; (*manodopera*) to employ; (*ingombrare*) to occupy, take up; **~rsi** *vr* to occupy o.s., keep o.s. busy; (*impiegarsi*) to get a job; **~rsi di** (*interessarsi*) to take an interest in; (*prendersi cura di*) to look after, take care of; **occu'pato, a** *ag* (MIL, POL) occupied; (*persona: affaccendato*) busy; (*posto, sedia*) taken; (*toilette, TEL*) engaged; **occupazi'one** *sf* occupation (*impiego, lavoro*) job; (ECON) employment

o'ceano [oˈtʃɛano] *sm* ocean

'ocra *sf* ochre

ocu'lare *ag* ocular, eye *cpd*; **testimone a ~** eye witness

ocu'lato, a *ag* (*attento*) cautious, prudent; (*accorto*) shrewd

ocu'lista, i, e *sm/f* eye specialist, oculist

'ode *sf* ode

odi'are *vt* to hate, detest

odi'erno, a *ag* today's, of today; (*attuale*) present

'odio *sm* hatred; **avere in ~ qc/qn** to hate o detest sth/sb; **odi'oso, a** *ag* hateful, odious

odo'rare *vt* (*annusare*) to smell; (*profumare*) to perfume, scent ♦ *vi*: **~ (di)** to smell (of); **odo'rato** *sm* sense of smell

o'dore *sm* smell; **gli ~i** *smpl* (CUC) (aromatic) herbs; **odo'roso, a** *ag* sweet-smelling

of'fendere *vt* to offend; (*violare*) to break, violate; (*insultare*) to insult; (*ferire*) to hurt; (*con senso reciproco*) to insult one another; (*risentirsi*): **~rsi (di)** to take offence (at), be offended (by); **offen'sivo, a** *ag, sf* offensive

offe'rente *sm* (*in aste*): **al maggior ~** to the highest bidder

of'ferta *sf* offer; (*donazione, anche* REL) offering; (*in gara d'appalto*) tender; (*in aste*) bid; (ECON) supply; **"~e d'impiego"** "situations vacant"; **fare un'~a** to make an offer; to tender; to bid

of'ferto, a *pp di* **offrire**

of'fesa *sf* insult, affront; (MIL) attack; (DIR) offence; *vedi anche* **offeso**

of'feso, a *pp di* **offendere** ♦ *ag* offended; (*fisicamente*) hurt, injured ♦ *sm/f* offended party; **essere ~ con qn** to be annoyed with sb; **parte ~a** (DIR) plaintiff

offi'cina [offiˈtʃina] *sf* workshop

of'frire *vt* to offer; (*proporsi*) to offer (o.s.), volunteer; (*occasione*) to present itself; (*esporsi*): **~rsi a** to expose o.s. to; **ti offro da bere** I'll buy you a drink

offus'care *vt* to obscure, darken; (*fig: intelletto*) to dim, cloud; (: *fama*) to obscure, overshadow; **~rsi** *vr* to grow dark; to cloud, grow dim; to be obscured

ogget'tivo, a [oddʒetˈtivo] *ag* objective

og'getto [odˈdʒetto] *sm* object; (*materia, argomento*) subject (matter); **~i smarriti** lost property *sg*

'oggi ['ɔddʒi] *av, sm* today; **~ a otto** a week today; **oggigi'orno** *av* nowadays

OGM *sigla m* (= *organismo geneticamente modificato*) GMO

'ogni ['oɲɲi] *det* every, each; (*tutti*) all; (*con valore distributivo*) every; **~ uomo è mortale** all men are mortal; **viene ~ due giorni** he comes every two days; **~ cosa** everything; **ad ~ costo** at all costs, at any price; **in ~ luogo** everywhere; **~ tanto** every so often; **~ volta che** every time that

Ognis'santi [oɲɲis'santi] *sm* All Saints' Day

o'gnuno [oɲ'ɲuno] *pron* everyone, everybody

'ohi *escl* oh!; (*esprimere dolore*) ow!

ohimè *escl* oh dear!

O'landa *sf*: **l'~** Holland; **olan'dese** *ag* Dutch ♦ *sm* (LING) Dutch ♦ *sm/f* Dutchman/woman; **gli Olandesi** the Dutch

oleo'dotto *sm* oil pipeline

ole'oso, a *ag* oily; (*che contiene olio*) oil-yielding

ol'fatto *sm* sense of smell

oli'are *vt* to oil

oli'era *sf* oil cruet

olim'piadi *sfpl* Olympic games; **o'limpico, a, ci, che** *ag* Olympic

'olio *sm* oil; **sott'~** (CUC) in oil; **~ di fegato di merluzzo** cod liver oil; **~ d'oliva** olive oil; **~ di semi** vegetable oil

o'liva *sf* olive; **oli'vastro, a** *ag* olive(-coloured); (*carnagione*) sallow; **oli'veto** *sm* olive grove; **o'livo** *sm* olive tree

'olmo *sm* elm

oltraggi'are [oltrad'dʒare] *vt* to outrage; to offend gravely

ol'traggio [ol'traddʒo] *sm* outrage; offence, insult; **~ al pudore** (DIR) indecent behaviour; **oltraggi'oso, a** *ag* offensive

ol'tralpe *av* beyond the Alps

ol'tranza [ol'trantsa] *sf*: **a ~** to the last, to the bitter end

'oltre *av* (*più in là*) further; (*di più: aspettare*) longer, more ♦ *prep* (*di là da*) beyond, over, on the other side of; (*più di*) more than, over; (*in aggiunta a*) besides; (*eccetto*): **~ a** except, apart from; **oltre'mare** *av* overseas; **oltre'modo** *av* extremely; **oltre-pas'sare** *vt* to go beyond, exceed

o'maggio [o'maddʒo] *sm* (*dono*) gift; (*segno di rispetto*) homage, tribute; **~i** *smpl* (*complimenti*) respects; **rendere ~ a** to pay homage o tribute to; **in ~** (*copia, biglietto*) complimentary

ombe'lico, chi *sm* navel

'ombra *sf* (*zona non assolata, fantasma*) shade; (*sagoma scura*) shadow; **sedere all'~** to sit in the shade; **restare nell'~** (*fig*) to remain in obscurity

om'brello *sm* umbrella; **ombrel'lone** *sm* beach umbrella

om'bretto *sm* eyeshadow

om'broso, a *ag* shady, shaded; (*cavallo*) nervous, skittish; (*persona*) touchy, easily offended

ome'lia *sf* (REL) homily, sermon

omeopa'tia *sf* homoeopathy

omertà *sf* conspiracy of silence

o'messo, a *pp di* **omettere**

o'mettere *vt* to omit, leave out; **~ di fare** to omit o fail to do

omi'cida, i, e [omi'tʃida] *ag* homicidal, murderous ♦ *sm/f* murderer/eress

omi'cidio [omi'tʃidjo] *sm* murder; **~ colposo** culpable homicide

omissi'one *sf* omission; **~ di soccorso** (DIR) failure to stop and give assistance

omogeneiz'zato [omodʒeneid'dzato] *sm* baby food

omo'geneo, a [omo'dʒɛneo] *ag* homogeneous

omolo'gare *vt* to approve, recognize; to ratify

o'monimo, a *sm/f* namesake ♦ *sm* (LING) homonym

omosessu'ale *ag, sm/f* homosexual

'oncia, ce ['ɔntʃa] *sf* ounce

'onda *sf* wave; **mettere** *o* **mandare in ~** (RADIO, TV) to broadcast; **andare in ~** (RADIO, TV) to go on the air; **~e corte/medie/lunghe** short/medium/long wave; **on'data** *sf* wave, billow; (fig) wave, surge; **a ondate** in waves; **ondata di caldo** heatwave

ondeggi'are [onded'dʒare] *vi* (acqua) to ripple; (muoversi sulle onde: barca) to rock, roll; (fig: muoversi come le onde, barcollare) to sway; (: essere incerto) to waver

'onere *sm* burden; **~i fiscali** taxes; **one'roso, a** *ag* (fig) heavy, onerous

ones'tà *sf* honesty

o'nesto, a *ag* (probo, retto) honest; (giusto) fair; (casto) chaste, virtuous

'onice ['ɔnitʃe] *sf* onyx

onnipo'tente *ag* omnipotent

ono'mastico, ci *sm* name-day

ono'ranze [ono'rantse] *sfpl* honours; **~ funebri** funeral (service)

ono'rare *vt* to honour; (far onore a) to do credit to; **~rsi** *vr*: **~rsi di** to feel honoured at, be proud of

ono'rario, a *ag* honorary ♦ *sm* fee

o'nore *sm* honour; **in ~ di** in honour of; **fare gli ~i di casa** to play host (or hostess); **fare ~ a** to honour; (pranzo) to do justice to; (famiglia) to be a credit to; **farsi ~** to distinguish o.s.; **ono'revole** *ag* honourable ♦ *sm/f* (POL) ≈ Member of Parliament (BRIT), ≈ Congressman/woman (US); **onorifi'cenza** *sf* honour; decoration; **ono'rifico, a, ci, che** *ag* honorary

'onta *sf* shame, disgrace

on'tano *sm* (BOT) alder

'O.N.U. *sf* sigla f (= Organizzazione delle Nazioni Unite) UN, UNO

o'paco, a, chi, che *ag* (vetro) opaque; (metallo) dull, matt

o'pale *sm o f* opal

'opera *sf* work; (azione rilevante) action, deed, work; (MUS) work; opus; (: melodramma) opera; (: teatro) opera house; (ente) institution, organization; **~ d'arte** work of art; **~ lirica** (grand) opera; **~e pubbliche** public works

ope'raio, a *ag* working-class; workers' ♦ *sm/f* worker; **classe ~a** working class

ope'rare *vt* to carry out, make; (MED) to operate on ♦ *vi* to operate, work; (rimedio) to act, work; (MED) to operate; **~rsi** *vr* (MED) to have an operation; **~rsi d'appendicite** to have one's appendix out; **opera'tivo, a** *ag* operative, operating; **opera'tore, 'trice** *sm/f* operator; (TV, CINEMA) cameraman; **operatore economico** agent, broker; **operatore turistico** tour operator; **opera'torio, a** *ag* (MED) operating; **operazi'one** *sf* operation

ope'retta *sf* (MUS) operetta, light opera

ope'roso, a *ag* busy, active, hard-working

opini'one *sf* opinion; **~ pubblica** public opinion

'oppio *sm* opium

oppo'nente *ag* opposing ♦ *sm/f* opponent

op'porre *vt* to oppose; **opporsi** *vr*: **opporsi (a qc)** to oppose (sth); to object (to sth); **~ resistenza/un rifiuto** to offer resistance/refuse

opportu'nista, i, e *sm/f* opportunist

opportunità *sf inv* opportunity; (convenienza) opportuneness, timeliness

oppor'tuno, a *ag* timely, opportune

opposi'tore, 'trice *sm/f* opposer, opponent

opposizi'one [oppozit'tsjone] *sf* opposition; (DIR) objection

op'posto, a *pp di* **opporre** ♦ *ag* opposite; (opinioni) conflicting ♦ *sm* opposite, contrary; **all'~** on the contrary

oppressi'one *sf* oppression

oppres'sivo, a *ag* oppressive

op'presso, a *pp di* **opprimere**

oppres'sore *sm* oppressor

op'primere *vt* (*premere, gravare*) to weigh down; (*estenuare: sog: caldo*) to suffocate, oppress; (*tiranneggiare: popolo*) to oppress

op'pure *cong* or (else)

op'tare *vi*: **~ per** to opt for

o'puscolo *sm* booklet, pamphlet

opzi'one [op'tsjone] *sf* option

'ora ^{1} *sf* (*60 minuti*) hour; (*momento*) time; **che ~ è?, che ~e sono?** what time is it?; **non veder l'~ di fare** to long to do, look forward to doing; **di buon'~** early; **alla buon'~!** at last!; **~ di cena** dinner time; **~ legale** *o* **estiva** summer time (*BRIT*), daylight saving time (*US*); **~ locale** local time; **~ di pranzo** lunchtime; **~ di punta** (*AUT*) rush hour

ora ^{2} *av* (*adesso*) now; (*poco fa*): **è uscito proprio ~** he's just gone out; (*tra poco*) presently, in a minute; (*correlativo*): **~ ... ~** now ... now; **d'~ in avanti** *o* **poi** from now on; **or ~** just now, a moment ago; **5 anni** *or* **sono** 5 years ago; **~ come ~** right now, at present

o'racolo *sm* oracle

'orafo *sm* goldsmith

o'rale *ag, sm* oral

ora'mai *av* = **ormai**

o'rario, a *ag* (*fuso, segnale*) time *cpd*; (*velocità*) per hour ♦ *sm* timetable, schedule; (*di ufficio, visite etc*) hours *pl*, time(s *pl*); **in ~** on time

o'rata *sf* (*ZOOL*) sea bream

ora'tore, 'trice *sm/f* speaker; orator

ora'toria *sf* (*arte*) oratory

ora'torio, a *ag* oratorical ♦ *sm* (*REL*) oratory; (*MUS*) oratorio

ora'zione [orat'tsjone] *sf* (*REL*) prayer; (*discorso*) speech, oration

or'bene *cong* so, well (then)

'orbita *sf* (*ASTR, FISICA*) orbit; (*ANAT*) (eye-)socket

or'chestra [or'kestra] *sf* orchestra; **orches'trare** *vt* to orchestrate; (*fig*) to mount, stage-manage

orchi'dea [orki'dea] *sf* orchid

'orco, chi *sm* ogre

'orda *sf* horde

or'digno [or'dinno] *sm* (*esplosivo*) explosive device

ordi'nale *ag, sm* ordinal

ordina'mento *sm* order, arrangement; (*regolamento*) regulations *pl*, rules *pl*; **~ scolastico/giuridico** education/legal system

ordi'nanza [ordi'nantsa] *sf* (*DIR, MIL*) order; (*persona: MIL*) orderly, batman; **d'~** (*MIL*) regulation *cpd*

ordi'nare *vt* (*mettere in ordine*) to arrange, organize; (*COMM*) to order; (*prescrivere: medicina*) to prescribe; (*comandare*): **~ a qn di fare qc** to order *o* command sb to do sth; (*REL*) to ordain

ordi'nario, a *ag* (*comune*) ordinary; everyday; standard; (*grossolano*) coarse, common ♦ *sm* ordinary; (*INS: di università*) full professor

ordi'nato, a *ag* tidy, orderly

ordinazi'one [ordinat'tsjone] *sf* (*COMM*) ordination; (*REL*) ordination; **eseguire qc su ~** to make sth to order

or'dine *sm* order; (*carattere*): **d'~ pratico** of a practical nature; **all'~** (*COMM: assegno*) to order; **di prim'~** first-class; **fino a nuovo ~** until further notice; **essere in ~** (*documenti*) to be in order; (*stanza, persona*) to be tidy; **mettere in ~** to put in order, tidy (up); **~ del giorno** (*di seduta*) agenda; (*MIL*) order of the day; **~ di pagamento** (*COMM*) order for payment; **l'~ pubblico** law and order; **~i (sacri)** (*REL*) holy orders

or'dire *vt* (*fig*) to plot, scheme; **or'dito** *sm* (*di tessuto*) warp

orec'chino [orek'kino] *sm* earring

o'recchio [o'rekkjo] (*pl(f)* **o'recchie**)

sm (ANAT) ear

orecchi'oni [orek'kjoni] *smpl* (MED) mumps *sg*

o'refice [o'refitʃe] *sm* goldsmith; jeweller; **orefice'ria** *sf* (*arte*) goldsmith's art; (*negozio*) jeweller's (shop)

'orfano, a *ag* orphan(ed) ♦ *sm/f* orphan; ~ **di padre/madre** fatherless/motherless; **orfano'trofio** *sm* orphanage

orga'netto *sm* barrel organ; (*fam: armonica a bocca*) mouth organ; (: *fisarmonica*) accordion

or'ganico, a, ci, che *ag* organic ♦ *sm* personnel, staff

organi'gramma, i *sm* organization chart

orga'nismo *sm* (BIOL) organism; (*corpo umano*) body; (AMM) body, organism

organiz'zare [organid'dzare] *vt* to organize; **~rsi** *vr* to get organized; **organizza'tore, 'trice** *ag* organizing ♦ *sm/f* organizer; **organizzazi'one** *sf* organization

'organo *sm* organ; (*di congegno*) part; (*portavoce*) spokesman, mouthpiece

or'gasmo *sm* (FISIOL) orgasm; (*fig*) agitation, anxiety

'orgia, ge ['ɔrdʒa] *sf* orgy

or'goglio [or'gɔʎʎo] *sm* pride; **orgogli'oso, a** *ag* proud

orien'tale *ag* oriental; eastern; east

orienta'mento *sm* positioning; orientation; direction; **senso di ~** sense of direction; **perdere l'~** to lose one's bearings; **~ professionale** careers guidance

orien'tare *vt* (*situare*) to position; (*fig*) to direct, orientate; **~rsi** *vr* to find one's bearings; (*fig*: *tendere*) to tend, lean; (: *indirizzarsi*): **~rsi verso** to take up, go in for

ori'ente *sm* east; **l'O~** the East, the Orient; **a ~** in the east

o'rigano *sm* oregano

origi'nale [oridʒi'nale] *ag* original;

(*bizzarro*) eccentric ♦ *sm* original; **originalità** *sf* originality; eccentricity

origi'nare [oridʒi'nare] *vt* to bring about, produce ♦ *vi*: ~ **da** to arise o spring from

origi'nario, a [oridʒi'narjo] *ag* original; **essere ~ di** to be a native of; (*provenire da*) to originate from; to be native to

o'rigine [o'ridʒine] *sf* origin; **all'~** originally; **d'~ inglese** of English origin; **dare ~ a** to give rise to

origli'are [oriʎ'ʎare] *vi*: ~ **(a)** to eavesdrop (on)

o'rina *sf* urine

ori'nare *vi* to urinate ♦ *vt* to pass; **orina'toio** *sm* (*public*) urinal

oriz'zontale [oriddzon'tale] *ag* horizontal

oriz'zonte [orid'dzonte] *sm* horizon

or'lare *vt* to hem

'orlo *sm* edge, border; (*di recipiente*) rim, brim; (*di vestito etc*) hem

'orma *sf* (*di persona*) footprint; (*di animale*) track; (*impronta, traccia*) mark, trace

or'mai *av* by now, by this time; (*adesso*) now; (*quasi*) almost, nearly

ormeggi'are [ormed'dʒare] *vt* (NAUT) to moor; **~rsi** *vr* (*di atto*) mooring *no pl*; (*luogo*) moorings *pl*

or'mone *sm* hormone

orna'mentale *ag* ornamental, decorative

orna'mento *sm* ornament, decoration

or'nare *vt* to adorn, decorate; **~rsi** *vr*: **~rsi (di)** to deck o.s. (out) (with); **or'nato, a** *ag* ornate

ornitolo'gia [ornitolo'dʒia] *sf* ornithology

'oro *sm* gold; **d'~, in ~** gold *cpd*; (*colore, occasione*) golden; (*persona*) marvellous

orologe'ria [orolodʒe'ria] *sf* watchmaking *no pl*; watchmaker's (shop); clockmaker's (shop); **bomba a ~** time bomb

orologi'aio [orolo'dʒajo] *sm* watchmaker; clockmaker

oro'logio [oro'lɔdʒo] *sm* clock; (*da tasca, da polso*) watch; **~ da polso** wristwatch; **~ al quarzo** quartz watch

o'roscopo [o'rɔskopo] *sm* horoscope

or'rendo, a *ag* (*spaventoso*) horrible, awful; (*bruttissimo*) hideous

or'ribile *ag* horrible

'orrido, a *ag* fearful, horrid

orripi'lante *ag* hair-raising, horrifying

or'rore *sm* horror; **avere in ~ qn/qc** to loathe o detest sb/sth; **mi fanno ~** I loathe o detest them

orsacchi'otto [orsak'kjɔtto] *sm* teddy bear

'orso *sm* bear; **~ bruno/bianco** brown/polar bear

or'taggio [or'taddʒo] *sm* vegetable

or'tensia *sf* hydrangea

or'tica, che *sf* (stinging) nettle

orti'caria *sf* nettle rash

'orto *sm* vegetable garden, kitchen garden; (*AGR*) market garden (*BRIT*), truck farm (*US*)

orto'dosso, a *ag* orthodox

ortogra'fia *sf* spelling

orto'lano, a *sm/f* (*venditore*) greengrocer (*BRIT*), produce dealer (*US*)

ortope'dia *sf* orthopaedics *sg*; **orto'pedico, a, ci, che** *ag* orthopaedic ♦ *sm* orthopaedic specialist

orzai'olo [ordza'jɔlo] *sm* (*MED*) stye

or'zata [or'dzata] *sf* barley water

'orzo ['ɔrdzo] *sm* barley

o'sare *vt, vi* to dare; **~ fare** to dare (to) do

oscenità [oʃʃeni'ta] *sf inv* obscenity

o'sceno, a [oʃ'ʃɛno] *ag* obscene; (*ripugnante*) ghastly

oscil'lare [oʃʃil'lare] *vi* (*pendolo*) to swing; (*dondolare: al vento etc*) to rock;

(*variare*) to fluctuate; (*TECN*) to oscillate; (*fig*): **~ fra** to waver o hesitate between; **oscillazi'one** *sf* oscillation; (*di prezzi, temperatura*) fluctuation

oscura'mento *sm* darkening, obscuring; (*in tempo di guerra*) blackout

oscu'rare *vt* to darken, obscure; (*fig*) to obscure; **~rsi** *vr* (*cielo*) to darken, cloud over; (*persona*): **si oscurò in volto** his face clouded over

os'curo, a *ag* dark; (*fig*) obscure; humble, lowly ♦ *sm*: **all'~** in the dark; **tenere qn all'~ di qc** to keep sb in the dark about sth

ospe'dale *sm* hospital; **ospedali'ero, a** *ag* hospital *cpd*

ospi'tale *ag* hospitable; **ospitalità** *sf* hospitality

ospi'tare *vt* to give hospitality to; (*sog: albergo*) to accommodate

'ospite *sm/f* (*persona che ospita*) host/ hostess; (*persona ospitata*) guest

os'pizio [os'pittsjo] *sm* (*per vecchi etc*) home

'ossa *sfpl vedi* **osso**

ossa'tura *sf* (*ANAT*) skeletal structure, frame; (*TECN, fig*) framework

'osseo, a *ag* bony; (*tessuto etc*) bone *cpd*

os'sequio *sm* deference, respect; **~i** *smpl* (*saluto*) respects, regards; **ossequi'oso, a** *ag* obsequious

osser'vanza [osser'vantsa] *sf* observance

osser'vare *vt* to observe, watch; (*esaminare*) to examine; (*notare, rilevare*) to notice, observe; (*DIR: la legge*) to observe, respect; (*mantenere: silenzio*) to keep, observe; **far ~ qc a qn** to point sth out to sb; **osserva'tore, 'trice** *ag* observant, perceptive ♦ *sm/f* observer; **osserva'torio** *sm* (*ASTR*) observatory; (*MIL*) observation post; **osservazi'one** *sf* observation; (*di legge etc*) observance; (*considerazione critica*) observation, remark; (*rimprovero*) reproof; **in osservazione** under observation

ossessio'nare vt to obsess, haunt; (*tormentare*) to torment, harass

ossessi'one sf obsession

os'sesso, a ag (*spiritato*) possessed

ossi'buchi [ossi'buki] smpl di **ossobuco**

ossi'dare vt to oxidize; **~rsi** vr to oxidize

'ossido sm oxide; **~ di carbonio** carbon monoxide

ossige'nare [ossidʒe'nare] vt to oxygenate; (*decolorare*) to bleach; **acqua ossigenata** hydrogen peroxide

os'sigeno sm oxygen

'osso (pl(f) **ossa** nel senso ANAT) sm bone; **d'~** (*bottone etc*) of bone, bone cpd

osso'buco (pl **ossi'buchi**) sm (CUC) marrowbone; (: *piatto*) stew made with knuckle of veal in tomato sauce

os'suto, a ag bony

ostaco'lare vt to block, obstruct

os'tacolo sm obstacle; (EQUITAZIONE) hurdle, jump

os'taggio [os'taddʒo] sm hostage

'oste, os'tessa sm/f innkeeper

osteggi'are [osted'dʒare] vt to oppose, be opposed to

os'tello sm: **~ della gioventù** youth hostel

osten'tare vt to make a show of, flaunt; **ostentazi'one** sf ostentation, show

oste'ria sf inn

os'tessa sf vedi **oste**

os'tetrica sf midwife; **os'tetrico, a, ci, che** ag obstetric ♦ sm obstetrician

'ostia sf (REL) host; (*per medicinali*) wafer

'ostico, a, ci, che ag (fig) harsh; hard, difficult; unpleasant

os'tile ag hostile; **ostilità** sf inv hostility ♦ sfpl (MIL) hostilities

osti'narsi vr to insist, dig one's heels in; **~ a fare** to persist (obstinately) in doing; **osti'nato, a** ag (*caparbio*) obstinate; (*tenace*) persistent, determined; **ostinazi'one** sf obstinacy; persistence

'ostrica, che sf oyster

ostru'ire vt to obstruct; block; **ostruzi'one** sf obstruction, blockage

'otre sm (*recipiente*) goatskin

otta'gonale ag octagonal

ot'tagono sm octagon

ot'tanta num eighty; **ottan'tesimo, a** num eightieth; **ottan'tina** sf: **una ottantina (di)** about eighty

ot'tava sf octave

ot'tavo, a num eighth

ottempe'rare vi: **~ a** to comply with, obey

otte'nere vt to obtain, get; (*risultato*) to achieve, obtain

'ottica sf (*scienza*) optics sg; (FOT: *lenti, prismi etc*) optics pl

'ottico, a, ci, che ag (*della vista: nervo*) optic; (*dell'ottica*) optical ♦ sm optician

ottima'mente av excellently, very well

otti'mismo sm optimism; **otti'mista, i, e** sm/f optimist

'ottimo, a ag excellent, very good

'otto num eight

ot'tobre sm October

otto'cento [otto'tʃɛnto] num eight hundred ♦ sm: **l'O~** the nineteenth century

ot'tone sm brass; **gli ~i** (MUS) the brass

ottu'rare vt to close (up); (*dente*) to fill; **ottura'tore** sm (FOT) shutter; (*nelle armi*) breechblock; **otturazi'one** sf closing (up); (*dentaria*) filling

ot'tuso, a pp di **OTTUNDERE** ♦ ag (MAT, fig) obtuse; (*suono*) dull

o'vaia sf (ANAT) ovary

o'vale ag, sm oval

o'vatta sf cotton wool; (*per imbottire*) padding; wadding; **ovat'tare** vt (fig: *smorzare*) to muffle

ovazi'one [ovat'tsjone] sf ovation

over'dose ['ouvadous] sf inv overdose

'ovest sm west

o'vile sm pen, enclosure

o'vino, a ag sheep cpd, ovine

ovulazi'one [ovulat'tsjone] sf ovulation

'ovulo sm (FISIOL) ovum

o'vunque av = **dovunque**

ov'vero cong (ossia) that is, to be precise; (oppure) or (else)

ovvi'are vi: **~ a** to obviate

'ovvio, a ag obvious

ozi'are [ott'tsjare] vi to laze, idle

'ozio ['ottsjo] sm idleness; (tempo libero) leisure; **ore d'~** leisure time; **stare in ~** to be idle; **ozi'oso, a** ag idle

o'zono [o'dzono] sm ozone

P, p

P abbr (= parcheggio) P; (AUT: = principiante) L

pa'cato, a ag quiet, calm

'pacca sf pat

pac'chetto [pak'ketto] sm packet; **~ azionario** (COMM) shareholding

pacchi'ano, a [pak'kjano] ag vulgar

'pacco, chi sm parcel; (involto) bundle

'pace ['patʃe] sf peace; **darsi ~** to resign o.s.; **fare la ~ con** to make it up with

pacifi'care [patʃifi'kare] vt (riconciliare) to reconcile, make peace between; (mettere in pace) to pacify

pa'cifico, a, ci, che [pa'tʃi:fiko] ag (persona) peaceable; (vita) peaceful; (fig: indiscusso) indisputable; (: ovvio) obvious, clear ♦ sm: **il P~, l'Oceano P~** the Pacific (Ocean)

paci'fista, i, a [patʃi'fista] sm/f pacifist

pa'della sf frying pan; (per infermi) bedpan

padigli'one [padiʎ'ʎone] sm pavilion

'Padova sf Padua

'padre sm father; **~i** smpl (antenati) forefathers

pa'drino sm godfather

padro'nanza [padro'nantsa] sf command, mastery

pa'drone, a sm/f master/mistress; (proprietario) owner; (datore di lavoro) employer; **essere ~ di sé** to be in control of o.s.; **~ di casa** (ospite) host/hostess; (per gli inquilini) landlord/lady; **padroneggi'are** vt (fig: sentimenti) to master, control; (: materia) to master, know thoroughly; **padroneggiarsi** vr to control o.s.

pae'saggio [pae'zaddʒo] sm landscape

pae'sano, a ag country cpd ♦ sm/f villager; countryman/woman

pa'ese sm (nazione) country, nation; (terra) country, land; (villaggio) village; (small) town; **~ di provenienza** country of origin; **i P~i Bassi** the Netherlands

paf'futo, a ag chubby, plump

'paga, ghe sf pay, wages pl

paga'mento sm payment

pa'gano, a ag, sm/f pagan

pa'gare vt to pay; (acquisto, fig: colpa) to pay for; (contraccambiare) to repay, pay back ♦ vi to pay; **quanto l'hai pagato?** how much did you pay for it?; **~ con carta di credito** to pay by credit card; **~ in contanti** to pay cash

pa'gella [pa'dʒella] sf (INS) report card

'paggio ['paddʒo] sm page(boy)

paghe'rò [page'rɔ] sm inv acknowledgement of a debt, IOU

'pagina ['padʒina] sf page; **~e gialle** Yellow Pages

'paglia ['paʎʎa] sf straw

pagliac'cetto [paʎʎat'tʃetto] sm (per bambini) rompers pl

pagli'accio [paʎ'ʎattʃo] sm clown

pagli'etta [paʎ'ʎetta] sf (cappello per uomo) (straw) boater; (per tegami etc) steel wool

pa'gnotta [paɲ'ɲɔtta] sf round loaf

'paio (pl(f) **'paia**) sm pair; **un ~ di**

(*alcuni*) a couple of

pai'olo *sm* (copper) pot

'pala *sf* shovel; (*di remo, ventilatore, elica*) blade; (*di ruota*) paddle

pa'lato *sm* palate

pa'lazzo [pa'lattso] *sm* (*reggia*) palace; (*edificio*) building; ~ **di giustizia** courthouse; ~ **dello sport** sports stadium

---
palazzi

Rome has a number of **palazzi**, which are now associated with various government departments and political figures or groups. Palazzo Chigi, in Piazza Colonna, dates from the 16th century and has, since 1961, been the Prime Minister's office and the place where the cabinet meets. Palazzo Madama, also built in the 16th century, has been the seat of the Senate since 1871. Palazzo di Montecitorio, which was completed in 1694, has housed the **Camera dei deputati** since 1870. Palazzo Viminale, which takes its name from the hill in Rome on which it stands, is the home of the Ministry of the Interior.

'palco, chi *sm* (*TEATRO*) box; (*tavolato*) platform, stand; (*ripiano*) layer

palco'scenico, ci [palko'ʃeniko] *sm* (*TEATRO*) stage

pale'sare *vt* to reveal, disclose; **~rsi** *vr* to reveal o show o.s.

pa'lese *ag* clear, evident

Pales'tina *sf*: **la** ~ Palestine

pa'lestra *sf* gymnasium; (*esercizio atletico*) exercise, training; (*fig*) training ground, school

pa'letta *sf* spade; (*per il focolare*) shovel; (*del capostazione*) signalling disc

pa'letto *sm* stake, peg; (*spranga*) bolt

'palio *sm* (*gara*): **il P~** horse race run at Siena; **mettere qc in** ~ to offer sth as

a prize

---
palio

The **palio** is a horse race which takes place in a number of Italian towns, the most famous being the one in Siena. This is usually held twice a year on 2 July and 16 August in the Piazza del Campo, Siena. 10 of the 17 **contrade** or districts take part, each represented by a horse and rider. The winner is the first horse to complete the course, whether it has a rider or not.

'palla *sf* ball; (*pallottola*) bullet; ~ **canestro** *sm* basketball; ~ **nuoto** *sm* water polo; ~ **ovale** rugby ball; ~ **volo** *sm* volleyball

palleggi'are [palled'dʒare] *vi* (*CALCIO*) to practise with the ball; (*TENNIS*) to knock up

pallia'tivo *sm* palliative; (*fig*) stopgap measure

'pallido, a *ag* pale

pal'lina *sf* (*bilia*) marble

pallon'cino [pallon'tʃino] *sm* balloon; (*lampioncino*) Chinese lantern

pal'lone *sm* (*palla*) ball; (*CALCIO*) football; (*aerostato*) balloon; **gioco del** ~ football

pal'lore *sm* pallor, paleness

pal'lottola *sf* pellet; (*proiettile*) bullet

'palma *sf* (*ANAT*) = **palmo**; (*BOT, simbolo*) palm; ~ **da datteri** date palm

'palmo *sm* (*ANAT*) palm; **restare con un** ~ **di naso** to be badly disappointed

'palo *sm* (*legno appuntito*) stake; (*sostegno*) pole; **fare da o il** ~ (*fig*) to act as look-out

palom'baro *sm* diver

pa'lombo *sm* (*pesce*) dogfish

pal'pare *vt* to feel, finger

'palpebra *sf* eyelid

palpi'tare *vi* (*cuore, polso*) to beat;

(: *più forte*) to pound, throb; (*fremere*) to quiver; **'palpito** *sm* (*del cuore*) beat; (*fig: d'amore etc*) throb

paltò *sm inv* overcoat

pa'lude *sf* marsh, swamp; **palu'doso, a** *ag* marshy, swampy

pa'lustre *ag* marsh *cpd*, swamp *cpd*

'pampino *sm* vine leaf

'panca, che *sf* bench

pancar'rè *sm* sliced square bread

pan'cetta [pan'tʃetta] *sf* (*CUC*) bacon

pan'chetto [pan'ketto] *sm* stool; footstool

pan'china [pan'kina] *sf* garden seat; (*di giardino pubblico*) (park) bench

'pancia, ce ['pantʃa] *sf* belly, stomach; **mettere** *o* **fare** ~ to be getting a paunch; **avere mal di** ~ to have stomachache *o* a sore stomach

panci'otto [pan'tʃɔtto] *sm* waistcoat

'pancreas *sm inv* pancreas

'panda *sm inv* panda

pande'monio *sm* pandemonium

'pane *sm* bread; (*pagnotta*) loaf (of bread); (*forma*): **un ~ di burro** a pat of butter; **guadagnarsi il ~** to earn one's living; **~ a cassetta** sliced bread; **~ di Spagna** sponge cake; **~ integrale** wholemeal bread; **~ tostato** toast

panette'ria *sf* (*forno*) bakery; (*negozio*) baker's (shop), bakery

panetti'ere, a *sm/f* baker

panet'tone *sm a kind of spiced brioche with sultanas, eaten at Christmas*

'panfilo *sm* yacht

pangrat'tato *sm* breadcrumbs *pl*

'panico, a, ci, che *ag, sm* panic

pani'ere *sm* basket

pani'ficio [pani'fitʃo] *sm* (*forno*) bakery; (*negozio*) baker's (shop), bakery

pa'nino *sm* roll; ~ **caldo** toasted sandwich; ~ **imbottito** filled roll; sandwich; **panino'teca** *sf* sandwich bar

'panna *sf* (*CUC*) cream; (*TECN*) = **panne**; ~ **da cucina** cooking cream;

~ **montata** whipped cream

'panne *sf inv:* **essere in** ~ (*AUT*) to have broken down

pan'nello *sm* panel; ~ **solare** solar panel

'panno *sm* cloth; ~**i** *smpl* (*abiti*) clothes; **mettiti nei miei** ~**i** (*fig*) put yourself in my shoes

pan'nocchia [pan'nɔkkja] *sf* (*di mais etc*) ear

panno'lino *sm* (*per bambini*) nappy (*BRIT*), diaper (*US*)

pano'rama, i *sm* panorama; **pano'ramico, a, ci, che** *ag* panoramic; **strada panoramica** scenic route

panta'loni *smpl* trousers (*BRIT*), pants (*US*), pair *sg* of trousers *o* pants

pan'tano *sm* bog

pan'tera *sf* panther

pan'tofola *sf* slipper

panto'mima *sf* pantomime

pan'zana [pan'tsana] *sf* fib, tall story

pao'nazzo, a [pao'nattso] *ag* purple

'papa, i *sm* pope

papà *sm inv* dad(dy)

pa'pale *ag* papal

pa'pato *sm* papacy

pa'pavero *sm* poppy

'papera *sf* (*fig*) slip of the tongue, blunder; *vedi anche* **papero**

'papero, a *sm/f* (*ZOOL*) gosling

pa'piro *sm* papyrus

'pappa *sf* baby cereal

pappa'gallo *sm* parrot; (*fig: uomo*) Romeo, wolf

pappa'gorgia, ge [pappa'gɔrdʒa] *sf* double chin

pap'pare *vt* (*fam: anche:* ~**rsi**) to gobble up

'para *sf:* **suole di** ~ crepe soles

pa'rabola *sf* (*MAT*) parabola; (*REL*) parable

para'brezza [para'breddza] *sm inv* (*AUT*) windscreen (*BRIT*), windshield (*US*)

paraca'dute *sm inv* parachute

para'carro *sm* kerbstone (*BRIT*),

curbstone (US)

para'diso sm paradise

parados'sale ag paradoxical

para'dosso sm paradox

para'fango, ghi sm mudguard

paraf'fina sf paraffin, paraffin wax

para'fulmine sm lightning conductor

pa'raggi [pa'raddʒi] smpl: **nei ~** in the vicinity, in the neighbourhood

parago'nare vt: ~ **con/a** to compare with/to

para'gone sm comparison; (esempio analogo) analogy, parallel; **reggere al ~** to stand comparison

pa'ragrafo sm paragraph

pa'ralisi sf paralysis; **para'litico, a, ci, che** ag, sm/f paralytic

paraliz'zare [paralid'dzare] vt to paralyze

paral'lela sf parallel (line); **~e** sfpl (attrezzo ginnico) parallel bars

paral'lelo, a ag parallel ♦ sm (GEO) parallel; (comparazione): **fare un ~ tra** to draw a parallel between

para'lume sm lampshade

pa'rametro sm parameter

para'noia sf paranoia; **para'noico, a, ci, che** ag, sm/f paranoid

para'occhi [para'ɔkki] smpl blinkers

para'petto sm balustrade

para'piglia [para'piʎʎa] sm commotion, uproar

pa'rare vt (addobbare) to adorn, deck; (proteggere) to shield, protect; (scansare: colpo) to parry; (CALCIO) to save ♦ vi: **dove vuole andare a ~?** what are you driving at?; **~rsi** vr (presentarsi) to appear, present o.s.

para'sole sm inv parasol, sunshade

paras'sita, i sm parasite

pa'rata sf (SPORT) save; (MIL) review, parade

para'tia sf (di nave) bulkhead

para'urti sm inv (AUT) bumper

para'vento sm folding screen; **fare da ~ a qn** (fig) to shield sb

par'cella [par'tʃella] sf account, fee (of

lawyer etc)

parcheggi'are [parked'dʒare] vt to park; **par'cheggio** sm parking no pl; (luogo) car park; (singolo posto) parking space

par'chimetro [par'kimetro] sm parking meter

'parco[1], chi sm park; (spazio per deposito) depot; (complesso di veicoli) fleet

'parco[2], a, chi, che ag: ~ (in) (sobrio) moderate (in); (avaro) sparing (with)

pa'recchio, a [pa'rekkjo] det quite a lot of; (tempo) quite a lot of, a long; **~i, e** det pl quite a lot of, several ♦ pron quite a lot, quite a bit; (tempo) quite a while, a long time; **~i, e** pron pl quite a lot, several ♦ av (con ag) quite, rather; (con vb) quite a lot, quite a bit

pareggi'are [pared'dʒare] vt to make equal; (terreno) to level, make level; (bilancio, conti) to balance ♦ vi (SPORT) to draw; **pa'reggio** sm (ECON) balance; (SPORT) draw

pa'rente sm/f relative, relation

paren'tela sf (vincolo di sangue, fig) relationship

pa'rentesi sf (segno grafico) bracket, parenthesis; (frase incisa) parenthesis; (digressione) parenthesis, digression

pa'rere sm (opinione) opinion; (consiglio) advice, opinion; **a mio ~** in my opinion ♦ vi to seem, appear ♦ vb impers: **pare che** it seems o appears that; **they say that; mi pare che** it seems to me that; **mi pare di sì** I think so; **fai come ti pare** do as you like; **che ti pare del mio libro?** what do you think of my book?

pa'rete sf wall

'pari ag inv (uguale) equal, same; (in giochi) equal; (drawn, tied; (MAT) even ♦ sm inv (POL: di Gran Bretagna) peer ♦ sm/f inv peer, equal; **copiato ~ ~** copied word for word; **alla ~** on the same level; **ragazza alla ~** au pair girl; **mettersi alla ~ con** to place o.s. on the same level as; **mettersi in ~ con** to catch up with; **andare di ~ passo con qn** to keep pace with sb

Pa'rigi [paˈridʒi] *sf* Paris

pa'riglia [paˈriʎʎa] *sf* pair; **rendere la ~** to give tit for tat

parità *sf* parity, equality; (SPORT) draw, tie

parlamen'tare *ag* parliamentary
♦ *sm/f* ≈ Member of Parliament (BRIT), ≈ Congressman/woman (US) ♦ *vi* to negotiate, parley

parla'mento *sm* parliament

parlan'tina (*fam*) *sf* talkativeness; **avere ~** to have the gift of the gab

par'lare *vi* to speak, talk; (*confidare cose segrete*) to talk ♦ *vt* to speak; **~ (a qn) di** to speak o talk (to sb) about; **parla'torio** *sm* (*di carcere etc*) visiting room; (REL) parlour

parmigi'ano [parmiˈdʒano] *sm* (*grana*) Parmesan (cheese)

paro'dia *sf* parody

pa'rola *sf* word; (*facoltà*) speech; **~e** *sfpl* (*chiacchiere*) talk *sg*; **chiedere la ~** to ask permission to speak; **prendere la ~** to take the floor; **~ d'onore** word of honour; **~ d'ordine** (MIL) password; **~e incrociate** crossword (puzzle) *sg*; **paro'laccia, ce** *sf* bad word, swearword

par'rocchia [parˈrɔkkja] *sf* parish; parish church

'parroco, ci *sm* parish priest

par'rucca, che *sf* wig

parruc'chiere, a [parrukˈkjɛre] *sm/f* hairdresser ♦ *sm* barber

parsi'monia *sf* frugality, thrift

'parso, a *pp di* **parere**

'parte *sf* part; (*lato*) side; (*quota spettante a ciascuno*) share; (*direzione*) direction; (POL) party; faction; (DIR) party; **a ~** *ag* separate ♦ *av* separately; **scherzi a ~** joking aside; **a ~ ciò** apart from that; **da ~** (*in disparte*) to one side, aside; **d'altra ~** on the other hand; **da ~ di** (*per conto di*) on behalf

of; **da ~ mia** as far as I'm concerned, as for me; **da ~ a ~** right through; **da ogni ~** on all sides, everywhere; (*moto da luogo*) from all sides; **da nessuna ~** nowhere; **da questa ~** (*in questa direzione*) this way; **prendere ~ a qc** to take part in sth; **mettere da ~** to put aside; **mettere qn a ~ di** to inform sb of

parteci'pare [partetʃiˈpare] *vi*: **~ a** to take part in, participate in; (*utili etc*) to share in; (*spese etc*) to contribute to; (*dolore, successo di qn*) to share (in); **partecipazi'one** *sf* participation; sharing; (ECON) interest; **partecipazione agli utili** profit-sharing; **partecipazioni di nozze** wedding announcement card; **par'tecipe** *ag* participating; **essere partecipe di** to take part in, participate in; to share (in); (*consapevole*) to be aware of

parteggi'are [partedˈdʒare] *vi*: **~ per** to side with, be on the side of

par'tenza [parˈtɛntsa] *sf* departure; (SPORT) start; **essere in ~** to be about to leave, be leaving

parti'cella [partiˈtʃɛlla] *sf* particle

parti'cipio [partiˈtʃipjo] *sm* participle

partico'lare *ag* (*specifico*) particular; (*proprio*) personal, private; (*speciale*) special, particular; (*caratteristico*) distinctive, characteristic; (*fuori dal comune*) peculiar ♦ *sm* detail, particular; **in ~** in particular, particularly; **particolarità** *sf inv* particularity; detail; characteristic, feature

partigi'ano, a [partiˈdʒano] *ag* partisan ♦ *sm* (MIL) partisan

par'tire *vi* to go, leave; (*allontanarsi*) to go (o drive *etc*) away o off; (*petardo, colpo*) to go off; (*fig: avere inizio, SPORT*) to start; **sono partita da Roma alle 7** I left Rome at 7; **il volo parte da Ciampino** the flight leaves from Ciampino; **a ~ da** from

par'tita *sf* (COMM) lot, consignment;

(ECON: registrazione) entry, item; (CARTE, SPORT: gioco) game; (: competizione) match, game; **~ di caccia** hunting party; **~ IVA** VAT registration number

par'tito sm (POL) party; (decisione) decision, resolution; (persona da maritare) match

parti'tura sf (MUS) score

'parto sm (MED) delivery, (child)birth; labour; **parto'rire** vt to give birth to; (fig) to produce

parzi'ale [par'tsjale] ag (limitato) partial; (non obiettivo) biased, partial

'pascere ['paʃʃere] vt (brucare) to graze on; (far pascolare) to graze, pasture; **pasci'uto, a** pp di **pascere**

pasco'lare vt, vi to graze

'pascolo sm pasture

'Pasqua sf Easter; **pas'quale** ag Easter cpd; **Pas'quetta** sf Easter Monday

pas'sabile ag fairly good, passable

pas'saggio [pas'saddʒo] sm passing no pl, passage; (traversata) crossing no pl, passage; (luogo, prezzo della traversata, brano di libro etc) passage; (su veicolo altrui) lift (BRIT), ride; (SPORT) pass; **di ~** (persona) passing through; **~ pedonale/a livello** pedestrian/level (BRIT) o grade (US) crossing

passaman'tagna [passamon'taɲɲa] sm inv balaclava

pas'sante sm/f passer-by ♦ sm loop

passa'porto sm passport

pas'sare vi (andare) to go; (veicolo, pedone) to pass (by), go by; (fare una breve sosta: postino etc) to come, call; (: amico: per fare una visita) to call o drop in; (sole, aria, luce) to get through; (trascorrere: giorni, tempo) to pass, go by; (fig: proposta di legge) to be passed; (: dolore) to pass, go away; (CARTE) to pass ♦ vt (attraversare) to cross; (trasmettere: messaggio): **~ qc a qn** to pass sth on to sb; (dare): **~ qc a qn** to pass sth to sb, give sb sth; (trascorrere: tempo) to spend; (superare: esame) to pass; (triturare: verdura) to

strain; (approvare) to pass, approve; (oltrepassare, sorpassare: anche fig) to go beyond, pass; (fig: subire) to go through; **~ da ... a** to pass from ... to; **~ di padre in figlio** to be handed down o to pass from father to son; **~ per** (anche fig) to go through; **~ per stupido/un genio** to be taken for a fool/a genius; **~ sopra** (anche fig) to pass over; **~ attraverso** (anche fig) to go through; **~ alla storia** to pass into history; **~ a un esame** to go up (to the next class) after an exam; **~ inosservato** to go unnoticed; **~ di moda** to go out of fashion; **le passo il Signor X** (al telefono) here is Mr X; I'm putting you through to Mr X; **lasciar ~ qn/qc** to let sb/sth through; **come la passi?** how are you getting on o along?

pas'sata sf: **dare una ~ di vernice a qc** to give sth a coat of paint; **dare una ~ al giornale** to have a look at the paper, skim through the paper

passa'tempo sm pastime, hobby

pas'sato, a ag past; (sfiorito) faded ♦ sm past; (LING) past (tense); **~ prossimo** (LING) present perfect; **~ remoto** (LING) past historic; **~ di verdura** (CUC) vegetable purée

passaver'dura sm inv vegetable mill

passeg'gero, a [passed'dʒero] ag passing ♦ sm/f passenger

passeggi'are [passed'dʒare] vi to go for a walk; (in veicolo) to go for a drive; **passeggi'ata** sf walk; (luogo) promenade; **fare una passeggiata** to go for a walk (o drive); **passeg'gino** sm pushchair (BRIT), stroller (US); **pas'seggio** sm walk, stroll; (luogo) promenade

passe'rella sf footbridge; (di nave, aereo) gangway; (pedana) catwalk

'passero sm sparrow

pas'sibile ag: **~ di** liable to

passi'one sf passion

pas'sivo, a ag passive ♦ sm (LING)

passive; (ECON) debit; (: complesso dei debiti) liabilities pl

'passo sm step; (andatura) pace; (rumore) (foot)step; (orma) footprint; (passaggio, fig: brano) passage; (valico) pass; a ~ d'uomo at walking pace; ~ (a) ~ step by step; fare due o quattro ~i to go for a walk o a stroll; di questo ~ at this rate; "~ carraio" "vehicle entrance — keep clear"

'pasta sf (CUC) dough; (: impasto per dolce) pastry; (: anche: ~ alimentare) pasta; (massa molle di materia) paste; (fig: indole) nature; ~e sfpl (pasticcini) pastries; ~ in brodo noodle soup

pastasci'utta [pasta]'futta] sf pasta

pas'tella sf batter

pas'tello sm pastel

pas'ticca, che sf = pastiglia

pasticce'ria [pastittfe'ria] sf (pasticcini) pastries pl, cakes pl; (negozio) cake shop; (arte) confectionery

pasticci'are [pastit'tfare] vt to mess up, make a mess of ♦ vi to make a mess

pasticci'ere, a [pastit'tfere] sm/f pastrycook; confectioner

pas'ticcio [pas'tittfo] sm (CUC) pie; (lavoro disordinato, imbroglio) mess; trovarsi nei ~i to get into trouble

pasti'ficio [pasti'fitfo] sm pasta factory

pas'tiglia [pas'tiλλa] sf pastille, lozenge

pas'tina sf small pasta shapes used in soup

'pasto sm meal

pas'tore sm shepherd; (REL) pastor, minister; (anche: cane ~) sheepdog; ~ tedesco (ZOOL) Alsatian, German shepherd

pastoriz'zare [pastorid'dzare] vt to pasteurize

pas'toso, a ag doughy; pasty; (fig: voce, colore) mellow, soft

pas'trano sm greatcoat

pa'tata sf potato; ~e fritte chips (BRIT), French fries; pata'tine sfpl (potato)

crisps; ~ fritte chips

pata'trac sm (crollo: anche fig) crash

paté sm inv pâté

pa'tella sf (ZOOL) limpet

pa'tema, i sm anxiety, worry

pa'tente sf licence; (anche: ~ di guida) driving licence (BRIT), driver's license (US)

paternità sf paternity, fatherhood

pa'terno, a ag (affetto, consigli) fatherly; (casa, autorità) paternal

pa'tetico, a, ci, che ag pathetic; (commovente) moving, touching

pa'tibolo sm gallows sg, scaffold

'patina sf (su rame etc) patina; (sulla lingua) fur, coating

pa'tire vt, vi to suffer

pa'tito, a sm/f enthusiast, fan, lover

patolo'gia [patolo'dʒia] sf pathology; pato'logico, a, ci, che ag pathological

'patria sf homeland

patri'arca, chi sm patriarch

pa'trigno [pa'trinno] sm stepfather

patri'monio sm estate, property; (fig) heritage

patri'ota, i, e sm/f patriot; patri'ottico, a, ci, che ag patriotic; patriot'tismo sm patriotism

patroci'nare [patrotʃi'nare] vt (DIR: difendere) to defend; (sostenere) to sponsor, support; patro'cinio sm defence; support, sponsorship

patro'nato sm patronage; (istituzione benefica) charitable institution o society

pa'trono sm (REL) patron saint; (socio di patronato) patron; (DIR) counsel

'patta sf flap; (dei pantaloni) fly

patteggia'mento [patteddʒa'mento] sm (DIR) plea bargaining

patteggi'are [patted'dʒare] vt, vi to negotiate; (DIR) to plea-bargain

patti'naggio [patti'naddʒo] sm skating

patti'nare vi to skate; ~ sul ghiaccio to ice-skate; pattina'tore, 'trice sm/f skater; 'pattino[1] sm skate; (di slitta) runner; (AER) skid; (TECN) sliding block;

pattini (da ghiaccio) (ice) skates;
pattini in linea Rollerblades ®;
pattini a rotelle roller skates;
pat'tino² sm (barca) kind of pedalo
with oars

'**patto** sm (accordo) pact, agreement;
(condizione) term, condition; **a ~ che**
on condition that

pat'tuglia [pat'tuʎʎa] sf (MIL) patrol

pattu'ire vt to reach an agreement on

pattumi'era sf (dust)bin (BRIT), ashcan
(US)

pa'ura sf fear; **aver ~ di/di fare/che**
to be frightened o afraid of/of doing/
that; **far ~ a** to frighten; **per ~ di/che**
for fear of/that; **pau'roso, a** ag (che ha
paura) frightening; (che ha
paura) fearful, timorous

'**pausa** sf (sosta) break; (nel parlare,
MUS) pause

pavi'mento sm floor

pa'vone sm peacock; **pavoneggi'arsi**
vr to strut about, show off

pazien'tare [pattsjen'tare] vi to be
patient

pazi'ente [pat'tsjɛnte] ag, sm/f
patient; **pazi'enza** sf patience

paz'zesco, a, schi, sche [pat'tsesko]
ag mad, crazy

paz'zia [pat'tsia] sf (MED) madness,
insanity; (azione) folly; (di azione,
decisione) madness, folly

'**pazzo, a** [pattso] ag (MED) mad,
insane; (strano) wild, mad ♦ sm/f
madman/woman; **~ di** (gioia, amore
etc) mad o crazy with; **~ per qc/qn**
mad o crazy about sth/sb

PCI sigla m = **Partito Comunista
Italiano**

'pecca, che sf defect, flaw, fault

peccami'noso, a ag sinful

pec'care vi to sin; (fig) to err

pec'cato sm sin; **è un ~ che** it's a pity
that; **che ~!** what a shame o pity!

pecca'tore, 'trice sm/f sinner

pece ['petʃe] sf pitch

Pe'chino [pe'kino] sf Beijing

'**pecora** sf sheep; **peco'raio** sm
shepherd; **peco'rino** sm sheep's milk
cheese

peculi'are ag: **~ di** peculiar to

pe'daggio [pe'daddʒo] sm toll

pedago'gia [pedago'dʒia] sf
pedagogy, educational methods pl

peda'lare vi to pedal; (andare in
bicicletta) to cycle

pe'dale sm pedal

pe'dana sf footboard; (SPORT: nel salto)
springboard; (: nella scherma) piste

pe'dante ag pedantic ♦ sm/f pedant

pe'data sf (impronta) footprint; (colpo)
kick; **prendere a ~e qn/qc** to kick
sb/sth

pede'rasta, i sm pederast; homosexual

pedi'atra, i, e sm/f paediatrician;
pedia'tria sf paediatrics sg

pedi'cure sm/f inv chiropodist

pe'dina sf (della dama) draughtsman
(BRIT), draftsman (US); (fig) pawn

pedi'nare vt to shadow, tail

pedo'nale ag pedestrian

pe'done, a sm/f pedestrian ♦ sm
(SCACCHI) pawn

'**peggio** ['pɛddʒo] av, ag inv worse
♦ sm o f: **il o la ~** the worst; **alla ~** at
worst, if the worst comes to the worst;
peggio'rare vt to make worse, worsen
♦ vi to grow worse, worsen;
peggiora'tivo, a ag pejorative;
peggi'ore ag (comparativo) worse;
(superlativo) worst ♦ sm/f: **il(la)
peggiore** the worst (person)

'**pegno** ['peɲɲo] sm (DIR) security,
pledge; (nei giochi di società) forfeit;
(fig) pledge, token; **dare in ~ qc** to
pawn sth

pe'lare vt (spennare) to pluck; (spellare)
to skin; (sbucciare) to peel; (fig) to
make pay through the nose; **~rsi** vr to
go bald

pe'lato, a ag: **pomodori ~i** tinned
tomatoes

pel'lame sm skins pl, hides pl

'**pelle** sf skin; (di animale) skin, hide; (cuoio) leather; **avere la ~ d'oca** to have goose pimples o goose flesh

pelle'grinaggio [pellegri'naddʒo] sm pilgrimage

pelle'grino, a sm/f pilgrim

pelle'rossa (pl pelli'rosse) sm/f Red Indian

pelle'tteria sf leather goods pl; (negozio) leather goods shop

pelli'cano sm pelican

pellic'ceria [pellittʃe'ria] sf (negozio) furrier's (shop)

pel'liccia, ce [pel'littʃa] sf (mantello di animale) coat, fur; (indumento) fur coat

pel'licola sf (membrana sottile) film, layer; (FOT, CINEMA) film

'pelo sm hair; (pelame) coat, hair; (pelliccia) fur; (di tappeto) pile; (di liquido) surface; **per un ~: per un ~ non ho perduto il treno** I very nearly missed the train; **c'è mancato un ~ che affogasse** he escaped drowning by the skin of his teeth; pe'loso, a ag hairy

'peltro sm pewter

pe'luria sf down

'**pena** sf (DIR) sentence; (punizione) punishment; (sofferenza) sadness no pl, sorrow; (fatica) trouble no pl, effort; (difficoltà) difficulty; **far ~** to be pitiful; **mi fai ~** I feel sorry for you; **prendersi** o **darsi la ~ di fare** to go to the trouble of doing; **~ di morte** death sentence; **~ pecuniaria** fine; pe'nale ag penal; penalità sf inv penalty; penaliz'zare vt (SPORT) to penalize

pe'nare vi (patire) to suffer; (faticare) to struggle

pen'dente ag hanging; leaning ♦ sm (ciondolo) pendant; (orecchino) drop earring; pen'denza sf slope, slant; (grado d'inclinazione) gradient; (ECON) outstanding account

'**pendere** vi (essere appeso): **~ da** to hang from; (essere inclinato) to lean;

(fig: incombere): **~ su** to hang over

pen'dice [pen'ditʃe] sf: **alle ~i del monte** at the foot of the mountain

pen'dio, 'dii sm slope, slant; (luogo in pendenza) slope

'**pendola** sf pendulum clock

pendo'lare sm/f commuter

pendo'lino sm high-speed train

'pendolo sm (peso) pendulum; (anche: orologio a ~) pendulum clock

'pene sm penis

pene'trante ag piercing, penetrating

pene'trare vi to come o get in ♦ vt to penetrate; **~ in** to enter; (sog: proiettile) to penetrate; (: acqua, aria) to go o come into

penicil'lina [penitʃil'lina] sf penicillin

pe'nisola sf peninsula

peni'tenza [peni'tentsa] sf penitence; (punizione) penance

penitenzi'ario [peniten'tsjarjo] sm prison

'**penna** sf (di uccello) feather; (per scrivere) pen; **~e** sfpl (CUC) quills (type of pasta); **~ stilografica/a sfera** fountain/ballpoint pen

penna'rello sm felt(-tip) pen

pennel'lare vi to paint

pen'nello sm brush; (per dipingere) (paint)brush; **a ~** (perfettamente) to perfection, perfectly; **~ per la barba** shaving brush

pen'nino sm nib

pen'none sm (NAUT) yard; (stendardo) banner, standard

pe'nombra sf half-light, dim light

pe'noso, a ag painful, distressing; (faticoso) tiring, laborious

pen'sare vi to think ♦ vt to think; (inventare, escogitare) to think out; **~ a** to think of; (amico, vacanze) to think of o about; (problema) to think about; **~ di fare qc** to think of doing sth; **ci penso io** I'll see to o take care of it

pensi'ero sm thought; (modo di pensare, dottrina) thinking no pl; (preoccupazione) worry, care, trouble;

stare in ~ per qn to be worried about sb; **pensie'roso, a** ag thoughtful

'**pensile** ag hanging

pensi'lina sf (per autobus) bus shelter

pensio'nante sm/f (presso una famiglia) lodger; (di albergo) guest

pensio'nato, a sm/f pensioner

pensi'one sf (al prestatore di lavoro) pension; (vitto e alloggio) board and lodging; (albergo) boarding house; **andare in ~** to retire; **mezza ~** half board; **~ completa** full board

pen'soso, a ag thoughtful, pensive, lost in thought

pentapar'tito sm five-party government

Pente'coste sf Pentecost, Whit Sunday (BRIT)

penti'mento sm repentance, contrition

pen'tirsi vr: **~ di** to repent of; (rammaricarsi) to regret, be sorry for

'**pentola** sf pot; **~ a pressione** pressure cooker

pe'nultimo, a ag last but one (BRIT), next to last, penultimate

pe'nuria sf shortage

penzo'lare [pendzo'lare] vi to dangle, hang loosely; **penzo'loni** av dangling, hanging down; **stare penzoloni** to dangle, hang down

'**pepe** sm pepper; **~ macinato/in grani** ground/whole pepper

pepe'rata sf (cuc) stewed peppers, tomatoes and onions

pepe'rone sm pepper, capsicum; (piccante) chili

pe'pita sf nugget

PAROLA CHIAVE

---

per prep **1** (moto attraverso luogo) through; **i ladri sono passati ~ la finestra** the thieves got in (o out) through the window; **l'ho cercato ~ tutta la casa** I've searched the whole house o all over the house for it

2 (moto a luogo) for, to; **partire ~ la Germania/il mare** to leave for Germany/the sea; **il treno ~ Roma** the Rome train, the train for o to Rome

3 (stato in luogo): **seduto/sdraiato ~ terra** sitting/lying on the ground

4 (tempo) for; **~ anni/lungo tempo** for years/a long time; **~ tutta l'estate** throughout the summer, all summer long; **lo rividi ~ Natale** I saw him again at Christmas; **lo faccio ~ lunedì** I'll do it for Monday

5 (mezzo, maniera) by; **~ lettera/via aerea/ferrovia** by letter/airmail/rail; **prendere qn ~ un braccio** to take sb by the arm

6 (causa, scopo) for; **assente ~ malattia** absent because of o through o owing to illness; **ottimo ~ il mal di gola** excellent for sore throats

7 (limitazione) for; **è troppo difficile ~ lui** it's too difficult for him; **~ quel che mi riguarda** as far as I'm concerned; **~ poco che sia** however little it may be; **~ questa volta ti perdono** I'll forgive you this time

8 (prezzo, misura) for; (distributivo) per; **venduto ~ 3 milioni** sold for 3 million; **1000 lire ~ persona** 1000 lire a o per person; **uno ~ volta** one at a time; **uno ~ uno** one by one; **5 ~ cento** 5 per cent; **3 ~ 4 fa 12** 3 times 4 equals 12; **dividere/moltiplicare 12 ~ 4** to divide/multiply 12 by 4

9 (in qualità di): (al posto di) for; **avere qn ~ professore** to have sb as a teacher; **ti ho preso ~ Mario** I mistook you for Mario, I thought you were Mario; **dare ~ morto qn** to give sb up for dead

10 (seguito da vb: finale): **~ fare qc** (so as) to do sth, in order to do sth; (: causale): **~ aver fatto qc** for having done sth; (: consecutivo): **è abbastanza grande ~ andarci da solo** he's big enough to go on his own

'**pera** sf pear

pe'raltro av moreover, what's more

per'bene ag inv respectable, decent
♦ av (con cura) properly, well

percentu'ale [pertʃentu'ale] sf percentage

perce'pire [pertʃe'pire] vt (sentire) to perceive; (ricevere) to receive; **percezi'one** sf perception

---

PAROLA CHIAVE

perché [per'ke] av why; ~ no? why not?; ~ **non vuoi andarci?** why don't you want to go?; **spiegami ~ l'hai fatto** tell me why you did it
♦ cong 1 (causale) because; **non posso uscire ~ ho da fare** I can't go out because o as I've a lot to do
2 (finale) in order that, so that; **te lo do ~ tu lo legga** I'm giving it to you so (that) you can read it
3 (consecutivo): **è troppo forte ~ si possa batterlo** he's too strong to be beaten
♦ sm inv reason; **il ~ di** the reason for

---

perciò [per'tʃɔ] cong so, for this (o that) reason

per'correre vt (luogo) to go all over; (: paese) to travel up and down, go all over; (distanza) to cover

per'corso, a pp di **percorrere** ♦ sm (tragitto) journey; (tratto) route

per'cossa sf blow

per'cosso, a pp di **percuotere**

percu'otere vt to hit, strike

percussi'one sf percussion; **strumenti a ~** (MUS) percussion instruments

'**perdere** vt to lose; (lasciarsi sfuggire) to miss; (sprecare: tempo, denaro) to waste ♦ vi to lose; (serbatoio etc) to leak; **~rsi** vr (smarrirsi) to get lost; (svanire) to disappear, vanish; **saper ~** to be a good loser; **lascia ~!** forget it!,

never mind!

perdigi'orno [perdi'dʒorno] sm/f inv idler, waster

'**perdita** sf loss; (spreco) waste; (fuoriuscita) leak; **siamo in ~** (COMM) we are running at a loss; **a ~ d'occhio** as far as the eye can see

perdo'nare vt to pardon, forgive; (scusare) to excuse, pardon

per'dono sm forgiveness; (DIR) pardon

perdu'rare vi to go on, last

perduta'mente av desperately, passionately

per'duto, a pp di **perdere**

peregri'nare vi to wander, roam

pe'renne ag eternal, perpetual, perennial; (BOT) perennial

peren'torio, a ag peremptory; (definitivo) final

per'fetto, a ag perfect ♦ sm (LING) perfect (tense)

perfezio'nare [perfettsjo'nare] vt to improve, perfect; **~rsi** vr to improve

perfezi'one [perfet'tsjone] sf perfection

'**perfido, a** ag perfidious, treacherous

per'fino av even

perfo'rare vt to perforate; to punch a hole (o holes) in; (banda, schede) to punch; (trivellare) to drill;

perfora'trice (TECN) boring o drilling machine; (INFORM) card punch;

perforazi'one sf perforation; punching; drilling; (INFORM) punch; (MED) perforation

perga'mena sf parchment

'**pergola** sf (per rampicanti) pergola

perico'lante ag precarious

pe'ricolo sm danger; **mettere in ~** to endanger, put in danger; **perico'loso, a** ag dangerous

perife'ria sf (di città) outskirts pl

pe'rifrasi sf circumlocution

pe'rimetro sm perimeter

peri'odico, a, ci, che ag periodic(al); (MAT) recurring ♦ sm periodical

pe'riodo sm period

peripe'zie [peripet'tsie] *sfpl* ups and downs, vicissitudes

pe'rire *vi* to perish, die

pe'rito, a *ag* expert, skilled ♦ *sm/f* expert; (*agronomo, navale*) surveyor; **un ~ chimico** a qualified chemist

pe'rizia [pe'rittsja] *sf* (*abilità*) ability; (*giudizio tecnico*) expert opinion; expert's report

'perla *sf* pearl; **per'lina** *sf* bead

perlus'trare *vt* to patrol

perma'loso, a *ag* touchy

perma'nente *ag* permanent ♦ *sm* permanent wave, perm; **perma'nenza** *sf* permanence; (*soggiorno*) stay

perma'nere *vi* to remain

perme'are *vt* to permeate

per'messo, a *pp di* **permettere** ♦ *sm* (*autorizzazione*) permission, leave; (*dato a militare, impiegato*) leave; (*licenza*) licence, permit; (MIL: *foglio*) pass; **~?, è ~?** (*posso entrare?*) may I come in?; (*posso passare?*) excuse me; **~ di lavoro/pesca** work/fishing permit; **~ di soggiorno** residence permit

per'mettere *vt* to allow, permit; **~ a qn qc/di fare** to allow sb sth/to do; **~rsi qc/di fare** to allow o.s. sth/to do; (*avere la possibilità*) to afford sth/to do

per'nacchia [per'nakkja] (*fam*) *sf*: **fare una ~** to blow a raspberry

per'nice [per'nitʃe] *sf* partridge

'perno *sm* pivot

pernot'tare *vi* to spend the night, stay overnight

'pero *sm* pear tree

però *cong* (*ma*) but; (*tuttavia*) however, nevertheless

pero'rare *vt* (DIR, *fig*): **~ la causa di qn** to plead sb's case

perpendico'lare *ag, sf* perpendicular

perpe'trare *vt* to perpetrate

perpetu'are *vt* to perpetuate

per'petuo, a *ag* perpetual

per'plesso, a *ag* perplexed; uncertain, undecided

perqui'sire *vt* to search; **perquisizi'one** *sf* (*police*) search

persecu'tore *sm* persecutor

persecuzi'one [persekut'tsjone] *sf* persecution

persegu'ire *vt* to pursue

persegui'tare *vt* to persecute

perseve'rante *ag* persevering

perseve'rare *vi* to persevere

'Persia *sf*: **la ~** Persia

persi'ana *sf* shutter; **~ avvolgibile** roller shutter

persi'ano, a *ag, sm/f* Persian

'persico, a, ci, che *ag*: **il golfo P~** the Persian Gulf

per'sino *av* = **perfino**

persis'tente *ag* persistent

per'sistere *vi* to persist; **~ a fare** to persist in doing; **persis'tito, a** *pp di* **persistere**

'perso, a *pp di* **perdere**

per'sona *sf* person; (*qualcuno*): **una ~** someone, somebody, *espressione interrogativa* +anyone *o* anybody; **~e** *sfpl* people; **non c'è ~ che** ... there's nobody who ..., there isn't anybody who ...

perso'naggio [perso'naddʒo] *sm* (*persona ragguardevole*) personality, figure; (*tipo*) character, individual; (LETTERATURA) character

perso'nale *ag* personal ♦ *sm* staff; personnel; (*figura fisica*) build

personalità *sf inv* personality

personifi'care *vt* to personify; to embody

perspi'cace [perspi'katʃe] *ag* shrewd, discerning

persu'adere *vt*: **~ qn (di qc/a fare)** to persuade sb (of sth/to do); **persuasi'one** *sf* persuasion; **persua'sivo, a** *ag* persuasive; **persu'aso, a** *pp di* **persuadere**

per'tanto *cong* (*quindi*) so, therefore

'pertica, che *sf* pole

perti'nente *ag*: **~ (a)** relevant (to), pertinent (to)

per'tosse sf whooping cough

per'tugio [per'tudʒo] sm hole, opening

perturbazi'one [perturbat'tsjone] sf disruption; perturbation; ~ **atmosferica** atmospheric disturbance

per'vadere vt to pervade; **per'vaso**, **a** pp di pervadere

perve'nire vi: ~ **a** to reach, arrive at, come to; (venire in possesso): **gli pervenne una fortuna** he inherited a fortune; **far** ~ **qc a** to have sth sent to; **perve'nuto**, **a** pp di pervenire

per'verso, **a** ag depraved; perverse

p. es. abbr (= per esempio) e.g.

'pesa sf weighing no pl; weighbridge

pe'sante ag heavy

pe'sare vt to weigh ♦ vi (avere un peso) to weigh; (essere pesante) to be heavy; (fig) to carry weight; ~ **su** (fig) to lie heavy on; to influence; to hang over

'pesca (pl **pesche**: frutto) sf peach; (il pescare) fishing; **andare a** ~ to go fishing; ~ **di beneficenza** (lotteria) lucky dip; ~ **con la lenza** angling

pes'care vt (pesce) to fish for; to catch; (qc nell'acqua) to fish out; (fig: trovare) to get hold of, find; **andare a** ~ to go fishing

pesca'tore sm fisherman; angler

'pesce ['peʃʃe] sm fish gen inv; **P~i** (dello zodiaco) Pisces; ~ **d'aprile!** April Fool!; ~ **spada** swordfish; **pesce'cane** sm shark

---

pesce d'aprile

Il **pesce d'aprile** is a practical joke played on 1 April. It takes its name from the traditional prank of surreptitiously sticking a paper fish on someone's back.

---

pesche'reccio [peske'rettʃo] sm fishing boat

pesche'ria [peske'ria] sf fishmonger's (shop) (BRIT), fish store (US)

pesci'vendolo, **a** [peʃʃi'vendolo] sm/f fishmonger (BRIT), fish merchant (US)

'pesco, **schi** sm peach tree

pes'coso, **a** ag abounding in fish

'peso sm weight; (SPORT) shot; **rubare sul** ~ to give short weight; **essere di** ~ **a qn** (fig) to be a burden to sb; ~ **lordo/netto** gross/net weight; ~ **piuma/mosca/gallo/medio/ massimo** (PUGILATO) feather/fly/ bantam/middle/heavyweight

pessi'mismo sm pessimism

pessi'mista, **i**, **e** ag pessimistic ♦ sm/f pessimist

'pessimo, **a** ag very bad, awful

pes'tare vt to tread on, trample on; (sale, pepe) to grind; (uva, aglio) to crush; (fig: picchiare): ~ **qn** to beat sb up

'peste sf plague; (persona) nuisance, pest

pe'stello sm pestle

pesti'lenza [pesti'lentsa] sf pestilence; (fetore) stench

'pesto, **a** ag: **c'è buio** ~ it's pitch-dark; **occhio** ~ black eye ♦ sm (CUC) sauce made with basil, garlic, cheese and oil

'petalo sm (BOT) petal

pe'tardo sm firecracker, banger (BRIT)

petizi'one [petit'tsjone] sf petition

'peto (fam!) sm fart (!)

petrol'chimica [petrol'kimika] sf petrochemical industry

petroli'era sf (nave) oil tanker

petro'lifero, **a** ag oil-bearing; oil cpd

pe'trolio sm oil, petroleum; (per lampada, fornello) paraffin

pettego'lare vi to gossip

pettego'lezzo [pettego'leddzo] sm gossip no pl; **fare** ~**i** to gossip

pet'tegolo, **a** ag gossipy ♦ sm/f gossip

petti'nare vt to comb (the hair of); ~**rsi** vr to comb one's hair; **petti'natura** sf (acconciatura) hairstyle

'pettine sm comb; (ZOOL) scallop

petti'rosso sm robin

'petto sm chest; (seno) breast, bust; (CUC: di carne bovina) brisket; (: di pollo etc) breast; **a doppio ~** (abito) double-breasted; **petto'ruto, a** ag broad-chested; full-breasted

petu'lante ag insolent

pe'tunia sf (BOT) petunia

'pezza ['pettsa] sf piece of cloth; (toppa) patch; (cencio) rag, cloth

pez'zato, a [pet'tsato] ag piebald

pez'zente [pet'tsɛnte] sm/f beggar

'pezzo ['pɛttso] sm (gen) piece; (brandello, frammento) piece, bit; (di macchina, arnese etc) part; (STAMPA) article; (di tempo): **aspettare un ~** to wait quite a while o some time; **in o a ~i** in pieces; **andare in ~i** to break into pieces; **un bel ~ d'uomo** a fine figure of a man; **abito a due ~i** two-piece suit; **~ di cronaca** (STAMPA) report; **~ grosso** (fig) bigwig; **~ di ricambio** spare part

pia'cente [pja'tʃɛnte] ag attractive

pia'cere [pja'tʃere] vi to please; **una ragazza che piace** a likeable girl; **an attractive girl; ~ a: mi piace** I like it; **quei ragazzi non mi piacciono** I don't like those boys; **gli piacerebbe andare al cinema** he would like to go to the cinema ♦ sm pleasure; (favore) favour; **"~!"** (nelle presentazioni) "pleased to meet you!"; **con ~** certainly, with pleasure; **per ~!** please; **fare un ~ a qn** to do sb a favour; **pia'cevole** ag pleasant, agreeable; **piaci'uto, a** pp di **piacere**

pi'aga, ghe sf (lesione) sore; (ferita: anche fig) wound; (fig: flagello) scourge, curse; (: persona) pest, nuisance

piagni'steo [pjaɲis'teo] sm whining, whimpering

piagnuco'lare [pjaɲɲuko'lare] vi to whimper

pi'alla sf (arnese) plane; **pial'lare** vt to plane

pi'ana sf stretch of level ground; (più estesa) plain

pianeggi'ante [pjaned'dʒante] ag flat, level

pia'neta sm (ASTR) planet

pi'angere ['pjandʒere] vi to cry, weep; (occhi) to water ♦ vt to cry, weep; (lamentare) to bewail, lament; **~ la morte di qn** to mourn sb's death

pianifi'care vt to plan;
pianificazi'one sf planning

pia'nista, i, e sm/f pianist

pi'ano, a ag (piatto) flat, level; (MAT) plane; (chiaro) clear, plain ♦ av (adagio) slowly; (a bassa voce) softly; (con cautela) slowly, carefully ♦ sm (MAT) plane; (GEO) plain; (livello) level, plane; (di edificio) floor; (programma) plan; (MUS) piano; **pian ~** very slowly; (poco a poco) little by little; **in primo/secondo ~** in the foreground/background; **di primo ~** (fig) prominent, high-ranking

piano'forte sm piano, pianoforte

pi'anta sf (BOT) plant; (ANAT: anche: ~ del piede) sole (of the foot); (grafico) plan; (topografica) map; (in ~ stabile) on the permanent staff; **piantagi'one** sf plantation; **pian'tare** vt to plant; (conficcare) to drive o hammer in; (tenda) to put up, pitch; (fig: lasciare) to leave, desert; **~rsi vr: ~rsi davanti a qn** to plant o.s. in front of sb; **piantala!** (fam) cut it out!

pianter'reno sm ground floor

pian'tina sf (carta) map

pi'anto, a pp di **piangere** ♦ sm tears pl, crying

pian'tone sm (vigilante) sentry, guard; (soldato) orderly; (AUT) steering column

pia'nura sf plain

pi'astra sf (lastra, di pietra) slab; (di fornello) hotplate; **~ di registrazione** tape deck; **panino alla ~** ≈ toasted sandwich

pias'trella sf tile

pias'trina sf (MIL) identity disc

piatta'forma sf (anche fig) platform

piat'tino sm saucer

pi'atto, a ag flat; (fig: scialbo) dull ♦ sm (recipiente, vivanda) dish; (portata) course; (parte piana) flat (part); **~i** smpl (MUS) cymbals; **~ fondo** soup dish; **~ forte** main course; **~ del giorno** dish of the day, plat du jour; **~ dei giradischi** turntable

pi'azza ['pjattsa] sf square; (COMM) market; **far ~ pulita** to make a clean sweep; **~ d'armi** (MIL) parade ground; **piaz'zale** sm (large) square

piaz'zare [pjat'tsare] vt to place; (COMM) to market, sell; **~rsi** vr (SPORT) to be placed

piaz'zista, i [pjat'tsista] sm (COMM) commercial traveller

piaz'zola [pjat'tsɔla] sf (AUT) lay-by

picca, che sf pike; **~che** sfpl (CARTE) spades

pic'cante ag hot, pungent; (fig) racy; biting

pic'carsi vr: **~ di fare** to pride o.s. on one's ability to do; **~ per qc** to take offence at sth

pic'chetto [pik'ketto] sm (MIL, di scioperanti) picket; (di tenda) peg

picchi'are [pik'kjare] vt (persona: colpire) to hit, strike; (: prendere a botte) to beat (up); (battere) to beat; (sbattere) to bang ♦ vi (bussare) to knock; (: con forza) to bang; (colpire) to hit, strike; (sole) to beat down; **picchi'ata** sf (AER) dive

picchiet'tare [pikkjet'tare] vt (punteggiare) to spot, dot; (colpire) to tap

'picchio ['pikkjo] sm woodpecker

pic'cino, a [pit'tʃino] ag tiny, very small

piccio'naia [pittʃo'naja] sf pigeon-loft; (TEATRO): **la ~** the gods sg

picci'one [pit'tʃone] sm pigeon

'picco, chi sm peak; **a ~** vertically

'piccolo, a ag small; (oggetto, mano, di

età: bambino) small, little (dav sostantivo); (di breve durata: viaggio) short; (fig) mean, petty ♦ sm/f child, little one; **~i** smpl (di animale) young pl; **in ~** in miniature

pic'cone sm pick(-axe)

pic'cozza [pik'kɔttsa] sf ice-axe

pic'nic sm inv picnic

pi'docchio [pi'dɔkkjo] sm louse

pi'ede sm foot; (di mobile) leg; **in ~i** standing; **a ~ on foot; a ~i nudi** barefoot; **su due ~i** (fig) at once; **prendere ~** (fig) to gain ground, catch on; **sul ~ di guerra** (MIL) ready for action; **~ di porco** crowbar

piedes'tallo sm pedestal

piedi'patti sm inv (peg) cop

pi'ega, ghe sf (piegatura, GEO) fold; (di gonna) pleat; (di pantaloni) crease; (grinza) wrinkle, crease; **prendere una brutta ~** (fig) to take a turn for the worse

pie'gare vt to fold; (braccia, gambe, testa) to bend ♦ vi to bend; **~rsi** vr to bend; (fig) to yield (to), submit (to); **pieghet'tare** vt to pleat; **pie'ghevole** ag pliable, flexible; (porta) folding

Pie'monte sm: **il ~** Piedmont

pi'ena sf (di fiume) flood, spate

pi'eno, a ag full; (muro, mattone) solid ♦ sm (colmo) height, peak; (carico) full load; **~ di** full of; **in ~ giorno** in broad daylight; **fare il ~** (di benzina) to fill up (with petrol)

pietà sf pity; (REL) piety; **senza ~** pitiless, merciless; **avere ~ di** (compassione) to pity, feel sorry for; (misericordia) to have pity o mercy on

pie'tanza [pje'tantsa] sf dish, course

pie'toso, a ag (compassionevole) pitying, compassionate; (che desta pietà) pitiful

pi'etra sf stone; **~ preziosa** precious stone, gem; **pie'traia** sf (terreno) stony ground; **pietrifi'care** vt to petrify; (fig) to transfix, paralyze

'piffero sm (MUS) pipe

pigi'ama, i [pi'dʒama] sm pyjamas pl

'pigia 'pigia [pidʒa'pidʒa] sm crowd, press

pigi'are [pi'dʒare] vt to press

pigi'one [pi'dʒone] sf rent

pigli'are [piʎ'ʎare] vt to take, grab; (afferrare) to catch

'piglio [piʎʎo] sm look, expression

pig'meo, a sm/f pygmy

'pigna [piɲɲa] sf pine cone

pi'gnolo, a [piɲ'ɲɔlo] ag pernickety

pigno'rare [piɲɲo'rare] vt to distrain

pigo'lare vi to cheep, chirp

pi'grizia [pi'grittsja] sf laziness

'pigro, a ag lazy

'pila sf (catasta, di ponte) pile; (ELETTR) battery; (torcia) torch (BRIT), flashlight

pi'lastro sm pillar

'pile ['pail] sm inv fleece

pil'lola sf pill; **prendere la ~** to be on the pill

pi'lone sm (di ponte) pier; (di linea elettrica) pylon

pi'lota, i, e sm/f pilot; (AUT) driver ♦ ag inv pilot cpd; **~ automatico** automatic pilot; **pilo'tare** vt to pilot; to drive

pinaco'teca, che sf art gallery

pi'neta sf pinewood

ping-'pong [piŋ'pɔŋ] sm table tennis

'pingue ag fat, corpulent

pingu'ino sm (ZOOL) penguin

'pinna sf (di pesce) fin; (di cetaceo, per nuotare) flipper

'pino sm pine (tree); **pi'nolo** sm pine kernel

'pinza ['pintsa] sf pliers pl; (MED) forceps pl; (ZOOL) pincer

pin'zette [pin'tsette] sfpl tweezers

'pio, a, 'pii, 'pie ag pious; (opere, istituzione) charitable, charity cpd

pi'oggia, ge [pi'ɔddʒa] sf rain; **~ acida** acid rain

piom'bare vi to fall heavily; (gettarsi con impeto): **~ su** to fall upon, assail ♦ vt (dente) to fill; **piomba'tura** sf (di

dente) filling

piom'bino sm (sigillo) (lead) seal; (del filo a piombo) plummet; (PESCA) sinker

pi'ombo sm (CHIM) lead; **a ~** (cadere) straight down; **senza ~** (benzina) unleaded

pioni'ere, a sm/f pioneer

pi'oppo sm poplar

pi'overe vb impers to rain ♦ vi (fig: scendere dall'alto) to rain down; (lettere, regali) to pour into; **pioviggi'nare** vb impers to drizzle; **pio'voso, a** ag rainy

pi'ovra sf octopus

'pipa sf pipe

pipì (fam) sf: **fare ~** to have a wee (wee)

pipis'trello sm (ZOOL) bat

pi'ramide sf pyramid

pi'rata, i sm pirate; **~ della strada** hit-and-run driver

Pire'nei smpl: **i ~** the Pyrenees

'pirico, a, ci, che ag: **polvere ~a** gunpowder

pi'rofila, a ag heat-resistant; **pi'rofila** sf heat-resistant dish

pi'roga, ghe sf dug-out canoe

pi'romane sm/f pyromaniac; arsonist

pi'roscafo sm steamer, steamship

pisci'are [piʃ'ʃare] (fam!) vi to piss (!), pee (!)

pi'scina [piʃ'ʃina] sf (swimming) pool; (stabilimento) swimming baths pl

pi'sello sm pea

piso'lino sm nap

'pista sf (traccia) track, trail; (di stadio) track; (di pattinaggio) rink; (da sci) run; (AER) runway; (di circo) ring; **~ da ballo** dance floor

pis'tacchio [pis'takkjo] sm pistachio (tree); pistachio (nut)

pis'tola sf pistol, gun

pis'tone sm piston

pi'tone sm python

pit'tore, 'trice sm/f painter; **pitto'resco, a, schi, sche** ag picturesque

pit'tura sf painting; **pittu'rare** vt to

paint

PAROLA CHIAVE

più av **1** (*in maggiore quantità*) more; ~ **del solito** more than usual; **in ~, di ~** more; **ne voglio di ~** I want some more; **ci sono 3 persone in** o **di ~** there are 3 more o extra people; ~ **o meno** more or less; **per di ~** (*inoltre*) what's more, moreover

2 (*comparativo*) more, *aggettivo corto* +...*er*; ~ ... **di/che** more ... than; **lavoro ~ di te/Paola** I work harder than you/Paola; **è ~ intelligente che ricco** he's more intelligent than rich

3 (*superlativo*) most, *aggettivo corto* +...*est*; **il ~ grande/intelligente** the biggest/most intelligent; **è quello che compro ~ spesso** that's the one I buy most often; **al ~ presto** as soon as possible; **al ~ tardi** at the latest

4 (*negazione*): **non ... ~** no more, no longer; **non ho ~ soldi** I've got no more money, I don't have any more money; **non lavoro ~** I'm no longer working, I don't work any more; **a ~ non posso** (*gridare*) at the top of one's voice; (*correre*) as fast as one can

5 (*MAT*) plus; **4 ~ 5 fa 9** 4 plus 5 equals 9; **~ 5 gradi** 5 degrees above freezing, plus 5

♦ *prep* plus

♦ *ag inv* **1**: ~ ... (**di**) more ... (than); ~ **denaro/tempo** more money/time; ~ **persone di quante ci aspettavamo** more people than we expected

2 (*numerosi, diversi*) several; **l'aspettai per ~ giorni** I waited for it for several days

♦ *sm* **1** (*la maggior parte*): **il ~ è fatto** most of it is done

2 (*MAT*) plus (sign)

3: **i ~** the majority

piucchepper'fetto [pjukkepper'fɛtto] *sm* (*LING*) pluperfect, past perfect

pi'uma *sf* feather; **piu'maggio** *sm* plumage, feathers *pl*; **piu'mino** *sm* (*eider*)down; (*per letto*) eiderdown; (: *tipo danese*) duvet, continental quilt; (*giacca*) quilted jacket (*with goose-feather padding*); (*per cipria*) powder puff; (*per spolverare*) feather duster

piut'tosto *av* rather; ~ **che** (*anziché*) rather than

pi'vello, a *sm/f* greenhorn

'pizza ['pittsa] *sf* pizza; **pizze'ria** *sf* place where pizzas are made, sold or eaten

pizzi'cagnolo, a [pittsi'kaɲɲolo] *sm/f* specialist grocer

pizzi'care [pittsi'kare] *vt* (*stringere*) to nip, pinch; (*pungere*) to sting; to bite; (*MUS*) to pluck ♦ *vi* (*prudere*) to itch, be itchy; (*cibo*) to be spicy

pizziche'ria [pittsike'ria] *sf* delicatessen (shop)

'pizzico, chi ['pittsiko] *sm* (*pizzicotto*) pinch, nip; (*piccola quantità*) pinch, dash; (*d'insetto*) sting; bite

pizzi'cotto [pittsi'kɔtto] *sm* pinch, nip

'pizzo ['pittso] *sm* (*merletto*) lace; (*barbetta*) goatee beard

pla'care *vt* to placate, soothe; **~rsi** *vr* to calm down

'placca, che *sf* plate; (*con iscrizione*) plaque; (*anche*: ~ *dentaria*) (dental) plaque; **plac'care** *vt* to plate; **placcato in oro/argento** gold-/silver-plated

'placido, a ['platʃido] *ag* placid, calm

plagi'are [pla'dʒare] *vt* (*copiare*) to plagiarize; **'plagio** *sm* plagiarism

pla'nare *vi* (*AER*) to glide

'plancia, ce ['plantʃa] *sf* (*NAUT*) bridge

plane'tario, a *ag* planetary ♦ *sm* (*locale*) planetarium

'plasma *sm* plasma

plas'mare *vt* to mould, shape

'plastica, che *sf* (*arte*) plastic arts *pl*; (*MED*) plastic surgery; (*sostanza*) plastic

'plastico, a, ci, che *ag* plastic ♦ *sm* (*rappresentazione*) relief model;

(*esplosivo*): **bomba al ~** plastic bomb

plasti'lina *sf* plasticine ®

'**platano** *sm* plane tree

pla'tea *sf* (*TEATRO*) stalls *pl*

'**platino** *sm* platinum

pla'tonico, a, ci, che *ag* platonic

plau'sibile *ag* plausible

'**plauso** *sm* (*fig*) approval

ple'baglia [ple'baʎʎa] (*peg*) *sf* rabble, mob

'**plebe** *sf* common people; **ple'beo, a** *ag* plebeian; (*volgare*) coarse, common

ple'nario, a *ag* plenary

pleni'lunio *sm* full moon

'**plettro** *sm* plectrum

pleu'rite *sf* pleurisy

'**plico, chi** *sm* (*pacco*) parcel; **in ~ a parte** (*COMM*) under separate cover

plo'tone *sm* (*MIL*) platoon; **~ d'esecuzione** firing squad

plumbeo, a *ag* leaden

plu'rale *ag, sm* plural; **pluralità** *sf* plurality; (*maggioranza*) majority

plusva'lore *sm* (*ECON*) surplus

pneu'matico, a, ci, che *ag* inflatable; pneumatic ♦ *sm* (*AUT*) tyre (*BRIT*), tire (*US*)

po' *av, sm vedi* **poco**

PAROLA CHIAVE

'**poco, a, chi, che** *ag* (*quantità*) little, not much; (*numero*) few, not many; **~ pane/denaro/spazio** little o not much bread/money/space; **~che persone/idee** few o not many people/ideas; **ci vediamo tra ~** (*sottinteso: tempo*) see you soon

♦ *av* **1** (*in piccola quantità*) little, not much; (*numero limitato*) few, not many; **guadagna ~** he doesn't earn much, he earns little

2 (*con ag, av*) (a) little, not very; **sta ~ bene** he isn't very well; **è ~ più vecchia di lui** she's a little o slightly older than him

3 (*tempo*): **~ dopo/prima** shortly afterwards/before; **il film dura ~** the

film doesn't last very long; **ci vediamo molto ~** we don't see each other very often, we hardly ever see each other

4: **un po'** a little, a bit; **è un po' corto** it's a little o a bit short; **arriverà fra un po'** he'll arrive shortly o in a little while

5: **a dir ~** to say the least; **a ~ a ~** little by little; **per ~ non cadevo** I nearly fell; **è una cosa da ~** it's nothing, it's of no importance; **una persona da ~** a worthless person

♦ *pron* (a) little; **~chi, che** *pron pl* (*persone*) few (people); (*cose*) few

♦ *sm* **1** little; **vive del ~ che ha** he lives on the little he has

2: **un po'** a little; **un po' di zucchero** a little sugar; **un bel po' di denaro** quite a lot of money; **un po' per ciascuno** a bit each

---

po'dere *sm* (*AGR*) farm

pode'roso, a *ag* powerful

podestà *sm inv* (*nel fascismo*) podesta, mayor

'**podio** *sm* dais, platform; (*MUS*) podium

po'dismo *sm* (*SPORT*) track events *pl*

po'ema, i *sm* poem

poe'sia *sf* (*arte*) poetry; (*componimento*) poem

po'eta, 'essa *sm/f* poet/poetess; **po'etico, a, ci, che** *ag* poetic(al)

poggi'are [pod'dʒare] *vt* to lean, rest; (*posare*) to lay, place; **poggia'testa** *sm inv* (*AUT*) headrest

'**poggio** ['poddʒo] *sm* hillock, knoll

poggi'olo [pod'dʒɔlo] *sm* balcony

'**poi** *av* then; (*alla fine*) finally, at last; **e ~** (*inoltre*) and besides; **questa ~ (è bella)!** (*ironico*) that's a good one!

poiché [poi'ke] *cong* since, as

'**poker** *sm* poker

po'lacco, a, chi, che *ag* Polish ♦ *sm/f* Pole

po'lare *ag* polar

po'lemica, che *sf* controversy

po'lemico, a, ci, che ag polemic(al), controversial

po'lenta sf (CUC) sort of thick porridge made with maize flour

poliambula'torio sm health centre

poli'clinico, ci sm general hospital, polyclinic

poli'estere sm polyester

'polio(mie'lite) sf polio(myelitis)

po'lipo sm polyp

polisti'rolo sm polystyrene

poli'tecnico, ci sm postgraduate technical college

po'litica, che sf politics sg; (linea di condotta) policy; vedi anche **politico**

politiciz'zare [politit∫id'dzare] vt to politicize

po'litico, a, ci, che ag political ♦ sm/f politician

poli'zia [polit'tsia] sf police; **~ giudiziaria** ≈ Criminal Investigation Department (BRIT); ≈ Federal Bureau of Investigation (US); **~ stradale** traffic police; **polizi'esco, a, schi, sche** ag police cpd; (film, romanzo) detective cpd; **polizi'otto** sm policeman; **cane poliziotto** police dog; **donna poliziotto** policewoman

┌─────────────────────┐
│ polizia di stato │
└─────────────────────┘

*The function of the polizia di stato
is to maintain public order, to uphold
the law and prevent and investigate
crime. They are a civil body, reporting
to the Minister of the Interior.*

'polizza ['polittsa] sf (COMM) bill; **~ di assicurazione** insurance policy; **~ di carico** bill of lading

pol'laio sm henhouse

pol'lame sm poultry

pol'lastro sm (ZOOL) cockerel

'pollice ['pollit∫e] sm thumb

'polline sm pollen

'pollo sm chicken

pol'mone sm lung; **~ d'acciaio** (MED) iron lung; **polmo'nite** sf pneumonia

'polo sm (GEO, FISICA) pole; (gioco) polo; **il ~ sud/nord** the South/North Pole

Po'lonia sf: **la ~** Poland

'polpa sf flesh, pulp; (carne) lean meat

pol'paccio [pol'patt∫o] sm (ANAT) calf

polpas'trello sm fingertip

pol'petta sf (CUC) meatball; **polpet'tone** sm (CUC) meatloaf

'polpo sm octopus

pol'poso, a ag fleshy

pol'sino sm cuff

'polso sm (ANAT) wrist; (pulsazione) pulse; (fig: forza) drive, vigour

pol'tiglia [pol'tiλλa] sf (composto) mash, mush; (di fango e neve) slush

pol'trire vi to laze about

pol'trona sf (TEATRO: posto) seat in the front stalls (BRIT) o orchestra (US)

pol'trone ag lazy, slothful

'polvere sf dust; (anche: ~ da sparo) (gun)powder; (sostanza ridotta minutissima) powder, dust; **latte in ~** dried o powdered milk; **caffè in ~** instant coffee; **sapone in ~** soap powder; **polveri'era** sf (MIL) (gun)powder magazine; **polveriz'zare** vt to pulverize; (nebulizzare) to atomize; (fig) to crush, pulverize; to smash; **polve'rone** sm thick cloud of dust; **polve'roso, a** ag dusty

po'mata sf ointment, cream

po'mello sm knob

pomeridi'ano, a ag afternoon cpd; **nelle ore ~e** in the afternoon

pome'riggio [pome'riddʒo] sm afternoon

'pomice ['pomit∫e] sf pumice

'pomo sm (mela) apple; (ornamentale) knob; (di sella) pommel; **~ d'Adamo** (ANAT) Adam's apple

pomo'doro sm tomato

'pompa sf pump; (sfarzo) pomp (and ceremony); **~e funebri** funeral parlour sg (BRIT); undertaker's sg; **pom'pare** vt to pump; (trarre) to pump out;

(gonfiare d'aria) to pump up

pom'pelmo *sm* grapefruit

pompi'ere *sm* fireman

pom'poso, a *ag* pompous

ponde'rare *vt* to ponder over, consider carefully

ponde'roso, a *ag (anche fig)* weighty

po'nente *sm* west

'ponte *sm* bridge; *(di nave)* deck; *(: anche: ~ di comando)* bridge; *(impalcatura)* scaffold; **fare il ~** *(fig)* to take the extra day off *(between 2 public holidays)*; **governo ~** interim government; **~ aereo** airlift; **~ sospeso** suspension bridge

pon'tefice [pon'tefitʃe] *sm (REL)* pontiff

pontifi'care *vi (anche fig)* to pontificate

ponti'ficio, a, ci, cie [ponti'fitʃo] *ag* papal

popo'lano, a *ag* popular, of the people

popo'lare *ag* popular; *(quartiere, clientela)* working-class ♦ *vt (rendere abitato)* to populate; **~rsi** *vr* to fill with people, get crowded; **popolarità** *sf* popularity; **popolazi'one** *sf* population

'popolo *sm* people; **popo'loso, a** *ag* densely populated

'poppa *sf (di nave)* stern; *(seno)* breast

pop'pare *vt* to suck

poppa'toio *sm (feeding)* bottle

porcel'lana [portʃel'lana] *sf* porcelain, china; piece of china

porcel'lino, a [portʃel'lino] *sf* piglet

porche'ria [porke'ria] *sf* filth, muck; *(fig: oscenità)* obscenity; *(: azione disonesta)* dirty trick; *(: cosa mal fatta)* rubbish

por'cile [por'tʃile] *sm* pigsty

por'cino, a [por'tʃino] *ag* of pigs, pork *cpd* ♦ *sm (fungo)* type of edible mushroom

'porco, ci *sm* pig; *(carne)* pork

porcos'pino *sm* porcupine

'porgere ['pɔrdʒere] *vt* to hand, give;

(tendere) to hold out

pornogra'fia *sf* pornography; **porno'grafico, a, ci, che** *ag* pornographic

'poro *sm* pore; **po'roso, a** *ag* porous

'porpora *sf* purple

'porre *vt (mettere)* to put; *(collocare)* to place; *(posare)* to lay (down), put (down); *(fig: supporre):* **poniamo (il caso) che ...** let's suppose that ...; **porsi** *vr (mettersi):* **porsi a sedere/in cammino** to sit down/set off; **~ una domanda a qn** to ask sb a question, put a question to sb

'porro *sm (BOT)* leek; *(MED)* wart

'porta *sf* door; *(SPORT)* goal; **~e** *sfpl (di città)* gates; **a ~e chiuse** *(DIR)* in camera

porta... *prefisso:* **portaba'gagli** *sm inv (facchino)* porter; *(AUT, FERR)* luggage rack; **porta'cenere** *sm inv* ashtray; **portachi'avi** *sm inv* keyring; **porta'cipria** *sm inv* powder compact; **porta'erei** *sf inv (nave)* aircraft carrier; **portafi'nestra** *(pl* **portefi'nestre)** *sf* French window; **porta'foglio** *sm (POL, BORSA)* wallet; *(POL, BORSA)* portfolio; **portafor'tuna** *sm inv* lucky charm; mascot; **portagi'oie** *sm inv* jewellery box

porta'lettere *sm/f inv* postman/ woman *(BRIT)*, mailman/woman *(US)*

porta'mento *sm* carriage, bearing

porta'monete *sm inv* purse

por'tante *ag (muro etc)* supporting, load-bearing

portan'tina *sf* sedan chair; *(per ammalati)* stretcher

por'tare *vt (sostenere, sorreggere: peso, bambino, pacco)* to carry; *(indossare: abito, occhiali)* to wear; *(: capelli lunghi)* to have; *(avere: nome, titolo)* to have, bear; *(recare):* **~ qc a qn** to take (o bring) sth to sb; *(fig: sentimenti)* to bear; **~rsi** *vr (recarsi)* to go; **~ avanti** *(discorso, idea)* to pursue; **~ via** to take away; *(rubare)* to take; **~ i bambini a**

spasso to take the children for a walk; ~ **fortuna** to bring good luck

portasiga'rette sm inv cigarette case

por'tata sf (vivanda) course; (AUT) carrying o (loading) capacity; (di arma) range; (volume d'acqua) (rate of) flow; (fig: limite) scope, capability; (: importanza) impact, import; **alla ~ di tutti** (conoscenza) within everybody's capabilities; (prezzo) within everybody's means; **a/fuori ~ (di)** within/out of reach (of); **a ~ di mano** within (arm's) reach

por'tatile ag portable

por'tato, a ag (incline): **~ a** inclined o apt to

porta'tore, 'trice sm/f (anche COMM) bearer; (MED) carrier

portau'ovo sm inv eggcup

porta'voce [porta'votʃe] sm/f inv spokesman/woman

por'tento sm wonder, marvel

porticc'iolo [portit'tʃolo] sm marina

'portico, ci sm portico

porti'era sf (AUT) door

porti'ere sm (portinaio) concierge, caretaker; (di hotel) porter; (nel calcio) goalkeeper

porti'naio, a sm/f concierge, caretaker

portine'ria sf caretaker's lodge

'porto, a pp di porgere ♦ sm (NAUT) harbour, port ♦ sm inv port (wine); **~ d'armi** (documento) gun licence

Porto'gallo sm: **il ~** Portugal

porto'ghese [porto'geze] ag, sm/f, sm Portuguese inv

por'tone sm main entrance, main door

portu'ale ag harbour cpd, port cpd ♦ sm dock worker

porzi'one [por'tsjone] sf portion, share; (di cibo) portion, helping

'posa sf (FOT) exposure; (atteggiamento, di modello) pose

posa'cenere [posa'tʃenere] sm inv ashtray

po'sare vt to put (down), lay (down) ♦ vi (ponte, edificio, teoria): **~ su** to rest

on; (FOT, atteggiarsi) to pose; **~rsi** vr (aereo) to land; (uccello) to alight; (sguardo) to settle

po'sata sf piece of cutlery; **~e** sfpl (servizio) cutlery sg

po'sato, a ag serious

pos'critto sm postscript

posi'tivo, a ag positive

posizi'one [pozit'tsjone] sf position; **prendere ~** (fig) to take a stand; **luci di ~** (AUT) sidelights

posolo'gia, 'gie [pozolo'dʒia] sf dosage, directions pl for use

pos'porre vt to place after; (differire) to postpone, defer; **pos'posto, a** pp di posporre

posse'dere vt to own, possess; (qualità, virtù) to have, possess; possedi'mento sm possession

posses'sivo, a ag possessive

pos'sesso sm ownership no pl; possession

posses'sore sm owner

pos'sibile ag possible ♦ sm: **fare tutto il ~** to do everything possible; **nei limiti del ~** as far as possible; **al più tardi ~** as late as possible; possibilità sf inv possibility ♦ sfpl (mezzi) means; **aver la possibilità di fare** to be in a position to do; to have the opportunity to do

possi'dente sm/f landowner

'posta sf (servizio) post, postal service; (corrispondenza) post, mail; (ufficio postale) post office; (nei giochi d'azzardo) stake; **~e** sfpl (amministrazione) post office; **~ aerea** airmail; **~ elettronica** E-mail, e-mail, electronic mail; **ministro delle P~e e Telecomunicazioni** Postmaster General; **posta'giro** sm post office cheque, postal giro (BRIT); **pos'tale** ag postal, post office cpd

post'bellico, a, ci, che ag postwar

posteggi'are [posted'dʒare] vt, vi to park; **posteggi'atore, 'trice** sm/f car park attendant; **pos'teggio** sm car park (BRIT), parking lot (US); (di taxi) rank (BRIT), stand (US)

postelegra'fonico, a, ci, che ag postal and telecommunications cpd

'**poster** sm inv poster

posteri'ore ag (dietro) back; (dopo) later ♦ sm (fam: sedere) behind

pos'ticcio, a, ci, ce [pos'tittʃo] ag false ♦ sm hairpiece

postici'pare [postitʃi'pare] vt to defer, postpone

pos'tilla sf marginal note

pos'tino sm postman (BRIT), mailman (US)

'**posto, a** pp di **porre** ♦ sm (sito, posizione) place; (impiego) job; (spazio libero) room, space; (di parcheggio) space; (sedile: al teatro, in treno etc) seat; (MIL) post; **a ~** (in ordine) in place, tidy; (fig) settled; (: persona) reliable; **al ~ di** in place of; **sul ~** on the spot; **mettere a ~** to tidy (up), put in order; (faccende) to straighten out; **~ di blocco** roadblock; **~ di polizia** police station

pos'tribolo sm brothel

'**postumo, a** ag posthumous; (tardivo) belated; **~i** smpl (conseguenze) after-effects, consequences

po'tabile ag drinkable; **acqua ~** drinking water

po'tare vt to prune

po'tassio sm potassium

po'tente ag (nazione) strong, powerful; (veleno, farmaco) potent, strong; **po'tenza** sf power; (forza) strength

potenzi'ale [poten'tsjale] ag, sm potential

PAROLA CHIAVE

po'tere sm power; **al ~** (partito etc) in power; **~ d'acquisto** purchasing power

♦ vb aus **1** (essere in grado di) can, be able to; **non ha potuto ripararlo** he couldn't o he wasn't able to repair it; **non è potuto venire** he couldn't o

he wasn't able to come; **spiacente di non poter aiutare** sorry not to be able to help

2 (avere il permesso) can, may, be allowed to; **posso entrare?** can o may I come in?; **si può sapere dove sei stato?** where on earth have you been?

3 (eventualità) may, might, could; **potrebbe essere vero** it might o could be true; **può aver avuto un incidente** he may o might o could have had an accident; **può darsi** perhaps; **può darsi** o **essere che non venga** he may o might not come

4 (augurio): **potessi almeno parlargli!** if only I could speak to him!

5 (suggerimento): **potresti almeno scusarti!** you could at least apologize! ♦ vt can, be able to; **può molto per noi** he can do a lot for us; **non ne posso più** (per stanchezza) I'm exhausted; (per rabbia) I can't take any more

---

potestà sf (potere) power; (DIR) authority

'**povero, a** ag poor; (disadorno) plain, bare ♦ sm/f poor man/woman; **i ~i** the poor; **~ di** lacking in, having little; **povertà** sf poverty

'**pozza** ['pottsa] sf pool

poz'zanghera [pot'tsangera] sf puddle

'**pozzo** ['pottso] sm well; (cava: di carbone) pit; (di miniera) shaft; **~ petrolifero** oil well

pran'zare [pran'dzare] vi to dine, have dinner; to lunch, have lunch

'**pranzo** ['prandzo] sm dinner; (a mezzogiorno) lunch

'**prassi** sf usual procedure

'**pratica, che** sf practice; (esperienza) experience; (conoscenza) knowledge, familiarity; (tirocinio) training, practice; (AMM: affare) matter, case; (: incartamento) file, dossier; **in ~**

(*praticamente*) in practice; **mettere in ~** to put into practice

prati'cabile *ag* (*progetto*) practicable, feasible; (*luogo*) passable, practicable

prati'cante *sm/f* apprentice, trainee; (*REL*) regular churchgoer

prati'care *vt* to practise; (*SPORT: tennis etc*) to play; (: *nuoto, scherma etc*) to go in for; (*eseguire: apertura, buco*) to make; **~ uno sconto** to give a discount

'pratico, a, ci, che *ag* practical; **~ di** (*esperto*) experienced o skilled in; (*familiare*) familiar with

'prato *sm* meadow; (*di giardino*) lawn

preav'viso *sm*: **telefonata con ~** personal o person to person call

pre'cario, a *ag* precarious; (*INS*) temporary

precauzi'one [prekaut'tsjone] *sf* caution, care; (*misura*) precaution

prece'dente [pretʃe'dɛnte] *ag* previous ♦ *sm* precedent; **il discorso/ film ~** the previous o preceding speech/film; **senza ~i** unprecedented; **~i penali** criminal record *sg*;

prece'denza *sf* priority, precedence; (*AUT*) right of way

pre'cedere [pre'tʃɛdere] *vt* to precede, go o come before

pre'cetto [pre'tʃɛtto] *sm* precept; (*MIL*) call-up notice

precet'tore [pretʃet'tore] *sm* (private) tutor

precipi'tare [pretʃipi'tare] *vi* (*cadere*) to fall headlong; (: *situazione*) to get out of control ♦ *vt* (*gettare dall'alto in basso*) to hurl, fling; (*fig: affrettare*) to rush; **~rsi** *vr* (*gettarsi*) to hurl o.s.; (*affrettarsi*) to rush;

precipitazi'one (*METEOR*) precipitation; (*fig*) haste; **precipi'toso, a** *ag* (*caduta, fuga*) headlong; (: *avventato*) rash, reckless; (: *affrettato*) hasty, rushed

preci'pizio [pretʃi'pittsjo] *sm* precipice; **a ~** (*fig: correre*) headlong

preci'sare [pretʃi'zare] *vt* to state, specify; (*spiegare*) to explain (in detail)

precisi'one [pretʃi'zjone] *sf* precision; accuracy

pre'ciso, a [pre'tʃizo] *ag* (*esatto*) precise; (*accurato*) accurate, precise; (*deciso: idee*) precise, definite; (*uguale*): **2 vestiti ~i** 2 dresses exactly the same; **sono le 9 ~e** it's exactly 9 o'clock

pre'cludere *vt* to block, obstruct;

pre'cluso, a *pp di* **precludere**

pre'coce [pre'kɔtʃe] *ag* early; (*bambino*) precocious; (*vecchiaia*) premature

precon'cetto [prekon'tʃɛtto] *sm* preconceived idea, prejudice

precur'sore *sm* forerunner, precursor

'preda *sf* (*bottino*) booty; (*animale, fig*) prey; **essere ~ di** to fall prey to; **essere in ~ a** to be prey to;

preda'tore *sm* predator

predeces'sore, a [predetʃes'sore] *sm/f* predecessor

predesti'nare *vt* to predestine

pre'detto, a *pp di* **predire**

'predica, che *sf* sermon; (*fig*) lecture, talking-to

predi'care *vt, vi* to preach

predi'cato *sm* (*LING*) predicate

predi'letto, a *pp di* **prediligere** ♦ *ag, sm/f* favourite

predilezi'one [predilet'tsjone] *sf* fondness, partiality; **avere una ~ per qc/qn** to be partial to sth/fond of sb

predi'ligere [predi'lidʒere] *vt* to prefer, have a preference for

pre'dire *vt* to foretell, predict

predis'porre *vt* to get ready, prepare; **~ qn a qc** to predispose sb to sth; **predis'posto, a** *pp di* **predisporre**

predizi'one [predit'tsjone] *sf* prediction

predomi'nare *vi* to predominate; **predo'minio** *sm* predominance, supremacy

prefabbri'cato, a *ag* (*EDIL*)

prefabricated

prefazi'one [prefat'tsjone] sf preface, foreword

prefe'renza [prefe'rentsa] sf preference; **preferenzi'ale** ag preferential; **corsia ~** bus and taxi lane

prefe'rire vt to prefer, like better; **~ il caffè al tè** to prefer coffee to tea, like coffee better than tea; **prefe'rito, a** ag favourite

pre'fetto sm prefect; **prefet'tura** sf prefecture

pre'figgersi [pre'fiddʒersi] vr: **~ uno scopo** to set o.s. a goal

pre'fisso, a pp di **prefiggere** ♦ sm (LING) prefix; (TEL) dialling (BRIT) o dial (US) code

pre'gare vi to pray ♦ vt (REL) to pray to; (implorare) to beg; (chiedere): **~ qn di fare** to ask sb to do; **farsi ~** to need coaxing o persuading

pre'gevole [pre'dʒevole] ag valuable

preghi'era [pre'gjɛra] sf (REL) prayer; (domanda) request

pregi'ato, a [pre'dʒato] ag (di valore) valuable; **vino ~** vintage wine

'pregio ['prɛdʒo] sm (stima) esteem, regard; (qualità) (good) quality, merit; (valore) value, worth

pregiudi'care [predʒudi'kare] vt to prejudice, harm, be detrimental to; **pregiudi'cato, a** sm/f (DIR) previous offender

pregiu'dizio [predʒu'dittsjo] sm (idea errata) prejudice; (danno) harm no pl

'pregno, a ['preɲɲo] ag (saturo): **~ di** full of, saturated with

'prego escl (a chi ringrazia) don't mention it!; (invitando qn ad accomodarsi) please sit down!; (invitando qn ad andare prima) after you!

pregus'tare vt to look forward to

preis'torico, a, ci, che ag prehistoric

pre'lato sm prelate

prele'vare vt (denaro) to withdraw; (campione) to take; (sog: polizia) to

take, capture

preli'evo sm (di denaro) withdrawal; (MED): **fare un ~ (di)** to take a sample (of)

prelimi'nare ag preliminary; **~i** smpl preliminary talks; preliminaries

pre'ludio sm prelude

pré-ma'man [prema'mã] sm inv maternity dress

prema'turo, a ag premature

premeditazi'one [premeditat'tsjone] sf (DIR) premeditation; **con ~** ag premeditated ♦ av with intent

'premere vt to press ♦ vi: **~ su** to press down on; (fig) to put pressure on; **~ a** (fig: importare) to matter to

pre'messa sf introductory statement, introduction

pre'messo, a pp di **premettere**

pre'mettere vt to put before; (dire prima) to start by saying, state first

premi'are vt to give a prize to; (fig: merito, onestà) to reward

'premio sm prize; (ricompensa) reward; (COMM) premium; (AMM: indennità) bonus

premu'nirsi vr: **~ di** to provide o.s. with; **~ contro** to protect o.s. from, guard o.s. against

pre'mura sf (fretta) haste, hurry; (riguardo) attention, care; **premu'roso, a** ag thoughtful, considerate

prena'tale ag antenatal

'prendere vt to take; (andare a prendere) to get, fetch; (ottenere) to get; (guadagnare) to get, earn; (catturare: ladro, pesce) to catch; (collaboratore, dipendente) to take on; (passeggero) to pick up; (chiedere: somma, prezzo) to charge, ask; (trattare: persona) to handle ♦ vi (colla, cemento) to set; (pianta) to take; (fuoco: nel camino) to catch; (voltare): **~ a destra** to turn (to the) right; **~rsi** vr (azzuffarsi): **~rsi a pugni** to come to blows; **prendi qualcosa?** (da bere, *da mangiare*) would you like something to eat (*o drink*)?; **prendo un caffè** I'll have a coffee; **~ qn/qc per** (*scambiare*) to take sb/sth for; **~ fuoco** to catch fire; **~ parte a** to take part in; **~rsi cura di qn/qc** to look after sb/ sth; **prendersela** (*adirarsi*) to get annoyed; (*preoccuparsi*) to get upset, worry

prendi'sole *sm inv* sundress

preno'tare *vt* to book, reserve; **prenotazi'one** *sf* booking, reservation

preoccu'pare *vt* to worry; to preoccupy; **~rsi** *vr*: **~rsi di qn/qc** to worry about sb/sth; **~rsi per qn** to be anxious for sb; **preoccupazi'one** *sf* worry, anxiety

prepa'rare *vt* to prepare; (*esame, concorso*) to prepare for; **~rsi** *vr* (*vestirsi*) to get ready; **~rsi a qc/a fare** to get ready o prepare (o.s.) for sth/to do; **~ da mangiare** to prepare a meal; **prepa'rato** *sm* (*prodotto*) preparation; **preparazi'one** *sf* preparation

preposizi'one [prepozit'tsjone] *sf* (LING) preposition

prepo'tente *ag* (*persona*) domineering, arrogant; (*bisogno, desiderio*) overwhelming, pressing ♦ *sm/f* bully; **prepo'tenza** *sf* arrogance; arrogant behaviour

'presa *sf* taking *no pl*; catching *no pl*; (*di città*) capture; (*indurimento: di cemento*) setting; (*appiglio, SPORT*) hold; (*di acqua, gas*) (supply) point; (ELETTR): **~ (di corrente)** socket; (: *al muro*) point; (*piccola quantità: di sale etc*) pinch; (CARTE) trick; **far ~** (*colla*) to set; **far ~ sul pubblico** to catch the public's imagination; **~ d'aria** air inlet; **essere alle ~e con** (*fig*) to be struggling with

pre'sagio [pre'zadʒo] *sm* omen

presa'gire [preza'dʒire] *vt* to foresee

'presbite *ag* long-sighted

presbi'terio *sm* presbytery

pre'scindere [preʃ'ʃindere] *vi*: **~ da** to leave out of consideration; **a ~ da** apart from

pres'critto, a *pp di* **prescrivere**

pres'crivere *vt* to prescribe; **prescrizi'one** *sf* (MED, DIR) prescription; (*norma*) rule, regulation

presen'tare *vt* to present; (*far conoscere*): **~ qn (a)** to introduce sb (to); (AMM: *inoltrare*) to submit; **~rsi** *vr* (*recarsi, farsi vedere*) to present o.s., appear; (*farsi conoscere*) to introduce o.s.; (*occasione*) to arise; **~rsi come candidato** (POL) to stand as a candidate; **~rsi bene/male** to have a good/poor appearance; **presentazi'one** *sf* presentation; introduction

pre'sente *ag* present; (*questo*) this ♦ *sm* present; **i ~i** those present; **aver ~ qc/qn** to remember sth/sb

presenti'mento *sm* premonition

pre'senza [pre'zɛntsa] *sf* presence; (*aspetto esteriore*) appearance; **~ di spirito** presence of mind

pre'sepe, pre'sepio *sm* crib

preser'vare *vt* to protect; to save; **preserva'tivo** *sm* sheath, condom

'preside *sm/f* (INS) head (teacher) (BRIT), principal (US); (*di facoltà universitaria*) dean

presi'dente *sm* (POL) president; (*di assemblea, COMM*) chairman; **~ del consiglio** prime minister; **presiden'tessa** *sf* president; president's wife; chairwoman; **presi'denza** *sf* presidency; office of president; chairmanship

presidi'are *vt* to garrison; **pre'sidio** *sm* garrison

presi'edere *vt* to preside over ♦ *vi*: **~ a** to direct, be in charge of

'preso, a *pp di* **prendere**

'pressa *sf* (TECN) press

pressap'poco *av* about, roughly

pres'sare *vt* to press

pressi'one *sf* pressure; **far ~ su qn** to

put pressure on sb; **~ sanguigna** blood pressure

'presso av (vicino) nearby, close at hand ♦ prep (vicino a) near; (accanto a) beside, next to; (in casa di): **~ qn** at sb's home; (nelle lettere) care of, c/o; (alle dipendenze di): **lavora ~ di noi** he works for o with us ♦ smpl: **nei ~i di** near, in the vicinity of

pressuriz'zare [pressurid'dzare] vt to pressurize

presta'nome (peg) sm/f inv figurehead

pres'tante ag good-looking

pres'tare vt: **~ (qc a qn)** to lend (sb sth o sth to sb); **~rsi** vr (offrirsi): **~rsi a fare** to offer to do; (essere adatto): **~rsi a** to lend itself to, be suitable for; **~ aiuto** to lend a hand; **~ attenzione** to pay attention; **~ fede** a qc/qn to give credence to sth/sb; **~ orecchio** to listen; **prestazi'one** sf (TECN, SPORT) performance; **prestazioni** sfpl (di persona: servizi) services

prestigia'tore, 'trice [prestidʒa'tore] sm/f conjurer

pres'tigio [pres'tidʒo] sm (fama) prestige; (illusione): **gioco di ~** conjuring trick

'prestito sm lending no pl; loan; **dar in ~** to lend; **prendere in ~** to borrow

'presto av (tra poco) soon; (in fretta) quickly; (di buon'ora) early; **a ~** see you soon; **fare ~ a fare qc** to hurry up and do sth; (non costare fatica) to have no trouble doing sth; **si fa ~ a criticare** it's easy to criticize

pre'sumere vt to presume, assume; **pre'sunto, a** pp di **presumere**

presuntu'oso, a ag presumptuous

presunzi'one [prezun'tsjone] sf presumption

presup'porre vt to suppose; to presuppose

'prete sm priest

preten'dente sm/f pretender ♦ sm (corteggiatore) suitor

pre'tendere vt (esigere) to demand,

require; (sostenere): **~ che** to claim that; **pretende di aver sempre ragione** he thinks he's always right

pretenzi'oso, a [preten'tsjoso] ag pretentious

pre'tesa sf (esigenza) claim, demand; (presunzione, sfarzo) pretentiousness; **senza ~e** unpretentious

pre'teso, a pp di **pretendere**

pre'testo sm pretext, excuse

pre'tore sm magistrate; **pre'tura** sf magistracy; (sede) magistrate's court

preva'lente ag prevailing; **preva'lenza** sf predominance

preva'lere vi to prevail; **pre'valso, a** pp di **prevalere**

preve'dere vt (indovinare) to foresee; (presagire) to foretell; (considerare) to make provision for

pre'vendita sf advance booking

preve'nire vt (anticipare) to forestall; to anticipate; (evitare) to avoid, prevent

preven'tivo, a ag preventive ♦ sm (COMM) estimate

prevenzi'one sf prevention; (preconcetto) prejudice

previ'dente ag showing foresight, prudent; **previ'denza** sf foresight; **istituto di previdenza** provident institution; **previdenza sociale** social security (BRIT), welfare (US)

previsi'one sf forecast, prediction; **~i meteorologiche** o **del tempo** weather forecast sg

pre'visto, a pp di **prevedere** ♦ sm: **più/meno del ~** more/less than expected

prezi'oso, a [pret'tsjozo] ag precious; invaluable ♦ sm jewel; valuable

prez'zemolo [pret'tsemolo] sm parsley

'prezzo ['prettso] sm price; **~ d'acquisto/di vendita** buying/selling price

prigi'one [pri'dʒone] sf prison; **prigio'nia** sf imprisonment; **prigioni'ero, a** ag captive ♦ sm/f prisoner

'**prima** sf (TEATRO) first night; (CINEMA) première; (AUT) first gear; vedi anche **primo** ♦ av before; (in anticipo) in advance, beforehand; (per l'addietro) at one time, formerly; (più presto) sooner, earlier; (in primo luogo) first ♦ cong: ~ **di fare/che parta** before doing/he leaves; ~ **di** before; ~ **o poi** sooner or later

pri'**mario, a** ag primary; (principale) chief, leading, primary ♦ sm (MED) chief physician

pri'**mato** sm supremacy; (SPORT) record

prima'**vera** sf spring; **primave'rile** ag spring cpd

primeggi'**are** [primed'dʒare] vi to excel, be one of the best

primi'**tivo, a** ag primitive; original

pri'**mizie** [pri'mittsje] sfpl early produce sg

'**primo, a** ag first; (fig) initial; basic; prime ♦ sm/f first (one) ♦ sm (CUC) first course; (in date): **il ~ luglio** the first of July; **le ~e ore del mattino** the early hours of the morning; **ai ~i di maggio** at the beginning of May; **viaggiare in ~a** to travel first-class; **in ~ luogo** first of all, in the first place; **di prim'ordine** o ~**a qualità** first-class, first-rate; **in un ~ tempo** at first; ~**a donna** leading lady; (di opera lirica) prima donna

primo'**genito, a** [primo'dʒɛnito] ag, sm/f firstborn

primordi'**ale** ag primordial

'**primula** sf primrose

princi'**pale** [printʃi'pale] ag main, principal ♦ sm manager, boss

princi'**pato** [printʃi'pato] sm principality

'**principe** ['printʃipe] sm prince; ~ **ereditario** crown prince;

princi'**pessa** sf princess

principi'**ante** [printʃi'pjante] sm/f beginner

prin'**cipio** [prin'tʃipjo] sm (inizio)

beginning, start; (origine) origin, cause; (concetto, norma) principle; **al o in ~** at first; **per ~** on principle

pri'**ore** sm (REL) prior

priorità sf priority

'**prisma, i** sm prism

pri'**vare** vt: ~ **qn di** to deprive sb of; ~**rsi di** to go o do without

pri'**vato, a** ag private ♦ sm/f private citizen; **in ~** in private

privazi'**one** [privat'tsjone] sf privation, hardship

privilegi'**are** [privile'dʒare] vt to grant a privilege to

privi'**legio** [privi'lɛdʒo] sm privilege

'**privo, a** ag: ~ **di** without, lacking

pro prep for, on behalf of ♦ sm inv (utilità) advantage, benefit; **a che ~?** what's the use?; **il ~ e il contro** the pros and cons

pro'**babile** ag probable, likely;

probabilità sf inv probability

pro'**blema, i** sm problem

pro'**boscide** [pro'bɔʃʃide] sf (di elefante) trunk

procacci'**are** [prokat'tʃare] vt to get, obtain

pro'**cedere** [pro'tʃɛdere] vi to proceed; (comportarsi) to behave; (iniziare): ~ **a** to start; ~ **contro** (DIR) to start legal proceedings against; **procedi'mento** sm (modo di condurre) procedure; (di avvenimenti) course; (TECN) process; **procedimento penale** (DIR) criminal proceedings; **proce'dura** sf (DIR) procedure

proces'**sare** [protʃes'sare] vt (DIR) to try

processi'**one** [protʃes'sjone] sf procession

pro'**cesso** [pro'tʃɛsso] sm (DIR) trial; proceedings pl; (metodo) process

pro'**cinto** [pro'tʃinto] sm: **in ~ di fare** about to do, on the point of doing

pro'**clama, i** sm proclamation

procla'**mare** vt to proclaim

procre'**are** vt to procreate

pro'cura sf (DIR) proxy; power of attorney; (ufficio) attorney's office

procu'rare vt: ~ **qc a qn** (fornire) to get o obtain sth for sb; (causare: noie etc) to bring o give sb sth

procura'tore, 'trice sm/f (DIR) ≈ solicitor; (: chi ha la procura) attorney; proxy; ~ **generale** (in corte d'appello) public prosecutor; (in corte di cassazione) Attorney General; ~ **della Repubblica** (in corte d'assise, tribunale) public prosecutor

prodi'gare vt to be lavish with; **~rsi per qn** to do all one can for sb

pro'digio [pro'didʒo] sm marvel, wonder; (persona) prodigy; **prodigi'oso, a** ag prodigious; phenomenal

'prodigo, a, ghi, ghe ag lavish, extravagant

pro'dotto, a pp di **produrre** ♦ sm product; **~i agricoli** farm produce sg

pro'durre vt to produce; **produttività** sf productivity; **produt'tivo, a** ag productive; **produt'tore, 'trice** sm/f producer; **produzi'one** sf production; (rendimento) output

pro'emio sm introduction, preface

Prof. abbr (= professore) Prof

profa'nare vt to desecrate

pro'fano, a ag (mondano) secular; profane; (sacrilego) profane

profe'rire vt to utter

profes'sare vt to profess; (medicina etc) to practise

professio'nale ag professional

professi'one sf profession; **professio'nista, i, e** sm/f professional

profes'sore, 'essa sm/f (INS) teacher; (: di università) lecturer; (: titolare di cattedra) professor

pro'feta, i sm prophet; **profe'zia** sf prophecy

pro'ficuo, a ag useful, profitable

profi'larsi vr to stand out, be silhouetted; to loom up

profi'lattico sm condom

pro'filo sm profile; (breve descrizione) sketch, outline; **di ~** in profile

pro'fitto sm advantage, profit, benefit; (fig: progresso) progress; (COMM) profit

profondità sf inv depth

pro'fondo, a ag deep; (rancore, meditazione) profound ♦ sm depth(s pl), bottom; ~ **8 metri** 8 metres deep

'profugo, a, ghi, ghe sm/f refugee

profu'mare vt to perfume ♦ vi to be fragrant; **~rsi** vr to put on perfume o scent

profume'ria sf perfumery; (negozio) perfume shop

pro'fumo sm (prodotto) perfume, scent; (fragranza) scent, fragrance

profusi'one sf profusion; **a ~** in plenty

proget'tare [prodʒet'tare] vt to plan; (edificio) to plan, design; **pro'getto** sm plan; (idea) plan, project; **progetto di legge** bill

pro'gramma, i sm programme; (TV, RADIO) programmes pl; (INS) syllabus, curriculum; (INFORM) program; **program'mare** vt (TV, RADIO) to put on; (INFORM) to program; (ECON) to plan; **programma'tore, 'trice** sm/f (INFORM) computer programmer

progre'dire vi to progress, make progress

progres'sivo, a ag progressive

pro'gresso sm progress no pl; **fare ~i** to make progress

proi'bire vt to forbid, prohibit; **proi'bitivo, a** ag prohibitive; **proibizi'one** sf prohibition

proiet'tare vt (gen, GEOM, CINEMA) to project; (: presentare) to show, screen; (luce, ombra) to throw, cast, project; **proi'ettile** sm projectile, bullet (o shell etc); **proiet'tore** sm (CINEMA) projector; (AUT) headlamp; (MIL) searchlight; **proiezi'one** sf (CINEMA) projection; showing

'prole sf children pl, offspring

prole'tario, a ag, sm proletarian

prolife'rare vi (fig) to proliferate

pro'lisso, a ag verbose
'prologo, ghi sm prologue
pro'lunga, ghe sf (di cavo etc)
extension
prolun'gare vt (discorso, attesa) to
prolong; (linea, termine) to extend
prome'moria sm inv memorandum
pro'messa sf promise
pro'messo, a pp di **promettere**
pro'mettere vt to promise ♦ vi to be o
look promising; **~ a qn di fare** to
promise sb that one will do
promi'nente ag prominent
promiscuità sf promiscuousness
promon'torio sm promontory,
headland
pro'mosso, a pp di **promuovere**
promo'tore, trice sm/f promoter,
organizer
promozi'one [promot'tsjone] sf
promotion
promul'gare vt to promulgate
promu'overe vt to promote
proni'pote sm/f (di nonni) great-
grandchild, great-grandson/
granddaughter; (di zii) great-nephew/
niece; **~i** smpl (discendenti)
descendants
pro'nome sm (LING) pronoun
pro'nostico, ci sm forecast, prediction
pron'tezza [pron'tettsa] sf readiness;
quickness, promptness
'pronto, a ag ready; (rapido) fast,
quick, prompt; **~!** (TEL) hello!; **~ all'ira**
quick-tempered; **~ soccorso** first aid
prontu'ario sm manual, handbook
pro'nuncia [pro'nuntʃa] sf
pronunciation
pronunci'are [pronun'tʃare] vt
(parola, sentenza) to pronounce; (dire)
to utter; (discorso) to deliver; **~rsi** vr to
declare one's opinion; **pronunci'ato,
a** ag (spiccato) pronounced, marked;
(sporgente) prominent
pro'nunzia etc [pro'nuntsja] =
pronuncia etc
propa'ganda sf propaganda

propa'gare vt (notizia, malattia) to
spread; (REL, BIOL) to propagate; **~rsi** vr
to spread; (BIOL) to propagate; (FISICA)
to be propagated
pro'pendere vi: **~ per** to favour, lean
towards; **propensi'one** sf inclination,
propensity; **pro'penso, a** pp di
propendere
propi'nare vt to administer
pro'pizio, a [pro'pittsjo] ag favourable
pro'porre vt (suggerire): **~ qc (a qn)** to
suggest sth (to sb); (candidato) to put
forward; (legge, brindisi) to propose;
~ di fare to suggest o propose doing;
proporsi di fare to propose o intend
to do; **proporsi una meta** to set o.s.
a goal
proporzio'nale [proportsjo'nale] ag
proportional
proporzio'nare [proportsjo'nare] vt:
~ qc a to proportion o adjust sth to
proporzi'one [propor'tsjone] sf
proportion; **in ~ a** in proportion to
pro'posito sm (intenzione) intention,
aim; (argomento) subject, matter; **a
~ di** regarding, with regard to; **di ~**
(apposta) deliberately, on purpose; **a ~**
by the way; **capitare a ~** (cosa,
persona) to turn up at the right time
proposizi'one [propozit'tsjone] sf
(LING) clause; (: periodo) sentence
pro'posta sf proposal; (suggerimento)
suggestion; **~a di legge** bill
pro'posto, a pp di **proporre**
proprietà sf inv (ciò che si possiede)
property gen no pl, estate;
(caratteristica) property; (correttezza)
correctness; **proprie'tario, a** sm/f
owner; (di albergo etc) proprietor,
owner; (per l'inquilino) landlord/lady
'proprio, a ag (possessivo) own;
(: impersonale) one's; (esatto) exact,
correct, proper; (senso, significato)
literal; (LING: nome) proper;
(particolare): **~ di** characteristic of,
peculiar to ♦ av (precisamente) just,
exactly; (davvero) really; (affatto): **non**

... ~ not ... at all; **l'ha visto con i (suoi) ~i occhi** he saw it with his own eyes

'**prora** sf (NAUT) bow(s pl), prow

'**proroga, ghe** sf extension; postponement; **proro'gare** vt to extend; (differire) to postpone, defer

pro'rompere vi to burst out; **pro'rotto, a** pp di **prorompere**

'**prosa** sf prose; **pro'saico, a, ci, che** ag (fig) prosaic, mundane

pro'sciogliere [proʃ'ʃɔʎʎere] vt to release; (DIR) to acquit; **prosci'olto, a** pp di **prosciogliere**

prosciu'gare [proʃʃu'gare] vt (terreni) to drain, reclaim; **~rsi** vr to dry up

prosci'utto [proʃ'ʃutto] sm ham; **~ cotto/crudo** cooked/cured ham

prosegui'mento sm continuation; **buon ~!** all the best!; (a chi viaggia) enjoy the rest of your journey!

prosegu'ire vt to carry on with, continue ♦ vi to carry on, go on

prospe'rare vi to thrive; **prosperità** sf prosperity; '**prospero, a** ag (fiorente) flourishing, thriving, prosperous; **prospe'roso, a** ag (robusto) hale and hearty; (: ragazza) buxom

prospet'tare vt (esporre) to point out, show; **~rsi** vr to look, appear

prospet'tiva sf (ARTE) perspective; (veduta) view; (fig: previsione, possibilità) prospect

pros'petto sm (DISEGNO) elevation; (veduta) view, prospect; (facciata) façade, front; (tabella) table; (sommario) summary

prospici'ente [prospi'tʃɛnte] ag: **~ qc** facing o overlooking sth

prossimità sf nearness, proximity; **in ~ di** near (to), close to

'**prossimo, a** ag (vicino): **~ a** near (to), close to; (che viene subito dopo) next; (parente) close ♦ sm neighbour, fellow man

prosti'tuta sf prostitute; **prostituzi'one** sf prostitution

pros'trare vt (fig) to exhaust, wear out; **~rsi** vr (fig) to humble o.s.

protago'nista, i, e sm/f protagonist

pro'teggere [pro'teddʒere] vt to protect

proteggi'slip [protedddʒi'zlip] sm inv panty liner

prote'ina sf protein

pro'tendere vt to stretch out; **pro'teso, a** pp di **protendere**

pro'testa sf protest

protes'tante vt, sm/f Protestant

protes'tare vt, vi to protest; **~rsi** vr: **~rsi innocente** etc to protest one's innocence o that one is innocent etc

protet'tivo, a ag protective

pro'tetto, a pp di **proteggere**

protet'tore, 'trice sm/f protector; (sostenitore) patron

protezi'one [protet'tsjone] sf protection; (patrocinio) patronage

protocol'lare vt to register ♦ ag formal; o protocol; **proto'collo** sm protocol; (registro) register of documents

pro'totipo sm prototype

pro'trarre vt (prolungare) to prolong; **pro'tratto, a** pp di **protrarre**

protube'ranza [protube'rantsa] sf protuberance, bulge

'**prova** sf (esperimento, cimento) test, trial; (tentativo) attempt, try; (MAT, testimonianza, documento etc) proof; (DIR) evidence no pl, proof; (INS) exam, test; (TEATRO) rehearsal; (di abito) fitting; **a ~ di** (in testimonianza di) as proof of; **a ~ di fuoco** fireproof; **fino a ~ contraria** until it is proved otherwise; **mettere alla ~** to put to the test; **giro di ~** test o trial run; **~ generale** (TEATRO) dress rehearsal

pro'vare vt (sperimentare) to test; (tentare) to try, attempt; (assaggiare) to try, taste; (sperimentare in sé) to experience; (sentire) to feel; (cimentare) to put to the test; (dimostrare) to prove; (abito) to try on; **~ a fare** to try o attempt to do

proveni'enza [prove'njentsa] sf origin, source

prove'nire vi: ~ **da** to come from

pro'venti smpl revenue sg

prove'nuto, a pp di **provenire**

pro'verbio sm proverb

pro'vetta sf test tube; **bambino in ~** test-tube baby

pro'vetto, a ag skilled, experienced

pro'vincia, ce o **cie** [pro'vintʃa] sf province; **provinci'ale** ag provincial; **(strada) provinciale** main road (BRIT), highway (US)

pro'vino sm (CINEMA) screen test; (campione) specimen

provo'cante ag (attraente) provocative

provo'care vt (causare) to cause, bring about; (eccitare: riso, pietà) to arouse; (irritare, sfidare) to provoke;
provoca'torio, a ag provocative;
provocazi'one sf provocation

provve'dere vi (disporre): ~ **(a)** to provide (for); (prendere un provvedimento) to take steps, act;
provvedi'mento sm measure; (di previdenza) precaution

provvi'denza [provvi'dɛntsa] sf: **la ~** providence; **provvidenzi'ale** ag providential

provvigi'one [provvi'dʒone] sf (COMM) commission

provvi'sorio, a ag temporary

prov'vista sf provision, supply

'prua sf (NAUT) = **prora**

pru'dente ag cautious, prudent; (assennato) sensible, wise; **pru'denza** sf prudence, caution; wisdom

'prudere vi to itch, be itchy

'prugna ['pruɲɲa] sf plum; ~ **secca** prune

prurigi'noso, a [pruridʒi'noso] ag itchy

pru'rito sm itchiness no pl; itch

P.S. abbr (= postscriptum) P.S.; (POLIZIA) = **Pubblica Sicurezza**

pseu'donimo sm pseudonym

PSI sigla m = **Partito Socialista Italiano**

psica'lista, i, e sm/f psychoanalyst

'psiche ['psike] sf (PSIC) psyche

psichi'atra, i, e ['psi'kjatra] sm/f psychiatrist; **psichi'atrico, a, ci, che** ag psychiatric

'psichico, a, ci, che ['psikiko] ag psychological

psico'logia [psikolo'dʒia] sf psychology; **psico'logico, a, ci, che** ag psychological; **psi'cologo, a, gi, ghe** sm/f psychologist

psico'patico, a, ci, che ag psychopathic ♦ sm/f psychopath

P.T. abbr = **Posta e Telegrafi**

pubbli'care vt to publish

pubblicazi'one [pubblikat'tsjone] sf publication; **~i (matrimoniali)** sfpl (marriage) banns

pubbli'cista, i, e [pubbli'tʃista] sm/f (STAMPA) occasional contributor

pubblicità [pubblitʃi'ta] sf (diffusione) publicity; (attività) advertising; (annunci nei giornali) advertisements pl;
pubblici'tario, a ag advertising cpd; (trovata, film) publicity cpd

'pubblico, a, ci, che ag public; (statale: scuola etc) state cpd ♦ sm public; (spettatori) audience; **in ~** in public; **~ funzionario** civil servant; **P~ Ministero** Public Prosecutor's Office; **la P~a Sicurezza** the police

'pube sm (ANAT) pubis

pubertà sf puberty

pu'dico, a, ci, che ag modest

pu'dore sm modesty

pueri'cultura sf paediatric nursing; infant care

pue'rile ag childish

pugi'lato [pudʒi'lato] sm boxing

'pugile ['pudʒile] sm boxer

pugna'lare [puɲɲa'lare] vt to stab

pu'gnale [puɲ'ɲale] sm dagger

'pugno ['puɲɲo] sm fist; (colpo) punch; (quantità) fistful

'pulce ['pultʃe] sf flea

pul'cino [pul'tʃino] sm chick

pu'ledro, a sm/f colt/filly
pu'leggia, ge [pu'leddʒa] sf pulley
pu'lire vt to clean; (*lucidare*) to polish;
pu'lita sf quick clean; **pu'lito, a** ag
(*anche fig*) clean; (*ordinato*) neat, tidy;
puli'tura sf cleaning; **pulitura a
secco** dry cleaning; **puli'zia** sf
cleaning; cleanness; **fare le pulizie** to
do the cleaning o the housework
'pullman sm inv coach
pul'lover sm inv pullover, jumper
pullu'lare vi to swarm, teem
pul'mino sm minibus
'pulpito sm pulpit
pul'sante sm (push-)button
pul'sare vi to pulsate, beat;
pulsazi'one sf beat
pul'viscolo sm fine dust
'puma sm inv puma
pun'gente [pun'dʒɛnte] ag prickly;
stinging; (*anche fig*) biting
'pungere ['pundʒere] vt to prick; (*sog:
insetto, ortica*) to sting; (: *freddo*) to
bite
pungigli'one [pundʒiʎ'ʎone] sm sting
pu'nire vt to punish; **punizi'one** sf
punishment; (*sport*) penalty
'punta sf point; (*parte terminale*) tip,
end; (*di monte*) peak; (*di costa*)
promontory; (*minima parte*) touch,
trace; **in ~ di piedi** on tip-toe; **ore di
~** peak hours; **uomo di ~** front-rank o
leading man
pun'tare vt (*piedi a terra, gomiti sul
tavolo*) to plant; (*dirigere: pistola*) to
point; (*scommettere*) to bet ♦ vi
(*mirare*): **~ a** to aim at; **~ su** (*dirigersi*)
to head o make for; (*fig: contare*) to
count o rely on
pun'tata sf (*gita*) short trip;
(*scommessa*) bet; (*parte di opera*)
instalment; **romanzo a ~e** serial
punteggia'tura [puntedddʒa'tura] sf
(*ling*) punctuation
pun'teggio [pun'teddʒo] sm score
puntel'lare vt to support
pun'tello sm prop, support

puntigli'oso, a [puntiʎ'ʎoso] ag
punctilious
pun'tina sf: **~ da disegno** drawing
pin
pun'tino sm dot; **fare qc a ~** to do
sth properly
'punto, a pp di **pungere** ♦ sm (*segno,
macchiolina*) dot; (*ling*) full stop; (*mat,
momento, di punteggio, fig: argomento*)
point; (*posto*) spot; (*a scuola*) mark;
(*nel cucire, nella maglia, med*) stitch
♦ av: **non ... ~** not at all; **due ~i**
(*ling*) colon; **sul ~ di fare** (just) about
to do; **fare il ~** (*naut*) to take a
bearing; (*fig*): **fare il ~ della
situazione** to take stock of the
situation; to sum up the situation; **alle
6 in ~** at 6 o'clock sharp o on the dot;
essere a buon ~ to have reached a
satisfactory stage; **mettere a ~** to
adjust; (*motore*) to tune; (*cannocchiale*)
to focus; (*fig*) to settle; **di ~ in bianco**
point-blank; **~ cardinale** point of the
compass, cardinal point; **~ debole**
weak point; **~ esclamativo/
interrogativo** exclamation/question
mark; **~ di riferimento** landmark; (*fig*)
point of reference; **~ di vendita** retail
outlet; **~ e virgola** semicolon; **~ di
vista** (*fig*) point of view; **~i di
sospensione** suspension points
puntu'ale ag punctual; **puntualità** sf
punctuality
pun'tura sf (*di ago*) prick; (*di insetto*)
sting, bite; (*med*) puncture; (: *iniezione*)
injection; (*dolore*) sharp pain
punzecchi'are [puntsek'kjare] vt to
prick; (*fig*) to tease
'pupa sf doll
pu'pazzo [pu'pattso] sm puppet
pu'pilla sf (*anat*) pupil
pu'pillo, a sm/f (*dir*) ward; (*prediletto*)
favourite, pet
purché [pur'ke] cong provided that, on
condition that
'pure cong (*tuttavia*) and yet,
nevertheless; (*anche se*) even if ♦ av

(*anche*) too, also; **pur di** (*al fine di*) just to; **faccia ~!** go ahead!, please do!

purè *sm* (*CUC*) purée; (: *di patate*) mashed potatoes

pu'rea *sf* = **purè**

pu'rezza [pu'rettsa] *sf* purity

'purga, ghe *sf* (*MED*) purging *no pl*; purge; (*POL*) purge

pur'gante *sm* (*MED*) purgative, purge

pur'gare *vt* (*MED, POL*) to purge; (*pulire*) to clean

purga'torio *sm* purgatory

purifi'care *vt* to purify; (*metallo*) to refine

puri'tano, a *ag, sm/f* puritan

'puro, a *ag* pure; (*acqua*) clear, limpid; (*vino*) undiluted; **puro'sangue** *sm/f inv* thoroughbred

pur'troppo *av* unfortunately

'pustola *sf* pimple

puti'ferio *sm* rumpus, row

putre'fare *vi* to putrefy, rot; **putre'fatto, a** *pp di* **putrefare**

'putrido, a *ag* putrid, rotten

put'tana (*fam!*) *sf* whore (!)

'puzza [puttsa] *sf* = **puzzo**

puz'zare [put'tsare] *vi* to stink

'puzzo [puttso] *sm* stink, foul smell

'puzzola [puttsola] *sf* polecat

puzzo'lente [puttso'lɛnte] *ag* stinking

Q, q

qua *av* here; **in ~** (*verso questa parte*) this way; **da un anno in ~** for a year now; **da quando in ~?** since when?; **per di ~** (*passare*) this way; **al di ~ di** (*fiume, strada*) on this side of; **~ dentro/fuori** *etc* in/out here *etc*; *vedi anche* **questo**

qua'derno *sm* notebook; (*per scuola*) exercise book

qua'drante *sm* quadrant; (*di orologio*) face

qua'drare *vi* (*bilancio*) to balance, tally; (*descrizione*) to correspond ♦ *vt* (*MAT*) to square; **non mi quadra** I don't like it; **qua'drato, a** *ag* square; (*fig: equilibrato*) level-headed, sensible; (: *peg*) square ♦ *sm* (*MAT*) square; (*PUGILATO*) ring; **5 al quadrato** 5 squared

qua'dretto *sm*: **a ~i** (*tessuto*) checked; (*foglio*) squared

quadri'foglio [kwadri'fɔʎʎo] *sm* four-leaf clover

'quadro *sm* (*pittura*) painting, picture; (*quadrato*) square; (*tabella*) table, chart; (*TECN*) board, panel; (*TEATRO*) scene; (*fig: scena, spettacolo*) sight; (: *descrizione*) outline, description; **~i** *smpl* (*POL*) party organizers; (*MIL*) cadres; (*COMM*) managerial staff; (*CARTE*) diamonds

'quadruplo, a *ag, sm* quadruple

quaggiù [kwad'dʒu] *av* down here

'quaglia ['kwaʎʎa] *sf* quail

PAROLA CHIAVE

'qualche ['kwalke] *det* **1** some, a few; (*in interrogative*) any; **ho comprato ~ libro** I've bought some o a few books; **~ volta** sometimes; **hai ~ sigaretta?** have you any cigarettes?

2 (*uno*): **c'è ~ medico?** is there a doctor?; **in ~ modo** somehow

3 (*un certo, parecchio*) some; **un personaggio di ~ rilievo** a figure of some importance

4: **~ cosa** = **qualcosa**

---

qualche'duno [kwalke'duno] *pron* = **qualcuno**

qual'cosa *pron* something; (*in espressioni interrogative*) anything; **qualcos'altro** something else; anything else; **~ di nuovo** something new; anything new; **~ da mangiare** something to eat; anything to eat; **c'è ~ che non va?** is there something o anything wrong?

qual'cuno *pron* (*persona*) someone, somebody; (: *in espressioni interrogative*) anyone, anybody; (*alcuni*) some; **~ è favorevole a noi** some are on our side; **qualcun altro** someone o somebody else; anyone o anybody else

PAROLA CHIAVE

'quale (*spesso troncato in* qual) **det 1**
(*interrogativo*) what; (: *scegliendo tra due o più cose o persone*) which;
~ uomo/denaro? what man/money?; which man/money?; **~i sono i tuoi programmi?** what are your plans?; **~ stanza preferisci?** which room do you prefer?

2 (*relativo*: come): **il risultato fu ~ ci si aspettava** the result was as expected

3 (*esclamativo*) what; **~ disgrazia!** what bad luck!

♦ **pron 1** (*interrogativo*) which; **~ dei due scegli?** which of the two do you want?

2 (*relativo*): **il(la) ~** (*persona: soggetto*) who; (: *oggetto, con preposizione*) whom; (: *cosa*) which; (*possessivo*) whose; **suo padre, il ~ è avvocato, ...** his father, who is a lawyer, ...; **il signore con il ~ parlavo** the gentleman to whom I was speaking; **l'albergo al ~ ci siamo fermati** the hotel where we stayed o which we stayed at; **la signora della ~ ammiriamo la bellezza** the lady whose beauty we admire

3 (*relativo*: *in elenchi*) such as, like; **piante ~i l'edera** plants like o such as ivy; **~ sindaco di questa città** as mayor of this town

qua'lifica, che *sf* qualification; (*titolo*) title

qualifi'care *vt* to qualify; (*definire*):
~ qn/qc come to describe sb/sth as;
~rsi *vr* (*anche* SPORT) to qualify;
qualifica'tivo, a *ag* qualifying;
qualificazi'one *sf*: **gara di qualificazione** (SPORT) qualifying event
qualità *sf inv* quality; **in ~ di** in one's

capacity as

qua'lora *cong* in case, if

qual'siasi *det inv* = **qualunque**

qua'lunque *det inv* any; (*quale che sia*) whatever; (*discriminativo*) whichever; (*posposto: mediocre*) poor, indifferent; ordinary; **mettiti un vestito ~** put on any old dress; **~ cosa** anything; **~ cosa accada** whatever happens; **a ~ costo** at any cost, whatever the cost; **l'uomo ~** the man in the street; **~ persona** anyone, anybody

'quando *cong, av* when; **~ sarò ricco** when I'm rich; **da ~** (*dacché*) since; (*interrogativo*): **da ~ sei qui?** how long have you been here?; **quand'anche** even if

quantità *sf inv* quantity; (*gran numero*) **una ~ di** a great deal of; a lot of; **in grande ~** in large quantities; **quantita'tivo** *sm* (COMM) amount, quantity

PAROLA CHIAVE

'quanto, a det 1 (*interrogativo*: *quantità*) how much; (: *numero*) how many; **~ pane/denaro?** how much bread/money?; **~i libri/ragazzi?** how many books/boys?; **~ tempo?** how long?; **~i anni hai?** how old are you?

2 (*esclamativo*: *quantità*): **~e storie!** what a lot of nonsense!; **~ tempo sprecato!** what a waste of time!

3 (*relativo*: *quantità*) as much ... as; (: *numero*) as many ... as; **ho ~ denaro mi occorre** I have as much money as I need; **prendi ~i libri vuoi** take as many books as you like

♦ **pron 1** (*interrogativo*: *quantità*) how much; (: *numero*) how many; (: *tempo*) how long; **~ mi dai?** how much will you give me?; **~i me ne hai portati?** how many did you bring me?; **da ~ sei qui?** how long have you been here?; **~i ne abbiamo oggi?** what's the date today?

2 (*relativo*: *quantità*) as much as;

(: *numero*) as many as; **farò ~ posso** I'll do as much as I can; **possono venire ~i sono stati invitati** all those who have been invited can come
♦ *av* **1** (*interrogativo: con ag, av*) how; (: *con vb*) how much; **~ stanco ti sembrava?** how tired did he seem to you?; **~ corre la tua moto?** how fast can your motorbike go?; **~ costa?** how much does it cost?; **quant'è?** how much is it?
2 (*esclamativo: con ag, av*) how; (: *con vb*) how much; **~ sono felice!** how happy I am!; **sapessi ~ abbiamo camminato!** if you knew how far we've walked!; **studierò ~ posso** I'll study as much as o all I can; **~ prima** as soon as possible
3: in ~ (*in qualità di*) as; (*perché, per il fatto che*) as, since; **(in) ~ a** (*per ciò che riguarda*) as for, as regards
4: per ~ (*nonostante, anche se*) however; **per ~ si sforzi, non ce la farà** try as he may, he won't manage it; **per ~ sia brava, fa degli errori** however good she may be, she makes mistakes; **per ~ io sappia** as far as I know

quan'tunque *cong* although, though
qua'ranta *num* forty
quaran'tena *sf* quarantine
quaran'tesimo, a *num* fortieth
quaran'tina *sf* (*età*) about forty
qua'resima *sf*: **la ~** Lent
'quarta *sf* (AUT) fourth (gear); *vedi anche* **quarto**
quar'tetto *sm* quartet(te)
quarti'ere *sm* district, area; (MIL) quarters *pl*; **~ generale** headquarters *pl*
'quarto, a *ag* fourth ♦ *sm* fourth; (*quarta parte*) quarter; **le 6 e un ~** a quarter past six; **~ d'ora** quarter of an hour; **~i di finale** quarter final
quarzo ['kwartso] *sm* quartz
'quasi *av* almost, nearly ♦ *cong* (*anche:*

~ che) as if; **(non) ... ~ mai** hardly ever; **~ ~ me ne andrei** I've half a mind to leave

quassù *av* up here
quatto, a *ag* crouched, squatting; (*silenzioso*) silent; **~ ~** very quietly; stealthily
quat'tordici [kwat'torditʃi] *num* fourteen
quat'trini *smpl* money *sg*, cash *sg*
'quattro *num* four; **in ~ e quatt'otto** in less than no time; **quattro'cento** *num* four hundred ♦ *sm*: **il Quattrocento** the fifteenth century; **quattro'mila** *num* four thousand

---

PAROLA CHIAVE

'quello, a (*dav sm* **quel** +C, **quell'** +V, **quello** +s *impura, gn, pn, ps, x, z; pl* **quei** +C, **quegli** +V *o s impura, gn, pn, ps, x, z; dav sf* **quella** +C, **quell'** +V; *pl* **quelle**) *det* that; those *pl*; **~a casa** that house; **quegli uomini** those men; **voglio ~a camicia** (li o là) I want that shirt
♦ *pron* **1** (*dimostrativo*) that (one); those (ones) *pl*; (*ciò*) that; **conosci ~a?** do you know that woman?; **prendo ~ bianco** I'll take the white one; **chi è ~?** who's that?; **prendi ~** (li o là) take that one (there)
2 (*relativo*): **~(a) che** (*persona*) the one (who); (*cosa*) the one (which), the one (that); **~i(e) che** (*persone*) those who; (*cose*) those which; **è lui ~ che non voleva venire** he's the one who didn't want to come; **ho fatto ~ che potevo** I did what I could

---

'quercia, ce ['kwertʃa] *sf* oak (tree); (*legno*) oak
que'rela (DIR) (*legal*) action;
quere'lare *vt* to bring an action against
que'sito *sm* question, query; problem
questio'nario *sm* questionnaire
questi'one *sf* problem; question;

(*controversia*) issue; (*litigio*) quarrel; **in ~ in question**; **è ~ di tempo** it's a matter o question of time

---
PAROLA CHIAVE

'questo, a *det* **1** (*dimostrativo*) this; these *pl*; (*qui o qua*) this book; **io prendo ~ cappotto, tu quello** I'll take this coat, you take that one; **quest'oggi** today; **~a sera** this evening

2 (*enfatico*): **non fatemi più prendere di ~e paure** don't frighten me like that again

♦ *pron* (*dimostrativo*) this (one); these (ones) *pl*; (*ciò*) this; **prendo ~** (*qui o qua*) I'll take this one; **preferisci ~i o quelli?** do you prefer these (ones) or those (ones)?; **~ intendevo io** this is what I meant; **vengono Paolo e Luca: ~ da Roma, quello da Palermo** Paolo and Luca are coming: the former from Palermo, the latter from Rome

---

ques'tore *sm* ≈ chief constable (*BRIT*), ≈ police commissioner (*US*)
'questua *sf* collection (of alms)
ques'tura *sf* police headquarters *pl*
qui *av* here; **da o di ~** from here; **di ~ in avanti** from now on; **di ~ a poco/una settimana** in a little while/a week's time; **~ dentro/sopra/vicino** in/up/near here; *vedi anche* **questo**
quie'tanza [kwje'tantsa] *sf* receipt
quie'tare *vt* to calm, soothe
qui'ete *sf* quiet, quietness; calmness; stillness; peace
qui'eto, a *ag* quiet; (*notte*) calm, still; (*mare*) calm
'quindi *av* then ♦ *cong* therefore, so
'quindici ['kwinditʃi] *num* fifteen; **~ giorni** a fortnight (*BRIT*), two weeks
quindi'cina [kwindi'tʃina] *sf* (*serie*): **una ~ (di)** about fifteen; **fra una ~ di giorni** in a fortnight

quin'quennio *sm* period of five years
quin'tale *sm* quintal (*100 kg*)
'quinte *sfpl* (*TEATRO*) wings
'quinto, a *num* fifth

Quirinale

The Quirinale, which takes its name from the hill in Rome on which it stands, is the official residence of the Presidente della Repubblica.

'quota *sf* (*parte*) quota, share; (*AER*) height, altitude; (*IPPICA*) odds *pl*; **prendere/perdere ~** (*AER*) to gain/ lose height o altitude; **~ d'iscrizione** enrolment fee; (*a club*) membership fee
quo'tare *vt* (*BORSA*) to quote; **quotazi'one** *sf* quotation
quotidi'ano, a *ag* daily; (*banale*) everyday ♦ *sm* (*giornale*) daily (paper)
quozi'ente [kwot'tsjɛnte] *sm* (*MAT*) quotient; **~ d'intelligenza** intelligence quotient, IQ

R, r

ra'barbaro *sm* rhubarb
'rabbia *sf* (*ira*) anger, rage; (*accanimento, furia*) fury; (*MED: idrofobia*) rabies *sg*
rab'bino *sm* rabbi
rabbi'oso, a *ag* angry, furious; (*facile all'ira*) quick-tempered; (*forze, acqua etc*) furious, raging; (*MED*) rabid, mad
rabbo'nire *vt* to calm down; **~rsi** *vr* to calm down
rabbrivi'dire *vi* to shudder, shiver
rabbui'arsi *vr* to grow dark
raccapez'zarsi [rakkapet'tsarsi] *vr*: **non ~** to be at a loss
raccapricci'ante [rakkaprit'tʃante] *ag* horrifying
raccatta'palle *sm inv* (*SPORT*) ballboy
raccat'tare *vt* to pick up
rac'chetta [rak'ketta] *sf* (*per tennis*)

racket; (per ping-pong) bat; ~ **da neve** snowshoe; ~ **da sci** ski stick

racchiudere [rak'kjudere] vt to contain; **racchi'uso, a** pp di **racchiudere**

rac'cogliere [rak'kɔʎʎere] vt to collect; (raccattare) to pick up; (frutti, fiori) to pick, pluck; (AGR) to harvest; (approvazione, voti) to win; ~**rsi** vr to gather; (fig) to gather one's thoughts; to meditate; **raccogli'mento** sm meditation; **raccogli'tore** sm (cartella) folder, binder; **raccoglitore ad anelli** ring binder

rac'colta sf collecting no pl; collection; (AGR) harvesting no pl, gathering no pl; harvest, crop; (adunata) gathering

rac'colto, a pp di **raccogliere** ♦ ag (persona: pensoso) thoughtful; (luogo: appartato) secluded, quiet ♦ sm (AGR) crop, harvest

raccoman'dare vt to recommend; (affidare) to entrust; (esortare): ~ **a qn di non fare** to tell o warn sb not to do; ~**rsi** vr: ~**rsi a qn** to commend o.s. to sb; **mi raccomando!** don't forget!; **raccoman'data** sf (anche: lettera raccomandata) recorded-delivery letter; **raccomandazi'one** sf recommendation

raccon'tare vt: ~ **(a qn)** (dire) to tell (sb); (narrare) to relate (to sb), tell (sb) about; **rac'conto** sm telling no pl, relating no pl; (fatto raccontato) story, tale

raccorci'are [rakkor'tʃare] vt to shorten

rac'cordo sm (TECN: giunto) connection, joint; (AUT: di autostrada) slip road (BRIT), entrance (o exit) ramp (US); ~ **anulare** (AUT) ring road (BRIT), beltway (US)

ra'chitico, a, ci, che [ra'kitiko] ag suffering from rickets; (fig) scraggy, scrawny

racimo'lare [ratʃimo'lare] vt (fig) to scrape together, glean

'**rada** sf (natural) harbour

'**radar** sm radar

raddol'cire [raddol'tʃire] vt (persona, carattere) to soften; ~**rsi** vr (tempo) to grow milder; (persona) to soften, mellow

raddoppi'are vt, vi to double

raddriz'zare [raddrit'tsare] vt to straighten; (fig: correggere) to put straight, correct

'**radere** vt (barba) to shave off; (mento) to shave; (fig: rasentare) to graze; to skim; ~**rsi** vr to shave (o.s.); ~ **al suolo** to raze to the ground

radi'are vt to strike off

radia'tore sm radiator

radiazi'one [radjat'tsjone] sf (FISICA) radiation; (cancellazione) striking off

radi'cale ag radical ♦ sm (LING) root

ra'dicchio [ra'dikkjo] sm chicory

radi'ce [ra'ditʃe] sf root

'**radio** sf inv radio ♦ sm (CHIM) radium; **radioat'tivo, a** ag radioactive; **radiodiffusi'one** sf (radio) broadcasting; **radiogra'fare** vt to X-ray; **radiogra'fia** sf radiography; (foto) X-ray photograph

radi'oso, a ag radiant

'**rado, a** ag (capelli) sparse, thin; (visite) infrequent; **di ~** rarely

radu'nare vt, to gather, assemble; ~**rsi** vr to gather, assemble; **ra'duno** sm meeting

ra'dura sf clearing

raffazzo'nato [raffattso'nato] ag patched up

raf'fermo, a ag stale

'**raffica, che** [meteor] gust (of wind); (di colpi: scarica) burst of gunfire

raffigu'rare vt to represent

raffi'nare vt to refine; **raffina'tezza** sf refinement; **raffi'nato, a** ag refined; **raffine'ria** sf refinery

raffor'zare [raffor'tsare] vt to reinforce

raffredda'mento sm cooling

raffred'dare vt to cool; (fig) to dampen, have a cooling effect on; ~**rsi**

vr to grow cool o cold; (*prendere un raffreddore*) to catch a cold; (*fig*) to cool (off)

raffred'dato, a *ag* (MED): **essere ~** to have a cold

raffred'dore *sm* (MED) cold

raf'fronto *sm* comparison

'rafia *sf* (*fibra*) raffia

ra'gazzo, a [ra'gattso] *sm/f* boy/girl; (*fam: fidanzato*) boyfriend/girlfriend

raggi'ante [rad'dʒante] *ag* radiant, shining

'raggio ['raddʒo] *sm* (*di sole etc*) ray; (MAT, *distanza*) radius; (*di ruota etc*) spoke; **~ d'azione** range; **~i X** X-rays

raggi'rare [raddʒi'rare] *vt* to take in, trick; **rag'giro** *sm* trick

raggi'ungere [rad'dʒundʒere] *vt* to reach; (*persona: riprendere*) to catch up (with); (*bersaglio*) to hit; (*fig: meta*) to achieve; **raggi'unto, a** *pp di* **raggiungere**

raggomi'tolarsi *vr* to curl up

raggranel'lare *vt* to scrape together

raggrup'pare *vt* to group (together)

raggu'aglio [rag'gwaʎʎo] *sm* (*informazione*) piece of information

ragguar'devole (*degno di riguardo*) distinguished, notable; (*notevole: somma*) considerable

ragiona'mento [radʒona'mento] *sm* reasoning *no pl*; arguing *no pl*; argument

ragio'nare [radʒo'nare] *vi* to reason; **~ di** (*discorrere*) to talk about

ragi'one [ra'dʒone] *sf* reason; (*dimostrazione, prova*) argument, reason; (*diritto*) right; **aver ~** to be right; **aver ~ di qn** to get the better of sb; **dare ~ a qn** to agree with sb; to prove sb right; **perdere la ~** to become insane; (*fig*) to take leave of one's senses; **in ~ di** at the rate of; to the amount of; according to; **a ~** o **con ~** rightly, justly; **~ sociale** (COMM) corporate name; **a ragion veduta** after due consideration

ragione'ria [radʒone'ria] *sf* accountancy; accounts department

ragio'nevole [radʒo'nevole] *ag* reasonable

ragioni'ere, a [radʒo'njere] *sm/f* accountant

ragli'are [raʎ'ʎare] *vi* to bray

ragna'tela [raɲɲa'tela] *sf* cobweb, spider's web

'ragno ['raɲɲo] *sm* spider

ragù *sm inv* (CUC) meat sauce; stew

RAI-TV [raiti'vu] *sigla f* = **Radio televisione italiana**

rallegra'menti *smpl* congratulations

ralle'grare *vt* to cheer up; **~rsi** *vr* to cheer up; (*provare allegrezza*) to rejoice; **~rsi con qn** to congratulate sb

rallen'tare *vt* to slow down; (*fig*) to lessen, slacken ♦ *vi* to slow down

raman'zina [raman'dzina] *sf* lecture, telling-off

'rame *sm* (CHIM) copper

rammari'carsi *vr*: **~ (di)** (*rincrescersi*) to be sorry (about), regret; (*lamentarsi*) to complain (about); **ram'marico, chi** *sm* regret

rammen'dare *vt* to mend; (*calza*) to darn; **ram'mendo** *sm* mending *no pl*; darning *no pl*; mend; darn

rammen'tare *vt* to remember, recall; (*richiamare alla memoria*): **~ qc a qn** to remind sb of sth; **~rsi** *vr*: **~rsi (di qc)** to remember (sth)

rammol'lire *vt* to soften ♦ *vi* (*anche:* **~rsi**) to go soft

'ramo *sm* branch

ramo'scello [ramoʃ'ʃello] *sm* twig

'rampa *sf* flight (*of stairs*); **~ di lancio** launching pad

rampi'cante *ag* (BOT) climbing

ram'pone *sm* harpoon; (ALPINISMO) crampon

'rana *sf* frog

'rancido, a ['rantʃido] *ag* rancid

ran'core *sm* rancour, resentment

ran'dagio, a, gi, gie o **ge** [ran'dadʒo] *ag* (*gatto, cane*) stray

ran'dello sm club, cudgel

'rango, ghi sm (condizione sociale, MIL: riga) rank

rannicchi'arsi [rannik'kjarsi] vr to crouch, huddle

rannuvo'larsi vr to cloud over, become overcast

ra'nocchio [ra'nɔkkjo] sm (edible) frog

'rantolo sm wheeze; (di agonizzanti) death rattle

'rapa sf (BOT) turnip

ra'pace [ra'patʃe] ag (animale) predatory; (fig) rapacious, grasping ♦ sm bird of prey

ra'pare vt (capelli) to crop, cut very short

'rapido (di fiume) rapid; vedi anche **rapido**

rapida'mente av quickly, rapidly

rapidità sf speed

'rapido, a ag fast; (esame, occhiata) quick, rapid ♦ sm (FERR) express (train)

rapi'mento sm kidnapping; (fig) rapture

ra'pina sf robbery; ~ **a mano armata** armed robbery; **rapi'nare** vt to rob; **rapina'tore, 'trice** sm/f robber

ra'pire vt (cose) to steal; (persone) to kidnap; (fig) to enrapture, delight; **rapi'tore, 'trice** sm/f kidnapper

rappor'tare vt (confrontare) to compare; (riprodurre) to reproduce

rap'porto sm (resoconto) report; (legame) relationship; (MAT, TECN) ratio; **~i** smpl (fra persone, paesi) relations; **~i sessuali** sexual intercourse sg

rap'prendersi vr to coagulate, clot; (latte) to curdle

rappre'saglia [rappre'saʎʎa] sf reprisal, retaliation

rappresen'tante sm/f representative; **rappresen'tanza** sf delegation, deputation; (COMM: ufficio, sede) agency

rappresen'tare vt to represent; (TEATRO) to perform;

rappresentazi'one sf representation; performing no pl; (spettacolo) performance

rap'preso, a pp di **rapprendere**

rapso'dia sf rhapsody

rara'mente av seldom, rarely

rare'fatto, a ag rarefied

'raro, a ag rare

ra'sare vt (barba etc) to shave off; (siepi, erba) to trim, cut; **~rsi** vr to shave (o.s.)

raschi'are [ras'kjare] vt to scrape; (macchia, fango) to scrape off ♦ vi to clear one's throat

rasen'tare vt (andar rasente) to keep close to; (sfiorare) to skim along (o over); (fig) to border on

ra'sente prep: ~ **(a)** close to, very near

'raso, a pp di **radere** ♦ ag (barba) shaved; (capelli) cropped; (con misure di capacità) level; (pieno: bicchiere) full to the brim ♦ sm (tessuto) satin; **~ terra** close to the ground; **un cucchiaio ~** a level spoonful

ra'soio sm razor; ~ **elettrico** electric shaver o razor

ras'segna [ras'seɲɲa] sf (MIL) inspection, review; (esame) inspection; (resoconto) review, survey; (pubblicazione letteraria etc) review; (mostra) exhibition, show; **passare in ~ (MIL, fig)** to review

rasse'gnare [rasseɲ'ɲare] vt: ~ **le dimissioni** to resign, hand in one's resignation; **~rsi** vr (accettare): **~rsi a qc/a fare** to resign o.s. (to sth/to doing); **rassegnazi'one** sf resignation

rassere'narsi vr (tempo) to clear up

rasset'tare vt to tidy, put in order; (aggiustare) to repair, mend

rassicu'rare vt to reassure

rasso'dare vt to harden, stiffen

rassomigli'anza [rassomiʎ'ʎantsa] sf resemblance

rassomigli'are [rassomiʎ'ʎare] vi: ~ **a** to resemble, look like

rastrel'lare vt to rake; (fig: perlustrare)

to comb

rastrelli'era sf rack; (per piatti) dish rack

ras'trello sm rake

'**rata** sf (quota) instalment; **pagare a ~e** to pay by instalments o on hire purchase (BRIT)

ratifi'care vt (DIR) to ratify

'**ratto** sm (DIR) abduction; (ZOOL) rat

rattop'pare vt to patch; **rat'toppo** sm patching no pl; patch

rattrap'pirsi vr to get stiff

rattris'tare vt to sadden; **~rsi** vr to become sad

'**rauco, a, chi, che** ag hoarse

rava'nello sm radish

ravi'oli smpl ravioli sg

ravve'dersi vr to mend one's ways

ravvici'nare [ravvit∫i'nare] vt (avvicinare): ~ **qc a** to bring sth nearer to; (: due tubi) to bring closer together; (riconciliare) to reconcile, bring together

ravvi'sare vt to recognize

ravvi'vare vt to revive; (fig) to brighten up, enliven; **~rsi** vr to revive; to brighten up

razio'cinio [ratsjo't∫injo] sm reasoning no pl; reason; (buon senso) common sense

razio'nale [rattsjo'nale] ag rational

razio'nare [rattsjo'nare] vt to ration

razi'one [rat'tsjone] sf ration; (porzione) portion, share

'**razza** ['rattsa] sf race; (ZOOL) breed; (discendenza, stirpe) stock, race; (sorta) sort, kind

raz'zia [rat'tsia] sf raid, foray

razzi'ale [rat'tsjale] ag racial

raz'zismo [rat'tsizmo] sm racism, racialism

raz'zista, i, e [rat'tsista] ag, sm/f racist, racialist

'**razzo** ['raddzo] sm rocket

razzo'lare [rattso'lare] vi (galline) to scratch about

re sm inv king; (MUS) D; (: solfeggiando)

re

rea'gire [rea'dʒire] vi to react

re'ale ag real; (di, da re) royal ♦ sm: **il ~** reality; **rea'lismo** sm realism; **rea'lista, i, e** sm/f realist; (POL) royalist

realiz'zare [realid'dzare] vt (progetto etc) to realize, carry out; (sogno, desiderio) to realize, fulfil; (scopo) to achieve; (COMM: titoli etc) to realize; (CALCIO etc) to score; **~rsi** vr to be realized; **realizzazi'one** sf realization; fulfilment; achievement

real'mente av really, actually

realtà sf inv reality

re'ato sm offence

reat'tore sm (FISICA) reactor; (AER: aereo) jet; (: motore) jet engine

reazio'nario, a [reattsjo'narjo] ag (POL) reactionary

reazi'one [reat'tsjone] sf reaction

recapi'tare vt to deliver

re'capito sm (indirizzo) address; (consegna) delivery

re'care vt (portare) to bring; (avere su di sé) to carry, bear; (cagionare) to cause, bring; **~rsi** vr to go

re'cedere [re't∫edere] vi to withdraw

recensi'one [ret∫en'sjone] sf review; **recen'sire** vt to review

re'cente [re't∫ɛnte] ag recent; **di ~** recently; **recente'mente** av recently

recessi'one [ret∫es'sjone] sf (ECON) recession

re'cidere [re't∫idere] vt to cut off, chop off

reci'divo, a [ret∫i'divo] sm/f (DIR) second (o habitual) offender, recidivist

re'cinto [re't∫into] sm enclosure; (ciò che recinge) fence; surrounding wall

recipi'ente [ret∫i'pjɛnte] sm container

re'ciproco, a, ci, che [re't∫iproko] ag reciprocal

re'ciso, a [re't∫izo] pp di **recidere**

re'cita [re't∫ita] sf performance

reci'tare [ret∫i'tare] vt (poesia, lezione) to recite; (dramma) to perform; (ruolo) to play o act (the part of);

recitazi'one sf recitation; (*di attore*) acting

recla'mare vi to complain ♦ vt (*richiedere*) to demand

ré'clame [re'klam] sf inv advertising no pl; advertisement, advert (*BRIT*), ad (*fam*)

re'clamo sm complaint

reclusi'one sf (*DIR*) imprisonment

'recluta sf recruit; **reclu'tare** vt to recruit

re'condito, a ag secluded; (*fig*) secret, hidden

recriminazi'one [rekriminat'tsjone] sf recrimination

recrude'scenza [rekrudeʃ'ʃentsa] sf fresh outbreak

recupe'rare vt = ricuperare

redargu'ire vt to rebuke

re'datto, a pp di redigere

redat'tore, 'trice sm/f (*STAMPA*) editor; (: *di articolo*) writer; (*di dizionario etc*) compiler; **redattore capo** chief editor; **redazi'one** sf editing; writing; (*sede*) editorial office(s); (*personale*) editorial staff; (*versione*) version

reddi'tizio, a [reddi'tittsjo] ag profitable

'reddito sm income; (*dello Stato*) revenue; (*di un capitale*) yield

re'dento, a pp di redimere

redenzi'one [reden'tsjone] sf redemption

re'digere [re'didʒere] vt to write; (*contratto*) to draw up

'redini sfpl reins

'reduce ['redutʃe] ag: ~ **da** returning from, back from ♦ sm/f survivor

refe'rendum sm inv referendum

refe'renza [refe'rɛntsa] sf reference

re'ferto sm medical report

refet'torio sm refectory

refrat'tario, a ag refractory

refrige'rare [refridʒe'rare] vt to refrigerate; (*rinfrescare*) to cool, refresh

rega'lare vt to give (as a present), make a present of

re'gale ag regal

re'galo sm gift, present

re'gata sf regatta

reg'gente [red'dʒɛnte] sm/f regent

'reggere ['rɛddʒere] vt (*tenere*) to hold; (*sostenere*) to support, bear, hold up; (*portare*) to carry, bear; (*resistere*) to withstand; (*dirigere: impresa*) to manage, run; (*governare*) to rule, govern; (*LING*) to take, be followed by ♦ vi (*resistere*): ~ **a** to stand up to, hold out against; (*sopportare*): ~ **a** to stand; (*durare*) to last; (*fig: teoria etc*) to hold water; ~**rsi** vr (*stare ritto*) to stand

'reggia, ge ['rɛddʒa] sf royal palace

reggi'calze [reddʒi'kaltse] sm inv suspender belt

reggi'mento [reddʒi'mento] sm (*MIL*) regiment

reggi'petto [reddʒi'pɛtto] sm bra

reggi'seno [reddʒi'seno] sm bra

re'gia, 'gie [re'dʒia] sf (*TV, CINEMA etc*) direction

re'gime [re'dʒime] sm (*POL*) regime; (*DIR: aureo, patrimoniale etc*) system; (*MED*) diet; (*TECN*) (engine) speed

re'gina [re'dʒina] sf queen

'regio, a, gi, gie ['rɛdʒo] ag royal

regio'nale [redʒo'nale] ag regional ♦ sm local train (*stopping frequently*)

regi'one [re'dʒone] sf region; (*territorio*) region, district, area

re'gista, i, e [re'dʒista] sm/f (*TV, CINEMA etc*) director

regis'trare [redʒis'trare] vt (*AMM*) to register; (*COMM*) to enter; (*notare*) to note, take note of; (*canzone, conversazione, sog: strumento di misura*) to record; (*mettere a punto*) to adjust, regulate; (*bagagli*) to check in; **registra'tore** sm (*strumento*) recorder, register; (*magnetofono*) tape recorder; **registratore di cassa** cash register; **registrazi'one** sf recording; (*AMM*) registration; (*COMM*) entry; (*di bagagli*) check-in

re'gistro [re'dʒistro] sm (*libro, MUS,*

TECH) register; ledger; logbook; (*DIR*) registry

re'gnare [reɲ'ɲare] *vi* to reign, rule

'regno ['reɲɲo] *sm* kingdom; (*periodo*) reign; (*fig*) realm; **il ~ animale/vegetale** the animal/vegetable kingdom; **il R~ Unito** the United Kingdom

'regola *sf* rule; **a ~ d'arte** duly; perfectly; **in ~** in order

rego'labile *ag* adjustable

regola'mento *sm* (*complesso di norme*) regulations *pl*; (*di debito*) settlement; **~ di conti** (*fig*) settling of scores

rego'lare *ag* regular; (*in regola: domanda*) in order, lawful ♦ *vt* to regulate, control; (*apparecchio*) to adjust, regulate; (*questione, conto, debito*) to settle; **~rsi** *vr* (*moderarsi*): **~rsi nel bere/nello spendere** to control one's drinking/spending; (*comportarsi*) to behave, act; **regolarità** *sf inv* regularity

'regolo *sm* ruler; **~ calcolatore** slide rule

reinte'grare *vt* (*energie*) to recover; (*in una carica*) to reinstate

rela'tivo, a *ag* relative

relazi'one [relat'tsjone] *sf* (*fra cose, persone*) relation(ship); (*resoconto*) report, account; **~i** *sfpl* (*conoscenze*) connections

rele'gare *vt* to banish; (*fig*) to relegate

religi'one [reli'dʒone] *sf* religion; **religi'oso, a** *ag* religious ♦ *sm/f* monk/nun

re'liquia *sf* relic

re'litto *sm* wreck; (*fig*) down-and-out

re'mare *vi* to row

remini'scenze [reminiʃ'ʃentse] *sfpl* reminiscences

remissi'one *sf* remission

remis'sivo, a *ag* submissive, compliant

'remo *sm* oar

re'moto, a *ag* remote

'rendere *vt* (*ridare*) to return, give

back; (: *saluto etc*) to return; (*produrre*) to yield, bring in; (*esprimere, tradurre*) to render; **~ qc possibile** to make sth possible; **~rsi utile** to make o.s. useful; **~rsi conto di qc** to realize sth

rendi'conto *sm* (*rapporto*) report, account; (*AMM, COMM*) statement of account

rendi'mento *sm* (*reddito*) yield; (*di manodopera, TECN*) efficiency; (*capacità di produrre*) output; (*di studenti*) performance

'rendita *sf* (*di individuo*) private *o* unearned income; (*COMM*) revenue; **~ annua** annuity

'rene *sm* kidney

'reni *sfpl* back *sg*

reni'tente *ag* reluctant, unwilling; **~ ai consigli di qn** unwilling to follow sb's advice; **essere ~ alla leva** (*MIL*) to fail to report for military service

'renna *sf* reindeer *inv*

'Reno *sm*: **il ~** the Rhine

'reo, a *sm/f* (*DIR*) offender

re'parto *sm* department, section; (*MIL*) detachment

repel'lente *ag* repulsive

repen'taglio [repen'taʎʎo] *sm*: **mettere a ~** to jeopardize, risk

repen'tino, a *ag* sudden, unexpected

repe'rire *vt* to find, trace

re'perto *sm* (*ARCHEOLOGIA*) find; (*MED*) report; (*DIR: anche:* **~ giudiziario**) exhibit

reper'torio *sm* (*TEATRO*) repertory; (*elenco*) index, (*alphabetical*) list

'replica *sf* (*ripetizione*) repetition; reply, answer; (*obiezione*) objection; (*TEATRO, CINEMA*) repeat performance; (*copia*) replica

repli'care *vt* (*ripetere*) to repeat; (*rispondere*) to answer, reply

repressi'one *sf* repression

re'presso, a *pp di* **reprimere**

re'primere *vt* to suppress, repress

re'pubblica, che *sf* republic; **repubbli'cano, a** *ag, sm/f* republican

repu'tare *vt* to consider, judge

reputazi'one [reputat'tsjone] *sf* reputation

'requie *sf*: **senza ~** unceasingly

requi'sire *vt* to requisition

requi'sito *sm* requirement

'resa *sf* (*l'arrendersi*) surrender; (*restituzione, rendimento*) return; **~ dei conti** rendering of accounts; (*fig*) day of reckoning

resi'dente *ag* resident; **resi'denza** *sf* residence; **residenzi'ale** (*CHIM*) residual

re'siduo, a *ag* residual, remaining ♦ *sm* remainder; (*CHIM*) residue

resina *sf* resin

resis'tente *ag* (*che resiste*): **~ a** resistant to; (*forte*) strong; (*duraturo*) long-lasting, durable; **~ al caldo** heat-resistant; **resis'tenza** *sf* resistance; (*di persona: fisica*) stamina, endurance; (: *mentale*) endurance, resistance

---
Resistenza

The **Resistenza** in Italy fought against the Nazis and the Fascists during the Second World War. Members of the Resistance spanned a wide political spectrum and played a vital role in the Liberation and in the formation of the new democratic government at the end of the war.

---

re'sistere *vi* to resist; **~ a** (*assalto, tentazioni*) to resist; (*dolore, sog: pianta*) to withstand; (*non patir danno*) to be resistant to; **resis'tito, a** *pp di* **resistere**

'reso, a *pp di* **rendere**

reso'conto *sm* report, account

res'pingere [res'pindʒere] *vt* to drive back, repel; (*rifiutare*) to reject; (*INS*: *bocciare*) to fail; **res'pinto, a** *pp di* **respingere**

respi'rare *vi* to breathe; (*fig*) to get one's breath; to breathe again ♦ *vt* to breathe (in), inhale; **respira'tore** *sm* respirator; **respirazi'one** *sf* breathing; **respirazione artificiale** artificial

respiration; **res'piro** *sm* breathing *no pl*; (*singolo atto*) breath; (*fig*) respite, rest; **mandare un respiro di sollievo** to give a sigh of relief

respon'sabile *ag* responsible ♦ *sm/f* person responsible; (*capo*) person in charge; **~ di** responsible for; (*DIR*) liable for; **responsabilità** *sf inv* responsibility; (*legale*) liability

res'ponso *sm* answer

'ressa *sf* crowd, throng

res'tare *vi* (*rimanere*) to remain, stay; (*avanzare*) to be left, remain; **~ orfano/cieco** to become o be left an orphan/become blind; **~ d'accordo** to agree; **non resta più niente** there's nothing left; **restano pochi giorni** there are only a few days left

restau'rare *vt* to restore; **restaurazi'one** *sf* (*POL*) restoration; **res'tauro** *sm* (*di edifici etc*) restoration

res'tio, a, 'tii, 'tie *ag*: **~ a** reluctant to

restitu'ire *vt* to return, give back; (*energie, forze*) to restore

'resto *sm* remainder, rest; (*denaro*) change; (*MAT*) remainder; **~i** *smpl* (*di cibo*) leftovers; (*di città*) ruins; **del ~** moreover, besides; **~i mortali** (*mortal*) remains

res'tringere [res'trindʒere] *vt* to reduce; (*vestito*) to take in; (*stoffa*) to shrink; (*fig*) to restrict, limit; **~rsi** *vr* (*strada*) to narrow; (*stoffa*) to shrink; **restrizi'one** *sf* restriction

'rete *sf* net; (*fig*) trap, snare; (*di recinzione*) wire netting; (*AUT, FERR, di spionaggio etc*) network; **segnare una ~** (*CALCIO*) to score a goal; **~ del letto** (*sprung*) bed base

reti'cente [reti'tʃɛnte] *ag* reticent

retico'lato *sm* grid; (*rete*) wire netting; (*di filo spinato*) barbed wire (fence)

'retina *sf* (*ANAT*) retina

re'torica *sf* rhetoric

re'torico, a, ci, che *ag* rhetorical

retribu'ire *vt* to pay; **retribuzi'one** *sf* payment

'**retro** *sm inv* back ♦ *av* (*dietro*): **vedi ~** see over/(leaf)

retro'cedere [retro'tʃɛdere] *vi* to withdraw ♦ *vt* (*CALCIO*) to relegate; (*MIL*) to degrade

re'trogrado, a *ag* (*fig*) reactionary, backward-looking

retro'marcia [retro'martʃa] *sf* (*AUT*) reverse; (: *dispositivo*) reverse gear

retro'scena [retro'ʃɛna] *sm inv* (*TEATRO*) backstage; **i ~** (*fig*) the behind-the-scenes activities

retrospet'tivo, a *ag* retrospective

retrovi'sore *sm* (*AUT*) (rear-view) mirror

'**retta** *sf* (*MAT*) straight line; (*di convitto*) charge for bed and board; (*fig*: *ascolto*): **dar ~ a** to listen to, pay attention to

rettango'lare *ag* rectangular

ret'tangolo, a *ag* right-angled ♦ *sm* rectangle

retti'fica, che *sf* rectification, correction

rettifi'care *vt* (*curva*) to straighten; (*fig*) to rectify, correct

'**rettile** *sm* reptile

retti'lineo, a *ag* rectilinear

retti'tudine *sf* rectitude, uprightness

'**retto, a** *pp di* **reggere** ♦ *ag* straight; (*MAT*): **angolo ~** right angle; (*onesto*) honest, upright; (*giusto, esatto*) correct, proper, right

ret'tore *sm* (*REL*) rector; (*di università*) ≈ chancellor

reuma'tismo *sm* rheumatism

reve'rendo, a *ag*: **il ~ padre Belli** the Reverend Father Belli

rever'sibile *ag* reversible

revisio'nare *vt* (*conti*) to audit; (*TECN*) to overhaul, service; (*DIR*: *processo*) to review

revisi'one *sf* auditing *no pl*; audit; servicing *no pl*; overhaul; review; revision

revi'sore *sm*: **~ di conti/bozze** auditor/proofreader

'**revoca** *sf* revocation

revo'care *vt* to revoke

re'volver *sm inv* revolver

riabili'tare *vt* to rehabilitate

riagganci'are [riaggan'tʃare] *vt* (*TEL*) to hang up

rial'zare [rial'tsare] *vt* to raise, lift; (*alzare di più*) to heighten, raise; (*aumentare: prezzi*) to increase, raise ♦ *vi* (*prezzi*) to rise, increase; **ri'alzo** *sm* (*di prezzi*) increase, rise; (*sporgenza*) rise

rianimazi'one [rianimat'tsjone] *sf* (*MED*) resuscitation; **centro di ~** intensive care unit

riap'pendere *vt* to rehang; (*TEL*) to hang up

ria'prire *vt* to reopen, open again; **~rsi** *vr* to reopen, open again

ri'armo *sm* (*MIL*) rearmament

rias'setto *sm* (*di stanza etc*) rearrangement; (*ordinamento*) reorganization

rias'sumere *vt* (*riprendere*) to resume; (*impiegare di nuovo*) to re-employ; (*sintetizzare*) to summarize; **rias'sunto, a** *pp di* **riassumere** ♦ *sm* summary

ria'vere *vt* to have again; (*avere indietro*) to get back; (*riacquistare*) to recover; **~rsi** *vr* to recover

riba'dire *vt* (*fig*) to confirm

ri'balta *sf* flap; (*TEATRO*: *proscenio*) front of the stage; (*fig*) limelight; **luci della ~** footlights *pl*

ribal'tabile *ag* (*sedile*) tip-up

ribal'tare *vt*, *vi* (*anche*: **~rsi**) to turn over, tip over

ribas'sare *vt* to lower, bring down ♦ *vi* to come down, fall; **ri'basso** *sm* reduction, fall

ri'battere *vt* to return, hit back; (*confutare*) to refute; **~ che** to retort that

ribel'larsi *vr*: **~ (a)** to rebel (against); **ri'belle** *ag* (*soldati*) rebel; (*ragazzo*) rebellious ♦ *sm/f* rebel; **ribelli'one** *sf* rebellion

'ribes *sm inv* currant; **~ nero** blackcurrant; **~ rosso** redcurrant

ribol'lire *vi* (*fermentare*) to ferment; (*fare bolle*) to bubble, boil; (*fig*) to seethe

ri'brezzo [ri'breddzo] *sm* disgust, loathing; **far ~ a** to disgust

ribut'tante *ag* disgusting, revolting

rica'dere *vi* to fall again; (*scendere a terra, fig: nel peccato etc*) to fall back; (*vestiti, capelli etc*) to hang (down); (*riversarsi: fatiche, colpe*): **~ su** to fall on; **rica'duta** *sf* (*MED*) relapse

rical'care *vt* (*disegni*) to trace; (*fig*) to follow faithfully

rica'mare *vt* to embroider

ricambi'are *vt* to change again; (*contraccambiare*) to repay, return; **ri'cambio** *sm* exchange, return; (*FISIOL*) metabolism; **ricambi** *smpl* (*TECN*) spare parts

ri'camo *sm* embroidery

ricapito'lare *vt* to recapitulate, sum up

ricari'care *vt* (*arma, macchina fotografica*) to reload; (*pipa*) to refill; (*orologio*) to rewind; (*batteria*) to recharge

ricat'tare *vt* to blackmail; **ricatta'tore, 'trice** *sm/f* blackmailer; **ri'catto** *sm* blackmail

rica'vare *vt* (*estrarre*) to draw out, extract; (*ottenere*) to obtain, gain; **ri'cavo** *sm* proceeds *pl*

ric'chezza [rik'kettsa] *sf* richness; **~e** *sfpl* (*beni*) wealth *sg*, riches

'riccio, a [ˈrittʃo] *ag* curly ♦ *sm* (*ZOOL*) hedgehog; (: *anche: ~ di mare*) sea urchin; **'ricciolo** *sm* curl; **ricci'uto, a** *ag* curly

'ricco, a, chi, che *ag* rich; (*persona, paese*) rich, wealthy ♦ *sm/f* rich person/woman; **i ~chi** the rich; **~ di** full of; rich in

ri'cerca, che [ri'tʃerka] *sf* search; (*indagine*) investigation, inquiry; (*studio*): **la ~** research; **una ~** piece of research

ricer'care [ritʃer'kare] *vt* (*motivi, cause*) to look for, try to determine; (*successo, piacere*) to pursue; (*onore, gloria*) to seek; **ricer'cato, a** *ag* (*apprezzato*) much sought-after; (*affettato*) studied, affected ♦ *sm/f* (*POLIZIA*) wanted man/woman

ri'cetta [ri'tʃetta] *sf* (*MED*) prescription; (*CUC*) recipe

ricettazi'one [ritʃettat'tsjone] *sf* (*DIR*) receiving (stolen goods)

ri'cevere [ri'tʃevere] *vt* to receive; (*stipendio, lettera*) to get, receive; (*accogliere: ospite*) to welcome; (*vedere: cliente, rappresentante etc*) to see; **ricevi'mento** *sm* receiving *no pl*; (*festa*) reception; **ricevi'tore** *sm* (*TECN*) receiver; **ricevito'ria** *sf* lottery o pools office; **rice'vuta** *sf* receipt; **ricevuta fiscale** receipt for tax purposes; **ricezi'one** *sf* (*RADIO, TV*) reception

richia'mare [rikja'mare] *vt* (*chiamare indietro, ritelefonare*) to call back; (*ambasciatore, truppe*) to recall; (*rimproverare*) to reprimand; (*attirare*) to attract, draw; **~rsi a** (*riferirsi a*) to refer to; **richi'amo** *sm* call; recall; reprimand; attraction

richi'edere [ri'kjedere] *vt* to ask again for; (*chiedere indietro*): **~ qc** to ask for sth back; (*chiedere: per sapere*) to ask; (: *per avere*) to ask for; (*AMM: documenti*) to apply for; (*esigere*) to need, require; **richi'esta** *sf* (*domanda*) request; (*AMM*) application, request; (*esigenza*) demand, request; **a richiesta** on request; **richi'esto, a** *pp di* **richiedere**

rici'clare [ritʃi'klare] *vt* to recycle

'ricino [ˈritʃino] *sm*: **olio di ~** castor oil

ricognizi'one [rikoɲɲit'tsjone] *sf* (*MIL*) reconnaissance; (*DIR*) recognition, acknowledgement

ricominci'are [rikomin'tʃare] *vt*, *vi* to start again, begin again

ricom'pensa *sf* reward

ricompen'sare *vt* to reward

riconcili'are |rikontʃi'ljare| vt to reconcile; **~rsi** vr to be reconciled; **riconciliazi'one** sf reconciliation

ricono'scente |rikonoʃ'ʃɛnte| ag grateful; **ricono'scenza** sf gratitude

rico'noscere |riko'noʃʃere| vt to recognize; (DIR: figlio, debito) to acknowledge; (ammettere: errore) to admit, acknowledge; **riconosci'mento** sm recognition; acknowledgement; (identificazione) identification; **riconosci'uto, a** pp di **riconoscere**

ricopi'are vt to copy

rico'prire vt (coprire) to cover; (occupare: carica) to hold

ricor'dare vt to remember, recall; (richiamare alla memoria): **~ qc a qn** to remind sb of sth; **~rsi** vr: **~rsi (di)** to remember; **~rsi di qc/di aver fatto** to remember sth/having done

ri'cordo sm memory; (regalo) keepsake, souvenir; (di viaggio) souvenir; **~i** smpl (memorie) memoirs

ricor'rente ag recurrent, recurring; **ricor'renza** sf recurrence; (festività) anniversary

ri'correre vi (ripetersi) to recur; **~ a** (rivolgersi) to turn to; (: DIR) to appeal to; (servirsi di) to have recourse to; **ri'corso, a** pp di **ricorrere** ♦ sm recurrence; (DIR) appeal; **far ricorso a** = **ricorrere a**

ricostitu'ente ag (MED): **cura ~** tonic

ricostru'ire vt (casa) to rebuild; (fatti) to reconstruct; **ricostruzi'one** sf rebuilding no pl; reconstruction

ri'cotta sf soft white unsalted cheese made from sheep's milk

ricove'rare vt to give shelter to; **~ qn in ospedale** to admit sb to hospital

ri'covero sm shelter, refuge; (MIL) shelter; (MED) admission to hospital

ricre'are vt to recreate; (fig: distrarre) to amuse

ricreazi'one |rikreat'tsjone| sf recreation, entertainment; (INS) break

ri'credersi vr to change one's mind

ricupe'rare vt (rientrare in possesso di) to recover, get back; (tempo perduto) to make up for; (NAUT) to salvage; (: naufraghi) to rescue; (delinquente) to rehabilitate; **~ lo svantaggio** (SPORT) to close the gap

ridacchi'are |ridak'kjare| vi to snigger

ri'dare vt to return, give back

'ridere vi to laugh; (deridere, beffare): **~ di** to laugh at, make fun of

ri'detto, a pp di **ridire**

ri'dicolo, a ag ridiculous, absurd

ridimensio'nare vt to reorganize; (fig) to see in the right perspective

ri'dire vt to repeat; (criticare) to find fault with; to object to; **trova sempre qualcosa da ~** he always manages to find fault

ridon'dante ag redundant

ri'dotto, a pp di **ridurre** ♦ ag (biglietto) reduced; (formato) small

ri'durre vt (prezzo, spese) to cut, reduce; (accorciare: opera letteraria) to abridge; (: RADIO, TV) to adapt; **ridursi** vr (diminuirsi) to be reduced, shrink; **ridursi a** to be reduced to; **ridursi pelle e ossa** to be reduced to skin and bone; **ridut'tore** sm (ELEC) adaptor; **riduzi'one** sf reduction; abridgement; adaptation

riem'pire vt to fill (up); (modulo) to fill in o out; **~rsi** vr to fill (up); **~ qc di** to fill sth (up) with

rien'tranza |rien'trantsa| sf recess; indentation

rien'trare vi (entrare di nuovo) to go (o come) back in; (tornare) to return; (fare una rientranza) to go in, curve inwards; to be indented; (riguardare): **~ in** to be included among, form part of; **ri'entro** sm (ritorno) return; (di astronave) re-entry

riepilo'gare vt to summarize ♦ vi to recapitulate

ri'fare vt to do again; (ricostruire) to

make again; (*nodo*) to tie again, do up again; (*imitare*) to imitate, copy; **~rsi** *vr* (*risarcirsi*) to make up for; (*vendicarsi*) **~rsi di qc su qn** to get one's own back on sb for sth; (*riferirsi*): **~rsi a** to go back to; to follow; **~ il letto** to make the bed; **~rsi una vita** to make a new life for o.s.; **ri'fatto, a** *pp di* **rifare**

riferi'mento *sm* reference; **in** o **con ~ a** with reference to

rife'rire *vt* (*riportare*) to report ♦ *vi* to do a report; **~rsi** *vr*, **~rsi a** to refer to

rifi'nire *vt* to finish off, put the finishing touches to; **rifini'tura** *sf* finishing touch; **rifiniture** *sfpl* (*di mobile, auto*) finish *sg*

rifiu'tare *vt* to refuse; **~ di fare** to refuse to do; **rifi'uto** *sm* refusal; **rifiuti** *smpl* (*spazzatura*) rubbish *sg*, refuse *sg*

riflessi'one *sf* (*FISICA, meditazione*) reflection; (*il pensare*) thought, reflection; (*osservazione*) remark

riflles'sivo, a *ag* (*persona*) thoughtful, reflective; (*LING*) reflexive

ri'flesso, a *pp di* **riflettere** ♦ *sm* (*di luce, allo specchio*) reflection; (*FISIOL*) reflex; **di** o **per ~** indirectly

ri'flettere *vt* to reflect ♦ *vi* to think; **~rsi** *vr* to be reflected; **~ su** to think over

riflet'tore *sm* reflector; (*proiettore*) floodlight; searchlight

ri'flusso *sm* flowing back; (*della marea*) ebb; **un'epoca di ~** an era of nostalgia

ri'fondere *vt* to refund, repay

ri'forma *sf* reform; **la R~** (*REL*) the Reformation

rifor'mare *vt* to re-form; (*REL, POL*) to reform; (*MIL: recluta*) to declare unfit for service; (*: soldato*) to invalid out, discharge; **riforma'torio** *sm* (*DIR*) community home (*BRIT*), reformatory (*US*)

riforni'mento *sm* supplying, providing; restocking; **~i** *smpl*

(*provviste*) supplies, provisions

rifor'nire *vt* (*provvedere*): **~ di** to supply o provide with; (*fornire di nuovo: casa etc*) to restock

rifrazi'one [rifrat'tsjone] *sf* refraction

rifu'gire [rifud'dʒire] *vi* to escape again; (*fig*): **~ da** to shun

rifugi'arsi [rifu'dʒarsi] *vr* to take refuge; **rifugi'ato, a** *sm/f* refugee

ri'fugio [ri'fudʒo] *sm* refuge, shelter; (*in montagna*) shelter; **~ antiaereo** air-raid shelter

'riga, ghe *sf* line; (*striscia*) stripe; (*di persone, cose*) line, row; (*regola*) ruler; (*scriminatura*) parting; **mettersi in ~** to line up; **a ~ghe** (*foglio*) lined; (*vestito*) striped

ri'gagnolo [ri'ɡaɲɲolo] *sm* rivulet

ri'gare (*foglio*) to rule ♦ *vi*: **~ diritto** (*fig*) to toe the line

rigatti'ere *sm* junk dealer

riget'tare [ridʒet'tare] *vt* (*gettare indietro*) to throw back; (*fig: respingere*) to reject; (*vomitare*) to bring o throw up; **ri'getto** *sm* (*anche MED*) rejection

rigidità [ridʒidi'ta] *sf* rigidity; stiffness; severity, rigours *pl*; strictness

'rigido, a ['ridʒido] *ag* rigid, stiff; (*membra etc: indurite*) stiff; (*METEOR*) harsh, severe; (*fig*) strict

rigi'rare [ridʒi'rare] *vt* to turn; **~rsi** *vr* to turn round; (*nel letto*) to turn over; **~ qc tra le mani** to turn sth over in one's hands; **~ il discorso** to change the subject

'rigo, ghi *sm* line; (*MUS*) staff, stave

rigogli'oso, a [riɡoʎʎoso] *ag* (*pianta*) luxuriant; (*fig: commercio, sviluppo*) thriving

ri'gonfio, a *ag* swollen

ri'gore (*METEOR*) harshness, rigours *pl*; (*fig*) severity, strictness; (*anche: calcio di ~*) penalty; **di ~** compulsory; **a rigor di termini** strictly speaking; **rigo'roso, a** *ag* (*severo: persona, ordine*) strict; (*preciso*) rigorous

rigover'nare *vt* to wash (up)

riguar'dare *vt* to look at again; (*considerare*) to regard, consider; (*concernere*) to regard, concern; **~rsi** *vr* (*aver cura di sé*) to look after o.s.

rigu'ardo *sm* (*attenzione*) care; (*considerazione*) regard, respect; **~ a** concerning, with regard to; **non aver ~i nell'agire/nel parlare** to act/speak freely

rilasci'are [rilaʃ'ʃare] *vt* (*rimettere in libertà*) to release; (*AMM: documenti*) to issue; **ri'lascio** *sm* release; issue

rilas'sare *vt* to relax; **~rsi** *vr* to relax; (*fig: disciplina*) to become slack

rile'gare *vt* (*libro*) to bind; **rilega'tura** *sf* binding

ri'leggere [ri'leddʒere] *vt* to reread, read again; (*rivedere*) to read over

ri'lento: a ~ *av* slowly

rileva'mento *sm* (*topografico, statistico*) survey; (*NAUT*) bearing

rile'vante *ag* considerable; important

rile'vare *vt* (*ricavare*) to find; (*notare*) to notice; (*mettere in evidenza*) to point out; (*venire a conoscere: notizia*) to learn; (*raccogliere: dati*) to gather, collect; (*TOPOGRAFIA*) to survey; (*MIL*) to relieve; (*COMM*) to take over

rili'evo *sm* (*ARTE, GEO*) relief; (*fig: rilevanza*) importance; (*TOPOGRAFIA*) survey; **dar ~ a** o **mettere in ~ qc** (*fig*) to bring sth out, highlight sth

rilut'tante *ag* reluctant; **rilut'tanza** *sf* reluctance

'rima *sf* rhyme; (*verso*) verse

riman'dare *vt* to send again; (*restituire, rinviare*) to send back, return; (*differire*): **~ qc (a)** to postpone sth o put sth off (till); (*fare riferimento*): **~ qn a** to refer sb to; **essere rimandato** (*INS*) to have to repeat one's exams

ri'mando *sm* (*rinvio*) return; (*dilazione*) postponement; (*riferimento*) cross-reference

rima'nente *ag* remaining ♦ *sm* rest, remainder; **i ~i** (*persone*) the rest of them, the others; **rima'nenza** *sf* rest,

remainder; **rimanenze** *sfpl* (*COMM*) unsold stock *sg*

rima'nere (*restare*) to remain, stay; (*avanzare*) to be left, remain; (*restare stupito*) to be amazed; (*restare, mancare*): **rimangono poche settimane a Pasqua** there are only a few weeks left till Easter; **rimane da vedere se** it remains to be seen whether; (*diventare*): **~ vedovo** to be left a widower; (*trovarsi*): **~ sorpreso** to be surprised

ri'mare *vt, vi* to rhyme

rimargi'nare [rimardʒi'nare] *vt, vi* (*anche: ~rsi*) to heal

ri'masto, a *pp di* **rimanere**

rima'sugli [rima'suʎʎi] *smpl* leftovers

rimbal'zare [rimbal'tsare] *vi* to bounce back, rebound; (*proiettile*) to ricochet; **rim'balzo** *sm* rebound; ricochet

rimbam'bito, a *ag* senile, in one's dotage

rimboc'care *vt* (*coperta*) to tuck in; (*maniche, pantaloni*) to turn o roll up

rimbom'bare *vi* to resound

rimbor'sare *vt* to pay back, repay; **rim'borso** *sm* repayment

rimedi'are *vi*: **~ a** to remedy ♦ *vt* (*fam: procurarsi*) to get o scrape together

ri'medio *sm* (*medicina*) medicine; (*cura, fig*) remedy, cure

rimesco'lare *vt* to mix well, stir well; (*carte*) to shuffle; **sentirsi ~ il sangue** (*per paura*) to feel one's blood run cold; (*per rabbia*) to feel one's blood boil

ri'messa *sf* (*locale: per veicoli*) garage; (: *per aerei*) hangar; (*COMM: di merce*) consignment; (: *di denaro*) remittance; (*TENNIS*) service; (*CALCIO: anche: ~ in gioco*) throw-in

ri'messo, a *pp di* **rimettere**

ri'mettere *vt* (*mettere di nuovo*) to put back; (*indossare di nuovo*): **~ qc** to put sth back on, put sth on again; (*affidare*) to entrust; (: *decisione*) to refer; (condonare) to remit; (COMM: merci) to deliver; (: denaro) to remit; (vomitare) to bring up; (perdere: anche: rimetterci) to lose; ~rsi al bello (tempo) to clear up; ~rsi in salute to get better, recover one's health

'rimmel ® sm inv mascara

rimoder'nare vt to modernize

rimon'tare vt (meccanismo) to reassemble; (: tenda) to put up again ♦ vi (salire di nuovo): ~ in (macchina, treno) to get back into; (SPORT) to close the gap

rimorchi'are [rimor'kjare] vt to tow; (fig: ragazza) to pick up

rimorchia'tore sm (NAUT) tug(boat)

ri'morchio [ri'mɔrkjo] sm tow; (veicolo) trailer

ri'morso sm remorse

rimozi'one [rimot'tsjone] sf removal; (da un impiego) dismissal; (PSIC) repression

rim'pasto sm (POL) reshuffle

rimpatri'are vi to return home ♦ vt to repatriate; rim'patrio sm repatriation

rimpi'angere [rim'pjandʒere] vt to regret; (persona) to miss; rimpi'anto, a pp di rimpiangere ♦ sm regret

rimpiat'tino sm hide-and-seek

rimpiaz'zare [rimpjat'tsare] vt to replace

rimpiccio'lire [rimpittʃo'lire] vt to make smaller ♦ vi (anche: ~rsi) to become smaller

rimpin'zare [rimpin'tsare] vt: ~ di to cram o stuff with

rimprove'rare vt to rebuke, reprimand; rim'provero sm rebuke, reprimand

rimugi'nare [rimudʒi'nare] vt (fig) to turn over in one's mind

rimunerazi'one [rimunerat'tsjone] sf remuneration; (premio) reward

rimu'overe vt to remove; (destituire) to dismiss

Rinasci'mento [rinaʃʃi'mento] sm: il ~ the Renaissance

ri'nascita [ri'naʃʃita] sf rebirth, revival

rinca'rare vt to increase the price of ♦ vi to go up, become more expensive

rinca'sare vi to go home

rinchi'udere [rin'kjudere] vt to shut (o lock) up; ~rsi vr: ~rsi in to shut o.s. up in; ~rsi in se stesso to withdraw into o.s.; rinchi'uso, a pp di rinchiudere

rin'correre vt to chase, run after; rin'corsa sf short run; (fig) rin'corso, a pp di rincorrere

rin'crescere [rin'kreʃʃere] vb impers: mi rincresce che/di non poter fare I'm sorry that/I can't do, I regret that/ being unable to do; rincresci'mento sm regret; rincresci'uto, a pp di rincrescere

rincu'lare vi (arma) to recoil

rinfacci'are [rinfat'tʃare] vt (fig): ~ qc a qn to throw sth in sb's face

rinfor'zare [rinfor'tsare] vt to reinforce, strengthen ♦ vi (anche: ~rsi) to grow stronger; rin'forzo sm: mettere un rinforzo a to strengthen; di rinforzo (asse, sbarra) strengthening; (esercito) supporting; (personale) extra, additional; rinforzi smpl (MIL) reinforcements

rinfran'care vt to encourage, reassure

rinfres'care vt (atmosfera, temperatura) to cool (down); (abito, pareti) to freshen up ♦ vi (tempo) to grow cooler; ~rsi vr (ristorarsi) to refresh o.s.; (lavarsi) to freshen up; rin'fresco, schi sm (festa) party; rinfreschi smpl refreshments

rin'fusa sf: alla ~ in confusion, higgledy-piggledy

ringhi'are [rin'gjare] vi to growl, snarl

ringhi'era [rin'gjɛra] sf railing; (delle scale) banister(s pl)

ringiova'nire [rindʒova'nire] vt (sog: vestito, acconciatura etc): ~ qn to make sb look younger; (: vacanze etc) to rejuvenate ♦ vi (anche: ~rsi) to become (o look) younger

ringrazia'mento [ringrattsja'mento] *sm* thanks *pl*

ringrazi'are [ringrat'tsjare] *vt* to thank; **~ qn di qc** to thank sb for sth

rinne'gare *vt* (*fede*) to renounce; (*figlio*) to disown, repudiate; **rinne'gato, a** *sm/f* renegade

rinnova'mento *sm* renewal; (*economico*) revival

rinno'vare *vt* to renew; (*ripetere*) to repeat, renew; **rin'novo** *sm* (*di contratto*) renewal; **"chiuso per rinnovo dei locali"** "closed for alterations"

rinoce'ronte [rinotʃe'ronte] *sm* rhinoceros

rino'mato, a *ag* renowned, celebrated

rinsal'dare *vt* to strengthen

rintoc'care *vi* (*campana*) to toll; (*orologio*) to strike

rintracci'are [rintrat'tʃare] *vt* to track down

rintro'nare *vi* to boom, roar ♦ *vt* (*assordare*) to deafen; (*stordire*) to stun

ri'nuncia [ri'nuntʃa] *etc* = **rinunzia** *etc*

ri'nunzia [ri'nuntsja] *sf* renunciation

rinunzi'are [rinun'tsjare] *vi*: **~ a** to give up, renounce

rinve'nire *vt* to find, recover; (*scoprire*) to discover, find out ♦ *vi* (*riprendere i sensi*) to come round; (*fiori*) to revive

rinvi'are *vt* (*rimandare indietro*) to send back, return; (*differire*): **~ qc (a)** to postpone sth o put sth off (till); to adjourn sth (till); (*fare un rimando*): **~ qn a** to refer sb to

rinvigo'rire *vt* to strengthen

rin'vio, 'vii *sm* (*rimando*) return; (*differimento*) postponement; (: *di seduta*) adjournment; (*in un testo*) cross-reference

ri'one *sm* district, quarter

riordi'nare *vt* (*rimettere in ordine*) to tidy; (*riorganizzare*) to reorganize

riorganiz'zare [riorganid'dzare] *vt* to reorganize

ripa'gare *vt* to repay

ripa'rare *vt* (*proteggere*) to protect, defend; (*correggere: male, torto*) to make up for; (: *errore*) to put right; (*aggiustare*) to repair ♦ *vi* (*mettere rimedio*): **~ a** to make up for; **~rsi** *vr* (*rifugiarsi*) to take refuge o shelter; **riparazi'one** *sf* (*di un torto*) reparation; (*di guasto, scarpe*) repairing *no pl*; repair; (*risarcimento*) compensation

ri'paro *sm* (*protezione*) shelter, protection; (*rimedio*) remedy

ripar'tire *vt* (*dividere*) to divide up; (*distribuire*) to share out ♦ *vi* to set off again; to leave again

ripas'sare *vi* to come (o go) back ♦ *vt* (*scritto, lezione*) to go over (again); **ri'passo** *sm* revision (*BRIT*), review (*US*)

ripen'sare *vi* to think; (*cambiare pensiero*) to change one's mind; (*tornare col pensiero*): **~ a** to recall

ripercuo'tersi *vr*: **~ su** (*fig*) to have repercussions on

ripercussi'one *sf* (*fig*): **avere una ~ o delle ~i su** to have repercussions on

ripes'care *vt* (*pesce*) to fish out; (*fig: ritrovare*) to dig out

ri'petere *vt* to repeat; (*ripassare*) to go over; **ripetizi'one** *sf* repetition; (*di lezione*) revision; **ripetizioni** *sfpl* (*INS*) private tutoring *o* coaching *sg*

ripi'ano *sm* (*CUC*) shelf

ri'picca *sf*: **per ~** out of spite

'ripido, a *ag* steep

ripie'gare *vt* to refold; (*piegare più volte*) to fold (up) ♦ *vi* (*MIL*) to retreat, fall back; (*fig: accontentarsi*): **~ su** to make do with; **~rsi** *vr* to bend; **ripi'ego, ghi** *sm* expedient

ripi'eno, a *ag* full; (*CUC*) stuffed; (: *panino*) filled ♦ *sm* (*CUC*) stuffing

ri'porre *vt* (*porre al suo posto*) to put back, replace; (*mettere via*) to put away; (*fiducia, speranza*): **~ qc in qn** to place o put sth in sb

ripor'tare vt (portare indietro) to bring (o take) back; (riferire) to report; (citare) to quote; (vittoria) to gain; (successo) to have; (MAT) to carry; **~rsi a** (anche fig) to go back to; (riferirsi a) to refer to; **~ danni** to suffer damage

ripo'sare vt, vi to rest; **~rsi** vr to rest; **ri'poso** sm rest; (MIL): **riposo!** at ease!; **a riposo** (in pensione) retired; **giorno di riposo** day off

ripos'tiglio [ripos'tiλλo] sm lumber-room

ri'posto, a pp di **riporre**

ri'prendere vt (prigioniero, fortezza) to recapture; (prendere indietro) to take back; (ricominciare: lavoro) to resume; (andare a prendere) to fetch, come back for; (riassumere: impiegati) to take on again, re-employ; (rimproverare) to tell off; (restringere: abito) to take in; (CINEMA) to shoot; **~rsi** vr to recover; (correggersi) to correct o.s.; **ri'presa** sf recapture; resumption; (economica, da malattia, emozione) recovery; (AUT) acceleration no pl; (TEATRO, CINEMA) rerun; (CINEMA: presa) shooting no pl; shot; (SPORT) second half; (PUGILATO) round; **a più riprese** on several occasions, several times; **ripreso, a** pp di **riprendere**

ripristi'nare vt to restore

ripro'durre vt to reproduce; **riprodursi** vr (BIOL) to reproduce; (riformarsi) to form again; **riproduzi'one** sf reproduction; **riproduzione vietata** all rights reserved

ripudi'are vt to repudiate, disown

ripu'gnante [ripuɲ'ɲante] ag disgusting, repulsive

ripu'gnare [ripuɲ'ɲare] vi: **~ a qn** to repel o disgust sb

ripu'lire vt to clean up; (sog: ladri) to clean out; (perfezionare) to polish, refine

ri'quadro sm square; (ARCHIT) panel

ri'saia sf paddy field

risa'lire vi (ritornare in su) to go back up; **~ a** (ritornare con la mente) to go back to; (datare da) to date back to, go back to

risal'tare vi (fig: distinguersi) to stand out; (ARCHIT) to project, jut out; **ri'salto** sm prominence; (sporgenza) projection; **mettere** o **porre in risalto qc** to make sth stand out

risa'nare vt (guarire) to heal, cure; (palude) to reclaim; (economia) to improve; (bilancio) to reorganize

risa'puto, a ag: **è ~ che ...** everyone knows that ..., it is common knowledge that ...

risarci'mento [risartʃi'mento] sm: **~ (di)** compensation (for)

risar'cire [risar'tʃire] vt (cose) to pay compensation for; (persona): **~ qn di qc** to compensate sb for sth

ri'sata sf laugh

riscalda'mento sm heating; **~ centrale** central heating

riscal'dare vt (scaldare) to heat; (: mani, persona) to warm; (minestra) to reheat; **~rsi** vr to warm up

riscat'tare vt (prigioniero) to ransom, pay a ransom for; (DIR) to redeem; **~rsi** vr (da disonore) to redeem o.s.; **ris'catto** sm ransom; redemption

rischia'rare [riskja'rare] vt (illuminare) to light up; (colore) to make lighter; **~rsi** vr (tempo) to clear up; (cielo) to clear; (fig: volto) to brighten up; **~rsi la voce** to clear one's throat

rischi'are [ris'kjare] vt o to risk ♦ vi: **~ di fare qc** to risk o run the risk of doing sth

'rischio ['riskjo] sm risk; **rischi'oso, a** ag risky, dangerous

risci'acquare [riʃʃa'kware] vt to rinse

riscon'trare vt (rilevare) to find; **ris'contro** sm confirmation; (lettera di risposta) reply

ris'cossa sf (riconquista) recovery, reconquest; vedi anche **riscosso**

riscossi'one sf collection

ris'cosso, a pp di **riscuotere**

ris'cuotere vt (ritirare: somma) to collect; (: stipendio) to draw, collect; (assegno) to cash; (fig: successo etc) to win, earn; ~**rsi** vr: ~**rsi (da)** to shake o.s. (out of), rouse o.s. (from)

risenti'mento sm resentment

risen'tire vt to hear again; (provare) to feel ♦ vi: ~**di** to feel (o show) the effects of; ~**rsi** vr: ~**rsi di** o **per** to take offence at, resent; **risen'tito, a** ag resentful

ri'serbo sm reserve

ri'serva sf reserve; (di caccia, pesca) preserve; (restrizione, di indigeni) reservation; **di ~** (provviste etc) in reserve

riser'vare vt (tenere in serbo) to keep, put aside; (prenotare) to book, reserve; ~**rsi** vr: ~**rsi di fare qc** to intend to do sth; **riserva'tezza** sf reserve; **riser'vato, a** ag (prenotato, fig: persona) reserved; (confidenziale) confidential

risi'edere vi: ~**a** o **in** to reside in

'**risma** sf (di carta) ream; (fig) kind, sort

'**riso** (pl(f) ~**a**: il ridere) sm: **il ~** laughter; (pianta) rice ♦ pp di **ridere**

riso'lino sm snigger

ri'solto, a pp di **risolvere**

risolu'tezza [risolu'tettsa] sf determination

riso'luto, a ag determined, resolute

risoluzi'one [risolut'tsjone] sf solving no pl; (MAT) solution; (decisione, di immagine) resolution

ri'solvere vt (difficoltà, controversia) to resolve; (problema) to solve; (decidere): ~**di fare** to resolve to do; ~**rsi** vr (decidersi): ~**rsi a fare** to make up one's mind to do; (andare a finire): ~**rsi in** to end up, turn out; ~**rsi in nulla** to come to nothing

riso'nanza [riso'nantsa] sf resonance; **aver vasta ~** (fig: fatto etc) to be known far and wide

riso'nare vt, vi = **risuonare**

ri'sorgere [ri'sɔrdʒere] vi to rise again; **risorgi'mento** sm revival; **il Risorgimento** (STORIA) the Risorgimento

ri'sorsa sf expedient, resort; ~**e** sfpl (naturali, finanziarie etc) resources; **persona piena di ~e** resourceful person

ri'sorto, a pp di **risorgere**

ri'sotto sm (cuc) risotto

risparmi'are vt to save; (non uccidere) to spare ♦ vi to save; ~**qc a qn** to spare sb sth

ris'parmio sm saving no pl; (denaro) savings pl

rispec'chiare [rispek'kjare] vt to reflect

rispet'tabile ag respectable

rispet'tare vt to respect; **farsi ~** to command respect

rispet'tivo, a ag respective

ris'petto sm respect; ~**i** smpl (saluti) respects, regards; **~a** (in paragone a) compared to; (in relazione a) as regards, as for; **rispet'toso, a** ag respectful

ris'plendere vi to shine

ris'pondere vi to answer, reply; (freni) to respond; **~a** (domanda) to answer, reply to; (persona) to answer; (invito) to reply to; (provocazione, sog: veicolo, apparecchio) to respond to; (corrispondere a) to correspond to; (: speranze, bisogno) to answer; **~di** to answer for; **ris'posta** sf answer, reply; **in risposta a** in reply to; **risposto, a** pp di **rispondere**

'**rissa** sf brawl

ristabi'lire vt to re-establish, restore;

(persona: sog: riposo etc) to restore to health; **~rsi** vr to recover

rista'gnare [ristaɲ'ɲare] vi (acqua) to become stagnant; (sangue) to cease flowing; (fig: industria) to stagnate; **ris'tagno** sm stagnation

ris'tampa sf reprinting no pl; reprint

risto'rante sm restaurant

risto'rarsi vr to have something to eat and drink; (riposarsi) to rest, have a rest; **ris'toro** sm (bevanda, cibo) refreshment; **servizio di ristoro** (FERR) refreshments pl

ristret'tezza [ristret'tettsa] sf (strettezza) narrowness; (fig: scarsezza) scarcity, lack; (: meschinità) meanness; **~e** sfpl (povertà) financial straits

ris'tretto, a pp di **restringere** ♦ ag (racchiuso) enclosed, hemmed in; (angusto) narrow; (limitato): **~ (a)** restricted o limited (to); (cuc: brodo) thick; (: caffè) extra strong

risucchi'are [risuk'kjare] vt to suck in

risul'tare vi (dimostrarsi) to prove (to be), turn out (to be); (riuscire): **~ vincitore** to emerge as the winner; **~ da** (provenire) to result from, be the result of; **mi risulta che ...** I understand that ...; **non mi risulta** not as far as I know; **risul'tato** sm result

risuo'nare vi (rimbombare) to resound

risurrezi'one [risurret'tsjone] sf (REL) resurrection

risusci'tare [risuʃʃi'tare] vt to resuscitate, restore to life; (fig) to revive, bring back ♦ vi to rise (from the dead)

ris'veglio [riz'veʎʎo] sm waking up; (fig) revival

ris'volto sm (di giacca) lapel; (di pantaloni) turn-up; (di manica) cuff; (di tasca) flap; (di libro) inside flap; (fig) implication

ritagli'are [ritaʎ'ʎare] vt (tagliar via) to cut out; **ri'taglio** sm (di giornale) cutting, clipping; (di stoffa etc) scrap;

nei ritagli di tempo in one's spare time

ritar'dare vi (persona, treno) to be late; (orologio) to be slow ♦ vt (rallentare) to slow down; (impedire) to delay, hold up; (differire) to postpone, delay; **ritarda'tario, a** sm/f latecomer

ri'tardo sm delay; (di persona aspettata) lateness no pl; (fig: mentale) backwardness; **in ~** late

ri'tegno [ri'teɲɲo] sm restraint

rite'nere vt (trattenere) to hold back; (: somma) to deduct; (giudicare) to consider, believe; **rite'nuta** sf (sul salario) deduction

riti'rare vt to withdraw; (POL: richiamare) to recall; (andare a prendere: pacco etc) to collect, pick up; **~rsi** vr to withdraw; (da un'attività) to retire; (stoffa) to shrink; (marea) to recede; **riti'rata** sf (MIL) retreat; (latrina) lavatory; **ri'tiro** sm withdrawal; recall; collection; (luogo appartato) retreat

'ritmo sm rhythm; (fig) rate; (: della vita) pace, tempo

'rito sm rite; **di ~** usual, customary

ritoc'care vt (disegno, fotografia) to touch up; (testo) to alter; **ri'tocco, chi** sm touching up no pl; alteration

ritor'nare vi to return, go (o come) back; (ripresentarsi) to recur; (ridiventare): **~ ricco** to become rich again ♦ vt (restituire) to return, give back

ritor'nello sm refrain

ri'torno sm return; **essere di ~** to be back; **avere un ~ di fiamma** (AUT) to backfire; (fig: persona) to be back in love again

ritorsi'one sf retaliation

ri'trarre vt (trarre indietro, via) to withdraw; (distogliere: sguardo) to turn away; (rappresentare) to portray, depict; (ricavare) to get, obtain

ritrat'tare vt (disdire) to retract, take back; (trattare nuovamente) to deal with again

ri'tratto, a pp di **ritrarre** ♦ sm portrait

ri'troso, a ag (restio): ~ **(a)** reluctant (to); (schivo) shy; **andare a ~** to go backwards

ritro'vare vt to find; (salute) to regain; (persona) to find; to meet again; **~rsi** vr (essere, capitare) to find o.s.; (raccapezzarsi) to find one's way; (con senso reciproco) to meet (again); **ri'trovo** sm meeting place; **ritrovo notturno** night club

'ritto, a ag (in piedi) standing, on one's feet; (levato in alto) erect, raised; (: capelli) standing on end; (posto verticalmente) upright

ritu'ale ag, sm ritual

riuni'one sf (adunanza) meeting; (riconciliazione) reunion

riu'nire vt (ricongiungere) to unite (together); (riconciliare) to reunite, bring together (again); **~rsi** vr (adunarsi) to meet; (tornare insieme) to be reunited

riu'scire [riuʃ'ʃire] vi (uscire di nuovo) to go out again, go back out; (aver esito: fatti, azioni) to go, turn out; (aver successo) to succeed, be successful; (essere, apparire) to be, prove; (raggiungere il fine) to manage, succeed; ~ **a fare qc** to manage to do o succeed in doing o be able to do sth; **riu'scita** sf (esito) result, outcome; (buon esito) success

'riva sf (di fiume) bank; (di lago, mare) shore

ri'vale sm/f rival; **rivalità** sf rivalry

ri'valsa sf (rivincita) revenge

rivalu'tare vt (ECON) to revalue

rivan'gare vt (ricordi etc) to dig up (again)

rive'dere vt to see again; (ripassare) to revise; (verificare) to check

rive'lare vt to reveal; (divulgare) to reveal, disclose; (dare indizio) to reveal, show; **~rsi** vr (manifestarsi) to be revealed; **~rsi onesto** etc to prove to

be honest etc; **rivela'tore** sm (TECN) detector; (FOT) developer; **rivelazi'one** sf revelation

rivendi'care vt to claim, demand

ri'vendita sf (bottega) retailer's (shop)

rivendi'tore, 'trice sm/f retailer; ~ **autorizzato** (COMM) authorized dealer

ri'verbero sm (di luce, calore) reflection; (di suono) reverberation

rive'renza [rive'rɛntsa] sf reverence; (inchino) bow; curtsey

rive'rire vt (rispettare) to revere; (salutare) to pay one's respects to

river'sare vt (anche fig) to pour; **~rsi** vr (fig: persone) to pour out

rivesti'mento sm covering; coating

rives'tire vt to dress again; (ricoprire) to cover; to coat; (fig: carica) to hold; **~rsi** vr to get dressed again; to change (one's clothes)

rivi'era sf coast; **la ~ ligure** the Italian Riviera

ri'vincita [ri'vintʃita] sf (SPORT) return match; (fig) revenge

rivis'suto, a pp di **rivivere**

ri'vista sf review; (periodico) magazine, review; (TEATRO) revue; variety show

ri'vivere vi (riacquistare forza) to come alive again; (tornare in uso) to be revived ♦ vt to relive

ri'volgere [ri'voldʒere] vt (attenzione, sguardo) to turn, direct; (parole) to address; **~rsi** vr to turn round; (fig: dirigersi per informazioni): **~rsi a** to go and see, go and speak to; (: ufficio) to enquire at

ri'volta sf revolt, rebellion

rivol'tare vt to turn over; (con l'interno all'esterno) to turn inside out; (disgustare: stomaco) to upset, turn; **~rsi** vr (ribellarsi): **~rsi (a)** to rebel (against)

rivol'tella sf revolver

ri'volto, a pp di **rivolgere**

rivoluzio'nare [rivoluttsjo'nare] vt to revolutionize

rivoluzio'nario, a [rivoluttsjo'narjo] *ag, sm/f* revolutionary

rivoluzi'one [rivolut'tsjone] *sf* revolution

riz'zare [rit'tsare] *vt* to raise, erect; **~rsi** *vr* to stand up; *(capelli)* to stand on end

'roba *sf* stuff, things *pl*; *(possessi, beni)* belongings *pl*, things *pl*, possessions *pl*; **~ da mangiare** things to eat; food; **~ da matti** sheer madness *o* lunacy

'robot *sm inv* robot

ro'busto, a *ag* robust, sturdy; *(solido: catena)* strong

'rocca, che *sf* fortress

rocca'forte *sf* stronghold

roc'chetto [rok'ketto] *sm* reel, spool

'roccia, ce ['rɔttʃa] *sf* rock; **fare ~** *(SPORT)* to go rock climbing; **roc'cioso, a** *ag* rocky

ro'daggio [ro'daddʒo] *sm* running *(BRIT)* *o* breaking *(US)* in; **in ~** running *(BRIT)* *o* breaking *(US)* in

'Rodano *sm*: **il ~** the Rhone

'rodere *vt* to gnaw (at); *(distruggere poco a poco)* to eat into

rodi'tore *sm (ZOOL)* rodent

rodo'dendro *sm (ZOOL)* rhododendron

'rogna ['rɔɲa] *sf (MED)* scabies *sg*; *(fig)* bother, nuisance

ro'gnone [roɲ'ɲone] *sm (CUC)* kidney

'rogo, ghi *sm (per cadaveri)* (funeral) pyre; *(supplizio)*: **il ~** the stake

rol'lio roll(ing)

'Roma *sf* Rome

Roma'nia *sf*: **la ~** Romania

ro'manico, a, ci, che *ag* Romanesque

ro'mano, a *ag, sm/f* Roman

romanti'cismo [romanti'tʃizmo] *sm* romanticism

ro'mantico, a, ci, che *ag* romantic

ro'manza [ro'mandza] *sf (MUS, LETTERATURA)* romance

roman'zesco, a, schi, sche [roman'dzesko] *ag (stile, personaggi)* fictional; *(fig)* storybook *cpd*

romanzi'ere [roman'dzjere] *sm*

novelist

ro'manzo, a [ro'mandzo] *ag (LING)* romance *cpd* ♦ *sm* novel; **~ d'appendice** serial (story)

rom'bare *vi* to rumble, thunder, roar

'rombo *sm* rumble, thunder, roar; *(MAT)* rhombus; *(ZOOL)* turbot; brill

ro'meno, a *ag, sm/f, sm* = **rumeno, a**

'rompere *vt* to break; *(fidanzamento)* to break off ♦ *vi* to break; **~rsi** *vr* to break; **mi rompe le scatole** *(fam)* he (*o* she) is a pain in the neck; **~rsi un braccio** to break an arm; **rompi'capo** *sm* worry, headache; *(indovinello)* puzzle; *(in enigmistica)* brainteaser; **rompighi'accio** *sm (NAUT)* icebreaker; **rompis'catole** *(fam)* *sm/f inv* pest, pain in the neck

'ronda *sf (MIL)* rounds *pl*, patrol

ron'della *sf (TECN)* washer

'rondine *sf (ZOOL)* swallow

ron'done *sm (ZOOL)* swift

ron'zare [ron'dzare] *vi* to buzz, hum

ron'zino [ron'dzino] *sm (peg: cavallo)* nag

ron'zio [ron'dzio] *sm* buzzing

'rosa *sf* rose ♦ *ag inv, sm inv* pink; **ro'saio** *sm (pianta)* rosebush, rose tree; *(giardino)* rose garden; **ro'sario** *sm (REL)* rosary; **ro'sato, a** *ag* pink, rosy ♦ *sm (vino)* rosé (wine); **ro'seo, a** *ag (anche fig)* rosy

rosicchi'are [rosik'kjare] *vt* to gnaw (at); *(mangiucchiare)* to nibble (at)

rosma'rino *sm* rosemary

'roso, a *pp di* **rodere**

roso'lare *vt (CUC)* to brown

roso'lia *sf (MED)* German measles *sg*, rubella

ro'sone *sm* rosette; *(vetrata)* rose window

'rospo *sm (ZOOL)* toad

ros'setto *sm (per labbra)* lipstick

'rosso, a *ag, sm, sm/f* red; **il mar R~** the Red Sea; **~ d'uovo** egg yolk; **ros'sore** *sm* flush, blush

rosticce'ria [rostittʃe'ria] *sf* shop selling

roast meat and other cooked food

ro'tabile *ag* (percorribile): **strada** ~
roadway; (FERR): **materiale** ~ rolling
stock

ro'taia *sf* rut, track; (FERR) rail

ro'tare *vt, vi* to rotate; **rotazi'one** *sf*
rotation

rote'are *vt, vi* to whirl; ~ **gli occhi** to
roll one's eyes

ro'tella *sf* small wheel; (*di mobile*)
castor

roto'lare *vt, vi* to roll; **~rsi** *vr* to roll
(about)

'rotolo *sm* roll; **andare a ~i** (*fig*) to go
to rack and ruin

ro'tonda *sf* rotunda

ro'tondo, a *ag* round

'rotta *sf* (AER, NAUT) course, route; (MIL)
rout; **a ~ di collo** at breakneck speed;
essere in ~ con qn to be on bad
terms with sb

rot'tame *sm* fragment, scrap, broken
bit; **~i** *smpl* (*di nave, aereo etc*)
wreckage *sg*

'rotto, a *pp di* **rompere ♦** *ag* broken;
(*calzoni*) torn, split; **per il ~ della
cuffia** by the skin of one's teeth

rot'tura *sf* breaking *no pl*; break;
breaking off; (MED) fracture, break

rou'lotte [ru'lɔt] *sf* caravan

ro'vente *ag* red-hot

'rovere *sm* oak

rovesci'are [rovef'ʃare] *vt* (*versare in
giù*) to pour; (: *accidentalmente*) to
spill; (*capovolgere*) to turn upside
down; (*gettare a terra*) to knock down;
(: *fig: governo*) to overthrow; (*piegare
all'indietro: testa*) to throw back; **~rsi** *vr*
(*sedia, macchina*) to overturn; (*barca*)
to capsize; (*liquido*) to spill; (*fig:
situazione*) to be reversed

ro'vescio, sci [ro'veʃʃo] *sm* other side,
wrong side; (*della mano*) back; (*di
moneta*) reverse; (*pioggia*) sudden
downpour; (MAGLIA): **anche: punto ~**) purl (stitch); (TENNIS)
backhand (stroke); **a ~** upside-down;

inside-out; **capire qc a ~** to
misunderstand sth

ro'vina *sf* ruin; **andare in ~** (*andare a
pezzi*) to collapse; (*fig*) to go to rack
and ruin

rovi'nare *vi* to collapse, fall down ♦ *vt*
(*danneggiare, fig*) to ruin; **rovi'noso, a**
ag disastrous; (*fig*) damaging; violent

rovis'tare *vt* (*casa*) to ransack; (*tasche*)
to rummage in (o through)

'rovo *sm* (BOT) blackberry bush,
bramble bush

'rozzo, a ['roddzo] *ag* rough, coarse

'ruba *sf*: **andare a ~** to sell like hot
cakes

ru'bare *vt* to steal; ~ **qc a qn** to steal
sth from sb

rubi'netto *sm* tap, faucet (US)

ru'bino *sm* ruby

'rubrica, che *sf* (STAMPA) column;
(*quadernetto*) index book; address book

'rude *ag* tough, rough

'rudere *sm* (*rovina*) ruins *pl*

rudimen'tale *ag* rudimentary, basic

rudi'menti *smpl* rudiments; basic
principles; basic knowledge *sg*

ruf'fiano *sm* pimp

'ruga, ghe *sf* wrinkle

'ruggine ['ruddʒine] *sf* rust

rug'gire [rud'dʒire] *vi* to roar

rugi'ada [ru'dʒada] *sf* dew

ru'goso, a *ag* wrinkled

rul'lare *vi* (*tamburo, nave*) to roll;
(*aereo*) to taxi

rul'lino *sm* (FOT) spool; (: *pellicola*) film

'rullo *sm* (*di tamburo*) roll; (*arnese
cilindrico, TIP*) roller; ~ **compressore**
steam roller; ~ **di pellicola** roll of film

rum *sm* rum

ru'meno, a *ag, sm/f, sm* Romanian

rumi'nare *vt* (ZOOL) to ruminate

ru'more *sm*: **un ~** a noise, a sound;
(*fig*) a rumour; **il ~** noise; **rumo'roso,
a** *ag* noisy

ru'olo *sm* (TEATRO, *fig*) role, part;
(*elenco*) roll, register, list; **di ~**
permanent, on the permanent staff

ru'ota sf wheel; ~ **anteriore/posteriore** front/back wheel; ~ **di scorta** spare wheel

ruo'tare vt, vi = **rotare**

'rupe sf cliff

ru'rale ag rural, country cpd

ru'scello [ruʃˈʃɛllo] sm stream

'ruspa sf excavator

rus'sare vi to snore

'Russia sf: **la ~** Russia; **'russo, a** ag, sm/f, sm Russian

'rustico, a, ci, che ag rustic; (fig) rough, unrefined

rut'tare vi to belch; **'rutto** sm belch

'ruvido, a ag rough, coarse

ruzzo'lare [ruttsoˈlare] vi to tumble down; **ruzzo'loni** av: **cadere ruzzoloni** to tumble down

S, s

S. abbr (= sud) S

sa vb vedi **sapere**

'sabato sm Saturday; **di o il ~ on Saturdays**

'sabbia sf sand; **~e mobili** quicksand(s); **sabbi'oso, a** ag sandy

sabo'taggio [saboˈtaddʒo] sm sabotage

sabo'tare vt to sabotage

'sacca, che sf bag; (bisaccia) haversack; ~ **da viaggio** travelling bag

sacca'rina sf saccharin(e)

saccheggi'are [sakkedˈdʒare] vt to sack, plunder; **sac'cheggio** sm sack(ing)

sac'chetto [sakˈketto] sm (small) bag; (small) sack

'sacco, chi sm bag; (per carbone etc) sack; (ANAT, BIOL) sac; (tela) sacking; (saccheggio) sack(ing); (fig: grande quantità): **un ~ di** lots of, heaps of; ~ **a pelo** sleeping bag; ~ **per i rifiuti** bin bag

sacer'dote [satʃerˈdɔte] sm priest; **sacer'dozio** sm priesthood

sacra'mento sm sacrament

sacrifi'care vt to sacrifice; **~rsi** vr to sacrifice o.s.; (privarsi di qc) to make sacrifices

sacri'ficio [sakriˈfitʃo] sm sacrifice

sacri'legio [sakriˈledʒo] sm sacrilege

'sacro, a ag sacred

'sadico, a, ci, che ag sadistic ♦ sm/f sadist

sa'etta sf arrow; (fulmine: anche fig) thunderbolt; flash of lightning

sa'fari sm inv safari

sa'gace [saˈgatʃe] ag shrewd, sagacious

sag'gezza [sadˈdʒettsa] sf wisdom

saggi'are [sadˈdʒare] vt (metalli) to assay; (fig) to test

'saggio, a, gi, ge ['saddʒo] ag wise ♦ sm (persona) sage; (esperimento) test; (fig: prova) proof; (campione) sample; (scritto) essay

Sagit'tario [sadʒitˈtarjo] sm Sagittarius

'sagoma sf (profilo) outline, profile; (forma) form, shape; (TECN) template; (bersaglio) target; (fig: persona) character

'sagra sf festival

sagres'tano sm sacristan; sexton

sagres'tia sf sacristy

Sa'hara [saˈara] sm: **il (deserto del) ~** the Sahara (Desert)

'sai vb vedi **sapere**

'sala sf hall; (stanza) room; ~ **d'aspetto** waiting room; ~ **da ballo** ballroom; ~ **per concerti** concert hall; ~ **da gioco** gaming room; ~ **operatoria** operating theatre; ~ **da pranzo** dining room

sa'lame sm salami no pl, salami sausage

sala'moia sf (CUC) brine

sa'lare vt to salt

sa'lario sm pay, wages pl

sa'lato, a ag (sapore) salty; (CUC) salted, salt cpd; (fig: prezzo) steep, stiff

sal'dare vt (congiungere) to join, bind;

(*parti metalliche*) to solder; (: *con saldatura autogena*) to weld; (*conto*) to settle, pay; **salda'tura** *sf* soldering; welding; (*punto saldato*) soldered joint; weld

sal'dezza [sal'dettsa] *sf* firmness; strength

'saldo, a *ag* (*resistente, forte*) strong, firm; (*fermo*) firm, steady, stable; (*fig*) firm, steadfast ♦ *sm* (*svendita*) sale; (*di conto*) settlement; (ECON) balance

'sale *sm* salt; (*fig*): **ha poco ~ in zucca** he doesn't have much sense; **~ fino/ grosso** table/cooking salt

'salice ['salitʃe] *sm* willow; **~ piangente** weeping willow

sali'ente *ag* (*fig*) salient, main

sali'era *sf* salt cellar

sa'lina *sf* saltworks *sg*

sa'lino, a *ag* saline

sa'lire *vi* to go (o come) up; (*aereo etc*) to climb, go up; (*passeggero*) to get on; (*sentiero, prezzi, livello*) to go up, rise ♦ *vt* (*scale, gradini*) to go (o come) up; **~ su** to climb (up); **~ sul treno/ sull'autobus** to board the train/the bus; **~ in macchina** to get into the car; **sa'lita** *sf* climb, ascent; (*erta*) hill, slope; **in salita** *ag, av* uphill

sa'liva *sf* saliva

'salma *sf* corpse

'salmo *sm* psalm

sal'mone *sm* salmon

sa'lone *sm* (*stanza*) sitting room, lounge; (*in albergo*) lounge; (*su nave*) lounge, saloon; (*mostra*) show, exhibition; **~ di bellezza** beauty salon

sa'lotto *sm* lounge, sitting room; (*mobilio*) lounge suite

sal'pare *vi* (NAUT) to set sail; (*anche*: **~ l'ancora**) to weigh anchor

'salsa *sf* (CUC) sauce; **~ di pomodoro** tomato sauce

sal'siccia, ce [sal'sittʃa] *sf* pork sausage

sal'tare *vi* to jump, leap; (*esplodere*) to blow up, explode; (: *valvola*) to blow;

(*venir via*) to pop off; (*non aver luogo: corso etc*) to be cancelled ♦ *vt* to jump (over), leap (over); (*fig: pranzo, capitolo*) to skip, miss (out); (CUC) to sauté; **far ~** to blow up; to burst open; **~ fuori** (*fig: apparire all'improvviso*) to turn up

saltim'banco *sm* acrobat

'salto *sm* jump; (SPORT) jumping; **fare un ~ to** jump, leap; **fare un ~ da qn** to pop over to sb's (place); **~ in alto/ lungo** high/long jump; **~ con l'asta** pole vaulting; **~ mortale** somersault

saltu'ario, a *ag* occasional, irregular

sa'lubre *ag* healthy, salubrious

salume'ria *sf* delicatessen

sa'lumi *smpl* salted pork meats

salu'tare *ag* healthy; (*fig*) salutary, beneficial ♦ *vt* (*incontrandosi*) to greet; (*congedandosi*) to say goodbye to; (MIL) to salute

sa'lute *sf* health; **~!** (*a chi starnutisce*) bless you!; (*nei brindisi*) cheers!; **bere alla ~ di qn** to drink (to) sb's health

sa'luto *sm* (*gesto*) wave; (*parola*) greeting; (MIL) salute; **~i** *smpl* (*formula di cortesia*) greetings; **cari ~i** best regards; **vogliate gradire i nostri più distinti ~i** Yours faithfully

salvacon'dotto *sm* (MIL) safe-conduct

salva'gente [salva'dʒɛnte] *sm* (NAUT) lifebuoy; (*ciambella*) life belt; (*giubbotto*) lifejacket; (*stradale*) traffic island

salvaguar'dare *vt* to safeguard

sal'vare *vt* to save; (*trarre da un pericolo*) to rescue; (*proteggere*) to protect; **~rsi** *vr* to save o.s.; to escape; **salva'taggio** *sm* rescue; **salva'tore, 'trice** *sm/f* saviour

'salve (*fam*) *escl* hi!

sal'vezza [sal'vettsa] *sf* salvation; (*sicurezza*) safety

'salvia *sf* (BOT) sage

salvi'etta *sf* napkin; **~ umidificata** baby wipe

'**salvo, a** *ag* safe, unhurt, unharmed; (*fuori pericolo*) safe, out of danger ♦ *sm*: **in ~ salvo** ♦ *prep* (*eccetto*) except; **mettere qc in ~** to put sth in a safe place; **~ che** (*a meno che*) unless; (*eccetto che*) except (that); **~ imprevisti** barring accidents

sam'buco *sm* elder (tree)

san *ag vedi* **santo**

sa'nare *vt* to heal, cure; (*economia*) to put right

san'cire [san't∫ire] *vt* to sanction

'sandalo *sm* (*bot*) sandalwood; (*calzatura*) sandal

'**sangue** *sm* blood; **farsi cattivo ~ to** fret, get in a state; **~ freddo** (*fig*) sang-froid, calm; **a ~ freddo** in cold blood; **sangu'igno, a** *ag* blood *cpd*; (*colore*) blood-red; **sangui'nare** *vi* to bleed; **sangui'noso, a** *ag* bloody; **sangui'suga** *sf* leech

sani'tà *sf* health; (*salubrità*) healthiness; **Ministero della S~** Department of Health; **~ mentale** sanity

sani'tario, a *ag* health *cpd*; (*condizioni*) sanitary ♦ *sm* (AMM) doctor; (**impianti**) **~i** *smpl* bathroom o sanitary fittings

'sanno *vb vedi* **sapere**

'**sano, a** *ag* healthy; (*denti, costituzione*) healthy, sound; (*integro*) whole, unbroken; (*fig: politica, consigli*) sound; **~ di mente** sane; **di ~ a pianta** completely, entirely; **~ e salvo** safe and sound

sant' *ag vedi* **santo**

santifi'care *vt* to sanctify; (*feste*) to observe

santi'tà *sf* sanctity; holiness; **Sua/ Vostra ~** (*titolo di Papa*) His/Your Holiness

'**santo, a** *ag* holy; (*fig*) saintly; (*seguito da nome proprio*) saint ♦ *sm/f* saint; **la S~a Sede** the Holy See

santu'ario *sm* sanctuary

sanzio'nare [santsjo'nare] *vt* to sanction

sanzi'one [san't sjone] *sf* sanction;

(*penale, civile*) sanction, penalty

sa'pere *vt* to know; (*essere capace di*): **so nuotare** I know how to swim, I can swim ♦ *vi*: **~ di** (*aver sapore*) to taste of; (*aver odore*) to smell of ♦ *sm* knowledge; **far ~ qc a qn** to inform sb about sth, let sb know sth; **mi sa che non sia vero** I don't think that's true

sapi'enza [sa'pjentsa] *sf* wisdom

sa'pone *sm* soap; **~ da bucato** washing soap; **sapo'netta** *sf* cake o bar o tablet of soap

sa'pore *sm* taste, flavour; **sapo'rito, a** *ag* tasty

sappi'amo *vb vedi* **sapere**

saraci'nesca [sarat∫i'neska] *sf* (*serranda*) rolling shutter

sar'casmo *sm* sarcasm *no pl*; sarcastic remark

Sar'degna [sar'de ŋŋa] *sf*: **la ~** Sardinia

sar'dina *sf* sardine

'**sardo, a** *ag, sm/f* Sardinian

'**sarto, a** *sm/f* tailor/dressmaker; **sarto'ria** *sf* tailor's (shop); dressmaker's (shop); (*casa di moda*) fashion house; (*arte*) couture

'**sasso** *sm* stone; (*ciottolo*) pebble; (*masso*) rock

sas'sofono *sm* saxophone

sas'soso, a *ag* stony; pebbly

'**Satana** *sm* Satan; **sa'tanico, a, ci, che** *ag* satanic, fiendish

sa'tellite *sm, ag* satellite

'satira *sf* satire

'saturo, a *ag* saturated; (*fig*): **~ di** full of

'**sauna** *sf* sauna

Sa'voia *sf* Savoy

savoi'ardo, a *ag* of Savoy, Savoyard ♦ *sm* (*biscotto*) sponge finger

sazi'are [sat'tsjare] *vt* to satisfy, satiate; **~rsi** *vr*: **~rsi (di)** to eat one's fill (of); (*fig*): **~rsi di** to grow tired o weary of

'**sazio, a** [ˈsattsjo] *ag*: **~ (di)** sated (with), full (of); (*fig: stufo*) fed up (with), sick (of)

sba'dato, a *ag* careless, inattentive

sbadigli'are [zbadiʎ'ʎare] *vi* to yawn; **sba'diglio** *sm* yawn

sbagli'are [zbaʎ'ʎare] *vt* to make a mistake in, get wrong ♦ *vi* to make a mistake, be mistaken, be wrong; *(operare in modo non giusto)* to err; **~rsi** *vr* to make a mistake, be mistaken, be wrong; **~ la mira/strada** to miss one's aim/take the wrong road; **'sbaglio** *sm* mistake, error; *(morale)* error; **fare uno sbaglio** to make a mistake

sbal'lare *vt (merce)* to unpack ♦ *vi (nel fare un conto)* to overestimate; *(fam: gergo della droga)* to get high

sballot'tare *vt* to toss about

sbalor'dire *vt* to stun, amaze ♦ *vi* to be stunned, be amazed; **sbalordi-'tivo, a** *ag* amazing; *(prezzo)* incredible, absurd

sbal'zare [zbal'tsare] *vt* to throw, hurl ♦ *vi (balzare)* to bounce; *(saltare)* to leap, bound; **'sbalzo** *sm (spostamento improvviso)* jolt, jerk; **a sbalzi** jerkily; *(fig)* in fits and starts; **uno sbalzo di temperatura** a sudden change in temperature

sban'dare *vi (NAUT)* to list; *(AER)* to bank; *(AUT)* to skid; **~rsi** *vr (folla)* to disperse

sbandie'rare *vt (bandiera)* to wave; *(fig)* to parade, show off

sbaragli'are [zbaraʎ'ʎare] *vt (MIL)* to rout; *(in gare sportive etc)* to beat, defeat

sba'raglio [zba'raʎʎo] *sm* rout; defeat; **gettarsi allo ~** to risk everything

sbaraz'zarsi [zbarat'tsarsi] *vr*: **~ di** to get rid of, rid o.s. of

sbar'care *vt (passeggeri)* to disembark; *(merci)* to unload ♦ *vi* to disembark; **'sbarco** *sm* disembarkation; unloading; *(MIL)* landing

'sbarra *sf* bar; *(di passaggio a livello)* barrier; *(DIR)*: **presentarsi alla ~** to

appear before the court

sbarra'mento *sm (stradale)* barrier; *(diga)* dam, barrage; *(MIL)* barrage

sbar'rare *vt (strada etc)* to block, bar; *(assegno)* to cross; **~ il passo** to bar the way; **~ gli occhi** to open one's eyes wide

'sbattere *vt (porta)* to slam, bang; *(tappeti, ali, cuc)* to beat; *(urtare)* to knock, hit ♦ *vi (porta, finestra)* to bang; *(agitarsi: ali, vele etc)* to flap; **me ne sbatto!** *(fam)* I don't give a damn!; **sbat'tuto, a** *ag (viso, aria)* dejected, worn out; *(uovo)* beaten

sba'vare *vi* to dribble; *(colore)* to smear, smudge

sbia'dire *vi, (anche: ~rsi)* to fade; **~rsi** *vr* to fade, **sbia'dito, a** *ag* faded; *(fig)* colourless, dull

sbian'care *vt* to whiten; *(tessuto)* to bleach ♦ *vi (impallidire)* to grow pale o white

sbi'eco, a, chi, che *ag (storto)* squint, askew; **di ~**: **guardare qn di ~** *(fig)* to look askance at sb; **tagliare una stoffa di ~** to cut a material on the bias

sbigot'tire *vt* to dismay, stun ♦ *vi (anche: ~rsi)* to be dismayed

sbilanci'are [zbilan'tʃare] *vt* to throw off balance; **~rsi** *vr (perdere l'equilibrio)* to overbalance, lose one's balance; *(fig: compromettersi)* to compromise o.s.

sbirci'are [zbir'tʃare] *vt* to cast sidelong glances at, eye

'sbirro *(peg)* *sm* cop

sbizzar'rirsi [zbiddzar'rirsi] *vr* to indulge one's whims

sbloc'care *vt* to unblock, free; *(freno)* to release; *(prezzi, affitti)* to decontrol

sboc'care *vi*: **~ in** *(fiume)* to flow into; *(strada)* to lead into; *(persona)* to come (out) into; *(fig: concludersi)* to end (up) in

sboc'cato, a *ag (persona)* foul-mouthed; *(linguaggio)* foul

sbocci'are [zbot'tʃare] *vi (fiore)* to

'sbocco, chi sm (di fiume) mouth; (di strada) end; (di tubazione, COMM) outlet; (uscita: anche fig) way out; **siamo in una situazione senza ~chi** there's no way out of this for us

sbol'lire vi (fig) to cool down, calm down

'sbornia (fam) sf: **prendersi una ~** to get plastered

sbor'sare vt (denaro) to pay out

sbot'tare vi: **~ in una risata/per la collera** to burst out laughing/explode with anger

sbotto'nare vt to unbutton, undo

sbrai'tare vi to yell, bawl

sbra'nare vt to tear to pieces

sbrici'olare [zbritʃo'lare] vt to crumble; **~rsi** vr to crumble

sbri'gare vt to deal with; **~rsi** vr to hurry (up); **sbri'gativo, a** ag (persona, modo) quick, expeditious; (giudizio) hasty

sbrindel'lato, a ag tattered, in tatters

sbro'dolare vt to stain, dirty

'sbronza ['zbrontsa] (fam) sf (ubriaco): **prendersi una ~** to get plastered

'sbronzo, a ['zbrontso] (fam) ag plastered

sbruf'fone, a sm/f boaster

sbu'care vi to come out, emerge; (improvvisamente) to pop out (o up)

sbucci'are [zbut'tʃare] vt (arancia, patata) to peel; (piselli) to shell; **~rsi un ginocchio** to graze one's knee

sbudel'larsi vr: **~ dalle risa** to split one's sides laughing

sbuf'fare vi (persona, cavallo) to snort; (: ansimare) to puff, pant; (treno) to puff; **'sbuffo** sm (di aria, fumo, vapore) puff; **maniche a sbuffo** puff(ed) sleeves

'scabbia sf (MED) scabies sg

sca'broso, a ag (fig: difficile) difficult, thorny; (: imbarazzante) embarrassing; (: sconcio) indecent

scacchi'era [skak'kjɛra] sf chessboard

scacci'are [skat'tʃare] vt to chase away o out, drive away o out

'scacco, chi sm (pezzo del gioco) chessman; (quadretto di scacchiera) square; (fig) setback, reverse; **~chi** smpl (gioco) chess sg; **a ~chi** (tessuto) check(ed); **scacco'matto** sm checkmate

sca'dente ag shoddy, of poor quality

sca'denza [ska'dɛntsa] sf (di cambiale, contratto) maturity; (di passaporto) expiry date; (di debito etc) expiry date; **a breve/lunga ~** short-/long-term; **data di ~** expiry date

sca'dere vi (contratto etc) to expire; (debito) to fall due; (valore, forze, peso) to decline, go down

sca'fandro sm (di palombaro) diving suit; (di astronauta) space-suit

scaf'fale sm shelf; (mobile) set of shelves

'scafo sm (NAUT, AER) hull

scagio'nare [skadʒo'nare] vt to exonerate, free from blame

'scaglia ['skaʎʎa] sf (ZOOL) scale; (scheggia) chip, flake

scagli'are [skaʎ'ʎare] vt (lanciare: anche fig) to hurl, fling; **~rsi su** o **contro** to hurl o fling o.s. at; (fig) to rail at

scaglio'nare [skaʎʎo'nare] vt (pagamenti) to space out, spread out; (MIL) to echelon; (GEO) to terrace; **a scaglioni** in groups

'scala sf (a gradini etc) staircase, stairs pl; (a pioli, di corda) ladder; (MUS, GEO, di colori, valori, fig) scale; **~e** sfpl (scalinata) stairs; **su vasta ~/~ ridotta** on a large/small scale; **~ a libretto** stepladder; **~ mobile** escalator; (ECON) sliding scale; **~ mobile (dei salari)** index-linked pay scale

Scala

Milan's world-famous **la Scala** theatre first opened its doors in 1778 with a performance of Salieri's opera,

"L'Europa riconosciuta". It suffered serious damage in the bombing of Milan in 1943 and reopened in 1946 with a concert conducted by Toscanini. It also has a famous classical dance school.

sca'lare vt (ALPINISMO, muro) to climb, scale; (debito) to scale down, reduce; **sca'lata** sf scaling no pl, climbing no pl; (arrampicata, fig) climb; **scala'tore, 'trice** sm/f climber

scalda'bagno [skalda'baɲɲo] sm water-heater

scal'dare vt to heat; **~rsi** vr to warm up, heat up; (al fuoco, al sole) to warm o.s.; (fig) to get excited

scal'fire vt to scratch

scali'nata sf staircase

sca'lino sm (anche fig) step; (di scala a pioli) rung

'scalo sm (NAUT) slipway; (: porto d'approdo) port of call; (AER) stopover; **fare ~ (a)** (NAUT) to call (at), put in (at); (AER) to land (at), make a stop (at); **~ merci** (FERR) goods (BRIT) o freight yard

scalop'pina sf (CUC) escalope

scal'pello sm chisel

scal'pore sm noise, row; **far ~** (notizia) to cause a sensation o a stir

'scaltro, a ag cunning, shrewd

'scalzo, a ['skaltso] ag barefoot

scambi'are vt to exchange; (confondere): **~ qn/qc per** to take o mistake sb/sth for; **mi hanno scambiato il cappello** they've given me the wrong hat

scambi'evole ag mutual, reciprocal

'scambio sm exchange; (FERR) points pl; **fare (uno) ~** to make a swap

scampa'gnata [skampaɲ'ɲata] sf trip to the country

scam'pare vt (salvare) to rescue, save; (evitare: morte, prigione) to escape ♦ vi: **~ (a qc)** to survive (sth), escape (sth); **scamparla bella** to have a narrow

escape

'scampo sm (salvezza) escape; (ZOOL) prawn; **cercare ~ nella fuga** to seek safety in flight

'scampolo sm remnant

scana'latura sf (incavo) channel, groove

scandagli'are [skanda⋌'⋌are] vt (NAUT) to sound; (fig) to sound out; to probe

scandaliz'zare [skandaliʣ'ʣare] vt to shock, scandalize; **~rsi** vr to be shocked

'scandalo sm scandal

Scandi'navia sf: **la ~** Scandinavia; **scandi'navo, a** ag, sm/f Scandinavian

scan'dire vt (versi) to scan; (parole) to articulate, pronounce distinctly; **~ il tempo** (MUS) to beat time

scan'nare vt (animale) to butcher, slaughter; (persona) to cut o slit the throat of

'scanno sm seat, bench

scansafa'tiche [skansafa'tike] sm/f inv idler, loafer

scan'sare vt (rimuovere) to move (aside), shift; (schivare: schiaffo) to dodge; (sfuggire) to avoid; **~rsi** vr to move aside

scan'sia sf shelves pl; (per libri) bookcase

'scanso sm: **a ~ di** in order to avoid, as a precaution against

scanti'nato sm basement

scanto'nare vi to turn the corner; (svignarsela) to sneak off

scapacci'one [skapat'tʃone] sm clout

scapes'trato, a ag dissolute

sca'pito sm: **a ~ di** to the detriment of

'scapola sf shoulder blade

'scapolo sm bachelor

scappa'mento sm (AUT) exhaust

scap'pare vi (fuggire) to escape; (andare via in fretta) to rush off; **lasciarsi ~ un'occasione** to let an opportunity go by; **~ di prigione** to escape from prison; **~ di mano** (*oggetto*) to slip out of one's hands; **~ di mente a qn** to slip sb's mind; **mi scappò detto** I let it slip; **scap'pata** *sf* quick visit o call; **scappa'tella** *sf* escapade; **scappa'toia** *sf* way out

scara'beo *sm* beetle

scarabocchi'are [skarabok'kjare] *vt* to scribble, scrawl; **scara'bocchio** *sm* scribble, scrawl

scara'faggio |skara'faddʒo| *sm* cockroach

scaraven'tare *vt* to fling, hurl

scarce'rare [skartʃe'rare] *vt* to release (from prison)

scardi'nare *vt*: **~ una porta** to take a door off its hinges

'scarica, che *sf* (*di più armi*) volley of shots; (*di sassi, pugni*) hail, shower; (*ELETTR*) discharge; **~ di mitra** burst of machine-gun fire

scari'care *vt* (*merci, camion etc*) to unload; (*passeggeri*) to set down, put off; (*arma*) to unload; (: *sparare, ELETTR*) to discharge; (*sog: corso d'acqua*) to empty, pour; (*fig: liberare da un peso*) to unburden, relieve; **~rsi** *vr* (*orologio*) to run o wind down; (*batteria, accumulatore*) to go flat o dead; (*fig: rilassarsi*) to unwind; (: *sfogarsi*) to let off steam; **scarica'tore** *sm* (*di porto*) docker

'scarico, a, chi, che *ag* unloaded; (*orologio*) run down; (*batteria*) dead, flat ♦ *sm* (*di merci, materiali*) unloading; (*di immondizie*) dumping, tipping (*BRIT*); (*TECN: deflusso*) draining; (: *dispositivo*) drain; (*AUT*) exhaust

scarlat'tina *sf* scarlet fever

scar'latto, a *ag* scarlet

'scarno, a *ag* thin, bony

'scarpa *sf* shoe; **~e da ginnastica/ tennis** gym/tennis shoes

scar'pata *sf* escarpment

scar'pone *sm* boot; **~i da sci** ski-boots

scarseggi'are [skarsed'dʒare] *vi* to be scarce; **~ di** to be short of, lack

scar'sezza [skar'settsa] *sf* scarcity, lack

'scarso, a *ag* (*insufficiente*) insufficient, meagre; (*povero: annata*) poor, lean; (*INS: voto*) poor; **~ di** lacking in; **3 chili ~i** just under 3 kilos, barely 3 kilos

scarta'mento *sm* (*FERR*) gauge; **~ normale/ridotto** standard/narrow gauge

scar'tare *vt* (*pacco*) to unwrap; (*idea*) to reject; (*MIL*) to declare unfit for military service; (*carte da gioco*) to discard; (*CALCIO*) to dodge (past) ♦ *vi* to swerve

'scarto *sm* (*cosa scartata, anche COMM*) reject; (*di veicolo*) swerve; (*differenza*) gap, difference

scassi'nare *vt* to break, force

'scasso *sm* *vedi* **furto**

scate'nare *vt* (*fig*) to incite, stir up; **~rsi** *vr* (*temporale*) to break; (*rivolta*) to break out; (*persona: infuriarsi*) to rage

'scatola *sf* box; (*di latta*) tin (*BRIT*), can; **cibi in ~** = tinned (*BRIT*) o canned foods; **~ cranica** cranium

scat'tare *vt* (*fotografia*) to take ♦ *vi* (*congegno, molla etc*) to be released; (*balzare*) to spring up; (*SPORT*) to put on a spurt; (*fig: per l'ira*) to fly into a rage; **~ in piedi** to spring to one's feet

'scatto *sm* (*dispositivo*) release; (: *di arma da fuoco*) trigger mechanism; (*rumore*) click; (*balzo*) jump, start; (*SPORT*) spurt; (*fig: di ira etc*) fit; (: *di stipendio*) increment; **di ~** suddenly

scatu'rire *vi* to gush, spring

scaval'care *vt* (*ostacolo*) to pass (o climb) over; (*fig*) to get ahead of, overtake

sca'vare *vt* (*terreno*) to dig; (*legno*) to hollow out; (*pozzo, galleria*) to bore; (*città sepolta etc*) to excavate

'scavo *sm* excavating *no pl*; excavation

'scegliere |'ʃeʎʎere| *vt* to choose, select

sce'icco, chi [ʃe'ikko] *sm* sheik

scelle'rato, a [ʃelle'rato] *ag* wicked, evil

scel'lino [ʃel'lino] *sm* shilling

'**scelta** ['ʃelta] *sf* choice; selection; **di prima ~** top grade o quality; **frutta o formaggi a ~** choice of fruit or cheese

'**scelto, a** ['ʃelto] *pp di* **scegliere ♦** *ag* (*gruppo*) carefully selected; (*frutta, verdura*) choice, top quality; (MIL: *specializzato*) crack *cpd*, highly skilled

sce'mare [ʃe'mare] *vt, vi* to diminish

'**scemo, a** ['ʃemo] *ag* stupid, silly

scempio ['ʃempjo] *sm* slaughter, massacre; (*fig*) ruin; **far ~ di** (*fig*) to play havoc with, ruin

'**scena** ['ʃena] *sf* (*gen*) scene; (*palcoscenico*) stage; **le ~e** (*fig: teatro*) the stage; **fare una ~** to make a scene; **andare in ~** to be staged o put on o performed; **mettere in ~** to stage

sce'nario [ʃe'narjo] *sm* scenery; (*di film*) scenario

sce'nata [ʃe'nata] *sf* row, scene

'**scendere** ['ʃendere] *vi* to go o (*o come*) down; (*strada, sole*) to go down; (*notte*) to fall; (*passeggero: fermarsi*) to get out, alight; (*fig: temperatura, prezzi*) to go o come down, fall, drop **♦** *vt* (*scale, pendio*) to go o (*o come*) down; **~ dalle scale** to go o (*o come*) down the stairs; **~ dal treno** to get off o out of the train; **~ dalla macchina** to get out of the car; **~ da cavallo** to dismount, get off one's horse

'**scenico, a, ci, che** ['ʃeniko] *ag* stage *cpd*, scenic

scervel'lato, a [ʃervel'lato] *ag* feather-brained, scatterbrained

'**sceso, a** ['ʃeso] *pp di* **scendere**

'**scettico, a, ci, che** ['ʃettiko] *ag* sceptical

'**scettro** ['ʃettro] *sm* sceptre

'**scheda** ['skeda] *sf* (*index*) card; **~ elettorale** ballot paper; **~ telefonica** phone card; **sche'dare** *vt* (*dati*) to file; (*libri*) to catalogue; (*registrare: anche POLIZIA*) to put on one's files; **sche'dario** *sm* file; (*mobile*)

filing cabinet

'**scheggia, ge** ['skeddʒa] *sf* splinter, sliver

'**scheletro** ['skeletro] *sm* skeleton

'**schema, i** ['skema] *sm* (*diagramma*) diagram, sketch; (*progetto, abbozzo*) outline, plan

'**scherma** ['skerma] *sf* fencing

scher'maglia [sker'maʎʎa] *sf* (*fig*) skirmish

'**schermo** ['skermo] *sm* shield, screen; (*CINEMA, TV*) screen

scher'nire [sker'nire] *vt* to mock, sneer at; '**scherno** *sm* mockery, derision

scher'zare [sker'tsare] *vi* to joke

'**scherzo** ['skertso] *sm* joke; (*tiro*) trick; (*MUS*) scherzo; **è uno ~!** (*una cosa facile*) it's child's play!, it's easy!; **per ~** in jest; for a joke o a laugh; **fare un brutto ~ a qn** to play a nasty trick on sb; **scher'zoso, a** *ag* (*tono, gesto*) playful; (*osservazione*) facetious; **è un tipo scherzoso** he likes a joke

schiaccia'noci [skjattʃa'notʃi] *sm inv* nutcracker

schiacci'are [skjat'tʃare] *vt* (*dito*) to crush; (*noci*) to crack; **~ un pisolino** to have a nap

schiaffeggi'are [skjaffeddʒ'dʒare] *vt* to slap

schi'affo ['skjaffo] *sm* slap

schiamaz'zare [skjamat'tsare] *vi* to squawk, cackle

schian'tare [skjan'tare] *vt* to break, tear apart; **~rsi** *vr* to break (up), shatter; **schi'anto** *sm* (*rumore*) crash; tearing sound; **è uno schianto!** (*fam*) it's (o he's o she's) terrific!; **di schianto** all of a sudden

schia'rire [skja'rire] *vt* to lighten, make lighter **♦** *vi* (*anche: ~rsi*) to grow lighter; (*tornar sereno*) to clear, brighten up; **~rsi la voce** to clear one's throat

schiavitù [skjavi'tu] *sf* slavery

schi'avo, a ['skjavo] *sm/f* slave

schi'ena ['skjɛna] *sf* (ANAT) back; **schie'nale** *sm* (*di sedia*) back

schi'era ['skjɛra] *sf* (MIL) rank; (*gruppo*) group, band

schiera'mento [skjera'mento] *sm* (MIL, SPORT) formation; (*fig*) alliance

schie'rare [skje'rare] *vt* (*esercito*) to line up, draw up, marshal; **~rsi** *vr* to line up; (*fig*): **~rsi con o dalla parte di/contro qn** to side with/oppose sb

schi'etto, a ['skjɛtto] *ag* (*puro*) pure; (*fig*) frank, straightforward; sincere

'schifo ['skifo] *sm* disgust; **fare ~** (*essere fatto male, dare pessimi risultati*) to be awful; **mi fa ~** it makes me sick, it's disgusting; **quel libro è uno ~** that book's rotten; **schi'foso, a** *ag* disgusting, revolting; (*molto scadente*) rotten, lousy

schioc'care [skjok'kare] *vt* (*frusta*) to crack; (*dita*) to snap; (*lingua*) to click; **~ le labbra** to smack one's lips

schi'udere ['skjudere] *vt* to open; **~rsi** *vr* to open

schi'uma ['skjuma] *sf* foam; (*di sapone*) lather; (*di latte*) froth; (*fig: feccia*) scum; **schiu'mare** *vt* to skim ♦ *vi* to foam

schi'uso, a ['skjuso] *pp di* **schiudere**

schi'vare [ski'vare] *vt* to dodge, avoid

'schivo, a ['skivo] *ag* (*ritroso*) standoffish, reserved; (*timido*) shy

schiz'zare [skit'tsare] *vt* (*spruzzare*) to spurt, squirt; (*sporcare*) to splash, spatter; (*fig: abbozzare*) to sketch ♦ *vi* to spurt, squirt; (*saltar fuori*) to dart up (*o off etc*)

schizzi'noso, a [skittsi'noso] *ag* fussy, finicky

'schizzo ['skittso] *sm* (*di liquido*) spurt; splash, spatter; (*abbozzo*) sketch

sci [ʃi] *sm* (*attrezzo*) ski; (*attività*) skiing; **~ nautico** water-skiing

'scia [ʃia] (*pl* **'scie**) *sf* (*di imbarcazione*) wake; (*di profumo*) trail

scià [ʃa] *sm inv* shah

sci'abola ['ʃabola] *sf* sabre

scia'callo [ʃa'kallo] *sm* jackal

sciac'quare [ʃak'kware] *vt* to rinse

scia'gura [ʃa'gura] *sf* disaster, calamity; misfortune; **sciagu'rato, a** *ag* unfortunate; (*malvagio*) wicked

scialac'quare [ʃalak'kware] *vt* to squander

scia'lare [ʃa'lare] *vi* to lead a life of luxury

sci'albo, a ['ʃalbo] *ag* pale, dull; (*fig*) dull, colourless

scia'luppa [ʃa'luppa] *sf* (*anche: ~ di salvataggio*) lifeboat

sci'ame ['ʃame] *sm* swarm

scian'cato, a [ʃan'kato] *ag* lame

sci'are [ʃi'are] *vi* to ski

sci'arpa ['ʃarpa] *sf* scarf; (*fascia*) sash

scia'tore, 'trice [ʃa'tore] *sm/f* skier

sci'atto, a ['ʃatto] *ag* (*persona*) slovenly, unkempt

scien'tifico, a, ci, che [ʃen'tifiko] *ag* scientific

sci'enza ['ʃɛntsa] *sf* science; (*sapere*) knowledge; **~e** *sfpl* (INS) science *sg*; **~e naturali** natural sciences; **scienzi'ato, a** *sm/f* scientist

sci'mmia ['ʃimmja] *sf* monkey; **scimmiot'tare** *vt* to ape, mimic

scimpanzé [ʃimpan'tse] *sm inv* chimpanzee

scimu'nito, a [ʃimu'nito] *ag* silly, idiotic

'scindere ['ʃindere] *vt* to split (up); **~rsi** *vr* to split (up)

scin'tilla [ʃin'tilla] *sf* spark; **scintil'lare** *vi* to sparkle; (*acqua, occhi*) to sparkle

scioc'chezza [ʃok'kettsa] *sf* stupidity *no pl*; stupid *o* foolish thing; **dire ~e** to talk nonsense

sci'occo, a, chi, che ['ʃɔkko] *ag* stupid, foolish

sci'ogliere ['ʃɔʎʎere] *vt* (*nodo*) to untie; (*capelli*) to loosen; (*persona, animale*) to untie, release; (*fig: persona*): **~ da** to release from; (*neve*) to melt; (*nell'acqua: zucchero etc*) to dissolve; (*fig: mistero*) to solve; (*porre fine a: contratto*) to cancel; (*: società, matrimonio*) to dissolve; (*: riunione*) to bring to an end; **~rsi** *vr* to loosen, come untied; to melt; to dissolve; (*assemblea etc*) to break up; **~ i muscoli** to limber up

sciol'tezza [ʃol'tettsa] *sf* agility; suppleness; ease

sci'olto, a [ˈʃɔlto] *pp di* **sciogliere** ♦ *ag* loose; (*agile*) agile, nimble; supple; (*disinvolto*) free and easy; **versi ~i** (*POESIA*) blank verse

sciope'rante [ʃope'rante] *sm/f* striker

sciope'rare [ʃope'rare] *vi* to strike, go on strike

sci'opero [ˈʃɔpero] *sm* strike; **fare ~** to strike; **~ bianco** work-to-rule (*BRIT*), slowdown (*US*); **~ selvaggio** wildcat strike; **~ a singhiozzo** on-off strike

scip'pare [ʃip'pare] *vt*: **~ qn** to snatch sb's bag; **mi hanno scippato** they snatched my bag

sci'rocco [ʃi'rɔkko] *sm* sirocco

sci'roppo [ʃi'rɔppo] *sm* syrup

'scisma, i [ˈʃizma] *sm* (*REL*) schism

scissi'one [ʃis'sjone] *sf* (*anche fig*) split, division; (*FISICA*) fission

'scisso, a [ˈʃisso] *pp di* **scindere**

sciu'pare [ʃu'pare] *vt* (*abito, libro, appetito*) to spoil, ruin; (*tempo, denaro*) to waste; **~rsi** *vr* to get spoilt o ruined; (*rovinarsi la salute*) to ruin one's health

scivo'lare [ʃivo'lare] *vi* to slide o glide along; (*involontariamente*) to slip, slide; **'scivolo** *sm* slide; (*TECN*) chute; **scivo'loso, a** *ag* slippery

scle'rosi *sf* sclerosis

scoc'care *vt* (*freccia*) to shoot ♦ *vi* (*guizzare*) to shoot up; (*battere: ora*) to strike

scocci'are [skot'tʃare] (*fam*) *vt* to bother, annoy; **~rsi** *vr* to be bothered o annoyed

sco'della *sf* bowl

scodinzo'lare [skodintso'lare] *vi* to

wag its tail

scogli'era [skoʎˈʎera] *sf* reef; cliff

'scoglio [ˈskɔʎʎo] *sm* (*al mare*) rock

scoi'attolo *sm* squirrel

scolapi'atti *sm inv* drainer (*for plates*)

sco'lare *ag*: **età ~** school age ♦ *vt* to drain ♦ *vi* to drip

scola'resca *sf* schoolchildren *pl*, pupils *pl*

sco'laro, a *sm/f* pupil, schoolboy/girl

sco'lastico, a, ci, che *ag* school *cpd*; scholastic

scol'lare *vt* (*staccare*) to unstick; **~rsi** *vr* to come unstuck

scolla'tura *sf* neckline

'scolo *sm* drainage

scolo'rire *vt* to fade; to discolour ♦ *vi* (*anche: ~rsi*) to fade; to become discoloured; (*impallidire*) to turn pale

scol'pire *vt* to carve, sculpt

scombi'nare *vt* to mess up, upset

scombus'solare *vt* to upset

scom'messa *sf* bet, wager

scom'messo, a *pp di* **scommettere**

scom'mettere *vt, vi* to bet

scomo'dare *vt* to trouble, bother; to disturb; **~rsi** *vr* to put o.s. out; **~rsi a fare** to go to the bother o trouble of doing

'scomodo, a *ag* uncomfortable; (*sistemazione, posto*) awkward, inconvenient

scompa'rire *vi* (*sparire*) to disappear, vanish; (*fig*) to be insignificant; **scom'parsa** *sf* disappearance; **scom'parso, a** *pp di* **scomparire**

scomparti'mento *sm* compartment

scom'parto *sm* compartment, division

scompigli'are [skompiʎˈʎare] *vt* (*cassetto, capelli*) to mess up, disarrange; (*fig: piani*) to upset; **scom'piglio** *sm* mess, confusion

scom'porre *vt* (*parola, numero*) to break up; (*CHIM*) to decompose; **scomporsi** *vr* (*fig*) to get upset, lose one's composure; **scom'posto, a** *pp di* **scomporre** ♦ *ag* (*gesto*) unseemly;

(capelli) ruffled, dishevelled

sco'munica sf excommunication

scomuni'care vt to excommunicate

sconcer'tare [skontʃer'tare] vt to disconcert, bewilder

'sconcio, a, ci, ce ['skontʃo] ag (osceno) indecent, obscene ♦ sm disgrace

sconfes'sare vt to renounce, disavow; to repudiate

scon'figgere [skon'fiddʒere] vt to defeat, overcome

sconfi'nare vi to cross the border; (in proprietà privata) to trespass; (fig): ~ **da** to stray o digress from; **sconfi'nato, a** ag boundless, unlimited

scon'fitta sf defeat

scon'fitto, a pp di **sconfiggere**

scon'forto sm despondency

scongiu'rare [skondʒu'rare] vt (implorare) to entreat, beseech, implore; (eludere: pericolo) to ward off, avert; **scongi'uro** sm entreaty; (esorcismo) exorcism; **fare gli scongiuri** to touch wood (BRIT), knock on wood (US)

scon'nesso, a ag incoherent

sconosci'uto, a [skono'ʃuto] ag unknown; new, strange ♦ sm/f stranger; unknown person

sconquas'sare vt to shatter, smash

sconside'rato, a ag thoughtless, rash

sconsigli'are [skonsiʎ'ʎare] vt: ~ **qc a qn** to advise sb against sth; ~ **qn dal fare qc** to advise sb not to do o against doing sth

sconso'lato, a ag inconsolable; desolate

scon'tare vt (COMM: detrarre) to deduct; (: debito) to pay off; (: cambiale) to discount; (pena) to serve; (colpa, errori) to pay for, suffer for

scon'tato, a ag (previsto) foreseen, taken for granted; **dare per ~ che** to take it for granted that

scon'tento, a ag: ~ **(di)** dissatisfied

(with) ♦ sm dissatisfaction

'sconto sm discount; **fare uno ~** to give a discount

scon'trarsi vr (treni etc) to crash, collide; (venire ad uno scontro, fig) to clash; ~ **con** to crash into, collide with

scon'trino sm ticket

'scontro sm clash, encounter; crash, collision

scon'troso, a ag sullen, surly; (permaloso) touchy

sconveni'ente ag unseemly, improper

scon'volgere [skon'vɔldʒere] vt to throw into confusion, upset; (turbare) to shake, disturb, upset; **scon'volto, a** pp di **sconvolgere**

'scopa sf broom; (CARTE) Italian card game; **sco'pare** vt to sweep

sco'perta sf discovery

sco'perto, a pp di **scoprire** ♦ ag uncovered; (capo) uncovered, bare; (macchina) open; (MIL) exposed, without cover; (conto) overdrawn

'scopo sm aim, purpose; **a che ~?** what for?

scoppi'are vi (spaccarsi) to burst; (esplodere) to explode; (fig) to break out; ~ **in pianto** o **a piangere** to burst out crying; ~ **dalle risa** o **dal ridere** to split one's sides laughing

scoppiet'tare vi to crackle

'scoppio sm explosion; (di tuono, arma etc) crash, bang; (fig: di risa, ira) fit, outburst; (: di guerra) outbreak; **a ~ ritardato** delayed-action

sco'prire vt to discover; (liberare da ciò che copre) to uncover; (: monumento) to unveil; **~rsi** vr to put on lighter clothes; (fig) to give o.s. away

scoraggi'are [skorad'dʒare] vt to discourage; **~rsi** vr to become discouraged, lose heart

scorcia'toia [skortʃa'toja] sf short cut

'scorcio ['skortʃo] sm (ARTE) foreshortening; (di secolo, periodo) end, close

scor'dare vt to forget; **~rsi** vr: **~rsi di**

qc/di fare to forget sth/to do

'scorgere ['skɔrdʒere] vt to make out, distinguish, see

sco'ria sf (di metalli) slag; (vulcanica) scoria; **~e radioattive** (FISICA) radioactive waste sg

'scorno sm ignominy, disgrace

scorpacci'ata [skorpat'tʃata] sf: **fare una ~ (di)** to stuff o.s. (with), eat one's fill (of)

scorpi'one sm scorpion; (dello zodiaco): **S~** Scorpio

scorraz'zare [skorrat'tsare] vi to run about

'scorrere vt (giornale, lettera) to run o skim through ♦ vi (liquido, fiume) to run, flow; (fune) to run; (cassetto, porta) to slide easily; (tempo) to pass (by)

scor'retto, a ag incorrect; (sgarbato) impolite; (sconveniente) improper

scor'revole ag (porta) sliding; (fig: stile) fluent, flowing

scorri'banda sf (MIL) raid; (escursione) trip, excursion

'scorsa sf quick look, glance

'scorso, a pp di **scorrere** ♦ ag last

scor'soio, a ag: **nodo ~** noose

'scorta sf (di personalità, convoglio) escort; (provvista) supply, stock; **scor'tare** vt to escort

scor'tese ag discourteous, rude; **scorte'sia** sf discourtesy, rudeness; (azione) discourtesy

scorti'care vt to skin

'scorto, a pp di **scorgere**

'scorza ['skɔrdza] sf (di albero) bark; (di agrumi) peel, skin

sco'sceso, a [skoʃ'feso] ag steep

'scossa sf jerk, jolt, shake; (ELETTR, fig) shock

'scosso, a pp di **scuotere** ♦ ag (turbato) shaken, upset

scos'tante ag (fig) off-putting (BRIT), unpleasant

scos'tare vt to move (away), shift; **~rsi** vr to move away

scostu'mato, a ag immoral, dissolute

scot'tare vt (ustionare) to burn; (: con liquido bollente) to scald ♦ vi to burn; (caffè) to be too hot; **scotta'tura** sf burn; scald

'scotto, a ag overcooked ♦ sm (fig): **pagare lo ~ (di)** to pay the penalty (for)

sco'vare vt to drive out, flush out; (fig) to discover

'Scozia ['skɔttsia] sf: **la ~** Scotland; **scoz'zese** ag Scottish ♦ sm/f Scot

scredi'tare vt to discredit

screpo'lare vt to crack; **~rsi** vr to crack; **screpola'tura** sf cracking no pl; crack

screzi'ato, a [skret'tsjato] ag streaked

'screzio ['skrettsjo] sm disagreement

scricchio'lare [skrikkjo'lare] vi to creak, squeak

scricci'olo [skrit'tʃɔlo] sm wren

'scrigno ['skrinno] sm casket

scrimina'tura sf parting

'scritta sf inscription

'scritto, a pp di **scrivere** ♦ ag written ♦ sm writing; (lettera) letter, note; **~i** smpl (letterari etc) writing sg

scrit'toio sm writing desk

scrit'tore, 'trice sm/f writer

scrit'tura sf writing; (COMM) entry; (contratto) contract; (REL): **la Sacra S~** the Scriptures pl; **~e** sfpl (COMM) accounts, books

scrittu'rare vt (TEATRO, CINEMA) to sign up, engage; (COMM) to enter

scriva'nia sf desk

'scrivere vt to write; **come si scrive?** how is it spelt?, how do you write it?

scroc'cone sm, sf/m scrounger

'scrofa sf (ZOOL) sow

scrol'lare vt to shake; **~rsi** vr (anche fig) to give o.s. a shake; **~ le spalle/il capo** to shrug one's shoulders/shake one's head

scrosci'are [skroʃ'fare] vi (pioggia) to pour down, pelt down; (torrente, fig: applausi) to thunder, roar; **'scroscio**

sm pelting; thunder, roar; *(di applausi)* burst

scros'tare *vt (intonaco)* to scrape off, strip; **~rsi** *vr* to peel off, flake off

'scrupolo *sm* scruple; *(meticolosità)* care, conscientiousness

scru'tare *vt* to scrutinize; *(intenzioni, causa)* to examine, scrutinize

scruti'nare *vt (voti)* to count;

scru'tinio *sm (votazione)* ballot; *(insieme delle operazioni)* poll; *(INS) (meeting for)* assignment of marks at end of a term or year

scu'cire [sku'tʃire] *vt (orlo etc)* to unpick, undo

scude'ria *sf* stable

scu'detto *sm (SPORT)* championship shield; *(distintivo)* badge

'scudo *sm* shield

scul'tore, 'trice *sm/f* sculptor

scul'tura *sf* sculpture

scu'ola *sf* school; **~ elementare/ materna/media** primary *(BRIT)* o grade *(US)*/nursery/secondary *(BRIT)* o high *(US)* school; **~ guida** driving school; **~ dell'obbligo** compulsory education; **~e serali** evening classes, night school *sg*; **~ tecnica** technical college

scu'otere *vt* to shake; **~rsi** *vr* to jump, be startled; *(fig: muoversi)* to rouse o.s., stir o.s.; *(: turbarsi)* to be shaken

'scure *sf* axe

'scuro, a *ag* dark; *(fig: espressione)* grim ♦ *sm* darkness; dark colour; *(imposta)* (window) shutter; **verde/ rosso** etc **~** dark green/red etc

scur'rile *ag* scurrilous

'scusa *sf* apology; *(pretesto)* excuse; **chiedere ~ a qn (per)** to apologize to sb (for); **chiedo ~** I'm sorry; *(disturbando etc)* excuse me

scu'sare *vt* to excuse; **~rsi** *vr*: **~rsi (di)** to apologize (for); **(mi) scusi** I'm sorry; *(per richiamare l'attenzione)* excuse me

sde'gnato, a [zdeɲ'ɲato] *ag*

indignant, angry

'sdegno [zdeɲɲo] *sm* scorn, disdain; **sde'gnoso, a** *ag* scornful, disdainful

sdoga'nare *vt (merci)* to clear through customs

sdolci'nato, a [zdoltʃi'nato] *ag* mawkish, oversentimental

sdrai'arsi *vr* to stretch out, lie down

'sdraio *sm*: **sedia a ~** deck chair

sdruccio'levole [zdruttʃo'levole] *ag* slippery

PAROLA CHIAVE

se *pron vedi* **si**

♦ *cong* **1** *(condizionale, ipotetica)* if; **~ nevica non vengo** I won't come if it snows; **sarei rimasto o me l'avessero chiesto** I would have stayed if they'd asked me; **non puoi fare altro ~ non telefonare** all you can do is phone; **~ mai** if, if ever; **siamo noi ~ mai che ti siamo grati** it is we who should be grateful to you; **~ no** *(altrimenti)* or (else), otherwise

2 *(in frasi dubitative, interrogative indirette)* if, whether; **non so ~ scrivere o telefonare** I don't know whether o if I should write or phone

sé *pron (gen)* oneself; *(esso, essa, lui, lei, loro)* itself; himself; herself; themselves; **~ stesso(a)** *pron* oneself; itself; himself; herself; **~ stessi(e)** *pron pl* themselves

seb'bene *cong* although, though

sec. *abbr (= secolo)* c

'secca *sf (del mare)* shallows *pl*; *vedi anche* **secco**

sec'care *vt* to dry; *(prosciugare)* to dry up; *(fig: importunare)* to annoy, bother ♦ *vi* to dry; to dry up; **~rsi** *vr* to dry; to dry up; *(fig)* to grow annoyed;

secca'tura *sf (fig)* bother *no pl*, trouble *no pl*

secchi'ello *sm* bucket; **~ del ghiaccio** ice bucket

'secchio ['sekkjo] *sm* bucket, pail

'secco, a, chi, che ag dry; (fichi, pesce) dried; (foglie, ramo) withered; (magro: persona) thin, skinny; (fig: risposta, modo di fare) curt, abrupt; (: colpo) clean, sharp ♦ sm (siccità) drought; **restarci ~** (fig: morire sul colpo) to drop dead; **mettere in ~** (barca) to beach; **rimanere a ~** (fig) to be left in the lurch

seco'lare ag age-old, centuries-old; (laico, mondano) secular

'secolo sm century; (epoca) age

se'conda sf (AUT) second (gear); **viaggiare in ~** to travel second-class; vedi anche **secondo**

secon'dario, a ag secondary

se'condo, a ag second ♦ sm second; (di pranzo) main course ♦ prep according to; (nel modo prescritto) in accordance with; **~ me** in my opinion, to my mind; **di ~a classe** second-class; **di ~a mano** second-hand; **a ~a di** according to; in accordance with

'sedano sm celery

seda'tivo, a ag sedative

'sede sf seat; (di ditta) head office; (di organizzazione) headquarters pl; **~ sociale** registered office

seden'tario, a ag sedentary

se'dere vi to sit, be seated; **~rsi** vr to sit down ♦ sm (deretano) behind, bottom

'sedia sf chair

sedi'cente [sedi'tʃɛnte] ag self-styled

'sedici ['seditʃi] num sixteen

se'dile sm seat; (panchina) bench

se'dotto, a pp di **sedurre**

sedu'cente [sedu'tʃɛnte] ag seductive; (proposta) very attractive

se'durre vt to seduce

se'duta sf session, sitting; (riunione) meeting; **~ spiritica** séance; **~ stante** (fig) immediately

seduzi'one [sedut'tsjone] sf seduction; (fascino) charm, appeal

'sega, ghe sf saw

'segale sf rye

se'gare vt to saw; (recidere) to saw off; **sega'tura** sf (residuo) sawdust

'seggio ['sɛddʒo] sm seat; **~ elettorale** polling station

seggi'ola ['sɛddʒola] sf chair; **seggio'lino** sm seat; (per bambini) child's chair; **seggio'lone** sm (per bambini) highchair

seggio'via [sɛddʒo'via] sf chairlift

seghe'ria [sege'ria] sf sawmill

segna'lare [senna'lare] vt (manovra etc) to signal; to indicate; (annunciare) to announce; to report; (fig: far conoscere) to point out; (: persona) to single out; **~rsi** vr (distinguersi) to distinguish o.s.

se'gnale [sen'nale] sm signal; (cartello): **~ stradale** road sign; **~ d'allarme** alarm; (FERR) communication cord; **~ orario** (RADIO) time signal; **segna'letica** sf signalling, signposting; **segnaletica stradale** road signs pl

segna'libro [senna'libro] sm bookmark

se'gnare [sen'nare] vt to mark; (prendere nota) to note; (indicare) to indicate, mark; (SPORT: goal) to score; **~rsi** vr (REL) to make the sign of the cross, cross o.s.

'segno ['senno] sm sign; (impronta, contrassegno) mark; (limite) limit, bounds pl; (bersaglio) target; **fare ~ di sì/no** to nod (one's head)/shake one's head; **fare ~ a qn di fermarsi** to motion (to) sb to stop; **cogliere** o **colpire nel ~** (fig) to hit the mark

segre'gare vt to segregate, isolate; **segregazi'one** sf segregation

segre'tario, a sm/f secretary; **~ comunale** town clerk; **S~ di Stato** Secretary of State

segrete'ria sf (di ditta, scuola) (secretary's) office; (d'organizzazione internazionale) secretariat; (POL etc: carica) office of Secretary; **~ telefonica** answering service

segre'tezza [segre'tettsa] sf secrecy

se'greto, a *ag* secret ♦ *sm* secret; secrecy *no pl*; **in ~** in secret, secretly

segu'ace [se'gwatʃe] *sm/f* follower, disciple

segu'ente *ag* following, next

segu'ire *vt* to follow; (*frequentare: corso*) to attend ♦ *vi* to follow; (*continuare: testo*) to continue

segui'tare *vt* to continue, carry on with ♦ *vi* to continue, carry on

'seguito *sm* (*scorta*) suite, retinue; (*discepoli*) followers *pl*; (*favore*) following; (*continuazione*) continuation; (*conseguenza*) result; **di ~** at a stretch, on end; **in ~** later on; **in ~ a, a ~ di** following; (*a causa di*) as a result of, owing to

'sei *vb vedi* **essere** ♦ *num* six

sei'cento [sei'tʃɛnto] *num* six hundred ♦ *sm*: **il S~** the seventeenth century

selci'ato [sel'tʃato] *sm* cobbled surface

selezio'nare [selettsjo'nare] *vt* to select

selezi'one [selet'tsjone] *sf* selection

'sella *sf* saddle; **sel'lare** *vt* to saddle

selvag'gina [selvad'dʒina] *sf* (*animali*) game

sel'vaggio, a, gi, ge [sel'vaddʒo] *ag* wild; (*tribù*) savage, uncivilized; (*fig*) savage, brutal ♦ *sm/f* savage

sel'vatico, a, ci, che *ag* wild

se'maforo *sm* (*AUT*) traffic lights *pl*

sem'brare *vi* to seem ♦ *vb impers*: **sembra che** it seems that; **mi sembra che** it seems to me that; I think (that); **~ di essere** to seem to be

'seme *sm* seed; (*sperma*) semen; (*CARTE*) suit

se'mestre *sm* half-year, six-month period

'semi... *prefisso* semi...; **semi'cerchio** *sm* semicircle; **semifi'nale** *sf* semifinal; **semi'freddo** *sm* ice-cream cake

'semina *sf* (*AGR*) sowing

semi'nare *vt* to sow

semi'nario *sm* seminar; (*REL*) seminary

seminter'rato *sm* basement; (*appartamento*) basement flat

sem'mai *= se mai*; *vedi* **se**

'semola *sf*: **~ di grano duro** durum wheat

semo'lino *sm* semolina

'semplice ['sɛmplitʃe] *ag* simple; (*di un solo elemento*) single; **semplice'mente** *av* simply; **semplicità** *sf* simplicity

'sempre *av* always; (*ancora*) still; **posso ~ tentare** I can always o still try; **da ~** always; **per ~** forever; **una volta per ~** once and for all; **~ che** provided (that); **~ più** more and more; **~ meno** less and less

sempre'verde *ag, sm o f* (*BOT*) evergreen

'senape *sf* (*CUC*) mustard

se'nato *sm* senate; **sena'tore, 'trice** *sm/f* senator

'senno *sm* judgment, (common) sense; **col ~ di poi** with hindsight

sennò *av = se no*; *vedi* **se**

'seno *sm* (*ANAT: petto, mammella*) breast; (*: grembo, fig*) womb; (*: cavità*) sinus

sen'sato, a *ag* sensible

sensazio'nale [sensattsjo'nale] *ag* sensational

sensazi'one [sensat'tsjone] *sf* feeling, sensation; **avere la ~ che** to have a feeling that; **fare ~** to cause a sensation, create a stir

sen'sibile *ag* sensitive; (*ai sensi*) perceptible; (*rilevante, notevole*) appreciable, noticeable; **~ a** sensitive to; **sensibilità** *sf* sensitivity

'senso *sm* (*FISIOL, istinto*) sense; (*impressione, sensazione*) feeling, sensation; (*significato*) meaning, sense; (*direzione*) direction; **~i** *smpl* (*coscienza*) consciousness *sg*; (*sensualità*) senses; **ciò non ha ~** that doesn't make sense; **fare ~ a** (*ripugnare*) to disgust, repel; **~ comune** common sense; **in ~ orario/antiorario** clockwise/

anticlockwise; **a ~ unico** (*strada*) one-way

sensu'ale *ag* sensual; sensuous; **sensualità** *sf* sensuality; sensuousness

sen'tenza [sen'tentsa] *sf* (*DIR*) sentence; (*massima*) maxim; **sentenzi'are** *vi* (*DIR*) to pass judgment

senti'ero *sm* path

sentimen'tale *ag* sentimental; (*vita, avventura*) love *cpd*

senti'mento *sm* feeling

senti'nella *sf* sentry

sen'tire *vt* (*percepire al tatto, fig*) to feel; (*udire*) to hear; (*ascoltare*) to listen to; (*odore*) to smell; (*avvertire con il gusto, assaggiare*) to taste ♦ *vi*: **~ di** (*avere sapore*) to taste of; (*avere odore*) to smell of; (*uso reciproco*) to be in touch; **~rsi bene/male** to feel well/unwell ♦ *ill*; **~rsi di fare qc** (*essere disposto*) to feel like doing sth

sen'tito, a *ag* (*sincero*) sincere, warm; **per ~ dire** by hearsay

'senza ['sentsa] *prep, cong* without; **~ dir nulla** without saying a word; **fare ~ qc** to do without sth; **~ di me** without me; **~ che io lo sapessi** without me or my knowing; **senz'altro** of course, certainly; **~ dubbio** no doubt; **~ scrupoli** unscrupulous; **~ amici** friendless

sepa'rare *vt* to separate; (*dividere*) to divide; (*tenere distinto*) to distinguish; **~rsi** *vr* (*coniugi*) to separate, part; (*amici*) to part, leave each other; **~rsi da** (*coniuge*) to separate or part from; (*amico, socio*) to part company with; (*oggetto*) to part with; **sepa'rato, a** *ag* (*letti, conto etc*) separate; (*coniugi*) separated; **separazi'one** *sf* separation

se'polcro *sm* sepulchre

se'polto, a *pp di* **seppellire**

seppel'lire *vt* to bury

'seppia *sf* cuttlefish ♦ *ag inv* sepia

se'quenza [se'kwɛntsa] *sf* sequence

seques'trare *vt* (*DIR*) to impound; (*rapire*) to kidnap; **se'questro** *sm* (*DIR*)

impoundment; **sequestro di persona** kidnapping

'sera *sf* evening; **di ~** in the evening; **domani ~** tomorrow evening, tomorrow night; **se'rale** *ag* evening *cpd*; **se'rata** *sf* evening; (*ricevimento*) party

ser'bare *vt* to keep; (*mettere da parte*) to put aside; **~ rancore/odio verso qn** to bear sb a grudge/hate sb

serba'toio *sm* tank; (*cisterna*) cistern

'serbo *sm*: **mettere/tenere** o **avere in ~ qc** to put/keep sth aside

se'reno, a *ag* (*tempo, cielo*) clear; (*fig*) serene, calm

ser'gente [ser'dʒɛnte] *sm* (*MIL*) sergeant

'serie *sf inv* (*successione*) series *inv*; (*gruppo, collezione*) set; (*SPORT*) division; league; (*COMM*) modello di **~/fuori ~** standard/custom-built model; **in ~** in quick succession; (*COMM*) mass *cpd*

serietà *sf* seriousness; reliability

'serio, a *ag* serious; (*impiegato*) responsible, reliable; (*ditta, cliente*) reliable, dependable; **sul ~** (*davvero*) really, truly; (*seriamente*) seriously

ser'mone *sm* sermon

serpeggi'are [serped'dʒare] *vi* to wind; (*fig*) to spread

ser'pente *sm* snake; **~ a sonagli** rattlesnake

'serra *sf* greenhouse; hothouse

ser'randa *sf* roller shutter

ser'rare *vt* to close, shut; (*a chiave*) to lock; (*stringere*) to tighten; **~ i pugni/i denti** to clench one's fists/teeth; **~ le file** to close ranks

serra'tura *sf* lock

'serva *sf vedi* **servo**

'server ['sɛrver] *sm inv* (*INFORM*) server

ser'vire *vt* to serve; (*clienti: al ristorante*) to wait on; (: *al negozio*) to serve, attend to; (*fig: giovare*) to aid, help; (*CARTE*) to deal ♦ *vi* (*TENNIS*) to serve; (*essere utile*): **~ a qn** to be of use to sb; **~ a qc/a fare** (*utensile etc*) to

be used for sth/for doing; ~ **(a qn) da**
to serve as (for sb); **~rsi** vr (usare): **~rsi
di** to use; (prendere: cibo): **~rsi (di)** to
help o.s. to (to); (essere cliente abituale):
~rsi da to be a regular customer at,
go to

servitù sf servitude; slavery; (personale di servizio) servants pl, domestic
staff

servizi'evole [servit'tsjevole] ag
obliging, willing to help

ser'vizio [ser'vittsjo] sm service; (al
ristorante: sul conto) service (charge);
(STAMPA, TV, RADIO) report; (da tè, caffè
etc) set, service; **~i** smpl (di casa)
kitchen and bathroom; (ECON) services;
essere di ~ to be on duty; **fuori ~**
(telefono etc) out of order;
~ compreso service included;
~ militare military service; **~i segreti**
secret service sg

'servo, a sm/f servant

ses'santa num sixty; **sessan'tesimo,
a** num sixtieth

sessan'tina sf: una **~ (di)** about sixty

sessi'one sf session

'sesso sm sex; **sessu'ale** ag sexual,
sex cpd

ses'tante sm sextant

'sesto, a ag, sm sixth

'seta sf silk

'sete sf thirst; **avere ~** to be thirsty

'setola sf bristle

'setta sf sect

set'tanta num seventy;
settan'tesimo, a num seventieth

settan'tina sf: una **~ (di)** about
seventy

'sette num seven

sette'cento [sette'tʃento] num seven
hundred ♦ sm: **il S~** the eighteenth
century

set'tembre sm September

settentrio'nale ag northern

settentri'one sm north

setti'mana sf week; **settima'nale** ag,
sm weekly

'settimo, a ag, sm seventh

set'tore sm sector

severità sf severity

se'vero, a ag severe

sevizi'are [sevit'tsjare] vt to torture

se'vizie [se'vittsje] sfpl torture pl

sezio'nare [settsjo'nare] vt to divide
into sections; (MED) to dissect

sezi'one [set'tsjone] sf section

sfaccen'dato, a [sfattʃen'dato] ag
idle

sfacci'ato, a [sfat'tʃato] ag
(maleducato) cheeky, impudent;
(vistoso) gaudy

sfa'celo [sfa'tʃelo] sm (fig) ruin,
collapse

sfal'darsi vr to flake (off)

sfa'mare vt to feed; (sog: cibo) to fill

'sfarzo ['sfartso] sm pomp, splendour

sfasci'are [sfaʃ'ʃare] vt (ferita) to
unbandage; (distruggere) to smash,
shatter; **~rsi** vr (rompersi) to smash,
shatter

sfa'tare vt (leggenda) to explode

sfavil'lare vi to spark, send out sparks;
(risplendere) to sparkle

sfavo'revole ag unfavourable

'sfera sf sphere; **'sferico, a, ci, che** ag
spherical

sfer'rare vt (fig: colpo) to land, deal;

(: *attacco*) to launch

sfer'zare [sfer'tsare] *vt* to whip; (*fig*) to lash out at

sfi'brare *vt* (*indebolire*) to exhaust, enervate

'sfida *sf* challenge

sfi'dare *vt* to challenge; (*fig*) to defy, brave

sfi'ducia [sfi'dutʃa] *sf* distrust, mistrust

sfigu'rare *vt* (*persona*) to disfigure; (*quadro, statua*) to deface ♦ *vi* (*far cattiva figura*) to make a bad impression

sfi'lare *vt* (*ago*) to unthread; (*abito, scarpe*) to slip off ♦ *vi* (*truppe*) to march past; (*atleti*) to parade; **~rsi** *vr* (*perle etc*) to come unstrung; (*orlo, tessuto*) to fray; (*calza*) to run, ladder; **sfi'lata** *sf* march past; parade; **sfilata di moda** fashion show

'sfinge ['sfindʒe] *sf* sphinx

sfi'nito, a *ag* exhausted

sfio'rare *vt* to brush (against); (*argomento*) to touch upon

sfio'rire *vi* to wither, fade

sfo'cato, a *ag* (FOT) out of focus

sfoci'are [sfo'tʃare] *vi*: **~ in** to flow into; (*fig: malcontento*) to develop into

sfode'rato, a *ag* (*vestito*) unlined

sfo'gare *vt* to vent, pour out; **~rsi** *vr* (*sfogare la propria rabbia*) to give vent to one's anger; (*confidarsi*): **~rsi (con)** to pour out one's feelings (to); **non sfogarti su di me!** don't take your bad temper out on me!

sfoggi'are [sfod'dʒare] *vt, vi* to show off

'sfoglia ['sfoʎʎa] *sf* sheet of pasta dough; **pasta ~** (*CUC*) puff pastry

sfogli'are [sfoʎ'ʎare] *vt* (*libro*) to leaf through

'sfogo, ghi *sm* (*eruzione cutanea*) rash; (*fig*) outburst; **dare ~ a** (*fig*) to give vent to

sfolgo'rante ['sfolgo'rante] *ag* (*luce*) blazing; (*fig: vittoria*) brilliant

sfol'lare *vt* to empty, clear ♦ *vi* to disperse; **~ da** (*città*) to evacuate

sfon'dare *vt* (*porta*) to break down; (*scarpe*) to wear a hole in; (*cesto, scatola*) to burst, knock the bottom out of; (*MIL*) to break through ♦ *vi* (*riuscire*) to make a name for o.s.

'sfondo *sm* background

sfor'mato *sm* (*CUC*) type of soufflé

sfor'nare *vt* (*pane etc*) to take out of the oven; (*fig*) to churn out

sfor'nito, a *ag*: **~ di** lacking in, without; (*negozio*) out of

sfor'tuna *sf* misfortune, ill luck *no pl*; **avere ~** to be unlucky; **sfortu'nato, a** *ag* unlucky; (*impresa, film*) unsuccessful

sfor'zare [sfor'tsare] *vt* to force; (*voce, occhi*) to strain; **~rsi** *vr* **~rsi di o a o per fare** to try hard to do

'sforzo ['sfɔrtso] *sm* effort; (*tensione eccessiva, TECN*) strain; **fare uno ~** to make an effort

sfrat'tare *vt* to evict; **'sfratto** *sm* eviction

sfrecci'are [sfret'tʃare] *vi* to shoot o flash past

sfregi'are [sfre'dʒare] *vt* to slash, gash; (*persona*) to disfigure; (*quadro*) to deface; **'sfregio** *sm* gash; scar; (*fig*) insult

sfre'nato, a *ag* (*fig*) unrestrained, unbridled

sfron'tato, a *ag* shameless

sfrutta'mento *sm* exploitation

sfrut'tare *vt* (*terreno*) to overwork, exhaust; (*miniera*) to exploit, work; (*fig: operai, occasione, potere*) to exploit

sfug'gire [sfud'dʒire] *vi* to escape; **~ a** (*custode*) to escape (from); (*morte*) to escape; **~ a qn** (*dettaglio, nome*) to escape sb; **~ di mano a qn** to slip out of sb's hand (o hands); **sfug'gita: di sfuggita** *ad* (*rapidamente, in fretta*) in passing

sfu'mare *vt* (*colori, contorni*) to soften, shade off ♦ *vi* to shade (off), fade; (*fig: svanire*) to vanish, disappear;

(: *speranze*) to come to nothing

sfuma'tura *sf* shading off *no pl*; (*tonalità*) shade, tone; (*fig*) touch, hint

sfuri'ata *sf* (*scatto di collera*) fit of anger; (*rimprovero*) sharp rebuke

sga'bello *sm* stool

sgabuz'zino [zgabud'dzino] *sm* lumber room

sgambet'tare *vi* to kick one's legs about

sgam'betto *sm*: **far lo ~ a qn** to trip sb up; (*fig*) to oust sb

sganasci'arsi [zgana∫'∫arsi] *vr*: **~ dalle risa** to roar with laughter

sganci'are [zgan't∫are] *vt* to unhook; (*FERR*) to uncouple; (*bombe: da aereo*) to release, drop; (*fig: fam: soldi*) to fork out; **~rsi** *vr* (*fig*): **~rsi (da)** to get away (from)

sganghe'rato, a [zgange'rato] *ag* (*porta*) off its hinges; (*auto*) ramshackle; (*risata*) wild, boisterous

sgar'bato, a *ag* rude, impolite

'sgarbo *sm*: **fare uno ~ a qn** to be rude to sb

sgattaio'lare *vi* to sneak away *o* off

sge'lare [zdʒe'lare] *vi, vt* to thaw

'sghembo, a [zgembo] *ag* (*obliquo*) slanting; (*storto*) crooked

sghignaz'zare [zgiɲɲat'tsare] *vi* to laugh scornfully

sgob'bare (*fam*) *vi* (*scolaro*) to swot; (*operaio*) to slog

sgoccio'lare [zgott∫o'lare] *vt* (*vuotare*) to drain (to the last drop) ♦ *vi* (*acqua*) to drip; (*recipiente*) to drain; **sgoccioli** *smpl*: **essere agli ~** (*provviste*) to be nearly finished; (*periodo*) to be nearly over

sgo'larsi *vr* to talk (*o* shout *o* sing) o.s. hoarse

sgomb(e)'rare *vt* to clear; (*andarsene da: stanza*) to vacate; (*evacuare*) to evacuate

'sgombro, a *ag*: **~ (di)** clear (of), free (from) ♦ *sm* (*ZOOL*) mackerel; (*anche*:

sgombero) clearing; vacating; evacuation; (: *trasloco*) removal

sgomen'tare *vt* to dismay;

sgo'mento, a *ag* dismayed ♦ *sm* dismay, consternation

sgonfi'are *vt* to let down, deflate; **~rsi** *vr* to go down

'sgorbio *sm* blot; scribble

sgor'gare *vi* to gush (out)

sgoz'zare [zgot'tsare] *vt* to cut the throat of

sgra'devole *ag* unpleasant, disagreeable

sgra'dito, a *ag* unpleasant, unwelcome

sgra'nare *vt* (*piselli*) to shell; **~ gli occhi** to open one's eyes wide

sgran'chirsi [zgran'kirsi] *vr* to stretch; **~ le gambe** to stretch one's legs

sgranocchi'are [zgranok'kjare] *vt* to munch

'sgravio *sm*: **~ fiscale** tax relief

sgrazi'ato, a [zgrat'tsjato] *ag* clumsy, ungainly

sgreto'lare *vt* to cause to crumble; **~rsi** *vr* to crumble

sgri'dare *vt* to scold; **sgri'data** *sf* scolding

sguai'ato, a *ag* coarse, vulgar

sgual'cire [zgwal't∫ire] *vt* to crumple (up), crease

sgual'drina (*peg*) *sf* slut

sgu'ardo *sm* (*occhiata*) look, glance; (*espressione*) look (*in* one's eye)

'sguattero, a *sm/f* dishwasher (*person*)

sguaz'zare [zgwat'tsare] *vi* (*nell'acqua*) to splash about; (*nella melma*) to wallow; **~ nell'oro** to be rolling in money

sguinzagli'are [zgwintsaʎ'ʎare] *vt* to let off the leash; (*fig: persona*): **~ qn dietro a qn** to set sb on sb

sgusci'are [zgu∫'∫are] *vt* to shell ♦ *vi* (*sfuggire di mano*) to slip; **~ via** to slip *o* slink away

'shampoo ['∫ampo] *sm inv* shampoo

shock [∫ɔk] *sm inv* shock

---

si[1] (*dav lo, la, li, le, ne diventa* **se**) *pron*
1 (*riflessivo: maschile*) himself;
(: *femminile*) herself; (: *neutro*) itself;
(: *impersonale*) oneself; (: *pl*)
themselves; **lavarsi** to wash (oneself);
~ è tagliato he has cut himself;
~ credono importanti they think a
lot of themselves

2 (*riflessivo: con complemento oggetto*):
lavarsi le mani to wash one's hands;
~ sta lavando i capelli he (*o* she) is
washing his (*o* her) hair

3 (*reciproco*) one another, each other;
si amano they love one another *o*
each other

4 (*passivo*): **~ ripara facilmente** it is
easily repaired

5 (*impersonale*): **~ dice che ...** they *o*
people say that ...; **~ vede che è
vecchio** one *o* you can see that it's
old

6 (*noi*) we; **tra poco ~ parte** we're
leaving soon

si[2] *sm* (*MUS*) B; (*solfeggiando la scala*) ti
sì *av* yes; **un giorno ~ e uno no** every
other day

'sia *cong*: **~ ... ~** (*o ... o*): **~ che lavori,
~ che non lavori** whether he works
or not; (*tanto ... quanto*): **verranno
~ Luigi ~ suo fratello** both Luigi and
his brother will be coming

si'amo *vb vedi* **essere**

sibi'lare *vi* to hiss; (*fischiare*) to whistle;
'sibilo *sm* hiss; whistle

si'cario *sm* hired killer

sicché [sik'ke] *cong* (*perciò*) so (that),
therefore; (*e quindi*) (and) so

siccità [sittʃi'ta] *sf* drought

sic'come *cong* since, as

Si'cilia [si'tʃilja] *sf*: **la ~** Sicily;
sicili'ano, a *ag, sm/f* Sicilian

si'cura *sf* safety catch; (*AUT*) safety lock

sicu'rezza [siku'rettsa] *sf* safety;
security; (*fiducia*) confidence; (*certezza*)

certainty; **di ~** safety *cpd*; **la
~ stradale** road safety

si'curo, a *ag* safe; (*ben difeso*) secure;
(*fiducioso*) confident; (*certo*) sure,
certain; (*notizia, amico*) reliable;
(*esperto*) skilled ♦ *av* (*anche: di ~*)
certainly; **essere/mettere al ~** to be
safe/put in a safe place; **~ di sé** self-
confident, sure of o.s.; **sentirsi ~** to
feel safe *o* secure

siderur'gia [siderur'dʒia] *sf* iron and
steel industry

'sidro *sm* cider

si'epe *sf* hedge

si'ero *sm* (*MED*) serum; **sieronega-
'tivo, a** *ag* HIV-negative; **sieropo-
si'tivo, a** *ag* HIV-positive

si'esta *sf* siesta, (afternoon) nap

si'ete *vb vedi* **essere**

si'filide *sf* syphilis

si'fone *sm* siphon

Sig. *abbr* (= *signore*) Mr

siga'retta *sf* cigarette

'sigaro *sm* cigar

Sigg. *abbr* (= *signori*) Messrs

sigil'lare [sidʒil'lare] *vt* to seal

si'gillo [si'dʒillo] *sm* seal

'sigla *sf* initials *pl*; acronym,
abbreviation; **~ automobilistica**
abbreviation of province on vehicle
number plate; **~ musicale** signature
tune

si'glare *vt* to initial

Sig.na *abbr* (= *signorina*) Miss

signifi'care [siɲɲifi'kare] *vt* to mean;
significa'tivo, a *ag* significant;
signifi'cato *sm* meaning

si'gnora [siɲ'ɲora] *sf* lady; **la ~ X** Mrs
X; **buon giorno S~/Signore/
Signorina** good morning; (*deferente*)
good morning Madam/Sir/Madam;
(*quando si conosce il nome*) good
morning Mrs/Mr/Miss X; **Gentile S~/
Signore/Signorina** (*in una lettera*)
Dear Madam/Sir/Madam; **il signor
Rossi e ~** Mr Rossi and his wife; **~e e
signori** ladies and gentlemen

si'gnore [siɲˈɲore] *sm* gentleman; (*padrone*) lord, master; (REL): **il S~** the Lord; **il signor X** Mr X; **i ~i Bianchi** (*coniugi*) Mr and Mrs Bianchi; *vedi anche* **signora**

signo'rile [siɲɲoˈrile] *ag* refined

signo'rina [siɲɲoˈrina] *sf* young lady; **la ~ X** Miss X; *vedi anche* **signora**

Sig.ra *abbr* (= *signora*) Mrs

silenzia'tore [silentsjaˈtore] *sm* silencer

si'lenzio [siˈlɛntsjo] *sm* silence; **fare ~** to be quiet, stop talking; **silenzi'oso, a** *ag* silent, quiet

si'licio [siˈlitʃo] *sm* silicon

'sillaba *sf* syllable

silu'rare *vt* to torpedo; (*fig: privare del comando*) to oust

si'luro *sm* torpedo

simboleggi'are [simboledˈdʒare] *vt* to symbolize

'simbolo *sm* symbol

'simile *ag* (*analogo*) similar; (*di questo tipo*): **un uomo ~** such a man, a man like this; **libri ~i** such books; **~ a** similar to; **i suoi ~i** one's fellow men; one's peers

simme'tria *sf* symmetry

simpa'tia *sf* (*qualità*) pleasantness; (*inclinazione*) liking; **avere ~ per qn** to like sb, have a liking for sb;
sim'patico, a, ci, che *ag* (*persona*) nice, pleasant, likeable; (*casa, albergo etc*) nice, pleasant

simpatiz'zare [simpatidˈdzare] *vi:* **~ con** to take a liking to

sim'posio *sm* symposium

simu'lare *vt* to sham, simulate; (TECN) to simulate; **simulazi'one** *sf* shamming; simulation

simul'taneo, a *ag* simultaneous

sina'goga, ghe *sf* synagogue

since'rità [sintʃeriˈta] *sf* sincerity

sin'cero, a [sinˈtʃero] *ag* sincere; genuine; heartfelt

'sincope *sf* syncopation; (MED) blackout

sinda'cale *ag* (trade-)union *cpd*;

sindaca'lista, i, e *sm/f* trade unionist

sinda'cato *sm* (*di lavoratori*) (trade) union; (AMM, ECON, DIR) syndicate, trust, pool

'sindaco, ci *sm* mayor

sinfo'nia *sf* (MUS) symphony

singhioz'zare [singjotˈtsare] *vi* to sob; to hiccup

singhi'ozzo [sinˈgjottso] *sm* sob; (MED) hiccup; **avere il ~** to have the hiccups; **a ~** (*fig*) by fits and starts

singo'lare *ag* (*insolito*) remarkable, singular; (LING) singular ♦ *sm* (LING) singular; (TENNIS): **~ maschile/femminile** men's/women's singles

'singolo, a *ag* single, individual ♦ *sm* (*persona*) individual; (TENNIS) = **singolare**

si'nistra *sf* (POL) left (wing); **a ~** on the left; (*direzione*) to the left

si'nistro, a *ag* left, left-hand; (*fig*) sinister ♦ *sm* (*incidente*) accident

'sino *prep* = **fino**

si'nonimo *sm* synonym; **~ di** synonymous with

sin'tassi *sf* syntax

'sintesi *sf* synthesis; (*riassunto*) summary, résumé

sin'tetico, a, ci, che *ag* synthetic

sintetiz'zare [sintetidˈdzare] *vt* to synthesize; (*riassumere*) to summarize

sinto'matico, a, ci, che *ag* symptomatic

'sintomo *sm* symptom

sinu'oso, a *ag* (*strada*) winding

si'pario *sm* (TEATRO) curtain

si'rena *sf* (*apparecchio*) siren; (*nella mitologia, fig*) siren, mermaid

'Siria *sf:* **la ~** Syria

si'ringa, ghe *sf* syringe

'sismico, a, ci, che *ag* seismic

sis'mografo *sm* seismograph

sis'tema, i *sm* system; method, way

siste'mare *vt* (*mettere a posto*) to tidy, put in order; (*risolvere: questione*) to sort out, settle; (*procurare un lavoro a*) to find a job for; (*dare un alloggio a*) to settle, find accommodation for; **~rsi** vr (problema) to be settled; (persona: trovare alloggio) to find accommodation (BRIT) o accommodations (US); (: trovarsi un lavoro) to get fixed up with a job; **ti sistemo io!** I'll soon sort you out!

siste'matico, a, ci, che ag systematic

sistemazi'one [sistemat'tsjone] sf arrangement, order; settlement; employment; accommodation (BRIT), accommodations (US)

'sito sm: **~ (Internet)** website

situ'are vt to site, situate; **situ'ato, a** ag: **situato a/su** situated at/on

situazi'one [situat'tsjone] sf situation

ski-lift ['ski:lift] sm inv ski tow

slacci'are [zlat'tʃare] vt to undo, unfasten

slanci'are [zlan'tʃare] ag slender

'slancio sm dash, leap; (fig) surge; **di ~** impetuously

sla'vato, a ag faded, washed out; (fig: viso, occhi) pale, colourless

'slavo, a ag Slav(onic), Slavic

sle'ale ag disloyal; (concorrenza etc) unfair

sle'gare vt to untie

slip [zlip] sm inv briefs pl

'slitta sf sledge; (trainata) sleigh

slit'tare vi to slip, slide; (AUT) to skid

slo'gare vt (MED) to dislocate

sloggi'are [zlod'dʒare] vt (inquilino) to turn out ♦ vi to move out

slo'vacco, a, chi, che ag, sm/f Slovak

Slovenia [zlo'venja] sf Slovenia

smacchi'are [zmak'kjare] vt to remove stains from; **smacchia'tore** sm stain remover

'smacco, chi sm humiliating defeat

smagli'ante [zmaʎ'ʎante] ag brilliant, dazzling

smagli'atura [zmaʎʎa'tura] sf (su maglia, calza) ladder; (della pelle) stretch mark

smalizi'ato, a [smalit'tsjato] ag shrewd, cunning

smal'tare vt to enamel; (ceramica) to glaze; (unghie) to varnish

smal'tire vt (merce) to sell off; (rifiuti) to dispose of; (cibo) to digest; (peso) to lose; (rabbia) to get over; **~ la sbornia** to sober up

'smalto sm (anche: di denti) enamel; (per ceramica) glaze; **~ per unghie** nail varnish

'smania sf agitation, restlessness; (fig): **~ di** thirst for, craving for; **avere la ~ addosso** to have the fidgets; **avere la ~ di fare** to be desperate to do

smantel'lare vt to dismantle

smarri'mento sm loss; (fig) bewilderment; dismay

smar'rire vt to lose; (non riuscire a trovare) to mislay; **~rsi** vr (perdersi) to lose one's way, get lost; (: oggetto) to go astray; **smar'rito, a** ag (sbigottito) bewildered

smasche'rare [zmaske'rare] vt to unmask

smemo'rato, a ag forgetful

smen'tire vt (negare) to deny; (testimonianza) to refute; **smen'tita** sf denial; retraction

sme'raldo sm emerald

smerci'are [zmer'tʃare] vt (COMM) to sell; (: svendere) to sell off

'smesso, a pp di **smettere**

'smettere vt to stop; (vestiti) to stop wearing ♦ vi to stop, cease; **~ di fare** to stop doing

'smilzo, a ['zmiltso] ag thin, lean

sminu'ire vt to diminish, lessen; (fig) to belittle

sminuz'zare [zminut'tsare] vt to break into small pieces; to crumble

smis'tare vt (pacchi etc) to sort; (FERR) to shunt

smisu'rato, a ag boundless, immeasurable; (grandissimo) immense, enormous

smobili'tare vt to demobilize

smo'dato, a ag immoderate

smoking ['sməukiŋ] sm inv dinner

jacket

smon'tare vt (mobile, macchina etc) to take to pieces, dismantle; (fig: scoraggiare) to dishearten ♦ vi (scendere: da cavallo) to dismount; (: da treno) to get off; (terminare il lavoro) to stop (work); **~rsi** vr to lose heart; to lose one's enthusiasm

'**smorfia** sf grimace; (atteggiamento lezioso) simpering; **fare ~e** to make faces; to simper; **smorfi'oso, a** ag simpering

'**smorto, a** ag (viso) pale, wan; (colore) dull

smor'zare [zmor'tsare] vt (suoni) to deaden; (colori) to tone down; (luce) to dim; (sete) to quench; (entusiasmo) to dampen; **~rsi** vr (suono, luce) to fade; (entusiasmo) to dampen

'**smosso, a** pp di **smuovere**

smotta'mento sm landslide

'**smunto, a** ag haggard, pinched

smu'overe vt to move, shift; (fig: commuovere) to move; (: dall'inerzia) to rouse, stir; **~rsi** vr to move, shift

smus'sare vt (angolo) to round off, smooth; (lama etc) to blunt; **~rsi** vr to become blunt

snatu'rato, a ag inhuman, heartless

'**snello, a** ag (agile) agile; (svelto) slender, slim

sner'vare vt to enervate, wear out

sni'dare vt to drive out, flush out

snob'bare vt to snub

sno'bismo sm snobbery

snoccio'lare [znottʃo'lare] vt (frutta) to stone; (fig: orazioni) to rattle off

sno'dare vt (rendere agile, mobile) to loosen; **~rsi** vr to come loose; (articolarsi) to bend; (strada, fiume) to wind

so vb vedi **sapere**

so'ave ag sweet, gentle, soft

sobbal'zare [sobbal'tsare] vi to jolt, jerk; (trasalire) to jump, start; **sob'balzo** sm jerk, jolt; jump, start; **sobbar'carsi** vr: **~ a** to take on,

undertake

sob'borgo, ghi sm suburb

sobil'lare vt to stir up, incite

'**sobrio, a** ag sober

socchi'udere [sok'kjudere] vt (porta) to leave ajar; (occhi) to half-close; **socchi'uso, a** pp di **socchiudere**

soc'correre vt to help, assist; **soc'corso, a** pp di **soccorrere** ♦ sm help, aid, assistance; **soccorsi** smpl relief sg, aid sg; **soccorso stradale** breakdown service

soci'ale [so'tʃale] ag social; (di associazione) club cpd, association cpd

socia'lismo [sotʃa'lizmo] sm socialism; **socia'lista, i, e** ag, sm/f socialist

società [sotʃe'ta] sf inv society; (sportiva) club; (COMM) company; **~ per azioni** limited (BRIT) o incorporated (US) company; **~ a responsabilità limitata** type of limited liability company

soci'evole [so'tʃevole] ag sociable

'**socio** ['sɔtʃo] sm (DIR, COMM) partner; (membro di associazione) member

'**soda** sf (CHIM) soda; (bibita) soda (water)

soda'lizio [soda'littsjo] sm association, society

soddisfa'cente [soddisfa'tʃɛnte] ag satisfactory

soddis'fare vt, vi: **~ a** to satisfy; (impegno) to fulfil; (debito) to pay off; (richiesta) to meet, comply with; **soddis'fatto, a** pp di **soddisfare** ♦ ag satisfied; **soddisfatto di** happy o satisfied with; pleased with; **soddisfazi'one** sf satisfaction

'**sodo, a** ag firm, hard; (uovo) hard-boiled ♦ av (picchiare, lavorare) hard; (dormire) soundly

sofà sm inv sofa

soffe'renza [soffe'rentsa] sf suffering

sof'ferto, a pp di **soffrire**

soffi'are vt to blow; (notizia, segreto) to whisper ♦ vi to blow; (sbuffare) to puff; **~rsi il naso** to blow one's nose; **~ qc/qn a qn** (fig) to pinch o steal sth/sb from sb; **~ via qc** to blow sth away

'soffice [ˈsɔffitʃe] *ag* soft

'soffio *sm* (*di vento*) breath; **~ al cuore** heart murmur

sof'fitta *sf* attic

sof'fitto *sm* ceiling

soffo'care *vi* (*anche: ~rsi*) to suffocate, choke ♦ *vt* to suffocate, choke; (*fig*) to stifle, suppress

sof'friggere [sofˈfriddʒere] *vt* to fry lightly

sof'frire *vt* to suffer, endure; (*sopportare*) to bear, stand ♦ *vi* to suffer; to be in pain; **~ (di) qc** (*MED*) to suffer from sth

sof'fritto, a *pp di* **soffriggere** ♦ *sm* (*CUC*) fried mixture of herbs, bacon and onions

sofisti'cato, a *ag* sophisticated; (*vino*) adulterated

sog'getto, a [sodˈdʒetto] *ag:* **~ a** (*sottomesso*) subject to; (*esposto: a variazioni, danni etc*) subject o liable to ♦ *sm* subject

soggezi'one [soddʒetˈtsjone] *sf* subjection; (*timidezza*) awe; **avere ~ di qn** to stand in awe of sb; to be ill at ease in sb's presence

sogghi'gnare [soggiɲˈɲare] *vi* to sneer

soggior'nare [soddʒorˈnare] *vi* to stay; **soggi'orno** *sm* (*invernale, marino*) stay; (*stanza*) living room

sog'giungere [sodˈdʒundʒere] *vt* to add

'soglia [ˈsɔʎʎa] *sf* doorstep; (*anche fig*) threshold

'sogliola [ˈsɔʎʎola] *sf* (*ZOOL*) sole

so'gnare [soɲˈɲare] *vt, vi* to dream; **~ a occhi aperti** to daydream; **sogna'tore, 'trice** *sm/f* dreamer

'sogno [ˈsoɲɲo] *sm* dream

'soia *sf* (*BOT*) soya

sol *sm* (*MUS*) G; (: *solfeggiando*) so(h)

so'laio *sm* (*soffitta*) attic

sola'mente *av* only, just

so'lare *ag* solar, sun *cpd*

'solco, chi *sm* (*scavo, fig: ruga*) furrow; (*incavo*) rut, track; (*di disco*) groove

sol'dato *sm* soldier; **~ semplice** private

'soldo *sm* (*fig*): **non avere un ~** to be penniless; **non vale un ~** it's not worth a penny; **~i** *smpl* (*denaro*) money *sg*

'sole *sm* sun; (*luce*) sun(light); (*tempo assolato*) sun(shine); **prendere il ~** to sunbathe

soleggi'ato, a [soledˈdʒato] *ag* sunny

so'lenne *ag* solemn; **solennità** *sf* solemnity; (*festività*) holiday, feast day

sol'fato *sm* (*CHIM*) sulphate

soli'dale *ag:* **essere ~ (con)** to be in agreement (with)

solidarietà *sf* solidarity

'solido, a *ag* solid; (*forte, robusto*) sturdy, solid; (*fig: ditta*) sound, solid ♦ *sm* (*MAT*) solid

soli'loquio *sm* soliloquy

so'lista, i, e *ag* solo ♦ *sm/f* soloist

solita'mente *av* usually, as a rule

soli'tario, a *ag* (*senza compagnia*) solitary, lonely; (*solo, isolato*) solitary, lone; (*deserto*) lonely ♦ *sm* (*gioiello, gioco*) solitaire

'solito, a *ag* usual; **essere ~ fare** to be in the habit of doing; **di ~** usually; **più tardi del ~** later than usual; **come al ~** as usual

soli'tudine *sf* solitude

solleci'tare [solletʃiˈtare] *vt* (*lavoro*) to speed up; (*persona*) to urge on; (*chiedere con insistenza*) to press for, request urgently; (*stimolare*) to stimulare; **~ qn a fare** to urge sb to do; **sollecitazi'one** *sf* entreaty, request; (*fig*) incentive; (*TECN*) stress

sol'lecito, a [solˈletʃito] *ag* prompt, quick ♦ *sm* (*lettera*) reminder; **solleci'tudine** *sf* promptness, speed

solleti'care vt to tickle

sol'letico sm tickling; **soffrire il ~** to be ticklish

solleva'mento sm raising; lifting; revolt; **~ pesi** (SPORT) weight-lifting

solle'vare vt to lift, raise; (fig: persona: alleggerire): **~ (da)** to relieve (of); (: dar conforto) to comfort, relieve; (: questione) to raise; (: far insorgere) to stir (to revolt); **~rsi** vr to rise; (fig: riprendersi) to recover; (: ribellarsi) to rise up

solli'evo sm relief; (conforto) comfort

'solo, a ag alone; (in senso spirituale: isolato) lonely; (unico): **un ~ libro** only one book, a single book; (con ag numerale): **veniamo noi tre ~i** just o only the three of us are coming ♦ av (soltanto) only, just; **non ~ ... ma anche** not only ... but also; **fare qc da ~** to do sth (all) by oneself

sol'tanto av only

so'lubile ag (sostanza) soluble

soluzi'one [solut'tsjone] sf solution

sol'vente ag, sm solvent

'soma sf: **bestia da ~** beast of burden

so'maro sm ass, donkey

somigli'anza [somiʎ'ʎantsa] sf resemblance

somigli'are [somiʎ'ʎare] vi: **~ a** to be like, resemble; (nell'aspetto fisico) to look like; **~rsi** vr to be (o look) alike

'somma sf (MAT) sum; (di denaro) sum (of money)

som'mare vt to add up; (aggiungere) to add; **tutto sommato** all things considered

som'mario, a ag (racconto, indagine) brief; (giustizia) summary ♦ sm summary

som'mergere [som'merdʒere] vt to submerge

sommer'gibile [sommer'dʒibile] sm submarine

som'merso, a pp di **sommergere**

som'messo, a ag (voce) soft, subdued

somminis'trare vt to give, administer

sommità sf inv summit, top; (fig) height

'sommo, a ag highest; (rispetto etc) highest, greatest; (poeta, artista) great, outstanding; **per ~i capi** briefly, covering the main points

som'mossa sf uprising

so'naglio [so'naddʒo] sm sounding; probe; boring, drilling; (indagine) survey; **~ d'opinioni** opinion poll

son'dare vt (NAUT) to sound; (atmosfera, spazio) to probe; (MINERALOGIA) to bore, drill; (fig: opinione etc) to survey, poll

so'netto sm sonnet

son'nambulo, a sm/f sleepwalker

sonnecchi'are [sonnek'kjare] vi to doze, nod

son'nifero sm sleeping drug (o pill)

'sonno sm sleep; **prendere ~** to fall asleep; **aver ~** to be sleepy

'sono vb vedi **essere**

so'noro, a ag (ambiente) resonant; (voce) sonorous, ringing; (onde, film) sound cpd

sontu'oso, a ag sumptuous; lavish

sopo'rifero, a ag soporific

soppe'sare vt to weigh in one's hand(s), feel the weight of; (fig) to weigh up

soppi'atto: di ~ av secretly; furtively

soppor'tare vt (reggere) to support; (subire: perdita, spese) to bear, sustain; (soffrire: dolore) to bear, endure; (: cosa: freddo) to withstand; (sog: persona: freddo, vino) to take; (tollerare) to put up with, tolerate

sop'presso, a pp di **sopprimere**

sop'primere vt (carica, privilegi, testimone) to do away with; (pubblicazione) to suppress; (parola, frase) to delete

'sopra prep (gen: al di sopra di, più in alto di) above; over; (riguardo a) on, about ♦ av on top; (attaccato, scritto)

soprabito *sm* overcoat

soprac'ciglio [soprat'tʃiʎʎo] (*pl(f)* **soprac'ciglia**) *sm* eyebrow

sopracco'perta *sf* (*di letto*) bedspread; (*di libro*) jacket

sopraf'fare *vt* to overcome, overwhelm; **sopraf'fatto, a** *pp di* **sopraffare**

sopraf'fino, a *ag* (*pranzo, vino*) excellent

sopraggi'ungere [soprad'dʒundʒere] *vi* (*giungere all'improvviso*) to arrive (unexpectedly); (*accadere*) to occur (unexpectedly)

sopral'luogo, ghi *sm* (*di esperti*) inspection; (*di polizia*) on-the-spot investigation

sopram'mobile *sm* ornament

soprannatu'rale *ag* supernatural

sopran'nome *sm* nickname

so'prano, a *sm/f* (*persona*) soprano ♦ *sm* (*voce*) soprano

soprappensi'ero *av* lost in thought

sopras'salto *sm*: **di ~** with a start; suddenly

soprasse'dere *vi*: **~ a** to delay, put off

soprat'tutto *av* (*anzitutto*) above all; (*specialmente*) especially

sopravvalu'tare *vt* to overestimate

soprav'vento *sm*: **avere/prendere il ~ su** to have/get the upper hand over

sopravvis'suto, a *pp di* **sopravvivere**

soprav'vivere *vi* to survive; (*continuare a vivere*): **~ (in)** to live on (in); **~ a** (*incidente etc*) to survive; (*persona*) to outlive

soprele'vata *sf* (*strada*) flyover; (*ferrovia*) elevated railway

soprinten'dente *sm/f* supervisor; (*statale: di belle arti etc*) keeper;

soprinten'denza *sf* supervision;

(*ente*): **soprintendenza alle Belle Arti** government department responsible for monuments and artistic treasures

so'pruso *sm* abuse of power; **subire un ~** to be abused

soq'quadro *sm*: **mettere a ~** to turn upside-down

sor'betto *sm* sorbet, water ice

sor'bire *vt* to sip; (*fig*) to put up with

'sorcio, ci ['sortʃo] *sm* mouse

'sordido, a *ag* sordid; (*fig: gretto*) stingy

sor'dina *sf*: **in ~** softly; (*fig*) on the sly

sordità *sf* deafness

'sordo, a *ag* deaf; (*rumore*) muffled; (*dolore*) dull; (*odio, rancore*) veiled ♦ *sm/f* deaf person; **sordo'muto, a** *ag* deaf-and-dumb ♦ *sm/f* deaf-mute

so'rella *sf* sister; **sorel'lastra** *sf* stepsister

sor'gente [sor'dʒente] *sf* (*d'acqua*) spring; (*di fiume, FISICA, fig*) source

'sorgere ['sordʒere] *vi* to rise; (*scaturire*) to spring; rise; (*fig: difficoltà*) to arise

sormon'tare *vt* (*fig*) to overcome, surmount

sorni'one, a *ag* sly

sorpas'sare *vt* (*AUT*) to overtake; (*fig*) to surpass; (: *eccedere*) to exceed, go beyond; **~ in altezza** to be higher than; (*persona*) to be taller than; **sor'passo** *sm* (*AUT*) overtaking

sorpren'dente *ag* surprising

sor'prendere *vt* (*cogliere: in flagrante etc*) to catch; (*stupire*) to surprise; **~rsi** *vr*: **~rsi (di)** to be surprised (at); **sor'presa** *sf* surprise; **fare una sorpresa a** to give sb a surprise; **sor'preso, a** *pp di* **sorprendere**

sor'reggere [sor'reddʒere] *vt* to support, hold up; (*fig*) to sustain; **sor'retto, a** *pp di* **sorreggere**

sor'ridere *vi* to smile; **sor'riso, a** *pp di* **sorridere** ♦ *sm* smile

'sorso *sm* sip

'sorta *sf* sort, kind; **di ~** whatever, of

any kind, at all

'**sorte** sf (fato) fate, destiny; (evento fortuito) chance; **tirare a ~** to draw lots

sor'**teggio** [sor'teddʒo] sm draw

sorti'**legio** [sorti'ledʒo] sm witchcraft no pl; (incantesimo) spell; **fare un ~ a qn** to cast a spell on sb

sor'**tita** sf (MIL) sortie

'**sorto, a** pp di **sorgere**

sorvegli'**anza** [sorveʎ'ʎantsa] sf watch; supervision; (POLIZIA, MIL) surveillance

sorvegli'**are** [sorveʎ'ʎare] vt (bambino, bagagli, prigioniero) to watch, keep an eye on; (malato) to watch over; (territorio, casa) to watch o keep watch over; (lavori) to supervise

sorvo'**lare** vt (territorio) to fly over ♦ vi: **~ su** (fig) to skim over

'**sosia** sm inv double

sos'**pendere** vt (appendere) to hang (up); (interrompere, privare di una carica) to suspend; (rimandare) to defer; (appendere) to hang; **sospensi'one** sf (anche CHIM, AUT) suspension; deferment; **sos'peso, a** pp di **sospendere** ♦ ag (appeso): **sospeso a** hanging on (o from); (treno, autobus) cancelled; **in sospeso** in abeyance; (conto) outstanding; **tenere in sospeso** (fig) to keep in suspense

sospet'**tare** vt to suspect ♦ vi: **~ di** to suspect; (diffidare) to be suspicious of

sos'**petto, a** ag suspicious ♦ sm suspicion; **sospet'toso, a** ag suspicious

sos'**pingere** [sos'pindʒere] vt to drive, push; **sos'pinto, a** pp di **sospingere**

sospi'**rare** vi to sigh ♦ vt to long for, yearn for; **sos'piro** sm sigh

'**sosta** sf (fermata) stop, halt; (pausa) pause, break; **senza ~** non-stop, without a break

sostan'**tivo** sm noun, substantive

sos'**tanza** [sos'tantsa] sf substance; **~e**

sfpl (ricchezze) wealth sg, possessions; **in ~** in short, to sum up;

sostanzi'**oso, a** ag (cibo) nourishing, substantial

sos'**tare** vi (fermarsi) to stop (for a while), stay; (fare una pausa) to take a break

sos'**tegno** [sos'teɲɲo] sm support

soste'**nere** vt to support; (prendere su di sé) to take on, bear; (resistere) to withstand, stand up to; (affermare): **~ che** to maintain that; **~rsi** vr to hold o.s. up, support o.s.; (fig) to keep up one's strength; **~ gli esami** to sit exams; **sosteni'tore, 'trice** sm/f supporter

sostenta'**mento** sm maintenance, support

soste'**nuto, a** ag (stile) elevated; (velocità, ritmo) sustained; (prezzo) high ♦ sm/f: **fare il(la) ~(a)** to be standoffish, keep one's distance

sostitu'**ire** vt (mettere al posto di): **~ qn/qc a** to substitute sb/sth for; (prendere il posto di: persona) to substitute for; (: cosa) to take the place of

sosti'**tuto, a** sm/f substitute

sostituzi'**one** [sostitut'tsjone] sf substitution; **in ~ di** as a substitute for, in place of

sotta'**ceti** [sotta'tʃeti] smpl pickles

sot'**tana** sf (sottoveste) underskirt; (gonna) skirt; (REL) soutane, cassock

sotter'**fugio** [sotter'fudʒo] sm subterfuge

sotter'**raneo, a** ag underground ♦ sm cellar

sotter'**rare** vt to bury

sottigli'**ezza** [sottiʎ'ʎettsa] sf thinness; slimness; (fig: acutezza) subtlety; shrewdness; **~e** sfpl (pedanteria) quibbles

sot'**tile** ag thin; (figura, caviglia) thin, slim, slender; (fine: polvere, capelli) fine; (fig: leggero) light; (: vista) sharp, keen; (: olfatto) fine, discriminating; (: mente) subtle; shrewd ♦ *sm:* **non andare per il ~** not to mince matters

sottin'tendere *vt* (*intendere qc non espresso*) to understand; (*implicare*) to imply; **sottin'teso, a** *pp di* **sottintendere** ♦ *sm* allusion; **parlare senza sottintesi** to speak plainly

'**sotto** *prep* (*gen*) under; (*più in basso di*) below ♦ *av* underneath, beneath; below; **(al piano) di ~** downstairs; **~ forma di** in the form of; **~ il monte** at the foot of the mountain; **siamo ~ Natale** it's nearly Christmas; **~ la pioggia/il sole** in the rain/sun(shine); **~ terra** underground; **chiuso ~ vuoto** vacuum-packed

sottoline'are *vt* to underline; (*fig*) to emphasize, stress

sottoma'rino, a *ag* (*flora*) submarine; (*cavo, navigazione*) underwater ♦ *sm* (NAUT) submarine

sotto'messo, a *pp di* **sottomettere**

sotto'mettere *vt* to subdue, subjugate; **~rsi** *vr* to submit

sottopas'saggio [sottopas'saddʒo] *sm* (AUT) underpass; (*pedonale*) subway, underpass

sotto'porre *vt* (*costringere*) to subject; (*fig: presentare*) to submit; **sottoporsi** *vr* to submit; **sottoporsi a** (*subire*) to undergo; **sotto'posto, a** *pp di* **sottoporre**

sottos'critto, a *pp di* **sottoscrivere**

sottos'crivere *vt* to sign ♦ **~ a** to subscribe to; **sottoscrizi'one** *sf* signing; subscription

sottosegre'tario *sm:* **~ di Stato** Under-Secretary of State (BRIT), Assistant Secretary of State (US)

sotto'sopra *av* upside-down

sotto'terra *av* underground

sotto'titolo *sm* subtitle

sottovalu'tare *vt* to underestimate

sotto'veste *sf* underskirt

sotto'voce [sotto'votʃe] *av* in a low voice

sot'trarre *vt* (MAT) to subtract, take

away; **~ qn/qc a** (*togliere*) to remove sb/sth from; (*salvare*) to save or rescue sb/sth from; **~ qc a qn** (*rubare*) to steal sth from sb; **sottrarsi** *vr:* **sottrarsi a** (*sfuggire*) to escape; (*evitare*) to avoid; **sot'tratto, a** *pp di* **sottrarre**; **sottrazi'one** *sf* subtraction; removal

sovi'etico, a, ci, che *ag* Soviet ♦ *sm/f* Soviet citizen

sovraccari'care *vt* to overload

sovrannatu'rale *ag* = **soprannaturale**

so'vrano, a *ag* sovereign; (*fig: sommo*) supreme ♦ *sm/f* sovereign, monarch

sovrap'porre *vt* to place on top of, put on top of

sovras'tare *vi:* **~ a** (*vallata, fiume*) to overhang; (*fig*) to hang over, threaten ♦ *vt* to overhang; to hang over, threaten

sovrinten'dente *etc* = **soprinten-dente** *etc*

sovru'mano, a *ag* superhuman

sovvenzi'one [sovven'tsjone] *sf* subsidy, grant

sovver'sivo, a *ag* subversive

'**sozzo, a** ['sottso] *ag* filthy, dirty

S.p.A. *abbr* = **società per azioni**

spac'care *vt* to split, break; (*legna*) to chop; **~rsi** *vr* to split, break; **spacca'tura** *sf* split

spacci'are [spat'tʃare] *vt* (*vendere*) to sell (off); (*mettere in circolazione*) to circulate; (*droga*) to peddle, push; **~rsi** *vr:* **~rsi per** (*farsi credere*) to pass o.s. off as, pretend to be; **spaccia'tore, 'trice** *sm/f* (*di droga*) pusher; (*di denaro falso*) dealer; **'spaccio** *sm* (*di merce rubata, droga*): **spaccio (di)** trafficking (in); (*in denaro falso*): **spaccio (di)** passing (of); (*vendita*) sale; (*bottega*) shop

'**spacco, chi** *sm* (*fenditura*) split, crack; (*strappo*) tear; (*di gonna*) slit

spac'cone *sm/f* boaster, braggart

'**spada** *sf* sword

spae'sato, a ag disorientated, lost

spa'ghetti [spa'getti] smpl (CUC) spaghetti sg

'Spagna ['spaɲɲa] sf: **la ~** Spain; **spa'gnolo, a** ag Spanish ♦ sm/f Spaniard ♦ sm (LING) Spanish; **gli Spagnoli** the Spanish

'spago, ghi sm string, twine

spai'ato, a ag (calza, guanto) odd

spalan'care vt to open wide; **~rsi** vr to open wide

spa'lare vt to shovel

'spalla sf shoulder; (fig: TEATRO) stooge; **~e** sfpl (dorso) back; **spalleggi'are** vt to back up, support

spalli'era sf (di sedia etc) back; (di letto: da capo) head(board); (: da piedi) foot(board); (GINNASTICA) wall bars pl

spal'lina sf (bretella) strap; (imbottita) shoulder pad

spal'mare vt to spread

'spalti smpl (di stadio) terracing

spandere vt (versare); (versare) to pour (out); **~rsi** vr to spread; **'spanto, a** pp di **spandere**

spa'rare vt to fire ♦ vi (far fuoco) to fire; (tirare) to shoot; **spara'toria** sf exchange of shots

sparecchi'are [sparek'kjare] vt: **~ (la tavola)** to clear the table

spa'reggio [spa'reddʒo] sm (SPORT) play-off

'spargere ['spardʒere] vt (sparpagliare) to scatter; (versare: vino) to spill; (: lacrime, sangue) to shed; (diffondere) to spread; (emanare) to give off (o out); **~rsi** vr to spread; **spargi'mento** sm scattering, strewing; spilling; shedding; **spargimento di sangue** bloodshed

spa'rire vi to disappear, vanish

spar'lare vi: **~ di** to run down, speak ill of

'sparo sm shot

sparpagli'are [sparpaʎ'ʎare] vt to scatter; **~rsi** vr to scatter

'sparso, a pp di **spargere** ♦ ag scattered; (sciolto) loose

spar'tire vt (eredità, bottino) to share out; (avversari) to separate

spar'tito sm (MUS) score

sparti'traffico sm inv (AUT) central reservation (BRIT), median (strip) (US)

spa'ruto, a ag (viso etc) haggard

sparvi'ero sm (ZOOL) sparrowhawk

spasi'mante sm suitor

'spasimo sm pang; **'spasmo** sm (MED) spasm; **spas'modico, a, ci, che** ag (angoscioso) agonizing; (MED) spasmodic

'spasso sm (divertimento) amusement, enjoyment; **andare a ~** to go out for a walk; **essere a ~** (fig) to be out of work; **mandare qn a ~** (fig) to give sb the sack

'spatola sf spatula; (di muratore) trowel

spauracchio [spau'rakkjo] sm scarecrow

spau'rire vt to frighten, terrify

spa'valdo, a ag arrogant, bold

spaventa'passeri sm inv scarecrow

spaven'tare vt to frighten, scare; **~rsi** vr to be frightened, be scared; to get a fright; **spa'vento** sm fear, fright; **far spavento a qn** to give sb a fright; **spaven'toso, a** ag frightening, terrible; (fig: fam) tremendous, fantastic

spazien'tire vi (anche: **~rsi**) to lose one's patience

'spazio ['spattsjo] sm space; **~ aereo** airspace; **spazi'oso, a** ag spacious

spazzaca'mino [spattsaka'mino] sm chimney sweep

spazza'neve [spattsa'neve] sm inv snowplough

spaz'zare [spat'tsare] vt to sweep; (foglie etc) to sweep up; (cacciare) to sweep away; **spazza'tura** sf sweepings pl; (immondizia) rubbish; **spaz'zino** sm street sweeper

'spazzola ['spattsola] sf brush; **~ per abiti** clothesbrush; **~ da capelli** hairbrush; **spazzo'lare** vt to brush;

spazzo'lino *sm* (small) brush;
spazzolino da denti toothbrush

specchi'arsi [spek'kjarsi] *vr* to look at
o.s. in a mirror; *(riflettersi)* to be
mirrored, be reflected

'specchio ['spekkjo] *sm* mirror

speci'ale [spe'tʃale] *ag* special;
specia'lista, i, e *sm/f* specialist;
specialità *sf inv* speciality; *(branca di
studio)* special field, speciality;
specializ'zarsi *vr*: **specializzarsi (in)**
to specialize (in); **special'mente** *av*
especially, particularly

'specie ['spetʃe] *sf inv* (BIOL, BOT, ZOOL)
species *inv*; *(tipo)* kind, sort ♦ *av*
especially, particularly; **una ~ di** a kind
of; **fare ~ a qn** to surprise sb; **la
~ umana** mankind

specifi'care [spetʃifi'kare] *vt* to
specify, state

spe'cifico, a, ci, che [spe'tʃifiko] *ag*
specific

specu'lare *vi*: **~ su** (COMM) to
speculate in; *(sfruttare)* to exploit;
(meditare) to speculate on;
speculazi'one *sf* speculation

spe'dire *vt* to send; **spedizi'one** *sf*
sending; *(collo)* consignment;
(scientifica etc) expedition

'spegnere ['spɛɲɲere] *vt* (fuoco,
sigaretta) to put out, extinguish;
(apparecchio elettrico) to turn o switch
off; *(gas)* to turn off; *(fig: suoni,
passioni)* to stifle; *(debito)* to extinguish;
~rsi *vr* to go out; to go off; *(morire)* to
pass away

spel'lare *vt* (scuoiare) to skin;
(scorticare) to graze; **~rsi** *vr* to peel

'spendere *vt* to spend

spen'nare *vt* to pluck

spensie'rato, a *ag* carefree

'spento, a *pp di* **spegnere** ♦ *ag*
(suono) muffled; *(colore)* dull;
(sigaretta) out; *(civiltà, vulcano)* extinct

spe'ranza [spe'rantsa] *sf* hope

spe'rare *vt* to hope for ♦ *vi*: **~ in** to
trust in; **~ che/di fare** to hope that/to

do; **lo spero, spero di sì** I hope so

sper'duto, a *ag* (isolato) out-of-the-
way; *(persona: smarrita, a disagio)* lost

spergi'uro, a [sper'dʒuro] *sm/f*
perjurer ♦ *sm* perjury

sperimen'tale *ag* experimental

sperimen'tare *vt* to experiment with,
test; *(fig)* to test, put to the test

'sperma, i *sm* sperm

spe'rone *sm* spur

sperpe'rare *vt* to squander

'spesa *sf (somma di denaro)* expense;
(costo) cost; *(acquisto)* purchase; *(fam:
acquisto del cibo quotidiano)* shopping;
~e *sfpl (soldi spesi)* expenses; (COMM)
costs; charges; **fare la ~** to do the
shopping; **a ~e di** *(a carico di)* at the
expense of; **~e generali** overheads; **~e
postali** postage *sg*; **~e di viaggio**
travelling expenses

'speso, a *pp di* **spendere**

'spesso, a *ag (fitto)* thick; *(frequente)*
frequent ♦ *av* often; **~e volte**
frequently, often

spes'sore *sm* thickness

spet'tabile *(abbr:* **Spett.***: in lettere)*
ag: **~ ditta X** Messrs X and Co.

spet'tacolo *sm (rappresentazione)*
performance, show; *(vista, scena)* sight;
dare ~ di sé to make an exhibition o
a spectacle of o.s.; **spetta'coloso, a**
ag spectacular

spet'tare *vi*: **~ a** *(decisione)* to be up
to; *(stipendio)* to be due; **spetta a te
decidere** it's up to you to decide

spetta'tore, 'trice *sm/f* (CINEMA,
TEATRO) member of the audience; *(di
avvenimento)* onlooker, witness

spetti'nare *vt*: **~ qn** to ruffle sb's hair;
~rsi *vr* to get one's hair in a mess

'spettro *sm (fantasma)* spectre; *(FISICA)*
spectrum

'spezie ['spɛttsje] *sfpl* (CUC) spices

spez'zare [spet'tsare] *vt* (rompere) to
break; *(fig: interrompere)* to break up;
~rsi *vr* to break

spezza'tino [spettsa'tino] *sm* (CUC)

stew

spezzet'tare [spettset'tare] vt to break up (o chop) into small pieces

'**spia** sf spy; (confidente della polizia) informer; (ELETTR) indicating light; warning light; (fessura) peep-hole; (fig: sintomo) sign, indication

spia'cente [spja'tʃɛnte] ag sorry; essere ~ di qc/di fare qc to be sorry about sth/for doing sth

spia'cevole [spja'tʃevole] ag unpleasant

spi'aggia, ge ['spjaddʒa] sf beach; ~ libera public beach

spia'nare vt (terreno) to level, make level; (edificio) to raze to the ground; (pasta) to roll out; (rendere liscio) to smooth (out)

spi'ano sm: a tutto ~ (lavorare) nonstop, without a break; (spendere) lavishly

spi'are vt to spy on

spi'azzo ['spjattso] sm open space; (radura) clearing

spic'care vt (assegno, mandato di cattura) to issue ♦ vi (risaltare) to stand out; ~ il volo to fly off; (fig) to spread one's wings; ~ un balzo to leap; spic'cato, a ag (marcato) marked, strong; (notevole) remarkable

'**spicchio** ['spikkjo] sm (di agrumi) segment; (di aglio) clove; (parte) piece, slice

spicci'are [spit'tʃare] vt to finish off quickly; ~rsi vr to hurry up

'spicciolo, a ['spittʃolo] ag: moneta ~a, ~i smpl (small) change

'spicco, chi sm: di ~ outstanding; (tema) main, principal; fare ~ to stand out

spie'dino sm (utensile) skewer; (pietanza) kebab

spi'edo sm (CUC) spit

spie'gare vt (far capire) to explain; (tovaglia) to unfold; (vele) to unfurl; ~rsi vr to explain o.s., make o.s. clear;

~ qc a qn to explain sth to sb; spiegazi'one sf explanation

spiegaz'zare [spjegat'tsare] vt to crease, crumple

spie'tato, a ag ruthless, pitiless

spiffe'rare (fam) vt to blurt out, blab

'spiga, ghe sf (BOT) ear

spigli'ato, a [spiʎ'ʎato] ag selfpossessed, self-confident

'spigolo sm corner; (MAT) edge

'spilla sf brooch; (da cravatta, cappello) pin; ~ di sicurezza o da balia safety pin

spil'lare vt (vino, fig) to tap; ~ denaro/notizie a qn to tap sb for money/information

'spillo sm pin

spi'lorcio, a, ci, ce [spi'lortʃo] ag mean, stingy

'spina sf (BOT) thorn; (ZOOL) spine, prickle; (di pesce) bone; (ELETTR) plug; (di botte) bunghole; birra alla ~ draught beer; ~ dorsale (ANAT) backbone

spi'nacio [spi'natʃo] sm spinach; (CUC): ~i spinach pl

'spingere ['spindʒere] vt to push; (condurre: anche fig) to drive; (stimolare): ~ qn a fare to urge o press sb to do; ~rsi vr (inoltrarsi) to push on, carry on; ~rsi troppo lontano (anche fig) to go too far

spi'noso, a ag thorny, prickly

'spinta sf (urto) push; (FISICA) thrust; (fig: stimolo) incentive, spur; (: appoggio) string-pulling no pl; dare una ~ a a qn (fig) to pull strings for sb

'spinto, a pp di spingere

spio'naggio [spio'naddʒo] sm espionage, spying

spi'overe vi to stop raining

'spira sf coil

spi'raglio [spi'raʎʎo] sm (fessura) chink, narrow opening; (raggio di luce, fig) glimmer, gleam

spi'rale sf spiral; (contraccettivo) coil; a ~ spiral(-shaped)

spi'rare vi (vento) to blow; (morire) to expire, pass away

spiri'tato, a ag possessed; (fig: persona, espressione) wild

spiri'tismo sm spiritualism

'spirito sm (REL, CHIM, disposizione d'animo, di legge etc, fantasma) spirit; (pensieri, intelletto) mind; (arguzia) wit; (umorismo) humour, wit; **lo S~ Santo** the Holy Spirit o Ghost

spirito'saggine [spirito'saddʒine] sf witticism; (peg) wisecrack

spiri'toso, a ag witty

spiritu'ale ag spiritual

'splendere vi to shine

'splendido, a ag splendid; (splendente) shining; (sfarzoso) magnificent, splendid

splen'dore sm splendour; (luce intensa) brilliance, brightness

spodes'tare vt to deprive of power; (sovrano) to depose

spogli'are [spoʎˈʎare] vt (svestire) to undress; (privare, fig: depredare): **~ qn di qc** to deprive sb of sth; (togliere ornamenti: anche fig): **~ qn/qc di** to strip sb/sth of; **~rsi** vr to undress, strip; **~rsi di** (ricchezze etc) to deprive o.s. of, give up; (pregiudizi) to rid o.s. of

spoglia'toio sm (dressing room; (di scuola etc) cloakroom; (SPORT) changing room; **'spoglie** ['spoʎʎe] sfpl (salma) remains; (preda) spoils, booty sg; vedi anche **spoglio**; **'spoglio, a** ag (pianta, terreno) bare; (privo): **spoglio di** stripped of; lacking in, without ♦ sm (di voti) counting

'spola sf (bobina di filo) cop; **fare la ~ (fra)** to go to and fro o shuttle (between)

spol'pare vt to strip the flesh off

spolve'rare vt (anche cuc) to dust; (con spazzola) to brush; (con battipanni) to beat; (fig) to polish off ♦ vi to dust

'sponda sf (di fiume) bank; (di mare, lago) shore; (bordo) edge

spon'taneo, a ag spontaneous; (persona) unaffected, natural

spopo'lare vt to depopulate ♦ vi (attirare folla) to draw the crowds; **~rsi** vr to become depopulated

spor'care vt to dirty, make dirty; (fig) to sully, soil; **~rsi** vr to get dirty

spor'cizia [spor'tʃittsja] sf (stato) dirtiness; (sudiciume) dirt, filth; (cosa sporca) dirt no pl, something dirty

'sporco, a, chi, che ag dirty, filthy

spor'genza [spor'dʒentsa] sf projection

'sporgere ['spordʒere] vt to put out, stretch out ♦ vi (venire in fuori) to stick out; **~rsi** vr to lean out; **~ querela contro qn** (DIR) to take legal action against sb

sport sm inv sport

'sporta sf shopping bag

spor'tello sm (di treno, auto etc) door; (di banca, ufficio) window, counter; **~ automatico** (BANCA) cash dispenser, automated telling machine

spor'tivo, a ag (gara, giornale, centro) sports cpd; (persona) sporty; (abito) casual; (spirito, atteggiamento) sporting

'sporto, a pp di **sporgere**

'sposa sf bride; (moglie) wife

spo'sare vt to marry; (fig: idea, fede) to espouse; **~rsi** vr to get married, marry; **~rsi con qn** to marry sb, get married to sb; **spo'sato, a** ag married

'sposo sm (bride)groom; (marito) husband; **gli ~i** smpl the newlyweds

spos'sato, a ag exhausted, weary

spos'tare vt to move, shift; (cambiare: orario) to change; **~rsi** vr to move

'spranga, ghe sf (sbarra) bar

'sprazzo ['sprattso] sm (di sole etc) flash; (fig: di gioia etc) burst

spre'care vt to waste; **~rsi** vr (persona) to waste one's energy; **'spreco** sm waste

spre'gevole [spre'dʒevole] ag

contemptible, despicable

spregiudi'cato, a [spredʒudi'kato] ag unprejudiced, unbiased; (peg) unscrupulous

'spremere vt to squeeze

spre'muta sf fresh juice; ~ **d'arancia** fresh orange juice

sprez'zante [spret'tsante] ag scornful, contemptuous

sprigio'nare [spridʒo'nare] vt to give off, emit; ~**rsi** vr to emanate; (uscire con impeto) to burst out

spriz'zare [sprit'tsare] vt, vi to spurt; ~ **gioia/salute** to be bursting with joy/health

sprofon'dare vi to sink; (casa) to collapse; (suolo) to give way, subside; ~**rsi** vr: ~**rsi in** (poltrona) to sink into; (fig) to become immersed o absorbed in

spro'nare vt to spur (on)

'sprone sm (sperone, fig) spur

sproporzio'nato, a [sproportsjo-'nato] ag disproportionate, out of all proportion

sproporzi'one [spropor'tsjone] sf disproportion

spropo'sito sm blunder; **a ~** at the wrong time; (rispondere, parlare) irrelevantly

sprovve'duto, a ag inexperienced, naïve

sprov'visto, a ag (mancante): ~ **di** lacking in, without; **alla ~a** unawares

spruz'zare [sprut'tsare] vt (a nebulizzazione) to spray; (aspergere) to sprinkle; (inzaccherare) to splash; **'spruzzo** sm spray; splash

'spugna ['spuɲɲa] sf (ZOOL) sponge; (tessuto) towelling; **spu'gnoso, a** ag spongy

'spuma sf (schiuma) foam; (bibita) fizzy drink

spu'mante sm sparkling wine

spumeggi'ante [spumed'dʒante] ag (birra) foaming; (vino, fig) sparkling

spu'mone sm (CUC) mousse

spun'tare vt (coltello) to break the point of; (capelli) to trim ♦ vi (uscire: germogli) to sprout; (: capelli) to begin to grow; (: denti) to come through; (apparire) to appear (suddenly); ~**rsi** vr to become blunt, lose its point; **spuntarla** (fig) to make it, win through

spun'tino sm snack

'spunto sm (TEATRO, MUS) cue; (fig) starting point; **dare lo ~ a** (fig) to give rise to

spur'gare vt (fogna) to clean, clear

spu'tare vt to spit out; (fig) to belch (out) ♦ vi to spit; **'sputo** sm spittle no pl, spit no pl

'squadra sf (strumento) (set) square; (gruppo) team, squad; (di operai) gang, squad; (MIL) squad; (: AER, NAUT) squadron; (SPORT) team; **lavoro a ~e** teamwork

squa'drare vt to square, make square; (osservare) to look at closely

squa'driglia [skwa'driʎʎa] sf (AER) flight; (NAUT) squadron

squa'drone sm squadron

squagli'arsi [skwaʎ'ʎarsi] vr to melt; (fig) to sneak off

squa'lifica sf disqualification

squalifi'care vt to disqualify

squal'lido, a ag wretched, bleak

squal'lore sm wretchedness, bleakness

'squalo sm shark

'squama sf scale; **squa'mare** vt to scale; **squamarsi** vr to flake o peel (off)

squarcia'gola [skwartʃa'gola]: **a ~** av at the top of one's voice

squarci'are [skwar'tʃare] vt to rip (open); (fig) to pierce

squar'tare vt to quarter, cut up

squattri'nato, a ag penniless

squili'brato, a ag (PSIC) unbalanced; **squi'librio** sm (differenza, sbilancio) imbalance; (PSIC) unbalance

squil'lante ag shrill, sharp

squil'lare vi (campanello, telefono) to ring (out); (tromba) to blare; **'squillo** sm ring, ringing no pl; blare; **ragazza f squillo** inv call girl

squi'sito, a ag exquisite; (cibo) delicious; (persona) delightful

squit'tire vi (uccello) to squawk; (topo) to squeak

sradi'care vt to uproot; (fig) to eradicate

sragio'nare [zradʒo'nare] vi to talk nonsense, rave

srego'lato, a ag (senza ordine: vita) disorderly; (smodato) immoderate; (dissoluto) dissolute

S.r.l. abbr = **società a responsabilità limitata**

'stabile ag stable, steady; (tempo: non variabile) settled; (TEATRO: compagnia) resident ♦ sm (edificio) building

stabili'mento sm (edificio) establishment; (fabbrica) plant, factory

stabi'lire vt to establish; (fissare: prezzi, data) to fix; (decidere) to decide; **~rsi** vr (prendere dimora) to settle

stac'care vt (levare) to detach, remove; (separare: anche fig) to separate, divide; (strappare) to tear off (o out); (staccare: parole) to pronounce clearly; (SPORT) to leave behind; **~rsi (da)** to come off; (scostarsi): **~rsi (da)** to move away (from); (fig: separarsi): **~rsi da** to leave; **non ~ gli occhi di dosso a qn** not to take one's eyes off sb

'stadio sm (SPORT) stadium; (periodo, fase) phase, stage

'staffa sf (di sella, TECN) stirrup; **perdere le ~e** (fig) to fly off the handle

staf'fetta sf (messo) dispatch rider; (SPORT) relay race

stagio'nale [stadʒo'nale] ag seasonal

stagio'nare [stadʒo'nare] vt (legno) to season; (formaggi, vino) to mature

stagi'one [sta'dʒone] sf season; **alta/**

bassa ~ high/low season

stagli'arsi [staʎ'ʎarsi] vr to stand out, be silhouetted

'stagno, a [staɲɲo] ag watertight; (a tenuta d'aria) airtight ♦ sm (acquitrino) pond; (CHIM) tin

sta'gnola [sta'ɲɔla] sf tinfoil

'stalla sf (per bovini) cowshed; (per cavalli) stable

stal'lone sm stallion

sta'mani av = **stamattina**

stamat'tina av this morning

stam'becco, chi sm ibex

'stampa sf (TIP, FOT: tecnica) printing; (impressione, copia fotografica) print; (insieme di quotidiani, giornalisti etc) press; **"~e"** sfpl "printed matter"

stam'pante sf (INFORM) printer

stam'pare vt to print; (pubblicare) to publish; (coniare) to strike, coin; (imprimere: anche fig) to impress

stampa'tello sm block letters pl

stam'pella sf crutch

'stampo sm mould; (fig: indole) type, kind, sort

sta'nare vt to drive out

stan'care vt to tire, make tired; (annoiare) to bore; (infastidire) to annoy; **~rsi** vr to get tired, tire o.s. out; **~rsi (di)** to grow weary (of), grow tired (of)

stan'chezza [stan'kettsa] sf tiredness, fatigue

'stanco, a, chi, che ag tired; **~ di** tired of, fed up with

'stanga, ghe sf (di carro) bar; (di carro) shaft

stan'gata sf (colpo: anche fig) blow; (cattivo risultato) poor result; (CALCIO) shot

sta'notte av tonight; (notte passata) last night

'stante prep: **a sé ~** (appartamento, casa) independent, separate

stan'tio, a, 'tii, 'tie ag stale; (burro) rancid; (fig) old

stan'tuffo sm piston

'stanza ['stantsa] sf room; (POESIA)

stanza; **~ da letto** bedroom

stanzi'are [stan'tsjare] *vt* to allocate

stap'pare *vt* to uncork; to uncap

'stare *vi* (*restare in un luogo*) to stay, remain; (*abitare*) to stay, live; (*essere situato*) to be, be situated; (*anche: ~ in piedi*) to be, stand; (*essere, trovarsi*) to be; (*dipendere*): **se stesse in me** if it were up to me, if it depended on me; (*seguito da gerundio*): **sta studiando** he's studying; **starci** (*esserci spazio*): **nel baule non ci sta più niente** there's no more room in the boot; (*accettare*) to accept; **ci stai?** is that okay with you?; **~ a** (*attenersi a*) to follow, stick to; (*seguito dall'infinito*): **stiamo a discutere** we're talking; (*toccare a*): **sta a te giocare** it's your turn to play; **~ per fare qc** to be about to do sth; **come stai?** how are you?; **io sto bene/male** I'm very well/not very well; **~ a qn** (*abiti etc*) to fit sb; **queste scarpe mi stanno strette** these shoes are tight for me; **il rosso ti sta bene** red suits you

starnu'tire *vi* to sneeze; **star'nuto** *sm* sneeze

sta'sera *av* this evening, tonight

sta'tale *ag* state *cpd*; government ♦ *sm/f* state employee, local authority employee; (*nell'amministrazione*) ≈ civil servant

sta'tista, i *sm* statesman

sta'tistica *sf* statistics *sg*

'stato, a *pp di* **essere; stare** ♦ *sm* (*condizione*) state, condition; (*POL*) state; (*DIR*) status; **essere in ~ d'accusa** (*DIR*) to be committed for trial; **~ d'assedio/d'emergenza** state of siege/emergency; **~ civile** (*AMM*) marital status; **~ maggiore** (*MIL*) staff; **gli S~i Uniti (d'America)** the United States (of America)

'statua *sf* statue

statuni'tense *ag* United States *cpd*, of the United States

sta'tura *sf* (*ANAT*) height, stature; (*fig*)

stature

sta'tuto *sm* (*DIR*) statute; constitution

sta'volta *av* this time

stazio'nario, a [stattsjo'narjo] *ag* stationary; (*fig*) unchanged

stazi'one [stat'tsjone] *sf* station; (*balneare, termale*) resort; **~ degli autobus** bus station; **~ balneare** seaside resort; **~ ferroviaria** railway (*BRIT*) o railroad (*US*) station; **~ invernale** winter sports resort; **~ di polizia** police station (*in small town*); **~ di servizio** service o petrol (*BRIT*) o filling station

'stecca, che *sf* stick; (*di ombrello*) rib; (*di sigarette*) carton; (*MED*) splint; (*stonatura*): **fare una ~** to sing (o play) a wrong note

stec'cato *sm* fence

stec'chito, a [stek'kito] *ag*: **lasciar ~ qn** (*fig*) to leave sb flabbergasted; **morto ~** stone dead

'stella *sf* star; **~ alpina** (*BOT*) edelweiss; **~ di mare** (*ZOOL*) starfish

'stelo *sm* stem; (*asta*) rod; **lampada a ~** standard lamp

'stemma, i *sm* coat of arms

stempe'rare *vt* to dilute; to dissolve; (*colori*) to mix

sten'dardo *sm* standard

'stendere *vt* (*braccia, gambe*) to stretch (out); (*tovaglia*) to spread (out); (*bucato*) to hang out; (*mettere a giacere*) to lay (down); (*spalmare: colore*) to spread; (*mettere per iscritto*) to draw up; **~rsi** *vr* (*coricarsi*) to stretch out, lie down; (*estendersi*) to extend, stretch

stenodatti'lografo, a *sm/f* shorthand typist (*BRIT*), stenographer (*US*)

stenogra'fare *vt* to take down in shorthand; **stenogra'fia** *sf* shorthand

sten'tare *vi*: **~ a fare** to find it hard to do, have difficulty doing

'stento, a (*fatica*) difficulty; **~i** *smpl* (*privazioni*) hardship *sg*, privation *sg*; **a ~** with difficulty, barely '**sterco** sm dung

'**stereo**('**fonico, a, ci, che**) ag stereo(phonic)

'**sterile** ag sterile; (*terra*) barren; (*fig*) futile, fruitless; **sterilità** sf sterility

sterili'zzare [sterilid'dzare] vt to sterilize; **sterilizzazi'one** sf sterilization

ster'lina sf pound (sterling)

stermi'nare vt to exterminate, wipe out

stermi'nato, a ag immense; endless

ster'minio sm extermination, destruction

'**sterno** sm (ANAT) breastbone

'**sterpo** sm dry twig; **~i** smpl brushwood sg

ster'zare [ster'tsare] vt, vi (AUT) to steer; '**sterzo** sm steering; (*volante*) steering wheel

'**steso, a** pp di **stendere**

'**stesso, a** ag same; (*rafforzativo: in persona, proprio*): **il re ~** the king himself o in person ♦ pron: **lo(la) ~(a)** the same (one); **i suoi ~i avversari lo ammirano** even his enemies admire him; **fa lo ~** it doesn't matter; **per me è lo ~** it's all the same to me, it doesn't matter to me; *vedi* **io; tu** etc

ste'sura sf drafting no pl, drawing up no pl; draft

'**stigmate** sfpl (REL) stigmata

sti'lare vt to draw up, draft

'**stile** sm style; stil'lista, i sm designer

stil'lare vi (*trasudare*) to ooze; (*gocciolare*) to drip; **stilli'cidio** sm (*fig*) continual pestering (o moaning etc)

stilo'grafica, che sf (*anche: penna* ~) fountain pen

'**stima** sf esteem; valuation; assessment, estimate

sti'mare vt (*persona*) to esteem, hold in high regard; (*terreno, casa* etc) to value; (*stabilire in misura approssimativa*) to estimate, assess; (*ritenere*): **~ che** to consider that; **~rsi fortunato** to consider o.s. (to be)

lucky

stimo'lare vt to stimulate; (*incitare*): **~ qn (a fare)** to spur sb on (to do)

'**stimolo** sm (*anche fig*) stimulus

'**stinco, chi** sm shin; shinbone

'**stingere** ['stindʒere] vt, vi (*anche:* ~*rsi*) to fade; '**stinto, a** pp di **stingere**

sti'pare vt to cram, pack; **~rsi** vr (*accalcarsi*) to crowd, throng

sti'pendio sm salary

'**stipite** sm (*di porta, finestra*) jamb

stipu'lare vt (*redigere*) to draw up

sti'rare vt (*abito*) to iron; (*distendere*) to stretch; (*strappare: muscolo*) to strain; **~rsi** vr to stretch (o.s.); **stira'tura** sf ironing

'**stirpe** sf birth, stock; descendants pl

stiti'chezza [stiti'kettsa] sf constipation

'**stitico, ci, che** ag constipated

'**stiva** sf (*di nave*) hold

sti'vale sm boot

'**stizza** ['stittsa] sf anger, vexation; **stiz'zirsi** vr to lose one's temper; **stiz'zoso, a** ag (*persona*) quick-tempered, irascible; (*risposta*) angry

stocca'fisso sm stockfish, dried cod

stoc'cata sf (*colpo*) stab, thrust; (*fig*) gibe, cutting remark

'**stoffa** sf material, fabric; (*fig*): **aver la ~ di** to have the makings of

'**stola** sf stole

'**stolto, a** ag stupid, foolish

'**stomaco, chi** sm stomach; **dare di ~** to vomit, be sick

sto'nare vt to sing (o play) out of tune ♦ vi to be out of tune, sing (o play) out of tune; (*fig*) to be out of place, jar; (: *colori*) to clash; **stona'tura** sf (*suono*) false note

stop sm inv (TEL) stop; (AUT: *cartello*) stop sign; (: *fanalino d'arresto*) brake-light

'**stoppa** sf tow

stop'pino sm wick; (*miccia*) fuse

'**storcere** ['stɔrtʃere] vt to twist; **~rsi** vr to writhe, twist; **~ il naso** (*fig*) to turn up one's nose; **~rsi la caviglia** to twist one's ankle

stor'dire vt (intontire) to stun, daze; **~rsi** vr: **~rsi col bere** to dull one's senses with drink; **stor'dito, a** ag stunned

'storia sf (scienza, avvenimenti) history; (racconto, bugia) story; (faccenda, questione) business no pl; (pretesto) excuse, pretext; **~e** sfpl (smancerie) fuss sg; **'storico, a, ci, che** ag historic(al) ♦ sm historian

stori'one sm (ZOOL) sturgeon

stor'mire vi to rustle

'stormo sm (di uccelli) flock

stor'nare vt (COMM) to transfer

'storno sm (ZOOL) starling

storpi'are vt to cripple, maim; (fig: parole) to mangle (: significato) to twist

'storpio, a ag crippled, maimed

'storta sf (distorsione) sprain, twist

'storto, a pp di **storcere** ♦ ag twisted, bent; (gamba, quadro) crooked

sto'viglie [sto'viʎʎe] sfpl dishes pl, crockery

strabico, a, ci, che ag squint-eyed; (occhi) squint

stra'bismo sm squinting

stra'carico, a, chi, che ag overloaded

strac'chino [strak'kino] sm type of soft cheese

stracci'are [strat'tʃare] vt to tear

'straccio, a, ci, ce [strat'tʃo] ag: **carta ~a** waste paper ♦ sm rag; (per pulire) cloth, duster

stra'cotto, a ag overcooked ♦ sm (CUC) beef stew

'strada sf road; (di città) street; (cammino, via, fig) way; **farsi ~** (fig) to do well for o.s.; **essere fuori ~** (fig) to be on the wrong track; **~ facendo** on the way; **~ senza uscita** dead end; **stra'dale** ag road cpd

strafalci'one [strafal'tʃone] sm blunder, howler

stra'fare vi to overdo it; **stra'fatto, a** pp di **strafare**

strafot'tente ag: **è ~** he doesn't give a damn, he couldn't care less

'strage ['stradʒe] sf massacre, slaughter

stralu'nato, a ag (occhi) rolling; (persona) beside o.s., very upset

stramaz'zare [stramat'tsare] vi to fall heavily

'strambo, a ag strange, queer

strampa'lato, a ag odd, eccentric

stra'nezza [stra'nettsa] sf strangeness

strango'lare vt to strangle; **~rsi** vr to choke

strani'ero, a ag foreign ♦ sm/f foreigner

'strano, a ag strange, odd

straordi'nario, a ag extraordinary; (treno etc) special ♦ sm (lavoro) overtime

strapaz'zare [strapat'tsare] vt to ill-treat; **~rsi** vr to tire o.s. out, overdo things; **stra'pazzo** sm strain, fatigue; **da strapazzo** (fig) third-rate

strapi'ombo sm overhanging rock; **a ~** overhanging

strapo'tere sm excessive power

strap'pare vt (gen) to tear, rip; (pagina etc) to tear off, tear out; (estrarre) to pull up; (togliere): **~ qc a qn** to snatch sth from sb; (fig) to wrest sth from sb; **~rsi** vr (lacerarsi) to rip, tear; (rompersi) to break; **~rsi un muscolo** to tear a muscle; **'strappo** sm pull, tug; tear, rip; **fare uno strappo alla regola** to make an exception to the rule; **strappo muscolare** torn muscle

strari'pare vi to overflow

strasci'care [straʃʃi'kare] vt to trail; (piedi) to drag; **~rsi** vr to drag o.s. along; **'strascico, chi** ['straʃʃiko] sm (di abito) train; (conseguenza) after-effect

strata'gemma, i [strata'dʒemma] sm stratagem

strate'gia, 'gie [strate'dʒia] sf strategy; **stra'tegico, a, ci, che** ag strategic

'**strato** sm layer; (rivestimento) coat, coating; (GEO, fig) stratum; (METEOR) stratus; ~ **di ozono** ozone layer

stra**va'gante** a ag strange, odd, eccentric; **strava'ganza** sf eccentricity

stra'**vecchio, a** [stra'vɛkkjo] ag very old

stra'**vizio** [stra'vittsjo] sm excess

stra**'volgere** [stra'vɔldʒere] vt (volto) to contort; (fig: animo) to trouble deeply; (: verità) to twist, distort; stra**'volto, a** pp di stravolgere

strazi**'are** [strat'tsjare] vt to torture, torment; **'strazio** sm torture; (fig: cosa fatta male): **essere uno ~** to be appalling

'**strega** sf witch

stre**'gare** vt to bewitch

stre'**gone** sm (mago) wizard; (di tribù) witch doctor

'**stregua** sf: **alla ~ di** by the same standard as

stre'**mare** vt to exhaust

'**stremo** sm very end; **essere allo ~** to be at the end of one's tether

'**strenna** sf Christmas present

strepi**'toso, a** ag clamorous, deafening; (fig: successo) resounding

stres'**sante** a ag stressful

'**stretta** sf (di mano) grasp; (finanziaria) squeeze; (fig: dolore, turbamento) pang; **una ~a di mano** a handshake; **essere alle ~e** to have one's back to the wall; vedi anche **stretto**

stretta'**mente** av tightly; (rigorosamente) strictly

stret'**tezza** [stret'tettsa] sf narrowness

'**stretto, a** pp di stringere ♦ ag (corridoio, limiti) narrow; (gonna, scarpe, nodo, curva) tight; (intimo: parente, amico) close; (rigoroso: osservanza) strict; (preciso: significato) precise, exact ♦ sm (braccio di mare) strait; **a denti ~i** with clenched teeth; **lo ~ necessario** the bare minimum; stret'**toia** sf bottleneck; (fig) tricky

situation

stri'**ato, a** ag streaked

'**stridere** vi (porta) to squeak; (animale) to screech, shriek; (colori) to clash; '**stridulo, a** ag shrill

stril**'lare** vt, vi to scream, shriek; '**strillo** sm scream, shriek

stril'**lone** sm newspaper seller

strimin'**zito, a** [strimin'tsito] ag (misero) shabby; (molto magro) skinny

strimpel'**lare** vt (MUS) to strum

'**stringa, ghe** sf lace

strin'**gato, a** ag (fig) concise

'**stringere** ['strindʒere] vt (avvicinare due cose) to press (together), squeeze (together); (tenere stretto) to hold tight, clasp, clutch; (pugno, mascella, denti) to clench; (labbra) to compress; (avvitare) to tighten; (abito) to take in; (sog: scarpe) to pinch, be tight for; (fig: concludere: patto) to make; (: accelerare: passo, tempo) to quicken ♦ vi (essere stretto) to be tight; (tempo: incalzare) to be pressing; **~rsi** vr (accostarsi) to press o.s. up against; **~ la mano a qn** to shake sb's hand; **~ gli occhi** to screw up one's eyes

'**striscia, sce** ['striʃʃa] sf (di carta, tessuto ecc) strip; (riga) stripe; **~sce (pedonali)** zebra crossing sg

strisci'**are** [striʃ'ʃare] vt (piedi) to drag; (muro, macchina) to graze ♦ vi to crawl, creep

'**striscio** ['striʃʃo] sm graze; (MED) smear; **colpire di ~** to graze

strito'**lare** vt to grind

striz'**zare** [strit'tsare] vt (panni) to wring (out); **~ l'occhio** to wink

'**strofa** sf strophe

strofi'**naccio** [strofi'nattʃo] sm duster, cloth; (per piatti) dishcloth; (per pavimenti) floorcloth

strofi'**nare** vt to rub

stron'**care** vt to break off; (fig: ribellione) to suppress, put down; (: film, libro) to tear to pieces

stropicci'are [stropit'tʃare] vt to rub

stroz'zare [strot'tsare] vt (soffocare): ~rsi vr to choke, strangle; (da vetri) bottleneck

strozza'tura sf (restringimento) narrowing; (di strada etc) bottleneck

'struggersi ['struddʒersi] vr (fig): ~ di to be consumed with

strumen'tale ag (MUS) instrumental

strumentaliz'zare [strumentalid-'dzare] vt to exploit, use to one's own ends

stru'mento sm (arnese, fig) instrument, tool; (MUS) instrument; ~ a corda o ad arco/a fiato stringed/ wind instrument

'strutto sm lard

strut'tura sf structure; **struttu'rare** vt to structure

'struzzo ['struttso] sm ostrich

stuc'care vt (muro) to plaster; (vetro) to putty; (decorare con stucchi) to stucco

stuc'chevole [stuk'kevole] ag nauseating; (fig) tedious, boring

'stucco, chi sm plaster; (da vetri) putty; (ornamentale) stucco; **rimanere di ~** (fig) to be dumbfounded

stu'dente, 'essa sm/f student; (scolaro) pupil, schoolboy/girl; **studen'tesco, a, schi, sche** ag student cpd; school cpd

studi'are vt to study

'studio sm studying; (ricerca, saggio, stanza) study; (di professionista) office; (di artista, CINEMA, TV, RADIO) studio; ~i smpl (INS) studies; ~ medico doctor's surgery (BRIT) o office (US)

studi'oso, a ag studious, hard-working ♦ sm/f scholar

'stufa sf stove; ~ elettrica electric fire o heater

stu'fare vt (CUC) to stew; (fig: fam) to bore; **stu'fato** sm (CUC) stew; **'stufo, a** (fam) ag: **essere stufo di** to be fed up with, be sick and tired of

stu'oia sf mat

stupefa'cente [stupefa'tʃɛnte] ag stunning, astounding ♦ sm drug, narcotic

stu'pendo, a ag marvellous, wonderful

stupi'daggine [stupi'daddʒine] sf stupid thing (to do o say)

stupidità sf stupidity

'stupido, a ag stupid

stu'pire vt to amaze, stun ♦ vi (anche: ~rsi): ~ (di) to be amazed (at), be stunned (by)

stu'pore sm amazement, astonishment

'stupro sm rape

stu'rare vt (lavandino) to clear

stuzzica'denti [stuttsika'denti] sm toothpick

stuzzi'care [stuttsi'kare] vt (ferita etc) to poke (at), prod (at); (fig) to tease; (: appetito) to whet; (: curiosità) to stimulate; ~ **i denti** to pick one's teeth

---

PAROLA CHIAVE

su (su +il = sul, su +lo = sullo, su +l' = sull', su +la = sulla, su +i = sui, su +gli = sugli, su +le = sulle) prep **1** (gen) on; (moto) on(to); (in cima a) on (top of); **mettilo sul tavolo** put it on the table; **un paesino sul mare** a village by the sea

2 (argomento) about, on; **un libro su Cesare** a book on o about Caesar

3 (circa) about; **costerà sui 3 milioni** it will cost about 3 million; **una ragazza sui 17 anni** a girl of about 17 (years of age)

4: ~ **misura** made to measure; ~ **richiesta** on request; **3 casi su dieci** 3 cases out of 10

♦ av **1** (in alto, verso l'alto) up; **vieni ~** come on up; **guarda ~** look up; ~ **le mani!** hands up!; **in ~** (verso l'alto) up(wards); (in poi) onwards; **dai 20 anni in ~** from the age of 20 onwards

2 (addosso) on; **cos'hai ~?** what have you got on?

♦ escl come on!; ~ **coraggio!** come on, cheer up!

'sua vedi **suo**

su'bacqueo, a ag underwater ♦ sm skindiver

sub'buglio [sub'buʎʎo] sm confusion, turmoil

subcosci'ente [subkoʃ'ʃɛnte] ag, sm subconscious

'subdolo, a ag underhand, sneaky

suben'trare vi: ~ **a qn in qc** to take over sth from sb

su'bire vt to suffer, endure

subis'sare vt (fig): ~ **di** to overwhelm with, load with

subi'taneo, a ag sudden

'subito av immediately, at once, straight away

subodo'rare vt (insidia etc) to smell, suspect

subordi'nato, a ag subordinate; (dipendente): ~ **a** dependent on, subject to

subur'bano, a ag suburban

suc'cedere [sut'tʃɛdere] vi (prendere il posto di qn): ~ **a** to succeed; (venire dopo): ~ **a** to follow; (accadere) to happen; ~**rsi** vr to follow each other; ~ **al trono** to succeed to the throne; **successi'one** sf succession; **succes'sivo, a** ag successive; **suc'cesso, a** pp di **succedere** ♦ sm (esito) outcome; (buona riuscita) success; **di successo** (libro, personaggio) successful

succhi'are [suk'kjare] vt to suck (up); **succhi'otto** sm (per bambino) dummy

suc'cinto, a [sut'tʃinto] ag (discorso) succinct; (abito) brief

'succo, chi sm juice; (fig) essence, gist; ~ **di frutta** fruit juice; **suc'coso, a** ag juicy; (fig) pithy

succur'sale sf branch (office)

sud sm south ♦ ag inv south; (lato) south, southern

Su'dafrica sm: **il** ~ South Africa; **sudafri'cano, a** ag, sm/f South African

Suda'merica sm: **il** ~ South America;

sudameri'cano, a ag, sm/f South American

su'dare vi to perspire, sweat; ~ **freddo** to come out in a cold sweat; **su'data** sf sweat; **ho fatto una bella sudata per finirlo in tempo** it was a real sweat to get it finished in time

sud'detto, a ag above-mentioned

sud'dito, a sm/f subject

suddi'videre vt to subdivide

su'dest sm south-east

'sudicio, a, ci, ce ['suditʃo] ag dirty, filthy; **sudici'ume** sm dirt, filth

su'dore sm perspiration, sweat

su'dovest sm south-west

'sue vedi **suo**

suffici'ente [suffi'tʃɛnte] ag enough, sufficient; (borioso) self-important; (ins) satisfactory; **suffici'enza** sf self-importance; pass mark; **a sufficienza** enough; **ne ho avuto a sufficienza!** I've had enough of this!

suf'fisso sm (ling) suffix

suf'fragio [suf'fradʒo] sm (voto) vote; ~ **universale** universal suffrage

suggel'lare [suddʒel'lare] vt (fig) to seal

suggeri'mento [suddʒeri'mento] sm suggestion; (consiglio) piece of advice, advice no pl

sugge'rire [suddʒe'rire] vt (risposta) to tell; (consigliare) to advise; (proporre) to suggest; (teatro) to prompt; **suggeri'tore, 'trice** sm/f (teatro) prompter

suggestio'nare [suddʒestjo'nare] vt to influence

suggesti'one [suddʒes'tjone] sf (psic) suggestion

sugges'tivo, a [suddʒes'tivo] ag (paesaggio) evocative; (teoria) interesting, attractive

'sughero ['sugero] sm cork

'sugli ['suʎʎi] prep +det vedi **su**

'sugo, ghi sm (succo) juice; (di carne) gravy; (condimento) sauce; (fig) gist, essence '**sui** prep +det vedi **su**

sui'cida, i, e [sui'tʃida] ag suicidal
♦ sm/f suicide

suici'darsi [suitʃi'darsi] vr to commit
suicide

sui'cidio [sui'tʃidjo] sm suicide

su'ino, a ag: **carne ~a** pork ♦ sm pig;
~i smpl swine sg

sul prep + det vedi **su**

sull' prep + det vedi **su**

'**sulla** prep + det vedi **su**

'**sulle** prep + det vedi **su**

'**sullo** prep + det vedi **su**

sulta'nina ag f: **(uva)** ~ sultana

sul'tano, a sm/f sultan/sultana

'**sunto** sm summary

'**suo** (f **'sua**, pl **'sue**, **'suoi**) det: **il** ~, **la
sua** (di lui) his; (di lei) her; (di esso)
its; (con valore indefinito) one's, his/her;
(forma di cortesia: anche: S~) your
♦ pron: **il** ~, **la sua** etc his; hers; yours;
i suoi his (o her o one's o your) family

su'ocero, a ['swɔtʃero] sm/f father/
mother-in-law; **i ~i** smpl father-and-
mother-in-law

su'oi vedi **suo**

su'ola sf (di scarpa) sole

su'olo sm (terreno) ground; (terra) soil

suo'nare vt (MUS) to play; (campana)
to ring; (ore) to strike; (clacson, allarme)
to sound ♦ vi to play; (telefono,
campana) to ring; (ore) to strike;
(clacson, fig: parole) to sound

suone'ria sf alarm

su'ono sm sound

su'ora sf (REL) sister

'**super** sf (anche: benzina ~) ≈ four-star
(petrol) (BRIT), premium (US)

supe'rare vt (oltrepassare: limite) to
exceed, surpass; (percorrere) to cover;
(attraversare: fiume) to cross; (sorpassare: veicolo) to overtake; (fig: essere più
bravo di) to surpass, outdo; (: difficoltà)
to overcome; (: esame) to get through;
~ **qn in altezza/peso** to be taller/
heavier than sb; **ha superato la cinquantina** he's over fifty (years of age)

su'perbia sf pride; **su'perbo, a** ag
proud; (fig) magnificent, superb

supera'lotto sm Italian national
lottery

superfici'ale [superfi'tʃale] ag
superficial

super'ficie, ci [super'fitʃe] sf surface

su'perfluo, a ag superfluous

superi'ore ag (piano, arto, classi)
upper; (più elevato: temperatura, livello):
~ **(a)** higher (than); (migliore): ~ **(a)**
superior (to); ~, **a** sm/f (anche REL)
superior; **superiorità** sf superiority

superla'tivo, a ag, sm superlative

supermer'cato sm supermarket

su'perstite ag surviving ♦ sm/f survivor

superstizi'one [superstit'tsjone] sf
superstition; **superstizi'oso, a** ag
superstitious

super'strada sf ≈ (toll-free) motorway

su'pino, a ag supine

suppel'lettile sf furnishings pl

suppergiù [supper'dʒu] av more or
less, roughly

supplemen'tare ag extra; (treno)
relief cpd; (entrate) additional

supple'mento sm supplement

sup'plente ag temporary member of
staff; supply (o substitute) teacher

'**supplica, che** sf (preghiera) plea;
(domanda scritta) petition, request

suppli'care vt to implore, beseech

sup'plire vi: ~ **a** to compensate for

sup'plizio [sup'plittsjo] sm torture

sup'porre vt to suppose

sup'porto sm (sostegno) support

sup'posta sf (MED) suppository

sup'posto, a pp di **supporre**

su'premo, a ag supreme

surge'lare [surdʒe'lare] vt to (deep-)
freeze; **surge'lati** smpl frozen food sg

sur'plus sm inv (ECON) surplus

surriscal'dare vt to overheat

surro'gato sm substitute

suscet'tibile [suʃʃet'tibile] ag
(sensibile) touchy, sensitive

susci'tare [suʃʃi'tare] vt to provoke,

arouse

su'sina *sf* plum; **su'sino** *sm* plum (tree)

sussegu'ire *vt* to follow; **~rsi** *vr* to follow one another

sus'sidio *sm* subsidy

sus'sistere *vi* to exist; *(essere fondato)* to be valid *o* sound

sussul'tare *vi* to shudder

sussur'rare *vt, vi* to whisper, murmur; **sus'surro** *sm* whisper, murmur

sutu'rare *vt (MED)* to stitch up, suture

sva'gare *vt (distrarre)* to distract; *(divertire)* to amuse; **~rsi** *vr* to amuse o.s.; to enjoy o.s.

'svago, ghi *sm (riposo)* relaxation; *(ricreazione)* amusement; *(passatempo)* pastime

svaligi'are [zvali'dʒare] *vt* to rob, burgle *(BRIT)*, burglarize *(US)*

svalu'tare *vt (distrarre)* to devalue; *(fig)* to belittle; **~rsi** *vr (ECON)* to be devalued; **svalutazi'one** *sf* devaluation

sva'nire *vi* to disappear, vanish

svan'taggio [zvan'taddʒo] *sm* disadvantage; *(inconveniente)* drawback, disadvantage

svapo'rare *vi* to evaporate

svari'ato, a *ag* varied; various

'svastica *sf* swastika

sve'dese *ag* Swedish ♦ *sm/f* Swede ♦ *sm (LING)* Swedish

'sveglia ['zveʎʎa] *sf* waking up; *(orologio)* alarm (clock); **~ telefonica** alarm call

svegli'are [zveʎ'ʎare] *vt* to wake up; *(fig)* to awaken, arouse; **~rsi** *vr* to wake up; *(fig)* to be revived, reawaken

'sveglio, a ['zveʎʎo] *ag* awake; *(fig)* quick-witted

sve'lare *vt* to reveal

'svelto, a *ag (passo)* quick; *(mente)* quick, alert; **alla ~** quickly

'svendita *sf (COMM)* clearance sale

sveni'mento *sm* fainting fit, faint

sve'nire *vi* to faint

sven'tare *vt* to foil, thwart

sven'tato, a *ag (distratto)* scatterbrained; *(imprudente)* rash

svento'lare *vt, vi* to wave, flutter

sven'trare *vt* to disembowel

sven'tura *sf* misfortune; **sventu'rato, a** *ag* unlucky, unfortunate

sve'nuto, a *pp di* **svenire**

svergo'gnato, a [zvergoɲ'ɲato] *ag* shameless

sver'nare *vi* to spend the winter

sves'tire *vt* to undress; **~rsi** *vr* to get undressed

'Svezia ['zvɛttsja] *sf:* **la ~** Sweden

svez'zare [zvet'tsare] *vt* to wean

svi'are *vt* to divert; *(fig)* to lead astray; **~rsi** *vr* to go astray

svi'gnarsela [zviɲ'ɲarsela] *vr* to slip away, sneak off

svilup'pare *vt* to develop; **~rsi** *vr* to develop

svi'luppo *sm* development

'svincolo *sm (stradale)* motorway *(BRIT)* o expressway *(US)* intersection

svisce'rare *vt (fig: argomento)* to examine in depth; **svisce'rato, a** *ag (amore)* passionate; *(lodi)* obsequious

'svista *sf* oversight

svi'tare *vt* to unscrew

'Svizzera ['zvittsera] *sf:* **la ~** Switzerland

'svizzero, a ['zvittsero] *ag, sm/f* Swiss

svogli'ato, a [zvoʎ'ʎato] *ag* listless; *(pigro)* lazy

svolaz'zare [zvolat'tsare] *vi* to flutter

'svolgere ['zvɔldʒere] *vt* to unwind; *(srotolare)* to unroll; *(fig: argomento)* to develop; *(: piano, programma)* to carry out; **~rsi** *vr* to unwind; to unroll; *(fig: aver luogo)* to take place; *(: procedere)* to go on; **svolgi'mento** *sm* development; carrying out; *(andamento)* course

'svolta *sf (atto)* turning *no pl*; *(curva)* turn, bend; *(fig)* turning-point

svol'tare *vi* to turn

'svolto, a *pp di* **svolgere**

svuo'tare vt to empty (out)

T, t

tabac'caio, a sm/f tobacconist

tabacche'ria [tabakke'ria] sf tobacconist's (shop)

ta'bacco, chi sm tobacco

ta'bella sf (tavola) table; (elenco) list

tabel'lone sm (pubblicitario) billboard; (con orario) timetable board

taber'nacolo sm tabernacle

tabu'lato sm (INFORM) printout

'tacca, che sf notch, nick

tac'cagno, a [tak'kaɲɲo] ag mean, stingy

tac'chino [tak'kino] sm turkey

tacci'are [tat'tʃare] vt: ~ qn di to accuse sb of

'tacco, chi sm heel; ~chi a spillo stiletto heels

taccu'ino sm notebook

ta'cere [ta'tʃere] vi to be silent o quiet; (smettere di parlare) to fall silent ♦ vt to keep to oneself, say nothing about; **far ~ qn** to make sb be quiet; (fig) to silence sb

ta'chimetro [ta'kimetro] sm speedometer

'tacito, a ['tatʃito, a] ag silent; (sottinteso) tacit, unspoken

ta'fano sm horsefly

taffe'ruglio [taffe'ruʎʎo] sm brawl, scuffle

taffettà sm taffeta

'taglia ['taʎʎa] sf (statura) height; (misura) size; (riscatto) ransom; (ricompensa) reward; ~ **forte** (di abito) large size

taglia'carte [taʎʎa'karte] sm inv paperknife

tagli'ando [taʎ'ʎando] sm coupon

tagli'are [taʎ'ʎare] vt to cut; (recidere, interrompere) to cut off; (intersecare) to cut across, intersect; (carne) to carve; (vini) to blend ♦ vi to cut; (prendere una scorciatoia) to take a short-cut; ~ **corto** (fig) to cut short

taglia'telle [taʎʎa'telle] sfpl tagliatelle pl

taglia'unghie [taʎʎa'ungje] sm inv nail clippers pl

tagli'ente [taʎ'ʎente] ag sharp

'taglio ['taʎʎo] sm cutting no pl; cut; (parte tagliente) cutting edge; (di abito) cut, style; (di stoffa: lunghezza) length; (di vini) blending; **di ~** on edge, edgeways; **banconote di piccolo/grosso ~** notes of small/large denomination

tagli'ola [taʎ'ʎola] sf trap, snare

tai'lleur [ta'jœr] sm inv suit (for women)

'talco sm talcum powder

'tale det 1 (simile, così grande) such; **un(a) ~** ... such (a) ...; **non accetto ~i discorsi** I won't allow such talk; **è di una ~ arroganza** he is so arrogant; **fa una ~ confusione!** he makes such a mess!

2 (persona o cosa indeterminata) such-and-such; **il giorno ~ all'ora ~** on such-and-such a day at such-and-such a time; **la tal persona** that person; **ha telefonato una ~ Giovanna** somebody called Giovanna phoned

3 (nelle similitudini): **tale ... ~** like ... like; **~ padre ~ figlio** like father, like son; **hai il vestito ~ quale il mio** your dress is just o exactly like mine

♦ pron (indefinito: persona): **un(a) ~** someone; **quel (o quella) ~** that person, that man (o woman); **il tal dei ~i** what's-his-name

ta'lento sm talent

talis'mano sm talisman

tallon'cino [tallon'tʃino] sm counterfoil

tal'lone sm heel

tal'mente av so

ta'lora av = **talvolta**

'talpa sf (ZOOL) mole

tal'volta av sometimes, at times

tambu'rello sm tambourine

tam'buro sm drum

Ta'migi [ta'midʒi] sm: **il ~** the Thames

tampona'mento sm (AUT) collision; **~ a catena** pile-up

tampo'nare vt (otturare) to plug; (urtare: macchina) to crash o ram into

tam'pone sm (MED) wad, pad; (per timbri) ink-pad; (respingente) buffer; **~ assorbente** tampon

'tana sf lair, den

'tanfo sm stench; musty smell

tan'gente [tan'dʒɛnte] ag (MAT): **~ a** tangential to ♦ sf tangent; (quota) share

---

Tangentopoli describes the corruption scandal involving a large number of politicians, industrialists and businessmen. Investigations exposed a complex system of bribes, some paid from public funds, to gain benefits for private individuals and political parties. The scandal began in Milan which was subsequently called Tangentopoli or "Bribesville".

---

tangenzi'ale [tandʒen'tsjale] sf (AUT) bypass

'tanica sf (contenitore) jerry can

tan'tino sm: **un ~** av a little, a bit

PAROLA CHIAVE

'tanto, a det **1** (molto: quantità) a lot of, much; (: numero) a lot of, many; (così ~: quantità) so much, such a lot of; (: numero) so many, such a lot of; **~e volte** so many times, so often; **~i auguri!** all the best!; **~e grazie** many thanks; **~ tempo** so long, such a long time; **ogni ~i chilometro** every so many kilometres

2: ~ ... quanto (quantità) as much ... as; (numero) as many ... as; **ho ~a pazienza quanta ne hai tu** I have as much patience as you have o as you; **ha ~i amici quanti nemici** he has as many friends as he has enemies

3 (rafforzativo) such; **ho aspettato per ~ tempo** I waited so long o for such a long time

♦ pron **1** (molto) much, a lot; (così ~) so much, such a lot; **~i, e** many, a lot; so many, such a lot; **credevo ce ne fosse ~** I thought there was (such) a lot, I thought there was plenty

2: ~ quanto (denaro) as much as; (cioccolatini) as many as; **ne ho ~ quanto basta** I have as much as I need; **due volte ~** twice as much

3 (indeterminato) so much; **~ per l'affitto, ~ per il gas** so much for the rent, so much for the gas; **costa un ~ al metro** it costs so much per metre; **di ~ in ~, ogni ~** every so often; **~ vale che ...** I (o we etc) may as well ...; **~ meglio!** so much the better!; **~ peggio per lui!** so much the worse for him!

♦ av **1** (molto) very; **vengo ~ volentieri** I'd be very glad to come; **non ci vuole ~ a capirlo** it doesn't take much to understand it

2 (così ~: con ag, av) so; (: con vb) so much, such a lot; **è ~ bella!** she's so beautiful!; **non urlare ~** don't shout so much; **sto ~ meglio adesso** I'm so much better now; **~ ... che** so ... (that); **~ ... da** so ... as

3: ~ ... quanto as ... as; conosco ~ Carlo quanto suo padre I know both Carlo and his father; **non è poi ~ complicato quanto sembri** it's not as difficult as it seems; **~ più insisti, ~ più non mollerà** the more you insist, the more stubborn he'll be; **quanto più ... ~ meno** the more ... the less

4 (solamente) only, just; **~ per cambiare/scherzare** just for a change/a joke; **una volta ~** for once

5 (a lungo) (for) long
♦ cong after all

'**tappa** sf (luogo di sosta, fermata) stop, halt; (parte di un percorso) stage, leg; (SPORT) lap; **a ~e** in stages

tap'pare vt to plug, stop up; (bottiglia) to cork

tap'peto sm carpet; (anche: tappetino) rug; (SPORT): **andare al ~** to go down for the count; **mettere sul ~** (fig) to bring up for discussion

tappez'zare [tappet'tsare] vt (con carta) to paper; (rivestire): **~ qc (di)** to cover sth (with); **tappezze'ria** sf (tessuto) tapestry; (carta da parati) wallpaper; (arte) upholstery; **far da tappezzeria** (fig) to be a wallflower; **tappezzi'ere** sm upholsterer

'**tappo** sm stopper; (in sughero) cork

tarchi'ato, a [tar'kjato] ag stocky, thickset

tar'dare vi to be late ♦ vt to delay; **~ a fare** to delay doing

'**tardi** av late; **più ~** later (on); **al più ~** at the latest; **sul ~** (verso sera) late in the day; **far ~** to be late; (restare alzato) to stay up late

tar'divo, a ag (primavera) late; (rimedio) belated, tardy; (fig) retarded

'**tardo, a** ag (lento, fig: ottuso) slow; (tempo: avanzato) late

'**targa, ghe** sf plate; (AUT) number (BRIT) o license (US) plate; **tar'ghetta** sf (su bagaglio) name tag; (su porta) nameplate

ta'riffa sf (gen) rate, tariff; (di trasporti) fare; (elenco) price list; tariff

'**tarlo** sm woodworm

'**tarma** sf moth

ta'rocco, chi sm tarot card; **~chi** smpl (gioco) tarot sg

tartagli'are [tartaʎ'ʎare] vi to stutter, stammer

'**tartaro** a ag, sm (in tutti i sensi) tartar

tarta'ruga, ghe sf tortoise; (di mare) turtle; (materiale) tortoiseshell

tar'tina sf canapé

tar'tufo sm (BOT) truffle

'**tasca, sche** sf pocket; **tas'cabile** ag (libro) pocket cpd; **tasca'pane** sm haversack; **tas'chino** sm breast pocket

'**tassa** sf (imposta) tax; (doganale) duty; (per iscrizione: a scuola etc) fee; **~ di circolazione/di soggiorno** road/tourist tax

tas'sametro sm taximeter

tas'sare vt to tax; to levy a duty on

tassa'tivo, a ag peremptory

tassazi'one [tassat'tsjone] sf taxation

tas'sello sm plug; wedge

tassi sm inv = taxi; tas'sista, i, e sm/f taxi driver

'**tasso** sm (di natalità, d'interesse etc) rate; (BOT) yew; (ZOOL) badger; **~ di cambio/d'interesse** rate of exchange/interest

tas'tare vt to feel; **~ il terreno** (fig) to see how the land lies

tasti'era sf keyboard

'**tasto** sm key; (tatto) touch, feel

tas'toni av: **procedere (a) ~** to grope one's way forward

'**tattica** sf tactics pl

'**tattico, a, ci, che** ag tactical

'**tatto** sm (senso) touch; (fig) tact; **duro al ~** hard to the touch; **aver ~** to be tactful, have tact

tatu'aggio [tatu'addʒo] sm tattooing; (disegno) tattoo

tatu'are vt to tattoo

'**tavola** sf table; (asse) plank, board; (lastra) tablet; (quadro) panel (painting); (illustrazione) plate; **~ calda** snack bar; **~ a vela** windsurfer

tavo'lato sm boarding; (pavimento) wooden floor

tavo'letta sf tablet, bar; **a ~** (AUT) flat out

tavo'lino sm small table; (scrivania) desk

'**tavolo** sm table

tavo'lozza [tavo'lɔttsa] sf (ARTE) palette

'**taxi** sm inv taxi

'tazza ['tattsa] *sf* cup; ~ **da caffè/tè** coffee/tea cup; **una ~ di caffè/tè** a cup of coffee/tea

te *pron* (*soggetto: in forme comparative, oggetto*) you

tè *sm inv* tea; (*trattenimento*) tea party

tea'trale *ag* theatrical

te'atro *sm* theatre

'tecnica, che *sf* technique; (*tecnologia*) technology

'tecnico, a, ci, che *ag* technical ♦ *sm/f* technician

tecnolo'gia [teknolo'dʒia] *sf* technology

te'desco, a, schi, sche *ag, sm/f, sm* German

'tedio *sm* tedium, boredom

te'game *sm* (*CUC*) pan

'teglia ['teʎʎa] *sf* (*per dolci*) (baking) tin; (*per arrosti*) (roasting) tin

'tegola *sf* tile

tei'era *sf* teapot

'tela *sf* (*tessuto*) cloth; (*per vele, quadri*) canvas; (*dipinto*) canvas, painting; **di ~** (*calzoni*) (heavy) cotton *cpd*; (*scarpe, borsa*) canvas *cpd*; **~ cerata** oilcloth

te'laio *sm* (*apparecchio*) loom; (*struttura*) frame

tele'camera *sf* television camera

teleco'mando *sm* remote control

telecopia'trice *sf* fax (machine)

tele'cronaca *sf* television report

tele'ferica, che *sf* cableway

telefo'nare *vi* to telephone, ring; to make a phone call ♦ *vt* to telephone; **~ a** to phone up, ring up, call up

telefo'nata *sf* (telephone) call; **~ a carico del destinatario** reverse charge (*BRIT*) o collect (*US*) call

tele'fonico, a, ci, che *ag* (tele)phone *cpd*

telefon'ino *sm* mobile phone

telefo'nista, i, e *sm/f* telephonist; (*d'impresa*) switchboard operator

te'lefono *sm* telephone; **~ a gettoni** ≈ pay phone

telegior'nale [teledʒor'nale] *sm*

television news (programme)

te'legrafo *sm* telegraph

tele'gramma, i *sm* telegram

telela'voro *sm* teleworking

tele'matica *sf* data transmission; telematics *sg*

teleobiet'tivo *sm* telephoto lens *sg*

telepa'tia *sf* telepathy

teles'copio *sm* telescope

teleselezi'one [teleselet'tsjone] *sf* direct dialling

telespetta'tore, 'trice *sm/f* (television) viewer

televisi'one *sf* television

televi'sore *sm* television set

'telex *sm inv* telex

'telo *sm* cloth; **~ da bagno** bath towel; **~ da spiaggia** beach towel

'tema, i *sm* theme; (*INS*) essay, composition

teme'rario, a *ag* rash, reckless

te'mere *vt* to fear, be afraid of; (*essere sensibile a: freddo, calore*) to be sensitive to ♦ *vi* to be afraid; (*essere preoccupato*): **~ per** to worry about, fear for; **~ di/che** to be afraid of/that

temperama'tite *sm inv* pencil sharpener

tempera'mento *sm* temperament

tempe'rato, a *ag* temperate

tempera'tura *sf* temperature

tempe'rino *sm* penknife

tem'pesta *sf* storm; **~ di sabbia/neve** sand/snowstorm

tempes'tare *vt*: **~ qn di domande** to bombard sb with questions; **~ qn di colpi** to rain blows on sb

tempes'tivo, a *ag* timely

tempes'toso, a *ag* stormy

'tempia (*ANAT*) temple

'tempio *sm* (*edificio*) temple

'tempo *sm* (*METEOR*) weather; (*cronologico*) time; (*epoca*) time, times *pl*; (*di film, gioco: parte*) part; (*MUS*) time; (*: battuta*) beat; (*LING*) tense; **un ~** once; **~ fa** some time ago; **al ~ stesso** o **a un ~** at the same time;

per ~ early; **ha fatto il suo** ~ it has had its day; ~ **libero** free time; **primo/secondo** ~ (TEATRO) first/ second part; (SPORT) first/second half; **in** ~ **utile** in due time o course; **a** ~ **pieno** full-time

tempo'rale ag temporal ♦ sm (METEOR) (thunder)storm

tempo'raneo, a ag temporary

temporeggi'are [tempored'dʒare] vi to play for time, temporize

tem'prare vt to temper

te'nace [te'natʃe] ag strong, tough; (fig) tenacious; **te'nacia** sf tenacity

te'naglie [te'naʎʎe] sfpl pincers pl

'tenda sf (riparo) awning; (di finestra) curtain; (per campeggio etc) tent

ten'denza [ten'dɛntsa] sf tendency; (orientamento) trend; **avere** ~ **a** o **per qc** to have a bent for sth

'tendere vt (allungare al massimo) to stretch, draw tight; (porgere: mano) to hold out; (fig: trappola) to lay, set ♦ vi: ~ **a qc/a fare** to tend towards sth/to do; ~ **l'orecchio** to prick up one's ears; **il tempo tende al caldo** the weather is getting hot; **un blu che tende al verde** a greenish blue

ten'dina sf curtain

'tendine sm tendon, sinew

ten'done sm (da circo) tent

'tenebre sfpl darkness sg; **tene'broso, a** ag dark, gloomy

te'nente sm lieutenant

te'nere vt to hold; (conservare, mantenere) to keep; (ritenere, considerare) to consider; (spazio: occupare) to take up, occupy; (seguire: strada) to keep to ♦ vi to hold; (colori) to be fast; (dare importanza): ~ **a** to care about; ~ **a fare** to want to do, be keen to do; ~**rsi** vr (stare in una determinata posizione) to stand; (stimarsi) to consider o.s.; (aggrapparsi): ~**rsi a** to hold on to; (attenersi): ~**rsi a** to stick to; ~ **una conferenza** to give a lecture; ~ **conto**

di qc to take sth into consideration; ~ **presente qc** to bear sth in mind

'tenero, a ag tender; (pietra, cera, colore) soft; (fig) tender, loving

'tenia sf tapeworm

'tennis sm tennis

te'nore sm (tono) tone; (MUS) tenor; ~ **di vita** (livello) standard of living

tensi'one sf tension

ten'tare vt (indurre) to tempt; (provare): ~ **qc/di fare** to attempt o try sth/to do; **tenta'tivo** sm attempt; **tentazi'one** sf temptation

tenten'nare vi to shake, be unsteady; (fig) to hesitate, waver

ten'toni av: **andare a** ~ (anche fig) to grope one's way

'tenue ag (sottile) fine; (colore) soft; (fig) slender, slight

te'nuta sf (capacità) capacity; (divisa) uniform; (abito) dress; (AGR) estate; **a** ~ **d'aria** airtight; ~ **di strada** roadholding power

teolo'gia [teolo'dʒia] sf theology; **te'ologo, gi** sm theologian

teo'rema, i sm theorem

teo'ria sf theory; **te'orico, a, ci, che** ag theoretic(al)

te'pore sm warmth

'teppa sf mob, hooligans pl; **tep'pismo** sm hooliganism; **tep'pista, i** sm hooligan

tera'pia sf therapy

tergicris'talle [terdʒikris'talle] sm windscreen (BRIT) o windshield (US) wiper

tergiver'sare [terdʒiver'sare] vi to shilly-shally

'tergo sm: **a** ~ behind; **vedi a** ~ please turn over

ter'male ag thermal; **stazione** sf ~ spa

'terme sfpl thermal baths

'termico, a, ci, che ag thermic; (unità) thermal

termi'nale ag, sm terminal

termi'nare vt to end; (lavoro) to finish ♦ vi to end

'**termine** sm term; (*fine, estremità*) end; (*di territorio*) boundary, limit;
 contratto a ~ (COMM) forward contract; **a breve/lungo ~** short-/long-term; **parlare senza mezzi ~i** to talk frankly, not to mince one's words

ter'**mometro** sm thermometer

termonucle'**are** ag thermonuclear

termosi'**fone** sm radiator

ter'**mostato** sm thermostat

'**terra** sf (GEN, ELETTR) earth; (*sostanza*) soil, earth; (*opposto al mare*) land *no pl*; (*regione, paese*) land; (*argilla*) clay; ~**e** sfpl (*possedimenti*) lands, land sg; **a o per ~** (*stato*) on the ground (o floor); (*moto*) to the ground, down; **mettere a ~** (ELETTR) to earth

terra'**cotta** sf terracotta; **vasellame** sm **di ~** earthenware

terra'**ferma** sf dry land, terra firma; (*continente*) mainland

terrapi'**eno** sm embankment, bank

ter'**razza** [ter'rattsa] sf terrace

ter'**razzo** [ter'rattso] sm = **terrazza**

terre'**moto** sm earthquake

ter'**reno, a** ag (*vita, beni*) earthly ♦ sm (*suolo, fig*) ground; (COMM) land *no pl*, plot (of land); site; (SPORT, MIL) field

ter'**restre** ag (*superficie*) of the earth, earth's; (*di terra: battaglia, animale*) land *cpd*; (REL) earthly, worldly

ter'**ribile** ag terrible, dreadful

terrifi'**cante** ag terrifying

ter'**rina** sf tureen

territori'**ale** ag territorial

terri'**torio** sm territory

ter'**rore** sm terror; terro'**rismo** sm terrorism; terro'**rista, i, e** sm/f terrorist

'**terso, a** ag clear

'**terzo, a** ['tertso] ag third ♦ sm (*frazione*) third; (DIR) third party; **la ~a pagina** (STAMPA) the Arts page

'**tesa** sf brim

'**teschio** ['teskjo] sm skull

'**tesi** sf thesis

'**teso, a** pp di **tendere** ♦ ag (*tirato*)

taut, tight; (*fig*) tense

tesore'**ria** sf treasury

tesori'**ere** sm treasurer

te'**soro** sm treasure; **il Ministero del T~** the Treasury

'**tessera** sf (*documento*) card

'**tessere** vt to weave; '**tessile** ag, sm textile; **tessi'tore, 'trice** sm/f weaver; **tessi'tura** sf weaving

tes'**suto** sf fabric, material; (BIOL) tissue

'**testa** sf head; (*di cose: estremità, parte anteriore*) head, front; **di ~** (*vettura etc*) front; **tenere ~ a qn** (*nemico etc*) to stand up to sb; **fare di ~ propria** to go one's own way; **in ~** (SPORT) in the lead; ~ **o croce?** heads or tails?; **avere la ~ dura** to be stubborn; ~ **di serie** (TENNIS) seed, seeded player

testa'**mento** sm (*atto*) will; **l'Antico/il Nuovo T~** (REL) the Old/New Testament

tes'**tardo, a** ag stubborn, pig-headed

tes'**tata** sf (*parte anteriore*) head; (*intestazione*) heading

'**teste** sm/f witness

tes'**ticolo** sm testicle

testi'**mone** sm/f (DIR) witness

testimoni'**anza** [testimo'njantsa] sf testimony

testimoni'**are** vt to testify; (*fig*) to bear witness to, to testify to ♦ vi to give evidence, testify

tes'**tina** sf (TECN) head

'**testo** sm text; **fare ~** (*opera, autore*) to be authoritative; **questo libro non fa ~** this book is not essential reading; **testu'ale** ag textual; literal, word for word

tes'**tuggine** [tes'tuddʒine] sf tortoise; (*di mare*) turtle

'**tetano** sm (MED) tetanus

'**tetro, a** ag gloomy

'**tetto** sm roof; **tet'toia** sf roofing; canopy

'**Tevere** sm: **il ~** the Tiber

Tg abbr = **telegiornale**

'**thermos** ® ['termos] *sm inv* vacuum o Thermos ® flask

ti *pron (dav lo, la, li, le, ne diventa* **te)** *pron (oggetto)* you; *(complemento di termine)* (to) you; *(riflessivo)* yourself

'**tibia** *sf* tibia, shinbone

tic *sm inv* tic, (nervous) twitch; *(fig)* mannerism

ticchet'tio [tikket'tio] *sm (di macchina da scrivere)* clatter; *(di orologio)* ticking; *(della pioggia)* patter

'**ticchio** ['tikkjo] *sm (ghiribizzo)* whim; *(tic)* tic, (nervous) twitch

'**ticket** *sm inv (su farmaci)* prescription charge

ti'**epido, a** *ag* lukewarm, tepid

ti'**fare** *vi:* ~ **per** to be a fan of; *(parteggiare)* to side with

'**tifo** *sm (MED)* typhus; *(fig):* **fare il** ~ **per** to be a fan of

tifoi'**dea** *sf* typhoid

ti'**fone** *sm* typhoon

ti'**foso, a** *sm/f (SPORT etc)* fan

'**tiglio** ['tiλλo] *sm* lime (tree), linden (tree)

'**tigre** *sf* tiger

tim'**ballo** *sm (strumento)* kettledrum; *(CUC)* timbale

'**timbro** *sm* stamp; *(MUS)* timbre, tone

'**timido, a** *ag* shy; timid

'**timo** *sm* thyme

ti'**mone** *sm (NAUT)* rudder; **timoni'ere** *sm* helmsman

ti'**more** *sm (paura)* fear; *(rispetto)* awe; **timo'roso, a** *ag* timid, timorous

'**timpano** *sm (ANAT)* eardrum; *(MUS):* ~**i** *smpl* kettledrums, timpani

ti'**nello** *sm* small dining room

'**tingere** ['tindʒere] *vt* to dye

'**tino** *sm* vat

ti'**nozza** [ti'nɔttsa] *sf* tub

'**tinta** *sf (materia colorante)* dye; *(colore)* colour, shade; **tinta'rella** *(fam) sf* (sun)tan

tintin'**nare** *vi* to tinkle

'**tinto, a** *pp di* **tingere**

tinto'**ria** *sf (lavasecco)* dry cleaner's

(shop)

tin'**tura** *sf (operazione)* dyeing; *(colorante)* dye; ~ **di iodio** tincture of iodine

'**tipico, a, ci, che** *ag* typical

'**tipo** *sm* type; *(genere)* kind, type; *(fam)* chap, fellow

tipogra'**fia** *sf* typography; *(procedimento)* letterpress (printing); *(officina)* printing house; **tipo'grafico, a, ci, che** *ag* typographic(al); letterpress *cpd;* **ti'pografo** *sm* typographer

ti'**ranno, a** *ag* tyrannical ♦ *sm* tyrant

ti'**rante** *sm (per tenda)* guy

ti'**rare** *vt (gen)* to pull; *(estrarre):* ~ **qc da** to take o pull sth out of; to get sth out of; to extract sth from; *(chiudere: tenda etc)* to draw, pull; *(tracciare, disegnare)* to draw, trace; *(lanciare: sasso, palla)* to throw; *(stampare)* to print; *(pistola, freccia)* to fire ♦ *vi (pipa, camino)* to draw; *(vento)* to blow; *(abito)* to be tight; *(fare fuoco)* to fire; *(fare del tiro, CALCIO)* to shoot; ~ **avanti** *vi* to struggle on ♦ *vt* to keep going; ~ **fuori** *(estrarre)* to take out, pull out; ~ **giù** *(abbassare)* to bring down; ~ **su** to pull up; *(capelli)* to put up; *(fig: bambino)* to bring up; ~**rsi indietro** to move back

tira'**tore** *sm* gunman; **un buon** ~ a good shot; ~ **scelto** marksman

tira'**tura** *sf (AZIONE)* printing; *(di libro)* (print) run; *(di giornale)* circulation

'**tirchio, a** ['tirkjo] *ag* mean, stingy

'**tiro** *sm* shooting *no pl,* firing *no pl;* *(colpo, sparo)* shot; *(di palla: lancio)* throwing *no pl;* throw; *(fig)* trick; **cavallo da** ~ draught *(BRIT)* o draft *(US)* horse; ~ **a segno** target shooting; *(luogo)* shooting range

tiro'**cinio** [tiro'tʃinjo] *sm* apprenticeship; *(professionale)* training

ti'**roide** *sf* thyroid (gland)

Tir'**reno** *sm:* **il (mar)** ~ the Tyrrhenian Sea

ti'sana sf herb tea

tito'lare sm/f incumbent; (proprietario) owner; (CALCIO) regular player

'titolo sm title; (di giornale) headline; (diploma) qualification; (COMM) security; (: azione) share; **a che ~?** for what reason?; **a ~ di amicizia** out of friendship; **a ~ di premio** as a prize; **~ di credito** share

titu'bante ag hesitant, irresolute

'tizio, a ['tittsjo] sm/f fellow, chap

tiz'zone [tit'tsone] sm brand

toast [toust] sm inv toasted sandwich (generally with ham and cheese)

toc'cante ag touching

toc'care vt to touch; (tastare) to feel; (fig: riguardare) to concern; (: commuovere) to touch, move; (: pungere) to hurt, wound; (: far cenno a: argomento) to touch on, mention ♦ vi: **~ a** (accadere) to happen to; (spettare) to be up to; **~ (il fondo)** (in acqua) to touch the bottom; **tocca a te difenderci** it's up to you to defend us; **a chi tocca?** whose turn is it?; **mi toccò pagare** I had to pay

'tocco, chi sm touch; (ARTE) stroke, touch

'toga, ghe sf toga; (di magistrato, professore) gown

'togliere ['tɔʎʎere] vt (rimuovere) to take away (o off), remove; (riprendere, non concedere più) to take away, remove; (MAT) to take away, subtract; **~ qc a qn** to take sth (away) from sb; **ciò non toglie che** nevertheless, be that as it may; **~rsi il cappello** to take off one's hat

toi'lette [twa'lɛt] sf inv toilet; (mobile) dressing table

to'letta sf = **toilette**

tolle'ranza [tolle'rantsa] sf tolerance

tolle'rare vt to tolerate

'tolto, a pp di **togliere**

to'maia sf (di scarpa) upper

'tomba sf tomb

tom'bino sm manhole cover

'tombola sf (gioco) tombola; (ruzzolone) tumble

'tomo sm volume

'tonaca, che sf (REL) habit

'tondo, a ag round

'tonfo sm splash; (rumore sordo) thud; (caduta): **fare un ~** to take a tumble

'tonico, a, ci, che ag, sm tonic

tonifi'care vt (muscoli, pelle) to tone up; (irrobustire) to invigorate, brace

tonnel laggio [tonnel'laddʒo] sm (NAUT) tonnage

tonnel lata sf ton

'tonno sm tuna (fish)

'tono sm (gen) tone; (MUS: di pezzo) key; (di colore) shade, tone

ton'silla sf tonsil; **tonsil'lite** sf tonsillitis

'tonto, a ag dull, stupid

to'pazio [to'pattsjo] sm topaz

'topo sm mouse

topogra'fia sf topography

'toppa sf (serratura) keyhole; (pezza) patch

to'race [to'ratʃe] sm chest

'torba sf peat

'torbido, a ag (liquido) cloudy; (: fiume) muddy; (fig) dark; troubled ♦ sm: **pescare nel ~** (fig) to fish in troubled water

'torcere ['tɔrtʃere] vt to twist; **~rsi** vr to twist, writhe

torchi'are [tor'kjare] vt to press; **'torchio** sm press

'torcia, ce ['tɔrtʃa] sf torch; **~ elettrica** torch (BRIT), flashlight (US)

torci'collo [tortʃi'kɔllo] sm stiff neck

'tordo sm thrush

To'rino sf Turin

tor'menta sf snowstorm

tormen'tare vt to torment; **~rsi** vr to fret, worry o.s.; **tor'mento** sm torment

torna'conto sm advantage, benefit

tor'nado sm tornado

tor'nante sm hairpin bend

tor'nare vi to return, go (o come)

back; (*ridiventare: anche fig*) to become (again); (*riuscire giusto, esatto: conto*) to work out; (*risultare*) to turn out (to be), prove (to be); **~ utile** to prove o turn out (to be) useful; **~ a casa** to go (o come) home

torna'sole *sm inv* litmus

tor'neo *sm* tournament

'tornio *sm* lathe

'toro *sm* bull; (*dello zodiaco*): **T~** Taurus

tor'pedine *sf* torpedo; **torpedini'era** *sf* torpedo boat

'torre *sf* tower; (*SCACCHI*) rook, castle; **~ di controllo** (*AER*) control tower

torrefazi'one [torrefat'tsjone] *sf* roasting

tor'rente *sm* torrent

tor'retta *sf* turret

torri'one *sm* keep

tor'rone *sm* nougat

torsi'one *sf* twisting; torsion

'torso *sm* torso, trunk; (*ARTE*) torso

'torsolo *sm* (*di cavolo etc*) stump; (*di frutta*) core

'torta *sf* cake

'torto, a *pp di* **torcere ♦** *ag* (*ritorto*) twisted; (*storto*) twisted, crooked ♦ *sm* (*ingiustizia*) wrong; (*colpa*) fault; **a ~** wrongly; **aver ~** to be wrong

'tortora *sf* turtle dove

tortu'oso, a *ag* (*strada*) twisting; (*fig*) tortuous

tor'tura *sf* torture; **tortu'rare** *vt* to torture

'torvo, a *ag* menacing, grim

tosa'erba *sm o f inv* (lawn)mower

to'sare *vt* (*pecora*) to shear; (*siepe*) to clip

Tos'cana *sf*: **la ~** Tuscany; **tos'cano, a** *ag, sm/f* Tuscan ♦ *sm* (*sigaro*) strong Italian cigar

'tosse *sf* cough

'tossico, a, ci, che *ag* toxic

tossicodipen'dente *sm/f* drug addict

tossi'comane *sm/f* drug addict

tos'sire *vi* to cough

tosta'pane *sm inv* toaster

tos'tare *vt* to toast; (*caffè*) to roast

'tosto, a *ag*: **faccia ~a** cheek

to'tale *ag* total; **totalità** *sf*: **la totalità** of all of, the total amount (*o* number) of; the whole +*sg*; **totaliz'zare** *vt* to total; (*SPORT: punti*) to score

toto'calcio [toto'kaltʃo] *sm* gambling pool betting on football results, ≈ (football) pools *pl* (*BRIT*)

to'vaglia [to'vaʎʎa] *sf* tablecloth; **tovagli'olo** *sm* napkin

'tozzo, a ['tɔttso] *ag* squat ♦ *sm*: **~ di pane** crust of bread

tra *prep* (*di due persone, cose*) between; (*di più persone, cose*) among(st); (*tempo: entro*) within, in; **~ 5 giorni** in 5 days' time; **sia detto ~ noi** ... between you and me ...; **litigano ~ (di) loro** they're fighting amongst themselves; **~ breve** soon; **~ sé e sé** (*parlare etc*) to oneself

trabal'lare *vi* to stagger, totter

traboc'care *vi* to overflow

traboc'chetto [trabok'ketto] *sm* (*fig*) trap

tracan'nare *vt* to gulp down

'traccia, ce ['trattʃa] *sf* (*segno, striscia*) trail, track; (*orma*) tracks *pl*; (*residuo, testimonianza*) trace, sign; (*abbozzo*) outline

tracci'are [trat'tʃare] *vt* to trace, mark (out); (*disegnare*) to draw; (*fig: abbozzare*) to outline; **tracci'ato** *sm* (*grafico*) layout, plan

tra'chea [tra'kɛa] *sf* windpipe, trachea

tra'colla *sf* shoulder strap; **borsa a ~** shoulder bag

tra'collo *sm* (*fig*) collapse, crash

tradi'mento *sm* betrayal; (*DIR, MIL*) treason

tra'dire *vt* to betray; (*coniuge*) to be unfaithful to; (*doveri: mancare*) to fail in; (*rivelare*) to give away, reveal; **tradi'tore, 'trice** *sm/f* traitor

tradizio'nale [tradittsjo'nale] *ag* traditional

tradizi'one [tradit'tsjone] sf tradition

tra'dotto, a pp di **tradurre**

tra'durre vt to translate; (spiegare) to render, convey; **tradut'tore, 'trice** sm/f translator; **traduzi'one** sf translation

trafe'lato, a ag out of breath

traffi'cante sm/f dealer; (peg) trafficker

traffi'care vi (commerciare): ~ (in) to trade (in), deal (in); (affaccendarsi) to busy o.s. ♦ vt (peg) to traffic in

'traffico, ci sm traffic; (commercio) trade, traffic

tra'figgere [tra'fiddʒere] vt to run through, stab; (fig) to pierce

tra'fitto, a pp di **trafiggere**

trafo'rare vt to bore, drill; **tra'foro** sm (azione) boring, drilling; (galleria) tunnel

tra'gedia [tra'dʒɛdja] sf tragedy

tra'ghetto [tra'getto] sm ferry(boat)

'tragico, a, ci, che ['tradʒiko] ag tragic

tra'gitto [tra'dʒitto] sm (passaggio) crossing; (viaggio) journey

tragu'ardo sm (SPORT) finishing line; (fig) goal, aim

traiet'toria sf trajectory

trai'nare vt to drag, haul; (rimorchiare) to tow; **'traino** sm (carro) wagon; (slitta) sledge; (carico) load

tralasci'are [tralaʃ'ʃare] vt (studi) to neglect; (dettagli) to leave out, omit

'tralcio ['traltʃo] sm (BOT) shoot

tra'liccio [tra'littʃo] sm (ELETTR) pylon

tram sm inv tram

'trama sf (filo) weft, woof; (fig: argomento, maneggio) plot

traman'dare vt to pass on, hand down

tra'mare vt (fig) to scheme, plot

tram'busto sm turmoil

trames'tio sm bustle

tramez'zino [tramed'dzino] sm sandwich

tra'mezzo [tra'meddzo] sm (EDIL) partition

'tramite prep through

tramon'tare vi to set, go down; (declinare) to decline

tra'monto sm setting; (del sole) sunset

tramor'tire vi to faint ♦ vt to stun

trampo'lino sm (per tuffi) springboard, diving board; (per lo sci) ski-jump

'trampolo sm stilt

tramu'tare vt: ~ **in** to change into, turn into

tra'nello sm trap

trangugi'are [trangu'dʒare] vt to gulp down

'tranne prep except (for), but (for); ~ **che** unless

tranquil'lante sm (MED) tranquillizer

tranquil'lità sf calm, stillness; quietness; peace of mind

tranquilliz'zare [trankwillid'dzare] vt to reassure

tran'quillo, a ag calm, quiet; (bambino, scolaro) quiet; (sereno) with one's mind at rest; **sta'** ~ don't worry

transat'lantico, ci sm transatlantic liner

---
transatlantico

The **transatlantico** is a room in the Palazzo di Montecitorio. The deputati relax in it between parliamentary sessions and give media interviews and press conferences there.

---

transazi'one [transat'tsjone] sf compromise; (DIR) settlement; (COMM) transaction, deal

tran'senna sf barrier

tran'sigere [tran'sidʒere] vi (venire a patti) to compromise, come to an agreement

tran'sistor sm inv transistor

transi'tabile ag passable

transi'tare vi to pass

transi'tivo, a ag transitive

'transito sm transit; **di** ~ (merci) in transit; (stazione) transit cpd; **''divieto**

di ~" "no entry"

transi'torio, a ag transitory, transient; (*provvisorio*) provisional

'**trapano** sm (*utensile*) drill; (: MED) trepan

trapas'sare vt to pierce

tra'passo sm passage

trape'lare vi to leak, drip; (*fig*) to leak out

tra'pezio [tra'pɛttsjo] sm (MAT) trapezium; (*attrezzo ginnico*) trapeze

trapian'tare vt to transplant; **trapi'anto** sm transplanting; (MED) transplant

'**trappola** sf trap

tra'punta sf quilt

'trarre vt to draw, pull; (*portare*) to take; (*prendere, tirare fuori*) to take (out), draw; (*derivare*) to obtain; ~ **origine da qc** to have its origins o originate in th

trasa'lire vi to start, jump

trasan'dato, a ag shabby

tras'bordo sm transfer

trasci'nare [traʃʃi'nare] vt to drag; **~rsi** vr to drag o.s. along; (*fig*) to drag on

tras'correre vt (*tempo*) to spend, pass ♦ vi to pass; **tras'corso, a** pp di **trascorrere**

tras'critto, a pp di **trascrivere**

tras'crivere vt to transcribe

trascu'rare vt to neglect; (*non considerare*) to disregard; **trascura'tezza** sf carelessness, negligence; **trascu'rato, a** ag (*casa*) neglected; (*persona*) careless, negligent

trasfe'ribile ag transferable; "**non ~**" (*su assegno*) "account payee only"

trasferi'mento sm transfer; (*trasloco*) removal, move

trasfe'rire vt to transfer; **~rsi** vr to move; **tras'ferta** sf transfer; (*indennità*) travelling expenses pl; (SPORT) away game

trasfigu'rare vt to transfigure

trasfor'mare vt to transform, change;

trasforma'tore sm (ELEC) transformer

trasfusi'one sf (MED) transfusion

trasgre'dire vt to disobey, contravene

tras'lato, a ag metaphorical, figurative

traslo'care vt to move, transfer; **~rsi** vr to move; **tras'loco, chi** sm removal

tras'messo, a pp di **trasmettere**

tras'mettere vt (*passare*): ~ **qc a qn** to pass sth on to sb; (*mandare*) to send; (TECN, TEL, MED) to transmit; (TV, RADIO) to broadcast; **trasmetti'tore** sm transmitter; **trasmissi'one** sf (*gen, FISICA, TECN*) transmission; (*passaggio*) transmission, passing on; (TV, RADIO) broadcast; **trasmit'tente** sf transmitting o broadcasting station

traso'gnato, a [trasoɲ'ɲato] ag dreamy

traspa'rente ag transparent

traspa'rire vi to show (through)

traspi'rare vi to perspire; (*fig*) to come to light, leak out; **traspirazi'one** sf perspiration

traspor'tare vt to carry, move; (*merce*) to transport, convey; **lasciarsi ~ (da qc)** (*fig*) to let o.s. be carried away (by sth); **tras'porto** sm transport

trastul'lare vt to amuse; **~rsi** vr to amuse o.s.

trasver'sale ag transverse, cross(-); running at right angles

trasvo'lare vt to fly over

'**tratta** sf (ECON) draft; (*di persone*): **la ~ delle bianche** the white slave trade

tratta'mento sm treatment; (*servizio*) service

trat'tare vt (*gen*) to treat; (*commerciare*) to deal in; (*svolgere: argomento*) to discuss, deal with; (*negoziare*) to negotiate ♦ vi: ~ **di** to deal with; ~ **con** (*persona*) to deal with; **si tratta di ...** it's about ...; **tratta'tive** sfpl negotiations; **trat'tato** sm (*testo*) treatise; (*accordo*) treaty; **trattazi'one** sf treatment

tratteggi'are [tratted'dʒare] vt (disegnare: a tratti) to sketch, outline; (: col tratteggio) to hatch

tratte'nere vt (far rimanere: persona) to detain; (intrattenere: ospiti) to entertain; (tenere, frenare, reprimere) to hold back, keep back; (astenersi dal consegnare) to hold, keep; (detrarre: somma) to deduct; **~rsi** vr (astenersi) to restrain o.s., stop o.s.; (soffermarsi) to stay, remain

tratteni'mento sm entertainment; (festa) party

tratte'nuta sf deduction

trat'tino sm dash; (in parole composte) hyphen

'tratto, a pp di **trarre** ♦ sm (di penna, matita) stroke; (parte) part, piece; (di strada) stretch; (di mare, cielo) expanse; (di tempo) period (of time); **~i** smpl (caratteristiche) features; (modo di fare) ways, manners; **a un ~, d'un ~** suddenly

trat'tore sm tractor

tratto'ria sf restaurant

'trauma, i sm trauma; **trau'matico, a, ci, che** ag traumatic

tra'vaglio [tra'vaʎʎo] sm (angoscia) pain, suffering; (MED) pains pl

trava'sare vt to decant

'trave sf beam

tra'versa sf (trave) crosspiece; (via) sidestreet; (FERR) sleeper (BRIT), (railroad) tie (US); (CALCIO) crossbar

traver'sare vt to cross; **traver'sata** sf crossing; (AER) flight, trip

traver'sie sfpl mishaps, misfortunes

traver'sina sf (FERR) sleeper (BRIT), (railroad) tie (US)

tra'verso, a ag oblique; **di ~** ag askew ♦ av sideways; **andare di ~** (cibo) to go down the wrong way; **guardare di ~** to look askance at

travesti'mento sm disguise

traves'tire vt to disguise; **~rsi** vr to disguise o.s.

travi'are vt (fig) to lead astray

travi'sare vt (fig) to distort, misrepresent

tra'volgere [tra'vɔldʒere] vt to sweep away, carry away; (fig) to overwhelm; **tra'volto, a** pp di **travolgere**

tre num three

trebbi'are vt to thresh

'treccia, ce ['trettʃa] sf plait, braid

tre'cento [tre'tʃento] num three hundred ♦ sm: **il T~** the fourteenth century

'tredici ['treditʃi] num thirteen

'tregua sf truce; (fig) respite

tre'mare vi: **~ di** (freddo etc) to shiver o tremble with; (paura, rabbia) to shake o tremble with

tre'mendo, a ag terrible, awful

tre'mila num three thousand

'tremito sm trembling no pl; shaking no pl; shivering no pl

tremo'lare vi to tremble; (luce) to flicker; (foglie) to quiver

tre'more sm tremor

'treno sm train; **~ di gomme** set of tyres (BRIT) o tires (US); **~ merci** goods (BRIT) o freight train; **~ viaggiatori** passenger train

'trenta num thirty; **tren'tesimo, a** num thirtieth; **tren'tina** sf: **una trentina (di)** thirty or so, about thirty

trepi'dante ag anxious

treppi'ede sm tripod; (CUC) trivet

'tresca, sche sf (fig) intrigue; (: relazione amorosa) affair

'trespolo sm trestle

tri'angolo sm triangle

tribù sf inv tribe

tri'buna sf (podio) platform; (in aule etc) gallery; (di stadio) stand

tribu'nale sm court

tribu'tare vt to bestow

tri'buto sm tax; (fig) tribute

tri'checo, chi [tri'kɛko] sm (ZOOL) walrus

tri'ciclo [tri'tʃiklo] sm tricycle

trico'lore ag three-coloured ♦ sm tricolour; (bandiera italiana) Italian flag

tri'dente sm trident

tri'foglio [tri'fɔʎʎo] sm clover

'triglia ['triʎʎa] sf red mullet

tril'lare vi (MUS) to trill

tri'mestre sm period of three months; (INS) term, quarter (US); (COMM) quarter

'trina sf lace

trin'cea [trin'tʃɛa] sf trench; **trince'rare** vt to entrench

trinci'are [trin'tʃare] vt to cut up

trion'fare vi to triumph, win; **~ su** to triumph over, overcome; **tri'onfo** sm triumph

tripli'care vt to triple

'triplice ['triplitʃe] ag triple; **in ~ copia** in triplicate

'triplo, a ag triple; treble ♦ sm: **il ~ (di)** three times as much (as); **la spesa è ~a** it costs three times as much

'trippa sf (CUC) tripe

'triste ag sad; (luogo) dreary, gloomy; **tris'tezza** sf sadness; gloominess

trita'carne sm inv mincer, grinder (US)

tri'tare vt to mince, grind (US)

'trito, a ag (tritato) minced, ground (US); **~ e ritrito** (fig) trite, hackneyed

trit'tico, ci sm (ARTE) triptych

trivel'lare vt to drill

trivi'ale ag vulgar, low

tro'feo sm trophy

'tromba sf (MUS) trumpet; (AUT) horn; **~ d'aria** whirlwind; **~ delle scale** stairwell

trom'bone sm trombone

trom'bosi sf thrombosis

tron'care vt to cut off; (spezzare) to break off

'tronco, a, chi, che ag cut off; broken off; (LING) truncated; (fig) cut short ♦ sm (BOT, ANAT) trunk; (fig: tratto) section; **licenziare qn a ~** to fire sb on the spot

troneggi'are [troned'dʒare] vi: **~ (su)** to tower (over)

'tronfio, a ag conceited

'trono sm throne

tropi'cale ag tropical

'tropico, ci sm tropic; **~ci** smpl (GEO) tropics

PAROLA CHIAVE

'troppo, a det (in eccesso: quantità) too much; (: numero) too many; **c'era ~a gente** there were too many people; **fa ~ caldo** it's too hot

♦ pron (in eccesso: quantità) too much; (: numero) too many; **ne hai messo ~** you've put in too much; **meglio ~i che pochi** better too many than too few

♦ av (eccessivamente: con ag, av) too; (: con vb) too much; **~ amaro/tardi** too bitter/late; **lavora ~** he works too much; **di ~** too much; **qualche tazza di ~** a few cups too many; **3000 lire di ~** 3000 lire too much; **essere di ~** to be in the way

---

'trota sf trout

trot'tare vi to trot; **trotterel'lare** vi to trot along; (bambino) to toddle; **'trotto** sm trot

'trottola sf spinning top

tro'vare vt to find; (giudicare): **trovo che** I find o think that; **~rsi** vr (reciproco: incontrarsi) to meet; (essere, stare) to be; (arrivare, capitare) to find o.s.; **andare a ~ qn** to go and see sb; **~ qn colpevole** to find sb guilty; **~rsi bene** (in un luogo, con qn) to get on well; **tro'vata** sf good idea

truc'care (falsare) to fake; (attore etc) to make up; (travestire) to disguise; (SPORT) to fix; (AUT) to soup up; **~rsi** vr to make up (one's face); **trucca'tore, 'trice** sm/f (CINEMA, TEATRO) make-up artist

'trucco, chi sm trick; (cosmesi) make-up

'truce ['trutʃe] ag fierce

truci'dare [trutʃi'dare] vt to slaughter

tru'ciolo ['trutʃolo] sm shaving

'truffa sf fraud, swindle; **truf'fare** vt to

swindle, cheat

'truppa sf troop

tu pron you; ~ **stesso(a)** you yourself; **dare del ~ a qn** to address sb as "tu"

'tua vedi **tuo**

'tuba sf (MUS) tuba; (cappello) top hat

tu'bare vi to coo

tu'betto sm tube

'tubo sm tube; pipe; ~ **digerente** (ANAT) alimentary canal, digestive tract; ~ **di scappamento** (AUT) exhaust pipe

'tue vedi **tuo**

tuf'fare vt to plunge, dip; **~rsi** vr to plunge, dive; **'tuffo** sm dive; (breve bagno) dip

tu'gurio sm hovel

tuli'pano sm tulip

tume'farsi vr (MED) to swell

'tumido, a ag swollen

tu'more sm (MED) tumour

tu'multo sm uproar, commotion; (sommossa) riot; (fig) turmoil; **tumultu'oso, a** ag rowdy, unruly; (fig) turbulent, stormy

'tunica, che sf tunic

Tuni'sia sf: **la** ~ Tunisia

'tuo (f **'tua**, pl **tu'oi**, **'tue**) det: **il ~, la tua** etc your ♦ pron: **il ~, la tua** etc yours

tuo'nare vi to thunder; **tuona** it is thundering, there's some thunder

tu'ono sm thunder

tu'orlo sm yolk

tu'racciolo [tu'rattʃolo] sm cap, top; (di sughero) cork

tu'rare vt to stop, plug; (con sughero) to cork; **~rsi il naso** to hold one's nose

turba'mento sm disturbance; (di animo) anxiety, agitation

tur'bante sm turban

tur'bare vt to disturb, trouble

'turbine sm whirlwind

turbo'lento, a ag turbulent; (ragazzo) boisterous, unruly

turbo'lenza [turbo'lentsa] sf

turbulence

tur'chese [tur'kese] sf turquoise

Tur'chia [tur'kia] sf: **la** ~ Turkey

tur'chino, a [tur'kino] ag deep blue

'turco, a, chi, che ag Turkish ♦ sm/f Turk/Turkish woman ♦ sm (LING) Turkish; **parlare** ~ (fig) to talk double-dutch

tu'rismo sm tourism; tourist industry; **tu'rista, i, e** sm/f tourist; **tu'ristico, a, ci, che** ag tourist cpd

'turno sm turn; (di lavoro) shift; **di** ~ (soldato, medico, custode) on duty; **a** ~ (rispondere) in turn; (lavorare) in shifts; **fare a** ~ **a fare qc** to take turns to do sth; **è il suo** ~ it's your (o his etc) turn

'turpe ag filthy, vile; **turpi'loquio** sm obscene language

'tuta sf overalls pl; (SPORT) tracksuit

tu'tela sf (DIR: di minore) guardianship; (: protezione) protection; (difesa) defence; **tute'lare** vt to protect, defend

tu'tore, 'trice sm/f (DIR) guardian

tutta'via cong nevertheless, yet

PAROLA CHIAVE

'tutto, a det **1** (intero) all; ~ **il latte** all the milk; **~a la notte** all night, the whole night; ~ **il libro** the whole book; **~a una bottiglia** a whole bottle **2** (pl, collettivo) all; every; **~i i libri** all the books; **~e le notti** every night; **~i i venerdì** every Friday; **~i gli uomini** all the men; (collettivo) all men; ~ **l'anno** all year long; **~i e due** both o each of us (o them o you); **~i e cinque** all five of us (o them o you) **3** (completamente): **era** ~ **a sporca** she was all dirty; **tremava** ~ he was trembling all over; **è ~a sua madre** she's just o exactly like her mother **4**: **a tutt'oggi** so far, up till now; **a ~a velocità** at full o top speed ♦ pron **1** (ogni cosa) everything, all; (qualsiasi cosa) anything; **ha mangiato** ~ he's eaten everything;

~ considerato all things considered; **in ~: 10.000 lire in ~** 10.000 lire in all; **in ~ eravamo 50** there were 50 of us in all
2: ~i, e (ognuno) all, everybody; **vengono ~i** they are all coming, everybody's coming; **~i quanti** all and sundry
♦ av (completamente) entirely, quite; **è ~ il contrario** it's quite o exactly the opposite; **tutt'al più: saranno stati tutt'al più una cinquantina** there were about fifty of them at the (very) most; **tutt'al più possiamo prendere un treno** if the worst comes to the worst we can take a train; **tutt'altro** on the contrary; **è tutt'altro che felice** he's anything but happy; **tutt'a un tratto** suddenly
♦ sm: **il ~** the whole lot, all of it

tutto'fare ag inv: **domestica ~** general maid; **ragazzo ~** office boy
♦ sm/f inv handyman/woman
tut'tora av still

U, u

ubbidi'ente ag obedient; **ubbidi'enza** sf obedience
ubbi'dire vi to obey; **~ a** to obey; (sog: veicolo, macchina) to respond to
ubria'care vi **~ qn** to get sb drunk; (sog: alcool) to make sb drunk; (fig) to make sb's head spin o reel; **~rsi** vr to get drunk; **~rsi di** (fig) to become intoxicated with
ubri'aco, a ag, sm/f drunk
uccelli'era [uttʃelˈljɛra] sf aviary
uccel'lino [uttʃelˈlino] sm baby bird, chick
uc'cello [utˈtʃɛllo] sm bird
uc'cidere [utˈtʃidere] vt to kill; **~rsi** vr (suicidarsi) to kill o.s.; (perdere la vita) to be killed; **uccisi'one** sf killing
uc'ciso, a pp di **uccidere**; **ucci'sore**

~ **considerato** sm killer
udi'enza [uˈdjɛntsa] sf audience; (DIR) hearing
u'dire vt to hear; **udi'tivo, a** ag auditory; **u'dito** sm (sense of) hearing; **udi'torio** sm (persone) audience
UE sigla f (= Unione Europea) EU
UEM sigla f (= Unione economica e monetaria) EMU
'uffa escl tut!
uffici'ale [uffiˈtʃale] ag official ♦ sm (AMM) official, officer; (MIL) officer; **~ di stato civile** registrar
uf'ficio [ufˈfitʃo] sm (gen) office; (dovere) duty; (mansione) task, function, job; (agenzia) agency, bureau; (REL) service; **d'~** ag office cpd; official o avofficially; **~ di collocamento** employment office; **~ informazioni** information bureau; **~ oggetti smarriti** lost property office (BRIT), lost and found (US); **~ postale** post office
uffici'oso, a [uffiˈtʃoso] ag unofficial
'UFO sm inv UFO
'ufo: a ~ free, for nothing
uguagli'anza [ugwaʎˈʎantsa] sf equality
uguagli'are [ugwaʎˈʎare] vt to make equal; (essere uguale) to equal, be equal to; (livellare) to level; **~rsi a o con qn** (paragonarsi) to compare o.s. to sb
ugu'ale ag equal; (identico) identical, the same; (uniforme) level, even ♦ av: **costano ~** they cost the same; **sono bravi ~** they're equally good; **ugual'mente** av equally; (lo stesso) all the same
'ulcera [ˈultʃera] sf ulcer
u'livo = **olivo**
ulteri'ore ag further
ulti'mare vt to finish, complete
'ultimo, a ag (finale) last; (estremo) farthest, utmost; (recente: notizia, moda) latest; (fig: sommo, fondamentale) ultimate ♦ sm/f last (one); **fino all'~** to the last, until the

end; **da ~**, **in ~** in the end; **abitare all'~ piano** to live on the top floor; **per ~** (*entrare, arrivare*) last

ulu'lare *vi* to howl; **ulu'lato** *sm* howling *no pl*; howl

umanità *sf* humanity; **umani'tario, a** *ag* humanitarian

u'mano, a *ag* human; (*comprensivo*) humane

umet'tare *vt* to dampen, moisten

umidità *sf* dampness; humidity

'umido, a *ag* damp; (*mano, occhi*) moist; (*clima*) humid ♦ *sm* dampness, damp; **carne in ~** stew

'umile *ag* humble

umili'are *vt* to humiliate; **~rsi** *vr* to humble o.s.; **umiliazi'one** *sf* humiliation

umiltà *sf* humility, humbleness

u'more *sm* (*disposizione d'animo*) mood; (*carattere*) temper; **di buon/ cattivo ~** in a good/bad mood

umo'rismo *sm* humour; **avere il senso dell'~** to have a sense of humour; **umo'ristico, a, ci, che** *ag* humorous, funny

un *vedi* **uno**

un' *vedi* **uno**

'una *vedi* **uno**

u'nanime *ag* unanimous; **unanimità** *sf* unanimity; **all'unanimità** unanimously

unci'netto [untʃi'netto] *sm* crochet hook

un'cino [un'tʃino] *sm* hook

'undici ['undit͡ʃi] *num* eleven

'ungere ['und͡ʒere] *vt* to grease, oil; (*REL*) to anoint; (*fig*) to flatter, butter up; **~rsi** *vr* (*sporcarsi*) to get covered in grease; **~rsi con la crema** to put on cream

unghe'rese [unge'rese] *ag, sm/f, sm* Hungarian

Unghe'ria [unge'ria] *sf*: **l'~** Hungary

'unghia ['ungja] *sf* (*ANAT*) nail; (*di animale*) claw; (*di rapace*) talon; (*di cavallo*) hoof; **unghi'ata** *sf* (*graffio*)

scratch

ungu'ento *sm* ointment

'unico, a, ci, che *ag* (*solo*) only; (*ineguagliabile*) unique; (*singolo: binario*) single; **figlio(a) ~(a)** only son/daughter, only child

unifamili'are *ag* one-family *cpd*

unificazi'one *sf* uniting; unification; standardization

uni'forme *ag* uniform; (*superficie*) even ♦ *sf* (*divisa*) uniform

unilate'rale *ag* one-sided; (*DIR*) unilateral

uni'one *sf* union; (*fig: concordia*) unity, harmony; **U~ Europea** European Union

u'nire *vt* to unite; (*congiungere*) to join, connect; (*: ingredienti, colori*) to combine; (*in matrimonio*) to unite, join together; **~rsi** *vr* to unite; (*in matrimonio*) to be joined together; **~ qc a** to unite sth with; to join o connect sth with; **to combine sth with**; **~rsi a** (*gruppo, società*) to join

unità *sf inv* (*unione, concordia*) unity; (*MAT, MIL, COMM, di misura*) unit; **uni'tario, a** *ag* unitary; **prezzo unitario** price per unit

u'nito, a *ag* (*paese*) united; (*amici, famiglia*) close; **in tinta ~a** plain, self-coloured

univer'sale *ag* universal; general

università *sf inv* university; **universi'tario, a** *ag* university *cpd* ♦ *sm/f* (*studente*) university student; (*insegnante*) academic, university lecturer

uni'verso *sm* universe

PAROLA CHIAVE

'uno, a (*dav sm* **un** +*C*, *V*, **uno** +*s impura, gn, pn, ps, x, z; dav sf* **un'** +*V*, **una** +*C*) *art indef* **1** a; (*dav vocale*) an; **un bambino** a child; **~a strada** a street; **~ zingaro** a gypsy

2 (*intensivo*): **ho avuto ~a paura!** I got such a fright!

♦ *pron* 1 one; **prendine ~** take one (of them); **l'~ o l'altro** either (of them); **l'~ e l'altro** both (of them); **aiutarsi l'un l'altro** to help one another o each other; **sono entrati l'~ dopo l'altro** they came in one after the other
2 (*un tale*) someone, somebody
3 (*con valore impersonale*) one, you; **se ~ vuole** if one wants, if you want
♦ *num* one; **~a mela e due pere** one apple and two pears; **~ più ~ fa due** one plus one equals two, one and one are two
♦ *sf*: **è l'~a** it's one (o'clock)

'**unto, a** *pp di* **ungere** ♦ *ag* greasy, oily ♦ *sf* grease; **untu'oso, a** *ag* greasy, oily

u'**omo** (*pl* **uomini**) *sm* man; **da ~** (*abito, scarpe*) men's, for men; **~ d'affari** businessman; **~ di paglia** stooge; **~ rana** frogman

u'**ovo** (*pl(f)* **uova**) *sm* egg; **~ affogato** poached egg; **~ al tegame** fried egg; **~ alla coque** boiled egg; **~ bazzotto/sodo** soft-/hard-boiled egg; **~ di Pasqua** Easter egg; **~ in camicia** poached egg; **~a strapazzate** scrambled eggs

ura'**gano** *sm* hurricane

urba'**nistica** *sf* town planning

ur'**bano, a** *ag* urban, city *cpd*, town *cpd*; (*TEL: chiamata*) local; (*fig*) urbane

ur'**gente** [ur'dʒɛnte] *ag* urgent; ur'**genza** *sf* urgency; **in caso d'urgenza** (in case of) an emergency; **d'urgenza** *ag* emergency ♦ *av* urgently, as a matter of urgency

u'**rina** *sf* = **orina**

ur'**lare** *vi* (*persona*) to scream, yell; (*animale, vento*) to howl ♦ *vt* to scream, yell

'**urlo** (*pl(m)* **urli,** *pl(f)* '**urla**) *sm* scream, yell; howl

'**urna** *sf* urn; (*elettorale*) ballot-box; **andare alle ~e** to go to the polls

urrà *escl* hurrah!

U.R.S.S. *abbr f*: **l'~** the USSR

ur'**tare** *vt* to bump into, knock against; (*fig: irritare*) to annoy ♦ *vi*: **~ contro o in** to bump into, knock against, crash into; (*fig: imbattersi*) to come up against, clash against; **~rsi** *vr* (*reciproco: scontrarsi*) to collide; (: *fig*) to clash; (*irritarsi*) to get annoyed; '**urto** *sm* (*colpo*) knock, bump; (*scontro*) crash, collision; (*fig*) clash

U.S.A. ['uza] *smpl*: **gli ~** the USA

u'**sanza** [u'zantsa] *sf* custom; (*moda*) fashion

u'**sare** *vt* to use, employ ♦ *vi* (*servirsi*): **~ di** to use; (*diritto*) to exercise; (*essere di moda*) to be fashionable; (*essere solito*): **~ fare** to be in the habit of doing, to be accustomed to doing ♦ *vb impers*: **qui usa così** it's the custom round here; u'**sato, a** *ag* used; (*consumato*) worn; (*di seconda mano*) used, second-hand ♦ *sm* second-hand goods *pl*

usci'**ere** [uʃ'ʃɛre] *sm* usher

'**uscio** ['uʃʃo] *sm* door

u'**scire** [uʃ'ʃire] *vi* (*gen*) to come out; (*partire, andare a passeggio, a uno spettacolo etc*) to go out; (*essere sorteggiato: numero*) to come up; **~ da** (*gen*) to leave; (*posto*) to go o come out of, leave; (*solco, vasca etc*) to come out of; (*muro*) to stick out of; (*competenza etc*) to be outside; (*infanzia, adolescenza*) to leave behind; (*famiglia nobile etc*) to come from; **~ da o di casa** to go out; (*fig*) to leave home; **~ in automobile** to go out in the car, go for a drive; **~ di strada** (*AUT*) to go off o leave the road

u'**scita** [uʃ'ʃita] *sf* (*passaggio, varco*) exit, way out; (*per divertimento*) outing; (*ECON: somma*) expenditure; (*TEATRO*) entrance; (*fig: battuta*) witty remark; **~ di sicurezza** emergency exit

usi'**gnolo** [uziɲ'ɲɔlo] *sm* nightingale

U.S.L. [uzl] *sigla f* (= unità sanitaria

locale) local health centre

'uso *sm (utilizzazione)* use; *(esercizio)* practice; *(abitudine)* custom; **a ~ di** for (the use of); **d'~** *(corrente)* in use; **fuori ~** out of use

usti'one *sf* burn

usu'ale *ag* common, everyday

u'sura *sf* usury; *(logoramento)* wear (and tear)

uten'sile [uten'sile] *sm* tool, implement; **~i da cucina** kitchen utensils

u'tente *sm/f* user

'utero *sm* uterus

'utile *ag* useful ♦ *sm (vantaggio)* advantage, benefit; *(ECON: profitto)* profit; **utilità** *sf* usefulness *no pl;* use; *(vantaggio)* benefit; **utili'taria** *sf (AUT)* economy car

utiliz'zare [utilid'dzare] *vt* to use, make use of, utilize

'uva *sf* grapes *pl;* **~ passa** raisins *pl;* **~ spina** gooseberry

V, v

v. *abbr (= vedi)* v

va *vb vedi* andare

va'cante *ag* vacant

va'canza [va'kantsa] *sf (l'essere vacante)* vacancy; *(riposo, ferie)* holiday(s *pl) (BRIT),* vacation *(US); (giorno di permesso)* day off, holiday; **~e** *sfpl (periodo di ferie)* holidays *(BRIT),* vacation *sg (US);* **essere/andare in ~** to be/go on holiday *o* vacation; **~e estive** summer holiday(s) *o* vacation

'vacca, che *sf* cow

vacci'nare [vattʃi'nare] *vt* to vaccinate

vac'cino [vat'tʃino] *sm (MED)* vaccine

vacil'lare [vatʃil'lare] *vi* to sway, wobble; *(luce)* to flicker; *(fig: memoria, coraggio)* to be failing, falter

'vacuo, a *ag (fig)* empty, vacuous

'vado *vb vedi* andare

vaga'bondo, a *sm/f* tramp, vagrant

va'gare *vi* to wander

va'gina [va'dʒina] *sf* vagina

va'gire [va'dʒire] *vi* to whimper

va'gito [va'dʒito] *sm* cry

'vaglia [ˈvaʎʎa] *sm inv* money order; **~ postale** postal order

vagli'are [vaʎˈʎare] *vt* to sift; *(fig)* to weigh up; **'vaglio** *sm* sieve

'vago, a, ghi, ghe *ag* vague

va'gone *sm (FERR: per passeggeri)* coach; *(: per merci)* truck, wagon; **~ letto** sleeper, sleeping car; **~ ristorante** dining *o* restaurant car

'vai *vb vedi* andare

vai'olo *sm* smallpox

va'langa, ghe *sf* avalanche

va'lente *ag* able, talented

va'lere *vi (avere forza, potenza)* to have influence; *(essere valido)* to be valid; *(avere vigore, autorità)* to hold, apply; *(essere capace: poeta, studente)* to be good, be able ♦ *vt (prezzo, sforzo)* to be worth; *(corrispondere)* to correspond to; *(procurare):* **~ qc a qn** to earn sb sth; **~rsi di** to make use of, take advantage of; **far ~** *(autorità etc)* to assert; **vale a dire** that is to say; **~ la pena** to be worth the effort *o* worth it

va'levole *ag* valid

vali'care *vt* to cross

'valico, chi *sm (passo)* pass

'valido, a *ag* valid; *(rimedio)* effective; *(aiuto)* real; *(persona)* worthwhile

valige'ria [validʒe'ria] *sf* leather goods *pl;* leather goods factory; leather goods shop

vali'getta [vali'dʒetta] *sf* briefcase

va'ligia, gie *o* **ge** [va'lidʒa] *sf* (suit)case; **fare le ~gie** to pack (up)

val'lata *sf* valley

'valle *sf* valley; **a ~** *(di fiume)* downstream; **scendere a ~** to go downhill

va'lore *sm (gen)* value; *(merito)* merit, worth; *(coraggio)* valour, courage; *(COMM: titolo)* security; **~i** *smpl (oggetti preziosi)* valuables

valoriz'zare [valorid'dzare] *vt*

(*terreno*) to develop; (*fig*) to make the most of

'**valso, a** *pp di* **valere**

va'**luta** *sf* currency, money; (*BANCA*): ~ **15 gennaio** interest to run from January 15th

valu'**tare** *vt* (*casa, gioiello, fig*) to value; (*stabilire: peso, entrate, fig*) to estimate; **valutazi'one** *sf* valuation; estimate

'**valvola** *sf* (*TECN, ANAT*) valve; (*ELETTR*) fuse

'**valzer** ['valtser] *sm inv* waltz

vam'**pata** *sf* (*di fiamma*) blaze; (*di calore*) blast; (: *al viso*) flush

'**vampiro** *sm* vampire

vanda'**lismo** *sm* vandalism

'**vandalo** *sm* vandal

vaneggi'**are** [vaned'dʒare] *vi* to rave

'**vanga, ghe** *sf* spade; van'**gare** *vt* to dig

van'**gelo** [van'dʒɛlo] *sm* gospel

va'**niglia** [va'niʎʎa] *sf* vanilla

vani'**tà** *sf* vanity; (*di promessa*) emptiness; (*di sforzo*) futility; **vani'toso, a** *ag* vain, conceited

'**vanno** *vb vedi* **andare**

'**vano, a** *ag* vain ♦ *sm* (*spazio*) space; (*apertura*) opening; (*stanza*) room

van'**taggio** [van'taddʒo] *sm* advantage; **essere/portarsi in ~** (*SPORT*) to be in/take the lead; **vantaggi'oso, a** *ag* advantageous, favourable

van'**tare** *vt* to praise, speak highly of; **~rsi** *vr*: **~rsi** (**di/di aver fatto**) to boast *o* brag (about/about having done); **vante'ria** *sf* boasting; '**vanto** *sm* boasting; (*merito*) virtue, merit; (*gloria*) pride

'**vanvera** *sf*: **a ~** haphazardly; **parlare a ~** to talk nonsense

va'**pore** *sm* vapour; (*anche*: ~ **acqueo**) steam; (*nave*) steamer; **a ~** (*turbina etc*) steam *cpd*; **al ~** (*CUC*) steamed; **vapo'retto** *sm* steamer; **vapori'zzare** *vt* to vaporize; **vapo'roso, a** *ag* (*tessuto*) filmy; (*capelli*) soft and full

va'**rare** *vt* (*NAUT, fig*) to launch; (*DIR*) to pass

var'**care** *vt* to cross

'**varco, chi** *sm* passage; **aprirsi un ~ tra la folla** to push one's way through the crowd

vari'**abile** *ag* variable; (*tempo, umore*) changeable, variable ♦ *sf* (*MAT*) variable

vari'**are** *vt, vi* to vary; ~ **di opinione** to change one's mind; **variazi'one** *sf* variation; change

va'**rice** [va'ritʃe] *sf* varicose vein

vari'**cella** [vari'tʃɛlla] *sf* chickenpox

vari'**coso, a** *ag* varicose

varie'**gato, a** *ag* variegated

varie'**tà** *sf inv* variety ♦ *sm inv* variety show

'**vario, a** *ag* varied; (*parecchi: col sostantivo al pl*) various; (*mutevole: umore*) changeable; **vario'pinto, a** *ag* multicoloured

'**varo** *sm* (*NAUT, fig*) launch; (*di leggi*) passing

va'**saio** *sm* potter

'**vasca, sche** *sf* basin; (*anche*: ~ **da bagno**) bathtub, bath

va'**scello** [va'ʃʃɛllo] *sm* vessel, ship

vase'**lina** *sf* vaseline

vasel'**lame** *sm* (*stoviglie*) crockery; (: *di porcellana*) china; ~ **d'oro/d'argento** gold/silver plate

'**vaso** *sm* (*recipiente*) pot; (: *barattolo*) jar; (: *decorativo*) vase; (*ANAT*) vessel; ~ **da fiori** vase; (*per piante*) flowerpot

vas'**soio** *sm* tray

'**vasto, a** *ag* vast, immense

Vati'**cano** *sm*: **il ~** the Vatican

ve *pron, av vedi* **vi**

vecchi'**aia** [vek'kjaja] *sf* old age

'**vecchio, a** ['vekkjo] *ag* old ♦ *sm/f* old man/woman; **i ~** the old

'**vece** ['vetʃe] *sf*: **in ~ di** in the place of, for; **fare le ~i di qn** to take sb's place

ve'**dere** *vt, vi* to see; **~rsi** *vr* to meet, see one another; **avere a che ~ con** to have something to do with; **far ~ qc a qn** to show sb sth; **farsi ~** to show o.s.; (*farsi vivo*) to show one's face; **vedi di non farlo** make sure o see you don't do it; **non (ci) si vede** (*è buio etc*) you can't see a thing; **non lo posso ~** (*fig*) I can't stand him

ve'detta *sf* (*sentinella, posto*) look-out; (NAUT) patrol boat

'vedovo, a *sm/f* widower/widow

ve'duta *sf* view

vee'mente *ag* vehement; violent

vege'tale [vedʒe'tale] *ag, sm* vegetable

vegetari'ano, a [vedʒeta'rjano] *ag, sm/f* vegetarian

'vegeto, a ['vedʒeto] *ag* (*pianta*) thriving; (*persona*) strong, vigorous

'veglia ['veʎʎa] *sf* wakefulness; (*sorveglianza*) watch; (*trattenimento*) evening gathering; **fare la ~ a un malato** to watch over a sick person

vegli'are [veʎ'ʎare] *vi* to be awake; to stay o sit up; (*stare vigile*) to watch; to keep watch ♦ *vt* (*malato, morto*) to watch over, sit up with

ve'icolo *sm* vehicle

'vela *sf* (NAUT: *tela*) sail; (*sport*) sailing

ve'lare *vt* to veil; **~rsi** *vr* (*occhi, luna*) to mist over; (*voce*) to become husky; **~rsi il viso** to cover one's face (with a veil); **ve'lato, a** *ag* veiled

veleggi'are [veled'dʒare] *vi* to sail; (AER) to glide

ve'leno *sm* poison; **vele'noso, a** *ag* poisonous

veli'ero *sm* sailing ship

ve'lina *sf* (*anche: carta ~*: *per imballare*) tissue paper

ve'livolo *sm* aircraft

velleità *sf inv* vain ambition, vain desire

vel'luto *sm* velvet; **~ a coste** cord

'velo *sm* veil; (*tessuto*) voile

ve'loce [ve'lotʃe] *ag* fast, quick ♦ *av* fast, quickly; **velo'cista, i, e** *sm/f* (*sport*) sprinter; **velo'cità** *sf* speed; **a forte velocità** at high speed; **velocità di crociera** cruising speed

'vena *sf* (*gen*) vein; (*filone*) vein, seam;

(*fig: ispirazione*) inspiration; (: *umore*) mood; **essere in ~ di qc** to be in the mood for sth

ve'nale *ag* (*prezzo, valore*) market *cpd*; (*fig*) venal; mercenary

ven'demmia *sf* (*raccolta*) grape harvest; (*quantità d'uva*) grape crop, grapes *pl*; (*vino ottenuto*) vintage; **vendemmi'are** *vt* to harvest ♦ *vi* to harvest the grapes

'vendere *vt* to sell; **"vendesi"** "for sale"

ven'detta *sf* revenge

vendi'care *vt* to avenge; **~rsi** *vr*: **~rsi (di)** to avenge o.s. (for); (*per rancore*) to take one's revenge (for); **~rsi su qn** to revenge o.s. on sb; **vendica'tivo, a** *ag* vindictive

'vendita *sf* sale; **la ~** (*attività*) selling; (*smercio*) sales *pl*; **in ~** on sale; **~ all'asta** sale by auction; **~ per telefono** telesales *sg*; **vendi'tore** *sm* seller, vendor; (*gestore di negozio*) trader, dealer

vene'rabile *ag* venerable

vene'rando, a *ag* = venerabile

vene'rare *vt* to venerate

venerdì *sm inv* Friday; **di o il ~** on Fridays; **V~ Santo** Good Friday

ve'nereo, a *ag* venereal

'veneto, a *ag, sm/f* Venetian

Ve'nezia [ve'nettsja] *sf* Venice; **venezi'ana** *sf* Venetian blind; **venezi'ano, a** *ag, sm/f* Venetian

ve'nire *vi* to come; (*riuscire: dolce, fotografia*) to turn out; (*come ausiliare: essere*): **viene ammirato da tutti** he is admired by everyone; **~ da** to come from; **quanto viene?** how much does it cost?; **far ~** (*mandare a chiamare*) to send for; **~ giù** to come down; **~ meno** (*svenire*) to faint; **~ meno a qc** not to fulfil sth; **~ su** to come up; **~ a trovare qn** to come and see sb; **~ via** to come away

ven'taglio [ven'taʎʎo] *sm* fan

ven'tata *sf* gust (of wind)

ven'tenne *ag*: una ragazza ~ a twenty-year-old girl, a girl of twenty

ven'tesimo, a *num* twentieth

'venti *num* twenty

venti'lare *vt* (*stanza*) to air, ventilate; (*fig: idea, proposta*) to air; **ventila'tore** *sm* ventilator, fan

ven'tina *sf*: una ~ (di) around twenty, twenty or so

venti'sette *num* twenty-seven

'vento *sm* wind

'ventola *sf* (*AUT, TECN*) fan

ven'tosa *sf* (*ZOOL*) sucker; (*di gomma*) suction pad

ven'toso, a *ag* windy

'ventre *sm* stomach

ven'tura *sf*: soldato di ~ mercenary

ven'turo, a *ag* next, coming

ve'nuta *sf* coming, arrival

ve'nuto, a *pp di* **venire**

vera'mente *av* really

ver'bale *ag* verbal ♦ *sm* (*di riunione*) minutes *pl*

'verbo *sm* (*LING*) verb; (*parola*) word; (*REL*): il **V**~ the Word

'verde *ag, sm* green; **essere al** ~ to be broke; ♦ **bottiglia/oliva** bottle/olive green

verde'rame *sm* verdigris

ver'detto *sm* verdict

ver'dura *sf* vegetables *pl*

'verga, ghe *sf* rod

'vergine ['verdʒine] *sf* virgin; (*dello zodiaco*): **V**~ Virgo ♦ *ag* virgin; (*ragazza*): **essere** ~ to be a virgin

ver'gogna [ver'ɡoɲɲa] *sf* shame; (*timidezza*) shyness, embarrassment; **vergo'gnarsi** *vr*: **vergognarsi (di)** to be o feel ashamed (of); to be shy (about), be embarrassed (about); **vergo'gnoso, a** *ag* ashamed; (*timido*) shy, embarrassed; (*causa di vergogna: azione*) shameful

ve'rifica, che *sf* checking *no pl*, check

verifi'care *vt* (*controllare*) to check; (*confermare*) to confirm, bear out

verità *sf inv* truth

veriti'ero, a *ag* (*che dice la verità*) truthful; (*conforme a verità*) true

'verme *sm* worm

vermi'celli [vermi'tʃelli] *smpl* vermicelli *pl*

ver'miglio [ver'miʎʎo] *sm* vermilion, scarlet

'vermut *sm inv* vermouth

ver'nice [ver'nitʃe] *sf* (*colorazione*) paint; (*trasparente*) varnish; (*pelle*) patent leather; "~ **fresca**" "wet paint"; **vernici'are** *vt* to paint; to varnish

'vero, a *ag* (*veridico: fatti, testimonianza*) true; (*autentico*) real ♦ *sm* (*verità*) truth; (*realtà*) real life; **un** ~ **e proprio delinquente** a real criminal, an out-and-out criminal

vero'simile *ag* likely, probable

ver'ruca, che *sf* wart

versa'mento *sm* (*pagamento*) payment; (*deposito di denaro*) deposit

ver'sante *sm* slopes *pl*, side

ver'sare *vt* (*fare uscire: vino, farina*) to pour (out); (*spargere: lacrime, sangue*) to shed; (*rovesciare*) to spill; (*ECON*) to pay; (: *depositare*) to deposit, pay in; **~rsi** *vr* (*rovesciarsi*) to spill; (*fiume, folla*): **~rsi (in)** to pour (into)

versa'tile *ag* versatile

ver'setto *sm* (*REL*) verse

versi'one *sf* version; (*traduzione*) translation

'verso *sm* (*di poesia*) verse, line; (*di animale, uccello*) cry; (*direzione*) direction; (*modo*) way; (*di foglio di carta*) verso; (*di moneta*) reverse; **~i** *smpl* (*poesia*) verse *sg*; **non c'è** ~ **di persuaderlo** there's no way of persuading him, he can't be persuaded ♦ *prep* (*in direzione di*) toward(s); (*nei pressi di*) near, around (about); (*in senso temporale*) about, around; (*nei confronti di*) for; ~ **di me** towards me; ~ **sera** towards evening

'vertebra *sf* vertebra

verti'cale *ag, sf* vertical

'vertice ['vertitʃe] sm summit, top; (MAT) vertex; **conferenza al ~** (POL) summit conference

ver'tigine [ver'tidʒine] sf dizziness no pl; dizzy spell; (MED) vertigo; **avere le ~i** to feel dizzy; **vertigi'noso, a** ag (altezza) dizzy; (fig) breathtakingly high (o deep etc)

ve'scica, che [veʃ'ʃika] sf (ANAT) bladder; (MED) blister

'vescovo sm bishop

'vespa sf wasp

'vespro sm (REL) vespers pl

ves'sillo sm standard; (bandiera) flag

ves'taglia [ves'taʎʎa] sf dressing gown

'veste sf garment; (rivestimento) covering; (qualità, facoltà) capacity; **in ~ ufficiale** (fig) in an official capacity; **in ~ di** in the guise of, as; **vesti'ario** sm wardrobe, clothes pl

ves'tire vt (bambino, malato) to dress; (avere indosso) to have on, wear; **~rsi** vr to dress, get dressed; **ves'tito, a** ag dressed ♦ sm garment; (da donna) dress; (da uomo) suit; **vestiti** smpl (indumenti) clothes; **vestito di bianco** dressed in white

Ve'suvio sm: **il ~** Vesuvius

vete'rano, a ag, sm/f veteran

veteri'naria sf veterinary medicine

veteri'nario, a ag veterinary ♦ sm veterinary surgeon (BRIT), veterinarian (US), vet

'veto sm inv veto

ve'traio sm glassmaker; glazier

ve'trata sf glass door (o window); (di chiesa) stained glass window

vetre'ria sf (stabilimento) glassworks sg; (oggetti di vetro) glassware

ve'trina sf (di negozio) (shop) window; (armadio) display cabinet; **vetri'nista, i, e** sm/f window dresser

vetri'olo sm vitriol

'vetro sm glass; (per finestra, porta) pane (of glass)

'vetta sf peak, summit, top

vet'tore sm (MAT, FISICA) vector; (chi trasporta) carrier

vetto'vaglie [vetto'vaʎʎe] sfpl supplies

vet'tura sf (carrozza) carriage; (FERR) carriage (BRIT), car (US); (auto) car (BRIT), automobile (US)

vezzeggia'tivo [vettseddʒa'tivo] sm (LING) term of endearment

'vezzo ['vettso] sm habit; **~i** smpl (smancerie) affected ways; (leggiadria) charms; **vez'zoso, a** ag (grazioso) charming, pretty; (lezioso) affected

vi (dav lo, la, li, le, ne diventa **ve**) pron (oggetto) you; (complemento di termine) (to) you; (riflessivo) yourselves; (reciproco) each other ♦ av (li) there; (qui) here; (per questo/quel luogo) through here/there; **~ è/sono** there is/are

'via sf (gen) way; (strada) street; (sentiero, pista) path, track; (AMM: procedimento) channels pl ♦ prep (passando per) via, by way of ♦ av away ♦ escl go away!; (suvvia) come on!; (SPORT) go! ♦ sm (SPORT) starting signal; **in ~ di guarigione** on the road to recovery; **per ~ di** (a causa di) because of, on account of; **in o per ~** on the way; **per ~ aerea** by air; (lettere) by airmail; **andare/essere ~** to go/be away; **~ ~ che** (a mano a mano) as; **dare il ~ a** (fig) to start; **V~ lattea** (ASTR) Milky Way; **~ di mezzo** middle course; **in ~ provvisoria** provisionally

viabilità sf (di strada) practicability; (rete stradale) roads pl, road network

via'dotto sm viaduct

viaggi'are [viad'dʒare] vi to travel; **viaggia'tore, 'trice** ag travelling ♦ sm traveller; (passeggero) passenger

vi'aggio ['vjaddʒo] sm travel(ling); (tragitto) journey, trip; **buon ~!** have a good trip!; **~ di nozze** honeymoon

vi'ale sm avenue

via'vai sm coming and going, bustle

vi'brare *vi* to vibrate

vi'cario *sm* (apostolico etc) vicar

vice ['vitʃe] *sm/f* deputy ♦ *prefisso*:
~**'console** *sm* vice-consul;
~**diret'tore** *sm* assistant manager

vi'cenda [vi'tʃɛnda] *sf* event; **a ~** in
turn; **vicen'devole** *ag* mutual,
reciprocal

vice'versa [vitʃe'vɛrsa] *av* vice versa;
da Roma a Pisa e ~ from Rome to
Pisa and back

vici'nanza [vitʃi'nantsa] *sf* nearness,
closeness; **~e** *sfpl* (paraggi)
neighbourhood, vicinity

vici'nato [vitʃi'nato] *sm*
neighbourhood; (vicini) neighbours
pl

vi'cino, a [vi'tʃino] *ag* (gen) near;
(nello spazio) near, nearby; (accanto)
next; (nel tempo) near, close at hand
♦ *sm/f* neighbour ♦ *av* near, close; **da
~** (guardare) close up; (esaminare,
seguire) closely; (conoscere) well,
intimately; **~ a** near (to), close to;
(accanto a) beside; **~ di casa**
neighbour

'vicolo *sm* alley; **~ cieco** blind alley

'video *sm inv* (TV: schermo) screen;
~**'camera** *sf* camcorder; ~**cas'setta** *sf*
videocassette; ~**registra'tore** *sm*
video (recorder)

vie'tare *vt* to forbid; (AMM) to prohibit;
~ a qn di fare to forbid sb to do; to
prohibit sb from doing; **"vietato
fumare/l'ingresso"** "no smoking/
admittance"

Viet'nam *sm*: **il ~** Vietnam;
vietna'mita, i e, ag, sm/f, sm
Vietnamese *inv*

vi'gente [vi'dʒɛnte] *ag* in force

vigi'lare [vidʒi'lare] *vt* to watch over,
keep an eye on; **~ che** to make sure
that, see to it that

'vigile ['vidʒile] *ag* watchful ♦ *sm*
(anche: **~ urbano**) policeman (in
towns); **~ del fuoco** fireman

vi'gilia [vi'dʒilja] *sf* (giorno

antecedente) eve; **la ~ di Natale**
Christmas Eve

vigli'acco, a, chi, che [viʎ'ʎakko] *ag*
cowardly ♦ *sm/f* coward

'vigna ['viɲɲa] *sf* = **vi'gneto**

vi'gneto [viɲ'ɲeto] *sm* vineyard

vi'gnetta [viɲ'ɲetta] *sf* cartoon

vi'gore *sm* vigour; (DIR): **essere/
entrare in ~** to be in/come into force;
vigo'roso, a *ag* vigorous

'vile *ag* (spregevole) low, mean, base;
(codardo) cowardly

vili'pendio *sm* contempt, scorn; public
insult

'villa *sf* villa

vil'laggio [vil'laddʒo] *sm* village

villa'nia *sf* rudeness, lack of manners;
fare o (dire) una ~ a qn to be rude
to sb

vil'lano, a *ag* rude, ill-mannered

villeggia'tura [villeddʒa'tura] *sf*
holiday(s *pl*) (BRIT), vacation (US)

vil'lino *sm* small house (with a garden),
cottage

vil'loso, a *ag* hairy

viltà *sf* cowardice *no pl*; cowardly act

'vimine *sm* wicker; **mobili di ~i** wicker
furniture *sg*

'vincere ['vintʃere] *vt* (in guerra, al
gioco, a una gara) to defeat, beat;
(premio, guerra, partita) to win; (fig) to
overcome, conquer ♦ *vi* to win; **~ qn
in bellezza** to be better-looking than
sb; **'vincita** *sf* win; (denaro vinto)
winnings *pl*; **vinci'tore** *sm* winner;
(MIL) victor

vinco'lare *vt* to bind; (COMM: denaro)
to tie up; **'vincolo** *sm* (fig) bond, tie;
(DIR: servitù) obligation

vi'nicolo, a *ag* wine *cpd*

'**vino** sm wine; ~ **bianco/rosso** white/red wine; ~ **da pasto** table wine

'**vinto, a** pp di **vincere**

vi'**ola** sf (BOT) violet; (MUS) viola ♦ ag, sm inv (colore) purple

vio'**lare** vt (chiesa) to desecrate, violate; (giuramento, legge) to violate

violen'**tare** vt to use violence on; (donna) to rape

vio'**lento, a** ag violent; vio'**lenza** sf violence; **violenza carnale** rape

vio'**letta** sf (BOT) violet

vio'**letto, a** ag, sm (colore) violet

violi'**nista, i, e** sm/f violinist

vio'**lino** sm violin

violon'**cello** [violon't∫ɛllo] sm cello

vi'**ottolo** sm path, track

'**vipera** sf viper, adder

vi'**rare** vi (NAUT, AER) to turn; (FOT) to tone; ~ **di bordo** (NAUT) to tack

'**virgola** sf (LING) comma; (MAT) point; **virgo'lette** sfpl inverted commas, quotation marks

vi'**rile** ag (proprio dell'uomo) masculine; (non puerile, da uomo) manly, virile

vi**rtù** sf inv virtue; **in o per ~ di** by virtue of, by

virtu'**ale** ag virtual

virtu'**oso, a** ag virtuous ♦ sm/f (MUS etc) virtuoso

'**virus** sm inv (anche COMPUT) virus

'**viscere** ['vi∫∫ere] sfpl (di animale) entrails pl; (fig) bowels pl

'**vischio** ['viskjo] sm (BOT) mistletoe; (pania) birdlime; **vischi'oso, a** ag sticky

'**viscido, a** ['vi∫∫ido] ag slimy

vi'**sibile** ag visible

visi'**bilio** sm: **andare in ~** to go into raptures

visibi'**lità** sf visibility

visi'**era** sf (di elmo) visor; (di berretto) peak

visi'**one** sf vision; **prendere ~ di qc** to examine sth, look sth over; **prima/seconda ~** (CINEMA) first/second showing

'**visita** sf visit; (MED) visit, call; (: esame) examination; **visi'tare** vt to visit; (MED) to visit, call on; (: esaminare) to examine; **visita'tore, 'trice** sm/f visitor

vi'**sivo, a** ag visual

'**viso** sm face

vi'**sone** sm mink

'**vispo, a** ag quick, lively

vis'**suto, a** pp di **vivere** ♦ ag (aria, modo di fare) experienced

'**vista** sf (facoltà) (eye)sight; (fatto di vedere): **la ~ di** the sight of; (veduta) view; **sparare a ~** to shoot on sight; **in ~** in sight; **perdere qn di ~** to lose sight of sb; (fig) to lose touch with sb; **a ~ d'occhio** as far as the eye can see; (fig) before one's very eyes; **far ~ di fare** to pretend to do

'**visto, a** pp di **vedere** ♦ sm visa; ~ **che** seeing (that)

vis'**toso, a** ag gaudy, garish; (ingente) considerable

visu'**ale** ag visual; **visualizza'tore** sm (INFORM) visual display unit, VDU

'**vita** sf life; (ANAT) waist; **a ~** for life

vi'**tale** ag vital; vita'**lizio, a** ag life cpd ♦ sm life annuity

vita'**mina** sf vitamin

'**vite** sf (BOT) vine; (TECN) screw

vi'**tello** sm (ZOOL) calf; (carne) veal; (pelle) calfskin

vi'**ticcio** [vi'titt∫o] sm (BOT) tendril

viticol'**tore** sm wine grower; viticol'**tura** sf wine growing

'**vitreo, a** ag vitreous; (occhio, sguardo) glassy

'**vittima** sf victim

'**vitto** sm food; (in un albergo etc) board; ~ **e alloggio** board and lodging

vit'**toria** sf victory

'**viva** escl: ~ **il re!** long live the king!

vi'**vace** [vi'vat∫e] ag (vivo, animato) lively; (: mente) lively, sharp; (colore) bright; **vivacità** sf vivacity; liveliness; brightness

vi'vaio sm (di pesci) hatchery; (AGR) nursery

vi'vanda sf food; (piatto) dish

vi'vente ag living, alive; **i ~i** the living

'vivere vi to live ♦ vt to live; (passare: brutto momento) to live through, go through; (sentire: gioie, pene di qn) to share ♦ sm life; (anche: modo di ~) way of life; **~i** smpl (cibo) food sg, provisions; **~ di** to live on

'vivido, a ag (colore) vivid, bright

'vivo, a ag (vivente) alive, living; : animale) live; (fig) lively; (: colore) bright, brilliant; **i ~i** the living; **~ e vegeto** hale and hearty; **farsi ~** to show one's face; to be heard from; **ritrarre dal ~** to paint from life; **pungere qn nel ~** (fig) to cut sb to the quick

vizi'are [vit'tsjare] vt (bambino) to spoil; (corrompere moralmente) to corrupt; **vizi'ato, a** ag spoilt; (aria, acqua) polluted

'vizio ['vittsjo] sm (morale) vice; (cattiva abitudine) bad habit; (imperfezione) flaw, defect; (errore) fault, mistake; **vizi'oso, a** ag depraved; defective; (inesatto) incorrect, wrong

vocabo'lario sm (dizionario) dictionary; (lessico) vocabulary

vo'cabolo sm word

vo'cale ag vocal ♦ sf vowel

vocazi'one [vokat'tsjone] sf vocation; (fig) natural bent

'voce ['votʃe] sf voice; (diceria) rumour; (di un elenco, in bilancio) item; **aver ~ in capitolo** (fig) to have a say in the matter

voci'are [vo'tʃare] vi to shout, yell

'voga sf (NAUT) rowing; (usanza): **essere in ~** to be in fashion o in vogue

vo'gare vi to row

'voglia ['vɔʎʎa] sf desire, wish; (macchia) birthmark; **aver ~ di qc/di fare** to feel like sth/like doing; (più

forte) to want sth/to do

'voi pron you; **vo'altri** pron you

vo'lano sm (SPORT) shuttlecock; (TECN) flywheel

vo'lante ag flying ♦ sm (steering) wheel

volan'tino sm leaflet

vo'lare vi (uccello, aereo, fig) to fly; (cappello) to blow away o off, fly away o off; **~ via** to fly away o off

vo'latile ag (CHIM) volatile ♦ sm (ZOOL) bird

volente'roso, a ag willing

volenti'eri av willingly; **"~"** "with pleasure", "I'd be glad to"

PAROLA CHIAVE

vo'lere sm will, wish(es); **contro il ~ di** against the wishes of; **per ~ di qn** in obedience to sb's will o wishes ♦ vt **1** (esigere, desiderare) to want; **voler fare/che qn faccia** to want to do/sb to do; **volete del caffè?** would you like o do you want some coffee? **vorrei questo/fare** I would o I'd like this/to do; **come vuoi** as you like; **senza ~** (inavvertitamente) without meaning to, unintentionally

2 (consentire): **vogliate attendere, per piacere** please wait; **vogliamo andare?** shall we go?; **vuole essere così gentile da ...?** would you be so kind as to ...?; **non ha voluto ricevermi** he wouldn't see me

3: **volerci** (essere necessario: materiale, attenzione) to need; (: tempo) to take: **quanta farina ci vuole per questa torta?** how much flour do you need for this cake?; **ci vuole un'ora per arrivare a Venezia** it takes an hour to get to Venice

4: **voler bene a qn** (amore) to love sb; (affetto) to be fond of sb, like sb very much; **voler male a qn** to dislike sb; **volerne a qn** to bear sb a grudge; **voler dire** to mean

vol'gare ag vulgar; **volgariz'zare** vt to popularize

'volgere ['vɔldʒere] vt to turn ♦ vi to turn; (tendere): ~ **a**: **il tempo volge al brutto** the weather is breaking; **un rosso che volge al viola** a red verging on purple; **~rsi** vr to turn; **~ al peggio** to take a turn for the worse; **~ al termine** to draw to an end

'volgo sm common people

voli'era sf aviary

voli'tivo, **a** ag strong-willed

'volo sm flight; **al ~**: **colpire qc al ~** to hit sth as it flies past; **capire al ~** to understand straight away

volontà sf will; **a ~** (mangiare, bere) as much as one likes; **buona/cattiva ~** goodwill/lack of goodwill

volon'tario, **a** ag voluntary ♦ sm (MIL) volunteer

'volpe sf fox

'volta sf (momento, circostanza) time; (turno, giro) turn; (curva) turn, bend; (ARCHIT) vault; (direzione): **partire alla ~ di** to set off for; **a mia** (o tua etc) **~** in turn; **una ~** once; **una ~ sola** only once; **due ~e** twice; **una cosa per ~** one thing at a time; **una ~ per tutte** once and for all; **a ~e** at times, sometimes; **una ~ che** (temporale) once; (causale) since; **3 ~e 4** 3 times 4

volta'faccia [vɔlta'fattʃa] sm inv (fig) volte-face

vol'taggio [vol'taddʒo] sm (ELETTR) voltage

vol'tare vt to turn; (girare: moneta) to turn over; (rigirare) to turn round ♦ vi to turn; **~rsi** vr to turn; to turn over; to turn round

volteggi'are [volted'dʒare] vi (volare) to circle; (in equitazione) to do trick riding; (in ginnastica) to vault; to perform acrobatics

'volto, **a** pp di **volgere** ♦ sm face

vo'lubile ag changeable, fickle

vo'lume sm volume; **volumi'noso**, **a**

ag voluminous, bulky

voluttà sf sensual pleasure o delight; **voluttu'oso**, **a** ag voluptuous

vomi'tare vt, vi to vomit; **'vomito** sm vomiting no pl; vomit

'vongola sf clam

vo'race [vo'ratʃe] ag voracious, greedy

vo'ragine [vo'radʒine] sf abyss, chasm

'vortice ['vɔrtitʃe] sm whirlpool; (fig) whirl

'vostro, **a** det: **il(la) ~(la)** etc your ♦ pron: **il(la) ~(la)** etc yours

vo'tante sm/f voter

vo'tare vi to vote ♦ vt (sottoporre a votazione) to take a vote on; (approvare) to vote for; (REL): **~ qc a** to dedicate sth to; **votazi'one** sf vote, voting; **votazioni** sfpl (POL) votes; (INS) marks

'voto sm (POL) vote; (INS) mark; (REL) vow; (: offerta) votive offering; **aver ~i belli/brutti** (INS) to get good/bad marks

vs. abbr (COMM) = **vostro**

vul'cano sm volcano

vulne'rabile ag vulnerable

vuo'tare vt to empty; **~rsi** vr to empty

vu'oto, **a** ag empty; (fig: privo): **~ di** (senso etc) devoid of ♦ sm empty space, gap; (spazio in bianco) blank; (FISICA) vacuum; (fig: mancanza) gap, void; **a mani ~e** empty-handed; **~ d'aria** air pocket; **~ a rendere** returnable bottle

W, X, Y

'water ['wɔːtəˀ] sm inv toilet

watt [vat] sm inv watt

'weekend ['wiːkɛnd] sm inv weekend

'whisky ['wiski] sm inv whisky

'windsurf ['windsəːf] sm inv (tavola) windsurfer; (sport) windsurfing

'würstel ['vyrstəl] sm inv frankfurter

xi'lofono [ksi'lɔfono] sm xylophone

yacht [jɔt] sm inv yacht

'yoghurt ['jɔgurt] *sm inv* yoghourt

Z, z

zabai'one [dzaba'jone] *sm* dessert made of egg yolks, sugar and marsala

zaf'fata [tsaf'fata] *sf (tanfo)* stench

zaffe'rano [dzaffe'rano] *sm* saffron

zaf'firo [dzaf'firo] *sm* sapphire

'zaino ['dzaino] *sm* rucksack

'zampa ['tsampa] *sf (di animale: gamba)* leg; *(: piede)* paw; **a quattro ~e** on all fours

zampil'lare [tsampil'lare] *vi* to gush, spurt; **zam'pillo** *sm* gush, spurt

zam'pogna [tsam'poɲɲa] *sf* instrument similar to bagpipes

'zanna ['tsanna] *sf (di elefante)* tusk; *(di carnivori)* fang

zan'zara [dzan'dzara] *sf* mosquito; **zanzari'era** *sf* mosquito net

'zappa ['tsappa] *sf* hoe; **zap'pare** *vt* to hoe

'zapping ['tsapiŋ] *sm (TV)* channel-hopping

zar, za'rina [tsar, tsa'rina] *sm/f* tsar/tsarina

'zattera ['dzattera] *sf* raft

za'vorra [dza'vɔrra] *sf* ballast

'zazzera ['tsattsera] *sf* shock of hair

'zebra ['dzɛbra] *sf* zebra; **~e** *sfpl (AUT)* zebra crossing *sg (BRIT)*, crosswalk *sg (US)*

'zecca, che ['tsekka] *sf (ZOOL)* tick; *(officina di monete)* mint

'zelo ['dzɛlo] *sm* zeal

ze'nit ['dzɛnit] *sm* zenith

zen'zero ['dzendzero] *sm* ginger

'zeppa ['tseppa] *sf* wedge

'zeppo, a ['tseppo] *ag:* **~ di** crammed o packed with

zer'bino [dzer'bino] *sm* doormat

'zero ['dzɛro] *sm* zero, nought; **vincere per tre a ~** *(SPORT)* to win three-nil

'zeta ['dzɛta] *sm o f* zed, (the letter) z

'zia ['tsia] *sf* aunt

zibel'lino [dzibel'lino] *sm* sable

'zigomo ['dzigomo] *sm* cheekbone

zig'zag [dzig'dzag] *sm inv* zigzag; **andare a ~** to zigzag

zim'bello [dzim'bɛllo] *sm (oggetto di burle)* laughing-stock

'zinco ['dzinko] *sm* zinc

'zingaro, a ['dzingaro] *sm/f* gipsy

'zio ['tsio] *(pl* **'zii)** *sm* uncle; **zii** *smpl (zio e zia)* uncle and aunt

zi'tella [dzi'tɛlla] *sf* spinster; *(peg)* old maid

'zitto, a ['tsitto] *ag* quiet, silent; **sta' ~!** be quiet!

ziz'zania [dzid'dzanja] *sf (fig):* **gettare** o **seminare ~** to sow discord

'zoccolo ['tsɔkkolo] *sm (calzatura)* clog; *(di cavallo etc)* hoof; *(basamento)* base; plinth

zo'diaco [dzo'diako] *sm* zodiac

'zolfo ['tsolfo] *sm* sulphur

'zolla ['dzɔlla] *sf* clod (of earth)

zol'letta [dzol'letta] *sf* sugar lump

'zona ['dzɔna] *sf* zone, area; **~ di depressione** *(METEOR)* trough of low pressure; **~ disco** *(AUT)* = meter zone; **~ pedonale** pedestrian precinct; **~ verde** *(di abitato)* green area

'zonzo ['dzondzo]: **a ~** *av:* **andare a ~** to wander about, stroll about

zoo ['dzɔo] *sm inv* zoo

zoolo'gia [dzoolo'dʒia] *sf* zoology

zoppi'care [tsoppi'kare] *vi* to limp; to be shaky, rickety

'zoppo, a ['tsɔppo] *ag* lame; *(fig: mobile)* shaky, rickety

zoti'cone [dzoti'kone] *sm* lout

'zucca, che ['tsukka] *sf (BOT)* marrow; pumpkin

zucche'rare [tsukke'rare] *vt* to put sugar in; **zucche'rato, a** *ag* sweet, sweetened

zuccheri'era [tsukke'rjera] *sf* sugar bowl

zucche'rino, a [tsukke'rino] *ag* sugary, sweet

'**zucchero** ['tsukkero] *sm* sugar

zuc'china [tsuk'kina] *sf* courgette (*BRIT*), zucchini (*US*)

zuc'chino [tsuk'kino] *sm* = **zucchina**

'**zuffa** ['tsuffa] *sf* brawl

'**zuppa** ['tsuppa] *sf* soup; (*fig*) mixture, muddle; **~ inglese** (*CUC*) *dessert made with sponge cake, custard and chocolate,* ≈ trifle (*BRIT*); **zuppi'era** *sf* soup tureen

'**zuppo, a** ['tsuppo] *ag:* **~ (di)** drenched (with), soaked (with)

ENGLISH - ITALIAN
INGLESE - ITALIANO

A, a

A [eɪ] n (MUS) la m; (letter) A, a f or m
inv; **~-road** n strada statale

KEYWORD
---

a [ə] (before vowel or silent h: **an**) indef
art **1** un (uno +s impure, gn, pn, ps, x,
z), f una (un' +vowel); **~ book** un libro; **~
mirror** uno specchio; **an apple** una
mela; **she's ~ doctor** è medico
2 (instead of the number ''one'') un(o),
f una; **~ year ago** un anno fa; **~
hundred/thousand** etc **pounds**
cento/mille etc sterline
3 (in expressing ratios, prices etc) a, per;
3 ~ day/week 3 al giorno/alla
settimana; **10 km an hour** 10 km
all'ora; **£5 ~ person** 5 sterline a
persona or per persona

A.A. n abbr (= Alcoholics Anonymous)
AA; (BRIT: = Automobile Association) ≈
A.C.I. f

A.A.A. (US) n abbr (= American
Automobile Association) ≈ A.C.I. m

aback [ə'bæk] adv: **to be taken ~**
essere sbalordito(a)

abandon [ə'bændən] vt abbandonare
♦ n: **with ~** sfrenatamente,
spensieratamente

abate [ə'beɪt] vi calmarsi

abattoir ['æbətwɑ:'] (BRIT) n mattatoio

abbey ['æbɪ] n abbazia, badia

abbot ['æbət] n abate m

abbreviation [əbri:vɪ'eɪʃən] n
abbreviazione f

abdicate ['æbdɪkeɪt] vt abdicare a ♦ vi
abdicare

abdomen ['æbdəmən] n addome m

abduct [æb'dʌkt] vt rapire

abide [ə'baɪd] vt: **I can't ~ it/him** non
lo posso soffrire or sopportare; **~ by** vt
fus conformarsi a

ability [ə'bɪlɪtɪ] n abilità f inv

abject ['æbdʒekt] adj (poverty)
abietto(a); (apology) umiliante

ablaze [ə'bleɪz] adj in fiamme

able ['eɪbl] adj capace; **to be ~ to do
sth** essere capace di fare qc, poter fare
qc; **~-bodied** adj robusto(a); **ably** adv
abilmente

abnormal [æb'nɔ:məl] adj anormale

aboard [ə'bɔ:d] adv a bordo ♦ prep a
bordo di

abode [ə'bəud] n: **of no fixed ~** senza
fissa dimora

abolish [ə'bɒlɪʃ] vt abolire

abominable [ə'bɒmɪnəbl] adj
abominevole

aborigine [æbə'rɪdʒɪnɪ] n aborigeno m

abort [ə'bɔ:t] vt abortire; **~ion**
[ə'bɔ:ʃən] n aborto; **to have an ~ion**
abortire; **~ive** adj abortivo(a)

abound [ə'baund] vi abbondare; **to ~
in** or **with** abbondare di

KEYWORD
---

about [ə'baut] adv **1** (approximately)
circa, quasi; **~ a hundred/thousand**
etc un centinaio/migliaio etc, circa
cento/mille etc; **it takes ~ 10 hours**
ci vogliono circa 10 ore; **at ~ 2
o'clock** verso le 2; **I've just
~ finished** ho quasi finito
2 (referring to place) qua e là, in giro;
to leave things lying ~ lasciare delle
cose in giro; **to run ~** correre qua e là;

to walk ~ camminare
3: to be ~ to do sth stare per fare qc
♦ prep 1 (relating to) su, di; a book
~ London un libro su Londra; what is
it ~? di che si tratta?; what is it
about? di cosa tratta?; we talked ~ it ne
abbiamo parlato; what or how
~ doing this? che ne dici di fare
questo?
2 (referring to place): to walk ~ the
town camminare per la città; his
clothes were scattered ~ the room
i suoi vestiti erano sparsi or in giro per
tutta la stanza

about-face n dietro front m inv
about-turn n dietro front m inv
above [ə'bʌv] adv, prep sopra;
mentioned ~ suddetto(a); ~ all
soprattutto; ~board adj aperto(a);
onesto(a)
abrasive [ə'breɪzɪv] adj abrasivo(a);
(fig) caustico(a)
abreast [ə'brɛst] adv di fianco; to
keep ~ of tenersi aggiornato su
abroad [ə'brɔːd] adv all'estero
abrupt [ə'brʌpt] adj (sudden)
improvviso(a); (gruff, blunt) brusco(a)
abscess ['æbsɪs] n ascesso
absence ['æbsəns] n assenza
absent ['æbsənt] adj assente; ~ee
[-'tiː] n assente m/f, ~-minded adj
distratto(a)
absolute ['æbsəluːt] adj assoluto(a);
~ly [-'luːtlɪ] adv assolutamente
absolve [əb'zɔlv] vt: to ~ sb (from)
(sin) assolvere qn (da); (oath) sciogliere
qn (da)
absorb [əb'zɔːb] vt assorbire; to be
~ed in a book essere immerso in un
libro; ~ent cotton (us) n cotone m
idrofilo
absorption [əb'sɔːpʃən] n
assorbimento
abstain [əb'steɪn] vi: to ~ (from)
astenersi (da)
abstract ['æbstrækt] adj astratto(a)

absurd [əb'sɜːd] adj assurdo(a)
abuse [n ə'bjuːs, vb ə'bjuːz] n abuso;
(insults) ingiurie fpl ♦ vt abusare di;
abusive adj ingiurioso(a)
abysmal [ə'bɪzməl] adj spaventoso(a)
abyss [ə'bɪs] n abisso
AC abbr (= alternating current) c.a.
academic [ækə'dɛmɪk] adj
accademico(a); (pej: issue) puramente
formale ♦ n universitario/a
academy [ə'kædəmɪ] n (learned body)
accademia; (school) scuola privata; ~ of
music conservatorio
accelerate [æk'sɛləreɪt] vt, vi
accelerare; acceleration n
accelerazione f; accelerator n
acceleratore n
accent ['æksɛnt] n accento
accept [ək'sɛpt] vt accettare; ~able
adj accettabile; ~ance n accettazione f
access ['æksɛs] n accesso; ~ible
[æk'sɛsəbl] adj accessibile
accessory [æk'sɛsərɪ] n accessorio;
(LAW): ~ to complice m/f di
accident ['æksɪdənt] n incidente m;
(chance) caso; by ~ per caso; ~al
[-'dɛntl] adj accidentale; ~ally
[-'dɛntəlɪ] adv per caso; ~ insurance
n assicurazione f contro gli infortuni;
~-prone adj: he's very ~-prone è un
vero passaguai
acclaim [ə'kleɪm] n acclamazione f
accommodate [ə'kɔmədeɪt] vt
alloggiare; (oblige, help) favorire
accommodating [ə'kɔmədeɪtɪŋ] adj
compiacente
accommodation [əkɔmə'deɪʃən] n
alloggio; ~s (us) npl alloggio
accompany [ə'kʌmpənɪ] vt
accompagnare
accomplice [ə'kʌmplɪs] n complice
m/f
accomplish [ə'kʌmplɪʃ] vt compiere;
(goal) raggiungere; ~ed adj esperto(a);
~ment n compimento; realizzazione f
accord [ə'kɔːd] n accordo ♦ vt
accordare; of his own ~ di propria

iniziativa; ~ance n: **in ~ance with** in conformità con; **~ing: ~ing to** prep secondo; **~ingly** adv in conformità

accordion [ə'kɔːdiən] n fisarmonica

account [ə'kaunt] n (COMM) conto; (report) descrizione f; **~s** npl (COMM) conti mpl; **of no ~** di nessuna importanza; **on ~** in acconto; **on no ~** per nessun motivo; **on ~ of** a causa di; **to take into ~, take ~ of** tener conto di; **~ for** vt fus spiegare; giustificare; **~able** adj: **~able (to)** responsabile (verso)

accountancy [ə'kauntənsɪ] n ragioneria

accountant [ə'kauntənt] n ragioniere/a

account number n numero di conto

accrued interest [ə'kruːd-] n interesse m maturato

accumulate [ə'kjuːmjuleɪt] vt accumulare ♦ vi accumularsi

accuracy ['ækjurəsɪ] n precisione f

accurate ['ækjurɪt] adj preciso(a); **~ly** adv precisamente

accusation [ækju'zeɪʃən] n accusa

accuse [ə'kjuːz] vt accusare; **~d** n accusato/a

accustom [ə'kʌstəm] vt abituare; **~ed** adj: **~ed to** abituato(a) a

ace [eɪs] n asso

ache [eɪk] n male m, dolore m ♦ vi (be sore) far male, dolere; **my head ~s** mi fa male la testa

achieve [ə'tʃiːv] vt (aim) raggiungere; (victory, success) ottenere; **~ment** n compimento; successo

acid ['æsɪd] adj acido(a) ♦ n acido; **~ rain** n pioggia acida

acknowledge [ək'nɔlɪdʒ] vt (letter: also: **~ receipt of**) confermare la ricevuta di; (fact) riconoscere; **~ment** n conferma; riconoscimento

acne ['æknɪ] n acne f

acorn ['eɪkɔːn] n ghianda

acoustic [ə'kuːstɪk] adj acustico(a); **~s** n, npl acustica

acquaint [ə'kweɪnt] vt: **to ~ sb with sth** far sapere qc a qn; **to be ~ed with** (person) conoscere; **~ance** n conoscenza; (person) conoscente m/f

acquire [ə'kwaɪə*] vt acquistare

acquit [ə'kwɪt] vt assolvere; **to ~ o.s. well** comportarsi bene; **~tal** n assoluzione f

acre ['eɪkə*] n acro (= 4047 m²)

acrid ['ækrɪd] adj acre; pungente

acrobat ['ækrəbæt] n acrobata m/f

across [ə'krɔs] prep (on the other side) dall'altra parte di; (crosswise) attraverso ♦ adv dall'altra parte; in larghezza; **to run/swim ~** attraversare di corsa/a nuoto; **~ from** di fronte a

acrylic [ə'krɪlɪk] adj acrilico(a)

act [ækt] n atto; (in music-hall etc) numero; (LAW) decreto ♦ vi agire; (THEATRE) recitare; (pretend) fingere ♦ vt (part) recitare; **to ~ as** agire da; **~ing** adj che fa le funzioni di ♦ n (of actor) recitazione f; (activity): **to do some ~ing** fare del teatro (or del cinema)

action ['ækʃən] n azione f; (MIL) combattimento; (LAW) processo; **out of ~** fuori combattimento; fuori servizio; **to take ~** agire; **~ replay** n (TV) replay m inv

activate ['æktɪveɪt] vt (mechanism) attivare

active ['æktɪv] adj attivo(a); **~ly** adv (participate) attivamente; (discourage, dislike) vivamente

activity [æk'tɪvɪtɪ] n attività f inv; **~ holiday** n vacanza organizzata con attività ricreative per ragazzi

actor ['æktə*] n attore m

actress ['æktrɪs] n attrice f

actual ['æktjuəl] adj reale, vero(a); **~ly** adv veramente; (even) addirittura

acute [ə'kjuːt] adj acuto(a); (mind, person) perspicace

ad [æd] n abbr = advertisement

A.D. adv abbr (= Anno Domini) d.C.

adamant ['ædəmənt] adj irremovibile

adapt [ə'dæpt] vt adattare ♦ vi: **to**

~ (to) adattarsi (a); **~able** adj (device) adattabile; (person) che sa adattarsi; **~er** or **~or** n (ELEC) adattatore m

add [æd] vt aggiungere; (figures: also: ~ up) addizionare ♦ vi: **to ~ to** (increase) aumentare; **it doesn't ~ up** (fig) non quadra, non ha senso

adder ['ædə*] n vipera

addict ['ædikt] n tossicomane m/f; (to) fanatico/a; **~ed** [ə'diktid] adj: **to be ~ed to** (drink etc) essere dedito(a) a; (fig: football etc) essere tifoso(a) di; **~ion** [ə'dikʃən] n (MED) tossicodipendenza; **~ive** [ə'diktiv] adj che dà assuefazione

addition [ə'diʃən] n aggiunta; (thing added) aggiunta; **in ~** inoltre; **in ~ to** oltre; **~al** adj supplementare

additive ['æditiv] n additivo

address [ə'drɛs] n indirizzo; (talk) discorso ♦ vt indirizzare; (speak to) fare un discorso a; (issue) affrontare

adept ['ædɛpt] adj: **~ at** esperto(a) in

adequate ['ædikwit] adj adeguato(a); sufficiente

adhere [əd'hiə*] vi: **to ~ to** aderire a; (fig: rule, decision) seguire

adhesive [əd'hi:ziv] n adesivo; **~ tape** n (BRIT: for parcels etc) nastro adesivo; (US: MED) cerotto adesivo

adjective ['ædʒɛktiv] n aggettivo

adjoining [ə'dʒɔɪnɪŋ] adj accanto inv, adiacente

adjourn [ə'dʒəːn] vt rimandare ♦ vi essere aggiornato(a)

adjust [ə'dʒʌst] vt aggiustare; (change) rettificare ♦ vi: **to ~ to** adattarsi (a); **~able** adj regolabile; **~ment** n (PSYCH) adattamento; (of machine) regolazione f; (of prices, wages) modifica

ad-lib [æd'lib] vt improvvisare ♦ vt adv: **ad lib** a piacere, a volontà

administer [əd'ministə*] vt amministrare; (justice, drug) somministrare

administration [ədminis'treiʃən] n amministrazione f

administrative [əd'ministrətiv] adj amministrativo(a)

admiral ['ædmərəl] n ammiraglio; **A~ty** (BRIT) n Ministero della Marina

admiration [ædmə'reiʃən] n ammirazione f

admire [əd'maiə*] vt ammirare

admission [əd'miʃən] n ammissione f; (to exhibition, night club etc) ingresso; (confession) confessione f

admit [əd'mit] vt ammettere; far entrare; (agree) riconoscere; **to ~ to** riconoscere; **~tance** n ingresso; **~tedly** adv bisogna pur riconoscere (che)

ad nauseam [æd'nɔːsiæm] adv fino alla nausea, a non finire

ado [ə'duː] n: **without (any) more ~** senza più indugi

adolescence [ædəu'lɛsns] n adolescenza

adolescent [ædəu'lɛsnt] adj, n adolescente m/f

adopt [ə'dɔpt] vt adottare; **~ed** adj adottivo(a); **~ion** [ə'dɔpʃən] n adozione f

adore [ə'dɔː*] vt adorare

Adriatic [eidri'ætik] n: **the ~ (Sea)** n mare Adriatico, l'Adriatico

adrift [ə'drift] adv alla deriva

adult ['ædʌlt] adj adulto(a); (work, education) per adulti ♦ n adulto/a

adultery [ə'dʌltəri] n adulterio

advance [əd'vɑːns] n avanzamento; (money) anticipo ♦ adj (booking etc) in anticipo ♦ vt (money) anticipare ♦ vi avanzare; **in ~** in anticipo; **~d** adj avanzato(a); (SCOL: studies) superiore

advantage [əd'vɑːntidʒ] n (also: TENNIS) vantaggio; **to take ~ of** approfittarsi di

advent ['ædvənt] n avvento; (REL): **A~** Avvento

adventure [əd'vɛntʃə*] n avventura

adverb ['ædvəːb] n avverbio

adverse ['ædvəːs] adj avverso(a)

advert ['ædvəːt] (BRIT) n abbr =

advertisement

advertise ['ædvətaiz] vi (vt) fare pubblicità or réclame (a); fare un'inserzione (per vendere); **to ~ for** (staff) mettere un annuncio sul giornale per trovare

advertisement [əd'və:tismənt] n (COMM) réclame f inv, pubblicità f inv; (in classified ads) inserzione f

advertising ['ædvətaiziŋ] n pubblicità

advice [əd'vais] n consigli mpl; (notification) avviso; **piece of ~** consiglio; **to take legal ~** consultare un avvocato

advisable [əd'vaizəbl] adj consigliabile

advise [əd'vaiz] vt consigliare; **to ~ sb of sth** informare qn di qc; **to ~ sb against sth/doing sth** sconsigliare qc a qn/a qn di fare qc; **~r** n consigliere/a; or **advisor** n consigliere/a; **advisory** [-əri] adj consultivo(a)

advocate [n 'ædvəkit, vb 'ædvəkeit] n (upholder) sostenitore/trice; (LAW) avvocato (difensore) ♦ vt propugnare

Aegean [i'dʒi:ən] n: **the ~ (Sea)** il mar Egeo, l'Egeo

aerial ['ɛəriəl] n antenna ♦ adj aereo(a)

aerobics [ɛə'rəubiks] n aerobica

aeroplane ['ɛərəplein] (BRIT) n aeroplano

aerosol ['ɛərəsɔl] (BRIT) n aerosol m inv

aesthetic [is'θɛtik] adj estetico(a)

afar [ə'fɑ:*] adv: **from ~** da lontano

affair [ə'fɛə*] n affare m; (also: love ~) relazione f amorosa; **~s** (business) affari mpl

affect [ə'fɛkt] vt toccare; (influence) influire su, incidere su; (feign) fingere; **~ed** adj affettato(a)

affection [ə'fɛkʃən] n affezione f; **~ate** adj affettuoso(a)

afflict [ə'flikt] vt affliggere

affluence ['æfluəns] n abbondanza; opulenza

affluent ['æfluənt] adj ricco(a); **the ~ society** la società del benessere

afford [ə'fɔ:d] vt permettersi; (provide) fornire

afloat [ə'fləut] adv a galla

afoot [ə'fut] adv: **there is something ~** si sta preparando qualcosa

afraid [ə'freid] adj impaurito(a); **to be ~ of or to/that** aver paura di/che; **I am ~ so/not** ho paura di sì/no

Africa ['æfrikə] n Africa; **~n** adj, n africano(a)

after ['ɑ:ftə*] prep, adv dopo ♦ conj dopo che; **what/who are you ~?** che/chi cerca?; **~ he left/having done** dopo che se ne fu andato/dopo aver fatto; **to name sb ~ sb** dare a qn il nome di qn; **it's twenty ~ eight** (US) sono le otto e venti; **to ask ~ sb** chiedere di qn; **~ all** dopotutto; **~ you!** dopo di lei!; **~effects** npl conseguenze fpl; (of illness) postumi mpl; **~math** n conseguenze fpl; **in the ~math of** nel periodo dopo; **~noon** n pomeriggio; **~s** n (inf: dessert) dessert m inv; **~-sales service** (BRIT) n servizio assistenza clienti; **~-shave (lotion)** n dopobarba m inv; **~-sun (lotion/cream)** n doposole m inv; **~thought** n: **as an ~thought** come aggiunta; **~wards** (US **~ward**) adv dopo

again [ə'gɛn] adv di nuovo; **to begin/see ~** ricominciare/rivedere; **not ... ~** non ... più; **~ and ~** ripetutamente

against [ə'gɛnst] prep contro

age [eidʒ] n età f inv ♦ vi, vt invecchiare; **it's been ~s since** sono secoli che; **he is 20 years of ~** ha 20 anni; **to come of ~** diventare maggiorenne; **~d 10** di 10 anni; **the ~d** ['eidʒid] gli anziani; **~ group** n generazione f; **~ limit** n limite m d'età

agency ['eidʒənsi] n agenzia

agenda [ə'dʒɛndə] n ordine m del giorno

agent ['eidʒənt] n agente m

aggravate ['ægrəveit] vt aggravare; (person) irritare

aggregate ['ægrigeit] n aggregato

aggressive [ə'grɛsiv] adj aggressivo(a)

agitate ['ædʒiteit] vt turbare; agitare

♦ vi: to ~ for agitarsi per

AGM n abbr = **annual general meeting**

ago [ə'gəu] adv: **2 days ~ 2** giorni fa; **not long ~** poco tempo fa; **how long ~?** quanto tempo fa?

agonizing [ˈægənaɪzɪŋ] adj straziante

agony [ˈægənɪ] n dolore m atroce; **to be in ~** avere dolori atroci

agree [ə'griː] vt (price) pattuire ♦ vi: **to ~ (with)** essere d'accordo (con); (LING) concordare (con); **to ~ to sth/to do sth** accettare qc/di fare qc; **to ~ that** (admit) ammettere che; **to ~ on sth** accordarsi su qc; **garlic doesn't ~ with me** l'aglio non mi va; **~able** adj gradevole; (willing) disposto/a; **~d** adj (time, place) stabilito(a); **~ment** n accordo; **in ~ment** d'accordo

agricultural [ægriˈkʌltʃərəl] adj agricolo/a

agriculture [ˈægrɪkʌltʃə*] n agricoltura

aground [ə'graund] adv: **to run ~** arenarsi

ahead [ə'hɛd] adv avanti; davanti; **~ of** davanti a; (fig: schedule etc) in anticipo su; **~ of time** in anticipo; **go right** o **straight ~** tiri dritto

aid [eɪd] n aiuto ♦ vt aiutare; **in ~ of** a favore di

aide [eɪd] n (person) aiutante m

AIDS [eɪdz] n abbr (= acquired immune deficiency syndrome) AIDS f; **~-related** adj (symptoms, illness) legato(a) all'AIDS; (research) sull'AIDS

aim [eɪm] vt: **to ~ sth at** (such as gun) mirare qc a, puntare qc a; (camera) rivolgere qc a; (missile) lanciare qc contro ♦ vi (also: to take ~) prendere la mira ♦ n mira; **to ~ at** mirare; **to ~ to do** aver l'intenzione di fare; **~less** adj senza scopo

ain't [eɪnt] (inf) = **am not**; **aren't**; **isn't**

air [ɛə*] n aria ♦ vt (room) arieggiare; (clothes) far prendere aria a; (grievances, ideas) esprimere

pubblicamente ♦ cpd (currents) d'aria; (attack) aereo(a); **to throw sth into the ~** lanciare qc in aria; **by ~** (travel) in aereo; **on the ~** (RADIO, TV) in onda; **~bed** n materassino; **~ conditioning** n condizionamento d'aria; **~craft** n inv apparecchio; **~craft carrier** n portaerei f inv; **~field** n campo d'aviazione; **A~ Force** n aviazione f militare; **~ freshener** n deodorante m per ambienti; **~gun** n fucile m ad aria compressa; **~ hostess** (BRIT) n hostess f inv; **~ letter** (BRIT) n aerogramma m; **~lift** n ponte m aereo; **~line** n linea aerea; **~liner** n aereo di linea; **~mail** n: **by ~mail** per via aerea; **~ mattress** n materassino gonfiabile; **~plane** (us) n aeroplano; **~port** n aeroporto; **~ raid** n incursione f aerea; **~sick** adj: **to be ~sick** soffrire di mal d'aria; **~tight** adj ermetico(a); **~ traffic controller** n controllore m del traffico aereo; **~y** adj arioso(a); (manners) noncurante

aisle [aɪl] n (of church) navata laterale, navata centrale; (of plane) corridoio; **~ seat** n (on plane) posto sul corridoio

ajar [ə'dʒɑː*] adj socchiuso(a)

alarm [ə'lɑːm] n allarme m ♦ vt allarmare; **~ call** n (in hotel etc) sveglia; **~ clock** n sveglia

alas [ə'læs] excl ohimè!, ahimè!

albeit [ɔːl'biːɪt] conj sebbene +sub, benché +sub

album [ˈælbəm] n album m inv

alcohol [ˈælkəhɔl] n alcool m; **~ic** [-'hɔlɪk] adj alcolico(a) ♦ n alcolizzato/a

ale [eɪl] n birra

alert [ə'ləːt] adj vigile ♦ n allarme m ♦ vt avvertire; mettere in guardia; **on the ~** all'erta

algebra [ˈældʒɪbrə] n algebra

alias [ˈeɪlɪəs] adv alias ♦ n pseudonimo, falso nome m

alibi [ˈælɪbaɪ] n alibi m inv

alien [ˈeɪlɪən] n straniero/a

(*extraterrestrial*) alieno/a ♦ *adj*: ~ (**to**) estraneo(a) (a); **~ate** *vt* alienare

alight [əˈlaɪt] *adj* acceso(a) ♦ *vi* scendere; (*bird*) posarsi

alike [əˈlaɪk] *adj* simile ♦ *adv* sia ... sia; **to look ~** assomigliarsi

alimony [ˈælɪmənɪ] *n* (*payment*) alimenti *mpl*

alive [əˈlaɪv] *adj* vivo(a); (*lively*) vivace

KEYWORD

all [ɔːl] *adj* tutto(a); ~ **day** tutto il giorno; ~ **night** tutta la notte; ~ **men** tutti gli uomini; ~ **five came** sono venuti tutti e cinque; ~ **the books** tutti i libri; ~ **the food** tutto il cibo; ~ **the time** sempre; tutto il tempo; ~ **his life** tutta la vita

♦ *pron* 1 tutto(a); **I ate it ~, I ate ~ of it** l'ho mangiato tutto; ~ **of us went** tutti noi siamo andati; ~ **of the boys went** tutti i ragazzi sono andati

2 (*in phrases*): **above** ~ soprattutto; **after** ~ dopotutto; **at ~: not at** ~ (*in answer to question*) niente affatto; (*in answer to thanks*) prego!, di niente!, s'immagini!; **I'm not at** ~ **tired** non sono affatto stanco(a); **anything at** ~ **will do** andrà bene qualsiasi cosa; ~ **in** ~ tutto sommato

♦ *adv*: **alone** tutto(a) solo(a); **it's not as hard as** ~ **that** non è poi così difficile; ~ **the more/the better** tanto più/meglio; ~ **but** quasi; **the score is two** ~ il punteggio è di due a due

allay [əˈleɪ] *vt* (*fears*) dissipare

all clear *n* (*also fig*) segnale *m* di cessato allarme

allegation [ælɪˈgeɪʃən] *n* asserzione *f*

allege [əˈledʒ] *vt* asserire; **~dly** [əˈledʒɪdlɪ] *adv* secondo quanto si asserisce

allegiance [əˈliːdʒəns] *n* fedeltà

allergic [əˈlɜːdʒɪk] *adj*: ~ **to** allergico(a) a

allergy [ˈælədʒɪ] *n* allergia

alleviate [əˈliːvɪeɪt] *vt* sollevare

alley [ˈælɪ] *n* vicolo

alliance [əˈlaɪəns] *n* alleanza

allied [ˈælaɪd] *adj* alleato(a)

all-in *adj* (*BRIT: also adv: charge*) tutto compreso

all-night *adj* aperto(a) (*or che dura*) tutta la notte

allocate [ˈæləkeɪt] *vt* assegnare

allot [əˈlɒt] *vt* assegnare; **~ment** *n* assegnazione f; (*garden*) lotto di terra

all-out *adj* (*effort etc*) totale ♦ *adv*: **to go all out for** mettercela tutta per

allow [əˈlaʊ] *vt* (*practice, behaviour*) permettere; (*sum to spend etc*) accordare; (*sum, time estimated*) dare; (*concede*): **to ~ that** ammettere che; **to ~ sb to do** permettere a qn di fare; **he is ~ed to** lo può fare; ~ **for** *vt fus* tener conto di; **~ance** *n* (*money received*) assegno; indennità f *inv*; (*TAX*) detrazione f di imposta; **to make ~ances for** tener conto di

alloy [ˈælɔɪ] *n* lega

all right *adv* (*feel, work*) bene; (*as answer*) va bene

all-round *adj* completo(a)

all-time *adj* (*record*) assoluto(a)

alluring [əˈljʊərɪŋ] *adj* seducente

ally [ˈælaɪ] *n* alleato

almighty [ɔːlˈmaɪtɪ] *adj* onnipotente; (*row etc*) colossale

almond [ˈɑːmənd] *n* mandorla

almost [ˈɔːlməʊst] *adv* quasi

alone [əˈləʊn] *adj, adv* solo(a); **to leave sb ~** lasciare qn in pace; **to leave sth ~** lasciare stare qc; **let ~ ...** figuriamoci poi ..., tanto meno ...

along [əˈlɒŋ] *prep* lungo ♦ *adv*: **is he coming ~?** viene con noi?; **he was limping ~** veniva zoppicando; ~ **with** insieme con; **all** ~ (*all the time*) sempre, fin dall'inizio; **~side** *prep* accanto a; lungo ♦ *adv* accanto

aloof [əˈluːf] *adj* distaccato(a) ♦ *adv*: **to stand ~** tenersi a distanza *or* in disparte

aloud [ə'laud] *adv* ad alta voce

alphabet ['ælfəbɛt] *n* alfabeto

alpine ['ælpaɪn] *adj* alpino(a)

Alps [ælps] *npl*: **the ~** le Alpi

already [ɔːl'rɛdɪ] *adv* già

alright ['ɔːl'raɪt] (*BRIT*) *adv* = **all right**

Alsatian [æl'seɪʃən] (*BRIT*) *n* (*dog*) pastore *m* tedesco, (cane *m*) lupo

also ['ɔːlsəu] *adv* anche

altar ['ɔːltə*] *n* altare *m*

alter ['ɔːltə*] *vt, vi* alterare

alternate [*adj* ɔl'təːnɪt, *vb* 'ɔltəːneɪt] *adj* alterno(a); (*US: plan etc*) alternativo(a) ♦ *vi*: **to ~ (with)** alternarsi (a); **on ~ days** ogni due giorni; **alternating** (*current*) alternato(a)

alternative [ɔl'təːnətɪv] *adj* alternativo(a) ♦ *n* (*choice*) alternativa; **~ly** *adv*: **~ly one could ...** come alternativa si potrebbe ...; **~ medicine** *n* medicina alternativa

alternator ['ɔltəːneɪtə*] *n* (*AUT*) alternatore *m*

although [ɔːl'ðəu] *conj* benché +*sub*, sebbene +*sub*

altitude ['æltɪtjuːd] *n* altitudine *f*

alto ['æltəu] *n* contralto; (*male*) contralto

altogether [ɔːltə'gɛðə*] *adv* del tutto, completamente; (*on the whole*) tutto considerato; (*in all*) in tutto

aluminium [ælju'mɪnɪəm] *n* alluminio

aluminum [ə'luːmɪnəm] (*US*) *n* = **aluminium**

always ['ɔːlweɪz] *adv* sempre

Alzheimer's ['æltshaɪməz-] *n* (malattia di) Alzheimer

AM *n abbr* (= (*Welsh*) *Assembly Member*) deputato/a del Parlamento gallese

am [æm] *vb see* **be**

a.m. *adv abbr* (= *ante meridiem*) della mattina

amalgamate [ə'mælgəmeɪt] *vt* amalgamare ♦ *vi* amalgamarsi

amateur ['æmətə*] *n* dilettante *m/f* ♦ *adj* (*SPORT*) dilettante; **~ish** (*pej*) *adj* da dilettante

amaze [ə'meɪz] *vt* stupire; **to be ~d (at)** essere sbalordito (da); **~ment** *n* stupore *m*; **amazing** *adj* sorprendente, sbalorditivo(a)

ambassador [æm'bæsədə*] *n* ambasciatore/trice

amber ['æmbə*] *n* ambra; **at ~** (*BRIT: AUT*) giallo

ambiguous [æm'bɪgjuəs] *adj* ambiguo(a)

ambition [æm'bɪʃən] *n* ambizione *f*

ambitious [æm'bɪʃəs] *adj* ambizioso(a)

ambulance ['æmbjuləns] *n* ambulanza

ambush ['æmbuʃ] *n* imboscata

amenable [ə'miːnəbl] *adj*: **~ to** (*advice etc*) ben disposto(a) a

amend [ə'mɛnd] *vt* (*law*) emendare; (*text*) correggere; **to make ~s** fare ammenda

amenities [ə'miːnɪtɪz] *npl* attrezzature *fpl* ricreative e culturali

America [ə'mɛrɪkə] *n* America; **~n** *adj*, *n* americano(a)

amiable ['eɪmɪəbl] *adj* amabile, gentile

amicable ['æmɪkəbl] *adj* amichevole

amid(st) [ə'mɪd(st)] *prep* in mezzo a

amiss [ə'mɪs] *adj*, *adv*: **there's something ~** c'è qualcosa che non va bene; **don't take it ~** non prendertela (a male)

ammonia [ə'məunɪə] *n* ammoniaca

ammunition [æmju'nɪʃən] *n* munizioni *fpl*

amok [ə'mɔk] *adv*: **to run ~** diventare pazzo(a) furioso(a)

amorous ['æmərəs] *adj* amoroso(a)

amount [ə'maunt] *n* somma; ammontare *m*; quantità *f inv* ♦ *vi*: **to ~ to** (*total*) ammontare a; (*be same as*) essere come

amp(ère) ['æmp(eə*)] *n* ampère *m inv*

ample ['æmpl] *adj* ampio(a); spazioso(a); (*enough*): **this is ~** questo è più che sufficiente

amplifier [ˈæmplɪfaɪə*] n amplificatore m

amuse [əˈmjuːz] vt divertire; **~ment** n divertimento; **~ment arcade** n sala giochi; **~ment park** n luna park m inv

an [æn] indef art see **a**

anaemic [əˈniːmɪk] adj anemico(a)

anaesthetic [ænɪsˈθetɪk] adj anestetico(a) ♦ n anestetico

analog(ue) [ˈænəlɔg] adj (watch, computer) analogico(a)

analyse [ˈænəlaɪz] (BRIT) vt analizzare

analysis [əˈnæləsɪs] (pl **analyses**) n analisi f inv

analyst [ˈænəlɪst] n (POL etc) analista m/f; (US) (psic)analista m/f

analyze [ˈænəlaɪz] (US) vt = **analyse**

anarchy [ˈænəkɪ] n anarchia

anatomy [əˈnætəmɪ] n anatomia

ancestor [ˈænsɪstə*] n antenato/a

anchor [ˈæŋkə*] n ancora ♦ vi (also: to drop ~) gettare l'ancora ♦ vt ancorare; **to weigh ~** salpare or levare l'ancora

anchovy [ˈæntʃəvɪ] n acciuga

ancient [ˈeɪnʃənt] adj antico(a); (person, car) vecchissimo(a)

ancillary [ænˈsɪlərɪ] adj ausiliario(a)

and [ænd] conj e (often ed before vowel); **~ so on** e così via; **try ~ come** cerca di venire; **he talked ~ talked** non la finiva di parlare; **better ~ better** sempre meglio

anemic [əˈniːmɪk] (US) adj = **anaemic**

anesthetic [ænɪsˈθetɪk] (US) adj, n = **anaesthetic**

anew [əˈnjuː] adv di nuovo

angel [ˈeɪndʒəl] n angelo

anger [ˈæŋgə*] n rabbia

angina [ænˈdʒaɪnə] n angina pectoris

angle [ˈæŋgl] n angolo; **from their ~** dal loro punto di vista

Anglican [ˈæŋglɪkən] adj, n anglicano(a)

angling [ˈæŋglɪŋ] n pesca con la lenza

Anglo- [ˈæŋgləʊ] prefix anglo....

angrily [ˈæŋgrɪlɪ] adv con rabbia

angry [ˈæŋgrɪ] adj arrabbiato(a), furioso(a); (wound) infiammato(a); **to be ~ with sb/at sth** essere in collera con qn/per qc; **to get ~** arrabbiarsi; **to make sb ~** fare arrabbiare qn

anguish [ˈæŋgwɪʃ] n angoscia

animal [ˈænɪməl] adj animale ♦ n animale m

animate [ˈænɪmɪt] adj animato(a)

animated [ˈænɪmeɪtɪd] adj animato(a)

aniseed [ˈænɪsiːd] n semi mpl di anice

ankle [ˈæŋkl] n caviglia; **~ sock** n calzino

annex [n ˈæneks, vb əˈneks] n (also: BRIT: annexe) (edificio) annesso ♦ vt annettere

anniversary [ænɪˈvɜːsərɪ] n anniversario

announce [əˈnauns] vt annunciare; **~ment** n annuncio; (letter, card) partecipazione f; **~r** n (RADIO, TV: between programmes) annunciatore/ trice; (: in a programme) presentatore/ trice

annoy [əˈnɔɪ] vt dare fastidio a; **don't get ~ed!** non irritarti!; **~ance** n fastidio; (cause of ~ance) noia; **~ing** adj noioso(a)

annual [ˈænjuəl] adj annuale ♦ n (BOT) pianta annua; (book) annuario

annul [əˈnʌl] vt annullare

annum [ˈænəm] n see **per**

anonymous [əˈnɔnɪməs] adj anonimo(a)

anorak [ˈænəræk] n giacca a vento

anorexia [ænəˈreksɪə] n (MED: also: ~ nervosa) anoressia

another [əˈnʌðə*] adj: **~ book** (one more) un altro libro, ancora un libro; (a different one) un altro libro ♦ pron un altro(un'altra), ancora uno(a); see also **one**

answer [ˈɑːnsə*] n risposta; soluzione f ♦ vi rispondere ♦ vt (reply to) rispondere a; (problem) risolvere; (prayer) esaudire; **in ~ to your letter** in risposta alla sua lettera; **to ~ the**

phone rispondere (al telefono); **to ~ the bell** rispondere al campanello; **to ~ the door** aprire la porta; **~ back** *vi* ribattere; **~ for** *vt fus* essere responsabile di; **~ to** *vt fus* (*description*) corrispondere a; **~able** *adj*: **~able (to sb/for sth)** responsabile (verso qn/di qc); **~ing machine** *n* segreteria (telefonica) automatica

ant [ænt] *n* formica

antagonism [æn'tægənɪzəm] *n* antagonismo

antagonize [æn'tægənaɪz] *vt* provocare l'ostilità di

Antarctic [ænt'ɑːktɪk] *n*: **the ~** l'Antartide *f*

antenatal ['æntɪ'neɪtl] *adj* prenatale; **~ clinic** *n* assistenza medica prenatale

anthem ['ænθəm] *n*: **national ~** inno nazionale

antibiotic ['æntɪbaɪ'ɔtɪk] *n* antibiotico

antibody ['æntɪbɔdɪ] *n* anticorpo

anticipate [æn'tɪsɪpeɪt] *vt* prevedere; pregustare; (*wishes, request*) prevenire

anticipation [æntɪsɪ'peɪʃən] *n* anticipazione *f*; (*expectation*) aspettative *fpl*

anticlimax ['æntɪ'klaɪmæks] *n*: **it was an ~** fu una completa delusione

anticlockwise ['æntɪ'klɔkwaɪz] *adj, adv* in senso antiorario

antics ['æntɪks] *npl* buffonerie *fpl*

antidepressant ['æntɪdɪ'prɛsnt] *n* antidepressivo

antifreeze ['æntɪ'friːz] *n* anticongelante *m*

antihistamine [æntɪ'hɪstəmɪn] *n* antistaminico

antique [æn'tiːk] *n* antichità *f inv* ♦ *adj* antico(a); **~ dealer** *n* antiquario/a; **~ shop** *n* negozio di antichità

anti-Semitism ['æntɪ'sɛmɪtɪzəm] *n* antisemitismo

antiseptic [æntɪ'sɛptɪk] *n* antisettico

antisocial ['æntɪ'səʊʃəl] *adj* asociale

antlers ['æntləz] *npl* palchi *mpl*

anvil ['ænvɪl] *n* incudine *f*

anxiety [æŋ'zaɪətɪ] *n* ansia; (*keenness*): **~ to do** smania di fare

anxious ['æŋkʃəs] *adj* ansioso(a), inquieto(a); (*worrying*) angosciante; (*keen*): **~ to do/that** impaziente di fare/che +*sub*

KEYWORD

any ['ɛnɪ] *adj* **1** (*in questions etc*): **have you ~ butter?** hai del burro?, hai un po' di burro?; **have you ~ children?** hai bambini?; **if there are ~ tickets left** se ci sono ancora (dei) biglietti, se c'è ancora qualche biglietto

2 (*with negative*): **I haven't ~ money/books** non ho soldi/libri

3 (*no matter which*) qualsiasi, qualunque; **choose ~ book you like** scegli un libro qualsiasi

4 (*in phrases*): **in ~ case** in ogni caso; **~ day now** da un giorno all'altro; **at ~ moment** in qualsiasi momento, da un momento all'altro; **at ~ rate** ad ogni modo

♦ *pron* **1** (*in questions, with negative*): **have you got ~?** ne hai?; **can ~ of you sing?** qualcuno di voi sa cantare?; **I haven't ~ (of them)** non ne ho

2 (*no matter which one(s)*): **take ~ of those books (you like)** prendi uno qualsiasi di quei libri

♦ *adv* **1** (*in questions etc*): **do you want ~ more soup/sandwiches?** vuoi ancora un po' di minestra/degli altri panini?; **are you feeling ~ better?** ti senti meglio?

2 (*with negative*): **I can't hear him ~ more** non lo sento più; **don't wait ~ longer** non aspettare più

---

anybody ['ɛnɪbɔdɪ] *pron* (*in questions etc*) qualcuno, nessuno; (*with negative*) nessuno; (*no matter who*) chiunque; **can you see ~?** vedi qualcuno or nessuno?; **if ~ should phone ...** se telefona qualcuno ...; **I can't see ~** non vedo nessuno; **could do it**

chiunque potrebbe farlo

anyhow ['enɪhaʊ] adv (at any rate) ad ogni modo, comunque; (haphazard): **do it ~ you like** fallo come ti pare; **I shall go** ~ ci andrò lo stesso or comunque; **she leaves things just ~** lascia tutto come capita

anyone ['enɪwʌn] pron = **anybody**

anything ['enɪθɪŋ] pron (in question etc) qualcosa, niente; (with negative) niente; (no matter what): **you can say ~ you like** puoi dire quello che ti pare; **can you see ~?** vedi niente or qualcosa?; **if ~ happens to me ...** se mi dovesse succedere qualcosa ...; **I can't see ~** non vedo niente or qualcosa; **~ will do** va bene qualsiasi cosa or tutto

anyway ['enɪweɪ] adv (at any rate) ad ogni modo, comunque; (besides) ad ogni modo

anywhere ['enɪwɛə*] adv (in questions etc) da qualche parte; (with negative) da nessuna parte; (no matter where) da qualsiasi or qualunque parte, dovunque; **can you see him ~?** lo vedi da qualche parte?; **I can't see him ~** non lo vedo da nessuna parte; **~ in the world** dovunque nel mondo

apart [ə'pɑːt] adv (to one side) a parte; (separately) separatamente; **with one's legs ~** con le gambe divaricate; **10 miles ~** a 10 miglia di distanza (l'uno dall'altro); **to take ~** smontare; **~ from** a parte, eccetto

apartheid [ə'pɑːteɪt] n apartheid f

apartment [ə'pɑːtmənt] n (US) appartamento; (room) locale m; **~ building** (US) n stabile m, caseggiato

ape [eɪp] n scimmia ♦ vt scimmiottare

apéritif [ə'perɪtɪv] n aperitivo

aperture ['æpətʃjʊə*] n apertura

APEX n abbr (= advance purchase excursion) APEX m inv

apologetic [əpɔlə'dʒetɪk] adj (tone, letter) di scusa

apologize [ə'pɔlədʒaɪz] vi: **to ~ (for sth to sb)** scusarsi (di qc a qn),

chiedere scusa (a qn per qc)

apology [ə'pɔlədʒɪ] n scuse fpl

apostle [ə'pɔsl] n apostolo

apostrophe [ə'pɔstrəfɪ] n (sign) apostrofo

appal [ə'pɔːl] vt scioccare; **~ling** adj spaventoso(a)

apparatus [æpə'reɪtəs] n apparato; (in gymnasium) attrezzatura

apparel [ə'pærl] (US) n abbigliamento, confezioni fpl

apparent [ə'pærənt] adj evidente; **~ly** adv evidentemente

appeal [ə'piːl] vi (LAW) appellarsi alla legge ♦ n (LAW) appello; (request) richiesta; (charm) attrattiva; **to ~ for** chiedere (con insistenza); **to ~ to** (subj: person) appellarsi a; (subj: thing) piacere a; **it doesn't ~ to me** mi dice poco; **~ing** adj (nice) attraente

appear [ə'pɪə*] vi apparire; (LAW) comparire; (publication) essere pubblicato(a); (seem) sembrare; **it would ~ that** sembra che; **~ance** n apparizione f; apparenza; (look, aspect) aspetto

appease [ə'piːz] vt calmare, appagare

appendicitis [əpendɪ'saɪtɪs] n appendicite f

appendix [ə'pendɪks] (pl **appendices**) n appendice f

appetite ['æpɪtaɪt] n appetito

appetizer ['æpɪtaɪzə*] n stuzzichino

applaud [ə'plɔːd] vt, vi applaudire

applause [ə'plɔːz] n applauso

apple ['æpl] n mela; **~ tree** n melo

appliance [ə'plaɪəns] n apparecchio

applicant ['æplɪkənt] n candidato/a

application [æplɪ'keɪʃən] n applicazione f; (for a job, grant etc) domanda; **~ form** n modulo per la domanda

applied [ə'plaɪd] adj applicato(a)

apply [ə'plaɪ] vt: **to ~ (to)** (paint, ointment) dare (a); (theory, technique) applicare (a) ♦ vi: **to ~ (for)** (job) rivolgersi a; (be suitable for, relevant to) riguardare, riferirsi a; **to ~ (for)** (permit, grant, job) fare domanda (per); **to ~ o.s.** dedicarsi a

appoint [ə'pɔɪnt] vt nominare; **~ed** adj: **at the ~ed time** all'ora stabilita; **~ment** n nomina; (arrangement to meet) appuntamento; **to make an ~ment (with)** prendere un appuntamento (con)

appraisal [ə'preɪzl] n valutazione f

appreciate [ə'priːʃieɪt] vt (like) apprezzare; (be grateful for) essere riconoscente di; (be aware of) rendersi conto di ♦ vi (FINANCE) aumentare; **I'd ~ your help** ti sono grato per l'aiuto

appreciation [əpriːʃi'eɪʃən] n apprezzamento; (FINANCE) aumento del valore

appreciative [ə'priːʃiətɪv] adj (person) sensibile; (comment) elogiativo(a)

apprehend [æprɪ'hend] vt (arrest) arrestare

apprehension [æprɪ'henʃən] n (fear) inquietudine f

apprehensive [æprɪ'hensɪv] adj apprensivo(a)

apprentice [ə'prentɪs] n apprendista m/f; **~ship** n apprendistato

approach [ə'prəutʃ] vi avvicinarsi ♦ vt (come near) avvicinare; (ask, apply to) rivolgersi a; (subject, passer-by) avvicinare ♦ n approccio; accesso; (to problem) modo di affrontare; **~able** adj accessibile

approach road n strada d'accesso

appropriate [adj ə'prəupriət, vb ə'prəuprieɪt] adj appropriato(a); adatto(a) ♦ vt (take) appropriarsi

approval [ə'pruːvl] n approvazione f; **on ~** (COMM) in prova, in esame

approve [ə'pruːv] vt, vi approvare; **~ of** vt fus approvare

approximate [ə'prɔksɪmɪt] adj approssimativo(a); **~ly** adv circa

apricot ['eɪprɪkɔt] n albicocca

April ['eɪprəl] n aprile m; **~ fool!** pesce d'aprile!

apron ['eɪprən] n grembiule m

apt [æpt] adj (suitable) adatto(a); (able) capace; (likely): **to be ~ to do** avere tendenza a fare

aquarium [ə'kwɛərɪəm] n acquario

Aquarius [ə'kwɛərɪəs] n Acquario

Arab ['ærəb] adj, n arabo/a

Arabian [ə'reɪbɪən] adj arabo(a)

Arabic ['ærəbɪk] adj arabico(a), arabo(a) ♦ n arabo; **~ numerals** numeri mpl arabi, numerazione f araba

arbitrary ['ɑːbɪtrərɪ] adj arbitrario(a)

arbitration [ɑːbɪ'treɪʃən] n (LAW) arbitrato; (INDUSTRY) arbitraggio

arcade [ɑː'keɪd] n portico; (passage with shops) galleria

arch [ɑːtʃ] n arco; (of foot) arco plantare ♦ vt inarcare

archaeologist [ɑːkɪ'ɔlədʒɪst] n archeologo/a

archaeology [ɑːkɪ'ɔlədʒɪ] n archeologia

archbishop [ɑːtʃ'bɪʃəp] n arcivescovo

archeology [ɑːkɪ'ɔlədʒɪ] etc (US) = **archaeology** etc

archery ['ɑːtʃərɪ] n tiro all'arco

architect ['ɑːkɪtekt] n architetto; **~ure** ['ɑːkɪtektʃə*] n architettura

archives ['ɑːkaɪvz] npl archivi mpl

Arctic ['ɑːktɪk] adj artico(a) ♦ n: **the ~** l'Artico

ardent ['ɑːdənt] adj ardente

are [ɑː*] vb see **be**

area ['ɛərɪə] n (GEOM) area; (zone) zona; (: smaller) settore m

aren't [ɑːnt] = **are not**

Argentina [ɑːdʒən'tiːnə] n Argentina;

Argentinian [-'tɪnɪən] adj, n
argentino(a)

arguably ['ɑːgjuəblɪ] adv: **it is ~** ... si
può sostenere che sia ....

argue ['ɑːgjuː] vi (quarrel) litigare;
(reason) ragionare; **to ~ that** sostenere
che

argument ['ɑːgjumənt] n (reasons)
argomento; (quarrel) lite f; **~ative**
[ɑːgju'mentətɪv] adj litigioso(a)

Aries ['ɛərɪz] n Ariete m

arise [ə'raɪz] (pt **arose**, pp **arisen**) vi
(opportunity, problem) presentarsi

aristocrat ['ærɪstəkræt] n
aristocratico/a

arithmetic [ə'rɪθmətɪk] n aritmetica

ark [ɑːk] n: **Noah's A~** l'arca di Noè

arm [ɑːm] n braccio ♦ vt armare; **~s**
npl (weapons) armi fpl; **~ in ~** a
braccetto

armaments ['ɑːməmənts] npl
armamenti mpl

arm: ~chair n poltrona; **~ed** adj
armato(a); **~ed robbery** n rapina a
mano armata

armour ['ɑːmə*] (US **armor**) n
armatura; (MIL: tanks) mezzi mpl
blindati; **~ed car** n autoblinda f inv

armpit ['ɑːmpɪt] n ascella

armrest ['ɑːmrɛst] n bracciolo

army ['ɑːmɪ] n esercito

aroma [ə'rəumə] n aroma; **~therapy**
n aromaterapia

arose [ə'rəuz] pt of **arise**

around [ə'raund] adv attorno, intorno
♦ prep intorno a; (fig: about): **~ £5/3
o'clock** circa 5 sterline/le 3; **is he ~?**
è in giro?

arrears [ə'rɪəz] npl arretrati mpl; **to be
in ~ with one's rent** essere in
arretrato con l'affitto

arrest [ə'rɛst] vt arrestare; (sb's
attention) attirare ♦ n arresto; **under ~**
in arresto

arrival [ə'raɪvl] n arrivo; (person)
arrivato/a; **a new ~** un nuovo venuto;
(baby) un neonato

arrive [ə'raɪv] vi arrivare

arrogant ['ærəgənt] adj arrogante

arrow ['ærəu] n freccia

arse [ɑːs] (inf!) n culo (!)

arson ['ɑːsn] n incendio doloso

art [ɑːt] n arte f; (craft) mestiere m;
A~s npl (scol) Lettere fpl

artery ['ɑːtərɪ] n arteria

art gallery n galleria d'arte

arthritis [ɑː'θraɪtɪs] n artrite f

artichoke ['ɑːtɪtʃəuk] n carciofo;
Jerusalem ~ topinambur m inv

article ['ɑːtɪkl] n articolo; **~s** npl (BRIT:
LAW: company) contratto di tirocinio; **~
of clothing** capo di vestiario

articulate [adj ɑː'tɪkjulɪt, vb
ɑː'tɪkjuleɪt] adj (person) che si esprime
forbitamente; (speech) articolato(a) ♦ vi
articolare; **~d lorry** (BRIT) n autotreno

artificial [ɑːtɪ'fɪʃl] adj artificiale;
~ respiration n respirazione f
artificiale

artist ['ɑːtɪst] n artista m/f; **~ic**
[ɑː'tɪstɪk] adj artistico(a); **~ry** n arte f

art school n scuola d'arte

KEYWORD

as [æz] conj **1** (referring to time) mentre;
~ the years went by col passare
degli anni; **he came in ~ I was
leaving** arrivò mentre stavo uscendo;
~ from tomorrow da domani
2 (in comparisons): **~ big** ... **~ big**
come; **twice ~ big ~** due volte più
grande di; **~ much/many ~** tanto
quanto/tanti quanti; **~ soon ~
possible** prima possibile
3 (since, because) dal momento che,

siccome

4 (referring to manner, way) come; **do ~ you wish** fa' come vuoi; **~ she said** come ha detto lei

5 (concerning): **~ for** or **to that** per quanto riguarda or quanto a quello

6: ~ if or **though** come se; **he looked ~ if he was ill** sembrava stare male; see also **long; such; well**
♦ prep: **he works ~ a driver** fa l'autista; **~ chairman of the company, he ...** come presidente della compagnia, lui ...; **he gave me it ~ a present** me lo ha regalato

a.s.a.p. abbr = **as soon as possible**

ascend [ə'sɛnd] vt salire

ascertain [æsə'teɪn] vt accertare

ash [æʃ] n (dust) cenere f; (wood, tree) frassino

ashamed [ə'ʃeɪmd] adj vergognoso(a); **to be ~ of** vergognarsi di

ashore [ə'ʃɔ:*] adv a terra

ashtray [æʃtreɪ] n portacenere m

Ash Wednesday n mercoledì m inv delle Ceneri

Asia ['eɪʃə] n Asia; **~n** adj, n asiatico(a)

aside [ə'saɪd] adv da parte ♦ n a parte m

ask [ɑ:sk] vt (question) domandare; (invite) invitare; **to ~ sb sth/sb to do sth** chiedere qc a qn/a qn di fare qc; **to ~ sb about sth** chiedere a qn di qc; **to ~ (sb) a question** fare una domanda (a qn); **to ~ sb out to dinner** invitare qn a mangiare fuori; **~ after** vt fus chiedere di; **~ for** vt fus chiedere; (trouble etc) cercare

asleep [ə'sli:p] adj addormentato(a); **to be ~** dormire; **to fall ~** addormentarsi

asparagus [əs'pærəgəs] n asparagi mpl

aspect ['æspɛkt] n aspetto

aspersions [əs'pə:ʃənz] npl: **to cast ~ on** diffamare

asphyxiation [æsfɪksɪ'eɪʃən] n asfissia

aspire [əs'paɪə*] vi: **to ~ to** aspirare a

aspirin ['æsprɪn] n aspirina

ass [æs] n asino; (inf) scemo/a; (US: inf!) culo (!)

assailant [ə'seɪlənt] n assalitore m

assassinate [ə'sæsɪneɪt] vt assassinare; **assassination** [əsæsɪ'neɪʃən] n assassinio

assault [ə'sɔ:lt] n (MIL) assalto; (gen: attack) aggressione f ♦ vt assaltare; aggredire; (sexually) violentare

assemble [ə'sɛmbl] vt riunire; (TECH) montare ♦ vi riunirsi

assembly [ə'sɛmbl] n (meeting) assemblea; (construction) montaggio; **~ line** n catena di montaggio

assent [ə'sɛnt] n assenso, consenso

assert [ə'sə:t] vt asserire; (insist on) far valere

assess [ə'sɛs] vt valutare; **~ment** n valutazione f

asset ['æsɛt] n vantaggio; **~s** npl (FINANCE: of individual) beni mpl; (: of company) attivo

assign [ə'saɪn] vt: **to ~ (to)** (task) assegnare a; (resources) riservare a; (cause, meaning) attribuire a; **to ~ a date to sth** fissare la data di qc; **~ment** n compito

assist [ə'sɪst] vt assistere, aiutare; **~ance** n assistenza, aiuto; **~ant** n assistente m/f; (BRIT: also: shop ~ant) commesso/a

associate [adj, n ə'səuʃɪɪt, vb ə'səuʃɪeɪt] adj associato(a); (member) aggiunto(a) ♦ n collega m/f ♦ vt associare ♦ vi: **to ~ with sb** frequentare qn

association [əsəusɪ'eɪʃən] n associazione f

assorted [ə'sɔ:tɪd] adj assortito(a)

assortment [ə'sɔ:tmənt] n assortimento

assume [ə'sju:m] vt supporre; (responsibilities etc) assumere; (attitude, name) prendere

assumption [ə'sʌmpʃən] n supposizione f, ipotesi f inv; (of power) assunzione f

assurance [ə'ʃuərəns] n assicurazione f; (self-confidence) fiducia in se stesso

assure [ə'ʃuə*] vt assicurare

asthma ['æsmə] n asma

astonish [ə'stɒnɪʃ] vt stupire; **~ment** n stupore m

astound [ə'staund] vt sbalordire

astray [ə'streɪ] adv: **to go ~** smarrirsi; **to lead ~** portare sulla cattiva strada

astride [ə'straɪd] prep a cavalcioni di

astrology [əs'trɒlədʒɪ] n astrologia

astronaut ['æstrənɔ:t] n astronauta m/f

astronomy [əs'trɒnəmɪ] n astronomia

asylum [ə'saɪləm] n asilo; (building) manicomio

┌─────────────┐
│ KEYWORD │
└─────────────┘

at [æt] prep 1 (referring to position, direction) a; **~ the top** in cima; **~ the desk** al banco, alla scrivania; **~ home/school** a casa/scuola; **~ the baker's** dal panettiere; **to look ~ sth** guardare qc; **to throw sth ~ sb** lanciare qc a qn

2 (referring to time) a; **~ 4 o'clock** alle 4; **~ night** di notte; **~ Christmas** a Natale; **~ times** a volte

3 (referring to rates, speed etc) a; **~ £1 a kilo** a 1 sterlina al chilo; **two ~ a time** due alla volta, due per volta; **~ 50 km/h** a 50 km/h

4 (referring to manner): **~ a stroke** d'un solo colpo; **~ peace** in pace

5 (referring to activity): **to be ~ work** essere al lavoro; **to play ~ cowboys** giocare ai cowboy; **to be good ~ sth/doing sth** essere bravo in qc/a fare qc

6 (referring to cause): **shocked/ surprised/annoyed ~ sth** colpito da/sorpreso da/arrabbiato per qc; **I went ~ his suggestion** ci sono andato dietro suo consiglio

ate [eɪt] pt of **eat**

atheist ['eɪθɪɪst] n ateo/a

Athens ['æθɪnz] n Atene f

athlete ['æθli:t] n atleta m/f

athletic [æθ'letɪk] adj atletico(a); **~s** n atletica

Atlantic [ət'læntɪk] adj atlantico(a) ♦ n: **the ~ (Ocean)** l'Atlantico, l'Oceano Atlantico

atlas ['ætləs] n atlante m

ATM n abbr (= automated telling machine) cassa automatica prelievi, sportello automatico

atmosphere ['ætməsfɪə*] n atmosfera

atom ['ætəm] n atomo; **~ic** [ə'tɒmɪk] adj atomico(a); **~(ic) bomb** n bomba atomica; **~izer** ['ætəmaɪzə*] n atomizzatore m

atone [ə'təun] vi: **to ~ for** espiare

atrocious [ə'trəuʃəs] adj pessimo(a), atroce

attach [ə'tætʃ] vt attaccare; (document, letter) allegare; (importance etc) attribuire; **to be ~ed to sb/sth** (to like) essere affezionato(a) a qn/qc

attaché case [ə'tæʃeɪ–] n valigetta per documenti

attachment [ə'tætʃmənt] n (tool) accessorio; (love): **~ (to)** affetto (per)

attack [ə'tæk] vt attaccare; (person) aggredire; (task etc) iniziare; (problem) affrontare ♦ n attacco; **heart ~** infarto; **~er** n aggressore m

attain [ə'teɪn] vt (also: **to ~ to**) arrivare a, raggiungere

attempt [ə'tempt] n tentativo ♦ vt tentare; **to make an ~ on sb's life** attentare alla vita di qn

attend [ə'tend] vt frequentare; (meeting, talk) andare a; (patient) assistere; **~ to** vt fus (needs, affairs etc) prendersi cura di; (customer) occuparsi di; **~ance** n (being present) presenza; (people present) gente f presente; **~ant** n custode m/f; persona di servizio ♦ adj concomitante

attention [ə'tenʃən] n attenzione f ♦ excl (MIL) attenti!; **for the ~ of**

(_ADMIN_) per l'attenzione di

attentive [ə'tɛntɪv] _adj_ attento(a); (_kind_) premuroso(a)

attic ['ætɪk] _n_ soffitta

attitude ['ætɪtjuːd] _n_ atteggiamento; posa

attorney [ə'tɜːnɪ] _n_ (_lawyer_) avvocato; (_having proxy_) mandatario; **A~ General** _n_ (_BRIT_) Procuratore _m_ Generale; (_US_) Ministro della Giustizia

attract [ə'trækt] _vt_ attirare; **~ion** [ə'trækʃən] _n_ (_gen pl: pleasant things_) attrattiva; (_PHYSICS, fig: towards sth_) attrazione _f_; **~ive** _adj_ attraente

attribute [_n_ 'ætrɪbjuːt, _vb_ ə'trɪbjuːt] _n_ attributo ♦ _vt_: **to ~ sth to** attribuire qc a

attrition [ə'trɪʃən] _n_: **war of ~** guerra di logoramento

aubergine ['əʊbəʒiːn] _n_ melanzana

auburn ['ɔːbən] _adj_ tizianesco(a)

auction ['ɔːkʃən] _n_ (_also: sale by ~_) asta ♦ _vt_ (_also: to sell by ~_) vendere all'asta; (_also: to put up for ~_) mettere all'asta; **~eer** [-'nɪə*] _n_ banditore _m_

audible ['ɔːdɪbl] _adj_ udibile

audience ['ɔːdɪəns] _n_ (_people_) pubblico; spettatori _mpl_; ascoltatori _mpl_; (_interview_) udienza

audio-typist ['ɔːdɪəʊ'taɪpɪst] _n_ dattilografo/a che trascrive da nastro

audio-visual ['ɔːdɪəʊ'vɪzjuəl] _adj_ audiovisivo(a); **~ aid** _n_ sussidio audiovisivo

audit ['ɔːdɪt] _vt_ rivedere, verificare

audition [ɔː'dɪʃən] _n_ audizione _f_

auditor ['ɔːdɪtə*] _n_ revisore _m_

augment [ɔːg'mɛnt] _vt, vi_ aumentare

augur ['ɔːgə*] _vi_: **it ~s well** promette bene

August ['ɔːgəst] _n_ agosto

aunt [ɑːnt] _n_ zia; **~ie** _n_ zietta; **~y** _n_ zietta

au pair ['əʊ'pɛə*] _n_ (_also: ~ girl_) (ragazza _f_) alla pari _inv_

auspicious [ɔːs'pɪʃəs] _adj_ propizio(a)

Australia [ɔs'treɪlɪə] _n_ Australia; **~n**

adj, n australiano(a)

Austria ['ɔstrɪə] _n_ Austria; **~n** _adj, n_ austriaco(a)

authentic [ɔː'θɛntɪk] _adj_ autentico(a)

author ['ɔːθə*] _n_ autore/trice

authoritarian [ɔːθɔrɪ'tɛərɪən] _adj_ autoritario(a)

authoritative [ɔː'θɔrɪtətɪv] _adj_ (_account etc_) autorevole; (_manner_) autoritario(a)

authority [ɔː'θɔrɪtɪ] _n_ autorità _f inv_; (_permission_) autorizzazione _f_; **the authorities** _npl_ (_government etc_) le autorità

authorize ['ɔːθəraɪz] _vt_ autorizzare

auto ['ɔːtəʊ] (_US_) _n_ auto _f inv_

autobiography [ɔːtəbaɪ'ɔgrəfɪ] _n_ autobiografia

autograph ['ɔːtəgrɑːf] _n_ autografo ♦ _vt_ firmare

automatic [ɔːtə'mætɪk] _adj_ automatico(a) ♦ _n_ (_gun_) arma automatica; (_washing machine_) lavatrice _f_ automatica; (_car_) automobile _f_ con cambio automatico; **~ally** _adv_ automaticamente

automation [ɔːtə'meɪʃən] _n_ automazione _f_

automobile ['ɔːtəməbiːl] (_US_) _n_ automobile _f_

autonomy [ɔː'tɔnəmɪ] _n_ autonomia

autumn ['ɔːtəm] _n_ autunno

auxiliary [ɔːg'zɪlɪərɪ] _adj_ ausiliario(a) ♦ _n_ ausiliare _m/f_

Av. _abbr_ = **avenue**

avail [ə'veɪl] _vt_: **to ~ o.s. of** servirsi di; approfittarsi di ♦ _n_: **to no ~** inutilmente

available [ə'veɪləbl] _adj_ disponibile

avalanche ['ævəlɑːnʃ] _n_ valanga

avant-garde ['ævɑ̃'gɑːd] _adj_ d'avanguardia

Ave. _abbr_ = **avenue**

avenge [ə'vɛndʒ] _vt_ vendicare

avenue ['ævənjuː] _n_ viale _m_; (_fig_) strada, via

average ['ævərɪdʒ] _n_ media ♦ _adj_

medio(a) ♦ vt (a certain figure) fare di
or in media; **on** ~ in media; **~ out** vi:
to ~ **out at** aggirarsi in media su,
essere in media di
averse [əˈvɜːs] adj: **to be** ~ **to sth/
doing** essere contrario a qc/a fare
avert [əˈvɜːt] vt evitare, prevenire;
(one's eyes) distogliere
aviary [ˈeɪvɪərɪ] n voliera, uccelliera
avid [ˈævɪd] adj (supporter etc)
accanito(a)
avocado [ævəˈkɑːdəʊ] n (also: BRIT:
~ **pear**) avocado m inv
avoid [əˈvɔɪd] vt evitare
await [əˈweɪt] vt aspettare
awake [əˈweɪk] (pt **awoke**, pp
awoken, awaked) adj sveglio(a) ♦ vt
svegliare ♦ vi svegliarsi; (fig): **~ (to)**
[əˈweɪknɪŋ] n risveglio
award [əˈwɔːd] n premio; (LAW)
risarcimento ♦ vt assegnare; (LAW:
damages) accordare
aware [əˈweə*] adj: **~ of** (conscious)
conscio(a), cosciente di; (informed)
informato(a) di; **to become** ~ **of**
accorgersi di; **~ness** n consapevolezza
away [əˈweɪ] adv via; lontano(a);
two kilometres ~ a due chilometri di
distanza; **two hours** ~ **by car** a due
ore di distanza in macchina; **the
holiday was two weeks** ~
mancavano due settimane alle vacanze;
he's ~ **for a week** è andato via per
una settimana; **to take** ~ togliere; **he
was working/pedalling** etc ~ la
particella indica la continuità a l'energia
dell'azione: lavorava/pedalava etc più
che poteva; **to fade/wither** etc ~ la
particella rinforza l'idea della
diminuzione; **~ game** n (SPORT) partita
fuori casa
awe [ɔː] n timore m; **~-inspiring**
imponente; **~some** adj imponente
awful [ˈɔːful] adj terribile; **an ~ lot of**
un mucchio di; **~ly** adv (very)
terribilmente
awkward [ˈɔːkwəd] adj (clumsy)

goffo(a); (inconvenient) scomodo(a);
(embarrassing) imbarazzante
awning [ˈɔːnɪŋ] n (of shop, hotel etc)
tenda
awoke [əˈwəʊk] pt of **awake**
awoken [əˈwəʊkən] pp of **awake**
awry [əˈraɪ] adv di traverso
axe [æks] (US **ax**) n scure f ♦ vt (project
etc) abolire; (jobs) sopprimere
axes [ˈæksiːz] npl of **axis**
axis [ˈæksɪs] (pl **axes**) n asse m
axle [ˈæksl] n (also: ~-**tree**) asse m
ay(e) [aɪ] excl (yes) sì

B, b

B [biː] n (MUS) si m; (letter) B, b f or m inv;
~-road n (BRIT: AUT) strada secondaria
B.A. n abbr = **Bachelor of Arts**
baby [ˈbeɪbɪ] n bambino/a; **~ carriage**
(US) n carrozzina; **~ food** n
omogeneizzati mpl; **~-sit** vi fare il (or
la) baby-sitter; **~-sitter** n baby-sitter
m/f inv; **~-sitting** n: **to go ~-sitting**
fare il (or la) baby-sitter; ~ **wipe** n
salvietta umidificata
bachelor [ˈbætʃələ*] n scapolo; **B~ of
Arts/Science** ≈ laureato/a in lettere/
scienze

back [bæk] n (of person, horse) dorso,
schiena; (as opposed to front) dietro; (of
hand) dorso; (of train) coda; (of chair)
schienale m; (of page) rovescio; (of
book) retro; (FOOTBALL) difensore m ♦ vt
(candidate: also: ~ **up**) appoggiare;
(horse: at races) puntare su; (car)
guidare a marcia indietro ♦ vi
indietreggiare; (car etc) fare marcia
indietro ♦ cpd posteriore, di dietro;
(AUT: seat, wheels) posteriore ♦ adv (not
forward) indietro; (returned): **he's** ~ è
tornato; **he ran** ~ tornò indietro di
corsa; (restitution): **throw the ball** ~
ritira la palla; **can I have it** ~? posso
riaverlo?; (again): **he called** ~ ha
richiamato; ~ **down** vi fare marcia

indietro; **~ out** vi (of promise) tirarsi indietro; **~ up** vt (support) appoggiare, sostenere; (COMPUT) fare una copia di riserva di; **~bencher** (BRIT) n membro del Parlamento senza potere amministrativo; **~bone** n spina dorsale; **~date** vt (letter) retrodatare; **~dated pay rise** aumento retroattivo; **~fire** vi (AUT) dar ritorni di fiamma; (plans) fallire; **~ground** n sfondo; (of events) background m inv; (basic knowledge) base f; (experience) esperienza; **family ~ground** ambiente m familiare; **~hand** n (TENNIS: also: ~hand stroke) rovescio; **~handed** adj (fig) ambiguo(a); **~hander** (BRIT) n (bribe) bustarella; **~ing** n (fig) appoggio; **~lash** n contraccolpo, ripercussione f; **~log** n: **~log of work** lavoro arretrato; **~ number** n (of magazine etc) numero arretrato; **~pack** n zaino; **~packer** n chi viaggia con zaino e sacco a pelo; **~ pay** n arretrato di paga; **~ payments** npl arretrati mpl; **~side** (inf) n sedere m; **~stage** adv nel retroscena; **~stroke** n nuoto sul dorso; **~up** adj (train, plane) supplementare; (COMPUT) di riserva ♦ n (support) appoggio, sostegno; (also: ~up file) file m inv di riserva; **~ward** adj (movement) indietro inv; (person) tardivo(a); (country) arretrato(a); **~wards** adv indietro; (fall, walk) all'indietro; **~yard** n cortile m dietro la casa

bacon ['beɪkən] n pancetta

bad [bæd] adj cattivo(a); (accident, injury) brutto(a); (meat, food) andato(a) a male; **his ~ leg** la sua gamba malata; **to go ~** andare a male

badge [bædʒ] n insegna; (of policeman) stemma m

badger ['bædʒə*] n tasso

badly ['bædlɪ] adv (work, dress etc) male; **~ wounded** gravemente ferito; **he needs it ~** ne ha un gran bisogno; **~ off** adj povero(a)

badminton ['bædmɪntən] n badminton m

bad-tempered ['bæd'tempəd] adj irritabile; di malumore

baffle ['bæfl] vt (puzzle) confondere

bag [bæg] n sacco; (handbag etc) borsa; **~s of** (inf: lots of) un sacco di; **~gage** n bagagli mpl; **~gage allowance** n franchigia f bagaglio inv; **~gage reclaim** n ritiro m bagaglio inv; **~gy** adj largo(a), sformato(a); **~pipes** npl cornamusa

bail [beɪl] n cauzione f ♦ vt (prisoner: also: grant ~ to) concedere la libertà provvisoria su cauzione a; (boat: also: ~ out) aggottare; **on ~** in libertà provvisoria su cauzione; **~ out** vt (prisoner) ottenere la libertà provvisoria su cauzione a; see also **bale**

bailiff ['beɪlɪf] n (LAW: BRIT) ufficiale m giudiziario; (: US) usciere m

bait [beɪt] n esca ♦ vt (hook) innescare; (trap) munire di esca; (fig) tormentare

bake [beɪk] vt cuocere al forno ♦ vi cuocersi al forno; **~d beans** npl fagioli mpl in salsa di pomodoro; **~d potato** n patata cotta al forno con la buccia; **~r** n fornaio/a, panettiere/a; **~ry** n panetteria; **baking** n cottura (al forno); **baking powder** n lievito in polvere

balance ['bæləns] n equilibrio; (COMM: sum) bilancio; (remainder) resto; (scales) bilancia ♦ vt tenere in equilibrio; (budget) far quadrare; (account) pareggiare; (compensate) contrappesare; **~ of trade/payments** bilancia commerciale/dei pagamenti; **~d** adj (personality, diet) equilibrato(a); **~ sheet** n bilancio

balcony ['bælkənɪ] n balcone m; (in theatre) balconata

bald [bɔːld] adj calvo(a); (tyre) liscio(a)

bale [beɪl] n balla; **~ out** vi (of a plane) gettarsi col paracadute

ball [bɔːl] n palla; (football) pallone m; (for golf) pallina; (of wool, string) gomitolo; (*dance*) ballo; **to play ~** (*fig*) stare al gioco

ballast ['bæləst] *n* zavorra

ball bearings *npl* cuscinetti a sfere

ballerina [bælə'riːnə] *n* ballerina

ballet ['bæleɪ] *n* balletto; **~ dancer** *n* ballerino(a) classico(a)

balloon [bə'luːn] *n* pallone *m*

ballot paper ['bælət-] *n* scheda

ball-point pen *n* penna a sfera

ballroom ['bɔːlrum] *n* sala da ballo

balm [bɑːm] *n* balsamo

ban [bæn] *n* interdizione *f* ♦ *vt* interdire

banana [bə'nɑːnə] *n* banana

band [bænd] *n* banda; (*at a dance*) orchestra; (*MIL*) fanfara; **~ together** *vi* collegarsi

bandage ['bændɪdʒ] *n* benda, fascia

Bandaid ® ['bændeɪd] (*US*) *n* cerotto

bandy-legged [-'legɪd] *adj* dalle gambe storte

bang [bæŋ] *n* (*of door*) lo sbattere; (*of gun, blow*) colpo ♦ *vt* battere (violentemente); (*door*) sbattere ♦ *vi* scoppiare; sbattere

Bangladesh [bæːŋglə'deʃ] *n* Bangladesh *m*

bangle ['bæŋgl] *n* braccialetto

bangs [bæŋz] (*US*) *npl* (*fringe*) frangia, frangetta

banish ['bænɪʃ] *vt* bandire

banister(s) ['bænɪstə(z)] *n(pl)* ringhiera

bank [bæŋk] *n* banca, banco; (*of river, lake*) riva, sponda; (*of earth*) banco ♦ *vi* (*AVIAT*) inclinarsi in virata; **~ on** *vt fus* contare su; **~ account** *n* conto in banca; **~ card** *n* carta *f* assegni *inv*; **~er** *n* banchiere *m*; **~er's card** (*BRIT*) *n* = **bank card**; **B~ holiday** (*BRIT*) *n* giorno di festa; **~ing** *n* attività bancaria; professione *f* di banchiere; **~note** *n* banconota; **~ rate** *n* tasso bancario

| bank holiday |

Una **bank holiday**, *in Gran*

Bretagna, è una giornata in cui banche e negozi sono chiusi. Generalmente le **bank holiday** *cadono di lunedì e molti ne approfittano per fare una breve vacanza fuori città.*

bankrupt ['bæŋkrʌpt] *adj* fallito(a); **to go ~** fallire; **~cy** *n* fallimento

bank statement *n* estratto conto

banner ['bænə*] *n* striscione *m*

baptism ['bæptɪzəm] *n* battesimo

bar [bɑː*] *n* (*place*) bar *m inv*; (*counter*) banco; (*rod*) barra; (*of window etc*) sbarra; (*of chocolate*) tavoletta; (*fig*) ostacolo; restrizione *f*; (*MUS*) battuta ♦ *vt* (*road, window*) sbarrare; (*person*) escludere; (*activity*) interdire; **~ of soap** saponetta; **the B~** (*LAW*) l'Ordine *m* degli avvocati; **behind ~s** (*prisoner*) dietro le sbarre; **~ none** senza eccezione

barbaric [bɑː'bærɪk] *adj* barbarico(a)

barbecue ['bɑːbɪkjuː] *n* barbecue *m inv*

barbed wire ['bɑːbd-] *n* filo spinato

barber ['bɑːbə*] *n* barbiere *m*

bar code *n* (*on goods*) codice *m* a barre

bare [beə*] *adj* nudo(a) ♦ *vt* scoprire, denudare; (*teeth*) mostrare; **the ~ necessities** lo stretto necessario; **~back** *adv* senza sella; **~faced** *adj* sfacciato(a); **~foot** *adj, adv* scalzo(a); **~ly** *adv* appena

bargain ['bɑːgɪn] *n* (*transaction*) contratto; (*good buy*) affare *m* ♦ *vi* trattare; **into the ~** per giunta; **~ for** *vt fus*: **he got more than he ~ed for** gli è andata peggio di quel che si aspettasse

barge [bɑːdʒ] *n* chiatta; **~ in** *vi* (*walk in*) piombare dentro; (*interrupt talk*) intromettersi a sproposito

bark [bɑːk] *n* (*of tree*) corteccia; (*of dog*) abbaio *vi* abbaiare

barley ['bɑːlɪ] *n* orzo

barmaid ['bɑːmeɪd] n cameriera al banco

barman ['bɑːmən] n barista m

bar meal n spuntino servito al bar

barn [bɑːn] n granaio

barometer [bə'rɒmɪtə*] n barometro

baron ['bærən] n barone m; **~ess** n baronessa

barracks ['bærəks] npl caserma

barrage ['bærɑːʒ] n (MIL, dam) sbarramento; (fig) fiume m

barrel ['bærəl] n barile m; (of gun) canna

barren ['bærən] adj sterile; (soil) arido(a)

barricade [bærɪ'keɪd] n barricata

barrier ['bærɪə*] n barriera

barring ['bɑːrɪŋ] prep salvo

barrister ['bærɪstə*] (BRIT) n avvocato/essa (con diritto di parlare davanti a tutte le corti)

barrow ['bærəu] n (cart) carriola

bartender ['bɑːtendə*] (US) n barista m

barter ['bɑːtə*] vt: **to ~ sth for** barattare qc con

base [beɪs] n base f ♦ vt: **to ~ sth on** basare qc su ♦ adj vile

baseball ['beɪsbɔːl] n baseball m

basement ['beɪsmənt] n seminterrato; (of shop) interrato

bases¹ ['beɪsiːz] npl of **basis**

bases² ['beɪsɪz] npl of **base**

bash [bæʃ] (inf) vt battere

bashful ['bæʃful] adj timido(a)

basic ['beɪsɪk] adj rudimentale; essenziale; **~ally** [-lɪ] adv fondamentalmente; sostanzialmente; **~s** npl: **the ~s** l'essenziale m

basil ['bæzl] n basilico

basin ['beɪsn] n (vessel, also GEO) bacino; (also: wash~) lavabo

basis ['beɪsɪs] (pl **bases**) n base f; **on a part-time ~** part-time; **on a trial ~** in prova

bask [bɑːsk] vi: **to ~ in the sun** crogiolarsi al sole

basket ['bɑːskɪt] n cesta; (smaller) cestino; (with handle) paniere m; **~ball** n pallacanestro f

bass [beɪs] n (MUS) basso

bassoon [bə'suːn] n fagotto

bastard ['bɑːstəd] n bastardo/a; (inf!) stronzo (!)

bat [bæt] n pipistrello; (for baseball etc) mazza; (BRIT: for table tennis) racchetta ♦ vt: **he didn't ~ an eyelid** non battè ciglio

batch [bætʃ] n (of bread) infornata; (of papers) cumulo

bated ['beɪtɪd] adj: **with ~ breath** col fiato sospeso

bath [bɑːθ] n bagno; (bathtub) vasca da bagno ♦ vt far fare il bagno a; **to have a ~** fare un bagno; see also **baths**

bathe [beɪð] vi fare il bagno ♦ vt (wound) lavare; **~r** n bagnante m/f

bathing ['beɪðɪŋ] n bagni mpl; **~ costume** (US **~ suit**) n costume m da bagno

bathrobe ['bɑːθrəub] n accappatoio

bathroom ['bɑːθrum] n stanza da bagno

baths [bɑːðz] npl bagni mpl pubblici

bath towel n asciugamano da bagno

baton ['bætən] n (MUS) bacchetta; (ATHLETICS) testimone m; (club) manganello

batter ['bætə*] vt battere ♦ n pastetta; **~ed** adj (hat) sformato(a); (pan) ammaccato(a)

battery ['bætərɪ] n batteria; (of torch) pila; **~ farming** n allevamento in batteria

battle ['bætl] n battaglia ♦ vi battagliare, lottare; **~field** n campo di battaglia; **~ship** n nave f da guerra

bawl [bɔːl] vi urlare

bay [beɪ] n (of sea) baia; **to hold sb at ~** tenere qn a bada; **~ leaf** n foglia d'alloro; **~ window** n bovindo

bazaar [bə'zɑː*] n bazar m inv; vendita di beneficenza

B. & B.

beard

B. & B. *abbr* (= bed and breakfast

BBC *n abbr* (= British Broadcasting Corporation) rete nazionale di radiotelevisione in Gran Bretagna

B.C. *adv abbr* (= before Christ) a.C.

KEYWORD
---

be [biː] (*pt* was, were, *pp* been) *aux vb* 1 (*with present participle: forming continuous tenses*): **what are you doing?** che fa?, che sta facendo?; **they're coming tomorrow** vengono domani; **I've been waiting for her for hours** sono ore che l'aspetto
2 (*with pp: forming passives*) essere; **to ~ killed** essere or venire ucciso(a); **the box had been opened** la scatola era stata aperta; **the thief was nowhere to ~ seen** il ladro non si trovava da nessuna parte
3 (*in tag questions*): **it was fun, wasn't it?** è stato divertente, no?; **he's good-looking, isn't he?** è un bell'uomo, vero?; **she's back, is she?** così è tornata, eh?
4 (+ *to* + *infinitive*): **the house is to ~ sold** abbiamo (or hanno *etc*) intenzione di vendere casa; **you're to ~ congratulated for all your work** dovremo farvi i complimenti per tutto il vostro lavoro; **he's not to open it** non deve aprirlo

♦ *vb + complement* 1 (*gen*) essere; **I'm English** sono inglese; **I'm tired** sono stanco(a); **I'm hot/cold** ho caldo/freddo; **he's a doctor** è medico; **2 and 2 are 4** 2 più 2 fa 4; **~ careful!** sta attento(a)!; **~ good!** sii buono(a)
2 (*of health*) stare; **how are you?** come sta?; **he's very ill** sta molto male
3 (*of age*): **how old are you?** quanti anni hai?; **I'm sixteen (years old)** ho sedici anni
4 (*cost*) costare; **how much was the meal?** quant'era or quanto costava il pranzo?; **that'll ~ £5, please** (fa) 5 sterline, per favore

♦ *vi* 1 (*exist, occur etc*) essere, esistere; **the best singer that ever was** il migliore cantante mai esistito or di tutti tempi; **~ that as it may** comunque sia, sia come sia; **so ~ it** sia pure, e sia
2 (*referring to place*) essere, trovarsi; **I won't ~ here tomorrow** non ci sarò domani; **Edinburgh is in Scotland** Edimburgo si trova in Scozia
3 (*referring to movement*): **where have you been?** dov'è stato?; **I've been to China** sono stato in Cina

♦ *impers vb* 1 (*referring to time, distance*) essere; **it's 5 o'clock** sono le 5; **it's the 28th of April** è il 28 aprile; **it's 10 km to the village** di qui al paese sono 10 km
2 (*referring to the weather*): **it's too hot/cold** fa troppo caldo/freddo; **it's windy** c'è vento
3 (*emphatic*): **it's me** sono io; **it was Maria who paid the bill** è stata Maria che ha pagato il conto

---

beach [biːtʃ] *n* spiaggia ♦ *vt* tirare in secco

beacon ['biːkən] *n* (*lighthouse*) faro; (*marker*) segnale *m*

bead [biːd] *n* perlina

beak [biːk] *n* becco

beaker ['biːkə*] *n* coppa

beam [biːm] *n* trave *f*; (*of light*) raggio ♦ *vi* brillare

bean [biːn] *n* fagiolo; (*of coffee*) chicco; **runner ~** fagiolino; **broad ~** fava; **~sprouts** *npl* germogli *mpl* di soia

bear [bεə*] (*pt* bore, *pp* borne) *n* orso ♦ *vt* portare; (*endure*) sopportare; (*produce*) generare ♦ *vi*: **to ~ right/left** piegare a destra/sinistra; **~ out** *vt* (*suspicions*) confermare, convalidare; (*person*) dare il proprio appoggio a; **~ up** *vi* (*person*) fare buon viso a cattiva sorte

beard [bɪəd] *n* barba

bearer ['bɛərə*] n portatore m

bearing ['bɛərɪŋ] n portamento; (connection) rapporto; **~s** npl (also: ball ~s) cuscinetti mpl a sfere; **to take a ~** fare un rilevamento; **to find one's ~s** orientarsi

beast [biːst] n bestia; **~ly** adj meschino(a); (weather) da cani

beat [biːt] (pt beat, pp beaten) n colpo; (of heart) battito; (MUS) tempo, battuta; (of policeman) giro ♦ vt battere; (eggs, cream) sbattere ♦ vi battere; **off the ~en track** fuori mano; **~ it!** (inf) fila!, fuori dai piedi!; **~ off** vt respingere; **~ up** vt (person) picchiare; (eggs) sbattere; **beaten** pp of beat; **~ing** n bastonata

beautiful ['bjuːtɪful] adj bello(a); **~ly** adv splendidamente

beauty ['bjuːtɪ] n bellezza; **~ salon** n istituto di bellezza; **~ spot** n (BRIT) n (TOURISM) luogo pittoresco

beaver ['biːvə*] n castoro

became [bɪˈkeɪm] pt of become

because [bɪˈkɔz] conj perché; **~ of** a causa di

beckon ['bekən] vt (also: ~ to) chiamare con un cenno

become [bɪˈkʌm] (irreg: like come) vt diventare; **to ~ fat/thin** ingrassarsi/ dimagrire

becoming [bɪˈkʌmɪŋ] adj (behaviour) che si conviene; (clothes) grazioso(a)

bed [bed] n letto; (of flowers) aiuola; (of coal, clay) strato; **single/double ~** letto a una piazza/a due piazze or matrimoniale; **~ and breakfast** n (place) ≈ pensione f familiare; (terms) camera con colazione; **~clothes** ['bedkləʊðz] npl biancheria e coperte fpl da letto; **~ding** n coperte e lenzuola fpl

---

bed and breakfast

I bed and breakfast, anche B & B, sono piccole pensioni a conduzione familiare, più economiche rispetto agli alberghi, dove al mattino viene servita la tradizionale colazione all'inglese.

bed linen n biancheria da letto

bedraggled [bɪˈdrægld] adj fradicio(a)

bed: ~ridden adj costretto(a) a letto; **~room** n camera da letto; **~side** n: at sb's **~side** al capezzale di qn; **~sit(ter)** (BRIT) n monolocale m; **~spread** n copriletto; **~time** n: it's **~time** è ora di andare a letto

bee [biː] n ape f

beech [biːtʃ] n faggio

beef [biːf] n manzo; **roast ~** arrosto di manzo; **~burger** n hamburger m inv; **B~eater** n guardia della Torre di Londra

beehive ['biːhaɪv] n alveare m

beeline ['biːlaɪn] n: to make a **~ for** buttarsi a capo fitto verso

been [biːn] pp of be

beer [bɪə*] n birra

beetle ['biːtl] n scarafaggio; coleottero

beetroot ['biːtruːt] (BRIT) n barbabietola

before [bɪˈfɔː*] prep (in time) prima di; (in space) davanti a ♦ conj prima che + sub; prima di ♦ adv prima; **~ going** prima di andare; **~ she goes** prima che vada; **the week ~** la settimana prima; **I've seen it ~** l'ho già visto; **I've never seen it ~** è la prima volta che lo vedo; **~hand** adv in anticipo

beg [beg] vi chiedere l'elemosina ♦ vt (also: ~ for) chiedere in elemosina; (: favour) chiedere; **to ~ sb to do** pregare qn di fare

began [bɪˈgæn] pt of begin

beggar ['begə*] n mendicante m/f

begin [bɪˈgɪn] (pt began, pp begun) vt, vi cominciare; **to ~ doing** or **to do sth** incominciare o iniziare a fare qc; **~ner** n principiante m/f; **~ning** n inizio, principio

begun [bɪˈgʌn] pp of begin

behalf [bɪˈhɑːf] n: **on ~ of** per conto di; a nome di

behave [bɪ'heɪv] vi comportarsi; (well: also: ~ o.s.)

behaviour [bɪ'heɪvjə*] (US **behavior**) n comportamento, condotta

behind [bɪ'haɪnd] prep dietro; (followed by pronoun) dietro di; (time) in ritardo con ♦ adv dietro; (leave, stay) indietro ♦ n didietro; **to be ~ (schedule)** essere in ritardo rispetto al programma; **~ the scenes** (fig) dietro le quinte

behold [bɪ'həʊld] (irreg: like hold) vt vedere, scorgere

beige [beɪʒ] adj beige inv

Beijing ['beɪ'dʒɪŋ] n Pechino f

being ['biːɪŋ] n essere m

Beirut [beɪ'ruːt] n Beirut f

Belarus [belə'rus] n Bielorussia

belated [bɪ'leɪtɪd] adj tardo(a)

belch [beltʃ] vi ruttare ♦ vt (gen: ~ out: smoke etc) eruttare

Belgian ['beldʒən] adj, n belga m/f

Belgium ['beldʒəm] n Belgio

belie [bɪ'laɪ] vt smentire

belief [bɪ'liːf] n (opinion) opinione f, convinzione f; (trust, faith) fede f

believe [bɪ'liːv] vt, vi credere; **to ~ in** (God) credere in; (ghosts) credere a; (method) avere fiducia in; **~r** n (REL) credente m/f; (in idea, activity): **to be a ~r in** credere in

belittle [bɪ'lɪtl] vt sminuire

bell [bel] n campana f; (small, on door, electric) campanello

belligerent [bɪ'lɪdʒərənt] adj bellicoso(a)

bellow ['beləʊ] vi muggire

bellows ['beləʊz] npl soffietto

belly ['belɪ] n pancia

belong [bɪ'lɒŋ] vi: **to ~ to** appartenere a; (club etc) essere socio di; **this book ~s here** questo libro va qui; **~ings** npl cose fpl, roba

beloved [bɪ'lʌvɪd] adj adorato(a)

below [bɪ'ləʊ] prep sotto, al di sotto di ♦ adv sotto, di sotto; giù; **see ~** vedi sotto or oltre

belt [belt] n cintura; (TECH) cinghia ♦ vt

(thrash) picchiare ♦ vi (inf) filarsela; **~way** (US) n (AUT: ring road) circonvallazione f; (: motorway) autostrada

bemused [bɪ'mjuːzd] adj perplesso(a), stupito(a)

bench [bentʃ] n panca; (in workshop, POL) banco; **the B~** (LAW) la Corte

bend [bend] (pt, pp **bent**) vt curvare; (leg, arm) piegare ♦ vi curvarsi; piegarsi ♦ n (BRIT: in road) curva; (in pipe, river) gomito; **~ down** vi chinarsi; **~ over** vi piegarsi

beneath [bɪ'niːθ] prep sotto, al di sotto di; (unworthy of) indegno(a) di ♦ adv sotto, di sotto

benefactor ['benɪfæktə*] n benefattore m

beneficial [benɪ'fɪʃəl] adj che fa bene; vantaggioso(a)

benefit ['benɪfɪt] n beneficio, vantaggio; (allowance of money) indennità f inv ♦ vt far bene a ♦ vi: **he'll ~ from it** ne trarrà beneficio or profitto

benevolent [bɪ'nevələnt] adj benevolo(a)

benign [bɪ'naɪn] adj (person, smile) benevolo(a); (MED) benigno(a)

bent [bent] pt, pp of bend ♦ n inclinazione f ♦ adj (inf: dishonest) losco(a); **to be ~ on** essere deciso(a) a

bequest [bɪ'kwest] n lascito

bereaved [bɪ'riːvd] n: **the ~** i familiari in lutto

beret ['bereɪ] n berretto

Berlin [bəː'lɪn] n Berlino f

berm [bəːm] (US) n (AUT) corsia d'emergenza

berry ['berɪ] n bacca

berserk [bə'səːk] adj: **to go ~** montare su tutte le furie

berth [bəːθ] n (bed) cuccetta; (for ship) ormeggio ♦ vi (in harbour) entrare in porto; (at anchor) gettare l'ancora

beseech [bɪ'siːtʃ] (pt, pp **besought**) vt implorare

beset [bɪ'set] (pt, pp **beset**) vt assalire

beside [bɪ'saɪd] prep accanto a; **to be ~ o.s. (with anger)** essere fuori di sé (dalla rabbia); **that's ~ the point** non c'entra

besides [bɪ'saɪdz] adv inoltre, per di più ♦ prep oltre a; a parte

besiege [bɪ'si:dʒ] vt (town) assediare; (fig) tempestare

best [best] adj migliore ♦ adv meglio; **the ~ part of** (quantity) la maggior parte di; **at ~** tutt'al più; **to make the ~ of sth** cavare il meglio possibile da qc; **to do one's ~** fare del proprio meglio; **to the ~ of my knowledge** per quel che ne so; **to the ~ of my ability** al massimo delle mie capacità; **~before date** n scadenza; **~ man** n testimone m dello sposo

bestow [bɪ'stəu] vt accordare; (title) conferire

bet [bet] (pt, pp **bet** or **betted**) n scommessa ♦ vt, vi scommettere; **to ~ sb sth** scommettere qc con qn

betray [bɪ'treɪ] vt tradire; **~al** n tradimento

better ['betə*] adj migliore ♦ adv meglio ♦ vt migliorare ♦ n: **to get the ~ of** avere la meglio su; **you had ~ do it** è meglio che lo faccia; **he thought ~ of it** cambiò idea; **to get ~** migliorare; **~ off** adj più ricco(a); (fig): **you'd be ~ off this way** starebbe meglio così

betting ['betɪŋ] n scommesse fpl; **~ shop** (BRIT) n ufficio dell'allibratore

between [bɪ'twi:n] prep tra ♦ adv in mezzo, nel mezzo

beverage ['bevərɪdʒ] n bevanda

beware [bɪ'wεə*] vt, vi: **to ~ (of)** stare attento(a) (a); "**~ of the dog**" "attenti al cane"

bewildered [bɪ'wɪldəd] adj sconcertato(a), confuso(a)

beyond [bɪ'jɒnd] prep (in space) oltre; (exceeding) al di sopra di ♦ adv di là; **~ doubt** senza dubbio; **~ repair**

irreparabile

bias ['baɪəs] n (prejudice) pregiudizio; (preference) preferenza; **~(s)ed** adj parziale

bib [bɪb] n bavaglino

Bible ['baɪbl] n Bibbia

bicarbonate of soda [baɪ'kɑ:bənɪt-] n bicarbonato (di sodio)

bicker ['bɪkə*] vi bisticciare

bicycle ['baɪsɪkl] n bicicletta

bid [bɪd] (pt **bade** or **bid**, pp **bidden** or **bid**) n offerta; (attempt) tentativo ♦ vi fare un'offerta ♦ vt fare un'offerta di; **to ~ sb good day** dire buon giorno a qn; **bidden** pp of **bid**; **~der** n: **the highest ~der** il maggior offerente; **~ding** n offerte fpl

bide [baɪd] vt: **to ~ one's time** aspettare il momento giusto

bifocals [baɪ'fəuklz] npl occhiali mpl bifocali

big [bɪg] adj grande; grosso(a)

big dipper [-'dɪpə*] n montagne fpl russe, otto m inv volante

bigheaded ['bɪg'hedɪd] adj presuntuoso(a)

bigot ['bɪgət] n persona gretta; **~ed** adj gretto(a); **~ry** n grettezza

big top n tendone m del circo

bike [baɪk] n bici f inv

bikini [bɪ'ki:nɪ] n bikini m inv

bilingual [baɪ'lɪŋgwəl] adj bilingue

bill [bɪl] n conto; (POL) atto; (US: banknote) banconota; (of show) locandina; "**post no ~s**" "divieto di affissione"; **to fit** or **fill the ~** (fig) fare al caso; **~board** n tabellone m

billet ['bɪlɪt] n alloggio

billfold ['bɪlfəuld] (US) n portafoglio

billiards ['bɪljədz] n biliardo

billion ['bɪljən] n (BRIT) bilione m; (US) miliardo

bimbo ['bɪmbəu] n (pej, col) pollastrella, svampitella

bin [bɪn] n (for coal, rubbish) bidone m; (for bread) cassetta; (dust~) pattumiera (litter ~) cestino

bind [baɪnd] (pt, pp bound) vt legare; (oblige) obbligare ♦ n (inf) scocciatura; **~ing** adj (contract) vincolante

binge [bɪndʒ] (inf) n: to go on a ~ fare baldoria

bingo ['bɪŋgəʊ] n gioco simile alla tombola

binoculars [bɪ'nɔkjʊləz] npl binocolo

bio... [baɪə'...] prefix: **~chemistry** n biochimica; **~degradable** adj biodegradabile; **~graphy** [baɪ'ɔgrəfɪ] n biografia; **~logical** adj biologico(a); **~logy** [baɪ'ɔlədʒɪ] n biologia

birch [bəːtʃ] n betulla

bird [bəːd] n uccello; (BRIT: inf: girl) bambola; **~'s eye view** n vista panoramica; **~ watcher** n ornitologo/a dilettante

Biro ® ['baɪrəʊ] n biro ® f inv

birth [bəːθ] n nascita; **to give ~** partorire; **~ certificate** n certificato di nascita; **~ control** n controllo delle nascite; contraccezione f; **~day** n compleanno ♦ cpd di compleanno; **~ rate** n indice m di natalità

biscuit ['bɪskɪt] n biscotto

bisect [baɪ'sɛkt] vt tagliare in due (parti)

bishop ['bɪʃəp] n vescovo

bit [bɪt] pt of **bite** ♦ n pezzo; (COMPUT) bit m inv; (of horse) morso; **a ~ of** un po' di; **a ~ mad** un po' matto; **~ by ~** a poco a poco

bitch [bɪtʃ] n (dog) cagna; (inf!) vacca

bite [baɪt] (pt bit, pp bitten) vt, vi mordere; (subj: insect) pungere ♦ n morso; (insect ~) puntura; (mouthful) boccone m; **let's have a ~ (to eat)** mangiamo un boccone; **to ~ one's nails** mangiarsi le unghie; **bitten** ['bɪtn] pp of **bite**

bitter ['bɪtə*] adj amaro(a); (wind, criticism) pungente ♦ n (BRIT: beer) birra amara; **~ness** n amarezza; gusto amaro

black [blæk] adj nero(a) ♦ n nero;

(person): **B~** negro/a ♦ vt (BRIT: INDUSTRY) boicottare; **to give sb a ~ eye** fare un occhio nero a qn; **in the ~** (bank account) in attivo; **~ and blue** adj tutto(a) pesto(a); **~berry** n mora; **~bird** n merlo; **~board** n lavagna; **~ coffee** n caffè m nero; **~currant** n ribes m inv; **~en** vt annerire; **~ ice** n strato trasparente di ghiaccio; **~leg** (BRIT) n crumiro/a; **~list** n lista nera; **~mail** n ricatto ♦ vt ricattare; **~ market** n mercato nero; **~out** n oscuramento; (TV, RADIO) interruzione f delle trasmissioni; (fainting) svenimento; **B~ Sea** n: **the B~ Sea** il Mar Nero; **~ sheep** n pecora nera; **~smith** n fabbro ferraio; **~ spot** n (AUT) luogo famigerato per gli incidenti; (for unemployment etc) zona critica

bladder ['blædə*] n vescica

blade [bleɪd] n lama; (of oar) pala; **~ of grass** filo d'erba

blame [bleɪm] n colpa ♦ vt: **to ~ sb/ sth for sth** dare la colpa di qc a qn/ qc; **who's to ~?** chi è colpevole?

bland [blænd] adj mite; (taste) blando(a)

blank [blæŋk] adj bianco(a); (look) distratto(a) ♦ n spazio vuoto; (cartridge) cartuccia a salve; **~ cheque** n assegno in bianco

blanket ['blæŋkɪt] n coperta

blare [blɛə*] vi strombettare

blasphemy ['blæsfɪmɪ] n bestemmia

blast [blɑːst] n (of wind) raffica; (of bomb etc) esplosione f ♦ vt far saltare; **~-off** n (SPACE) lancio

blatant ['bleɪtənt] adj flagrante

blaze [bleɪz] n (fire) incendio; (fig) vampata; splendore m ♦ vi (fire) ardere, fiammeggiare; (guns) sparare senza sosta; (fig: eyes) ardere ♦ vt: **to ~ a trail** (fig) tracciare una via nuova; **in a ~ of publicity** circondato da grande pubblicità

blazer ['bleɪzə*] n blazer m inv

bleach [bliːtʃ] n (also: household ~) varechina ♦ vt (material) candeggiare; ~ed adj (hair) decolorato(a); ~ers n (US) npl (SPORT) posti mpl di gradinata

bleak [bliːk] adj tetro(a)

bleat [bliːt] vi belare

bled [bled] pt, pp of **bleed**

bleed [bliːd] (pt, pp **bled**) vi sanguinare; **my nose is ~ing** mi viene fuori sangue dal naso

bleeper ['bliːpə*] n (device) cicalino

blemish ['blemɪʃ] n macchia

blend [blend] n miscela ♦ vt mescolare ♦ vi (colours etc: also: ~ **in**) armonizzare

bless [bles] (pt, pp **blessed** or **blest**) vt benedire; ~ **you!** (after sneeze) salute!; ~ing n benedizione f; fortuna; **blest** [blest] pt, pp of **bless**

blew [bluː] pt of **blow**

blight [blaɪt] vt (hopes etc) deludere; (life) rovinare

blimey ['blaɪmɪ] (BRIT: inf) excl accidenti!

blind [blaɪnd] adj cieco(a) ♦ n (for window) avvolgibile m; (Venetian ~) veneziana ♦ vt accecare; **the** ~ npl i ciechi; ~ **alley** n vicolo cieco; ~ **corner** n (BRIT) n svolta cieca; ~**fold** n benda ♦ adj, adv bendato(a) ♦ vt bendare gli occhi a; ~**ly** adv ciecamente; ~**ness** n cecità; ~ **spot** n (AUT etc) punto cieco; (fig) punto debole

blink [blɪŋk] vi battere gli occhi; (light) lampeggiare; ~**ers** npl paraocchi mpl

bliss [blɪs] n estasi f

blister ['blɪstə*] n (on skin) vescica; (on paintwork) bolla ♦ vi (paint) coprirsi di bolle

blizzard ['blɪzəd] n bufera di neve

bloated ['bləutɪd] adj gonfio(a)

blob [blɔb] n (drop) goccia; (stain, spot) macchia

bloc [blɔk] n (POL) blocco

block [blɔk] n blocco; (in pipes) ingombro; (toy) cubo; (of buildings) isolato ♦ vt bloccare; ~**ade** [-'keɪd] n

blocco; ~**age** n ostacolo; ~**buster** n (film, book) grande successo; ~ **letters** npl stampatello; ~ **of flats** (BRIT) n caseggiato.

bloke [bləuk] (BRIT: inf) n tizio

blond(e) [blɔnd] adj, n biondo(a)

blood [blʌd] n sangue m; ~ **donor** n donatore/trice di sangue; ~ **group** n gruppo sanguigno; ~**hound** n segugio; ~ **poisoning** n setticemia; ~ **pressure** n pressione f sanguigna; ~**shed** n spargimento di sangue; ~**shot** adj: ~**shot eyes** occhi iniettati di sangue; ~**stream** n flusso del sangue; ~ **test** n analisi f inv del sangue; ~**thirsty** adj assetato(a) di sangue; ~**y** adj (fight) sanguinoso(a); (nose) sanguinante; (BRIT: inf!): **this ~y** ... questo maledetto ...; ~**y awful/good** (inf!) veramente terribile/forte; ~**y-minded** (BRIT: inf) adj indispensabile

bloom [bluːm] n fiore m ♦ vi (tree) essere in fiore; (flower) aprirsi

blossom ['blɔsəm] n fiore m; (with pl sense) fiori mpl ♦ vi essere in fiore

blot [blɔt] n macchia ♦ vt macchiare; ~ **out** vt (memories) cancellare; (view) nascondere

blotchy ['blɔtʃɪ] adj (complexion) coperto(a) di macchie

blotting paper ['blɔtɪŋ-] n carta assorbente

blouse [blauz] n (feminine garment) camicetta

blow [bləu] (pt **blew**, pp **blown**) n colpo ♦ vi soffiare ♦ vt (fuse) far saltare; (subj: wind) spingere; (instrument) suonare; **to ~ one's nose** soffiarsi il naso; **to ~ a whistle** fischiare; ~ **away** vt portare via; ~ **down** vt abbattere; ~ **off** vt far volare via; ~ **out** vi scoppiare; ~ **over** vi calmarsi; ~ **up** vi saltare in aria ♦ vt far saltare in aria; (tyre) gonfiare; (PHOT) ingrandire; ~-**dry** n messa in piega a föhn; ~**lamp** (BRIT) n lampada a benzina per saldare; **blown** pp of **blow**; ~-**out** n (of tyre) scoppio; **~torch** n = **~lamp**

blue [blu:] *adj* azzurro(a); (*depressed*) giù *inv*; **~ film/joke** film/ barzelletta pornografico(a); **out of the ~** (*fig*) all'improvviso; **~bell** n giacinto dei boschi; **~bottle** n moscone m; **~print** n (*fig*) **~print (for)** formula (di)

bluff [blʌf] *vi* bluffare ♦ n bluff m *inv* ♦ *adj* (*person*) brusco(a); **to call sb's ~** mettere alla prova il bluff di qn

blunder ['blʌndə*] n abbaglio ♦ *vi* prendere un abbaglio

blunt [blʌnt] *adj* smussato(a); spuntato(a); (*person*) brusco(a)

blur [blə:*] n forma indistinta ♦ *vt* offuscare

blush [blʌʃ] *vi* arrossire ♦ n rossore m

blustering ['blʌstərɪŋ] *adj* infuriato(a)

blustery ['blʌstərɪ] *adj* (*weather*) burrascoso(a)

boar [bɔ:*] n cinghiale m

board [bɔ:d] n tavola; (*on wall*) tabellone m; (*committee*) consiglio, comitato; (*in firm*) consiglio d'amministrazione; (*NAUT, AVIAT*): **on ~** a bordo ♦ *vt* (*ship*) salire a bordo di; (*train*) salire su; **full ~** (*BRIT*) pensione completa; **half ~** (*BRIT*) mezza pensione; **~ and lodging** vitto e alloggio; **which goes by the ~** (*fig*) che viene abbandonato; **~ up** *vt* (*door*) chiudere con assi; **~er** n (*SCOL*) convittore/trice; **~ing card** n = **~ing pass**; **~ing house** n pensione f; **~ing pass** n (*AVIAT, NAUT*) carta d'imbarco; **~ing school** n collegio; **~ room** n sala del consiglio

boast [bəust] *vi*: **to ~ (about** *or* **of)** vantarsi (di)

boat [bəut] n nave f; (*small*) barca; **~swain** ['bəusn] n nostromo

bob [bɔb] *vi* (*boat, cork on water*: *also*: **~ up and down**) andare su e giù; **~ up** *vi* saltare fuori

bobby ['bɔbɪ] (*BRIT*: *inf*) n poliziotto

bobsleigh ['bɔbsleɪ] n bob m *inv*

bode [bəud] *vi*: **to ~ well/ill (for)**

essere di buon/cattivo auspicio (per)

bodily ['bɔdɪlɪ] *adj* fisico(a), corporale ♦ *adv* corporalmente; interamente; in persona

body ['bɔdɪ] n corpo; (*of car*) carrozzeria; (*of plane*) fusoliera; (*fig*: *group*) gruppo; (: *organization*) organizzazione f; (: *quantity*) quantità f *inv*; **~-building** n culturismo; **~guard** n guardia del corpo; **~work** n carrozzeria

bog [bɔg] n palude f ♦ *vt*: **to get ~ged down** (*fig*) impantanarsi

bogus ['bəugəs] *adj* falso(a); finto(a)

boil [bɔɪl] *vt, vi* bollire ♦ n (*MED*) foruncolo; **to come to the** (*BRIT*) *or* **a** (*US*) **~** raggiungere l'ebollizione; **~ down to** *vi* (*fig*) ridursi a; **~ over** *vi* traboccare (bollendo); **~ed egg** n uovo alla coque; **~ed potatoes** *npl* patate *fpl* bollite *or* lesse; **~er** n caldaia; **~er suit** (*BRIT*) n tuta; **~ing point** n punto di ebollizione

boisterous ['bɔɪstərəs] *adj* chiassoso(a)

bold [bəuld] *adj* audace; (*child*) impudente; (*colour*) deciso(a)

bollard ['bɔləd] (*BRIT*) n (*AUT*) colonnina luminosa

bolt [bəult] n chiavistello; (*with nut*) bullone m ♦ *adv*: **~ upright** diritto(a) come un fuso ♦ *vt* serrare; (*also*: **~ together**) imbullonare; (*food*) mangiare in fretta ♦ *vi* scappare via

bomb [bɔm] n bomba ♦ *vt* bombardare

bombastic [bɔm'bæstɪk] *adj* magniloquente

bomb: ~ disposal unit n corpo degli artificieri; **~er** n (*AVIAT*) bombardiere m; **~shell** n (*fig*) notizia bomba

bond [bɔnd] n legame m; (*binding promise, FINANCE*) obbligazione f; (*COMM*): **in ~** in attesa di sdoganamento

bondage ['bɔndɪdʒ] n schiavitù f

bone [bəun] n osso; (*of fish*) spina, lisca ♦ *vt* disossare; togliere le spine a;

~ **idle** adj pigrissimo(a); ~ **marrow** n midollo osseo

bonfire ['bɔnfaɪə*] n falò m inv

bonnet ['bɔnɪt] n cuffia; (BRIT: of car) cofano

bonus ['bəʊnəs] n premio; (fig) sovrappiù m inv

bony ['bəʊnɪ] adj (MED: tissue) osseo(a); (arm, face) ossuto(a); (meat) pieno(a) di ossi; (fish) pieno(a) di spine

boo [bu:] excl ba! ♦ vt fischiare

booby trap ['bu:bɪ-] n trappola

book [buk] n libro; (of stamps etc) blocchetto ♦ vt (ticket, seat, room) prenotare; (driver) multare; (football player) ammonire; ~s npl (COMM) conti mpl; ~**case** n scaffale m; ~**ing office** (BRIT) n (RAIL) biglietteria; (THEATRE) botteghino; ~-**keeping** n contabilità; ~**let** n libricino; ~**maker** n allibratore m; ~**seller** n libraio; ~**shop**, ~**store** n libreria

boom [bu:m] n (noise) rimbombo; (in prices etc) boom m inv ♦ vi rimbombare; andare a gonfie vele

boon [bu:n] n vantaggio

boost [bu:st] n spinta ♦ vt spingere; ~**er** n (MED) richiamo

boot [bu:t] n stivale m; (for hiking) scarpone m da montagna; (for football etc) scarpa; (BRIT: of car) portabagagli m inv ♦ vt (COMPUT) inizializzare; **to** ~ (in addition) per giunta, in più

booth [bu:ð] n cabina; (at fair) baraccone m

booty ['bu:tɪ] n bottino

booze [bu:z] (inf) n alcool m

border ['bɔ:də*] n orlo; margine m; (of a country) frontiera; (for flowers) aiuola (laterale) ♦ vt (road) costeggiare; (another country: also: ~ **on**) confinare con; **the B~s** la zona di confine tra l'Inghilterra e la Scozia; ~ **on** vt fus (fig: insanity etc) sfiorare; ~**line** n (fig): **on the** ~**line** incerto(a); ~**line case** n caso incerto

bore [bɔ:*] pt of **bear** ♦ vt (hole etc)

scavare; (person) annoiare ♦ n (person) seccatore/trice; (of gun) calibro; **to be** ~**d** annoiarsi; ~**dom** n noia; **boring** adj noioso(a)

born [bɔ:n] adj: **to be** ~ nascere; **I was** ~ **in 1960** sono nato nel 1960

borne [bɔ:n] pp of **bear**

borough ['bʌrə] n comune m

borrow ['bɔrəʊ] vt: **to** ~ **sth (from sb)** prendere in prestito qc (da qn)

Bosnia-(Herzegovina) ['bɔznɪə(hɜːzə'gəʊviːnə)] n Bosnia-Erzegovina

Bosnian ['bɔznɪən] n, adj bosniaco(a) m/f

boss [bɔs] n capo ♦ vt comandare; ~**y** adj prepotente

bosun ['bəʊsn] n nostromo

botany ['bɔtənɪ] n botanica

botch [bɔtʃ] vt (also: ~ **up**) fare un pasticcio di

both [bəʊθ] adj entrambi(e), tutt'e due ♦ pron: ~ **(of them)** entrambi(e); ~ **of us went, we** ~ **went** ci siamo andati tutt'e due ♦ adv: **they sell** ~ **meat and poultry** vendono insieme la carne ed il pollame

bother ['bɔðə*] vt (worry) preoccupare; (annoy) infastidire ♦ vi (also: ~ **o.s.**) preoccuparsi ♦ n: **it is a** ~ **to have to do** è una seccatura dover fare; **it's no** ~ non c'è problema; **to** ~ **doing sth** darsi la pena di fare qc

bottle ['bɔtl] n bottiglia; (baby's) biberon m inv ♦ vt imbottigliare; ~ **up** vt contenere; ~ **bank** n contenitore m per la raccolta del vetro; ~**neck** n imbottigliamento; ~-**opener** n apribottiglie m inv

bottom ['bɔtəm] n fondo; (buttocks) sedere m ♦ adj più basso(a); ultimo(a); **at the** ~ **of** in fondo a

bough [baʊ] n ramo

bought [bɔ:t] pt, pp of **buy**

boulder ['bəʊldə*] n masso (tondeggiante)

bounce [baʊns] vi (ball) rimbalzare;

bound
337
brand

(*cheque*) essere restituito(a) ♦ *vt* far rimbalzare ♦ *n* (*rebound*) rimbalzo; **~r** (*inf*) *n* buttafuori *m inv*

bound [baʊnd] *pt, pp* of **bind** ♦ *n* (*gen pl*) limite *m*; (*leap*) salto ♦ *vi* saltare ♦ *vt* (*limit*) delimitare ♦ *adj*: **~ by law** obbligato(a) per legge; **to be ~ to do sth** (*obliged*) essere costretto(a) a fare qc; **he's ~ to fail** (*likely*) è destinato di certo; **~ for** diretto(a) a; **out of ~s** il cui accesso è vietato

boundary ['baʊndrɪ] *n* confine *m*

boundless ['baʊndlɪs] *adj* senza limiti

bourgeois ['bʊəʒwɑ:] *adj* borghese

bout [baʊt] *n* periodo; (*of malaria etc*) attacco; (*BOXING etc*) incontro

bow¹ [baʊ] *n* nodo; (*weapon*) arco; (*MUS*) archetto

bow² [baʊ] *n* (*with body*) inchino; (*NAUT: also*: **~s**) prua ♦ *vi* inchinarsi; (*yield*): **to ~ to** or **before** sottomettersi a

bowels ['baʊəlz] *npl* intestini *mpl*; (*fig*) viscere *fpl*

bowl [baʊl] *n* (*for eating*) scodella; (*for washing*) bacino; (*ball*) boccia ♦ *vi* (*CRICKET*) servire (la palla)

bow-legged ['baʊ'legɪd] *adj* dalle gambe storte

bowler ['baʊlə*] *n* (*CRICKET, BASEBALL*) lanciatore *m*; (*BRIT: also*: **~ hat**) bombetta

bowling ['baʊlɪŋ] *n* (*game*) gioco delle bocce; **~ alley** *n* pista da bowling; **~ green** *n* campo di bocce

bowls [baʊlz] *n* gioco delle bocce

bow tie *n* cravatta a farfalla

box [bɒks] *n* scatola; (*also*: *cardboard* **~**) cartone *m*; (*THEATRE*) palco ♦ *vt* inscatolare ♦ *vi* fare del pugilato; **~er** *n* (*person*) pugile *m*; **~ing** *n* (*SPORT*) pugilato; **B~ing Day** (*BRIT*) *n* ≈ Santo Stefano; **~ing gloves** *npl* guantoni *mpl* da pugile; **~ing ring** *n* ring *m inv*; **~ office** *n* biglietteria; **~ room** *n* ripostiglio

boy [bɔɪ] *n* ragazzo

boycott ['bɔɪkɒt] *n* boicottaggio ♦ *vt* boicottare

boyfriend ['bɔɪfrɛnd] *n* ragazzo

boyish ['bɔɪʃ] *adj* da ragazzo

B.R. *abbr* (*formerly*) = **British Rail**

bra [brɑ:] *n* reggipetto, reggiseno

brace [breɪs] *n* (*on teeth*) apparecchio correttore; (*tool*) trapano ♦ *vt* rinforzare, sostenere; **~s** (*BRIT*) *npl* (*DRESS*) bretelle *fpl*; **to ~ o.s.** (*also fig*) tenersi forte

bracelet ['breɪslɪt] *n* braccialetto

bracing ['breɪsɪŋ] *adj* invigorante

bracken ['brækən] *n* felce *f*

bracket ['brækɪt] *n* (*TECH*) mensola; (*group*) gruppo; (*TYP*) parentesi *f inv* ♦ *vt* mettere fra parentesi

brag [bræg] *vi* vantarsi

braid [breɪd] *n* (*trimming*) passamano; (*of hair*) treccia

brain [breɪn] *n* cervello; **~s** *npl* (*intelligence*) cervella *fpl*; **he's got ~s** è intelligente; **~wash** *vt* fare un lavaggio di cervello a; **~wave** *n* lampo di genio; **~y** *adj* intelligente

braise [breɪz] *vt* brasare

brake [breɪk] *n* (*on vehicle*) freno ♦ *vi* frenare; **~ fluid** *n* liquido dei freni; **~ light** *n* (*fanalino dello*) stop *m inv*

bramble ['bræmbl] *n* rovo

bran [bræn] *n* crusca

branch [brɑ:ntʃ] *n* ramo; (*COMM*) succursale *f*; **~ out** *vi* (*fig*) intraprendere una nuova attività

brand [brænd] *n* (*also*: **~** *name*) marca; (*fig*) tipo ♦ *vt* (*cattle*) marcare (a ferro rovente)

brand-new adj nuovo(a) di zecca

brandy ['brændı] n brandy m inv

brash [bræʃ] adj sfacciato(a)

brass [brɑːs] n ottone m; **the ~** (MUS) gli ottoni; **~ band** n fanfara

brat [bræt] (pej) n marmocchio, monello/a

bravado [brə'vɑːdəu] n spavalderia

brave [breɪv] adj coraggioso(a) ♦ vt affrontare; **~ry** n coraggio

brawl [brɔːl] n rissa

brawny ['brɔːnı] adj muscoloso(a)

bray [breɪ] vi ragliare

brazen ['breɪzn] adj sfacciato(a) ♦ vt: **to ~ it out** fare lo sfacciato

brazier ['breɪzɪə*] n braciere m

Brazil [brə'zıl] n Brasile m

breach [briːtʃ] vt aprire una breccia in ♦ n (gap) breccia, varco; (breaking): **~ of contract** rottura di contratto; **~ of the peace** violazione f dell'ordine pubblico

bread [brɛd] n pane m; **~ and butter** n pane e burro; (fig) mezzi mpl di sussistenza; **~bin** n cassetta f portapane inv; **~crumbs** npl briciole fpl; (CULIN) pangrattato; **~line** n: **to be on the ~line** avere appena il denaro per vivere

breadth [brɛtθ] n larghezza; (fig: of knowledge etc) ampiezza

breadwinner ['brɛdwınə*] n chi guadagna il pane per tutta la famiglia

break [breɪk] (pt broke, pp broken) vt rompere; (law) violare; (record) battere ♦ vi rompersi; (storm) scoppiare; (weather) cambiare; (dawn) spuntare; (news) saltare fuori ♦ n (gap) breccia; (fracture) rottura; (rest, also SCOL) intervallo; (: short) pausa; (chance) possibilità f inv; **to ~ one's leg** etc rompersi la gamba etc; **to ~ the news to sb** comunicare per primo la notizia a qn; **to ~ even** coprire le spese; **to ~ free or loose** spezzare i legami; **to ~ open** (door etc) sfondare; **~ down**

vt (figures, data) analizzare ♦ vi (person) avere un esaurimento (nervoso); (AUT) guastarsi; **~ in** vt (horse etc) domare ♦ vi (burglar) fare irruzione; (interrupt) interrompere; **~ into** vt fus (house) fare irruzione in; **~ off** vi (speaker) interrompersi; (branch) troncarsi; **~ out** vi evadere; (war, fight) scoppiare; **to ~ out in spots** coprirsi di macchie; **~ up** vi (ship) sfondarsi; (meeting) sciogliersi; (crowd) disperdersi; (marriage) andare a pezzi; (SCOL) chiudere ♦ vt fare a pezzi, spaccare; (fight etc) interrompere, far cessare; **~age** n rottura; (object broken) cosa rotta; **~down** n (AUT) guasto; (in communications) interruzione f; (of marriage) rottura; (MED: also: nervous ~down) esaurimento nervoso; (of statistics) resoconto; **~down van** (BRIT) n carro m attrezzi inv; **~er** n frangente m

breakfast ['brɛkfəst] n colazione f

break: **~-in** n irruzione f; **~ing and entering** n (LAW) violazione f di domicilio con scasso; **~through** n (fig) passo avanti; **~water** n frangiflutti m inv

breast [brɛst] n (of woman) seno; (chest, CULIN) petto; **~-feed** (irreg: like feed) vt, vi allattare (al seno); **~-stroke** n nuoto a rana

breath [brɛθ] n respiro; **out of ~** senza fiato

Breathalyser ® ['brɛθəlaɪzə*] (BRIT) n alcoltest m inv

breathe [briːð] vt, vi respirare; **~ in** vt, vi inspirare ♦ vi (weather) cambiare; **~ out** vt, vi espirare; **~r** n attimo di respiro; **breathing** n respiro, respirazione f

breathless ['brɛθlıs] adj senza fiato

breathtaking ['brɛθteɪkıŋ] adj mozzafiato inv

bred [brɛd] pt, pp of **breed**

breed [briːd] (pt, pp bred) vt allevare ♦ vi riprodursi ♦ n razza; (type, class) varietà f inv; **~ing** n riproduzione f;

allevamento; (*upbringing*) educazione f

breeze [bri:z] *n* brezza

breezy ['bri:zɪ] *adj* allegro(a); ventilato(a)

brew [bru:] *vt* (*tea*) fare un infuso di; (*beer*) fare ♦ *vi* (*storm, fig: trouble etc*) prepararsi; **~ery** *n* fabbrica di birra

bribe [braɪb] *n* bustarella ♦ *vt* comprare; **~ry** *n* corruzione f

brick [brɪk] *n* mattone m; **~layer** *n* muratore m

bridal ['braɪdl] *adj* nuziale

bride [braɪd] *n* sposa; **~groom** *n* sposo; **~smaid** *n* damigella d'onore

bridge [brɪdʒ] *n* ponte m; (*NAUT*) ponte di comando; (*of nose*) dorso; (*CARDS*) bridge *m inv* ♦ *vt* (*fig: gap*) colmare

bridle ['braɪdl] *n* briglia; **~ path** *n* sentiero (per cavalli)

brief [bri:f] *adj* breve ♦ *n* (*LAW*) comparsa; (*gen*) istruzioni *fpl* ♦ *vt* mettere al corrente; **~s** *npl* (*underwear*) mutande *fpl*; **~case** *n* cartella; **~ing** *n* briefing *m inv*; **~ly** *adv* (*glance*) di sfuggita; (*explain, say*) brevemente

bright [braɪt] *adj* luminoso(a); (*clever*) sveglio(a); (*lively*) vivace; **~en** (*also: ~en up*) *vt* (*room*) rendere luminoso(a) ♦ *vi* schiarirsi; (*person*) rallegrarsi

brilliance ['brɪljəns] *n* splendore m

brilliant ['brɪljənt] *adj* brillante; (*light, smile*) radioso(a); (*inf*) splendido(a)

brim [brɪm] *n* orlo

brine [braɪn] *n* (*CULIN*) salamoia

bring [brɪŋ] (*pt, pp* **brought**) *vt* portare; **~ about** *vt* causare; **~ back** *vt* riportare; **~ down** *vt* portare giù; abbattere; **~ forward** *vt* (*proposal*) avanzare; (*meeting*) anticipare; **~ off** *vt* (*task, plan*) portare a compimento; **~ out** *vt* tirar fuori; (*meaning*) mettere in evidenza; (*book, album*) far uscire; **~ round** *vt* (*unconscious person*) far rinvenire; **~ up** *vt* (*carry up*) portare su; (*child*) allevare; (*question*) introdurre; (*food: vomit*) rimettere, rigurgitare

brink [brɪŋk] *n* orlo

brisk [brɪsk] *adj* (*manner*) spiccio(a); (*trade*) vivace; (*pace*) svelto(a)

bristle ['brɪsl] *n* setola ♦ *vi* rizzarsi; **bristling with** irto(a) di

Britain ['brɪtən] *n* (*also: Great ~*) Gran Bretagna

British ['brɪtɪʃ] *adj* britannico(a); **the ~** *npl* i Britannici; **the ~ Isles** *npl* le Isole Britanniche; **~ Rail** *n* compagnia ferroviaria britannica, ≈ Ferrovie *fpl* dello Stato

Briton ['brɪtən] *n* britannico/a

brittle ['brɪtl] *adj* fragile

broach [brəʊtʃ] *vt* (*subject*) affrontare

broad [brɔ:d] *adj* largo(a); (*distinction*) generale; (*accent*) spiccato(a); in **~ daylight** in pieno giorno; **~cast** (*pt, pp* **~cast**) *n* trasmissione f ♦ *vt* trasmettere per radio (*or* per televisione) ♦ *vi* fare una trasmissione; **~en** *vt* allargare ♦ *vi* allargarsi; **~ly** *adv* (*fig*) in generale; **~-minded** *adj* di mente aperta

broccoli ['brɒkəlɪ] *n* broccoli *mpl*

brochure ['brəʊʃjʊə*] *n* dépliant *m inv*

broil [brɔɪl] *vt* cuocere a fuoco vivo

broke [brəʊk] *pt of* **break** ♦ *adj* (*inf*) squattrinato(a)

broken ['brəʊkn] *pp of* **break** ♦ *adj* rotto(a); **a ~ leg** una gamba rotta; in **~ English** in un inglese stentato; **~-hearted** *adj*: **to be ~-hearted** avere il cuore spezzato

broker ['brəʊkə*] *n* agente m

brolly ['brɒlɪ] (*BRIT: inf*) *n* ombrello

bronchitis [brɒŋ'kaɪtɪs] *n* bronchite f

bronze [brɒnz] *n* bronzo

brooch [brəʊtʃ] *n* spilla

brood [bru:d] *n* covata ♦ *vi* (*person*) rimuginare

brook [brʊk] *n* ruscello

broom [brʊm] *n* scopa; (*BOT*) ginestra

Bros. *abbr* (= *Brothers*) F.lli

broth [brɔθ] *n* brodo

brothel ['brɒθl] *n* bordello

brother ['brʌðə*] *n* fratello; **~-in-law** *n* cognato

brought [brɔːt] pt, pp of **bring**

brow [brau] n fronte f; (rare, gen: eye~) sopracciglio; (of hill) cima

brown [braun] adj bruno(a), marrone; (tanned) abbronzato(a) ♦ n (colour) color m bruno or marrone ♦ vt (CULIN) rosolare; (of meat) rosolarsi; **~ bread** n pane m integrale, pane nero

Brownie ['brauni] n giovane esploratrice f; **b~** (US: cake) dolce al cioccolato e nocciole

brown paper n carta da pacchi or da imballaggio

brown sugar n zucchero greggio

browse [brauz] vi (among books) curiosare fra i libri; **to ~ through a book** sfogliare un libro; **~r** n (COMPUT) browser m inv

bruise [bruːz] n (on person) livido ♦ vt farsi un livido a

brunette [bruːˈnɛt] n bruna

brunt [brʌnt] n: **the ~ of** (attack, criticism etc) il peso maggiore di

brush [brʌʃ] n spazzola; (for painting, shaving) pennello; (quarrel) schermaglia ♦ vt spazzolare; (also: ~ against) sfiorare; **~ aside** vt scostare; **~ up** vt (knowledge) rinfrescare; **~wood** n macchia

Brussels ['brʌslz] n Bruxelles f; **~ sprout** n cavolo di Bruxelles

brutal ['bruːtl] adj brutale

brute [bruːt] n bestia ♦ adj: **by ~ force** con la forza, a viva forza

B.Sc. n abbr (UNIV) **= Bachelor of Science**

BSE n abbr (= bovine spongiform encephalopathy) encefalite f bovina spongiforme

bubble ['bʌbl] n bolla ♦ vi ribollire; (sparkle, fig) essere effervescente; **~ bath** n bagnoschiuma m inv; **~ gum** n gomma americana

buck [bʌk] n maschio (di camoscio, caprone, coniglio etc); (US: inf) dollaro ♦ vi sgropparsi; **to pass the ~ (to sb)** scaricare (su di qn) la propria

responsabilità; **~ up** vi (cheer up) rianimarsi

bucket ['bʌkɪt] n secchio

Buckingham Palace

Buckingham Palace è la residenza ufficiale a Londra del sovrano britannico. Fu costruita nel 1703 per il duca di Buckingham.

---

buckle ['bʌkl] n fibbia ♦ vt allacciare ♦ vi (wheel etc) piegarsi

bud [bʌd] n gemma; (of flower) bocciolo ♦ vi germogliare; (flower) sbocciare

Buddhism ['budɪzəm] n buddismo

budding ['bʌdɪŋ] adj (poet etc) in erba

buddy ['bʌdɪ] (US) n compagno

budge [bʌdʒ] vt scostare; (fig) smuovere ♦ vi spostarsi; smuoversi

budgerigar ['bʌdʒərɪgɑːʳ] n pappagallino

budget ['bʌdʒɪt] n bilancio preventivo ♦ vi: **to ~ for sth** fare il bilancio per qc

budgie ['bʌdʒɪ] n **= budgerigar**

buff [bʌf] adj color camoscio ♦ n (inf: enthusiast) appassionato/a

buffalo ['bʌfələu] (pl ~ or ~es) n bufalo; (US) bisonte m

buffer ['bʌfəʳ] n respingente m; (COMPUT) memoria tampone, buffer m inv

buffet[1] ['bufei] n (food, BRIT: bar) buffet m inv; **~ car** (BRIT) n (RAIL) ≈ servizio ristoro

buffet[2] ['bʌfit] vt sferzare

bug [bʌg] n (esp US: insect) insetto; (COMPUT, fig: germ) virus m inv; (spy device) microfono spia ♦ vt mettere sotto controllo; (inf: annoy) scocciare

buggy ['bʌgɪ] n (baby ~) passeggino

bugle ['bjuːgl] n tromba

build [bɪld] (pt, pp **built**) n (of person) corporatura ♦ vt costruire; **~ up** vt accumulare; aumentare; **~er** n costruttore m; **~ing** n costruzione f; edificio; (industry) edilizia; **~ing**

society (BRIT) n società f inv
immobiliare

built [bɪlt] pt, pp of **build** ♦ adj: **~-in**
(cupboard, oven) n device
incorporato(a); **~-up area** n abitato

bulb [bʌlb] n (BOT) bulbo; (ELEC)
lampadina

bulge [bʌldʒ] n rigonfiamento ♦ vi
essere protuberante or rigonfio(a); **to
be bulging with** essere pieno(a) or
zeppo(a) di

bulk [bʌlk] n massa, volume m; **in ~ a**
pacchi (or cassette etc); (COMM)
all'ingrosso; **the ~ of** il grosso di; **~y**
adj grosso(a); voluminoso(a)

bull [bul] n toro; (male elephant, whale)
maschio; **~dog** n bulldog m inv

bulldozer ['buldəʊzə*] n bulldozer m
inv

bullet [bulɪt] n pallottola

bulletin ['bulɪtɪn] n bollettino

bulletproof ['bulɪtpru:f] adj (car)
blindato(a); (vest etc) antiproiettile inv

bullfight ['bulfaɪt] n corrida; **~er** n
torero; **~ing** n tauromachia

bullion ['buljən] n oro or argento in
lingotti

bullock ['bulək] n manzo

bullring ['bulrɪŋ] n arena (per corride)

bull's-eye ['bulzaɪ] n centro del
bersaglio

bully ['bulɪ] n prepotente m ♦ vt
angariare; (frighten) intimidire

bum [bʌm] (inf) n (backside) culo;
(tramp) vagabondo/a

bumblebee ['bʌmblbi:] n bombo

bump [bʌmp] n (in car) piccolo
tamponamento; (jolt) scossa; (on road
etc) protuberanza; (on head)
bernoccolo ♦ vt battere; **~ into** vt fus
scontrarsi con; (person) imbattersi in;
~er n paraurti m inv ♦ adj: **~er
harvest** raccolto eccezionale; **~er
cars** npl autoscontri mpl

bumpy ['bʌmpɪ] adj (road)
dissestato(a)

bun [bʌn] n focaccia; (of hair) crocchia

bunch [bʌntʃ] n (of flowers, keys)
mazzo; (of bananas) casco; (of people)
gruppo; **~ of grapes** grappolo d'uva;
~es npl (in hair) codine fpl

bundle ['bʌndl] n fascio ♦ vt (also:
~ up) legare in un fascio; (put): **to
~ sth/sb into** spingere qc/qn in

bungalow ['bʌŋgələʊ] n bungalow m
inv

bungle ['bʌŋgl] vt fare un pasticcio di

bunion ['bʌnjən] n callo (al piede)

bunk [bʌŋk] n cuccetta; **~ beds** npl
letti mpl a castello

bunker ['bʌŋkə*] n (coal store)
ripostiglio per il carbone; (MIL, GOLF)
bunker m inv

bunny ['bʌnɪ] n (also: **~ rabbit**)
coniglietto

bunting ['bʌntɪŋ] n pavesi mpl,
bandierine fpl

buoy [bɔɪ] n boa; **~ant** adj
galleggiante; (fig) vivace

burden ['bə:dn] n carico, fardello ♦ vt:
to ~ sb with caricare qn di

bureau [bjuə'rəu] (pl **bureaux**) n (BRIT:
writing desk) scrivania; (US: chest of
drawers) cassettone m; (office) ufficio,
agenzia

bureaucracy [bjuə'rɔkrəsɪ] n
burocrazia

bureaux [bjuə'rəuz] npl of **bureau**

burglar ['bə:glə*] n scassinatore m;
~ alarm n campanello antifurto; **~y**
n furto con scasso

burial ['berɪəl] n sepoltura

burly ['bə:lɪ] adj robusto(a)

Burma ['bə:mə] n Birmania

burn [bə:n] (pt, pp **burned** or **burnt**)
vt, vi bruciare ♦ n bruciatura,
scottatura; **~ down** vt distruggere col
fuoco; **~er** n (on cooker) fornello; (TECH)
bruciatore m, becco a (gas); **~ing** adj
in fiamme; (sand) che scotta;
(ambition) bruciante; **burnt** pt, pp of
burn

burrow ['bʌrəu] n tana ♦ vt scavare

bursary ['bə:sərɪ] (BRIT) n (SCOL) borsa

di studio

burst [bə:st] (pt, pp burst) vt far
scoppiare ♦ vi esplodere; (tyre)
scoppiare ♦ n scoppio; (also: ~ pipe)
rottura nel tubo, perdita; **a ~ of
speed** uno scatto di velocità; **to
~ into flames/tears** scoppiare in
fiamme/lacrime; **to ~ out laughing**
scoppiare a ridere; **to be ~ing with**
scoppiare di; **~ into** vt fus (room etc)
irrompere in

bury ['bɛrɪ] vt seppellire

bus [bʌs] (pl ~es) n autobus m inv

bush [buʃ] n cespuglio; (scrub land)
macchia; **to beat about the ~**
menare il cane per l'aia

bushy ['buʃɪ] adj cespuglioso(a)

busily ['bɪzɪlɪ] adv con impegno,
alacremente

business ['bɪznɪs] n (matter) affare m;
(trading) affari mpl; (firm) azienda; (job,
duty) lavoro; **to be away on ~** essere
andato via per affari; **it's none of my
~** questo non mi riguarda; **he means
~** non scherza; **~like** adj serio(a);
efficiente; **~man/woman** (irreg) n
uomo/donna d'affari; **~ trip** n viaggio
d'affari

busker ['bʌskə*] (BRIT) n suonatore/
trice ambulante

bus: ~ shelter n pensilina (alla fermata
dell'autobus); **~ station** n stazione f
delle corriere, autostazione f; **~-stop** n
fermata d'autobus

bust [bʌst] n busto; (ANAT) seno ♦ adj
(inf: broken) rotto(a); **to go ~** fallire

bustle ['bʌsl] n movimento, attività
♦ vi darsi da fare; **bustling** adj
movimentato(a)

busy ['bɪzɪ] adj occupato(a); (shop,
street) molto frequentato(a) ♦ vt: **to
~ o.s.** darsi da fare; **~body** n ficcanaso
m/f inv; **~ signal** (US) n (TEL) segnale m
di occupato

but [bʌt] conj ma; **I'd love to come,**

~ I'm busy vorrei tanto venire, ma ho
da fare
♦ prep (apart from, except) eccetto,
tranne, meno; **he was nothing
~ trouble** non dava altro che guai;
no-one ~ him can do it nessuno può
farlo tranne lui; **~ for you/your help**
se non fosse per te/per il tuo aiuto;
anything ~ that tutto ma non questo
♦ adv (just, only) solo, soltanto; **she's
~ a child** è solo una bambina; **had I
~ known** se solo avessi saputo; **I can
~ try** tentar non nuoce; **all ~ finished**
quasi finito

butcher ['butʃə*] n macellaio ♦ vt
macellare; **~'s (shop)** n macelleria

butler ['bʌtlə*] n maggiordomo

butt [bʌt] n (cask) grossa botte f; (of
gun) calcio; (of cigarette) mozzicone m;
(BRIT: fig: target) oggetto ♦ vt cozzare;
~ in vi (interrupt) interrompere

butter ['bʌtə*] n burro ♦ vt imburrare;
~cup n ranuncolo

butterfly ['bʌtəflaɪ] n farfalla;
(SWIMMING: also: ~ stroke) (nuoto a)
farfalla

buttocks ['bʌtəks] npl natiche fpl

button ['bʌtn] n bottone m; (us:
badge) distintivo ♦ vt (also: ~ up)
abbottonare ♦ vi abbottonarsi

buttress ['bʌtrɪs] n contrafforte f

buy [baɪ] (pt, pp bought) vt comprare
♦ n acquisto; **to ~ sb sth/sth from
sb** comprare qc per qn/qc da qn; **to
~ sb a drink** offrire da bere a qn; **~er**
n compratore/trice

buzz [bʌz] n ronzio; (inf: phone call)
colpo di telefono ♦ vi ronzare

buzzer ['bʌzə*] n cicalino

buzz word (inf) n termine m di gran
moda

by [baɪ] prep **1** (referring to cause,
agent) da; **killed ~ lightning** ucciso
da un fulmine; **surrounded ~ a fence**

circondato da uno steccato; **a ~ painting** ~ Picasso un quadro di Picasso

2 (*referring to method, manner, means*): **~ bus/car/train** in autobus/macchina/treno, con l'autobus/la macchina/il treno; **to pay ~ cheque** pagare con (un) assegno; **~ moonlight** al chiaro di luna; **~ saving hard, he …** risparmiando molto, lui …

3 (*via, through*) per; **we came ~ Dover** siamo venuti via Dover

4 (*close to, past*) accanto a; **the house ~ the river** la casa sul fiume; **a holiday ~ the sea** una vacanza al mare; **she sat ~ his bed** si sedette accanto al suo letto; **she rushed ~ me** mi è passata accanto correndo; **I go ~ the post office every day** passo davanti all'ufficio postale ogni giorno

5 (*not later than*) per, entro; **~ 4 o'clock** per or entro le 4; **~ this time tomorrow** domani a quest'ora; **~ the time I got here it was too late** quando sono arrivato era ormai troppo tardi

6 (*during*): **~ day/night** di giorno/notte

7 (*amount*) a; **~ the kilo/metre** a chili/metri; **paid ~ the hour** pagato all'ora; **one ~ one** uno per uno; **little ~ little** a poco a poco

8 (*MATH, measure*): **to divide/multiply ~ 3** dividere/moltiplicare per 3; **it's broader ~ a metre** è un metro più largo, è più largo di un metro

9 (*according to*) per; **to play ~ the rules** attenersi alle regole; **it's all right ~ me** per me va bene

10: **(all) ~ oneself** *etc* (tutto(a)) solo(a); **he did it (all) ~ himself** lo ha fatto (tutto) da solo

11: **~ the way** a proposito, **this wasn't my idea ~ the way** tra l'altro l'idea non è stata mia

♦ *adv* **1** *see* **go**; **pass** *etc*

2: **~ and ~** (*in past*) poco dopo; (*in future*) fra breve; **~ and large** nel complesso

bye(-bye) ['baɪ('baɪ)] *excl* ciao!, arrivederci!

by(e)-law *n* legge *f* locale

by-election (*BRIT*) *n* elezione *f* straordinaria

bygone ['baɪɡɒn] *adj* passato(a) ♦ *n*: **let ~ be ~s** mettiamoci una pietra sopra

bypass ['baɪpɑːs] *n* circonvallazione *f*; (*MED*) by-pass *m inv* ♦ *vt* fare una deviazione intorno a

by-product *n* sottoprodotto; (*fig*) conseguenza secondaria

bystander ['baɪstændə*] *n* spettatore/trice

byte [baɪt] *n* (*COMPUT*) byte *m inv*, bicarattere *m*

byword ['baɪwɜːd] *n*: **to be a ~ for** essere sinonimo di

C, c

C [siː] *n* (*MUS*) do

C. *abbr* (= *centigrade*) C.

C.A. *n abbr* = **chartered accountant**

cab [kæb] *n* taxi *m inv*; (*of train, truck*) cabina

cabaret ['kæbəreɪ] *n* cabaret *m inv*

cabbage ['kæbɪdʒ] *n* cavolo

cabin ['kæbɪn] *n* capanna; (*on ship*) cabina; **~ crew** *n* equipaggio; **~ cruiser** *n* cabinato

cabinet ['kæbɪnɪt] *n* (*POL*) consiglio dei ministri; (*furniture*) armadietto; (*also:* **display ~**) vetrinetta

cable ['keɪbl] *n* cavo; fune *f*; (*TEL*) cablogramma *m* ♦ *vt* telegrafare; **~-car** *n* funivia; **~ television** *n* televisione *f* via cavo

cache [kæʃ] *n* deposito segreto

cackle ['kækl] *vi* schiamazzare

cactus ['kæktəs] (pl **cacti**) n cactus m inv

cadet [kə'dɛt] n (MIL) cadetto

cadge [kædʒ] (inf) vt scroccare

café ['kæfeɪ] n caffè m inv

cafeteria [kæfɪ'tɪərɪə] n self-service m inv

cage [keɪdʒ] n gabbia

cagey ['keɪdʒɪ] (inf) adj chiuso(a); guardingo(a)

cagoule [kə'guːl] n K-way ® m inv

cajole [kə'dʒəʊl] vt allettare

cake [keɪk] n (large) torta; (small) pasticcino; **~ of soap** saponetta; **~d** adj: **~d with** incrostato(a) di

calculate ['kælkjʊleɪt] vt calcolare; **calculation** [-'leɪʃən] n calcolo; **calculator** n calcolatrice f

calendar ['kæləndə*] n calendario; **~ year** n anno civile

calf [kɑːf] (pl **calves**) n (of cow) vitello; (of other animals) piccolo; (also: **~skin**) (pelle f di) vitello; (ANAT) polpaccio

calibre ['kælɪbə*] (US **caliber**) n calibro

call [kɔːl] vt (gen, also TEL) chiamare; (meeting) indire ♦ vi chiamare; (visit: also: **~ in, ~ round**) passare ♦ n (shout) grido, urlo; (TEL) telefonata; **to be ~ed** (person, object) chiamarsi; **to be on ~** essere a disposizione; **~ back** vi (return) ritornare; (TEL) ritelefonare, richiamare; **~ for** vt fus richiedere; (fetch) passare a prendere; **~ off** vt disdire; **~ on** vt fus (visit) passare da; (appeal to) chiedere a; **~ out** vi (in pain) urlare; (to person) chiamare; **~ up** vt (MIL) richiamare; (TEL) telefonare a; **~box** (BRIT) n cabina telefonica; **~ centre** n centro informazioni telefoniche; **~er** n persona che chiama; visitatore/trice; **~ girl** n ragazza f squillo inv; **~-in** (US) n (phone-in) trasmissione f a filo diretto con gli ascoltatori; **~ing** n vocazione f; **~ing card** (US) n biglietto da visita

callous ['kæləs] adj indurito(a), insensibile

calm [kɑːm] adj calmo(a) ♦ n calma ♦ vt calmare; **~ down** vi calmarsi ♦ vt calmare

Calor gas ® ['kælə*-] n butano

calorie ['kælərɪ] n caloria

calves [kɑːvz] npl of **calf**

Cambodia [kæm'bəʊdɪə] n Cambogia

camcorder ['kæmkɔːdə*] n camcorder f inv

came [keɪm] pt of **come**

camel ['kæməl] n cammello

camera ['kæmərə] n macchina fotografica; (CINEMA, TV) cinepresa; **in ~** a porte chiuse; **~man** (irreg) n cameraman m inv

camouflage ['kæməflɑːʒ] n (MIL, ZOOL) mimetizzazione f ♦ vt mimetizzare

camp [kæmp] n campeggio; (MIL) campo ♦ vi accamparsi ♦ adj effeminato(a)

campaign [kæm'peɪn] n (MIL, POL etc) campagna ♦ vi (also fig) fare una campagna

camp bed (BRIT) n brandina

camper ['kæmpə*] n campeggiatore/ trice; (vehicle) camper m inv

camping ['kæmpɪŋ] n campeggio; **to go ~** andare in campeggio

campsite ['kæmpsaɪt] n campeggio

campus ['kæmpəs] n campus m inv

can¹ [kæn] n (of milk) scatola; (of oil) bidone m; (of water) tanica; (tin) scatola ♦ vt mettere in scatola

---

KEYWORD

---

can² [kæn] (negative **cannot**, **can't**; conditional and pt **could**) aux vb 1 (be able to) potere; **I ~'t go any further** non posso andare oltre; **you ~ do it if you try** sei in grado di farlo — basta provarci; **I'll help you all I ~** ti aiuterò come potrò; **I ~'t see you** non ti vedo 2 (know how to) sapere, essere capace di; **I ~ swim** so nuotare; **~ you speak French?** parla francese? 3 (may) potere; **could I have a word with you?** posso parlarle un momento? 4 (expressing disbelief, puzzlement etc):

it ~'t be true! non può essere vero!; what CAN he want? cosa può mai volere?

5 (expressing possibility, suggestion etc): **he could be in the library** può darsi che sia in biblioteca; **she could have been delayed** può aver avuto un contrattempo

Canada ['kænədə] n Canada m
Canadian [kə'neɪdɪən] adj, n canadese m/f
canal [kə'næl] n canale m
canary [kə'nɛərɪ] n canarino
cancel ['kænsəl] vt annullare; (train) sopprimere; (cross out) cancellare; **~lation** [-'leɪʃən] n annullamento; soppressione f; cancellazione f; (TOURISM) prenotazione f annullata
cancer ['kænsə*] n cancro; **C~** (sign) Cancro
candid ['kændɪd] adj onesto(a)
candidate ['kændɪdeɪt] n candidato/a
candle ['kændl] n candela; (in church) cero; **~light** n: **by ~light** a lume di candela; **~stick** n (also: **bigger, ornate**) candeliere m
candour ['kændə*] (US **candor**) n sincerità
candy ['kændɪ] n zucchero candito; (US) caramella; caramelle fpl; **~floss** (BRIT) n zucchero filato
cane [keɪn] n canna; (for furniture) bambù m; (stick) verga ♦ vt (BRIT: SCOL) punire a colpi di verga
canister ['kænɪstə*] n scatola metallica
cannabis ['kænəbɪs] n canapa indiana
canned ['kænd] adj (food) in scatola
cannon ['kænən] (pl ~ or ~s) n (gun) cannone m
cannot ['kænɒt] = **can not**
canny ['kænɪ] adj furbo(a)
canoe [kə'nuː] n canoa; **~ing** n canottaggio
canon ['kænən] n (clergyman) canonico; (standard) canone m
can opener [-'əʊpnə*] n apriscatole m

inv

canopy ['kænəpɪ] n baldacchino
cant [kænt] n gergo ♦ vt inclinare ♦ vi inclinarsi
can't [kænt] = **can not**
canteen [kæn'tiːn] n mensa; (BRIT: of cutlery) portaposate m inv
canter ['kæntə*] vi andare al piccolo galoppo
canvas ['kænvəs] n tela
canvass ['kænvəs] vi (POL): **to ~ for** raccogliere voti per ♦ vt fare un sondaggio di
cap [kæp] n (hat) berretto; (of pen) coperchio; (of bottle, toy gun) tappo; (contraceptive) diaframma m ♦ vt (out-do) superare; (limit) fissare un tetto (a)
capability [keɪpə'bɪlɪtɪ] n capacità f inv, abilità f inv
capable ['keɪpəbl] adj capace
capacity [kə'pæsɪtɪ] n capacità f inv; (of lift etc) capienza
cape [keɪp] n (garment) cappa; (GEO) capo
caper ['keɪpə*] n (CULIN) cappero; (prank) scherzetto
capital ['kæpɪtl] n (also: **~ city**) capitale f; (money) capitale m; (also: **~ letter**) (lettera) maiuscola; **~ gains tax** n imposta sulla plusvalenza; **~ism** n capitalismo; **~ist** adj, n capitalista (m/f); **~ize**: **to ~ize on** vt fus trarre vantaggio da; **~ punishment** n pena capitale
Capitol ['kæpɪtl] n: **the ~** il Campidoglio

Il *Capitol* è l'edificio dove si svolgono le riunioni del Congresso degli Stati Uniti. È situato sull'omonimo colle, Capitol Hill, a Washington D.C.

Capricorn ['kæprɪkɔːn] n Capricorno
capsize [kæp'saɪz] vt capovolgere ♦ vi capovolgersi

capsule ['kæpsju:l] n capsula

captain ['kæptɪn] n capitano

caption ['kæpʃən] n leggenda

captivate ['kæptɪveɪt] vt avvincere

captive ['kæptɪv] adj, n prigioniero(a)

captivity [kæp'tɪvɪtɪ] n cattività

capture ['kæptʃə*] vt catturare; (COMPUT) registrare ♦ n cattura; (data ~) registrazione f or rilevazione f di dati

car [ka:*] n (AUT) macchina, automobile f; (RAIL) vagone m

carafe [kə'ræf] n caraffa

caramel ['kærəməl] n caramello

caravan ['kærəvæn] n (BRIT) roulotte f inv; (of camels) carovana; **~ning** n vacanze fpl in roulotte; **~ site** (BRIT) n campeggio per roulotte

carbohydrates [ka:bəu'haɪdreɪts] npl (foods) carboidrati mpl

carbon ['ka:bən] n carbonio; **~ paper** n carta carbone

car boot sale n mercatino dell'usato dove la merce viene esposta nei bagagliai delle macchine

carburettor [ka:bju'retə*] (US **carburetor**) n carburatore m

card [ka:d] n carta; (visiting ~ etc) biglietto; (Christmas ~ etc) cartolina; **~board** n cartone m; **~ game** n gioco di carte

cardiac ['ka:dɪæk] adj cardiaco(a)

cardigan ['ka:dɪgən] n cardigan m inv

cardinal ['ka:dɪnl] adj cardinale ♦ n cardinale m

card index n schedario

cardphone ['ka:dfəun] n telefono a scheda

care [kɛə*] n cura, attenzione f; (worry) preoccupazione f ♦ vi: **to ~ about** curarsi di; (thing, idea) interessarsi di; **~ of** presso; **in sb's ~** alle cure di qn; **to take ~ (to do)** fare attenzione (a fare); **to take ~ of** curarsi di; (bill, problem) occuparsi di; **I don't ~** non me ne importa; **I couldn't ~ less** non m'interessa affatto; **~ for** vt fus aver cura di; (like) volere bene a

career [kə'rɪə*] n carriera ♦ vi (also: ~ along) andare di (gran) carriera

carefree ['kɛəfri:] adj sgombro(a) di preoccupazioni

careful ['kɛəful] adj attento(a); (cautious) cauto(a); **(be) ~!** attenzione!; **~ly** adv con cura, cautamente

careless ['kɛəlɪs] adj negligente; (heedless) spensierato(a)

carer ['kɛərə*] n assistente m/f (di persone malate o handicappate)

caress [kə'rɛs] n carezza ♦ vt accarezzare

caretaker ['kɛəteɪkə*] n custode m

car-ferry n traghetto

cargo ['ka:gəu] (pl **~es**) n carico

car hire n autonoleggio

Caribbean [kærɪ'bi:ən] adj: **the ~ (Sea)** il Mar dei Caraibi

caring ['kɛərɪŋ] adj (person) premuroso(a); (society, organization) umanitario(a)

carnage ['ka:nɪdʒ] n carneficina

carnation [ka:'neɪʃən] n garofano

carnival ['ka:nɪvəl] n (public celebration) carnevale m; (US: funfair) luna park m inv

carol ['kærəl] n: **(Christmas) ~** canto di Natale

carp [ka:p] n (fish) carpa

car park (BRIT) n parcheggio

carpenter ['ka:pɪntə*] n carpentiere m

carpentry ['ka:pɪntrɪ] n carpenteria

carpet ['ka:pɪt] n tappeto ♦ vt coprire con tappeto

car phone n telefonino per auto, cellulare m per auto

car rental (US) n autonoleggio

carriage ['kærɪdʒ] n vettura; (of goods) trasporto; **~way** (BRIT) n (part of road) carreggiata

carrier ['kærɪə*] n (of disease) portatore/trice; (COMM) impresa di trasporti; **~ bag** (BRIT) n sacchetto

carrot ['kærət] n carota

carry ['kærɪ] vt (subj: person) portare;

(: *vehicle*) trasportare; (*involve: responsibilities etc*) comportare; (MED) essere portatore/trice di ♦ *vi* (*sound*) farsi sentire; **to be** or **get carried away** (*fig*) entusiasmarsi; **~ on** *vi*: **to ~ on with sth/doing** continuare qc/a fare ♦ *vt* mandare avanti; **~ out** *vt* (*orders*) eseguire; (*investigation*) svolgere; **~cot** (BRIT) *n* culla portabile; **~-on** (*inf*) *n* (*fuss*) casino, confusione *f*

cart [kɑ:t] *n* carro ♦ *vt* (*inf*) trascinare

carton ['kɑ:tən] *n* (*box*) scatola di cartone; (*of yogurt*) cartone *m*; (*of cigarettes*) stecca

cartoon [kɑ:'tu:n] *n* (PRESS) disegno umoristico; (*comic strip*) fumetto; (CINEMA) disegno animato

cartridge ['kɑ:trɪdʒ] *n* (*for gun, pen*) cartuccia; (*music tape*) cassetta

carve [kɑ:v] *vt* (*meat*) trinciare; (*wood, stone*) intagliare; **~ up** *vt* (*fig: country*) suddividere; **carving** *n* (*in wood etc*) scultura; **carving knife** *n* trinciante *m*

car wash *n* lavaggio auto

cascade [kæs'keɪd] *n* cascata

case [keɪs] *n* caso; (LAW) causa, processo; (*box*) valigia; (BRIT: *also: suit~*) valigia; **in ~ of** in caso di; **in ~ he** caso mai lui; **in any ~** in ogni caso; **just in ~** in caso di bisogno

cash [kæʃ] *n* denaro; (*coins, notes*) denaro liquido ♦ *vt* incassare; **to pay (in) ~** pagare in contanti; **~ on delivery** pagamento alla consegna; **~book** *n* giornale *m* di cassa; **~ card** (BRIT) *n* tesserino di prelievo; **~ desk** (BRIT) *n* cassa; **~ dispenser** (BRIT) *n* sportello automatico

cashew [kæ'ʃu:] *n* (*also: ~ nut*) anacardio

cashier [kæ'ʃɪə*] *n* cassiere/a

cashmere ['kæʃmɪə*] *n* cachemire *m*

cash register *n* registratore *m* di cassa

casing ['keɪsɪŋ] *n* rivestimento

casino [kə'si:nəu] *n* casinò *m inv*

cask [kɑ:sk] *n* botte *f*

casket ['kɑ:skɪt] *n* cofanetto; (US:

coffin) bara

casserole ['kæsərəul] *n* casseruola; (*food*): **chicken ~** pollo in casseruola

cassette [kæ'set] *n* cassetta; **~ player** *n* riproduttore *m* a cassette; **~ recorder** *n* registratore *m* a cassette

cast [kɑ:st] (*pt, pp* **cast**) *vt* (*throw*) gettare; (*metal*) gettare, fondere; (THEATRE): **to ~ sb as Hamlet** scegliere qn per la parte di Amleto ♦ *n* (THEATRE) cast *m inv*; (*also: plaster ~*) ingessatura; **to ~ one's vote** votare, dare il voto; **~ off** *vi* (NAUT) salpare; (KNITTING) calare; **~ on** *vi* (KNITTING) avviare le maglie

castaway ['kɑ:stəwei] *n* naufrago/a

caster sugar ['kɑ:stə*-] (BRIT) *n* zucchero semolato

casting vote ['kɑ:stɪŋ-] (BRIT) *n* voto decisivo

cast iron *n* ghisa

castle ['kɑ:sl] *n* castello

castor oil ['kɑ:stə*-] *n* olio di ricino

casual ['kæʒjul] *adj* (*by chance*) casuale, fortuito(a); (*irregular: work etc*) avventizio(a); (*unconcerned*) noncurante, indifferente; **~ wear** casual *m*; **~ly** *adv* (*in a relaxed way*) con noncuranza; (*dress*) casual

casualty ['kæʒjultɪ] *n* ferito/a; (*dead*) morto/a, vittima; (MED: *department*) pronto soccorso

cat [kæt] *n* gatto

catalogue ['kætəlɔg] (US **catalog**) *n* catalogo ♦ *vt* catalogare

catalyst ['kætəlɪst] *n* catalizzatore *m*

catalytic convertor [kætəlɪtɪk-] *n* marmitta catalitica, catalizzatore *m*

catapult ['kætəpʌlt] *n* catapulta; fionda

cataract ['kætərækt] *n* (*also* MED) cateratta

catarrh [kə'tɑ:*] *n* catarro

catastrophe [kə'tæstrəfɪ] *n* catastrofe *f*

catch [kætʃ] (*pt, pp* **caught**) *vt* prendere; (*ball*) afferrare; (*surprise: person*) sorprendere; (*attention*) attirare (*comment, whisper*) cogliere; (*person: also: ~ up*) raggiungere ♦ *vi* (*fire*) prendere ♦ *n* (*fish etc caught*) retata; (*of ball*) presa; (*trick*) inganno; (*TECH*) gancio; (*game*) catch *m inv*; **to ~ fire** prendere fuoco; **to ~ sight of** scorgere; **to ~ on** *vi* capire; (*become popular*) affermarsi, far presa; **~ up** *vi* mettersi in pari ♦ *vt* (*also: ~ up with*) raggiungere

catching ['kætʃɪŋ] *adj* (*MED*) contagioso(a)

catchment area ['kætʃmənt-] (*BRIT*) *n* (*SCOL*) circoscrizione *f* scolare

catch phrase *n* slogan *m inv*; frase *f* fatta

catchy ['kætʃɪ] *adj* orecchiabile

category ['kætɪgərɪ] *n* categoria

cater ['keɪtə*] *vi*: **~ for** (*BRIT: needs*) provvedere a; (: *readers, consumers*) incontrare i gusti di; (*COMM: provide food*) provvedere alla ristorazione di; **~er** *n* fornitore *m*; **~ing** *n* approvvigionamento

caterpillar ['kætəpɪlə*] *n* bruco

cathedral [kə'θi:drəl] *n* cattedrale *f*, duomo

catholic ['kæθəlɪk] *adj* universale, aperto(a); eclettico(a); **C~** *adj*, *n* (*REL*) cattolico(a)

CAT scan *n* (= *computerized axial tomography*) TAC *f inv*

Catseye ® ['kæts'aɪ] (*BRIT*) *n* (*AUT*) catarifrangente *m*

cattle ['kætl] *npl* bestiame *m*, bestie *fpl*

catty ['kætɪ] *adj* maligno(a), dispettoso(a)

caucus ['kɔ:kəs] *n* (*POL: group*) comitato di dirigenti; (: *US*) (riunione *f* del) comitato elettorale

caught [kɔ:t] *pt, pp of* **catch**

cauliflower ['kɔlɪflauə*] *n* cavolfiore *m*

cause [kɔ:z] *n* causa ♦ *vt* causare

caution ['kɔ:ʃən] *n* prudenza; (*warning*) avvertimento ♦ *vt* avvertire; ammonire

cautious ['kɔ:ʃəs] *adj* cauto(a), prudente

cavalry ['kævəlrɪ] *n* cavalleria

cave [keɪv] *n* caverna, grotta; **~ in** *vi* (*roof etc*) crollare; **~man** (*irreg*) *n* uomo delle caverne

caviar(e) ['kævɪɑ:*] *n* caviale *m*

CB *n abbr* (= *Citizens' Band (Radio)*): **~ radio (set)** baracchino

CBI *n abbr* (= *Confederation of British Industries*) ≈ Confindustria

cc *abbr* = *cubic centimetres*; *carbon copy*

CCTV *n abbr* = *closed-circuit television* televisione *f* a circuito chiuso

CD *abbr* (*disc*) CD *m inv*; (*player*) lettore *m* CD *inv*

CDI *n abbr* (= *compact disk interactive*) CD-I *m inv*, compact disc *m inv* interattivo

CD player *n* lettore *m* CD

CD-ROM [-rɔm] *n abbr* CD-ROM *m inv*

cease [si:s] *vt, vi* cessare; **~fire** *n* cessate il fuoco *m inv*; **~less** *adj* incessante, continuo(a)

cedar ['si:də*] *n* cedro

ceiling ['si:lɪŋ] *n* soffitto; (*on wages etc*) tetto

celebrate ['sɛlɪbreɪt] *vt, vi* celebrare; **~d** *adj* celebre; **celebration** [-'breɪʃən] *n* celebrazione *f*

celery ['sɛlərɪ] *n* sedano

cell [sɛl] *n* cella; (*of revolutionaries, BIOL*) cellula; (*ELEC*) elemento (di batteria)

cellar ['sɛlə*] *n* sottosuolo; cantina

'cello ['tʃɛləu] *n* violoncello

cellphone [sɛl,fəun] *n* cellulare *m*

Celt [kɛlt, sɛlt] *n* celta *m/f*

Celtic ['kɛltɪk, 'sɛltɪk] *adj* celtico(a)

cement [sə'mɛnt] *n* cemento; **~ mixer** *n* betoniera

cemetery ['sɛmɪtrɪ] *n* cimitero

censor ['sɛnsə*] *n* censore *m* ♦ *vt* censurare; **~ship** *n* censura

censure ['sɛnʃə*] *vt* riprovare, censurare

census ['sɛnsəs] *n* censimento

cent [sɛnt] *n* (*US: coin*) centesimo (= *1:100 di un dollaro*); *see also* **per**

centenary [sɛn'ti:nərɪ] *n* centenario

center ['sɛntə*] (*US*) *n, vt* = **centre**

centigrade ['sɛntɪgreɪd] *adj* centigrado(a)

centimetre ['sɛntɪmiːtə*] (*us* **centimeter**) *n* centimetro

centipede ['sɛntɪpiːd] *n* centopiedi *m inv*

central ['sɛntrəl] *adj* centrale; **C~ America** *n* America centrale; **~ heating** *n* riscaldamento centrale; **~ize** *vt* accentrare

centre ['sɛntə*] (*us* **center**) *n* centro ♦ *vt* centrare; **~-forward** *n* (*SPORT*) centroavanti *m inv*; **~-half** *n* (*SPORT*) centromediano

century ['sɛntjʊrɪ] *n* secolo; **20th ~** ventesimo secolo

ceramic [sɪ'ræmɪk] *adj* ceramico(a); **~s** *npl* ceramica

cereal ['siːrɪəl] *n* cereale *m*

ceremony ['sɛrɪmənɪ] *n* cerimonia; **to stand on ~** fare complimenti

certain ['sɜːtən] *adj* certo(a); **to make ~ of** assicurarsi di; **for ~** per certo, di sicuro; **~ly** *adv* certamente, certo; **~ty** *n* certezza

certificate [sə'tɪfɪkɪt] *n* certificato; diploma *m*

certified ['sɜːtɪfaɪd]: **~ mail** (*us*) *n* posta raccomandata con ricevuta di ritorno; **~ public accountant** (*us*) *n* ≈ commercialista *m/f*

certify ['sɜːtɪfaɪ] *vt* certificare; (*award diploma to*) conferire un diploma a; (*declare insane*) dichiarare pazzo(a)

cervical ['sɜːvɪkl] *adj*: **~ cancer** cancro della cervice; **~ smear** Pap-test *m inv*

cervix ['sɜːvɪks] *n* cervice *f*

cf. *abbr* (= *compare*) cfr

CFC *n* (= *chlorofluorocarbon*) CFC *m inv*

ch. *abbr* (= *chapter*) cap

chafe [tʃeɪf] *vt* fregare, irritare

chain [tʃeɪn] *n* catena ♦ *vt* (*also:* **~ up**) incatenare; **~ reaction** *n* reazione *f* a catena; **~-smoke** *vi* fumare una sigaretta dopo l'altra; **~ store** *n* negozio a catena

chair [tʃeə*] *n* sedia; (*armchair*)

poltrona; (*of university*) cattedra; (*of meeting*) presidenza ♦ *vt* (*meeting*) presiedere; **~-lift** *n* seggiovia; **~man** (*irreg*) *n* presidente *m*

chalet ['ʃæleɪ] *n* chalet *m inv*

chalk [tʃɔːk] *n* gesso

challenge ['tʃælɪndʒ] *n* sfida ♦ *vt* sfidare; (*statement, right*) mettere in dubbio; **to ~ sb to do** sfidare qn a fare; **challenging** *adj* (*task*) impegnativo(a); (*look*) di sfida

chamber ['tʃeɪmbə*] *n* camera; **~ of commerce** *n* camera di commercio; **~maid** *n* cameriera; **~ music** *n* musica da camera

chamois ['ʃæmwɑː] *n* camoscio; (*also:* **~ leather**) panno in pelle di camoscio

champagne [ʃæm'peɪn] *n* champagne *m inv*

champion ['tʃæmpɪən] *n* campione/ essa; **~ship** *n* campionato

chance [tʃɑːns] *n* caso; (*opportunity*) occasione *f*; (*likelihood*) possibilità *f inv* ♦ *vt*: **to ~ it** rischiare, provarci ♦ *adj* fortuito(a), casuale; **to take a ~** rischiare; **by ~** per caso

chancellor ['tʃɑːnsələ*] *n* cancelliere *m*; **C~ of the Exchequer** (*BRIT*) *n* Cancelliere dello Scacchiere

chandelier [ʃændə'lɪə*] *n* lampadario

change [tʃeɪndʒ] *vt* cambiare; (*transform*): **to ~ sb into** trasformare qn in ♦ *vi* cambiare; (*~ one's clothes*) cambiarsi; (*be transformed*): **to ~ into** trasformarsi in ♦ *n* cambiamento; (*of clothes*) cambio; (*money*) resto; **to ~ one's mind** cambiare idea; **for a ~** tanto per cambiare; **~able** *adj* (*weather*) variabile; **~ machine** *n* distributore automatico di monete; **~over** *n* cambiamento, passaggio

changing ['tʃeɪndʒɪŋ] *adj* che cambia; (*colours*) cangiante; **~ room** *n* (*BRIT*: in shop) camerino; (: *SPORT*) spogliatoio

channel ['tʃænl] *n* canale *m*; (*of river, sea*) alveo ♦ *vt* canalizzare; **the (English) C~** *n* la Manica; **~-hopping**

n (TV) zapping *m inv*; **the C~ Islands** *npl* le Isole Normanne; **the C~ Tunnel** *n* il tunnel sotto la Manica

chant [tʃɑːnt] *n* canto; salmodia ♦ *vt* cantare; salmodiare

chaos ['keɪɒs] *n* caos *m*

chap [tʃæp] (BRIT: inf) *n* (man) tipo

chapel ['tʃæpəl] *n* cappella

chaperone ['ʃæpərəʊn] *n* accompagnatrice *f* ♦ *vt* accompagnare

chaplain ['tʃæplɪn] *n* cappellano

chapped [tʃæpt] *adj* (skin, lips) screpolato/a

chapter ['tʃæptə*] *n* capitolo

char [tʃɑː*] *vt* (burn) carbonizzare

character ['kærɪktə*] *n* carattere *m*; (in novel, film) personaggio; **~istic** [-'rɪstɪk] *adj* caratteristico(a) ♦ *n* caratteristica

charcoal ['tʃɑːkəʊl] *n* carbone *m* di legna

charge [tʃɑːdʒ] *n* accusa; (cost) prezzo; (responsibility) responsabilità ♦ *vt* (gun, battery, MIL: enemy) caricare; (customer) fare pagare a; (sum) fare pagare; (LAW): **to ~ sb (with)** accusare qn (di) ♦ *vi* (gen with: up, along etc) lanciarsi; **~s** *npl* (bank ~s etc) tariffe *fpl*; **to reverse the ~s** (TEL) fare una telefonata a carico del destinatario; **to take ~ of** incaricarsi di; **to be in ~ of** essere responsabile per; **how much do you ~?** quanto chiedete?; **to ~ an expense (up) to sb** addebitare una spesa a qn; **~ card** *n* carta *f* clienti *inv*

charitable ['tʃærɪtəbl] *adj* caritatevole

charity ['tʃærɪtɪ] *n* carità; (organization) opera pia

charm [tʃɑːm] *n* fascino; (on bracelet) ciondolo ♦ *vt* affascinare, incantare; **~ing** *adj* affascinante

chart [tʃɑːt] *n* tabella; grafico; (map) carta nautica ♦ *vt* fare una carta nautica di; **~s** *npl* (MUS) hit parade *f*

charter ['tʃɑːtə*] *vt* (plane) noleggiare ♦ *n* (document) carta; **~ed**

accountant (BRIT) *n* ragioniere/a professionista; **~ flight** *n* volo *m* charter *inv*

charwoman ['tʃɑːwʊmən] *n* = **charlady**

chase [tʃeɪs] *vt* inseguire; (also: ~ away) cacciare ♦ *n* caccia

chasm ['kæzəm] *n* abisso

chassis ['ʃæsɪ] *n* telaio

chat [tʃæt] *vi* (also: have a ~) chiacchierare ♦ *n* chiacchierata; **~ show** (BRIT) *n* talk show *m inv*

chatter ['tʃætə*] *vi* (person) ciarlare; (bird) cinguettare; (teeth) battere ♦ *n* ciarle *fpl*; cinguettio; **~box** (inf) *n* chiacchierone/a

chatty ['tʃætɪ] *adj* (style) familiare; (person) chiacchierino/a

chauffeur ['ʃəʊfə*] *n* autista *m*

chauvinist ['ʃəʊvɪnɪst] *n* (male ~) maschilista *m*; (nationalist) sciovinista *m/f*

cheap [tʃiːp] *adj* a buon mercato; (joke) grossolano(a); (poor quality) di cattiva qualità ♦ *adv* a buon mercato; **~ day return** *n* biglietto ridotto di andata e ritorno valido in giornata; **~er** *adj* meno caro(a); **~ly** *adv* a buon prezzo, a buon mercato

cheat [tʃiːt] *vi* imbrogliare; (at school) copiare ♦ *vt* ingannare ♦ *n* imbroglione *m*; **to ~ sb out of sth** defraudare qn di qc

check [tʃek] *vt* verificare; (passport, ticket) controllare; (halt) fermare; (restrain) contenere ♦ *n* verifica, controllo; (curb) freno; (us: bill) conto; (pattern: gen pl) quadretti *mpl*; (US) = **cheque** ♦ *adj* (pattern, cloth) a quadretti; **~ in** *vi* (in hotel) registrare; (at airport) presentarsi all'accettazione ♦ *vt* (luggage) depositare; **~ out** *vi* (in hotel) saldare il conto; **~ up** *vi*: **to ~ up (on sth)** investigare (qc); **to ~ up on sb** informarsi sul conto di qn; **~ered** (us) *adj* = **chequered**; **~ers** (us) *n* dama; **~-in (desk)** *n* check-in *m* *inv*, accettazione f (bagagli *inv*); **~ing account** (*US*) n conto corrente; **~mate** n scaccomatto; **~out** n (*in supermarket*) cassa; **~point** n posto di blocco; **~room** (*US*) n deposito m bagagli *inv*; **~up** n (*MED*) controllo medico

cheek [tʃiːk] n guancia; (*impudence*) faccia tosta; **~bone** n zigomo; **~y** *adj* sfacciato(a)

cheep [tʃiːp] vi pigolare

cheer [tʃɪə*] vt applaudire; (*gladden*) rallegrare ♦ vi applaudire ♦ n grido (di incoraggiamento); **~s** *npl* (*of approval, encouragement*) applausi *mpl*; evviva *mpl*; **~s!** salute!; **~ up** vi rallegrarsi, farsi animo ♦ vt rallegrare; **~ful** *adj* allegro(a)

cheerio [tʃɪərɪ'əu] (*BRIT*) *excl* ciao!

cheese [tʃiːz] n formaggio; **~board** n piatto del (*or* per il) formaggio

cheetah [tʃiːtə] n ghepardo

chef [ʃef] n capocuoco

chemical ['kemɪkəl] *adj* chimico(a) ♦ n prodotto chimico

chemist ['kemɪst] n (*BRIT: pharmacist*) farmacista m/f; (*scientist*) chimico/a; **~ry** n chimica; **~'s (shop)** (*BRIT*) n farmacia

cheque [tʃek] (*BRIT*) n assegno; **~book** n libretto degli assegni; **~ card** n carta f assegni *inv*

chequered ['tʃekəd] (*US* **checkered**) *adj* (*fig*) movimentato(a)

cherish ['tʃerɪʃ] vt aver caro

cherry ['tʃerɪ] n ciliegia; (*also: ~ tree*) ciliegio

chess [tʃes] n scacchi *mpl*; **~board** n scacchiera

chest [tʃest] n petto; (*box*) cassa; **~ of drawers** n cassettone m

chestnut ['tʃesnʌt] n castagna; (*also: ~ tree*) castagno

chew [tʃuː] vt masticare; **~ing gum** n chewing gum m

chic [ʃiːk] *adj* elegante

chick [tʃɪk] n pulcino; (*inf*) pollastrella

chicken ['tʃɪkɪn] n pollo; (*inf: coward*) coniglio; **~ out** (*inf*) vi avere fifa; **~pox** n varicella

chicory ['tʃɪkərɪ] n cicoria

chief [tʃiːf] n capo ♦ *adj* principale; **~ executive** n direttore m generale; **~ly** *adv* per lo più, soprattutto

chilblain ['tʃɪlbleɪn] n gelone m

child [tʃaɪld] (*pl* **~ren**) n bambino/a; **~birth** n parto; **~hood** n infanzia; **~ish** *adj* puerile; **~like** *adj* fanciullesco(a); **~ minder** (*BRIT*) n bambinaia

children ['tʃɪldrən] *npl of* **child**

child seat n seggiolino per bambini (*in auto*)

Chile ['tʃɪlɪ] n Cile m

chill [tʃɪl] n freddo; (*MED*) infreddatura ♦ vt raffreddare

chilli ['tʃɪlɪ] n peperoncino

chilly ['tʃɪlɪ] *adj* freddo(a), fresco(a); **to feel ~** sentirsi infreddolito(a)

chime [tʃaɪm] n carillon m *inv* ♦ vi suonare, scampanare

chimney ['tʃɪmnɪ] n camino; **~ sweep** n spazzacamino

chimpanzee [tʃɪmpæn'ziː] n scimpanzé m *inv*

chin [tʃɪn] n mento

China ['tʃaɪnə] n Cina

china ['tʃaɪnə] n porcellana

Chinese [tʃaɪ'niːz] *adj* cinese ♦ n *inv* cinese m/f; (*LING*) cinese m

chink [tʃɪŋk] n (*opening*) fessura; (*noise*) tintinnio

chip [tʃɪp] n (*gen pl: CULIN*) patatina fritta; (*US: also: potato ~*) patatina; (*of wood, glass, stone*) scheggia; (*also: micro~*) chip m *inv* ♦ vt (*cup, plate*) scheggiare

---

chip shop

I **chip shops**, anche chiamati "fish and chip shops", sono friggitorie che vendono principalmente filetti di pesce impanati e patatine fritte.

chiropodist [kɪ'rɒpədɪst] (BRIT) n pedicure m/f inv

chirp [tʃə:p] vi cinguettare; fare cri cri

chisel [tʃɪzl] n cesello

chit [tʃɪt] n biglietto

chitchat [tʃɪttʃæt] n chiacchiere fpl

chivalry ['ʃɪvəlrɪ] n cavalleria; cortesia

chives [tʃaɪvz] npl erba cipollina

chock-a-block ['tʃɒk-] adj pieno(a); zeppo(a)

chock-full ['tʃɒk-] adj = **chock-a-block**

chocolate ['tʃɒklɪt] n (substance) cioccolato, cioccolata; (drink) cioccolata; (a sweet) cioccolatino

choice [tʃɔɪs] n scelta ♦ adj scelto(a)

choir ['kwaɪə*] n coro; ~boy n corista m fanciullo

choke [tʃəuk] vi soffocare ♦ vt soffocare; (block): **to be ~d with** essere intasato(a) di ♦ n (AUT) valvola dell'aria

cholera ['kɒlərə] n colera m

cholesterol [kə'lɛstərɒl] n colesterolo

choose [tʃu:z] (pt chose, pp chosen) vt scegliere; **to ~ to do** decidere di fare; preferire fare

choosy ['tʃu:zɪ] adj schizzinoso(a)

chop [tʃɒp] vt (wood) spaccare ♦ n (CULIN: also: ~ up) tritare ♦ n (CULIN) costoletta; **~s** npl (jaws) mascelle fpl

chopper ['tʃɒpə*] n (helicopter) elicottero

choppy ['tʃɒpɪ] adj (sea) mosso(a)

chopsticks ['tʃɒpstɪks] npl bastoncini mpl cinesi

choral ['kɔ:rəl] adj corale

chord [kɔ:d] n (MUS) accordo

chore [tʃɔ:*] n faccenda; **household ~s** faccende fpl domestiche

chortle ['tʃɔ:tl] vi ridacchiare

chorus ['kɔ:rəs] n coro; (repeated part of song, also fig) ritornello

chose [tʃəuz] pt of **choose**

chosen ['tʃəuzn] pp of **choose**

chowder ['tʃaudə*] n (esp US) zuppa di pesce

Christ [kraɪst] n Cristo

christen ['krɪsn] vt battezzare

Christian ['krɪstɪən] adj, n cristiano(a); **~ity** [-'ænɪtɪ] n cristianesimo; **~ name** n nome m (di battesimo)

Christmas ['krɪsməs] n Natale m; **Merry ~!** Buon Natale!; **~ card** n cartolina di Natale; **~ Day** n il giorno di Natale; **~ Eve** n la vigilia di Natale; **~ tree** n albero di Natale

chrome [krəum] n cromo

chromium ['krəumɪəm] n cromo

chronic ['krɒnɪk] adj cronico(a)

chronological [krɒnə'lɒdʒɪkəl] adj cronologico(a)

chrysanthemum [krɪ'sænθəməm] n crisantemo

chubby ['tʃʌbɪ] adj paffuto(a)

chuck [tʃʌk] (inf) vt buttare, gettare; (BRIT: also: ~ up) piantare; **~ out** vt buttar fuori

chuckle ['tʃʌkl] vi ridere sommessamente

chug [tʃʌg] vi fare ciuf ciuf

chum [tʃʌm] n compagno/a

chunk [tʃʌŋk] n pezzo

church [tʃə:tʃ] n chiesa; **~yard** n sagrato

churn [tʃə:n] n (for butter) zangola; (for milk) bidone m; **~ out** vt sfornare

chute [ʃu:t] n (also: rubbish ~) canale m di scarico; (BRIT: children's slide) scivolo

chutney ['tʃʌtnɪ] n salsa piccante (di frutta, zucchero e spezie)

CIA (US) n abbr (= Central Intelligence Agency) CIA f

CID (BRIT) n abbr (= Criminal Investigation Department) ≈ polizia giudiziaria

cider ['saɪdə*] n sidro

cigar [sɪ'gɑ:*] n sigaro

cigarette [sɪgə'rɛt] n sigaretta; **~ case** n portasigarette m inv; **~ end** n mozzicone m

Cinderella [sɪndə'rɛlə] n Cenerentola

cinders ['sɪndəz] npl ceneri fpl

cine camera ['sɪnɪ-] (BRIT) n cinepresa

cine film ['sɪnɪ-] (BRIT) n pellicola

cinema ['sɪnəmə] n cinema m inv

cinnamon ['sɪnəmən] n cannella

cipher ['saɪfə*] n cifra

circle ['sə:kl] n cerchio; (of friends etc) circolo; (in cinema) galleria ♦ vi girare in circolo ♦ vt (surround) circondare; (move round) girare intorno a

circuit ['sə:kɪt] n circuito; **~ous** [sə:'kjuɪtəs] adj indiretto(a)

circular ['sə:kjulə*] adj circolare ♦ n circolare f

circulate ['sə:kjuleɪt] vi circolare ♦ vt far circolare; **circulation** [-'leɪʃən] n circolazione f; (of newspaper) tiratura

circumstances ['sə:kəmstənsɪz] npl circostanze fpl; (financial condition) condizioni fpl finanziarie

circus ['sə:kəs] n circo

CIS n abbr (= Commonwealth of Independent States) CSI f

cistern ['sɪstən] n cisterna; (in toilet) serbatoio d'acqua

citizen ['sɪtɪzn] n cittadino/a; (of town) abitante m/f; **~ship** n cittadinanza

citrus fruit ['sɪtrəs-] n agrume m

city ['sɪtɪ] n città f inv; **the C~** la Città di Londra (centro commerciale)

civic ['sɪvɪk] adj civico(a); **~ centre** (BRIT) n centro civico

civil ['sɪvɪl] adj civile; **~ engineer** n ingegnere m civile; **~ian** [sɪ'vɪlɪən] adj, n borghese m/f

civilization [sɪvɪlaɪ'zeɪʃən] n civiltà f inv

civilized ['sɪvɪlaɪzd] adj civilizzato(a); (fig) cortese

civil: **~ law** n codice m civile; (study) diritto civile; **~ servant** n impiegato/a statale; **C~ Service** n amministrazione f statale; **~ war** n guerra civile

clad [klæd] adj: **~ (in)** vestito(a) di

claim [kleɪm] vt (assert): **to ~ (that)/ to be** sostenere (che)/di essere; (credit, rights etc) rivendicare; (damages)

richiedere ♦ vi (for insurance) fare una domanda d'indennizzo ♦ n pretesa; rivendicazione f; richiesta; **~ant** n (ADMIN, LAW) richiedente m/f

clairvoyant [kleə'vɔɪənt] n chiaroveggente m/f

clam [klæm] n vongola

clamber ['klæmbə*] vi arrampicarsi

clammy ['klæmɪ] adj (weather) caldo(a) umido(a); (hands) viscido(a)

clamour ['klæmə*] vi: **to ~ for** chiedere a gran voce

clamp [klæmp] n pinza; morsa ♦ vt stringere con una morsa; (AUT: wheel) applicare i ceppi bloccaruote a; **~ down on** vt fus dare un giro di vite

clan [klæn] n clan m inv

clang [klæŋ] vi emettere un suono metallico

clap [klæp] vi applaudire; **~ping** n applausi mpl

claret ['klærət] n vino di Bordeaux

clarify ['klærɪfaɪ] vt chiarificare, chiarire

clarinet [klærɪ'net] n clarinetto

clarity ['klærɪtɪ] n chiarità

clash [klæʃ] n frastuono; (fig) scontro ♦ vi scontrarsi; cozzare

clasp [klɑːsp] n (hold) stretta; (on necklace, bag) fermaglio, fibbia ♦ vt stringere

class [klɑːs] n classe f ♦ vt classificare

classic ['klæsɪk] adj classico(a) ♦ n classico; **~al** adj classico(a)

classified ['klæsɪfaɪd] adj (information) segreto(a), riservato(a); **~ advertisement** n annuncio economico

classmate ['klɑːsmeɪt] n compagno/a di classe

classroom ['klɑːsrum] n aula

clatter ['klætə*] n tintinnio; scalpitio ♦ vi tintinnare; scalpitare

clause [klɔːz] n clausola; (LING) proposizione f

claw [klɔː] n (of bird of prey) artiglio; (of lobster) pinza

clay [kleɪ] *n* argilla

clean [kliːn] *adj* pulito(a); (*clear, smooth*) liscio(a) ♦ *vt* pulire; ~ **out** *vt* ripulire; ~ **up** *vt* (*also fig*) ripulire; ~-**cut** *adj* (*man*) curato(a); ~**er** *n* (*person*) donna delle pulizie; ~**er's** *n* (*also: dry ~er's*) tintoria; ~**ing** *n* pulizia; ~**liness** ['klɛnlɪnɪs] *n* pulizia

cleanse [klɛnz] *vt* pulire; purificare; ~**r** *n* detergente *m*

clean-shaven [-'ʃeɪvn] *adj* sbarbato(a)

cleansing department ['klɛnzɪŋ-] (*BRIT*) *n* nettezza urbana

clear [klɪə*] *adj* chiaro(a); (*glass etc*) trasparente; (*road, way*) libero(a); (*conscience*) pulito(a) ♦ *vt* sgombrare; liberare; (*table*) sparecchiare; (*cheque*) fare la compensazione di; (*LAW: suspect*) discolpare; (*obstacle*) superare ♦ *vi* (*weather*) rasserenarsi; (*fog*) andarsene ♦ *adv*: ~ **of** distante da; ~ **up** *vt* mettere in ordine; (*mystery*) risolvere; ~**ance** *n* (*removal*) sgombro; (*permission*) autorizzazione *f*, permesso; ~-**cut** *adj* ben delineato(a), distinto(a); ~**ing** *n* radura; ~**ing bank** (*BRIT*) *n* banca (che fa uso della camera di compensazione); ~**ly** *adv* chiaramente, in modo evidente; ~**way** (*BRIT*) *n* strada con divieto di sosta

cleaver ['kliːvə*] *n* mannaia

clef [klɛf] *n* (*MUS*) chiave *f*

cleft [klɛft] *n* (*in rock*) crepa, fenditura

clench [klɛntʃ] *vt* stringere

clergy ['kləːdʒɪ] *n* clero; ~**man** (*irreg*) *n* ecclesiastico

clerical ['klɛrɪkəl] *adj* d'impiegato; (*REL*) clericale

clerk [klɑːk, (*US*) kləːrk] *n* (*BRIT*) impiegato/a; (*US*) commesso/a

clever ['klɛvə*] *adj* (*mentally*) intelligente; (*deft, skilful*) abile; (*device, arrangement*) ingegnoso(a)

click [klɪk] *vi* scattare ♦ *vt* (*heels etc*) battere; (*tongue*) far schioccare; ~ **on** *vt* (*COMPUT*) cliccare su

client ['klaɪənt] *n* cliente *m/f*

cliff [klɪf] *n* scogliera scoscesa, rupe *f*

climate ['klaɪmɪt] *n* clima *m*

climax ['klaɪmæks] *n* culmine *m*; (*sexual*) orgasmo

climb [klaɪm] *vi* salire; (*clamber*) arrampicarsi ♦ *vt* (*CLIMBING*) scalare ♦ *n* salita; arrampicata; scalata; ~-**down** *n* marcia indietro; ~**er** *n* rocciatore/trice; alpinista *m/f*; ~**ing** *n* alpinismo

clinch [klɪntʃ] *vt* (*deal*) concludere

cling [klɪŋ] (*pt, pp* **clung**) *vi*: **to** ~ (**to**) aggrapparsi a; (*of clothes*) aderire strettamente a

clinic ['klɪnɪk] *n* clinica; ~**al** *adj* clinico(a); (*fig*) distaccato(a); (*: room*) freddo(a)

clink [klɪŋk] *vi* tintinnare

clip [klɪp] *n* (*for hair*) forcina; (*also: paper* ~) graffetta; (*TV, CINEMA*) sequenza ♦ *vt* attaccare insieme; (*hair, nails*) tagliare; (*hedge*) tosare; ~**pers** *npl* (*for gardening*) cesoie *fpl*; (*also: nail* ~*pers*) forbicine *fpl* per le unghie; ~**ping** *n* (*from newspaper*) ritaglio

clique [kliːk] *n* cricca

cloak [kləʊk] *n* mantello ♦ *vt* avvolgere; ~**room** *n* (*for coats etc*) guardaroba *m inv*; (*BRIT: W.C.*) gabinetti *mpl*

clock [klɔk] *n* orologio; ~ **in** *or* **on** *vi* timbrare il cartellino (all'entrata); ~ **off** *or* **out** *vi* timbrare il cartellino (all'uscita); ~**wise** *adv* in senso orario; ~**work** *n* movimento *or* meccanismo a orologeria ♦ *adj* a molla

clog [klɔg] *n* zoccolo ♦ *vt* intasare ♦ *vi* (*also: ~ up*) intasarsi, bloccarsi

cloister ['klɔɪstə*] *n* chiostro

clone [kləʊn] *n* clone *m*

close¹ [kləʊs] *adj*: ~ (**to**) vicino(a) (a); (*watch, link, relative*) stretto(a); (*examination*) attento(a); (*contest*) combattuto(a), (*weather*) afoso(a) ♦ *adv* vicino, dappresso; ~ **to** vicino a; ~ **by**, ~ **at hand** a portata di mano; **a** ~ **friend** un amico intimo; **to have a** ~ **shave** (*fig*) scamparla bella

close² [kləuz] vt chiudere ♦ vi (shop etc) chiudere; (lid, door etc) chiudersi; (end) finire ♦ n (end) fine f; ~ **down** vi cessare (definitivamente); ~**d** adj chiuso(a); ~**d shop** n azienda o fabbrica che impiega solo aderenti ai sindacati

close-knit [kləus'nɪt] adj (family, community) molto unito(a)

closely ['kləuslɪ] adv (examine, watch) da vicino; (related) strettamente

closet ['klɒzɪt] n (cupboard) armadio

close-up ['kləusʌp] n primo piano

closure ['kləuʒə*] n chiusura

clot [klɒt] n (also: blood ~) coagulo; (inf: idiot) scemo/a ♦ vi coagularsi

cloth [klɒθ] n (material) tessuto, stoffa; (rag) strofinaccio

clothe [kləuð] vt vestire; ~**s** npl abiti mpl, vestiti mpl; ~**s brush** n spazzola per abiti; ~**s line** n corda (per stendere il bucato); ~**s peg** (US ~**s pin**) n molletta

clothing ['kləuðɪŋ] n = **clothes**

cloud [klaud] n nuvola; ~**burst** n acquazzone m; ~**y** adj nuvoloso(a); (liquid) torbido(a)

clout [klaut] vt dare un colpo a

clove [kləuv] n chiodo di garofano; ~ **of garlic** spicchio d'aglio

clover ['kləuvə*] n trifoglio

clown [klaun] n pagliaccio ♦ vi (also: ~ about, ~ around) fare il pagliaccio

cloying ['klɔɪɪŋ] adj (taste, smell) nauseabondo(a)

club [klʌb] n (society) club m inv, circolo; (weapon, GOLF) mazza ♦ vt bastonare ♦ vi: **to ~ together** associarsi; ~**s** npl (CARDS) fiori mpl; ~ **class** n (AVIAT) classe f club inv; ~**house** n sede f del circolo

cluck [klʌk] vi chiocciare

clue [kluː] n indizio; (in crosswords) definizione f; **I haven't a ~** non ho la minima idea

clump [klʌmp] n (of flowers, trees) gruppo; (of grass) ciuffo

clumsy ['klʌmzɪ] adj goffo(a)

clung [klʌŋ] pt, pp of **cling**

cluster ['klʌstə*] n gruppo ♦ vi raggrupparsi

clutch [klʌtʃ] n (grip, grasp) presa, stretta; (AUT) frizione f ♦ vt afferrare, stringere forte

clutter ['klʌtə*] vt ingombrare

CND n abbr = **Campaign for Nuclear Disarmament**

Co. abbr = **county; company**

c/o abbr (= care of) presso

coach [kəutʃ] n (bus) pullman m inv; (horse-drawn, of train) carrozza; (SPORT) allenatore/trice; (tutor) chi dà ripetizioni ♦ vt allenare; dare ripetizioni a; ~ **trip** n viaggio in pullman

coal [kəul] n carbone m; ~**-face** n fronte f; ~**-field** n bacino carbonifero

coalition [kəuə'lɪʃən] n coalizione f

coalman ['kəulmən] (irreg) n negoziante m di carbone

coalmine ['kəulmaɪn] n miniera di carbone

coarse [kɔːs] adj (salt, sand etc) grosso(a); (cloth, person) rozzo(a)

coast [kəust] n costa ♦ vi (with cycle etc) scendere a ruota libera; ~**al** adj costiero(a); ~**guard** n guardia costiera; ~**line** n linea costiera

coat [kəut] n cappotto; (of animal) pelo; (of paint) mano f ♦ vt coprire; ~ **of arms** n stemma m; ~ **hanger** n attaccapanni m inv; ~**ing** n rivestimento

coax [kəuks] vt indurre (con moine)

cobbler ['kɒblə*] n calzolaio

cobbles ['kɒblz] npl ciottoli mpl

cobblestones ['kɒblstəunz] npl ciottoli mpl

cobweb ['kɒbweb] n ragnatela

cocaine [kə'keɪn] n cocaina

cock [kɒk] n (rooster) gallo; (male bird) maschio ♦ vt (gun) armare; ~**erel** n galletto

cockle ['kɒkl] n cardio

cockney ['kɒknɪ] n cockney m/f inv

(abitante dei quartieri popolari dell'East End di Londra)

cockpit ['kɔkpɪt] *n* abitacolo

cockroach ['kɔkrəʊtʃ] *n* blatta

cocktail ['kɔkteɪl] *n* cocktail *m inv*;
~ **cabinet** *n* mobile *m* bar *inv*;
~ **party** *n* cocktail *m inv*

cocoa ['kəʊkəʊ] *n* cacao

coconut ['kəʊkənʌt] *n* noce *f* di cocco

cocoon [kə'ku:n] *n* bozzolo

cod [kɔd] *n* merluzzo

C.O.D. *abbr* = **cash on delivery**

code [kəʊd] *n* codice *m*

cod-liver oil *n* olio di fegato di merluzzo

coercion [kəʊ'ə:ʃən] *n* coercizione *f*

coffee ['kɔfɪ] *n* caffè *m inv*; ~ **bar** (BRIT) *n* caffè *m inv*; ~ **break** *n* pausa per il caffè; ~**pot** *n* caffettiera; ~ **table** *n* tavolino

coffin ['kɔfɪn] *n* bara

cog [kɔg] *n* dente *m*

cogent ['kəʊdʒənt] *adj* convincente

coherent [kəʊ'hɪərənt] *adj* coerente

coil [kɔɪl] *n* rotolo; (ELEC) bobina;
(contraceptive) spirale *f* ♦ *vt* avvolgere

coin [kɔɪn] *n* moneta ♦ *vt* (word) coniare; ~**age** *n* sistema *m* monetario;
~**-box** (BRIT) *n* telefono a gettoni

coincide [kəʊɪn'saɪd] *vi* coincidere;
coincidence [kəʊ'ɪnsɪdəns] *n* combinazione *f*

Coke ® [kəʊk] *n* coca

coke [kəʊk] *n* coke *m*

colander ['kɔləndə*] *n* colino

cold [kəʊld] *adj* freddo ♦ *n* freddo;
(MED) raffreddore *m*; **it's** ~ fa freddo;
to be ~ *(person)* aver freddo; *(object)* essere freddo(a); **to catch** ~ prendere freddo; **to catch a** ~ prendere un raffreddore; **in** ~ **blood** a sangue freddo; ~**-shoulder** *vt* trattare con freddezza; ~ **sore** *n* erpete *m*

coleslaw ['kəʊlslɔ:] *n* insalata di cavolo bianco

colic ['kɔlɪk] *n* colica

collapse [kə'læps] *vi* crollare ♦ *n* crollo;

(MED) collasso

collapsible [kə'læpsəbl] *adj* pieghevole

collar ['kɔlə*] *n* (of coat, shirt) colletto;
(of dog, cat) collare *m*; ~**bone** *n* clavicola

collateral [kə'lætərl] *n* garanzia

colleague ['kɔli:g] *n* collega *m/f*

collect [kə'lɛkt] *vt* (gen) raccogliere;
(as a hobby) fare collezione di; (BRIT: call and pick up) prendere; (money owed, pension) riscuotere; (donations, subscriptions) fare una colletta di ♦ *vi* adunarsi, riunirsi; ammucchiarsi; **to call** ~ (US: TEL) fare una chiamata a carico del destinatario; ~**ion** [kə'lɛkʃən] *n* raccolta; collezione *f*; (for money) colletta

collector [kə'lɛktə*] *n* collezionista *m/f*

college ['kɔlɪdʒ] *n* college *m inv*; (of technology etc) istituto superiore

collide [kə'laɪd] *vi*: **to** ~ **(with)** scontrarsi (con)

colliery ['kɔlɪərɪ] (BRIT) *n* miniera di carbone

collision [kə'lɪʒən] *n* collisione *f*, scontro

colloquial [kə'ləʊkwɪəl] *adj* familiare

colon ['kəʊlən] *n* (sign) due punti *mpl*;
(MED) colon *m inv*

colonel ['kə:nl] *n* colonnello

colonial [kə'ləʊnɪəl] *adj* coloniale

colony ['kɔlənɪ] *n* colonia

colour ['kʌlə*] (US **color**) *n* colore *m* ♦ *vt* colorare; (tint, dye) tingere; (fig: affect) influenzare ♦ *vi* (blush) arrossire; ~**s** *npl* (of party, club) colori *mpl*; **in** ~ a colori; ~ **in** *vt* colorare; ~ **bar** *n* discriminazione *f* razziale (in locali etc); ~**-blind** *adj* daltonico(a); ~**ed** *adj* (photo) a colori; (person) di colore; ~ **film** *n* (for camera) pellicola a colori; ~**ful** *adj* pieno(a) di colore, a vivaci colori; (personality) colorato(a); ~**ing** *n* (substance) colorante *m*; (complexion) colorito; ~ **scheme** *n* combinazione *f* di colori; ~ **television** *n* televisione *f* a colori

colt [kəʊlt] n puledro

column [ˈkɔləm] n colonna; **~ist** [ˈkɔləmnɪst] n articolista m/f

coma [ˈkəʊmə] n coma m inv

comb [kəʊm] n pettine m ♦ vt (hair) pettinare; (area) battere a tappeto

combat [ˈkɔmbæt] n combattimento ♦ vt combattere, lottare contro

combination [kɔmbɪˈneɪʃən] n combinazione f

combine [vb kəmˈbaɪn, n ˈkɔmbaɪn] vt: **to ~ (with)** combinare (con); (one quality with another) unire (a) ♦ vi unirsi; (CHEM) combinarsi ♦ n (ECON) associazione f; **~ (harvester)** n mietitrebbia

come [kʌm] (pt came, pp come) vi venire; arrivare; **to ~ to** (decision etc) raggiungere; **I've ~ to like him** ho cominciato a piacermi; **to ~ undone** slacciarsi; **to ~ loose** allentarsi; **~ about** vi succedere; **~ across** vt fus trovare per caso; **~ away** vi venire via; staccarsi; **~ back** vi ritornare; **~ by** vt fus (acquire) ottenere; procurarsi; **~ down** vi scendere; (prices) calare; (buildings) essere demolito(a); **~ forward** vi farsi avanti; presentarsi; **~ from** vt fus venire da; provenire da; **~ in** vi entrare; **~ in for** vt fus (criticism etc) ricevere; **~ into** vt fus (money) ereditare; **~ off** vi (button) staccarsi; (stain) andar via; (attempt) riuscire; **~ on** vi (pupil, work, project) fare progressi; (lights) accendersi; (electricity) entrare in funzione; **~ on!** avanti!, andiamo!, forza!; **~ out** vi uscire; (stain) andare via; **~ round** vi (after faint, operation) riprendere conoscenza, rinvenire; **~ to** vi rinvenire; **~ up** vi (sun) salire; (problem) sorgere; (event) essere in arrivo; (in conversation) saltar fuori; **~ up against** vt fus (resistance, difficulties) urtare contro; **~ up with** vt fus: **he came up with an idea** venne fuori con un'idea; **~ upon** vt fus trovare per

caso; **~back** n (THEATRE etc) ritorno

comedian [kəˈmiːdɪən] n comico

comedienne [kəmiːdɪˈɛn] n attrice f comica

comedy [ˈkɔmɪdɪ] n commedia

comeuppance [kʌmˈʌpəns] n: **to get one's ~** ricevere ciò che si merita

comfort [ˈkʌmfət] n comodità f inv, benessere m; (relief) consolazione f, conforto ♦ vt consolare, confortare; **~s** npl comodità fpl; **~able** adj comodo(a); (financially) agiato(a); **~ably** adv (sit etc) comodamente; (live) bene; **~ station** (US) n gabinetti mpl

comic [ˈkɔmɪk] adj (also: **~al**) comico(a) ♦ n comico; (magazine) giornaletto; **~ strip** n fumetto

coming [ˈkʌmɪŋ] n arrivo ♦ adj (next) prossimo(a); (future) futuro(a); **~(s) and going(s)** n(pl) andirivieni m inv

comma [ˈkɔmə] n virgola

command [kəˈmɑːnd] n ordine m, comando; (MIL: authority) comando; (mastery) padronanza ♦ vt comandare; **to ~ sb to do** ordinare a qn di fare; **~eer** [kɔmənˈdɪə*] vt requisire; **~er** n capo; (MIL) comandante m

commando [kəˈmɑːndəʊ] n commando m inv; membro di un commando

commence [kəˈmɛns] vt, vi cominciare

commend [kəˈmɛnd] vt lodare; raccomandare

commensurate [kəˈmɛnʃərɪt] adj: **~ with** proporzionato(a) a

comment [ˈkɔmɛnt] n commento ♦ vi: **to ~ (on)** fare commenti (su); **~ary** [ˈkɔməntərɪ] n commentario; (SPORT) radiocronaca; telecronaca; **~ator** [ˈkɔməntteɪtə*] n commentatore/trice; radiocronista m/f; telecronista m/f

commerce [ˈkɔməːs] n commercio

commercial [kəˈmɜːʃəl] adj commerciale ♦ n (TV, RADIO: advertisement) pubblicità f inv; **~ radio/television** n radio f inv/ televisione f privata

commiserate [kə'mɪzəreɪt] vi: to ~ with partecipare al dolore di

commission [kə'mɪʃən] n commissione f ♦ vt (work of art) commissionare; **out of ~** (NAUT) in disarmo; **~aire** [kəmɪʃə'nɛə*] (BRIT) n (at shop, cinema etc) portiere m in livrea; **~er** n (POLICE) questore m

commit [kə'mɪt] vt (act) commettere; (to sb's care) affidare; to ~ o.s. (to do) impegnarsi (a fare); to ~ suicide suicidarsi; **~ment** n impegno; promessa

committee [kə'mɪtɪ] n comitato

commodity [kə'mɔdɪtɪ] n prodotto, articolo

common ['kɔmən] adj comune; (pej) volgare; (usual) normale ♦ n terreno comune; **the C~s** (BRIT) npl la Camera dei Comuni; **in ~** in comune; **~er** n cittadino/a (non nobile); **~ law** n diritto consuetudinario; **~ly** adv comunemente, usualmente; **C~ Market** n Mercato Comune; **~place** adj banale, ordinario(a); **~room** n sala di riunione; (SCOL) sala dei professori; **~ sense** n buon senso; **the C~wealth** n il Commonwealth

commotion [kə'məuʃən] n confusione f, tumulto

communal ['kɔmju:nl] adj (for common use) pubblico(a)

commune [n 'kɔmju:n, vb kə'mju:n] n (group) comune f ♦ vi: to ~ with mettersi in comunione con

communicate [kə'mju:nɪkeɪt] vt comunicare, trasmettere ♦ vi: to ~ (with) comunicare (con)

communication [kəmju:nɪ'keɪʃən] n comunicazione f; **~ cord** (BRIT) n segnale m d'allarme

communion [kə'mju:nɪən] n (also: Holy C~) comunione f

communiqué [kə'mju:nɪkeɪ] n comunicato

communism ['kɔmjunɪzəm] n comunismo; **communist** adj, n comunista m/f

community [kə'mju:nɪtɪ] n comunità f inv; **~ centre** n circolo ricreativo; **~ chest** (US) n fondo di beneficenza

commutation ticket [kɔmju'teɪʃən-] (US) n biglietto di abbonamento

commute [kə'mju:t] vi fare il pendolare ♦ vt (LAW) commutare; **~r** n pendolare m/f

compact [adj kəm'pækt, n 'kɔmpækt] adj compatto(a) ♦ n (also: powder ~) portacipria m inv; **~ disc** n compact disc m inv; **~ disc player** n lettore m CD inv

companion [kəm'pænɪən] n compagno/a; **~ship** n compagnia

company ['kʌmpənɪ] n (also COMM, MIL, THEATRE) compagnia; to keep sb ~ tenere compagnia a qn; **~ secretary** (BRIT) n segretario/a generale

comparable ['kɔmpərəbl] adj simile

comparative [kəm'pærətɪv] adj relativo(a); (adjective etc) comparativo(a); **~ly** adv relativamente

compare [kəm'pɛə*] vt: to ~ sth/sb with/to confrontare qc/qn con/a ♦ vi: to ~ (with) reggere il confronto (con); **comparison** [-'pærɪsn] n confronto; **in comparison (with)** in confronto (a)

compartment [kəm'pɑ:tmənt] n compartimento; (RAIL) scompartimento

compass ['kʌmpəs] n bussola; **~es** npl (MATH) compasso

compassion [kəm'pæʃən] n compassione f

compatible [kəm'pætɪbl] adj compatibile

compel [kəm'pɛl] vt costringere, obbligare

compensate ['kɔmpənseɪt] vt risarcire ♦ vi: to ~ for compensare; **compensation** [-'seɪʃən] n compensazione f; (money) risarcimento

compère ['kɔmpɛə*] n presentatore/ trice

compete [kəm'pi:t] vi (take part)

concorrere; (vie): **to ~ (with)** fare concorrenza (a)

competent ['kɔmpɪtənt] adj competente

competition [kɔmpɪ'tɪʃən] n gara; concorso; (ECON) concorrenza

competitive [kəm'petɪtɪv] adj (ECON) concorrenziale; (sport) agonistico(a); (person) che ha spirito di competizione; che ha spirito agonistico

competitor [kəm'petɪtə*] n concorrente m/f

complacency [kəm'pleɪsnsɪ] n compiacenza di sé

complain [kəm'pleɪn] vi lagnarsi, lamentarsi; **~t** n lamento; (in shop etc) reclamo; (MED) malattia

complement [n 'kɔmplɪmənt, vb 'kɔmplɪment] n complemento; (especially of ship's crew etc) effettivo ♦ vt (enhance) accompagnarsi bene a; **~ary** [kɔmplɪ'mentərɪ] adj complementare

complete [kəm'pliːt] adj completo(a) ♦ vt completare; (a form) riempire; **~ly** adv completamente; **completion** [-'pliːʃən] n completamento

complex ['kɔmpleks] adj complesso(a) ♦ n (PSYCH, buildings etc) complesso

complexion [kəm'plekʃən] n (of face) carnagione f

compliance [kəm'plaɪəns] n acquiescenza; **in ~ with** (orders, wishes etc) in conformità con

complicate ['kɔmplɪkeɪt] vt complicare; **~d** adj complicato(a); **complication** [-'keɪʃən] n complicazione f

compliment [n 'kɔmplɪmənt, vb 'kɔmplɪment] n complimento ♦ vt fare un complimento a; **~s** npl (greetings) complimenti mpl; rispetti mpl; **to pay sb a ~** fare un complimento a qn; **~ary** [-'mentərɪ] adj complimentoso(a), elogiativo(a); (free) in omaggio; **~ary ticket** n biglietto omaggio

comply [kəm'plaɪ] vi: **to ~ with** assentire a; conformarsi a

component [kəm'pəunənt] a componente ♦ n componente m

compose [kəm'pəuz] vt (form): **to be ~d of** essere composto di; (music, poem etc) comporre; **to ~ o.s.** ricomporsi; **~d** adj calmo(a); **~r** n (MUS) compositore/trice

composition [kɔmpə'zɪʃən] n composizione f

composure [kəm'pəuʒə*] n calma

compound ['kɔmpaund] n (CHEM, LING) composto; (enclosure) recinto ♦ adj composto(a); **~ fracture** n frattura esposta

comprehend [kɔmprɪ'hend] vt comprendere, capire; **comprehension** [-'henʃən] n comprensione f

comprehensive [kɔmprɪ'hensɪv] adj comprensivo(a); **~ policy** n (INSURANCE) polizza che copre tutti i rischi; **~ (school)** (BRIT) n scuola secondaria aperta a tutti

compress [vb kəm'pres, n 'kɔmpres] vt comprimere ♦ n (MED) compressa

comprise [kəm'praɪz] vt (also: **be ~d of**) comprendere

compromise ['kɔmprəmaɪz] n compromesso ♦ vt compromettere ♦ vi venire in un compromesso

compulsion [kəm'pʌlʃən] n costrizione f

compulsive [kəm'pʌlsɪv] adj (liar, gambler) che non riesce a controllarsi; (viewing, reading) cui non si può fare a meno

compulsory [kəm'pʌlsərɪ] adj obbligatorio(a)

computer [kəm'pjuːtə*] n computer m inv, elaboratore m elettronico; **~ game** n gioco per computer; **~-generated** adj realizzato(a) al computer; **~ize** vt computerizzare; **~ programmer** n programmatore/trice; **~ programming** n

programmazione f di computer;
~ science n informatica; **computing**
n informatica

comrade ['kɒmrɪd] n compagno/a;
~ship n cameratismo

con [kɒn] (inf) vt truffare ♦ n truffa

conceal [kən'si:l] vt nascondere

concede [kən'si:d] vt ammettere

conceit [kən'si:t] n presunzione f,
vanità; **~ed** adj presuntuoso(a),
vanitoso(a)

conceive [kən'si:v] vt concepire ♦ vi
concepire un bambino

concentrate ['kɒnsəntreɪt] vi
concentrarsi ♦ vt concentrare

concentration [kɒnsən'treɪʃən] n
concentrazione f; **~ camp** n campo di
concentramento

concept ['kɒnsept] n concetto

concern [kən'sɜ:n] n affare m; (COMM)
azienda, ditta; (anxiety) preoccupazione
f ♦ vt riguardare; **to be ~ed (about)**
preoccuparsi (di); **~ing** prep riguardo
a, circa

concert ['kɒnsət] n concerto; **~ed**
[kən'sɜ:tɪd] adj concertato(a); **~ hall** n
sala da concerti

concertina [kɒnsə'ti:nə] n piccola
fisarmonica

conclude [kən'klu:d] vt concludere;
conclusion [-'klu:ʒən] n conclusione
f; **conclusive** [-'klu:sɪv] adj
conclusivo(a)

concoct [kən'kɒkt] vt inventare; **~ion**
[-'kɒkʃən] n miscuglio

concourse ['kɒŋkɔ:s] n (hall) atrio

concrete ['kɒŋkri:t] n calcestruzzo
♦ adj concreto(a); di calcestruzzo

concur [kən'kɜ:*] vi concordare

concurrently [kən'kʌrntlɪ] adv
simultaneamente

concussion [kən'kʌʃən] n
commozione f cerebrale

condemn [kən'dem] vt condannare;
(building) dichiarare pericoloso(a)

condensation [kɒndən'seɪʃən] n
condensazione f

condense [kən'dens] vi condensarsi
♦ vt condensare; **~d milk** n latte m
condensato

condescending [kɒndɪ'sendɪŋ] adj
(person) che ha un'aria di superiorità

condition [kən'dɪʃən] n condizione f;
(MED) malattia ♦ vt condizionare; **on
~ that** a condizione che + sub, a
condizione di; **~er** n (for hair) balsamo;
(for fabrics) ammorbidente m

condolences [kən'dəʊlənsɪz] npl
condoglianze fpl

condom ['kɒndəm] n preservativo

condominium [kɒndə'mɪnɪəm] n (US) n
condominio

conducive [kən'dju:sɪv] adj: **~ to**
favorevole a

conduct [n 'kɒndʌkt, vb kən'dʌkt] n
condotta ♦ vt condurre; (manage)
dirigere; amministrare; (MUS) dirigere;
to ~ o.s. comportarsi; **~ed tour** n
gita accompagnata; **~or** n (of
orchestra) direttore m d'orchestra; (on
bus) bigliettaio; (US: on train)
controllore m; (ELEC) conduttore m;
~ress n (on bus) bigliettaia

cone [kəʊn] n cono; (BOT) pigna;
(traffic ~) birillo

confectioner [kən'fekʃənə*] n
pasticciere m; **~'s (shop)** n ≈
pasticceria; **~y** n dolciumi mpl

confer [kən'fɜ:*] vt: **to ~ sth on**
conferire qc a ♦ vi conferire

conference ['kɒnfərəns] n congresso

confess [kən'fes] vt confessare,
ammettere ♦ vi confessarsi; **~ion**
[-'feʃən] n confessione f

confetti [kən'fetɪ] n coriandoli mpl

confide [kən'faɪd] vi: **to ~ in** confidarsi
con

confidence ['kɒnfɪdns] n (also:
(trust) fiducia; (self-assurance) sicurezza
di sé; **in ~** (speak, write) in confidenza,
confidenzialmente; **~ trick** n truffa;
confident adj sicuro(a); sicuro(a) di
sé; **confidential** [kɒnfɪ'denʃəl] adj
riservato(a), confidenziale

confine [kən'faɪn] vt limitare; (shut up) rinchiudere; **~d** adj (space) ristretto(a); **~ment** n prigionia; **~s** ['kɒnfaɪnz] npl confini mpl

confirm [kən'fəːm] vt confermare; **~ation** [kɒnfə'meɪʃən] n conferma; (REL) cresima; **~ed** adj inveterato(a)

confiscate ['kɒnfɪskeɪt] vt confiscare

conflict [n 'kɒnflɪkt, vb kən'flɪkt] n conflitto ♦ vi essere in conflitto; **~ing** adj contrastante

conform [kən'fɔːm] vi: to ~ (to) conformarsi (a)

confound [kən'faund] vt confondere

confront [kən'frʌnt] vt (enemy, danger) affrontare; **~ation** [kɒnfrən'teɪʃən] n scontro

confuse [kən'fjuːz] vt (one thing with another) confondere; **~d** adj confuso(a); **confusing** adj che fa confondere; **confusion** [-'fjuːʒən] n confusione f

congeal [kən'dʒiːl] vi (blood) congelarsi

congenial [kən'dʒiːnɪəl] adj (person) simpatico(a); (thing) congeniale

congested [kən'dʒestɪd] adj congestionato(a)

congestion [kən'dʒestʃən] n congestione f

congratulate [kən'grætjuleɪt] vt: to ~ sb (on) congratularsi con qn (per o di); **congratulations** [-'leɪʃənz] npl auguri mpl; (on success) complimenti mpl, congratulazioni fpl

congregate ['kɒŋgrɪgeɪt] vi congregarsi, riunirsi

congress ['kɒŋgres] n congresso; **C~man** (US) n membro del Congresso

conjunction [kən'dʒʌŋkʃən] n congiunzione f

conjunctivitis [kəndʒʌŋktɪ'vaɪtɪs] n congiuntivite f

conjure ['kʌndʒə*] vi fare giochi di prestigio; ~ **up** vt (ghost, spirit) evocare; (memories) rievocare; **~r** n prestidigitatore/trice, prestigiatore/trice

conk out [kɒŋk-] (inf) vi andare in panne

con man n truffatore m

connect [kə'nekt] vt connettere, collegare; (ELEC, TEL) collegare; (fig) associare ♦ vi (train): to ~ with essere in coincidenza con; to be ~ed with (associated) aver rapporti con; **~ion** [-ʃən] n relazione f, rapporto; (ELEC) connessione f; (train, plane) coincidenza f; (TEL) collegamento

connive [kə'naɪv] vi: to ~ at essere connivente in

connoisseur [kɒnɪ'sə*] n conoscitore/trice

conquer ['kɒŋkə*] vt conquistare; (feelings) vincere

conquest ['kɒŋkwest] n conquista

cons [kɒnz] npl see convenience; pro

conscience ['kɒnʃəns] n coscienza

conscientious [kɒnʃɪ'enʃəs] adj coscienzioso(a)

conscious ['kɒnʃəs] adj consapevole; (MED) cosciente; **~ness** n consapevolezza; coscienza

conscript ['kɒnskrɪpt] n coscritto; **~ion** [-'skrɪpʃən] n arruolamento (obbligatorio)

consent [kən'sent] n consenso ♦ vi: to ~ (to) acconsentire (a)

consequence ['kɒnsɪkwəns] n conseguenza, risultato; importanza

consequently ['kɒnsɪkwəntlɪ] adv di conseguenza, dunque

conservation [kɒnsə'veɪʃən] n conservazione f

conservative [kən'səːvətɪv] adj conservatore(trice); (cautious) cauto(a); **C~** (BRIT) adj, n (POL) conservatore(trice)

conservatory [kən'səːvətrɪ] n (greenhouse) serra; (MUS) conservatorio

conserve [kən'səːv] vt conservare ♦ n conserva

consider [kən'sɪdə*] vt considerare; (take into account) tener conto di; to ~ doing sth considerare la possibilità di fare qc

considerable [kən'sɪdərəbl] adj considerevole, notevole; **considerably** adv notevolmente, decisamente

considerate [kən'sɪdərɪt] adj premuroso/a

consideration [kənsɪdə'reɪʃən] n considerazione f

considering [kən'sɪdərɪŋ] prep in considerazione di

consign [kən'saɪn] vt: **to ~ to** (sth unwanted) relegare in; (person: to sb's care) consegnare a; (: to poverty) condannare a; **~ment** n (of goods) consegna; spedizione f

consist [kən'sɪst] vi: **~ of** constare di, essere composto/a di

consistency [kən'sɪstənsɪ] n consistenza; (fig) coerenza

consistent [kən'sɪstənt] adj coerente

consolation [kɔnsə'leɪʃən] n consolazione f

console[1] [kən'səul] vt consolare

console[2] ['kɔnsəul] n quadro di comando

consonant ['kɔnsənənt] n consonante f

consortium [kən'sɔːtɪəm] n consorzio

conspicuous [kən'spɪkjuəs] adj cospicuo/a

conspiracy [kən'spɪrəsɪ] n congiura, cospirazione f

constable ['kʌnstəbl] (BRIT) n ≈ poliziotto, agente m di polizia; **chief ~** ≈ questore m

constabulary [kən'stæbjulərɪ] n forze fpl dell'ordine

constant ['kɔnstənt] adj costante; continuo/a; **~ly** adv costantemente, continuamente

constipated ['kɔnstɪpeɪtɪd] adj stitico/a

constipation [kɔnstɪ'peɪʃən] n stitichezza

constituency [kən'stɪtjuənsɪ] n collegio elettorale

constituent [kən'stɪtjuənt] n

elettore/trice; (part) elemento componente

constitution [kɔnstɪ'tjuːʃən] n costituzione f; **~al** adj costituzionale

constraint [kən'streɪnt] n costrizione f

construct [kən'strʌkt] vt costruire; **~ion** [-ʃən] n costruzione f; **~ive** adj costruttivo/a

consul ['kɔnsl] n console m; **~ate** ['kɔnsjulɪt] n consolato

consult [kən'sʌlt] vt consultare; **~ant** n (MED) consulente m medico; (other specialist) consulente; **~ation** [-'teɪʃən] n (MED) consulto; (discussion) consultazione f; **~ing room** (BRIT) n ambulatorio

consume [kən'sjuːm] vt consumare; **~r** n consumatore/trice; **~r goods** npl beni mpl di consumo; **~r society** n società dei consumi

consumption [kən'sʌmpʃən] n consumo

cont. abbr = **continued**

contact ['kɔntækt] n contatto; (person) conoscenza ♦ vt mettersi in contatto con; **~ lenses** npl lenti fpl a contatto

contagious [kən'teɪdʒəs] adj (also fig) contagioso/a

contain [kən'teɪn] vt contenere; **to ~ o.s.** contenersi; **~er** n recipiente m; (for shipping etc) container m inv

contaminate [kən'tæmɪneɪt] vt contaminare

cont'd abbr = **continued**

contemplate ['kɔntəmpleɪt] vt contemplare; (consider) pensare a (or di)

contemporary [kən'tempərərɪ] adj, n contemporaneo/a

contempt [kən'tempt] n disprezzo; **~ of court** (LAW) oltraggio alla Corte; **~ible** adj deprecabile

contend [kən'tend] vt: **to ~ that** sostenere che ♦ vi: **to ~ with** lottare contro; **~er** n contendente m/f; concorrente m/f

content[1] ['kɔntent] n contenuto; **~s**

npl (of box, case etc) contenuto; **(table of)** ~**s** indice *m*

content² [kən'tent] *adj* contento(a), soddisfatto(a) ♦ *vt* contentare, soddisfare; ~**ed** *adj* contento(a), soddisfatto(a)

contention [kən'tenʃən] *n* contesa; *(assertion)* tesi *f inv*

contentment [kən'tentmənt] *n* contentezza

contest [*n* 'kɔntest, *vb* kən'test] *n* lotta; *(competition)* gara, concorso ♦ *vt* contestare; impugnare; *(compete for)* essere in lizza per; ~**ant** [kən'testənt] *n* concorrente *m/f*; *(in fight)* avversario *m*

context ['kɔntekst] *n* contesto

continent ['kɔntinənt] *n* continente *m*; **the C~** *(BRIT)* l'Europa continentale; ~**al** [-'nentl] *adj* continentale; ~**al breakfast** *n* colazione *f* all'europea *(senza piatti caldi)*; ~**al quilt** *(BRIT) n* piumino

contingency [kən'tindʒənsɪ] *n* eventualità *f inv*

continual [kən'tinjuəl] *adj* continuo(a)

continuation [kəntinju'eɪʃən] *n* continuazione *f*; *(after interruption)* ripresa; *(of story)* seguito

continue [kən'tinju:] *vi* continuare ♦ *vt* continuare; *(start again)* riprendere

continuity [kɔntɪ'nju:ɪtɪ] *n* continuità; *(TV, CINEMA)* (ordine *m* della) sceneggiatura

continuous [kən'tinjuəs] *adj* continuo(a); ininterrotto(a)

contort [kən'tɔ:t] *vt* contorcere

contour ['kɔntuə*] *n* contorno, profilo; *(also:* ~ **line)** curva di livello

contraband ['kɔntrəbænd] *n* contrabbando

contraceptive [kɔntrə'septiv] *adj* contraccettivo(a) ♦ *n* contraccettivo

contract [*n* 'kɔntrækt, *vb* kən'trækt] *n* contratto ♦ *vi (become smaller)* contrarsi; *(COMM):* **to ~ to do sth** fare un contratto per fare qc ♦ *vt (illness)*

contrarre; ~**ion** [-ʃən] *n* contrazione *f*; ~**or** *n* imprenditore *m*

contradict [kɔntrə'dɪkt] *vt* contraddire

contraflow ['kɔntrəfləu] *n (AUT)* senso unico alternato

contraption [kən'træpʃən] *(pej) n* aggeggio

contrary¹ ['kɔntrərɪ] *adj* contrario(a); *(unfavourable)* avverso, contrario(a) ♦ *n* contrario; **on the ~** al contrario; **unless you hear to the ~** salvo contrordine

contrary² [kən'trɛərɪ] *adj (perverse)* bisbetico(a)

contrast [*n* 'kɔntrɑ:st, *vb* kən'trɑ:st] *n* contrasto ♦ *vt* mettere in contrasto; **in ~ to** contrariamente a

contribute [kən'trɪbju:t] *vi* contribuire ♦ *vt:* **to ~ £10/an article** to dare 10 sterline/un articolo a; **to ~ to** contribuire a; *(newspaper)* scrivere per; ~**contribution** [kɔntrɪ'bju:ʃən] *n* contributo; **contributor** *n (to newspaper)* collaboratore/trice

contrivance [kən'traɪvəns] *n* congegno; espediente *m*

contrive [kən'traɪv] *vi:* **to ~ to do** fare in modo di fare

control [kən'trəul] *vt* controllare; *(firm, operation etc)* dirigere ♦ *n* controllo; ~**s** *npl (of vehicle etc)* comandi *mpl*; *(governmental)* controlli *mpl*; **under ~** sotto controllo; **to be in ~ of** avere il controllo di; **to go out of ~** *(car)* non rispondere ai comandi; *(situation)* sfuggire di mano; ~**led substance** *n* sostanza stupefacente; ~ **panel** *n* quadro dei comandi; ~ **room** *n (NAUT, MIL)* sala di controllo; *(RADIO, TV)* sala di regia; ~ **tower** *n (AVIAT)* torre *f* di controllo

controversial [kɔntrə'və:ʃl] *adj* controverso(a), polemico(a)

controversy ['kɔntrəvə:sɪ] *n* controversia, polemica

convalesce [kɔnvə'les] *vi* rimettersi in salute

convene [kən'vi:n] *vt* convocare ♦ *vi* convenire, adunarsi

convenience [kən'vi:niəns] *n* comodità *f inv*; **at your ~s** (BRIT) **all mod cons** tutte le comodità moderne

convenient [kən'vi:niənt] *adj* conveniente, comodo(a)

convent ['kɔnvənt] *n* convento

convention [kən'venʃən] *n* convenzione *f*; (*meeting*) convegno; **~al** *adj* convenzionale

conversant [kən'və:sənt] *adj*: **to be ~ with** essere a corrente di, essere pratico(a) di

conversation [kɔnvə'seɪʃən] *n* conversazione *f*; **~al** *adj* non formale

converse[1] [kən'və:s] *vi* conversare

converse[2] ['kɔnvə:s] *n* contrario, opposto; **~ly** [-'və:slɪ] *adv* al contrario, per contro

convert [*vb* kən'və:t, *n* 'kɔnvə:t] *vt* (COMM, REL) convertire; (*alter*) trasformare ♦ *n* convertito/a; **~ible** *n* macchina decappottabile

convex ['kɔnveks] *adj* convesso(a)

convey [kən'veɪ] *vt* trasportare; (*thanks*) comunicare; (*idea*) dare; **~or belt** *n* nastro trasportatore

convict [*vb* kən'vɪkt, *n* 'kɔnvɪkt] *vt* dichiarare colpevole ♦ *n* carcerato/a; **~ion** [-ʃən] *n* condanna; (*belief*) convinzione *f*

convince [kən'vɪns] *vt* convincere, persuadere; **convincing** *adj* convincente

convoluted [kɔnvə'lu:tɪd] *adj* (*argument etc*) involuto(a)

convoy ['kɔnvɔɪ] *n* convoglio

convulse [kən'vʌls] *vt*: **to be ~d with laughter** contorcersi dalle risa

cook [kuk] *vt* cucinare, cuocere ♦ *vi* cuocere; (*person*) cucinare ♦ *n* cuoco/a; **~book** *n* libro di cucina; **~er** *n* fornello, cucina; **~ery** *n* cucina; **~ery book** (BRIT) *n* = **~book**; **~ie** (US) *n* biscotto; **~ing** *n* cucina

cool [ku:l] *adj* fresco(a); (*not afraid, calm*) calmo(a); (*unfriendly*) freddo(a) ♦ *vt* raffreddare; (*room*) rinfrescare ♦ *vi* (*water*) raffreddarsi; (*air*) rinfrescarsi

coop [ku:p] *n* stia ♦ *vt*: **to ~ up** (*fig*) rinchiudere

cooperate [kəu'ɔpəreɪt] *vi* cooperare, collaborare; **cooperation** [-'reɪʃən] *n* cooperazione *f*, collaborazione *f*

cooperative [kəu'ɔpərətɪv] *adj* cooperativo(a) ♦ *n* cooperativa

coordinate [*vb* kəu'ɔ:dɪneɪt, *n* kəu'ɔ:dɪnət] *vt* coordinare ♦ *n* (MATH) coordinata; **~s** *npl* (*clothes*) coordinati *mpl*

co-ownership [kəu'əunəʃɪp] *n* comproprietà

cop [kɔp] (*inf*) *n* sbirro

cope [kəup] *vi*: **to ~ with** (*problems*) far fronte a

copper ['kɔpə*] *n* rame *m*; (*inf*: *policeman*) sbirro; **~s** *npl* (*coins*) spiccioli *mpl*

copse [kɔps] *n* bosco ceduo

copy ['kɔpɪ] *n* copia ♦ *vt* copiare; **~right** *n* diritto d'autore

coral ['kɔrəl] *n* corallo

cord [kɔ:d] *n* corda; (ELEC) filo

cordial ['kɔ:dɪəl] *adj* cordiale ♦ *n* (BRIT) cordiale *m*

cordon ['kɔ:dn] *n* cordone *m*; **~ off** *vt* fare cordone a

corduroy ['kɔ:dərɔɪ] *n* fustagno

core [kɔ:*] *n* (*of fruit*) torsolo; (*of organization etc*) cuore *m* ♦ *vt* estrarre il torsolo da

cork [kɔ:k] *n* sughero; (*of bottle*) tappo; **~screw** *n* cavatappi *m inv*

corn [kɔ:n] *n* (BRIT: *wheat*) grano; (US: *maize*) granturco; (*on foot*) callo; **~ on the cob** (CULIN) pannocchia cotta

corned beef ['kɔ:nd-] *n* carne *f* di manzo in scatola

corner ['kɔ:nə*] *n* angolo; (AUT) curva ♦ *vt* intrappolare; mettere con le spalle al muro; (COMM: *market*) accaparrare ♦ *vi* prendere una curva; **~stone** *n* pietra angolare

cornet ['kɔ:nɪt] n (MUS) cornetta; (BRIT: of ice-cream) cono

cornflakes ['kɔ:nfleɪks] npl fiocchi mpl di granturco

cornflour ['kɔ:nflauə*] (BRIT) n farina finissima di granturco

cornstarch ['kɔ:nstɑ:tʃ] (US) n = **cornflour**

Cornwall ['kɔ:nwəl] n Cornovaglia

corny ['kɔ:nɪ] (inf) adj trito(a)

coronary ['kɔrənərɪ] n:
~ **(thrombosis)** trombosi f coronaria

coronation [kɔrə'neɪʃən] n incoronazione f

coroner ['kɔrənə*] n magistrato incaricato di indagare la causa di morte in circostanze sospette

coronet ['kɔrənɪt] n diadema m

corporal ['kɔ:pərl] n caporalmaggiore m ♦ adj: ~ **punishment** pena corporale

corporate ['kɔ:pərɪt] adj costituito(a) (in corporazione); comune

corporation [kɔ:pə'reɪʃən] n (of town) consiglio comunale; (COMM) ente m

corps [kɔ:*, pl kɔ:z] n inv corpo

corpse [kɔ:ps] n cadavere m

correct [kə'rekt] adj (accurate) corretto(a), esatto(a); (proper) corretto(a) ♦ vt correggere; ~ion [-ʃən] n correzione f

correspond [kɔrɪs'pɔnd] vi corrispondere; ~**ence** n corrispondenza; ~**ence course** n corso per corrispondenza; ~**ent** n corrispondente m/f

corridor ['kɔrɪdɔ:*] n corridoio

corrode [kə'rəud] vt corrodere ♦ vi corrodersi

corrugated ['kɔrəgeɪtɪd] adj increspato(a); ondulato(a); ~ **iron** n lamiera di ferro ondulata

corrupt [kə'rʌpt] adj corrotto(a); (COMPUT) alterato(a) ♦ vt corrompere

corset ['kɔ:sɪt] n busto

Corsica ['kɔ:sɪkə] n Corsica

cosh [kɔʃ] (BRIT) n randello (corto)

cosmetic [kɔz'metɪk] n cosmetico ♦ adj (fig: measure etc) superficiale

cost [kɔst] (pt, pp cost) n costo ♦ vi costare; (find out the ~ of) stabilire il prezzo di; ~s npl (COMM, LAW) spese fpl; **how much does it ~?** quanto costa?; **at all ~s** a ogni costo

co-star ['kau-] n attore/trice della stessa importanza del protagonista

cost-effective adj conveniente

costly ['kɔstlɪ] adj costoso(a), caro(a)

cost-of-living adj: ~ **allowance** indennità f inv di contingenza

cost price (BRIT) n prezzo all'ingrosso

costume ['kɔstju:m] n costume m; (lady's suit) tailleur m inv; (BRIT: also: swimming ~) costume da bagno; ~ **jewellery** n bigiotteria

cosy ['kəuzɪ] (US **cozy**) adj intimo(a); **I'm very ~ here** sto proprio bene qui

cot [kɔt] n (BRIT: child's) lettino; (US: campbed) brandina

cottage ['kɔtɪdʒ] n cottage m inv; ~ **cheese** n fiocchi mpl di latte magro

cotton ['kɔtn] n cotone m; ~ **on to** (inf) vt fus afferrare; ~ **candy** (US) n zucchero filato; ~ **wool** (US) n cotone idrofilo

couch [kautʃ] n sofà m inv

couchette [ku:'ʃet] n (on train, boat) cuccetta

cough [kɔf] vi tossire ♦ n tosse f; ~ **drop** n pasticca per la tosse

could [kud] pt of can²; ~**n't** = could not

council ['kaunsl] n consiglio; **city** or **town** ~ consiglio comunale; ~ **estate** (BRIT) n quartiere m di case popolari; ~ **house** (BRIT) n casa popolare; ~**lor** n consigliere/a

counsel ['kaunsl] n avvocato; consultazione f ♦ vt consigliare; ~**lor** (~**or**) n consigliere/a; (US) avvocato

count [kaunt] vt, vi contare ♦ n (of votes etc) conteggio; (of pollen etc) livello; (nobleman) conte m; ~ **on** vt fus contare su; **~down** n conto alla rovescia

countenance ['kauntɪnəns] n volto, aspetto ♦ vt approvare

counter ['kauntə*] n banco ♦ vt opporsi a ♦ adv: **~ to** contro; in opposizione a; **~act** vt agire in opposizione a; (poison etc) annullare gli effetti di; **~espionage** n controspionaggio

counterfeit ['kauntəfɪt] n contraffazione f, falso ♦ vt contraffare, falsificare ♦ adj falso(a)

counterfoil ['kauntəfɔɪl] n matrice f

counterpart ['kauntəpɑ:t] n (of document etc) copia; (of person) corrispondente m/f

counter-productive [-prə'dʌktɪv] adj controproducente

countersign ['kauntəsaɪn] vt controfirmare

countess ['kauntɪs] n contessa

countless ['kauntlɪs] adj innumerevole

country ['kʌntrɪ] n paese m; (native land) patria; (as opposed to town) campagna; (region) regione f; **~ dancing** (BRIT) n danza popolare; **~ house** (BRIT) n villa in campagna; **~man** (irreg) n (national) compatriota m; (rural) contadino; **~side** n campagna

county ['kauntɪ] n contea

coup [ku:] (pl **coups**) n colpo; (also: **~ d'état**) colpo di Stato

couple ['kʌpl] n coppia; **a ~ of** un paio di

coupon ['ku:pɔn] n buono; (detachable form) coupon m inv

courage ['kʌrɪdʒ] n coraggio

courgette [kuə'ʒɛt] (BRIT) n zucchina

courier ['kurɪə*] n corriere m; (for tourists) guida

course [kɔ:s] n corso; (of ship) rotta; (for golf) campo; (part of meal) piatto; **of ~** senz'altro, naturalmente; **~ of action** modo d'agire; **a ~ of treatment** (MED) una cura

court [kɔ:t] n corte f; (TENNIS) campo

♦ vt (woman) fare la corte a; **to take to ~** citare in tribunale

courteous ['kɜ:tɪəs] adj cortese

courtesy ['kɜ:təsɪ] n cortesia; **(by) ~ of** per gentile concessione di; **~ bus, ~ coach** n autobus m inv gratuito (di hotel, aeroporto)

court-house (US) n palazzo di giustizia

courtier ['kɔ:tɪə*] n cortigiano/a

court-martial [-'mɑ:ʃəl] (pl **courts-martial**) n corte f marziale

courtroom ['kɔ:trum] n tribunale m

courtyard ['kɔ:tjɑ:d] n cortile m

cousin ['kʌzn] n cugino/a; **first ~** cugino di primo grado

cove [kəuv] n piccola baia

covenant ['kʌvənənt] n accordo

cover ['kʌvə*] vt coprire; (book, table) rivestire; (include) comprendere; (PRESS) fare un servizio su ♦ n (of pan) coperchio; (over furniture) fodera; (of bed) copriletto; (of book) copertina; (shelter) riparo; (COMM, INSURANCE, of spy) copertura; **to take ~** (shelter) ripararsi; **under ~** al riparo; **under ~ of darkness** protetto dall'oscurità; **under separate ~** (COMM) a parte, in plico separato; **~ up** vi: **to ~ up for sb** coprire qn; **~age** n (PRESS, RADIO, TV): **to give full ~age to sth** fare un ampio servizio su qc; **~ charge** n coperto; **~ing** n copertura; **~ing letter** (US **~ letter**) n lettera d'accompagnamento; **~ note** n (INSURANCE) polizza f (di assicurazione) provvisoria

covert ['kʌvət] adj (hidden) nascosto(a); (glance) furtivo(a)

cover-up n occultamento (di informazioni)

cow [kau] n vacca ♦ vt (person) intimidire

coward ['kauəd] n vigliacco/a; **~ice** [-ɪs] n vigliaccheria; **~ly** adj vigliacco(a)

cowboy ['kaubɔɪ] n cow-boy m inv

cower ['kauə*] vi acquattarsi

coxswain ['kɔksn] (abbr: **cox**) n

timoniere m

coy [kɔɪ] adj falsamente timido(a)

cozy ['kəʊzɪ] (US) adj = **cosy**

CPA (US) n abbr = **certified public accountant**

crab [kræb] n granchio; ~ **apple** n mela selvatica

crack [kræk] n fessura, crepa; incrinatura; (noise) scoppio; (: of gun) scoppio; (drug) crack m inv ♦ vt spaccare; incrinare; (whip) schioccare; (nut) schiacciare; (problem) risolvere; (code) decifrare ♦ adj (troops) fuori classe; **to ~ a joke** fare una battuta; ~ **down on** vt fus porre freno a; ~ **up** vi crollare; **~er** n cracker m inv; petardo

crackle ['krækl] vi crepitare

cradle ['kreɪdl] n culla

craft [krɑːft] n mestiere m; (cunning) astuzia; (boat) naviglio; (: of plane) aereo ♦ n artigiano; **~smanship** n abilità; **~y** adj furbo(a), astuto(a)

crag [kræg] n roccia

cram [kræm] vt (fill): **to ~ sth with** riempire qc di; (put): **to ~ sth into** stipare qc in ♦ vi (for exams) prepararsi (in gran fretta)

cramp [kræmp] n crampo; **~ed** adj ristretto(a)

crampon ['kræmpən] n (CLIMBING) rampone m

cranberry ['krænbərɪ] n mirtillo

crane [kreɪn] n gru f inv

crank [kræŋk] n manovella; (person) persona stramba

cranny ['krænɪ] n see **nook**

crash [kræʃ] n fragore m; (of car) incidente m; (of plane) caduta; (: of business etc) crollo ♦ vt fracassare ♦ vi (plane) fracassarsi; (car) avere un incidente; (two cars) scontrarsi; (business etc) fallire, andare in rovina; ~ **course** n corso intensivo; ~ **helmet** n casco; ~ **landing** n atterraggio di fortuna

crate [kreɪt] n cassa

cravat(e) [krə'væt] n fazzoletto da collo

crave [kreɪv] vt, vi: **to ~ (for)** desiderare ardentemente

crawl [krɔːl] vi strisciare carponi; (vehicle) avanzare lentamente ♦ n (SWIMMING) crawl m

crayfish ['kreɪfɪʃ] n inv (freshwater) gambero (d'acqua dolce); (saltwater) gambero

crayon ['kreɪən] n matita colorata

craze [kreɪz] n mania

crazy ['kreɪzɪ] adj matto(a); (inf: keen): ~ **about sb** pazzo(a) di qn; ~ **about sth** matto(a) per qc

creak [kriːk] vi cigolare, scricchiolare

cream [kriːm] n crema; (fresh) panna ♦ adj (colour) color crema inv; ~ **cake** n torta alla panna; ~ **cheese** n formaggio fresco; **~y** adj cremoso(a)

crease [kriːs] n grinza; (deliberate) piega ♦ vt sgualcire ♦ vi sgualcirsi

create [kriː'eɪt] vt creare; **creation** [-ʃən] n creazione f; **creative** adj creativo(a)

creature ['kriːtʃə*] n creatura

crèche [krɛʃ] n asilo infantile

credence ['kriːdns] n: **to lend** or **give ~ to** prestar fede a

credentials [krɪ'dɛnʃlz] npl credenziali fpl

credit ['krɛdɪt] n credito; onore m ♦ vt (COMM) accreditare; (believe: also: **give ~ to**) credere, prestar fede a; **~s** npl (CINEMA) titoli mpl; **to ~ sb with** (fig) attribuire a qn; **to be in ~** (person) essere creditore (trice); (bank account) essere coperto(a); ~ **card** n carta di credito; **~or** n creditore/trice

creed [kriːd] n credo; dottrina

creek [kriːk] n insenatura; (US) piccolo fiume m

creep [kriːp] (pt, pp **crept**) vi avanzare furtivamente (or pian piano); **~er** n pianta rampicante; **~y** adj (frightening) che fa accapponare la pelle

crematorium [krɛmə'tɔːrɪəm] (pl

crematoria n forno crematorio

crêpe [kreɪp] n crespo; **~ bandage** (BRIT) n fascia elastica

crept [krept] pt, pp of **creep**

crescent ['kresnt] n (shape) mezzaluna; (street) strada semicircolare

cress [krɛs] n crescione m

crest [krɛst] n cresta; (of coat of arms) cimiero; **~fallen** adj mortificato(a)

Crete [kriːt] n Creta

crevasse [krɪ'væs] n crepaccio

crevice ['krɛvɪs] n fessura, crepa

crew [kruː] n equipaggio; **~-cut** to **have a ~-cut** avere i capelli a spazzola; **~-neck** n girocollo

crib [krɪb] n culla ♦ vt (inf) copiare

crick [krɪk] n crampo

cricket ['krɪkɪt] n (insect) grillo; (game) cricket m

crime [kraɪm] n crimine m; **criminal** ['krɪmɪnl] adj, n criminale m/f

crimson ['krɪmzn] adj color cremisi inv

cringe [krɪndʒ] vi acquattarsi; (in embarrassment) sentirsi sprofondare

crinkle ['krɪŋkl] vt arricciare, increspare

cripple ['krɪpl] n zoppo/a ♦ vt azzoppare

crises [kraɪsiːz] npl of **crisis**

crisis ['kraɪsɪs] (pl **crises**) n crisi f inv

crisp [krɪsp] adj croccante; (fig) frizzante; vivace; deciso(a); **~s** (BRIT) npl patatine fpl

criss-cross ['krɪs-] adj incrociato(a)

criteria [kraɪ'tɪərɪə] npl of **criterion**

criterion [kraɪ'tɪərɪən] (pl **criteria**) n criterio

critic ['krɪtɪk] n critico; **~al** adj critico(a); **~ally** adv (speak etc) criticamente; **~ally ill** gravemente malato; **~ism** ['krɪtɪsɪzm] n critica; **~ize** ['krɪtɪsaɪz] vt criticare

croak [krəʊk] vi gracchiare; (frog) gracidare

Croatia [krəʊ'eɪʃə] n Croazia

crochet ['krəʊʃeɪ] n lavoro all'uncinetto

crockery ['krɒkərɪ] n vasellame m

crocodile ['krɒkədaɪl] n coccodrillo

crocus ['krəʊkəs] n croco

croft [krɒft] (BRIT) n piccolo podere m

crony ['krəʊnɪ] n (inf: pej) compare m

crook [krʊk] n truffatore m; (of shepherd) bastone m; **~ed** ['krʊkɪd] adj curvo(a), storto(a); (action) disonesto(a)

crop [krɒp] n (produce) coltivazione f; (amount produced) raccolto; (riding ~) frustino ♦ vt (hair) rapare; **~ up** vi presentarsi

croquette [krə'kɛt] n crocchetta

cross [krɒs] n croce f; (BIOL) incrocio ♦ vt (street etc) attraversare; (arms, legs, BIOL) incrociare; (cheque) sbarrare ♦ adj di cattivo umore; **~ out** vt cancellare; **~ over** vi attraversare; **~bar** n traversa; **~country (race)** n cross-country n inv; **~-examine** vt (LAW) interrogare in contraddittorio; **~-eyed** adj strabico(a); **~fire** n fuoco incrociato; **~ing** n incrocio; (sea passage) traversata; (also: pedestrian ~ing) passaggio pedonale; **~ing guard** (US) n dipendente comunale che aiuta i bambini ad attraversare la strada; **~ purposes** npl: **to be at ~ purposes** non parlare della stessa cosa; **~-reference** n rinvio, rimando; **~roads** n incrocio;

~ section n sezione f trasversale; (in population) settore m rappresentativo; **~walk** (US) n strisce fpl pedonali, passaggio pedonale; **~wind** n vento di traverso; **~word** n cruciverba m inv

crotch [krɒtʃ] n (ANAT) inforcatura; (of garment) pattina

crotchet ['krɒtʃɪt] n (MUS) semiminima

crouch [kraʊtʃ] vi acquattarsi; rannicchiarsi

crow [krəʊ] n (bird) cornacchia; (of cock) canto del gallo ♦ vi (cock) cantare

crowbar ['krəʊbɑː*] n piede m di porco

crowd [kraʊd] n folla ♦ vt affollare, stipare ♦ vi: **to ~ round/in** affollarsi intorno a/in; **~ed** adj affollato(a); **~ed with** stipato(a) di

crown [kraʊn] n corona; (of head)

calotta cranica; (of hat) cocuzzolo; (of hill) cima ♦ vt incoronare; (fig: career) coronare; ~ **jewels** npl gioielli mpl della Corona; ~ **prince** n principe m ereditario

crow's feet npl zampe fpl di gallina

crucial ['kru:ʃl] adj cruciale, decisivo(a)

crucifix ['kru:sıfıks] n crocifisso; ~**ion** [-'fıkʃən] n crocifissione f

crude [kru:d] adj (materials) greggio(a); non raffinato(a); (fig: basic) crudo(a), primitivo(a); (: vulgar) rozzo(a), grossolano(a); ~ **(oil)** n (petrolio) greggio

cruel ['kruəl] adj crudele; ~**ty** n crudeltà f inv

cruise [kru:z] n crociera ♦ vi andare a velocità di crociera; (taxi) circolare; ~**r** n incrociatore m

crumb [krʌm] n briciola

crumble ['krʌmbl] vt sbriciolare ♦ vi sbriciolarsi; (plaster etc) sgretolarsi; (land, earth) franare; (building, fig) crollare; **crumbly** adj friabile

crumpet ['krʌmpıt] n specie di frittella

crumple ['krʌmpl] vt raggrinzare, spiegazzare

crunch [krʌntʃ] vt sgranocchiare; (underfoot) scricchiolare ♦ n (fig) punto or momento cruciale; ~**y** adj croccante

crusade [kru:'seıd] n crociata

crush [krʌʃ] n folla; (love): **to have a ~ on sb** avere una cotta per qn; (drink): **lemon ~** spremuta di limone ♦ vt schiacciare; (crumple) sgualcire

crust [krʌst] n crosta

crutch [krʌtʃ] n gruccia

crux [krʌks] n nodo

cry [kraı] vi piangere; (shout: also: ~ **out**) urlare ♦ n urlo, grido; ~ **off** vi ritirarsi

cryptic ['krıptık] adj ermetico(a)

crystal ['krıstl] n cristallo; ~-**clear** adj cristallino(a)

cub [kʌb] n cucciolo; (also: ~ **scout**) lupetto

Cuba ['kju:bə] n Cuba

cube [kju:b] n cubo ♦ vt (MATH) elevare al cubo; **cubic** adj cubico(a); (metre, foot) cubo(a); **cubic capacity** n cilindrata

cubicle ['kju:bıkl] n scompartimento separato; cabina

cuckoo ['kuku:] n cucù m inv; ~ **clock** n orologio a cucù

cucumber ['kju:kʌmbə*] n cetriolo

cuddle ['kʌdl] vt abbracciare, coccolare ♦ vi abbracciarsi

cue [kju:] n (snooker ~) stecca; (THEATRE etc) segnale m

cuff [kʌf] n (BRIT: of shirt, coat etc) polsino; (US: of trousers) risvolto; **off the ~** improvvisando; ~**link** n gemello

cuisine [kwı'zi:n] n cucina

cul-de-sac ['kʌldəsæk] n vicolo cieco

cull [kʌl] vt (ideas etc) scegliere ♦ n (of animals) abbattimento selettivo

culminate ['kʌlmıneıt] vi: **to ~ in** culminare con; **culmination** [-'neıʃən] n culmine m

culottes [kju:'lɒts] npl gonna f pantalone inv

culpable ['kʌlpəbl] adj colpevole

culprit ['kʌlprıt] n colpevole m/f

cult [kʌlt] n culto

cultivate ['kʌltıveıt] vt (also fig) coltivare; **cultivation** [-'veıʃən] n coltivazione f

cultural ['kʌltʃərəl] adj culturale

culture ['kʌltʃə*] n (also fig) cultura; ~**d** adj colto(a)

cumbersome ['kʌmbəsəm] adj ingombrante

cunning ['kʌnıŋ] n astuzia, furberia ♦ adj astuto(a), furbo(a)

cup [kʌp] n tazza; (prize, of bra) coppa

cupboard ['kʌbəd] n armadio

cup-tie (BRIT) n partita di coppa

curate ['kjuərıt] n cappellano

curator [kjuə'reıtə*] n direttore m (di museo etc)

curb [kə:b] vt tenere a freno ♦ n freno; (US) bordo del marciapiede

curdle ['kə:dl] vt cagliare

cure [kjuə*] vt guarire; (CULIN) trattare; affumicare; essiccare ♦ n rimedio

curfew [ˈkəːfjuː] n coprifuoco

curiosity [kjuərɪˈɒsɪtɪ] n curiosità

curious [ˈkjuərɪəs] adj curioso(a)

curl [kəːl] n riccio ♦ vt ondulare; (tightly) arricciare ♦ vi arricciarsi; ~ **up** vi rannicchiarsi; **~er** n bigodino

curly [ˈkəːlɪ] adj ricciuto(a)

currant [ˈkʌrnt] n (dried) sultanina; (bush, fruit) ribes m inv

currency [ˈkʌrnsɪ] n moneta; **to gain ~** (fig) acquistare larga diffusione

current [ˈkʌrnt] adj corrente ♦ n corrente f; **~ account** (BRIT) n conto corrente; **~ affairs** npl attualità fpl; **~ly** adv attualmente

curricula [kəˈrɪkjulə] npl of **curriculum**

curriculum [kəˈrɪkjuləm] (pl **~s** or **curricula**) n curriculum m inv; **~ vitae** n curriculum vitae m inv

curry [ˈkʌrɪ] n curry m inv ♦ vt: **to ~ favour with** cercare di attirarsi i favori di; **~ powder** n curry m

curse [kəːs] vt maledire ♦ vi bestemmiare ♦ n maledizione f; bestemmia

cursor [ˈkəːsə*] n (COMPUT) cursore m

cursory [ˈkəːsərɪ] adj superficiale

curt [kəːt] adj secco(a)

curtail [kəːˈteɪl] vt (visit etc) accorciare; (expenses etc) ridurre

curtain [ˈkəːtn] n tenda; (THEATRE) sipario

curts(e)y [ˈkəːtsɪ] vi fare un inchino or una riverenza

curve [kəːv] n curva ♦ vi curvarsi

cushion [ˈkuʃən] n cuscino ♦ vt (shock) fare da cuscinetto a

custard [ˈkʌstəd] n (for pouring) crema

custodian [kʌsˈtəudɪən] n custode m/f

custody [ˈkʌstədɪ] n (of child) tutela; **to take into ~** (suspect) mettere in detenzione preventiva

custom [ˈkʌstəm] n costume m, consuetudine f; (COMM) clientela; **~ary**

adj consueto(a)

customer [ˈkʌstəmə*] n cliente m/f

customized [ˈkʌstəmaɪzd] adj (car etc) fuoriserie inv

custom-made adj (clothes) fatto(a) su misura; (other goods) fatto(a) su ordinazione

customs [ˈkʌstəmz] npl dogana; **~ duty** n tassa doganale; **~ officer** n doganiere m

cut [kʌt] (pt, pp **cut**) vt tagliare; (shape, make) intagliare; (reduce) ridurre ♦ vi tagliare ♦ n taglio; (in salary etc) riduzione f; **to ~ a tooth** mettere un dente; **~ down** vt (tree etc) abbattere ♦ vt fus (also: ~ down on) ridurre; **~ off** vt tagliare; (fig) isolare; **~ out** vt tagliare fuori; eliminare; ritagliare; **~ up** vt tagliare a pezzi; **~back** n riduzione f

cute [kjuːt] adj (sweet) carino(a)

cuticle [ˈkjuːtɪkl] n (on nail) pellicina, cuticola

cutlery [ˈkʌtlərɪ] n posate fpl

cutlet [ˈkʌtlɪt] n costoletta; (nut etc ~) cotoletta vegetariana

cut: **~out** n interruttore m; (cardboard ~out) ritaglio; **~-price** (US **~-rate**) adj a prezzo ridotto; **~throat** n assassino ♦ adj (competition) spietato(a)

cutting [ˈkʌtɪŋ] adj tagliente ♦ n (from newspaper) ritaglio (di giornale); (from plant) talea

CV n abbr = curriculum vitae

cwt abbr = hundredweight(s)

cyanide [ˈsaɪənaɪd] n cianuro

cybercafé [ˈsaɪbəkæfeɪ] n cybercaffè m inv

cycle [ˈsaɪkl] n ciclo; (bicycle) bicicletta ♦ vi andare in bicicletta; **~ hire** n noleggio m biciclette inv; **~ lane**, **~ path** n pista ciclabile

cycling [ˈsaɪklɪŋ] n ciclismo

cyclist [ˈsaɪklɪst] n ciclista m/f

cygnet [ˈsɪgnɪt] n cigno giovane

cylinder [ˈsɪlɪndə*] n cilindro; **~-head gasket** n guarnizione f della testata del cilindro

cymbals ['sɪmblz] *npl* cembali *mpl*

cynic ['sɪnɪk] *n* cinico(a); **~al** *adj* cinico(a); **~ism** ['sɪnɪsɪzəm] *n* cinismo

Cyprus ['saɪprəs] *n* Cipro

cyst [sɪst] *n* cisti *f inv*

cystitis [sɪs'taɪtɪs] *n* cistite *f*

czar [zɑ:*] *n* zar *m inv*

Czech [tʃek] *adj* ceco(a) ♦ *n* ceco/a; (LING) ceco

Czech Republic *n*: **the ~** la Repubblica Ceca

D, d

D [di:] *n* (MUS) re *m*

dab [dæb] *vt* (eyes, wound) tamponare; (paint, cream) applicare (con leggeri colpetti)

dabble ['dæbl] *vi*: **to ~ in** occuparsi (da dilettante) di

dad(dy) [dæd(ɪ)] (*inf*) *n* babbo, papà *m inv*

daffodil ['dæfədɪl] *n* trombone *m*, giunchiglia

daft [dɑ:ft] *adj* sciocco(a)

dagger ['dægə*] *n* pugnale *m*

daily ['deɪlɪ] *adj* quotidiano(a), giornaliero(a) ♦ *n* quotidiano ♦ *adv* tutti i giorni

dainty ['deɪntɪ] *adj* delicato(a), grazioso(a)

dairy ['dɛərɪ] *n* (BRIT: shop) latteria; (on farm) caseificio ♦ *adj* caseario(a); **~ farm** *n* caseificio; **~ products** *npl* latticini *mpl*; **~ store** (US) *n* latteria

daisy ['deɪzɪ] *n* margherita

dale [deɪl] (BRIT) *n* valle *f*

dam [dæm] *n* diga ♦ *vt* sbarrare; costruire dighe su

damage ['dæmɪdʒ] *n* danno, danni *mpl*; (fig) danno ♦ *vt* danneggiare; **~s** *npl* (LAW) danni

damn [dæm] *vt* condannare; (curse) maledire ♦ *n* (inf): **I don't give a ~** non me ne frega niente ♦ *adj* (inf: also: **~ed**): **this ~ ...** questo maledetto ...; **~**

(it)! accidenti!; **~ing** *adj* (evidence) schiacciante

damp [dæmp] *adj* umido(a) ♦ *n* umidità, umido ♦ *vt* (also: **~en**: cloth, rag) inumidire, bagnare; (: enthusiasm etc) spegnere

damson ['dæmzən] *n* susina damaschina

dance [dɑ:ns] *n* danza, ballo; (ball) ballo ♦ *vi* ballare; **~ hall** *n* dancing *m inv*, sala da ballo; **~r** *n* danzatore/trice; (professional) ballerino/a

dancing ['dɑ:nsɪŋ] *n* danza, ballo

dandelion ['dændɪlaɪən] *n* dente *m* di leone

dandruff ['dændrəf] *n* forfora

Dane [deɪn] *n* danese *m/f*

danger ['deɪndʒə*] *n* pericolo; **there is a ~ of fire** c'è pericolo di incendio; **in ~** in pericolo; **he was in ~ of falling** rischiava di cadere; **~ous** *adj* pericoloso(a)

dangle ['dæŋgl] *vt* dondolare; (fig) far balenare ♦ *vi* pendolare

Danish ['deɪnɪʃ] *adj* danese ♦ *n* (LING) danese *m*

dare [dɛə*] *vt*: **to ~ sb to do** sfidare qn a fare ♦ *vi*: **to ~ (to) do sth** osare fare qc; **I ~ say** (I suppose) immagino (che); **daring** *adj* audace, ardito(a) ♦ *n* audacia

dark [dɑ:k] *adj* (night, room) buio(a), scuro(a); (colour, complexion) scuro(a); (fig) cupo(a), tetro(a), nero(a) ♦ *n*: **in the ~** al buio; **in the ~ about** (fig) all'oscuro di; **after ~** a notte fatta; **~en** *vt* (colour) scurire ♦ *vi* (sky, room) oscurarsi; **~ glasses** *npl* occhiali *mpl* scuri; **~ness** *n* oscurità, buio; **~room** *n* camera oscura

darling ['dɑ:lɪŋ] *adj* caro(a) ♦ *n* tesoro

darn [dɑ:n] *vt* rammendare

dart [dɑ:t] *n* freccetta; (SEWING) pince *f inv* ♦ *vi*: **to ~ towards** precipitarsi verso; **to ~ away/along** sfrecciare via/lungo; **~board** *n* bersaglio (per freccette); **~s** *n* tiro al bersaglio (con freccette)

dash [dæʃ] *n* (*sign*) lineetta; (*small quantity*) punta ♦ *vt* (*missile*) gettare; (*hopes*) infrangere ♦ *vi*: **to ~ towards** precipitarsi verso; **~ away** *or* **off** *vi* scappare via

dashboard ['dæʃbɔːd] *n* (AUT) cruscotto

dashing ['dæʃɪŋ] *adj* ardito(a)

data ['deɪtə] *npl* dati *mpl*; **~base** *n* base *f* di dati, data base *m inv*; **~ processing** *n* elaborazione *f* (elettronica) dei dati

date [deɪt] *n* data; appuntamento; (*fruit*) dattero ♦ *vt* datare; (*person*) uscire con; **~ of birth** data di nascita; **to ~** (*until now*) fino a oggi; **~d** *adj* passato(a), di moda; **~ rape** stupro perpetrato da persona conosciuta

daub [dɔːb] *vt* imbrattare

daughter ['dɔːtə*] *n* figlia; **~-in-law** *n* nuora

daunting ['dɔːntɪŋ] *adj* non invidiabile

dawdle ['dɔːdl] *vi* bighellonare

dawn [dɔːn] *n* alba ♦ *vi* (*day*) spuntare; (*fig*): **it ~ed on him that** ... gli è venuto in mente che ....

day [deɪ] *n* giorno; (*as duration*) giornata; (*period of time, age*) tempo, epoca; **the ~ before** il giorno avanti *or* prima; **the ~ after, the following ~** il giorno dopo *or* seguente; **the ~ after tomorrow** dopodomani; **the ~ before yesterday** l'altroieri; **by ~** di giorno; **~break** *n* spuntar *m* del giorno; **~dream** *vi* sognare a occhi aperti; **~light** *n* luce *f* del giorno; **~ return** (BRIT) *n* biglietto giornaliero di andata e ritorno; **~time** *n* giorno; **~-to-~** *adj* (*life, organization*) quotidiano(a)

daze [deɪz] *vt* (*subject: drug*) inebetire; (*: blow*) stordire ♦ *n*: **in a ~** inebetito(a); stordito(a)

dazzle ['dæzl] *vt* abbagliare

DC *abbr* (= *direct current*) c.c.

D-day *n* giorno dello sbarco alleato in Normandia

dead [dɛd] *adj* morto(a); (*numb*) intirizzito(a); (*telephone*) muto(a); (*battery*) scarico(a) ♦ *adv* assolutamente, perfettamente ♦ *npl*: **the ~** i morti; **he was shot ~** fu colpito a morte; (*telephone*) muto(a) morto(a); **to stop ~** fermarsi di colpo; **~en** *vt* (*blow, sound*) ammortire; **~ end** *n* vicolo cieco; **~ heat** *n* (SPORT): **to finish in a ~ heat** finire alla pari; **~line** *n* scadenza; **~lock** *n* punto morto; **~ loss** *n*: **to be a ~ loss** (*inf: person, thing*) non valere niente; **~ly** *adj* mortale; (*weapon, poison*) micidiale; **~pan** *adj* a faccia impassibile

deaf [dɛf] *adj* sordo(a); **~en** *vt* assordare; **~ness** *n* sordità

deal [diːl] (*pt, pp* **dealt**) *n* accordo; (*business ~*) affare *m* ♦ *vt* (*blow, cards*) dare; **a great ~ (of)** molto(a); **~ in** *vt fus* occuparsi di; **~ with** *vt fus* (COMM) fare affari con, trattare con; (*handle*) occuparsi di; (*be about: book etc*) trattare di; **~er** *n* commerciante *m/f*; **~ings** *npl* (COMM) relazioni *fpl*; (*relations*) rapporti *mpl*; **dealt** [dɛlt] *pt, pp of* **deal**

dean [diːn] *n* (REL) decano; (SCOL) preside *m* di facoltà (*or* di collegio)

dear [dɪə*] *adj* caro(a) ♦ *n*: **my ~** caro mio/cara mia ♦ *excl*: **~ me!** Dio mio!; **D~ Sir/Madam** (*in letter*) Egregio Signore/Egregia Signora; **D~ Mr/Mrs X** Gentile Signor/Signora X; **~ly** *adv* (*love*) moltissimo; (*pay*) a caro prezzo

death [dɛθ] *n* morte *f*; (ADMIN) decesso; **~ certificate** *n* atto di decesso; **~ly** *adj* di morte; **~ penalty** *n* pena di morte; **~ rate** *n* indice *m* di mortalità; **~ toll** *n* vittime *fpl*

debacle [dɪˈbækl] *n* fiasco

debase [dɪˈbeɪs] *vt* (*currency*) adulterare; (*person*) degradare

debatable [dɪˈbeɪtəbl] *adj* discutibile

debate [dɪˈbeɪt] *n* dibattito ♦ *vt* dibattere; discutere

debit 373 default

debit ['dɛbɪt] n debito ♦ vt: **to ~ a
sum to sb** or **to sb's account**
addebitare una somma a qn

debris ['dɛbriː] n detriti mpl

debt [dɛt] n debito; **to be in ~** essere
indebitato(a); **~or** n debitore/trice

début ['deɪbjuː] n debutto

decade ['dɛkeɪd] n decennio

decadence ['dɛkədəns] n decadenza

decaff ['diːkæf] (inf) n decaffeinato

decaffeinated [dɪ'kæfɪneɪtɪd] adj
decaffeinato(a)

decanter [dɪ'kæntə*] n caraffa

decay [dɪ'keɪ] n decadimento; (also:
tooth ~) carie f ♦ vi (rot) imputridire

deceased [dɪ'siːst] adj morto(a)

deceit [dɪ'siːt] n inganno; **~ful** adj
ingannevole, perfido(a)

deceive [dɪ'siːv] vt ingannare

December [dɪ'sɛmbə*] n dicembre m

decent ['diːsənt] adj decente;
(respectable) per bene; (kind) gentile

deception [dɪ'sɛpʃən] n inganno

deceptive [dɪ'sɛptɪv] adj ingannevole

decide [dɪ'saɪd] vt (person) far prendere
una decisione a; (question, argument)
risolvere, decidere ♦ vi decidere,
decidersi; **to ~ to do/that** decidere di
fare/che; **to ~ on** decidere per; **~d** adj
(resolute) deciso(a); (clear, definite)
netto(a), chiaro(a); **~dly** [-dɪdlɪ] adv
indubbiamente; decisamente

decimal ['dɛsɪməl] adj decimale ♦ n
decimale m; **~ point** n virgola

decipher [dɪ'saɪfə*] vt decifrare

decision [dɪ'sɪʒən] n decisione f

decisive [dɪ'saɪsɪv] adj deciso(a);
(person) deciso(a)

deck [dɛk] n (NAUT) ponte m; (of bus):
top ~ imperiale m; (record ~) piatto;
(of cards) mazzo; **~chair** n sedia a
sdraio

declaration [dɛklə'reɪʃən] n
dichiarazione f

declare [dɪ'klɛə*] vt dichiarare

decline [dɪ'klaɪn] n (decay) declino;
(lessening) ribasso ♦ vt declinare;

rifiutare ♦ vi declinare; diminuire

decode [diː'kəud] vt decifrare

decoder [diː'kəudə*] n (TV)
decodificatore m

decompose [diːkəm'pəuz] vi
decomporre

décor ['deɪkɔ:*] n decorazione f

decorate ['dɛkəreɪt] vt (adorn, give a
medal to) decorare; (paint and paper)
tinteggiare e tappezzare; **decoration**
[-'reɪʃən] n (medal etc, adornment)
decorazione f; **decorator** n decoratore
m

decorum [dɪ'kɔ:rəm] n decoro

decoy ['diːkɔɪ] n zimbello

decrease [n 'diːkri:s, vb diː'kri:s] n
diminuzione f ♦ vt, vi diminuire

decree [dɪ'kri:] n decreto; **~ nisi**
[-'naɪsaɪ] n sentenza provvisoria di
divorzio

dedicate ['dɛdɪkeɪt] vt consacrare;
(book etc) dedicare

dedication [dɛdɪ'keɪʃən] n (devotion)
dedizione f; (in book etc) dedica

deduce [dɪ'dju:s] vt dedurre

deduct [dɪ'dʌkt] vt: **to ~ sth (from)**
dedurre qc (da); **~ion** n (amount, of
tax) deduzione f; (LAW) atto

deed [di:d] n (gen) azione f, atto; (LAW) atto

deep [di:p] adj profondo(a); **4 metres
~** profondo(a) 4 metri ♦ adv:
spectators stood 20 ~ c'erano 20
file di spettatori; **~en** vt (hole)
approfondire ♦ vi approfondirsi;
(darkness) farsi più buio; **~ end** n: the
~ end (of swimming pool) la parte più
profonda; **~-freeze** n congelatore m;
~-fry vt friggere in olio abbondante;
~ly adv profondamente; **~-sea diving**
n immersione f in alto mare; **~-seated**
adj radicato(a)

deer [dɪə*] n inv: **the ~** i cervidi; (red)
~ cervo; (fallow) **~** daino; (roe) **~**
capriolo; **~skin** n pelle f di daino

deface [dɪ'feɪs] vt imbrattare

default [dɪ'fɔ:lt] n (COMPUT: also:
~ value) default m inv; **by ~** (SPORT) per

abbandono

defeat [dɪˈfiːt] *n* sconfitta ♦ *vt* (team, opponents) sconfiggere; **~ist** *adj*, *n* disfattista *m/f*

defect [*n* ˈdiːfekt, *vb* dɪˈfekt] *n* difetto ♦ *vi*: **to ~ to the enemy** passare al nemico; **~ive** [dɪˈfektɪv] *adj* difettoso/a

defence [dɪˈfɛns] (*US* **defense**) *n* difesa; **~less** *adj* senza difesa

defend [dɪˈfɛnd] *vt* difendere; **~ant** *n* imputato/a; **~er** *n* difensore/a

defense [dɪˈfɛns] (*US*) *n* = **defence**

defensive [dɪˈfɛnsɪv] *adj* difensivo(a) ♦ *n*: **on the ~** sulla difensiva

defer [dɪˈfəː*] *vt* (postpone) differire, rinviare

defiance [dɪˈfaɪəns] *n* sfida; **in ~ of** a dispetto di

defiant [dɪˈfaɪənt] *adj* (attitude) di sfida; (person) ribelle

deficiency [dɪˈfɪʃənsɪ] *n* deficienza; carenza

deficit [ˈdɛfɪsɪt] *n* deficit *m inv*

define [dɪˈfaɪn] *vt* definire

definite [ˈdɛfɪnɪt] *adj* (fixed) definito(a), preciso(a); (clear, obvious) ben definito(a), esatto(a); (LING) determinativo(a); **he was ~ about it** ne era sicuro; **~ly** *adv* indubbiamente

definition [dɛfɪˈnɪʃən] *n* definizione *f*

deflate [diːˈfleɪt] *vt* sgonfiare

deflect [dɪˈflɛkt] *vt* deflettere, deviare

deformed [dɪˈfɔːmd] *adj* deforme

defraud [dɪˈfrɔːd] *vt* defraudare

defrost [diːˈfrɔst] *vt* (fridge) disgelare; **~er** (*US*) *n* (demister) sbrinatore *m*

deft [dɛft] *adj* svelto(a), destro(a)

defunct [dɪˈfʌŋkt] *adj* che non esiste più

defuse [diːˈfjuːz] *vt* disinnescare; (fig) distendere

defy [dɪˈfaɪ] *vt* sfidare; (efforts etc) resistere a; **it defies description** supera ogni descrizione

degenerate [*vb* dɪˈdʒɛnəreɪt, *adj* dɪˈdʒɛnərɪt] *vi* degenerare ♦ *adj*

degenere

degree [dɪˈgriː] *n* grado; (SCOL) laurea (universitaria); **a (first) ~ in maths** una laurea in matematica; **by ~s** (gradually) gradualmente, a poco a poco; **to some ~** fino a un certo punto, in certa misura

dehydrated [diːhaɪˈdreɪtɪd] *adj* disidratato(a); (milk, eggs) in polvere

de-ice [diːˈaɪs] *vt* (windscreen) disgelare

deign [deɪn] *vi*: **to ~ to do** degnarsi di fare

deity [ˈdiːɪtɪ] *n* divinità *f inv*

dejected [dɪˈdʒɛktɪd] *adj* abbattuto(a), avvilito(a)

delay [dɪˈleɪ] *vt* ritardare ♦ *vi*: **to ~ (in doing sth)** ritardare (a fare qc) ♦ *n* ritardo; **to be ~ed** subire un ritardo; (person) essere trattenuto(a)

delectable [dɪˈlɛktəbl] *adj* (person, food) delizioso/a

delegate [*n* ˈdɛlɪgɪt, *vb* ˈdɛlɪgeɪt] *n* delegato/a ♦ *vt* delegare; **delegation** [-ˈgeɪʃən] *n* (group) delegazione *f*; (by manager) delega

delete [dɪˈliːt] *vt* cancellare

deliberate [*adj* dɪˈlɪbərɪt, *vb* dɪˈlɪbəreɪt] *adj* (intentional) intenzionale; (slow) misurato(a) ♦ *vi* deliberare, riflettere; **~ly** *adv* (on purpose) deliberatamente

delicacy [ˈdɛlɪkəsɪ] *n* delicatezza

delicate [ˈdɛlɪkɪt] *adj* delicato(a)

delicatessen [dɛlɪkəˈtɛsn] *n* ≈ salumeria

delicious [dɪˈlɪʃəs] *adj* delizioso(a), squisito(a)

delight [dɪˈlaɪt] *n* delizia, gran piacere *m* ♦ *vt* dilettare; **to take (a) ~ in** dilettarsi in; **~ed** *adj*: **~ed (at** *or* **with)** contentissimo(a) (di), felice (di); **~ed to do** felice di fare; **~ful** *adj* delizioso(a); incantevole

delinquent [dɪˈlɪŋkwənt] *adj*, *n* delinquente *m/f*

delirious [dɪˈlɪrɪəs] *adj*: **to be ~** delirare

deliver [dɪ'lɪvə*] vt (mail) distribuire; (goods) consegnare; (speech) pronunciare; (MED) far partorire; **~y** n distribuzione f; consegna; (of speaker) dizione f; (MED) parto

delude [dɪ'lu:d] vt illudere

deluge ['delju:dʒ] n diluvio

delusion [dɪ'lu:ʒən] n illusione f

demand [dɪ'mɑ:nd] vt richiedere; (rights) rivendicare ♦ n domanda; (claim) rivendicazione f; **in ~** ricercato(a), richiesto(a); **on ~** a richiesta; **~ing** adj (boss) esigente; (work) impegnativo(a)

demean [dɪ'mi:n] vt: **to ~ o.s.** umiliarsi

demeanour [dɪ'mi:nə*] (US **demeanor**) n comportamento; contegno

demented [dɪ'mentɪd] adj demente, impazzito(a)

demise [dɪ'maɪz] n decesso

demister [di:'mɪstə*] (BRIT) n (AUT) sbrinatore m

demo ['deməu] (inf) n abbr (= demonstration) manifestazione f

democracy [dɪ'mɒkrəsɪ] n democrazia

democrat ['deməkræt] n democratico(a); **~ic** [demə'krætɪk] adj democratico(a)

demolish [dɪ'mɒlɪʃ] vt demolire

demonstrate ['demənstreɪt] vt dimostrare, provare ♦ vi dimostrare, manifestare; **demonstration** [-'streɪʃən] n dimostrazione f; (POL) dimostrazione, manifestazione f; **demonstrator** n (POL) dimostrante m/f; (COMM) dimostratore/trice

demote [dɪ'məut] vt far retrocedere

demure [dɪ'mjuə*] adj contegnoso(a)

den [den] n tana, covo; (room) buco

denial [dɪ'naɪəl] n diniego; rifiuto

denim ['denɪm] n tessuto di cotone ritorto; **~s** npl (jeans) blue jeans mpl

Denmark ['denmɑ:k] n Danimarca

denomination [dɪnɒmɪ'neɪʃən] n (money) valore m; (REL) confessione f

denounce [dɪ'nauns] vt denunciare

dense [dens] adj fitto(a); (smoke) denso(a); (inf: person) ottuso(a), duro(a)

density ['densɪtɪ] n densità f inv

dent [dent] n ammaccatura ♦ vt (also: **make a ~ in**) ammaccare

dental ['dentl] adj dentale; **~ surgeon** n medico/a dentista

dentist ['dentɪst] n dentista m/f

dentures ['dentʃəz] npl dentiera

deny [dɪ'naɪ] vt negare; (refuse) rifiutare

deodorant [di:'əudərənt] n deodorante m

depart [dɪ'pɑ:t] vi partire; **to ~ from** (fig) deviare da

department [dɪ'pɑ:tmənt] n (COMM) reparto; (SCOL) sezione f, dipartimento f; (POL) ministero; **~ store** n grande magazzino

departure [dɪ'pɑ:tʃə*] n partenza; (fig): **~ from** deviazione f da; **a new ~** una svolta (decisiva); **~ lounge** n (at airport) sala d'attesa

depend [dɪ'pend] vi: **to ~ on** (rely on) contare su; (financially) dipendere da; (rely on) contare su; **it ~s** dipende; **~ing on the result ...** a seconda del risultato ...; **~able** adj (person etc) fidato(a); (car etc) affidabile; **~ant** n persona a carico; **~ent** adj: **to be ~ent on** dipendere da; (child, relative) essere a carico di ♦ n = **~ant**

depict [dɪ'pɪkt] vt (in picture) dipingere; (in words) descrivere

depleted [dɪ'pli:tɪd] adj diminuito(a)

deploy [dɪ'plɔɪ] vt dispiegare

depopulation ['di:pɒpju'leɪʃən] n spopolamento

deport [dɪ'pɔ:t] vt deportare; espellere

deportment [dɪ'pɔ:tmənt] n portamento

deposit [dɪ'pɒzɪt] n (COMM, GEO) deposito; (of ore, oil) giacimento; (CHEM) sedimento; (part payment) acconto; (for hired goods etc) cauzione f ♦ vt depositare; dare in acconto;

mettere or lasciare in deposito; **~ account** n conto vincolato

depot ['depəʊ] n deposito; (US) stazione f ferroviaria

depreciate [dɪ'priːʃɪeɪt] vi svalutarsi

depress [dɪ'pres] vt deprimere; (price, wages) abbassare; (press down) premere; **~ed** adj (person) depresso(a), abbattuto(a); (price) in ribasso; (industry) in crisi; **~ing** adj deprimente; **~ion** [dɪ'preʃən] n depressione f

deprivation [deprɪ'veɪʃən] n privazione f

deprive [dɪ'praɪv] vt: **to ~ sb of** privare qn di; **~d** adj disgraziato(a)

depth [depθ] n profondità f inv; **in the ~s of** nel profondo di; nel cuore di; **out of one's ~** (in water) dove non si tocca; (fig) a disagio

deputize ['depjutaɪz] vi: **to ~ for** svolgere le funzioni di

deputy ['depjutɪ] adj: **~ head** (BRIT: SCOL) vicepreside m/f ♦ n (assistant) vice m/f inv; (US: also: **~ sheriff**) vice-sceriffo

derail [dɪ'reɪl] vt: **to be ~ed** deragliare

deranged [dɪ'reɪndʒd] adj: **to be (mentally) ~** essere pazzo(a)

derby ['dɜːbɪ] (US) n (bowler hat) bombetta

derelict ['derɪlɪkt] adj abbandonato(a)

derisory [dɪ'raɪsərɪ] adj (sum) irrisorio(a); (laughter, person) beffardo(a)

derive [dɪ'raɪv] vt: **to ~ sth from** derivare qc da; trarre qc da ♦ vi: **to ~ from** derivare da

derogatory [dɪ'rɔgətərɪ] adj denigratorio(a)

derv [dɜːv] (BRIT) n gasolio

descend [dɪ'send] vt, vi discendere, scendere; **to ~ from** discendere da; **to ~ to** (lying, begging) abbassarsi a; **~ant** n discendente m/f

descent [dɪ'sent] n discesa f; (origin) discendenza, famiglia

describe [dɪs'kraɪb] vt descrivere;

description [dɪ'skrɪpʃən] n descrizione f; (sort) genere m, specie f

desecrate ['desɪkreɪt] vt profanare

desert [n 'dezət, vb dɪ'zɜːt] n deserto ♦ vt lasciare, abbandonare ♦ vi (MIL) disertare; **~er** n disertore m; **~ion** [dɪ'zɜːʃən] n (MIL) diserzione f; (LAW) abbandono del tetto coniugale; **~ island** n isola deserta; **~s** ['dezəts] npl: **to get one's just ~s** avere ciò che si merita

deserve [dɪ'zɜːv] vt meritare; **deserving** adj (person) meritevole, degno(a); (cause) meritorio(a)

design [dɪ'zaɪn] n (art, sketch) disegno; (layout, shape) linea; (pattern) fantasia; (intention) intenzione f ♦ vt disegnare; progettare

designer [dɪ'zaɪnə*] n (ART, TECH) disegnatore/trice; (of fashion) modellista m/f

desire [dɪ'zaɪə*] n desiderio, voglia ♦ vt desiderare, volere

desk [desk] n (in office) scrivania; (for pupil) banco; (BRIT: in shop, restaurant) cassa; (in hotel) ricevimento; (at airport) accettazione f

desolate ['desələt] adj desolato(a)

despair [dɪs'peə*] n disperazione f ♦ vi: **to ~ of** disperare di

despatch [dɪs'pætʃ] n, vt = **dispatch**

desperate ['despərət] adj disperato(a); (fugitive) capace di tutto; **to be ~ for sth/to do** volere disperatamente qc/ fare; **~ly** adv disperatamente; (very) terribilmente, estremamente

desperation [despə'reɪʃən] n disperazione f

despicable [dɪs'pɪkəbl] adj disprezzabile

despise [dɪs'paɪz] vt disprezzare, sdegnare

despite [dɪs'paɪt] prep malgrado, a dispetto di, nonostante

despondent [dɪs'pɔndənt] adj abbattuto(a), scoraggiato(a)

dessert [dɪ'zɜːt] n dolce m; frutta;

~spoon n cucchiaio da dolci

destination [destɪˈneɪʃən] n destinazione f

destined ['destɪnd] adj: **to be ~ to do/for** essere destinato(a) a fare/per

destiny ['destɪnɪ] n destino

destitute ['destɪtjuːt] adj indigente, bisognoso(a)

destroy [dɪsˈtrɔɪ] vt distruggere; **~er** n (NAUT) cacciatorpediniere m

destruction [dɪsˈtrʌkʃən] n distruzione f

detach [dɪˈtætʃ] vt staccare, distaccare; **~ed** adj (attitude) distante; **~ed house** n villa; **~ment** n (MIL) distaccamento m; (fig) distacco

detail ['diːteɪl] n particolare m, dettaglio ♦ vt dettagliare, particolareggiare; **in ~** nei particolari; **~ed** adj particolareggiato(a)

detain [dɪˈteɪn] vt trattenere; (in captivity) detenere

detect [dɪˈtekt] vt scoprire, scorgere; (MED, POLICE, RADAR etc) individuare; **~ion** [dɪˈtekʃən] n scoperta; individuazione f; **~ive** n investigatore/trice; **~ive story** n giallo

détente [deɪˈtɑːnt] n (POL) distensione f

detention [dɪˈtenʃən] n detenzione f; (SCOL) permanenza forzata per punizione

deter [dɪˈtəː*] vt dissuadere

detergent [dɪˈtəːdʒənt] n detersivo

deteriorate [dɪˈtɪərɪəreɪt] vi deteriorarsi

determine [dɪˈtəːmɪn] vt determinare; **~d** adj (person) risoluto(a), deciso(a); **~d to do** deciso(a) a fare

detour ['diːtuə*] n deviazione f

detract [dɪˈtrækt] vi: **to ~ from** detrarre da

detriment ['detrɪmənt] n: **to the ~ of** a detrimento di; **~al** [detrɪˈmentl] adj: **~al to** dannoso(a) a, nocivo(a) a

devaluation [diːvæljuˈeɪʃən] n svalutazione f

devastate ['devəsteɪt] vt devastare;

(fig): **~d by** sconvolto(a) da;

devastating adj devastatore(trice); sconvolgente

develop [dɪˈveləp] vt sviluppare; (habit) prendere (gradualmente) ♦ vi svilupparsi; (facts, symptoms: appear) manifestarsi, rivelarsi; **~er** n (also: property **~er**) costruttore m edile; **~ing country** n paese m in via di sviluppo; **~ment** n sviluppo

device [dɪˈvaɪs] n (apparatus) congegno

devil ['devl] n diavolo; demonio

devious ['diːvɪəs] adj (person) subdolo(a)

devise [dɪˈvaɪz] vt escogitare, concepire

devoid [dɪˈvɔɪd] adj: **~ of** privo(a) di

devolution [diːvəˈluːʃən] n (POL) decentramento m

devote [dɪˈvəut] vt: **to ~ sth to** dedicare qc a; **~d** adj devoto(a); **to be ~d to sb** essere molto affezionato(a) a qn; **~e** [devəuˈtiː] n (MUS, SPORT) appassionato/a

devotion [dɪˈvəuʃən] n devozione f, attaccamento m; (REL) atto di devozione, preghiera

devour [dɪˈvauə*] vt divorare

devout [dɪˈvaut] adj pio(a), devoto(a)

dew [djuː] n rugiada

dexterity [deksˈterɪtɪ] n destrezza

diabetes [daɪəˈbiːtiːz] n diabete m; **diabetic** [-ˈbetɪk] adj, n diabetico/a

diabolical [daɪəˈbɒlɪkl] (inf) adj (weather, behaviour) orribile

diagnosis [daɪəgˈnəusɪs] (pl **diagnoses**) n diagnosi f inv

diagonal [daɪˈægənl] adj diagonale ♦ n diagonale f

diagram ['daɪəgræm] n diagramma m

dial ['daɪəl] n quadrante m; (on radio) lancetta; (on telephone) disco combinatore ♦ vt (number) fare

dialect ['daɪəlekt] n dialetto

dialling code ['daɪəlɪŋ-] (US **area code**) n prefisso

dialling tone ['daɪəlɪŋ-] (US **dial tone**) n segnale m di linea libera

dialogue ['daɪəlɔg] (US **dialog**) n dialogo

diameter [daɪ'æmɪtə*] n diametro

diamond ['daɪəmənd] n diamante m; (shape) rombo; **~s** npl (CARDS) quadri mpl

diaper ['daɪəpə*] (US) n pannolino

diaphragm ['daɪəfræm] n diaframma m

diarrhoea [daɪə'riːə] (US **diarrhea**) n diarrea

diary ['daɪərɪ] n (daily account) diario; (book) agenda

dice [daɪs] n inv dado ♦ vt (CULIN) tagliare a dadini

Dictaphone ® ['dɪktəfəʊn] n dittafono ®

dictate [dɪk'teɪt] vt dettare

dictation [dɪk'teɪʃən] n dettatura; (SCOL) dettato

dictator [dɪk'teɪtə*] n dittatore m; **~ship** n dittatura

dictionary ['dɪkʃənrɪ] n dizionario

did [dɪd] pt of **do**

didn't = **did not**

die [daɪ] vi morire; **to be dying for sth/to do sth** morire dalla voglia di qc/di fare qc; **~ away** vi spegnersi a poco a poco; **~ down** vi abbassarsi; **~ out** vi estinguersi

diesel ['diːzəl] n (vehicle) diesel m inv; **~ engine** n motore m diesel inv; **~ (oil)** n gasolio (per motori diesel), diesel m inv

diet ['daɪət] n alimentazione f; (restricted food) dieta ♦ vi (also: **be on a ~**) stare a dieta

differ ['dɪfə*] vi: **to ~ from sth** differire da qc; essere diverso(a) da qc; **to ~ from sb over sth** essere in disaccordo con qn su qc; **~ence** n differenza; (disagreement) screzio; **~ent** adj diverso(a); **~entiate** [-'renʃɪeɪt] vi: **to ~entiate between** discriminare or fare differenza fra

difficult ['dɪfɪkəlt] adj difficile; **~y** n difficoltà f inv

diffident ['dɪfɪdənt] adj sfiduciato(a)

diffuse [adj dɪ'fjuːs, vb dɪ'fjuːz] adj diffuso(a) ♦ vt diffondere

dig [dɪg] (pt, pp **dug**) vt (hole) scavare; (garden) vangare ♦ n (prod) gomitata; (archaeological) scavo; (fig) frecciata; **~ into** vt fus (savings) scavare in; **to ~ one's nails into** conficcare le unghie in; **~ up** vt (tree etc) sradicare; (information) scavare fuori

digest [vb daɪ'dʒest, n 'daɪdʒest] vt digerire ♦ n compendio; **~ion** [dɪ'dʒestʃən] n digestione f; **~ive** adj (juices, system) digerente

digit ['dɪdʒɪt] n cifra; (finger) dito; **~al** adj digitale; **~al camera** n macchina fotografica digitale; **~al TV** n televisione f digitale

dignified ['dɪgnɪfaɪd] adj dignitoso(a)

dignity ['dɪgnɪtɪ] n dignità

digress [daɪ'gres] vi: **to ~ from** divagare da

digs [dɪgz] (BRIT: inf) npl camera ammobiliata

dike [daɪk] n = **dyke**

dilapidated [dɪ'læpɪdeɪtɪd] adj cadente

dilemma [daɪ'lemə] n dilemma m

diligent ['dɪlɪdʒənt] adj diligente

dilute [daɪ'luːt] vt diluire; (with water) annacquare

dim [dɪm] adj (light) debole; (shape etc) vago(a); (room) in penombra; (inf: person) tonto(a) ♦ vt (light) abbassare

dime [daɪm] (US) n = 10 cents

dimension [daɪ'menʃən] n dimensione f

diminish [dɪ'mɪnɪʃ] vi, vt diminuire

diminutive [dɪ'mɪnjʊtɪv] adj minuscolo(a) ♦ n (LING) diminutivo

dimmers ['dɪməz] (US) npl (AUT) anabbaglianti mpl; luci fpl di posizione

dimple ['dɪmpl] n fossetta

din [dɪn] n chiasso, fracasso

dine [daɪn] vi pranzare; **~r** n (person) cliente m/f; (US: place) tavola calda

dinghy ['dɪŋgɪ] n battello pneumatico; (also: rubber ~) gommone m

dingy ['dɪndʒɪ] adj grigio(a)

dining car ['daɪnɪŋ-] (BRIT) n vagone m ristorante

dining room ['daɪnɪŋ-] n sala da pranzo

dinner ['dɪnə*] n (lunch) pranzo; (evening meal) cena; (public) banchetto; ~ **jacket** n smoking m inv; ~ **party** n cena; ~ **time** n ora di pranzo (or cena)

dip [dɪp] n discesa; (in sea) bagno; (CULIN) salsetta ♦ vt immergere; bagnare; (BRIT: AUT: lights) abbassare ♦ vi abbassarsi

diploma [dɪ'pləumə] n diploma m

diplomacy [dɪ'pləuməsɪ] n diplomazia

diplomat ['dɪpləmæt] n diplomatico; ~**ic** [dɪplə'mætɪk] adj diplomatico(a)

diprod ['dɪprɒd] (US) n = dipstick

dipstick ['dɪpstɪk] n (AUT) indicatore m di livello dell'olio

dipswitch ['dɪpswɪtʃ] (BRIT) n (AUT) levetta dei fari

dire [daɪə*] adj terribile; estremo(a)

direct [daɪ'rɛkt] adj diretto(a) ♦ vt dirigere; (order): **to ~ sb to do sth** dare direttive a qn di fare qc ♦ adv direttamente; **can you ~ me to ...?** mi può indicare la strada per ...?

direction [dɪ'rɛkʃən] n direzione f; ~**s** npl (advice) chiarimenti mpl; **sense of** ~ senso dell'orientamento; ~**s for use** istruzioni fpl

directly [dɪ'rɛktlɪ] adv (in straight line) direttamente; (at once) subito

director [dɪ'rɛktə*] n direttore/trice; amministratore/trice; (THEATRE, CINEMA) regista m/f

directory [dɪ'rɛktərɪ] n elenco; ~ **enquiries**, ~ **assistance** (US) n informazioni fpl elenco abbonati inv

dirt [də:t] n sporcizia; immondizia; (earth) terra; ~-**cheap** adj da due soldi; ~**y** adj sporco(a) ♦ vt sporcare; ~**y trick** n brutto scherzo

disability [dɪsə'bɪlɪtɪ] n invalidità f inv;

(LAW) incapacità f inv

disabled [dɪs'eɪbld] adj invalido(a); (mentally) ritardato(a) ♦ npl: **the ~** gli invalidi

disadvantage [dɪsəd'vɑ:ntɪdʒ] n svantaggio

disagree [dɪsə'gri:] vi (differ) discordare; (be against, think otherwise): **to ~ (with)** essere in disaccordo (con), dissentire (da); ~**able** adj sgradevole; (person) antipatico(a); ~**ment** n disaccordo; (argument) dissapore m

disallow [dɪsə'lau] vt (appeal) respingere

disappear [dɪsə'pɪə*] vi scomparire; ~**ance** n scomparsa

disappoint [dɪsə'pɔɪnt] vt deludere; ~**ed** adj deluso(a); ~**ing** adj deludente; ~**ment** n delusione f

disapproval [dɪsə'pru:vəl] n disapprovazione f

disapprove [dɪsə'pru:v] vi: **to ~ of** disapprovare

disarm [dɪs'ɑ:m] vt disarmare; ~**ament** n disarmo

disarray [dɪsə'reɪ] n: **in ~** (army) in rotta; (organization) in uno stato di confusione; (clothes, hair) in disordine

disaster [dɪ'zɑ:stə*] n disastro

disband [dɪs'bænd] vt sbandare; (MIL) congedare ♦ vi sciogliersi

disbelief ['dɪsbə'li:f] n incredulità

disc [dɪsk] n disco; (COMPUT) = **disk**

discard [dɪs'kɑ:d] vt (old things) scartare; (fig) abbandonare

discern [dɪ'sə:n] vt scorgere, distinguere; ~**ing** adj perspicace

discharge [vb dɪs'tʃɑ:dʒ, n 'dɪstʃɑ:dʒ] vt (duties) compiere; (ELEC, waste etc) scaricare; (MED) emettere; (patient) dimettere; (employee) licenziare; (soldier) congedare; (defendant) liberare ♦ n (ELEC) scarica; (MED) emissione f; (dismissal) licenziamento; congedo; liberazione f

disciple [dɪ'saɪpl] n discepolo

discipline ['dɪsɪplɪn] n disciplina ♦ vt

disc jockey n disc jockey m inv

disclaim [dɪs'kleɪm] vt negare, smentire

disclose [dɪs'kləuz] vt rivelare, svelare; **disclosure** [-'kləuʒə*] n rivelazione f

disco ['dɪskəu] n abbr = **discotheque**

discoloured [dɪs'kʌləd] (US **discolored**) adj scolorito(a); ingiallito(a)

discomfort [dɪs'kʌmfət] n disagio; (lack of comfort) scomodità f inv

disconcert [dɪskən'sə:t] vt sconcertare

disconnect [dɪskə'nekt] vt sconnettere, staccare; (ELEC, RADIO) staccare; (gas, water) chiudere

discontent [dɪskən'tent] n scontentezza; **~ed** adj scontento(a)

discontinue [dɪskən'tɪnju:] vt smettere, cessare; "**~d**" (COMM) "fuori produzione"

discord ['dɪskɔ:d] n disaccordo; (MUS) dissonanza

discotheque ['dɪskəutek] n discoteca

discount [n 'dɪskaunt, vt-'kaunt] n sconto ♦ vt scontare; (idea) non badare a

discourage [dɪs'kʌrɪdʒ] vt scoraggiare

discourteous [dɪs'kə:tɪəs] adj scortese

discover [dɪs'kʌvə*] vt scoprire; **~y** n scoperta

discredit [dɪs'kredɪt] vt screditare; mettere in dubbio

discreet [dɪ'skri:t] adj discreto(a)

discrepancy [dɪ'skrepənsɪ] n discrepanza

discriminate [dɪ'skrɪmɪneɪt] vi: to ~ between distinguere tra; to ~ against discriminare contro; **discriminating** adj fine, giudizioso(a); **discrimination** [-'neɪʃən] n discriminazione f; (judgment) discernimento

discuss [dɪ'skʌs] vt discutere; (debate) dibattere; **~ion** [dɪ'skʌʃən] n discussione f

disdain [dɪs'deɪn] n disdegno

disease [dɪ'zi:z] n malattia

disembark [dɪsɪm'bɑ:k] vt, vi sbarcare

disentangle [dɪsɪn'tæŋgl] vt liberare; (wool etc) sbrogliare

disfigure [dɪs'fɪgə*] vt sfigurare

disgrace [dɪs'greɪs] n vergogna; (disfavour) disgrazia ♦ vt disonorare, far cadere in disgrazia; **~ful** adj scandaloso(a), vergognoso(a)

disgruntled [dɪs'grʌntld] adj scontento(a), di cattivo umore

disguise [dɪs'gaɪz] n travestimento ♦ vt: to ~ (as) travestire (da); in ~ travestito(a)

disgust [dɪs'gʌst] n disgusto, nausea ♦ vt disgustare, far schifo a; **~ing** adj disgustoso(a); ripugnante

dish [dɪʃ] n piatto; to do or wash the **~es** fare i piatti; ~ **out** vt distribuire; ~ **up** vt servire; **~cloth** n strofinaccio

dishearten [dɪs'hɑ:tn] vt scoraggiare

dishevelled [dɪ'ʃevəld] (US **disheveled**) adj arruffato(a); scapigliato(a)

dishonest [dɪs'ɔnɪst] adj disonesto(a)

dishonour [dɪs'ɔnə*] (US **dishonor**) n disonore m; **~able** adj disonorevole

dishtowel ['dɪʃtauəl] (US) n strofinaccio dei piatti

dishwasher ['dɪʃwɔʃə*] n lavastoviglie f inv

disillusion [dɪsɪ'lu:ʒən] vt disilludere, disingannare

disinfect [dɪsɪn'fekt] vt disinfettare; **~ant** n disinfettante m

disintegrate [dɪs'ɪntɪgreɪt] vi disintegrarsi

disinterested [dɪs'ɪntrəstɪd] adj disinteressato(a)

disjointed [dɪs'dʒɔɪntɪd] adj sconnesso(a)

disk [dɪsk] n (COMPUT) disco; **single-/double-sided** ~ disco a facciata singola/doppia; ~ **drive** n lettore m; **~ette** (US) n = **disk**

dislike [dɪs'laɪk] n antipatia, avversione f; (gen pl) cosa che non piace ♦ vt: he

~s it non gli piace

dislocate ['dɪsləkeɪt] *vt* slogare

dislodge [dɪs'lɔdʒ] *vt* rimuovere

disloyal [dɪs'lɔɪəl] *adj* sleale

dismal ['dɪzml] *adj* triste, cupo(a)

dismantle [dɪs'mæntl] *vt (machine)* smontare

dismay [dɪs'meɪ] *n* costernazione *f* ♦ *vt* sgomentare

dismiss [dɪs'mɪs] *vt* congedare; *(employee)* licenziare; *(idea)* scacciare; *(LAW)* respingere; **~al** *n* congedo; licenziamento

dismount [dɪs'maunt] *vi* scendere

disobedience [dɪsə'biːdɪəns] *n* disubbidienza

disobedient [dɪsə'biːdɪənt] *adj* disubbidiente

disobey [dɪsə'beɪ] *vt* disubbidire a

disorder [dɪs'ɔːdə*] *n* disordine *m; (rioting)* tumulto; *(MED)* disturbo; **~ly** *adj* disordinato(a); *(rioting)* tumultuoso(a)

disorientated [dɪs'ɔːrɪenteɪtɪd] *adj* disorientato(a)

disown [dɪs'əun] *vt* rinnegare

disparaging [dɪs'pærɪdʒɪŋ] *adj* spregiativo(a), sprezzante

dispassionate [dɪs'pæʃənət] *adj* calmo(a), freddo(a); imparziale

dispatch [dɪs'pætʃ] *vt* spedire, inviare ♦ *n* spedizione *f*, invio; *(MIL, PRESS)* dispaccio

dispel [dɪs'pel] *vt* dissipare, scacciare

dispense [dɪs'pens] *vt* distribuire, amministrare; **~ with** *vt fus* fare a meno di; *(container)* distributore *m*; **dispensing chemist** *(BRIT)* farmacista *m/f*

disperse [dɪs'pɜːs] *vt* disperdere; *(knowledge)* disseminare ♦ *vi* disperdersi

dispirited [dɪs'pɪrɪtɪd] *adj* scoraggiato(a), abbattuto(a)

displace [dɪs'pleɪs] *vt* spostare; **~d person** *n (POL)* profugo/a

display [dɪs'pleɪ] *n* esposizione *f*; *(of feeling etc)* manifestazione *f*; *(screen)*

schermo ♦ *vt* mostrare; *(goods)* esporre; *(pej)* ostentare

displease [dɪs'pliːz] *vt* dispiacere a, scontentare; **~d with** scontento di; **displeasure** [-'pleʒə*] *n* dispiacere *m*

disposable [dɪs'pəuzəbl] *adj (pack etc)* a perdere; *(income)* disponibile; **~ nappy** *n* pannolino di carta

disposal [dɪs'pəuzl] *n* eliminazione *f*, *(of property)* cessione *f*; **at one's ~** alla sua disposizione

dispose [dɪs'pəuz] *vi:* **~ of** sbarazzarsi di; **~d** *adj:* **~d to do** disposto(a) a fare; **disposition** [-'zɪʃən] *n* disposizione *f*; *(temperament)* carattere *m*

disproportionate [dɪsprə'pɔːʃənət] *adj* sproporzionato(a)

disprove [dɪs'pruːv] *vt* confutare

dispute [dɪs'pjuːt] *n* disputa; *(also: industrial ~)* controversia *(sindacale)* ♦ *vt* contestare; *(matter)* discutere; *(victory)* disputare

disqualify [dɪs'kwɔlɪfaɪ] *vt (SPORT)* squalificare; **to ~ sb from sth/from doing** rendere qn incapace a qc/da fare; squalificare qn da qc/da fare; **to ~ sb from driving** ritirare la patente a qn

disquiet [dɪs'kwaɪət] *n* inquietudine *f*

disregard [dɪsrɪ'gɑːd] *vt* non far caso a, non badare a

disrepair [dɪsrɪ'peə*] *n:* **to fall into ~** *(building)* andare in rovina; *(machine)* deteriorarsi

disreputable [dɪs'repjutəbl] *adj* poco raccomandabile; indecente

disrupt [dɪs'rʌpt] *vt* disturbare; creare scompiglio in

dissatisfaction [dɪssætɪs'fækʃən] *n* scontentezza, insoddisfazione *f*

dissect [dɪ'sekt] *vt* sezionare

dissent [dɪ'sent] *n* dissenso

dissertation [dɪsə'teɪʃən] *n* tesi *f inv*, dissertazione *f*

disservice [dɪs'sɜːvɪs] *n:* **to do sb a ~** fare un cattivo servizio a qn

dissimilar [dɪ'sɪmɪlə*] *adj:* **~ (to)**

dissimile or diverso(a) (da)

dissipate ['dɪsɪpeɪt] vt dissipare

dissolve [dɪ'zɔlv] vt dissolvere, sciogliere; (POL, marriage etc) sciogliere ♦ vi dissolversi, sciogliersi

distance ['dɪstns] n distanza; **in the ~** in lontananza

distant ['dɪstnt] adj lontano(a), distante; (manner) riservato(a), freddo(a)

distaste [dɪs'teɪst] n ripugnanza; **~ful** adj ripugnante, sgradevole

distended [dɪs'tɛndɪd] adj (stomach) dilatato(a)

distil [dɪs'tɪl] (US **distill**) vt distillare; **~lery** n distilleria

distinct [dɪs'tɪŋkt] adj distinto(a); **as ~ from** a differenza di; **~ion** [dɪs'tɪŋkʃən] n distinzione f; (in exam) lode f; **~ive** adj distintivo(a)

distinguish [dɪs'tɪŋgwɪʃ] vt distinguere, discernere; **~ed** adj (eminent) eminente; **~ing** adj (feature) distinto(a), caratteristico(a)

distort [dɪs'tɔːt] vt distorcere; (TECH) deformare

distract [dɪs'trækt] vt distrarre; **~ed** adj distratto(a); **~ion** [dɪs'trækʃən] n distrazione f

distraught [dɪs'trɔːt] adj stravolto(a)

distress [dɪs'trɛs] n angoscia ♦ vt affliggere; **~ing** adj doloroso(a); **~ signal** n segnale m di soccorso

distribute [dɪs'trɪbjuːt] vt distribuire; **distribution** [-'bjuːʃən] n distribuzione f; **distributor** n distributore m

district ['dɪstrɪkt] n (of country) regione f; (of town) quartiere m; (ADMIN) distretto; **~ attorney** (US) n ≈ sostituto procuratore m della Repubblica; **~ nurse** (BRIT) n infermiera di quartiere

distrust [dɪs'trʌst] n diffidenza, sfiducia ♦ vt non aver fiducia in

disturb [dɪs'tɜːb] vt disturbare; **~ance** n disturbo; (political etc) disordini mpl;

~ed adj (worried, upset) turbato(a); **emotionally ~ed** con turbe emotive; **~ing** adj sconvolgente

disuse [dɪs'juːs] n: **to fall into ~** cadere in disuso

disused [dɪs'juːzd] adj abbandonato(a)

ditch [dɪtʃ] n fossa ♦ vt (inf) piantare in asso

dither ['dɪðə*] (pej) vi vacillare

ditto ['dɪtəu] adv idem

dive [daɪv] n tuffo; (of submarine) immersione f ♦ vi tuffarsi; immergersi; **~r** n tuffatore/trice; palombaro

diverse [daɪ'vəːs] adj vario(a)

diversion [daɪ'vəːʃən] n (BRIT: AUT) deviazione f; (distraction) divertimento

divert [daɪ'vəːt] vt deviare

divide [dɪ'vaɪd] vt dividere; (separate) separare ♦ vi dividersi; **~d highway** (US) n strada a doppia carreggiata

dividend ['dɪvɪdɛnd] n dividendo; (fig): **to pay ~s** dare dei frutti

divine [dɪ'vaɪn] adj divino(a)

diving ['daɪvɪŋ] n tuffo; **~ board** n trampolino

divinity [dɪ'vɪnɪtɪ] n divinità f inv; teologia

division [dɪ'vɪʒən] n divisione f; separazione f; (esp FOOTBALL) serie f

divorce [dɪ'vɔːs] n divorzio ♦ vt divorziare da; (dissociate) separare; **~d** adj divorziato(a); **~e** [-'siː] n divorziato/a

D.I.Y. (BRIT) n abbr = **do-it-yourself**

dizzy ['dɪzɪ] adj: **to feel ~** avere il capogiro

DJ n abbr = **disc jockey**

KEYWORD

do [duː] (pt **did**, pp **done**) n (inf: party etc) festa; **it was rather a grand ~** è stato un ricevimento piuttosto importante

♦ vb **1** (in negative constructions) non tradotto; **I don't understand** non capisco

2 (to form questions) non tradotto;

didn't you know? non lo sapevi?;
why didn't you come? perché non
sei venuto?

3 (for emphasis, in polite questions):
she does seem rather late sembra
essere piuttosto in ritardo; **~ sit down**
si accomodi la prego, prego si sieda;
~ take care! mi raccomando, sta
attento!

4 (used to avoid repeating vb): **she
swims better than I ~** lei nuota
meglio di me; **~ you agree? — yes, I
~/no, I don't** sei d'accordo? — sì/no;
she lives in Glasgow — so ~ I lei
vive a Glasgow — anch'io; **he asked
me to help him and I did** mi ha
chiesto di aiutarlo ed io l'ho fatto

5 (in question tags): **you like him,
don't you?** ti piace, vero?; **I don't
know him, ~ I?** non lo conosco,
vero?

♦ vt (gen, carry out, perform etc) fare;
what are you ~ing tonight? che fai
stasera?; **to ~ the cooking** cucinare;
to ~ the washing-up fare i piatti; **to
~ one's teeth** lavarsi i denti; **to
~ one's hair/nails** farsi i capelli/le
unghie; **the car was ~ing 100** la
macchina faceva i 100 all'ora

♦ vi **1** (act, behave) fare; **~ as I ~** faccia
come me, faccia come faccio io

2 (get on, fare) andare; **he's ~ing
well/badly at school** va bene/male a
scuola; **how ~ you ~?** piacere!

3 (suit) andare bene; **this room will
~** questa stanza va bene

4 (be sufficient) bastare; **will £10 ~?**
basteranno 10 sterline?; **that'll ~** basta
così; **that'll ~!** basta!; **to make ~ (with)** arrangiarsi
(con)

do away with vt fus (kill) far fuori;
(abolish) abolire

do up vt (laces) allacciare; (dress,
buttons) abbottonare; (renovate: room,
house) rimettere a nuovo, ristrutturare

do with vt fus (need) aver bisogno di;

(be connected): **what has it got to
~ with you?** e tu che c'entri?; **I
won't have anything to ~ with it**
non voglio avere niente a che farci; **it
has to ~ with money** si tratta di
soldi

do without vi fare senza ♦ vt fus fare
a meno di

dock [dɔk] n (NAUT) bacino; (LAW)
banco degli imputati ♦ vi entrare in
bacino; (SPACE) agganciarsi; **~s** npl
(NAUT) dock m inv; **~er** n scaricatore m;
~yard n cantiere m (navale)

doctor ['dɔktə*] n medico/a; (Ph.D.
etc) dottore/essa ♦ vt (drink etc)
adulterare; **D~ of Philosophy** n
dottorato di ricerca; (person) titolare
m/f di un dottorato di ricerca

doctrine ['dɔktrɪn] n dottrina

document ['dɔkjumənt] n
documento; **~ary** [-'mentərɪ] adj
(evidence) documentato(a) ♦ n
documentario

dodge [dɔdʒ] n trucco; schivata ♦ vt
schivare, eludere

dodgems ['dɔdʒəmz] (BRIT) npl
autoscontri mpl

doe [dəu] n (deer) femmina di daino;
(rabbit) coniglia

does [dʌz] vb see **do**; **doesn't** = **does
not**

dog [dɔg] n cane m ♦ vt (follow closely)
pedinare; (fig: memory etc)
perseguitare; **~ collar** n collare m di
cane; (fig) collarino; **~-eared** adj
(book) con orecchie

dogged ['dɔgɪd] adj ostinato(a), tenace

dogsbody ['dɔgzbɔdɪ] (BRIT: inf) n
factotum m inv

doing ['du:ɪŋ] n: **this is your ~** è
opera tua, sei stato tu

do-it-yourself n il far da sé

doldrums ['dɔldrəmz] npl (fig): **to be
in the ~** essere un brutto periodo

dole [dəul] (BRIT) n il sussidio di
disoccupazione; **to be on the ~** vivere

del sussidio; **~ out** vt distribuire

doll [dɔl] n bambola; **~ed up** (inf) in ghingheri

dollar ['dɔlə*] n dollaro

dolly ['dɔlɪ] n bambola

dolphin ['dɔlfɪn] n delfino

domain [də'meɪn] n dominio

dome [dəum] n cupola

domestic [də'mestɪk] adj (duty, happiness, animal) domestico(a); (policy, affairs, flights) nazionale; **~ated** adj addomesticato(a)

dominant ['dɔmɪnənt] adj dominante

dominate ['dɔmɪneɪt] vt dominare

domineering [dɔmɪ'nɪərɪŋ] adj dispotico(a), autoritario(a)

dominion [də'mɪnɪən] n dominio; sovranità; dominion m inv

domino ['dɔmɪnəu] (pl **~es**) n domino; **~es** n (game) gioco del domino

don [dɔn] n (BRIT) n docente m/f universitario(a)

donate [də'neɪt] vt donare

done [dʌn] pp of **do**

donkey ['dɔŋkɪ] n asino

donor ['dəunə*] n donatore/trice; **~ card** n tessera di donatore di organi

don't [dəunt] = **do not**

doodle ['du:dl] vi scarabocchiare

doom [du:m] n destino; rovina ♦ vt: **to be ~ed (to failure)** essere predestinato(a) (a fallire)

door [dɔ:*] n porta; **~bell** n campanello; **~ handle** n maniglia; **~man** (irreg) n (in hotel) portiere m in livrea; **~mat** n stuoia della porta; **~step** n gradino della porta; **~way** n porta

dope [dəup] n (inf: drugs) roba ♦ vt (horse etc) drogare

dormant ['dɔ:mənt] adj inattivo(a)

dormitory ['dɔ:mɪtrɪ] n dormitorio; (US) casa dello studente

dormouse ['dɔ:maus] (pl **dormice**) n ghiro

dosage ['dəusɪdʒ] n posologia

dose [dəus] n dose f; (bout) attacco

doss house [dɔs-] (BRIT) n asilo notturno

dot [dɔt] n punto; macchiolina ♦ vt: **~ted with** punteggiato(a) di; **on the ~** in punto

dotted line ['dɔtɪd-] n linea punteggiata

double ['dʌbl] adj doppio(a) ♦ adv (twice): **to cost ~** (sth) costare il doppio (di qc) ♦ n sosia m inv ♦ vt raddoppiare; (fold) piegare doppio or in due ♦ vi raddoppiarsi; **at the ~** (BRIT), **on the ~** a passo di corsa; **~ bass** n contrabbasso; **~ bed** n letto matrimoniale; **~-breasted** adj a doppio petto; **~cross** vt fare il doppio gioco con; **~decker** n autobus m inv a due piani; **~ glazing** (BRIT) n doppi vetri mpl; **~ room** n camera per due; **~s** n (TENNIS) doppio; **doubly** adv doppiamente

doubt [daut] n dubbio ♦ vt dubitare di; **to ~** that dubitare che ♦ sub; **~ful** adj dubbioso(a), incerto(a); (person) equivoco(a); **~less** adv indubbiamente

dough [dəu] n pasta, impasto; **~nut** n bombolone m

dove [dʌv] n colombo/a

Dover ['dəuvə*] n Dover f

dovetail ['dʌvteɪl] vi (fig) combaciare

dowdy ['daudɪ] adj trasandato(a); malvestito(a)

down [daun] n piume fpl ♦ adv giù, di sotto ♦ prep giù per ♦ vt (inf: drink) scolarsi; **~ with X!** abbasso X!; **~-and-out** n barbone m; **~-at-heel** adj scalcagnato(a); **~cast** adj abbattuto(a); **~fall** n caduta; rovina; **~hearted** adj scoraggiato(a); **~hill** adv: **to go ~hill** andare in discesa; (fig) lasciarsi andare; andare a rotoli; **~load** vt (COMPUT) scaricare; **~ payment** n acconto; **~pour** n scroscio di pioggia; **~right** adj franco(a); (refusal) assoluto(a); **~size** vi (ECON: company) ridurre il personale; **~stairs** adv di sotto; al piano inferiore; **~stream** adv a valle;

~-to-earth adj pratico(a); **~town** adv
in città; **~ under** adv (Australia etc)
agli antipodi; **~ward** ['daʊnwəd] adj,
adv in giù, in discesa; **~wards**
['daʊnwədz] adv = **~ward**

Downing Street

Al numero 10 di **Downing Street**,
nel quartiere di Westminster a
Londra, si trova la residenza del
primo ministro inglese, al numero 11
quella del Chancellor of the
Exchequer.

---

dowry ['daʊrɪ] n dote f
doz. abbr = **dozen**
doze [dəʊz] vi sonnecchiare; **~ off** vi
appisolarsi
dozen ['dʌzn] n dozzina; **a ~ books**
una dozzina di libri; **~s of** decine fpl
di
Dr. abbr (= doctor) dott.; (in street
names) = drive n
drab [dræb] adj tetro(a), grigio(a)
draft [drɑːft] n abbozzo; (POL) bozza;
(COMM) tratta; (US: call-up) leva ♦ vt
abbozzare; see also **draught**
draftsman ['drɑːftsmən] (US) n =
draughtsman
drag [dræg] vt trascinare; (river)
dragare ♦ vi trascinarsi ♦ n (inf)
noioso/a; noia, fatica; (women's
clothing): **in ~** travestito (da donna);
~ on vi tirar avanti lentamente
dragon ['drægən] n drago
dragonfly ['drægənflaɪ] n libellula
drain [dreɪn] n (for sewage) fogna; (on
resources) salasso ♦ vt (land, marshes)
prosciugare; (vegetables) scolare ♦ vi
(water) defluire (via); **~age** n
prosciugamento; fognatura; **~ing
board** (US **~board**) n piano del lavello;
~pipe n tubo di scarico
drama ['drɑːmə] n (art) dramma m,
teatro; (play) commedia; (event)
dramma; **~tic** [drə'mætɪk] adj
drammatico(a); **~tist** ['dræmətɪst] n

drammaturgo/a; **~tize** vt (events)
drammatizzare
drank [dræŋk] pt of **drink**
drape [dreɪp] vt drappeggiare; **~r** (BRIT)
n negoziante m/f di stoffe; **~s** (US) npl
(curtains) tende fpl
drastic ['dræstɪk] adj drastico(a)
draught [drɑːft] (US **draft**) n corrente f
d'aria; (NAUT) pescaggio; **on ~** (beer)
alla spina; **~ beer** n birra alla spina;
~board (BRIT) n scacchiera; **~s** (BRIT) n
(gioco della) dama
draughtsman ['drɑːftsmən] (US
draftsman) n (irreg) n disegnatore m
draw [drɔː] (pt **drew**, pp **drawn**) vt
tirare; (take out) estrarre; (attract)
attirare; (picture) disegnare; (line, circle)
tracciare; (money) ritirare ♦ vi (SPORT)
pareggiare ♦ n pareggio; (in lottery)
estrazione f; **to ~ near** avvicinarsi;
~ out vi (lengthen) allungarsi ♦ vt
(money) ritirare; **~ up** vi (stop)
arrestarsi, fermarsi ♦ vt (chair)
avvicinare; (document) compilare;
~back n svantaggio, inconveniente m;
~bridge n ponte m levatoio
drawer [drɔː*] n cassetto
drawing ['drɔːɪŋ] n disegno; **~ board**
n tavola da disegno; **~ pin** (BRIT) n
puntina da disegno; **~ room** n salotto
drawl [drɔːl] n pronuncia strascicata
drawn [drɔːn] pp of **draw**
dread [dred] n terrore m ♦ vt tremare
all'idea di; **~ful** adj terribile
dream [driːm] (pt, pp **dreamed** or
dreamt) n sogno ♦ vt, vi sognare; **~y**
adj sognante
dreary ['drɪərɪ] adj tetro(a);
monotono(a)
dredge [dredʒ] vt dragare
dregs [dregz] npl feccia
drench [drentʃ] vt inzuppare
dress [dres] n vestito; (no pl: clothing)
abbigliamento ♦ vt vestire; (wound)
fasciare ♦ vi vestirsi; **to get ~ed**
vestirsi; **~ up** vi vestirsi a festa; (in fancy
dress) vestirsi in costume; **~ circle**

(BRIT) n prima galleria; **~er** n (BRIT: cupboard) credenza; (US) cassettone m; **~ing** n (MED) benda; (CULIN) condimento; **~ing gown** (BRIT) n vestaglia; **~ing room** n (THEATRE) camerino; (SPORT) spogliatoio; **~ing table** n toilette f inv; **~maker** n sarta; **~ rehearsal** n prova generale; **~y** (inf) adj elegante

drew [dru:] pt of **draw**

dribble ['drɪbl] vi (baby) sbavare ♦ vt (ball) dribblare

dried [draɪd] adj (fruit, beans) secco(a); (eggs, milk) in polvere

drier ['draɪə*] n = **dryer**

drift [drɪft] n (of current etc) direzione f; forza; (of snow) cumulo; turbine m; (general meaning) senso ♦ vi (boat) essere trasportato(a) dalla corrente; (sand, snow) ammucchiarsi; **~wood** n resti mpl della mareggiata

drill [drɪl] n trapano; (MIL) esercitazione f ♦ vt trapanare; (troops) addestrare ♦ vi (for oil) fare trivellazioni

drink [drɪŋk] (pt drank, pp drunk) n bevanda, bibita; (alcoholic) bicchierino; (sip) sorso ♦ vt, vi bere; **to have a ~** bere qualcosa; **a ~ of water** un po' d'acqua; **~er** n bevitore/trice; **~ing water** n acqua potabile

drip [drɪp] n goccia; gocciolamento; (MED) fleboclisi f inv ♦ vi gocciolare; (tap) sgocciolare; **~-dry** adj (shirt) che non si stira; **~ping** n grasso d'arrosto

drive [draɪv] (pt drove, pp driven) n passeggiata or giro in macchina; (also: **~way**) viale m d'accesso; (energy) energia; (campaign) campagna; (also: disk **~**) lettore m ♦ vt guidare; (nail) piantare; (push) cacciare, spingere; (TECH: motor) azionare; (: to function ♦ vi (AUT: at controls) guidare; (: travel) andare in macchina; **left-/right-hand ~** guida a sinistra/destra; **to ~ sb mad** far impazzire qn

drivel ['drɪvl] (inf) n idiozie fpl

driven ['drɪvn] pp of **drive**

driver ['draɪvə*] n conducente m/f; (of taxi) tassista m; (chauffeur, of bus) autista m/f; **~'s license** (US) n patente f di guida

driveway ['draɪvweɪ] n viale m d'accesso

driving ['draɪvɪŋ] n guida; **~ instructor** n istruttore/trice di scuola guida; **~ lesson** n lezione f di guida; **~ licence** (BRIT) n patente f di guida; **~ mirror** n specchietto retrovisore; **~ school** n scuola f guida inv; **~ test** n esame m di guida

drizzle ['drɪzl] n pioggerella

drool [dru:l] vi sbavare

droop [dru:p] vi (flower) appassire; (head, shoulders) chinarsi

drop [drɒp] n (of water) goccia; (lessening) diminuzione f; (fall) caduta ♦ vt lasciar cadere; (voice, eyes, price) abbassare; (set down from car) far scendere; (name from list) lasciare fuori ♦ vi cascare; (wind) abbassarsi; **~s** npl (MED) gocce fpl; **~ off** vi (sleep) addormentarsi ♦ vt (passenger) far scendere; **~ out** vi (withdraw) ritirarsi; (student etc) smettere di studiare; **~-out** n (from society/from university) chi ha abbandonato (la società/gli studi); **~per** n contagocce m inv; **~pings** npl sterco

drought [draut] n siccità f inv

drove [drəuv] pt of **drive**

drown [draun] vt affogare; (fig: noise) soffocare ♦ vi affogare

drowsy ['drauzɪ] adj sonnolento(a), assonnato(a)

drudgery [not present]

drug [drʌg] n farmaco; (narcotic) droga ♦ vt drogare; **to be on ~s** drogarsi; (MED) prendere medicinali; **hard/soft ~s** droghe pesanti/leggere; **~ addict** n tossicomane m/f; **~gist** n persona che gestisce un drugstore; **~store** (US) n drugstore m inv

drum [drʌm] n tamburo; (for oil, petrol) fusto ♦ vi tamburellare; **~s** npl (set of ~s) batteria; **~mer** n batterista m/f

drunk [drʌŋk] *pp of* **drink** ♦ *adj*
ubriaco(a); ebbro(a) ♦ *n* (*also:* ~ard)
ubriacone/a; **~en** *adj* ubriaco(a); da
ubriaco

dry [draɪ] *adj* secco(a); (*day, clothes*)
asciutto(a) ♦ *vt* seccare; (*clothes, hair,
hands*) asciugare ♦ *vi* asciugarsi; ~ **up**
vi seccarsi; **~-cleaner's** *n* lavasecco *m
inv*; **~-cleaning** *n* pulitura a secco; **~er**
n (*for hair*) föhn *m inv*, asciugacapelli *m
inv*; (*for clothes*) asciugabiancheria; (*US:
spin-dryer*) centrifuga; **~ goods store**
(*US*) *n* negozio di stoffe; **~ rot** *n* fungo
del legno

DSS *n abbr* (= *Department of Social
Security*) ministero della Previdenza
sociale

DTP *n abbr* (= *desk-top publishing*)
desktop publishing *m inv*

dual [ˈdjuəl] *adj* doppio(a);
~ **carriageway** (*BRIT*) *n* strada a
doppia carreggiata; **~-purpose** *adj* a
doppio uso

dubbed [dʌbd] *adj* (*CINEMA*)
doppiato(a)

dubious [ˈdjuːbɪəs] *adj* dubbio(a)

Dublin [ˈdʌblɪn] *n* Dublino *f*

duchess [ˈdʌtʃɪs] *n* duchessa

duck [dʌk] *n* anatra ♦ *vi* abbassare la
testa; **~ling** *n* anatroccolo

duct [dʌkt] *n* condotto; (*ANAT*) canale
m

dud [dʌd] *n* (*object, tool*): **it's a ~** è
inutile, non funziona ♦ *adj*: ~ **cheque**
(*BRIT*) assegno a vuoto

due [djuː] *adj* dovuto(a); (*expected*)
atteso(a); (*fitting*) giusto(a) ♦ *n* dovuto
♦ *adv*: ~ **north** diritto verso nord; **~s**
npl (*for club, union*) quota; (*in harbour*)
diritti *mpl* di porto; **in ~ course** a
tempo debito; finalmente; **~ to** dovuto
a; a causa di; **to be ~ to do** dover fare

duet [djuːˈet] *n* duetto

duffel bag [ˈdʌfl-] *n* sacca da viaggio
di tela

duffel coat [ˈdʌfl-] *n* montgomery *m
inv*

dug [dʌg] *pt, pp of* **dig**

duke [djuːk] *n* duca *m*

dull [dʌl] *adj* (*light*) debole; (*boring*)
noioso(a); (*slow-witted*) ottuso(a);
(*sound, pain*) sordo(a); (*weather, day*)
fosco(a), scuro(a) ♦ *vt* (*pain, grief*)
attutire; (*mind, senses*) intorpidire

duly [ˈdjuːlɪ] *adv* (*on time*) a tempo
debito; (*as expected*) debitamente

dumb [dʌm] *adj* muto(a); (*pej*)
stupido(a); **~founded** [dʌmˈfaʊndɪd]
adj stupito(a), stordito(a)

dummy [ˈdʌmɪ] *n* (*tailor's model*)
manichino; (*TECH, COMM*) riproduzione
f; (*BRIT: for baby*) tettarella ♦ *adj*
falso(a), finto(a)

dump [dʌmp] *n* (*also: rubbish ~*)
discarica di rifiuti; (*inf: place*) buco *m*
(*put down*) scaricare; mettere giù; (*get
rid of*) buttar via

dumpling [ˈdʌmplɪŋ] *n* specie di
gnocco

dumpy [ˈdʌmpɪ] *adj* tracagnotto(a)

dunce [dʌns] *n* (*SCOL*) somaro/a

dung [dʌŋ] *n* concime *m*

dungarees [dʌŋgəˈriːz] *npl* tuta

dungeon [ˈdʌndʒən] *n* prigione *f*
sotterranea

dupe [djuːp] *n* zimbello ♦ *vt* gabbare,
ingannare

duplex [ˈdjuːpleks] (*US*) *n* (*house*) casa
con muro divisorio in comune con
un'altra; (*apartment*) appartamento su
due piani

duplicate [*n* ˈdjuːplɪkət, *vb*
ˈdjuːplɪkeɪt] *n* doppio ♦ *vt* duplicare;
in ~ in doppia copia

durable [ˈdjuərəbl] *adj* durevole;
(*clothes, metal*) resistente

duration [djuəˈreɪʃən] *n* durata

during [ˈdjuərɪŋ] *prep* durante, nel
corso di

dusk [dʌsk] *n* crepuscolo

dust [dʌst] *n* polvere *f* ♦ *vt* (*furniture*)
spolverare; (*cake etc*): **to ~ with**
cospargere con; **~bin** (*BRIT*) *n*
pattumiera; **~er** *n* straccio per la

polvere; **~man** (BRIT irreg) n
netturbino; **~y** adj polveroso(a)

Dutch [dʌtʃ] adj olandese ♦ n (LING)
olandese m; **the ~** npl gli Olandesi; **to
go ~** (inf) fare alla romana; **~man/
woman** (irreg) n olandese m/f

duty ['djuːtɪ] n dovere m; (tax) dazio,
tassa; **on ~** di servizio; **off ~** libero(a),
fuori servizio; **~-free** adj esente da dazio

duvet ['duːveɪ] (BRIT) n piumino,
piumone m

DVD n abbr (= digital versatile disk)
DVD m inv

dwarf [dwɔːf] n nano/a ♦ vt far
apparire piccolo

dwell [dwel] (pt, pp dwelt) vi
dimorare; **~ on** vt fus indugiare su

dwindle ['dwɪndl] vi diminuire

dye [daɪ] n tinta ♦ vt tingere

dying ['daɪɪŋ] adj morente,
moribondo(a)

dyke [daɪk] (BRIT) n diga

dynamic [daɪ'næmɪk] adj dinamico(a)

dynamite ['daɪnəmaɪt] n dinamite f

dynamo ['daɪnəməʊ] n dinamo f inv

dyslexia [dɪs'leksɪə] n dislessia

E, e

E [iː] n (MUS) mi m

each [iːtʃ] adj ogni, ciascuno(a) ♦ pron
ciascuno(a), ognuno(a); **~ one**
ognuno(a); **~ other** si (or ci etc);
they hate ~ other si odiano (l'un l'altro);
you are jealous of ~ other siete
gelosi l'uno dell'altro; **they have 2
books ~** hanno 2 libri ciascuno

eager ['iːgə*] adj impaziente; deside-
roso(a); ardente; **to be ~ for** essere
desideroso di, aver gran voglia di

eagle ['iːgl] n aquila

ear [ɪə*] n orecchio m; (of corn)
pannocchia; **~ache** n mal m d'orecchi;
~drum n timpano

earl [əːl] (BRIT) n conte m

earlier ['əːlɪə*] adj precedente ♦ adv
prima

early ['əːlɪ] adv presto, di buon'ora;
(ahead of time) in anticipo ♦ adj (near
the beginning) primo(a); (sooner than
expected) prematuro(a); (quick: reply)
veloce; **at an ~ hour** di buon'ora; **to
have an ~ night** andare a letto
presto; **in the ~ or ~ in the spring/
19th century** all'inizio della
primavera/dell'Ottocento;
~ retirement n ritiro anticipato

earmark ['ɪəmɑːk] vt: **to ~ sth for**
destinare qc a

earn [əːn] vt guadagnare; (rest, reward)
meritare

earnest ['əːnɪst] adj serio(a); **in ~** sul
serio

earnings ['əːnɪŋz] npl guadagni mpl;
(salary) stipendio

earphones ['ɪəfəʊnz] npl cuffia

earring ['ɪərɪŋ] n orecchino

earshot ['ɪəʃɔt] n: **within ~** a portata
d'orecchio

earth [əːθ] n terra ♦ vt (BRIT: ELEC)
mettere a terra; **~enware** n terracotta;
stoviglie fpl di terracotta; **~quake** n
terremoto; **~y** adj (fig) grossolano(a)

ease [iːz] n agio, comodo ♦ vt (soothe)
calmare; (loosen) allentare; **to ~ sth
out/in** tirare fuori/infilare qc con
qc; **at ~** a proprio agio; (MIL) a riposo;
~ off or **up** vi diminuire; (slow down)
rallentare

easel ['iːzl] n cavalletto

easily ['iːzɪlɪ] adv facilmente

east [iːst] n est m ♦ adj dell'est ♦ adv a
oriente; **the E~** l'Oriente m; (POL) l'Est

Easter ['iːstə*] n Pasqua; **~ egg** n uovo
di Pasqua

easterly ['iːstəlɪ] adj dell'est, d'oriente

eastern ['iːstən] adj orientale,
d'oriente; dell'est

East Germany n Germania dell'Est

eastward(s) ['iːstwəd(z)] adv verso
est, verso levante

easy ['iːzɪ] adj facile; (manner) disinvolto(a) ♦ adv: **to take it** or **things ~** prendersela con calma; **~ chair** n poltrona; **~-going** adj accomodante

eat [iːt] (pt **ate**, pp **eaten**) vt, vi mangiare; **~ away at** vt fus rodere; **~ into** vt fus rodere

eaves [iːvz] npl gronda

eavesdrop ['iːvzdrɒp] vi: **to ~ (on a conversation)** origliare (una conversazione)

ebb [ɛb] n riflusso ♦ vi rifluire; (fig: also: **~ away**) declinare

ebony ['ɛbənɪ] n ebano

EC n abbr (= European Community) CEE f

ECB n abbr (= European Central Bank) BCE f

eccentric [ɪk'sɛntrɪk] adj, n eccentrico(a)

echo ['ɛkəʊ] (pl **~es**) n eco m or f ♦ vt ripetere; fare eco ♦ vi echeggiare; dare un eco

éclair [eɪ'klɛə*] n ≈ bignè m inv

eclipse [ɪ'klɪps] n eclissi f inv

ecology [ɪ'kɒlədʒɪ] n ecologia

e-commerce n commercio elettronico

economic [iːkə'nɒmɪk] adj economico(a); **~al** adj economico(a); (person) economo(a); **~s** n economia ♦ npl lato finanziario

economize [ɪ'kɒnəmaɪz] vi risparmiare, fare economia

economy [ɪ'kɒnəmɪ] n economia; **~ class** n (AVIAT) classe f turistica; **~ size** n (COMM) confezione f economica

ecstasy ['ɛkstəsɪ] n estasi f inv

ECU ['eɪkjuː] n abbr (= European Currency Unit) ECU m inv

eczema ['ɛksɪmə] n eczema m

edge [ɛdʒ] n margine m; (of table, plate, cup) orlo; (of knife etc) taglio ♦ vt bordare; **on** ~ (fig) = **on edge**; **to ~ away from** sgattaiolare da; **~ways** adv: **he couldn't get a word in ~ways** non riuscì a dire una parola;

edgy adj nervoso(a)

edible ['ɛdɪbl] adj commestibile; (meal) mangiabile

edict ['iːdɪkt] n editto

Edinburgh ['ɛdɪnbərə] n Edimburgo f

edit ['ɛdɪt] vt curare; **~ion** [ɪ'dɪʃən] n edizione f; **~or** n (in newspaper) redattore/trice; redattore/trice capo; (of sb's work) curatore/trice; **~orial** [-'tɔːrɪəl] adj redazionale, editoriale ♦ n editoriale m

educate ['ɛdjukeɪt] vt istruire; educare

education [ɛdju'keɪʃən] n educazione f; (schooling) istruzione f; **~al** adj pedagogico(a); scolastico(a); istruttivo(a)

EEC n abbr = **EC**

eel [iːl] n anguilla

eerie ['ɪərɪ] adj che fa accapponare la pelle

effect [ɪ'fɛkt] n effetto ♦ vt effettuare; **to take ~** (law) entrare in vigore; (drug) fare effetto; **in ~** effettivamente; **~ive** adj efficace; (actual) effettivo(a); **~ively** adv efficacemente; effettivamente; **~iveness** n efficacia

effeminate [ɪ'fɛmɪnɪt] adj effeminato(a)

efficiency [ɪ'fɪʃənsɪ] n efficienza; rendimento effettivo

efficient [ɪ'fɪʃənt] adj efficiente

effort ['ɛfət] n sforzo

effusive [ɪ'fjuːsɪv] adj (handshake, welcome) caloroso(a)

e.g. adv abbr (= exempli gratia) per esempio, p.es.

egg [ɛg] n uovo; **hard-boiled/soft-boiled ~** uovo sodo/alla coque; **~ on** vt incitare; **~cup** n portauovo m inv; **~plant** n (especially US) melanzana; **~shell** n guscio d'uovo

ego ['iːgəʊ] n ego m inv

egotism ['ɛgəutɪzəm] n egotismo

Egypt ['iːdʒɪpt] n Egitto; **~ian** [ɪ'dʒɪpʃən] adj, n egiziano(a)

eiderdown ['aɪdədaʊn] n piumino

eight [eɪt] num otto; **~een** num diciotto; **eighth** [eɪtθ] num ottavo(a); **~y** num ottanta

Eire ['ɛərə] n Repubblica d'Irlanda

either ['aɪðə*] adj l'uno(a) o l'altro(a); (both, each) ciascuno(a) ♦ pron: ~ (of them) (o) l'uno(a) o l'altro(a) ♦ adv neanche ♦ conj: ~ good or bad o buono o cattivo; on ~ side su ciascun lato; I don't like ~ non mi piace né l'uno né l'altro; no, I don't ~ no, neanch'io

eject [ɪ'dʒɛkt] vt espellere; lanciare

elaborate [adj ɪ'læbərɪt, vb ɪ'læbəreɪt] adj elaborato(a), minuzioso(a) ♦ vt elaborare ♦ vi fornire i particolari

elastic [ɪ'læstɪk] adj elastico(a) ♦ n elastico; ~ band (BRIT) n elastico

elated [ɪ'leɪtɪd] adj pieno(a) di gioia

elbow ['ɛlbəu] n gomito

elder ['ɛldə*] adj maggiore, più vecchio(a) ♦ n (tree) sambuco; one's ~s i più anziani; ~ly adj anziano(a) ♦ npl: the ~ly gli anziani

eldest ['ɛldɪst] adj, n: the ~ (child) il(la) maggiore (dei bambini)

elect [ɪ'lɛkt] vt eleggere ♦ adj: the president ~ il presidente designato; to ~ to do decidere di fare; ~ion [ɪ'lɛkʃən] n elezione f; ~ioneering [ɪlɛkʃə'nɪərɪŋ] n propaganda elettorale; ~or n elettore/trice; ~orate n elettorato

electric [ɪ'lɛktrɪk] adj elettrico(a); ~al adj elettrico(a); ~ blanket n coperta elettrica; ~ fire n stufa elettrica

electrician [ɪlɛk'trɪʃən] n elettricista m

electricity [ɪlɛk'trɪsɪtɪ] n elettricità

electrify [ɪ'lɛktrɪfaɪ] vt (RAIL) elettrificare; (audience) elettrizzare

electrocute [ɪ'lɛktrəukjuːt] vt fulminare

electronic [ɪlɛk'trɒnɪk] adj elettronico(a); ~ mail n posta elettronica; ~s n elettronica

elegant ['ɛlɪgənt] adj elegante

element ['ɛlɪmənt] n elemento; (of heater, kettle etc) resistenza; ~ary [-'mɛntərɪ] adj elementare

elephant ['ɛlɪfənt] n elefante/essa

elevation [ɛlɪ'veɪʃən] n elevazione f

elevator ['ɛlɪveɪtə*] n elevatore m; (US: lift) ascensore m

eleven [ɪ'lɛvn] num undici; ~ses (BRIT) n caffè m a metà mattina; ~th adj undicesimo(a)

elicit [ɪ'lɪsɪt] vt: to ~ (from) trarre (da), cavare fuori (da)

eligible ['ɛlɪdʒəbl] adj eleggibile; (for membership) che ha i requisiti

elm [ɛlm] n olmo

elocution [ɛlə'kjuːʃən] n dizione f

elongated ['iːlɒŋgeɪtɪd] adj allungato(a)

elope [ɪ'ləup] vi (lovers) scappare; ~ment n fuga

eloquent ['ɛləkwənt] adj eloquente

else [ɛls] adv altro; something ~ qualcos'altro; somewhere ~ altrove; everywhere ~ in qualsiasi altro luogo; nobody ~ nessun altro; where ~? in quale altro luogo?; little ~ poco altro; ~where adv altrove

elude [ɪ'luːd] vt eludere

elusive [ɪ'luːsɪv] adj elusivo(a)

emaciated [ɪ'meɪsɪeɪtɪd] adj emaciato(a)

E-mail, e-mail n abbr (= electronic mail) posta elettronica ♦ vti mandare un messaggio di posta elettronica a

emancipate [ɪ'mænsɪpeɪt] vt emancipare

embankment [ɪm'bæŋkmənt] n (of road, railway) terrapieno

embark [ɪm'baːk] vi: to ~ (on) imbarcarsi (su) ♦ vt imbarcare; to ~ on (fig) imbarcarsi in; ~ation [ɛmbaː'keɪʃən] n imbarco

embarrass [ɪm'bærəs] vt imbarazzare; ~ed adj imbarazzato(a); ~ing adj imbarazzante; ~ment n imbarazzo

embassy ['ɛmbəsɪ] n ambasciata

embedded [ɪm'bɛdɪd] adj incastrato(a)

embellish [ɪm'bɛlɪʃ] vt abbellire

embers ['ɛmbəz] npl braci fpl

embezzle [ɪm'bɛzl] vt appropriarsi

indebitamente di

embitter [ɪm'bɪtə*] vt amareggiare; inasprire

embody [ɪm'bɔdɪ] vt (features) racchiudere, comprendere; (ideas) dar forma concreta a, esprimere

embossed [ɪm'bɔst] adj in rilievo; goffrato(a)

embrace [ɪm'breɪs] vt abbracciare ♦ vi abbracciarsi ♦ n abbraccio

embroider [ɪm'brɔɪdə*] vt ricamare; **~y** n ricamo

embryo ['embrɪəʊ] n embrione m

emerald ['emərəld] n smeraldo

emerge [ɪ'mɜːdʒ] vi emergere

emergency [ɪ'mɜːdʒənsɪ] n emergenza; **in an ~** in caso di emergenza; **~ cord** (US) n segnale m d'allarme; **~ exit** n uscita di sicurezza; **~ landing** n atterraggio forzato; **~ services** npl (fire, police, ambulance) servizi mpl di pronto intervento

emery board ['emərɪ-] n limetta di carta smerigliata

emigrate ['emɪgreɪt] vi emigrare

eminent ['emɪnənt] adj eminente

emissions [ɪ'mɪʃənz] npl emissioni fpl

emit [ɪ'mɪt] vt emettere

emotion [ɪ'məʊʃən] n emozione f; **~al** adj (person) emotivo(a); (scene) commovente; (tone, speech) carico(a) d'emozione

emperor ['empərə*] n imperatore m

emphasis ['emfəsɪs] (pl **-ases**) n enfasi f inv; importanza

emphasize ['emfəsaɪz] vt (word, point) sottolineare; (feature) mettere in evidenza

emphatic [em'fætɪk] adj (strong) vigoroso(a); (unambiguous, clear) netto(a)

empire ['empaɪə*] n impero

employ [ɪm'plɔɪ] vt impiegare; **~ee** [-'iː] n impiegato/a; **~er** n principale m/f, datore m di lavoro; **~ment** n impiego; **~ment agency** n agenzia di collocamento

empower [ɪm'paʊə*] vt: **to ~ sb to do** concedere autorità a qn di fare

empress ['emprɪs] n imperatrice f

emptiness ['emptɪnɪs] n vuoto

empty ['emptɪ] adj (threat, promise) vano(a) ♦ vt vuotare ♦ vi vuotarsi; (liquid) scaricarsi; **~-handed** adj a mani vuote

EMU n abbr (= economic and monetary union) unione f economica e monetaria

emulate ['emjʊleɪt] vt emulare

emulsion [ɪ'mʌlʃən] n emulsione f; **~ (paint)** n colore m a tempera

enable [ɪ'neɪbl] vt: **to ~ sb to do** permettere a qn di fare

enamel [ɪ'næməl] n smalto; (also: **~ paint**) vernice f a smalto

enchant [ɪn'tʃɑːnt] vt incantare; (subj: magic spell) catturare; **~ing** adj incantevole, affascinante

encircle [ɪn'sɜːkl] vt accerchiare

encl. abbr (= enclosed) all

enclave ['enkleɪv] n enclave f

enclose [ɪn'kləʊz] vt (land) circondare, recingere; (letter etc): **to ~ (with)** allegare (con); **please find ~d** trovi qui accluso

enclosure [ɪn'kləʊʒə*] n recinto

encompass [ɪn'kʌmpəs] vt comprendere

encore [ɔŋ'kɔː*] excl bis ♦ n bis m inv

encounter [ɪn'kaʊntə*] n incontro ♦ vt incontrare

encourage [ɪn'kʌrɪdʒ] vt incoraggiare; **~ment** n incoraggiamento

encroach [ɪn'krəʊtʃ] vi: **to ~ (up)on** (rights) usurpare; (time) abusare di; (land) oltrepassare i limiti di

encyclop(a)edia [ensaɪkləʊ'piːdɪə] n enciclopedia

end [end] n fine f; (aim) fine m; (of table) bordo estremo; (of pointed object) punta ♦ vt finire; (also: **bring to an ~, put an ~ to**) mettere fine a ♦ vi finire; **in the ~** alla fine; **on ~** (object) ritto(a); **to stand on ~** (hair) rizzarsi; **for hours on ~** per ore ed ore; **~ up**

vi: **to ~ up in** finire in

endanger [ɪnˈdeɪndʒə*] *vt* mettere in pericolo

endearing [ɪnˈdɪərɪŋ] *adj* accattivante

endeavour [ɪnˈdevə*] (*US* **endeavor**) *n* sforzo, tentativo ♦ *vi*: **to ~ to do** cercare or sforzarsi di fare

ending [ˈendɪŋ] *n* fine *f*, conclusione *f*; (*LING*) desinenza

endive [ˈendaɪv] *n* (*curly*) indivia (riccia); (*smooth, flat*) indivia belga

endless [ˈendlɪs] *adj* senza fine

endorse [ɪnˈdɔːs] *vt* (*cheque*) girare; (*approve*) approvare, appoggiare; **~ment** *n* approvazione *f*; (*on driving licence*) contravvenzione registrata sulla patente

endurance [ɪnˈdjuərəns] *n* resistenza; pazienza

endure [ɪnˈdjuə*] *vt* sopportare, resistere a ♦ *vi* durare

enemy [ˈenəmɪ] *adj, n* nemico(a)

energetic [enəˈdʒetɪk] *adj* energico(a); attivo(a)

energy [ˈenədʒɪ] *n* energia

enforce [ɪnˈfɔːs] *vt* (*LAW*) applicare, far osservare

engage [ɪnˈgeɪdʒ] *vt* (*hire*) assumere; (*lawyer*) incaricare; (*attention, interest*) assorbire; (*TECH*): **to ~ gear/the clutch** innestare la marcia/la frizione ♦ *vi* (*TECH*): **to ~ in** impegnarsi in; **~d** (*BRIT*: busy, in use) occupato(a); (*betrothed*) fidanzato(a); **to get ~d** fidanzarsi; **~d tone** (*BRIT*) *n* (*TEL*) segnale *m* di occupato; **~ment** *n* impegno, obbligo; appuntamento; (*to marry*) fidanzamento; **~ment ring** *n* anello di fidanzamento

engaging [ɪnˈgeɪdʒɪŋ] *adj* attraente

engine [ˈendʒɪn] *n* (*AUT*) motore *m*; (*RAIL*) locomotiva *f*; **~ driver** *n* (*of train*) macchinista *m*

engineer [endʒɪˈnɪə*] *n* ingegnere *m*; (*BRIT*: for repairs) tecnico; (*on ship, US*: *RAIL*) macchinista *m*; **~ing** *n* ingegneria

England [ˈɪŋglənd] *n* Inghilterra

English [ˈɪŋglɪʃ] *adj* inglese ♦ *n* (*LING*) inglese *m*; **the ~** *npl* gli Inglesi; **the ~ Channel** *n* la Manica; **~man/woman** (*irreg*) *n* inglese *m/f*

engraving [ɪnˈgreɪvɪŋ] *n* incisione *f*

engrossed [ɪnˈgrəust] *adj*: **~ in** assorbito(a) da, preso(a) da

engulf [ɪnˈgʌlf] *vt* inghiottire

enhance [ɪnˈhɑːns] *vt* accrescere

enjoy [ɪnˈdʒɔɪ] *vt* godere; (*have*: success, fortune*) avere; **to ~ o.s.** godersela, divertirsi; **~able** *adj* piacevole; **~ment** *n* piacere *m*, godimento

enlarge [ɪnˈlɑːdʒ] *vt* ingrandire ♦ *vi*: **to ~ on** (*subject*) dilungarsi su

enlighten [ɪnˈlaɪtn] *vt* illuminare; dare schiarimenti a; **~ed** *adj* illuminato(a); **~ment** *n*: **the E~ment** (*HISTORY*) l'Illuminismo

enlist [ɪnˈlɪst] *vt* arruolare; (*support*) procurare ♦ *vi* arruolarsi

enmity [ˈenmɪtɪ] *n* inimicizia

enormous [ɪˈnɔːməs] *adj* enorme

enough [ɪˈnʌf] *adj, n*: **~ time/books** assai tempo/libri; **have you got ~?** ne ha abbastanza *or* a sufficienza? ♦ *adv*: **big ~** abbastanza grande; **he has not worked ~** non ha lavorato abbastanza; **~! basta!; that's ~,** **thanks** basta così, grazie; **I've had ~ of him** ne ho abbastanza di lui; ... **which, funnily** *or* **oddly ~** ... che, strano a dirsi

enquire [ɪnˈkwaɪə*] *vt, vi* = **inquire**

enrage [ɪnˈreɪdʒ] *vt* fare arrabbiare

enrich [ɪnˈrɪtʃ] *vt* arricchire

enrol [ɪnˈrəul] (*US* **enroll**) *vt* iscrivere ♦ *vi* iscriversi; **~ment** (*US* **enrollment**) *n* iscrizione *f*

en suite [ɒnˈswiːt] *adj*: **room with ~ bathroom** camera con bagno

ensure [ɪnˈʃuə*] *vt* assicurare; garantire

entail [ɪnˈteɪl] *vt* comportare

entangled [ɪnˈtæŋgld] *adj*: **to become ~ (in)** impigliarsi (in)

enter [ˈentə*] *vt* entrare in; (*army*)

arruolarsi in; (*competition*) partecipare a; (*sb for a competition*) iscrivere; (*write down*) registrare; (*COMPUT*) inserire ♦ vi entrare; **~ for** vt fus iscriversi a; **~ into** vt fus (*explanation*) cominciare a dare; (*debate*) partecipare a; (*agreement*) concludere

enterprise ['entəpraız] n (*undertaking, company*) impresa; (*spirit*) iniziativa; **free ~** liberalismo economico; **private ~** iniziativa privata

enterprising ['entəpraızıŋ] adj intraprendente

entertain [entə'teın] vt divertire; (*invite*) ricevere; (*idea, plan*) nutrire; **~er** n comico/a; **~ing** adj divertente; **~ment** n (*amusement*) divertimento; (*show*) spettacolo

enthralled [ın'θrɔːld] adj affascinato(a)

enthusiasm [ın'θuːzıæzəm] n entusiasmo

enthusiast [ın'θuːzıæst] n entusiasta m/f; **~ic** [-'æstık] adj entusiasta, entusiastico(a); **to be ~ic about sth/sb** essere appassionato(a) di qc/entusiasta di qn

entire [ın'taıə*] adj intero(a); **~ly** adv completamente, interamente; **~ty** [ın'taıərətı] n: **in its ~ty** nel suo complesso

entitle [ın'taıtl] vt (*give right*): **to ~ sb to sth/to do** dare diritto a qn a qc/a fare; **~d** adj (*book*) che si intitola; **to be ~d to do** avere il diritto di fare

entrails ['entreılz] npl interiora fpl

entrance [n 'entrns, vb ın'trɑːns] n entrata, ingresso; (*of person*) entrata ♦ vt incantare, rapire; **to gain ~ to** (*university etc*) essere ammesso a; **~ examination** n esame m di ammissione; **~ fee** n tassa d'iscrizione; (*to museum etc*) prezzo d'ingresso; **~ ramp** (*us*) n (*AUT*) rampa di accesso

entrant ['entrnt] n partecipante m/f; concorrente m/f

entreat [ın'triːt] vt supplicare

entrenched [en'trentʃt] adj radicato(a)

entrepreneur [ɔntrəprə'nə:*] n imprenditore m

entrust [ın'trʌst] vt: **to ~ sth to** affidare qc a

entry ['entrı] n entrata; (*way in*) entrata, ingresso; (*item: on list*) iscrizione f; (*in dictionary*) voce f; **no ~** vietato l'ingresso; (*AUT*) divieto di accesso; **~ form** n modulo d'iscrizione; **~ phone** n citofono

envelop [ın'veləp] vt avvolgere, avviluppare

envelope ['envələup] n busta

envious ['envıəs] adj invidioso(a)

environment [ın'vaıərnmənt] n ambiente m; **~al** [-'mentl] adj ecologico(a); ambientale; **~-friendly** adj che rispetta l'ambiente

envisage [ın'vızıdʒ] vt immaginare; prevedere

envoy ['envɔı] n inviato/a

envy ['envı] n invidia ♦ vt invidiare; **to ~ sb sth** invidiare qn per qc

epic ['epık] n poema m epico ♦ adj epico(a)

epidemic [epı'demık] n epidemia

epilepsy ['epılepsı] n epilessia

episode ['epısəud] n episodio

epistle [ı'pısl] n epistola

epitome [ı'pıtəmı] n epitome f, quintessenza; **epitomize** vt (*fig*) incarnare

equal ['iːkwl] adj uguale ♦ n pari m/f inv ♦ vt uguagliare; **~ to** (*task*) all'altezza di; **~ity** [ı:'kwɔlıtı] n uguaglianza; **~ize** vi pareggiare; **~ly** adv ugualmente

equanimity [ekwə'nımıtı] n serenità

equate [ı'kweıt] vt: **to ~ sth with** considerare qc uguale a; (*compare*) paragonare qc con; **equation** [ı'kweıʃən] n (*MATH*) equazione f

equator [ı'kweıtə*] n equatore m

equilibrium [i:kwı'lıbrıəm] n equilibrio

equip [ı'kwıp] vt equipaggiare, attrezzare; **to ~ sb/sth with** fornire qn/qc di; **to be well ~ped** (office etc) essere ben attrezzato(a); **he is well ~ped for the job** ha i requisiti necessari per quel lavoro; **~ment** n attrezzatura; (electrical etc) apparecchiatura

equitable ['ekwɪtəbl] adj equo(a), giusto(a)

equities ['ekwɪtɪz] (BRIT) npl (COMM) azioni fpl ordinarie

equivalent [ɪ'kwɪvəlnt] adj equivalente ♦ n equivalente m; **to be ~ to** equivalere a

era ['ɪərə] n era, età f inv

eradicate [ɪ'rædɪkeɪt] vt sradicare

erase [ɪ'reɪz] vt cancellare; **~r** n gomma

erect [ɪ'rekt] adj eretto(a) ♦ vt costruire; (assemble) montare; **~ion** [ɪ'rekʃən] n costruzione f; montaggio; (PHYSIOL) erezione f

ERM n (= Exchange Rate Mechanism) ERM m

ermine ['ə:mɪn] n ermellino

erode [ɪ'rəud] vt erodere; (metal) corrodere

erotic [ɪ'rɔtɪk] adj erotico(a)

errand ['ernd] n commissione f

erratic [ɪ'rætɪk] adj imprevedibile; (person, mood) incostante

error ['erə*] n errore m

erupt [ɪ'rʌpt] vi (volcano) mettersi (or essere) in eruzione; (war, crisis) scoppiare; **~ion** [ɪ'rʌpʃən] n eruzione f; scoppio

escalate ['eskəleɪt] vi intensificarsi

escalator ['eskəleɪtə*] n scala mobile

escapade [eskə'peɪd] n scappatella; avventura

escape [ɪ'skeɪp] n evasione f; fuga; (of gas etc) fuga, fuoriuscita f ♦ vi fuggire; (from jail) evadere, scappare; (leak) uscire ♦ vt sfuggire a; **to ~ from** (place) fuggire da; (person) sfuggire a; **~escapism** n evasione f (dalla realtà)

escort [n 'eskɔ:t, vb ɪ'skɔ:t] n scorta; (male companion) cavaliere m ♦ vt

scortare; accompagnare

Eskimo ['eskɪməu] n eschimese m/f

especially [ɪ'speʃlɪ] adv specialmente; soprattutto; espressamente

espionage ['espɪənɑ:ʒ] n spionaggio

esplanade [esplə'neɪd] n lungomare m inv

Esq. abbr = **Esquire**

Esquire [ɪ'skwaɪə*] n: **J. Brown, ~** Signor J. Brown

essay ['eseɪ] n (SCOL) composizione f; (LITERATURE) saggio

essence ['esns] n essenza

essential [ɪ'senʃl] adj essenziale ♦ n elemento essenziale; **~ly** adv essenzialmente

establish [ɪ'stæblɪʃ] vt stabilire; (business) mettere su; (one's power etc) affermare; **~ed** adj (business etc) affermato(a), **~ment** n stabilimento; **the E~ment** la classe dirigente, l'establishment m

estate [ɪ'steɪt] n proprietà f inv; beni mpl, patrimonio; (BRIT: also: housing ~) complesso edilizio; **~ agent** (BRIT) n agente m immobiliare; **~ car** (BRIT) n giardiniera

esteem [ɪ'sti:m] n stima ♦ vt (think highly of) stimare; (consider) considerare

esthetic [ɪs'θetɪk] (US) adj = **aesthetic**

estimate [n 'estɪmət, vb 'estɪmeɪt] n stima; (COMM) preventivo ♦ vt stimare, valutare; **estimation** [-'meɪʃən] n stima; opinione f

estranged [ɪs'treɪndʒd] adj separato(a)

etc abbr (= et cetera) etc, ecc

eternal [ɪ'tə:nl] adj eterno(a)

eternity [ɪ'tə:nɪtɪ] n eternità

ether ['i:θə*] n etere m

ethical ['eθɪkl] adj etico(a), morale

ethics ['eθɪks] n etica ♦ npl morale f

Ethiopia [i:θɪ'əupɪə] n Etiopia

ethnic ['eθnɪk] adj etnico(a); **~ minority** n minoranza etnica

ethos ['i:θɔs] n norma di vita

etiquette ['etɪket] n etichetta

EU n abbr (= European Union) UE

euro ['juərəʊ] n (currency) euro m inv

Eurocheque ['juərəʊtʃɛk] n eurochèque m inv

Euroland ['juərəʊlænd] n Eurolandia

Europe ['juərəp] n Europa; **European** [-'pi:ən] adj, n europeo(a); **European Community** n Comunità Europea

evacuate [ɪ'vækjueɪt] vt evacuare

evade [ɪ'veɪd] vt (tax) evadere; (duties etc) sottrarsi a; (person) schivare

evaluate [ɪ'væljueɪt] vt valutare

evaporate [ɪ'væpəreɪt] vi evaporare; **~d milk** n latte m concentrato

evasion [ɪ'veɪʒən] n evasione f

evasive [ɪ'veɪsɪv] adj evasivo(a)

eve [iːv] n: **on the ~ of** alla vigilia di

even ['iːvn] adj regolare; (number) pari inv ♦ adv anche, perfino; **~ if, ~ though** anche se; **~ more** ancora di più; **~ so** ciò nonostante; **not ~** nemmeno; **to get ~ with sb** dare la pari a qn

evening ['iːvnɪŋ] n sera; (as duration, event) serata; **in the ~** la sera; **~ class** n corso serale; **~ dress** n (woman's) abito da sera; **in ~ dress** (man) in abito scuro; (woman) in abito lungo

event [ɪ'vɛnt] n avvenimento m; (SPORT) gara; **in the ~ of** in caso di; **~ful** adj denso(a) di eventi

eventual [ɪ'vɛntʃuəl] adj finale; **~ity** [-'ælɪtɪ] n possibilità f inv, eventualità f inv; **~ly** adv alla fine

ever ['ɛvə*] adv (at all times) sempre; **the best ~** il migliore che ci sia mai stato; **have you ~ seen it?** l'ha mai visto?; **~ since** adv da allora ♦ conj sin da quando; **~ so pretty** così bello(a); **~green** n sempreverde m; **~lasting** adj eterno(a)

every ['ɛvrɪ] adj ogni; **~ day** tutti i giorni, ogni giorno; **~ other/third day** ogni due/tre giorni; **~ other car** una macchina su due; **~ now and then** ogni tanto, di quando in quando; **~body** pron **~one**; **~day** adj quotidiano(a); di ogni giorno; **~one**

pron ognuno, tutti pl; **~thing** pron tutto, ogni cosa; **~where** adv (gen) dappertutto; (wherever) ovunque

evict [ɪ'vɪkt] vt sfrattare

evidence ['ɛvɪdns] n (proof) prova; (of witness) testimonianza; (sign): **to show ~ of** dare segni di; **to give ~** deporre

evident ['ɛvɪdnt] adj evidente; **~ly** adv evidentemente

evil ['iːvl] adj cattivo(a), maligno(a) ♦ n male m

evoke [ɪ'vəʊk] vt evocare

evolution [iːvə'luːʃən] n evoluzione f

evolve [ɪ'vɔlv] vt elaborare ♦ vi sviluparsi, evolversi

ewe [juː] n pecora

ex- [ɛks] prefix ex

exacerbate [ɛks'æsəbeɪt] vt aggravare

exact [ɪg'zækt] adj esatto(a) ♦ vt: **to ~ sth (from)** estorcere qc (da); esigere qc (da); **~ing** adj esigente; (work) faticoso(a); **~ly** adv esattamente

exaggerate [ɪg'zædʒəreɪt] vt, vi esagerare; **exaggeration** [-'reɪʃən] n esagerazione f

exalted [ɪg'zɔːltɪd] adj esaltato(a); elevato(a)

exam [ɪg'zæm] n abbr (SCOL) = **examination**

examination [ɪgzæmɪ'neɪʃən] n (SCOL) esame m; (MED) controllo

examine [ɪg'zæmɪn] vt esaminare; **~r** n esaminatore/trice

example [ɪg'zɑːmpl] n esempio; **for ~** ad or per esempio

exasperate [ɪg'zɑːspəreɪt] vt esasperare; **exasperating** adj esasperante; **exasperation** [-'reɪʃən] n esasperazione f

excavate ['ɛkskəveɪt] vt scavare

exceed [ɪk'siːd] vt superare; (one's powers, time limit) oltrepassare; **~ingly** adv eccessivamente

excellent ['ɛksələnt] adj eccellente

except [ɪk'sɛpt] prep (also: **~ for, ~ing**) salvo, all'infuori di, eccetto ♦ vt escludere; **~ if/when** salvo se/quando;

~ **that** salvo che; **~ion** [ɪkˈsɛpʃən] n eccezione f; **to take ~ion to** trovare a ridire su; **~ional** [ɪkˈsɛpʃənl] adj eccezionale

excerpt [ˈɛksɜːpt] n estratto

excess [ɪkˈsɛs] n eccesso; ~ **baggage** n bagaglio in eccedenza; ~ **fare** n supplemento; **~ive** adj eccessivo(a)

exchange [ɪksˈtʃeɪndʒ] n scambio; (also: telephone ~) centralino ♦ vt: **to ~ (for)** scambiare (con); ~ **rate** n tasso di cambio

Exchequer [ɪksˈtʃɛkə*] n: **the ~** (BRIT) lo Scacchiere, ≈ il ministero delle Finanze

excise [ˈɛksaɪz] n imposta, dazio

excite [ɪkˈsaɪt] vt eccitare; **to get ~d** eccitarsi; **~ment** n eccitazione f, agitazione f; **exciting** adj avventuroso(a); (film, book) appassionante

exclaim [ɪkˈskleɪm] vi esclamare; **exclamation** [ɛksklǝˈmeɪʃǝn] n esclamazione f; **exclamation mark** n punto esclamativo

exclude [ɪkˈskluːd] vt escludere

exclusive [ɪkˈskluːsɪv] adj esclusivo(a); ~ **of VAT** I.V.A. esclusa

excommunicate [ɛkskǝˈmjuːnɪkeɪt] vt scomunicare

excruciating [ɪkˈskruːʃɪeɪtɪŋ] adj straziante, atroce

excursion [ɪkˈskɜːʃǝn] n escursione f, gita

excuse [n ɪkˈskjuːs, vb ɪkˈskjuːz] n scusa f ♦ vt scusare; **to ~ sb from** (activity) dispensare qn da; ~ **me!** mi scusi!; **now, if you will ~ me ...** ora, mi scusi ma ....

ex-directory (BRIT) adj (TEL): **to be ~** non essere sull'elenco

execute [ˈɛksɪkjuːt] vt (prisoner) giustiziare; (plan etc) eseguire

execution [ɛksɪˈkjuːʃǝn] n esecuzione f; **~er** n boia m inv

executive [ɪgˈzɛkjutɪv] n (COMM) dirigente m; (POL) esecutivo ♦ adj

esecutivo(a)

exemplify [ɪgˈzɛmplɪfaɪ] vt esemplificare

exempt [ɪgˈzɛmpt] adj esentato(a) ♦ vt: **to ~ sb from** esentare qn da; **~ion** [ɪgˈzɛmpʃǝn] n esenzione f

exercise [ˈɛksǝsaɪz] n (keep fit) moto; (SCOL, MIL etc) esercizio ♦ vt esercitare; (patience) usare; (dog) portar fuori ♦ vi (also: take ~) fare del moto; **~bike** n cyclette f inv; ~ **book** n quaderno

exert [ɪgˈzɜːt] vt esercitare; **to ~ o.s.** sforzarsi; **~ion** [-ʃǝn] n sforzo

exhale [ɛksˈheɪl] vt, vi espirare

exhaust [ɪgˈzɔːst] n (also: ~ fumes) scappamento; (also: ~ pipe) tubo di scappamento ♦ vt esaurire; **~ed** adj esaurito(a); **~ion** [ɪgˈzɔːstʃǝn] n esaurimento; **nervous ~ion** sovraffaticamento mentale; **~ive** adj esauriente

exhibit [ɪgˈzɪbɪt] n (ART) oggetto esposto; (LAW) documento or oggetto esibito ♦ vt esporre; (courage, skill) dimostrare; **~ion** [ɛksɪˈbɪʃǝn] n mostra, esposizione f

exhilarating [ɪgˈzɪlǝreɪtɪŋ] adj esilarante; stimolante

exhort [ɪgˈzɔːt] vt esortare

exile [ˈɛksaɪl] n esilio; (person) esiliato/a ♦ vt esiliare

exist [ɪgˈzɪst] vi esistere; **~ence** n esistenza; **~ing** adj esistente

exit [ˈɛksɪt] n uscita ♦ vi (THEATRE, COMPUT) uscire; ~ **poll** n exit poll m inv; ~ **ramp** (US) n (AUT) rampa di uscita

exodus [ˈɛksǝdǝs] n esodo

exonerate [ɪgˈzɔnǝreɪt] vt: **to ~ from** discolpare da

exotic [ɪgˈzɔtɪk] adj esotico(a)

expand [ɪkˈspænd] vt espandere; estendere; allargare ♦ vi (business, gas) espandersi; (metal) dilatarsi

expanse [ɪkˈspæns] n distesa, estensione f

expansion [ɪkˈspænʃǝn] n (gen)

espansione f; (of town, economy) sviluppo; (of metal) dilatazione f

expect [ɪk'spɛkt] vt (anticipate) prevedere, aspettarsi, prevedere or aspettarsi che + sub; (require) richiedere, esigere; (suppose) supporre; (await, also baby) aspettare ♦ vi: **to be ~ing** essere in stato interessante; **to ~ sb to do** aspettarsi che qn faccia; **~ancy** n (anticipation) attesa; **life ~ancy** n probabilità fpl di vita; **~ant mother** n gestante f; **~ation** [ɛkspɛk'teɪʃən] n aspettativa; speranza f

expediency [ɪk'spiːdɪənsɪ] n convenienza

expedient [ɪk'spiːdɪənt] adj conveniente; vantaggioso(a) ♦ n espediente m

expedition [ɛkspə'dɪʃən] n spedizione f

expel [ɪk'spɛl] vt espellere

expend [ɪk'spɛnd] vt spendere; (use up) consumare; **~iture** [ɪk'spɛndɪtʃə*] n spesa

expense [ɪk'spɛns] n spesa; (high cost) costo; **~s** npl (COMM) spese fpl, indennità fpl; **at the ~ of** a spese di; **~ account** n conto m spese inv

expensive [ɪk'spɛnsɪv] adj caro(a), costoso(a)

experience [ɪk'spɪərɪəns] n esperienza ♦ vt (pleasure) provare; (hardship) soffrire; **~d** adj esperto(a)

experiment [n ɪk'spɛrɪmənt, vb ɪk'spɛrɪmɛnt] n esperimento, esperienza ♦ vi: **to ~ (with/on)** fare esperimenti (con/su)

expert ['ɛkspə:t] adj, n esperto(a); **~ise** [-'tiːz] n competenza

expire [ɪk'spaɪə*] vi (period of time, licence) scadere; **expiry** n scadenza

explain [ɪk'spleɪn] vt spiegare; **explanation** [ɛksplə'neɪʃən] n spiegazione f; **explanatory** [ɪk'splænətrɪ] adj esplicativo(a)

explicit [ɪk'splɪsɪt] adj esplicito(a)

explode [ɪk'spləud] vi esplodere

exploit [n 'ɛksplɔɪt, vb ɪk'splɔɪt] n impresa f ♦ vt sfruttare; **~ation** [-'teɪʃən] n sfruttamento

exploratory [ɪk'splɔrətrɪ] adj esplorativo(a)

explore [ɪk'splɔ:*] vt esplorare; (possibilities) esaminare; **~r** n esploratore/trice

explosion [ɪk'spləuʒən] n esplosione f

explosive [ɪk'spləusɪv] adj esplosivo(a) ♦ n esplosivo

exponent [ɪk'spəunənt] n esponente m/f

export [vb ɛk'spɔ:t, n 'ɛkspɔ:t] vt esportare ♦ n esportazione f; articolo di esportazione ♦ cpd d'esportazione; **~er** n esportatore m

expose [ɪk'spəuz] vt esporre; (unmask) smascherare; **~d** adj (position) esposto(a)

exposure [ɪk'spəuʒə*] n esposizione f; (PHOT) posa; (MED) assideramento; **~ meter** n esposimetro

express [ɪk'sprɛs] adj (definite) chiaro(a), espresso(a); (BRIT: letter etc) espresso inv ♦ n (train) espresso ♦ vt esprimere; **~ion** [ɪk'sprɛʃən] n espressione f; **~ive** adj espressivo(a); **~ly** adv espressamente; **~way** (US) n (urban motorway) autostrada che attraversa la città

exquisite [ɛk'skwɪzɪt] adj squisito(a)

extend [ɪk'stɛnd] vt (visit) protrarre; (road, deadline) prolungare; (building) ampliare; (offer) offrire, porgere ♦ vi (land, period) estendersi

extension [ɪk'stɛnʃən] n (of road, term) prolungamento; (of contract, deadline) proroga; (building) annesso; (to wire, table) prolunga; (telephone) interno; (: in private house) apparecchio supplementare

extensive [ɪk'stɛnsɪv] adj esteso(a), ampio(a); (damage) su larga scala; (coverage, discussion) esauriente; (use) grande; **~ly** adv: **he's travelled ~ly** ha viaggiato molto

extent [ɪk'stɛnt] n estensione f; **to some ~** fino a un certo punto; **to such an ~ that ...** in un tal punto che ...; **to what ~?** fino a che punto?; **the ~ of ...** fino al punto di ...

extenuating [ɪks'tɛnjueɪtɪŋ] adj: **~ circumstances** attenuanti fpl

exterior [ɛk'stɪərɪə•] adj esteriore, esterno(a) ♦ n esteriore m, esterno, aspetto (esteriore)

exterminate [ɪk'stə:mɪneɪt] vt sterminare

external [ɛk'stə:nl] adj esterno(a), esteriore

extinct [ɪk'stɪŋkt] adj estinto(a)

extinguish [ɪk'stɪŋgwɪʃ] vt estinguere; **~er** n estintore m

extort [ɪk'stɔ:t] vt: **to ~ sth (from)** estorcere qc (da); **~ionate** [ɪk'stɔ:ʃnət] adj esorbitante

extra ['ɛkstrə] adj extra inv, supplementare ♦ adv (in addition) di più ♦ n extra m inv, (surcharge) supplemento; (CINEMA, THEATRE) comparsa

extra... ['ɛkstrə] prefix extra...

extract [vb ɪk'strækt, n 'ɛkstrækt] vt estrarre; (money, promise) strappare ♦ n estratto; (passage) brano

extracurricular ['ɛkstrəkə'rɪkjulə•] adj extrascolastico(a)

extradite ['ɛkstrədaɪt] vt estradare

extramarital [ɛkstrə'mærɪtl] adj extraconiugale

extramural [ɛkstrə'mjuərl] adj fuori dell'università

extraordinary [ɪk'strɔ:dnrɪ] adj straordinario(a)

extravagance [ɪk'strævəgəns] n sperpero; stravaganza

extravagant [ɪk'strævəgənt] adj (lavish) prodigo(a); (wasteful) dispendioso(a)

extreme [ɪk'stri:m] adj estremo(a) ♦ n estremo; **~ly** adv estremamente

extricate ['ɛkstrɪkeɪt] vt: **to ~ sth (from)** districare qc (da)

extrovert ['ɛkstrəvə:t] n estroverso/a

exude [ɪg'zju:d] vt trasudare; (fig) emanare

eye [aɪ] n occhio; (of needle) cruna ♦ vt osservare; **to keep an ~ on** tenere d'occhio; **~brow** n sopracciglio; **~drops** npl gocce fpl oculari, collirio; **~lash** n ciglio; **~lid** n palpebra; **~liner** n eye-liner m inv; **~opener** n rivelazione f; **~shadow** n ombretto; **~sight** n vista; **~sore** n pugno nell'occhio; **~ witness** n testimone m/f oculare

F, f

F [ɛf] n (MUS) fa m

fable ['feɪbl] n favola

fabric ['fæbrɪk] n stoffa, tessuto

fabulous ['fæbjuləs] adj favoloso(a); (super) favoloso(a), fantastico(a)

façade [fə'sɑ:d] n (also fig) facciata

face [feɪs] n faccia, viso, volto; (expression) faccia; (of clock) quadrante m; (of building) facciata ♦ vt essere di fronte a; (facts, situation) affrontare; **~ down** a faccia in giù; **to make** or **pull a ~** fare una smorfia; **in the ~ of** (difficulties etc) di fronte a; **on the ~ of it** a prima vista; **~ to ~** faccia a faccia; **~ up to** vt fus affrontare, far fronte a; **~ cloth** (BRIT) n guanto di spugna; **~ cream** n crema per il viso; **~ lift** n lifting m inv; (of façade etc) ripulita; **~ powder** n cipria; **~saving** adj per salvare la faccia

facet ['fæsɪt] n sfaccettatura

facetious [fə'si:ʃəs] adj faceto(a)

face value n (of coin) valore m facciale or nominale; **to take sth at ~** (fig) giudicare qc dalle apparenze

facial ['feɪʃl] adj del viso

facile ['fæsaɪl] adj superficiale

facilities [fə'sɪlɪtɪz] npl attrezzature fpl; **credit ~** facilitazioni fpl di credito

facing ['feɪsɪŋ] prep di fronte a

facsimile [fæk'sɪmɪlɪ] n facsimile m inv;
~ **machine** n telecopiatrice f

fact [fækt] n fatto; **in** ~ infatti

factor ['fæktə*] n fattore m

factory ['fæktərɪ] n fabbrica,
stabilimento

factual ['fæktjuəl] adj che si attiene ai
fatti

faculty ['fækəltɪ] n facoltà f inv; (us)
corpo insegnante

fad [fæd] n mania; capriccio

fade [feɪd] vi sbiadire, sbiadirsi; (light,
sound, hope) attenuarsi, affievolirsi;
(flower) appassire

fag [fæg] (BRIT: inf) n (cigarette) cicca

fail [feɪl] vt (exam) non superare;
(candidate) bocciare; (subj: courage,
memory) mancare a ♦ vi fallire;
(student) essere respinto/a; (eyesight,
health, light) venire a mancare; **to** ~ **to
do sth** (neglect) mancare di fare qc;
(be unable) non riuscire a fare qc;
without ~ senza fallo; certamente;
~**ing** n difetto ♦ prep in mancanza di;
~**ure** ['feɪljə*] n fallimento; (person)
fallito/a; (mechanical etc) guasto

faint [feɪnt] adj debole; (recollection)
vago/a; (mark) indistinto/a ♦ n (MED)
svenimento ♦ vi svenire; **to feel** ~
sentirsi svenire

fair [feə*] adj (person, decision)
giusto/a, equo/a; (quite large, quite
good) discreto/a; (hair etc) biondo/a;
(skin, complexion) chiaro/a; (weather)
bello/a, clemente ♦ adv (play)
lealmente ♦ n fiera; (BRIT: funfair) luna
park m inv; ~**ly** adv equamente; (quite)
abbastanza; ~**ness** n equità, giustizia;
~ **play** n correttezza

fairy ['feərɪ] n fata; ~ **tale** n fiaba

faith [feɪθ] n fede f; (trust) fiducia;
(sect) religione f, fede f; ~**ful** adj
fedele; ~**fully** adv fedelmente; **yours
~fully** (BRIT: in letters) distinti saluti

fake [feɪk] n imitazione f; (picture) falso;
(person) impostore/a ♦ adj falso/a ♦ vt
(accounts) falsificare; (illness) fingere;

(painting) contraffare

fall [fɔːl] (pt **fell**, pp **fallen**) n caduta;
(in temperature) abbassamento; (in
price) ribasso; (us: autumn) autunno
♦ vi cadere; (temperature, price, night)
scendere; ~**s** npl (waterfall) cascate fpl;
to ~ **flat** (on one's face) cadere
bocconi; (joke) fare cilecca; (plan)
fallire; ~ **back** vi (retreat)
indietreggiare; (MIL) ritirarsi; ~ **back
on** vt fus (remedy etc) ripiegare su;
~ **behind** vi rimanere indietro; ~
down vi (person) cadere; (building)
crollare; ~ **for** vt fus (person) prendere
una cotta per; **to** ~ **for a trick** (or a
story etc) cascarci; ~ **in** vi crollare;
(MIL) mettersi in riga; ~ **off** vi cadere;
(diminish) diminuire, abbassarsi; ~ **out**
vi (hair, teeth) cadere; (friends etc)
litigare; ~ **through** vi (plan, project)
fallire

fallacy ['fæləsɪ] n errore m

fallen ['fɔːlən] pp of **fall**

fallout ['fɔːlaut] n fall-out m

fallow ['fæləu] adj incolto/a, a
maggese

false [fɔːls] adj falso/a; **under**
~ **pretences** con l'inganno; ~ **teeth**
(BRIT) npl denti mpl finti

falter ['fɔːltə*] vi esitare, vacillare

fame [feɪm] n fama, celebrità

familiar [fə'mɪlɪə*] adj familiare; (close)
intimo/a; **to be** ~ **with** (subject)
conoscere; ~**ize** [fə'mɪlɪəraɪz] vt: **to**
~**ize o.s. with** familiarizzare con

family ['fæmɪlɪ] n famiglia; ~
business n ditta a conduzione
familiare

famine ['fæmɪn] n carestia

famished ['fæmɪʃt] adj affamato/a

famous ['feɪməs] adj famoso/a; ~**ly**
adv (get on) a meraviglia

fan [fæn] n (folding) ventaglio; (ELEC)
ventilatore m; (person) ammiratore/
trice; tifoso/a ♦ vt far vento a; (fire,
quarrel) alimentare

fanatic [fə'nætɪk] n fanatico/a

fan belt n cinghia del ventilatore

fanciful ['fænsɪful] adj fantasioso(a)

fancy ['fænsɪ] n immaginazione f,
fantasia; (whim) capriccio ♦ adj (hat)
stravagante; (hotel, food) speciale ♦ vt
(feel like, want) aver voglia di; (imagine,
think) immaginare; **to take a ~ to**
incapricciarsi di; **he fancies her** (inf)
gli piace; **~ dress** n costume m (per
maschera); **~-dress ball** n ballo in
maschera

fang [fæŋ] n zanna; (of snake) dente m

fantastic [fæn'tæstɪk] adj fantastico(a)

fantasy ['fæntəsɪ] n fantasia,
immaginazione f, fantasticheria;
chimera

far [fɑː*] adj lontano(a) ♦ adv lontano;
(much, greatly) molto; **~ away, ~ off**
lontano, distante; **~ better** assai
migliore; **~ from** lontano da; **by ~** di
gran lunga; **go as ~ as the farm**
vada fino alla fattoria; **as ~ as I know**
per quel che so; **how ~?** quanto
lontano?; (referring to activity etc) fino a
dove?; **~away** adj lontano(a)

farce [fɑːs] n farsa

fare [fɛə*] n (on trains, buses) tariffa; (in
taxi) prezzo della corsa; (food) vitto,
cibo; **half ~** metà tariffa; **full ~** tariffa
intera

Far East n: **the ~** l'Estremo Oriente m

farewell [fɛə'wɛl] excl, n addio

farm [fɑːm] n fattoria, podere m ♦ vt
coltivare; **~er** n coltivatore/trice;
agricoltore/trice; **~hand** n bracciante
m agricolo; **~house** n fattoria; **~ing** n
(gen) agricoltura; (of crops) coltivazione
f; (of animals) allevamento; **~land** n
terreno coltivabile; **~ worker** n =
~hand; **~yard** n aia

far-reaching [-'riːtʃɪŋ] adj di vasta
portata

fart [fɑːt] (inf!) vi scoreggiare (!)

farther ['fɑːðə*] adv più lontano ♦ adj
più lontano(a)

farthest ['fɑːðɪst] superl of **far**

fascinate ['fæsɪneɪt] vt affascinare;

fascinating [-neɪtɪŋ] adj affascinante;

fascination [-'neɪʃən] n fascino

fascism ['fæʃɪzəm] n fascismo

fashion ['fæʃən] n moda; (manner)
maniera, modo ♦ vt foggiare, formare;
in ~ alla moda; **out of ~** passato(a) di
moda; **~able** adj alla moda, di moda;
~ show n sfilata di moda

fast [fɑːst] adj rapido(a), svelto(a),
veloce; (clock): **to be ~** andare avanti;
(dye, colour) solido(a) ♦ adv
rapidamente; (stuck, held) saldamente
♦ n digiuno ♦ vi digiunare; **~ asleep**
profondamente addormentato

fasten ['fɑːsn] vt chiudere, fissare;
(coat) abbottonare, allacciare ♦ vi
chiudersi, fissarsi; abbottonarsi,
allacciarsi; **~er** n fermaglio, chiusura;
~ing n = **~er**

fast food n fast food m

fastidious [fæs'tɪdɪəs] adj esigente,
difficile

fat [fæt] adj grasso(a); (book, profit etc)
grosso(a) ♦ n grasso

fatal ['feɪtl] adj fatale; mortale;
disastroso(a); **~ity** [fə'tælɪtɪ] n (road
death etc) morto/a, vittima; **~ly** adv a
morte

fate [feɪt] n destino; (of person) sorte f;
~ful adj fatidico(a)

father ['fɑːðə*] n padre m; **~-in-law** n
suocero; **~ly** adj paterno(a)

fathom ['fæðəm] n braccio (= 1828
mm) ♦ vt (mystery) penetrare, sondare

fatigue [fə'tiːɡ] n stanchezza

fatten ['fætn] vt, vi ingrassare

fatty ['fætɪ] adj (food) grasso(a) ♦ n
(inf) ciccione/a

fatuous ['fætjuəs] adj fatuo(a)

faucet ['fɔːsɪt] (US) n rubinetto

fault [fɔːlt] n colpa; (TENNIS) fallo;
(defect) difetto; (GEO) faglia ♦ vt
criticare; **it's my ~** è colpa mia; **to
find ~ with** trovare da ridire su; **at ~**
in fallo; **~y** adj difettoso(a)

fauna ['fɔːnə] n fauna

favour ['feɪvə*] (US **favor**) n favore m

♦ vt (*proposition*) favorire, essere favorevole a; (*pupil etc*) favorire; (*team, horse*) dare per vincente; **to do sb a ~** fare un favore or una cortesia a qn; **to find ~ with** (*subj: person*) entrare nelle buone grazie di; (: *suggestion*) avere l'approvazione di; **in ~ of** in favore di; **~able** adj favorevole; **~ite** [-rɪt] adj, n favorito(a)

fawn [fɔ:n] n daino ♦ adj (*also*: **~-coloured**) marrone chiaro inv ♦ vi: **to ~ (up)on** adulare servilmente

fax [fæks] n (*document*) facsimile m inv, telecopia; (*machine*) telecopiatrice f ♦ vt telecopiare, trasmettere in facsimile

FBI (*us*) n abbr (= *Federal Bureau of Investigation*) F.B.I. f

fear [fɪə*] n paura, timore m ♦ vt aver paura di, temere; **for ~ of** per paura di; **~ful** adj pauroso(a); (*sight, noise*) terribile, spaventoso(a)

feasible ['fi:zəbl] adj possibile, realizzabile

feast [fi:st] n festa, banchetto; (*REL: also*: ~ *day*) festa ♦ vi banchettare

feat [fi:t] n impresa, fatto insigne

feather ['feðə*] n penna

feature ['fi:tʃə*] n caratteristica; (*PRESS, TV*) articolo ♦ vt (*subj: film*) avere come protagonista ♦ vi figurare; **~s** npl (*of face*) fisionomia; **~ film** n film m inv principale

February ['februərɪ] n febbraio

fed [fed] pt, pp of **feed**

federal ['fedərəl] adj federale

fed-up adj: **to be ~** essere stufo(a)

fee [fi:] n pagamento; (*of doctor, lawyer*) onorario; (*for examination*) tassa d'esame; **school ~s** tasse fpl scolastiche

feeble ['fi:bl] adj debole

feed [fi:d] (pt, pp **fed**) n (*of baby*) pappa; (*of animal*) mangime m; (*on printer*) meccanismo di alimentazione ♦ vt nutrire; (*baby*) allattare; (*horse etc*) dare da mangiare a; (*fire, machine*)

alimentare; (*data, information*): **to ~ into** inserire in; **~ on** vt fus nutrirsi di; **~back** n feed-back m

feel [fi:l] (pt, pp **felt**) n consistenza; (*sense of touch*) tatto ♦ vt toccare; palpare; tastare; (*cold, pain, anger*) sentire; (*think, believe*): **to ~ (that)** pensare che; **to ~ hungry/cold** aver fame/freddo; **to ~ lonely/better** sentirsi solo/meglio; **I don't ~ well** non mi sento bene; **it ~s soft** è morbido al tatto; **to ~ like** (*want*) aver voglia di; **to ~ about** or **around** for cercare a tastoni; **~er** n (*of insect*) antenna; **~ing** n sensazione f; (*emotion*) sentimento

feet [fi:t] npl of **foot**

feign [feɪn] vt fingere, simulare

fell [fel] pt of **fall** ♦ vt (*tree*) abbattere

fellow ['feləu] n individuo, tipo; compagno; (*of learned society*) membro ♦ cpd: **~ citizen** n concittadino/a; **~ countryman** (*irreg*) n compatriota m; **~ men** npl simili mpl; **~ship** n associazione f; compagnia; *specie di borsa di studio universitaria*

felony ['felənɪ] n reato, crimine m

felt [felt] pt, pp of **feel** ♦ n feltro; **~-tip pen** n pennarello

female ['fi:meɪl] n (*zool*) femmina; (*pej: woman*) donna, femmina ♦ adj (*BIOL, ELEC*) femmina inv; (*sex, character*) femminile; (*vote etc*) di donne

feminine ['femɪnɪn] adj femminile

feminist ['femɪnɪst] n femminista m/f

fence [fens] n recinto ♦ vt (*also*: ~ in) recingere ♦ vi (*SPORT*) tirare di scherma; **fencing** n (*SPORT*) scherma

fend [fend] vi: **to ~ for o.s.** arrangiarsi; **~ off** vt (*attack, questions*) respingere, difendersi da

fender ['fendə*] n parafuoco; (*on boat*) parabordo; (*us*) parafango; parurti m inv

ferment [vb fə'ment, n 'fə:ment] vi fermentare ♦ n (*fig*) agitazione f, eccitazione f

fern [fəːn] *n* felce *f*

ferocious [fəˈrəʊʃəs] *adj* feroce

ferret [ˈfɛrɪt] *n* furetto; **~ out** *vt* (*information*) scovare

ferry [ˈfɛrɪ] *n* (*small*) traghetto; (*large: also: ~boat*) nave *f* traghetto *inv* ♦ *vt* traghettare

fertile [ˈfəːtaɪl] *adj* fertile; (*BIOL*) fecondo(a); **fertilizer** [ˈfəːtɪlaɪzə*] *n* fertilizzante *m*

fester [ˈfɛstə*] *vi* suppurare

festival [ˈfɛstɪvəl] *n* (*REL*) festa; (*ART*, *MUS*) festival *m inv*

festive [ˈfɛstɪv] *adj* di festa; **the ~ season** (*BRIT: Christmas*) il periodo delle feste

festivities [fɛsˈtɪvɪtɪz] *npl* festeggiamenti *mpl*

festoon [fɛsˈtuːn] *vt*: **to ~ with** ornare di

fetch [fɛtʃ] *vt* andare a prendere; (*sell for*) essere venduto(a) per

fête [feɪt] *n* festa

fetus [ˈfiːtəs] (*US*) *n* = **foetus**

feud [fjuːd] *n* contesa, lotta

feudal [ˈfjuːdl] *adj* feudale

fever [ˈfiːvə*] *n* febbre *f*; **~ish** *adj* febbrile

few [fjuː] *adj* pochi(e); **a ~** qualche *inv* ♦ *pron* alcuni(e); **~er** *adj* meno *inv*; meno numerosi(e); **~est** *adj* il minor numero di

fiancé [fiˈɑːnseɪ] *n* fidanzato; **~e** *n* fidanzata

fib [fɪb] *n* piccola bugia

fibre [ˈfaɪbə*] (*US* **fiber**) *n* fibra; **F~glass** ® *n* fibra di vetro

fickle [ˈfɪkl] *adj* incostante, capriccioso(a)

fiction [ˈfɪkʃən] *n* narrativa, romanzi *mpl*; (*sth made up*) finzione *f*; **~al** *adj* immaginario(a)

fictitious [fɪkˈtɪʃəs] *adj* fittizio(a)

fiddle [ˈfɪdl] *n* (*MUS*) violino; (*cheating*) imbroglio; truffa ♦ *vt* (*BRIT: accounts*) falsificare, falsare; **~ with** *vt fus* gingillarsi con

fidelity [fɪˈdɛlɪtɪ] *n* fedeltà; (*accuracy*) esattezza

fidget [ˈfɪdʒɪt] *vi* agitarsi

field [fiːld] *n* campo; **~ marshal** *n* feldmaresciallo; **~work** *n* ricerche *fpl* esterne

fiend [fiːnd] *n* demonio

fierce [fɪəs] *adj* (*animal, person, fighting*) feroce; (*loyalty*) assoluto(a); (*wind*) furioso(a); (*heat*) intenso(a)

fiery [ˈfaɪərɪ] *adj* ardente; infocato(a)

fifteen [fɪfˈtiːn] *num* quindici

fifth [fɪfθ] *num* quinto(a)

fifty [ˈfɪftɪ] *num* cinquanta; **~-~** *adj*: **a ~-~ chance** una possibilità su due ♦ *adv* fifty-fifty, metà per ciascuno

fig [fɪg] *n* fico

fight [faɪt] (*pt, pp* **fought**) *n* zuffa, rissa; (*MIL*) battaglia, combattimento; (*against cancer etc*) lotta ♦ *vt* (*person*) azzuffarsi con; (*enemy: also: MIL*) combattere; (*cancer, alcoholism, emotion*) lottare contro, combattere; (*election*) partecipare a ♦ *vi* combattere; **~er** *n* combattente *m*; (*plane*) aeroplano da caccia; **~ing** *n* combattimento

figment [ˈfɪgmənt] *n*: **a ~ of the imagination** un parto della fantasia

figurative [ˈfɪgjʊrətɪv] *adj* figurato(a)

figure [ˈfɪgə*] *n* figura; (*number, cipher*) cifra ♦ *vt* (*think: esp US*) pensare ♦ *vi* (*appear*) figurare; **~ out** *vt* riuscire a capire; calcolare; **~head** *n* (*NAUT*) polena; (*pej*) prestanome *m/f inv*; **~ of speech** *n* figura retorica

file [faɪl] *n* (*tool*) lima; (*dossier*) incartamento; (*folder*) cartella; (*COMPUT*) archivio; (*row*) fila ♦ *vt* (*nails, wood*) limare; (*papers*) archiviare; (*LAW: claim*) presentare; passare agli atti; **~ in/out** *vi* entrare/uscire in fila

filing cabinet [ˈfaɪlɪŋ-] *n* casellario

fill [fɪl] *vt* riempire; (*job*) coprire ♦ *n*: **to eat one's ~** mangiare a sazietà; **~ in** *vt* (*hole*) riempire; (*form*) compilare; **~ up** *vt* riempire ♦ *vi* (*AUT*) fare il pieno

fillet ['fılıt] n filetto; ~ **steak** n bistecca di filetto

filling ['fılıŋ] n (CULIN) impasto, ripieno; (for tooth) otturazione f; ~ **station** n stazione f di rifornimento

film [fılm] n (CINEMA) film m inv; (PHOT) pellicola; (of powder, liquid) sottile strato ♦ vt, vi girare; ~ **star** n diva/o dello schermo

filter ['fıltə*] n filtro ♦ vt filtrare; ~ **lane** (BRIT) n (AUT) corsia di svincolo; ~-**tipped** adj con filtro

filth [fılθ] n sporcizia; ~**y** adj lordo(a), sozzo(a); (language) osceno(a)

fin [fın] n (of fish) pinna

final ['faınl] adj finale, ultimo(a); definitivo(a) ♦ n (SPORT) finale f; ~**s** npl (SCOL) esami mpl finali

finale [fı'nɑːlı] n finale m

finalize ['faınəlaız] vt mettere a punto

finally ['faınəlı] adv (lastly) alla fine; (eventually) finalmente

finance [faı'næns] n finanza; (capital) capitale m ♦ vt finanziare; ~**s** npl (funds) finanze fpl

financial [faı'nænʃəl] adj finanziario(a)

financier [faı'nænsıə*] n finanziatore m

find [faınd] (pt, pp found) vt trovare; (lost object) ritrovare ♦ n trovata, scoperta; to ~ **sb guilty** (LAW) giudicare qn colpevole; ~ **out** vt (truth, secret) scoprire; (person) cogliere in fallo; to ~ **out about** informarsi su; (by chance) scoprire; ~**ings** npl (LAW) sentenza, conclusioni fpl; (of report) conclusioni

fine [faın] adj bello(a); ottimo(a); (thin, subtle) fine ♦ adv (well) molto bene ♦ n (LAW) multa ♦ vt (LAW) multare; to be ~ (person) stare bene; (weather) far bello; ~ **arts** npl belle arti fpl

finery ['faınərı] n abiti mpl eleganti

finger ['fıŋgə*] n dito ♦ vt toccare, tastare; **little/index** ~ mignolo/(dito) indice m; ~**nail** n unghia; ~**print** n impronta digitale; ~**tip** n punta del dito

finish ['fınıʃ] n fine f; (polish etc) finitura f; (of race) arrivo m ♦ vt, vi finire; to ~ **doing sth** finire di fare qc; to ~ **third** arrivare terzo(a); ~ **off** vt compiere; (kill) uccidere; ~ **up** vi, vt finire; ~**ing line** n linea d'arrivo

finite ['faınaıt] adj limitato(a); (verb) finito(a)

Finland ['fınlənd] n Finlandia

Finn [fın] n finlandese m/f; ~**ish** adj finlandese ♦ n (LING) finlandese m

fir [fəː*] n abete m

fire [faıə*] n (destructive) incendio; (gas -, electric ~) stufa ♦ vt (gun) far fuoco con; (arrow) sparare; (fig) infiammare; (inf: dismiss) licenziare ♦ vi sparare, far fuoco; **on** ~ in fiamme; ~ **alarm** n allarme m d'incendio; ~**arm** n arma da fuoco; ~ **brigade** (US ~ **department**) n (corpo dei) pompieri mpl; ~ **engine** n autopompa; ~ **escape** n scala di sicurezza; ~ **extinguisher** n estintore m; ~**guard** n parafuoco; ~**man** (irreg) n pompiere m; ~**place** n focolare m; ~**side** n angolo del focolare; ~ **station** n caserma dei pompieri; ~**wood** n legna; ~**works** npl fuochi mpl d'artificio

firing squad ['faıərıŋ-] n plotone m d'esecuzione

firm [fəːm] adj fermo(a) ♦ n ditta, azienda; ~**ly** adv fermamente

first [fəːst] adj primo(a) ♦ adv (before others) il primo, la prima; (before other things) per primo; (when listing reasons etc) per prima cosa ♦ n (person: in race) primo/a; (BRIT: SCOL) laurea con lode; (AUT) prima; **at** ~ dapprima, all'inizio; ~ **of all** prima di tutto; ~ **aid** n pronto soccorso; ~-**aid kit** n cassetta pronto soccorso; ~-**class** adj di prima classe; ~ **floor** n il primo piano (BRIT); (US) pianterreno (US); ~-**hand** adj di prima mano; ~ **lady** (US) n moglie f del presidente; ~**ly** adv in primo luogo; ~ **name** n prenome m; ~-**rate** adj di prima qualità, ottimo(a)

fish [fɪʃ] n inv pesce m ♦ vt (river, area) pescare in ♦ vi pescare; **to go ~ing** andare a pesca; **~erman** n pescatore m; **~ farm** n vivaio; **~ fingers** (BRIT) npl bastoncini mpl di pesce (surgelati); **~ing boat** n barca da pesca; **~ing line** n lenza; **~ing rod** n canna da pesca; **~monger** n pescivendolo; **~monger's (shop)** n pescheria; **~ sticks** (US) npl = **~ fingers**; **~y** (inf) adj (tale, story) sospetto(a)

fist [fɪst] n pugno

fit [fɪt] adj (MED, SPORT) in forma; (proper) adatto(a), appropriato(a); conveniente ♦ vt (subj: clothes) stare bene a; (put in, attach) mettere; installare; (equip) fornire, equipaggiare ♦ vi (clothes) stare bene; (parts) andare bene, adattarsi; (in space, gap) entrare ♦ n (MED) accesso, attacco; **~ to** in grado di; **~ for** adatto(a) a; degno(a) di; **a ~ of anger** un accesso d'ira; **this dress is a good ~** questo vestito sta bene; **by ~s and starts** a sbalzi; **~ in** vi accordarsi; adattarsi; **~ful** adj saltuario(a); **~ness** n (MED) forma fisica; **~ted carpet** n moquette f; **~ted kitchen** n cucina componibile; **~ter** n aggiustatore m or montatore m meccanico; **~ting** adj appropriato(a) ♦ n (of dress) prova; (of piece of equipment) montaggio, aggiustaggio; **~tings** npl (in building) impianti mpl; **~ting room** n camerino

five [faɪv] num cinque; **~r** (inf) n (BRIT) biglietto da cinque sterline; (US) biglietto da cinque dollari

fix [fɪks] vt fissare; (mend) riparare; (meal, drink) preparare ♦ n: **to be in a ~** essere nei guai; **~ up** vt (meeting) fissare; **to ~ sb up with sth** procurare qc a qn; **~ation** n fissazione f; **~ed** [fɪkst] adj (prices etc) fisso(a); **~ture** ['fɪkstʃə*] n impianto (fisso); (SPORT) incontro del calendario sportivo

fizzy ['fɪzɪ] adj frizzante; gassato(a)

flabbergasted ['flæbəɡɑːstɪd] adj sbalordito(a)

flabby ['flæbɪ] adj flaccido(a)

flag [flæɡ] n bandiera; (also: **~stone**) pietra da lastricare ♦ vi stancarsi; affievolirsi; **~ down** vt fare segno (di fermarsi) a

flagpole ['flæɡpəʊl] n albero

flagship ['flæɡʃɪp] n nave f ammiraglia

flair [fleə*] n (for business etc) fiuto; (for languages etc) facilità; (style) stile m

flak [flæk] n (MIL) fuoco d'artiglieria; (inf: criticism) critiche fpl

flake [fleɪk] n (of rust, paint) scaglia; (of snow, soap powder) fiocco ♦ vi (also: **~ off**) sfaldarsi

flamboyant [flæm'bɔɪənt] adj sgargiante

flame [fleɪm] n fiamma

flamingo [fləˈmɪŋɡəʊ] n fenicottero, fiammingo

flammable ['flæməbl] adj infiammabile

flan [flæn] (BRIT) n flan m inv

flank [flæŋk] n fianco ♦ vt fiancheggiare

flannel ['flænl] n (BRIT: also: **face ~**) guanto di spugna; (fabric) flanella

flap [flæp] n (of pocket) patta; (of envelope) lembo ♦ vt (wings) battere ♦ vi (sail, flag) sbattere; (inf: also: **be in a ~**) essere in agitazione

flare [fleə*] n razzo; (in skirt etc) svasatura; **~ up** vi andare in fiamme; (fig: person) infiammarsi di rabbia; (: revolt) scoppiare

flash [flæʃ] n vampata; (also: **news ~**) notizia f lampo inv; (PHOT) flash m inv ♦ vt accendere e spegnere; (send: message) trasmettere; (: look, smile) lanciare ♦ vi brillare; (light on ambulance, eyes etc) lampeggiare; **in a ~** in un lampo; **to ~ one's headlights** lampeggiare; **he ~ed by** or **past** ci passò davanti come un lampo; **~bulb** n cubo m flash inv; **~cube** n flash m inv; **~light** n lampadina tascabile

flashy ['flæ∫ɪ] (pej) adj vistoso(a)

flask [flɑ:sk] n fiasco; (also: vacuum ~) thermos ® m inv

flat [flæt] adj piatto(a); (tyre) sgonfio(a), a terra; (battery) scarico(a); (beer) svampito(a); (denial) netto(a); (MUS) bemolle inv; (: voice) stonato(a); (rate, fee) unico(a) ♦ n (BRIT: rooms) appartamento; (AUT) pneumatico sgonfio; (MUS) bemolle m; **to work ~ out** lavorare a più non posso; **~ly** adv categoricamente; **~ten** vt (also: ~ten out) appiattire; (building, city) spianare

flatter ['flætə*] vt lusingare; **~ing** adj lusinghiero(a); (dress) che dona; **~y** n adulazione f

flaunt [flɔ:nt] vt fare mostra di

flavour ['fleɪvə*] (US **flavor**) n gusto ♦ vt insaporire, aggiungere sapore a; **strawberry-~ed** al gusto di fragola; **~ing** n essenza (artificiale)

flaw [flɔ:] n difetto

flax [flæks] n lino

flea [fli:] n pulce f

fleck [flɛk] n (mark) macchiolina; (pattern) screziatura

fled [flɛd] pt, pp of **flee**

flee [fli:] (pt, pp **fled**) vt fuggire da ♦ vi fuggire, scappare

fleece [fli:s] n vello ♦ vt (inf) pelare

fleet [fli:t] n flotta; (of lorries etc) convoglio; parco

fleeting ['fli:tɪŋ] adj fugace, fuggitivo(a); (visit) volante

Flemish ['flɛmɪ∫] adj fiammingo(a)

flesh [flɛ∫] n carne f; (of fruit) polpa; **~ wound** n ferita superficiale

flew [flu:] pt of **fly**

flex [flɛks] n filo (flessibile) ♦ vt flettere; (muscles) contrarre; **~ible** adj flessibile

flick [flɪk] n colpetto; scarto ♦ vt dare un colpetto a; **~ through** vt fus sfogliare

flicker ['flɪkə*] vi tremolare

flier ['flaɪə*] n aviatore m

flight [flaɪt] n volo; (escape) fuga; (also: ~ of steps) scalinata; **~ attendant** (US) n steward m inv, hostess f inv; **~ deck** n (AVIAT) cabina di controllo; (NAUT) ponte m di comando

flimsy ['flɪmzɪ] adj (shoes, clothes) leggero(a); (building) poco solido(a); (excuse) che non regge

flinch [flɪnt∫] vi ritirarsi; **to ~ from** tirarsi indietro di fronte a

fling [flɪŋ] (pt, pp **flung**) vt lanciare, gettare

flint [flɪnt] n selce f; (in lighter) pietrina

flip [flɪp] vt (switch) far scattare; (coin) lanciare in aria

flippant ['flɪpənt] adj senza rispetto, irriverente

flipper ['flɪpə*] n pinna

flirt [flɜ:t] vi flirtare ♦ n civetta

float [fləʊt] n galleggiante m; (in procession) carro; (money) somma ♦ vi galleggiare

flock [flɒk] n (of sheep, REL) gregge m; (of birds) stormo ♦ vi: **to ~ to** accorrere in massa a

flog [flɒg] vt flagellare

flood [flʌd] n alluvione m; (of letters etc) marea ♦ vt allagare; (subj: people) invadere ♦ vi (place) allagarsi; (people): **to ~ into** riversarsi in; **~ing** n inondazione f; **~light** n riflettore m ♦ vt illuminare a giorno

floor [flɔ:*] n pavimento; (storey) piano; (of sea, valley) fondo ♦ vt (subj: blow) atterrare; (: question) ridurre al silenzio; **ground ~**, (US) **first ~** pianterreno; **first ~**, (US) **second ~** primo piano; **~board** n tavellone m di legno; **~ show** n spettacolo di varietà

flop [flɒp] n fiasco ♦ vi far fiasco; (fall) lasciarsi cadere

floppy ['flɒpɪ] adj floscio(a), molle; **~ (disk)** n (COMPUT) floppy disk m inv

Florence ['flɒrəns] n Firenze f; **Florentine** ['flɒrəntaɪn] adj fiorentino(a)

florid ['flɒrɪd] adj (complexion)

florido(a); (style) fiorito(a)

florist ['flɒrɪst] n fioraio/a

flounder ['flaʊndə*] vi annaspare ♦ n (ZOOL) passera di mare

flour ['flaʊə*] n farina

flourish ['flʌrɪʃ] vi fiorire ♦ n (bold gesture): with a ~ con ostentazione; **~ing** adj florido(a)

flout [flaʊt] vt (order) contravvenire a

flow [fləʊ] n flusso; circolazione f ♦ vi fluire; (traffic, blood in veins) circolare; (hair) scendere; **~ chart** n schema m di flusso

flower ['flaʊə*] n fiore m ♦ vi fiorire; **~ bed** n aiuola; **~pot** n vaso da fiori; **~y** adj (perfume) di fiori; (pattern) a fiori; (speech) fiorito(a)

flown [fləʊn] pp of fly

flu [fluː] n influenza

fluctuate ['flʌktjʊeɪt] vi fluttuare, oscillare

fluent ['fluːənt] adj (speech) facile, sciolto(a); corrente; he speaks ~ **Italian, he's ~ in Italian** parla l'italiano correntemente

fluff [flʌf] n lanugine f; **~y** adj lanuginoso(a); (toy) di peluche

fluid ['fluːɪd] adj fluido(a) ♦ n fluido

fluke [fluːk] (inf) n colpo di fortuna

flung [flʌŋ] pt, pp of fling

fluoride ['flʊəraɪd] n fluoruro; **~ toothpaste** dentifricio al fluoro

flurry ['flʌrɪ] n (of snow) tempesta; a ~ **of activity** uno scoppio di attività

flush [flʌʃ] n rossore m; (fig: of youth, beauty etc) rigoglio, pieno vigore ♦ vt ripulire con un getto d'acqua ♦ vi arrossire ♦ adj: ~ **with** a livello di, pari a; **to ~ the toilet** tirare l'acqua; **~ed** adj tutto(a) rosso(a)

flustered ['flʌstəd] adj sconvolto(a)

flute [fluːt] n flauto

flutter ['flʌtə*] n agitazione f; (of wings) battito ♦ vi (bird) battere le ali

flux [flʌks] n: in a state of ~ in continuo mutamento

fly [flaɪ] (pt flew, pp flown) n (insect)

mosca; (on trousers: also: flies) chiusura ♦ vt pilotare; (passengers, cargo) trasportare (in aereo); (distances) percorrere ♦ vi volare; (passengers) andare in aereo; (escape) fuggire; (flag) sventolare; ~ **away** or **off** vi volare via; **~ing** n (activity) aviazione f; (action) volo ♦ adj: **~ing visit** visita volante; **with ~ing colours** con risultati brillanti; **~ing saucer** n disco volante; **~ing start** n: **to get off to a ~ing start** partire come un razzo; **~over** (BRIT) n (bridge) cavalcavia m inv; **~sheet** n (for tent) soprattetto

foal [fəʊl] n puledro

foam [fəʊm] n schiuma; (also: ~ **rubber**) gommapiuma ® ♦ vi schiumare; (soapy water) fare la schiuma

fob [fɒb] vt: **to ~ sb off with** rifilare a qn

focus ['fəʊkəs] (pl ~es) n fuoco; (of interest) centro ♦ vt (field glasses etc) mettere a fuoco ♦ vi: **to ~ on** (with camera) mettere a fuoco; (person) fissare lo sguardo su; **in ~** a fuoco; **out of ~** sfocato(a)

fodder ['fɒdə*] n foraggio

foe [fəʊ] n nemico

foetus ['fiːtəs] (US **fetus**) n feto

fog [fɒg] n nebbia; **~gy** adj: **it's ~gy** c'è nebbia; **~ lamp** (US **~ light**) n (AUT) faro m antinebbia inv

foil [fɔɪl] vt confondere, frustrare ♦ n lamina di metallo; (kitchen ~) foglio di alluminio; (FENCING) fioretto; **to act as a ~ to** (fig) far risaltare

fold [fəʊld] n (bend, crease) piega; (AGR) ovile m; (fig) gregge m ♦ vt (material) piegare; (arms) incrociare; **~ up** vi (map, bed, table) piegarsi; (business) crollare ♦ vt (map etc) piegare, ripiegare; **~er** n (for papers) cartella, cartellina; **~ing** adj (chair, bed) pieghevole

foliage ['fəʊlɪdʒ] n fogliame m

folk [fəʊk] npl gente f ♦ adj popolare; **~s** npl (family) famiglia; **~lore**

['fəʊkləː*] *n* folclore *m*; **~ song** *n* canto popolare

follow ['fɒləʊ] *vt* seguire ♦ *vi* seguire; (*result*) conseguire, risultare; **to ~ suit** fare lo stesso; **~ up** *vt* (*letter, offer*) fare seguito a; (*case*) seguire; **~er** *n* seguace *m/f*, discepolo/a; **~ing** *adj* seguente ♦ *n* seguito, discepoli *mpl*; **~-on call** *n* chiamata successiva

folly ['fɒlɪ] *n* pazzia, follia

fond [fɒnd] *adj* (*memory, look*) tenero(a), affettuoso(a); **to be ~ of sb** volere bene a qn; **he's ~ of walking** gli piace fare camminate

fondle ['fɒndl] *vt* accarezzare

font [fɒnt] *n* (*in church*) fonte *m* battesimale; (*TYP*) caratteri *mpl*

food [fuːd] *n* cibo; **~ mixer** *n* frullatore *m*; **~ poisoning** *n* intossicazione *f*; **~ processor** *n* tritatutto *m* inv elettrico; **~stuffs** *npl* generi *fpl* alimentari

fool [fuːl] *n* sciocco/a; (*CULIN*) frullato ♦ *vt* ingannare ♦ *vi* (*gen: ~ around*) fare lo sciocco; **~hardy** *adj* avventato(a); **~ish** *adj* scemo(a), stupido(a); imprudente; **~proof** *adj* (*plan etc*) sicurissimo(a)

foot [fʊt] (*pl* **feet**) *n* piede *m*; (*measure*) piede (= 304 mm; 12 inches); (*of animal*) zampa ♦ *vt* (*bill*) pagare; **on ~** a piedi; **~age** *n* (*CINEMA: length*) ≈ metraggio; (: *material*) sequenza; **~ball** *n* pallone *m*; (*sport: ball*) calcio; (: *US*) football *m* americano; **~ball player** *n* (*BRIT: also: ~baller*) calciatore *m*; (*US*) giocatore *m* di football americano; **~brake** *n* freno a pedale; **~bridge** *n* passerella; **~hills** *npl* contrafforti *fpl*; **~hold** *n* punto d'appoggio; **~ing** *n* (*fig*) posizione *f*; **to lose one's ~ing** mettere un piede in fallo; **~lights** *npl* luci *fpl* della ribalta; **~note** *n* nota (a piè di pagina); **~path** *n* sentiero; (*in street*) marciapiede *m*; **~print** *n* orma, impronta; **~step** *n* passo; (*~print*)

orma, impronta; **~wear** *n* calzatura

KEYWORD

---

for [fɔː*] *prep* **1** (*indicating destination, intention, purpose*) per; **the train ~ London** il treno per Londra; **he went ~ the paper** è andato a prendere il giornale; **it's time ~ lunch** è ora di pranzo; **what's it ~?** a che serve?; **what ~?** (*why*) perché?

2 (*on behalf of, representing*) per; **to work ~ sb/sth** lavorare per qn/qc; **I'll ask him ~ you** glielo chiederò a nome tuo; **G ~ George** G come George

3 (*because of*) per, a causa di; **~ this reason** per questo motivo

4 (*with regard to*) per; **it's cold ~ July** è freddo per luglio; **~ everyone who voted yes, 50 voted no** per ogni voto a favore ce n'erano 50 contro

5 (*in exchange for*) per; **I sold it ~ £5** l'ho venduto per 5 sterline

6 (*in favour of*) per, a favore di; **are you ~ or against us?** è con noi o contro di noi?; **I'm all ~ it** sono completamente a favore

7 (*referring to distance, time*) per; **there are roadworks ~ 5 km** ci sono lavori in corso per 5 km; **he was away ~ 2 years** è stato via per 2 anni; **she will be away ~ a month** starà via un mese; **it hasn't rained ~ 3 weeks** non piove da 3 settimane; **can you do it ~ tomorrow?** può farlo per domani?

8 (*with infinitive clauses*): **it is not ~ me to decide** non sta a me decidere; **it would be best ~ you to leave** sarebbe meglio che lei se ne andasse; **there is still time ~ you to do it** ha ancora tempo per farlo; **~ this to be possible ...** perché ciò sia possibile ...

9 (*in spite of*) nonostante; **~ all his complaints, he's very fond of her** nonostante tutte le sue lamentele, le

vuole molto bene
♦ *conj* (*since, as: rather formal*) dal momento che, poiché

forage ['fɒrɪdʒ] *vi*: **to ~ (for)** andare in cerca (di)

foray ['fɒreɪ] *n* incursione *f*

forbid [fə'bɪd] (*pt* **forbad(e)**, *pp* **forbidden**) *vt* vietare, interdire; **to ~ sb to do sth** proibire a qn di fare qc; **~ding** *adj* minaccioso(a)

force [fɔːs] *n* forza ♦ *vt* forzare; **the F~s** (*BRIT*) *npl* le forze armate; **to ~ o.s. to do** costringersi a fare; **in ~** (*in large numbers*) in gran numero; (*law*) in vigore; **~d** *adj* forzato(a); **~-feed** *vt* (*animal, prisoner*) sottoporre ad alimentazione forzata; **~ful** *adj* forte, vigoroso(a)

forceps ['fɔːseps] *npl* forcipe *m*

forcibly ['fɔːsəblɪ] *adv* con la forza; (*vigorously*) vigorosamente

ford [fɔːd] *n* guado

fore [fɔː*] *n*: **to come to the ~** mettersi in evidenza

forearm ['fɔːrɑːm] *n* avambraccio

foreboding [fɔː'bəudɪŋ] *n* cattivo presagio

forecast ['fɔːkɑːst] (*irreg: like* **cast**) *n* previsione *f* ♦ *vt* prevedere

forecourt ['fɔːkɔːt] *n* (*of garage*) corte *f* esterna

forefinger ['fɔːfɪŋɡə*] *n* (dito) indice *m*

forefront ['fɔːfrʌnt] *n*: **in the ~ of** all'avanguardia in

forego [fɔː'ɡəu] (*irreg: like* **go**) *vt* rinunciare a

foregone ['fɔːɡɒn] *pp of* **forego** ♦ *adj*: **it's a ~ conclusion** è una conclusione scontata

foreground ['fɔːɡraund] *n* primo piano

forehead ['fɒrɪd] *n* fronte *f*

foreign ['fɒrɪn] *adj* straniero(a); (*trade*) estero(a); (*object, matter*) estraneo(a); **~er** *n* straniero/a; **~ exchange** *n* cambio con l'estero; (*currency*) valuta

estera; **F~ Office** (*BRIT*) *n* Ministero degli Esteri; **F~ Secretary** (*BRIT*) *n* ministro degli Affari esteri

foreleg ['fɔːleg] *n* zampa anteriore

foreman ['fɔːmən] (*irreg*) *n* caposquadra *m*

foremost ['fɔːməust] *adj* principale; più in vista ♦ *adv*: **first and ~** innanzitutto

forensic [fə'rensɪk] *adj*: **~ medicine** medicina legale

forerunner ['fɔːrʌnə*] *n* precursore *m*

foresee [fɔː'siː] (*irreg: like* **see**) *vt* prevedere; **~able** *adj* prevedibile; **foreseen** *pp of* **foresee**

foreshadow [fɔː'ʃædəu] *vt* presagire, far prevedere

foresight ['fɔːsaɪt] *n* previdenza

forest ['fɒrɪst] *n* foresta

forestry ['fɒrɪstrɪ] *n* silvicoltura

foretaste ['fɔːteɪst] *n* pregustazione *f*

foretell [fɔː'tel] (*irreg: like* **tell**) *vt* predire; **foretold** [fɔː'təuld] *pt, pp of* **foretell**

forever [fə'revə*] *adv* per sempre; (*endlessly*) sempre, di continuo

foreword ['fɔːwəːd] *n* prefazione *f*

forfeit ['fɔːfɪt] *vt* perdere; (*one's happiness, health*) giocarsi

forgave [fə'ɡeɪv] *pt of* **forgive**

forge [fɔːdʒ] *n* fucina ♦ *vt* (*signature, money*) contraffare, falsificare; (*wrought iron*) fucinare, foggiare; **to ~ ahead** *vi* tirare avanti; **~ry** *n* falso; (*activity*) contraffazione *f*

forget [fə'ɡet] (*pt* **forgot**, *pp* **forgotten**) *vt, vi* dimenticare; **~ful** *adj* di corta memoria; **~ful of** dimentico(a) di; **~-me-not** *n* nontiscordardimé *m inv*

forgive [fə'ɡɪv] (*pt* **forgave**, *pp* **forgiven**) *vt* perdonare; **to ~ sb for sth** perdonare qc a qn; **~ness** *n* perdono

forgo [fɔː'ɡəu] = **forego**

forgot [fə'ɡɒt] *pt of* **forget**

forgotten [fə'ɡɒtn] *pp of* **forget**

fork [fɔ:k] n (for eating) forchetta; (for gardening) forca; (of roads, rivers, railways) biforcazione f ♦ vi (road etc) biforcarsi; ~ **out** (inf) vt (pay) sborsare; **~-lift truck** n carrello elevatore

forlorn [fə'lɔ:n] adj (person) sconsolato(a); (place) abbandonato(a); (attempt) disperato(a); (hope) vano(a)

form [fɔ:m] n forma; (SCOL) classe f; (questionnaire) scheda ♦ vt formare; **in top ~** in gran forma

formal ['fɔ:məl] adj formale; (gardens) simmetrico(a), regolare; **~ly** adv formalmente

format ['fɔ:mæt] n formato ♦ vt (COMPUT) formattare

formation [fɔ:'meɪʃən] n formazione f

formative ['fɔ:mətɪv] adj: **~ years** anni mpl formativi

former ['fɔ:mə*] adj vecchio(a) (before n), ex inv (before n); **the ~ ... the latter** quello ... questo; **~ly** adv in passato

formula ['fɔ:mjulə] n formula

forsake [fə'seɪk] (pt forsook, pp forsaken) vt abbandonare

fort [fɔ:t] n forte m

forth [fɔ:θ] adv in avanti; **back and ~** avanti e indietro; **and so ~** e così via; **~coming** adj (event) prossimo(a); (help) disponibile; (character) aperto(a), comunicativo(a); **~right** adj franco(a), schietto(a); **~with** adv immediatamente, subito

fortify ['fɔ:tɪfaɪ] vt (city) fortificare; (person) armare

fortitude ['fɔ:tɪtju:d] n forza d'animo

fortnight ['fɔ:tnaɪt] (BRIT) n quindici giorni mpl, due settimane fpl; **~ly** adj bimensile ♦ adv ogni quindici giorni

fortress ['fɔ:trɪs] n fortezza, rocca

fortunate ['fɔ:tʃənɪt] adj fortunato(a); **it is ~ that** è una fortuna che; **~ly** adv fortunatamente

fortune ['fɔ:tʃən] n fortuna; **~-teller** n indovino/a

forty ['fɔ:tɪ] num quaranta

forum ['fɔ:rəm] n foro

forward ['fɔ:wəd] adj (ahead of schedule) in anticipo; (movement, position) in avanti; (not shy) aperto(a); diretto(a) ♦ n (SPORT) avanti m inv ♦ vt (letter) inoltrare; (parcel, goods) spedire; (career, plans) promuovere, appoggiare; **to move ~** avanzare; **~(s)** adv avanti

fossil ['fɔsl] adj fossile ♦ n fossile m

foster ['fɔstə*] vt incoraggiare, nutrire; (child) avere in affidamento; **~ child** n bambino/a preso(a) in affidamento

fought [fɔ:t] pt, pp of **fight**

foul [faul] adj (smell, food, temper etc) cattivo(a); (weather) brutto(a); (language) osceno(a) ♦ n (SPORT) fallo ♦ vt sporcare; **~ play** n (LAW): **the police suspect ~ play** la polizia sospetta un atto criminale

found [faund] pt, pp of **find** ♦ vt (establish) fondare; **~ation** [-'deɪʃən] n (act) fondazione f; (base) base f; (also: **~ation cream**) fondo tinta; **~ations** npl (of building) fondamenta fpl

founder ['faundə*] n fondatore/trice ♦ vi affondare

foundry ['faundrɪ] n fonderia

fountain ['fauntɪn] n fontana; **~ pen** n penna stilografica

four [fɔ:*] num quattro; **on all ~s** a carponi; **~-poster** n (also: **~-poster bed**) letto a quattro colonne; **~teen** num quattordici; **~th** num quarto(a)

fowl [faul] n pollame m; volatile m

fox [fɔks] n volpe f ♦ vt confondere

foyer ['fɔɪeɪ] n atrio; (THEATRE) ridotto

fraction ['frækʃən] n frazione f

fracture ['fræktʃə*] n frattura

fragile ['frædʒaɪl] adj fragile

fragment ['frægmənt] n frammento

fragrant ['freɪgrənt] adj fragrante, profumato(a)

frail [freɪl] adj debole, delicato(a)

frame [freɪm] n (of building) armatura; (of human, animal) ossatura, corpo; (of picture) cornice f; (of door, window)

telaio; (of spectacles: also: ~s)
montatura ♦ vt (picture) incorniciare;
~ **of mind** n stato d'animo; ~**work** n
struttura

France [frɑːns] n Francia

franchise ['fræntʃaɪz] n (POL) diritto di
voto; (COMM) concessione f

frank [fræŋk] adj franco(a), aperto(a)
♦ vt (letter) affrancare; ~**ly** adv
francamente, sinceramente

frantic ['fræntɪk] adj frenetico(a)

fraternity [frə'tɜːnɪtɪ] n (club)
associazione f; (spirit) fratellanza

fraud [frɔːd] n truffa; (LAW) frode f;
(person) impostore/a

fraught [frɔːt] adj: ~ **with** pieno(a) di,
intriso(a) da

fray [freɪ] vt logorare ♦ vi logorarsi

freak [friːk] n fenomeno, mostro

freckle ['frekl] n lentiggine f

free [friː] adj libero(a); (gratis)
gratuito(a) ♦ vt (prisoner, jammed
person) liberare; (jammed object)
districare; ~ (**of charge**), **for** ~
gratuitamente; ~**dom** ['friːdəm] n
libertà; F~**fone** ® n numero verde; ~-
for-all n parapiglia m generale; ~ **gift**
n regalo, omaggio; ~**hold** n proprietà
assoluta; ~ **kick** n calcio libero; ~**lance**
adj indipendente; ~**ly** adv liberamente;
(liberally) liberamente; F~**mason** n
massone m; F~**post** ® n affrancatura
a carico del destinatario; ~-**range** adj
(hen) ruspante; (eggs) di gallina
ruspante; ~**style** n (SPORT) stile m
libero; ~ **trade** n libero scambio;
~**way** (US) n superstrada; ~ **will** n
libero arbitrio; **of one's own** ~ **will** di
spontanea volontà

freeze [friːz] (pt **froze**, pp **frozen**) vi
gelare ♦ vt gelare; (food) congelare;
(prices, salaries) bloccare ♦ n gelo;
blocco; ~-**dried** adj liofilizzato(a); ~**r** n
congelatore m

freezing ['friːzɪŋ] adj (wind, weather)
gelido(a), (water) ghiacciato; ~
point n punto di
congelamento; **3 degrees below**

~ **point 3** gradi sotto zero

freight [freɪt] n (goods) merce f, merci
fpl; (money charged) spese fpl di
trasporto; ~ **train** (US) n treno m merci

French [frentʃ] adj francese ♦ n (LING)
francese m; **the** ~ npl i Francesi;
~ **bean** n fagiolino; ~ **fried potatoes**
(US ~ **fries**) npl patate fpl fritte; ~**man**
(irreg) n francese m; ~ **window** n
portafinestra; ~**woman** (irreg) n
francese f

frenzy ['frenzɪ] n frenesia

frequency ['friːkwənsɪ] n frequenza

frequent [adj 'friːkwənt, vb frɪ'kwent]
adj frequente ♦ vt frequentare; ~**ly** adv
frequentemente, spesso

fresco ['freskəʊ] n affresco

fresh [freʃ] adj fresco(a); (new)
nuovo(a); (cheeky) sfacciato(a); ~**en** vi
(wind, air) rinfrescare; ~**en up** vi
rinfrescarsi; ~**er** (BRIT: inf) n (SCOL)
matricola; ~**ly** adv di recente, di fresco;
~**man** (irreg) (US) n = ~**er**; ~**ness** n
freschezza; ~**water** adj (fish) d'acqua
dolce

fret [fret] vi agitarsi, affliggersi

friar ['fraɪə*] n frate m

friction ['frɪkʃən] n frizione f, attrito

Friday ['fraɪdɪ] n venerdì m inv

fridge [frɪdʒ] (BRIT) n frigo, frigorifero

fried [fraɪd] pt, pp of **fry** ♦ adj fritto(a)

friend [frend] n amico/a; ~**ly** adj
amichevole; ~**ly fire** n (MIL) fuoco
amico; ~**ship** n amicizia

frieze [friːz] n fregio

fright [fraɪt] n paura, spavento; **to
take** ~ spaventarsi; ~**en** vt spaventare,
far paura a; ~**ened** adj spaventato(a);
~**ening** adj spaventoso(a), pauroso(a);
~**ful** adj orribile

frill [frɪl] n balza

fringe [frɪndʒ] n (decoration, BRIT: of
hair) frangia; (edge: of forest etc)
margine m; ~ **benefits** npl vantaggi
mpl

frisk [frɪsk] vt perquisire

frisky ['frɪskɪ] adj vivace, vispo(a)

fritter ['frɪtə*] n frittella f; ~ **away** vt sprecare

frivolous ['frɪvələs] adj frivolo(a)

frizzy ['frɪzɪ] adj crespo(a)

fro [frəu] see **to**

frock [frɒk] n vestito

frog [frɒg] n rana; **~man** (irreg) n uomo m rana inv

frolic ['frɒlɪk] vi sgambettare

KEYWORD

from [frɒm] prep **1** (indicating starting place, origin etc) da; **where do you come ~?, where are you ~?** da dove viene?, di dov'è?; ~ **London to Glasgow** da Londra a Glasgow; **a letter ~ my sister** una lettera da mia sorella; **tell him ~ me that ...** gli dica da parte mia che ...

2 (indicating time) da; ~ **one o'clock to** or **until** or **till two** dall'una alle due; ~ **January (on)** da gennaio, a partire da gennaio

3 (indicating distance) da; **the hotel is 1 km ~ the beach** l'albergo è a 1 km dalla spiaggia

4 (indicating price, number etc) da; **prices range ~ £10 to £50** i prezzi vanno dalle 10 alle 50 sterline

5 (indicating difference) da; **he can't tell red ~ green** non sa distinguere il rosso dal verde

6 (because of, on the basis of): ~ **what he says** da quanto dice lui; **weak ~ hunger** debole per la fame

front [frʌnt] n (of house, dress) davanti m inv; (of train) testa; (of book) copertina; (promenade: also: **sea ~**) lungomare m inv; (MIL, POL, METEOR) fronte m; (fig: appearances) fronte f ♦ adj primo(a); anteriore, davanti inv; **in ~ of** davanti a, di fronte a; ~ **door** n porta d'entrata; (of car) sportello anteriore; **~ier** ['frʌntɪə*] n frontiera; ~ **page** n prima pagina; ~ **room** (BRIT) n salotto;

~-wheel drive n trasmissione f anteriore

frost [frɒst] n gelo; (also: **hoar~**) brina; **~bite** n congelamento; **~ed** adj (glass) smerigliato(a); **~y** adj (weather, look) gelido(a)

froth ['frɒθ] n spuma; schiuma

frown [fraun] vi accigliarsi

froze [frəuz] pt of **freeze**; **frozen** pp of **freeze**

fruit [fruːt] n inv (also fig) frutto; (collectively) frutta; **~erer** n fruttivendolo; **~erer's (shop)** n: **at the ~erer's (shop)** dal fruttivendolo; **~ful** adj fruttuoso(a); **~ion** [fruː'ɪʃən] n: **to come to ~ion** realizzarsi; ~ **juice** n succo di frutta; ~ **machine** (BRIT) n macchina f mangiasoldi inv; ~ **salad** n macedonia

frustrate [frʌs'treɪt] vt frustrare

fry [fraɪ] (pt, pp **fried**) vt friggere; see also **small**; **~ing pan** n padella

ft. abbr = **foot**; **feet**

fudge [fʌdʒ] n (CULIN) specie di caramella a base di latte, burro e zucchero

fuel [fjuəl] n (for heating) combustibile m; (for propelling) carburante m; ~ **tank** n deposito m nafta inv; (on vehicle) serbatoio (della benzina)

fugitive ['fjuːdʒɪtɪv] n fuggitivo/a, profugo/a

fulfil [ful'fɪl] vt (function) compiere; (order) eseguire; (wish, desire) soddisfare, appagare; **~ment** (US **fulfillment**) n (of wishes) soddisfazione f, appagamento; **sense of ~ment** soddisfazione

full [ful] adj pieno(a); (details, skirt) ampio(a) ♦ adv: **to know ~ well that** sapere benissimo che; **I'm ~ (up)** sono pieno; **a ~ two hours** due ore intere; **at ~ speed** a tutta velocità; **in ~** per intero; ~ **board** (BRIT) n pensione f completa; ~ **employment** n piena occupazione; **~-length** adj (film) a lungometraggio; (coat, novel) lungo(a);

(portrait) in piedi; **~ moon** n luna piena; **~-scale** adj *(attack, war)* su larga scala; *(model)* in grandezza naturale; **~ stop** n punto; **~-time** adj, adv *(work)* a tempo pieno; **~y** work) interamente, pienamente, completamente; *(at least)* almeno; **~y-fledged** adj *(teacher, member etc)* a tutti gli effetti; **~y licensed** adj *(hotel, restaurant)* autorizzato(a) alla vendita di alcolici

fumble ['fʌmbl] vi: **to ~ with sth** armeggiare con qc

fume [fju:m] vi essere furioso(a); **~s** npl esalazioni fpl, vapori mpl

fun [fʌn] n divertimento, spasso; **to have ~** divertirsi; **for ~** per scherzo; **to make ~ of** prendersi gioco di

function ['fʌŋkʃən] n funzione f; cerimonia, ricevimento ♦ vi funzionare; **~al** adj funzionale

fund [fʌnd] n fondo, cassa; *(source)* fondo; *(store)* riserva; **~s** npl *(money)* fondi mpl

fundamental [fʌndə'mɛntl] adj fondamentale

funeral ['fju:nərəl] n funerale m; **~ parlour** n impresa di pompe funebri; **~ service** n ufficio funebre

fun fair (BRIT) n luna park m inv

fungus ['fʌŋgəs] *(pl* fungi) n fungo; *(mould)* muffa

funnel ['fʌnl] n imbuto; *(of ship)* ciminiera

funny ['fʌni] adj divertente, buffo(a); *(strange)* strano(a), bizzarro(a)

fur [fə:*] n pelo; pelliccia; *(BRIT: in kettle etc)* deposito calcare; **~ coat** n pelliccia

furious ['fjuəriəs] adj furioso(a); *(effort)* accanito(a)

furlong ['fə:lɔŋ] n = 201.17 m *(termine ippico)*

furnace ['fə:nis] n fornace f

furnish ['fə:niʃ] vt ammobiliare; *(supply)* fornire; **~ings** npl mobili mpl, mobilia

furniture ['fə:nitʃə*] n mobili mpl;

piece of ~ mobile m

furrow ['fʌrəu] n solco

furry ['fə:ri] adj *(animal)* peloso(a)

further ['fə:ðə*] adj supplementare, altro(a); nuovo(a); più lontano(a) ♦ adv più lontano; *(more)* di più; *(moreover)* inoltre ♦ vt favorire, promuovere; **college of ~ education** n istituto statale con corsi specializzati di formazione professionale, aggiornamento professionale etc); **~more** [fə:ðə'mɔ:*] adv inoltre, per di più

furthest ['fə:ðist] superl of **far**

fury ['fjuəri] n furore m

fuse [fju:z] n fusibile m; *(for bomb etc)* miccia, spoletta ♦ vt fondere ♦ vi fondersi; **to ~ the lights** *(BRIT: ELEC)* far saltare i fusibili; **~ box** n cassetta dei fusibili

fuselage ['fju:zəla:ʒ] n fusoliera

fuss [fʌs] n agitazione f; *(complaining)* storie fpl; **to make a ~** fare delle storie; **~y** adj *(person)* puntiglioso(a), esigente; che fa le storie; *(dress)* carico(a) di fronzoli; *(style)* elaborato(a)

future ['fju:tʃə*] adj futuro(a) ♦ n futuro, avvenire m; *(LING)* futuro; **in ~** in futuro

fuze [fju:z] (US) = **fuse**

fuzzy ['fʌzi] adj *(PHOT)* indistinto(a), sfocato(a); *(hair)* crespo(a)

G, g

G [dʒi:] n *(MUS)* sol m

G7 abbr (= Group of Seven) G7

gabble ['gæbl] vi borbottare; farfugliare

gable ['geibl] n frontone m

gadget ['gædʒit] n aggeggio

Gaelic ['geilik] adj gaelico(a) ♦ n *(LING)* gaelico

gag [gæg] n bavaglio; *(joke)* facezia, scherzo ♦ vt imbavagliare

gaiety ['geiəti] n gaiezza

gaily ['geili] adv allegramente

gain [gein] n guadagno, profitto ♦ vt

gal. *abbr* = **gallon**

galaxy ['gæləksɪ] *n* galassia

gale [geɪl] *n* vento forte; burrasca

gallant ['gælənt] *adj* valoroso(a); (*towards ladies*) galante, cortese

gall bladder ['gɔːl-] *n* cistifellea

gallery ['gælərɪ] *n* galleria

gallon ['gælən] *n* gallone *m* (= 8 pints; BRIT: = 4.543 l; US = 3.785 l)

gallop ['gæləp] *n* galoppo ♦ *vi* galoppare

gallows ['gæləuz] *n* forca

gallstone ['gɔːlstəun] *n* calcolo biliare

galore [gə'lɔː*] *adv* a iosa, a profusione

galvanize ['gælvənaɪz] *vt* galvanizzare

gambit ['gæmbɪt] *n* (*fig*): (*opening*) ~ prima mossa

gamble ['gæmbl] *n* azzardo, rischio calcolato ♦ *vt, vi* giocare; **to ~ on** (*fig*) giocare su; **~r** *n* giocatore/trice d'azzardo; **gambling** *n* gioco d'azzardo

game [geɪm] *n* gioco; (*event*) partita; (TENNIS) game *m inv*; (CULIN, HUNTING) selvaggina ♦ *adj* selvatico(a); **to be ~ (for sth/to do)** essere pronto(a) (a qc/a fare); **big ~** selvaggina grossa; **~keeper** *n* guardacaccia *m inv*

gammon ['gæmən] *n* (*bacon*) quarto di maiale; (*ham*) prosciutto affumicato

gamut ['gæmət] *n* gamma

gang [gæŋ] *n* banda, squadra ♦ *vi*: **to ~ up on sb** far combutta contro qn

gangrene ['gæŋgriːn] *n* cancrena

gangster ['gæŋstə*] *n* gangster *m inv*

gangway ['gæŋweɪ] *n* passerella; (BRIT: of bus) corridoio

gaol [dʒeɪl] (BRIT) *n, vt* = **jail**

gap [gæp] *n* (*space*) buco; (*in time*) intervallo; (*difference*): ~ **(between)** divario (tra)

gape [geɪp] *vi* (*person*) restare a bocca

aperta; (*shirt, hole*) essere spalancato(a); **gaping** *adj* spalancato(a)

garage ['gærɑːʒ] *n* garage *m inv*

garbage ['gɑːbɪdʒ] *n* (US) immondizie *fpl*, rifiuti *mpl*; (*inf*) sciocchezze *fpl*; ~ **can** (US) *n* bidone *m* della spazzatura

garbled ['gɑːbld] *adj* deformato(a); ingarbugliato(a)

garden ['gɑːdn] *n* giardino; ~**s** *npl* (*public park*) giardini pubblici; ~**er** *n* giardiniere/a; ~**ing** *n* giardinaggio

gargle ['gɑːgl] *vi* fare gargarismi

garish ['gɛərɪʃ] *adj* vistoso(a)

garland ['gɑːlənd] *n* ghirlanda; corona

garlic ['gɑːlɪk] *n* aglio

garment ['gɑːmənt] *n* indumento

garnish ['gɑːnɪʃ] *vt* (*food*) guarnire

garrison ['gærɪsn] *n* guarnigione *f*

garter ['gɑːtə*] *n* giarrettiera

gas [gæs] *n* gas *m inv*; (US: *gasoline*) benzina ♦ *vt* asfissiare con il gas; ~ **cooker** (BRIT) *n* cucina a gas; ~ **cylinder** *n* bombola del gas; ~ **fire** (BRIT) *n* radiatore *m* a gas

gash [gæʃ] *n* sfregio ♦ *vt* sfregiare

gasket ['gæskɪt] *n* (AUT) guarnizione *f*

gas mask *n* maschera *f* antigas *inv*

gas meter *n* contatore *m* del gas

gasoline ['gæsəliːn] (US) *n* benzina

gasp [gɑːsp] *n* respiro affannoso, ansito ♦ *vi* ansare, ansimare; (*in surprise*) restare senza fiato

gas station (US) *n* distributore *m* di benzina

gassy ['gæsɪ] *adj* gassoso(a)

gate [geɪt] *n* cancello; (*at airport*) uscita; ~**crash** (BRIT) *vt* partecipare senza invito a; ~**way** *n* porta

gather ['gæðə*] *vt* (*flowers, fruit*) cogliere; (*pick up*) raccogliere; (*assemble*) radunare; raccogliere; (*understand*) capire; (SEWING) increspare ♦ *vi* (*assemble*) radunarsi; **to ~ speed** acquistare velocità; ~**ing** *n* adunanza

gauche [gəuʃ] *adj* goffo(a), maldestro(a)

gaudy ['gɔːdɪ] adj vistoso(a)

gauge [geɪdʒ] n (instrument) indicatore m ♦ vt misurare; (fig) valutare

gaunt [gɔːnt] adj scarno(a); (grim, desolate) desolato(a)

gauntlet ['gɔːntlɪt] n guanto; (fig): **to run the ~ through an angry crowd** passare sotto il fuoco di una folla ostile; **to throw down the ~** gettare il guanto

gauze [gɔːz] n garza

gave [geɪv] pt of **give**

gay [geɪ] adj (homosexual) omosessuale; (cheerful) gaio(a), allegro(a); (colour) vivace, vivo(a)

gaze [geɪz] n sguardo fisso ♦ vi: **to ~ at** guardare fisso

GB abbr = **Great Britain**

GCE (BRIT) n abbr (= General Certificate of Education) ≈ maturità

GCSE (BRIT) n abbr = General Certificate of Secondary Education

gear [gɪə*] n attrezzi mpl, equipaggiamento; (TECH) ingranaggio; (AUT) marcia ♦ vt (fig: adapt): **to ~ sth to** adattare qc a; **in top** or (US) **high/ low ~** in quarta (or quinta)/seconda; **in ~** in marcia; **~ box** n scatola del cambio; **~ lever** (US **~ shift**) n leva del cambio

geese [giːs] npl of **goose**

gel [dʒel] n gel m inv

gem [dʒem] n gemma

Gemini ['dʒemɪnaɪ] n Gemelli mpl

gender ['dʒendə*] n genere m

general ['dʒenərl] n generale m ♦ adj generale; **in ~** in genere; **~ delivery** (US) n fermo posta m; **~ election** n elezioni fpl generali; **~ly** adv generalmente

general practitioner n medico generico

generate ['dʒenəreɪt] vt generare

generation [dʒenə'reɪʃən] n generazione f

generator ['dʒenəreɪtə*] n generatore m

generosity [dʒenə'rɔsɪtɪ] n generosità

generous ['dʒenərəs] adj generoso(a); (copious) abbondante

genetic engineering [dʒɪ'netɪkendʒɪ'nɪərɪŋ] n ingegneria genetica

genetic fingerprinting n rilevamento delle impronte genetiche

Geneva [dʒɪ'niːvə] n Ginevra

genial ['dʒiːnɪəl] adj geniale, cordiale

genitals ['dʒenɪtlz] npl genitali mpl

genius ['dʒiːnɪəs] n genio

Genoa ['dʒenəuə] n Genova

gent [dʒent] n abbr = **gentleman**

genteel [dʒen'tiːl] adj raffinato(a), distinto(a)

gentle ['dʒentl] adj delicato(a); (person) dolce

gentleman ['dʒentlmən] n signore m; (well-bred man) gentiluomo

gently ['dʒentlɪ] adv delicatamente

gentry ['dʒentrɪ] n nobiltà minore

gents [dʒents] n W.C. m (per signori)

genuine ['dʒenjuɪn] adj autentico(a); sincero(a)

geography [dʒɪ'ɔgrəfɪ] n geografia

geology [dʒɪ'ɔlədʒɪ] n geologia

geometric(al) [dʒɪə'metrɪk(l)] adj geometrico(a)

geometry [dʒɪ'ɔmətrɪ] n geometria

geranium [dʒɪ'reɪnjəm] n geranio

geriatric [dʒerɪ'ætrɪk] adj geriatrico(a)

germ [dʒəːm] n (MED) microbo; (BIOL, fig) germe m

German ['dʒəːmən] adj tedesco(a) ♦ n tedesco/a; (LING) tedesco; **~ measles** (BRIT) n rosolia

Germany ['dʒəːmənɪ] n Germania

gesture ['dʒestjə*] n gesto

KEYWORD

---

get [get] (pt, pp **got**, (US) pp **gotten**) vi 1 (become, get) diventare, farsi; **to ~ old** invecchiare; **to ~ tired** stancarsi; **to ~ drunk** ubriacarsi; **to ~ killed** venire or rimanere ucciso(a); **when did you ~ married?** quando vi siete sposati?; **to ~ paid?** quando mi pagate?; **it's**

~ting late si sta facendo tardi

2 (go): **to ~ to/from** andare a/da; **to ~ home** arrivare o tornare a casa; **how did you ~ here?** come sei venuto?

3 (begin) mettersi a, cominciare a; **to ~ to know sb** incominciare a conoscere qn; **let's ~ going** or **started** muoviamoci

4 (modal aux vb): **you've got to do it** devi farlo

♦ vt **1: to ~ sth done** (do) fare qc; (have done) far fare qc; **to ~ one's hair cut** farsi tagliare i capelli; **to ~ sb to do sth** far fare qc a qn

2 (obtain: money, permission, results) ottenere; (find: job, flat) trovare; (fetch: person, doctor) chiamare; (: object) prendere; **to ~ sth for sb** prendere o procurare qc a qn; **~ me Mr Jones, please** (TEL) mi passi il signor Jones, per favore; **can I ~ you a drink?** le posso offrire da bere?

3 (receive: present, letter, prize) ricevere; (acquire: reputation) farsi; **how much did you ~ for the painting?** quanto le hanno dato per il quadro?

4 (catch) prendere; (hit: target etc) colpire; **to ~ sb by the arm/throat** afferrare qn per un braccio/alla gola; **~ him!** prendetelo!

5 (take, move) portare; **to ~ sth to sb** far avere qc a qn; **do you think we'll ~ it through the door?** pensi che riusciremo a farlo passare per la porta?

6 (catch, take: plane, bus etc) prendere

7 (understand) afferrare; (hear) sentire; **I've got it!** ci sono arrivato!, ci sono!; **I'm sorry, I didn't ~ your name** scusi, non ho capito (or sentito) il suo nome

8 (have, possess): **to have got** avere; **how many have you got?** quanti ne ha?

get about vi muoversi; (news) diffondersi

get along vi (agree) andare

d'accordo; (depart) andarsene; (manage) = **get by**

get at vt fus (attack) prendersela con; (reach) raggiungere, arrivare a

get away vi partire, andarsene; (escape) scappare

get away with vt fus cavarsela; farla franca

get back vi (return) ritornare, tornare ♦ vt riottenere, riavere

get by vi (pass) passare; (manage) farcela

get down vi, vt fus scendere ♦ vt far scendere; (depress) buttare giù

get down to vt fus (work) mettersi a (fare)

get in vi entrare; (train) arrivare (arrive home) ritornare, tornare

get into vt fus entrare in; **to ~ into a rage** incavolarsi

get off vi (from train etc) scendere; (depart: person, car) andare via; (escape) cavarsela ♦ vt (remove: clothes, stain) levare ♦ vt fus (train, bus) scendere da

get on vi (at exam etc) andare; (agree): **to ~ on (with)** andare d'accordo (con) ♦ vt montare in; (horse) montare su

get out vi uscire; (of vehicle) scendere ♦ vt tirar fuori, far uscire

get out of vt fus uscire da; (duty etc) evitare

get over vt fus (illness) riaversi da

get round vt fus aggirare; (fig: person) rigirare

get through vi (TEL) avere la linea

get through to vt fus (TEL) parlare a

get together vi riunirsi ♦ vt raccogliere; (people) adunare

get up vi (rise) alzarsi ♦ vt fus salire su; per

get up to vt fus (reach) raggiungere; (prank etc) fare

getaway ['getəweɪ] n fuga

geyser ['gi:zə*] n (BRIT) scaldabagno;

(GEO) geyser m inv

Ghana ['gɑːnə] n Ghana m

ghastly ['gɑːstlɪ] adj orribile, orrendo(a); (pale) spettrale

gherkin ['gɜːkɪn] n cetriolino

ghetto blaster ['getəublɑːstə*] n maxistereo m inv portatile

ghost [gəust] n fantasma m, spettro

giant ['dʒaɪənt] n gigante m ♦ adj gigantesco(a), enorme

gibberish ['dʒɪbərɪʃ] n parole fpl senza senso

gibe [dʒaɪb] n = **jibe**

giblets ['dʒɪblɪts] npl frattaglie fpl

Gibraltar [dʒɪ'brɔːltə*] n Gibilterra

giddy ['gɪdɪ] adj (dizzy): **to be ~** aver le vertigini

gift [gɪft] n regalo; (donation, ability) dono; **~ed** adj dotato(a); **~ token** n buono m omaggio inv; **~ voucher** n = **~ token**

gigantic [dʒaɪ'gæntɪk] adj gigantesco(a)

giggle ['gɪgl] vi ridere scioccamente

gill [dʒɪl] n (measure) = 0.25 pints (BRIT = 0.148l, US = 0.118l)

gills [gɪlz] npl (of fish) branchie fpl

gilt [gɪlt] n doratura ♦ adj dorato(a); **~-edged** adj (COMM) della massima sicurezza

gimmick ['gɪmɪk] n trucco

gin [dʒɪn] n (liquor) gin m inv

ginger ['dʒɪndʒə*] n zenzero; **~ ale**, **~ beer** n bibita gassosa allo zenzero; **~bread** n pan m di zenzero

gingerly ['dʒɪndʒəlɪ] adv cautamente

gipsy ['dʒɪpsɪ] n zingaro/a

giraffe [dʒɪ'rɑːf] n giraffa

girder ['gɜːdə*] n trave f

girl [gɜːl] n ragazza; (young unmarried woman) signorina; (daughter) figlia, figliola; **~friend** n (of girl) amica; (of boy) ragazza; **~ish** adj da ragazza

giro ['dʒaɪrəu] n (bank ~) versamento bancario; (post office ~) postagiro; (BRIT: welfare cheque) assegno del sussidio di assistenza sociale

gist [dʒɪst] n succo

give [gɪv] (pt gave, pp given) vt dare ♦ vi cedere; **to ~ sb sth, ~ sth to sb** dare qc a qn; **I'll ~ you £5 for it** te lo pago 5 sterline; **to ~ a cry/sigh** emettere un grido/sospiro; **to ~ a speech** fare un discorso; **~ away** vt dare via; (disclose) rivelare; (bride) condurre all'altare; **~ back** vt rendere; **~ in** vi cedere ♦ vt consegnare; **~ off** vt emettere; **~ out** vt distribuire; annunciare; **~ up** vi rinunciare ♦ vt rinunciare a; **to ~ up smoking** smettere di fumare; **to ~ o.s. up** arrendersi; **~ way** vi cedere; (BRIT: AUT) dare la precedenza

glacier ['glæsɪə*] n ghiacciaio

glad [glæd] adj lieto(a), contento(a)

gladly ['glædlɪ] adv volentieri

glamorous ['glæmərəs] adj affascinante, seducente

glamour ['glæmə*] n fascino

glance [glɑːns] n occhiata, sguardo ♦ vi: **to ~ at** dare un'occhiata a; **to ~ off** (bullet) rimbalzare su; **glancing** adj (blow) che colpisce di striscio

gland [glænd] n ghiandola

glare [glɛə*] n (of anger) sguardo furioso; (of light) riverbero, luce f abbagliante; (of publicity) chiasso ♦ vi abbagliare; **to ~ at** guardare male; **glaring** adj (mistake) madornale

glass [glɑːs] n (substance) vetro; (tumbler) bicchiere m; **~es** npl (spectacles) occhiali mpl; **~ware** n vetrame m; **~y** adj (eyes) vitreo(a)

glaze [gleɪz] vt (door) fornire di vetri; (pottery) smaltare ♦ n smalto; **~d** adj (eyes) vitreo(a); (pottery) smaltato(a)

glazier ['gleɪzɪə*] n vetraio

gleam [gliːm] vi luccicare

glean [gliːn] vt (information) racimolare

glee [gliː] n allegrezza, gioia

glen [glɛn] n valletta

glib [glɪb] adj dalla parola facile; facile

glide [glaɪd] vi scivolare; (AVIAT, birds) planare; **~r** n (AVIAT) aliante m; **gliding**

n (AVIAT) volo a vela

glimmer ['glɪmə*] *n* barlume *m*

glimpse [glɪmps] *n* impressione *f*
fugace ♦ *vt* vedere al volo

glint [glɪnt] *vi* luccicare

glisten ['glɪsn] *vi* luccicare

glitter ['glɪtə*] *vi* scintillare

gloat [gləʊt] *vi* gongolare

global ['gləʊbl] *adj* globale;
~ **warming** *n* effetto *m* serra *inv*

globe [gləʊb] *n* globo, sfera

gloom [gluːm] *n* oscurità, buio;
(*sadness*) tristezza, malinconia; ~**y** *adj*
scuro(a); fosco(a), triste

glorious ['glɔːrɪəs] *adj* glorioso(a);
magnifico(a)

glory ['glɔːrɪ] *n* gloria; splendore *m*

gloss [glɔs] *n* (*shine*) lucentezza; (*also*:
~ **paint**) vernice *f* a olio; ~ **over** *vt fus*
scivolare su

glossary ['glɔsərɪ] *n* glossario

glossy ['glɔsɪ] *adj* lucente

glove [glʌv] *n* guanto; ~ **compartment** *n* (AUT) vano portaoggetti

glow [gləʊ] *vi* ardere; (*face*) essere
luminoso(a)

glower ['glaʊə*] *vi*: **to** ~ (**at sb**)
guardare (qn) in cagnesco

glucose ['gluːkəʊs] *n* glucosio

glue [gluː] *n* colla ♦ *vt* incollare

glum [glʌm] *adj* abbattuto(a)

glut [glʌt] *n* eccesso

glutton ['glʌtn] *n* ghiottone/a; **a ~ for
work** *n* un(a) patito(a) del lavoro

GM *adj abbr* (= *genetically modified*)
geneticamente modificato(a)

gnat [næt] *n* moscerino

gnaw [nɔː] *vt* rodere

go [gəʊ] (*pt* **went**, *pp* **gone**; *pl* ~**es**) *vi*
andare; (*depart*) partire, andarsene;
(*work*) funzionare; (*time*) passare;
(*break etc*) rompersi; (*be sold*): **to ~ for
£10** essere venduto per 10 sterline; (*fit,
suit*): **to ~ with** andare bene con;
(*become*): **to ~ pale** diventare
pallido(a); **to ~ mouldy** ammuffire
♦ *n*: **to have a ~ (at)** provare; **to be**

on the ~ essere in moto; **whose ~ is
it?** a chi tocca?; **he's going to do**
far per fare; **to ~ for a walk** andare a
fare una passeggiata; **to ~ dancing/
shopping** andare a ballare/fare la
spesa; **just then the bell went**
proprio allora suonò il campanello;
how did it ~? com'è andato?; **to
~ round the back/by the shop**
passare da dietro/davanti al negozio;
~ **about** *vi* (*also*: ~ **round**: *rumour*)
correre, circolare ♦ *vt fus*: **how do I
~ about this?** qual'è la prassi per
questo?; ~ **ahead** *vi* andare avanti;
~ **along** *vi* andare, avanzare ♦ *vt fus*
percorrere; **to ~ along with** (*plan,
idea*) appoggiare; ~ **away** *vi* partire,
andarsene; ~ **back** *vi* tornare,
ritornare; ~ **back on** *vt fus* (*promise*)
non mantenere; ~ **by** *vi* (*years, time*)
scorrere ♦ *vt fus* attenersi a, seguire
(alla lettera); prestar fede a; ~ **down** *vi*
scendere; (*ship*) affondare; (*sun*)
tramontare ♦ *vt fus* scendere; ~ **for** *vt
fus* (*fetch*) andare a prendere; (*like*)
andar matto(a) per; (*attack*) attaccare;
saltare addosso a; ~ **in** *vi* entrare; ~ **in
for** *vt fus* (*competition*) iscriversi a; (*be
interested in*) interessarsi di; ~ **into** *vt
fus* entrare in; (*investigate*) indagare,
esaminare; (*embark on*) lanciarsi in;
~ **off** *vi* partire, andar via; (*food*)
guastarsi; (*explode*) esplodere,
scoppiare; (*event*) passare ♦ *vt fus*: **I've
gone off chocolate** la cioccolata non
mi piace più; **the gun went off** il
fucile si scaricò; ~ **on** *vi* continuare;
(*happen*) succedere; **to ~ on doing**
continuare a fare; ~ **out** *vi* uscire;
(*couple*): **they went out for 3 years**
sono stati insieme per 3 anni; (*fire,
light*) spegnersi; ~ **over** *vi* (*ship*)
ribaltarsi ♦ *vt fus* (*check*) esaminare;
~ **through** *vt fus* (*town etc*)
attraversare; (*files, papers*) passare in
rassegna; (*examine: list etc*) leggere da
cima a fondo; ~ **up** *vi* salire;

~ without vt fus fare a meno di

goad [gəʊd] vt spronare

go-ahead adj intraprendente ♦ n via m

goal [gəʊl] n (SPORT) gol m, rete f; (: place) porta; (fig: aim) fine m, scopo; **~keeper** n portiere m; **~-post** n palo (della porta)

goat [gəʊt] n capra

gobble ['gɔbl] vt (also: ~ down, ~ up) ingoiare

go-between n intermediario/a

god [gɔd] n dio; **G~** n Dio; **~child** n figlioccio/a; **~daughter** n figlioccia; **~dess** n dea; **~father** n padrino; **~-forsaken** adj desolato(a), sperduto(a); **~mother** n madrina; **~send** n dono del cielo; **~son** n figlioccio

goggles ['gɔglz] npl occhiali mpl (di protezione)

going ['gəʊɪŋ] n (conditions) andare m, stato del terreno ♦ adj: **the ~ rate** la tariffa in vigore

gold [gəʊld] n oro ♦ adj d'oro; **~en** adj (made of ~) d'oro; (~ in colour) dorato(a); **~fish** n pesce m dorato or rosso; **~mine** n (also fig) miniera d'oro; **~-plated** adj placcato(a) oro inv; **~smith** n orefice m, orafo

golf [gɔlf] n golf m; **~ ball** n (for game) pallina da golf; (on typewriter) pallina; **~ club** n circolo di golf; (stick) bastone m or mazza da golf; **~ course** n campo da golf; **~er** n giocatore/trice di golf

gondola ['gɔndələ] n gondola

gone [gɔn] pp of **go** ♦ adj partito(a)

gong [gɔŋ] n gong m inv

good [gʊd] adj buono(a); (kind) buono(a), gentile; (child) bravo(a) ♦ n bene m; **~s** npl (COMM etc) beni mpl, merci fpl; **~!** bene!, ottimo!; **to be ~ at** essere bravo(a) in; **to be ~ for** andare bene per; **it's ~ for you** fa bene; **would you be ~ enough to ...?** avrebbe la gentilezza di ...?; **a ~ deal (of)** molto(a), una buona quantità (di); **a ~ many** molti(e); **to**

make ~ (loss, damage) compensare; **it's no ~ complaining** non serve a niente; **for ~** per sempre, definitivamente; **~ morning!** buon giorno!; **~ afternoon/evening!** buona sera!; **~ night!** buona notte!; **~bye** excl arrivederci!; **G~ Friday** n Venerdì Santo; **~-looking** adj bello(a); **~-natured** adj (person) bonario(a); **~ness** n (of person) bontà; **for ~ness sake!** per amor di Dio!; **~ness gracious!** santo cielo!, mamma mia!; **~s train** (BRIT) n treno m merci inv; **~will** n amicizia, benevolenza

goose [gu:s] (pl **geese**) n oca

gooseberry ['gʊzbəri] n uva spina; **to play ~** (BRIT) tenere la candela

gooseflesh ['gu:sfleʃ] n pelle f d'oca

goose pimples npl pelle f d'oca

gore [gɔ:*] vt incornare ♦ n sangue m (coagulato)

gorge [gɔ:dʒ] n gola ♦ vt: **to ~ o.s. (on)** ingozzarsi (di)

gorgeous ['gɔ:dʒəs] adj magnifico(a)

gorilla [gə'rɪlə] n gorilla m inv

gorse [gɔ:s] n ginestrone m

gory ['gɔ:rɪ] adj sanguinoso(a)

go-slow n (BRIT) rallentamento dei lavori (per agitazione sindacale)

gospel ['gɔspl] n vangelo

gossip ['gɔsɪp] n chiacchiere fpl; pettegolezzi mpl; (person) pettegolo/a ♦ vi chiacchierare

got [gɔt] pt, pp of **get**; **~ten** (US) pp of **get**

gout [gaʊt] n gotta

govern ['gʌvən] vt governare

governess ['gʌvənɪs] n governante f

government ['gʌvnmənt] n governo

governor ['gʌvənə*] n (of state, bank) governatore m; (of school, hospital) amministratore m; (BRIT: of prison) direttore/trice

gown [gaʊn] n vestito lungo; (of teacher, BRIT: of judge) toga

G.P. n abbr = **general practitioner**

grab [græb] vt afferrare, arraffare;

(*property, power*) impadronirsi di ♦ *vi*:
to ~ at cercare di afferrare

grace [greɪs] *n* grazia ♦ *vt* onorare; **5
days'** ~ dilazione *f* di 5 giorni; **~ful**
adj elegante, aggraziato(a); **gracious**
['greɪʃəs] *adj* grazioso(a);
misericordioso(a)

grade [greɪd] *n* (COMM) qualità *f inv*;
classe *f*; categoria; (*in hierarchy*) grado;
(SCOL: *mark*) voto; (US: *school class*)
classe ♦ *vt* classificare; ordinare;
graduate; ~ **crossing** (US) *n* passaggio
a livello; ~ **school** (US) *n* scuola
elementare

gradient ['greɪdɪənt] *n* pendenza,
inclinazione *f*

gradual ['grædjʊəl] *adj* graduale; **~ly**
adv man mano, a poco a poco

graduate [*n* 'grædjʊət, *vb* 'grædjʊeɪt]
n (*of university*) laureato/a; (US: *of high
school*) diplomato/a ♦ *vi* laurearsi;
diplomarsi; **graduation** [-'eɪʃən] *n*
(*ceremony*) consegna delle lauree (*or*
dei diplomi)

graffiti [grə'fiːtɪ] *npl* graffiti *mpl*

graft [grɑːft] *n* (AGR, MED) innesto;
(*bribery*) corruzione *f*; (BRIT: *hard work*):
it's hard ~ è un lavoraccio ♦ *vt*
innestare

grain [greɪn] *n* grano; (*of sand*)
granello; (*of wood*) venatura

gram [græm] *n* gramm

grammar ['græmə*] *n* grammatica;
~ **school** (BRIT) *n* ≈ liceo

grammatical [grə'mætɪkl] *adj*
grammaticale

gramme [græm] *n* = **gram**

grand [grænd] *adj* grande,
magnifico(a); grandioso(a); **~children**
npl nipoti *mpl*; **~dad** (*inf*) *n* nonno;
~daughter *n* nipote *f*; **~eur**
['grændjə*] *n* grandiosità; **~father** *n*
nonno; **~ma** (*inf*) *n* nonna; **~mother**
n nonna; **~pa** (*inf*) *n* = **~dad**;
~parents *npl* nonni *mpl*; ~ **piano** *n*
pianoforte *m* a coda; **~son** *n* nipote *m*;
~stand *n* (SPORT) tribuna

granite ['grænɪt] *n* granito

granny ['grænɪ] (*inf*) *n* nonna

grant [grɑːnt] *vt* accordare; (*a request*)
accogliere; (*admit*) ammettere,
concedere ♦ *n* (SCOL) borsa; (ADMIN)
sussidio, sovvenzione *f*; **to take sth
for ~ed** dare qc per scontato; **to take
sb for ~ed** dare per scontata la
presenza di qn

granulated ['grænjʊleɪtɪd] *adj*:
~ **sugar** zucchero cristallizzato

granule ['grænjuːl] *n* granello

grape [greɪp] *n* chicco d'uva, acino

grapefruit ['greɪpfruːt] *n* pompelmo

graph [grɑːf] *n* grafico; **~ic** *adj*
grafico(a); (*vivid*) vivido(a); **~ics** *n*
grafica ♦ *npl* illustrazioni *fpl*

grapple ['græpl] *vi*: **to ~ with** essere
alle prese con

grasp [grɑːsp] *vt* afferrare ♦ *n* (*grip*)
presa; (*fig*) potere *m*; comprensione *f*;
~ing *adj* avido(a)

grass [grɑːs] *n* erba; **~hopper** *n*
cavalletta; **~-roots** *adj* di base

grate [greɪt] *n* graticola (del focolare)
♦ *vi* cigolare, stridere ♦ *vt* (CULIN)
grattugiare

grateful ['greɪtfʊl] *adj* grato(a),
riconoscente

grater ['greɪtə*] *n* grattugia

grating ['greɪtɪŋ] *n* (*iron bars*) grata
♦ *adj* (*noise*) stridente, stridulo(a)

gratitude ['grætɪtjuːd] *n* gratitudine *f*

gratuity [grə'tjuːɪtɪ] *n* mancia

grave [greɪv] *n* tomba ♦ *adj* grave,
serio(a)

gravel ['grævl] *n* ghiaia

gravestone ['greɪvstəʊn] *n* pietra
tombale

graveyard ['greɪvjɑːd] *n* cimitero

gravity ['grævɪtɪ] *n* (PHYSICS) gravità;
pesantezza; (*seriousness*) gravità, serietà

gravy ['greɪvɪ] *n* intingolo della carne;
salsa

gray [greɪ] *adj* = **grey**

graze [greɪz] *vi* pascolare, pascere ♦ *vt*
(*touch lightly*) sfiorare; (*scrape*)

escoriare ♦ n (MED) escoriazione f

grease [gri:s] n (fat) grasso; (lubricant) lubrificante m ♦ vt ingrassare; lubrificare; **~proof paper** (BRIT) n carta oleata; **greasy** adj grasso(a), untuoso(a)

great [greɪt] adj grande; (inf) magnifico(a), meraviglioso(a); **G~ Britain** n Gran Bretagna; **~grandfather** n bisnonno; **~grandmother** n bisnonna; **~ly** adv molto; **~ness** n grandezza

Greece [gri:s] n Grecia

greed [gri:d] n (also: ~iness) avarizia; (for food) golosità, ghiottoneria; **~y** adj avido(a), goloso(a), ghiotto(a)

Greek [gri:k] adj greco(a) ♦ n greco/a; (LING) greco

green [gri:n] adj verde; (inexperienced) inesperto(a), ingenuo(a) ♦ n verde m; (stretch of grass) prato; (on golf course) green m inv; **~s** npl (vegetables) verdura; **~ belt** n (round town) cintura di verde; **~ card** n (BRIT: AUT) carta verde; (US: ADMIN) permesso di soggiorno e di lavoro; **~ery** n verde m; **~grocer** (BRIT) n fruttivendolo/a, erbivendolo/a; **~house** n serra; **~house effect** n effetto serra; **~house gas** n gas responsabile dell'effetto serra; **~ish** adj verdastro(a)

Greenland [ˈgriːnlənd] n Groenlandia

greet [gri:t] vt salutare; **~ing** n saluto; **~ing(s) card** n cartolina d'auguri

gregarious [grəˈgɛərɪəs] adj (person) socievole

grenade [grəˈneɪd] n (also: hand ~) granata

grew [gru:] pt of **grow**

grey [greɪ] adj grigio(a); **~haired** adj dai capelli grigi; **~hound** n levriere m

grid [grɪd] n grata; (ELEC) rete f

gridlock [ˈgrɪdlɒk] n (traffic jam) paralisi f inv del traffico; **~ed** adj paralizzato(a) dal traffico; (talks etc) in fase di stallo

grief [gri:f] n dolore m

grievance [ˈgriːvəns] n lagnanza

grieve [gri:v] vi addolorarsi; rattristarsi ♦ vt addolorare; **to ~ for sb** (dead person) piangere qn

grievous [ˈgriːvəs] adj: **~ bodily harm** (LAW) aggressione f

grill [grɪl] n (on cooker) griglia; (also: mixed ~) grigliata mista ♦ vt (BRIT) cuocere ai ferri; (inf: question) interrogare senza sosta

grille [grɪl] n griglia; (AUT) griglia

grim [grɪm] adj sinistro(a), brutto(a)

grimace [grɪˈmeɪs] n smorfia ♦ vi fare smorfie; fare boccacce

grime [graɪm] n sudiciume m

grin [grɪn] n sorriso smagliante ♦ vi fare un gran sorriso

grind [graɪnd] (pt, pp **ground**) vt macinare; (make sharp) arrotare ♦ n (work) sgobbata

grip [grɪp] n impugnatura; presa; (holdall) borsa da viaggio ♦ vt (object) afferrare; (attention) catturare; **to come to ~s with** affrontare; cercare di risolvere

gripping [ˈgrɪpɪŋ] adj avvincente

grisly [ˈgrɪzlɪ] adj macabro(a), orrido(a)

gristle [ˈgrɪsl] n cartilagine f

grit [grɪt] n ghiaia; (courage) fegato ♦ vt (road) coprire di sabbia; **to ~ one's teeth** stringere i denti

groan [grəun] n gemito ♦ vi gemere

grocer [ˈgrəusə*] n negoziante m di generi alimentari; **~ies** npl provviste fpl; **~'s (shop)** n negozio di (generi) alimentari

groggy [ˈgrɒgɪ] adj barcollante

groin [grɔɪn] n inguine m

groom [gru:m] n palafreniere m; (also: bride~) sposo ♦ vt (horse) strigliare; (fig): **to ~ sb for** avviare qn a; **well-~ed** (person) curato(a)

groove [gru:v] n scanalatura, solco

grope [grəup] vi: **to ~ for** cercare a tastoni

gross [grəus] adj grossolano(a); (COMM) lordo(a); **~ly** adv (greatly) molto

grotesque [grəʊˈtɛsk] adj grottesco(a)

grotto [ˈgrɒtəʊ] n grotta

grotty [ˈgrɒtɪ] (inf) adj terribile

ground [graʊnd] pt, pp of **grind** ♦ n suolo, terra; (land) terreno; (SPORT) campo; (reason: gen pl) ragione f; (US: also: ~ wire) terra ♦ vt (plane) tenere a terra; (US: ELEC) mettere la presa a terra a; ~s npl (of coffee etc) fondi mpl; (gardens etc) terreno, giardini mpl; **on/to the** ~ per/a terra; **to gain/lose** ~ guadagnare/perdere terreno; ~ **cloth** (US) n = ~**sheet**; ~**ing** n (in education) basi fpl; ~**less** adj infondato(a); ~**sheet** (BRIT) n telone m impermeabile; ~ **staff** n personale m di terra; ~**work** n preparazione f

group [gruːp] n gruppo ♦ vt (also: ~ together) raggruppare ♦ vi (also: ~ together) raggrupparsi

grouse [graʊs] n inv (bird) tetraone m ♦ vi (complain) brontolare

grove [grəʊv] n boschetto

grovel [ˈgrɒvl] vi (fig): **to** ~ (**before**) strisciare (di fronte a)

grow [grəʊ] (pt **grew**, pp **grown**) vi crescere; (increase) aumentare; (develop) svilupparsi; (become): **to** ~ **rich/weak** arricchirsi/indebolirsi ♦ vt coltivare, far crescere; ~ **up** vi farsi grande, crescere; ~**er** n coltivatore/trice; ~**ing** adj (fear, amount) crescente

growl [graʊl] vi ringhiare

grown [grəʊn] pp of **grow**; ~**-up** n adulto/a, grande m/f

growth [grəʊθ] n crescita, sviluppo; (what has grown) crescita; (MED) escrescenza, tumore m

grub [grʌb] n larva; (inf: food) roba (da mangiare)

grubby [ˈgrʌbɪ] adj sporco(a)

grudge [grʌdʒ] n rancore m ♦ vt: **to** ~ **sb sth** dare qc a qn di malavoglia; invidiare qc a qn; **to bear sb a** ~ (**for**) serbar rancore a qn (per)

gruelling [ˈgruəlɪŋ] (US **grueling**) adj estenuante

gruesome [ˈgruːsəm] adj orribile

gruff [grʌf] adj rozzo(a)

grumble [ˈgrʌmbl] vi brontolare, lagnarsi

grumpy [ˈgrʌmpɪ] adj scorbutico(a)

grunt [grʌnt] vi grugnire

G-string n tanga m inv

guarantee [gærənˈtiː] n garanzia ♦ vt garantire

guard [gɑːd] n guardia; (one man) guardia, sentinella; (BRIT: RAIL) capotreno; (on machine) schermo protettivo; (also: fire~) parafuoco ♦ vt fare la guardia a; (protect): **to** ~ (**against**) proteggere (da); **to be on one's** ~ stare in guardia; ~ **against** vt fus guardarsi da; ~**ed** adj (fig) cauto(a), guardingo(a); ~**ian** n custode m/f; (of minor) tutore/trice; ~'**s van** (BRIT) n (RAIL) vagone m di servizio

guerrilla [gəˈrɪlə] n guerrigliero

guess [gɛs] vi indovinare ♦ vi indovinare; (US) credere, pensare ♦ n: **to take** or **have a** ~ provare a indovinare; ~**work** n: **I got the answer by** ~**work** ho azzeccato la risposta

guest [gɛst] n ospite m/f; (in hotel) cliente m/f; ~~**house** n pensione f; ~ **room** n camera degli ospiti

guffaw [gʌˈfɔː] vi scoppiare in una risata sonora

guidance [ˈgaɪdəns] n guida, direzione f

guide [gaɪd] n (person, book etc) guida; (BRIT: also: girl ~) giovane esploratrice f ♦ vt guidare; ~**book** n guida; ~ **dog** n cane m guida inv; ~**lines** npl (fig) indicazioni fpl, linee fpl direttive

guild [gɪld] n arte f, corporazione f; associazione f

guillotine [ˈgɪlətiːn] n ghigliottina; (for paper) taglierina

guilt [gɪlt] n colpevolezza; ~**y** adj colpevole

guinea pig [ˈgɪnɪ-] n cavia

guise [gaɪz] n maschera

guitar [gɪ'tɑ:*] n chitarra
gulf [gʌlf] n golfo; (abyss) abisso
gull [gʌl] n gabbiano
gullible ['gʌlɪbl] adj credulo(a)
gully ['gʌlɪ] n burrone m; gola; canale m
gulp [gʌlp] vi deglutire; (from emotion) avere il nodo in gola ♦ vt (also: ~ down) tracannare, inghiottire
gum [gʌm] n (ANAT) gengiva; (glue) colla; (also: ~drop) caramella gommosa; (also: chewing ~) chewing-gum m ♦ vt: **to ~ (together)** incollare; **~boots** (BRIT) npl stivali mpl di gomma
gumption ['gʌmpʃən] n spirito d'iniziativa, buonsenso
gun [gʌn] n fucile m; (small) pistola, rivoltella; (rifle) carabina; (shotgun) fucile da caccia; (cannon) cannone m; **~boat** n cannoniera; **~fire** n spari mpl; **~man** n bandito armato; **~point** n: **at ~point** sotto minaccia di fucile; **~powder** n polvere f da sparo; **~shot** n sparo
gurgle ['gə:gl] vi gorgogliare
gush [gʌʃ] vi sgorgare; (fig) abbandonarsi ad effusioni
gusset ['gʌsɪt] n gherone m
gust [gʌst] n (of wind) raffica; (of smoke) buffata
gusto ['gʌstəu] n entusiasmo
gut [gʌt] n intestino, budello; **~s** (ANAT) interiora fpl; (courage) fegato
gutter ['gʌtə*] n (of roof) grondaia; (in street) cunetta
guy [gaɪ] n (inf: man) tipo, elemento; (also: ~rope) cavo or corda di fissaggio; (figure) effigie di Guy Fawkes

| Guy Fawkes' Night |

Il 5 novembre si festeggia con falò e fuochi d'artificio la Guy Fawkes' Night, la notte in cui, nel 1605, fallì la Congiura delle Polveri contro Giacomo I; Guy Fawkes era il nome di uno dei cospiratori.

guzzle ['gʌzl] vt tranguggiare
gym [dʒɪm] n (also: gymnasium) palestra; (also: gymnastics) ginnastica
gymnast ['dʒɪmnæst] n ginnasta m/f; **~ics** [-'næstɪks] n, npl ginnastica
gym shoes npl scarpe fpl da ginnastica
gym slip (BRIT) n grembiule m da scuola (per ragazze)
gynaecologist [gaɪnɪ'kɔlədʒɪst] (US **gynecologist**) n ginecologo/a
gypsy ['dʒɪpsɪ] n = **gipsy**
gyrate [dʒaɪ'reɪt] vi girare

H, h

haberdashery ['hæbə'dæʃərɪ] (BRIT) n merceria
habit ['hæbɪt] n abitudine f; (costume) abito; (REL) tonaca
habitual [hə'bɪtjuəl] adj abituale; (drinker, liar) inveterato/a
hack [hæk] vt tagliare, fare a pezzi ♦ n (pej: writer) scribacchino/a
hacker ['hækə*] n (COMPUT) pirata m informatico
hackney cab ['hæknɪ-] n carrozza a nolo
hackneyed ['hæknɪd] adj comune, trito(a)
had [hæd] pt, pp of **have**
haddock ['hædək] (pl ~ or ~s) n eglefino
hadn't ['hædnt] = **had not**
haemorrhage ['hemərɪdʒ] (US **hemorrhage**) n emorragia
haemorrhoids ['hemərɔɪdz] (US **hemorrhoids**) npl emorroidi fpl
haggard ['hægəd] adj smunto(a)
haggle ['hægl] vi mercanteggiare
Hague [heɪg] n: **The ~** L'Aia
hail [heɪl] n grandine f; (of criticism etc) pioggia ♦ vt (call) chiamare; (flag down: taxi) fermare; (greet) salutare ♦ vi grandinare; **~stone** n chicco di grandine
hair [heə*] n capelli mpl; (single hair: on

hake   423   hand

head) capello; (: on body) pelo; **to do one's ~** pettinarsi; **~brush** n spazzola per capelli; **~cut** n taglio di capelli; **~do** ['hɛːduː] n acconciatura, pettinatura; **~dresser** n parrucchiere/a; **~dryer** n asciugacapelli m inv; **~grip** n forcina; **~net** n retina per capelli; **~pin** n forcina; **~pin bend** (us **~pin curve**) n tornante m; **~raising** adj orripilante; **~ removing cream** n crema depilatoria; **~spray** n lacca per capelli; **~style** n pettinatura, acconciatura; **~y** adj irsuto(a); peloso(a); (inf: frightening) spaventoso(a)

hake [heɪk] (pl ~ or ~s) n nasello

half [hɑːf] (pl **halves**) n mezzo, metà f inv ♦ adj mezzo(a) ♦ adv a mezzo, a metà; **~ an hour** mezz'ora; **~ a dozen** mezza dozzina; **~ a pound** mezza libbra; **two and a ~** due e mezzo; **a week and a ~** una settimana e mezza; **~ (of it)** la metà; **~ (of)** la metà di; **to cut sth in ~** tagliare qc in due; **~ asleep** addormentato(a); **~-baked** adj (scheme) che non sta in piedi; **~ board** (BRIT) n mezza pensione; **~-caste** ['hɑːfkɑːst] n meticcio/a; **~ fare** n tariffa a metà prezzo; **~-hearted** adj tiepido(a); **~-hour** n mezz'ora; **~-mast**: **at ~-mast** adv (flag) a mezz'asta; **~-penny** ['heɪpnɪ] (BRIT) n mezzo penny m inv; **~-price** adj, adv a metà prezzo; **~ term** (BRIT) n (SCOL) vacanza a or di metà trimestre; **~-time** n (SPORT) intervallo; **~way** adv a metà strada

halibut ['hælɪbət] n inv ippoglosso

hall [hɔːl] n sala, salone m; (entrance way) entrata; **~ of residence** (BRIT) n casa dello studente

hallmark ['hɔːlmɑːk] n marchio di garanzia; (fig) caratteristica

hallo [ha'ləu] excl = **hello**

Hallowe'en [hæləu'iːn] n vigilia d'Ognissanti

Hallowe'en

Negli Stati Uniti e in Scozia il 31 ottobre si festeggia **Hallowe'en**, la notte delle streghe e dei fantasmi; i bambini, travestiti da fantasmi e con lanterne ricavate da zucche, bussano alle porte e raccolgono dolci e piccoli doni.

---

hallucination [həluːsɪˈneɪʃən] n allucinazione f

hallway ['hɔːlweɪ] n corridoio; (entrance) ingresso

halo ['heɪləu] n (of saint etc) aureola

halt [hɔːlt] n fermata ♦ vt fermare ♦ vi fermarsi

halve [hɑːv] vt (apple etc) dividere a metà; (expense) ridurre di metà

halves [hɑːvz] npl of **half**

ham [hæm] n prosciutto

Hamburg ['hæmbəːg] n Amburgo f

hamburger ['hæmbəːgə*] n hamburger m inv

hamlet ['hæmlɪt] n paesetto

hammer ['hæmə*] n martello ♦ vt martellare ♦ vi: **to ~ on or at the door** picchiare alla porta

hammock ['hæmək] n amaca

hamper ['hæmpə*] vt impedire ♦ n cesta

hamster ['hæmstə*] n criceto

hand [hænd] n mano f; (of clock) lancetta; (handwriting) scrittura; (at cards) mano; (: game) partita; (worker) operaio/a ♦ vt dare, passare; **to give sb a ~** dare una mano a qn; **at ~** a portata di mano; **in ~** a disposizione; (work) in corso; on ~ (person) disponibile; (services) pronto(a) a intervenire; **to ~** (information etc) a portata di mano; **on the one ~ ...**, **on the other ~** da un lato ..., dall'altro; **~ in** vt consegnare; **~ out** vt distribuire; **~ over** vt passare; cedere; **~bag** n borsetta; **~book** n manuale m; **~brake** n freno a mano; **~cuffs** npl manette *fpl*; **~ful** *n* manciata, pugno

handicap ['hændɪkæp] *n* handicap *m inv* ♦ *vt* handicappare; **to be physically ~ped** essere handicappato(a); **to be mentally ~ped** essere una(a) handicappato(a) mentale

handicraft ['hændɪkrɑːft] *n* lavoro d'artigiano

handiwork ['hændɪwəːk] *n* opera

handkerchief ['hæŋkətʃɪf] *n* fazzoletto

handle ['hændl] *n* (*of door etc*) maniglia; (*of cup etc*) ansa; (*of knife etc*) impugnatura; (*for winding*) manovella ♦ *vt* toccare, maneggiare; (*deal with*) occuparsi di; (*treat: people*) trattare; **"~ with care"** "fragile"; **to fly off the ~** (*fig*) perdere le staffe, uscire dai gangheri; **~bar(s)** *n(pl)* manubrio

hand: **~ luggage** *n* bagagli *mpl* a mano; **~made** *adj* fatto a mano; **~out** *n* (*money, food*) elemosina; (*leaflet*) volantino; (*at lecture*) prospetto; **~rail** *n* corrimano; **~set** *n* (*TEL*) ricevitore *m*; **please replace the ~set** riaganciare il ricevitore; **~shake** *n* stretta di mano

handsome ['hænsəm] *adj* bello(a); (*profit, fortune*) considerevole

handwriting ['hændraɪtɪŋ] *n* scrittura

handy ['hændɪ] *adj* (*person*) bravo(a); (*close at hand*) a portata di mano; (*convenient*) comodo(a)

hang [hæŋ] (*pt, pp hung*) *vt* appendere; (*criminal: pt, pp hanged*) impiccare ♦ *vt* (*painting*) essere appeso(a); (*hair*) scendere; (*drapery*) cadere; **to get the ~ of sth** (*inf*) capire come qc funziona; **~ about** *or* **around** *vi* bighellonare, ciondolare; **~ on** *vi* (*wait*) aspettare; **~ up** *vi* (*TEL*) riattaccare ♦ *vt* appendere

hangar ['hæŋə*] *n* hangar *m inv*

hanger ['hæŋə*] *n* gruccia

hanger-on *n* parassita *m*

hang-gliding [-'glaɪdɪŋ] *n* volo col

deltaplano

hangover ['hæŋəʊvə*] *n* (*after drinking*) postumi *mpl* di sbornia

hang-up *n* complesso

hanker ['hæŋkə*] *vi*: **to ~ after** bramare

hankie ['hæŋkɪ] *n abbr* = **handkerchief**

hanky ['hæŋkɪ] *n abbr* = **handkerchief**

haphazard [hæp'hæzəd] *adj* a casaccio, alla carlona

happen ['hæpən] *vi* accadere, succedere; (*chance*): **to ~ to do sth** fare qc per caso; **as it ~s** guarda caso; **~ing** *n* avvenimento

happily ['hæpɪlɪ] *adv* felicemente; fortunatamente

happiness ['hæpɪnɪs] *n* felicità, contentezza

happy ['hæpɪ] *adj* felice, contento(a); **~ with** (*arrangements etc*) soddisfatto(a); (*to be ~ to do* (*willing*) fare volentieri; **~ birthday!** buon compleanno!; **~-go-lucky** *adj* spensierato(a); **~ hour** *n* orario in cui i bar hanno prezzi ridotti

harangue [hə'ræŋ] *vt* arringare

harass ['hærəs] *vt* molestare; **~ment** *n* molestia

harbour ['hɑːbə*] (*US* **harbor**) *n* porto ♦ *vt* (*hope, fear*) nutrire; (*criminal*) dare rifugio a

hard [hɑːd] *adj* duro(a) ♦ *adv* (*work*) sodo; (*think, try*) bene; **to look ~ at** guardare fissamente; esaminare attentamente; **no ~ feelings!** senza rancore!; **to be ~ of hearing** essere duro(a) d'orecchio; **to be ~ done by** essere trattato(a) ingiustamente; **~back** *n* libro rilegato; **~ cash** *n* denaro in contanti; **~ disk** *n* (*COMPUT*) disco rigido; **~en** *vt, vi* indurire; **~-headed** *adj* pratico(a); **~ labour** *n* lavori forzati *mpl*

hardly ['hɑːdlɪ] *adv* (*scarcely*) appena; **it's ~ the case** non è proprio il caso;

~ **anyone/anywhere** quasi nessuno/ da nessuna parte; ~ **ever** quasi mai

hardship ['hɑːdʃɪp] n avversità f inv; privazioni fpl

hard shoulder (BRIT) n (AUT) corsia d'emergenza

hard-up (inf) adj al verde

hardware ['hɑːdwɛə*] n ferramenta fpl; (COMPUT) hardware m inv; (MIL) armamenti mpl; ~ **shop** n (negozio di) ferramenta fpl

hard-wearing [-'wɛərɪŋ] adj resistente; (shoes) robusto(a)

hard-working [-'wəːkɪŋ] adj lavoratore(trice)

hardy ['hɑːdɪ] adj robusto(a); (plant) resistente al gelo

hare [hɛə*] n lepre f; ~**-brained** adj folle; scervellato(a)

harm [hɑːm] n male m; (wrong) danno ♦ vt (person) fare male a; (thing) danneggiare; **out of ~'s way** al sicuro; ~**ful** adj dannoso(a); (plant) innocuo(a), inoffensivo(a)

harmonica [hɑːˈmɒnɪkə] n armonica f

harmonious [hɑːˈməʊnɪəs] adj armonioso(a)

harmony ['hɑːmənɪ] n armonia f

harness ['hɑːnɪs] n (for horse) bardatura, finimenti mpl; (for child) briglie fpl; (safety ~) imbracatura ♦ vt (horse) bardare; (resources) sfruttare

harp [hɑːp] n arpa ♦ vi: **to ~ on about** insistere tediosamente su

harpoon [hɑːˈpuːn] n arpione m

harrowing ['hærəʊɪŋ] adj straziante

harsh [hɑːʃ] adj (life, winter) duro(a); (judge, criticism) severo(a); (sound) rauco(a); (light) violento(a)

harvest ['hɑːvɪst] n raccolto; (of grapes) vendemmia ♦ vt fare il raccolto di, raccogliere; vendemmiare

has [hæz] vb see **have**

hash [hæʃ] n (CULIN) specie di spezzatino fatto con carne già cotta; (fig: mess) pasticcio

hasn't ['hæznt] = **has not**

hassle ['hæsl] (inf) n sacco di problemi

haste [heɪst] n fretta; precipitazione f; ~**n** ['heɪsn] vt affrettare ♦ vi: **to ~n (to)** affrettarsi (a); **hastily** adv in fretta; precipitosamente; **hasty** adj affrettato(a); precipitoso(a)

hat [hæt] n cappello

hatch [hætʃ] n (NAUT: also: ~**way**) boccaporto; (also: **service ~**) portello di servizio ♦ vi (bird) uscire dal guscio; (egg) schiudersi

hatchback ['hætʃbæk] n (AUT) tre (or cinque) porte f inv

hatchet ['hætʃɪt] n accetta

hate [heɪt] vt odiare, detestare ♦ n odio; ~**ful** adj odioso(a), detestabile

hatred ['heɪtrɪd] n odio

haughty ['hɔːtɪ] adj altero(a), arrogante

haul [hɔːl] vt trascinare, tirare ♦ n (of fish) pescata; (of stolen goods etc) bottino; ~**age** n trasporto; autotrasporto; ~**ier** (US ~**er**) n trasportatore m

haunch [hɔːntʃ] n anca; (of meat) coscia

haunt [hɔːnt] vt (subj: fear) pervadere; (: person) frequentare ♦ n rifugio; **this house is ~ed** questa casa è abitata da un fantasma

┌─────────────────────────┐
│ KEYWORD │
└─────────────────────────┘

have [hæv] (pt, pp **had**) aux vb 1 (gen) avere; essere; **to ~ arrived/gone** essere arrivato/andato(a); **to ~ eaten/slept** aver mangiato/ dormito; **he has been kind/ promoted** è stato gentile/promosso; **having finished** or **when he had finished, he left** dopo aver finito, se n'è andato

2 (in tag questions): **you've done it, ~n't you?** l'hai fatto, (non è) vero?; **he hasn't done it, has he?** non l'ha fatto, vero?

3 (in short answers and questions): **you've made a mistake — no I**

~n't/so I ~ ha fatto un errore — ma
no, niente affatto/sì, è vero; **we ~n't
paid — yes we ~!** non abbiamo
pagato — ma sì che abbiamo pagato!;
I've been there before, ~ you? ci
sono già stato, e lei?

♦ *modal aux vt* (*be obliged*): **to ~ (got)
to do sth** dover fare qc; **I ~n't got or
I don't ~ to wear glasses** non ho
bisogno di portare gli occhiali

♦ *vt* **1** (*possess, obtain*) avere; **he has
(got) blue eyes/dark hair** ha gli
occhi azzurri/i capelli scuri; **do you ~
or** *or* **you got a car/phone?** ha la
macchina/il telefono?; **may I ~ your
address?** potrebbe darmi il suo
indirizzo?; **you can ~ it for £5** te lo
lascio per 5 sterline
2 (+ *noun: take, hold etc*): **to ~
breakfast/a swim/a bath** fare
colazione/una nuotata/un bagno; **to
~ lunch** pranzare; **to ~ dinner** cenare;
to ~ a drink bere qualcosa; **to ~ a
cigarette** fumare una sigaretta
3: **to ~ sth done** far fare qc; **to
~ one's hair cut** farsi tagliare i capelli;
to ~ sb do sth far fare qc a qn
4 (*experience, suffer*) avere; **to ~ a
cold/flu** avere il raffreddore/
l'influenza; **she had her bag stolen**
le hanno rubato la borsa
5 (*inf: dupe*): **you've been had!** ci sei
cascato!

have out *vt*: **to ~ it out with sb**
(*settle a problem etc*) mettere le cose in
chiaro con qn

haven ['heɪvn] *n* porto; (*fig*) rifugio
haven't ['hævnt] = **have not**
havoc ['hævək] *n* caos *m*
hawk [hɔːk] *n* falco
hay [heɪ] *n* fieno; **~ fever** *n* febbre *f* da
fieno; **~stack** *n* pagliaio
haywire ['heɪwaɪə*] (*inf*) *adj*: **to go ~**
impazzire
hazard ['hæzəd] *n* azzardo, ventura;
pericolo, rischio ♦ *vt* (*guess etc*)

azzardare; **~ous** *adj* pericoloso(a);
~ (warning) lights *npl* (*AUT*) luci *fpl* di
emergenza
haze [heɪz] *n* foschia
hazelnut ['heɪzlnʌt] *n* nocciola
hazy ['heɪzɪ] *adj* fosco(a); (*idea*)
vago(a)

he [hiː] *pronoun* lui, egli; **it is ~ who
... è lui che ...**

head [hed] *n* testa; (*leader*) capo; (*of
school*) preside *m/f* ♦ *vt* (*list*) essere in
testa a; (*group*) essere a capo di; **~s (o
tails)** testa (o croce), pari (o dispari);
~ first a capofitto, di testa; **~ over
heels in love** pazzamente
innamorato(a); **to ~ the ball** colpire
una palla di testa; **~ for** *vt fus* dirigersi
verso; **~ache** *n* mal *m* di testa; **~dress**
(*BRIT*) *n* (*of bride*) acconciatura; **~ing**
n titolo; intestazione *f*; **~lamp** (*BRIT*) *n* =
~light; **~land** *n* promontorio; **~light**
n fanale *m*; **~line** *n* titolo; **~long** *adv*
(*fall*) a capofitto; (*rush*)
precipitosamente; **~master/mistress**
n preside *m/f*; **~ office** *n* sede *f*
(centrale); **~-on** *adj* (*collision*) frontale;
~phones *npl* cuffia; **~quarters** *npl*
ufficio centrale; (*MIL*) quartiere *m*
generale; **~rest** *n* poggiacapo;
~room *n* (*in car*) altezza dell'abitacolo;
(*under bridge*) altezza limite; **~scarf** *n*
foulard *m inv*; **~strong** *adj* testardo(a);
~ waiter *n* capocameriere *m*; **~way**
n: **to make ~way** fare progressi;
~wind *n* controvento; **~y** *adj*
(*experience, period*) inebriante

heal [hiːl] *vt, vi* guarire
health [helθ] *n* salute *f*; **~ centre** (*BRIT*)
n poliambulatorio; **~ food(s)** *n(pl)* cibo
macrobiotico; **~ food store** *n* negozio
di alimenti dietetici e macrobiotici; **the
H~ Service** (*BRIT*) *n* ≈ il Servizio
Sanitario Statale; **~y** *adj* (*person*)
sano(a), in buona salute; (*climate*)
salubre; (*appetite, economy etc*) sano(a)

heap [hiːp] *n* mucchio ♦ *vt* (*stones,
sand*): **to ~ (up)** ammucchiare; (*plate,*

sink): **to ~ sth with** riempire qc di; **~s of** (*inf*) un mucchio di

hear [hɪə*] (*pt, pp* **heard**) *vt* sentire; (*news*) ascoltare ♦ *vi* sentire; **to ~ about** avere notizie di; sentire parlare di; **to ~ from sb** ricevere notizie da qn; **~ing** *n* (*sense*) udito; (*of witnesses*) audizione *f*; (*of a case*) udienza; **~ing aid** *n* apparecchio acustico; **~say** *n* dicerie *fpl*, chiacchiere *fpl*

hearse [hə:s] *n* carro funebre

heart [hɑ:t] *n* cuore *m*; **~s** *npl* (*CARDS*) cuori *mpl*; **to take ~** farsi coraggio; **at ~** in fondo; **by ~** (*learn, know*) a memoria; **~ attack** *n* attacco di cuore; **~beat** *n* battito del cuore; **~breaking** *adj* straziante; **~broken** *adj*: **to be ~broken** avere il cuore spezzato; **~burn** *n* bruciore *m* di stomaco; **~ failure** *n* arresto cardiaco; **~felt** *adj* sincero(a)

hearth [hɑ:θ] *n* focolare *m*

heartland ['hɑ:tlænd] *n* regione *f* centrale

heartless ['hɑ:tlɪs] *adj* senza cuore

hearty ['hɑ:tɪ] *adj* caloroso(a), robusto(a), sano(a); vigoroso(a)

heat [hi:t] *n* calore *m*; (*fig*) ardore *m*, fuoco; (*SPORT: also: qualifying ~*) prova eliminatoria ♦ *vt* scaldare; **~ up** *vi* (*liquids*) scaldarsi; (*room*) riscaldarsi ♦ *vt* riscaldare; **~ed** *adj* riscaldato(a); (*argument*) acceso(a); **~er** *n* radiatore *m*; (*stove*) stufa

heath [hi:θ] (*BRIT*) *n* landa

heathen ['hi:ðn] *n* pagano/a

heather ['hɛðə*] *n* erica

heating ['hi:tɪŋ] *n* riscaldamento

heatstroke ['hi:tstrəuk] *n* colpo di sole

heatwave ['hi:tweɪv] *n* ondata di caldo

heave [hi:v] *vt* (*pull*) tirare (con forza); (*push*) spingere (con forza); (*lift*) sollevare (con forza) ♦ *vi* sollevarsi;

(*retch*) aver conati di vomito ♦ *n* (*push*) grande spinta; **to ~ a sigh** emettere un sospiro

heaven ['hɛvn] *n* paradiso, cielo; **~ly** *adj* divino(a), celeste

heavily ['hɛvɪlɪ] *adv* pesantemente; (*drink, smoke*) molto

heavy ['hɛvɪ] *adj* pesante; (*sea*) grosso(a); (*rain, blow*) forte; (*weather*) afoso(a); (*drinker, smoker*) gran (*before noun*); **~ goods vehicle** *n* veicolo per trasporti pesanti; **~weight** *n* (*SPORT*) peso massimo

Hebrew ['hi:bru:] *adj* ebreo(a) ♦ *n* (*LING*) ebraico

Hebrides ['hɛbrɪdi:z] *npl*: **the ~** le Ebridi

heckle ['hɛkl] *vt* interpellare e dare noia a (*un oratore*)

hectic ['hɛktɪk] *adj* movimentato(a)

he'd [hi:d] = **he would; he had**

hedge [hɛdʒ] *n* siepe *f* ♦ *vi* essere elusivo(a); **to ~ one's bets** (*fig*) coprirsi dai rischi

hedgehog ['hɛdʒhɔg] *n* riccio

heed [hi:d] *vt* (*also: take ~ of*) badare a, far conto di; **~less** *adj*: **~less (of)** sordo(a) (a)

heel [hi:l] *n* (*ANAT*) calcagno; (*of shoe*) tacco ♦ *vt* (*shoe*) rifare i tacchi a

hefty ['hɛftɪ] *adj* (*person*) robusto(a); (*parcel*) pesante; (*profit*) grosso(a)

heifer ['hɛfə*] *n* giovenca

height [haɪt] *n* altezza; (*high ground*) altura; (*fig: of glory*) apice *m*; (: *of stupidity*) colmo; **~en** *vt* (*fig*) accrescere

heir [ɛə*] *n* erede *m*; **~ess** *n* erede *f*; **~loom** *n* mobile *m* (*or* gioiello *m* *or* quadro) di famiglia

held [hɛld] *pt, pp of* **hold**

helicopter ['hɛlɪkɔptə*] *n* elicottero

heliport ['hɛlɪpɔ:t] *n* eliporto

helium ['hi:lɪəm] *n* elio

hell [hɛl] *n* inferno; **~!** (*inf*) porca miseria!, accidenti!

he'll [hi:l] = **he will; he shall**

hellish ['hɛlɪʃ] (*inf*) *adj* infernale

hello [hə'ləu] *excl* buon giorno!; ciao! (*to sb one addresses as "tu"*); (*surprise*) ~! ma guarda!

helm [helm] *n* (NAUT) timone *m*

helmet ['helmɪt] *n* casco

help [help] *n* aiuto; (*charwoman*) donna di servizio ♦ *vt* aiutare; ~! aiuto!; ~ **yourself (to bread)** si serva (del pane); **he can't** ~ **it** non ci può far niente; ~**er** *n* aiutante *m/f*, assistente *m/f*; ~**ful** *adj* di grande aiuto; (*useful*) utile; ~**ing** *n* porzione *f*; ~**less** *adj* impotente; debole

hem [hem] *n* orlo ♦ *vt* fare l'orlo a; ~ **in** *vt* cingere

hemisphere ['hemɪsfɪə*] *n* emisfero *m*

hemorrhage ['hemərɪdʒ] (*US*) *n* = **haemorrhage**

hemorrhoids ['hemərɔɪdz] (*US*) *npl* = **haemorrhoids**

hen [hen] *n* gallina; (*female bird*) femmina

hence [hens] *adv* (*therefore*) dunque; **2 years** ~ di qui a 2 anni; ~**forth** *adv* d'ora in poi

henpecked ['henpekt] *adj* dominato dalla moglie

hepatitis [hepə'taɪtɪs] *n* epatite *f*

her [hə:*] *pron* (*direct*) la, l' + *vowel*; (*indirect*) le; (*stressed, after prep*) lei ♦ *adj* il(la) suo(a), i(le) suoi(sue); *see also* **me; my**

herald ['herəld] *n* araldo ♦ *vt* annunciare

heraldry ['herəldrɪ] *n* araldica

herb [hə:b] *n* erba

herd [hə:d] *n* mandria

here [hɪə*] *adv* qui, qua ♦ *excl* ehi!; ~! (*at roll call*) presente!; ~ **is/are** ~ **he/she is** eccolo/eccola; ~**after** *adv* in futuro; dopo questo; ~**by** *adv* (*in letter*) con la presente

hereditary [hɪ'redɪtrɪ] *adj* ereditario(a)

heresy ['herəsɪ] *n* eresia

heretic ['herətɪk] *n* eretico/a

heritage ['herɪtɪdʒ] *n* eredità; (*fig*) retaggio

hermetically [hə:'metɪklɪ] *adv*: ~ **sealed** ermeticamente chiuso(a)

hermit ['hə:mɪt] *n* eremita *m*

hernia ['hə:nɪə] *n* ernia

hero ['hɪərəu] (*pl* ~**es**) *n* eroe *m*

heroin ['herəuɪn] *n* eroina

heroine ['herəuɪn] *n* eroina

heron ['herən] *n* airone *m*

herring ['herɪŋ] *n* aringa

hers [hə:z] *pron* il(la) suo(a), i(le) suoi(sue); *see also* **mine¹**

herself [hə:'self] *pron* (*reflexive*) si; (*emphatic*) lei stessa; (*after prep*) se stessa, sé; *see also* **oneself**

he's [hi:z] = **he is**; **he has**

hesitant ['hezɪtənt] *adj* esitante, indeciso(a)

hesitate ['hezɪteɪt] *vi*: **to** ~ (**about/to do**) esitare (su/a fare); **hesitation** [-'teɪʃən] *n* esitazione *f*

heterosexual ['hetərəu'seksjuəl] *adj*, *n* eterosessuale *m/f*

hexagonal [hek'sægənəl] *adj* esagonale

heyday ['heɪdeɪ] *n*: **the** ~ **of** i bei giorni di, l'età d'oro di

HGV *n abbr* = **heavy goods vehicle**

hi [haɪ] *excl* ciao!

hiatus [haɪ'eɪtəs] *n* vuoto; (*LING*) iato

hibernate ['haɪbəneɪt] *vi* ibernare

hiccough ['hɪkʌp] *vi* singhiozzare; ~**s** *npl*: **to have** ~**s** avere il singhiozzo

hiccup ['hɪkʌp] *n* = **hiccough**

hid [hɪd] *pt of* **hide**; ~**den** ['hɪdn] *pp of* **hide**

hide [haɪd] (*pt* **hid**, *pp* **hidden**) *n* (*skin*) pelle *f* ♦ *vt*: **to** ~ **sth (from sb)** nascondere qc (a qn) ♦ *vi*: **to** ~ (**from sb**) nascondersi (da qn); ~-**and-seek** *n* rimpiattino

hideous ['hɪdɪəs] *adj* laido(a); orribile

hiding ['haɪdɪŋ] *n* (*beating*) bastonata; **to be in** ~ (*concealed*) tenersi nascosto(a)

hierarchy ['haɪərɑːkɪ] *n* gerarchia

hi-fi ['haɪfaɪ] *n* stereo ♦ *adj* ad alta fedeltà, hi-fi *inv*

high [haɪ] adj alto(a); (speed, respect, number) grande; (wind) forte; (voice) acuto(a) ♦ adv alto, in alto; **20m** ~ alto/a 20m; ~**brow** adj, n intellettuale m/f; ~**chair** n seggiolone m; ~**er education** n studi mpl superiori; ~-**handed** adj prepotente; ~-**heeled** adj con i tacchi alti; ~-**jump** n (SPORT) salto in alto; **the H~lands** npl le Highlands scozzesi; ~**light** n (fig: of event) momento culminante; (in hair) colpo di sole ♦ vt mettere in evidenza; ~**ly** adv molto; **to speak ~ly of** parlare molto bene di; ~**ly strung** adj teso(a) di nervi, eccitabile; ~**ness** n: **Her H~ness** Sua Altezza; ~-**pitched** adj acuto(a); ~-**rise block** n palazzone m; ~ **school** n scuola secondaria; (US) istituto superiore d'istruzione; ~ **season** (BRIT) n alta stagione; ~ **street** (BRIT) n strada principale

highway ['haɪweɪ] n strada maestra; **H~ Code** (BRIT) n codice m della strada

hijack ['haɪdʒæk] vt dirottare; ~**er** n dirottatore/trice

hike [haɪk] vi fare un'escursione a piedi ♦ n escursione f a piedi; ~**r** n escursionista m/f; **hiking** n escursioni fpl a piedi

hilarious [hɪ'leərɪəs] adj (behaviour, event) spassosissimo(a)

hill [hɪl] n collina, colle m; (fairly high) montagna; (on road) salita; ~**side** n fianco della collina; ~ **walking** n escursioni fpl in collina; ~**y** adj collinoso(a); montagnoso(a)

hilt [hɪlt] n (of sword) elsa; **to the** ~ (fig: support) fino in fondo

him [hɪm] pron (direct) lo, l' + vowel; (indirect) gli; (stressed, after prep) lui; see also **me**; ~**self** pron (reflexive) si; (emphatic) lui stesso; (after prep) se stesso, sé; see also **oneself**

hinder ['hɪndə*] vt ostacolare; **hindrance** ['hɪndrəns] n ostacolo, impedimento

hindsight ['haɪndsaɪt] n: **with** ~ con il

senno di poi

Hindu ['hɪnduː] n indù m/f inv

hinge [hɪndʒ] n cardine m ♦ vi (fig): **to** ~ **on** dipendere da

hint [hɪnt] n (suggestion) allusione f; (advice) consiglio; (sign) accenno ♦ vt: **to** ~ **that** lasciar capire che ♦ vi: **to** ~ **at** alludere a

hip [hɪp] n anca, fianco

hippopotamus [hɪpə'pɒtəməs] (pl ~**es** or **hippopotami**) n ippopotamo

hire ['haɪə*] vt (BRIT: car, equipment) noleggiare; (worker) assumere, dare lavoro a ♦ n nolo, noleggio; **for** ~ da nolo; (taxi) libero(a); ~**(d) car** (BRIT) n macchina a nolo; ~ **purchase** (BRIT) n acquisto (or vendita) rateale

his [hɪz] adj, pron il(la) suo(a), i(le) suoi(sue); see also **my**; **mine**[1]

hiss [hɪs] vi fischiare; (cat, snake) sibilare

historic(al) [hɪ'stɔrɪk(l)] adj storico(a)

history ['hɪstərɪ] n storia

hit [hɪt] (pt, pp **hit**) vt colpire, picchiare; (knock against) battere; (reach: target) raggiungere; (collide with: car) urtare contro; (fig: affect) colpire; (find: problem etc) incontrare ♦ n colpo; (success, song) successo; **to** ~ **it off with sb** andare molto d'accordo con qn; ~-**and-run driver** n pirata m della strada

hitch [hɪtʃ] vt (fasten) attaccare; (also: ~ **up**) tirare su ♦ n (difficulty) intoppo, difficoltà f inv; **to** ~ **a lift** fare l'autostop

hitch-hike vi fare l'autostop; ~**r** n autostoppista m/f; **hitch-hiking** n autostop m

hi-tech ['haɪtek] adj di alta tecnologia ♦ n alta tecnologia

hitherto [hɪðə'tuː] adv in precedenza

HIV abbr: **HIV-negative/-positive** adj sieronegativo(a)/sieropositivo(a)

hive [haɪv] n alveare m

H.M.S. abbr = **His(Her) Majesty's Ship**

hoard [hɔːd] n (of food) provviste fpl; (of money) gruzzolo ♦ vt ammassare

hoarding ['hɔːdɪŋ] (BRIT) n (for posters) tabellone m per affissioni

hoarse [hɔːs] adj rauco(a)

hoax [həʊks] n scherzo; falso allarme

hob [hɔb] n piastra (con fornelli)

hobble ['hɔbl] vi zoppicare

hobby ['hɔbɪ] n hobby m inv, passatempo

hobo ['həʊbəʊ] (US) n vagabondo

hockey ['hɔkɪ] n hockey m

hoe [həʊ] n zappa

hog [hɔg] n maiale m ♦ vt (fig) arraffare; **to go the whole ~** farlo fino in fondo

hoist [hɔɪst] n paranco ♦ vt issare

hold [həʊld] (pt, pp held) vt tenere; (contain) contenere; (keep back) trattenere; (believe) mantenere; considerare; (possess) avere, possedere; detenere ♦ vi (withstand pressure) tenere; (be valid) essere valido(a) ♦ n presa; (control): **to have a ~ over** avere controllo su; (NAUT) stiva; ~ **the line!** (TEL) resti in linea!; **to ~ one's own** (fig) difendersi bene; **to catch or get (a) ~ of** afferrare; ~ **back** vt trattenere; (secret) tenere celato(a); ~ **down** vt (person) tenere a terra; (job) tenere; ~ **off** vt tener lontano; ~ **on** vi tenere fermo; (wait) aspettare; ~ **on!** (TEL) resti in linea!; **to ~ on to** vt fus tenersi stretto(a) a; (keep) conservare; ~ **out** vt offrire ♦ vi (resist) resistere; ~ **up** vt (raise) alzare; (support) sostenere; (delay) ritardare; (rob) assaltare; ~**all** (BRIT) n borsone m; ~**er** n (of container) contenitore m; (of ticket, title) possessore/posseditrice; (of office etc) incaricato/a; (of record) detentore/trice; ~**ing** n (share) azioni fpl, titoli mpl; (farm) podere m, tenuta; ~**up** n (robbery) rapina a mano armata; (delay) ritardo; (BRIT: in traffic) blocco

hole [həʊl] n buco, buca

holiday ['hɔlədɪ] n vacanza; (day off)

giorno di vacanza; (public) giorno festivo; **on ~** in vacanza; ~ **camp** (BRIT) n (also: ~ centre) ≈ villaggio (di vacanze); ~-**maker** (BRIT) n villeggiante m/f; ~ **resort** n luogo di villeggiatura

holiness ['həʊlɪnɪs] n santità

Holland ['hɔlənd] n Olanda

hollow ['hɔləʊ] adj cavo(a); (container, claim) vuoto(a); (laugh, sound) cupo(a) ♦ n cavità f inv; (in land) valletta, depressione f ♦ vt: **to ~ out** scavare

holly ['hɔlɪ] n agrifoglio

holocaust ['hɔləkɔːst] n olocausto

holster ['həʊlstə*] n fondina (di pistola)

holy ['həʊlɪ] adj santo(a); (bread, ground) benedetto(a), consacrato(a)

homage ['hɔmɪdʒ] n omaggio; **to pay ~ to** rendere omaggio a

home [həʊm] n casa; (country) patria; (institution) casa, ricovero ♦ cpd familiare; (cooking etc) casalingo(a); (ECON, POL) nazionale, interno(a); (SPORT) di casa ♦ adv a casa; in patria; (right in: nail etc) fino in fondo; **at ~** a casa; (in situation) a proprio agio; **to go (or come) ~** tornare a casa (or in patria); **make yourself at ~** si metta a suo agio; ~ **address** n indirizzo di casa; ~**land** n patria; ~**less** adj senza tetto; spiantato(a); ~**ly** adj semplice, alla buona; accogliente; ~-**made** adj casalingo(a); H~ **Office** (BRIT) n ministero degli Interni; ~**page** n (COMPUT) home page f inv; ~ **rule** n autogoverno; H~ **Secretary** (BRIT) n ministro degli Interni; ~**sick** adj: **to be ~sick** avere la nostalgia; ~ **town** n città f inv natale; ~**ward** ['həʊmwəd] adj (journey) di ritorno; ~**work** n compiti mpl (per casa)

homicide ['hɔmɪsaɪd] (US) n omicidio

homoeopathic [həʊmɪəʊˈpæθɪk] (US **homeopathic**) adj omeopatico(a)

homosexual [hɔməʊˈsɛksjuəl] adj, n omosessuale m/f

honest ['ɔnɪst] adj onesto(a);

sincero(a); **~ly** adv onestamente;
sinceramente; **~y** n onestà

honey ['hʌnɪ] n miele m; **~comb** n
favo; **~moon** n luna di miele, viaggio
di nozze; **~suckle** n (BOT) caprifoglio

honk [hɒŋk] vi suonare il clacson

honorary ['ɒnərərɪ] adj onorario(a);
(duty, title) onorifico(a)

honour ['ɒnə*] (US **honor**) vt onorare
♦ n onore m; **~able** adj onorevole; **~s
degree** n (SCOL) laurea specializzata

hood [hud] n cappuccio; (on cooker)
cappa; (BRIT: AUT) capote f; (US: AUT)
cofano

hoodlum ['hu:dləm] n teppista m/f

hoof [hu:f] (pl **hooves**) n zoccolo

hook [huk] n gancio; (for fishing) amo
♦ vt uncinare; (dress) agganciare

hooligan ['hu:lɪɡən] n giovinastro,
teppista m

hoop [hu:p] n cerchio

hooray [hu:'reɪ] excl = **hurray**

hoot [hu:t] vi (AUT) suonare il clacson;
(siren) ululare; (owl) gufare; **~er** n (BRIT:
AUT) clacson m inv; (NAUT) sirena

Hoover ® ['hu:və*] (BRIT) n
aspirapolvere m inv ♦ vt: **h~** pulire con
l'aspirapolvere

hooves [hu:vz] npl di **hoof**

hop [hɒp] vi saltellare, saltare; (on one
foot) saltare su una gamba

hope [həup] vt: **~ that/to do**
sperare che/di fare ♦ vi sperare ♦ n
speranza; **I ~ so/not** spero di sì/no;
~ful adj (person) pieno(a) di speranza;
(situation) promettente; **~fully** adv con
speranza; **~fully he will recover**
speriamo che si riprenda; **~less** adj
senza speranza, disperato(a); (useless)
inutile

hops [hɒps] npl luppoli mpl

horde [hɔ:d] n orda

horizon [hə'raɪzn] n orizzonte m; **~tal**
[hɔrɪ'zɒntl] adj orizzontale

hormone ['hɔ:məun] n ormone m

horn [hɔ:n] n (ZOOL, MUS) corno; (AUT)
clacson m inv

hornet ['hɔ:nɪt] n calabrone m

horoscope ['hɒrəskəup] n oroscopo

horrendous [hə'rendəs] adj
orrendo(a)

horrible ['hɒrɪbl] adj orribile,
tremendo(a)

horrid ['hɒrɪd] adj orrido(a); (person)
odioso(a)

horrify ['hɒrɪfaɪ] vt scandalizzare

horror ['hɒrə*] n orrore m; **~ film** n
film m inv dell'orrore

hors d'œuvre [ɔ:'də:vrə] n antipasto

horse [hɔ:s] n cavallo; **~back: on
~back** adj, adv a cavallo; **~ chestnut**
n ippocastano; **~man** (irreg) n
cavaliere m; **~power** n cavallo
(vapore); **~-racing** n ippica; **~radish**
n rafano; **~shoe** n ferro di cavallo;
~woman (irreg) n amazzone f

horticulture ['hɔ:tɪkʌltʃə*] n
orticoltura

hose [həuz] n (also: **~pipe**) tubo; (also:
garden **~**) tubo per annaffiare

hosiery ['həuʒərɪ] n maglieria

hospice ['hɒspɪs] n ricovero, ospizio

hospitable [hɒs'pɪtəbl] adj ospitale

hospital ['hɒspɪtl] n ospedale m

hospitality [hɒspɪ'tælɪtɪ] n ospitalità

host [həust] n ospite m; (REL) ostia;
(large number): **a ~ of** una schiera di

hostage ['hɒstɪdʒ] n ostaggio/a

hostel ['hɒstl] n ostello; (also: **youth ~**)
ostello della gioventù

hostess ['həustɪs] n ospite f; (BRIT: air
~) hostess f inv

hostile ['hɒstaɪl] adj ostile

hostility [hɒ'stɪlɪtɪ] n ostilità f inv

hot [hɒt] adj caldo(a); (as opposed to
only warm) molto caldo(a); (spicy)
piccante; (fig) accanito(a); ardente;
violento(a), focoso(a); **to be ~** (person)
aver caldo; (object) essere caldo(a);
(weather) far caldo ♦ n (fig)
focolaio; **~ dog** n hot dog m inv

hotel [həu'tel] n albergo; **~ier** n
albergatore/trice

hot: ~house n serra; **~ line** n (POL)

telefono rosso; **~ly** adv violentemente; **~plate** n (on cooker) piastra riscaldante; **~pot** (BRIT) n stufato coperto da uno strato di patate; **~water bottle** n borsa dell'acqua calda

hound [haund] vt perseguitare ♦ n segugio

hour ['auə*] n ora; **~ly** adv all'ora

house [n haus, pl 'hauziz, vb hauz] n (also: firm) casa; (POL) camera; (THEATRE) sala; pubblico; spettacolo; (dynasty) casata ♦ vt (person) ospitare, alloggiare; **on the ~** (fig) offerto(a) dalla casa; **~ arrest** n arresti mpl domiciliari; **~boat** n house boat f inv; **~bound** adj confinato(a) in casa; **~breaking** n furto con scasso; **~hold** n famiglia; casa; **~keeper** n governante f; **~keeping** n (work) governo della casa; (money) soldi mpl per le spese di casa; **~-warming party** n festa per inaugurare la casa nuova; **~wife** (irreg) n massaia, casalinga; **~work** n faccende fpl domestiche

housing ['hauziŋ] n alloggio; **~ development** (BRIT = **estate**) n zona residenziale con case popolari e/o private

hovel ['hɔvl] n casupola

hover ['hɔvə*] vi (bird) librarsi; **~craft** n hovercraft m inv

how [hau] adv come; **~ are you?** come sta?; **~ do you do?** piacere!; **~ far is it to the river?** quanto è lontano il fiume?; **~ long have you been here?** da quando è qui?; **~ lovely/awful!** che bello!/orrore!; **~ many?** quanti(e)?; **~ much?** quanto(a)?; **~ much milk?** quanto latte?; **~ many people?** quante persone?; **~ old are you?** quanti anni ha?; **~ever** adv in qualsiasi modo o maniera che; (+ adjective) per quanto + sub; (in questions) come ♦ conj comunque, però

howl [haul] vi ululare; (baby, person) urlare

H.P. abbr = **hire purchase**;

horsepower

h.p. n abbr = **H.P.**

HQ n abbr = **headquarters**

HTML abbr (= hypertext markup language) HTML m inv

hub [hʌb] n (of wheel) mozzo; (fig) fulcro

hubcap ['hʌbkæp] n coprimozzo

huddle ['hʌdl] vi: **to ~ together** rannicchiarsi l'uno contro l'altro

hue [hju:] n tinta

huff [hʌf] n: **in a ~** stizzito(a)

hug [hʌg] vt abbracciare; (shore, kerb) stringere

huge [hju:dʒ] adj enorme, immenso(a)

hulk [hʌlk] n (ship) nave f in disarmo; (building, car) carcassa; (person) mastodonte m

hull [hʌl] n (of ship) scafo

hullo [hə'ləu] excl = **hello**

hum [hʌm] vt (tune) canticchiare ♦ vi canticchiare; (insect, tool) ronzare

human ['hju:mən] adj umano(a) ♦ n essere m umano

humane [hju:'mein] adj umanitario(a)

humanitarian [hju:mænɪ'tɛərɪən] adj umanitario(a)

humanity [hju:'mænɪtɪ] n umanità

humble ['hʌmbl] adj umile, modesto(a) ♦ vt umiliare

humdrum ['hʌmdrʌm] adj monotono(a), tedioso(a)

humid ['hju:mɪd] adj umido(a)

humiliate [hju:'mɪlɪeɪt] vt umiliare; **humiliation** [-'eɪʃən] n umiliazione f

humility [hju:'mɪlɪtɪ] n umiltà

humorous ['hju:mərəs] adj umoristico(a); (person) buffo(a)

humour ['hju:mə*] (US **humor**) n umore m ♦ vt accontentare

hump [hʌmp] n gobba

hunch [hʌntʃ] n (premonition) intuizione f; **~ed** adj incurvato(a)

hundred ['hʌndrəd] num cento; **~s of** centinaia fpl di; **~weight** n (BRIT) = 50.8 kg; 112 lb; (US) = 45.3 kg; 100 lb

hung [hʌŋ] pt, pp of **hang**

Hungary ['hʌŋgərɪ] n Ungheria

hunger ['hʌŋgə*] n fame f ♦ vi: **to ~ for** desiderare ardentemente; **~ strike** n sciopero della fame

hungry ['hʌŋgrɪ] adj affamato(a); **to be ~** aver fame

hunk [hʌŋk] n (of bread etc) bel pezzo

hunt [hʌnt] vt (seek) cercare; (SPORT) cacciare ♦ vi: **to ~ (for)** andare a caccia (di) ♦ n caccia; **~er** n cacciatore m; **~ing** n caccia

hurdle ['hə:dl] n (SPORT, fig) ostacolo

hurl [hə:l] vt lanciare con violenza

hurrah [hu'rɑ:] excl = **hurray**

hurray [hu'reɪ] excl urrà!, evviva!

hurricane ['hʌrɪkən] n uragano

hurried ['hʌrɪd] adj affrettato(a); (work) fatto(a) in fretta; **~ly** adv in fretta

hurry ['hʌrɪ] n fretta ♦ vi (also: **~ up**) affrettarsi ♦ vt (also: **~ up**) (person) affrettare; (: work) far in fretta; **to be in a ~** aver fretta

hurt [hə:t] (pt, pp **hurt**) vt (cause pain to) far male a; (injure, fig) ferire ♦ vi far male; **~ful** adj (remark) che ferisce

hurtle ['hə:tl] vi: **to ~ past/down** passare/scendere a razzo

husband ['hʌzbənd] n marito

hush [hʌʃ] n silenzio, calma ♦ vt zittire; **~ up** vt (scandal) mettere a tacere

husk [hʌsk] n (of wheat) cartoccio; (of rice, maize) buccia

husky ['hʌskɪ] adj roco(a) ♦ n cane m eschimese

hustle ['hʌsl] vt spingere, incalzare ♦ n: **~ and bustle** trambusto

hut [hʌt] n rifugio; (shed) ripostiglio

hutch [hʌtʃ] n gabbia

hyacinth ['haɪəsɪnθ] n giacinto

hybrid ['haɪbrɪd] n ibrido

hydrant ['haɪdrənt] n (also: fire ~) idrante m

hydraulic [haɪ'drɔ:lɪk] adj idraulico(a)

hydroelectric [haɪdrəʊɪ'lektrɪk] adj idroelettrico(a)

hydrofoil ['haɪdrəʊfɔɪl] n aliscafo

hydrogen ['haɪdrədʒən] n idrogeno

hyena [haɪ'i:nə] n iena

hygiene ['haɪdʒi:n] n igiene f

hymn [hɪm] n inno; cantica

hype [haɪp] (inf) n campagna pubblicitaria

hypermarket ['haɪpəmɑ:kɪt] (BRIT) n ipermercato

hypertext ['haɪpətekst] n (COMPUT) ipertesto

hyphen ['haɪfn] n trattino

hypnotize ['hɪpnətaɪz] vt ipnotizzare

hypocrisy [hɪ'pɒkrɪsɪ] n ipocrisia

hypocrite ['hɪpəkrɪt] n ipocrita m/f; **hypocritical** [-'krɪtɪkl] adj ipocrita

hypothermia [haɪpəʊ'θə:mɪə] n ipotermia

hypothesis [haɪ'pɒθɪsɪs] (pl **hypotheses**) n ipotesi f inv

hypothetical [haɪpəʊ'θetɪkl] adj ipotetico(a)

hysterical [hɪ'sterɪkl] adj isterico(a)

hysterics [hɪ'sterɪks] npl accesso di isteria; (laughter) attacco di riso

I, i

I [aɪ] pron io

ice [aɪs] n ghiaccio; (on road) gelo; (~ cream) gelato ♦ vt (cake) glassare ♦ vi (also: **~ over**) ghiacciare; (also: **~ up**) gelare; **~berg** n iceberg m inv; **~box** n (US) frigorifero; (BRIT) reparto ghiaccio; (insulated box) frigo portatile; **~ cream** n gelato; **~ hockey** n hockey m su ghiaccio

Iceland ['aɪslənd] n Islanda

ice: ~ lolly (BRIT) n ghiacciolo; **~ rink** n pista di pattinaggio; **~ skating** n pattinaggio sul ghiaccio

icicle ['aɪsɪkl] n ghiacciolo

icing ['aɪsɪŋ] n (CULIN) glassa; **~ sugar** (BRIT) n zucchero a velo

icon ['aɪkɒn] n icona

icy ['aɪsɪ] adj ghiacciato(a); (weather, temperature) gelido(a)

I'd [aɪd] = **I would**; **I had**

idea [aɪ'dɪə] n idea

ideal [aɪˈdɪəl] *adj* ideale ♦ *n* ideale *m*

identical [aɪˈdɛntɪkl] *adj* identico(a)

identification [aɪdɛntɪfɪˈkeɪʃən] *n* identificazione *f*; **(means of)** ~ carta d'identità

identify [aɪˈdɛntɪfaɪ] *vt* identificare

Identikit picture ® [aɪˈdɛntɪkɪt-] *n* identikit *m inv*

identity [aɪˈdɛntɪtɪ] *n* identità *f inv*; ~ **card** *n* carta d'identità

ideology [aɪdɪˈɒlədʒɪ] *n* ideologia *f*

idiom [ˈɪdɪəm] *n* idioma *m*; **(phrase)** espressione *f* idiomatica

idiot [ˈɪdɪət] *n* idiota *m/f*; ~**ic** [-ˈɔtɪk] *adj* idiota

idle [ˈaɪdl] *adj* inattivo(a); **(lazy)** pigro(a), ozioso(a); **(unemployed)** disoccupato(a); **(question, pleasures)** ozioso(a) ♦ *vi* **(engine)** girare al minimo

idol [ˈaɪdl] *n* idolo; **~ize** *vt* idoleggiare

i.e. *adv abbr* (= *that is*) cioè

if [ɪf] *conj* se; ~ **I were you** ... se fossi in te ..., io al tuo posto ...; **~ so** se è così; **~ not** se no; **~ only** se solo or soltanto

ignite [ɪgˈnaɪt] *vt* accendere ♦ *vi* accendersi

ignition [ɪgˈnɪʃən] *n* (AUT) accensione *f*; **to switch on/off the ~** accendere/ spegnere il motore; **~ key** *n* (AUT) chiave *f* dell'accensione

ignorant [ˈɪgnərənt] *adj* ignorante; **to be ~ of** **(subject)** essere ignorante in; **(events)** essere ignaro(a) di

ignore [ɪgˈnɔː*] *vt* non tener conto di; **(person, fact)** ignorare

I'll [aɪl] = **I will**; **I shall**

ill [ɪl] *adj* **(sick)** malato(a); **(bad)** cattivo(a) ♦ *n* male *m* ♦ *adv*: **to speak** *etc* ~ **of sb** parlare *etc* male di qn; **to take** *or* **be taken** ~ ammalarsi; **~-advised** *adj* **(decision)** poco giudizioso(a); **(person)** mal consigliato(a); **~-at-ease** *adj* a disagio

illegal [ɪˈliːgl] *adj* illegale

illegible [ɪˈlɛdʒɪbl] *adj* illeggibile

illegitimate [ɪlɪˈdʒɪtɪmət] *adj* illegittimo(a)

ill-fated [ɪlˈfeɪtɪd] *adj* nefasto(a)

ill feeling *n* rancore *m*

illiterate [ɪˈlɪtərət] *adj* analfabeta, illetterato(a); **(letter)** scorretto(a)

ill-mannered [ɪlˈmænəd] *adj* maleducato(a)

illness [ˈɪlnɪs] *n* malattia

ill-treat *vt* maltrattare

illuminate [ɪˈluːmɪneɪt] *vt* illuminare; **illumination** [-ˈneɪʃən] *n* illuminazione *f*; **illuminations** *npl* **(decorative)** luminarie *fpl*

illusion [ɪˈluːʒən] *n* illusione *f*

illustrate [ˈɪləstreɪt] *vt* illustrare

illustration [ɪləˈstreɪʃən] *n* illustrazione *f*

I'm [aɪm] = **I am**

image [ˈɪmɪdʒ] *n* immagine *f*; **(public face)** immagine (pubblica); **~ry** *n* immagini *fpl*

imaginary [ɪˈmædʒɪnərɪ] *adj* immaginario(a)

imagination [ɪmædʒɪˈneɪʃən] *n* immaginazione *f*, fantasia

imaginative [ɪˈmædʒɪnətɪv] *adj* immaginoso(a)

imagine [ɪˈmædʒɪn] *vt* immaginare

imbalance [ɪmˈbæləns] *n* squilibrio

imbue [ɪmˈbjuː] *vt*: **to ~ sb/sth with** permeare qn/qc di

imitate [ˈɪmɪteɪt] *vt* imitare; **imitation** [-ˈteɪʃən] *n* imitazione *f*

immaculate [ɪˈmækjulət] *adj* immacolato(a); **(dress, appearance)** impeccabile

immaterial [ɪməˈtɪərɪəl] *adj* immateriale, indifferente

immature [ɪməˈtjuə*] *adj* immaturo(a)

immediate [ɪˈmiːdɪət] *adj* immediato(a); **~ly** *adv* **(at once)** subito, immediatamente; **~ly next to** proprio accanto a

immense [ɪˈmɛns] *adj* immenso(a); enorme

immerse [ɪˈməːs] *vt* immergere

immersion heater [ɪˈməːʃən-] (BRIT) *n*

scaldacqua *m inv* a immersione

immigrant ['ɪmɪɡrənt] *n* immigrante *m/f*; immigrato/a

immigration [ɪmɪ'ɡreɪʃən] *n* immigrazione *f*

imminent ['ɪmɪnənt] *adj* imminente

immoral [ɪ'mɔrl] *adj* immorale

immortal [ɪ'mɔːtl] *adj*, *n* immortale *m/f*

immune [ɪ'mjuːn] *adj*: ~ (to) immune (da); **immunity** *n* immunità *f*

impact ['ɪmpækt] *n* impatto *m*

impair [ɪm'peə*] *vt* danneggiare

impart [ɪm'pɑːt] *vt* (*make known*) comunicare; (*bestow*) impartire

impartial [ɪm'pɑːʃl] *adj* imparziale

impassable [ɪm'pɑːsəbl] *adj* insuperabile; (*road*) impraticabile

impassive [ɪm'pæsɪv] *adj* impassibile

impatience [ɪm'peɪʃəns] *n* impazienza

impatient [ɪm'peɪʃənt] *adj* impaziente; **to get** *or* **grow ~** perdere la pazienza

impeccable [ɪm'pekəbl] *adj* impeccabile

impede [ɪm'piːd] *vt* impedire

impediment [ɪm'pedɪmənt] *n* impedimento; (*also: speech ~*) difetto di pronuncia

impending [ɪm'pendɪŋ] *adj* imminente

imperative [ɪm'perətɪv] *adj* imperativo(a); necessario(a), urgente; (*voice*) imperioso(a) ♦ *n* (*LING: also: ~ tense*) imperativo

imperfect [ɪm'pəːfɪkt] *adj* imperfetto(a); (*goods etc*) difettoso(a) ♦ *n* (*LING: also: ~ tense*) imperfetto

imperial [ɪm'pɪərɪəl] *adj* imperiale; (*measure*) legale

impersonal [ɪm'pəːsənl] *adj* impersonale

impersonate [ɪm'pəːsəneɪt] *vt* impersonare; (*THEATRE*) fare la mimica di

impertinent [ɪm'pəːtɪnənt] *adj* insolente, impertinente

impervious [ɪm'pəːvɪəs] *adj* (*fig*): ~ **to** insensibile a; impassibile di fronte a

impetuous [ɪm'petjuəs] *adj*

impetuoso(a), precipitoso(a)

impetus ['ɪmpətəs] *n* impeto

impinge on [ɪm'pɪndʒ-] *vt fus* (*person*) colpire; (*rights*) ledere

implement [*n* 'ɪmplɪmənt, *vb* 'ɪmplɪment] *n* attrezzo; (*for cooking*) utensile *m* ♦ *vt* effettuare

implicit [ɪm'plɪsɪt] *adj* implicito(a); (*complete*) completo(a)

imply [ɪm'plaɪ] *vt* insinuare; suggerire

impolite [ɪmpə'laɪt] *adj* scortese

import [*vb* ɪm'pɔːt, *n* 'ɪmpɔːt] *vt* importare ♦ *n* (*COMM*) importazione *f*

importance [ɪm'pɔːtns] *n* importanza

important [ɪm'pɔːtnt] *adj* importante; **it's not ~** non ha importanza

importer [ɪm'pɔːtə*] *n* importatore/trice

impose [ɪm'pəuz] *vt* imporre ♦ *vi*: **to ~ on sb** sfruttare la bontà di qn

imposing [ɪm'pəuzɪŋ] *adj* imponente

imposition [ɪmpə'zɪʃən] *n* (*of tax etc*) imposizione *f*; **to be an ~ on** (*person*) abusare della gentilezza di

impossibility [ɪmpɒsə'bɪlɪtɪ] *n* impossibilità

impossible [ɪm'pɒsɪbl] *adj* impossibile

impotent ['ɪmpətnt] *adj* impotente

impound [ɪm'paund] *vt* confiscare

impoverished [ɪm'pɒvərɪʃt] *adj* impoverito(a)

impracticable [ɪm'præktɪkəbl] *adj* inattuabile

impractical [ɪm'præktɪkl] *adj* non pratico(a)

impress [ɪm'pres] *vt* impressionare; (*mark*) imprimere, stampare; **to ~ sth on sb** far capire qc a qn

impression [ɪm'preʃən] *n* impressione *f*; **to be under the ~ that** avere l'impressione che

impressive [ɪm'presɪv] *adj* notevole

imprint ['ɪmprɪnt] *n* (*of hand etc*) impronta; (*PUBLISHING*) sigla editoriale

imprison [ɪm'prɪzn] *vt* imprigionare; **~ment** *n* imprigionamento

improbable [ɪm'prɒbəbl] *adj*

improbabile; *(excuse)* inverosimile
impromptu [ɪmˈprɒmptjuː] *adj* improvvisato(a)
improper [ɪmˈprɒpə*] *adj* scorretto(a); *(unsuitable)* inadatto(a), improprio(a); sconveniente, indecente
improve [ɪmˈpruːv] *vt* migliorare ♦ *vi* migliorare; *(pupil etc)* fare progressi; **~ment** *n* miglioramento; progresso
improvise [ˈɪmprəvaɪz] *vt, vi* improvvisare
impudent [ˈɪmpjudnt] *adj* impudente, sfacciato(a)
impulse [ˈɪmpʌls] *n* impulso; **on ~** d'impulso, impulsivamente
impulsive [ɪmˈpʌlsɪv] *adj* impulsivo(a)

KEYWORD

in [ɪn] *prep* 1 *(indicating place, position)* in; **~ the house/garden** in casa/giardino; **~ the box** nella scatola; **~ the fridge** nel frigorifero; **I have it ~ my hand** ce l'ho in mano; **~ town/the country** in città/ campagna; **~ school** a scuola; **~ here/there** qui/lì dentro
2 *(with place names: of town, region, country)*: **~ London** a Londra; **~ England** in Inghilterra; **~ the United States** negli Stati Uniti; **~ Yorkshire** nello Yorkshire
3 *(indicating time: during, in the space of)* in; **~ spring/summer** in primavera/estate; **~ 1988** nel 1988; **~ May** a o maggio; **I'll see you ~ July** ci vediamo a luglio; **~ the afternoon** nel pomeriggio; **at 4 o'clock ~ the afternoon** alle 4 del pomeriggio; **I did it ~ 3 hours/days** l'ho fatto in 3 ore/giorni; **I'll see you ~ 2 weeks** o **~ 2 weeks' time** ci vediamo tra 2 settimane
4 *(indicating manner etc)* a; **~ a loud/ soft voice** a voce alta/bassa; **~ pencil** a matita; **~ English/French** in inglese/francese; **the boy ~ the blue shirt** il ragazzo con la camicia blu

5 *(indicating circumstances)*: **~ the sun** al sole; **~ the shade** all'ombra; **~ the rain** sotto la pioggia; **a rise ~ prices** un aumento dei prezzi
6 *(indicating mood, state)*: **~ tears** in lacrime; **~ anger** per la rabbia; **~ despair** disperato(a); **~ good condition** in buono stato, in buone condizioni; **to live ~ luxury** vivere nel lusso
7 *(with ratios, numbers)*: **1 ~ 10** 1 su 10; **20 pence ~ the pound** 20 pence per sterlina; **they lined up ~ twos** si misero in fila a due a due
8 *(referring to people, works)* in; **the disease is common ~ children** la malattia è comune nei bambini; **~ (the works of) Dickens** in Dickens
9 *(indicating profession etc)* in; **to be ~ teaching** fare l'insegnante, insegnare; **to be ~ publishing** essere nell'editoria
10 *(after superlative)* di; **the best ~ the class** il migliore della classe
11 *(with present participle)*: **~ saying this** dicendo questo, nel dire questo
♦ *adv*: **to be ~** *(person: at home, work)* esserci; *(train, ship, plane)* essere arrivato(a); *(in fashion)* essere di moda; **to ask sb ~** invitare qn ad entrare; **to run/limp** *etc* **~** entrare di corsa/ zoppicando *etc*
♦ *n*: **the ~s and outs of the problem** tutti i particolari del problema

in. *abbr* = **inch**
inability [ɪnəˈbɪlɪtɪ] *n*: **~ (to do)** incapacità (di fare)
inaccurate [ɪnˈækjurət] *adj* inesatto(a), impreciso(a)
inadequate [ɪnˈædɪkwət] *adj* insufficiente
inadvertently [ɪnədˈvəːtntlɪ] *adv* senza volerlo
inadvisable [ɪnədˈvaɪzəbl] *adj* sconsigliabile

inane [ɪ'neɪn] *adj* vacuo(a), stupido(a)

inanimate [ɪn'ænɪmət] *adj* inanimato(a)

inappropriate [ɪnə'prəʊprɪət] *adj* non adatto(a); *(word, expression)* improprio(a)

inarticulate [ɪnɑː'tɪkjʊlət] *adj (person)* che si esprime male; *(speech)* inarticolato(a)

inasmuch as [ɪnəz'mʌtʃæz] *adv* in quanto che; *(insofar as)* poiché

inaudible [ɪn'ɔːdɪbl] *adj* che non si riesce a sentire

inauguration [ɪnɔːgjʊ'reɪʃən] *n* inaugurazione *f*; insediamento in carica

in-between [ɪnbɪ'twiːn] *adj* (or le) due

inborn [ɪn'bɔːn] *adj* innato(a)

inbred [ɪn'bred] *adj* innato(a); *(family)* connaturato(a)

Inc. *(us) abbr* (= **incorporated**) S.A

incapable [ɪn'keɪpəbl] *adj* incapace

incapacitate [ɪnkə'pæsɪteɪt] *vt*: **to ~ sb from doing** rendere qn incapace di fare

incense [*n* 'ɪnsens, *vb* ɪn'sens] *n* incenso ♦ *vt (anger)* infuriare

incentive [ɪn'sentɪv] *n* incentivo

incessant [ɪn'sesnt] *adj* incessante; **~ly** *adv* di continuo, senza sosta

inch [ɪntʃ] *n* pollice *m* (= 25 mm; 12 in a foot); **within an ~ of** a un pelo da; **he didn't give an ~** non ha ceduto di un millimetro

incidence ['ɪnsɪdns] *n (of crime, disease)* incidenza

incident ['ɪnsɪdnt] *n* incidente *m*; *(in book)* episodio

incidental [ɪnsɪ'dentl] *adj* accessorio(a), d'accompagnamento; *(unplanned)* incidentale; **~ to** marginale a; **~ly** [-'dentəlɪ] *adv (by the way)* a proposito

inclination [ɪnklɪ'neɪʃən] *n* inclinazione *f*

incline [*n* 'ɪnklaɪn, *vb* ɪn'klaɪn] *n* pendenza, pendio ♦ *vt* inclinare ♦ *vi (surface)* essere inclinato(a); **to be ~d**

to do tendere a fare; essere propenso(a) a fare

include [ɪn'kluːd] *vt* includere, comprendere; **including** *prep* compreso(a), incluso(a)

inclusive [ɪn'kluːsɪv] *adj* incluso(a), compreso(a); **~ of tax** *etc* tasse *etc* comprese

incoherent [ɪnkəʊ'hɪərənt] *adj* incoerente

income ['ɪnkʌm] *n* reddito; **~ tax** *n* imposta sul reddito

incoming ['ɪnkʌmɪŋ] *adj (flight, mail)* in arrivo; *(government)* subentrante; *(tide)* montante

incompetent [ɪn'kɒmpɪtnt] *adj* incompetente, incapace

incomplete [ɪnkəm'pliːt] *adj* incompleto(a)

incongruous [ɪn'kɒŋgruəs] *adj* poco appropriato(a); *(remark, act)* incongruo(a)

inconsiderate [ɪnkən'sɪdərət] *adj* sconsiderato(a)

inconsistency [ɪnkən'sɪstənsɪ] *n* incoerenza

inconsistent [ɪnkən'sɪstnt] *adj* incoerente; **~ with** non coerente con

inconspicuous [ɪnkən'spɪkjuəs] *adj* incospicuo(a); *(colour)* poco appariscente; *(dress)* dimesso(a)

inconvenience [ɪnkən'viːnjəns] *n* inconveniente *m*; *(trouble)* disturbo ♦ *vt* disturbare

inconvenient [ɪnkən'viːnjənt] *adj* scomodo(a)

incorporate [ɪn'kɔːpəreɪt] *vt* incorporare; *(contain)* contenere; **~d** *adj*: **~d company** *(us)* società *f inv* anonima

incorrect [ɪnkə'rekt] *adj* scorretto(a); *(statement)* inesatto(a)

increase [*n* 'ɪnkriːs, *vb* ɪn'kriːs] *n* aumento ♦ *vi, vt* aumentare

increasing [ɪn'kriːsɪŋ] *adj (number)* crescente; **~ly** *adv* sempre più

incredible [ɪn'kredɪbl] *adj* incredibile

increment ['ɪnkrɪmənt] n aumento, incremento

incriminate [ɪn'krɪmɪneɪt] vt compromettere

incubator ['ɪnkjubeɪtə*] n incubatrice f

incumbent [ɪn'kʌmbənt] adj: **to be ~ on sb** spettare a qn

incur [ɪn'kə:*] vt (expenses) incorrere; (anger, risk) esporsi a; (debt) contrarre; (loss) subire

indebted [ɪn'detɪd] adj: **to be ~ to sb (for)** essere obbligato(a) verso qn (per)

indecent [ɪn'di:snt] adj indecente; **~ assault** (BRIT) n aggressione f a scopo di violenza sessuale; **~ exposure** n atti mpl osceni in luogo pubblico

indecisive [ɪndɪ'saɪsɪv] adj indeciso(a)

indeed [ɪn'di:d] adv infatti; veramente; **yes ~!** certamente!

indefinite [ɪn'defɪnɪt] adj indefinito(a); (answer) vago(a); (period, number) indeterminato(a); **~ly** adv (wait) indefinitamente

indemnity [ɪn'demnɪtɪ] n (insurance) assicurazione f; (compensation) indennità, indennizzo

independence [ɪndɪ'pendns] n indipendenza

Independence Day

*Negli Stati Uniti il 4 luglio si festeggia l'***Independence Day***, giorno in cui, nel 1776, 13 colonie britanniche proclamarono la propria indipendenza dalla Gran Bretagna ed entrarono ufficialmente a far parte degli Stati Uniti d'America.*

independent [ɪndɪ'pendnt] adj indipendente

index ['ɪndeks] n (pl **-es**) (in book) indice m; (: in library etc) catalogo; (pl **indices**: ratio, sign) indice m; **~ card** n scheda; **~ finger** n (dito) indice m; **~-linked** (US **-ed**) adj legato(a) al costo

della vita

India ['ɪndɪə] n India; **~n** adj, n indiano(a)

indicate ['ɪndɪkeɪt] vt indicare; **~ion** [-'keɪʃən] n indicazione f, segno

indicative [ɪn'dɪkətɪv] adj: **~ of** indicativo(a) di

indicator ['ɪndɪkeɪtə*] n indicatore m; (AUT) freccia

indices ['ɪndɪsi:z] npl of **index**

indictment [ɪn'daɪtmənt] n accusa

indifference [ɪn'dɪfrəns] n indifferenza

indifferent [ɪn'dɪfrənt] adj indifferente; (poor) mediocre

indigenous [ɪn'dɪdʒɪnəs] adj indigeno(a)

indigestion [ɪndɪ'dʒestʃən] n indigestione f

indignant [ɪn'dɪgnənt] adj: **~ (at sth/with sb)** indignato(a) (per qc/ contro qn)

indignity [ɪn'dɪgnɪtɪ] n umiliazione f

indigo ['ɪndɪgəʊ] n indaco

indirect [ɪndɪ'rekt] adj indiretto(a)

indiscreet [ɪndɪ'skri:t] adj indiscreto(a); (rash) imprudente

indiscriminate [ɪndɪ'skrɪmɪnət] adj indiscriminato(a)

indisputable [ɪndɪ'spju:təbl] adj incontestabile, indiscutibile

individual [ɪndɪ'vɪdjuəl] n individuo ♦ adj individuale; (characteristic) particolare, originale

indoctrination [ɪndɒktrɪ'neɪʃən] n indottrinamento

Indonesia [ɪndə'ni:zɪə] n Indonesia

indoor ['ɪndɔ:*] adj da interno; (plant) d'appartamento; (swimming pool) coperto(a); (sport, games) fatto(a) al coperto; **~s** [ɪn'dɔ:z] adv all'interno

induce [ɪn'dju:s] vt persuadere; (bring about, MED) indurre

indulge [ɪn'dʌldʒ] vt (whim) compiacere, soddisfare; (child) viziare ♦ vi: **to ~ in sth** concedersi qc; abbandonarsi a qc; **~nce** n lusso (che

uno si permette); (*leniency*) indulgenza;
~**nt** *adj* indulgente

industrial [ɪn'dʌstrɪəl] *adj* industriale;
(*injury*) sul lavoro; ~ **action** *n* azione *f*
rivendicativa; ~ **estate** (*BRIT*) *n* zona
industriale; ~ **park** (*US*) *n* = ~ **estate**

industrious [ɪn'dʌstrɪəs] *adj*
industrioso(a), assiduo(a)

industry ['ɪndəstrɪ] *n* industria;
(*diligence*) operosità

inedible [ɪn'ɛdɪbl] *adj* immangiabile;
(*poisonous*) non commestibile

ineffective [ɪnɪ'fɛktɪv] *adj* inefficace;
incompetente

ineffectual [ɪnɪ'fɛktʃuəl] *adj* inefficace;
incompetente

inefficient [ɪnɪ'fɪʃənt] *adj* inefficiente

inept [ɪ'nɛpt] *adj* inetto(a)

inequality [ɪnɪ'kwɔlɪtɪ] *n*
ineguaglianza

inescapable [ɪnɪ'skeɪpəbl] *adj*
inevitabile

inevitable [ɪn'ɛvɪtəbl] *adj* inevitabile;
inevitably *adv* inevitabilmente

inexact [ɪnɪɡ'zækt] *adj* inesatto(a)

inexcusable [ɪnɪks'kju:zəbl] *adj*
ingiustificabile

inexpensive [ɪnɪk'spɛnsɪv] *adj* poco
costoso(a)

inexperienced [ɪnɪks'pɪərɪənst] *adj*
inesperto(a), senza esperienza

infallible [ɪn'fælɪbl] *adj* infallibile

infamous ['ɪnfəməs] *adj* infame

infancy ['ɪnfənsɪ] *n* infanzia

infant ['ɪnfənt] *n* bambino/a; ~ **school**
(*BRIT*) scuola elementare (*per bambini
dall'età di 5 a 7 anni*)

infantry ['ɪnfəntrɪ] *n* fanteria

infatuated [ɪn'fætjueɪtɪd] *adj*: ~ **with**
infatuato(a) di

infatuation [ɪnfætju'eɪʃən] *n*
infatuazione *f*

infect [ɪn'fɛkt] *vt* infettare; ~**ion**
[ɪn'fɛkʃən] *n* infezione *f*; ~**ious**
[ɪn'fɛkʃəs] *adj* (*disease*) infettivo(a),
contagioso(a); (*person, fig: enthusiasm*)
contagioso(a)

infer [ɪn'fə:*] *vt* inferire, dedurre

inferior [ɪn'fɪərɪə*] *adj* inferiore;
(*goods*) di qualità scadente ♦ *n*
inferiore *m/f*; (*in rank*) subalterno/a;
~**ity** [ɪnfɪərɪ'ɔrɪtɪ] *n* inferiorità; ~**ity
complex** *n* complesso di inferiorità

infertile [ɪn'fə:taɪl] *adj* sterile

in-fighting ['ɪnfaɪtɪŋ] *n* lotte *fpl*
intestine

infiltrate ['ɪnfɪltreɪt] *vt* infiltrarsi in

infinite ['ɪnfɪnɪt] *adj* infinito(a)

infinitive [ɪn'fɪnɪtɪv] *n* infinito

infinity [ɪn'fɪnɪtɪ] *n* infinità; (*also MATH*)
infinito

infirmary [ɪn'fə:mərɪ] *n* ospedale *m*;
(*in school, factory*) infermeria

inflamed [ɪn'fleɪmd] *adj* infiammato(a)

inflammable [ɪn'flæməbl] *adj*
infiammabile

inflammation [ɪnflə'meɪʃən] *n*
infiammazione *f*

inflatable [ɪn'fleɪtəbl] *adj* gonfiabile

inflate [ɪn'fleɪt] *vt* (*tyre, balloon*)
gonfiare; (*fig*) esagerare; gonfiare;
inflation [ɪn'fleɪʃən] *n* (*ECON*)
inflazione *f*; **inflationary** [ɪn'fleɪʃnərɪ]
adj inflazionistico(a)

inflict [ɪn'flɪkt] *vt*: **to ~ on** infliggere a

influence ['ɪnfluəns] *n* influenza ♦ *vt*
influenzare; **under the ~ of alcohol**
sotto l'effetto dell'alcool

influential [ɪnflu'ɛnʃl] *adj* influente

influenza [ɪnflu'ɛnzə] *n* (*MED*)
influenza

influx ['ɪnflʌks] *n* afflusso

inform [ɪn'fɔ:m] *vt*: **to ~ sb (of)**
informare qn (di) ♦ *vi*: **to ~ on sb**
denunciare qn

informal [ɪn'fɔ:ml] *adj* informale;
(*announcement, invitation*) non ufficiale;
~**ity** [-'mælɪtɪ] *n* informalità; carattere
m non ufficiale

informant [ɪn'fɔ:mənt] *n*
informatore/trice

information [ɪnfə'meɪʃən] *n*
informazioni *fpl*; particolari *mpl*; **a
piece of ~** un'informazione; ~ **desk** *n*

banco m informazioni inv; ~ **office** n ufficio m informazioni inv

informative [ɪnˈfɔːmətɪv] adj istruttivo(a)

informer [ɪnˈfɔːməˀ] n (also: police ~) informatore/trice

infringe [ɪnˈfrɪndʒ] vt infrangere ♦ vi: **to ~ on** calpestare; ~**ment** n infrazione f

infuriating [ɪnˈfjuərieɪtɪŋ] adj molto irritante

ingenious [ɪnˈdʒiːnjəs] adj ingegnoso(a)

ingenuity [ɪndʒɪˈnjuːɪtɪ] n ingegnosità f

ingenuous [ɪnˈdʒɛnjuəs] adj ingenuo(a)

ingot [ˈɪŋgət] n lingotto

ingrained [ɪnˈgreɪnd] adj radicato(a)

ingratiate [ɪnˈgreɪʃieɪt] vt: **to ~ o.s. with sb** ingraziarsi qn

ingredient [ɪnˈgriːdiənt] n ingrediente m; elemento

inhabit [ɪnˈhæbɪt] vt abitare

inhabitant [ɪnˈhæbɪtnt] n abitante m/f

inhale [ɪnˈheɪl] vt inalare ♦ vi (in smoking) aspirare

inherent [ɪnˈhɪərənt] adj: ~ (**in** or **to**) inerente (a)

inherit [ɪnˈhɛrɪt] vt ereditare; ~**ance** n eredità f

inhibit [ɪnˈhɪbɪt] vt (PSYCH) inibire; ~**ion** [-ˈbɪʃən] n inibizione f

inhospitable [ɪnhɔsˈpɪtəbl] adj inospitale

inhuman [ɪnˈhjuːmən] adj inumano(a)

initial [ɪˈnɪʃl] adj iniziale ♦ n iniziale f ♦ vt siglare; ~**s** npl (of name) iniziali fpl; (as signature) sigla; ~**ly** adv inizialmente, all'inizio

initiate [ɪˈnɪʃieɪt] vt (start) avviare; intraprendere; iniziare; (person) iniziare; **to ~ sb into a secret** mettere qn a parte di un segreto; **to ~ proceedings against sb** (LAW) intentare causa contro qn

initiative [ɪˈnɪʃətɪv] n iniziativa f

inject [ɪnˈdʒɛkt] vt (liquid) iniettare;

(patient): **to ~ sb with sth** fare a qn un'iniezione di qc; (funds) immettere; ~**ion** [ɪnˈdʒɛkʃən] n iniezione f, puntura

injure [ˈɪndʒəˀ] vt ferire; (damage: reputation etc) nuocere a; ~**d** adj ferito(a)

injury [ˈɪndʒərɪ] n ferita f; ~ **time** n (SPORT) tempo di recupero

injustice [ɪnˈdʒʌstɪs] n ingiustizia f

ink [ɪŋk] n inchiostro

inkling [ˈɪŋklɪŋ] n sentore m, vaga idea

inlaid [ˈɪnleɪd] adj incrostato(a); (table etc) intarsiato(a)

inland [adj ˈɪnlənd, adv ɪnˈlænd] adj interno(a), interiore ♦ adv all'interno; **I~ Revenue** (BRIT) n Fisco

in-laws [ˈɪnlɔːz] npl suoceri mpl; famiglia del marito (o della moglie)

inlet [ˈɪnlɛt] n (GEO) insenatura, baia

inmate [ˈɪnmeɪt] n (in prison) carcerato/a; (in asylum) ricoverato/a

inn [ɪn] n locanda

innate [ɪˈneɪt] adj innato(a)

inner [ˈɪnəˀ] adj interno(a), interiore; ~ **city** n centro di una zona urbana; ~ **tube** n camera d'aria

innings [ˈɪnɪŋz] n (CRICKET) turno di battuta

innocence [ˈɪnəsns] n innocenza

innocent [ˈɪnəsnt] adj innocente

innocuous [ɪˈnɔkjuəs] adj innocuo(a)

innuendo [ɪnjuˈɛndəu] (pl ~**es**) n insinuazione f

innumerable [ɪˈnjuːmrəbl] adj innumerevole

in-patient [ˈɪnpeɪʃənt] n ricoverato/a

input [ˈɪnput] n input m

inquest [ˈɪnkwɛst] n inchiesta

inquire [ɪnˈkwaɪəˀ] vi informarsi ♦ vt domandare, informarsi su; ~ **about** vt fus informarsi di or su; ~ **into** vt fus fare indagini su; ~**ry** n domanda; (LAW) indagine f, investigazione f; "**inquiries**" "informazioni"; **inquiry office** (BRIT) n ufficio m informazioni inv

inquisitive [ɪn'kwɪzɪtɪv] *adj* curioso(a)

ins. *abbr* = **inches**

insane [ɪn'seɪn] *adj* matto(a), pazzo(a); (MED) alienato(a)

insanity [ɪn'sænɪtɪ] *n* follia; (MED) alienazione *f* mentale

inscription [ɪn'skrɪpʃən] *n* iscrizione *f*; dedica

insect ['ɪnsekt] *n* insetto; **~icide** [ɪn'sektɪsaɪd] *n* insetticida *m*; **~ repellent** *n* insettifugo

insecure [ɪnsɪ'kjuə*] *adj* malsicuro(a); (person) insicuro(a)

insemination [ɪnsemɪ'neɪʃən] *n*: **artificial ~** fecondazione *f* artificiale

insensible [ɪn'sensɪbl] *adj* (unconscious) privo(a) di sensi

insensitive [ɪn'sensɪtɪv] *adj* insensibile

insert [ɪn'sə:t] *vt* inserire, introdurre; **~ion** [ɪn'sə:ʃən] *n* inserzione *f*

in-service *adj* (training, course) durante l'orario di lavoro

inshore [ɪn'ʃɔ:*] *adj* costiero(a) ♦ *adv* presso la riva; verso la riva

inside ['ɪn'saɪd] *n* interno, parte *f* interiore ♦ *adj* interno(a), interiore ♦ *adv* dentro, all'interno ♦ *prep* dentro, all'interno di; (of time): **~ 10 minutes** entro 10 minuti; **~s** *npl* (inf: stomach) ventre *m*; **~ forward** *n* (SPORT) mezzala, interno; **~ lane** *n* (AUT) corsia di marcia; **~ out** *adv* (turn) a rovescio; (know) in fondo

insider dealing [ɪn'saɪdə'di:lɪŋ] *n* insider dealing *m inv*

insider trading [ɪn'saɪdə'treɪdɪŋ] *n* insider trading *m inv*

insight ['ɪnsaɪt] *n* acume *m*, perspicacia; (glimpse, idea) percezione *f*

insignia [ɪn'sɪgnɪə] *npl* insegne *fpl*

insignificant [ɪnsɪg'nɪfɪkənt] *adj* insignificante

insincere [ɪnsɪn'sɪə*] *adj* insincero(a)

insinuate [ɪn'sɪnjueɪt] *vt* insinuare

insist [ɪn'sɪst] *vi* insistere; **to ~ on doing** insistere per fare; **to ~ that** insistere perché + *sub*; (claim)

sostenere che; **~ent** *adj* insistente

insole ['ɪnsəul] *n* soletta

insolent ['ɪnsələnt] *adj* insolente

insomnia [ɪn'sɒmnɪə] *n* insonnia

inspect [ɪn'spekt] *vt* ispezionare; (BRIT: ticket) controllare; **~ion** [ɪn'spekʃən] *n* ispezione *f*; controllo; **~or** *n* ispettore/trice; (BRIT: on buses, trains) controllore *m*

inspire [ɪn'spaɪə*] *vt* ispirare

install [ɪn'stɔ:l] *vt* installare; **~ation** [ɪnstə'leɪʃən] *n* installazione *f*

instalment [ɪn'stɔ:lmənt] (US **installment**) *n* rata; (of TV serial etc) puntata; **in ~s** (pay) a rate; (receive) una parte per volta; (: publication) a fascicoli

instance ['ɪnstəns] *n* esempio, caso; **for ~** per or ad esempio; **in the first ~** in primo luogo

instant ['ɪnstənt] *n* istante *m*, attimo ♦ *adj* immediato(a); urgente; (coffee, food) in polvere; **~ly** *adv* immediatamente, subito

instead [ɪn'sted] *adv* invece; **~ of** invece di

instep ['ɪnstep] *n* collo del piede; (of shoe) collo della scarpa

instil [ɪn'stɪl] *vt*: **to ~ (into)** inculcare (in)

instinct ['ɪnstɪŋkt] *n* istinto

institute ['ɪnstɪtjuːt] *n* istituto ♦ *vt* istituire, stabilire; (inquiry) avviare; (proceedings) iniziare

institution [ɪnstɪ'tjuːʃən] *n* istituzione *f*; (educational ~, mental ~) istituto

instruct [ɪn'strʌkt] *vt*: **to ~ sb in sth** insegnare qc a qn; **to ~ sb to do** dare ordini a qn di fare; **~ion** [ɪn'strʌkʃən] *n* istruzione *f*; **~ions (for use)** istruzioni per l'uso; **~or** *n* istruttore/trice; (for skiing) maestro/a

instrument ['ɪnstrəmənt] *n* strumento; **~al** [-'mentl] *adj* (MUS) strumentale; **to be ~al in** essere d'aiuto in; **~ panel** *n* quadro *m* portastrumenti *inv*

insufferable [ɪn'sʌfərəbl] *adj* insopportabile

insufficient [ɪnsə'fɪʃənt] *adj* insufficiente

insular ['ɪnsjulə*] *adj* insulare; (*person*) di mente ristretta

insulate ['ɪnsjuleɪt] *vt* isolare; **insulation** [-'leɪʃən] *n* isolamento

insulin ['ɪnsjulɪn] *n* insulina

insult [*n* 'ɪnsʌlt, *vb* ɪn'sʌlt] *n* insulto, affronto ♦ *vt* insultare; **~ing** *adj* offensivo(a), ingiurioso(a)

insuperable [ɪn'sjuːprəbl] *adj* insormontabile, insuperabile

insurance [ɪn'ʃuərəns] *n* assicurazione f; **fire/life** ~ assicurazione contro gli incendi/sulla vita; ~ **policy** n polizza d'assicurazione

insure [ɪn'ʃuə*] *vt* assicurare

intact [ɪn'tækt] *adj* intatto(a)

intake ['ɪnteɪk] *n* (*TECH*) immissione f; (*of food*) consumo; (*BRIT: of pupils etc*) afflusso

integral ['ɪntɪɡrəl] *adj* integrale; (*part*) integrante

integrate ['ɪntɪɡreɪt] *vt* integrare ♦ *vi* integrarsi

integrity [ɪn'tɛɡrɪtɪ] *n* integrità

intellect ['ɪntɪlekt] *n* intelletto; **~ual** [-'lektjuəl] *adj, n* intellettuale *m/f*

intelligence [ɪn'telɪdʒəns] *n* intelligenza; (*MIL etc*) informazioni *fpl*; ~ **service** *n* servizio segreto

intelligent [ɪn'telɪdʒənt] *adj* intelligente

intend [ɪn'tend] *vt* (*gift etc*): **to** ~ **sth for** destinare qc a; **to** ~ **to do** aver l'intenzione di fare; **~ed** *adj* (*effect*) voluto(a)

intense [ɪn'tens] *adj* intenso(a); (*person*) di forti sentimenti; **~ly** *adv* intensamente; profondamente

intensive [ɪn'tensɪv] *adj* intensivo(a); ~ **care unit** *n* reparto terapia intensiva

intent [ɪn'tent] *n* intenzione f ♦ *adj*: ~ (**on**) intento(a), immerso(a) (in); **to all** ~**s and purposes** a tutti gli

effetti; **to be** ~ **on doing sth** essere deciso a fare qc

intention [ɪn'tenʃən] *n* intenzione f; ~**al** *adj* intenzionale, deliberato(a); ~**ally** *adv* apposta

intently [ɪn'tentlɪ] *adv* attentamente

interact [ɪntər'ækt] *vi* interagire

interactive *adj* (*COMPUT*) interattivo(a)

interchange [*n* 'ɪntətʃeɪndʒ] *n* (*exchange*) scambio; (*on motorway*) incrocio pluridirezionale; ~**able** [-'tʃeɪndʒəbl] *adj* intercambiabile

intercom ['ɪntəkɔm] *n* interfono

intercourse ['ɪntəkɔːs] *n* rapporti *mpl*

interest ['ɪntrɪst] *n* interesse *m*; (*COMM: stake, share*) interessi *mpl* ♦ *vt* interessare; ~**ed** *adj* interessato(a); **to be** ~**ed in** interessarsi di; ~**ing** *adj* interessante; ~ **rate** *n* tasso di interesse

interface ['ɪntəfeɪs] *n* (*COMPUT*) interfaccia

interfere [ɪntə'fɪə*] *vi*: **to** ~ **in** (*quarrel, other people's business*) immischiarsi in; **to** ~ **with** (*object*) toccare; (*plans, duty*) interferire con

interference [ɪntə'fɪərəns] *n* interferenza

interim ['ɪntərɪm] *adj* provvisorio(a) ♦ *n*: **in the** ~ nel frattempo

interior [ɪn'tɪərɪə*] *n* interno; (*of country*) degli entroterra ♦ *adj* interno(a); (*minister*) degli Interni; ~ **designer** *n* arredatore/trice

interlock [ɪntə'lɔk] *vi* ingranarsi

interlude ['ɪntəluːd] *n* intervallo; (*THEATRE*) intermezzo

intermediate [ɪntə'miːdɪət] *adj* intermedio(a)

intermission [ɪntə'mɪʃən] *n* pausa; (*THEATRE, CINEMA*) intermissione f, intervallo

intern [*vb* ɪn'tɜːn, *n* 'ɪntɜːn] *vt* internare ♦ *n* (*US*) medico interno

internal [ɪn'tɜːnl] *adj* interno(a); ~**ly** *adv*: "**not to be taken** ~**ly**" "per uso esterno"; **I~ Revenue Service** (*US*) *n* Fisco

international [ɪntəˈnæʃənl] *adj*
internazionale ♦ *n* (BRIT: SPORT) incontro
internazionale

Internet [ˈɪntənɛt] *n*: **the ~** Internet *f*;
~ café *n* cybercaffè *m inv*

interplay [ˈɪntəpleɪ] *n* azione e
reazione *f*

interpret [ɪnˈtəːprɪt] *vt* interpretare
♦ *vi* fare da interprete; **~er** *n* interprete
m/f

interrogate [ɪnˈtɛrəgeɪt] *vt*
interrogare; **interrogation** [-ˈgeɪʃən] *n*
interrogazione *f*; (of suspect etc)
interrogatorio

interrupt [ɪntəˈrʌpt] *vt, vi*
interrompere; **~ion** [-ˈrʌpʃən] *n*
interruzione *f*

intersect [ɪntəˈsɛkt] *vi* (roads)
incrociarsi; **~ion** [-ˈsɛkʃən] *n*
intersezione *f*; (of roads) incrocio

intersperse [ɪntəˈspəːs] *vt*: **to ~ with**
costellare di

intertwine [ɪntəˈtwaɪn] *vi* intrecciarsi

interval [ˈɪntəvl] *n* intervallo; **at ~s** a
intervalli

intervene [ɪntəˈviːn] *vi* (time)
intercorrere; (event, person) intervenire;
intervention [-ˈvɛnʃən] *n* intervento

interview [ˈɪntəvjuː] *n* (RADIO, TV etc)
intervista; (for job) colloquio ♦ *vt*
intervistare; avere un colloquio con;
~er *n* intervistatore/trice

intestine [ɪnˈtɛstɪn] *n* intestino

intimacy [ˈɪntɪməsɪ] *n* intimità

intimate [adj ˈɪntɪmət, vb ˈɪntɪmeɪt]
adj intimo(a); (knowledge) profondo(a)
♦ *vt* lasciar capire

into [ˈɪntuː] *prep* dentro, in; **come
~ the house** entra in casa; **he
worked late ~ the night** lavorò fino
a tarda notte; **~ Italian** in italiano

intolerable [ɪnˈtɔlərəbl] *adj*
intollerabile

intolerance [ɪnˈtɔlərns] *n* intolleranza

intolerant [ɪnˈtɔlərnt] *adj*: **~ of**
intollerante di

intoxicated [ɪnˈtɔksɪkeɪtɪd] *adj*

inebriato(a)

intractable [ɪnˈtræktəbl] *adj*
intrattabile

intranet [ˈɪntrənɛt] *n* intranet *f*

intransitive [ɪnˈtrænsɪtɪv] *adj*
intransitivo(a)

intravenous [ɪntrəˈviːnəs] *adj*
endovenoso(a)

in-tray *n* contenitore *m* per la
corrispondenza in arrivo

intricate [ˈɪntrɪkət] *adj* intricato(a),
complicato(a)

intrigue [ɪnˈtriːg] *n* intrigo ♦ *vt*
affascinare; **intriguing** *adj* affascinante

intrinsic [ɪnˈtrɪnsɪk] *adj* intrinseco(a)

introduce [ɪntrəˈdjuːs] *vt* introdurre;
to ~ sb (to sb) presentare qn (a qn);
to ~ sb to (pastime, technique) iniziare
qn a; **introduction** [-ˈdʌkʃən] *n* introduzione *f*; (of person) presentazione *f*;
(to new experience) iniziazione *f*;
introductory *adj* introduttivo(a)

intrude [ɪnˈtruːd] *vi* (person): **to ~ (on)**
intromettersi (in); **~r** *n* intruso/a

intuition [ɪntjuːˈɪʃən] *n* intuizione *f*

inundate [ˈɪnʌndeɪt] *vt*: **to ~ with**
inondare di

invade [ɪnˈveɪd] *vt* invadere

invalid [*n* ˈɪnvəlɪd, *adj* ɪnˈvælɪd] *n*
malato/a; (with disability) invalido/a
♦ *adj* (not valid) invalido(a), non
valido(a)

invaluable [ɪnˈvæljuəbl] *adj*
prezioso(a); inestimabile

invariably [ɪnˈvɛərɪəblɪ] *adv*
invariabilmente; sempre

invasion [ɪnˈveɪʒən] *n* invasione *f*

invent [ɪnˈvɛnt] *vt* inventare; **~ion**
[ɪnˈvɛnʃən] *n* invenzione *f*; **~ive** *adj*
inventivo(a); **~or** *n* inventore *m*

inventory [ˈɪnvəntrɪ] *n* inventario

invert [ɪnˈvəːt] *vt* invertire; (cup, object)
rovesciare; **~ed commas** (BRIT) *npl*
virgolette *fpl*

invest [ɪnˈvɛst] *vt* investire ♦ *vi*: **to
~ (in)** investire (in)

investigate [ɪnˈvɛstɪgeɪt] *vt*

investigare, indagare; (crime) fare indagini su; **investigation** [-'geɪʃən] n investigazione f; (of crime) indagine f

investment [ɪn'vɛstmənt] n investimento

investor [ɪn'vɛstə*] n investitore/trice; azionista m/f

invidious [ɪn'vɪdɪəs] adj odioso(a); (task) spiacevole

invigilator [ɪn'vɪdʒɪleɪtə*] n (in exam) sorvegliante m/f

invigorating [ɪn'vɪgəreɪtɪŋ] adj stimolante; vivificante

invisible [ɪn'vɪzɪbl] adj invisibile

invitation [ɪnvɪ'teɪʃən] n invito

invite [ɪn'vaɪt] vt invitare; (opinions etc) sollecitare; **inviting** adj invitante, attraente

invoice ['ɪnvɔɪs] n fattura ♦ vt fatturare

involuntary [ɪn'vɔləntrɪ] adj involontario(a)

involve [ɪn'vɔlv] vt (entail) richiedere, comportare; (associate): **to ~ sb (in)** implicare qn (in); coinvolgere qn (in); **~d** adj involuto(a), complesso(a); **to be ~d in** essere coinvolto(a) in; **~ment** n implicazione f; coinvolgimento

inward ['ɪnwəd] adj (movement) verso l'interno; (thought, feeling) interiore, intimo(a); **~(s)** adv verso l'interno

I/O abbr (COMPUT: = input/output) I/O

iodine ['aɪəʊdiːn] n iodio

ioniser ['aɪənaɪzə*] n ionizzatore m

iota [aɪ'əʊtə] n (fig) briciolo

IOU n abbr (= I owe you) pagherò m inv

IQ n abbr (= intelligence quotient) quoziente m d'intelligenza

IRA n abbr (= Irish Republican Army) IRA f

Iran [ɪ'rɑːn] n Iran m; **~ian** adj, n iraniano(a)

Iraq [ɪ'rɑːk] n Iraq m; **~i** adj, n iracheno(a)

irate [aɪ'reɪt] adj adirato(a)

Ireland ['aɪələnd] n Irlanda

iris ['aɪrɪs] (pl **~es**) n iride f; (BOT) giaggiolo, iride

Irish ['aɪrɪʃ] adj irlandese ♦ npl: **the ~** gli Irlandesi; **~man** (irreg) n irlandese m; **~ Sea** n Mar m d'Irlanda; **~woman** (irreg) n irlandese f

irksome ['əːksəm] adj seccante

iron ['aɪən] n ferro; (for clothes) ferro da stiro ♦ adj di o in ferro ♦ vt (clothes) stirare; **~ out** vt (crease) appianare; (fig) spianare; far sparire

ironic(al) [aɪ'rɔnɪk(l)] adj ironico(a)

ironing ['aɪənɪŋ] n (activity) stirare m; (clothes) roba da stirare; **~ board** n asse f da stiro

ironmonger's (shop) ['aɪənmʌŋgəz-] (BRIT) n negozio di ferramenta

irony ['aɪrənɪ] n ironia

irrational [ɪ'ræʃənl] adj irrazionale

irregular [ɪ'regjulə*] adj irregolare

irrelevant [ɪ'reləvənt] adj non pertinente

irreplaceable [ɪrɪ'pleɪsəbl] adj insostituibile

irrepressible [ɪrɪ'presəbl] adj irrefrenabile

irresistible [ɪrɪ'zɪstɪbl] adj irresistibile

irrespective [ɪrɪ'spektɪv]: **~ of** prep senza riguardo a

irresponsible [ɪrɪ'spɔnsɪbl] adj irresponsabile

irrigate ['ɪrɪgeɪt] vt irrigare; **irrigation** [-'geɪʃən] n irrigazione f

irritable ['ɪrɪtəbl] adj irritabile

irritate ['ɪrɪteɪt] vt irritare; **irritating** adj (person, sound etc) irritante; **irritation** [-'teɪʃən] n irritazione f

IRS (US) n abbr = **Internal Revenue Service**

is [ɪz] vb see **be**

Islam ['ɪzlɑːm] n Islam m

island ['aɪlənd] n isola; **~er** n isolano/a

isle [aɪl] n isola

isn't ['ɪznt] = **is not**

isolate ['aɪsəleɪt] vt isolare; **~d** adj isolato(a); **isolation** [-'leɪʃən] n isolamento

ISP n abbr (= Internet Service Provider) provider m inv

Israel ['izreil] n Israele m; **~i** [iz'reili] adj, n israeliano(a)

issue ['iʃju:] n questione f, problema m; (of banknotes etc) emissione f; (of newspaper etc) numero ♦ vt (statement) rilasciare; (rations, equipment) distribuire; (book) pubblicare; (banknotes, cheques, stamps) emettere; **at ~** in gioco, in discussione; **to take ~ with sb (over sth)** prendere posizione contro qn (riguardo a qc); **to make an ~ of sth** fare un problema di qc

---

KEYWORD

---

it [it] pron 1 (specific: subject) esso(a); (: direct object) lo(la), l'; (: indirect object) gli(le); **where's my book?** — **~'s on the table** dov'è il mio libro? — è sulla tavola; **I can't find ~** non lo (or la) trovo; **give ~ to me** dammelo (or dammela); **did you learn from ~?** ne hai tratto?; **I'm proud of ~** ne sono fiero; **did you go to ~?** ci sei andato?; **put the book in ~** mettici il libro

2 (impers): **~'s raining** piove; **~'s Friday tomorrow** domani è venerdì; **~'s 6 o'clock** sono le 6; **who is ~?** — **~'s me** chi è? — sono io

Italian [i'tæljən] adj italiano(a) ♦ n italiano/a; (LING) italiano; **the ~s** gli Italiani

italics [i'tæliks] npl corsivo

Italy ['itəli] n Italia f

itch [itʃ] n prurito ♦ vi (person) avere il prurito; (part of body) prudere; **to ~ to do sth** aver una gran voglia di fare qc; **~y** adj che prude; **to be ~y** = to ~

it'd ['itd] = **it would; it had**

item ['aitəm] n articolo; (on agenda) punto; (also: news ~) notizia; **~ize** vt specificare, dettagliare

itinerant [i'tinərənt] adj ambulante

itinerary [ai'tinərəri] n itinerario

it'll ['itl] = **it will; it shall**

its [its] adj il(la) suo(a), i(le) suoi(sue)

it's [its] = **it is; it has**

itself [it'self] pron (emphatic) esso(a) stesso(a); (reflexive) si

ITV (BRIT) n abbr (= Independent Television) rete televisiva in concorrenza con la BBC

I.U.D. n abbr (= intra-uterine device) spirale f

I've [aiv] = **I have**

ivory ['aivəri] n avorio

ivy ['aivi] n edera

J, j

jab [dʒæb] vt dare colpetti a ♦ n (MED: inf) puntura; **to ~ sth into** affondare or piantare qc dentro

jack [dʒæk] n (AUT) cricco; (CARDS) fante m; **~ up** vt sollevare col cricco

jackal ['dʒækl] n sciacallo

jackdaw ['dʒækdɔ:] n taccola

jacket ['dʒækit] n giacca; (of book) copertura

jack-knife vi: **the lorry ~d** l'autotreno si è piegato su se stesso

jack plug n (ELEC) jack m inv

jackpot ['dʒækpɔt] n primo premio (in denaro)

jade [dʒeid] n (stone) giada

jaded ['dʒeidid] adj sfinito(a), spossato(a)

jagged ['dʒægid] adj seghettato(a); (cliffs etc) frastagliato(a)

jail [dʒeil] n prigione f ♦ vt mandare in prigione

jam [dʒæm] n marmellata; (also: traffic ~) ingorgo; (inf) pasticcio ♦ vt (passage etc) ingombrare, ostacolare; (mechanism, drawer etc) bloccare; (RADIO) disturbare con interferenze ♦ vi incepparsi; **to ~ sth into** forzare qc dentro; infilare qc a forza dentro

Jamaica [dʒə'meɪkə] n Giamaica

jangle ['dʒæŋgl] vi risuonare; (bracelet) tintinnare

janitor ['dʒænɪtə*] n (caretaker) portiere m; (: SCOL) bidello

January ['dʒænjuərɪ] n gennaio

Japan [dʒə'pæn] n Giappone m; **~ese** [dʒæpə'niːz] adj giapponese ♦ n inv giapponese m/f; (LING) giapponese m

jar [dʒɑː*] n (glass) barattolo, vasetto ♦ vi (sound) stridere; (colours etc) stonare

jargon ['dʒɑːgən] n gergo

jasmin(e) ['dʒæzmɪn] n gelsomino

jaundice ['dʒɔːndɪs] n itterizia

jaunt [dʒɔːnt] n gita

javelin ['dʒævlɪn] n giavellotto

jaw [dʒɔː] n mascella

jay [dʒeɪ] n ghiandaia

jaywalker ['dʒeɪwɔːkə*] n pedone(a) indisciplinato(a)

jazz [dʒæz] n jazz m; **~ up** vt rendere vivace

jealous ['dʒeləs] adj geloso(a); **~y** n gelosia

jeans [dʒiːnz] npl (blue-)jeans mpl

jeer [dʒɪə*] vi: **to ~ (at)** fischiare; beffeggiare

jelly ['dʒelɪ] n gelatina; **~fish** n medusa

jeopardy ['dʒepədɪ] n: **in ~** in pericolo

jerk [dʒɜːk] n sobbalzo, scossa; sussulto; (inf: idiot) tonto/a ♦ vt dare una scossa a ♦ vi (vehicles) sobbalzare

jersey ['dʒɜːzɪ] n maglia; (fabric) jersey m

jest [dʒest] n scherzo

Jesus ['dʒiːzəs] n Gesù m

jet [dʒet] n (of gas, liquid) getto; (AVIAT) aviogetto; **~-black** adj nero(a) come l'ebano, corvino(a); **~ engine** n motore m a reazione; **~ lag** n (problemi mpl dovuti allo) sbalzo dei fusi orari

jettison ['dʒetɪsn] vt gettare in mare

jetty ['dʒetɪ] n molo

Jew [dʒuː] n ebreo

jewel ['dʒuːəl] n gioiello; **~ler** (US **~er**) n orefice m, gioielliere/a; **~(l)er's (shop)** n oreficeria, gioielleria; **~lery** (US **~ery**) n gioielli mpl

Jewess ['dʒuːɪs] n ebrea

Jewish ['dʒuːɪʃ] adj ebreo(a), ebraico(a)

jibe [dʒaɪb] n beffa

jiffy ['dʒɪfɪ] (inf) n: **in a ~** in un batter d'occhio

jig [dʒɪg] n giga

jigsaw ['dʒɪgsɔː] n (also: ~ puzzle) puzzle m inv

jilt [dʒɪlt] vt piantare in asso

jingle ['dʒɪŋgl] n (for advert) sigla pubblicitaria ♦ vi tintinnare, scampanellare

jinx [dʒɪŋks] n iettatura; (person) iettatore/trice

jitters ['dʒɪtəz] (inf) npl: **to get the ~** aver fifa

job [dʒɔb] n lavoro; (employment) impiego, posto; **it's not my ~** (duty) non è compito mio; **it's a good ~ that ...** meno male che ...; **just the ~!** proprio quello che ci vuole; **~ centre** (BRIT) n ufficio di collocamento; **~less** adj senza lavoro, disoccupato(a)

jockey ['dʒɔkɪ] n fantino, jockey m inv ♦ vi: **to ~ for position** manovrare per una posizione di vantaggio

jog [dʒɔg] vt urtare ♦ vi (SPORT) fare footing, fare jogging; **to ~ sb's memory** rinfrescare la memoria a qn; **to ~ along** trottare; (fig) andare avanti piano piano; **~ging** n footing m, jogging m

join [dʒɔɪn] vt unire, congiungere; (become member of) iscriversi a; (meet) raggiungere; riunirsi a ♦ vi (roads, rivers) confluire ♦ n giuntura; **~ in** vi partecipare ♦ vt fus unirsi a; **~ up** vi incontrarsi; (MIL) arruolarsi

joiner ['dʒɔɪnə*] (BRIT) n falegname m

joint [dʒɔɪnt] n (TECH) giunto; giunto; (ANAT) articolazione f, giuntura; (BRIT: CULIN) arrosto; (inf: place) locale m; (: of

cannabis) spinello ♦ adj comune;
~ **account** n (at bank etc) conto in
partecipazione, conto comune

joist [dʒɔɪst] n trave f

joke [dʒəuk] n scherzo; (funny story)
barzelletta; (also: practical ~) beffa ♦ vi
scherzare; **to play a ~ on sb** fare uno
scherzo a qn; **~r** n (CARDS) matta, jolly
m inv

jolly ['dʒɔlɪ] adj allegro(a), gioioso(a)
♦ adv (BRIT: inf) veramente, proprio

jolt [dʒəult] n scossa, sobbalzo ♦ vt
urtare

Jordan ['dʒɔːdən] n (country)
Giordania; (river) Giordano

jostle ['dʒɔsl] vt spingere coi gomiti

jot [dʒɔt] n: **not one** ~ nemmeno un
po'; ~ **down** vt annotare in fretta,
buttare giù; **~ter** n (BRIT) n blocco

journal ['dʒɜːnl] n giornale m; rivista;
diario; **~ism** n giornalismo; **~ist** n
giornalista m/f

journey ['dʒɜːnɪ] n viaggio; (distance
covered) tragitto

joy [dʒɔɪ] n gioia; **~ful** adj gioioso(a),
allegro(a); **~rider** n chi ruba un'auto
per farvi un giro; **~stick** n (AVIAT) barra
di comando; (COMPUT) joystick m inv

JP n abbr = **Justice of the Peace**

Jr abbr = **junior**

jubilant ['dʒuːbɪlnt] adj giubilante;
trionfante

jubilee ['dʒuːbɪliː] n giubileo; **silver** ~
venticinquesimo anniversario

judge [dʒʌdʒ] n giudice m/f ♦ vt
giudicare; (gu)**ement** n giudizio

judiciary [dʒuː'dɪʃərɪ] n magistratura

judo ['dʒuːdəu] n judo

jug [dʒʌɡ] n brocca, bricco

juggernaut ['dʒʌɡənɔːt] n (huge
truck) bestione m

juggle ['dʒʌɡl] vi fare giochi di
destrezza; **~r** n giocoliere/a

juice [dʒuːs] n succo

juicy ['dʒuːsɪ] adj succoso(a)

jukebox ['dʒuːkbɔks] n juke-box m
inv

July [dʒuː'laɪ] n luglio

jumble ['dʒʌmbl] n miscuglio ♦ vt
(also: ~ **up**) mischiare; ~ **sale** (BRIT) n
vendita di beneficenza

---

jumble sale

Una **jumble sale** è un mercatino di
oggetti di seconda mano organizzato
in chiese, scuole o in circoli ricreativi,
i cui proventi vengono devoluti in
beneficenza.

---

jumbo (jet) ['dʒʌmbəu-] n jumbo-jet
m inv

jump [dʒʌmp] vi saltare, balzare; (start)
sobbalzare; (increase) rincarare ♦ vt
saltare ♦ n salto; balzo; sobbalzo

jumper ['dʒʌmpə*] n (BRIT: pullover)
maglione m, pullover m inv; (US: dress)
scamiciato; ~ **cables** (US) npl = **jump
leads**

jump leads (BRIT) npl cavi mpl per
batteria

jumpy ['dʒʌmpɪ] adj nervoso(a),
agitato(a)

Jun. abbr = **junior**

junction ['dʒʌŋkʃən] n (BRIT: of roads)
incrocio; (of rails) nodo ferroviario

juncture ['dʒʌŋktʃə*] n: **at this** ~ in
questa congiuntura

June [dʒuːn] n giugno

jungle ['dʒʌŋgl] n giungla

junior ['dʒuːnɪə*] adj, n: **he's** ~ **to me
(by 2 years), he's my** ~ **(by 2
years)** è più giovane di me (di 2 anni);
he's ~ **to me** (seniority) è al di sotto
di me, ho più anzianità di lui;
~ **school** (BRIT) n scuola elementare
(da 8 a 11 anni)

junk [dʒʌŋk] n cianfrusaglie fpl; (cheap
goods) robaccia; ~ **food** n porcherie fpl

junkie ['dʒʌŋkɪ] (inf) n drogato/a

junk mail n stampe fpl pubblicitarie

junk shop n chincaglieria

Junr abbr = **junior**

juror ['dʒuərə*] n giurato/a

jury ['dʒuərɪ] n giuria

just [dʒʌst] *adj* giusto(a) ♦ *adv*: **he's ~ right/left** lo ha appena fatto/è appena partito; **~ right** proprio giusto; **~ 2 o'clock** le 2 precise; **she's ~ as clever as you is** in gamba proprio male tu; **it's ~ as well that ...** meno male che ...; **~ as I arrived** proprio mentre arrivavo; **it was ~ before/enough/here** era poco prima/appena assai/proprio qui; **it's ~ me** sono solo io; **~ missed/caught** appena perso/preso; **~ listen to this!** senta un po' questo!

justice ['dʒʌstɪs] *n* giustizia; **J~ of the Peace** *n* giudice *m* conciliatore

justify ['dʒʌstɪfaɪ] *vt* giustificare

jut [dʒʌt] *vi* (*also*: **~ out**) sporgersi

juvenile ['dʒuːvənaɪl] *adj* giovane, giovanile; (*court*) dei minorenni; (*books*) per ragazzi ♦ *n* giovane *m/f*, minorenne *m/f*

juxtapose ['dʒʌkstəpəʊz] *vt* giustapporre

K, k

K *abbr* (= *one thousand*) mille; (= *kilobyte*) K

Kampuchea [kæmpʊ'tʃɪə] *n* Cambogia

kangaroo [kæŋgə'ruː] *n* canguro

karate [kə'rɑːtɪ] *n* karatè *m*

kebab [kə'bæb] *n* spiedino

keel [kiːl] *n* chiglia; **on an even ~** (*fig*) in uno stato normale

keen [kiːn] *adj* (*interest, desire*) vivo(a); (*eye, intelligence*) acuto(a); (*competition*) serrato(a); (*edge*) affilato(a); (*eager*) entusiasta; **to be ~ to do** *or* **on doing sth** avere una gran voglia di fare qc; **to be ~ on sth** essere appassionato(a) di qc; **to be ~ on sb** avere un debole per qn

keep [kiːp] (*pt, pp* **kept**) *vt* tenere; (*hold back*) trattenere; (*feed: one's family etc*) mantenere, sostentare; (*a promise*) mantenere; (*chickens, bees, pigs etc*) allevare ♦ *vi* (*food*) mantenersi; (*remain: in a certain state or place*) restare ♦ *n* (*of castle*) maschio; (*food etc*): **enough for his ~** abbastanza per vitto e alloggio; (*inf*): **for ~s** per sempre; **to ~ doing sth** continuare a fare qc; fare qc di continuo; **to ~ sb from doing** impedire a qn di fare; **to ~ sb busy/a place tidy** tenere qn occupato(a)/un luogo in ordine; **to ~ sth to o.s.** tenere qc per sé; **to ~ sth (back) from sb** celare qc a qn; **to ~ time** (*clock*) andar bene; **~ on** *vi*: **to ~ on doing** continuare a fare; **to ~ on (about sth)** continuare a insistere (su qc); **~ out** *vt* tener fuori; **"~ out"** "vietato l'accesso"; **~ up** *vt* continuare, mantenere ♦ *vi*: **to ~ up with** tener dietro a, andare di pari passo con; (*work etc*) farcela a seguire; **~er** *n* custode *m/f*, guardiano/a; **~-fit** *n* ginnastica; **~ing** *n* (*care*) custodia; **in ~ing with** in armonia con; in accordo con; **~sake** *n* ricordo

kennel ['kɛnl] *n* canile *m*; **to put a dog in ~s** mettere un cane al canile

kept [kɛpt] *pt, pp of* **keep**

kerb [kɜːb] (*BRIT*) *n* orlo del marciapiede

kernel ['kɜːnl] *n* nocciolo

kettle ['kɛtl] *n* bollitore *m*

kettle drum *n* timpano

key [kiː] *n* (*gen, MUS*) chiave *f*; (*of piano, typewriter*) tasto ♦ *adj* chiave *inv* ♦ *vt* (*also*: **~ in**) digitare; **~board** *n* tastiera; **~ed up** *adj* (*person*) agitato(a); **~hole** *n* buco della serratura; **~hole surgery** *n* chirurgia non invasiva; **~note** *n* (*MUS*) tonica; (*fig*) nota dominante; **~ring** *n* portachiavi *m inv*

khaki ['kɑːkɪ] *adj* cachi ♦ *n* cachi *m*

kick [kɪk] *vt* calciare, dare calci a; (*inf: habit etc*) liberarsi de ♦ *vi* (*horse*) tirar calci ♦ *n* calcio; (*thrill*): **he does it for ~s** lo fa giusto per il piacere di farlo; **~ off** *vi* (*SPORT*) dare il primo calcio

kid [kɪd] *n* (*inf: child*) ragazzino/a;

(animal, leather) capretto ♦ vi (inf) scherzare

kidnap ['kɪdnæp] vt rapire, sequestrare; **~per** n rapitore/trice; killer m inv; **~ping** n sequestro (di persona)

kidney ['kɪdnɪ] n (ANAT) rene m; (CULIN) rognone m

kill [kɪl] vt uccidere, ammazzare ♦ n uccisione f; **~er** n uccisore m, killer m inv; assassino/a; **~ing** n assassinio; to make a **~ing** (inf) fare un bel colpo; **~joy** n guastafeste m/f inv

kiln [kɪln] n forno

kilo ['kiːləʊ] n chilo; **~byte** n (COMPUT) kilobyte m inv; **~gram(me)** ['kɪləʊgræm] n chilogrammo; **~metre** ['kɪləmiːtə*] (US **~meter**) n chilometro; **~watt** ['kɪləʊwɔt] n chilowatt m inv

kilt [kɪlt] n gonnellino scozzese

kin [kɪn] n see **next**; **kith**

kind [kaɪnd] adj gentile, buono(a) ♦ n sorta, specie f; (species) genere m; to be two of a **~** essere molto simili; in **~** (COMM) in natura

kindergarten ['kɪndəgɑːtn] n giardino d'infanzia

kind-hearted [-'hɑːtɪd] adj di buon cuore

kindle ['kɪndl] vt accendere, infiammare

kindly ['kaɪndlɪ] adj pieno(a) di bontà, benevolo(a) ♦ adv con bontà, gentilmente; **will you ...** vuole ... per favore

kindness ['kaɪndnɪs] n bontà, gentilezza

king [kɪŋ] n re m inv; **~dom** n regno, reame m; **~fisher** n martin m inv pescatore; **~-size** adj super inv; gigante

kiosk ['kiːɔsk] n edicola, chiosco; (BRIT: TEL) cabina (telefonica)

kipper ['kɪpə*] n aringa affumicata

kiss [kɪs] n bacio ♦ vt baciare; to **~ (each other)** baciarsi; **~ of life** n respirazione f bocca a bocca

kit [kɪt] n equipaggiamento, corredo;

(set of tools etc) attrezzi mpl; (for assembly) scatola di montaggio

kitchen ['kɪtʃɪn] n cucina; **~ sink** n acquaio

kite [kaɪt] n (toy) aquilone m

kitten ['kɪtn] n gattino/a, micino/a

kitty ['kɪtɪ] n (money) fondo comune

knack [næk] n: to have the **~** of avere l'abilità di

knapsack ['næpsæk] n zaino, sacco da montagna

knead [niːd] vt impastare

knee [niː] n ginocchio; **~cap** n rotula

kneel [niːl] (pt, pp **knelt**) vi (also: **~ down**) inginocchiarsi

knew [njuː] pt of **know**

knickers ['nɪkəz] (BRIT) npl mutandine fpl

knife [naɪf] (pl **knives**) n coltello ♦ vt accoltellare, dare una coltellata a

knight [naɪt] n cavaliere m; (CHESS) cavallo; **~hood** n (title): to get a **~hood** essere fatto cavaliere

knit [nɪt] vt fare a maglia ♦ vi lavorare a maglia; (broken bones) saldarsi; to **~ one's brows** aggrottare le sopracciglia; **~ting** n lavoro a maglia; **~ting machine** n macchina per maglieria; **~ting needle** n ferro da calza); **~wear** n maglieria

knives [naɪvz] npl of **knife**

knob [nɔb] n bottone m; manopola

knock [nɔk] vt colpire; urtare; (fig: inf) criticare ♦ vi (at door etc): to **~ at/on** bussare a ♦ n bussata; colpo, botta; **~ down** vt abbattere; **~ off** vi (inf: finish) smettere (di lavorare) ♦ vt (from price) far abbassare; (inf: steal) sgraffignare; **~ out** vt stendere; (BOXING) mettere K.O.; (defeat) battere; **~ over** vt (person) investire; (object) far cadere; **~er** n (on door) battente m; **~out** n (BOXING) knock out m inv ♦ cpd a eliminazione

knot [nɔt] n nodo ♦ vt annodare

know [nəʊ] (pt **knew**, pp **known**) vt sapere; (person, author, place) conoscere; **to ~ how to do** sapere fare; **to ~ about or of sth/sb** conoscere qc/qn; **~all** n sapientone(a); **~-how** n tecnica; pratica; **~ing** adj (look etc) d'intesa; **~ingly** adv (purposely) consapevolmente; (smile, look) con aria d'intesa

knowledge ['nɒlɪdʒ] n consapevolezza; (learning) conoscenza, sapere m; **~able** adj ben informato(a)

known [nəun] pp of **know**

knuckle ['nʌkl] n nocca

Koran [kɔ'rɑːn] n Corano

Korea [kə'rɪə] n Corea

kosher ['kəuʃə*] adj kasher inv

L, l

L (BRIT) abbr = **learner driver**

lab [læb] n abbr (= laboratory) laboratorio

label ['leɪbl] n etichetta, cartellino; (brand: of record) casa ♦ vt etichettare

labor etc ['leɪbə*] (US) = **labour** etc

laboratory [lə'bɒrətərɪ] n laboratorio

labour ['leɪbə*] (US **labor**) n (task) lavoro; (workmen) manodopera; (MED): **to be in ~** avere le doglie ♦ vi: **to ~ (at)** lavorare duro; **L~**, **the L~ party** (BRIT) il partito laburista, i laburisti; **hard ~** lavori mpl forzati; **~ed** adj (breathing) affannoso(a); **~er** n manovale m; **farm ~er** lavoratore m agricolo

lace [leɪs] n merletto, pizzo; (of shoe etc) laccio ♦ vt (shoe: also: **~ up**) allacciare

lack [læk] n mancanza ♦ vt mancare di; **through or for ~ of** per mancanza di; **to be ~ing** mancare; **to be ~ing in** mancare in

lackadaisical [lækə'deɪzɪkl] adj disinteressato(a), noncurante

lacquer ['lækə*] n lacca

lad [læd] n ragazzo, giovanotto

ladder ['lædə*] n scala; (BRIT: in tights) smagliatura

laden ['leɪdn] adj: **~ (with)** carico(a) or caricato(a) (di)

ladle ['leɪdl] n mestolo

lady ['leɪdɪ] n signora; dama; **L~ Smith** lady Smith; **the ladies' (room)** i gabinetti per signore; **~bird** (US **~bug**) n coccinella; **~like** adj da signora, distinto(a); **~ship** n: **your ~ship** signora contessa (or baronessa etc)

lag [læg] n (of time) lasso, intervallo ♦ vi (also: **~ behind**) trascinarsi ♦ vt (pipes) rivestire di materiale isolante

lager ['lɑːɡə*] n lager m inv

lagoon [lə'ɡuːn] n laguna

laid [leɪd] pt, pp of **lay**; **~ back** (inf) rilassato(a), tranquillo(a); **~ up** adj: **~ up (with)** costretto(a) a letto (da)

lain [leɪn] pp of **lie**

lair [leə*] n covo, tana

lake [leɪk] n lago

lamb [læm] n agnello

lame [leɪm] adj zoppo(a); (excuse etc) zoppicante

lament [lə'ment] n lamento ♦ vt lamentare, piangere

laminated ['læmɪneɪtɪd] adj laminato(a)

lamp [læmp] n lampada

lamppost ['læmppəust] (BRIT) n lampione m

lampshade ['læmpʃeɪd] n paralume m

lance [lɑːns] vt (MED) incidere

land [lænd] n (as opposed to sea) terra (ferma); (country) paese m; (soil) terreno; suolo; (estate) terreni mpl, terre fpl ♦ vi (from ship) sbarcare; (AVIAT) atterrare; (fig: fall) cadere ♦ vt (passengers) sbarcare; (goods) scaricare; **to ~ sb with sth** affibbiare qc a qn; **~ up** vi andare a finire; **~fill site** n discarica; **~ing** n atterraggio; (of staircase) pianerottolo; **~ing gear** n carrello di atterraggio; **~lady** n padrona or proprietaria di casa; **~locked** adj senza sbocco sul mare;

~lord n padrone m or proprietario di casa; (of pub etc) padrone m; **~mark** n punto di riferimento; (fig) pietra miliare; **~owner** n proprietario(a) terriero(a); **~scape** n paesaggio; **~slide** n (GEO) frana; (fig: POL) valanga

lane [leɪn] n stradina; (AUT, in race) corsia; "get in lane" "immettersi in corsia"

language ['læŋgwɪdʒ] n lingua; (way one speaks) linguaggio; **bad ~** linguaggio volgare; **~ laboratory** n laboratorio linguistico

languid ['læŋgwɪd] adj languido(a)

lank [læŋk] adj (hair) liscio(a) e opaco(a)

lanky ['læŋkɪ] adj allampanato(a)

lantern ['læntn] n lanterna

lap [læp] n (of track) giro; (of body): **in** or **on one's ~** in grembo ♦ vt (also: **~ up**) papparsi, leccare ♦ vi (waves) sciabordare; **~ up** vt (fig) bearsi di

lapel [lə'pel] n risvolto

Lapland ['læplænd] n Lapponia

lapse [læps] n lapsus m inv; (longer) caduta ♦ vi (law) cadere; (membership, contract) scadere; **to ~ into bad habits** pigliare cattive abitudini; **~ of time** spazio di tempo

laptop (computer) ['læptɒp] n laptop m inv

larch [lɑːtʃ] n larice m

lard [lɑːd] n lardo

larder ['lɑːdə*] n dispensa

large [lɑːdʒ] adj grande; (person, animal) grosso(a); **at ~** (free) in libertà; (generally) in generale; nell'insieme; **~ly** adv in gran parte

largesse [lɑː'ʒes] n generosità

lark [lɑːk] n (bird) allodola; (joke) scherzo, gioco

laryngitis [lærɪn'dʒaɪtɪs] n laringite f

laser ['leɪzə*] n laser m; **~ printer** n stampante f laser inv

lash [læʃ] n frustata; (also: **eye~**) ciglio ♦ vt frustare; (tie): **to ~ to/together** legare a insieme; **~ out** vi: **to ~ out** (at or against sb) attaccare violentemente (qn)

lass [læs] n ragazza

lasso [læ'suː] n laccio

last [lɑːst] adj ultimo(a); (week, month, year) scorso(a), passato(a) ♦ adv per ultimo ♦ vi durare; **~ week** la settimana scorsa, la settimana scorsa; **~ night** ieri sera, la notte scorsa; **at ~** finalmente, alla fine; **~ but one** penultimo(a); **~-ditch** adj (attempt) estremo(a); **~ing** adj durevole; **~ly** adv infine, per finire; **~-minute** adj fatto(a) (or preso(a) etc) all'ultimo momento

latch [lætʃ] n chiavistello

late [leɪt] adj (not on time) in ritardo; (far on in day etc) tardi inv; tardo(a); (former) ex; (dead) defunto(a) ♦ adv tardi; (behind time, schedule) in ritardo; **of ~** di recente; **in the ~ afternoon** nel tardo pomeriggio; **in ~ May** verso la fine di maggio; **~comer** n ritardatario/a; **~ly** adv recentemente

later ['leɪtə*] adj (date etc) posteriore; (version etc) successivo(a) ♦ adv più tardi; **~ on** più avanti

lateral ['lætərl] adj laterale

latest ['leɪtɪst] adj ultimo(a), più recente; **at the ~** al più tardi

lathe [leɪð] n tornio

lather ['lɑːðə*] n schiuma di sapone ♦ vt insaponare

Latin ['lætɪn] n latino ♦ adj latino(a); **~ America** n America Latina; **~-American** adj, n sudamericano/a

latitude ['lætɪtjuːd] n latitudine f; (fig) libertà d'azione

latter ['lætə*] adj secondo(a); più recente ♦ n: **the ~** quest'ultimo, il secondo; **~ly** adv recentemente, negli ultimi tempi

lattice ['lætɪs] n traliccio; graticolato

laudable ['lɔːdəbl] adj lodevole

laugh [lɑːf] n risata ♦ vi ridere; **~ at** vt fus (misfortune etc) ridere di; **~ off** vt prendere alla leggera; **~able** adj ridicolo(a); **~ing stock** n: **the ~ing**

stock of lo zimbello di; **~ter** n riso; risate fpl

launch [lɔːntʃ] n (of rocket, COMM) lancio; (of new ship) varo; (also: motor ~) lancia ♦ vt (rocket, COMM) lanciare; (ship, plan) varare; **~ into** vt fus lanciarsi in; **~(ing) pad** n rampa di lancio

launder ['lɔːndə*] vt lavare e stirare

launderette [lɔːn'drɛt] (BRIT) n lavanderia (automatica)

Laundromat ® ['lɔːndrəmæt] (US) n lavanderia automatica

laundry ['lɔːndrɪ] n lavanderia; (clothes) biancheria; (: dirty) panni mpl da lavare

laurel ['lɔrl] n lauro

lava ['lɑːvə] n lava

lavatory ['lævətərɪ] n gabinetto

lavender ['lævəndə*] n lavanda

lavish ['lævɪʃ] adj copioso(a); abbondante; (giving freely): **~ with** prodigo(a) di, largo(a) in ♦ vt: **to ~ sth on sb** colmare qn di qc

law [lɔː] n legge f; civil/criminal **~** diritto civile/penale; **~-abiding** adj ubbidiente alla legge; **~ and order** n l'ordine m pubblico; **~ court** n tribunale m, corte f di giustizia; **~ful** adj legale; lecito(a); **~less** adj che non conosce nessuna legge

lawn [lɔːn] n tappeto erboso; **~ mower** n tosaerba m or f inv; **~ tennis** n tennis m su prato

law school n facoltà f inv di legge

lawsuit ['lɔːsuːt] n processo, causa

lawyer ['lɔːjə*] n (for sales, wills etc) n notaio; (partner, in court) ≈ avvocato/essa

lax [læks] adj rilassato(a); negligente

laxative ['læksətɪv] n lassativo

lay [leɪ] (pt, pp **laid**) pt of **lie** ♦ adj laico(a); (not expert) inesperto(a) ♦ vt posare, mettere; (eggs) fare; (trap) tendere; (plans) fare, elaborare; **to ~ the table** apparecchiare la tavola; **~ aside** or **by** vt mettere da parte;

~ down vt mettere giù; (rules etc) formulare, fissare; **to ~ down the law** dettar legge; **to ~ down one's life** dare la propria vita; **~ off** vt (workers) licenziare; **~ on** vt (provide) fornire; **~ out** vt (display) presentare, disporre; **~about** n sfaccendato/a, fannullone/a; **~-by** (BRIT) n piazzola (di sosta)

layer ['leɪə*] n strato

layman ['leɪmən] n laico; profano

layout ['leɪaut] n lay-out m inv, disposizione f; (PRESS) impaginazione f

laze [leɪz] vi oziare

lazy ['leɪzɪ] adj pigro(a)

lb. abbr = **pound** (weight)

lead[1] [liːd] (pt, pp **led**) n (front position) posizione f di testa; (distance, time ahead) vantaggio; (clue) indizio; (ELEC) filo (elettrico); (for dog) guinzaglio; (THEATRE) parte f principale ♦ vt guidare, condurre; (induce) indurre; (be leader of) essere a capo di ♦ vi condurre; (SPORT) essere in testa; **in the ~** in testa; **to ~ the way** fare strada; **~ away** vt condurre via; **~ back** vt: **to ~ back to** ricondurre a; **~ on** vt (tease) tenere sulla corda; **~ to** vt fus condurre a; portare a; **~ up to** vt fus portare a

lead[2] [lɛd] n (metal) piombo; (in pencil) mina; **~ed petrol** n benzina con piombo

leaden ['lɛdn] adj (sky, sea) plombeo(a)

leader ['liːdə*] n capo; leader m inv; (in newspaper) articolo di fondo; (SPORT) chi è in testa; **~ship** n direzione f; capacità di comando

leading ['liːdɪŋ] adj primo(a); principale; **~ light** n (person) personaggio di primo piano; **~ man/lady** n (THEATRE) primo attore/prima attrice

lead singer n cantante alla testa di un gruppo

leaf [liːf] (pl **leaves**) n foglia ♦ vi: **to ~ through sth** sfogliare qc; **to turn**

over a new ~ cambiar vita
leaflet ['li:flɪt] n dépliant m inv; (POL,
REL) volantino
league [li:g] n lega; (FOOTBALL)
campionato; **to be in ~ with** essere in
lega con
leak [li:k] n (out) fuga; (in) infiltrazione
f; (security) fuga d'informazioni ♦ vi
(roof, bucket) perdere; (liquid) uscire;
(shoes) lasciar passare l'acqua ♦ vt
(information) divulgare; **~ out** vi uscire;
(information) trapelare
lean [li:n] (pt, pp **leaned** or **leant**) adj
magro ♦ vt: **to ~ sth on sth**
appoggiare qc su qc ♦ vi (slope)
pendere; (rest): **to ~ against**
appoggiarsi contro; **to ~ on** appoggiarsi
a; **~ back/forward** vi sporgersi
indietro/in avanti; **~ out** vi sporgersi;
~ over vi inclinarsi; **~ing** n: **~ing**
(towards) propensione f (per)
leap [li:p] (pt, pp **leaped** or **leapt**) n
salto, balzo ♦ vi saltare, balzare; **~frog**
n gioco della cavallina; **~ year** n anno
bisestile
learn [lə:n] (pt, pp **learned** or **learnt**)
vt, vi imparare; **to ~ about sth** (hear,
read) apprendere qc; **to ~ to do sth**
imparare a fare qc; **~ed** ['lə:nɪd] adj
erudito(a), dotto(a); **~er** n principiante
m/f; apprendista m/f; (BRIT: also: **~er
driver**) guidatore/trice principiante;
~ing n erudizione f, sapienza
lease [li:s] n contratto d'affitto ♦ vt
affittare
leash [li:ʃ] n guinzaglio
least [li:st] adj: **the ~** (+ noun) il(la)
più piccolo(a), il(la) minimo(a);
(smallest amount of) il(la) meno ♦ adv
(+ verb) meno; **the ~** (+ adjective):
the ~ beautiful girl la ragazza meno
bella; **the ~ possible effort** il minimo
sforzo possibile; **I have the ~ money**
ho meno denaro di tutti; **at ~** almeno;
not in the ~ affatto, per nulla
leather ['lɛðə*] n cuoio

leave [li:v] (pt, pp **left**) vt lasciare; (go
away from) partire da ♦ vi partire,
andarsene; (bus, train) partire ♦ n (time
off) congedo; (MIL, also: consent)
licenza; **to be left** rimanere; **there's
some milk left over** c'è rimasto del
latte; **on ~** in congedo; **~ behind** vt
(person, object) lasciare; (: forget)
dimenticare; **~ out** vt omettere,
tralasciare; **~ of absence** n congedo
leaves [li:vz] npl of **leaf**
Lebanon ['lɛbənən] n Libano
lecherous ['lɛtʃərəs] adj lascivo(a),
lubrico(a)
lecture ['lɛktʃə*] n conferenza; (SCOL)
lezione f ♦ vi fare conferenze; fare
lezioni ♦ vt (scold): **to ~ sb on** or
about sth rimproverare qn or fare una
ramanzina a qn per qc; **to give a
~ on** tenere una conferenza su
lecturer ['lɛktʃərə*] (BRIT) n (at
university) professore/essa, docente m/f
led [lɛd] pt, pp of **lead**
ledge [lɛdʒ] n (of window) davanzale
m; (on wall etc) sporgenza; (of
mountain) cornice f, cengia
ledger ['lɛdʒə*] n libro maestro,
registro
lee [li:] n lato sottovento
leech [li:tʃ] n sanguisuga
leek [li:k] n porro
leer [lɪə*] vi: **to ~ at sb** gettare uno
sguardo voglioso (or maligno) su qn
leeway ['li:weɪ] n (fig): **to have some
~** avere una certa libertà di azione
left [lɛft] pt, pp of **leave** ♦ adj
sinistro(a) ♦ adv a sinistra ♦ n sinistra;
on the ~, to the ~ a sinistra; **the L~**
(POL) la sinistra; **~-hand** adj; **~-hand
drive** guida a sinistra; **~-handed** adj
mancino(a); **~-hand side** n lato or
fianco sinistro; **~-luggage locker** n
armadietto per deposito bagagli;
~ luggage (office) (BRIT) n deposito
m bagagli inv; **~overs** npl avanzi mpl,
resti mpl; **~-wing** adj (POL) di sinistra
leg [lɛg] n gamba; (of animal) zampa;

(of furniture) piede m; (CULIN: of chicken) coscia; (of journey) tappa; **1st/2nd ~** (SPORT) partita di andata/ritorno

legacy ['lɛgəsɪ] n eredità f inv

legal ['li:gl] adj legale; **~ holiday** (US) n giorno festivo, festa nazionale; **~ tender** n moneta legale

legend ['lɛdʒənd] n leggenda

legislation [lɛdʒɪs'leɪʃən] n legislazione f; **legislature** ['lɛdʒɪslətʃə*] n corpo legislativo

legitimate [lɪ'dʒɪtɪmət] adj legittimo(a)

leg-room n spazio per le gambe

leisure ['lɛʒə*] n agio, tempo libero; ricreazioni fpl; **at ~** con comodo; **~ centre** n centro di ricreazione; **~ly** adj tranquillo(a); fatto(a) con comodo or senza fretta

lemon ['lɛmən] n limone m; **~ade** [-'neɪd] n limonata f; **~ tea** n tè m inv al limone

lend [lɛnd] (pt, pp lent) vt: **to ~ sth (to sb)** prestare qc (a qn); **~ing library** n biblioteca che consente prestiti di libri

length [lɛŋθ] n lunghezza; (distance) distanza; (section: of road, pipe etc) pezzo, tratto; (of time) periodo; **at ~** (at last) finalmente, alla fine; (lengthily) a lungo; **~en** vt allungare, prolungare ♦ vi allungarsi; **~ways** adv per il lungo; **~y** adj molto lungo(a)

lenient ['li:nɪənt] adj indulgente, clemente

lens [lɛnz] n lente f; (of camera) obiettivo

Lent [lɛnt] n Quaresima

lent [lɛnt] pt, pp of **lend**

lentil ['lɛntl] n lenticchia

Leo ['li:əʊ] n Leone m

leotard ['li:ətɑ:d] n calzamaglia

leprosy ['lɛprəsɪ] n lebbra

lesbian ['lɛzbɪən] n lesbica

less [lɛs] adj, pron, adv meno ♦ prep: **~ tax/10% discount** meno tasse/il 10% di sconto; **~ than ever** meno

che mai; **~ than half** meno della metà; **~ and ~** sempre meno; **the ~ he works ...** meno lavora ....

lessen ['lɛsn] vi diminuire, attenuarsi ♦ vt diminuire, ridurre

lesser ['lɛsə*] adj minore, più piccolo(a); **to a ~ extent** in grado or misura minore

lesson ['lɛsn] n lezione f; **to teach sb a ~** dare una lezione a qn

let [lɛt] (pt, pp let) vt lasciare; (BRIT: lease) dare in affitto; **to ~ sb do sth** lasciar fare qc a qn, lasciare che qn faccia qc; **to ~ sb know sth** far sapere qc a qn; **~'s go** andiamo; **~ him come** lo lasci venire; **"to ~"** "affittasi"; **~ down** vt (lower) abbassare; (dress) allungare; (hair) sciogliere; (tyre) sgonfiare; (disappoint) deludere; **~ go** vt, vi mollare; **~ in** vt lasciare entrare; (visitor) far entrare; **~ off** vt (allow to go) lasciare andare; (firework etc) far partire; **~ on** (inf) vi dire; **~ out** vt lasciare uscire; (scream) emettere; **~ up** vi diminuire

lethal ['li:θl] adj letale, mortale

lethargic [lɛ'θɑ:dʒɪk] adj letargico(a)

letter ['lɛtə*] n lettera; **~ bomb** n lettera esplosiva; **~box** (BRIT) n buca delle lettere; **~ing** n iscrizione f; caratteri mpl

lettuce ['lɛtɪs] n lattuga, insalata

let-up ['lɛtʌp] n pausa

leukaemia [lu:'ki:mɪə] (US **leukemia**) n leucemia

level ['lɛvl] adj piatto(a), piano(a), orizzontale ♦ adv: **to draw ~ with** mettersi alla pari di ♦ n livello ♦ vt livellare, spianare; **to be ~ with** essere alla pari di; **A ~s** (BRIT) npl ≈ esami mpl di maturità; **O ~s** (BRIT) npl esami fatti in Inghilterra all'età di 16 anni; **on the ~** onesto(a); (fig) onesto(a); **~ off** or **out** vi (prices etc) stabilizzarsi; **~ crossing** (BRIT) n passaggio a livello; **~-headed** adj equilibrato(a)

lever ['li:və*] n leva; **~age** n: **~age**

(on or with) forza (su); (fig) ascendente m (su)

levy ['lɛvɪ] n tassa, imposta ♦ vt imporre

lewd [lu:d] adj osceno(a), lascivo(a)

liability [laɪə'bɪlɪtɪ] n responsabilità f inv; (handicap) peso; **liabilities** npl debiti mpl; (on balance sheet) passivo

liable ['laɪəbl] adj (subject): ~ to soggetto(a) a; passibile di; (responsible): ~ (for) responsabile di; (likely): ~ to do propenso(a) a fare

liaise [li:'eɪz] vi: to ~ (with) mantenere i contatti (con)

liaison [li:'eɪzɔn] n relazione f; (MIL) collegamento

liar ['laɪə*] n bugiardo/a

libel ['laɪbl] n libello, diffamazione f ♦ vt diffamare

liberal ['lɪbərl] adj liberale; (generous): to be ~ with distribuire liberamente

liberation [lɪbə'reɪʃən] n liberazione f

liberty ['lɪbətɪ] n libertà f inv; at ~ (criminal) in libertà; at ~ to do libero(a) di fare

Libra ['li:brə] n Bilancia

librarian [laɪ'brɛərɪən] n bibliotecario/a

library ['laɪbrərɪ] n biblioteca

Libya ['lɪbɪə] n Libia; **~n** adj, n libico(a)

lice [laɪs] npl of louse

licence ['laɪsns] (US **license**) n autorizzazione f, permesso; (COMM) licenza; (RADIO, TV) canone m, abbonamento; (also: driving ~, (US) driver's ~) patente f di guida; (excessive freedom) licenza; ~ **number** n numero di targa; ~ **plate** n targa

license ['laɪsns] n (US) = **licence** ♦ vt dare una licenza a; **~d** adj (for alcohol) che ha la licenza di vendere bibite alcoliche

lick [lɪk] vt leccare; (inf: defeat) stracciare; to ~ **one's lips** (fig) leccarsi i baffi

licorice ['lɪkərɪs] (US) n = **liquorice**

lid [lɪd] n coperchio; (eye~) palpebra

lie [laɪ] (pt **lay**, pp **lain**) vi (rest)

giacere; star disteso(a); (of object: be situated) trovarsi, essere; (tell lies: pt, pp **lied**) mentire, dire bugie ♦ n bugia, menzogna; to ~ **low** (fig) latitare; ~ **about** or **around** vi (things) essere in giro; (person) bighellonare; **~-down** (BRIT) n: to have a ~-down sdraiarsi, riposarsi; **~-in** (BRIT) n: to have a ~-in rimanere a letto

lieu [lu:]: in ~ of prep invece di, al posto di

lieutenant [lɛf'tɛnənt, (US) lu:'tɛnənt] n tenente m

life [laɪf] (pl **lives**) n vita ♦ cpd di vita; della vita; to come to ~ rianimarsi; ~ **assurance** (BRIT) n = ~ **insurance**; **~belt** (BRIT) n salvagente m; **~boat** n scialuppa di salvataggio; **~guard** n bagnino; ~ **imprisonment** n carcere m a vita; ~ **insurance** n assicurazione f sulla vita; ~ **jacket** n giubbotto di salvataggio; **~less** adj senza vita; **~like** adj verosimile; rassomigliante; **~long** adj per tutta la vita; ~ **preserver** (US) n salvagente m; giubbotto di salvataggio; ~ **sentence** n ergastolo; **~-size(d)** adj a grandezza naturale; ~ **span** n (durata della) vita; **~style** n stile m di vita; ~ **support system** n respiratore m automatico; **~time** n: in his ~time durante la sua vita; once in a ~time una volta nella vita

lift [lɪft] vt sollevare; (ban, rule) levare ♦ vi (fog) alzarsi ♦ n (BRIT: elevator) ascensore m; to give sb a ~ (BRIT) dare un passaggio a qn; **~-off** n decollo

light [laɪt] (pt, pp **lighted** or **lit**) n luce f, lume m; (daylight) luce f, giorno; (lamp) lampada; (AUT: rear) luce f di posizione; (: headlamp) fanale m; (for cigarette etc) have you got a ~? ha da accendere?; **~s** npl (AUT: traffic ~s) semaforo ♦ vt (candle, cigarette, fire) accendere; (room): to be lit by essere illuminato(a) da ♦ adj (room, colour) chiaro(a); (*not heavy, also fig*) leggero(a); **to come to ~** venire alla luce, emergere; **~ up** *vi* illuminarsi ♦ *vt* illuminare; **~ bulb** *n* lampadina; **~en** *vt* (*make less heavy*) alleggerire; **~er** *n* (*also: cigarette ~er*) accendino; **~-headed** *adj* stordito(a); **~-hearted** *adj* gioioso(a), gaio(a); **~house** *n* faro; **~ing** *n* illuminazione f; **~ly** *adv* leggermente; **to get off ~ly** cavarsela a buon mercato; **~ meter** *n* (*PHOT*) esposimetro; **~ness** *n* chiarezza f; (*in weight*) leggerezza

lightning ['laɪtnɪŋ] *n* lampo, fulmine m; **~ conductor** (*US ~ rod*) *n* parafulmine m

light pen *n* penna ottica

lightweight ['laɪtweɪt] *adj* (*suit*) leggero(a) ♦ *n* (*BOXING*) peso leggero

light year *n* anno *m* luce *inv*

like [laɪk] *vt* (*person*) volere bene a; (*activity, object, food*): **I ~ swimming/ that book/chocolate** mi piace nuotare/quel libro/il cioccolato ♦ *prep* come ♦ *adj* simile, uguale ♦ *n*: **the ~** uno(a) uguale; **his ~s and dislikes** i suoi gusti; **I would ~, I'd ~** mi piacerebbe, vorrei; **would you ~ a coffee?** gradirebbe un caffè?; **to be/ look ~ sb/sth** somigliare a qn/qc; **what does it look/taste ~?** che aspetto/gusto ha?; **what does it sound ~?** come fa?; **that's just ~ him** è proprio da lui; **do it ~ this** fallo così; **it is nothing ~ ...** non è affatto come ...; **~able** *adj* simpatico(a)

likelihood ['laɪklɪhud] *n* probabilità

likely ['laɪklɪ] *adj* probabile; plausibile; **he's ~ to leave** probabilmente partirà, è probabile che parta; **not ~!** neanche per sogno!

likeness ['laɪknɪs] *n* somiglianza

likewise ['laɪkwaɪz] *adv* similmente, nello stesso modo

liking ['laɪkɪŋ] *n*: **~ (for)** debole m (per); **to be to sb's ~** piacere a qn

lilac ['laɪlək] *n* lilla *m inv*

lily ['lɪlɪ] *n* giglio; **~ of the valley** *n* mughetto

limb [lɪm] *n* arto

limber up ['lɪmbə*-] *vi* riscaldarsi i muscoli

limbo ['lɪmbəu] *n*: **to be in ~** (*fig*) essere lasciato(a) nel dimenticatoio

lime [laɪm] *n* (*tree*) tiglio; (*fruit*) limetta; (*GEO*) calce f

limelight ['laɪmlaɪt] *n*: **in the ~** (*fig*) alla ribalta, in vista

limerick ['lɪmərɪk] *n* poesiola umoristica di 5 versi

limestone ['laɪmstəun] *n* pietra calcarea; (*GEO*) calcare m

limit ['lɪmɪt] *n* limite m ♦ *vt* limitare; **~ed** *adj* limitato(a), ristretto(a); **to be ~ed to** limitarsi a; **~ed (liability) company** (*BRIT*) *n* ≈ società f *inv* a responsabilità limitata

limp [lɪmp] *n*: **to have a ~** zoppicare ♦ *vi* zoppicare ♦ *adj* floscio(a), flaccido(a)

limpet ['lɪmpɪt] *n* patella

line [laɪn] *n* linea; (*rope*) corda; (*for fishing*) lenza; (*wire*) filo; (*of people*) fila; (*row, series*) fila, riga; coda; (*on face*) ruga ♦ *vt* (*clothes*): **to ~ (with)** foderare (di); (*box*): **to ~ (with)** rivestire or foderare (di); (*subj: trees, crowd*) fiancheggiare; **~ of business** settore m or ramo d'attività; **in ~ with** in linea con; **~ up** *vi* allinearsi, mettersi in fila ♦ *vt* mettere in fila; (*event, celebration*) preparare

lined [laɪnd] *adj* (*face*) rugoso(a); (*paper*) a righe, rigato(a)

linen ['lɪnɪn] *n* biancheria, panni *mpl*; (*cloth*) tela di lino

liner ['laɪnə*] *n* nave f di linea; (*for bin*) sacchetto

linesman ['laɪnzmən] *n* guardalinee *m inv*

line-up *n* allineamento, fila; (*SPORT*) formazione f di gioco

linger ['lɪŋgə*] *vi* attardarsi; indugiare;

(smell, tradition) persistere

lingerie ['læŋʒəriː] n biancheria intima femminile

linguistics [lɪŋ'gwɪstɪks] n linguistica

lining ['laɪnɪŋ] n fodera

link [lɪŋk] n (of a chain) anello; *(relationship)* legame m; *(connection)* collegamento ♦ vt collegare, unire, congiungere; *(associate):* to ~ with or to collegare a; ~s npl (GOLF) pista or terreno da golf; ~ up vt collegare, unire ♦ vi riunirsi; associarsi

lino ['laɪnəʊ] n = **linoleum**

linoleum [lɪ'nəʊlɪəm] n linoleum m inv

lion ['laɪən] n leone m; ~ess n leonessa

lip [lɪp] n labbro; (of cup etc) orlo

liposuction ['lɪpəʊsʌkʃən] n liposuzione f

lip: ~read vi leggere sulle labbra; ~ salve n burro di cacao; ~ service n: to pay ~ service to sth essere favorevole a qc solo a parole; ~stick n rossetto

liqueur [lɪ'kjʊə*] n liquore m

liquid ['lɪkwɪd] n liquido ♦ adj liquido(a)

liquidize ['lɪkwɪdaɪz] vt (CULIN) passare al frullatore; ~r n frullatore m (a brocca)

liquor ['lɪkə*] n alcool m

liquorice ['lɪkərɪs] (BRIT) n liquirizia

liquor store (US) n negozio di liquori

lisp [lɪsp] n pronuncia blesa della "s"

list [lɪst] n lista, elenco ♦ vt (write down) mettere in lista; fare una lista di; *(enumerate)* elencare; ~ed building (BRIT) n edificio sotto la protezione delle Belle Arti

listen ['lɪsn] vi ascoltare; to ~ to ascoltare; ~er n ascoltatore/trice

listless ['lɪstlɪs] adj apatico(a)

lit [lɪt] pt, pp of **light**

liter ['liːtə*] (US) n = **litre**

literacy ['lɪtərəsɪ] n il sapere leggere e scrivere

literal ['lɪtərl] adj letterale; ~ly adv alla lettera, letteralmente

literary ['lɪtərərɪ] adj letterario(a)

literate ['lɪtərət] adj che sa leggere e scrivere

literature ['lɪtərɪtʃə*] n letteratura; *(brochures etc)* materiale m

lithe [laɪð] adj agile, snello(a)

litigation [lɪtɪ'geɪʃən] n causa

litre ['liːtə*] (US liter) n litro

litter ['lɪtə*] n (rubbish) rifiuti mpl; *(young animals)* figliata; ~ bin (BRIT) n cestino per rifiuti; ~ed adj: ~ed with coperto(a) di

little ['lɪtl] adj (small) piccolo(a); (not much) poco(a) ♦ adv poco; a ~ un po' (di); a ~ bit un pochino; ~ by ~ a poco a poco; ~ finger n mignolo

live¹ [lɪv] vi vivere; *(reside)* vivere, abitare; ~ down vt far dimenticare (alla gente); ~ on vt fus (food) vivere di; ~ together vi vivere insieme, convivere; ~ up to vt fus tener fede a, non venir meno a

live² [laɪv] adj (animal) vivo(a); (wire) sotto tensione; *(bullet, missile)* inesploso(a); *(broadcast)* diretto(a); *(performance)* dal vivo

livelihood ['laɪvlɪhʊd] n mezzi mpl di sostentamento

lively ['laɪvlɪ] adj vivace, vivo(a)

liven up ['laɪvn'ʌp] vt (discussion, evening) animare ♦ vi ravvivarsi

liver ['lɪvə*] n fegato

lives [laɪvz] npl of **life**

livestock ['laɪvstɒk] n bestiame m

livid ['lɪvɪd] adj livido(a); *(furious)* livido(a) di rabbia, furibondo(a)

living ['lɪvɪŋ] adj vivo(a), vivente ♦ n: to earn or make a ~ guadagnarsi la vita; ~ conditions npl condizioni fpl di vita; ~ room n soggiorno; ~ standards npl tenore m di vita; ~ wage n salario sufficiente per vivere

lizard ['lɪzəd] n lucertola

load [ləʊd] n (weight) peso; *(thing carried)* carico ♦ vt (also: ~ up) to ~ (with) (lorry, ship) caricare di); (to gun, camera, COMPUT) caricare (con); a ~ of,

~s of (fig) un sacco di; **~ed** adj (vehicle): **~ed (with)** carico/a (di); (question) capzioso(a); (inf: rich) carico(a) di soldi

loaf [ləuf] (pl **loaves**) n pane m, pagnotta

loan [ləun] n prestito ♦ vt dare in prestito; **on ~** in prestito

loath [ləuθ] adj: **to be ~ to do** essere restio(a) a fare

loathe [ləuð] vt detestare, aborrire

loaves [ləuvz] npl of **loaf**

lobby ['lɔbɪ] n atrio, vestibolo; (POL: pressure group) gruppo di pressione ♦ vt fare pressione su

lobster ['lɔbstə*] n aragosta

local ['ləukl] adj locale ♦ n (BRIT: pub) ≈ bar m inv all'angolo; the **~s** npl (local inhabitants) la gente della zona; **~ anaesthetic** n anestesia locale; **~ authority** n ente m locale; **~ call** n (TEL) telefonata urbana; **~ government** n amministrazione f locale

locality [ləu'kælɪtɪ] n località f inv; (position) posto, luogo

locally ['ləukəlɪ] adv da queste parti; nel vicinato

locate [ləu'keɪt] vt (find) trovare; (situate) collocare; situare

location [ləu'keɪʃən] n posizione f; **on ~** (CINEMA) all'esterno

loch [lɔx] n lago

lock [lɔk] n (of door, box) serratura; (of canal) chiusa; (of hair) ciocca, riccio ♦ vt (with key) chiudere a chiave ♦ vi (door etc) chiudersi; (wheels) bloccarsi, incepparsi; **~ in** vt chiudere dentro (a chiave); **~ out** vt chiudere fuori; **~ up** vt (criminal, mental patient) rinchiudere; (house) chiudere (a chiave) ♦ vi chiudere tutto (a chiave)

locker ['lɔkə*] n armadietto

locket ['lɔkɪt] n medaglione m

locksmith ['lɔksmɪθ] n magnano

lockup ['lɔkʌp] n (US) prigione f; guardina

locum ['ləukəm] n (MED) medico sostituto

locust ['ləukəst] n locusta

lodge [lɔdʒ] n casetta, portineria; (hunting ~) casotto di caccia ♦ vi (person): **to ~ (with)** essere a pensione (presso or da); (bullet etc) conficcarsi ♦ vt (appeal etc) presentare, fare; **to ~ a complaint** presentare un reclamo; **~r** n affittuario/a; (with room and meals) pensionante m/f

lodgings ['lɔdʒɪŋz] npl camera d'affitto; camera ammobiliata

loft [lɔft] n solaio, soffitta

lofty ['lɔftɪ] adj alto(a); (haughty) altezzoso(a)

log [lɔg] n (of wood) ceppo; (book) = **logbook** ♦ vt registrare; **~ in** or **on** vi (COMPUT) collegarsi; **~ off** or **out** vi (COMPUT) scollegarsi

logbook ['lɔgbuk] n (NAUT, AVIAT) diario di bordo; (AUT) libretto di circolazione

loggerheads ['lɔgəhedz] npl: **at ~ (with)** ai ferri corti (con)

logic ['lɔdʒɪk] n logica; **~al** adj logico(a)

loin [lɔɪn] n (CULIN) lombata

loiter ['lɔɪtə*] vi attardarsi

loll [lɔl] vi (also: **~ about**) essere stravaccato(a)

lollipop ['lɔlɪpɔp] n lecca lecca m inv; **~ man/lady** (BRIT irreg) n see box

---
lollipop man/lady

In Gran Bretagna il **lollipop man** e la **lollipop lady** sono persone incaricate di aiutare i bambini ad attraversare la strada in prossimità delle scuole; usano una paletta la cui forma ricorda quella di un lecca lecca, in inglese **lollipop**.

London ['lʌndən] n Londra; **~er** n londinese m/f

lone [ləun] adj solitario(a)

loneliness ['ləunlɪnɪs] n solitudine f, isolamento

lonely ['ləunlı] *adj* solo(a); solitario(a), isolato(a)

long [lɒŋ] *adj* lungo(a) ♦ *adv* a lungo, per molto tempo ♦ *vi*: **to ~ for sth/to do** desiderare qc/di fare; non veder l'ora di aver qc/di fare; **so** *or* **as ~ as** (*while*) finché; (*provided that*) sempre che + *sub*; **don't be ~!** fai presto!; **how ~ is this river/course?** quanto è lungo questo fiume/corso?; **6 metres ~** lungo 6 metri; **6 months ~** che dura 6 mesi, di 6 mesi; **all night ~** tutta la notte; **he no ~er comes** non viene più; **~ before** molto tempo prima; **before ~** (+ *future*) presto, fra poco; (+ *past*) poco tempo dopo; **at ~ last** finalmente; **~-distance** *adj* (*race*) di fondo; (*call*) interurbano(a); **~-haired** *adj* dai capelli lunghi; **~hand** *n* scrittura normale; **~ing** *n* desiderio, voglia, brama

longitude ['lɒŋgɪtjuːd] *n* longitudine *f*

long: **~ jump** *n* salto in lungo; **~-life** *adj* (*milk*) a lunga conservazione; (*batteries*) di lunga durata; **~lost** *adj* perduto(a) da tempo; **~-range** *adj* a lunga portata; **~-sighted** *adj* presbite; **~-standing** *adj* di vecchia data; **~-suffering** *adj* estremamente paziente; infinitamente tollerante; **~-term** *adj* a lungo termine; **~ wave** *n* onde *fpl* lunghe; **~-winded** *adj* prolisso(a), interminabile

loo [luː] (*BRIT*) *n* W.C. *m inv*, cesso

look [luk] *vi* guardare; (*seem*) sembrare, parere; (*building etc*): **to ~ south/on to the sea** dare a sud/sul mare ♦ *n* sguardo; (*appearance*) aspetto, aria; **~s** *npl* (*good ~s*) bellezza; **~ after** *vt fus* occuparsi di, prendere cura di; (*keep an eye on*) guardare, badare a; **~ at** *vt fus* guardare; **~ back** *vi*: **to ~ back on** (*event etc*) ripensare a; **~ down on** *vt fus* (*fig*) guardare dall'alto, disprezzare; **~ for** *vt fus* cercare; **~ forward to** *vt fus* non veder l'ora di; (*in letters*): **we**

~ forward to hearing from you in attesa di una vostra gentile risposta; **~ into** *vt fus* esaminare; **~ on** *vi* fare da spettatore; **~ out** *vi* stare in guardia (*beware*); **~ out (for)** stare in guardia (per); **~ out for** *vt fus* cercare; **~ round** *vi* (*turn*) girarsi, voltarsi; (*in shop*) dare un'occhiata; **~ to** *vt fus* (*rely on*) contare su; **~ up** *vi* alzare gli occhi; (*improve*) migliorare ♦ *vt* (*word*) cercare; (*friend*) andare a trovare; **~ up to** *vt fus* avere rispetto per; **~out** *n* posto d'osservazione; guardia; **to be on the ~out (for)** stare in guardia (per)

loom [luːm] *n* telaio ♦ *vi* (*also*: **~ up**) apparire minaccioso(a); (*event*) essere imminente

loony ['luːnɪ] (*inf*) *n* pazzo/a

loop [luːp] *n* cappio ♦ *vt*: **to ~ sth round sth** passare qc intorno a qc; **~hole** *n* via d'uscita; scappatoia

loose [luːs] *adj* (*knot*) sciolto(a); (*screw*) allentato(a); (*stone*) cadente; (*clothes*) ampio(a), largo(a); (*animal*) in libertà, scappato(a); (*life, morals*) dissoluto(a) ♦ *n*: **to be on the ~** essere in libertà; **~ change** *n* spiccioli *mpl*, moneta; **~ chippings** *npl* (*on road*) ghiaino; **~ end** *n*: **to be at a ~ end** (*BRIT*) *or* **at ~ ends** (*US*) non saper che fare; **~ly** *adv* senza stringere; approssimativamente; **~n** *vt* sciogliere; (*belt etc*) allentare

loot [luːt] *n* bottino ♦ *vt* saccheggiare

lop [lɒp] *vt* (*also*: **~ off**) tagliare via, recidere

lop-sided ['lɒp'saɪdɪd] *adj* non equilibrato(a), asimmetrico(a)

lord [lɔːd] *n* signore *m*; **L~ Smith** lord Smith; **the L~** il Signore; **good L~!** buon Dio!; **the (House of) L~s** (*BRIT*) la Camera dei Lord; **~ship** *n*: **your L~ship** Sua Eccellenza

lore [lɔː] *n* tradizioni *fpl*

lorry ['lɒrɪ] (*BRIT*) *n* camion *m inv*; **~ driver** (*BRIT*) *n* camionista *m*

lose [luːz] (pt, pp **lost**) vt perdere ♦ vi perdere; **to ~ (time)** (clock) ritardare; **~r** n perdente m/f

loss [lɒs] n perdita; **to be at a ~** essere perplesso(a)

lost [lɒst] pt, pp of **lose** ♦ adj perduto(a); **~ property** n (US **~ and found**) n oggetti mpl smarriti

lot [lɒt] n (at auctions) lotto; (destiny) destino, sorte f; **the ~** tutto(a) quanto(a); tutti(e) quanti(e); **a ~** molto; **a ~ of** una gran quantità di, un sacco di; **~s of** molto(a); **to draw ~s (for sth)** tirare a sorte (per qc)

lotion ['ləʊʃən] n lozione f

lottery ['lɒtərɪ] n lotteria

loud [laʊd] adj forte, alto(a); (gaudy) vistoso(a), sgargiante ♦ adv (speak etc) forte; **out ~** (read etc) ad alta voce; **~hailer** (BRIT) n portavoce m inv; **~ly** adv fortemente, ad alta voce; **~speaker** n altoparlante m

lounge [laʊndʒ] n salotto, soggiorno; (at airport, station) sala d'attesa; (BRIT: also: **~ bar**) bar m inv con servizio a tavolino ♦ vi oziare; **~ about** or **around** vi starsene colle mani in mano

louse [laʊs] (pl **lice**) n pidocchio

lousy ['laʊzɪ] (inf) adj orrendo(a), schifoso(a); **to feel ~** stare da cani

lout [laʊt] n zoticone m

lovable ['lʌvəbl] adj simpatico(a), carino(a); amabile

love [lʌv] n amore m ♦ vt amare; voler bene a; **to ~ to do:** **I ~ to do** mi piace fare; **to be/fall in ~ with** essere innamorato(a)/innamorarsi di; **to make ~** fare l'amore; **"15 ~"** (TENNIS) "15 a zero"; **~ affair** n relazione f; **~ life** n vita sentimentale

lovely ['lʌvlɪ] adj bello(a); (delicious: smell, meal) buono(a)

lover ['lʌvə*] n amante m/f; (person in love) innamorato/a; (amateur): **a ~ of** un(un')amante di; un(un')appassiona-to(a) di

loving ['lʌvɪŋ] adj affettuoso(a)

low [ləʊ] adj basso(a) ♦ adv in basso ♦ n (METEOR) depressione f; **to be ~ on** (supplies etc) avere scarsità di; **to feel ~** sentirsi giù; **~-alcohol** adj a basso contenuto alcolico; **~-calorie** adj a basso contenuto calorico; **~-cut** adj (dress) scollato(a); **~er** adj (bottom: of 2 things) più basso; (less important) meno importante ♦ vt calare; (prices, eyes, voice) abbassare; **~-fat** adj magro(a); **~lands** npl (GEO) pianura; **~ly** adj umile, modesto(a)

loyal ['lɔɪəl] adj fedele, leale; **~ty** n fedeltà, lealtà; **~ty card** n carta che offre sconti a clienti abituali

lozenge ['lɒzɪndʒ] n (MED) pastiglia

L.P. n abbr = **long-playing record**

L-plates (BRIT) npl contrassegno P principiante

Ltd abbr (= **limited**) ≈ S.r.l.

lubricate ['luːbrɪkeɪt] vt lubrificare

luck [lʌk] n fortuna, sorte f; **bad ~** sfortuna, mala sorte f; **good ~!** buona fortuna!; **~ily** adv fortunatamente, per fortuna; **~y** adj fortunato(a); (number etc) che porta fortuna

ludicrous ['luːdɪkrəs] adj ridicolo(a)

lug [lʌɡ] (inf) vt trascinare

luggage ['lʌɡɪdʒ] n bagagli mpl; **~ rack** n portabagagli m inv

lukewarm ['luːkwɔːm] adj tiepido(a)

lull [lʌl] n intervallo di calma ♦ vt: **to ~ sb to sleep** cullare qn finché si addormenta

lullaby ['lʌləbaɪ] n ninnananna

lumbago [lʌm'beɪɡəʊ] n lombaggine f

lumber ['lʌmbə*] n (wood) legname m; (junk) roba vecchia; ~ **with** vt: **to be ~ed with sth** doversi sorbire qc; **~jack** n boscaiolo

luminous ['lu:mɪnəs] adj luminoso(a)

lump [lʌmp] n pezzo; (in sauce) grumo; (swelling) gonfiore m; (also: sugar ~) zolletta ♦ vt (also: ~ together) riunire, mettere insieme; **a ~ sum** una somma globale; **~y** adj (sauce) pieno(a) di grumi; (bed) bitorzoluto(a)

lunatic ['lu:nətɪk] adj pazzo(a), matto(a)

lunch [lʌntʃ] n pranzo, colazione f

luncheon ['lʌntʃən] n pranzo; **~ voucher** (BRIT) n buono m pasto inv

lunch time n ora di pranzo

lung [lʌŋ] n polmone m

lunge [lʌndʒ] vi (also: ~ forward) fare un balzo in avanti; **to ~ at** balzare su

lurch [lə:tʃ] vi vacillare, barcollare ♦ n scatto improvviso; **to leave sb in the ~** piantare in asso qn

lure [luə*] n richiamo; lusinga ♦ vt attirare (con l'inganno)

lurid ['luərɪd] adj sgargiante; (details etc) impressionante

lurk [lə:k] vi stare in agguato

luscious ['lʌʃəs] adj succulento(a); delizioso(a)

lush [lʌʃ] adj lussureggiante

lust [lʌst] n lussuria; cupidigia; desiderio, (fig): **~ for** sete f di

lusty ['lʌstɪ] adj vigoroso(a), robusto(a)

Luxembourg ['lʌksəmbə:g] n (state) Lussemburgo m; (city) Lussemburgo f

luxuriant [lʌg'zjuərɪənt] adj lussureggiante; (hair) folto(a)

luxurious [lʌg'zjuərɪəs] adj sontuoso(a), di lusso

luxury ['lʌkʃərɪ] n lusso ♦ cpd di lusso

lying ['laɪɪŋ] n bugie fpl, menzogne fpl ♦ adj bugiardo(a)

lynch [lɪntʃ] vt linciare

lyrical ['lɪrɪkl] adj lirico(a); (fig) entusiasta

lyrics ['lɪrɪks] npl (of song) parole fpl

M, m

m. abbr = metre; mile; million

M.A. abbr = Master of Arts

mac [mæk] (BRIT) n impermeabile m

macaroni [mækə'rəunɪ] n maccheroni mpl

machine [mə'ʃi:n] n macchina ♦ vt (TECH) lavorare a macchina; (dress etc) cucire a macchina; **~ gun** n mitragliatrice f; **~ry** n macchinario, macchine fpl; (fig) macchina

mackerel ['mækrl] n inv sgombro

mackintosh ['mækɪntɔʃ] (BRIT) n impermeabile m

mad [mæd] adj matto(a), pazzo(a); (foolish) sciocco(a); (angry) furioso(a); **to be ~ about** (keen) andare pazzo(a) per

madam ['mædəm] n signora

madden ['mædn] vt fare infuriare

made [meɪd] pt, pp of **make**

Madeira [mə'dɪərə] n (GEO) Madera (f); (wine) madera

made-to-measure (BRIT) adj fatto(a) su misura

madly ['mædlɪ] adv follemente

madman ['mædmən] (irreg) n pazzo, alienato

madness ['mædnɪs] n pazzia

magazine [mægə'zi:n] n (PRESS) rivista; (RADIO, TV) rubrica

maggot ['mægət] n baco, verme m

magic ['mædʒɪk] n magia ♦ adj magico(a); **~al** adj magico(a); **~ian** [mə'dʒɪʃən] n mago/a

magistrate ['mædʒɪstreɪt] n magistrato; giudice m/f

magnet ['mægnɪt] n magnete m, calamita; **~ic** ['nɛtɪk] adj magnetico(a)

magnificent [mæg'nɪfɪsnt] adj magnifico(a)

magnify ['mægnɪfaɪ] vt ingrandire; **~ing glass** n lente f d'ingrandimento

magnitude ['mægnɪtju:d] n

grandezza; importanza

magpie ['mægpaɪ] n gazza

mahogany [mə'hɔgənɪ] n mogano

maid [meɪd] n domestica; (in hotel) cameriera

maiden ['meɪdn] n fanciulla ♦ adj (aunt etc) nubile; (speech, voyage) inaugurale; **~ name** n nome m da nubile or da ragazza

mail [meɪl] n posta ♦ vt spedire (per posta); **~box** (US) n cassetta delle lettere; **~ing list** n elenco m d'indirizzi; **~-order** n vendita (or acquisto) per corrispondenza

maim [meɪm] vt mutilare

main [meɪn] adj principale ♦ n (pipe) conduttura principale; **the ~s** npl (ELEC) la linea principale; **in the ~** nel complesso, nell'insieme; **~frame** n (COMPUT) mainframe m inv; **~land** n continente m; **~ly** adv principalmente, soprattutto; **~ road** n strada principale; **~stay** n (fig) sostegno principale; **~stream** n (fig) corrente f principale

maintain [meɪn'teɪn] vt mantenere; (affirm) sostenere; **maintenance** ['meɪntənəns] n manutenzione f; (alimony) alimenti mpl

maize [meɪz] n granturco, mais m

majestic [mə'dʒestɪk] adj maestoso(a)

majesty ['mædʒɪstɪ] n maestà f inv

major ['meɪdʒə*] n (MIL) maggiore m ♦ adj (greater, MUS) maggiore; (in importance) principale, importante

Majorca [mə'jɔːkə] n Maiorca

majority [mə'dʒɔrɪtɪ] n maggioranza

make [meɪk] (pt, pp **made**) vt fare; (manufacture) fare, fabbricare; (cause to be): **to ~ sb sad** etc rendere qn triste etc; (force): **to ~ sb do sth** costringere qn a fare qc, far fare qc a qn; (equal): **2 and 2 ~ 4** 2 più 2 fa 4 ♦ n fabbricazione f; (brand) marca; **to ~ a fool of sb** far fare a qn la figura dello scemo; **to ~ a profit** realizzare un profitto; **to ~ a loss** subire una

perdita; **to ~ it** (arrive) arrivare; (achieve sth) farcela; **what time do you ~ it?** che ora fai?; **to ~ do with** arrangiarsi con; **~ for** vt fus (place) avviarsi verso; **~ out** vt (write out) scrivere; (: cheque) emettere; (understand) capire; (see) distinguere; (: numbers) decifrare; **~ up** vt (constitute) formare; (invent) inventare; (parcel) fare ♦ vi conciliarsi; (with cosmetics) truccarsi; **~ up for** vt fus compensare; ricuperare; **~-believe** n: **a world of ~-believe** un mondo di favole; **it's just ~-believe** è tutta un'invenzione; **~r** n (of programme etc) creatore/trice; (manufacturer) fabbricante m; **~shift** adj improvvisato(a); **~up** n trucco; **~up remover** n struccatore m

making ['meɪkɪŋ] n (fig): **in the ~** in formazione; **to have the ~s of** (actor, athlete etc) avere la stoffa di

maladjusted [mælə'dʒʌstɪd] adj disadattato(a)

malaria [mə'leərɪə] n malaria

Malaysia [mə'leɪzɪə] n Malaysia

male [meɪl] n (BIOL) maschio ♦ adj maschile; maschio(a)

malfunction [mæl'fʌŋkʃən] n funzione f difettosa

malice ['mælɪs] n malevolenza; **malicious** [mə'lɪʃəs] adj malevolo(a); (LAW) doloso(a)

malignant [mə'lɪgnənt] adj (MED) maligno(a)

mall [mɔːl] n (also: shopping ~) centro commerciale

mallet ['mælɪt] n maglio

malnutrition [mælnjuː'trɪʃən] n denutrizione f

malpractice [mæl'præktɪs] n prevaricazione f; negligenza

malt [mɔːlt] n malto

Malta ['mɔːltə] n Malta

mammal ['mæml] n mammifero

mammoth ['mæməθ] adj enorme, gigantesco(a)

man [mæn] (pl **men**) n uomo ♦ vt
fornire d'uomini; stare a; **an old ~** un
vecchio; **~ and wife** marito e moglie

manage ['mænɪdʒ] vi farcela ♦ vt (be
in charge of) occuparsi di; gestire; **to
~ to do sth** riuscire a far qc; **~able**
adj maneggevole; fattibile; **~ment** n
amministrazione f, direzione f; **~r** n
direttore m; (of artist, restaurant)
gerente m; (of artist, SPORT) manager m
inv; **~ress** [-ə'rɛs] n direttrice f,
gerente f; **~rial** [-ə'dʒɪərɪəl] adj
dirigenziale; **managing director** n
amministratore m delegato

mandarin ['mændərɪn] n (person, fruit)
mandarino

mandatory ['mændətərɪ] adj
obbligatorio(a); ingiuntivo(a)

mane [meɪn] n criniera

maneuver etc [mə'nu:və*] (US) =
manoeuvre etc

manfully ['mænfəlɪ] adv
valorosamente

mangle ['mæŋgl] vt straziare; mutilare

mango ['mæŋgəʊ] (pl **~es**) n mango

mangy ['meɪndʒɪ] adj rognoso(a)

manhandle ['mænhændl] vt
malmenare

manhole ['mænhəʊl] n botola stradale

manhood ['mænhʊd] n età virile;
virilità

man-hour n ora di lavoro

manhunt ['mænhʌnt] n caccia
all'uomo

mania ['meɪnɪə] n mania; **~c**
['meɪnɪæk] n maniaco/a

manic ['mænɪk] adj (behaviour, activity)
maniacale

manicure ['mænɪkjʊə*] n manicure f
inv; **~ set** n trousse f inv della
manicure

manifest ['mænɪfɛst] vt manifestare
♦ adj manifesto(a), palese

manifesto [mænɪ'fɛstəʊ] n manifesto

manipulate [mə'nɪpjʊleɪt] vt
manipolare

mankind [mæn'kaɪnd] n umanità,

genere m umano

manly ['mænlɪ] adj virile; coraggioso(a)

man-made adj sintetico(a); artificiale

manner ['mænə*] n maniera, modo;
(behaviour) modo di fare; (type, sort):
all ~ of things ogni genere di cosa;
~s npl (conduct) maniere fpl; **bad ~s**
maleducazione f; **~ism** n vezzo, tic m
inv

manoeuvre [mə'nu:və*] (US
maneuver) vt manovrare ♦ vi far
manovre ♦ n manovra

manor ['mænə*] n (also: **~ house**)
maniero

manpower ['mænpaʊə*] n
manodopera

mansion ['mænʃən] n casa signorile

manslaughter ['mænslɔːtə*] n
omicidio preterintenzionale

mantelpiece ['mæntlpiːs] n mensola
del caminetto

manual ['mænjʊəl] adj manuale ♦ n
manuale m

manufacture [mænjʊ'fæktʃə*] vt
fabbricare ♦ n fabbricazione f,
manifattura; **~r** n fabbricante m

manure [mə'njʊə*] n concime m

manuscript ['mænjʊskrɪpt] n
manoscritto

many ['mɛnɪ] adj molti(e) ♦ pron
molti(e); **a great ~** moltissimi(e), un
gran numero (di); **~ a time** molte
volte

map [mæp] n carta (geografica); **~ out**
vt tracciare un piano di

maple ['meɪpl] n acero

mar [mɑː*] vt sciupare

marathon ['mærəθən] n maratona

marauder [mə'rɔːdə*] n
saccheggiatore m

marble ['mɑːbl] n marmo; (toy)
pallina, bilia

March [mɑːtʃ] n marzo

march [mɑːtʃ] vi marciare; sfilare ♦ n
marcia

mare [mɛə*] n giumenta

margarine [mɑːdʒə'riːn] n margarina

margin ['mɑːdʒɪn] n margine m; ~al (seat) n (POL) seggio elettorale ottenuto con una stretta maggioranza

marigold ['mærɪɡəʊld] n calendola f

marina [mə'riːnə] n marina

marine [mə'riːn] adj (animal, plant) marino(a); (forces, engineering) marittimo(a) ♦ n (BRIT) fante m di marina; (US) marine m inv

marital ['mærɪtl] adj maritale, coniugale; ~ **status** n stato coniugale

mark [mɑːk] n segno; (stain) macchia; (of skid etc) traccia; (BRIT: SCOL) voto; (SPORT) bersaglio; (currency) marco ♦ vt segnare; (stain) macchiare; (indicate) indicare; (BRIT: SCOL) dare un voto a; correggere; **to ~ time** segnare il passo; **~ed** adj spiccato(a), chiaro(a) ♦; **~er** n (sign) segno; (bookmark) segnalibro

market ['mɑːkɪt] n mercato ♦ vt (COMM) mettere in vendita; ~ **garden** (BRIT) n orto industriale; **~ing** n marketing m; ~ **place** n piazza del mercato; (COMM) piazza, mercato; ~ **research** n indagine f or ricerca di mercato

marksman ['mɑːksmən] n tiratore m scelto

marmalade ['mɑːməleɪd] n marmellata d'arance

maroon [mə'ruːn] vt (also fig): **to be ~ed (in or at)** essere abbandonato(a) (in) ♦ adj bordeaux inv

marquee [mɑː'kiː] n padiglione m

marquess ['mɑːkwɪs] n = **marquis**

marquis ['mɑːkwɪs] n marchese m

marriage ['mærɪdʒ] n matrimonio; ~ **certificate** n certificato di matrimonio

married ['mærɪd] adj sposato(a); (life, love) coniugale, matrimoniale

marrow ['mærəʊ] n midollo; (vegetable) zucca

marry ['mærɪ] vt sposare, sposarsi con; (subj: vicar, priest etc) dare in matrimonio ♦ vi (also: get married)

sposarsi

Mars [mɑːz] n (planet) Marte m

marsh [mɑːʃ] n palude f

marshal ['mɑːʃl] n maresciallo; (US: fire) capo; (: police) capitano ♦ vt (thoughts, support) ordinare; (soldiers) adunare

martyr ['mɑːtə*] n martire m/f; ~**dom** n martirio

marvel ['mɑːvl] n meraviglia ♦ vi: **to ~ (at)** meravigliarsi (di); ~**lous** (US ~**ous**) adj meraviglioso(a)

Marxist ['mɑːksɪst] adj, n marxista m/f

marzipan ['mɑːzɪpæn] n marzapane m

mascara [mæs'kɑːrə] n mascara m

masculine ['mæskjʊlɪn] adj maschile; (woman) mascolino(a)

mash [mæʃ] vt passare, schiacciare; ~**ed potatoes** npl purè m di patate

mask [mɑːsk] n maschera f ♦ vt mascherare

mason ['meɪsn] n (also: stone~) scalpellino; (also: free~) massone m; ~**ry** n muratura

masquerade [mæskə'reɪd] vi: **to ~ as** farsi passare per

mass [mæs] n moltitudine f, massa; (PHYSICS) massa; (REL) messa ♦ cpd di massa ♦ vi ammassarsi; **the ~es** npl (ordinary people) le masse; ~**es of** (inf) una montagna di

massacre ['mæsəkə*] n massacro

massage ['mæsɑːʒ] n massaggio

masseur [mæ'sə:*] n massaggiatore m; **masseuse** [-'sə:z] n massaggiatrice f

massive ['mæsɪv] adj enorme, massiccio(a)

mass media npl mass media mpl

mass-production n produzione f in serie

mast [mɑːst] n albero

master ['mɑːstə*] n padrone m; (ART etc, teacher: in primary school) maestro; (: in secondary school) professore m; (title for boys) Signorino X ♦ vt domare; (learn) imparare a fondo; (understand) conoscere a fondo; ~ **key**

n chiave *f* maestra; **~ly** *adj* magistrale;
~mind *n* mente *f* superiore ♦ *vt* essere
il cervello di; **M~ of Arts/Science** *n*
Master *m inv* in lettere/scienze; **~piece**
n capolavoro; **~y** *n* dominio;
padronanza

mat [mæt] *n* stuoia; (*also: door~*)
stoino, zerbino; (*also: table ~*)
sottopiatto ♦ *adj* = **matt**

match [mætʃ] *n* fiammifero; (*game*)
partita, incontro; (*fig*) uguale *m/f*;
matrimonio; partito ♦ *vt* intonare; (*go
well with*) andare benissimo con; (*equal*)
uguagliare; (*correspond to*)
corrispondere a; (*pair: also: ~ up*)
accoppiare ♦ *vi* combaciare; **to be a
good ~** andare bene; **~box** *n* scatola
per fiammiferi; **~ing** *adj* ben
assortito(a)

mate [meɪt] *n* compagno/a di lavoro;
(*inf: friend*) amico/a; (*animal*)
compagno/a; (*in merchant navy*)
secondo ♦ *vi* accoppiarsi

material [mə'tɪərɪəl] *n* (*substance*)
materiale *m*, materia; (*cloth*) stoffa
♦ *adj* materiale; **~s** *npl* (*equipment*)
materiali *mpl*

maternal [mə'tɜːnl] *adj* materno(a)

maternity [mə'tɜːnɪtɪ] *n* maternità;
~ dress *n* vestito *m* pre-maman *inv*;
~ hospital *n* ≈ clinica ostetrica

math [mæθ] (*US*) *n* = **maths**

mathematical [mæθə'mætɪkl] *adj*
matematico(a)

mathematics [mæθə'mætɪks] *n*
matematica

maths [mæθs] (*US* **math**) *n*
matematica

matinée ['mætɪneɪ] *n* matinée *f
inv*

mating call ['meɪtɪŋ-] *n* richiamo
sessuale

matriculation [mətrɪkju'leɪʃən] *n*
immatricolazione *f*

matrimonial [mætrɪ'məunɪəl] *adj*
matrimoniale, coniugale

matrimony ['mætrɪmənɪ] *n*

matrimonio

matron ['meɪtrən] *n* (*in hospital*)
capoinfermiera; (*in school*) infermiera

matt(ed) [mæt] *adj* opaco(a)

matted ['mætɪd] *adj* ingarbugliato(a)

matter ['mætə*] *n* questione *f*; (*PHYSICS*)
materia, sostanza; (*content*) contenuto;
(*MED: pus*) pus *m* ♦ *vi* importare; **it
doesn't ~** non importa; (*I don't mind*)
non fa niente; **what's the ~?** che cosa
c'è?; **no ~ what** qualsiasi cosa accada;
as a ~ of course come cosa naturale;
as a ~ of fact in verità; **~-of-fact** *adj*
prosaico(a)

mattress ['mætrɪs] *n* materasso

mature [mə'tjuə*] *adj* maturo(a);
(*cheese*) stagionato(a) ♦ *vi* maturare;
stagionare

maul [mɔːl] *vt* lacerare

mauve [məuv] *adj* malva *inv*

maxim ['mæksɪm] *n* massima

maximum ['mæksɪməm] (*pl* **maxima**)
adj massimo(a) ♦ *n* massimo

May [meɪ] *n* maggio

may [meɪ] (*conditional:* **might**) *vi*
(*indicating possibility*): **he ~ come** può
darsi che venga; (*be allowed to*): **~ I
smoke?** posso fumare?; (*wishes*):
~ God bless you! Dio la benedica!;
you ~ as well go tanto vale che tu te
ne vada

maybe ['meɪbiː] *adv* forse, può darsi;
~ he'll ... può darsi che lui ... + *sub*,
forse lui ...

May Day *n* il primo maggio

mayhem ['meɪhem] *n* cagnara

mayonnaise [meɪə'neɪz] *n* maionese *f*

mayor [mεə*] *n* sindaco; **~ess** *n*
sindaco (*donna*); moglie *f* del sindaco

maze [meɪz] *n* labirinto, dedalo

M.D. *abbr* = **Doctor of Medicine**

me [miː] *pron* mi, m' + *vowel or silent
'h';* (*stressed, after prep*) me; **he
heard ~** mi ha *or* m'ha sentito; **give
~ a book** dammi (*or* mi dia) un libro;
it's ~ sono io; **with ~** con me;
without ~ senza di me

meadow ['mɛdəu] n prato

meagre ['mi:gə*] (US **meager**) adj magro(a)

meal [mi:l] n pasto; (flour) farina;
~**time** n l'ora di mangiare

mean [mi:n] (pt, pp **meant**) adj (with money) avaro(a), gretto(a); (unkind) meschino(a), maligno(a); (shabby) misero(a); (average) medio(a) ♦ vt (signify) significare, voler dire; (intend): **to ~ to do** aver l'intenzione di fare ♦ n mezzo; (MATH) media; ~**s** npl (way, money) mezzi mpl; **by ~s of** per mezzo di; **by all ~s** prego, certo; **to be meant for** essere destinato(a) a; **do you ~ it?** dice sul serio?; **what do you ~?** che cosa vuol dire?

meander [mi'ændə*] vi far meandri

meaning ['mi:niŋ] n significato, senso;
~**ful** adj significativo(a); ~**less** adj senza senso

means [mi:nz] npl mezzi mpl; **by ~ of** per mezzo di; (person) a mezzo di; **by all ~** ma certo, prego

meant [mɛnt] pt, pp of **mean**

meantime ['mi:ntaim] adv (also: in the ~) nel frattempo

meanwhile ['mi:nwail] adv nel frattempo

measles ['mi:zlz] n morbillo

measure ['mɛʒə*] vt, vi misurare ♦ n misura; (also: tape ~) metro; ~**ments** npl (size) misure fpl

meat [mi:t] n carne f; **cold ~** affettato;
~**ball** n polpetta di carne; ~ **pie** n pasticcio di carne in crosta

Mecca ['mɛkə] n (also fig) la Mecca

mechanic [mi'kænik] n meccanico;
~**al** adj meccanico(a); ~**s** n meccanica ♦ npl meccanismo

mechanism ['mɛkənizəm] n meccanismo

medal ['mɛdl] n medaglia; ~**lion** [mi'dæliən] n medaglione m; ~**list** (US ~**ist**) n (SPORT): **to be a gold ~list** essere medaglia d'oro

meddle ['mɛdl] vi: **to ~ in** immischiarsi in, mettere le mani in; **to ~ with** toccare

media ['mi:diə] npl media mpl

mediaeval [mɛdi'i:vl] adj = **medieval**

median ['mi:diən] (US) n (also: ~ strip) banchina f spartitraffico

mediate ['mi:dieit] vi fare da mediatore/trice

Medicaid ® ['mɛdikeid] (US) n assistenza medica ai poveri

medical ['mɛdikl] adj medico(a) ♦ n visita medica

Medicare ® ['mɛdikeə*] (US) n assistenza medica agli anziani

medication [mɛdi'keiʃən] n medicinali mpl, farmaci mpl

medicine ['mɛdsin] n medicina

medieval [mɛdi'i:vl] adj medievale

mediocre [mi:di'əukə*] adj mediocre

meditate ['mɛditeit] vi: **to ~ (on)** meditare (su)

Mediterranean [mɛditə'reiniən] adj mediterraneo(a); **the ~ (Sea)** il (mare) Mediterraneo

medium ['mi:diəm] (pl **media**) adj medio(a) ♦ n (means) mezzo; (pl **mediums**: person) medium m inv;
~ **wave** n onde fpl medie

meek [mi:k] adj dolce, umile

meet [mi:t] (pt, pp **met**) vt incontrare; (for the first time) fare la conoscenza di; (go and fetch) andare a prendere; (fig) affrontare; soddisfare; raggiungere ♦ vi incontrarsi; (in session) riunirsi; (join: objects) unirsi; ~ **with** vt fus incontrare;
~**ing** n incontro; (session: of club etc) riunione f; (interview) intervista; **she's at a ~ing** (COMM) è in riunione

megabyte ['mɛgəbait] n (COMPUT) megabyte m inv

megaphone ['mɛgəfəun] n megafono

melancholy ['mɛlənkəli] n malinconia ♦ adj malinconico(a)

mellow ['mɛləu] adj (wine, sound) ricco(a); (light) dolce; (colour) caldo(a) ♦ vi (person) addolcirsi

melody ['mɛlədɪ] n melodia

melon ['mɛlən] n melone m

melt [mɛlt] vi (gen) sciogliersi, struggersi; (metals) fondersi ♦ vt sciogliere, struggere; fondere; ~ **down** vt fondere; **~down** n (in nuclear reactor) fusione f (dovuta a surriscaldamento); **~ing pot** n (fig) crogiolo

member ['mɛmbə*] n membro; **M~ of the European Parliament** (BRIT) n eurodeputato/a; **M~ of Parliament** (BRIT) n deputato/a; **M~ of the Scottish Parliament** (BRIT) n deputato/a del Parlamento scozzese; **~ship** n iscrizione f; (number d')iscritti mpl; membri mpl; **~ship card** n tessera (di iscrizione)

memento [mə'mɛntəu] n ricordo, souvenir m inv

memo ['mɛməu] n appunto; (COMM etc) comunicazione f di servizio

memoirs ['mɛmwɑːz] npl memorie fpl, ricordi mpl

memoranda [mɛmə'rændə] npl of **memorandum**

memorandum [mɛmə'rændəm] (pl **memoranda**) n appunto; (COMM etc) comunicazione f di servizio

memorial [mɪ'mɔːrɪəl] n monumento commemorativo ♦ adj commemorativo(a)

memorize ['mɛmərɑɪz] vt memorizzare

memory ['mɛmərɪ] n (also COMPUT) memoria; (recollection) ricordo

men [mɛn] npl of **man**

menace ['mɛnəs] n minaccia ♦ vt minacciare

mend [mɛnd] vt aggiustare, riparare; (darn) rammendare ♦ n: **on the ~** in via di guarigione

menial ['miːnɪəl] adj da servo, domestico(a); umile

meningitis [mɛnɪn'dʒɑɪtɪs] n meningite f

menopause ['mɛnəupɔːz] n menopausa

menstruation [mɛnstru'eɪʃən] n mestruazione f

mental ['mɛntl] adj mentale

mentality [mɛn'tælɪtɪ] n mentalità f inv

menthol ['mɛnθɔl] n mentolo

mention ['mɛnʃən] n menzione f ♦ vt menzionare, far menzione di; **don't ~ it!** non c'è di che!, prego!

menu ['mɛnjuː] n (set ~, COMPUT) menù m inv; (printed) carta

MEP n abbr = **Member of the European Parliament**

merchandise ['mɜːtʃəndɑɪz] n merci fpl

merchant ['mɜːtʃənt] n mercante m, commerciante m; **~ bank** (BRIT) n banca d'affari; **~ navy** (US **~ marine**) n marina mercantile

merciful ['mɜːsɪful] adj pietoso(a), clemente

merciless ['mɜːsɪlɪs] adj spietato(a)

mercury ['mɜːkjurɪ] n mercurio

mercy ['mɜːsɪ] n pietà; (REL) misericordia; **at the ~ of** alla mercè di

mere [mɪə*] adj semplice; **by a ~ chance** per mero caso; **~ly** adv semplicemente, non ... che

merge [mɜːdʒ] vt unire ♦ vi fondersi, unirsi; (COMM) fondersi; **~r** n (COMM) fusione f

meringue [mə'ræŋ] n meringa

merit ['mɛrɪt] n merito, valore m ♦ vt meritare

mermaid ['mɜːmeɪd] n sirena

merry ['mɛrɪ] adj gaio(a), allegro(a); **M~ Christmas!** Buon Natale!; **~-go-round** n carosello

mesh [mɛʃ] n maglia; rete f

mesmerize ['mɛzmərɑɪz] vt ipnotizzare; affascinare

mess [mɛs] n confusione f, disordine m; (fig) pasticcio; (dirt) sporcizia; (MIL) mensa; **~ about** (inf) vi (also: ~ around) trastullarsi; **~ about with** (inf) vt fus (also: ~ around with) gingillarsi con; (plans) fare un pasticcio di; **~ up** vt sporcare; fare un pasticcio di; rovinare

message ['mɛsɪdʒ] n messaggio

messenger ['mɛsɪndʒə*] n messaggero/a

Messrs ['mɛsəz] abbr (on letters) Spett

messy ['mɛsɪ] adj sporco(a); disordinato(a)

met [mɛt] pt, pp of meet

metal ['mɛtl] n metallo; **~lic** [-'tælɪk] adj metallico(a)

metaphor ['mɛtəfə*] n metafora

meteorology [miːtɪə'rɔlədʒɪ] n meteorologia

meter ['miːtə*] n (instrument) contatore m; (parking =) parchimetro; (US: unit) = **metre**

method ['mɛθəd] n metodo; **~ical** [mɪ'θɔdɪkl] adj metodico(a)

Methodist ['mɛθədɪst] n metodista m/f

meths [mɛθs] (BRIT) n = **methylated spirit**

methylated spirit ['mɛθɪleɪtɪd-] (BRIT) n alcool m denaturato

metre ['miːtə*] (US meter) n metro

metric ['mɛtrɪk] adj metrico(a)

metropolitan [mɛtrə'pɔlɪtən] adj metropolitano(a); **the M~ Police** (BRIT) n la polizia di Londra

mettle ['mɛtl] n: **to be on one's ~** essere pronto(a) a dare il meglio di se stesso(a)

mew [mjuː] vi (cat) miagolare

mews [mjuːz] (BRIT) n: **~ flat** appartamento ricavato da un'antica scuderia

Mexico ['mɛksɪkəu] n Messico

miaow [miːˈau] vi miagolare

mice [maɪs] npl of **mouse**

micro... ['maɪkrəu] prefix micro...; **~chip** n microcircuito integrato; **~(computer)** n microcomputer m inv; **~phone** n microfono; **~scope** n microscopio; **~wave** n (also: **~wave oven**) forno a microonde

mid [mɪd] adj: **~ May** metà maggio;

~ afternoon metà pomeriggio; **in ~ air** a mezz'aria; **~day** n mezzogiorno

middle ['mɪdl] n mezzo; centro; (waist) vita ♦ adj di mezzo; **in the ~ of the night** nel bel mezzo della notte; **the ~ class(es)** n(pl) ≈ la borghesia; **the M~ Ages** npl il Medioevo; **~class** adj ≈ borghese; **M~ East** n Medio Oriente m; **~man** (irreg) n intermediario; agente m rivenditore; **~ name** n secondo nome m; **~-of-the-road** adj moderato(a); **~weight** n (BOXING) peso medio

middling ['mɪdlɪŋ] adj medio(a)

midge [mɪdʒ] n moscerino

midget ['mɪdʒɪt] n nano/a

Midlands ['mɪdləndz] npl contee del centro dell'Inghilterra

midnight ['mɪdnaɪt] n mezzanotte f

midriff ['mɪdrɪf] n diaframma m

midst [mɪdst] n: **in the ~ of** in mezzo a

midsummer [mɪd'sʌmə*] n mezza or piena estate f

midway [mɪd'weɪ] adj, adv: **~ (between)** a mezza strada (fra); **~ (through)** a metà (di)

midweek [mɪd'wiːk] adv a metà settimana

midwife ['mɪdwaɪf] (pl midwives) n levatrice f

might [maɪt] vb see **may** ♦ n potere m, forza; **~y** adj forte, potente

migraine ['miːgreɪn] n emicrania

migrant ['maɪgrənt] adj (bird) migratore(trice); (worker) emigrato/a

migrate [maɪ'greɪt] vi (bird) migrare; (person) emigrare

mike [maɪk] n abbr (= microphone) microfono

Milan [mɪ'læn] n Milano f

mild [maɪld] adj mite; (person, voice) dolce; (flavour) delicato(a); (illness) leggero(a); (interest) blando(a) ♦ n (beer) birra leggera

mildew ['mɪldju:] n muffa

mildly ['maɪldlɪ] adv mitemente;
dolcemente; delicatamente;
leggermente; blandamente; **to put it
~** a dire poco

mile [maɪl] n miglio; **~age** n distanza
in miglia, ≈ chilometraggio

mileometer [maɪ'lɒmɪtə*] n ≈
contachilometri m inv

milestone ['maɪlstəʊn] n pietra miliare

milieu ['mi:ljɜ:] n ambiente m

militant ['mɪlɪtnt] adj militante

military ['mɪlɪtərɪ] adj militare

milk [mɪlk] n latte m ♦ vt (cow)
mungere; (fig) sfruttare; **~ chocolate**
n cioccolato al latte; **~man** (irreg) n
lattaio; **~ shake** n frappé m inv; **~y**
adj lattiginoso(a); (colour) latteo(a); **M~y
Way** n Via Lattea

mill [mɪl] n mulino; (small: for coffee,
pepper etc) macinino; (factory) fabbrica;
(spinning ~) filatura ♦ vt macinare ♦ vi
(also: ~ about) brulicare

millennia [mɪ'lenɪə] npl of
millennium

millennium [mɪ'lenɪəm] (pl **~s** or
millennia) n millennio; **~ bug** n baco
di fine millennio

miller ['mɪlə*] n mugnaio

milli... ['mɪlɪ] prefix: **~gram(me)** n
milligrammo; **~metre** (US **~meter**) n
millimetro

million ['mɪljən] n milione m; **~aire**
n milionario, ≈ miliardario

milometer [maɪ'lɒmɪtə*] n =
mileometer

mime [maɪm] n mimo ♦ vt, vi mimare

mimic ['mɪmɪk] n imitatore/trice ♦ vt
fare la mimica di

min. abbr = **minute(s)**; **minimum**

mince [mɪns] vt tritare, macinare ♦ n
(BRIT: CULIN) carne f tritata or macinata;
~meat n frutta secca tritata per uso in
pasticceria; (US) carne f tritata or
macinata; **~ pie** n specie di torta con
frutta secca; **~r** n tritacarne m inv

mind [maɪnd] n mente f ♦ vt (attend

to, look after) badare a, occuparsi di;
(be careful) fare attenzione a, stare
attento(a) a; (object to): **I don't ~ the
noise** il rumore non mi dà alcun
fastidio; **I don't ~** non m'importa; **it is
on my ~** mi preoccupa; **to my ~**
secondo me, a mio parere; **to be out
of one's ~** essere uscito(a) di mente;
to keep or **bear sth in ~** non
dimenticare qc; **to make up one's ~**
decidersi; **~ you,** ... sì, però va detto
che ...; **never ~** non importa, non fa
niente; (don't worry) non preoccuparti;
"~ the step" "attenzione allo
scalino"; **~er** n (child ~er) bambinaia;
(bodyguard) guardia del corpo; **~less**
adj idiota

mine [maɪn] pron il(la) mio(a), pl i(le)
miei(mie); **that book is ~** quel libro è
mio; **yours is red, ~ is green** il tuo è
rosso, il mio è verde; **a friend of ~** un
mio amico

mine² [maɪn] n miniera; (explosive)
mina ♦ vt (coal) estrarre; (ship, beach)
minare; **~field** n (also fig) campo
minato

miner ['maɪnə*] n minatore m

mineral ['mɪnərəl] adj minerale ♦ n
minerale m; **~s** npl (BRIT: soft drinks)
bevande fpl gasate; **~ water** n acqua
minerale

mingle ['mɪŋgl] vi: **to ~ with**
mescolarsi a, mischiarsi con

miniature ['mɪnətʃə*] adj in miniatura
♦ n miniatura

minibus ['mɪnɪbʌs] n minibus m inv

minim ['mɪnɪm] n (MUS) minima

minimum ['mɪnɪməm] (pl **minima**) n
minimo ♦ adj minimo(a)

mining ['maɪnɪŋ] n industria mineraria

miniskirt ['mɪnɪskɜ:t] n minigonna

minister ['mɪnɪstə*] n (BRIT: POL)
ministro; (REL) pastore m

ministry ['mɪnɪstrɪ] n ministero

mink [mɪŋk] n visone m

minnow ['mɪnəʊ] n pesciolino d'acqua
dolce

minor ['maɪnə*] *adj* minore, di poca importanza; (*MUS*) minore ♦ *n* (*LAW*) minorenne *m/f*

minority [maɪ'nɒrɪtɪ] *n* minoranza

mint [mɪnt] *n* (*plant*) menta; (*sweet*) pasticca di menta ♦ *vt* (*coins*) battere; **the (Royal) M~** (*BRIT*), **the (US) M~** (*US*) la Zecca; **in ~ condition** come nuovo(a) di zecca

minus ['maɪnəs] *n* (*also*: ~ **sign**) segno meno ♦ *prep* meno

minute [*adj* maɪ'njuːt, *n* 'mɪnɪt] *adj* minuscolo(a); (*detail*) minuzioso(a) ♦ *n* minuto; **~s** *npl* (*of meeting*) verbale *m*

miracle ['mɪrəkl] *n* miracolo

mirage ['mɪrɑːʒ] *n* miraggio

mirror ['mɪrə*] *n* specchio; (*in car*) specchietto

mirth [mɜːθ] *n* ilarità

misadventure [mɪsəd'ventʃə*] *n* disavventura; **death by ~** morte *f* accidentale

misapprehension ['mɪsæprɪ'henʃən] *n* malinteso

misappropriate [mɪsə'prəuprɪeɪt] *vt* appropriarsi indebitamente di

misbehave [mɪsbɪ'heɪv] *vi* comportarsi male

miscarriage ['mɪskærɪdʒ] *n* (*MED*) aborto spontaneo; **~ of justice** errore *m* giudiziario

miscellaneous [mɪsɪ'leɪnɪəs] *adj* (*items*) vario(a); (*selection*) misto(a)

mischance [mɪs'tʃɑːns] *n* sfortuna

mischief ['mɪstʃɪf] *n* (*naughtiness*) birichineria; (*maliciousness*) malizia; **mischievous** *adj* birichino(a)

misconception ['mɪskən'sepʃən] *n* idea sbagliata

misconduct [mɪs'kɒndʌkt] *n* cattiva condotta; **professional ~** reato professionale

misdemeanour [mɪsdɪ'miːnə*] (*US* **misdemeanor**) *n* misfatto; infrazione *f*

miser ['maɪzə*] *n* avaro

miserable ['mɪzərəbl] *adj* infelice; (*wretched*) miserabile; (*weather*)

depriment; (*offer, failure*) misero(a)

miserly ['maɪzəlɪ] *adj* avaro(a)

misery ['mɪzərɪ] *n* (*unhappiness*) tristezza; (*wretchedness*) miseria

misfire [mɪs'faɪə*] *vi* far cilecca; (*car engine*) perdere colpi

misfit ['mɪsfɪt] *n* (*person*) spostato/a

misfortune [mɪs'fɔːtʃən] *n* sfortuna

misgiving [mɪs'gɪvɪŋ] *n* apprensione *f*; **to have ~s about** avere dei dubbi per quanto riguarda

misguided [mɪs'gaɪdɪd] *adj* sbagliato(a); poco giudizioso(a)

mishandle [mɪs'hændl] *vt* (*mismanage*) trattare male

mishap ['mɪshæp] *n* disgrazia

misinterpret [mɪsɪn'tɜːprɪt] *vt* interpretare male

misjudge [mɪs'dʒʌdʒ] *vt* giudicare male

mislay [mɪs'leɪ] (*irreg*) *vt* smarrire

mislead [mɪs'liːd] (*irreg*) *vt* sviare; **~ing** *adj* ingannevole

mismanage [mɪs'mænɪdʒ] *vt* gestire male

misplace [mɪs'pleɪs] *vt* smarrire

misprint ['mɪsprɪnt] *n* errore *m* di stampa

Miss [mɪs] *n* Signorina

miss [mɪs] *vt* (*fail to get*) perdere; (*fail to hit*) mancare; (*fail to see*): **you can't ~ it** non puoi non vederlo; (*regret the absence of*): **I ~ him** sento la sua mancanza ♦ *vi* mancare ♦ *n* (*shot*) colpo mancato; **~ out** (*BRIT*) *vt* omettere

misshapen [mɪs'ʃeɪpən] *adj* deforme

missile ['mɪsaɪl] *n* (*MIL*) missile *m*; (*object thrown*) proiettile *m*

missing ['mɪsɪŋ] *adj* perso(a), smarrito(a); (*person*) scomparso(a); (: *after disaster, MIL*) disperso(a); (*removed*) mancante; **to be ~** mancare

mission ['mɪʃən] *n* missione *f*; **~ary** *n* missionario/a

mist [mɪst] *n* nebbia, foschia ♦ *vi* (*also*: ~ **over**, ~ **up**) annebbiarsi; (: *BRIT*:

windows) apparnarsi

mistake [mɪs'teɪk] (*irreg: like* **take**) *n* sbaglio, errore *m* ♦ *vt* sbagliarsi di; fraintendere; **to make a ~** fare uno sbaglio, sbagliare; **by ~** per sbaglio; **to ~ for** prendere per; **mistaken** *pp of* **mistake** ♦ *adj* (*idea etc*) sbagliato(a); **to be mistaken** sbagliarsi

mister ['mɪstə*] (*inf*) *n* signore *m*; *see* **Mr**

mistletoe ['mɪsltəu] *n* vischio

mistook [mɪs'tuk] *pt of* **mistake**

mistress ['mɪstrɪs] *n* padrona; (*lover*) amante *f*; (*BRIT: SCOL*) insegnante *f*

mistrust [mɪs'trʌst] *vt* diffidare di

misty ['mɪstɪ] *adj* nebbioso(a), brumoso(a)

misunderstand [mɪsʌndə'stænd] (*irreg*) *vt, vi* capire male, fraintendere; **~ing** *n* malinteso, equivoco

misuse [*n* mɪs'juːs, *vb* mɪs'juːz] *n* cattivo uso; (*of power*) abuso ♦ *vt* far cattivo uso di; abusare di

mitigate ['mɪtɪgeɪt] *vt* mitigare

mitt(en) ['mɪt(n)] *n* mezzo guanto; manopola

mix [mɪks] *vt* mescolare ♦ *vi* (*people*): **to ~ with** avere a che fare con ♦ *n* mescolanza; preparato; **~ up** *vt* mescolare; (*confuse*) confondere; **~ed** *adj* misto(a); **~ed-up** *adj* (*confused*) confuso(a); **~er** *n* (*for food: electric*) frullatore *m*; (*: hand*) frullino; (*person*): **he is a good ~er** è molto socievole; **~ture** *n* mescolanza; (*blend: of tobacco etc*) miscela; (*MED*) sciroppo; **~-up** *n* confusione *f*

moan [məun] *n* gemito ♦ *vi* (*inf: complain*): **to ~ (about)** lamentarsi (di)

moat [məut] *n* fossato

mob [mɔb] *n* calca ♦ *vt* accalcarsi intorno a

mobile ['məubaɪl] *adj* mobile ♦ *n* (*decoration*) mobile *m*; **~ home** *n* grande roulotte *f inv* (*utilizzata come domicilio*); **~ phone** telefono portatile, telefonino

mock [mɔk] *vt* deridere, burlarsi di ♦ *adj* falso(a); **~ery** *n* derisione *f*; **to make a ~ery of** burlarsi di; (*exam*) rendere una farsa; **~-up** *n* modello

mod [mɔd] *adj see* **convenience**

mode [məud] *n* modo

model ['mɔdl] *n* modello; (*person: for fashion*) indossatore/trice; (*: for artist*) modello/a ♦ *adj* (*small-scale: railway etc*) in miniatura; (*child, factory*) modello *inv* ♦ *vt* modellare ♦ *vi* fare l'indossatore (*or* l'indossatrice); **to ~ clothes** presentare degli abiti

modem ['məudem] *n* modem *m inv*

moderate [*adj* 'mɔdərət, *vb* 'mɔdəreɪt] *adj* moderato(a) ♦ *vi* moderarsi, placarsi ♦ *vt* moderare

modern ['mɔdən] *adj* moderno(a); **~ize** *vt* modernizzare

modest ['mɔdɪst] *adj* modesto(a); **~y** *n* modestia

modify ['mɔdɪfaɪ] *vt* modificare

mogul ['məugl] *n* (*fig*) magnate *m*, pezzo grosso

mohair ['məuhɛə*] *n* mohair *m*

moist [mɔɪst] *adj* umido(a); **~en** ['mɔɪsn] *vt* inumidire; **~ure** ['mɔɪstʃə*] *n* umidità; (*on glass*) goccioline *fpl* di vapore; **~urizer** ['mɔɪstʃəraɪzə*] *n* idratante *f*

molar ['məulə*] *n* molare *m*

mold [məuld] (*US*) *n, vt* = **mould**

mole [məul] *n* (*animal, fig*) talpa; (*spot*) neo

molest [məu'lest] *vt* molestare

mollycoddle ['mɔlɪkɔdl] *vt* coccolare, vezzeggiare

molt [məult] (*US*) *vi* = **moult**

molten ['məultən] *adj* fuso(a)

mom [mɔm] (*US*) *n* = **mum**

moment ['məumənt] *n* momento, istante *m*; **at that ~** in quel momento; **at the ~** al momento, in questo momento; **~ary** *adj* momentaneo(a), passeggero(a); **~ous** [-'mentəs] *adj* di grande importanza

momentum [məu'mentəm] *n*

(*PHYSICS*) momento; (*fig*) impeto; **to gather** ~ aumentare di velocità

mommy ['mɒmɪ] (*US*) *n* = **mummy**

Monaco ['mɒnəkəʊ] *n* Principato di Monaco

monarch ['mɒnək] *n* monarca *m*; **~y** *n* monarchia

monastery ['mɒnəstərɪ] *n* monastero

Monday ['mʌndɪ] *n* lunedì *m inv*

monetary ['mʌnɪtərɪ] *adj* monetario(a)

money ['mʌnɪ] *n* denaro, soldi *mpl*; ~ **belt** *n* marsupio (*per soldi*); ~ **order** *n* vaglia *m inv*; **~-spinner** (*inf*) *n* miniera d'oro (*fig*)

mongol ['mɒŋgəl] *adj*, *n* (*MED*) mongoloide *m/f*

mongrel ['mʌŋgrəl] *n* (*dog*) cane *m* bastardo

monitor ['mɒnɪtə*] *n* (*TV, COMPUT*) monitor *m inv* ♦ *vt* controllare

monk [mʌŋk] *n* monaco

monkey ['mʌŋkɪ] *n* scimmia; ~ **nut** (*BRIT*) *n* nocciolina americana; ~ **wrench** *n* chiave *f* a rullino

mono ['mɒnəʊ] *adj* (*recording*) (in) mono *inv*

monopoly [məˈnɒpəlɪ] *n* monopolio

monotone ['mɒnətəʊn] *n* pronunzia (*or voce f*) monotona

monotonous [məˈnɒtənəs] *adj* monotono(a)

monsoon [mɒnˈsuːn] *n* monsone *m*

monster ['mɒnstə*] *n* mostro

monstrous ['mɒnstrəs] *adj* mostruoso(a); (*huge*) gigantesco(a)

month [mʌnθ] *n* mese *m*; **~ly** *adj* mensile ♦ *adv* al mese; ogni mese

monument ['mɒnjumənt] *n* monumento

moo [muː] *vi* muggire, mugghiare

mood [muːd] *n* umore *m*; **to be in a good/bad** ~ essere di buon/cattivo umore; **~y** *adj* (*variable*) capriccioso(a), lunatico(a); (*sullen*) imbronciato(a)

moon [muːn] *n* luna; **~light** *n* chiaro di luna; **~lighting** *n* lavoro nero; **~lit** *adj*: **a ~lit night** una notte rischiarata dalla luna

Moor [mʊə*] *n* moro/a

moor [mʊə*] *n* brughiera ♦ *vt* (*ship*) ormeggiare ♦ *vi* ormeggiarsi

moorland ['mʊələnd] *n* brughiera

moose [muːs] *n inv* alce *m*

mop [mɒp] *n* lavapavimenti *m inv*; (*also*: ~ **of hair**) zazzera ♦ *vt* lavare con lo straccio; (*face*) asciugare; ~ **up** *vt* asciugare con uno straccio

mope [məʊp] *vi* fare il broncio

moped ['məʊpɛd] *n* (*BRIT*) ciclomotore *m*

moral ['mɒrl] *adj* morale ♦ *n* morale *f*; **~s** *npl* (*principles*) moralità

morality [məˈrælɪtɪ] *n* moralità

morass [məˈræs] *n* palude *f*, pantano

morbid ['mɔːbɪd] *adj* morboso(a)

KEYWORD

more [mɔː*] *adj* **1** (*greater in number etc*) più; ~ **people/letters than we expected** più persone/lettere di quante ne aspettavamo; **I have** ~ **wine/money than you** ho più vino/soldi di te; **I have** ~ **wine than beer** ho più vino che birra

2 (*additional*) altro(a), ancora; **do you want (some) ~ tea?** vuole dell'altro tè?, vuole ancora del tè?; **I have no** or **I don't have any** ~ **money** non ho più soldi

♦ *pron* **1** (*greater amount*) più; ~ **than 10** più di 10; **it cost** ~ **than we expected** è costato più di quanto ci aspettavamo

2 (*further or additional amount*) ancora; **is there any ~?** ce n'è ancora?; **there's no** ~ non ce n'è più; **a little** ~ ancora un po'; **many/much** ~ molti(e)/molto(a) di più

♦ *adv*: ~ **dangerous/easily (than)** più pericoloso/facilmente (di); ~ **and** ~ sempre di più; ~ **and** ~ **difficult** sempre più difficile; ~ **or less** più o meno; ~ **than ever** più che mai

moreover [mɔːˈrəʊvə*] adv inoltre, di più

morgue [mɔːg] n obitorio

morning [ˈmɔːnɪŋ] n mattina, mattino; (duration) mattinata ♦ cpd del mattino; **in the ~** la mattina; **7 o'clock in the ~** le 7 di mattina o della mattina; **~ sickness** n nausee fpl mattutine

Morocco [məˈrɒkəʊ] n Marocco

moron [ˈmɔːrɒn] (inf) n deficiente m/f

morose [məˈrəʊs] adj cupo(a), tetro(a)

Morse [mɔːs] n (also: **~ code**) alfabeto Morse

morsel [ˈmɔːsl] n boccone m

mortal [ˈmɔːtl] adj mortale ♦ n mortale m

mortgage [ˈmɔːgɪdʒ] n ipoteca; (loan) prestito ipotecario ♦ vt ipotecare; **~ company** (US) n società f inv di credito immobiliare

mortuary [ˈmɔːtjʊərɪ] n camera mortuaria; obitorio

mosaic [məʊˈzeɪɪk] n mosaico

Moscow [ˈmɒskəʊ] n Mosca

Moslem [ˈmɒzləm] adj, n = **Muslim**

mosque [mɒsk] n moschea

mosquito [mɒsˈkiːtəʊ] (pl **~es**) n zanzara

moss [mɒs] n muschio

most [məʊst] adj (almost all) la maggior parte di; (largest, greatest): **who has (the) ~ money?** chi ha più soldi di tutti? ♦ pron la maggior parte ♦ adv più; (work, sleep etc) di più; (very) molto, estremamente; **the ~** (also: + adjective) il(la) più; **~ of** la maggior parte di; **~ of them** quasi tutti; **I saw (the) ~** ho visto più di; **at the (very) ~** al massimo; **to make the ~ of** trarre il massimo vantaggio da; **a ~ interesting book** un libro estremamente interessante; **~ly** adv per lo più

MOT (BRIT) n abbr (= Ministry of Transport): **the ~ (test)** revisione annuale obbligatoria degli autoveicoli

motel [məʊˈtel] n motel m inv

moth [mɒθ] n farfalla notturna; tarma

mother [ˈmʌðə*] n madre f ♦ vt (care for) fare da madre a; **~hood** n maternità; **~-in-law** n suocera; **~ly** adj materno(a); **~-of-pearl** [mʌðərəvˈpɜːl] n madreperla; **~-to-be** [mʌðətəˈbiː] n futura mamma; **~ tongue** n madrelingua

motion [ˈməʊʃən] n movimento; moto; (gesture) gesto; (at meeting) mozione f ♦ vt, vi: **to ~ (to) sb to do** fare cenno a qn di fare; **~less** adj immobile; **~ picture** n film m inv

motivated [ˈməʊtɪveɪtɪd] adj motivato(a)

motive [ˈməʊtɪv] n motivo

motley [ˈmɒtlɪ] adj eterogeneo(a), molto vario(a)

motor [ˈməʊtə*] n motore m; (BRIT: inf: vehicle) macchina ♦ cpd automobilistico(a); **~bike** n moto f inv; **~boat** n motoscafo; **~car** (BRIT) n automobile f; **~cycle** n motocicletta; **~cyclist** n motociclista m/f; **~ing** (BRIT) n turismo automobilistico; **~ist** n automobilista m/f; **~ racing** (BRIT) n corse fpl automobilistiche; **~way** (BRIT) n autostrada

mottled [ˈmɒtld] adj chiazzato(a), marezzato(a)

motto [ˈmɒtəʊ] (pl **~es**) n motto

mould [məʊld] (US **mold**) n forma, stampo; (mildew) muffa ♦ vt formare; (fig) foggiare; **~y** adj ammuffito(a); (smell) di muffa

moult [məʊlt] (US **molt**) vi far la muta

mound [maʊnd] n rialzo, collinetta; (heap) mucchio

mount [maʊnt] n (GEO) monte m ♦ vt montare; (horse) montare a ♦ vi (increase) aumentare; **~ up** vi (build up) accumularsi

mountain [ˈmaʊntɪn] n montagna ♦ cpd di montagna; **~ bike** n mountain bike f inv; **~eer** [-ˈnɪə*] n alpinista m/f; **~eering** [-ˈnɪərɪŋ] n alpinismo; **~ous** adj montagnoso(a),

~ rescue team n squadra di soccorso alpino; **~side** n fianco della montagna

mourn [mɔːn] vt piangere, lamentare ♦ vi: **to ~ (for sb)** piangere (la morte di qn); **~er** n parente m/f or amico/a del defunto; **~ing** n lutto; **in ~ing** in lutto

mouse [maus] (pl **mice**) n topo; (COMPUT) mouse m inv; **~ mat**, **~ pad** n (COMPUT) tappetino del mouse; **~trap** n trappola per i topi

mousse [muːs] n mousse f inv

moustache [məs'tɑːʃ] (US **mustache**) n baffi mpl

mousy ['mausɪ] adj (hair) né chiaro/a né scuro/a

mouth [mauθ, pl mauðz] n bocca; (of river) bocca, foce f; (of bottle) imboccatura; (opening) orifizio; **~ful** n boccata; **~ organ** n armonica; **~piece** n (of MUS) imboccatura, bocchino; (spokesman) portavoce m/f inv; **~wash** n collutorio; **~watering** adj che fa venire l'acquolina in bocca

movable ['muːvəbl] adj mobile

move [muːv] n (movement) movimento; (in game) mossa; (: turn to play) turno; (change: of house) trasloco; (: of job) cambiamento ♦ vt muovere, spostare; (emotionally) commuovere; (POL: resolution etc) proporre ♦ vi (gen) muoversi, spostarsi; (also: ~ house) cambiar casa, traslocare; **to get a ~ on** affrettarsi, sbrigarsi; **to ~ sb to do sth** indurre or spingere qn a fare qc; **to ~ towards** andare verso; **~ about** or **around** vi spostarsi; **~ along** vi muoversi avanti; **~ away** vi allontanarsi, andarsene; **~ back** vi (return) ritornare; **~ forward** vi avanzare; **~ in** vi (to a house) entrare (in una nuova casa); **~ on** vi riprendere la strada; **~ out** vi (of house) sgombrare; **~ over** vi spostarsi; **~ up** vi avanzare

moveable ['muːvəbl] adj = **movable**

movement ['muːvmənt] n (gen) movimento; (gesture) gesto; (of stars,

water, physical) moto

movie ['muːvɪ] n film m inv; **the ~s** il cinema

moviecamera n cinepresa

moving ['muːvɪŋ] adj mobile; (causing emotion) commovente

mow [məu] (pt **mowed**, pp **mowed** or **mown**) vt (grass) tagliare; (corn) mietere; **~ down** vt falciare; **~er** n (also: lawnmower) tagliaerba m inv

MP n abbr = **Member of Parliament**

m.p.h. n abbr = miles per hour (60 m.p.h. = 96 km/h)

Mr ['mɪstə*] (US **Mr.**) n: **~ X** Signor X, Sig. X

Mrs ['mɪsɪz] (US **Mrs.**) n: **~ X** Signora X, Sig.ra X

Ms [mɪz] (US **Ms.**) n (= Miss or Mrs): **~ X** Signora X, Sig.ra X

M.Sc. abbr = **Master of Science**

MSP n abbr = **Member of the Scottish Parliament**

much [mʌtʃ] adj, pron molto(a); he's done so ~ work ha lavorato così tanto; **I have as ~ money as you** ho tanti soldi quanti ne hai tu; **how ~ is it?** quant'è?; **it costs too ~** costa troppo; **as ~ as you want** quanto vuoi ♦ adv 1 (greatly) molto, tanto; **thank you very ~** molte grazie; **he's very ~ the gentleman** è il vero gentiluomo; **I read as ~ as I can** leggo quanto posso; **as ~ as you** tanto quanto te 2 (by far) molto; **it's ~ the biggest company in Europe** è di gran lunga la più grossa società in Europa 3 (almost) grossomodo, praticamente; **they're ~ the same** sono praticamente uguali

muck [mʌk] n (dirt) sporcizia; **~ about** or **around** (inf) vi fare lo stupido; (waste time) gingillarsi; **~ up** (inf) vt (ruin) rovinare

mud [mʌd] n fango

muddle ['mʌdl] n confusione f, disordine m; pasticcio f ♦ vt (also: ~ up) confondere; ~ **through** vi cavarsela alla meno peggio

muddy ['mʌdɪ] adj fangoso(a)

mudguard ['mʌdɡɑːd] n parafango

muesli ['mjuːzlɪ] n muesli m

muffin ['mʌfɪn] n specie di pasticcino soffice da tè

muffle ['mʌfl] vt (sound) smorzare, attutire; (against cold) imbaccuare

muffler ['mʌflə*] (US) n (AUT) marmitta; (: on motorbike) silenziatore m

mug [mʌɡ] n (cup) tazzone m; (for beer) boccale m; (inf: face) muso; (: fool) scemo/a ♦ vt (assault) assalire; **~ging** n assalto

muggy ['mʌɡɪ] adj afoso(a)

mule [mjuːl] n mulo

multi-level ['mʌltɪ-] (US) adj = **multistorey**

multiple ['mʌltɪpl] adj multiplo(a), molteplice ♦ n multiplo; ~ **sclerosis** n sclerosi f a placche

multiplex cinema ['mʌltɪpleks-] n cinema m inv multisala inv

multiplication [mʌltɪplɪ'keɪʃən] n moltiplicazione f

multiply ['mʌltɪplaɪ] vt moltiplicare ♦ vi moltiplicarsi

multistorey ['mʌltɪ'stɔːrɪ] (BRIT) adj (building, car park) a più piani

mum [mʌm] (BRIT: inf) n mamma ♦ adj: **to keep** ~ non aprire bocca

mumble ['mʌmbl] vt, vi borbottare

mummy ['mʌmɪ] n (BRIT: mother) mamma; (embalmed) mummia

mumps [mʌmps] n orecchioni mpl

munch [mʌntʃ] vt, vi sgranocchiare

mundane [mʌn'deɪn] adj terra a terra inv

municipal [mjuː'nɪsɪpl] adj municipale

mural ['mjuərl] n dipinto murale

murder ['məːdə*] n assassinio, omicidio ♦ vt assassinare; **~er** n omicida m, assassino; **~ous** adj omicida

murky ['məːkɪ] adj tenebroso(a)

murmur ['məːmə*] n mormorio ♦ vt, vi mormorare

muscle ['mʌsl] n muscolo; (fig) forza; ~ **in** vi immischiarsi

muscular ['mʌskjulə*] adj muscolare; (person, arm) muscoloso(a)

muse [mjuːz] vi meditare, sognare ♦ n musa

museum [mjuː'zɪəm] n museo

mushroom ['mʌʃrum] n fungo ♦ vi crescere in fretta

music ['mjuːzɪk] n musica; (fig) musicale; (person) portato(a) per la musica ♦ n (show) commedia musicale; **~al instrument** n strumento musicale; **~ hall** n teatro di varietà; **~ian** [-'zɪʃən] n musicista m/f

Muslim ['mʌzlɪm] adj, n musulmano(a)

muslin ['mʌzlɪn] n mussola

mussel ['mʌsl] n cozza

must [mʌst] aux vb (obligation): **I ~ do it** devo farlo; (probability): **he ~ be there by now** dovrebbe essere arrivato ormai; **I ~ have made a mistake** devo essermi sbagliato ♦ n: **it's a ~** è d'obbligo

mustache ['mʌstæʃ] (US) n = **moustache**

mustard ['mʌstəd] n senape f, mostarda

muster ['mʌstə*] vt radunare

mustn't ['mʌsnt] = **must not**

musty ['mʌstɪ] adj che sa di muffa or di rinchiuso

mute [mjuːt] adj, n muto(a)

muted ['mjuːtɪd] adj smorzato(a)

mutiny ['mjuːtɪnɪ] n ammutinamento

mutter ['mʌtə*] vt, vi borbottare, brontolare

mutton ['mʌtn] n carne f di montone

mutual ['mjuːtʃuəl] adj mutuo(a), reciproco(a); **~ly** adv reciprocamente

muzzle ['mʌzl] n muso; (protective device) museruola; (of gun) bocca ♦ vt mettere la museruola a

my [maɪ] *adj* il(la) mio(a), *pl* i(le)
miei(mie); **~ house** la mia casa;
~ books i miei libri; **~ brother** mio
fratello; **I've washed ~ hair/cut
~ finger** mi sono lavato i capelli/
tagliato il dito

myself [maɪ'sɛlf] *pron* (*reflexive*) mi;
(*emphatic*) io stesso(a); (*after prep*) me;
see also **oneself**

mysterious [mɪs'tɪərɪəs] *adj*
misterioso(a)

mystery ['mɪstərɪ] *n* mistero

mystify ['mɪstɪfaɪ] *vt* mistificare;
(*puzzle*) confondere

mystique [mɪs'tiːk] *n* fascino

myth [mɪθ] *n* mito

mythology [mɪ'θɒlədʒɪ] *n*
mitologia

N, n

n/a *abbr* = **not applicable**

nag [næg] *vt* tormentare ♦ *vi* brontolare
in continuazione; **~ging** *adj* (*doubt,
pain*) persistente

nail [neɪl] *n* (*human*) unghia; (*metal*)
chiodo ♦ *vt* inchiodare; **to ~ sb down
to (doing) sth** costringere qn a (fare)
qc; **~brush** *n* spazzolino da or per
unghie; **~file** *n* lima da or per unghie;
~ polish *n* smalto da or per unghie;
~ polish remover *n* acetone *m*,
solvente *m*; **~ scissors** *npl* forbici *fpl*
da or per unghie; **~ varnish** (*BRIT*) *n* =
~ polish

naïve [naɪ'iːv] *adj* ingenuo(a)

naked ['neɪkɪd] *adj* nudo(a)

name [neɪm] *n* nome *m*; (*reputation*)
nome, reputazione *f* ♦ *vt* (*baby etc*)
chiamare; (*plant, illness*) nominare;
(*person, object*) identificare; (*price, date*)
fissare; **what's your ~?** come si
chiama?; **by ~** di nome; **she knows
them all by ~** li conosce tutti per
nome; **~ly** *adv* cioè; **~sake** *n*
omonimo

nanny ['nænɪ] *n* bambinaia

nap [næp] *n* (*sleep*) pisolino; (*of cloth*)
peluria; **to be caught ~ping** essere
preso alla sprovvista

nape [neɪp] *n*: **~ of the neck** nuca

napkin ['næpkɪn] *n* (*also*: **table ~**)
tovagliolo

nappy ['næpɪ] (*BRIT*) *n* pannolino;
~ rash *n* arrossamento (causato dal
pannolino)

narcissus [naː'sɪsəs] (*pl* **narcissi**) *n*
narciso

narcotic [naː'kɒtɪk] *n* narcotico ♦ *adj*
narcotico(a)

narrative ['nærətɪv] *n* narrativa

narrow ['nærəu] *adj* stretto(a); (*fig*)
limitato(a), ristretto(a) ♦ *vi* restringersi;
to have a ~ escape farcela per un
pelo; **to ~ sth down to** ridurre qc a;
~ly *adv* per un pelo; (*time*) per poco;
~-minded *adj* meschino(a)

nasty ['naːstɪ] *adj* (*person, remark:
unpleasant*) cattivo(a); (: *rude*)
villano(a); (*smell, wound, situation*)
brutto(a)

nation ['neɪʃən] *n* nazione *f*

national ['næʃənl] *adj* nazionale ♦ *n*
cittadino(a); **~ dress** *n* costume *m*
nazionale; **N~ Health Service** (*BRIT*) *n*
servizio nazionale di assistenza sanitaria,
≈ S.S.N. *m*; **N~ Insurance** (*BRIT*) *n* ≈
Previdenza Sociale; **~ism** *n*
nazionalismo; **~ity** [-'nælɪtɪ] *n*
nazionalità *f inv*; **~ize** *vt* nazionalizzare;
~ly *adv* a livello nazionale; **~ park** *n*
parco nazionale

National Trust

Fondato nel 1895, il **National Trust**
*è un'organizzazione che si occupa
della tutela e della salvaguardia di
luoghi di interesse storico o
ambientale*

---

nationwide ['neɪʃənwaɪd] *adj*
diffuso(a) in tutto il paese ♦ *adv* in
tutto il paese

native ['neɪtɪv] *n* abitante *m/f* del paese ♦ *adj* indigeno(a); (*country*) natio(a); (*ability*) innato(a); **a ~ of Russia** un nativo della Russia; **a ~ speaker of French** una persona di madrelingua francese; **N~ American** *n* discendente di tribù dell'America settentrionale; **~ language** *n* madrelingua

Nativity [nə'tɪvɪtɪ] *n*: **the ~** la Natività

NATO ['neɪtəu] *n abbr* (= *North Atlantic Treaty Organization*) N.A.T.O. f

natural ['nætʃrəl] *adj* naturale; (*ability*) innato(a); (*manner*) semplice; **~ gas** *n* gas *m* metano; **~ly** *adv* naturalmente; (*by nature*) di natura

nature ['neɪtʃə*] *n* natura; (*character*) natura, indole f; **by ~** di natura

naught [nɔːt] *n* = **nought**

naughty ['nɔːtɪ] *adj* (*child*) birichino(a), cattivello(a); (*story, film*) spinto(a)

nausea ['nɔːsɪə] *n* (*MED*) nausea; (*fig: disgust*) schifo

nautical ['nɔːtɪkl] *adj* nautico(a)

naval ['neɪvl] *adj* navale; **~ officer** *n* ufficiale *m* di marina

nave [neɪv] *n* navata centrale

navel ['neɪvl] *n* ombelico

navigate ['nævɪgeɪt] *vt* percorrere navigando ♦ *vi* navigare; (*AUT*) fare da navigatore; **navigation** [-'geɪʃən] *n* navigazione f; **navigator** *n* (*NAUT, AVIAT*) ufficiale *m* di rotta; (*explorer*) navigatore *m*; (*AUT*) copilota *m/f*

navvy ['nævɪ] (*BRIT*) *n* manovale *m*

navy ['neɪvɪ] *n* marina; **~(-blue)** *adj* blu scuro *inv*

Nazi ['nɑːtsɪ] *n* nazista *m/f*

NB *abbr* (= *nota bene*) N.B.

near [nɪə*] *adj* vicino(a); (*relation*) prossimo(a) ♦ *adv* vicino ♦ *prep* (*also: ~ to*) vicino a, presso; (*: time*) verso ♦ *vt* avvicinarsi a; **~by** [nɪə'baɪ] *adj* vicino(a) ♦ *adv* vicino; **~ly** *adv* quasi; **I ~ly fell** per poco non sono caduto; **~ miss** *n*: **that was a ~ miss** c'è mancato poco; **~side** *n* (*AUT: in Britain*)

lato sinistro; (*: in US, Europe etc*) lato destro; **~-sighted** [nɪə'saɪtd] *adj* miope

neat [niːt] *adj* (*person, room*) ordinato(a); (*work*) pulito(a); (*solution, plan*) ben indovinato(a), azzeccato(a); (*spirits*) liscio(a); **~ly** *adv* con ordine; (*skilfully*) abilmente

necessarily ['nɛsɪsrɪlɪ] *adv* necessariamente

necessary ['nɛsɪsrɪ] *adj* necessario(a)

necessity [nɪ'sɛsɪtɪ] *n* necessità f *inv*

neck [nɛk] *n* collo; (*of garment*) colletto ♦ *vi* (*inf*) pomiciare, sbaciucchiarsi; **~ and ~** testa a testa

necklace ['nɛklɪs] *n* collana

neckline ['nɛklaɪn] *n* scollatura

necktie ['nɛktaɪ] *n* cravatta

née [neɪ] *adj*: **~ Scott** nata Scott

need [niːd] *n* bisogno ♦ *vt* aver bisogno di; **to ~ to do** dover fare; aver bisogno di fare; **you don't ~ to go** non devi andare, non c'è bisogno che tu vada

needle ['niːdl] *n* ago; (*on record player*) puntina ♦ *vt* punzecchiare

needless ['niːdlɪs] *adj* inutile

needlework ['niːdlwəːk] *n* cucito

needn't ['niːdnt] = **need not**

needy ['niːdɪ] *adj* bisognoso(a)

negative ['nɛgətɪv] (*LING*) negazione f; (*PHOT*) negativo ♦ *adj* negativo(a); **~ equity** *n* situazione in cui l'ammontare del mutuo su un immobile supera il suo valore sul mercato

neglect [nɪ'glɛkt] *vt* trascurare ♦ *n* (*of person, duty*) negligenza; (*of child, house etc*) scarsa cura; **state of ~** stato di abbandono

negligence ['nɛglɪdʒəns] *n* negligenza

negligible ['nɛglɪdʒɪbl] *adj* insignificante, trascurabile

negotiable [nɪ'gəujɪəbl] *adj* (*cheque*) trasferibile

negotiate [nɪ'gəujɪeɪt] *vi*: **to ~ (with)** negoziare (con) ♦ *vt* (*COMM*) negoziare; (*obstacle*) superare; **negotiation**

[-'eɪʃən] n negoziato, trattativa

Negro ['niːgrəʊ] (pl **~es**) n negro/a

neigh [neɪ] vi nitrire

neighbour ['neɪbə*] (US **neighbor**) n vicino/a; **~hood** n vicinato; **~ing** adj vicino/a; **~ly** adj: he is a ~ly person è un buon vicino

neither ['naɪðə*] adj, pron né l'uno/a né l'altro/a, nessuno/a dei(delle) due ♦ conj neanche, nemmeno, neppure ♦ adv: ~ **good nor bad** né buono né cattivo; **I didn't move and ~ did Claude** io non mi mossi e nemmeno Claude; ...; **~ did I refuse** ..., ma non ho nemmeno rifiutato

neon light ['niːɔn-] n luce f al neon

nephew ['nɛvjuː] n nipote m

nerve [nɜːv] n nervo; (fig) coraggio; (impudence) faccia tosta; **a fit of ~s** una crisi di nervi; **~-racking** adj che spezza i nervi

nervous ['nɜːvəs] adj nervoso/a; (anxious) agitato/a, in apprensione; ~ **breakdown** n esaurimento nervoso

nest [nɛst] n nido ♦ vi fare il nido, nidificare; ~ **egg** n (fig) gruzzolo

nestle ['nɛsl] vi accoccolarsi

net [nɛt] n rete ♦ adj netto/a ♦ vt (fish etc) prendere con la rete; (profit) ricavare un utile netto di; **the N~** (Internet) Internet f; **~ball** n specie di pallacanestro

Netherlands ['nɛðələndz] npl: **the ~** i Paesi Bassi

nett [nɛt] adj = **net**

netting ['nɛtɪŋ] n (for fence etc) reticolato

nettle ['nɛtl] n ortica

network ['nɛtwɜːk] n rete f

neurotic [njuə'rɔtɪk] adj, n nevrotico/a)

neuter ['njuːtə*] adj neutro/a) ♦ vt (cat etc) castrare

neutral ['njuːtrəl] adj neutro/a); (person, nation) neutrale ♦ n (AUT): **in ~** in folle; **~ize** vt neutralizzare

never ['nɛvə*] adv (non...) mai;

~ **again** mai più; **I'll ~ go there again** non ci vado più; ~ **in my life** mai in vita mia; see also **mind**; **~-ending** adj interminabile; **~theless** [nɛvəðə'lɛs] adv tuttavia, ciò nonostante, ciò nondimeno

new [njuː] adj nuovo/a); (brand new) nuovo/a) di zecca; **N~ Age** n New Age f inv; **~born** adj neonato/a); **~comer** ['njuːkʌmə*] n nuovo/a venuto/a); **~fangled** ['njuːfæŋgld] (pej) adj stramoderno/a); **~found** adj nuovo/a); **~ly** adv di recente; **~ly-weds** npl sposini mpl, sposi mpl novelli

news [njuːz] n notizie fpl; (RADIO) giornale m radio; (TV) telegiornale m; **a piece of ~** una notizia; **~ agency** n agenzia di stampa; **~agent** (BRIT) n giornalaio; **~caster** n (RADIO, TV) annunciatore/trice; **~flash** n notizia f lampo inv; **~letter** n bollettino; **~paper** n giornale m; **~print** n carta da giornale; **~reader** n = **~caster**; **~reel** n cinegiornale m; **~ stand** n edicola

newt [njuːt] n tritone m

New Year n Anno Nuovo; **~'s Day** n il Capodanno; **~'s Eve** n la vigilia di Capodanno

New York [-'jɔːk] n New York f

New Zealand [-'ziːlənd] n Nuova Zelanda; **~er** n neozelandese m/f

next [nɛkst] adj prossimo/a) ♦ adv accanto; (in time) dopo; **the ~ day** il giorno dopo, l'indomani; ~ **time** la prossima volta; ~ **year** l'anno prossimo; **when do we meet ~?** quando ci rincontriamo?; ~ **to** accanto a; ~ **to nothing** quasi niente; ~ **please!** (avanti) il prossimo!; ~ **door** adv, adj accanto inv; **~-of-kin** n parente m/f prossimo/a)

NHS n abbr = **National Health Service**

nib [nɪb] n (of pen) pennino

nibble ['nɪbl] vt mordicchiare

Nicaragua [nɪkə'ræɡjuə] n Nicaragua

m

nice [naɪs] *adj (holiday, trip)* piacevole; *(flat, picture)* bello(a); *(person)* simpatico(a), gentile; **~ly** *adv* bene

niceties ['naɪsɪtɪz] *npl* finezze *fpl*

nick [nɪk] *n* taglietto; tacca ♦ *vt (inf)* rubare; **in the ~ of time** appena in tempo

nickel ['nɪkl] *n* nichel *m*; *(US)* moneta da cinque centesimi di dollaro

nickname ['nɪkneɪm] *n* soprannome *m*

niece [niːs] *n* nipote *f*

Nigeria [naɪ'dʒɪərɪə] *n* Nigeria *f*

niggling ['nɪglɪŋ] *adj* insignificante; *(annoying)* irritante

night [naɪt] *n* notte *f*; *(evening)* sera; **at ~** la sera; **by ~** di notte; **the ~ before last** l'altro ieri notte (*or* sera); **~cap** *n* bicchierino prima di andare a letto; **~ club** *n* locale *m* notturno; **~dress** *n* camicia da notte; **~fall** *n* crepuscolo; **~gown** *n* = **~dress**; **~ie** ['naɪtɪ] *n* = **~dress**

nightingale ['naɪtɪŋgeɪl] *n* usignolo

nightlife ['naɪtlaɪf] *n* vita notturna

nightly ['naɪtlɪ] *adj* di ogni notte *or* sera; *(by night)* notturno(a) ♦ *adv* ogni notte *or* sera

nightmare ['naɪtmeə*] *n* incubo

night: ~ porter *n* portiere *m* di notte; **~ school** *n* scuola serale; **~ shift** *n* turno di notte; **~-time** *n* notte *f*

nil [nɪl] *n* nulla *m*; *(BRIT: SPORT)* zero

Nile [naɪl] *n*: **the ~** il Nilo

nimble ['nɪmbl] *adj* agile

nine [naɪn] *num* nove; **~teen** *num* diciannove; **~ty** *num* novanta

ninth [naɪnθ] *adj* nono(a)

nip [nɪp] *vt* pizzicare; *(bite)* mordere

nipple ['nɪpl] *n (ANAT)* capezzolo

nitrogen ['naɪtrədʒən] *n* azoto

KEYWORD
---

no [nəʊ] *(pl* **~es)** *adv (opposite of "yes")* no; **are you coming? —** **~ (I'm not)** viene? — no (non vengo);

would you like some more? — **~ thank you** ne vuole ancora un po'? — no, grazie

♦ *adj (not any)* nessuno(a); **I have ~ money/time/books** non ho soldi/ tempo/libri; **~ student would have done it** nessuno studente lo avrebbe fatto; **"~ parking"** "divieto di sosta"; **"~ smoking"** "vietato fumare"

♦ *n* no *m inv*

---

nobility [nəʊ'bɪlɪtɪ] *n* nobiltà

noble ['nəʊbl] *adj* nobile

nobody ['nəʊbədɪ] *pron* nessuno

nod [nɒd] *vi* accennare col capo, fare un cenno; *(in agreement)* annuire con un cenno del capo; *(sleep)* sonnecchiare ♦ *vt*: **to ~ one's head** fare di sì col capo ♦ *n* cenno; **~ off** *vi* assopirsi

noise [nɔɪz] *n* rumore *m*; *(din, racket)* chiasso; **noisy** *adj (street, car)* rumoroso(a); *(person)* chiassoso(a)

nominal ['nɒmɪnl] *adj* nominale; *(rent)* simbolico(a)

nominate ['nɒmɪneɪt] *vt (propose)* proporre come candidato; *(elect)* nominare

nominee [nɒmɪ'niː] *n* persona nominata; candidato/a

non... [nɒn] *prefix* non...; **~-alcoholic** *adj* analcolico(a)

nonchalant ['nɒnʃələnt] *adj* disinvolto(a), noncurante

non-committal ['nɒnkə'mɪtl] *adj* evasivo(a)

nondescript ['nɒndɪskrɪpt] *adj* qualunque *inv*

none [nʌn] *pron (not one thing)* niente; *(not one person)* nessuno(a); **~ of you** nessuno(a) di voi; **I've ~ left** non ho più; **he's ~ the worse for it** non ne ha risentito

nonentity [nɒ'nentɪtɪ] *n* persona insignificante

nonetheless [nʌnðə'les] *adv* nondimeno

non-existent [-ig'zistənt] *adj* inesistente

non-fiction *n* saggistica

nonplussed [nɔn'plʌst] *adj* sconcertato(a)

nonsense ['nɔnsəns] *n* sciocchezze *fpl*

non-: ~**smoker** *n* non fumatore/trice; ~**smoking** *adj* (*person*) che non fuma; (*area*, *section*) per non fumatori; ~**stick** *adj* antiaderente, antiadesivo(a); ~**stop** *adj* continuo(a); (*train*, *bus*) direttissimo(a) ♦ *adv* senza sosta

noodles ['nu:dlz] *npl* taglierine *mpl*

nook [nuk] *n*: ~**s and crannies** angoli *mpl*

noon [nu:n] *n* mezzogiorno

no one ['nəuwʌn] *pron* = **nobody**

noose [nu:s] *n* nodo scorsoio; (*hangman's*) cappio

nor [nɔ:*] *conj* = **neither** ♦ *adv see* **neither**

norm [nɔ:m] *n* norma

normal ['nɔ:ml] *adj* normale; ~**ly** *adv* normalmente

north [nɔ:θ] *n* nord *m*, settentrione *m* ♦ *adj* nord *inv*, del nord, settentrionale ♦ *adv* verso nord; **N~ America** *n* America del Nord; ~**east** *n* nord-est *m*; ~**erly** ['nɔ:ðəli] *adj* (*point*, *direction*) verso nord; ~**ern** ['nɔ:ðən] *adj* del nord, settentrionale; **N~ern Ireland** *n* Irlanda del Nord; **N~ Pole** *n* Polo Nord; **N~ Sea** *n* Mare *m* del Nord; ~**ward(s)** ['nɔ:θwəd(z)] *adv* verso nord; ~**west** *n* nord-ovest *m*

Norway ['nɔ:wei] *n* Norvegia

Norwegian [nɔ:'wi:dʒən] *adj* norvegese ♦ *n* norvegese *m/f*; (*LING*) norvegese *m*

nose [nəuz] *n* naso; (*of animal*) muso ♦ *vi*: **to ~ about** aggirarsi; ~**bleed** *n* emorragia nasale; ~**dive** *n* picchiata; ~**y** (*inf*) *adj* = **nosy**

nostalgia [nɔs'tældʒiə] *n* nostalgia

nostril ['nɔstril] *n* narice *f*; (*of horse*) froglia

nosy ['nəuzi] (*inf*) *adj* curioso(a)

not [nɔt] *adv* non; **he is ~** or **isn't here** non è qui, non c'è; **you must ~** or **you mustn't do that** non devi fare quello; **it's too late, isn't it** or **is it ~?** è troppo tardi, vero?; ~ **that I don't like him** non che lui (non) mi piaccia; ~ **yet/now** non ancora/ora; *see also* **all; only**

notably ['nəutəbli] *adv* (*markedly*) notevolmente; (*particularly*) in particolare

notary ['nəutəri] *n* notaio

notch [nɔtʃ] *n* tacca; (*in saw*) dente *m*

note [nəut] *n* nota; (*letter*, *banknote*) biglietto ♦ *vt* (*also*: ~ **down**) prendere nota di; **to take ~s** prendere appunti; ~**book** *n* taccuino; ~**d** ['nəutid] *adj* celebre; ~**pad** *n* bloc-notes *m inv*; ~**paper** *n* carta da lettere

nothing ['nʌθiŋ] *n* nulla *m*, niente *m*; (*zero*) zero; **he does ~** non fa niente; ~ **new/much** *etc* niente di nuovo/ speciale *etc*; **for ~** per niente

notice ['nəutis] *n* avviso; (*of leaving*) preavviso ♦ *vt* notare, accorgersi di; **to take ~ of** fare attenzione a; **to bring sth to sb's ~** far notare qc a qn; **at short ~** con un breve preavviso; **until further ~** fino a nuovo avviso; **to hand in one's ~** licenziarsi; ~**able** *adj* evidente; ~ **board** (*BRIT*) *n* tabellone *m* per affissi

notify ['nəutifai] *vt*: **to ~ sth to sb** far sapere qc a qn; **to ~ sb of sth** avvisare qn di qc

notion ['nəuʃən] *n* idea; (*concept*) nozione *f*

notorious [nəu'tɔ:riəs] *adj* famigerato(a)

nougat ['nu:ga:] *n* torrone *m*

nought [nɔːt] *n* zero

noun [naun] *n* nome *m*, sostantivo

nourish ['nʌriʃ] *vt* nutrire

novel ['nɔvl] *n* romanzo ♦ *adj* nuovo(a); ~**ist** *n* romanziere/a; ~**ty** *n* novità *f inv*

November [nəu'vɛmbə*] n novembre m

novice ['nɒvɪs] n principiante m/f; (REL) novizio/a

now [nau] adv ora, adesso ♦ conj: ~ (**that**) adesso che, ora che; **by** ~ ormai; **just** ~ proprio ora; **right** ~ subito, immediatamente; ~ **and then**, ~ **and again** ogni tanto; **from** ~ **on** da ora in poi; **~adays** ['nauədeɪz] adv oggidì

nowhere ['nəuwɛə*] adv in nessun luogo, da nessuna parte

nozzle ['nɒzl] n (of hose etc) boccaglio; (of fire extinguisher) lancia

nuance ['njuːɑːns] n sfumatura

nuclear ['njuːklɪə*] adj nucleare

nucleus ['njuːklɪəs] (pl **nuclei**) n nucleo

nude [njuːd] adj nudo(a) ♦ n (ART) nudo; **in the** ~ tutto(a) nudo(a)

nudge [nʌdʒ] vt dare una gomitata a

nudist ['njuːdɪst] n nudista m/f

nuisance ['njuːsns] n: **it's a** ~ è una seccatura; **he's a** ~ è uno scocciatore

null [nʌl] adj: ~ **and void** nullo(a)

numb [nʌm] adj: ~ (**with**) (with cold) intorpidito(a) (da); (with fear) impietrito(a) (da); ~ **with cold** intirizzito(a) (dal freddo)

number ['nʌmbə*] n numero ♦ vt numerare; (include) contare; **a** ~ **of** un certo numero di; **to be ~ed among** venire annoverato(a) tra; **they were 10 in** ~ erano in tutto 10; ~ **plate** (BRIT) n (AUT) targa

numeral ['njuːmərəl] n numero, cifra

numerate ['njuːmərɪt] adj: **to be** ~ avere nozioni di aritmetica

numerical [njuː'mɛrɪkl] adj numerico(a)

numerous ['njuːmərəs] adj numeroso(a)

nun [nʌn] n suora, monaca

nurse [nəːs] n infermiere/a; (also: ~maid) bambinaia ♦ vt (patient, cold) curare; (baby: BRIT) cullare; (: US)

allattare, dare il latte a

nursery ['nəːsərɪ] n (room) camera dei bambini; (institution) asilo; (for plants) vivaio; ~ **rhyme** n filastrocca; ~ **school** n scuola materna; ~ **slope** (BRIT) n (SKI) pista per principianti

nursing ['nəːsɪŋ] n (profession) professione f di infermiere (or di infermiera); (care) cura; ~ **home** n casa di cura

nurture ['nəːtʃə*] vt allevare; nutrire

nut [nʌt] n (of metal) dado; (fruit) noce f; **~crackers** npl schiaccianoci m inv

nutmeg ['nʌtmɛg] n noce f moscata

nutritious [njuː'trɪʃəs] adj nutriente

nuts [nʌts] (inf) adj matto(a)

nutshell ['nʌtʃɛl] n: **in a** ~ in poche parole

nylon ['naɪlɒn] n nailon m ♦ adj di nailon

O, o

oak [əuk] n quercia ♦ adj di quercia

O.A.P. (BRIT) n abbr = **old age pensioner**

oar [ɔː*] n remo

oasis [əu'eɪsɪs] (pl **oases**) n oasi f inv

oath [əuθ] n giuramento; (swear word) bestemmia

oatmeal ['əutmiːl] n farina d'avena

oats [əuts] npl avena

obedience [ə'biːdɪəns] n ubbidienza

obedient [ə'biːdɪənt] adj ubbidiente

obey [ə'beɪ] vt ubbidire a; (instructions, regulations) osservare

obituary [ə'bɪtjuərɪ] n necrologia

object [n 'ɒbdʒɪkt, vb əb'dʒɛkt] n oggetto; (purpose) scopo, intento; (LING) complemento oggetto ♦ vi: **to** ~ **to** (attitude) disapprovare; (proposal) protestare contro, sollevare delle obiezioni contro; **expense is no** ~ non si bada a spese; **to** ~ **that** obiettare che; **I ~!** mi oppongo!; **~ion** [əb'dʒɛkʃən] n obiezione f; **~ionable**

[əb'dʒɛkʃənəbl] *adj* antipatico(a); (*language*) sboluggiarsi(a); **~ive** *n* obiettivo

obligation [ɒblɪ'geɪʃən] *n* obbligo, dovere *m*; **without ~** senza impegno

oblige [ə'blaɪdʒ] *vt* (*force*): **to ~ sb to do** costringere qn a fare; (*do a favour*) fare una cortesia a qn per qc; **to be ~d to sb for sth** essere grato a qn per qc; **obliging** *adj* servizievole, compiacente

oblique [ə'bli:k] *adj* obliquo(a); (*allusion*) indiretto(a)

obliterate [ə'blɪtəreɪt] *vt* cancellare

oblivion [ə'blɪvɪən] *n* oblio

oblivious [ə'blɪvɪəs] *adj*: **~ of** incurante di; inconscio(a) di

oblong ['ɒblɒŋ] *adj* oblungo(a) ♦ *n* rettangolo

obnoxious [əb'nɒkʃəs] *adj* odioso(a); (*smell*) disgustoso(a), ripugnante

oboe ['əubəu] *n* oboe *m*

obscene [əb'si:n] *adj* osceno(a)

obscure [əb'skjuə*] *adj* oscuro(a) ♦ *vt* oscurare; (*hide: sun*) nascondere

observant [əb'zə:vnt] *adj* attento(a)

observation [ɒbzə'veɪʃən] *n* osservazione f; (*by police etc*) sorveglianza

observatory [əb'zə:vatrɪ] *n* osservatorio

observe [əb'zə:v] *vt* osservare; (*remark*) fare osservare; **~r** *n* osservatore/trice

obsess [əb'ses] *vt* ossessionare; **~ive** *adj* ossessivo(a)

obsolescence [ɒbsə'lɛsns] *n* obsolescenza

obsolete ['ɒbsəli:t] *adj* obsoleto(a)

obstacle ['ɒbstəkl] *n* ostacolo

obstinate ['ɒbstɪnɪt] *adj* ostinato(a)

obstruct [əb'strʌkt] *vt* (*block*) ostruire, ostacolare; (*halt*) fermare; (*hinder*) impedire

obtain [əb'teɪn] *vt* ottenere; **~able** *adj* ottenibile

obvious ['ɒbvɪəs] *adj* ovvio(a), evidente; **~ly** *adv* ovviamente; certo

occasion [ə'keɪʒən] *n* occasione f;

(*event*) avvenimento; **~al** *adj* occasionale; **~ally** *adv* ogni tanto

occupation [ɒkju'peɪʃən] *n* occupazione f; (*job*) mestiere m, professione f; **~al hazard** *n* rischio del mestiere

occupier ['ɒkjupaɪə*] *n* occupante m/f

occupy ['ɒkjupaɪ] *vt* occupare; **to o.s. in doing** occuparsi a fare

occur [ə'kə:*] *vi* accadere, capitare; **to ~ to sb** venire in mente a qn; **~rence** *n* caso, fatto; (*of error etc*) il verificarsi

ocean ['əuʃən] *n* oceano

o'clock [ə'klɒk] *adv*: **it is 5 ~** sono le 5

OCR *n abbr* (= *optical character recognition*) lettura ottica; (= *optical character reader*) lettore *m* ottico

octave ['ɒktɪv] *n* ottava

October [ɒk'təubə*] *n* ottobre m

octopus ['ɒktəpəs] *n* polpo, piovra

odd [ɒd] *adj* (*strange*) strano(a), bizzarro(a); (*number*) dispari *inv*; (*not of a set*) spaiato(a); **60~** 60 e oltre; **at ~ times** di tanto in tanto; **the ~ one out** l'eccezione f; **~ity** *n* bizzarria; (*person*) originale m; **~job man** *n* tuttofare m *inv*; **~jobs** *npl* lavori *mpl* occasionali; **~ly** *adv* stranamente; **~ments** *npl* (COMM) rimanenze *fpl*; **~s** *npl* (*in betting*) quota; **~s and ends** *npl* avanzi *mpl*; **it makes no ~s** non importa; **at ~s** in contesa

odometer [ɒ'dɒmɪtə*] *n* odometro

odour ['əudə*] (*US* **odor**) *n* odore m; (*unpleasant*) cattivo odore

┌──────────────────┐
│ **KEYWORD**   │
└──────────────────┘

of [ɒv, əv] *prep* 1 (*gen*) di; **a boy ~ 10** un ragazzo di 10 anni; **a friend ~ ours** un nostro amico; **that was kind ~ you** è stato molto gentile da parte sua

2 (*expressing quantity, amount, dates etc*) di; **a kilo ~ flour** un chilo di farina; **how much ~ this do you need?** quanto gliene serve?; **there were 3 ~ them** (*people*) erano in 3;

(objects) ce n'erano 3; **3 ~ us went** 3 di noi se n'erano andati; **the 5th ~ July** il 5 luglio

3 (from, out of) di, in; **made ~ wood** (fatto) di or in legno

---

KEYWORD

---

off [ɔf] adv **1** (distance, time): **it's a long way ~** è lontano; **the game is 3 days ~** la partita è tra 3 giorni **2** (departure, removal) via; **to go ~ to Paris** andarsene a Parigi; **I must be ~** devo andare via; **to take ~ one's coat** togliersi il cappotto; **the button came ~** il bottone è venuto via or si è staccato; **10% ~** con lo sconto del 10%

3 (not at work): **to have a day ~** avere un giorno libero; **to be ~ sick** essere assente per malattia
♦ adj (engine) spento(a); (tap) chiuso(a); (cancelled) sospeso(a); (BRIT: food) andato(a) a male; **on the ~ chance** nel caso; **to have an ~ day** non essere in forma
♦ prep (motion, removal etc) da; (distant from) a poca distanza da; **a street ~ the square** una strada che parte dalla piazza
2: to be ~ meat non mangiare più la carne

offal ['ɔfl] n (CULIN) frattaglie fpl

off-colour (BRIT) adj (ill) malato(a), indisposto(a)

offence [ə'fɛns] (US **offense**) n (LAW) contravvenzione f; (: more serious) reato; **to take ~ at** offendersi per

offend [ə'fɛnd] vt (person) offendere; **~er** n delinquente m/f; (against regulations) contravventore/trice

offense [ə'fɛns] (US) n = **offence**

offensive [ə'fɛnsɪv] adj offensivo(a); (smell etc) sgradevole, ripugnante ♦ n (MIL) offensiva

offer ['ɔfə*] n offerta, proposta ♦ vt

offrire; **"on ~"** (COMM) "in offerta speciale"; **~ing** n offerta

office ['ɔfɪs] n (place) ufficio; (position) carica; **doctor's ~** studio; **to take ~** entrare in carica; **~ automation** n automazione f d'ufficio; burotica; **~ block** (US **~ building**) n complesso di uffici; **~ hours** npl orario d'ufficio; (US: MED) orario di visite

officer ['ɔfɪsə*] n (MIL etc) ufficiale m; (also: police **~**) agente m di polizia; (of organization) funzionario

office worker n impiegato/a d'ufficio

official [ə'fɪʃl] adj (authorized) ufficiale ♦ n ufficiale m; (civil servant) impiegato/a statale; funzionario

officiate [ə'fɪʃieɪt] vi presenziare

officious [ə'fɪʃəs] adj invadente

offing ['ɔfɪŋ] n: **in the ~** (fig) in vista

off: **~-licence** (BRIT) n (shop) spaccio di bevande alcoliche; **~-line** adj, adv (COMPUT) off-line inv, fuori linea; (: switched off) spento(a); **~-peak** adj (ticket, heating etc) a tariffa ridotta; (time) non di punta; **~-putting** (BRIT) adj sgradevole, antipatico(a); **~-road vehicle** n fuoristrada m inv; **~-season** adj, adv fuori stagione

---

off-licence

In Gran Bretagna e in Irlanda, gli **off-licence** sono rivendite di vini, liquori e superalcolici, spesso aperti fino a tarda ora.

---

offset ['ɔfsɛt] (irreg) vt (counteract) controbilanciare, compensare

offshoot ['ɔfʃuːt] n (fig) diramazione f

offshore [ɔf'ʃɔː*] adj (breeze) di terra; (island) vicino alla costa; (fishing) costiero(a)

offside ['ɔf'saɪd] adj (SPORT) fuori gioco; (AUT: in Britain) destro(a); (: in Italy etc) sinistro(a)

offspring ['ɒfsprɪŋ] n inv prole f, discendenza

off: ~**stage** adv dietro le quinte; ~-**the-peg** (US ~-**the-rack**) adv prêt-à-porter; ~-**white** adj bianco sporco inv

often ['ɒfn] adv spesso; **how ~ do you go?** quanto spesso ci vai?

oh [əu] excl oh!

oil [ɔɪl] n olio; (petroleum) petrolio; (for central heating) nafta ♦ vt (machine) lubrificare; ~**can** n oliatore m a mano; (for storing) latta da olio; ~**field** n giacimento petrolifero; ~ **filter** n filtro dell'olio; ~ **painting** n quadro a olio; ~ **refinery** [-rɪ'faɪnərɪ] n raffineria di petrolio; ~ **rig** n derrick m inv; (at sea) piattaforma per trivellazioni subacquee; ~ **tanker** n (ship) petroliera; (truck) autocisterna per petrolio; ~ **well** n pozzo petrolifero; ~**y** adj unto/a, oleoso(a); (food) grasso/a

ointment ['ɔɪntmənt] n unguento

O.K. ['əu'keɪ] excl d'accordo! ♦ adj non male inv ♦ vt approvare; **is it ~?, are you ~?** tutto bene?

okay ['əu'keɪ] excl, adj, vt = **O.K.**

old [əuld] adj vecchio(a); (ancient) antico(a), vecchio(a); (person) vecchio(a), anziano(a); **how ~ are you?** quanti anni hai?; **he's 10 years ~** ha 10 anni; ~**er brother** fratello maggiore; ~ **age** n vecchiaia; ~ **age pensioner** (BRIT) n pensionato/a, ~-**fashioned** adj antiquato(a), fuori moda; (person) all'antica

olive ['ɒlɪv] n (fruit) oliva; (tree) olivo ♦ adj (also: ~-**green**) verde oliva inv; ~ **oil** n olio d'oliva

Olympic [əu'lɪmpɪk] adj olimpico(a); **the ~ Games, the ~s** i giochi olimpici, le Olimpiadi

omelet(te) ['ɒmlɪt] n omelette f inv

omen ['əumən] n presagio, augurio

ominous ['ɒmɪnəs] adj minaccioso(a); (event) di malaugurio

omit [əu'mɪt] vt omettere

KEYWORD

on [ɒn] prep 1 (indicating position) su; ~ **the wall** sulla parete; ~ **the left** a or sulla sinistra

2 (indicating means, method, condition etc): ~ **foot** a piedi; ~ **the train/plane** in treno/aereo; ~ **the telephone** al telefono; ~ **the radio/television** alla radio/televisione; **to be ~ drugs** drogarsi; ~ **holiday** in vacanza

3 (of time): ~ **Friday** venerdì; ~ **Fridays** il or di venerdì; ~ **June 20th** il 20 giugno; ~ **Friday, June 20th** venerdì, 20 giugno; **a week** ~ **Friday** venerdì a otto; ~ **his arrival** al suo arrivo; ~ **seeing this** vedendo ciò

4 (about, concerning) su, di; **information** ~ **train services** informazioni sui collegamenti ferroviari; **a book** ~ **Goldoni/physics** un libro su Goldoni/di or sulla fisica

♦ adv 1 (referring to dress, covering): **to have one's coat** ~ avere indosso il cappotto; **to put one's coat** ~ mettersi il cappotto; **what's she got** ~? cosa indossa?; **she put her boots/gloves/hat** ~ si mise gli stivali/i guanti/il cappello; **screw the lid** ~ **tightly** avvita bene il coperchio

2 (further, continuously): **to walk** ~, **go** ~ etc continuare, proseguire etc; **to read** ~ continuare a leggere; ~ **and off** ogni tanto

♦ adj 1 (in operation): machine, TV, light) acceso(a); (: tap) aperto(a); (: brake) inserito(a); **is the meeting still** ~? (in progress) è ancora in corso?; (not cancelled) è confermato l'incontro?; **there's a good film** ~ **at the cinema** danno un buon film al cinema

2 (inf): **that's not** ~! (not acceptable) non si fa così!; (not possible) non se ne parla neanche!

once [wʌns] *adv* una volta ♦ *conj* non appena, quando; ~ **he had left/it was done** dopo che se n'era andato/ fu fatto; **at** ~ subito; *(simultaneously)* a un tempo; ~ **a week** una volta per settimana; ~ **more** ancora una volta; ~ **and for all** una volta per sempre; ~ **upon a time** c'era una volta

oncoming ['ɔnkʌmɪŋ] *adj (traffic)* che viene in senso opposto

one [wʌn] *num* uno(a); ~ **hundred and fifty** centocinquanta; ~ **day** un giorno
♦ *adj* **1** *(sole)* unico(a); **the** ~ **book which** l'unico libro che; **the** ~ **man who** l'unico che
2 *(same)* stesso(a); **they came in the** ~ **car** sono venuti nella stessa macchina
♦ *pron* **1**: **this** ~ questo/a; **that** ~ quello/a; **I've already got** ~**/a red** ~ ne ho già uno/uno rosso; ~ **by** ~ uno per uno
2: ~ **another** l'un l'altro; **to look at** ~ **another** guardarsi; **to help** ~ **another** aiutarsi l'un l'altro a vicenda
3 *(impersonal)* si; ~ **never knows** non si sa mai; **to cut** ~'s **finger** tagliarsi un dito; ~ **needs to eat** bisogna mangiare

one: ~-**day excursion** *(US) n* biglietto giornaliero di andata e ritorno; ~-**man** *adj (business)* diretto(a) *etc* da un solo uomo; ~-**man band** *n* suonatore ambulante con vari strumenti; ~-**off** *(BRIT: inf) n* fatto eccezionale

oneself [wʌn'sɛlf] *pron (reflexive)* si; *(after prep)* se stesso(a), sé; **to do sth (by)** ~ fare qc da sé; **to hurt** ~ farsi male; **to keep sth for** ~ tenere qc per sé; **to talk to** ~ parlare da solo

one: ~-**sided** *adj (argument)* unilaterale; ~-**to**~ *adj (relationship)*

univocal(e) ['juːnɪ'vəukl]; ~-**way** *adj (street, traffic)* a senso unico

ongoing ['ɔngəuɪŋ] *adj* in corso; in attuazione

onion ['ʌnjən] *n* cipolla

on-line *adj, adv (COMPUT)* on-line *inv*

onlooker ['ɔnlukə*] *n* spettatore/trice

only ['əunlɪ] *adv* solo, soltanto ♦ *adj* solo(a), unico(a) ♦ *conj* solo che, ma; **an** ~ **child** un figlio unico; **not** ~ ... **but also** non solo ... ma anche

onset ['ɔnsɛt] *n* inizio

onshore ['ɔnʃɔ:*] *adj (wind)* di mare

onslaught ['ɔnslɔ:t] *n* attacco, assalto

onto ['ɔntu] *prep* = **on to**

onus ['əunəs] *n* onere *m*, peso

onward(s) ['ɔnwəd(z)] *adv (move)* in avanti; **from that time** ~ da quella volta in poi

onyx ['ɔnɪks] *n* onice *f*

ooze [u:z] *vi* stillare

OPEC ['əupɛk] *n abbr* (= *Organization of Petroleum-Exporting Countries*) O.P.E.C. *f*

open ['əupn] *adj* aperto(a); *(road)* libero(a); *(meeting)* pubblico(a) ♦ *vt* aprire ♦ *vi (eyes, door, debate)* aprirsi; *(flower)* sbocciare; *(shop, bank, museum)* aprire; *(book etc. commence)* cominciare; **in the** ~ **(air)** all'aperto; ~ **on to** *vt fus (subj: room, door)* dare su; ~ **up** *vt* aprire; *(blocked road)* sgombrare ♦ *vi (shop, business)* aprire; ~**ing** *adj (speech)* di apertura ♦ *n* apertura; *(opportunity)* occasione f, opportunità f *inv*; sbocco; ~**ing hours** *npl* orario di apertura; ~**ing learning centre** *n* sistema educativo nel quale lo studente ha maggiore controllo e gestione delle modalità di apprendimento; ~**ly** *adv* apertamente; ~-**minded** *adj* che ha la mente aperta; ~-**necked** *adj* col collo slacciato; ~-**plan** *adj* senza pareti divisorie

La **Open University**, *fondata in*

Gran Bretagna nel 1969, organizza corsi universitari per corrispondenza, basati anche su lezioni trasmesse per radio e per televisione e su corsi estivi.

opera ['ɔpərə] *n* opera

operate ['ɔpəreɪt] *vt* (*machine*) azionare, far funzionare; (*system*) usare ♦ *vi* funzionare; (*drug*) essere efficace; **to ~ on sb (for)** (*MED*) operare qn (di)

operatic [ɔpə'rætɪk] *adj* dell'opera, lirico(a)

operating ['ɔpəreɪtɪŋ] *adj*: **~ table** tavolo operatorio; **~ theatre** sala operatoria

operation [ɔpə'reɪʃən] *n* operazione *f*; **to be in ~** (*machine*) essere in azione or funzionamento; (*system*) essere in vigore; **to have an ~** (*MED*) subire un'operazione; **~al** *adj* in funzione; d'esercizio

operative ['ɔpərətɪv] *adj* (*measure*) operativo(a)

operator ['ɔpəreɪtə*] *n* (*of machine*) operatore/trice; (*TEL*) centralinista *m/f*

opinion [ə'pɪnɪən] *n* opinione *f*, parere *m*; **in my ~** secondo me, a mio avviso; **~ated** *adj* dogmatico(a); **~ poll** *n* sondaggio di opinioni

opium ['əupɪəm] *n* oppio

opponent [ə'pəunənt] *n* avversario/a

opportunist [ɔpə'tjuːnɪst] *n* opportunista *m/f*

opportunity [ɔpə'tjuːnɪtɪ] *n* opportunità *f* inv, occasione *f*; **to take the ~ of doing** cogliere l'occasione per fare

oppose [ə'pəuz] *vt* opporsi a; **~d to** contrario a; **as ~d to** in contrasto con; **opposing** *adj* opposto(a); (*team*) avversario(a)

opposite ['ɔpəzɪt] *adj* opposto(a); (*house etc*) di fronte ♦ *adv* di fronte, dirimpetto ♦ *prep* di fronte a ♦ *n*: **the ~** il contrario, l'opposto; **the ~ sex** l'altro sesso

opposition [ɔpə'zɪʃən] *n* opposizione

f

opt [ɔpt] *vi*: **to ~ for** optare per; **to ~ to do** scegliere di fare; **~ out** *vi*: **to ~ out of** ritirarsi da

optical ['ɔptɪkl] *adj* ottico(a)

optician [ɔp'tɪʃən] *n* ottico

optimist ['ɔptɪmɪst] *n* ottimista *m/f*; **~ic** [-'mɪstɪk] *adj* ottimistico(a)

optimum ['ɔptɪməm] *adj* ottimale

option ['ɔpʃən] *n* scelta; (*SCOL*) materia facoltativa; (*COMM*) opzione *f*; **~al** *adj* facoltativo(a); (*COMM*) a scelta

or [ɔː*] *conj* o, oppure; (*with negative*): **he hasn't seen ~ heard anything** non ha visto né sentito niente; **~ else** se no, altrimenti; oppure

oral ['ɔːrəl] *adj* orale ♦ *n* esame *m* orale

orange ['ɔrɪndʒ] *n* (*fruit*) arancia ♦ *adj* arancione

orbit ['ɔːbɪt] *n* orbita ♦ *vt* orbitare intorno a

orbital (motorway) ['ɔːbɪtl-] *n* raccordo anulare

orchard ['ɔːtʃəd] *n* frutteto

orchestra ['ɔːkɪstrə] *n* orchestra; (*US: seating*) platea

orchid ['ɔːkɪd] *n* orchidea

ordain [ɔː'deɪn] *vt* (*REL*) ordinare; (*decide*) decretare

ordeal [ɔː'diːl] *n* prova, travaglio

order ['ɔːdə*] *n* ordine *m*; (*COMM*) ordinazione *f* ♦ *vt* ordinare; **in ~** in ordine; (*of document*) in regola; **in (working) ~** funzionante; **in ~ to do** per fare; **in ~ that** affinché + *sub*; **on ~** (*COMM*) in ordinazione; **out of ~** non in ordine; (*not working*) guasto; **to ~ sb to do** ordinare a qn di fare; **~ form** *n* modulo d'ordinazione; **~ly** *n* (*MIL*) attendente *m*; (*MED*) inserviente *m* ♦ *adj* (*room*) in ordine; (*mind*) metodico(a); (*person*) ordinato(a), metodico(a)

ordinary ['ɔːdnrɪ] *adj* normale, comune; (*pej*) mediocre; **out of the ~** diverso dal solito, fuori dell'ordinario

Ordnance Survey ['ɔːdnəns-] (*BRIT*)

istituto cartografico britannico

ore [ɔ:*] *n* minerale *m* grezzo

organ ['ɔ:gən] *n* organo; **~ic**
[ɔ:'gænɪk] *adj* organico(a); (*of food*)
biologico(a)

organization [ɔ:gənaɪ'zeɪʃən] *n*
organizzazione *f*

organize ['ɔ:gənaɪz] *vt* organizzare; **to
get ~d** organizzarsi; **~r** *n*
organizzatore/trice

orgasm ['ɔ:gæzəm] *n* orgasmo

orgy ['ɔ:dʒɪ] *n* orgia

Orient ['ɔ:rɪənt] *n*: **the ~** l'Oriente *m*;
oriental [-'ɛntl] *adj*, *n* orientale *m/f*

origin ['ɔrɪdʒɪn] *n* origine *f*

original [ə'rɪdʒɪnl] *adj* originale;
(*earliest*) originario(a) ♦ *n* originale *m*;
~ly *adv* (*at first*) all'inizio

originate [ə'rɪdʒɪneɪt] *vi*: **to ~ from**
essere originario(a) di; (*suggestion*)
provenire da; **to ~ in** avere origine in

Orkneys ['ɔ:knɪz] *npl*: **the ~** (*also: the
Orkney Islands*) le Orcadi

ornament ['ɔ:nəmənt] *n* ornamento;
(*trinket*) ninnolo; **~al** [-'mɛntl] *adj*
ornamentale

ornate [ɔ:'neɪt] *adj* molto ornato(a)

orphan ['ɔ:fn] *n* orfano/a

orthodox ['ɔ:θədɔks] *adj* ortodosso(a);
~y *n* ortodossia

orthopaedic [ɔ:θə'pi:dɪk] (*us*
orthopedic) *adj* ortopedico(a)

ostensibly [ɔs'tɛnsɪblɪ] *adv*
all'apparenza

ostentatious [ɔstɛn'teɪʃəs] *adj*
pretenzioso(a); ostentato(a)

ostrich ['ɔstrɪtʃ] *n* struzzo

other ['ʌðə*] *adj* altro(a) ♦ *pron*: **the
~** (*one*) l'altro(a); **~s** (*~ people*) altri
mpl; **~ than** altro che; a parte; **~wise**
adv, *conj* altrimenti

otter ['ɔtə*] *n* lontra

ouch [autʃ] *excl* ohi!, ahi!

ought [ɔ:t] (*pt* ought) *aux vb*: **I ~ to
do it** dovrei farlo; **this ~ to have
been corrected** questo avrebbe
dovuto essere corretto; **he ~ to win**
dovrebbe vincere

ounce [auns] *n* oncia (= 28.35 *g*; 16 in
a pound)

our ['auə*] *adj* il(la) nostro(a), *pl* i(le)
nostri(e); *see also* **my**; **~s** *pron* il(la)
nostro(a), *pl* i(le) nostri(e); *see also*
mine; **~selves** *pron pl* (*reflexive*) ci;
(*after preposition*) noi; (*emphatic*) noi
stessi(e); *see also* **oneself**

oust [aust] *vt* cacciare, espellere

KEYWORD

out [aut] *adv* (*gen*) fuori; **~ here/there**
qui/là fuori; **to speak ~ loud** parlare
forte; **to have a night ~** uscire una
sera; **the boat was 10 km ~** la barca
era a 10 km dalla costa; **3 days
~ from Plymouth** a 3 giorni da
Plymouth

♦ *adj*: **to be ~** (*gen*) essere fuori;
(*unconscious*) aver perso i sensi; (*style,
singer*) essere fuori moda; **before the
week was ~** prima che la settimana
fosse finita; **to be ~ to do sth** avere
intenzione di fare qc; **to be ~ in
one's calculations** aver sbagliato i
calcoli

♦ **out of** *prep* **1** (*outside, beyond*) fuori
di; **to go ~ the house** uscire di
casa; **to look ~ the window**
guardare fuori dalla finestra
2 (*because of*) per
3 (*origin*) da; **to drink ~ of a cup**
bere da una tazza
4 (*from among*) **~ of 10** su 10
5 (*without*) senza; **~ of petrol** senza
benzina

out-and-out *adj* (*liar, thief etc*) vero(a)
e proprio(a)

outback ['autbæk] *n* (*in Australia*)
interno, entroterra

outboard ['autbɔ:d] *n*: **~ (motor)**
(motore *m*) fuoribordo

outbreak ['autbreɪk] *n* scoppio;
epidemia

outburst ['autbə:st] *n* scoppio

outcast ['autkɑ:st] *n* esule *m/f*;

(socially) paria m inv

outcome ['autkʌm] n esito, risultato

outcrop ['autkrɔp] n (of rock) affioramento

outcry ['autkraɪ] n protesta, clamore m

outdated [aut'deɪtɪd] adj (custom, clothes) fuori moda; (idea) sorpassato(a)

outdo [aut'duː] (irreg) vt sorpassare

outdoor [aut'dɔː*] adj all'aperto; ~s adv fuori; all'aria aperta

outer ['autə*] adj esteriore; ~ space n spazio cosmico

outfit ['autfɪt] n (clothes) completo; (: for sport) tenuta

outgoing ['autgəuɪŋ] adj (character) socievole; ~s (BRIT) npl (expenses) spese fpl, uscite fpl

outgrow [aut'grəu] (irreg) vt: **he has ~n his clothes** tutti i vestiti gli sono diventati piccoli

outhouse ['authaus] n costruzione f annessa

outing ['autɪŋ] n gita; escursione f

outlaw ['autlɔː] n fuorilegge m/f ♦ vt bandire

outlay ['autleɪ] n spese fpl; (investment) sborsa, spesa

outlet ['autlet] n (for liquid etc) sbocco, scarico; (US: ELEC) presa di corrente; (also: retail ~) punto di vendita

outline ['autlaɪn] n contorno, profilo; (summary) abbozzo, grandi linee fpl ♦ vt (fig) descrivere a grandi linee

outlive [aut'lɪv] vt sopravvivere a

outlook ['autluk] n prospettiva, vista

outlying ['autlaɪŋ] adj periferico(a)

outmoded [aut'məudɪd] adj passato(a) di moda; antiquato(a)

outnumber [aut'nʌmbə*] vt superare in numero

out-of-date adj (passport) scaduto(a); (clothes) fuori moda

out-of-the-way adj (place) fuori mano inv

outpatient ['autpeɪʃənt] n paziente m/f esterno(a)

outpost ['autpəust] n avamposto

output ['autput] n produzione f; (COMPUT) output m inv

outrage ['autreɪdʒ] n oltraggio; scandalo ♦ vt oltraggiare; **~ous** [-'reɪdʒəs] adj oltraggioso(a); scandaloso(a)

outreach worker ['autriːtʃ-] n assistente sociale che opera direttamente nei luoghi di aggregazione di emarginati, tossicodipendenti ecc

outright [adv aut'raɪt, adj 'autraɪt] adv completamente; schiettamente; apertamente; sul colpo ♦ adj completo(a); schietto(a) e netto(a)

outset ['autset] n inizio

outside [aut'saɪd] n esterno, esteriore m ♦ adj esterno(a), esteriore ♦ adv fuori, all'esterno ♦ prep fuori di, all'esterno di; **at the ~** (fig) al massimo; **~ lane** n (AUT) corsia di sorpasso; **~ line** n (TEL) linea esterna; **~r** n (in race etc) outsider m inv; (stranger) estraneo/a

outsize ['autsaɪz] adj (clothes) per taglie forti

outskirts ['autskəːts] npl sobborghi mpl

outspoken [aut'spəukən] adj molto franco(a)

outstanding [aut'stændɪŋ] adj eccezionale, di rilievo; (unfinished) non completo(a); (non evaso(a); non regolato(a)

outstay [aut'steɪ] vt: to ~ **one's welcome** diventare un ospite sgradito

outstretched [aut'stretʃt] adj (hand) teso(a); (body) disteso(a)

outstrip [aut'strɪp] vt (competitors, demand) superare

out-tray n contenitore m per la corrispondenza in partenza

outward ['autwəd] adj (sign, appearances) esteriore; (journey) d'andata

outweigh [aut'weɪ] vt avere maggior peso di

outwit [aut'wɪt] vt superare in astuzia

oval ['əuvl] adj ovale ♦ n ovale m

Oval Office

L'**Oval Office** è una grande sala di forma ovale nella **White House**, la Casa Bianca, dove ha sede l'ufficio del Presidente degli Stati Uniti

---

ovary ['əuvərɪ] n ovaia

oven ['ʌvn] n forno; **~proof** adj da forno

over ['əuvə*] adv al di sopra ♦ adj (or adv) (finished) finito; (BRIT) terminale ♦ (too) troppo; (remaining) che avanza ♦ prep su; sopra; (above) al di sopra di; (on the other side of) di là di; (more than) più di; (during) durante; **~ here** qui; **~ there** là; **all ~** (everywhere) dappertutto; (finished) finito(a); **~ and ~ (again)** più e più volte; **~ and above** oltre (a); **to ask sb ~** invitare qn (a passare)

overall [adj, n 'əuvərɔːl, adv əuvər'ɔːl] adj totale ♦ n (BRIT) grembiule m ♦ adv nell'insieme, complessivamente; **~s** npl (worker's ~s) tuta (da lavoro)

overawe [əuvər'ɔː] vt intimidire

overbalance [əuvə'bæləns] vi perdere l'equilibrio

overboard ['əuvəbɔːd] adv (NAUT) fuori bordo, in mare

overbook [əuvə'buk] vt: **the hotel was ~ed** le prenotazioni all'albergo superavano i posti disponibili

overcast ['əuvəkɑːst] adj (sky) coperto(a)

overcharge [əuvə'tʃɑːdʒ] vt: **to ~ sb for sth** far pagare troppo caro a qn per qc

overcoat ['əuvəkəut] n soprabito, cappotto

overcome [əuvə'kʌm] (irreg) vt superare; sopraffare

overcrowded [əuvə'kraudɪd] adj sovraffollato(a)

overdo [əuvə'duː] (irreg) vt esagerare;

(overcook) cuocere troppo

overdose ['əuvədəus] n dose f eccessiva

overdraft ['əuvədrɑːft] n scoperto (di conto)

overdrawn [əuvə'drɔːn] adj (account) scoperto(a)

overdue [əuvə'djuː] adj in ritardo

overestimate [əuvər'estɪmeɪt] vt sopravvalutare

overflow [vb əuvə'fləu, n 'əuvəfləu] vi traboccare ♦ n (also: ~ pipe) troppopieno

overgrown [əuvə'grəun] adj (garden) ricoperto(a) di vegetazione

overhaul [vb əuvə'hɔːl, n 'əuvəhɔːl] vt revisionare ♦ n revisione f

overhead [adv əuvə'hed, adj, n 'əuvəhed] adv di sopra ♦ adj aereo(a); (lighting) verticale ♦ n (US) = **~s**; **~s** npl spese fpl generali

overhear [əuvə'hɪə*] (irreg) vt sentire (per caso)

overheat [əuvə'hiːt] vi (engine) surriscaldare

overjoyed [əuvə'dʒɔɪd] adj pazzo(a) di gioia

overlap [əuvə'læp] vi sovrapporsi

overleaf [əuvə'liːf] adv a tergo

overload [əuvə'ləud] vt sovraccaricare

overlook [əuvə'luk] vt (have view of) dare su; (miss) trascurare; (forgive) passare sopra a

overnight [əuvə'naɪt] adv (happen) durante la notte; (fig) tutto ad un tratto ♦ adj di notte; **he stayed there ~** ci ha passato la notte

overpass ['əuvəpɑːs] n cavalcavia m inv

overpower [əuvə'pauə*] vt sopraffare; **~ing** adj irresistibile; (heat, stench) soffocante

overrate [əuvə'reɪt] vt sopravvalutare

override [əuvə'raɪd] (irreg: like **ride**) vt (order, objection) passar sopra a; (decision) annullare; **overriding** adj preponderante

overrule [əuvə'ru:l] vt (decision) annullare; (claim) respingere

overrun [əuvə'rʌn] (irreg: like run) vt (country) invadere; (time limit) superare

overseas [əuvə'si:z] adv oltremare; (abroad) all'estero ♦ adj (trade) estero(a); (visitor) straniero(a)

overshadow [əuvə'ʃædəu] vt far ombra su; (fig) eclissare

overshoot [əuvə'ʃu:t] (irreg) vt superare

oversight ['əuvəsaɪt] n omissione f, svista

oversleep [əuvə'sli:p] (irreg) vt dormire troppo a lungo

overstep [əuvə'stɛp] vt: **to ~ the mark** superare ogni limite

overt [əu'vɛ:t] adj palese

overtake [əuvə'teɪk] (irreg) vt sorpassare

overthrow [əuvə'θrəu] (irreg) vt (government) rovesciare

overtime ['əuvətaɪm] n (lavoro) straordinario

overtone ['əuvətəun] n sfumatura

overture ['əuvətʃuə*] n (MUS) ouverture f inv; (fig) approccio

overturn [əuvə'tɛ:n] vt rovesciare ♦ vi rovesciarsi

overweight [əuvə'weɪt] adj (person) troppo grasso(a)

overwhelm [əuvə'wɛlm] vt sopraffare; sommergere; schiacciare; **~ing** adj (victory, defeat) schiacciante; (heat, desire) intenso(a)

overwrought [əuvə'rɔːt] adj molto agitato(a)

owe [əu] vt: **to ~ sb sth**, **to ~ sth to sb** dovere qc a qn; **owing to** prep a causa di

owl [aul] n gufo

own [əun] vt possedere ♦ adj proprio(a); **a room of my ~** la mia propria camera; **to get one's ~ back** vendicarsi; **on one's ~** tutto(a) solo(a); **~ up** vi confessare; **~er** n proprietario/a; **~ership** n possesso

ox [ɔks] pl **oxen** n bue m

oxen ['ɔksn] npl of **ox**

oxtail ['ɔksteɪl] n: **~ soup** minestra di coda di bue

oxygen ['ɔksɪdʒən] n ossigeno; **~ mask/tent** n maschera/tenda ad ossigeno

oyster ['ɔɪstə*] n ostrica

oz. abbr = **ounce(s)**

ozone ['əuzəun] n ozono; **~-friendly** adj che non danneggia l'ozono; **~ hole** n buco nell'ozono

P, p

p [pi:] abbr = **penny; pence**

P.A. n abbr = **personal assistant; public address system**

p.a. abbr = **per annum**

pa [pɑ:] (inf) n papà m, babbo

pace [peɪs] n passo; (speed) passo; velocità ♦ vi: **to ~ up and down** camminare su e giù; **to keep ~ with** camminare di pari passo a; (events) tenersi al corrente di; **~maker** n (MED) segnapasso; (SPORT: also: **~ setter**) battistrada m inv

pacific [pə'sɪfɪk] n: **the P~ (Ocean)** il Pacifico, l'Oceano Pacifico

pacify ['pæsɪfaɪ] vt calmare, placare

pack [pæk] n pacco; (US: of cigarettes) pacchetto; (back~) zaino; (of hounds) muta; (of thieves etc) banda; (of cards) mazzo ♦ vt (in suitcase etc) mettere; (box) riempire; (cram) stipare, pigiare; **to ~ (one's bags)** fare la valigia; **to ~ sb off** spedire via qn; **~ it in!** (inf) dacci un taglio!

package ['pækɪdʒ] n pacco; balla; (also: **~ deal**) pacchetto; forfait m inv; **~ holiday** n vacanza organizzata; **~ tour** n viaggio organizzato

packed lunch n pranzo al sacco

packet ['pækɪt] n pacchetto

packing ['pækɪŋ] n imballaggio; **~ case** n cassa da imballaggio

pact [pækt] *n* patto, accordo; trattato

pad [pæd] *n* blocco; (to prevent friction) cuscinetto; (inf: flat) appartamentino ♦ *vt* imbottire; **~ding** *n* imbottitura

paddle ['pædl] *n* (oar) pagaia; (us: for table tennis) racchetta da ping-pong ♦ *vi* sguazzare ♦ *vt*: **to ~ a canoe** etc vogare con la pagaia; **paddling pool** (BRIT) *n* piscina per bambini

paddock ['pædək] *n* prato recintato; (at racecourse) paddock *m inv*

padlock ['pædlɔk] *n* lucchetto

paediatrics [pi:dɪ'ætrɪks] (us **pediatrics**) *n* pediatria

pagan ['peɪgən] *adj, n* pagano(a)

page [peɪdʒ] *n* pagina; (also: ~ **boy**) paggio ♦ *vt* (in hotel etc) (far) chiamare

pageant ['pædʒənt] *n* spettacolo storico; grande cerimonia; **~ry** *n* pompa

pager ['peɪdʒə*] *n* (TEL) cercapersone *m inv*

paging device ['peɪdʒɪŋ-] *n* (TEL) cercapersone *m inv*

paid [peɪd] *pt, pp of* **pay** ♦ *adj* (work, official) rimunerato(a); **to put ~ to** (BRIT) mettere fine a

pail [peɪl] *n* secchio

pain [peɪn] *n* dolore *m*; **to be in ~** soffrire, aver male; **to take ~s to do** mettercela tutta per fare; **~ed** *adj* addolorato(a), afflitto(a); **~ful** *adj* doloroso(a), che fa male; difficile, penoso(a); **~fully** *adv* (fig: very) fin troppo; **~killer** *n* antalgico, antidolorifico; **~less** *adj* indolore

painstaking ['peɪnzteɪkɪŋ] *adj* (person) sollecito(a); (work) accurato(a)

paint [peɪnt] *n* vernice *f*, colore *m* ♦ *vt* dipingere; (walls, door etc) verniciare; **to ~ the door blue** verniciare la porta di azzurro; **~brush** *n* pennello; **~er** *n* (artist) pittore *m*; (decorator) imbianchino; **~ing** *n* pittura; verniciatura; (picture) dipinto, quadro; **~work** *n* tinta; (of car) vernice *f*

pair [peə*] *n* (of shoes, gloves etc) paio;

(of people) coppia; duo *m inv*; **a ~ of scissors/trousers** un paio di forbici/pantaloni

pajamas [pɪ'dʒɑ:məz] (us) *npl* pigiama *m*

Pakistan [pɑ:kɪ'stɑ:n] *n* Pakistan *m*; **~i** *adj, n* pakistano(a)

pal [pæl] (inf) *n* amico/a, compagno/a

palace ['pæləs] *n* palazzo

palatable ['pælɪtəbl] *adj* gustoso(a)

palate ['pælɪt] *n* palato

palatial [pə'leɪʃəl] *adj* sontuoso(a), sfarzoso(a)

pale [peɪl] *adj* pallido(a) ♦ *n*: **to be beyond the ~** aver oltrepassato ogni limite

Palestine ['pælɪstaɪn] *n* Palestina; **Palestinian** [-'tɪnɪən] *adj, n* palestinese *m/f*

palette ['pælɪt] *n* tavolozza

palings ['peɪlɪŋz] *npl* (fence) palizzata

pallet ['pælɪt] *n* (for goods) paletta

pallid ['pælɪd] *adj* pallido(a), smorto(a)

pallor ['pælə*] *n* pallore *m*

palm [pɑ:m] *n* (ANAT) palma, palmo; (also: ~ **tree**) palma ♦ *vt*: **to ~ sth off on sb** (inf) rifilare qc a qn; **P~ Sunday** *n* Domenica delle Palme

paltry ['pɔ:ltrɪ] *adj* irrisorio(a); insignificante

pamper ['pæmpə*] *vt* viziare, coccolare

pamphlet ['pæmflət] *n* dépliant *m inv*

pan [pæn] *n* (also: **sauce~**) casseruola; (also: **frying ~**) padella

panache [pə'næʃ] *n* stile *m*

pancake ['pænkeɪk] *n* frittella

pancreas ['pæŋkrɪəs] *n* pancreas *m inv*

panda ['pændə] *n* panda *m inv*; **~ car** (BRIT) *n* auto *f* della polizia

pandemonium [pændɪ'məʊnɪəm] *n* pandemonio

pander ['pændə*] *vi*: **to ~ to** lusingare; concedere tutto a

pane [peɪn] *n* vetro

panel ['pænl] *n* (of wood, cloth etc) pannello; (RADIO, TV) giuria; **~ling** (us **~ing**) *n* rivestimento a pannelli

pang [pæŋ] n: **a ~ of regret** un senso di rammarico; **hunger ~s** morsi mpl della fame

panic ['pænɪk] n panico ♦ vi perdere il sangue freddo; **~ky** adj (person) pauroso(a); **~-stricken** adj (person) preso(a) dal panico, in preda al panico; (look) terrorizzato(a)

pansy ['pænzɪ] n (BOT) viola del pensiero, pensée f; (inf: pej) femminuccia

pant [pænt] vi ansare

panther ['pænθə*] n pantera

panties ['pæntɪz] npl slip m, mutandine fpl

pantihose ['pæntɪhəʊz] (US) n collant m inv

pantomime ['pæntəmaɪm] (BRIT) n pantomima

---

pantomime

In Gran Bretagna la **pantomime** è una sorta di libera interpretazione delle favole più conosciute, che vengono messe in scena a teatro durante il periodo natalizio. È uno spettacolo per tutta la famiglia che prevede la partecipazione del pubblico.

---

pantry ['pæntrɪ] n dispensa

pants [pænts] npl mutande fpl, slip m; (US: trousers) pantaloni mpl

papal ['peɪpəl] adj papale, pontificio(a)

paper ['peɪpə*] n carta; (also: wall~) carta da parati, tappezzeria; (also: news~) giornale m; (study, article) saggio; (exam) prova scritta ♦ adj di carta ♦ vt tappezzare; **~s** npl (also: identity ~s) carte fpl, documenti mpl; **~back** n tascabile m; edizione f economica; **~ bag** n sacchetto di carta; **~ clip** n graffetta, clip f inv; **~ hankie** n fazzolettino di carta; **~weight** n fermacarte m inv; **~work** n lavoro amministrativo

papier-mâché ['pæpɪeɪ'mæʃeɪ] n cartapesta

par [pɑ:*] n parità, pari f; (GOLF) norma; **on a ~ with** alla pari con

parachute ['pærəʃu:t] n paracadute m inv

parade [pə'reɪd] n parata ♦ vt (fig) fare sfoggio di ♦ vi sfilare in parata

paradise ['pærədaɪs] n paradiso

paradox ['pærədɒks] n paradosso; **~ically** [-'dɒksɪklɪ] adv paradossalmente

paraffin ['pærəfɪn] (BRIT) n: **~ (oil)** paraffina

paragon ['pærəgən] n modello di perfezione or di virtù

paragraph ['pærəgrɑ:f] n paragrafo

parallel ['pærəlɛl] adj parallelo(a); (fig) analogo(a) ♦ n (line) parallela; (fig, GEO) parallelo

paralyse ['pærəlaɪz] (US **paralyze**) vt paralizzare

paralysis [pə'rælɪsɪs] n paralisi f inv

paralyze ['pærəlaɪz] (US) vt = **paralyse**

paramount ['pærəmaunt] adj: **of ~ importance** di capitale importanza

paranoid ['pærənɔɪd] adj paranoico(a)

paraphernalia [pærəfə'neɪlɪə] n attrezzi mpl, roba

parasol ['pærəsɔl] n parasole m

paratrooper ['pærətru:pə*] n paracadutista m (soldato)

parcel ['pɑ:sl] n pacco, pacchetto ♦ vt (also: ~ up) impaccare

parched [pɑ:tʃt] adj (person) assetato(a)

parchment ['pɑ:tʃmənt] n pergamena

pardon ['pɑ:dn] n perdono; grazia ♦ vt perdonare; (LAW) graziare; **~ me!** mi scusi!; **I beg your ~!** scusi!; **I beg your ~?** (BRIT), **~ me?** (US) prego?

parent ['pɛərənt] n genitore m; **~s** npl (mother and father) genitori mpl; **~al** [pə'rɛntl] adj dei genitori

parentheses [pə'rɛnθɪsi:z] npl of **parenthesis**

parenthesis [pə'rɛnθɪsɪs] (pl

parentheses) n parentesi f inv

Paris ['pærɪs] n Parigi f

parish ['pærɪʃ] n parrocchia; (BRIT: civil) ≈ municipio

park [pɑːk] n parco ♦ vt, vi parcheggiare

parka ['pɑːkə] n eskimo

parking ['pɑːkɪŋ] n parcheggio; "no ~" "sosta vietata"; ~ **lot** (US) n posteggio, parcheggio; ~ **meter** n parchimetro; ~ **ticket** n multa per sosta vietata

parliament ['pɑːləmənt] n parlamento

parliamentary [pɑːlə'mɛntərɪ] adj parlamentare

parlour ['pɑːlə*] (US **parlor**) n salotto

parochial [pə'rəʊkɪəl] (pej) adj provinciale

parole [pə'rəʊl] n: **on** ~ in libertà per buona condotta

parrot ['pærət] n pappagallo

parry ['pærɪ] vt parare

parsley ['pɑːslɪ] n prezzemolo

parsnip ['pɑːsnɪp] n pastinaca

parson ['pɑːsn] n prete m; (Church of England) parroco

part [pɑːt] n parte f; (of machine) pezzo; (US: in hair) scriminatura ♦ adj in parte ♦ adv = **partly** ♦ vt separare ♦ vi (people) separarsi; **to take** ~ in prendere parte a; **for my** ~ per parte mia; **to take sth in good** ~ prendere bene qc; **to take sb's** ~ parteggiare per o prendere le parti di qn; **for the most** ~ in generale; nella maggior parte dei casi; ~ **with** vt fus separarsi da; rinunciare a; ~ **exchange** (BRIT) n: **in** ~ **exchange** in pagamento parziale

partial ['pɑːʃl] adj parziale; **to be** ~ **to** avere un debole per

participate [pɑː'tɪsɪpeɪt] vi: **to** ~ (**in**) prendere parte a, partecipare (a); **participation** [-'peɪʃən] n partecipazione f

participle ['pɑːtɪsɪpl] n participio

particle ['pɑːtɪkl] n particella

particular [pə'tɪkjulə*] adj particolare; speciale; (fussy) difficile; meticoloso(a); **in** ~ in particolare, particolarmente; ~**ly** adv particolarmente; in particolare; ~**s** npl particolari mpl, dettagli mpl; (information) informazioni fpl

parting ['pɑːtɪŋ] n separazione f; (BRIT: in hair) scriminatura ♦ adj d'addio

partisan [pɑːtɪ'zæn] n partigiano/a ♦ adj partigiano(a); di parte

partition [pɑː'tɪʃən] n (POL) partizione f; (wall) tramezzo

partly ['pɑːtlɪ] adv parzialmente; in parte

partner ['pɑːtnə*] n (COMM) socio/a; (wife, husband etc, SPORT) compagno/a; (at dance) cavaliere/dama; ~**ship** n associazione f; (COMM) società f inv

partridge ['pɑːtrɪdʒ] n pernice f

part-time adj, adv a orario ridotto

party ['pɑːtɪ] n (POL) partito; (group) gruppo; (LAW) parte f; (celebration) ricevimento; serata; festa ♦ cpd (POL) del partito, di partito; ~ **dress** n vestito da festa

pass [pɑːs] vt (gen) passare; (place) passare davanti a; (exam) passare, superare; (candidate) promuovere; (overtake, surpass) sorpassare, superare; (approve) approvare ♦ vi passare ♦ n (permit) lasciapassare m inv; permesso; (in mountains) passo, gola; (SPORT) passaggio; (SCOL): **to get a** ~ prendere la sufficienza; **to** ~ **sth through a hole** etc far passare qc attraverso un buco etc; **to make a** ~ **at sb** (inf) fare delle proposte o delle avances a qn; ~ **away** vi morire; ~ **by** vi passare ♦ vt trascurare; ~ **on** vt passare; ~ **out** vi svenire; ~ **up** vt (opportunity) lasciarsi sfuggire, perdere; ~**able** adj (road) praticabile; (work) accettabile

passage ['pæsɪdʒ] n (gen) passaggio; (also: ~**way**) corridoio; (in book) brano, passo; (by boat) traversata

passbook ['pɑːsbuk] n libretto di risparmio

passenger ['pæsɪndʒə*] n passeggero/a

passer-by [pɑːsə'baɪ] n passante m/f

passing ['pɑːsɪŋ] adj (fig) fuggevole; **to mention sth in ~** accennare a qc di sfuggita; **~ place** n (AUT) piazzola di sosta

passion ['pæʃən] n passione f; amore m; **~ate** adj appassionato/a

passive ['pæsɪv] adj (also LING) passivo/a; **~ smoking** n fumo passivo

Passover ['pɑːsəʊvə*] n Pasqua ebraica

passport ['pɑːspɔːt] n passaporto; **~ control** n controllo m passaporti inv; **~ office** n ufficio m passaporti inv

password ['pɑːswɜːd] n parola d'ordine

past [pɑːst] prep (further than) oltre, di là di; dopo; (later than) dopo ♦ adj passato/a; (president etc) ex inv ♦ n passato; **he's ~ forty** ha più di quarant'anni; **ten ~ eight** le otto e dieci; **for the ~ few days** da qualche giorno; in questi ultimi giorni; **to run ~** passare di corsa

pasta ['pæstə] n pasta

paste [peɪst] n (glue) colla; (CULIN) pâté m inv; pasta ♦ vt colare

pastel ['pæstl] adj pastello inv

pasteurized ['pæstəraɪzd] adj pastorizzato/a

pastille ['pæstl] n pastiglia

pastime ['pɑːstaɪm] n passatempo

pastry ['peɪstrɪ] n pasta

pasture ['pɑːstʃə*] n pascolo

pasty¹ ['pæstɪ] n pasticcio di carne

pasty² ['peɪstɪ] adj (face etc) smorto/a

pat [pæt] vt accarezzare, dare un colpetto (affettuoso) a

patch [pætʃ] n (of material, on tyre) toppa; (eye ~) benda; (spot) macchia ♦ vt (clothes) rappezzare; **(to go through) a bad ~** (attraversare) un brutto periodo; **~ up** vt rappezzare; (quarrel) appianare; **~y** adj irregolare

pâté ['pæteɪ] n pâté m inv

patent ['peɪtnt] n brevetto ♦ vt brevettare ♦ adj patente, manifesto(a); **~ leather** n cuoio verniciato

paternal [pə'tɜːnl] adj paterno(a)

path [pɑːθ] n sentiero, viottolo; viale m; (fig) via, strada; (of planet, missile) traiettoria

pathetic [pə'θetɪk] adj (pitiful) patetico(a); (very bad) penoso(a)

pathological [pæθə'lɔdʒɪkl] adj patologico(a)

pathway ['pɑːθweɪ] n sentiero

patience ['peɪʃns] n pazienza; (BRIT: CARDS) solitario

patient ['peɪʃnt] n paziente m/f; malato/a ♦ adj paziente

patio ['pætɪəʊ] n terrazza

patriot ['peɪtrɪət] n patriota m/f; **~ic** [pætrɪ'ɔtɪk] adj patriottico(a); **~ism** n patriottismo

patrol [pə'trəʊl] n pattuglia ♦ vt pattugliare; **~ car** n autoradio f inv (della polizia); **~man** (US irreg) n poliziotto

patron ['peɪtrən] n (in shop) cliente m/f; (of charity) benefattore/trice; **~ of the arts** mecenate m/f; **~ize** ['pætrənaɪz] vt essere cliente abituale di; (fig) trattare dall'alto in basso

patter ['pætə*] n picchiettio; (sales talk) propaganda di vendita ♦ vi picchiettare; **a ~ of footsteps** un rumore di passi

pattern ['pætən] n modello, (design) disegno, motivo

pauper ['pɔːpə*] n indigente m/f

pause [pɔːz] n pausa ♦ vi fare una pausa, arrestarsi

pave [peɪv] vt pavimentare; **to ~ the way for** aprire la via a

pavement ['peɪvmənt] (BRIT) n marciapiede m

pavilion [pə'vɪlɪən] n (SPORT) edificio annesso a campo sportivo

paving ['peɪvɪŋ] n pavimentazione f; **~ stone** n lastra di pietra

paw [pɔː] n zampa

pawn [pɔːn] n (CHESS) pedone m; (fig) pedina ♦ vt dare in pegno; **~broker** n prestatore m su pegno; **~shop** n monte m di pietà

pay [peɪ] (pt, pp **paid**) n stipendio, paga ♦ vt pagare ♦ vi (be profitable) rendere; **to ~ attention (to)** fare attenzione (a); **to ~ sb a visit** far visita a qn; **to ~ one's respects to sb** porgere i propri rispetti a qn; **~ back** vt rimborsare; **~ for** vt fus pagare; **~ in** vt versare; **~ off** vt (debt) saldare; (person) pagare e licenziare; (employee) pagare e licenziare ♦ vi (scheme, decision) dare dei frutti; **~ up** vt saldare; **~able** adj pagabile; **~ee** n beneficiario/a; **~ envelope** (US) n = **~ packet; ~ing** adj: **~ing guest** ospite m/f pagante, pensionante m/f; **~ment** n pagamento; versamento; saldo; **~ packet** (BRIT) n busta f paga inv; **~ phone** n cabina telefonica; **~roll** n ruolo (organico); **~ slip** n foglio m paga inv; **~ television** n televisione f a pagamento, pay-tv f inv

PC n abbr = **personal computer**; adv abbr = **politically correct**

p.c. abbr = **per cent**

pea [piː] n pisello

peace [piːs] n pace f; **~ful** adj pacifico(a), calmo(a)

peach [piːtʃ] n pesca

peacock [ˈpiːkɔk] n pavone m

peak [piːk] n (of mountain) cima, vetta; (mountain itself) picco; (of cap) visiera; (fig) apice m, culmine m; **~ hours** npl ore fpl di punta; **~ period** n = **~ hours**

peal [piːl] n (of bells) scampanio, carillon m inv; **~s of laughter** scoppi mpl di risa

peanut [ˈpiːnʌt] n arachide f, nocciolina americana; **~ butter** n burro di arachidi

pear [pɛəˈ] n pera

pearl [pɔːl] n perla

peasant [ˈpɛznt] n contadino/a

peat [piːt] n torba

pebble [ˈpɛbl] n ciottolo

peck [pɛk] vt (also: ~ at) beccare ♦ n colpo di becco; (kiss) bacetto; **~ing order** n ordine m gerarchico; **~ish** (BRIT: inf) adj: **I feel ~ish** ho un languorino

peculiar [pɪˈkjuːlɪəˈ] adj strano(a), bizzarro(a); peculiare; **~ to** peculiare di

pedal [ˈpɛdl] n pedale m ♦ vi pedalare

pedantic [pɪˈdæntɪk] adj pedantesco(a)

peddler [ˈpɛdləˈ] n (also: drug ~) spacciatore/trice

pedestal [ˈpɛdəstl] n piedestallo

pedestrian [pɪˈdɛstrɪən] n pedone/a ♦ adj pedonale; (fig) prosaico(a), pedestre; **~ crossing** (BRIT) n passaggio pedonale; **~ precinct** (BRIT), **~ zone** (US) n zona pedonale

pediatrics [piːdɪˈætrɪks] (US) n = **paediatrics**

pedigree [ˈpɛdɪgriː] n (of animal) pedigree m inv; (fig) background m inv ♦ cpd (animal) di razza

pee [piː] (inf) vi pisciare

peek [piːk] vi guardare furtivamente

peel [piːl] n (of orange, lemon) scorza ♦ vt sbucciare ♦ vi (paint etc) staccarsi

peep [piːp] n (BRIT: look) sguardo furtivo, sbirciata; (sound) pigolio ♦ vi (BRIT) guardare furtivamente; **~ out** vi mostrarsi furtivamente; **~hole** n spioncino

peer [pɪəˈ] vi: **to ~ at** scrutare ♦ n (noble) pari m inv; (equal) pari m/f inv, uguale m/f; (contemporary) contemporaneo/a; **~age** n dignità di pari; pari mpl

peeved [piːvd] adj stizzito(a)

peevish [ˈpiːvɪʃ] adj stizzoso(a)

peg [pɛg] n caviglia; (for coat etc) attaccapanni m inv; (BRIT: also: clothes ~) molletta

Peking [piːˈkɪŋ] n Pechino f

pelican [ˈpɛlɪkən] n pellicano; **~ crossing** (BRIT) n (AUT) *attraversamento pedonale con semaforo a controllo manuale*

pellet ['pɛlɪt] *n* pallottola, pallina

pelt [pɛlt] *vt*: **to ~ sb (with)** bombardare qn (con) ♦ *vi (rain)* piovere a dirotto; *(inf: run)* filare ♦ *n* pelle *f*

pelvis ['pɛlvɪs] *n* pelvi *f inv*, bacino

pen [pɛn] *n* penna; *(for sheep)* recinto

penal ['piːnl] *adj* penale; **~ize** *vt* punire; *(SPORT, fig)* penalizzare

penalty ['pɛnltɪ] *n* penalità *f inv*; sanzione *f* penale; *(fine)* ammenda; *(SPORT)* penalizzazione *f*; **~ (kick)** *n* *(SPORT)* calcio di rigore

penance ['pɛnəns] *n* penitenza

pence [pɛns] *(BRIT)* npl of **penny**

pencil ['pɛnsl] *n* matita; **~ case** *n* astuccio per matite; **~ sharpener** *n* temperamatite *m inv*

pendant ['pɛndnt] *n* pendaglio

pending ['pɛndɪŋ] *prep* in attesa di ♦ *adj* in sospeso

pendulum ['pɛndjuləm] *n* pendolo

penetrate ['pɛnɪtreɪt] *vt* penetrare

penfriend ['pɛnfrɛnd] *(BRIT)* *n* corrispondente *m/f*

penguin ['pɛŋgwɪn] *n* pinguino

penicillin [pɛnɪ'sɪlɪn] *n* penicillina

peninsula [pə'nɪnsjulə] *n* penisola

penis ['piːnɪs] *n* pene *m*

penitentiary [pɛnɪ'tɛnʃərɪ] *(US)* *n* carcere *m*

penknife ['pɛnnaɪf] *n* temperino

pen name *n* pseudonimo

penniless ['pɛnɪlɪs] *adj* senza un soldo

penny ['pɛnɪ] *(pl* **pennies** *or* **pence** *(BRIT))* *n* penny *m*; *(US)* centesimo

penpal ['pɛnpæl] *n* corrispondente *m/f*

pension ['pɛnʃən] *n* pensione *f*; **~er** *(BRIT)* *n* pensionato/a

pensive ['pɛnsɪv] *adj* pensoso(a)

penthouse ['pɛnthaus] *n* appartamento (di lusso) nell'attico

pent-up ['pɛntʌp] *adj* *(feelings)* represso(a)

people ['piːpl] npl gente *f*; persone fpl;

(citizens) popolo ♦ *n* *(nation, race)* popolo; **4/several ~ came** 4/ parecchie persone sono venute; **~ say that ...** si dice che ....

pep [pɛp] *(inf)*: **~ up** *vt* vivacizzare; *(food)* rendere più gustoso(a)

pepper ['pɛpə*] *n* pepe *m*; *(vegetable)* peperone *m* ♦ *vt* *(fig)*: **to ~ with** spruzzare di; **~mint** *n* *(sweet)* pasticca di menta

peptalk ['pɛptɔːk] *(inf)* *n* discorso di incoraggiamento

per [pə:*] *prep per*; a; **~ hour** all'ora; **~ kilo** *etc* il chilo *etc*; **~ day** al giorno; **~ annum** *adv* all'anno; **~ capita** *adj*, *adv* pro capite *inv*

perceive [pə'siːv] *vt* percepire; *(notice)* accorgersi di

per cent [pə:'sɛnt] *adv* per cento

percentage [pə'sɛntɪdʒ] *n* percentuale *f*

perception [pə'sɛpʃən] *n* percezione *f*; sensibilità; perspicacia

perceptive [pə'sɛptɪv] *adj* percettivo(a); perspicace

perch [pə:tʃ] *n* *(fish)* pesce *m* persico; *(for bird)* sostegno, ramo ♦ *vi* appollaiarsi

percolator ['pə:kəleɪtə*] *n* *(also: coffee ~)* caffettiera a pressione; caffettiera elettrica

percussion [pə'kʌʃən] *n* percussione *f*; *(MUS)* strumenti mpl a percussione

perennial [pə'rɛnɪəl] *adj* perenne

perfect [*adj, n* 'pə:fɪkt, *vb* pə'fɛkt] *adj* perfetto(a) ♦ *n* *(also: ~ tense)* perfetto, passato prossimo ♦ *vt* perfezionare; mettere a punto; **~ly** *adv* perfettamente; alla perfezione

perforate ['pə:fəreɪt] *vt* perforare; **perforation** [-'reɪʃən] *n* perforazione *f*

perform [pə'fɔːm] *vt* *(carry out)* eseguire, fare; *(symphony etc)* suonare; *(play, ballet)* dare; *(opera)* fare ♦ *vi* suonare; recitare; **~ance** *n* esecuzione *f*; *(at theatre etc)* rappresentazione *f*, spettacolo; *(of an artist)* interpretazione f; (of player etc) performance f; (of car, engine) prestazione f; **~er** n artista m/f

perfume ['pə:fju:m] n profumo

perhaps [pə'hæps] adv forse

peril ['peril] n pericolo

perimeter [pə'rimitə*] n perimetro

period ['piəriəd] n periodo; (SCOL) lezione f, (full stop) punto; (MED) mestruazioni fpl ♦ adj (costume, furniture) d'epoca; **~ic(al)** [-'ɔdik(l)] adj periodico(a); **~ical** [-'ɔdikl] n periodico

peripheral [pə'nfərəl] adj periferico(a) ♦ n (COMPUT) unità f periferica

perish ['periʃ] vi perire, morire; (decay) deteriorarsi; **~able** adj deperibile

perjury ['pə:dʒəri] n spergiuro

perk [pə:k] (inf) n vantaggio; **~ up** vi (cheer up) rianimarsi

perm [pə:m] n (for hair) permanente f

permanent ['pə:mənənt] adj permanente

permeate ['pə:mieit] vi penetrare ♦ vt permeare

permissible [pə'misibl] adj permissibile, ammissibile

permission [pə'miʃən] n permesso

permissive [pə'misiv] adj permissivo(a)

permit [n 'pə:mit, vb pə'mit] n permesso ♦ vt permettere; **to ~ sb to do** permettere a qn di fare

perpendicular [pə:pən'dikjulə*] adj perpendicolare ♦ n perpendicolare f

perplex [pə'pleks] vt lasciare perplesso(a)

persecute ['pə:sikju:t] vt perseguitare

persevere [pə:si'viə*] vi perseverare

Persian ['pə:ʃən] adj persiano(a) ♦ n (LING) persiano; **the (~) Gulf** n il Golfo Persico

persist [pə'sist] vi: **to ~ (in doing)** persistere (nel fare); ostinarsi (a fare); **~ent** adj persistente; ostinato(a)

person ['pə:sn] n persona; **in ~** di or in persona, personalmente; **~al** adj personale; individuale; **~al assistant** n

segretaria personale; **~al column** n ≈ messaggi mpl personali; **~al computer** n personal computer m inv; **~ality** [-'næliti] n personalità f inv; **~ally** adv personalmente; **to take sth ~ally** prendere qc come una critica personale; **~al organizer** n (Filofax ®) Fulltime ®; (electronic) agenda elettronica; **~al stereo** n Walkman ® m inv

personnel [pə:sə'nel] n personale m

perspective [pə'spektiv] n prospettiva

Perspex ® ['pə:speks] (BRIT) n tipo di resina termoplastica

perspiration [pə:spi'reiʃən] n traspirazione f, sudore m

persuade [pə'sweid] vt: **to ~ sb to do sth** persuadere qn a fare qc

perturb [pə'tə:b] vt turbare

pervert [n 'pə:və:t, vb pə'və:t] n pervertito/a ♦ vt pervertire

pessimism ['pesimizəm] n pessimismo

pessimist ['pesimist] n pessimista m/f; **~ic** [-'mistik] adj pessimistico(a)

pest [pest] n animale m (or insetto) pestifero; (fig) peste f

pester ['pestə*] vt tormentare, molestare

pet [pet] n animale m domestico ♦ cpd favorito(a) ♦ vt accarezzare; **teacher's ~** favorito/a del maestro

petal ['petl] n petalo

peter ['pi:tə*]: **to ~ out** vi esaurirsi; estinguersi

petite [pə'ti:t] adj piccolo(a) e aggraziato(a)

petition [pə'tiʃən] n petizione f

petrified ['petrifaid] adj (fig) morto(a) di paura

petrol ['petrəl] (BRIT) n benzina; **two/four-star ~** ≈ benzina normale/super; **~ can** n tanica per benzina

petroleum [pə'trəuliəm] n petrolio

petrol: ~ pump (BRIT) n (in car, at garage) pompa di benzina; **~ station** (BRIT) n stazione f di rifornimento; **~ tank** (BRIT) n serbatoio della benzina

petticoat ['petɪkəut] n sottana

petty ['petɪ] adj (mean) meschino(a); (unimportant) insignificante; ~ **cash** n piccola cassa; ~ **officer** n sottufficiale m di marina

petulant ['petjulənt] adj irritabile

pew [pju:] n panca (di chiesa)

pewter ['pju:tə*] n peltro

phallic ['fælɪk] adj fallico(a)

phantom ['fæntəm] n fantasma m

pharmaceutical [fɑ:mə'sju:tɪkl] adj farmaceutico(a)

pharmacy ['fɑ:məsɪ] n farmacia

phase [feɪz] n fase f, periodo ♦ vt: to ~ **sth in/out** introdurre/eliminare qc progressivamente

Ph.D. n abbr = **Doctor of Philosophy**

pheasant ['feznt] n fagiano

phenomena [fə'nɔmɪnə] npl of **phenomenon**

phenomenon [fə'nɔmɪnən] (pl **phenomena**) n fenomeno

Philippines ['fɪlɪpi:nz] npl: **the** ~ le Filippine

philosophical [fɪlə'sɔfɪkl] adj filosofico(a)

philosophy [fɪ'lɔsəfɪ] n filosofia

phobia ['fəubjə] n fobia

phone [fəun] n telefono ♦ vi: **to be on the** ~ avere il telefono; (be calling) essere al telefono; ~ **back** vt, vi richiamare; ~ **up** vt telefonare a ♦ vi telefonare; ~ **book** n guida del telefono, elenco telefonico; ~ **booth** n = ~ **box**; ~ **box** n cabina telefonica; ~ **call** n telefonata; ~**card** n scheda telefonica; ~-**in** n (BRIT: RADIO, TV) trasmissione f a filo diretto con gli ascoltatori

phonetics [fə'netɪks] n fonetica

phoney ['fəunɪ] adj falso(a), fasullo(a)

phosphorus ['fɔsfərəs] n fosforo

photo ['fəutəu] n foto f inv

photo... ['fəutəu] prefix: ~**copier** n fotocopiatrice f; ~**copy** n fotocopia ♦ vt fotocopiare; ~**graph** n fotografia ♦ vt fotografare; ~**grapher**

[fə'tɔgrəfə*] n fotografo; ~**graphy** [fə'tɔgrəfɪ] n fotografia

phrase [freɪz] n espressione f; (LING) locuzione f; (MUS) frase f ♦ vt esprimere; ~ **book** n vocabolarietto

physical ['fɪzɪkl] adj fisico(a); ~ **education** n educazione f fisica; ~**ly** adv fisicamente

physician [fɪ'zɪʃən] n medico

physicist ['fɪzɪsɪst] n fisico

physics ['fɪzɪks] n fisica

physiology [fɪzɪ'ɔlədʒɪ] n fisiologia

physique [fɪ'zi:k] n fisico; costituzione f

pianist ['pi:ənɪst] n pianista m/f

piano [pɪ'ænəu] n pianoforte m

piccolo ['pɪkələu] n ottavino

pick [pɪk] n (tool: also: ~-axe) piccone m ♦ vt scegliere; (gather) cogliere; (remove) togliere; (lock) far scattare; **take your** ~ scelga; **to** ~ **the** ♦ il fior fiore di; **to** ~ **one's nose** mettersi le dita nel naso; **to** ~ **one's teeth** pulirsi i denti con lo stuzzicadenti; **to** ~ **a quarrel** attaccar briga; ~ **at** vt fus: **to** ~ **at one's food** piluccare; ~ **on** vt fus (person) avercela con; ~ **out** vt scegliere; (distinguish) distinguere; ~ **up** vi (improve) migliorarsi ♦ vt raccogliere; (POLICE, RADIO) prendere; (collect) passare a prendere; (AUT: give lift to) far salire; (person: for sexual encounter) rimorchiare; (learn) imparare; **to** ~ **up speed** acquistare velocità; **to** ~ **o.s. up** rialzarsi

picket ['pɪkɪt] n (in strike) scioperante m/f che fa parte di un picchetto; picchetto ♦ vt picchettare

pickle ['pɪkl] n (also: ~s: as condiment) sottaceti mpl; (fig: mess) pasticcio ♦ vt mettere sottaceto; mettere in salamoia

pickpocket ['pɪkpɔkɪt] n borsaiolo

pickup ['pɪkʌp] n (small truck) camioncino

picnic ['pɪknɪk] n picnic m inv

picture ['pɪktʃə*] n quadro; (painting) pittura; (photograph) foto(grafia);

(*drawing*) disegno; (*film*) film m inv ♦ vt raffigurarsi; **~s** (*BRIT*) npl (*cinema*): **the ~s** il cinema; **~ book** n libro illustrato

picturesque [pɪktʃə'rɛsk] adj pittoresco(a)

pie [paɪ] n torta; (*of meat*) pasticcio

piece [piːs] n pezzo; (*of land*) appezzamento; (*item*): **a ~ of furniture/advice** un mobile/consiglio ♦ vt: **to ~ together** mettere insieme; **to take to ~s** smontare; **~ by ~** pezzo a pezzo, a spizzico; **~work** n (lavoro a) cottimo

pie chart n grafico a torta

pier [pɪə*] n molo; (*of bridge etc*) pila

pierce [pɪəs] vt forare; (*with arrow etc*) trafiggere

piercing [ˈpɪəsɪŋ] adj (*cry*) acuto(a); (*eyes*) penetrante; (*wind*) pungente

pig [pɪg] n maiale m, porco

pigeon [ˈpɪdʒən] n piccione m; **~hole** n casella

piggy bank [ˈpɪgɪ-] n salvadanaro

pigheaded [ˈpɪgˈhɛdɪd] adj caparbio(a), cocciuto(a)

piglet [ˈpɪglɪt] n porcellino

pigskin [ˈpɪgskɪn] n cinghiale m

pigsty [ˈpɪgstaɪ] n porcile m

pigtail [ˈpɪgteɪl] n treccina

pike [paɪk] n (*fish*) luccio

pilchard [ˈpɪltʃəd] n specie di sardina

pile [paɪl] n (*pillar, of books*) pila; (*heap*) mucchio; (*of carpet*) pelo ♦ vt (*also: ~ up*) ammucchiare ♦ vi (*also: ~ up*) ammucchiarsi; **to ~ into** (*car*) stiparsi or ammucchiarsi in

piles [paɪlz] npl emorroidi fpl

pile-up [ˈpaɪlʌp] n (*AUT*) tamponamento a catena

pilfering [ˈpɪlfrɪŋ] n rubacchiare m

pilgrim [ˈpɪlgrɪm] n pellegrino/a; **~age** n pellegrinaggio

pill [pɪl] n pillola; **the ~** la pillola

pillage [ˈpɪlɪdʒ] n saccheggiare

pillar [ˈpɪlə*] n colonna; **~ box** (*BRIT*) n cassetta postale

pillion [ˈpɪljən] n: **to ride ~** (*on motor*

cycle) viaggiare dietro

pillow [ˈpɪləu] n guanciale m; **~case** n federa

pilot [ˈpaɪlət] n pilota m/f ♦ cpd (*scheme etc*) pilota inv ♦ vt pilotare; **~ light** n fiamma pilota

pimp [pɪmp] n mezzano

pimple [ˈpɪmpl] n foruncolo

pin [pɪn] n spillo; (*TECH*) perno ♦ vt attaccare con uno spillo; **~s and needles** formicolio; **to ~ sb down** (*fig*) obbligare qn a pronunziarsi; **to ~ sth on sb** (*fig*) addossare la colpa di qc a qn

pinafore [ˈpɪnəfɔː*] n (*also: ~ dress*) grembiule m (senza maniche)

pinball [ˈpɪnbɔːl] n flipper m inv

pincers [ˈpɪnsəz] npl pinzette fpl

pinch [pɪntʃ] n pizzicotto, pizzico ♦ vt pizzicare; (*inf: steal*) grattare; **at a ~** in caso di bisogno

pincushion [ˈpɪnkuʃən] n puntaspilli m inv

pine [paɪn] n (*also: ~ tree*) pino ♦ vi: **to ~ for** struggersi dal desiderio di; **~ away** vi languire

pineapple [ˈpaɪnæpl] n ananas m inv

ping [pɪŋ] n (*noise*) tintinnio; **~-pong** ® n ping-pong ®

pink [pɪŋk] adj rosa inv ♦ n (*colour*) rosa m inv; (*BOT*) garofano

PIN (number) [pɪn-] n abbr codice m segreto

pinpoint [ˈpɪnpɔɪnt] vt indicare con precisione

pint [paɪnt] n pinta (*BRIT* = 0.57l; *US* = 0.47l); (*BRIT: inf*) ≈ birra da mezzo

pioneer [paɪəˈnɪə*] n pioniere/a

pious [ˈpaɪəs] adj pio(a)

pip [pɪp] n (*seed*) seme m; (*BRIT: time signal on radio*) segnale m orario

pipe [paɪp] n tubo; (*for smoking*) pipa ♦ vt portare per mezzo di tubazione; **~s** npl (*also: bag~s*) cornamusa (scozzese); **~ cleaner** n scovolino; **~ dream** n vana speranza; **~line** n conduttura; (*for oil*) oleodotto; **~r** n piffero; suonatore/trice di cornamusa

piping ['paɪpɪŋ] *adv:* ~ **hot** caldo bollente

pique [piːk] *n* picca

pirate ['paɪərət] *n* pirata *m* ♦ *vt* riprodurre abusivamente

Pisces ['paɪsiːz] *n* Pesci *mpl*

piss [pɪs] (*inf*) *vi* pisciare; ~**ed** (*inf*) *adj* (*drunk*) ubriaco(a) fradicio(a)

pistol ['pɪstl] *n* pistola

piston ['pɪstən] *n* pistone *m*

pit [pɪt] *n* buca, fossa; (*also: coal* ~) miniera; (*quarry*) cava ♦ *vt:* **to** ~ **sb against sb** opporre qn a qn; ~**s** *npl* (*AUT*) box *m*

pitch [pɪtʃ] *n* (*BRIT: SPORT*) campo; (*MUS*) tono; (*tar*) pece *f*; (*fig*) grado, punto ♦ *vt* (*throw*) lanciare ♦ *vi* (*fall*) cascare; **to** ~ **a tent** piantare una tenda; ~**ed battle** *n* battaglia campale

pitfall ['pɪtfɔːl] *n* trappola

pith [pɪθ] *n* (*of plant*) midollo; (*of orange*) parte *f* interna della scorza; (*fig*) essenza, succo; vigore *m*

pithy ['pɪθɪ] *adj* conciso(a); vigoroso(a)

pitiful ['pɪtɪful] *adj* (*touching*) pietoso(a)

pitiless ['pɪtɪlɪs] *adj* spietato(a)

pittance ['pɪtns] *n* miseria, magro salario

pity ['pɪtɪ] *n* pietà ♦ *vt* aver pietà di; **what a** ~! che peccato!

pivot ['pɪvət] *n* perno

pizza ['piːtsə] *n* pizza

placard ['plækɑːd] *n* affisso

placate [plə'keɪt] *vt* placare, calmare

place [pleɪs] *n* posto, luogo; (*proper position, rank, seat*) posto; (*house*) casa, alloggio; (*home*): **at/to his** ~ a casa sua ♦ *vt* (*object*) posare, mettere; (*identify*) riconoscere; individuare; **to take** ~ aver luogo; succedere; **to change** ~**s with sb** scambiare il posto con qn; **out of** ~ (*not suitable*) inopportuno(a); **in the first** ~ in primo luogo; **to** ~ **an order** dare un'ordinazione; **to be** ~**d** (*in race,*

exam) classificarsi

placid ['plæsɪd] *adj* placido(a), calmo(a)

plagiarism ['pleɪdʒjərɪzəm] *n* plagio

plague [pleɪg] *n* peste *f* ♦ *vt* tormentare

plaice [pleɪs] *n inv* pianuzza

plaid [plæd] *n* plaid *m inv*

plain [pleɪn] *adj* (*clear*) chiaro(a), palese; (*simple*) semplice; (*frank*) franco(a), aperto(a); (*not handsome*) bruttino(a); (*without seasoning etc*) scondito(a); naturale; (*in one colour*) tinta unita *m inv* ♦ francamente, chiaramente ♦ *n* pianura; ~ **chocolate** *n* cioccolato fondente; ~ **clothes** **in** ~ **clothes** (*police*) in borghese; ~**ly** *adv* chiaramente; (*frankly*) francamente

plaintiff ['pleɪntɪf] *n* attore/trice

plaintive ['pleɪntɪv] *adj* (*cry, voice*) dolente, lamentoso(a)

plait [plæt] *n* treccia

plan [plæn] *n* progetto; (*scheme*) progetto, piano ♦ *vt* (*think in advance*) progettare; (*prepare*) organizzare ♦ *vi* far piani *or* progetti; **to** ~ **to do** progettare di fare

plane [pleɪn] *n* (*AVIAT*) aereo; (*tree*) platano; (*tool*) pialla; (*ART, MATH etc*) piano ♦ *adj* piano(a), piatto(a) ♦ *vt* (*with tool*) piallare

planet ['plænɪt] *n* pianeta *m*

plank [plæŋk] *n* tavola, asse *f*

planner ['plænə*] *n* pianificatore/trice

planning ['plænɪŋ] *n* progettazione *f*; **family** ~ pianificazione *f* delle nascite; ~ **permission** *n* permesso di costruzione

plant [plɑːnt] *n* pianta; (*machinery*) impianto; (*factory*) fabbrica ♦ *vt* piantare; (*bomb*) mettere

plantation [plæn'teɪʃən] *n* piantagione *f*

plaque [plæk] *n* placca

plaster ['plɑːstə*] *n* intonaco; (*also:* ~ *of Paris*) gesso; (*BRIT: also: sticking* ~) cerotto ♦ *vt* intonacare; ingessare

(cover): **to ~ with** coprire di; **~ed** *(inf)*
adj ubriaco(a) fradicio(a)

plastic ['plæstɪk] *n* plastica ♦ *adj (made
of ~)* di o in plastica; **~ bag** *n*
sacchetto di plastica

Plasticine ® ['plæstɪsi:n] *n* plastilina
®

plastic surgery *n* chirurgia plastica

plate [pleɪt] *n (dish)* piatto; *(in book)*
tavola; *(dental ~)* dentiera; **gold/silver
~** vasellame *m* d'oro/d'argento

plateau ['plætəʊ] *(pl* **~s** *or* **~x)** *n*
altipiano

plateaux ['plætəʊz] *npl of* **plateau**

plate glass *n* vetro piano

platform ['plætfɔ:m] *n (stage, at
meeting)* palco; *(RAIL)* marciapiede *m*;
(BRIT: of bus) piattaforma

platinum ['plætɪnəm] *n* platino

platitude ['plætɪtju:d] *n* luogo
comune

platoon [plə'tu:n] *n* plotone *m*

platter ['plætə*] *n* piatto

plausible ['plɔ:zɪbl] *adj* plausibile,
credibile; *(person)* convincente

play [pleɪ] *n* gioco; *(THEATRE)* commedia
♦ *vt (game)* giocare a; *(team, opponent)*
giocare contro; *(instrument, piece of
music)* suonare; *(record, tape)* ascoltare;
(role, part) interpretare ♦ *vi* giocare;
suonare; recitare; **to ~ safe** giocare sul
sicuro; **~ down** *vt* minimizzare; **~ up**
vi (cause trouble) fare i capricci; **~boy** *n*
playboy *m inv*; **~er** *n* giocatore/trice;
(THEATRE) attore/trice; *(MUS)* musicista
m/f; **~ful** *adj* giocoso(a); **~ground** *n*
(in school) cortile *m* per la ricreazione;
(in park) parco *m* giochi *inv*; **~group** *n*
giardino d'infanzia; **~ing card** *n* carta
da gioco; **~ing field** *n* campo
sportivo; **~mate** *n* compagno/a di
gioco; **~-off** *n (SPORT)* bella; **~pen** *n*
box *m inv*; **~thing** *n* giocattolo; **~time**
n (SCOL) ricreazione *f*; **~wright** *n*
drammaturgo *f*

plc *abbr (= public limited company)*
società per azioni a responsabilità

limitata quotata in borsa

plea [pli:] *n (request)* preghiera,
domanda; *(LAW)* (argomento di) difesa;
~ bargaining *n (LAW)* patteggiamento
(della pena)

plead [pli:d] *vt* patrocinare; *(give as
excuse)* addurre a pretesto ♦ *vi (LAW)*
perorare la causa; *(beg)*: **to ~ with sb**
implorare qn

pleasant ['pleznt] *adj* piacevole,
gradevole; **~ries** *npl (polite remarks)*:
to exchange ~ries scambiarsi i
convenevoli

please [pli:z] *excl* per piacere!, per
favore!; *(acceptance)*: **yes, ~** sì, grazie
♦ *vt* piacere a ♦ *vi* piacere; *(think fit)*:
do as you ~ faccia come le pare;
~ yourself! come ti (or le) pare!; **~d**
adj: **~d (with)** contento(a) (di); **~d to
meet you!** piacere!; **pleasing** *adj*
piacevole, che fa piacere

pleasure ['pleʒə*] *n* piacere *m*; **"it's a
~"** "prego"

pleat [pli:t] *n* piega

pledge [pledʒ] *n* pegno; *(promise)*
promessa ♦ *vt* impegnare; promettere

plentiful ['plentɪful] *adj* abbondante,
copioso(a)

plenty ['plentɪ] *n*: **~ of** tanto(a),
molto(a); un'abbondanza di

pleurisy ['pluərɪsɪ] *n* pleurite *f*

pliable ['plaɪəbl] *adj* flessibile; *(fig:
person)* malleabile

pliant ['plaɪənt] *adj* = **pliable**

pliers ['plaɪəz] *npl* pinza

plight [plaɪt] *n* situazione *f* critica

plimsolls ['plɪmsəlz] *(BRIT)* *npl* scarpe
fpl da tennis

plinth [plɪnθ] *n* plinto; piedistallo

plod [plɒd] *vi* camminare a stento; *(fig)*
sgobbare

plonk [plɒŋk] *(inf)* *n (BRIT: wine)* vino
da poco ♦ *vt*: **to ~ sth down** buttare
giù qc bruscamente

plot [plɒt] *n* congiura, cospirazione *f*;
(of story, play) trama; *(of land)* lotto
♦ *vt (mark out)* fare la pianta di;

rilevare; (: *diagram etc*) tracciare; (*conspire*) congiurare, cospirare ♦ *vi* congiurare

plough [plau] (US **plow**) *n* aratro ♦ *vt* (*earth*) arare; **to ~ money into** (*company etc*) investire denaro in; **~ through** *vt fus* (*snow etc*) procedere a fatica in; **~man's lunch** (BRIT) *n* pasto a base di pane, formaggio e birra

ploy [plɔɪ] *n* stratagemma *m*

pluck [plʌk] *vt* (*fruit*) cogliere; (*musical instrument*) pizzicare; (*bird*) spennare; (*hairs*) togliere ♦ *n* coraggio, fegato; **to ~ up courage** farsi coraggio

plug [plʌg] *n* tappo; (ELEC) spina; (AUT: *also:* **spark(ing) ~**) candela ♦ *vt* (*hole*) tappare; (*inf: advertise*) spingere; **~ in** *vt* (ELEC) attaccare a una presa

plum [plʌm] *n* (*fruit*) susina

plumb [plʌm] *vt:* **to ~ the depths** (*fig*) toccare il fondo

plumber ['plʌmə*] *n* idraulico

plumbing ['plʌmɪŋ] *n* (*trade*) lavoro di idraulico; (*piping*) tubature *fpl*

plummet ['plʌmɪt] *vi:* **to ~ (down)** cadere a piombo

plump [plʌmp] *adj* grassoccio(a) ♦ *vt:* **to ~ for** (*inf: choose*) decidersi per; **~ up** *vt* (*cushion etc*) sprimacciare

plunder ['plʌndə*] *n* saccheggio ♦ *vt* saccheggiare

plunge [plʌndʒ] *n* tuffo; (*fig*) caduta ♦ *vt* immergere ♦ *vi* (*fall*) cadere, precipitare; (*dive*) tuffarsi; **to take the ~** saltare il fosso; **plunging** *adj* (*neckline*) profondo(a)

pluperfect [pluː'pəːfɪkt] *n* piuccheperfetto

plural ['pluərl] *adj* plurale ♦ *n* plurale *m*

plus [plʌs] *n* (*also:* **~ sign**) segno più ♦ *prep* più; **ten/twenty ~** più di dieci/venti

plush [plʌʃ] *adj* lussuoso(a)

ply [plaɪ] *vt* (*a trade*) esercitare ♦ *vi* (*ship*) fare il servizio ♦ *n* (*of wool, rope*) capo; **to ~ sb with drink** dare di bere continuamente a qn; **~wood** *n* legno

compensato

P.M. *n abbr* = **prime minister**

p.m. *adv abbr* (= *post meridiem*) del pomeriggio

pneumatic drill [njuː'mætɪk-] *n* martello pneumatico

pneumonia [njuː'məunɪə] *n* polmonite *f*

poach [pəutʃ] *vt* (*cook: egg*) affogare; (: *fish*) cuocere in bianco; (*steal*) cacciare (or pescare) di frodo ♦ *vi* fare il bracconiere; **~er** *n* bracconiere *m*

P.O. Box *n abbr* = **Post Office Box**

pocket ['pɔkɪt] *n* tasca ♦ *vt* intascare; **to be out of ~** (BRIT) rimetterci; **~book** (US) *n* (*wallet*) portafoglio; **~ knife** *n* temperino; **~ money** *n* paghetta, settimana

pod [pɔd] *n* guscio

podgy ['pɔdʒɪ] *adj* grassoccio(a)

podiatrist [pɔ'diːətrɪst] (US) *n* callista *m/f*, pedicure *m/f*

poem ['pəuɪm] *n* poesia

poet ['pəuɪt] *n* poeta/essa; **~ic** [-'ɛtɪk] *adj* poetico(a); **~ry** *n* poesia

poignant ['pɔɪnjənt] *adj* struggente

point [pɔɪnt] *n* (*gen*) punto; (*tip: of needle etc*) punta; (*in time*) punto, momento; (SCOL) voto; (*main idea, important part*) nocciolo; (ELEC) presa (di corrente); (*also: decimal ~*): **2 ~ 3 (2.3)** 2 virgola 3 (2,3) ♦ *vt* (*show*) indicare; (*gun etc*): **to ~ sth at** puntare qc contro ♦ *vi:* **to ~ at** mostrare a dito; **~s** *npl* (AUT) puntine *fpl*; (RAIL) scambio; **to be on the ~ of doing sth** essere sul punto di or stare per fare qc; **to make a ~** fare un'osservazione; **to get/miss the ~** capire/non capire; **to come to the ~** venire al dunto; **there's no ~ (in doing)** è inutile (fare); **~ out** *vt* far notare; **~ to** *vt fus* indicare; (*fig*) dimostrare; **~-blank** *adv* (*also: at ~-blank range*) a bruciapelo; (*fig*) categoricamente; **~ed** *adj* (*shape*) aguzzo(a), appuntito(a); (*remark*) specifico(a); **~edly** adv in maniera inequivocabile; **~er** n (needle) lancetta; (fig) indicazione f, consiglio; **~less** adj inutile, vano(a); **~ of view** n punto di vista

poise [pɔɪz] n (composure) portamento; **~d** adj: **to be ~d to** essere pronto(a) a fare

poison ['pɔɪzn] n veleno ♦ vt avvelenare; **~ing** n avvelenamento; **~ous** adj velenoso(a)

poke [pəuk] vt (fire) attizzare; (jab with finger, stick etc) punzecchiare; (put): to ~ **sth in(to)** spingere qc dentro; ~ **about** vi frugare

poker ['pəukə*] n attizzatoio; (CARDS) poker m

poky ['pəukɪ] adj piccolo(a) e stretto(a)

Poland ['pəulənd] n Polonia

polar ['pəulə*] adj polare; ~ **bear** n orso bianco

Pole [pəul] n polacco/a

pole [pəul] n (of wood) palo; (ELEC, GEO) polo; ~ **bean** n (US) (runner bean) fagiolino; ~ **vault** n salto con l'asta

police [pə'li:s] n polizia ♦ vt mantenere l'ordine in; ~ **car** n macchina della polizia; **~man** (irreg) n poliziotto, agente m di polizia; ~ **station** n posto di polizia; **~woman** (irreg) n donna f poliziotto inv

policy ['pɔlɪsɪ] n politica; (also: insurance ~) polizza (d'assicurazione)

polio ['pəulɪəu] n polio f

Polish ['pəulɪʃ] adj polacco(a) ♦ n (LING) polacco

polish ['pɔlɪʃ] n (for shoes) lucido; (for floor) cera; (for nails) smalto; (shine) lucentezza, lustro; (fig: refinement) raffinatezza ♦ vt lucidare; (fig: improve) raffinare; ~ **off** vt (food) mangiarsi; **~ed** adj (fig) raffinato(a)

polite [pə'laɪt] adj cortese; **~ness** n cortesia

political [pə'lɪtɪkl] adj politico(a); **~ly** adv politicamente; **~ly correct** politicamente corretto(a)

politician [pɔlɪ'tɪʃən] n politico

politics ['pɔlɪtɪks] n politica ♦ npl (views, policies) idee fpl politiche

poll [pəul] n scrutinio; (votes cast) voti mpl; (also: opinion ~) sondaggio (d'opinioni) ♦ vt ottenere

pollen ['pɔlən] n polline m

polling day ['pəulɪŋ-] (BRIT) n giorno delle elezioni

polling station ['pəulɪŋ-] (BRIT) n sezione f elettorale

pollute [pə'lu:t] vt inquinare

pollution [pə'lu:ʃən] n inquinamento

polo ['pəuləu] n polo; **~-necked** adj a collo alto risvoltato; ~ **shirt** n polo f inv

polyester [pɔlɪ'estə*] n poliestere m

polystyrene [pɔlɪ'staɪri:n] n polistirolo

polytechnic [pɔlɪ'teknɪk] n (college) istituto superiore ad indirizzo tecnologico

polythene ['pɔlɪθi:n] n politene m; ~ **bag** n sacco di plastica

pomegranate ['pɔmɪɡrænɪt] n melagrana

pomp [pɔmp] n pompa, fasto

pompom ['pɔmpɔm] n pompon m inv

pompon ['pɔmpɔn] n = **pompom**

pompous ['pɔmpəs] adj pomposo(a)

pond [pɔnd] n pozza; stagno

ponder ['pɔndə*] vt ponderare, riflettere su; **~ous** adj ponderoso(a), pesante

pong [pɔŋ] (BRIT: inf) n puzzo

pony ['pəunɪ] n pony m inv; **~tail** n coda di cavallo; ~ **trekking** (BRIT) n escursione f a cavallo

poodle ['pu:dl] n barboncino, barbone m

pool [pu:l] n (puddle) pozza; (pond) stagno; (also: swimming ~) piscina; (fig: of light) cerchio; (billiards) specie di biliardo a buca ♦ vt mettere in comune; **~s** npl (football ~s) ≈ totocalcio; **typing** ~ n servizio comune di dattilografia

poor [puə*] adj povero(a); (mediocre) mediocre, cattivo(a) ♦ npl: **the ~ i**

poveri; **~ in** povero(a) di; **~ly** adv
poveramente; male ♦ adj indisposto(a),
malato(a)

pop [pɔp] n (noise) schiocco; (MUS)
musica pop; (drink) bibita gasata; (US:
inf: father) babbo ♦ vt (put) mettere (in
fretta) ♦ vi scoppiare; (cork) schioccare;
~ in vi passare; **~ out** vi fare un salto
fuori; **~ up** vi apparire, sorgere; **~corn**
n pop-corn m

pope [pəup] n papa m

poplar ['pɔplə*] n pioppo

popper ['pɔpə*] n bottone m a
pressione

poppy ['pɔpi] n papavero

Popsicle ® ['pɔpsikl] (US) n (ice lolly)
ghiacciolo

populace ['pɔpjuləs] n popolino

popular ['pɔpjulə*] adj popolare;
(fashionable) in voga; **~ity** [-'læriti] n
popolarità

population [pɔpju'leiʃən] n
popolazione f

porcelain ['pɔːslin] n porcellana

porch [pɔːtʃ] n veranda

porcupine ['pɔːkjupain] n porcospino

pore [pɔː*] n poro ♦ vi: **to ~ over**
essere immerso(a) in

pork [pɔːk] n carne f di maiale

pornographic [pɔːnə'græfik] adj
pornografico(a)

pornography [pɔː'nɔgrəfi] n
pornografia

porpoise ['pɔːpəs] n focena

porridge ['pɔridʒ] n porridge m

port [pɔːt] n (gen, wine) porto; (NAUT:
left side) babordo; **~ of call** (porto di)
scalo

portable ['pɔːtəbl] adj portatile

porter ['pɔːtə*] n (for luggage)
facchino, portabagagli m inv;
(doorkeeper) portiere m, portinaio

portfolio [pɔːt'fəuliəu] n (case)
cartella; (POL, FINANCE) portafoglio; (of
artist) raccolta dei propri lavori

porthole ['pɔːthəul] n oblò m inv

portion ['pɔːʃən] n porzione f

portrait ['pɔːtreit] n ritratto

portray [pɔː'trei] vt fare il ritratto di;
(character on stage) rappresentare; (in
writing) ritrarre

Portugal [pɔː'tjugl] n Portogallo

Portuguese [pɔːtju'giːz] adj
portoghese ♦ n inv portoghese m/f;
(LING) portoghese m

pose [pəuz] n posa ♦ vi posare;
(pretend): **to ~ as** atteggiarsi a, posare
a ♦ vt porre

posh [pɔʃ] (inf) adj elegante; (family)
per bene

position [pə'ziʃən] n posizione f; (job)
posto ♦ vt sistemare

positive ['pɔzitiv] adj positivo(a);
(certain) sicuro(a), certo(a); (definite)
preciso(a); definitivo(a)

posse ['pɔsi] (US) n drappello

possess [pə'zes] vt possedere; **~ion**
[pə'zeʃən] n possesso; **~ions** npl
(belongings) beni mpl; **~ive** adj
possessivo(a)

possibility [pɔsi'biliti] n possibilità f
inv

possible ['pɔsibl] adj possibile; **as big
as ~** il più grande possibile

possibly ['pɔsibli] adv (perhaps) forse;
if you ~ can se le è possibile; **I
cannot ~ come** proprio non posso
venire

post [pəust] n (BRIT) posta; (: collection)
levata; (job, situation) posto; (MIL)
postazione f; (pole) palo ♦ vt (BRIT: send
by post) impostare; (: appoint): **to ~** to
assegnare a; **~age** n affrancatura;
~age stamp n francobollo; **~al order**
n vaglia m inv postale; **~box** (BRIT) n
cassetta postale; **~card** n cartolina;
~ code (BRIT) n codice m (di
avviamento) postale

poster ['pəustə*] n manifesto, affisso

poste restante [pəust'rɛstɑ̃nt] (BRIT)
n fermo posta m

postgraduate ['pəust'grædjuət] n
laureato/a che continua gli studi

posthumous ['pɔstjuməs] adj

postumo(a)

postman ['pəustmən] (*irreg*) *n* postino

postmark ['pəustmɑ:k] *n* bollo or timbro postale

post-mortem [-'mɔ:təm] *n* autopsia

post office *n* (*building*) ufficio postale; (*organization*): **the Post Office** ≈ le Poste e Telecomunicazioni; **Post Office Box** *n* casella postale

postpone [pəs'pəun] *vt* rinviare

postscript ['pəustskript] *n* poscritto

posture ['pɔstʃə*] *n* portamento; (*pose*) posa, atteggiamento

postwar ['pəust'wɔ:*] *adj* del dopoguerra

posy ['pəuzi] *n* mazzetto di fiori

pot [pɔt] *n* (*for cooking*) pentola; casseruola; (*tea~*) teiera; (*coffee~*) caffettiera; (*for plants, jam*) vaso; (*inf: marijuana*) erba ♦ *vt* (*plant*) piantare in vaso; **a ~ of tea for two** tè per due; **to go to ~** (*inf: work, performance*) andare in malora

potato [pə'teitəu] (*pl* **~es**) *n* patata; **~ peeler** *n* sbucciapatate *m inv*

potent ['pəutnt] *adj* potente, forte

potential [pə'tenʃl] *adj* potenziale ♦ *n* possibilità *fpl*

pothole ['pɔthəul] *n* (*in road*) buca; (*BRIT: underground*) caverna; **potholing** (*BRIT*) *n*: **to go potholing** fare speleologia

potluck ['pɔt'lʌk] *n*: **to take ~** tentare la sorte

potted ['pɔtid] *adj* (*food*) in conserva; (*plant*) in vaso; (*account etc*) condensato(a)

potter ['pɔtə*] *n* vasaio ♦ *vi*: **to ~ around, ~ about** (*BRIT*) lavoracchiare; **~y** *n* ceramica *fpl*; (*factory*) fabbrica di ceramiche

potty ['pɔti] *adj* (*inf: mad*) tocco(a) ♦ *n* (*child's*) vasino

pouch [pautʃ] *n* borsa; (*ZOOL*) marsupio

poultry ['pəultri] *n* pollame *m*

pounce [pauns] *vi*: **to ~ (on)** piombare (su)

pound [paund] *n* (*weight*) libbra; (*money*) (*lira*) sterlina ♦ *vt* (*beat*) battere; (*crush*) pestare, polverizzare ♦ *vi* (*beat*) battere, martellare; **~ sterling** *n* sterlina (inglese)

pour [pɔ:*] *vt* versare ♦ *vi* riversarsi; (*rain*) piovere a dirotto; **~ away** *vt* vuotare; **~ in** *vi* affluire in gran quantità; **~ off** *vt* vuotare; **~ out** *vi* (*people*) uscire a fiumi ♦ *vt* vuotare; versare; (*fig*) sfogare; **~ing** *adj*: **~ing rain** pioggia torrenziale

pout [paut] *vi* sporgere le labbra; fare il broncio

poverty ['pɔvəti] *n* povertà, miseria; **~-stricken** *adj* molto povero(a), misero(a)

powder ['paudə*] *n* polvere *f* ♦ *vt*: **to ~ one's face** incipriarsi il viso; **~ compact** *n* portacipria *m inv*; **~ed milk** *n* latte *m* in polvere; **~ room** *n* toilette *f inv* (*per signore*)

power ['pauə*] *n* (*strength*) potenza, forza; (*ability, POL: of party, leader*) potere *m*; (*ELEC*) corrente *f*; **to be in ~** (*POL etc*) essere al potere; **~ cut** (*BRIT*) *n* interruzione *f* or mancanza di corrente; **~ed** *adj*: **~ed by** azionato(a) da; **~ failure** *n* interruzione *f* della corrente elettrica; **~ful** *adj* potente, forte; **~less** *adj* impotente; **~less to do** impossibilitato(a) a fare; **~ point** (*BRIT*) *n* presa di corrente; **~ station** *n* centrale *f* elettrica

p.p. *abbr* (*= per procurationem*): **~ J. Smith** per J. Smith; (*= pages*) p.p.

PR *abbr* = **public relations**

practicable ['præktikəbl] *adj* (*scheme*) praticabile

practical ['præktikl] *adj* pratico(a); **~ity** [-'kæliti] *n* (*no pl*) *n* (*of situation etc*) lato pratico; **~ joke** *n* beffa; **~ly** *adv* praticamente

practice ['præktis] *n* pratica; (*of profession*) esercizio; (*at football etc*) allenamento; (*business*) gabinetto; clientela ♦ *vt*, *vi* (*US*) = **practise**; **in ~**

(in reality) in pratica; **out of ~** fuori esercizio

practise ['præktɪs] *(US* **practice)** *vt (work at: piano, one's backhand etc)* esercitarsi a; *(train for: skiing, running etc)* allenarsi a; *(a sport, religion)* praticare; *(method)* usare; *(profession)* esercitare ♦ *vi* esercitarsi; *(train)* allenarsi; *(lawyer, doctor)* esercitare; **practising** *adj (Christian etc)* praticante; *(lawyer)* che esercita la professione

practitioner [præk'tɪʃənə*] *n* professionista *m/f*

pragmatic [præg'mætɪk] *adj* pragmatico(a)

prairie ['prɛərɪ] *n* prateria

praise [preɪz] *n* elogio, lode ♦ *vt* elogiare, lodare; **~worthy** *adj* lodevole

pram [præm] *(BRIT) n* carrozzina

prank [præŋk] *n* burla

prawn [prɔ:n] *n* gamberetto

pray [preɪ] *vi* pregare

prayer [prɛə*] *n* preghiera

preach [pri:tʃ] *vt, vi* predicare

precarious [prɪ'kɛərɪəs] *adj* precario(a)

precaution [prɪ'kɔ:ʃən] *n* precauzione *f*

precede [prɪ'si:d] *vt* precedere

precedent ['prɛsɪdənt] *n* precedente *m*

precept ['pri:sɛpt] *n* precetto

precinct ['pri:sɪŋkt] *n (US)* circoscrizione *f*; **~s** *npl (of building)* zona recintata; **pedestrian ~** *(BRIT)* zona pedonale; **shopping ~** *(BRIT)* centro commerciale *(chiuso al traffico)*

precious ['prɛʃəs] *adj* prezioso(a)

precipitate [prɪ'sɪpɪteɪt] *vt* precipitare

precise [prɪ'saɪs] *adj* preciso(a); **~ly** *adv* precisamente

precocious [prɪ'kəuʃəs] *adj* precoce

precondition [pri:kən'dɪʃən] *n* condizione *f* necessaria

predecessor ['pri:dɪsɛsə*] *n* predecessore/a

predicament [prɪ'dɪkəmənt] *n*

situazione *f* difficile

predict [prɪ'dɪkt] *vt* predire; **~able** *adj* prevedibile

predominantly [prɪ'dɔmɪnəntlɪ] *adv* in maggior parte; soprattutto

predominate [prɪ'dɔmɪneɪt] *vi* predominare

pre-empt [pri:'ɛmpt] *vt* pregiudicare

preen [pri:n] *vt:* **to ~ itself** *(bird)* lisciarsi le penne; **to ~ o.s.** agghindarsi

prefab ['pri:fæb] *n* casa prefabbricata

preface ['prɛfəs] *n* prefazione *f*

prefect ['pri:fɛkt] *n (BRIT: in school)* studente/essa con funzioni disciplinari; *(French etc, ADMIN)* prefetto

prefer [prɪ'fə:*] *vt* preferire; **to ~ doing** *or* **to do** preferire fare; **~ably** ['prɛfrəblɪ] *adv* preferibilmente; **~ence** ['prɛfrəns] *n* preferenza; **~ential** [prɛfə'rɛnʃəl] *adj* preferenziale

prefix ['pri:fɪks] *n* prefisso

pregnancy ['prɛgnənsɪ] *n* gravidanza

pregnant ['prɛgnənt] *adj* incinta *af*

prehistoric ['pri:hɪs'tɔrɪk] *adj* preistorico(a)

prejudice ['prɛdʒudɪs] *n* pregiudizio; *(harm)* torto, danno; **~d** *adj:* **~d (against)** prevenuto(a) (contro); **~d (in favour of)** ben disposto(a) (verso)

preliminary [prɪ'lɪmɪnərɪ] *adj* preliminare

premarital ['pri:'mærɪtl] *adj* prematrimoniale

premature ['prɛmətʃuə*] *adj* prematuro(a)

premenstrual syndrome [pri:'mɛnstruəl-] *n (MED)* sindrome *f* premestruale

premier ['prɛmɪə*] *adj* primo(a) ♦ *n (POL)* primo ministro

première ['prɛmɪɛə*] *n* prima

premise ['prɛmɪs] *n* premessa; **~s** *npl (of business, institution)* locale *m;* **on the ~s** sul posto

premium ['pri:mɪəm] *n* premio; **to be at a ~** essere ricercatissimo; **~ bond** *(BRIT) n* obbligazione *f* a premio

premonition [premə'nɪʃən] n premonizione f

preoccupied [pri:'ɔkjupaɪd] adj preoccupato(a)

prep [prep] n (SCOL: study) studio

prepaid [pri:'peɪd] adj pagato(a) in anticipo

preparation [prepə'reɪʃən] n preparazione f, preparativo(a); ~s npl (for trip, war) preparativi mpl

preparatory [prɪ'pærətərɪ] adj preparatorio(a); ~ school n scuola elementare privata

prepare [prɪ'peə*] vt preparare ♦ vi: to ~ for prepararsi a; ~d to pronto(a) a

preposition [prepə'zɪʃən] n preposizione f

preposterous [prɪ'pɔstərəs] adj assurdo(a)

prep school n = preparatory school

prerequisite [pri:'rekwɪzɪt] n requisito indispensabile

prescribe [prɪ'skraɪb] vt (MED) prescrivere

prescription [prɪ'skrɪpʃən] n prescrizione f; (MED) ricetta

presence ['prezns] n presenza; ~ of mind presenza di spirito

present [adj, n 'preznt, vb prɪ'zent] adj presente; (wife, residence, job) attuale ♦ n (actuality): the ~ il presente; (gift) regalo m ♦ vt presentare; (give): to ~ sb with sth offrire qc a qn; to give sb a ~ fare un regalo a qn; at ~ al momento; ~ation [-'teɪʃən] n presentazione f; (ceremony) consegna ufficiale; ~-day adj attuale, d'oggigiorno; ~er n (RADIO, TV) presentatore/trice; ~ly adv (soon) fra poco, presto; (at present) al momento

preservative [prɪ'zɜ:vətɪv] n conservante m

preserve [prɪ'zɜ:v] vt (keep safe) preservare, proteggere; (maintain) conservare; (food) mettere in conserva ♦ n (often pl: jam) marmellata f; (: fruit) frutta sciroppata

preside [prɪ'zaɪd] vi: to ~ (over) presiedere (a)

president ['prezɪdənt] n presidente m; ~ial [-'denʃl] adj presidenziale

press [pres] n (newspapers etc): the P~ la stampa; (tool, machine) pressa; (for wine) torchio ♦ vt (push) premere, pigiare; (squeeze) spremere; (: hand) stringere; (clothes: iron) stirare; (pursue) incalzare; (insist): to ~ sth on sb far accettare qc da qn ♦ vi premere; ~ on vi continuare; ~ conference n conferenza f stampa inv; ~ing adj urgente; ~ stud (BRIT) n bottone m a pressione; ~-up (BRIT) n flessione f sulle braccia

pressure ['preʃə*] n pressione f; to put ~ on sb (to do) mettere qn sotto pressione (affinché faccia); ~ cooker n pentola a pressione; ~ gauge n manometro; ~ group n gruppo di pressione

prestige [pres'ti:ʒ] n prestigio

presumably [prɪ'zju:məblɪ] adv presumibilmente

presume [prɪ'zju:m] vt supporre

presumption [prɪ'zʌmpʃən] n presunzione f

presumptuous [prɪ'zʌmpʃəs] adj presuntuoso(a)

pretence [prɪ'tens] (US **pretense**) n (claim) pretesa; to make a ~ of doing far finta di fare; under false ~s con l'inganno

pretend [prɪ'tend] vt (feign) fingere ♦ vi far finta; to ~ to do far finta di fare

pretense [prɪ'tens] (US) n = pretence

pretentious [prɪ'tenʃəs] adj pretenzioso(a)

pretext ['pri:tekst] n pretesto

pretty ['prɪtɪ] adj grazioso(a), carino(a) ♦ adv abbastanza, assai

prevail [prɪ'veɪl] vi (win, be usual) prevalere; (persuade): to ~ (up)on sb

to do persuadere qn a fare; **~ing** adj
dominante

prevalent ['prɛvələnt] adj (belief)
predominante; (customs) diffuso(a);
(fashion) corrente; (disease) comune

prevent [prɪ'vɛnt] vt: **to ~ sb from
doing** impedire a qn di fare; **to ~ sth
from happening** impedire che qc
succeda; **~ative** adj = **~ive**; **~ion**
[-'vɛnʃən] n prevenzione f; **~ive** adj
preventivo(a)

preview ['priːvjuː] n (of film)
anteprima

previous ['priːvɪəs] adj precedente;
anteriore; **~ly** adv prima

prewar ['priː'wɔː*] adj anteguerra inv

prey [preɪ] n preda ♦ vi: **to ~ on** far
preda di; **it was ~ing on his mind** lo
stava ossessionando

price [praɪs] n prezzo m ♦ vt (goods)
fissare il prezzo di; valutare; **~less** adj
inapprezzabile; **~ list** n listino (dei)
prezzi

prick [prɪk] n puntura ♦ vt pungere; **to
~ up one's ears** drizzare gli orecchi

prickle ['prɪkl] n (of plant) spina;
(sensation) pizzicore m

prickly ['prɪklɪ] adj spinoso(a); **~ heat**
n sudamina

pride [praɪd] n orgoglio m; superbia ♦ vt:
to ~ o.s. on essere orgoglioso di;
vantarsi di

priest [priːst] n prete m, sacerdote m;
~hood n sacerdozio

prim [prɪm] adj pudico(a);
contegnoso(a)

primarily ['praɪmərɪlɪ] adv
principalmente, essenzialmente

primary ['praɪmərɪ] adj primario(a);
(first in importance) primo(a) ♦ n (us:
election) primarie fpl; **~ school** (BRIT) n
scuola elementare

prime [praɪm] adj primario(a),
fondamentale; (excellent) di prima
qualità ♦ vt (wood) preparare; (fig)
mettere al corrente ♦ n: **in the ~ of
life** nel fiore della vita; **P~ Minister** n

primo ministro

primeval [praɪ'miːvl] adj primitivo(a)

primitive ['prɪmɪtɪv] adj primitivo(a)

primrose ['prɪmrəʊz] n primavera

primus (stove) ® ['praɪməs(-)] (BRIT)
n fornello a petrolio

prince [prɪns] n principe m

princess [prɪn'sɛs] n principessa

principal ['prɪnsɪpl] adj principale ♦ n
(headmaster) preside m

principle ['prɪnsɪpl] n principio; **in ~**
in linea di principio; **on ~** per principio

print [prɪnt] n (mark) impronta; (letters)
caratteri mpl; (fabric) tessuto stampato;
(ART, PHOT) stampa ♦ vt imprimere;
(publish) stampare, pubblicare; (write in
capitals) scrivere in stampatello; **out of
~** esaurito(a); **~ed matter** n stampe
fpl; **~er** n tipografo; (machine)
stampante f; **~ing** n stampa; **~-out** n
(COMPUT) tabulato

prior ['praɪə*] adj precedente; (claim
etc) più importante; **~ to doing** prima
di fare

priority [praɪ'ɔrɪtɪ] n priorità f inv;
precedenza

prise [praɪz] vt: **to ~ open** forzare

prison ['prɪzn] n prigione f ♦ cpd
(system) carcerario(a); (conditions, food)
nelle o delle prigioni; **~er** n
prigioniero/a

pristine ['prɪstiːn] adj immacolato(a)

privacy ['prɪvəsɪ] n solitudine f,
intimità

private ['praɪvɪt] adj privato(a);
personale ♦ n soldato semplice; **"~"**
(on envelope) "riservata"; (on door)
"privato"; **in ~** in privato;
~ enterprise n iniziativa privata;
~ eye n investigatore m privato; **~ly**
adv in privato; (within oneself) dentro
di sé; **~ property** n proprietà privata;
privatize vt privatizzare

privet ['prɪvɪt] n ligustro

privilege ['prɪvɪlɪdʒ] n privilegio

privy ['prɪvɪ] adj: **to be ~ to** essere al
corrente di

prize [praɪz] n premio ♦ adj (example,
idiot) perfetto(a); (bull, novel)
premiato(a) ♦ vt apprezzare, pregiare;
~giving n premiazione f; **~winner** n
premiato/a

pro [prəʊ] n (SPORT) professionista m/f
♦ prep pro; **the ~s and cons** il pro e il
contro

probability [prɒbə'bɪlɪtɪ] n probabilità
f inv; **in all ~** con tutta probabilità

probable ['prɒbəbl] adj probabile;
probably adv probabilmente

probation [prə'beɪʃən] n: **on ~**
(employee) in prova; (LAW) in libertà
vigilata

probe [prəʊb] n (MED, SPACE) sonda;
(enquiry) indagine f, investigazione f
♦ vt sondare, esplorare; indagare

problem ['prɒbləm] n problema m

procedure [prə'siːdʒə*] n (ADMIN, LAW)
procedura; (method) metodo,
procedimento

proceed [prə'siːd] vi (go forward)
avanzare, andare avanti; (go about it)
procedere; (continue): **to ~ (with)**
continuare; **to ~ to** andare a; passare
a; **to ~ to do** mettersi a fare; **~ings**
npl misure fpl; (LAW) procedimento;
(meeting) riunione f; (records)
rendiconti mpl, atti mpl; **~s** ['prəʊsiːdz]
npl profitto, incasso

process ['prəʊses] n processo;
(method) metodo, sistema m ♦ vt
trattare; (information) elaborare; **~ing** n
trattamento; elaborazione f

procession [prə'seʃən] n processione f,
corteo; **funeral ~** corteo funebre

pro-choice [prəʊ'tʃɔɪs] adj per la
libertà di scelta di gravidanza

proclaim [prə'kleɪm] vt proclamare,
dichiarare

procrastinate [prəʊ'kræstɪneɪt] vi
procrastinare

prod [prɒd] vt dare un colpetto a;
pungolare ♦ n colpetto

prodigal ['prɒdɪgl] adj prodigo(a)

prodigy ['prɒdɪdʒɪ] n prodigio

produce [n 'prɒdjuːs, vb prə'djuːs] n
(AGR) prodotto, prodotti mpl ♦ vt
produrre; (to show) esibire, mostrare;
(cause) cagionare, causare; (THEATRE)
rappresentare; **~r** n (THEATRE) regista m/f; (AGR, CINEMA)
produttore m

product ['prɒdʌkt] n prodotto

production [prə'dʌkʃən] n produzione
f; **~ line** n catena di lavorazione

productivity [prɒdʌk'tɪvɪtɪ] n
produttività

profane [prə'feɪn] adj profano(a);
(language) empio(a)

profess [prə'fes] vt (claim) dichiarare;
(opinion etc) professare

profession [prə'feʃən] n professione f;
~al n professionista m/f ♦ adj
professionale; (work) da professionista

professor [prə'fesə*] n professore m
(titolare di una cattedra); (US)
professore/essa

proficiency [prə'fɪʃənsɪ] n
competenza, abilità

profile ['prəʊfaɪl] n profilo

profit ['prɒfɪt] n profitto; beneficio ♦ vi:
to ~ (by or from) approfittare (di);
~ability [-'bɪlɪtɪ] n redditività; **~able**
adj redditizio(a)

profound [prə'faʊnd] adj profondo(a)

profusely [prə'fjuːslɪ] adv con grande
effusione

programme ['prəʊgræm] (US
program) n programma m ♦ vt
programmare; **~r** (US **programmer**) n
programmatore/trice

progress [n 'prəʊgres, vb prə'gres] n
progresso ♦ vi avanzare, procedere; **in
~** in corso; **to make ~** far progressi;
~ive [-'gresɪv] adj progressivo(a);
(person) progressista

prohibit [prə'hɪbɪt] vt proibire, vietare;
~ion [prəʊɪ'bɪʃən] n proibizione f,
divieto; (US): **P~ion** proibizionismo;
~ive adj (price etc) proibitivo(a)

project [n 'prɒdʒekt, vb prə'dʒekt] n
(plan) piano; (venture) progetto; (SCOL)
studio ♦ vt proiettare ♦ vi (stick out)

sporgere

projectile [prəˈdʒektail] n proiettile m

projector [prəˈdʒektə*] n proiettore m

pro-life [prəʊˈlaif] adj per il diritto alla vita

prolific [prəˈlifik] adj (artist etc) fecondo/a

prolong [prəˈlɒŋ] vt prolungare

Prom

In Gran Bretagna i **Prom** (promenade concert) sono concerti di musica classica, i più noti dei quali sono quelli eseguiti nella Royal Albert Hall a Londra. Un tempo il pubblico seguiva i concerti in piedi, passeggiando. Negli Stati Uniti, invece, con prom si intende il ballo studentesco di un'università o di un college.

---

prom [prɒm] n abbr = **promenade**; (US: ball) ballo studentesco

promenade [prɒməˈnɑːd] n (by sea) lungomare m; **~ concert** n concerto (con posti in piedi)

prominent [ˈprɒminənt] adj (standing out) prominente; (important) importante

promiscuous [prəˈmiskjuəs] adj (sexually) di facili costumi

promise [ˈprɒmis] n promessa ♦ vt, vi promettere; **to ~ sb sth**, **~ sth to sb** promettere qc a qn; **to ~ (sb) that/to do sth** promettere (a qn) che/di fare qc; **promising** adj promettente

promote [prəˈməut] vt promuovere; (venture, event) organizzare; **~r** n (of sporting event) promotore/trice; **promotion** [-ˈməuʃən] n promozione f

prompt [prɒmpt] adj rapido/a, svelto/a; (reply) sollecito/a ♦ adv (punctually) in punto ♦ n (COMPUT) prompt m ♦ vt incitare, provocare; (THEATRE) suggerire a; **to ~ sb to do sth** incitare qn a fare; **~ly** adv

prontamente; puntualmente

prone [prəun] adj (lying) prono(a); **~ to** propenso/a, incline a

prong [prɒŋ] n rebbio, punta

pronoun [ˈprəunaun] n pronome m

pronounce [prəˈnauns] vt pronunciare

pronunciation [prənʌnsiˈeiʃən] n pronuncia

proof [pruːf] n prova f, prova; (of book) bozza; (PHOT) provino ♦ adj: **~ against** a prova di

prop [prɒp] n sostegno, appoggio ♦ vt (also: **~ up**) sostenere, appoggiare; (lean): **to ~ sth against** appoggiare qc contro o a

propaganda [prɒpəˈgændə] n propaganda

propel [prəˈpel] vt spingere (in avanti), muovere; **~ler** n elica

propensity [prəˈpensiti] n tendenza

proper [ˈprɒpə*] adj (suited, right) adatto/a, appropriato/a; (seemly) decente; (authentic) vero(a); (inf: real) noun + vero(a) e proprio(a); **~ly** [ˈprɒpəli] adv (eat, study) bene; (behave) come si deve; **~ noun** n nome m proprio

property [ˈprɒpəti] n (things owned) beni mpl; (land, building) proprietà f inv; (CHEM etc: quality) proprietà f; **~ owner** n proprietario/a

prophecy [ˈprɒfisi] n profezia

prophesy [ˈprɒfisai] vt predire

prophet [ˈprɒfit] n profeta m

proportion [prəˈpɔːʃən] n proporzione f; (share) parte f; **~al** adj proporzionale; **~ate** adj proporzionato/a

proposal [prəˈpəuzl] n proposta; (plan) progetto; (of marriage) proposta di matrimonio

propose [prəˈpəuz] vt proporre, suggerire ♦ vi fare una proposta di matrimonio; **to ~ to do** proporsi di fare, aver l'intenzione di fare

proposition [prɒpəˈziʃən] n proposizione f; (offer) proposta

proprietor [prəˈpraiətə*] n

proprietario/a

propriety [prə'praɪətɪ] n (seemliness) decoro, rispetto delle convenienze sociali

pro rata ['prəu'rɑ:tə] adv in proporzione

prose [prəuz] n prosa

prosecute ['prɔsɪkjuːt] vt processare; **prosecution** [-'kjuːʃən] n processo; (accusing side) accusa; **prosecutor** n (also: **public prosecutor**) ≈ procuratore m della Repubblica

prospect [n 'prɔspekt, vb prə'spekt] n prospettiva; (hope) speranza ♦ vi: **to ~ for** cercare; **~s** npl (for work etc) prospettive fpl; **~ive** [-'spektɪv] adj possibile; futuro(a)

prospectus [prə'spektəs] n prospetto, programma m

prosperity [prɔ'spɛrɪtɪ] n prosperità

prostitute ['prɔstɪtjuːt] n prostituta; **male ~** uomo che si prostituisce

protect [prə'tɛkt] vt proteggere, salvaguardare; **~ed** n specie f protetta; **~ion** n protezione f; **~ive** adj protettivo(a)

protégé ['prəutɛʒeɪ] n protetto

protein ['prəutiːn] n proteina

protest [n 'prəutɛst, vb prə'tɛst] n protesta ♦ vt, vi protestare

Protestant ['prɔtɪstənt] adj, n protestante m/f

protester [prə'tɛstə*] n dimostrante m/f

prototype ['prəutətaɪp] n prototipo

protracted [prə'træktɪd] adj tirato(a) per le lunghe

protrude [prə'truːd] vi sporgere

proud [praud] adj fiero(a), orgoglioso(a); (pej) superbo(a)

prove [pruːv] vt provare, dimostrare ♦ vi: **to ~ (to be) correct** etc risultare vero(a) etc; **to ~ o.s.** mostrare le proprie capacità

proverb ['prɔvəːb] n proverbio

provide [prə'vaɪd] vt fornire, provvedere; **to ~ sb with sth** fornire

or provvedere qn di qc; **~ for** vt fus provvedere a; (future event) prevedere; **~d (that)** conj purché + sub, a condizione che + sub

providing [prə'vaɪdɪŋ] conj purché + sub, a condizione che + sub

province ['prɔvɪns] n provincia; **provincial** [prə'vɪnʃəl] adj provinciale

provision [prə'vɪʒən] n (supply) riserva; (supplying) provvista; (stipulation) condizione f; rifornimento; **~s** npl (food) provviste fpl; **~al** adj provvisorio(a)

proviso [prə'vaɪzəu] n condizione f

provocative [prə'vɔkətɪv] adj (aggressive) provocatorio(a); (thought-provoking) stimolante; (seductive) provocante

provoke [prə'vəuk] vt provocare; incitare

prowess ['prauɪs] n prodezza

prowl [praul] vi (also: ~ about, ~ around) aggirarsi ♦ n: **to be on the ~** aggirarsi; **~er** n tipo sospetto (che s'aggira con l'intenzione di rubare, aggredire etc)

proximity [prɔk'sɪmɪtɪ] n prossimità

proxy ['prɔksɪ] n: **by ~** per procura

prude [pruːd] n puritano/a

prudent ['pruːdnt] adj prudente

prudish ['pruːdɪʃ] adj puritano(a)

prune [pruːn] n prugna secca ♦ vt potare

pry [praɪ] vi: **to ~ into** ficcare il naso in

PS abbr (= postscript) P.S.

psalm [sɑːm] n salmo

pseudonym ['sjuːdənɪm] n pseudonimo

psyche ['saɪkɪ] n psiche f

psychiatric [saɪkɪ'ætrɪk] adj psichiatrico(a)

psychiatrist [saɪ'kaɪətrɪst] n psichiatra m/f

psychic ['saɪkɪk] adj (also: ~al) psichico(a); (person) dotato(a) di qualità telepatiche

psychoanalyst [saɪkəu'ænəlɪst] n

psicanalista m/f

psychological [saikə'lɒdʒikl] adj psicologico(a)

psychologist [sai'kɒlədʒist] n psicologo/a

psychology [sai'kɒlədʒi] n psicologia

psychopath ['saikəupæθ] n psicopatico/a

P.T.O. abbr (= please turn over) v.r.

pub [pʌb] n abbr (= public house) pub m inv

---

pub

In Gran Bretagna e in Irlanda i pub sono locali dove vengono servite bevande alcoliche e analcoliche e dove spesso è possibile anche mangiare, giocare a biliardo o a frecette e guardare la televisione.

---

pubic ['pju:bik] adj pubico(a), del pube

public ['pʌblik] adj pubblico(a) ♦ n pubblico; **in ~** in pubblico; **~ address system** n impianto di amplificazione

publican ['pʌblikən] n proprietario di un pub

publication [pʌbli'keiʃən] n pubblicazione f

publicity [pʌb'lisiti] n pubblicità

publicize ['pʌblisaiz] vt rendere pubblico(a)

publicly ['pʌblikli] adv pubblicamente

public: ~ opinion n opinione f pubblica; **~ relations** npl pubbliche relazioni fpl; **~ school** n (BRIT) scuola privata; (US) scuola statale; **~-spirited** adj che ha senso civico; **~ transport** n mezzi mpl pubblici

publish ['pʌbliʃ] vt pubblicare; **~er** n editore m; **~ing** n (industry) editoria;

(of a book) pubblicazione f

pub lunch n pranzo semplice ed economico servito nei pub

puce [pju:s] adj marroncino rosato inv

pucker ['pʌkə*] vt corrugare

pudding ['pudiŋ] n budino; (BRIT: dessert) dolce m; **black ~**, (US) **blood ~** sanguinaccio

puddle ['pʌdl] n pozza, pozzanghera

puff [pʌf] n sbuffo ♦ vt: **to ~ one's pipe** tirare sboccate di fumo ♦ vi (pant) ansare; **~ out** (cheeks etc) gonfiare; **~ pastry** n pasta sfoglia; **~y** adj gonfio(a)

pull [pul] n (tug): **to give sth a ~** tirare su qc ♦ vt tirare; (muscle) strappare; (trigger) premere ♦ vi tirare; **to ~ to pieces** fare a pezzi; **to ~ one's punches** (BOXING) risparmiare l'avversario; **to ~ one's weight** dare il proprio contributo; **to ~ o.s. together** ricomporsi, riprendersi; **to ~ sb's leg** prendere in giro qn; **~ apart** vt (break) fare a pezzi; **~ down** vt (house) demolire; (tree) abbattere; **~ in** vi (AUT: at the kerb) accostarsi; (RAIL) entrare in stazione; **~ off** vt (clothes) togliere; (deal etc) portare a compimento; **~ out** vi partire; (AUT: come out of line) spostarsi sulla mezzeria ♦ vt staccare; far uscire; (withdraw) ritirare; **~ over** vi (AUT) accostare; **~ through** vi farcela; **~ up** vi (stop) fermarsi ♦ vt (raise) sollevare; (uproot) sradicare

pulley ['puli] n puleggia, carrucola

pullover ['puləuvə*] n pullover m inv

pulp [pʌlp] n (of fruit) polpa

pulpit ['pulpit] n pulpito

pulsate [pʌl'seit] vi battere, palpitare

pulse [pʌls] n polso; (BOT) legume m

pummel ['pʌml] vt dare pugni a

pump [pʌmp] n pompa; (shoe) scarpetta ♦ vt pompare; **~ up** vt gonfiare

pumpkin ['pʌmpkin] n zucca

pun [pʌn] n gioco di parole

punch [pʌntʃ] n (blow) pugno; (tool)

punctual 513 put

punzone m; (*drink*) ponce m ♦ *vt* (*hit*):
to ~ sb/sth dare un pugno a qn/qc;
~ line *n* (*of joke*) battuta finale; **~up**
(*BRIT: inf*) *n* rissa

punctual ['pʌŋktjuəl] *adj* puntuale

punctuation [pʌŋktju'eɪʃən] *n*
interpunzione f, punteggiatura

puncture ['pʌŋktʃə*] *n* foratura ♦ *vt*
forare

pundit ['pʌndɪt] *n* sapientone/a

pungent ['pʌndʒənt] *adj* pungente

punish ['pʌnɪʃ] *vt* punire; **~ment** *n*
punizione f

punk [pʌŋk] *n* (*also*: ~ *rocker*) punk m/f
inv; (*also*: ~ *rock*) musica punk, punk
rock m; (*us: inf: hoodlum*) teppista m

punt [pʌnt] *n* (*boat*) barchino

punter ['pʌntə*] (*BRIT*) *n* (*gambler*)
scommettitore/trice; (: *inf*) cliente m/f

puny ['pjuːnɪ] *adj* gracile

pup [pʌp] *n* cucciolo/a

pupil ['pjuːpl] *n* allievo/a; (*ANAT*) pupilla

puppet ['pʌpɪt] *n* burattino

puppy ['pʌpɪ] *n* cucciolo/a, cagnolino/
a

purchase ['pɜːtʃɪs] *n* acquisto,
compera ♦ *vt* comprare; **~r** *n*
compratore/trice

pure [pjuə*] *adj* puro(a)

purée ['pjuəreɪ] *n* (*of potatoes*) purè m;
(*of tomatoes*) passato; (*of apples*) crema

purely ['pjuəlɪ] *adv* puramente

purge [pɜːdʒ] *n* (*MED*) purga; (*POL*)
epurazione f ♦ *vt* purgare

puritan ['pjuərɪtən] *adj*, *n* puritano(a)

purity ['pjuərɪtɪ] *n* purezza

purple ['pɜːpl] *adj* di porpora; viola *inv*

purpose ['pɜːpəs] *n* intenzione f,
scopo; **on ~** apposta; **~ful** *adj*
deciso(a), risoluto(a)

purr [pɜː*] *vi* fare le fusa

purse [pɜːs] *n* (*BRIT*) borsellino; (*US*)
borsetta ♦ *vt* contrarre

purser ['pɜːsə*] (*NAUT*) *n* commissario
di bordo

pursue [pə'sjuː] *vt* inseguire; (*fig*:
activity etc) continuare con; (: *aim etc*)

perseguire

pursuit [pə'sjuːt] *n* inseguimento; (*fig*)
ricerca; (*pastime*) passatempo

push [puʃ] *n* spinta; (*effort*) grande
sforzo; (*drive*) energia ♦ *vt* spingere;
(*button*) premere; (*thrust*) fare; **to ~ sth
(into)** ficcare qc (in); (*fig*) fare
pubblicità a ♦ *vi* spingere; premere; **to
~ for** (*fig*) insistere per; **~ aside** *vt*
scostare; **~ off** (*inf*) *vi* filare; **~ on** *vi*
(*continue*) continuare; **~ through** *vi*
farsi largo spingendo ♦ *vt* (*measure*) far
approvare; **~ up** *vt* (*total, prices*) far
salire; **~chair** (*BRIT*) *n* passeggino; **~er**
n (*drug ~er*) spacciatore/trice; **~over**
(*inf*) *n*: **it's a ~over** è un lavoro da
bambini; **~up** (*US*) *n* (*press-up*)
flessione f sulle braccia; **~y** (*pej*) *adj*
opportunista

puss [pus] (*inf*) *n* = **pussy(-cat)**

pussy(-cat) ['pusi(-)] (*inf*) *n* micio

put [put] (*pt, pp* **put**) *vt* mettere, porre;
(*say*) dire, esprimere; (*a question*) fare;
(*estimate*) stimare; **~ about** *or* **around**
vt (*rumour*) diffondere; **~ across** *vt*
(*ideas etc*) comunicare; far capire; **~
away** *vt* (*return*) rimettere a posto; **~
back** *vt* (*replace*) rimettere (a posto);
(*postpone*) rimandare; (*delay*) ritardare;
~ by *vt* (*money*) mettere da parte; **~
down** *vt* (*parcel etc*) posare, mettere
giù; (*pay*) versare; (*in writing*) mettere
per iscritto; (*revolt, animal*) sopprimere;
(*attribute*) attribuire; **~ forward** *vt*
(*ideas*) avanzare, proporre; **~ in** *vt*
(*application, complaint*) presentare;
(*time, effort*) mettere; **~ off** *vt*
(*postpone*) rimandare, rinviare;
(*discourage*) dissuadere; **~ on** *vt*
(*clothes, lipstick etc*) mettere; (*light etc*)
accendere; (*play etc*) mettere in scena;
(*food, meal*) mettere su; (*brake*)
mettere; **to ~ on weight** ingrassare;
to ~ on airs darsi delle arie; **~ out** *vt*
mettere fuori; (*one's hand*) porgere;
(*light etc*) spegnere; (*person:
inconvenience*) scomodare; **~ through**

vt (*TEL: call*) passare; (: *person*) mettere in comunicazione; (*plan*) far approvare; **~ up** *vt* (*raise*) sollevare, alzare; (: *umbrella*) aprire; (: *tent*) montare; (*pin up*) affiggere; (*hang*) appendere; (*build*) costruire, erigere; (*increase*) aumentare; (*accommodate*) alloggiare; **~ up with** *vt fus* sopportare

putt [pʌt] *n* colpo leggero; **~ing green** *n* green *m inv*; campo da putting

putty ['pʌtɪ] *n* stucco

puzzle ['pʌzl] *n* enigma *m*, mistero; (*jigsaw*) puzzle *m*; (*also: crossword ~*) parole *fpl* incrociate, cruciverba *m inv* ♦ *vt* confondere, rendere perplesso(a) ♦ *vi* scervellarsi

pyjamas [pɪ'dʒɑ:məz] (*BRIT*) *npl* pigiama *m*

pylon ['paɪlən] *n* pilone *m*

pyramid ['pɪrəmɪd] *n* piramide *f*

Pyrenees [pɪrɪ'ni:z] *npl*: **the ~** i Pirenei

Q, q

quack [kwæk] *n* (*of duck*) qua qua *m inv*; (*pej: doctor*) dottoruccio/a

quad [kwɔd] *n abbr* = **quadrangle**; **quadruplet**

quadrangle ['kwɔdræŋgl] *n* (*courtyard*) cortile *m*

quadruple [kwɔ'drupl] *vt* quadruplicare ♦ *vi* quadruplicarsi

quadruplets [kwɔ'dru:plɪts] *npl* quattro gemelli *mpl*

quail [kweɪl] *n* (*ZOOL*) quaglia ♦ *vi* (*person*): **to ~ at** *or* **before** perdersi d'animo davanti a

quaint [kweɪnt] *adj* bizzarro(a); (*old-fashioned*) antiquato(a); grazioso(a), pittoresco(a)

quake [kweɪk] *vi* tremare ♦ *n abbr* = **earthquake**

Quaker ['kweɪkə*] *n* quacchero/a

qualification [kwɔlɪfɪ'keɪʃən] *n* (*degree etc*) qualifica, titolo; (*ability*)

competenza, qualificazione *f*; (*limitation*) riserva, restrizione *f*

qualified ['kwɔlɪfaɪd] *adj* qualificato(a); (*able*): **~ to** competente in, qualificato(a) a; (*limited*) condizionato(a)

qualify ['kwɔlɪfaɪ] *vt* abilitare; (*limit: statement*) modificare, precisare ♦ *vi*: **to ~ (as)** qualificarsi (come); **to ~ (for)** acquistare i requisiti necessari (per); (*SPORT*) qualificarsi (per *o* a)

quality ['kwɔlɪtɪ] *n* qualità *f inv*

quality press

Il termine **quality press** si riferisce ai quotidiani e ai settimanali che offrono un'informazione più seria ed approfondita rispetto ai **tabloid**, i giornali popolari; vedi anche **tabloid press**.

qualm [kwɑ:m] *n* dubbio; scrupolo

quandary ['kwɔndrɪ] *n*: **in a ~** in un dilemma

quantity ['kwɔntɪtɪ] *n* quantità *f inv*

quantity surveyor [-sə'veɪə*] *n* geometra *m* (*specializzato nel calcolare la quantità e il costo del materiale da costruzione*)

quarantine ['kwɔrntiːn] *n* quarantena

quarrel ['kwɔrl] *n* lite *f*, disputa ♦ *vi* litigare

quarry ['kwɔrɪ] *n* (*for stone*) cava; (*animal*) preda

quart [kwɔːt] *n* ≈ litro

quarter ['kwɔːtə*] *n* quarto; (*US: coin*) quarto di dollaro; (*of year*) trimestre *m*; (*district*) quartiere *m* ♦ *vt* dividere in quattro; (*MIL*) alloggiare; **~s** *npl* (*living ~s*) alloggio; (*MIL*) alloggi *mpl*; quadrato; **a ~ of an hour** un quarto d'ora; **~ final** *n* quarto di finale; **~ly** *adj* trimestrale ♦ *adv* trimestralmente

quartet(te) [kwɔː'tet] *n* quartetto

quartz [kwɔːts] *n* quarzo

quash [kwɔʃ] *vt* (*verdict*) annullare

quaver ['kweɪvə*] *n* (*BRIT: MUS*) croma

♦ vi tremolare

quay [ki:] n (also: ~side) banchina

queasy ['kwi:zɪ] adj (stomach) delicato(a); **to feel ~** aver la nausea

queen [kwi:n] n (gen) regina; (CARDS etc) regina, donna; **~ mother** n regina madre

queer [kwɪə*] adj strano(a), curioso(a) ♦ n (inf) finocchio

quell [kwel] vt domare

quench [kwentʃ] vt: **to ~ one's thirst** dissetarsi

query ['kwɪərɪ] n domanda, questione f ♦ vt mettere in questione

quest [kwest] n cerca, ricerca

question ['kwestʃən] n domanda, questione f ♦ vt (person) interrogare; (plan, idea) mettere in questione or in dubbio; **it's a ~ of doing** si tratta di fare; **beyond ~** fuori di dubbio; **out of the ~** fuori discussione, impossibile; **~able** adj discutibile; **~ mark** n punto interrogativo

questionnaire [kwestʃə'nɛə*] n questionario

queue [kju:] (BRIT) n coda, fila ♦ vi fare la coda

quibble ['kwɪbl] vi cavillare

quiche [ki:ʃ] n torta salata a base di uova, formaggio, prosciutto o altro

quick [kwɪk] adj rapido(a), veloce; (reply) pronto(a); (mind) pronto(a), acuto(a) ♦ n: **cut to the ~** (fig) toccato(a) sul vivo; **be ~!** fa presto!; **~en** vt accelerare, affrettare ♦ vi accelerare, affrettarsi; **~ly** adv rapidamente, velocemente; **~sand** n sabbie fpl mobili; **~-witted** adj pronto(a) d'ingegno

quid [kwɪd] (BRIT: inf) n inv sterlina

quiet ['kwaɪət] adj tranquillo(a), quieto(a); (ceremony) semplice ♦ n tranquillità, calma ♦ vt, vi (US) = **~en**; **keep ~!** sta zitto!; **~en** (also: **~en down**) vi calmarsi, chetarsi ♦ vt calmare, chetare; **~ly** adv tranquillamente, calmamente;

sommessamente

quilt [kwɪlt] n trapunta; (continental ~) piumino

quin [kwɪn] n abbr = **quintuplet**

quintuplets [kwɪn'tju:plɪts] npl cinque gemelli mpl

quip [kwɪp] n frizzo

quirk [kwə:k] n ghiribizzo

quit [kwɪt] (pt, pp quit or quitted) vt mollare; (premises) lasciare, partire da ♦ vi (give up) mollare; (resign) dimettersi

quite [kwaɪt] adv (rather) assai; (entirely) completamente, del tutto; **I ~ understand** capisco perfettamente; **that's not ~ big enough** non è proprio sufficiente; **~ a few of them** non pochi di loro; **~ (so)!** esatto!

quits [kwɪts] adj: **~ (with)** pari (con); **let's call it ~** adesso siamo pari

quiver ['kwɪvə*] vi tremare, fremere

quiz [kwɪz] n (game) quiz m inv; indovinello ♦ vt interrogare; **~zical** adj enigmatico(a)

quota ['kwəʊtə] n quota

quotation [kwəʊ'teɪʃən] n citazione f; (of shares etc) quotazione f; (estimate) preventivo; **~ marks** npl virgolette fpl

quote [kwəʊt] n citazione f ♦ vt (sentence) citare; (price) dare, fissare; (shares) quotare ♦ vi: **to ~ from** citare; **~s** npl = **quotation marks**

R, r

rabbi ['ræbaɪ] n rabbino

rabbit ['ræbɪt] n coniglio; **~ hutch** n conigliera

rabble ['ræbl] (pej) n canaglia, plebaglia

rabies ['reɪbi:z] n rabbia

RAC (BRIT) n abbr = **Royal Automobile Club**

rac(c)oon [rə'ku:n] n procione m

race [reɪs] n razza; (competition, rush) corsa ♦ vt (horse) far correre ♦ vi

correre; (*engine*) imballarsi; **~ car** (*US*)
n = **racing car**; **~ car driver** (*US*) *n* =
racing driver; **~course** *n* campo di
corse, ippodromo; **~horse** *n* cavallo
da corsa; **~track** *n* pista
racial ['reɪʃl] *adj* razziale
racing ['reɪsɪŋ] *n* corsa; **~ car** (*BRIT*) *n*
macchina da corsa; **~ driver** (*BRIT*) *n*
corridore *m* automobilista
racism ['reɪsɪzəm] *n* razzismo; **racist**
adj, *n* razzista *m/f*
rack [ræk] *n* rastrelliera; (*also*: **luggage
~**) rete *f*, portabagagli *m inv*; (*also*: **roof
~**) portabagagli; (*dish~*) scolapiatti *m
inv* ♦ *vt*: **~ed by** torturato/a da; **to
~ one's brains** scervellarsi
racket ['rækɪt] *n* (*for tennis*) racchetta; (*noise*) fracasso; baccano; (*swindle*)
imbroglio, truffa; (*organized crime*)
racket *m inv*
racoon [rə'ku:n] *n* = **raccoon**
racquet ['rækɪt] *n* racchetta
racy ['reɪsɪ] *adj* brioso/a; piccante
radar ['reɪda:*] *n* radar *m*
radial ['reɪdɪəl] *adj* (*also*: **~-ply**) radiale
radiant ['reɪdɪənt] *adj* raggiante;
(*PHYSICS*) radiante
radiate ['reɪdɪeɪt] *vt* (*heat*) irraggiare,
irradiare ♦ *vi* (*lines*) irradiarsi
radiation [reɪdɪ'eɪʃən] *n* irradiamento *m*;
(*radioactive*) radiazione *f*
radiator ['reɪdɪeɪtə*] *n* radiatore *m*
radical ['rædɪkl] *adj* radicale
radii ['reɪdɪaɪ] *npl of* **radius**
radio ['reɪdɪəu] *n* radio *f inv*; **on the ~**
alla radio
radioactive [reɪdɪəu'æktɪv] *adj*
radioattivo/a
radio station *n* stazione *f* radio *inv*
radish ['rædɪʃ] *n* ravanello
radius ['reɪdɪəs] (*pl* **radii**) *n* raggio
RAF *n abbr* = **Royal Air Force**
raffle ['ræfl] *n* lotteria
raft [rɑ:ft] *n* zattera; (*also*: **life ~**) zattera
di salvataggio
rafter ['rɑ:ftə*] *n* trave *f*
rag [ræg] *n* straccio, cencio; (*pej*:

newspaper) giornalaccio, bandiera; (*for
charity*) iniziativa studentesca a scopo
benefico; **~s** *npl* (*torn clothes*) stracci
mpl, brandelli *mpl*; **~ doll** *n* bambola
di pezza
rage [reɪdʒ] *n* (*fury*) collera, furia ♦ *vi*
(*person*) andare su tutte le furie; (*storm*)
infuriare; **it's all the ~** fa furore
ragged ['rægɪd] *adj* (*clothes*) logoro/a;
(*appearance*) irregolare; (*edge*)
pezzente
raid [reɪd] *n* (*MIL*) incursione *f*; (*criminal*)
rapina; (*by police*) irruzione *f* ♦ *vt* fare
un'incursione in; rapinare; fare
irruzione in
rail [reɪl] *n* (*on stair*) ringhiera; (*on
bridge, balcony*) parapetto; (*of ship*)
battagliola; **~s** *npl* (*for train*) binario,
rotaie *fpl*; **by ~** per ferrovia; **~ing(s)**
n(pl) ringhiere *fpl*; **~road** (*US*) *n* =
~way; **~way** (*BRIT*) *n* ferrovia; **~way
line** (*BRIT*) *n* linea ferroviaria; **~wayman** (*BRIT irreg*) *n* ferroviere *m*;
~way station (*BRIT*) *n* stazione *f*
ferroviaria
rain [reɪn] *n* pioggia ♦ *vi* piovere; **in
the ~** sotto la pioggia; **it's ~ing** piove;
~bow *n* arcobaleno; **~coat** *n*
impermeabile *m*; **~drop** *n* goccia di
pioggia; **~fall** *n* pioggia;
(*measurement*) piovosità; **~forest** *n*
foresta pluviale; **~y** *adj* piovoso/a
raise [reɪz] *n* aumento ♦ *vt* (*lift*) alzare;
sollevare; (*increase*) aumentare; (*a
protest, doubt, question*) sollevare;
(*cattle, family*) allevare; (*crop*) coltivare;
(*army, funds*) raccogliere; (*loan*)
ottenere; **to ~ one's voice** alzare la
voce
raisin ['reɪzn] *n* uva secca
rake [reɪk] *n* (*tool*) rastrello ♦ *vt*
(*garden*) rastrellare
rally ['rælɪ] *n* (*POL etc*) riunione *f*; (*AUT*)
rally *m inv*; (*TENNIS*) scambio ♦ *vt*
riunire, radunare ♦ *vi* (*sick person, Stock
Exchange*) riprendersi; **~ round** *vt fus*
raggrupparsi intorno a; venire in aiuto

di

RAM [ræm] n abbr (= random access memory) memoria ad accesso casuale

ram [ræm] n montone m, ariete m ♦ vt conficcare; (crash into) cozzare, sbattere contro; percuotere; speronare

ramble ['ræmbl] n escursione f ♦ vi (pej: also: ~ on) divagare; **~r** n escursionista m/f; **rambling** adj (speech) sconnesso(a); (house) tutto(a) a nicchie e corridoi; (BOT) rampicante

ramp [ræmp] n rampa; **on/off** ~ (US: AUT) raccordo di entrata/uscita

rampage [ræm'peɪdʒ] n: **to go on the** ~ scatenarsi in modo violento

rampant ['ræmpənt] adj (disease etc) che infierisce

rampart ['ræmpɑːt] n bastione m

ram raiding il rapinare un negozio o una banca sfondandone la vetrina con un'auto-ariete

ramshackle ['ræmʃækl] adj (house) cadente; (car etc) sgangherato(a)

ran [ræn] pt of **run**

ranch [rɑːntʃ] n ranch m inv; **~er** n proprietario di un ranch; cowboy m inv

rancid ['rænsɪd] adj rancido(a)

rancour ['ræŋkə*] (US **rancor**) n rancore m

random ['rændəm] adj fatto(a) o detto(a) per caso; (COMPUT, MATH) casuale ♦ n: **at** ~ a casaccio; ~ **access** (COMPUT) accesso casuale

randy ['rændɪ] (BRIT: inf) adj arrapato(a); lascivo(a)

rang [ræŋ] pt of **ring**

range [reɪndʒ] n (of mountains) catena; (of missile, voice) portata; (of proposals, products) gamma; (MIL: also: shooting ~) campo di tiro; (also: kitchen ~) fornello, cucina economica ♦ vt disporre ♦ vi: **to** ~ **over** coprire; **to** ~ **from ... to** andare da ... a

ranger ['reɪndʒə*] n guardia forestale

rank [ræŋk] n fila; (status, MIL) grado; (BRIT: also: taxi ~) posteggio di taxi ♦ vi:

to ~ **among** essere tra ♦ adj puzzolente; vero(a) e proprio(a); **the** ~ **and file** (fig) la gran massa

ransack ['rænsæk] vt rovistare; (plunder) saccheggiare

ransom ['rænsəm] n riscatto; **to hold sb to** ~ (fig) esercitare pressione su qn

rant [rænt] vi vociare

rap [ræp] vt bussare a; picchiare su ♦ n (music) rap m inv

rape [reɪp] n violenza carnale, stupro; (BOT) ravizzone m ♦ vt violentare; **~(seed) oil** n olio di ravizzone

rapid ['ræpɪd] adj rapido(a); **~s** npl (GEO) rapida; **~ly** adv rapidamente

rapist ['reɪpɪst] n violentatore m

rapport [ræ'pɔː*] n rapporto

rare [rɛə*] adj raro(a); (CULIN: steak) al sangue

rarely ['rɛəlɪ] adv raramente

raring ['rɛərɪŋ] adj: **to be** ~ **to go** (inf) non veder l'ora di cominciare

rascal ['rɑːskl] n mascalzone m

rash [ræʃ] adj imprudente, sconsiderato(a) ♦ n (MED) eruzione f; (of events etc) scoppio

rasher ['ræʃə*] n fetta sottile (di lardo or prosciutto)

raspberry ['rɑːzbərɪ] n lampone m

rasping ['rɑːspɪŋ] adj stridulo(a)

rat [ræt] n ratto

rate [reɪt] n (proportion) tasso, percentuale f; (speed) velocità f inv; (price) tariffa ♦ vt giudicare; stimare; **~s** npl (BRIT: property tax) imposte fpl comunali; (fees) tariffe fpl; **to** ~ **sb/sth as** valutare qn/qc come; **~able value** (BRIT) n valore m imponibile or locativo (di una proprietà); **~payer** (BRIT) n contribuente m/f (che paga le imposte comunali)

rather ['rɑːðə*] adv piuttosto; **it's** ~ **expensive** è piuttosto caro; (too) è un po' caro; **there's** ~ **a lot** ce n'è parecchio; **I would** or **I'd** ~ **go** preferirei andare

rating ['reɪtɪŋ] n (assessment)

valutazione f; (score) punteggio di merito

ratio [ˈreɪʃiəʊ] n proporzione f, rapporto

ration [ˈræʃən] n (gen pl) razioni fpl
♦ vt razionare

rational [ˈræʃənl] adj razionale, ragionevole; (solution, reasoning) logico(a); **~e** [-ˈnɑːl] n fondamento logico; giustificazione f; **~ize** vt razionalizzare

rat race n carrierismo, corsa al successo

rattle [ˈrætl] n tintinnio; (louder) strepito; (for baby) sonaglino ♦ vi risuonare, tintinnare; fare un rumore di ferraglia ♦ vt scuotere (con strepito); **~snake** n serpente m a sonagli

raucous [ˈrɔːkəs] adj rumoroso(a), fragoroso(a)

ravage [ˈrævɪdʒ] vt devastare; **~s** npl danni mpl

rave [reɪv] vi (in anger) infuriarsi; (with enthusiasm) andare in estasi; (MED) delirare ♦ (BRIT: inf) n (party) rave m inv

raven [ˈreɪvən] n corvo

ravenous [ˈrævənəs] adj affamato(a)

ravine [rəˈviːn] n burrone m

raving [ˈreɪvɪŋ] adj: **~ lunatic** pazzo(a) furioso(a)

ravishing [ˈrævɪʃɪŋ] adj incantevole

raw [rɔː] adj (uncooked) crudo(a); (not processed) greggio(a); (sore) vivo(a); (inexperienced) inesperto(a); (weather, day) gelido(a); **~ deal** (inf) n bidonata; **~ material** n materia prima

ray [reɪ] n raggio; **a ~ of hope** un barlume di speranza

rayon [ˈreɪɔn] n raion m

raze [reɪz] vt radere, distruggere

razor [ˈreɪzə*] n rasoio; **~ blade** n lama di rasoio

Rd abbr = **road**

re [riː] prep con riferimento a

reach [riːtʃ] n portata; (of river etc) tratto ♦ vt raggiungere; arrivare a ♦ vi stendersi; **out of/within ~** fuori/a portata di mano; **within ~ of the**

shops/station vicino ai negozi/alla stazione; **~ out** vt (hand) allungare
♦ vi: **to ~ out for** stendere la mano per prendere

react [riːˈækt] vi reagire; **~ion** [-ˈækʃən] n reazione f

reactor [riːˈæktə*] n reattore m

read [riːd, pt, pp red] (pt, pp **read**) vi leggere ♦ vt leggere; (understand) intendere, interpretare; (study) studiare; **~ out** vt leggere ad alta voce; **~able** adj (writing) leggibile; (book etc) che si legge volentieri; **~er** n lettore/trice; (BRIT: at university) professore con funzioni preminenti di ricerca; **~ership** n (of paper etc) numero di lettori

readily [ˈrɛdɪlɪ] adv volentieri; (easily) facilmente; (quickly) prontamente

readiness [ˈrɛdɪnɪs] n prontezza; **in ~** (prepared) pronto(a)

reading [ˈriːdɪŋ] n lettura; (understanding) interpretazione f; (on instrument) indicazione f

readjust [riːəˈdʒʌst] vt riaggiustare ♦ vi (person): **to ~ (to)** riadattarsi (a)

ready [ˈrɛdɪ] adj pronto(a); (willing) pronto(a), disposto(a); (available) disponibile ♦ n: **at the ~** (MIL) pronto a sparare; **to get ~** vi prepararsi ♦ vt preparare; **~-made** adj prefabbricato(a); (clothes) confezionato(a); **~ reckoner** n prontuario di calcolo; **~-to-wear** adj prêt-à-porter inv

reaffirm [riːəˈfɜːm] vt riaffermare

real [rɪəl] adj reale; vero(a); **in ~ terms** in realtà; **~ estate** n beni mpl immobili; **~ism** n (also ART) realismo; **~ist** n realista m/f; **~istic** [-ˈlɪstɪk] adj realistico(a)

reality [rɪˈælɪtɪ] n realtà f inv

realization [rɪələˈzeɪʃən] n presa di coscienza; realizzazione f

realize [ˈrɪəlaɪz] vt (understand) rendersi conto di

really [ˈrɪəlɪ] adv veramente, davvero; **~!** (indicating annoyance) oh, insomma!

realm [rɛlm] n reame m, regno

Realtor ® [ˈrɪəltɔ:*] (US) n agente m immobiliare

reap [ri:p] vt mietere; (fig) raccogliere

reappear [ri:əˈpɪə*] vi ricomparire, riapparire

rear [rɪə*] adj di dietro; (AUT: wheel etc) posteriore ♦ n didietro, parte f posteriore ♦ vt (cattle, family) allevare ♦ vi (also: ~ up: animal) impennarsi

rearmament [ri:ˈɑːməmənt] n riarmo

rearrange [ri:əˈreɪndʒ] vt riordinare

rear-view: ~ **mirror** n (AUT) specchio retrovisore

reason [ˈri:zn] n ragione f; (cause, motive) ragione, motivo ♦ vi: to ~ **with sb** far ragionare qn; **it stands to** ~ **that** è ovvio che; ~**able** adj ragionevole; (not bad) accettabile; ~**ably** adv ragionevolmente; ~**ed** adj: **a well-~ed argument** una forte argomentazione; ~**ing** n ragionamento

reassurance [ri:əˈʃuərəns] n rassicurazione f

reassure [ri:əˈʃuə*] vt rassicurare; **to** ~ **sb of** rassicurare qn di or su

rebate [ˈri:beɪt] n (on tax etc) sgravio

rebel [n ˈrɛbl, vb rɪˈbɛl] n ribelle m/f ♦ vi ribellarsi; ~**lion** n ribellione f; ~**lious** adj ribelle

rebound [vb rɪˈbaʊnd, n ˈri:baʊnd] vi (ball) rimbalzare ♦ n: **on the** ~ di rimbalzo

rebuff [rɪˈbʌf] n secco rifiuto

rebuke [rɪˈbju:k] vt rimproverare

rebut [rɪˈbʌt] vt rifiutare

recall [rɪˈkɔ:l] vt richiamare; (remember) ricordare, richiamare alla mente ♦ n richiamo

recap [ˈri:kæp], **recapitulate** [ri:kəˈpɪtjuleɪt] vt ricapitolare ♦ vi riassumere

rec'd abbr = **received**

recede [rɪˈsi:d] vi allontanarsi; ritirarsi; calare; **receding** adj (forehead, chin) sfuggente; **he's got a receding hairline** sta stempiando

receipt [rɪˈsi:t] n (document) ricevuta; (act of receiving) ricevimento; ~**s** npl (COMM) introiti mpl

receive [rɪˈsi:v] vt ricevere; (guest) ricevere, accogliere

receiver [rɪˈsi:və*] n (TEL) ricevitore m; (RADIO, TV) apparecchio ricevente; (of stolen goods) ricettatore/trice; (COMM) curatore m fallimentare

recent [ˈri:snt] adj recente; ~**ly** adv recentemente

receptacle [rɪˈsɛptɪkl] n recipiente m

reception [rɪˈsɛpʃən] n ricevimento; (welcome) accoglienza; (TV etc) ricezione f; ~ **desk** n (in hotel) accettazione f; (in offices etc) portineria; ~**ist** n receptionist m/f inv

receptive [rɪˈsɛptɪv] adj ricettivo(a)

recess [rɪˈsɛs] n (in room, secret place) alcova; (POL etc: holiday) vacanze fpl; ~**ion** [-ˈsɛʃən] n recessione f

recharge [ri:ˈtʃɑːdʒ] vt (battery) ricaricare

recipe [ˈrɛsɪpɪ] n ricetta

recipient [rɪˈsɪpɪənt] n beneficiario/a; (of letter) destinatario/a

recital [rɪˈsaɪtl] n recital m inv

recite [rɪˈsaɪt] vt (poem) recitare

reckless [ˈrɛkləs] adj (driver etc) spericolato(a); (spending) folle

reckon [ˈrɛkən] vt (count) calcolare; (think): **I** ~ **that** ... penso che ...; ~ **on** vt fus contare su; ~**ing** n conto; stima

reclaim [rɪˈkleɪm] vt (demand back) richiedere, reclamare; (land) bonificare; (materials) recuperare; **reclamation** [rɛkləˈmeɪʃən] n bonifica

recline [rɪˈklaɪn] vi stare sdraiato(a); **reclining** adj (seat) ribaltabile

recognition [rɛkəgˈnɪʃən] n riconoscimento; **transformed beyond** ~ irriconoscibile

recognize [ˈrɛkəgnaɪz] vt: **to** ~ (**by/as**) riconoscere (a da/come)

recoil [rɪˈkɔɪl] vi (person): **to** ~ **from doing sth** rifuggire dal fare qc ♦ n (of gun) rinculo

recollect [rekə'lekt] vt ricordare; **~ion** [-'lekʃən] n ricordo

recommend [rekə'mend] vt raccomandare; (advise) consigliare

reconcile ['rekənsaɪl] vt (two people) riconciliare; (two facts) conciliare, quadrare; **to ~ o.s.** to rassegnarsi a

recondition [ri:kən'dɪʃən] vt rimettere a nuovo

reconnoitre [rekə'nɔɪtə*] (US **reconnoiter**) vt (MIL) fare una ricognizione di

reconstruct [ri:kən'strʌkt] vt ricostruire

record [n 'rekɔːd, vb ri'kɔːd] n ricordo, documento; (of meeting etc) nota, verbale m; (register) registro; (file) pratica, dossier m inv; (COMPUT) record m inv; (also: criminal ~) fedina penale sporca; (MUS: disc) disco; (SPORT) record m inv, primato ♦ vt (set down) prendere nota di, registrare; (MUS: song etc) registrare; **in ~ time** a tempo di record; **off the ~** adj ufficioso(a) ♦ adv ufficiosamente; **~ card** n (in file) scheda; **~ed delivery** (BRIT) n (POST): **~ed delivery letter** etc lettera etc raccomandata; **~er** n (MUS) flauto diritto; **~ holder** n (SPORT) primatista m/f; **~ing** n (MUS) registrazione f; **~ player** n giradischi m inv

recount [ri'kaunt] vt raccontare, narrare

re-count ['ri:kaunt] n (POL: of votes) nuovo computo

recoup [ri'ku:p] vt ricuperare

recourse [ri'kɔːs] n: **to have ~ to** ricorrere a, far ricorso a

recover [ri'kʌvə*] vt ricuperare ♦ vi: **to ~ (from)** riprendersi (da)

recovery [ri'kʌvəri] n ricupero; ristabilimento; ripresa

recreation [rekri'eɪʃən] n ricreazione f; svago; **~al drug** n sostanza stupefacente usata a scopo ricreativo

recrimination [rɪkrɪmɪ'neɪʃən] n recriminazione f

recruit [ri'kru:t] n recluta; (in company) nuovo(a) assunto(a) ♦ vt reclutare

rectangle ['rektæŋgl] n rettangolo; **rectangular** [-'tæŋgjulə*] adj rettangolare

rectify ['rektɪfaɪ] vt (error) rettificare; (omission) riparare

rector ['rektə*] n (REL) parroco (anglicano); **~y** n presbiterio

recuperate [ri'kju:pəreɪt] vi ristabilirsi

recur [ri'kɜː*] vi riaccadere; (symptoms) ripresentarsi; **~rent** adj ricorrente, periodico(a)

recycle [ri:'saɪkl] vt riciclare

red [red] n rosso; (POL: pej) rosso/a ♦ adj rosso(a); **in the ~** (account) scoperto; (business) in deficit; **~ carpet treatment** n cerimonia col gran pavese; **R~ Cross** n Croce f Rossa; **~currant** n ribes m inv; **~den** vt arrossare ♦ vi arrossire

redeem [ri'di:m] vt (debt) riscattare; (sth in pawn) ritirare; (fig, also REL) redimere; **~ing** adj: **~ing feature** unico aspetto positivo

redeploy [ri:dɪ'plɔɪ] vt (resources) riorganizzare

red-haired [-'heəd] adj dai capelli rossi

red-handed [-'hændɪd] adj: **to be caught ~** essere preso(a) in flagrante or con le mani nel sacco

redhead ['redhed] n rosso/a

red herring n (fig) falsa pista

red-hot adj arroventato(a)

redirect [ri:daɪ'rekt] vt (mail) far seguire

red light n: **to go through a ~** (AUT) passare col rosso; **red-light district** n quartiere m a luci rosse

redo [ri:'du:] (irreg) vt rifare

redouble [ri:'dʌbl] vt: **to ~ one's efforts** raddoppiare gli sforzi

redress [ri'dres] vt riparare

Red Sea n: **the ~** il Mar Rosso

redskin ['redskɪn] n pellerossa m/f

red tape n (fig) burocrazia

reduce [rɪ'djuːs] vt ridurre; (lower) ridurre, abbassare; **"~ speed now"** (AUT) "rallentare"; **at a ~d price** scontato(a); **reduction** [rɪ'dʌkʃən] n riduzione f; (of price) ribasso; (discount) sconto

redundancy [rɪ'dʌndənsɪ] n licenziamento

redundant [rɪ'dʌndnt] adj (worker) licenziato(a); (detail, object) superfluo(a); **to be made ~** essere licenziato (per eccesso di personale)

reed [riːd] n (BOT) canna; (MUS: of clarinet etc) ancia

reef [riːf] n (at sea) scogliera

reek [riːk] vi: **to ~ (of)** puzzare (di)

reel [riːl] n bobina, rocchetto; (FISHING) mulinello; (CINEMA) rotolo; (dance) danza veloce scozzese ♦ vi (sway) barcollare; **~ in** tirare su

ref [rɛf] (inf) n abbr (= referee) arbitro

refectory [rɪ'fɛktərɪ] n refettorio

refer [rɪ'fəː*] vt: **to ~ sth to** (dispute, decision) deferire qc a; **to ~ sb to** (inquirer, MED: patient) indirizzare qn a; (reader: to text) rimandare qn a ♦ vi: **~ to** (allude to) accennare a; (consult) rivolgersi a

referee [rɛfə'riː] n arbitro; (BRIT: for job application) referenza ♦ vt arbitrare

reference ['rɛfrəns] n riferimento; (mention) menzione f, allusione f; (for job application) referenza; **with ~ to** (COMM: in letter) in o con riferimento a; **~ book** n libro di consultazione; **~ number** n numero di riferimento

referenda [rɛfə'rɛndə] npl of **referendum**

referendum [rɛfə'rɛndəm] (pl **referenda**) n referendum m inv

refill [vb riː'fɪl, n 'riːfɪl] vt riempire di nuovo; (pen, lighter etc) ricaricare ♦ n (for pen etc) ricambio

refine [rɪ'faɪn] vt raffinare; **~d** adj (person, taste) raffinato(a)

reflect [rɪ'flɛkt] vt (light, image)

riflettere; (fig) rispecchiare ♦ vi (think) riflettere, considerare; **it ~s badly/ well on him** si ripercuote su di lui in senso negativo/positivo; **~ion** [-'flɛkʃən] n riflessione f; (image) riflesso; (criticism): **~ion on** giudizio su; **on ~ion** pensandoci sopra

reflex ['riːflɛks] adj riflesso(a) ♦ n riflesso; **~ive** [rɪ'flɛksɪv] adj (LING) riflessivo(a)

reform [rɪ'fɔːm] n (of sinner etc) correzione f; (of law etc) riforma ♦ vt correggere; riformare; (sinner) ravvedersi; **~atory** (US) n riformatorio

refrain [rɪ'freɪn] vi: **to ~ from doing** trattenersi dal fare ♦ n ritornello

refresh [rɪ'frɛʃ] vt rinfrescare; (subj: food, sleep) ristorare; **~er course** (BRIT) n corso di aggiornamento; **~ing** adj (drink) rinfrescante; (sleep) riposante, ristoratore(trice); **~ments** npl rinfreschi mpl

refrigerator [rɪ'frɪdʒəreɪtə*] n frigorifero

refuel [riː'fjuəl] vi far rifornimento (di carburante)

refuge ['rɛfjuːdʒ] n rifugio; **to take ~ in** rifugiarsi in

refugee [rɛfju'dʒiː] n rifugiato/a, profugo/a

refund [n 'riːfʌnd, vb rɪ'fʌnd] n rimborso ♦ vt rimborsare

refurbish [riː'fəːbɪʃ] vt rimettere a nuovo

refusal [rɪ'fjuːzəl] n rifiuto; **to have first ~** n avere il diritto d'opzione su

refuse [n 'rɛfjuːs, vb rɪ'fjuːz] n rifiuti mpl ♦ vt, vi rifiutare; **to ~ to do** rifiutare di fare; **~ collection** n raccolta di rifiuti

refute [rɪ'fjuːt] vt confutare

regain [rɪ'geɪn] vt riguadagnare; riacquistare, ricuperare

regal ['riːɡl] adj regale; **~ia** [rɪ'ɡeɪlɪə] n insegne fpl regie

regard [rɪ'ɡɑːd] n riguardo, stima ♦ vt considerare, stimare; **to give one's ~s**

to porgere i suoi saluti a; **"with kindest ~s"** "cordiali saluti"; **~ing, as ~s, with ~** to riguardo a; **~less** adv lo stesso; **~less of** a dispetto di, nonostante

regenerate [rɪ'dʒenəreɪt] vt rigenerare

régime [reɪ'ʒiːm] n regime m

regiment ['redʒɪmənt] n reggimento; **~al** [-'mentl] adj reggimentale

region ['riːdʒən] n regione f; **in the ~ of** (fig) all'incirca di; **~al** adj regionale

register ['redʒɪstə*] n registro; (also: electoral ~) lista elettorale ♦ vt registrare; (vehicle) immatricolare; (letter) assicurare; (subj: instrument) segnare ♦ vi iscriversi; (at hotel) firmare il registro; (make impression) entrare in testa; **~ed** (BRIT) adj (letter) assicurato(a); **~ed trademark** n marchio depositato

registrar ['redʒɪstrɑː*] n ufficiale m di stato civile; segretario

registration [redʒɪs'treɪʃən] n (act) registrazione f, iscrizione f; (AUT: also: ~ number) numero di targa

registry ['redʒɪstrɪ] n ufficio del registro; **~ office** (BRIT) n anagrafe f; **to get married in a ~ office** ≈ sposarsi in municipio

regret [rɪ'gret] n rimpianto, rincrescimento ♦ vt rimpiangere; **~fully** adv con rincrescimento; **~table** adj deplorevole

regular ['regjulə*] adj regolare; (usual) abituale, normale; (soldier) dell'esercito regolare ♦ n (client etc) cliente m/f abituale; **~ly** adv regolarmente

regulate ['regjuleɪt] vt regolare; **regulation** [-'leɪʃən] n regolazione f; (rule) regola, regolamento

rehabilitation ['riːhəbɪlɪ'teɪʃən] n (of offender) riabilitazione f; (of disabled) riadattamento

rehearsal [rɪ'hɜːsəl] n prova

rehearse [rɪ'hɜːs] vt provare

reign [reɪn] n regno ♦ vi regnare

reimburse [riːɪm'bɜːs] vt rimborsare

rein [reɪn] n (for horse) briglia

reindeer ['reɪndɪə*] n inv renna

reinforce [riːɪn'fɔːs] vt rinforzare; **~d concrete** n cemento armato; **~ment** n rinforzo; **~ments** npl (MIL) rinforzi mpl

reinstate [riːɪn'steɪt] vt reintegrare

reiterate [riː'ɪtəret] vt reiterare, ripetere

reject [n 'riːdʒekt, vb rɪ'dʒekt] n (COMM) scarto ♦ vt rifiutare, respingere; (COMM: goods) scartare; **~ion** [rɪ'dʒekʃən] n rifiuto

rejoice [rɪ'dʒɔɪs] vi: **to ~ (at or over)** provare diletto in

rejuvenate [rɪ'dʒuːvəneɪt] vt ringiovanire

relapse [rɪ'læps] n (MED) ricaduta

relate [rɪ'leɪt] vt (tell) raccontare; (connect) collegare ♦ vi: **to ~ to** (connect) riferirsi a; (get on with) stabilire un rapporto con; **relating to** che riguarda, rispetto a; **~d** adj: **~d (to)** imparentato(a (con); collegato(a) or connesso(a) (a)

relation [rɪ'leɪʃən] n (person) parente m/f; (link) rapporto, relazione f; **~ship** n rapporto; (personal ties) rapporti mpl, relazioni fpl; (also: family ~ship) legami mpl di parentela

relative ['relətɪv] n parente m/f ♦ adj relativo(a); (respective) rispettivo(a); **~ly** adv relativamente; (fairly, rather) abbastanza

relax [rɪ'læks] vi rilassarsi; (person: unwind) rilassarsi ♦ vt rilasciare; (mind, person) rilassare; **~ation** [riːlæk'seɪʃən] n rilassamento; rilassamento; (entertainment) ricreazione f, svago; **~ed** adj rilassato(a); **~ing** adj rilassante

relay ['riːleɪ] n (SPORT) corsa a staffetta ♦ vt (message) trasmettere

release [rɪ'liːs] n (from prison) rilascio; (from obligation) liberazione f; (of gas etc) emissione f; (of film etc) distribuzione f; (record) disco; (device) disinnesto ♦ vt (*prisoner*) rilasciare; (*from obligation, wreckage etc*) liberare; (*book, film*) fare uscire; (*news*) rendere pubblico(a); (*gas etc*) emettere; (*TECH: catch, spring etc*) disinnestare

relegate ['relɪgeɪt] vt relegare; (*BRIT: SPORT*): **to be ~d** essere retrocesso(a)

relent [rɪ'lent] vi cedere; **~less** adj implacabile

relevant ['reləvənt] adj pertinente; (*chapter*) in questione; **~ to** pertinente a

reliability [rɪlaɪə'bɪlɪtɪ] n (*of person*) serietà; (*of machine*) affidabilità

reliable [rɪ'laɪəbl] adj (*person, firm*) fidato(a), che dà affidamento; (*method*) sicuro(a); (*machine*) affidabile; **reliably** adv: **to be reliably informed** sapere da fonti sicure

reliance [rɪ'laɪəns] n: **~ (on)** fiducia (in); bisogno (di)

relic ['relɪk] n (*REL*) reliquia; (*of the past*) resto

relief [rɪ'liːf] n (*from pain, anxiety*) sollievo; (*help, supplies*) soccorsi mpl; (*ART, GEO*) rilievo

relieve [rɪ'liːv] vt (*pain, patient*) sollevare; (*bring help*) soccorrere; (*take over from: gen*) sostituire; (*: guard*) rilevare; **to ~ sb of sth** (*load*) alleggerire qn di qc; **to ~ o.s.** fare i propri bisogni

religion [rɪ'lɪdʒən] n religione f; **religious** adj religioso(a)

relinquish [rɪ'lɪŋkwɪʃ] vt abbandonare; (*plan, habit*) rinunziare a

relish ['relɪʃ] n (*CULIN*) condimento; (*enjoyment*) gran piacere m ♦ vt (*food etc*) godere; **to ~ doing** adorare fare

relocate ['riːləu'keɪt] vt trasferire ♦ vi trasferirsi

reluctance [rɪ'lʌktəns] n riluttanza

reluctant [rɪ'lʌktənt] adj riluttante, mal disposto(a); **~ly** adv di mala voglia, a malincuore

rely [rɪ'laɪ]: **to ~ on** vt fus contare su;

(*be dependent*) dipendere da

remain [rɪ'meɪn] vi restare, rimanere; **~der** n resto; (*COMM*) rimanenza; **~ing** adj che rimane; **~s** npl resti mpl

remand [rɪ'mɑːnd] n: **on ~** in detenzione preventiva ♦ vt: **to ~ in custody** rinviare in carcere; trattenere a disposizione della legge; **~ home** (*BRIT*) n riformatorio, casa di correzione

remark [rɪ'mɑːk] n osservazione f ♦ vt osservare, dire; **~able** adj notevole; eccezionale

remedial [rɪ'miːdɪəl] adj (*tuition, classes*) di riparazione; (*exercise*) correttivo(a)

remedy ['remədɪ] n: **~ (for)** rimedio (per) ♦ vt rimediare a

remember [rɪ'membə*] vt ricordare, ricordarsi di; **~ me to him** salutalo da parte mia; **remembrance** n memoria; ricordo; **Remembrance Day** n 11 novembre, giorno della commemorazione dei caduti in guerra

---

Remembrance Day

In Gran Bretagna, il **Remembrance Day** *è un giorno di commemorazione dei caduti in guerra. Si celebra ogni anno la domenica più vicina all'11 novembre, anniversario della firma dell'armistizio con la Germania nel 1918.*

---

remind [rɪ'maɪnd] vt: **to ~ sb of sth** ricordare qc a qn; **to ~ sb to do** ricordare a qn di fare; **~er** n richiamo; (*note etc*) promemoria m inv

reminisce [remɪ'nɪs] vi: **to ~ (about)** abbandonarsi ai ricordi (di)

reminiscent [remɪ'nɪsnt] adj: **~ of** che fa pensare a, che richiama

remiss [rɪ'mɪs] adj negligente

remission [rɪ'mɪʃən] n remissione f

remit [rɪ'mɪt] vt (*send: money*) rimettere; **~tance** n rimessa

remnant ['remnənt] n resto, avanzo; **~s** npl (*COMM*) scampoli mpl; fine f serie

remorse [rɪ'mɔːs] n rimorso; **~ful** adj pieno(a) di rimorsi; **~less** adj (fig) spietato(a)

remote [rɪ'məut] adj remoto(a), lontano(a); (person) distaccato(a); **~ control** n telecomando; **~ly** adv remotamente; (slightly) vagamente

remould ['riːməuld] (BRIT) n (tyre) gomma rivestita

removable [rɪ'muːvəbl] adj (detachable) staccabile

removal [rɪ'muːvl] n (taking away) rimozione f; soppressione f; (BRIT: from house) trasloco; (from office: dismissal) destituzione f; (MED) ablazione f; **~ van** (BRIT) n furgone m per traslochi

remove [rɪ'muːv] vt togliere, rimuovere; (employee) destituire; (stain) far sparire; (doubt, abuse) sopprimere, eliminare; **~rs** (BRIT) npl (company) ditta o impresa di traslochi

Renaissance [rɪ'neɪsɑ̃ːns] n: **the ~** il Rinascimento

render ['rendə*] vt rendere; **~ing** n (MUS etc) interpretazione f

rendez-vous ['rɔndɪvuː] n appuntamento; (place) luogo d'incontro; (meeting) incontro

renegade ['renɪgeɪd] n rinnegato/a

renew [rɪ'njuː] vt rinnovare; (negotiations) riprendere; **~able** adj rinnovabile; **~al** n rinnovo; ripresa

renounce [rɪ'nauns] vt rinunziare a

renovate ['renəveɪt] vt rinnovare; (art work) restaurare; **renovation** [-'veɪʃən] n rinnovamento; restauro

renown [rɪ'naun] n rinomanza; **~ed** adj rinomato(a)

rent [rent] n affitto ♦ vt (take for ~) prendere in affitto; (also: ~ out) dare in affitto; **~al** n (for television, car) fitto

renunciation [rɪnʌnsɪ'eɪʃən] n rinunzia

rep [rep] n abbr (COMM: = representative) rappresentante m/f; (THEATRE: = repertory) teatro di repertorio

repair [rɪ'pɛə*] n riparazione f ♦ vt riparare; **in good/bad ~** in buone/cattive condizioni; **~ kit** n corredo per riparazioni

repatriate [riː'pætrɪeɪt] vt rimpatriare

repay [riː'peɪ] (irreg) vt (money, creditor) rimborsare, ripagare; (sb's efforts) ricompensare; (favour) ricambiare; **~ment** n pagamento; rimborso

repeal [rɪ'piːl] n (of law) abrogazione f ♦ vt abrogare

repeat [rɪ'piːt] n (RADIO, TV) replica f ♦ vt ripetere; (pattern) riprodurre; (promise, attack, also COMM: order) rinnovare ♦ vi ripetere; **~edly** adv ripetutamente, spesso

repel [rɪ'pel] vt respingere; (disgust) ripugnare a; **~lent** adj repellente ♦ n: **insect ~lent** prodotto m anti-insetti inv

repent [rɪ'pent] vi: **to ~ (of)** pentirsi (di); **~ance** n pentimento

repertoire ['repətwɑː*] n repertorio

repertory ['repətərɪ] n (also: ~ theatre) teatro di repertorio

repetition [repɪ'tɪʃən] n ripetizione f

repetitive [rɪ'petɪtɪv] adj (movement) che si ripete; (work) monotono(a); (speech) pieno(a) di ripetizioni

replace [rɪ'pleɪs] vt (put back) rimettere a posto; (take the place of) sostituire; **~ment** n rimessa; sostituzione f; (person) sostituto/a

replay ['riːpleɪ] n (of match) partita ripetuta; (of tape, film) replay m inv

replenish [rɪ'plenɪʃ] vt (glass) riempire; (stock etc) rifornire

replete [rɪ'pliːt] adj (well-fed) sazio(a)

replica ['replɪkə] n replica, copia

reply [rɪ'plaɪ] n risposta ♦ vi rispondere; **~ coupon** n buono di risposta

report [rɪ'pɔːt] n rapporto; (PRESS etc) cronaca; (BRIT: also: school ~) pagella; (of gun) sparo ♦ vt riportare; (PRESS etc) fare una cronaca su; (bring to notice: occurrence) segnalare; (: person) denunciare ♦ vi (make a report) fare un rapporto (or una cronaca); (present o.s.): **to ~ (to sb)** presentarsi a (qn); **~ card** (US, SCOTTISH) n pagella; **~edly** adv stando a quanto si dice; **he ~edly told them to ...** avrebbe detto loro di ...; **~er** n reporter m inv

repose [rɪ'pəuz] n: **in ~** (face, mouth) in riposo

reprehensible [reprɪ'hensɪbl] adj riprovevole

represent [reprɪ'zent] vt rappresentare; **~ation** [-'teɪʃən] n rappresentazione f; (petition) rappresentanza f; **~ations** npl (protest) protesta; **~ative** n rappresentante m/f; (US: POL) deputato/a ♦ adj rappresentativo(a)

repress [rɪ'pres] vt reprimere; **~ion** [-'preʃən] n repressione f

reprieve [rɪ'priːv] n (LAW) sospensione f dell'esecuzione della condanna; (fig) dilazione f

reprimand ['reprɪmaːnd] n rimprovero ♦ vt rimproverare

reprint ['riːprɪnt] n ristampa

reprisal [rɪ'praɪzl] n rappresaglia

reproach [rɪ'prəutʃ] n rimprovero ♦ vt: **to ~ sb for sth** rimproverare qn di qc; **~ful** adj di rimprovero

reproduce [riːprə'djuːs] vt riprodurre ♦ vi riprodursi; **reproduction** [-'dʌkʃən] n riproduzione f

reproof [rɪ'pruːf] n riprovazione f

reprove [rɪ'pruːv] vt: **to ~ (for)** biasimare (per)

reptile ['reptaɪl] n rettile m

republic [rɪ'pʌblɪk] n repubblica; **~an** adj, n repubblicano(a)

repudiate [rɪ'pjuːdɪeɪt] vt (accusation) respingere

repulse [rɪ'pʌls] vt respingere

repulsive [rɪ'pʌlsɪv] adj ripugnante, ripulsivo(a)

reputable ['repjutəbl] adj di buona reputazione; (occupation) rispettabile

reputation [repju'teɪʃən] n

reputazione f

reputed [rɪ'pjuːtɪd] adj reputato(a); **~ly** adv secondo quanto si dice

request [rɪ'kwest] n domanda; (formal) richiesta ♦ vt: **to ~ (of or from sb)** chiedere (a qn); **~ stop** (BRIT) n (for bus) fermata facoltativa o a richiesta

require [rɪ'kwaɪə*] vt (need: subj: person) aver bisogno di; (: thing, situation) richiedere; (want) volere; esigere; (order): **to ~ sb to do sth** ordinare a qn di fare qc; **~ment** n esigenza; bisogno; requisito

requisition [rekwɪ'zɪʃən] n: **~ (for)** richiesta (di) ♦ vt (MIL) requisire

rescue ['reskjuː] n salvataggio; (help) soccorso ♦ vt salvare; **~ party** n squadra di salvataggio; **~r** n salvatore/trice

research [rɪ'sɜːtʃ] n ricerca, ricerche fpl ♦ vt fare ricerche su; **~er** n ricercatore/trice

resemblance [rɪ'zembləns] n somiglianza

resemble [rɪ'zembl] vt assomigliare a

resent [rɪ'zent] vt risentirsi di; **~ful** adj pieno(a) di risentimento; **~ment** n risentimento

reservation [rezə'veɪʃən] n (booking) prenotazione f; (doubt) dubbio; (protected area) riserva; (BRIT: on road: also: central ~) spartitraffico m inv

reserve [rɪ'zɜːv] n riserva ♦ vt (seats etc) prenotare; **~s** npl (MIL) riserve fpl; **in ~** in serbo; **~d** adj (shy) riservato(a)

reservoir ['rezəvwaː*] n serbatoio

reshuffle [riː'ʃʌfl] n: **Cabinet ~** (POL) rimpasto governativo

reside [rɪ'zaɪd] vi risiedere

residence ['rezɪdəns] n residenza; **~ permit** (BRIT) n permesso di soggiorno

resident ['rezɪdənt] n residente m/f; (in hotel) cliente m/f fisso ♦ adj residente; (doctor) fisso(a); (course, college) a tempo pieno con pernottamento; **~ial** [-'denʃəl] adj di residenza; (area) residenziale

residue [ˈrɛzɪdjuː] n resto; (CHEM, PHYSICS) residuo

resign [rɪˈzaɪn] vt (one's post) dimettersi da ♦ vi dimettersi; **to ~ o.s. to** rassegnarsi a; **~ation** [rɛzɪgˈneɪʃən] n dimissioni fpl; rassegnazione f; **~ed** adj rassegnato(a)

resilience [rɪˈzɪlɪəns] n (of material) elasticità, resilienza; (of person) capacità di recupero

resilient [rɪˈzɪlɪənt] adj elastico(a); (person) che si riprende facilmente

resin [ˈrɛzɪn] n resina

resist [rɪˈzɪst] vt resistere a; **~ance** n resistenza

resolution [rɛzəˈluːʃən] n risoluzione f

resolve [rɪˈzɔlv] n risoluzione f ♦ vi (decide): **to ~ to do** decidere di fare ♦ vt (problem) risolvere

resort [rɪˈzɔːt] n (town) stazione f; (recourse) ricorso ♦ vi: **to ~ to** aver ricorso a; **in the last ~** come ultima risorsa

resounding [rɪˈzaundɪŋ] adj risonante; (fig) clamoroso(a)

resource [rɪˈzɔːs] n risorsa; **~s** npl (coal, iron etc) risorse fpl; **~ful** adj pieno(a) di risorse, intraprendente

respect [rɪsˈpɛkt] n rispetto ♦ vt rispettare; **~s** npl (greetings) ossequi mpl; **with ~ to** rispetto a, riguardo a; **in this ~** per questo riguardo; **~able** adj rispettabile; **~ful** adj rispettoso(a)

respective [rɪsˈpɛktɪv] adj rispettivo(a)

respite [ˈrɛspaɪt] n respiro, tregua

respond [rɪsˈpɔnd] vi rispondere

response [rɪsˈpɔns] n risposta

responsibility [rɪspɔnsɪˈbɪlɪtɪ] n responsabilità f inv

responsible [rɪsˈpɔnsɪbl] adj (trustworthy) fidato(a); (job) di (grande) responsabilità; **~ (for)** responsabile (di)

responsive [rɪsˈpɔnsɪv] adj che reagisce

rest [rɛst] n riposo; (stop) sosta, pausa; (MUS) pausa; (object: to support sth)

appoggio, sostegno; (remainder) resto, avanzi mpl ♦ vi riposarsi; (be supported): **to ~ on** appoggiarsi su ♦ vt (far) riposare; (lean): **to ~ sth on/against** appoggiare qc su/contro; **the ~ of them** gli altri; **it ~s with him to decide** sta a lui decidere

restaurant [ˈrɛstərɔŋ] n ristorante m; **~ car** (BRIT) n vagone m ristorante

restful [ˈrɛstful] adj riposante

rest home n casa di riposo

restitution [rɛstɪˈtjuːʃən] n: **to make ~ to sb for sth** compensare qn di qc

restive [ˈrɛstɪv] adj agitato(a), impaziente

restless [ˈrɛstlɪs] adj agitato(a), irrequieto(a)

restoration [rɛstəˈreɪʃən] n restauro; restituzione f

restore [rɪsˈtɔː] vt (building, to power) restaurare; (sth stolen) restituire; (peace, health) ristorare

restrain [rɪsˈtreɪn] vt (feeling, growth) contenere, frenare; (person): **to ~ (from doing)** trattenere (dal fare); **~ed** adj (style) contenuto(a), sobrio(a); (person) riservato(a); **~t** n (restriction) limitazione f; (moderation) ritegno; (of style) contenutezza

restrict [rɪsˈtrɪkt] vt restringere, limitare; **~ion** [-kʃən] n: **~ion (on)** restrizione f (di), limitazione f

rest room (US) n toletta

restructure [riːˈstrʌktʃə*] vt ristrutturare

result [rɪˈzʌlt] n risultato ♦ vi: **to ~ in** avere per risultato; **as a ~ of** in or di conseguenza a, in seguito a

resume [rɪˈzjuːm] vt, vi (work, journey) riprendere

résumé [ˈreɪzjumeɪ] n riassunto; (US) curriculum m inv vitae

resumption [rɪˈzʌmpʃən] n ripresa

resurgence [rɪˈsɜːdʒəns] n rinascita

resurrection [rɛzəˈrɛkʃən] n risurrezione f

resuscitate [rɪ'sʌsɪteɪt] vt (MED) risuscitare; **resuscitation** [-'teɪʃən] n rianimazione f

retail ['riːteɪl] adj, adv al minuto ♦ vt vendere al minuto; **~er** n commerciante m/f al minuto, dettagliante m/f; **~ price** n prezzo al minuto

retain [rɪ'teɪn] vt (keep) tenere, serbare; **~er** n (fee) onorario

retaliate [rɪ'tælɪeɪt] vi: **to ~ (against)** vendicarsi (di); **retaliation** [-'eɪʃən] n rappresaglie fpl

retarded [rɪ'tɑːdɪd] adj ritardato(a)

retch [retʃ] vi aver conati di vomito

retire [rɪ'taɪə*] vi (give up work) andare in pensione; (withdraw) ritirarsi, andarsene; (go to bed) andare a letto, ritirarsi; **~d** adj (person) pensionato(a); **~ment** n pensione f; (act) pensionamento; **retiring** adj (leaving) uscente; (shy) riservato(a)

retort [rɪ'tɔːt] vi rimbeccare

retrace [riː'treɪs] vt: **to ~ one's steps** tornare sui passi

retract [rɪ'trækt] vt (statement) ritrattare; (claws, undercarriage, aerial) ritrarre, ritirare

retrain [riː'treɪn] vt (worker) riaddestrare

retread ['riːtred] n (tyre) gomma rigenerata

retreat [rɪ'triːt] n (withdrawal) ritirata; (place) rifugio ♦ vi battere in ritirata

retribution [retrɪ'bjuːʃən] n castigo

retrieval [rɪ'triːvəl] n (see vb) ricupero; riparazione f

retrieve [rɪ'triːv] vt (sth lost) ricuperare, ritrovare; (situation, honour) salvare; (error, loss) rimediare a; **~r** n cane m da riporto

retrospect ['retrəspekt] n: **in ~** guardando indietro; **~ive** [-'spektɪv] adj retrospettivo(a); (law) retroattivo(a)

return [rɪ'tɜːn] n (going or coming back) ritorno; (of sth stolen etc) restituzione f; (FINANCE: from land,

shares) profitto, reddito ♦ cpd (journey, match) di ritorno; (BRIT: ticket) di andata e ritorno ♦ vi tornare, ritornare ♦ vt rendere, restituire; (bring back) riportare; (send back) mandare indietro; (put back) rimettere; (POL: candidate) eleggere; **~s** npl (COMM) incassi mpl; profitti mpl; **in ~ (for)** in cambio (di); **by ~ of post** a stretto giro di posta; **many happy ~s (of the day)!** cento di questi giorni!

reunion [riː'juːnɪən] n riunione f

reunite [riːjuː'naɪt] vt riunire

rev [rev] n abbr (AUT: = revolution) giro ♦ vt (also: ~ up) imballare

revamp ['riː'væmp] vt (firm) riorganizzare

reveal [rɪ'viːl] vt (make known) rivelare, svelare; (display) rivelare, mostrare; **~ing** adj rivelatore(trice); (dress) scollato(a)

revel ['revl] vi: **to ~ in sth/in doing** dilettarsi di qc/a fare

revelation [revə'leɪʃən] n rivelazione f

revenge [rɪ'vendʒ] n vendetta ♦ vt vendicare; **to take ~ on** vendicarsi di

revenue ['revənjuː] n reddito

reverberate [rɪ'vɜːbəreɪt] vi (sound) rimbombare; (light) riverberarsi; (fig) ripercuotersi

revere [rɪ'vɪə*] vt venerare

reverence ['revərəns] n venerazione f, riverenza

Reverend ['revərənd] adj (in titles) reverendo(a)

reverie ['revərɪ] n fantasticheria

reversal [rɪ'vɜːsl] n capovolgimento

reverse [rɪ'vɜːs] n contrario, opposto; (back, defeat) rovescio; (AUT: also: ~ gear) marcia indietro ♦ adj (order, direction) contrario(a), opposto(a) ♦ vt (turn) invertire, rivoltare; (change) capovolgere, rovesciare; (LAW: judgment) cassare; (car) fare marcia indietro con ♦ vi (BRIT: AUT, person etc) fare marcia indietro; **~-charge call** (BRIT) n (TEL) telefonata con addebito al

ricevente; **reversing lights** (BRIT) npl
(AUT) luci fpl per la retromarcia

revert [rɪ'vəːt] vi: **to ~ to** tornare a

review [rɪ'vjuː] n rivista; (of book, film)
recensione f; (of situation) esame m
♦ vt passare in rivista; fare la
recensione di; fare il punto di; **~er** n
recensore/a

revise [rɪ'vaɪz] vt (manuscript) rivedere,
correggere; (opinion) emendare,
modificare; (study: subject, notes)
ripassare; **revision** [rɪ'vɪʒən] n
revisione f; ripasso

revitalize [riː'vaɪtəlaɪz] vt ravvivare

revival [rɪ'vaɪvəl] n ripresa;
ristabilimento; (of faith) risveglio

revive [rɪ'vaɪv] vt (person) rianimare;
(custom) far rivivere; (hope, courage,
economy) ravvivare; (play, fashion)
riesumare ♦ vi (person) rianimarsi;
(hope) ravvivarsi; (activity) riprendersi

revolt [rɪ'vəult] n rivolta, ribellione f
♦ vi rivoltarsi, ribellarsi ♦ vt (far)
rivoltare; **~ing** adj ripugnante

revolution [revə'luːʃən] n rivoluzione
f; (of wheel etc) rivoluzione, giro; **~ary**
adj, n rivoluzionario(a)

revolve [rɪ'vɔlv] vi girare

revolver [rɪ'vɔlvə*] n rivoltella

revolving [rɪ'vɔlvɪŋ] adj girevole

revue [rɪ'vjuː] n (THEATRE) rivista

revulsion [rɪ'vʌlʃən] n ripugnanza

reward [rɪ'wɔːd] n ricompensa, premio
♦ vt ricompensare (per);
~ing adj (fig) gratificante

rewind [riː'waɪnd] (irreg) vt (watch)
ricaricare; (ribbon etc) riavvolgere

rewire [riː'waɪə*] vt (house) rifare
l'impianto elettrico di

reword [riː'wəːd] vt formulare or
esprimere con altre parole

rheumatism ['ruːmətɪzəm] n
reumatismo

Rhine [raɪn] n: **the ~** il Reno

rhinoceros [raɪ'nɔsərəs] n rinoceronte
m

rhododendron [rəudə'dendrən] n

rododendro

Rhone [rəun] n: **the ~** il Rodano

rhubarb ['ruːbɑːb] n rabarbaro

rhyme [raɪm] n rima; (verse) poesia

rhythm ['rɪðm] n ritmo

rib [rɪb] n (ANAT) costola ♦ vt (tease)
punzecchiare

ribbon ['rɪbən] n nastro; **in ~s** (torn) a
brandelli

rice [raɪs] n riso; **~ pudding** n budino
di riso

rich [rɪtʃ] adj ricco(a); (clothes)
sontuoso(a); (abundant) ricco(a)
di; **~ in** ricco(a) di; **the ~** npl (wealthy people) i ricchi;
~es npl ricchezze fpl; **~ly** adv
riccamente; (dressed) sontuosamente;
(deserved) pienamente

rickets ['rɪkɪts] n rachitismo

ricochet ['rɪkəʃeɪ] vi rimbalzare

rid [rɪd] (pt, pp **rid**) vt: **to ~ sb of**
sbarazzare o liberare qn di; **to get
~ of** sbarazzarsi di

ridden ['rɪdn] pp of **ride**

riddle ['rɪdl] n (puzzle) indovinello ♦ vt:
to be ~d with (holes) essere
crivellato(a) di; (doubts) essere pieno(a)
di

ride [raɪd] (pt **rode**, pp **ridden**) n (on
horse) cavalcata; (outing) passeggiata;
(distance covered) cavalcata; corsa ♦ vi
(as sport) cavalcare; (go somewhere: on
horse, bicycle) andare (a cavallo or in
bicicletta etc); (journey: on bicycle,
motorcycle, bus) andare, viaggiare ♦ vt
(a horse) montare, cavalcare; **to take
sb for a ~** (fig) prendere in giro qn;
fregare qn; **to ~ a horse/bicycle/
camel** montare a cavallo/in bicicletta/
in groppa a un cammello; **~r** n
cavalcatore/trice; (in race) fantino; (on
bicycle) ciclista m/f; (on motorcycle)
motociclista m/f

ridge [rɪdʒ] n (of hill) cresta; (of roof)
colmo; (on object) riga (in rilievo)

ridicule ['rɪdɪkjuːl] n ridicolo; scherno
♦ vt mettere in ridicolo

ridiculous [rɪ'dɪkjuləs] adj ridicolo(a)

riding ['raɪdɪŋ] n equitazione f;
~ **school** n scuola d'equitazione

rife [raɪf] adj diffuso(a); **to be ~ with**
abbondare di

riffraff ['rɪfræf] n canaglia

rifle ['raɪfl] n carabina ♦ vt vuotare;
~ **through** vt fus frugare tra; ~ **range**
n campo di tiro; (at fair) tiro a segno

rift [rɪft] n fessura, crepatura; (fig:
disagreement) incrinatura, disaccordo

rig [rɪg] n (also: oil ~: on land) derrick m
inv; (: at sea) piattaforma di
trivellazione ♦ vt (election etc) truccare;
~ **out** (BRIT) vt: **to ~ out as/in** vestire
da/in; ~ **up** vt allestire; ~**ging** n (NAUT)
attrezzatura

right [raɪt] adj giusto(a); (suitable)
appropriato(a); (not left) destro(a) ♦ n
giusto; (title, claim) diritto; (not left)
destra ♦ adv (answer) correttamente;
(not on the left) a destra ♦ vt
raddrizzare; (fig) riparare ♦ excl bene!;
to be ~ (person) aver ragione; (answer)
essere giusto(a) or corretto(a); **by ~s** di
diritto; **on the ~** a destra; **to be in the
~** aver ragione, essere nel giusto; ~
now proprio adesso; subito; ~ **away**
subito; ~ **angle** n angolo retto; ~**eous**
['raɪtʃəs] adj retto(a), virtuoso(a);
(anger) giusto(a), giustificato(a); ~**ful**
adj (heir) legittimo(a); ~**-handed** adj
(person) che adopera la mano destra; ~**-
hand man** n braccio destro; ~**-
hand side** n il lato destro; ~**ly** adv
bene, correttamente; (with reason) a
ragione; ~ **of way** n diritto di
passaggio; (AUT) precedenza; ~**-wing**
adj (POL) di destra

rigid ['rɪdʒɪd] adj rigido(a); (principle)
rigoroso(a)

rigmarole ['rɪgmərəul] n tiritera,
commedia

rile [raɪl] vt irritare, seccare

rim [rɪm] n orlo; (of spectacles)
montatura; (of wheel) cerchione m

rind [raɪnd] n (of bacon) cotenna; (of
lemon etc) scorza

ring [rɪŋ] (pt rang, pp rung) n anello;
(of people, objects) cerchio; (of spies)
giro; (of smoke etc) spirale m; (arena)
pista, arena; (for boxing) ring m;
(sound of bell) scampanio ♦ vi (person,
bell, telephone) suonare; (also: ~ out:
voice, words) risuonare; (TEL) telefonare;
(ears) fischiare ♦ vt (BRIT: TEL) telefonare
a; (bell, doorbell) suonare; **to give sb a
~** (BRIT: TEL) dare un colpo di telefono a
qn; ~ **back** vt, vi (TEL) richiamare; ~
off (BRIT) vi (TEL) mettere giù,
riattaccare; ~ **up** (BRIT) vt (TEL)
telefonare a; ~**ing** n (of bell)
scampanio; (of telephone) squillo; (in
ears) ronzio; ~**ing tone** n (TEL)
segnale m di libero; ~**leader** n (of
gang) capobanda m

ringlets ['rɪŋlɪts] npl boccoli mpl

ring road (BRIT) n raccordo anulare

rink [rɪŋk] n (also: ice ~) pista di
pattinaggio

rinse [rɪns] n risciacquatura; (hair tint)
cachet m inv ♦ vt sciacquare

riot ['raɪət] n sommossa, tumulto; (of
colours) orgia ♦ vi tumultuare; **to run
~** creare disordine; ~**ous** adj
tumultuoso(a); (living) sfrenato(a);
(party) scatenato(a)

rip [rɪp] n strappo ♦ vt strappare ♦ vi
strapparsi; ~**cord** n cavo di sfilamento

ripe [raɪp] adj (fruit, grain) maturo(a);
(cheese) stagionato(a); ~**n** vt maturare
♦ vi maturarsi

ripple ['rɪpl] n increspamento,
ondulazione f; mormorio ♦ vi
incresparsi

rise [raɪz] (pt rose, pp risen) n (slope)
salita, pendio; (hill) altura; (increase: in
wages: BRIT) aumento; (: in prices,
temperature) rialzo, aumento; (fig: to
power etc) ascesa ♦ vi alzarsi, levarsi;
(prices) aumentare; (waters, river)
crescere; (sun, wind, person: from chair,
bed) levarsi; (also: ~ up: building)
ergersi; (: rebel) insorgere; ribellarsi; (in
rank) salire; **to give ~ to** provocare,

dare origine a; **to ~ to the occasion** essere all'altezza; **risen** ['rɪzn] *pp of* **rise; rising** *adj (increasing: number)* sempre crescente; (: *prices)* in aumento; *(tide)* montante; *(sun, moon)* nascente, che sorge

risk [rɪsk] *n* rischio; pericolo ♦ *vt* rischiare; **to take** *or* **run the ~ of doing** correre il rischio di fare; **at one's own ~** a proprio rischio e pericolo; **~y** *adj* rischioso(a)

risqué ['ri:skeɪ] *adj (joke)* spinto(a)

rissole ['rɪsəʊl] *n* crocchetta

rite [raɪt] *n* rito; **last ~s** l'estrema unzione

ritual ['rɪtjʊəl] *adj* rituale ♦ *n* rituale *m*

rival ['raɪvl] *n* rivale *m/f*; *(in business)* concorrente *m/f* ♦ *adj* rivale; che fa concorrenza ♦ *vt* essere in concorrenza con; **to ~ sb/sth in** competere con qn/qc in; **~ry** *n* rivalità; concorrenza

river ['rɪvə*] *n* fiume *m* ♦ *cpd (port, traffic)* fluviale; **up/down ~** a monte/valle; **~bank** *n* argine *m*; **~bed** *n* letto di fiume

rivet ['rɪvɪt] *n* rivetto, ribattino ♦ *vt (fig)* concentrare, fissare

Riviera [rɪvɪ'eərə] *n*: **the (French) ~** la Costa Azzurra; **the Italian ~** la Riviera

road [rəʊd] *n* strada; *(small)* cammino; *(in town)* via ♦ *cpd* stradale; **major/minor ~** strada con/senza diritto di precedenza; **~ accident** *n* incidente stradale; **~block** *n* blocco stradale; **~hog** *n* guidatore *m* egoista e spericolato; **~ map** *n* carta stradale; **~ rage** *n* comportamento aggressivo al volante; **~ safety** *n* sicurezza sulle strade; **~side** *n* margine *m* della strada; **~sign** *n* cartello stradale; **~ user** *n* chi usa la strada; **~way** *n* carreggiata; **~works** *npl* lavori *mpl* stradali; **~worthy** *adj* in buono stato di marcia

roam [rəʊm] *vi* errare, vagabondare

roar [rɔ:*] *n* ruggito; *(of crowd)* tumulto; *(of thunder, storm)* muggito;

(of laughter) scoppio ♦ *vi* ruggire; tumultuare; muggire; **to ~ with laughter** scoppiare dalle risa; **to do a ~ing trade** fare affari d'oro

roast [rəʊst] *n* arrosto ♦ *vt* arrostire; *(coffee)* tostare, torrefare; **~ beef** *n* arrosto di manzo

rob [rɔb] *vt (person)* rubare; *(bank)* svaligiare; **to ~ sb of sth** derubare qn di qc; *(fig: deprive)* privare qn di qc; **~ber** *n* ladro; *(armed)* rapinatore *m*; **~bery** *n* furto; rapina

robe [rəʊb] *n (for ceremony etc)* abito; *(also: bath ~)* accappatoio; *(us: also: lap ~)* coperta

robin ['rɔbɪn] *n* pettirosso

robot ['rəʊbɔt] *n* robot *m inv*

robust [rəʊ'bʌst] *adj* robusto(a); *(economy)* solido(a)

rock [rɔk] *n (substance)* roccia; *(boulder)* masso; roccia; *(in sea)* scoglio; *(us: pebble)* sassolino; *(BRIT: sweet)* zucchero candito ♦ *vt (swing gently: cradle)* dondolare; (: *child)* cullare; *(shake)* scrollare, far tremare ♦ *vi* dondolarsi; scrollarsi, tremare; **on the ~s** *(drink)* col ghiaccio; *(marriage etc)* in crisi; **~ and roll** *n* rock and roll *m*; **~-bottom** *adj* bassissimo(a); **~ery** *n* giardino roccioso

rocket ['rɔkɪt] *n* razzo

rock fall *n* parete *f* della roccia

rocking ['rɔkɪŋ]: **~ chair** *n* sedia a dondolo; **~ horse** *n* cavallo a dondolo

rocky ['rɔkɪ] *adj (hill)* roccioso(a); *(path)* sassoso(a); *(marriage etc)* instabile

rod [rɔd] *n (metallic, TECH)* asta; *(wooden)* bacchetta; *(also: fishing ~)* canna da pesca

rode [rəʊd] *pt of* **ride**

rodent ['rəʊdnt] *n* roditore *m*

rodeo ['rəʊdɪəʊ] *n* rodeo

roe [rəʊ] *n (species: also: ~ deer)* capriolo; *(of fish, also: hard ~)* uova *fpl* di pesce; **soft ~** latte *m* di pesce

rogue [rəʊg] *n* mascalzone *m*

role [rəʊl] n ruolo

roll [rəʊl] n rotolo; (of banknotes) mazzo; (also: bread ~) panino; (register) lista; (sound: of drums etc) rullo ♦ vt rotolare; (also: ~ up: string) aggomitolare; (also: ~ up: sleeves) rimboccare; (cigarettes) arrotolare ♦ vi (eyes) roteare; (cheese: also: ~ out: pastry) stendere; (lawn, road etc) spianare ♦ vi rotolare; (wheel) girare; (drum) rullare; (vehicle: also: ~ along) avanzare; (ship) rollare; **~ about** or **around** vi rotolare qua e là; (person) rotolarsi; **~ by** (time) passare; **~ over** vi rivoltarsi; **~ up** (inf) vi (arrive) arrivare ♦ vt (carpet) arrotolare; **~ call** n appello; **~er** n rullo; (wheel) rotella; (for hair) bigodino; **~er blades** npl pattini mpl in linea; **~er coaster** n montagne fpl russe; **~er skates** npl pattini mpl a rotelle

rolling ['rəʊlɪŋ] adj (landscape) ondulato(a); **~ pin** n matterello; **~ stock** n (RAIL) materiale m rotabile

ROM [rɔm] n abbr (= read only memory) memoria di sola lettura

Roman ['rəʊmən] adj, n romano(a); **~ Catholic** adj, n cattolico(a)

romance [rə'mæns] n storia or avventura or film m inv romantico(a); (charm) poesia; (love affair) idillio

Romania [rəʊ'meɪnɪə] n = **Rumania**

Roman numeral n numero romano

romantic [rə'mæntɪk] adj romantico(a); sentimentale

Rome [rəʊm] n Roma

romp [rɔmp] n gioco rumoroso ♦ vi (also: ~ about) far chiasso, giocare in un modo rumoroso

rompers ['rɔmpəz] npl pagliaccetto

roof [ru:f] n tetto; (of tunnel, cave) volta ♦ vt coprire (con un tetto); **~ of the mouth** palato; **~ing** n materiale m per copertura; **~ rack** n (AUT) portabagagli m inv

rook [ruk] n (bird) corvo nero; (CHESS) torre f

room [ru:m] n (in house) stanza; (bed~, in hotel) camera; (in school etc) sala; (space) posto, spazio; **~s** npl (lodging) alloggio; **"~s to let"** (BRIT), **"~s for rent"** (US) "si affittano camere"; **there is ~ for improvement** si potrebbe migliorare; **~ing house** (US) n casa in cui si affittano camere o appartamentini ammobiliati; **~mate** n compagno/a di stanza; **~ service** n servizio da camera; **~y** adj spazioso(a); (garment) ampio(a)

roost [ru:st] vi appollaiarsi

rooster ['ru:stə*] n gallo

root [ru:t] n radice f ♦ vi (plant, belief) attecchire; **~ about** vi (fig) frugare; **~ for** vt fus fare il tifo per; **~ out** vt estirpare

rope [rəʊp] n corda, fune f; (NAUT) cavo ♦ vt (box) legare; (climbers) legare in cordata; (area: also: ~ off) isolare cingendo con cordoni; **to know the ~s** (fig) conoscere i trucchi del mestiere; **~ in** vt (fig) coinvolgere; **~ ladder** n scala a corda

rosary ['rəʊzərɪ] n rosario; roseto

rose [rəʊz] pt of **rise** ♦ n rosa; (also: ~ bush) rosaio; (on watering can) rosetta

rosé ['rəʊzeɪ] n vino rosato

rosebud ['rəʊzbʌd] n bocciolo di rosa

rosebush ['rəʊzbʊʃ] n rosaio

rosemary ['rəʊzmərɪ] n rosmarino

rosette [rəʊ'zet] n coccarda

roster ['rɔstə*] n: **duty ~** ruolino di servizio

rostrum ['rɔstrəm] n tribuna

rosy ['rəʊzɪ] adj roseo(a)

rot [rɔt] n (decay) putrefazione f; (inf: nonsense) stupidaggini fpl ♦ vt, vi imputridire, marcire

rota ['rəʊtə] n tabella dei turni

rotary ['rəʊtərɪ] adj rotante

rotate [rəʊ'teɪt] vt (revolve) far girare; (change round: jobs) fare a turno ♦ vi (revolve) girare; **rotating** adj (movement) rotante

rotten ['rɔtn] adj (decayed) putrido(a), marcio(a); (dishonest) corrotto(a); (inf: bad) brutto(a); (: action) vigliacco(a); **to feel ~** (ill) sentirsi da cani

rouble ['ru:bl] (US **ruble**) n rublo

rouge [ru:ʒ] n belletto

rough [rʌf] adj (skin, surface) ruvido(a); (terrain, road) accidentato(a); (voice) rauco(a); (person, manner: coarse) rozzo(a), aspro(a); (: violent) brutale; (district) malfamato(a); (weather) cattivo(a); (sea) mosso(a); (plan) abbozzato(a); (guess) approssimativo(a) ♦ n (GOLF) macchia; **to ~ it** far vita dura; **to sleep ~** (BRIT) dormire all'addiaccio; **~age** n alimenti mpl ricchi in cellulosa; **~-and-ready** adj rudimentale; **~cast** n intonaco grezzo; **~ copy** n brutta copia; **~ly** adv (handle) rudemente, brutalmente; (make) grossolanamente; (speak) bruscamente; (approximately) approssimativamente; **~ness** n ruvidità; (of manner) rozzezza

roulette [ru:'let] n roulette f

Roumania [ru:'meɪnɪə] n = **Rumania**

round [raund] adj rotondo(a); (figures) tondo(a) ♦ n (BRIT: of toast) fetta; (duty: of policeman, milkman etc) giro; (: of doctor) visite fpl; (game: of cards, golf, in competition) partita; (of ammunition) cartuccia; (BOXING) round m inv; (of talks) serie f inv ♦ vt (corner) girare; (bend) prendere ♦ prep intorno a ♦ adv: **all ~** tutt'attorno; **to go the long way ~** fare il giro più lungo; **all the year ~** tutto l'anno; **it's just ~ the corner** (also fig) è dietro l'angolo; **~ the clock** ininterrottamente; **to go ~ to sb's house** andare a da qn; **go ~ the back** passi dietro; **enough to go ~** abbastanza per tutti; **~ of applause** applausi mpl; **~ of drinks** giro di bibite; **~ of sandwiches** sandwich m inv; **~ off** vt (speech etc) finire; **~ up** vt radunare; (criminals) fare una retata di

(prices) arrotondare; **~about** n (BRIT: AUT) rotatoria; (: at fair) giostra ♦ adj (route, means) indiretto(a); **~ers** npl (game) gioco simile al baseball; **~ly** adv (fig) chiaro e tondo; **~ trip** n (viaggio di) andata e ritorno; **~up** n raduno; (of criminals) retata

rouse [rauz] vt (wake up) svegliare; (stir up) destare; provocare; **rousing** adj (speech, applause) entusiastico(a)

route [ru:t] n itinerario; (of bus) percorso

routine [ru:'ti:n] adj (work) corrente, abituale; (procedure) solito(a) ♦ n (pej) routine f, tran tran m; (THEATRE) numero

rove [rəuv] vt vagabondare per

row¹ [rəu] n (line) riga, fila; (KNITTING) ferro; (behind one another: of cars, people) fila; (in boat) remata ♦ vi (in boat) remare, (as sport) vogare ♦ vt (boat) manovrare a remi; **in a ~** (fig) di fila

row² [rau] n (racket) baccano, chiasso; (dispute) lite f; (scolding) sgridata ♦ vi (argue) litigare

rowboat ['rəubəut] (US) n barca a remi

rowdy ['raudɪ] adj chiassoso(a); turbolento(a) ♦ n teppista m/f

rowing ['rəuɪŋ] n canottaggio; **~ boat** (BRIT) n barca a remi

royal ['rɔɪəl] adj reale; **R~ Air Force** n aeronautica militare britannica

royalty ['rɔɪəltɪ] n (royal persons) (membri mpl della) famiglia reale; (payment: to author) diritti mpl d'autore

r.p.m. abbr (= revolutions per minute) giri/min

R.S.V.P. abbr (= répondez s'il vous plaît) R.S.V.P.

Rt Hon. (BRIT) abbr (= Right Honourable) ≈ Onorevole

rub [rʌb] n: **to give sth a ~** strofinare qc; (sore place) massaggiare qc ♦ vt strofinare; massaggiare; (hands: also: **~ together**) sfregarsi; **to ~ sb up** (BRIT) or **~ sb the wrong way** (US) lisciare

qn contro pelo; ~ **off** vi andare via;
~ **off** on vt fus lasciare una traccia su;
~ **out** vt cancellare

rubber ['rʌbə*] n gomma; ~ **band** n
elastico; ~ **plant** n ficus m inv

rubbish ['rʌbɪʃ] n (from household)
immondizie fpl, rifiuti mpl; (fig: pej)
cose fpl senza valore; robaccia;
sciocchezze fpl; ~ **bin** (BRIT) n
pattumiera; ~ **dump** n (in town)
immondezzaio

rubble ['rʌbl] n macerie fpl; (smaller)
pietrisco

ruble ['ru:bl] (US) n = **rouble**

ruby ['ru:bɪ] n rubino

rucksack ['rʌksæk] n zaino

rudder ['rʌdə*] n timone m

ruddy ['rʌdɪ] adj (face) rubicondo(a);
(inf: damned) maledetto(a)

rude [ru:d] adj (impolite: person)
scortese, rozzo(a); (: word, manners)
grossolano(a), rozzo(a); (shocking)
indecente; ~**ness** n scortesia;
grossolanità

ruffle ['rʌfl] vt (hair) scompigliare;
(clothes, water) increspare; (fig: person)
turbare

rug [rʌg] n tappeto; (BRIT: for knees)
coperta

rugby ['rʌgbɪ] n (also: ~ **football**) rugby
m

rugged ['rʌgɪd] adj (landscape)
aspro(a); (features, determination)
duro(a); (character) brusco(a)

ruin ['ru:ɪn] n rovina ♦ vt rovinare; ~**s**
npl (of building, castle etc) rovine fpl,
ruderi mpl; ~**ous** adj rovinoso(a);
(expenditure) inverosimile

rule [ru:l] n regola; (regulation)
regolamento, regola; (government)
governo; (~r) riga ♦ vt (country)
governare; (person) dominare ♦ vi
regnare; decidere; (LAW) dichiarare; **as
a** ~ normalmente; ~ **out** vt escludere;
~**d** adj (paper) vergato(a); ~**r** n
(sovereign) sovrano(a); (for measuring)
regolo, riga; **ruling** adj (party) al

potere; (class) dirigente ♦ n (LAW)
decisione f

rum [rʌm] n rum m

Rumania [ruː'meɪnɪə] n Romania

rumble ['rʌmbl] n rimbombo;
brontolio ♦ vi rimbombare; (stomach,
pipe) brontolare

rummage ['rʌmɪdʒ] vi frugare

rumour ['ru:mə*] (US **rumor**) n voce f
♦ vt: **it is ~ed that** corre voce che

rump [rʌmp] n groppa; ~ **steak** n
bistecca di girello

rumpus ['rʌmpəs] (inf) n baccano;
(quarrel) rissa

run [rʌn] (pt **ran**, pp **run**) n corsa; (in
car) gita f (in macchina); (distance
travelled) percorso, tragitto; (SKI) pista;
(CRICKET, BASEBALL) meta; (series) serie f;
(THEATRE) periodo di rappresentazione;
(in tights, stockings) smagliatura ♦ vt
(distance) correre; (operate: business)
gestire, dirigere; (: competition, course)
organizzare; (: hotel) gestire; (: house)
governare; (COMPUT) eseguire; (water,
bath) far scorrere; (force through: rope,
pipe): **to** ~ **sth through** far passare qc
attraverso; (pass: hand, finger): **to**
~ **sth over** passare qc su; (PRESS:
feature) presentare ♦ vi correre; (flee)
scappare; (pass: road etc) passare;
(work: machine, factory) funzionare,
andare; (bus, train: operate) far servizio;
(: travel) circolare; (continue: play,
contract) durare; (slide: drawer; flow:
river, bath) scorrere; (colours, washing)
stemperarsi; (in election) presentarsi
candidato; (nose) colare; **there was a
~ on ...** c'era una corsa a ...; **in the
long** ~ a lungo andare; **on the** ~ in
fuga; **to** ~ **a race** partecipare ad una
gara; **I'll** ~ **you to the station** la
porto alla stazione; **to** ~ **a risk** correre
un rischio; ~ **about** or **around** vi
(children) correre qua e là; ~ **across** vt
fus (find) trovare per caso; ~ **away** vi
fuggire; ~ **down** vt (production) ridurre
gradualmente; (factory) rallentare

l'attività di; (AUT) investire; (criticize)
criticare; **to be ~ down** (person: tired)
essere esausto(a); **~ in** (BRIT) vt (car)
rodare, fare il rodaggio di; **~ into** vt
fus (meet: person) incontrare per caso;
(: trouble) incontrare, trovare; (collide
with) andare a sbattere contro; **~ off** vi
fuggire ♦ vt (water) far scolare; (copies)
fare; **~ out** vi (person) uscire di corsa;
(liquid) colare; (lease) scadere; (money)
esaurirsi; **~ out of** vt fus rimanere a
corto di; **~ over** vt (AUT) investire,
mettere sotto ♦ vt fus (revise) rivedere;
~ through vt fus (instructions) dare
una scorsa a; (rehearse: play) riprovare,
ripetere; **~ up** vt (debt) lasciar
accumulare; **to ~ up against**
(difficulties) incontrare; **~away** adj
(person) fuggiasco(a); (horse) in libertà;
(truck) fuori controllo

rung [rʌŋ] pp of **ring** ♦ n (of ladder)
piolo

runner ['rʌnə*] n (in race) corridore m;
(: horse) partente m/f; (on sledge)
pattino; (for drawer etc) guida; **~ bean**
(BRIT) n fagiolo rampicante; **~-up** n
secondo(a) arrivato(a)

running ['rʌnɪŋ] n corsa; direzione f;
organizzazione f; funzionamento m ♦ adj
(water) corrente; (commentary)
simultaneo(a); **to be in/out of the
~ for sth** essere/non essere più in lizza
per qc; **6 days ~** 6 giorni di seguito;
~ costs npl costi mpl d'esercizio; (of
car) spese fpl di mantenimento

runny ['rʌnɪ] adj che cola

run-of-the-mill adj solito(a), banale

runt [rʌnt] n (also pej) omuncolo m;
(ZOOL) animale m più piccolo del
normale

run-through n prova

run-up n: **~ to** (election etc) periodo
che precede

runway ['rʌnweɪ] n (AVIAT) pista (di
decollo)

rupture ['rʌptʃə*] n (MED) ernia

rural ['ruərəl] adj rurale

ruse [ru:z] n trucco

rush [rʌʃ] n corsa precipitosa; (hurry)
furia, fretta; (sudden demand): **~ for**
corsa a; (current) flusso; (of emotion)
impeto; (BOT) giunco ♦ vt mandare o
spedire velocemente; (attack: town etc)
prendere d'assalto ♦ vi precipitarsi;
~ hour n ora di punta

rusk [rʌsk] n biscotto

Russia ['rʌʃə] n Russia; **~n** adj russo(a)
♦ n russo/a; (LING) russo

rust [rʌst] n ruggine f ♦ vi arrugginirsi

rustic ['rʌstɪk] adj rustico(a)

rustle ['rʌsl] vi frusciare ♦ vt (paper) far
frusciare

rustproof ['rʌstpru:f] adj inossidabile

rusty ['rʌstɪ] adj arrugginito(a)

rut [rʌt] n solco; (ZOOL) fregola; **to get
into a ~** (fig) adagiarsi troppo

ruthless ['ru:θlɪs] adj spietato(a)

rye [raɪ] n segale f; **~ bread** n pane m
di segale

S, s

Sabbath ['sæbəθ] n (Jewish) sabato;
(Christian) domenica

sabotage ['sæbətɑ:ʒ] n sabotaggio
♦ vt sabotare

saccharin(e) ['sækərɪn] n saccarina

sachet ['sæʃeɪ] n bustina

sack [sæk] n (bag) sacco ♦ vt (dismiss)
licenziare, mandare a spasso; (plunder)
saccheggiare; **to get the ~** essere
mandato a spasso; **~ing** n tela di
sacco; (dismissal) licenziamento

sacrament ['sækrəmənt] n
sacramento

sacred ['seɪkrɪd] adj sacro(a)

sacrifice ['sækrɪfaɪs] n sacrificio ♦ vt
sacrificare

sad [sæd] adj triste

saddle ['sædl] n sella ♦ vt (horse)
sellare; **to be ~d with sth** (inf) avere
qc sulle spalle; **~bag** n (on bicycle)
borsa

sadistic [sə'dɪstɪk] *adj* sadico(a)

sadness ['sædnɪs] *n* tristezza

s.a.e. *n abbr* = **stamped addressed envelope**

safe [seɪf] *adj* sicuro(a); (*out of danger*) salvo(a), al sicuro; (*cautious*) prudente ♦ *n* cassaforte *f*; **~ from** al sicuro da; **~ and sound** sano(a) e salvo(a); (*just*) **to be on the ~ side** per non correre rischi; **~-conduct** *n* salvacondotto; **~-deposit** *n* (*vault*) caveau *m inv*; (*box*) cassetta di sicurezza; **~guard** *n* salvaguardia ♦ *vt* salvaguardare; **~keeping** *n* custodia; **~ly** *adv* sicuramente; sano(a) e salvo(a); prudentemente; **~ sex** *n* sesso sicuro

safety ['seɪftɪ] *n* sicurezza; **~ belt** *n* cintura di sicurezza; **~ pin** *n* spilla di sicurezza; **~ valve** *n* valvola di sicurezza

saffron ['sæfrən] *n* zafferano

sag [sæg] *vi* incurvarsi; afflosciarsi

sage [seɪdʒ] *n* (*herb*) salvia; (*man*) saggio

Sagittarius [sædʒɪ'tɛərɪəs] *n* Sagittario

Sahara [sə'hɑːrə] *n*: **the ~ (Desert)** il (deserto del) Sahara

said [sɛd] *pt, pp of* **say**

sail [seɪl] *n* (*on boat*) vela; (*trip*): **to go for a ~** fare un giro in barca a vela ♦ *vt* (*boat*) condurre, governare ♦ *vi* (*travel: ship*) navigare; (: *passenger*) viaggiare per mare; (*set off*) salpare; (*sport*) fare della vela; **they ~ed into Genoa** entrarono nel porto di Genova; **~ through** *vt fus* (*fig*) superare senza difficoltà; **~boat** (*US*) *n* barca a vela; **~ing** *n* (*sport*) vela; **to go ~ing** fare della vela; **~ing boat** *n* barca a vela; **~ing ship** *n* veliero; **~or** *n* marinaio

saint [seɪnt] *n* santo/a; **~ly** *adj* santo(a)

sake [seɪk] *n*: **for the ~ of** per, per amore di

salad ['sæləd] *n* insalata; **~ bowl** *n* insalatiera; **~ cream** (*BRIT*) *n* (tipo di) maionese *f*; **~ dressing** *n* condimento per insalata

salami [sə'lɑːmɪ] *n* salame *m*

salary ['sælərɪ] *n* stipendio

sale [seɪl] *n* vendita; (*at reduced prices*) svendita, liquidazione *f*; (*auction*) vendita all'asta; **"for ~"** "in vendita"; **on ~** in vendita; **on ~ or return** da vendere o rimandare; **~room** *n* sala delle aste; **~s assistant** (*US* **~s clerk**) *n* commesso/a; **~sman/swoman** (*irreg*) *n* commesso/a; (*representative*) rappresentante *m/f*

salmon ['sæmən] *n inv* salmone *m*

saloon [sə'luːn] *n* (*US*) saloon *m inv*, bar *m inv*; (*BRIT: AUT*) berlina; (*ship's lounge*) salone *m*

salt [sɔːlt] *n* sale *m* ♦ *vt* salare; **~ cellar** *n* saliera; **~water** *adj* di mare; **~y** *adj* salato(a)

salute [sə'luːt] *n* saluto ♦ *vt* salutare

salvage ['sælvɪdʒ] *n* (*saving*) salvataggio; (*things saved*) beni *mpl* salvati *or* recuperati ♦ *vt* salvare, mettere in salvo

salvation [sæl'veɪʃən] *n* salvezza; **S~ Army** *n* Esercito della Salvezza

same [seɪm] *adj* stesso(a), medesimo(a) ♦ *pron*: **the ~** la(lo) stesso(a), gli(le) stessi(e); **the ~ book** lo stesso libro di (*o* che); **at the ~ time** allo stesso tempo; **all** *or* **just the ~** tuttavia; **to do the ~ as sb** fare come qn; **the ~ to you!** altrettanto a te!

sample ['sɑːmpl] *n* campione *m* ♦ *vt* (*food*) assaggiare; (*wine*) degustare

sanction ['sæŋkʃən] *n* sanzione *f* ♦ *vt* sancire, sanzionare

sanctity ['sæŋktɪtɪ] *n* santità

sanctuary ['sæŋktjuərɪ] *n* (*holy place*) santuario; (*refuge*) rifugio; (*for wildlife*) riserva

sand [sænd] *n* sabbia ♦ *vt* (*also: ~ down*) cartavetrare

sandal ['sændl] *n* sandalo

sandbox ['sændbɔks] (*US*) *n* = **sandpit**

sandcastle ['sændkɑːsl] *n* castello di sabbia

sandpaper ['sændpeɪpə*] n carta
vetrata

sandpit ['sændpɪt] n (for children) buca
di sabbia

sandstone ['sændstəun] n arenaria

sandwich ['sændwɪtʃ] n tramezzino,
panino, sandwich m inv ♦ vt: **~ed
between** incastrato/a fra; **cheese/
ham ~** sandwich al formaggio/
prosciutto; **~ course** (BRIT) n corso di
formazione professionale

sandy ['sændɪ] adj sabbioso(a); (colour)
color sabbia inv, biondo(a) rossiccio(a)

sane [seɪn] adj (person) sano(a) di
mente; (outlook) sensato(a)

sang [sæŋ] pt of **sing**

sanitary ['sænɪtərɪ] adj (system,
arrangements) sanitario(a); (clean)
igienico(a); **~ towel** (US **~ napkin**) n
assorbente m (igienico)

sanitation [sænɪ'teɪʃən] n (in house)
impianti mpl sanitari; (in town)
fognature fpl; **~ department** (US) n
nettezza urbana

sanity ['sænɪtɪ] n sanità mentale;
(common sense) buon senso

sank [sæŋk] pt of **sink**

Santa Claus [sæntə'klɔːz] n Babbo
Natale

sap [sæp] n (of plants) linfa ♦ vt
(strength) fiaccare

sapling ['sæplɪŋ] n alberello

sapphire ['sæfaɪə*] n zaffiro

sarcasm ['sɑːkæzm] n sarcasmo

sardine [sɑː'diːn] n sardina

Sardinia [sɑː'dɪnɪə] n Sardegna

sash [sæʃ] n fascia

sat [sæt] pt, pp of **sit**

Satan ['seɪtən] n Satana m

satchel ['sætʃl] n cartella

satellite ['sætəlaɪt] adj satellite ♦ n
satellite m; **~ dish** n antenna
parabolica; **~ television** n televisione f
via satellite

satin ['sætɪn] n raso ♦ adj di raso

satire ['sætaɪə*] n satira

satisfaction [sætɪs'fækʃən] n

soddisfazione f

satisfactory [sætɪs'fæktərɪ] adj
soddisfacente

satisfy ['sætɪsfaɪ] vt soddisfare;
(convince) convincere; **~ing** adj
soddisfacente

Saturday ['sætədɪ] n sabato

sauce [sɔːs] n salsa; (containing meat,
fish) sugo; **~pan** n casseruola

saucer ['sɔːsə*] n sottocoppa m,
piattino

Saudi ['saʊdɪ]: **~ Arabia** n Arabia
Saudita; **~ (Arabian)** adj, n arabo(a)
saudita

sauna ['sɔːnə] n sauna

saunter ['sɔːntə*] vi andare a zonzo,
bighellonare

sausage ['sɒsɪdʒ] n salsiccia; **~ roll** n
rotolo di pasta sfoglia ripieno di salsiccia

sauté ['səʊteɪ] adj: **~ potatoes** patate
fpl saltate in padella

savage ['sævɪdʒ] adj (cruel, fierce)
selvaggio(a), feroce; (primitive)
primitivo(a) ♦ n selvaggio/a ♦ vt
attaccare selvaggiamente

save [seɪv] vt (person, belongings,
COMPUT) salvare; (money) risparmiare,
mettere da parte; (time) risparmiare;
(food) conservare; (avoid: trouble)
evitare; (SPORT) parare ♦ vi (also: **~ up**)
economizzare ♦ n (SPORT) parata ♦ prep
salvo, a eccezione di

saving ['seɪvɪŋ] n risparmio ♦ adj: **the
~ grace of** l'unica cosa buona di; **~s**
npl (money) risparmi mpl; **~s account**
n libretto di risparmio; **~s bank** n
cassa di risparmio

saviour ['seɪvjə*] (US **savior**) n
salvatore m

savour ['seɪvə*] (US **savor**) vt gustare;
~y adj (dish: not sweet) salato(a)

saw [sɔː] (pt **sawed**, pp **sawed** or
sawn) pt of **see** ♦ n (tool) sega ♦ vt
segare; **~dust** n segatura; **~mill** n
segheria; **sawn** pp of **saw**; **~n-off
shotgun** n fucile m a canne mozze

saxophone ['sæksəfəun] n sassofono

say [seɪ] (pt, pp **said**) n: to have one's ~ fare sentire il proprio parere; **to have** a or **some** ~ avere voce in capitolo ♦ vt dire; **could you** ~ **that again?** potrebbe ripeterlo?; **that goes without** ~**ing** va da sé; ~**ing** n proverbio, detto

scab [skæb] n crosta; (pej) crumiro/a

scaffold ['skæfəʊld] n (gallows) patibolo; ~**ing** n impalcatura

scald [skɔːld] n scottatura ♦ vt scottare

scale [skeɪl] n scala; (of fish) squama ♦ vt (mountain) scalare; ~**s** npl (for weighing) bilancia; **on a large** ~ su vasta scala; ~ **of charges** tariffa; ~ **down** vt ridurre (proporzionalmente)

scallop ['skɒləp] n (ZOOL) pettine m; (SEWING) smerlo

scalp [skælp] n cuoio capelluto ♦ vt scotennare

scalpel ['skælpl] n bisturi m inv

scampi ['skæmpɪ] npl scampi mpl

scan [skæn] vt scrutare; (glance at quickly) scorrere, dare un'occhiata a; (TV) analizzare; (RADAR) esplorare ♦ n (MED) ecografia

scandal ['skændl] n scandalo; (gossip) pettegolezzi mpl

Scandinavia [skændɪ'neɪvɪə] n Scandinavia; ~**n** adj, n scandinavo(a)

scant [skænt] adj scarso(a); ~**y** adj insufficiente; (swimsuit) ridotto(a)

scapegoat ['skeɪpgəʊt] n capro espiatorio

scar [skɑː] n cicatrice f ♦ vt sfregiare

scarce [skɛəs] adj scarso(a); (copy, edition) raro(a); **to make o.s.** ~ (inf) squagliarsela; ~**ly** adv appena; **scarcity** n scarsità, mancanza

scare [skɛə*] n spavento; panico ♦ vt spaventare, atterrire; **there was a bomb** ~ **at the bank** hanno evacuato la banca per paura di un attentato dinamitardo; **to** ~ **sb stiff** spaventare a morte qcn; ~ **off** or **away** vt mettere in fuga; ~**crow** n spaventapasseri m

inv; ~**d** adj: **to be** ~**d** aver paura

scarf [skɑːf] (pl **scarves** or ~**s**) n (long) sciarpa; (square) fazzoletto da testa, foulard m inv

scarlet ['skɑːlɪt] adj scarlatto(a); ~ **fever** n scarlattina

scarves [skɑːvz] npl of **scarf**

scary ['skɛərɪ] adj che spaventa

scathing ['skeɪðɪŋ] adj aspro(a)

scatter ['skætə*] vt spargere; (crowd) disperdere ♦ vi disperdersi; ~**brained** adj sbadato(a)

scavenger ['skævəndʒə*] n (person) accattone/a

scenario [sɪ'nɑːrɪəʊ] n (THEATRE, CINEMA) copione m; (fig) situazione f

scene [siːn] n (THEATRE, fig etc) scena; (of crime, accident) scena, luogo; (sight, view) vista, veduta; ~**ry** n (THEATRE) scenario; (landscape) panorama m; **scenic** adj scenico(a); panoramico(a)

scent [sent] n profumo; (sense of smell) olfatto, odorato; (fig: track) pista

sceptical ['skeptɪkl] (US **skeptical**) adj scettico(a)

sceptre ['septə*] (US **scepter**) n scettro

schedule ['ʃedjuːl, (US) 'skedjuːl] n programma m, piano; (of trains) orario; (of prices etc) lista, tabella ♦ vt fissare; **on** ~ in orario; **to be ahead of/behind** ~ essere in anticipo/ritardo sul previsto; ~**d flight** n volo di linea

scheme [skiːm] n piano, progetto; (method) sistema m; (dishonest plan, plot) intrigo, trama; (arrangement) disposizione f, sistemazione f; (pension ~ etc) programma m ♦ vi fare progetti; (intrigue) complottare; **scheming** adj intrigante ♦ n intrighi mpl, macchinazioni fpl

schism ['skɪzəm] n scisma m

scholar ['skɒlə*] n erudito/a; (pupil) scolaro/a; ~**ship** n erudizione f; (grant) borsa di studio

school [skuːl] n (primary, secondary) scuola; (university: US) università f inv ♦ cpd scolare, scolastico(a) ♦ vt (*animal*) addestrare; **~ age** n età scolare; **~bag** n cartella; **~book** n libro scolastico; **~boy** n scolaro; **~children** npl scolari mpl; **~girl** n scolara; **~ing** n istruzione f; **~master** n (*primary*) maestro; (*secondary*) insegnante m; **~mistress** n maestra; insegnante f; **~teacher** n insegnante m/f, docente m/f; (*primary*) maestro/a

sciatica [sar'ætɪkə] n sciatica

science ['saɪəns] n scienza; **~ fiction** n fantascienza; **scientific** [-'tɪfɪk] adj scientifico(a); **scientist** n scienziato/a

scissors ['sɪzəz] npl forbici fpl

scoff [skɔf] vt tranguiare, ingozzare ♦ vi: **to ~ (at)** (*mock*) farsi beffe di

scold [skəuld] vt rimproverare

scone [skɔn] n focaccina da tè

scoop [sku:p] n mestolo; (*for ice cream*) cucchiaio dosatore; (*PRESS*) colpo giornalistico, notizia (in) esclusiva; **~ out** vt scavare; **~ up** vt tirare su, sollevare

scooter ['sku:tə*] n (*motor cycle*) motoretta, scooter m inv; (*toy*) monopattino

scope [skəup] n (*capacity: of plan, undertaking*) portata f; (: *of person*) capacità fpl; (*opportunity*) possibilità fpl

scorch [skɔtʃ] vt (*clothes*) strinare, bruciacchiare; (*earth, grass*) bruciare

score [skɔ:*] n punti mpl, punteggio; (*MUS*) partitura, spartito; (*twenty*) venti ♦ vt (*goal, point*) segnare, fare; (*success*) ottenere ♦ vi segnare; (*FOOTBALL*) fare un goal; (*keep score*) segnare i punti; **~s of** (*very many*) un sacco di; **on that ~** a questo riguardo; **to ~ 6 out of 10** prendere 6 su 10; **~ out** vt cancellare con un segno; **~board** n tabellone m segnapunti

scorn [skɔ:n] n disprezzo ♦ vt disprezzare

scornful ['skɔ:nful] adj sprezzante

Scorpio ['skɔ:pɪəu] n Scorpione m

scorpion ['skɔ:pɪən] n scorpione m

Scot [skɔt] n scozzese m/f

Scotch [skɔtʃ] n whisky m scozzese, scotch m

scot-free adv: **to get off ~** farla franca

Scotland ['skɔtlənd] n Scozia

Scots [skɔts] adj scozzese; **~man/woman** (*irreg*) n scozzese m/f

Scottish ['skɔtɪʃ] adj scozzese; **~ Parliament** n Parlamento scozzese

scoundrel ['skaundrl] n farabutto/a; (*child*) furfantello/a

scour ['skauə*] vt (*search*) battere, perlustrare

scout [skaut] n (*MIL*) esploratore m; (*also: boy ~*) giovane esploratore, scout m inv; **~ around** vi cercare in giro; **girl ~** (*us*) n giovane esploratrice f

scowl [skaul] vi accigliarsi, aggrottare le sopracciglia; **to ~** guardare torvo

scrabble ['skræbl] vi (*claw*): **to ~ (at)** graffiare, grattare; (*also: ~ around: search*) cercare a tentoni ♦ n: **S~** ® Scarabeo ®

scraggy ['skrægɪ] adj scarno(a), molto magro(a)

scram [skræm] (*inf*) vi filare via

scramble ['skræmbl] n arrampicata ♦ vi inerpicarsi; **to ~ out** etc uscire etc in fretta; **to ~ for** azzuffarsi per; **~d eggs** npl uova fpl strapazzate

scrap [skræp] n pezzo, pezzetto; (*fight*) zuffa; (*also: ~ iron*) rottami mpl di ferro, ferraglia ♦ vt demolire; (*fig*) scartare ♦ vi: **to ~ (with sb)** fare a pezzi (con qn); **~s** npl (*waste*) scarti mpl; **~book** n album m inv di ritagli; **~ dealer** n commerciante m di ferraglia

scrape [skreip] vt (*clean*) raschiare, grattare ♦ n: **to get into a ~** cacciarsi in un guaio; **~ through** vi farcela per un pelo; **~ together** vt (*money*) raggranellare; **~r** n raschietto

scrap: ~ heap n: **on the ~ heap** (*fig*) nel dimenticatoio; **~ merchant** (*BRIT*) n commerciante m di ferraglia; **~ paper** n cartaccia

scratch [skrætʃ] n graffio ♦ cpd:

~ team squadra raccogliticcia ♦ vt graffiare, rigare or grattare; (paint, car) graffiare; **to start from ~** cominciare or partire da zero; **to be up to ~** essere all'altezza

scrawl [skrɔːl] n scarabocchio ♦ vi scarabocchiare

scrawny ['skrɔːnɪ] adj scarno(a), pelle e ossa inv

scream [skriːm] n grido, urlo ♦ vi urlare, gridare

scree [skriː] n ghiaione m

screech [skriːtʃ] vi stridere

screen [skriːn] n schermo; (fig) muro, cortina, velo ♦ vt schermare, fare schermo a; (from the wind etc) riparare; (film) proiettare; (book) adattare per lo schermo; (candidates etc) selezionare; **~ing** n (MED) dépistage m inv; **~play** n sceneggiatura; **~ saver** n (COMPUT) screen saver m inv

screw [skruː] n vite f ♦ vt avvitare; **~ up** vt (paper etc) spiegazzare; (inf: ruin) rovinare; **to ~ up one's eyes** strizzare gli occhi; **~driver** n cacciavite m

scribble ['skrɪbl] n scarabocchio ♦ vt scribacchiare in fretta ♦ vi scarabocchiare

script [skrɪpt] n (CINEMA etc) copione m; (in exam) elaborato or compito d'esame

scripture(s) ['skrɪptʃə(z)] n(pl) sacre Scritture fpl

scroll [skrəul] n rotolo di carta

scrounge [skraundʒ] (inf) vt: **to ~ sth (off or from sb)** scroccare qc (a qn) ♦ n: **on the ~** a sbafo

scrub [skrʌb] n (land) boscaglia ♦ vt pulire strofinando; (reject) annullare

scruff [skrʌf] n: **by the ~ of the neck** per la collottola

scruffy ['skrʌfɪ] adj sciatto(a)

scrum(mage) ['skrʌm(ɪdʒ)] n mischia

scruple ['skruːpl] n scrupolo

scrutiny ['skruːtɪnɪ] n esame m accurato

scuff [skʌf] vt (shoes) consumare

strascicando

scuffle ['skʌfl] n baruffa, tafferuglio

sculptor ['skʌlptə*] n scultore m

sculpture ['skʌlptʃə*] n scultura

scum [skʌm] n schiuma; (pej: people) feccia

scupper ['skʌpə*] (BRIT: inf) vt far naufragare

scurry ['skʌrɪ] vi sgambare, affrettarsi; **~ off** vi andarsene a tutta velocità

scuttle ['skʌtl] n (also: **coal ~**) secchio del carbone ♦ vt (ship) autoaffondare ♦ vi (scamper): **to ~ away, ~ off** darsela a gambe, scappare

scythe [saɪð] n falce f

SDP (BRIT) n abbr = **Social Democratic Party**

sea [siː] n mare m ♦ cpd marino(a), del mare; (bird, fish) di mare; (route, transport) marittimo(a); **by ~** (travel) per mare; **on the ~** (boat) in mare; (town) di mare; **to be all at ~** (fig) non sapere che pesci pigliare; **out to ~** al largo; (out) **at ~** in mare; **~board** n costa; **~food** n frutti mpl di mare; **~ front** n lungomare m; **~gull** n gabbiano

seal [siːl] n (animal) foca; (stamp) sigillo; (impression) impronta del sigillo ♦ vt sigillare; **~ off** vt (close) sigillare; (forbid entry to) bloccare l'accesso a

sea level n livello del mare

seam [siːm] n cucitura; (of coal) filone m

seaman ['siːmən] (irreg) n marinaio

seance ['seɪɔns] n seduta spiritica

seaplane ['siːpleɪn] n idrovolante m

seaport ['siːpɔːt] n porto di mare

search [səːtʃ] n ricerca; (LAW: at sb's home) perquisizione f ♦ vt frugare ♦ vi: **to ~ for** ricercare; **in ~ of** alla ricerca di; **~ through** vt fus frugare; **~ engine** n (COMPUT) motore m di ricerca; **~ing** adj minuzioso(a); penetrante; **~light** n proiettore m; **~ party** n squadra di soccorso; **~ warrant** n mandato di perquisizione

seashore ['siːʃɔː*] n spiaggia

seasick ['si:sɪk] *adj* che soffre il mal di mare

seaside ['si:saɪd] *n* spiaggia; ~ **resort** *n* stazione *f* balneare

season ['si:zn] *n* stagione *f* ♦ *vt* condire, insaporire; ~**al** *adj* stagionale; ~**ed** *adj* (*fig*) con esperienza; ~**ing** *n* condimento; ~ **ticket** *n* abbonamento

seat [si:t] *n* sedile *m*; (*in bus, train: place*) posto; (*PARLIAMENT*) seggio; (*buttocks*) didietro; (*of trousers*) fondo ♦ *vt* far sedere; (*have room for*) avere o essere fornito(a) di posti a sedere per; **to be** ~**ed** essere seduto(a); ~ **belt** *n* cintura di sicurezza

sea water *n* acqua di mare

seaweed ['si:wi:d] *n* alghe *fpl*

seaworthy ['si:wə:ðɪ] *adj* atto(a) alla navigazione

sec. *abbr* = **second(s)**

secluded [sɪ'klu:dɪd] *adj* isolato(a), appartato(a)

seclusion [sɪ'klu:ʒən] *n* isolamento

second¹ [sɪ'kɔnd] (*BRIT*) *vt* (*worker*) distaccare

second² ['sɛkənd] *num* secondo(a) ♦ *adv* (*in race etc*) al secondo posto ♦ *n* (*unit of time*) secondo; (*AUT: also*: ~ *gear*) seconda; (*COMM: imperfect*) scarto; (*BRIT: SCOL: degree*) laurea con punteggio discreto ♦ *vt* (*motion*) appoggiare; ~**ary** *adj* secondario(a); ~**ary school** *n* scuola secondaria; ~**class** *adj* di seconda classe ♦ *adv* in seconda classe; ~**er** *n* sostenitore/trice; ~**hand** *adj* di seconda mano, usato(a); ~ **hand** *n* (*on clock*) lancetta dei secondi; ~**ly** *adv* in secondo luogo; ~**rate** *adj* scadente; ~ **thoughts** *npl* ripensamenti *mpl*; **on** ~ **thoughts** (*BRIT*) *or* **thought** (*US*) ripensandoci bene

secrecy ['si:krəsɪ] *n* segretezza

secret ['si:krɪt] *adj* segreto(a) ♦ *n* segreto; **in** ~ in segreto

secretarial [sɛkrɪ'tɛərɪəl] *adj* di segretario(a)

secretariat [sɛkrɪ'tɛərɪət] *n* segretariato

secretary ['sɛkrətrɪ] *n* segretario/a; **S~ of State (for)** (*BRIT: POL*) ministro (di)

secretive ['si:krətɪv] *adj* riservato(a)

sect [sɛkt] *n* setta; ~**arian** [-'tɛərɪən] *adj* settario(a)

section ['sɛkʃən] *n* sezione *f*

sector ['sɛktə*] *n* settore *m*

secure [sɪ'kjuə*] *adj* sicuro(a); (*firmly fixed*) assicurato(a), ben fermato(a); (*in safe place*) al sicuro ♦ *vt* (*fix*) fissare, assicurare; (*get*) ottenere, assicurarsi

security [sɪ'kjuərɪtɪ] *n* sicurezza; (*for loan*) garanzia

sedate [sɪ'deɪt] *adj* posato(a); calmo(a) ♦ *vt* calmare

sedation [sɪ'deɪʃən] *n* (*MED*) effetto dei sedativi

sedative ['sɛdɪtɪv] *n* sedativo, calmante *m*

seduce [sɪ'dju:s] *vt* sedurre; **seduction** [-'dʌkʃən] *n* seduzione *f*; **seductive** [-'dʌktɪv] *adj* seducente

see [si:] (*pt* **saw**, *pp* **seen**) *vt* vedere; (*accompany*): **to** ~ **sb to the door** accompagnare qn alla porta ♦ *vi* vedere; (*understand*) capire ♦ *n* sede *f* vescovile; **to** ~ **that** (*ensure*) badare che + *sub*, fare in modo che + *sub*; ~ **you soon!** a presto!; ~ **about** *vt fus* occuparsi di; ~ **off** *vt* salutare alla partenza; ~ **through** *vt* portare a termine ♦ *vt fus* non lasciarsi ingannare da; ~ **to** *vt fus* occuparsi di

seed [si:d] *n* seme *m*; (*fig*) germe *m*; (*TENNIS etc*) testa di serie; **to go to** ~ fare seme; (*fig*) scadere; ~**ling** *n* piantina di semenzaio; ~**y** *adj* (*shabby: person*) sciatto(a); (: *place*) cadente

seeing ['si:ɪŋ] *conj*: ~ (**that**) visto che

seek [si:k] (*pt, pp* **sought**) *vt* cercare

seem [si:m] *vi* sembrare, parere; **there** ~**s to be** ... sembra che ci sia ...; ~**ingly** *adv* apparentemente

seen [si:n] *pp of* **see**

seep [si:p] vi filtrare, trapelare

seesaw ['si:sɔ:] n altalena a bilico

seethe [si:ð] vi ribollire; **to ~ with anger** fremere di rabbia

see-through adj trasparente

segregate ['sɛgrɪgeɪt] vt segregare, isolare

seize [si:z] vt (grasp) afferrare; (take possession of) impadronirsi di; (LAW) sequestrare; **~ (up)on** vt fus ricorrere a; **~ up** vi (TECH) grippare

seizure ['si:ʒə*] n (MED) attacco; (LAW) confisca, sequestro

seldom ['sɛldəm] adv raramente

select [sɪ'lɛkt] adj scelto(a) ♦ vt scegliere, selezionare; **~ion** [-'lɛkʃən] n selezione f, scelta

self [sɛlf] n: **the ~** l'io m ♦ prefix auto...; **~-assured** adj sicuro(a) di sé; **~-catering** (BRIT) adj in cui ci si cucina da sé; **~-centred** (US **~-centered**) adj egocentrico(a); **~-confidence** n sicurezza di sé; **~-conscious** adj timido(a); **~-contained** (BRIT) adj (flat) indipendente; **~-control** n autocontrollo; **~-defence** (US **~-defense**) n autodifesa; (LAW) legittima difesa; **~-discipline** n autodisciplina; **~-employed** adj che lavora in proprio; **~-evident** adj evidente; **~-governing** adj autonomo(a); **~-indulgent** adj indulgente verso se stesso(a); **~-interest** n interesse m personale; **~ish** adj egoista; **~ishness** n egoismo; **~less** adj dimentico(a) di sé, altruista; **~-pity** n autocommiserazione f; **~-portrait** n autoritratto; **~-possessed** adj controllato(a); **~-preservation** n istinto di conservazione f; **~-respect** n rispetto di sé, amor proprio; **~-righteous** adj soddisfatto(a) di sé; **~-sacrifice** n abnegazione f; **~-satisfied** adj compiaciuto(a) di sé; **~-service** adj: autoservizio, self-service m; **~-sufficient** adj autosufficiente; **~-taught** adj autodidatta

sell [sɛl] (pt, pp **sold**) vt vendere ♦ vi vendersi; **to ~ at** or **for 1000 lire** essere in vendita a 1000 lire; **~ off** vt svendere, liquidare; **~ out** vi: **to ~ out (of sth)** esaurire (qc); **the tickets are all sold out** i biglietti sono esauriti; **~-by date** n data di scadenza; **~er** n venditore/trice; **~ing price** n prezzo di vendita

Sellotape ® ['sɛləʊteɪp] (BRIT) n nastro adesivo, scotch ® m

selves [sɛlvz] npl of **self**

semaphore ['sɛməfɔ:*] n segnalazioni fpl con bandierine; (RAIL) semaforo (ferroviario)

semblance ['sɛmbləns] n parvenza, apparenza

semen ['si:mən] n sperma m

semester [sɪ'mɛstə*] (US) n semestre m

semi... ['sɛmɪ] prefix semi...; **~circle** n semicerchio; **~colon** n punto e virgola; **~detached (house)** (BRIT) n casa gemella; **~final** n semifinale f

seminar ['sɛmɪnɑ:*] n seminario

seminary ['sɛmɪnərɪ] n (REL) seminario

semiskilled ['sɛmɪ'skɪld] adj (worker) parzialmente qualificato(a); (work) che richiede una qualificazione parziale

semi-skimmed ['sɛmɪ'skɪmd] adj (milk) parzialmente scremato(a)

senate ['sɛnɪt] n senato; **senator** n senatore/trice

send [sɛnd] (pt, pp **sent**) vt mandare; **~ away** vt (letter, goods) spedire; (person) mandare via; **~ away for** vt fus richiedere per posta, farsi spedire; **~ back** vt rimandare; **~ for** vt fus mandare a chiamare, far venire; **~ off** vt (goods) spedire; (BRIT: SPORT: player) espellere; **~ out** vt (invitation) diramare; **~ up** vt (person, price) far salire; (BRIT: parody) mettere in ridicolo; **~er** n mittente m/f; **~-off** n: **to give sb a good ~-off** festeggiare la partenza di qn

senior ['si:nɪə*] adj (older) più vecchio(a); (of higher rank) di grado più elevato; **~ citizen** n persona anziana; **~ity** [-'ɔːriti] n anzianità

sensation [sen'seɪʃən] n sensazione f; **~al** adj sensazionale; (marvellous) eccezionale

sense [sens] n senso; (feeling) sensazione f, senso; (meaning) senso, significato; (wisdom) buonsenso ♦ vt sentire, percepire; **it makes ~** ha senso; **~less** adj sciocco(a); (unconscious) privo(a) di sensi

sensible ['sensibl] adj sensato(a), ragionevole

sensitive ['sensitiv] adj sensibile; (skin, question) delicato(a)

sensual ['sensjuəl] adj sensuale

sensuous ['sensjuəs] adj sensuale

sent [sent] pt, pp of **send**

sentence ['sentns] n (LING) frase f; (LAW: judgment) sentenza; (: punishment) condanna ♦ vt: **to ~ sb to death/to 5 years** condannare qn a morte/a 5 anni

sentiment ['sentimənt] n sentimento; (opinion) opinione f; **~al** [-'mentl] adj sentimentale

sentry ['sentri] n sentinella

separate [adj 'seprit, vb 'sepəreit] adj separato(a) ♦ vt separare ♦ vi separarsi; **~ly** adv separatamente; **~s** npl (clothes) coordinati mpl; **separation** [-'reiʃən] n separazione f

September [sep'tembə*] n settembre m

septic ['septik] adj settico(a); (wound) infettato(a); **~ tank** n fossa settica

sequel ['siːkwl] n conseguenza f; (of story) seguito; (of film) sequenza

sequence ['siːkwəns] n (series) serie f; (order) ordine m

sequin ['siːkwin] n lustrino, paillette f inv

serene [sə'riːn] adj sereno(a), calmo(a)

sergeant ['saːdʒənt] n sergente m; (POLICE) brigadiere m

serial ['siəriəl] n (PRESS) romanzo a puntate; (RADIO, TV) trasmissione f a puntate, serial m inv; **~ize** vt

pubblicare (or trasmettere) a puntate; **~ killer** n serial-killer m/f inv; **~ number** n numero di serie

series ['siəriːz] n inv serie f inv; (PUBLISHING) collana

serious ['siəriəs] adj serio(a), grave; **~ly** adv seriamente

sermon ['səːmən] n sermone m

serrated [si'reitid] adj seghettato(a)

serum ['siərəm] n siero

servant ['səːvənt] n domestico/a

serve [səːv] vt (employer etc) servire, essere a servizio di; (purpose) servire a; (customer, food, meal) servire; (apprenticeship) fare; (prison term) scontare ♦ vi (also TENNIS) servire; (be useful): **to ~ as/for/to do** servire da/per/per fare ♦ n (TENNIS) servizio; **it ~s him right** ben gli sta, se l'è meritata; **~ out, ~ up** vt (food) servire

service ['səːvis] n servizio; (AUT: maintenance) assistenza, revisione f ♦ vt (car, washing machine) revisionare; **the S~s** le forze armate; **to be of ~ to sb** essere d'aiuto a qn; **~ included/not included** servizio compreso/escluso; **~able** adj pratico(a), utile; **~ area** n (on motorway) area di servizio; **~ charge** (BRIT) n servizio; **~man** (irreg) n militare m; **~ station** n stazione f di servizio

serviette [səːvi'et] (BRIT) n tovagliolo

session ['seʃən] n (sitting) seduta, sessione f; (SCOL) anno scolastico (or accademico)

set [set] (pt, pp set) n (of cutlery etc) servizio; (RADIO, TV) apparecchio; (TENNIS) set m inv; (group of people) mondo, ambiente m; (CINEMA) scenario; (THEATRE: stage) scene fpl; (: scenery) scenario; (MATH) insieme m; (HAIRDRESSING) messa in piega ♦ adj (fixed) stabilito(a), determinato(a); (ready) pronto(a) ♦ vt (place) posare, mettere; (arrange) sistemare; (fix) fissare; (adjust) regolare; (decide: rules etc) stabilire, fissare ♦ vi (sun) tramontare; (jam, jelly) rapprendersi; (concrete) fare presa; **to be ~ on doing** essere deciso a fare; **to ~ on music** mettere in musica; **to ~ on fire** dare fuoco a; **to ~ free** liberare; **to ~ sth going** mettere in moto qc; **to ~ sail** prendere il mare; **to ~ about** vt fus (task) intraprendere, mettersi a; **~ aside** vt mettere da parte; **~ back** vt (in time): **to ~ back (by)** mettere indietro (di); (inf: cost): **it ~ me back £5** mi è costato la bellezza di 5 sterline; **~ off** vi partire ♦ vt (bomb) far scoppiare; (cause to start) mettere in moto; (show up well) dare risalto a; **~ out** vi partire ♦ vt (arrange) disporre; (state) esporre, presentare; **to ~ out to do** proporsi di fare; **~ up** vt (organization) fondare, costituire; **~back** n (hitch) contrattempo, inconveniente m; **~ menu** n menù m inv fisso

settee [se'ti:] n divano, sofà m inv

setting ['sɛtɪŋ] n (background) ambiente m; (of controls) posizione f; (of sun) tramonto; (of jewel) montatura f

settle ['sɛtl] vt (argument, matter) appianare; (accounts) regolare; (MED: calm) calmare ♦ vi (bird, dust etc) posarsi; (sediment) depositarsi; (also: ~ down) sistemarsi, stabilirsi; calmarsi; **to ~ for sth** accontentarsi di qc; **to ~ on sth** decidersi per qc; **~ in** vi sistemarsi; **~ up** vi: **to ~ up with sb** regolare i conti con qn; **~ment** n (payment) pagamento, saldo; (agreement) accordo; (colony) colonia; (village etc) villaggio, comunità f inv; **~r** n colonizzatore/trice

setup ['sɛtʌp] n (arrangement) sistemazione f; (situation) situazione f

seven ['sɛvn] num sette; **~teen** num diciassette; **~th** num settimo(a); **~ty** num settanta

sever ['sɛvə*] vt recidere, tagliare; (relations) troncare

several ['sɛvərl] adj, pron alcuni(e),

diversi(e); **~ of us** alcuni di noi

severance ['sɛvərəns] n (of relations) rottura; **~ pay** n indennità di licenziamento

severe [sɪ'vɪə*] adj severo(a); (serious) serio(a), grave; (hard) duro(a); (plain) semplice, sobrio(a); **severity** [sɪ'vɛrɪtɪ] n severità; gravità; (of weather) rigore m

sew [səu] (pt **sewed**, pp **sewn**) vt, vi cucire; **~ up** vt ricucire

sewage ['su:ɪdʒ] n acque fpl di scolo

sewer ['su:ə*] n fogna

sewing ['səuɪŋ] n cucitura; cucito; **~ machine** n macchina da cucire

sewn [səun] pp of **sew**

sex [sɛks] n sesso; **to have ~ with** avere rapporti sessuali con; **~ist** adj, n sessista m/f

sexual ['sɛksjuəl] adj sessuale

sexy ['sɛksɪ] adj provocante, sexy inv

shabby ['ʃæbɪ] adj malandato(a); (behaviour) vergognoso(a)

shack [ʃæk] n baracca, capanna

shackles ['ʃæklz] npl ferri mpl, catene fpl

shade [ʃeɪd] n ombra; (for lamp) paralume m; (of colour) tonalità f inv; (small quantity): **a ~ (more/too large)** un po' (di più/troppo grande) ♦ vt ombreggiare, fare ombra a; **in the ~** all'ombra

shadow ['ʃædəu] n ombra ♦ vt (follow) pedinare; **~ cabinet** (BRIT) n (POL) governo m ombra inv; **~y** adj ombreggiato(a), ombroso(a); (dim) vago(a), indistinto(a)

shady ['ʃeɪdɪ] adj ombroso(a); (fig: dishonest) losco(a), equivoco(a)

shaft [ʃɑ:ft] n (of arrow, spear) asta; (AUT, TECH) albero; (of mine) pozzo; (of lift) tromba; (of light) raggio

shaggy ['ʃægɪ] adj ispido(a)

shake [ʃeɪk] (pt **shook**, pp **shaken**) vt scuotere; (bottle, cocktail) agitare ♦ vi tremare; **to ~ one's head** (in refusal, dismay) scuotere la testa; **to ~ hands**

with sb stringere *or* dare la mano a qn; ~ **off** vt scrollare (via); (fig) sbarazzarsi di; ~ **up** vt scuotere; ~**n** pp of **shake**; **shaky** *adj* (hand, voice) tremante; (building) traballante

shall [ʃæl] *aux vb*: **I ~ go** andrò; ~ **I open the door?** apro io la porta?; **I'll get some, ~ I?** ne prendo un po', va bene?

shallow ['ʃæləu] *adj* poco profondo(a); (fig) superficiale

sham [ʃæm] *n* finzione *f*, messinscena; (jewellery, furniture) imitazione *f*

shambles ['ʃæmblz] *n* confusione *f*, baraonda, scompiglio

shame [ʃeim] *n* vergogna ♦ *vt* far vergognare; **it is a ~ (that/to do)** è un peccato (che + *sub*/fare); **what a ~!** che peccato!; ~**ful** *adj* vergognoso(a); ~**less** *adj* sfrontato(a); (immodest) spudorato(a)

shampoo [ʃæm'pu:] *n* shampoo *m inv* ♦ *vt* fare lo shampoo a; ~ **and set** *n* shampoo e messa in piega

shamrock ['ʃæmrɔk] *n* trifoglio (simbolo nazionale dell'Irlanda)

shandy ['ʃændɪ] *n* birra con gassosa

shan't [ʃɑ:nt] = **shall not**

shanty town ['ʃæntɪ-] *n* bidonville *f inv*

shape [ʃeip] *n* forma *f* ♦ *vt* formare; (statement) formulare; (sb's ideas) condizionare; **to take ~** prendere forma; ~ **up** *vi* (events) andare, mettersi; (person) cavarsela, **-shaped** *suffix*: **heart-shaped** a forma di cuore; ~**less** *adj* senza forma, informe; ~**ly** *adj* ben proporzionato(a)

share [ʃeə*] *n* (thing received, contribution) parte *f*; (COMM) azione *f* ♦ *vt* dividere; (have in common) condividere, avere in comune; ~ **out** *vi* dividere; ~**holder** *n* azionista *m/f*

shark [ʃɑ:k] *n* squalo, pescecane *m*

sharp [ʃɑ:p] *adj* (razor, knife) affilato(a); (point) acuto(a), acuminato(a); (nose, chin) aguzzo(a); (outline, contrast)

netto(a); (cold, pain) pungente; (voice) stridulo(a); (person: quick-witted) sveglio(a); (: unscrupulous) disonesto(a); (MUS): **C ~** do diesis ♦ *n* (MUS) diesis *m inv* ♦ *adv*: **at 2 o'clock** ~ alle due in punto; ~**en** *vt* affilare; (pencil) fare la punta a; (fig) acuire; ~**ener** *n* (also: **pencil ~ener**) temperamatite *m inv*; ~**eyed** *adj* dalla vista acuta; ~**ly** *adv* (turn, stop) bruscamente; (stand out, contrast) nettamente; (criticize, retort) duramente, aspramente

shatter ['ʃætə*] *vt* mandare in frantumi, frantumare; (fig: upset) distruggere; (: ruin) rovinare ♦ *vi* frantumarsi, andare in pezzi

shave [ʃeiv] *vt* radere, rasare ♦ *vi* radersi, farsi la barba ♦ *n*: **to have a ~!** che peccato!; ~**r** *n* (also: **electric ~r**) rasoio elettrico

shaving ['ʃeivɪŋ] *n* (action) rasatura; ~**s** *npl* (of wood etc) trucioli *mpl*; ~ **brush** *n* pennello da barba; ~ **cream** *n* crema da barba; ~ **foam** *n* = ~ **cream**

shawl [ʃɔ:l] *n* scialle *m*

she [ʃi:] *pron* ella, lei; ~-**cat** gatta; ~-**elephant** elefantessa

sheaf [ʃi:f] (*pl* **sheaves**) *n* covone *m*; (of papers) fascio

shear [ʃiə*] (*pt* ~**ed**, *pp* ~**ed** *or* **shorn**) *vt* (sheep) tosare; ~**s** *npl* (for hedge) cesoie *fpl*

sheath [ʃi:θ] *n* fodero, guaina; (contraceptive) preservativo

sheaves [ʃi:vz] *npl of* **sheaf**

shed [ʃed] (*pt*, *pp* **shed**) *n* capannone *m* ♦ *vt* (leaves, fur etc) perdere; (tears, blood) versare; (workers) liberarsi di

she'd [ʃi:d] = **she had**; **she would**

sheen [ʃi:n] *n* lucentezza

sheep [ʃi:p] *n inv* pecora; ~**dog** *n* cane *m* da pastore; ~**skin** *n* pelle *f* di pecora

sheer [ʃiə*] *adj* (utter) vero(a) (e proprio(a)); (steep) a picco, perpendicolare; (almost transparent) sottile ♦ *adv* a picco

sheet [ʃiːt] n (on bed) lenzuolo; (of paper) foglio; (of glass, ice) lastra; (of metal) foglio, lamina; **~ lightning** n lampo diffuso

sheik(h) [ʃeɪk] n sceicco

shelf [ʃelf] (pl **shelves**) n scaffale m, mensola

shell [ʃel] n (on beach) conchiglia; (of egg, nut etc) guscio; (explosive) granata; (of building) scheletro ♦ vt (peas) sgranare; (MIL) bombardare; **~ suit** n (lightweight) tuta di acetato; (heavier) tuta di trilobato

she'll [ʃiːl] = **she will; she shall**

shellfish [ʃelfɪʃ] n inv (crab etc) crostaceo; (scallop etc) mollusco; (pl: as food) crostacei; molluschi

shelter [ʃeltə*] n riparo, rifugio ♦ vt riparare, proteggere; (give lodging to) dare rifugio or asilo a ♦ vi ripararsi, mettersi al riparo; **~ed** adj riparato(a); **~ed housing** n alloggi dotati di strutture per anziani o handicappati

shelve [ʃelv] vt (fig) accantonare, rimandare; **~s** npl of **shelf**

shepherd [ʃepəd] n pastore m ♦ vt (guide) guidare; **~'s pie** (BRIT) n timballo di carne macinata e purè di patate

sheriff [ʃerɪf] (US) n sceriffo

sherry [ʃerɪ] n sherry m inv

she's [ʃiːz] = **she is; she has**

Shetland [ʃetlənd] n (also: the ~s, the ~ Isles) le isole Shetland, le Shetland

shield [ʃiːld] n scudo; (trophy) scudetto; (protection) schermo ♦ vt: **~ (from)** riparare (da), proteggere (da or contro)

shift [ʃɪft] n (change) cambiamento; (of workers) turno ♦ vt spostare, muovere; (remove) rimuovere ♦ vi spostarsi, muoversi; **~ work** n lavoro a squadre; **~y** adj ambiguo(a); (eyes) sfuggente

shilling [ʃɪlɪŋ] (BRIT) n scellino (= 12 old pence; 20 in a pound)

shimmer [ʃɪmə*] vi brillare, luccicare

shin [ʃɪn] n tibia

shine [ʃaɪn] (pt, pp **shone**) n splendore m, lucentezza ♦ vi splendere, brillare ♦ vt far brillare, far risplendere; (torch): **to ~ sth on** puntare qc verso

shingle [ʃɪŋgl] n (on beach) ciottoli mpl; **~s** n (MED) herpes zoster m

shiny [ʃaɪnɪ] adj lucente, lucido(a)

ship [ʃɪp] n nave f ♦ vt trasportare (via mare); (send) spedire (via mare); **~building** n costruzione f navale; **~ment** n carico; **~ping** n (ships) naviglio; (traffic) navigazione f; **~shape** adj in perfetto ordine; **~wreck** n relitto; (event) naufragio ♦ vt: **to be ~wrecked** naufragare, fare naufragio; **~yard** n cantiere m navale

shire [ʃaɪə*] (BRIT) n contea

shirt [ʃɜːt] n camicia; **in ~ sleeves** in maniche di camicia

shit [ʃɪt] (inf!) excl merda (!)

shiver [ʃɪvə*] n brivido ♦ vi rabbrividire, tremare

shoal [ʃəʊl] n (of fish) banco; (fig) massa

shock [ʃɔk] n (impact) urto, colpo; (ELEC) scossa; (emotional) colpo m, shock m inv; (MED) shock m ♦ vt colpire, scioccare; scandalizzare; **~ absorber** n ammortizzatore m; **~ing** adj scioccante, traumatizzante; scandaloso(a)

shoddy [ʃɔdɪ] adj scadente

shoe [ʃuː] (pt, pp **shod**) n scarpa; (also: horse~) ferro di cavallo ♦ vt (horse) ferrare; **~brush** n spazzola per scarpe; **~lace** n stringa; **~ polish** n lucido per scarpe; **~shop** n calzoleria; **~string** n (fig): **on a ~string** con quattro soldi

shone [ʃɔn] pt, pp of **shine**

shook [ʃuk] pt of **shake**

shoot [ʃuːt] (pt, pp **shot**) n (on branch, seedling) germoglio ♦ vt (game) cacciare, andare a caccia di; (person) sparare a; (execute) fucilare; (film) girare ♦ vi (with gun): **to ~** sparare (a), fare fuoco (su); (with bow): **to ~ (at)** tirare (su); (FOOTBALL) sparare,

tirare (forte); **~ down** vt (plane)
abbattere; **~ in/out** vi entrare/uscire
come una freccia; **~ up** vi (fig) salire
alle stelle; **~ing** n (shots) sparatoria;
(HUNTING) caccia; **~ing star** n stella
cadente

shop [ʃɒp] n negozio; (workshop)
officina ♦ vi (also: **go ~ping**) fare spese;
~ assistant (BRIT) n commesso/a;
~ floor n officina; (BRIT: fig) operai mpl,
maestranza fpl; **~keeper** n negoziante
m/f, bottegaio/a; **~lifting** n
taccheggio; **~per** n compratore/trice;
~ping n (goods) spesa, acquisti mpl;
~ping bag n borsa per la spesa;
~ping centre (US **~ping center**) n
centro commerciale; **~-soiled** adj
sciupato/a a forza di stare in vetrina;
~ steward (BRIT) n (INDUSTRY)
rappresentante m sindacale;
~ window n vetrina

shore [ʃɔː*] n (of sea) riva, spiaggia; (of
lake) riva ♦ vt: **to ~ (up)** puntellare; **on
~** a riva

shorn [ʃɔːn] pp of **shear**

short [ʃɔːt] adj (not long) corto(a);
(soon finished) breve; (person) basso(a);
(curt) brusco(a), secco(a); (insufficient)
insufficiente ♦ n (also: ~ film)
cortometraggio; **(a pair of) ~s** (i)
calzoncini; **to be ~ of sth** essere a
corto di or mancare di qc; **in ~** in
breve; **~ of doing** a meno che non si
faccia; **everything ~ of** tutto fuorché;
it is ~ for è l'abbreviazione or il
diminutivo di; **to cut ~** (speech, visit)
accorciare, abbreviare; **to fall ~ of**
venir meno a; non soddisfare; **to run
~ of** rimanere senza; **to stop ~**
fermarsi di colpo; **to stop ~ of** non
arrivare fino a; **~age** n scarsezza,
carenza; **~bread** n biscotto di pasta
frolla; **~change** vt **to ~change sb**
imbrogliare qn sul resto; **~circuit** n
cortocircuito; **~coming** n difetto;
~(crust) pastry (BRIT) n pasta frolla;
~cut n scorciatoia; **~en** vt accorciare,

ridurre; **~fall** n deficit m; **~hand** (BRIT)
n stenografia; **~hand typist** (BRIT) n
stenodattilografo/a; **~ list** (BRIT) n (for
job) rosa dei candidati; **~-lived** adj di
breve durata; **~ly** adv fra poco; **~-
sighted** (BRIT) adj miope; **~-staffed** adj
a corto di personale; **~-stay** adj
(car park) a tempo limitato; **~ story** n
racconto, novella; **~-tempered** adj
irascibile; **~-term** adj (effect) di or a
breve durata; (borrowing) a breve
scadenza; **~ wave** n (RADIO) onde fpl
corte

shot [ʃɒt] n, pp of **shoot** ♦ n sparo,
colpo; (try) prova; (FOOTBALL) tiro;
(injection) iniezione f; (PHOT) foto f inv;
like a ~ come un razzo; (very readily)
immediatamente; **~gun** n fucile m da
caccia

should [ʃud] aux vb: **I ~ go now**
dovrei andare ora; **he ~ be there
now** dovrebbe essere arrivato ora; **I
~ go if I were you** se fossi in te
andrei; **I ~ like to** mi piacerebbe

shoulder [ʃəuldə*] n spalla; (BRIT: of
road): **hard ~** banchina ♦ vt (fig)
addossarsi, prendere sulle proprie
spalle; **~ bag** n borsa a tracolla; **~
blade** n scapola

shouldn't [ʃudnt] = **should not**

shout [ʃaut] n urlo, grido ♦ vt gridare
♦ vi (also: ~ out) urlare, gridare;
~ down vt zittire gridando; **~ing** n
urli mpl

shove [ʃʌv] vt spingere; (inf: put): **to
~ sth in** ficcare qc in; **~ off** (inf) vi
sloggiare, smammare

shovel [ʃʌvl] n pala ♦ vt spalare

show [ʃəu] (pt **~ed**, pp **shown**) n (of
emotion) dimostrazione f,
manifestazione f; (semblance)
apparenza; (exhibition) mostra,
esposizione f; (THEATRE, CINEMA)
spettacolo ♦ vt far vedere, mostrare;
(courage etc) dimostrare, dar prova di;
(exhibit) esporre ♦ vi vedersi, essere
visibile; **for ~** per fare scena; **on ~**

(exhibits etc) esposto(a); **~ in** vt
(person) far entrare; **~ off** vi (pej)
esibirsi, mettersi in mostra ♦ vt (display)
mettere in risalto; (pej) mettere in
mostra; **~ out** vt (person)
accompagnare alla porta; **~ up** vi
(stand out) essere ben visibile; (inf: turn
up) farsi vedere ♦ vt mettere in risalto;
~ business n industria dello
spettacolo; **~down** n prova di forza

shower ['ʃauə*] n (rain) acquazzone m;
(of stones etc) pioggia; (also: **~bath**)
doccia ♦ vi fare la doccia ♦ vt: **to ~ sb
with** (gifts, abuse etc) coprire qn di;
(missiles) lanciare contro qn una
pioggia di; **to have a ~** fare la doccia;
~proof adj impermeabile

showing ['ʃəuɪŋ] n (of film) proiezione
f

show jumping n concorso ippico (di
salto ad ostacoli)

shown [ʃəun] pp of **show**

show-off (inf) n (person) esibizionista
m/f

showpiece ['ʃəupi:s] n pezzo forte

showroom ['ʃəurum] n sala
d'esposizione

shrank [ʃræŋk] pt of **shrink**

shrapnel ['ʃræpnl] n shrapnel m

shred [ʃrɛd] n (gen pl) brandello ♦ vt
fare a brandelli; (CULIN) sminuzzare,
tagliuzzare; **~der** n (vegetable ~der)
grattugia; (document ~der) distruttore
m di documenti

shrewd [ʃru:d] adj astuto(a), scaltro(a)

shriek [ʃri:k] n strillo ♦ vi strillare

shrill [ʃrɪl] adj acuto(a), stridulo(a),
stridente

shrimp [ʃrɪmp] n gamberetto

shrine [ʃraɪn] n reliquario; (place)
santuario

shrink [ʃrɪŋk] (pt shrank, pp shrunk)
vi restringersi; (fig) ridursi; (also:
~ away) ritrarsi ♦ vt (wool) far
restringere ♦ n (inf: pej) psicanalista m/
f; **to ~ from** rifuggire dal
fare qc; **~wrap** vt confezionare con

pellicola di plastica

shrivel ['ʃrɪvl] (also: **~ up**) vt
raggrinzare, avvizzire ♦ vi raggrinzirsi,
avvizzire

shroud [ʃraud] n lenzuolo funebre ♦ vt:
~ed in mystery avvolto(a) nel mistero

Shrove Tuesday ['ʃrəuv-] n martedì
m grasso

shrub [ʃrʌb] n arbusto; **~bery** n arbusti
mpl

shrug [ʃrʌg] n scrollata di spalle ♦ vt,
vi: **to ~ (one's shoulders)** alzare le
spalle, fare spallucce; **~ off** vt passare
sopra a

shrunk [ʃrʌŋk] pp of **shrink**

shudder ['ʃʌdə*] n brivido ♦ vi
rabbrividire

shuffle ['ʃʌfl] vt (cards) mescolare; **to
~ (one's feet)** strascicare i piedi

shun [ʃʌn] vt sfuggire, evitare

shunt [ʃʌnt] vt (RAIL: direct) smistare;
(: divert) deviare; (object) spostare

shut [ʃʌt] (pt, pp shut) vt chiudere ♦ vi
chiudersi, chiudere; **~ down** vt, vi
chiudere definitivamente; **~ off** vt
fermare, bloccare; **~ up** vi (inf: keep
quiet) stare zitto(a), fare silenzio ♦ vt
(close) chiudere; (silence) far tacere;
~ter n imposta; (PHOT) otturatore m

shuttle ['ʃʌtl] n spola, navetta; (space
~) navetta (spaziale); (also: ~ service)
servizio m navetta inv

shuttlecock ['ʃʌtlkɔk] n volano

shuttle diplomacy n la gestione dei
rapporti diplomatici caratterizzata da
frequenti viaggi e incontri dei
rappresentanti del governo

shy [ʃaɪ] adj timido(a)

Sicily ['sɪsɪlɪ] n Sicilia

sick [sɪk] adj (ill) malato(a); (vomiting):
to be ~ vomitare; (humour)
macabro(a); **to feel ~** avere la nausea;
to be ~ of (fig) averne abbastanza di;
~ bay n infermeria; **~en** vt nauseare
♦ vi: **to be ~ening for sth** (cold etc)
covare qc

sickle ['sɪkl] n falcetto

sick: ~ **leave** n congedo per malattia; ~**ly** adj malaticcio(a); (causing nausea) nauseante; ~**ness** n malattia; (vomiting) vomito; ~ **pay** n sussidio per malattia

side [saɪd] n lato; (of lake) riva; (team) squadra ♦ cpd (door, entrance) laterale ♦ vi: **to** ~ **with sb** parteggiare per qn, prendere le parti di qn; **by the** ~ **of** a fianco di; (road) sul ciglio di; ~ **by** ~ fianco a fianco; **from** ~ **to** ~ da una parte all'altra; **to take** ~**s (with)** schierarsi (con); ~**board** n credenza; ~**burns** (BRIT ~**boards**) npl (whiskers) basette fpl; ~ **effect** n (MED) effetto collaterale; ~**light** n (AUT) luce f di posizione; ~**line** n (SPORT) linea laterale; (fig) attività secondaria; ~**long** adj obliquo(a); ~ **order** n contorno (pietanza); ~ **show** n attrazione f; ~**step** vt (question) eludere; (problem) scavalcare; ~ **street** n strada laterale; ~**track** vt (fig) distrarre; ~**walk** (US) n marciapiede m; ~**ways** adv (move) di lato, di fianco

siding ['saɪdɪŋ] n (RAIL) binario di raccordo

siege [siːdʒ] n assedio

sieve [sɪv] n setaccio ♦ vt setacciare

sift [sɪft] vt passare al crivello; (fig) vagliare

sigh [saɪ] n sospiro ♦ vi sospirare

sight [saɪt] n (faculty) vista; (spectacle) spettacolo; (on gun) mira ♦ vt avvistare; **in** ~ in vista; **on** ~ a vista; **out of** ~ non visibile; ~**seeing** n giro turistico; **to go** ~**seeing** visitare una località

sign [saɪn] n segno; (with hand etc) segno, gesto; (notice) insegna, cartello ♦ vt firmare; (player) ingaggiare; ~ **on** vi (MIL) arruolarsi; (as unemployed) iscriversi sulla lista (dell'ufficio di collocamento) ♦ vt (MIL) arruolare; (employee) assumere; ~ **over** vt: **to** ~ **sth over to sb** cedere qc con scrittura legale a qn; ~ **up** vi (MIL) arruolarsi; (for course) iscriversi ♦ vt

(player) ingaggiare; (recruits) reclutare

signal ['sɪgnl] n segnale m ♦ vi segnalare, mettere la freccia ♦ vt (person) fare segno a; (message) comunicare per mezzo di segnali; ~**man** (irreg) n (RAIL) deviatore m

signature ['sɪgnətʃə*] n firma; ~ **tune** n sigla musicale

signet ring ['sɪgnət-] n anello con sigillo

significance [sɪg'nɪfɪkəns] n significato; importanza

significant [sɪg'nɪfɪkənt] adj significativo(a)

sign language n linguaggio dei muti

signpost ['saɪnpəʊst] n cartello indicatore

silence ['saɪləns] n silenzio ♦ vt tacere, ridurre al silenzio; ♦ n (on gun, BRIT: AUT) silenziatore m

silent ['saɪlnt] adj silenzioso(a); (film) muto(a); **to remain** ~ tacere, stare zitto; ~ **partner** n (COMM) socio inattivo

silhouette [sɪluː'et] n silhouette f inv

silicon chip ['sɪlɪkən-] n piastrina di silicio

silk [sɪlk] n seta ♦ adj di seta; ~**y** adj di seta

silly ['sɪlɪ] adj stupido(a), sciocco(a)

silt [sɪlt] n limo

silver ['sɪlvə*] n argento; (money) monete da 5, 10 or 50 pence; (also: ~ware) argenteria ♦ adj d'argento; ~ **paper** (BRIT) n carta argentata, (carta) stagnola; ~**plated** adj argentato(a); ~**smith** n argentiere m; ~**y** adj (colour) argenteo(a); (sound) argentino(a)

similar ['sɪmɪlə*] adj: ~ **(to)** simile (a); ~**ly** adv allo stesso modo; così pure

simmer ['sɪmə*] vi cuocere a fuoco lento

simple ['sɪmpl] adj semplice; **simplicity** [-'plɪsɪtɪ] n semplicità; **simply** adv semplicemente

simultaneous [sɪməl'teɪnɪəs] adj

simultaneo(a)

sin [sɪn] n peccato ♦ vi peccare

since [sɪns] adv da allora ♦ prep da (♦ conj (time) da quando; (because) poiché, dato che; ~ then, ever ~ da allora

sincere [sɪn'sɪə*] adj sincero(a); **~ly** adv: **yours ~ly** (in letters) distinti saluti; **sincerity** [-'serɪtɪ] n sincerità

sinew ['sɪnjuː] n tendine m

sing [sɪŋ] (pt **sang**, pp **sung**) vt, vi cantare

singe [sɪndʒ] vt bruciacchiare

singer ['sɪŋə*] n cantante m/f

singing ['sɪŋɪŋ] n canto

single ['sɪŋgl] adj solo(a), unico(a); (unmarried: man) celibe; (: woman) nubile; (not double) semplice ♦ n (BRIT: also: ~ ticket) biglietto di (sola) andata; (record) 45 giri m inv; ~s npl (TENNIS) singolo m; ~ **out** vt scegliere; (distinguish) distinguere; **~-bed** n letto singolo; **~-breasted** adj a un petto; **~ file** n: **in ~ file** in fila indiana; **~-handed** adv senza aiuto, da solo(a); **~-minded** adj tenace, risoluto(a); **~ parent** n (mother) ragazza f madre inv; (father) ragazzo m padre inv; **~ room** n camera singola; **~-track road** n strada a una carreggiata

singly ['sɪŋglɪ] adv separatamente

singular ['sɪŋgjulə*] adj (exceptional, LING) singolare ♦ n (LING) singolare m

sinister ['sɪnɪstə*] adj sinistro(a)

sink [sɪŋk] (pt **sank**, pp **sunk**) n lavandino, acquaio ♦ vt (ship) (fare) affondare, colare a picco; (foundations) scavare; (piles etc): **to ~ sth into** conficcare qc in ♦ vi affondare, andare a fondo; (ground etc) cedere, avvallarsi; **my heart sank** mi sentii venir meno; **~ in** vi penetrare

sinner ['sɪnə*] n peccatore/trice

sinus ['saɪnəs] n (ANAT) seno

sip [sɪp] n sorso ♦ vt sorseggiare

siphon ['saɪfən] n sifone m; **~ off** vt travasare (con un sifone)

sir [sə*] n signore m; S~ **John Smith** Sir John Smith; **yes** ~ sì, signore

sirloin ['sɜːlɔɪn] n controfiletto

sissy ['sɪsɪ] (inf) n femminuccia

sister ['sɪstə*] n sorella; (nun) suora; (BRIT: nurse) infermiera f caposala inv; **~-in-law** n cognata

sit [sɪt] (pt, pp **sat**) vi sedere, sedersi; (assembly) essere in seduta; (for painter) posare ♦ vt (exam) sostenere, dare; ~ **down** vi sedersi; ~ **in on** vt fus assistere a; ~ **up** vi tirarsi su a sedere; (not go to bed) stare alzato(a) fino a tardi

sitcom ['sɪtkəm] n abbr (= situation comedy) commedia di situazione; (TV) telefilm m inv comico d'interni

site [saɪt] n posto; (also: building ~) cantiere m ♦ vt situare

sit-in n (demonstration) sit-in m inv

sitting ['sɪtɪŋ] n (of assembly etc) seduta; (in canteen) turno; **~ room** n soggiorno

situated ['sɪtjueɪtɪd] adj situato(a)

situation [sɪtju'eɪʃən] n situazione f; (job) lavoro; (location) posizione f; "~s **vacant**" (BRIT) "offerte fpl di impiego"

six [sɪks] num sei; **~teen** num sedici; **~th** num sesto(a); **~ty** num sessanta

size [saɪz] n dimensioni fpl; (of clothing) taglia, misura; (of shoes) numero; (glue) colla; ~ **up** vt giudicare, farsi un'idea di; **~able** adj considerevole

sizzle ['sɪzl] vi sfrigolare

skate [skeɪt] n pattino; (fish: pl inv) razza ♦ vi pattinare; **~board** n skateboard m inv; **~r** n pattinatore/trice; **skating** n pattinaggio; **skating rink** n pista di pattinaggio

skeleton ['skelɪtn] n scheletro; ~ **staff** n personale m ridotto

skeptical ['skeptɪkl] (US) adj = **sceptical**

sketch [sketʃ] n (drawing) schizzo, abbozzo; (THEATRE) scenetta comica, sketch m inv ♦ vt abbozzare, schizzare; ~ **book** n album m inv per schizzi; **~y**

adj incompleto(a), lacunoso(a)

skewer ['skjuːə*] *n* spiedo

ski [skiː] *n* sci *m inv* ♦ *vi* sciare; ~ **boot** *n* scarpone *m* da sci

skid [skɪd] *n* slittamento ♦ *vi* slittare

skier ['skiːə*] *n* sciatore/trice

skiing ['skiːɪŋ] *n* sci *m*

ski jump *n* (ramp) trampolino; (event) salto con gli sci

skilful ['skɪlful] (US **skillful**) *adj* abile

ski lift ['skiːlɪft] *n* sciovia

skill [skɪl] *n* abilità *f inv*, capacità *f inv*; ~**ed** *adj* esperto(a); (worker) qualificato(a), specializzato(a); ~**ful** (US) *adj* = **skilful**

skim [skɪm] *vt* (milk) scremare; (glide over) sfiorare ♦ *vi*: **to ~ through** (fig) scorrere, dare una scorsa a; ~**med milk** *n* latte *m* scremato

skimp [skɪmp] *vt* (work: also: ~ **on**) fare alla carlona; (cloth: also) lesinare; ~**y** *adj* misero(a); striminzito(a); frugale

skin [skɪn] *n* pelle *f* ♦ *vt* (fruit etc) sbucciare; (animal) scuoiare, spellare; ~ **cancer** *n* cancro alla pelle; ~**-deep** *adj* superficiale; ~ **diving** *n* nuoto subacqueo; ~**ny** *adj* molto magra(a), pelle e ossa *inv*; ~**tight** *adj* (dress etc) aderente

skip [skɪp] *n* saltello, balzo; (BRIT: container) benna ♦ *vi* saltare; (with rope) saltare la corda ♦ *vt* saltare

ski pass *n* ski pass *m inv*

ski pole *n* racchetta (da sci)

skipper ['skɪpə*] *n* (NAUT, SPORT) capitano

skipping rope ['skɪpɪŋ-] (BRIT) *n* corda per saltare

skirmish ['skəːmɪʃ] *n* scaramuccia

skirt [skəːt] *n* gonna, sottana ♦ *vt* fiancheggiare, costeggiare; ~**ing board** (BRIT) *n* zoccolo

ski slope *n* pista da sci

ski suit *n* tuta da sci

skit [skɪt] *n* parodia; scenetta satirica

ski tow *n* sciovia, ski-lift *m inv*

skittle ['skɪtl] *n* birillo; ~**s** *n* (game)

(gioco dei) birilli *mpl*

skive [skaɪv] (BRIT: inf) *vi* fare il lavativo

skull [skʌl] *n* cranio, teschio

skunk [skʌŋk] *n* moffetta

sky [skaɪ] *n* cielo; ~**light** *n* lucernario; ~**scraper** *n* grattacielo

slab [slæb] *n* lastra; (of cake, cheese) fetta

slack [slæk] *adj* (loose) allentato(a); (slow) lento(a); (careless) negligente; ~**en** (also: ~**en off**) *vi* rallentare, diminuire ♦ *vt* allentare; (speed) diminuire; ~**s** *npl* (trousers) pantaloni *mpl*

slag heap [slæg-] *n* ammasso di scorie

slag off [slæg-] (BRIT: inf) *vt* sparlare di

slam [slæm] *vt* (door) sbattere; (throw) scaraventare; (criticize) stroncare ♦ *vi* sbattere

slander ['slɑːndə*] *n* calunnia; diffamazione *f*

slang [slæŋ] *n* gergo, slang *m*

slant [slɑːnt] *n* pendenza, inclinazione *f*; (fig) angolazione *f*, punto di vista; ~**ed** *adj* in pendenza, inclinato(a); (eyes) obliquo(a); ~**ing** *adj* = ~**ed**

slap [slæp] *n* manata, pacca; (on face) schiaffo ♦ *vt* dare una manata a; schiaffeggiare ♦ *adv* (directly) in pieno; ~ **a coat of paint on it** dagli una mano di vernice; ~**dash** *adj* negligente; (work) raffazzonato(a); ~**stick** *n* (comedy) farsa grossolana; ~**up** (BRIT) *adj*: **a** ~**up meal** un pranzo (or una cena) coi fiocchi

slash [slæʃ] *vt* tagliare; (face) sfregiare; (fig: prices) ridurre drasticamente, tagliare

slat [slæt] *n* (of wood) stecca; (of plastic) lamina

slate [sleɪt] *n* ardesia; (piece) lastra di ardesia ♦ *vt* (fig: criticize) stroncare, distruggere

slaughter ['slɔːtə*] *n* strage *f*, massacro; (of animal) macellare; (people) trucidare, massacrare

slave [sleɪv] *n* schiavo/a ♦ *vi* (also: ~ **away**) lavorare come uno schiavo;

~ry n schiavitù f; **slavish** adj servile; (copy) pedissequo(a)

slay [sleɪ] (pt **slew**, pp **slain**) vt (formal) uccidere

sleazy ['sliːzɪ] adj trasandato(a)

sledge [sledʒ] n slitta; **~hammer** n mazza, martello da fabbro

sleek [sliːk] adj (hair, fur) lucido(a), lucente; (car, boat) slanciato(a), affusolato(a)

sleep [sliːp] (pt, pp **slept**) n sonno ♦ vi dormire; **to go to ~** addormentarsi; **~ around** vi andare a letto con tutti; **~ in** vi (oversleep) dormire fino a tardi; **~er** (BRIT) n (RAIL: on track) traversina; (: train) treno di vagoni letto; **~ing bag** n sacco a pelo; **~ing car** n vagone m letto inv, carrozza f letto inv; **~ing partner** (BRIT) n (COMM) socio inattivo; **~ing pill** n sonnifero; **~less** adj: **a ~less night** una notte in bianco; **~walker** n sonnambulo/a; **~y** adj assonnato(a), sonnolento(a); (fig) addormentato(a)

sleet [sliːt] n nevischio

sleeve [sliːv] n manica; (of record) copertina

sleigh [sleɪ] n slitta

sleight [slaɪt] n: **~ of hand** gioco di destrezza

slender ['slendə*] adj snello(a), sottile; (not enough) scarso(a), esiguo(a)

slept [slept] pt, pp of **sleep**

slew [sluː] pt of **slay** ♦ vi (BRIT) girare

slice [slaɪs] n fetta ♦ vt affettare, tagliare a fette

slick [slɪk] adj (skilful) brillante; (clever) furbo(a) ♦ n (also: oil ~) chiazza di petrolio

slide [slaɪd] (pt, pp **slid**) n scivolone m; (in playground) scivolo; (PHOT) diapositiva; (BRIT: also: hair ~) fermaglio (per capelli) ♦ vt far scivolare ♦ vi scivolare; **~ rule** n regolo calcolatore; **sliding** adj (door) scorrevole; **sliding scale** n scala mobile

slight [slaɪt] adj (slim) snello(a), sottile;

(frail) delicato(a), fragile; (trivial) insignificante; (small) piccolo(a), n offesa, affronto; **not in the ~est** affatto, neppure per sogno; **~ly** adv lievemente, un po'

slim [slɪm] adj magro(a), snello(a) ♦ vi dimagrire; fare (o seguire) una dieta dimagrante

slime [slaɪm] n limo, melma; viscidume m

slimming ['slɪmɪŋ] adj (diet) dimagrante; (food) ipocalorico(a)

sling [slɪŋ] (pt, pp **slung**) n (MED) fascia al collo; (for baby) marsupio ♦ vt lanciare, tirare

slip [slɪp] n scivolata, scivolone m; (mistake) sbaglio n, sbaglio; (underskirt) sottoveste f; (of paper) striscia di carta; tagliando, scontrino ♦ vt (slide) far scivolare ♦ vi (slide) scivolare; (move smoothly): **to ~ into/out of** scivolare in/fuori da; (decline) declinare; **to ~ sth on/off** infilarsi/togliersi qc; **to give sb the ~** sfuggire qn; **a ~ of the tongue** un lapsus linguae; **~ away** vi svignarsela; **~ in** vt infilare ♦ vi (error) scivolare; **~ out** vi scivolare fuori; **~ up** vi sbagliarsi; **~ped disc** n spostamento delle vertebre

slipper ['slɪpə*] n pantofola

slippery ['slɪpərɪ] adj scivoloso(a)

slip road (BRIT) n (to motorway) rampa di accesso

slip-up n granchio (fig)

slipway ['slɪpweɪ] n scalo di costruzione

slit [slɪt] (pt, pp **slit**) n fessura, fenditura; (cut) taglio ♦ vt fendere; tagliare

slither ['slɪðə*] vi scivolare, sdrucciolare

sliver ['slɪvə*] n (of glass, wood) scheggia; (of cheese etc) fettina

slob [slɔb] (inf) n sciattone/a

slog [slɔg] (BRIT) n faticata f ♦ vi lavorare con accanimento, sgobbare

slogan ['sləʊgən] n motto, slogan m inv

slope [sləup] n pendio; (*side of mountain*) versante m; (*ski* ~) pista; (*of roof*) pendenza; (*of floor*) inclinazione f ♦ vi: **to ~ down** declinare; **to ~ up** essere in salita; **sloping** adj inclinato(a)

sloppy ['slɔpɪ] adj (*work*) tirato(a) via; (*appearance*) sciatto(a)

slot [slɔt] n fessura ♦ vt: **to ~ sth into** infilare qc in

sloth [sləuθ] n (*laziness*) pigrizia, accidia

slot machine n (*BRIT: vending machine*) distributore m automatico; (*for gambling*) slot-machine f inv

slouch [slautʃ] vi (*when walking*) camminare dinoccolato(a); **she was ~ing in a chair** era sprofondata in una poltrona

Slovenia [sləu'vi:nɪə] n Slovenia

slovenly ['slʌvənlɪ] adj sciatto(a), trasandato(a)

slow [sləu] adj lento(a), (*watch*): **to be** ~ essere indietro ♦ adv lentamente ♦ vi (*also*: ~ **down**, ~ **up**) rallentare; "**~**" (*road sign*) "rallentare"; **~ly** adv lentamente; **~ motion** n: **in ~ motion** al rallentatore

sludge [slʌdʒ] n fanghiglia

slug [slʌg] n lumaca; (*bullet*) pallottola; **~gish** adj lento(a); (*trading*) stagnante

sluice [slu:s] n chiusa

slum [slʌm] n catapecchia

slumber ['slʌmbə*] n sonno

slump [slʌmp] n crollo, caduta; (*economic*) depressione f, crisi f inv ♦ vi crollare

slung [slʌŋ] pt, pp of **sling**

slur [slə:*] n (*fig*): ~ (**on**) calunnia (su) ♦ vt pronunciare in modo indistinto

slush [slʌʃ] n neve f mista a fango; ~ **fund** n fondi mpl neri

slut [slʌt] n donna trasandata, sciattona

sly [slaɪ] adj (*smile, remark*) sornione(a); (*person*) falso(a)

smack [smæk] n (*slap*) pacca; (*on face*) schiaffo ♦ vt schiaffeggiare; (*child*)

picchiare ♦ vi: **to ~ of** puzzare di

small [smɔ:l] adj piccolo(a); the ~ (*BRIT*) npl piccola pubblicità; ~ **change** n moneta, spiccioli mpl; ~**holder** n piccolo proprietario; ~ **hours** npl: **in the ~ hours** alle ore piccole; ~**pox** n vaiolo; ~ **talk** n chiacchiere fpl

smart [smɑ:t] adj elegante; (*fashionable*) alla moda; (*clever*) intelligente, (*quick*) sveglio(a) ♦ vi bruciare; ~ **ads** npl carta intelligente; ~**en up** vi farsi bello(a) ♦ vt (*people*) fare bello(a); (*things*) abbellire

smash [smæʃ] n (*also*: ~-**up**) scontro, collisione f; (~ *hit*) successone m ♦ vt frantumare, fracassare; (*SPORT: record*) battere ♦ vi frantumarsi, andare in pezzi; ~**ing** (*inf*) adj favoloso(a), formidabile

smattering ['smætərɪŋ] n: **a ~ of** un'infarinatura di

smear [smɪə*] n macchia; (*MED*) striscio ♦ vt spalmare; (*make dirty*) sporcare; ~ **campaign** n campagna diffamatoria

smell [smɛl] (*pt, pp* **smelt** or **smelled**) n odore m; (*sense*) olfatto, odorato ♦ vt sentire (l')odore di ♦ vi (*food etc*): **to ~ (of)** avere odore (di); (*pej*) puzzare, avere un cattivo odore; ~**y** adj puzzolente

smile [smaɪl] n sorriso ♦ vi sorridere

smirk [smə:k] n sorriso furbo; sorriso compiaciuto

smog [smɔg] n smog m

smoke [sməuk] n fumo ♦ vt, vi fumare; ~**d** adj (*bacon, glass*) affumicato(a); ~**r** n (*person*) fumatore/trice; (*RAIL*) carrozza per fumatori; ~ **screen** n (*MIL*) cortina fumogena or di fumo; (*fig*) copertura; **smoking** n fumo; "**no smoking**" (*sign*) "vietato fumare"; **smoking compartment** (*BRIT*); **smoking car** (*US*) n scompartimento (per) fumatori; **smoky** adj fumoso(a); (*taste*) affumicato(a)

smolder ['sməuldə*] (*US*) vi = **smoulder**

smooth [smuːð] *adj* liscio(a); (*sauce*) omogeneo(a); (*flavour, whisky*) amabile; (*movement*) regolare; (*person*) mellifluo(a) ♦ *vt* (*also*: ~ **out**) lisciare, spianare; (: *difficulties*) appianare

smother ['smʌðə*] *vt* soffocare

smoulder ['smǝuldǝ*] (*US* **smolder**) *vi* covare sotto la cenere

smudge [smʌdʒ] *n* macchia; sbavatura ♦ *vt* imbrattare, sporcare

smug [smʌg] *adj* soddisfatto(a), compiaciuto(a)

smuggle ['smʌgl] *vt* contrabbandare; ~**r** *n* contrabbandiere/a; **smuggling** *n* contrabbando

smutty ['smʌtɪ] *adj* (*fig*) osceno(a), indecente

snack [snæk] *n* spuntino; ~ **bar** *n* tavola calda, snack bar *m inv*

snag [snæg] *n* intoppo, ostacolo imprevisto

snail [sneɪl] *n* chiocciola

snake [sneɪk] *n* serpente *m*

snap [snæp] *n* (*sound*) schianto, colpo secco; (*photograph*) istantanea ♦ *adj* improvviso(a) ♦ *vi* (*far*) schioccare; (*break*) spezzare di netto ♦ *vt* spezzarsi con un rumore secco; (*fig: person*) parlare con tono secco; to ~ **shut** chiudersi di scatto; ~ **at** *vt fus* (*subj: dog*) cercare di mordere; ~ **off** *vt* (*break*) spezzare; ~ **up** *vt* afferrare; ~**py** (*inf*) *adj* (*answer, slogan*) d'effetto; **make it** ~**py!** (*hurry up!*) sbrigati!, svelto!; ~**shot** *n* istantanea

snare [snɛǝ*] *n* trappola

snarl [snɑːl] *vi* ringhiare

snatch [snætʃ] *n* (*small amount*) frammento ♦ *vt* strappare (con violenza); (*fig*) rubare

sneak [sniːk] (*pt* (*US*) **snuck**) *vi*: to ~ **in/out** entrare/uscire di nascosto ♦ *vi* spione/a; to ~ **up on sb** avvicinarsi quatto quatto a qn; ~**ers** *npl* scarpe *fpl* da ginnastica

sneer [snɪǝ*] *vi* sogghignare; to ~ **at** farsi beffe di

sneeze [sniːz] *n* starnuto ♦ *vi* starnutire

sniff [snɪf] *n* fiutata, annusata ♦ *vi* tirare su col naso ♦ *vt* fiutare, annusare

snigger ['snɪgǝ*] *vi* ridacchiare, ridere sotto i baffi

snip [snɪp] *n* pezzetto; (*bargain*) (buon) affare *m*, occasione *f* ♦ *vt* tagliare

sniper ['snaɪpǝ*] *n* (*marksman*) franco tiratore *m*, cecchino

snippet ['snɪpɪt] *n* frammento

snob [snɔb] *n* snob *m/f inv*; ~**bery** *n* snobismo; ~**bish** *adj* snob *inv*

snooker ['snuːkǝ*] *n* tipo di gioco del biliardo

snoop ['snuːp] *vi*: to ~ **about** curiosare

snooze [snuːz] *n* sonnellino, pisolino ♦ *vi* fare un sonnellino

snore [snɔː*] *vi* russare

snorkel ['snɔːkl] *n* (*of swimmer*) respiratore *m* a tubo

snort [snɔːt] *n* sbuffo ♦ *vi* sbuffare

snout [snaut] *n* muso

snow [snǝu] *n* neve *f* ♦ *vi* nevicare; ~**ball** *n* palla di neve ♦ *vi* (*fig*) crescere a vista d'occhio; ~**bound** *adj* bloccato(a) dalle nevi; ~**drift** *n* cumulo di neve (ammucchiato dal vento); ~**drop** *n* bucaneve *m inv*; ~**fall** *n* nevicata; ~**flake** *n* fiocco di neve; ~**man** (*irreg*) *n* pupazzo di neve; ~**plough** (*US* ~**plow**) *n* spazzaneve *m inv*; ~**shoe** *n* racchetta da neve; ~**storm** *n* tormenta

snub [snʌb] *vt* snobbare ♦ *n* offesa, affronto; ~**-nosed** *adj* dal naso camuso

snuff [snʌf] *n* tabacco da fiuto

snug [snʌg] *adj* comodo(a); (*room, house*) accogliente, comodo(a)

snuggle ['snʌgl] *vi*: to ~ **up to sb** stringersi a qn

KEYWORD

so [sǝu] *adv* **1** (*thus, likewise*) così; **if** ~ se è così, quand'è così; **I didn't do it — you did** ~! non l'ho fatto io — sì che l'hai fatto!; ~ **do I**, ~ **am I** *etc*

anch'io; **it's 5 o'clock — ~ it is!** sono le 5 — davvero!; **I hope ~ it is** lo spero; **I think ~** penso di sì; **~ far** finora, fin qui; *(in past)* fino ad allora
2 *(in comparisons etc: to such a degree)* così; **~ big (that)** così grande (che); **she's not ~ clever as her brother** lei non è (così) intelligente come suo fratello
3: **~ much** *adj* tanto(a) ♦ *adv* tanto; **I've got ~ much work/money** ho tanto lavoro/tanti soldi; **I love you ~ much** ti amo tanto; **~ many** tanti(e)
4 *(phrases)*: **10 or ~** circa 10; **~ long!** *(inf: goodbye)* ciao!, ci vediamo!
♦ *conj* 1 *(expressing purpose)*: **~ as to** do in modo or così da fare; **we hurried ~ as not to be late** ci affrettammo per non fare tardi; **~ (that)** affinché + *sub*, perché + *sub*
2 *(expressing result)*: **he didn't arrive ~ I left** non è venuto così me ne sono andata; **~ you see, I could have gone** vedi, sarei potuto andare

soak |səuk| *vt* inzuppare; *(clothes)* mettere a mollo ♦ *vi (clothes etc)* essere a mollo; **~ in** *vi* penetrare; **~ up** *vt* assorbire
soap |səup| *n* sapone *m*; **~flakes** *npl* sapone *m* in scaglie; **~ opera** *n* soap opera *f inv*; **~ powder** *n* detersivo; **~y** *adj* insaponato(a)
soar |sɔː*| *vi* (*bird*) alzarsi in volo; *(price etc)* salire alle stelle; *(building)* ergersi
sob |sɔb| *n* singhiozzo ♦ *vi* singhiozzare
sober |'səubə*| *adj* sobrio(a); *(not drunk)* non ubriaco(a); *(moderate)* moderato(a); **~ up** *vt* far passare la sbornia ♦ *vi* farsi passare la sbornia
so-called |'səu'kɔːld| *adj* cosiddetto(a)
soccer |'sɔkə*| *n* calcio
sociable |'səuʃəbl| *adj* socievole
social |'səuʃl| *adj* sociale ♦ *n* festa, serata; **~ club** *n* club *m inv* sociale; **~ism** *n* socialismo; **~ist** *adj*, *n* socialista *m/f*; **~ize** *vi*: **to ~ize (with)**

socializzare (con); **~ security** *(BRIT)* *n* previdenza sociale *f*; **~ work** *n* servizio sociale; **~ worker** *n* assistente *m/f* sociale
society |sə'saɪətɪ| *n* società *f inv*; *(club)* società, associazione *f*; *(also: high ~)* alta società
sociology |səusɪ'ɔlədʒɪ| *n* sociologia
sock |sɔk| *n* calzino
socket |'sɔkɪt| *n* cavità *f inv*; *(of eye)* orbita; *(BRIT: ELEC: also: wall ~)* presa di corrente
sod |sɔd| *n (of earth)* zolla erbosa; *(BRIT: inf!)* bastardo/a (!)
soda |'səudə| *n (CHEM)* soda; *(also: ~ water)* acqua di seltz; *(US: also: ~ pop)* gassosa
sodium |'səudɪəm| *n* sodio
sofa |'səufə| *n* sofà *m inv*
soft |sɔft| *adj (not rough)* morbido(a); *(not hard)* soffice; *(not loud)* sommesso(a); *(not bright)* tenue; *(kind)* gentile; **~ drink** *n* analcolico; **~en** |'sɔfn| *vt* ammorbidire; addolcire; attenuare ♦ *vi* ammorbidirsi; addolcirsi; attenuarsi; **~ly** *adv* dolcemente; morbidamente; **~ness** *n* dolcezza; morbidezza
software |'sɔftwɛə*| *n (COMPUT)* software *m*
soggy |'sɔgɪ| *adj* inzuppato(a)
soil |sɔɪl| *n* terreno ♦ *vt* sporcare
solar |'səulə*| *adj* solare; **~ panel** *n* pannello solare; **~ power** *n* energie solare
sold |səuld| *pt*, *pp* *of* **sell**; **~ out** *adj (COMM)* esaurito(a)
solder |'səuldə*| *vt* saldare ♦ *n* saldatura
soldier |'səuldʒə*| *n* soldato, militare *m*
sole |səul| *n (of foot)* pianta (del piede); *(of shoe)* suola; *(fish: pl inv)* sogliola ♦ *adj* solo(a), unico(a)
solemn |'sɔləm| *adj* solenne
sole trader *n (COMM)* commerciante *m* in proprio

solicit [sə'lɪsɪt] *vt* (request) richiedere, sollecitare ♦ *vi* (prostitute) adescare i passanti

solicitor [sə'lɪsɪtə*] (*BRIT*) *n* (for wills etc) ≈ notaio; (in court) ≈ avvocato

solid ['sɒlɪd] *adj* solido(a); (not hollow) pieno(a); (meal) sostanzioso(a) ♦ *n* solido

solidarity [sɒlɪ'dærɪtɪ] *n* solidarietà

solitaire [sɒlɪ'teə*] *n* (games, gem) solitario

solitary ['sɒlɪtərɪ] *adj* solitario(a); **~ confinement** *n* (LAW) isolamento

solo ['səuləu] *n* assolo; **~ist** *n* solista *m/f*

soluble ['sɒljubl] *adj* solubile

solution [sə'lu:ʃən] *n* soluzione *f*

solve [sɒlv] *vt* risolvere

solvent ['sɒlvənt] *adj* (COMM) solvibile ♦ *n* (CHEM) solvente *m*

sombre ['sɒmbə*] (*US* **somber**) *adj* scuro(a); (mood, person) triste

---

KEYWORD

some [sʌm] *adj* **1** (a certain amount or number of): **~ tea/water/cream** del tè/dell'acqua/della panna; **~ children/apples** dei bambini/delle mele

2 (certain: in contrasts) certo(a); **~ people say that ...** alcuni dicono che ..., certa gente dice che ...

3 (unspecified) un(a) certo(a), qualche; **~ woman was asking for you** una tale chiedeva di lei; **~ day** un giorno; **~ day next week** un giorno della prossima settimana

♦ *pron* **1** (a certain number) alcuni(e), certi(e); **I've got ~** (books etc) ne ho alcuni; **~ (of them) have been sold** alcuni sono stati venduti

2 (a certain amount) un po'; **I've got ~** (money, milk) ne ho un po'; **I've read ~ of the book** ho letto parte del libro

♦ *adv*: **~ 10 people** circa 10 persone

somebody ['sʌmbədɪ] *pron* =

someone

somehow ['sʌmhau] *adv* in un modo o nell'altro, in qualche modo; (for some reason) per qualche ragione

someone ['sʌmwʌn] *pron* qualcuno

someplace ['sʌmpleɪs] (*US*) *adv* = **somewhere**

somersault ['sʌməsɔ:lt] *n* capriola; salto mortale ♦ *vi* fare una capriola (or un salto mortale); (car) cappottare

something ['sʌmθɪŋ] *pron* qualcosa, qualche cosa; **~ nice** qualcosa di bello; **~ to do** qualcosa da fare

sometime ['sʌmtaɪm] *adv* (in future) una volta o l'altra; (in past): **~ last month** durante il mese scorso

sometimes ['sʌmtaɪmz] *adv* qualche volta

somewhat ['sʌmwɒt] *adv* piuttosto

somewhere ['sʌmweə*] *adv* in or da qualche parte

son [sʌn] *n* figlio

song [sɒŋ] *n* canzone *f*

sonic ['sɒnɪk] *adj* (boom) sonico(a)

son-in-law ['sʌnɪnlɔ:] *n* genero

sonnet ['sɒnɪt] *n* sonetto

sonny ['sʌnɪ] (inf) *n* ragazzo mio

soon [su:n] *adv* presto, fra poco; (early, a short time after) presto; **~ afterwards** poco dopo; see also **as**; **~er** *adv* (time) prima; (preference): **I would ~er do** preferirei fare; **~er or later** prima o poi

soot [sut] *n* fuliggine *f*

soothe [su:ð] *vt* calmare

sophisticated [sə'fɪstɪkeɪtɪd] *adj* sofisticato(a); raffinato(a); complesso(a)

sophomore ['sɒfəmɔ:*] (*US*) *n* studente/essa del secondo anno

sopping ['sɒpɪŋ] *adj* (also: **~ wet**) bagnato(a) fradicio(a)

soppy ['sɒpɪ] (pej) *adj* sentimentale

soprano [sə'prɑ:nəu] *n* (voice) soprano *m*; (singer) soprano *m/f*

sorcerer ['sɔ:sərə*] *n* stregone *m*, mago

sore [sɔ:*] *adj* (painful) dolorante ♦ *n*

piaga; **~ly** adv (tempted) fortemente
sorrow ['sɔrəu] n dolore m; **~ful** adj
doloroso(a)
sorry ['sɔrɪ] adj spiacente; (condition,
excuse) misero(a); **~!** scusa! (or scusi! or
scusate!); **to feel ~ for sb** rincrescersi
per qn
sort [sɔ:t] n specie f, genere m ♦ vt
(also: **~ out**: papers) classificare;
ordinare; (: letters etc) smistare;
(: problems) risolvere; **~ing office** n
ufficio m smistamento
SOS n abbr (= save our souls) S.O.S. m
inv
so-so adv così così
sought [sɔ:t] pt, pp of **seek**
soul [səul] n anima; **~ful** adj pieno(a)
di sentimento
sound [saund] adj (healthy) sano(a);
(safe, not damaged) solido(a), in buono
stato; (reliable, not superficial) solido(a);
(sensible) giudizioso(a), di buon senso
♦ adv: **~ asleep** profondamente
addormentato ♦ n suono; (noise)
rumore m; (GEO) stretto ♦ vt (alarm)
suonare ♦ vi suonare; (fig: seem)
sembrare; **to ~ like** rassomigliare a;
~ out vt sondare; **~ barrier** n muro
del suono; **~bite** n dichiarazione breve
ed incisiva (preparata per radio o per
TV); **~ effects** npl effetti sonori; **~ly**
adv (sleep) profondamente; (beat)
duramente; **~proof** adj
insonorizzato(a), isolato(a)
acusticamente; **~track** n (of film)
colonna sonora
soup [su:p] n minestra; brodo; zuppa;
~ plate n piatto fondo; **~spoon** n
cucchiaio da minestra
sour ['sauə*] adj aspro(a); (fruit)
acerbo(a); (milk) acido(a); (fig)
acrigno(a); acido(a); **it's ~ grapes** è
soltanto invidia
source [sɔ:s] n fonte f, sorgente f; (fig)
fonte f
south [sauθ] n sud m, meridione m,
mezzogiorno ♦ adj del sud, sud inv,

meridionale ♦ adv verso sud;
S~ Africa n Sudafrica m; **S~ African**
adj, n sudafricano(a); **S~ America** n
Sudamerica m, America del sud;
S~ American adj, n sudamericano(a);
~-east n sud-est m; **~erly** ['sʌðəlɪ]
adj del sud; **~ern** ['sʌðən] adj del sud,
meridionale; esposto(a) a sud; **S~ Pole**
n Polo Sud; **~ward(s)** adv verso sud;
~-west n sud-ovest m
souvenir [su:və'nɪə*] n ricordo,
souvenir m inv
sovereign ['sɔvrɪn] adj, n sovrano(a)
soviet ['səuvɪət] adj sovietico(a); **the
S~ Union** l'Unione f Sovietica
sow1 [sau] (pt **~ed**, pp **sown**) vt
seminare
sow2 [sau] n scrofa
sown [səun] pp of **sow**
soya ['sɔɪə] (US **soy**) n: **~ bean** n seme
m di soia; **~ sauce** n salsa di soia
spa [spa:] n (resort) stazione f termale;
(US: also: health ~) centro di cure
estetiche
space [speɪs] n spazio; (room) posto;
spazio; (length of time) intervallo ♦ cpd
spaziale ♦ vt (also: **~ out**) distanziare;
~craft n inv veicolo spaziale; **~man/
woman** (irreg) n astronauta m/f,
cosmonauta m/f; **~ship** n = **~craft**;
spacing n spaziatura
spacious ['speɪʃəs] adj spazioso(a),
ampio(a)
spade [speɪd] n (tool) vanga; pala;
(child's game) paletta; **~s** npl (CARDS) picche
fpl
Spain [speɪn] n Spagna
span [spæn] n (of bird, plane) apertura
alare; (of arch) campata; (in time)
periodo; durata ♦ vt attraversare; (fig)
abbracciare
Spaniard ['spænjəd] n spagnolo/a
spaniel ['spænjəl] n spaniel m inv
Spanish ['spænɪʃ] adj spagnolo(a) ♦ n
(LING) spagnolo; **the ~** npl gli Spagnoli
spank [spæŋk] vt sculacciare

spanner ['spænə*] (BRIT) n chiave f inglese

spare [speə*] adj di riserva, di scorta; (surplus) in più, d'avanzo ♦ n (part) pezzo di ricambio ♦ vt (do without) fare a meno di; (afford to give) concedere; (refrain from hurting, using) risparmiare; **to ~** (surplus) d'avanzo; **~ part** n pezzo di ricambio; **~ time** n tempo libero; **~ wheel** n (AUT) ruota di scorta

sparingly ['speərɪŋlɪ] adv moderatamente

spark [spɑːk] n scintilla; **~(ing) plug** n candela

sparkle ['spɑːkl] n scintillio, sfavillio ♦ vi scintillare, sfavillare; **sparkling** adj scintillante, sfavillante; (conversation, wine, water) frizzante

sparrow ['spærəu] n passero

sparse [spɑːs] adj sparso(a), rado(a)

spartan ['spɑːtən] adj (fig) spartano(a)

spasm ['spæzəm] n (MED) spasmo; (fig) accesso, attacco; **~odic** [spæz'mɔdɪk] adj spasmodico(a); (fig) intermittente

spastic ['spæstɪk] n spastico/a

spat [spæt] pt, pp of **spit**

spate [speɪt] n (fig): **~ of** di diluvio di fiume m di

spawn [spɔːn] vi deporre le uova ♦ n uova fpl

speak [spiːk] (pt **spoke**, pp **spoken**) vt (language) parlare; (truth) dire ♦ vi parlare; **to ~ to sb/of** or **about sth** parlare a qn/di qc; **~ up!** parla più forte!; **~er** n (in public) oratore/trice; (also: loud~er) altoparlante m; (POL): **the S~er** il presidente della Camera dei Comuni (BRIT) or dei Rappresentanti (US)

spear [spɪə*] n lancia ♦ vt infilzare; **~head** vt (attack etc) condurre

spec [spek] (inf) n: **on ~** sperando bene

special ['spɛʃl] adj speciale; **~ist** n specialista m/f; **~ity** [spɛʃɪ'ælɪtɪ] n specialità f inv; **~ize** vi: **to ~ize (in)** specializzarsi (in); **~ly** adv specialmente, particolarmente;

~ needs adj: **~ needs children** bambini mpl con difficoltà di apprendimento; **~ty** n = **speciality**

species ['spiːʃiːz] n inv specie f inv

specific [spə'sɪfɪk] adj specifico(a); preciso(a); **~ally** adv esplicitamente; (especially) appositamente

specimen ['spesɪmən] n esemplare m, modello; (MED) campione m

speck [spek] n puntino, macchiolina; (particle) granello

speckled ['spekld] adj macchiettato(a)

specs [speks] (inf) npl occhiali mpl

spectacle ['spektəkl] n spettacolo; **~s** npl (glasses) occhiali mpl; **spectacular** [-'tækjulə*] adj spettacolare

spectator [spek'teɪtə*] n spettatore m

spectra ['spektrə] npl of **spectrum**

spectre ['spektə*] (US **specter**) n spettro

spectrum ['spektrəm] (pl **spectra**) n spettro

speculation [spekju'leɪʃən] n speculazione f; congettura fpl

speech [spiːtʃ] n (faculty) parola; (talk, THEATRE) discorso; (manner of speaking) parlata; **~less** adj ammutolito(a), muto(a)

speed [spiːd] n velocità f inv; (promptness) prontezza; **at full** or **top ~** a tutta velocità; **~ up** vi, vt accelerare; **~boat** n motoscafo; **~ily** adv velocemente; prontamente; **~ing** n (AUT) eccesso di velocità; **~ limit** n limite m di velocità; **~ometer** [spɪ'dɔmɪtə*] n tachimetro; **~way** n (sport) corsa motociclistica (su pista); **~y** adj veloce, rapido(a); pronto(a)

spell [spel] (pt, pp **spelt** (BRIT) or **~ed**) n (also: magic ~) incantesimo; (period of time) (breve) periodo ♦ vt (in writing) scrivere (lettera per lettera); (aloud) dire lettera per lettera; **to cast a ~ on sb** fare un incantesimo a qn; **he can't ~** fa errori di ortografia; **~bound** adj incantato(a); affascinato(a); **~ing** n ortografia; **spelt**

spend (BRIT) pt, pp of **spell**

spend [spɛnd] (pt, pp **spent**) vt (money) spendere; (time, life) passare; **~thrift** n spendaccione/a; **spent** pt, pp of **spend**

sperm [spə:m] n sperma m

sphere [sfɪə*] n sfera

spice [spais] n spezia ♦ vt aromatizzare

spicy ['spaisi] adj piccante

spider ['spaidə*] n ragno

spike [spaik] n punta

spill [spil] (pt, pp **spilt** or **~ed**) vt versare, rovesciare ♦ vi versarsi, rovesciarsi; **~ over** vi (liquid) versarsi; (crowd) riversarsi; **spilt** pt, pp of **spill**

spin [spin] (pt, pp **spun**) n (revolution of wheel) rotazione f; (AVIAT) avvitamento; (trip in car) giretto ♦ vt (wool etc) filare; (wheel) far girare ♦ vi girare

spinach ['spinitʃ] n spinacio; (as food) spinaci mpl

spinal ['spainl] adj spinale; **~ cord** n midollo spinale

spin doctor (inf) n esperto di comunicazioni responsabile dell'immagine di un partito politico

spin-dryer (BRIT) n centrifuga

spine [spain] n spina dorsale; (thorn) spina

spinning ['spinin] n filatura; **~ top** n trottola

spin-off n (product) prodotto secondario

spinster ['spinstə*] n nubile f; zitella

spiral ['spaiərl] n spirale f ♦ vi (fig) salire a spirale; **~ staircase** n scala a chiocciola

spire [spaiə*] n guglia

spirit ['spirit] n spirito; (ghost) spirito, fantasma m; (mood) stato d'animo, umore m; (courage) coraggio; **~s** (drink) alcolici mpl; **in good ~s** di buon umore; **~ed** adj vivace, vigoroso(a); (horse) focoso(a); **~ level** n livella a bolla d'aria

spiritual ['spiritjuəl] adj spirituale

spit [spit] (pt, pp **spat**) n (for roasting) spiedo; (saliva) sputo; saliva ♦ vi sputare; (fire, fat) scoppiettare

spite [spait] n dispetto ♦ vt contrariare, far dispetto a; **in ~ of** nonostante, malgrado; **~ful** adj dispettoso(a)

spittle ['spitl] n saliva; sputo

splash [splæʃ] n spruzzo; (sound) splash m inv; (of colour) schizzo ♦ vt spruzzare ♦ vi (also: ~ about) sguazzare

spleen [spli:n] n (ANAT) milza

splendid ['splendid] adj splendido(a), magnifico(a)

splint [splint] n (MED) stecca

splinter ['splintə*] n scheggia ♦ vi scheggiarsi

split [split] (pt, pp **split**) n spaccatura; (fig: division, quarrel) scissione f ♦ vt spaccare; (party) dividere; (work, profits) spartire, ripartire ♦ vi (divide) dividersi; **~ up** vi (couple) separarsi, rompere; (meeting) sciogliersi

spoil [spɔil] (pt, pp **spoilt** or **~ed**) vt (damage) rovinare, guastare; (mar) sciupare; (child) viziare; **~s** npl bottino; **~sport** n guastafeste m/f inv; **spoilt** pt, pp of **spoil**

spoke [spəuk] pt of **speak** ♦ n raggio

spoken ['spəukn] pp of **speak**

spokesman ['spəuksmən] (irreg) n portavoce m inv

spokeswoman ['spəukswumən] (irreg) n portavoce f inv

sponge [spʌndʒ] n spugna; (also: ~ cake) pan m di spagna ♦ vt spugnare, pulire con una spugna ♦ vi: **to ~ off** or **on** scroccare a; **~ bag** (BRIT) n nécessaire m inv

sponsor ['spɔnsə*] n (RADIO, TV, SPORT etc) sponsor m inv; (POL: of bill) promotore/trice ♦ vt sponsorizzare; (bill) presentare; **~ship** n sponsorizzazione f

spontaneous [spɔn'teiniəs] adj spontaneo(a)

spooky ['spu:ki] (inf) adj che fa accapponare la pelle

spool [spu:l] *n* bobina

spoon [spu:n] *n* cucchiaio; **~-feed** *vt* nutrire con il cucchiaio; (*fig*) imboccare; **~ful** *n* cucchiaiata

sport [spɔ:t] *n* sport *m inv*; (*person*) persona di spirito ♦ *vt* sfoggiare; **~ing** *adj* sportivo(a); **to give sb a ~ing chance** dare a qn una possibilità (di vincere); **~ jacket** (*US*) *n* = **~s jacket**; **~s car** *n* automobile *f* sportiva; **~s jacket** (*BRIT*) *n* giacca sportiva; **~smanship** *n* spirito sportivo; **~swear** *n* abiti *mpl* sportivi; **~swoman** (*irreg*) *n* sportiva; **~y** *adj* sportivo(a)

spot [spɔt] *n* punto; (*mark*) macchia; (*dot: on pattern*) pallino; (*pimple*) foruncolo; (*place*) posto; (*RADIO, TV*) spot *m inv*; (*small amount*): **a ~ of** un po' di ♦ *vt* (*notice*) individuare, distinguere; **on the ~** sul posto; (*immediately*) su due piedi; (*in difficulty*) nei guai; **~ check** *n* controllo senza preavviso; **~less** *adj* immacolato(a); **~light** *n* proiettore *m*; (*AUT*) faro ausiliario; **~ted** *adj* macchiato(a); a puntini, a pallini; **~ty** *adj* (*face*) foruncoloso(a)

spouse [spauz] *n* sposo/a

spout [spaut] *n* (*of jug*) beccuccio; (*of pipe*) scarico ♦ *vi* zampillare

sprain [spreɪn] *n* storta, distorsione *f* ♦ *vt*: **to ~ one's ankle** storcersi una caviglia

sprang [spræŋ] *pt of* **spring**

sprawl [sprɔ:l] *vi* sdraiarsi (in modo scomposto); (*place*) estendersi (disordinatamente)

spray [spreɪ] *n* spruzzo; (*container*) nebulizzatore *m*, spray *m inv*; (*of flowers*) mazzetto ♦ *vt* spruzzare; (*crops*) irrorare

spread [spred] (*pt, pp* **spread**) *n* diffusione *f*; (*distribution*) distribuzione *f*; (*CULIN*) pasta (da spalmare); (*inf: food*) banchetto ♦ *vt* (*cloth*) stendere, distendere; (*butter etc*) spalmare;

(*disease, knowledge*) propagare, diffondere ♦ *vt* stendersi, distendersi; spalmarsi; propagarsi, diffondersi; **~ out** *vi* (*move apart*) separarsi; **~-eagled** ['spredɪ:gld] *adj* a gambe e braccia aperte; **~sheet** *n* foglio elettronico ad espansione

spree [spri:] *n*: **to go on a ~** fare baldoria

sprightly ['spraɪtlɪ] *adj* vivace

spring [sprɪŋ] (*pt* **sprang**, *pp* **sprung**) *n* (*leap*) salto, balzo; (*coiled metal*) molla; (*season*) primavera; (*of water*) sorgente *f* ♦ *vi* saltare, balzare; **~ up** *vi* (*problem*) presentarsi; **~board** *n* trampolino; **~-clean(ing)** *n* grandi pulizie *fpl* di primavera; **~time** *n* primavera

sprinkle ['sprɪŋkl] *vt* spruzzare; spargere; **to ~ water** *etc* on, **~ with water** *etc* spruzzare dell'acqua *etc* su; **~r** *n* (*for lawn*) irrigatore *m*; (*to put out fire*) sprinkler *m inv*

sprint [sprɪnt] *n* scatto ♦ *vi* scattare; **~er** *n* (*SPORT*) velocista *m/f*

sprout [spraut] *vi* germogliare; **~s** *npl* (*also: Brussels ~*) cavolini *mpl* di Bruxelles

spruce [spru:s] *n inv* abete *m* rosso ♦ *adj* lindo(a); azzimato(a)

sprung [sprʌŋ] *pp of* **spring**

spun [spʌn] *pt, pp of* **spin**

spur [spə:*] *n* sperone *m*; (*fig*) sprone *m*, incentivo *m ♦ vt* (*also: ~ on*) spronare; **on the ~ of the moment** lì per lì

spurious ['spjuərɪəs] *adj* falso(a)

spurn [spə:n] *vt* rifiutare con disprezzo, sdegnare

spurt [spə:t] *n* (*of water*) getto; (*of energy*) scatto ♦ *vi* sgorgare

spy [spaɪ] *n* spia ♦ *vi*: **to ~ on** spiare ♦ *vt* (*see*) scorgere; **~ing** *n* spionaggio

sq. *abbr* = **square**

squabble ['skwɔbl] *vi* bisticciarsi

squad [skwɔd] *n* (*MIL*) plotone *m*; (*POLICE*) squadra

squadron ['skwɔdrn] *n* (*MIL*)

squadrone m; (AVIAT, NAUT) squadriglia

squalid ['skwɔlɪd] adj squallido(a)

squall [skwɔ:l] n raffica; burrasca

squalor ['skwɔlə*] n squallore m

squander ['skwɔndə*] vt dissipare

square [skwεə*] n quadrato; (in town) piazza ♦ vt quadrato(a); (inf: ideas, person) di vecchio stampo ♦ vt (arrange) regolare; (MATH) elevare al quadrato; (reconcile) conciliare; **all ~** pari; **a ~ meal** un pasto abbondante; **2 metres ~** di 2 metri per 2; **1 ~ metre** 1 metro quadrato; **~ly** adv diritto; fermamente

squash [skwɔʃ] n (SPORT) squash m; (BRIT: drink): **lemon/orange ~** sciroppo di limone/arancia; (US) zucca; (SPORT) squash m ♦ vt schiacciare

squat [skwɔt] adj tarchiato(a), tozzo(a) ♦ vi (also: **~ down**) accovacciarsi; **~ter** n occupante m/f abusivo(a)

squeak [skwi:k] vi squittire

squeal [skwi:l] vi strillare

squeamish ['skwi:mɪʃ] adj schizzinoso(a); disgustato(a)

squeeze [skwi:z] n pressione f; (also ECON) stretta ♦ vt premere; (hand, arm) stringere; **~ out** vt spremere

squelch [skweltʃ] vi fare ciac; sguazzare

squid [skwɪd] n calamaro

squiggle ['skwɪgl] n ghirigoro

squint [skwɪnt] vi essere strabico(a) ♦ n: **he has a ~** è strabico

squirm [skwə:m] vi contorcersi

squirrel ['skwɪrəl] n scoiattolo

squirt [skwə:t] vi schizzare; zampillare ♦ vt spruzzare

Sr abbr = **senior**

St abbr = **saint**; **street**

stab [stæb] n (with knife etc) pugnalata; (of pain) fitta; (inf: try): **to have a ~ at (doing) sth** provare a (fare) qc ♦ vt pugnalare

stable ['steɪbl] n (for horses) scuderia; (for cattle) stalla ♦ adj stabile

stack [stæk] n catasta, pila ♦ vt accatastare, ammucchiare

stadium ['steɪdɪəm] n stadio

staff [stɑ:f] n (work force: gen) personale m; (: BRIT: SCOL) personale insegnante ♦ vt fornire di personale

stag [stæg] n cervo

stage [steɪdʒ] n palcoscenico; (profession): **the ~** il teatro, la scena; (point) punto; (platform) palco ♦ vt (play) allestire, mettere in scena; (demonstration) organizzare; **in ~s** per gradi; a tappe; **~coach** n diligenza; **~ manager** n direttore m di scena

stagger ['stægə*] vi barcollare ♦ vt (person) sbalordire; (hours, holidays) scaglionare; **~ing** adj (amazing) sbalorditivo(a)

stagnate [stæg'neɪt] vi stagnare

stag party n festa di addio al celibato

staid [steɪd] adj posato(a), serio(a)

stain [steɪn] n macchia; (colouring) colorante m ♦ vt macchiare; (wood) tingere; **~ed glass window** n vetrata; **~less** adj (steel) inossidabile; **~ remover** n smacchiatore m

stair [stεə*] n (step) gradino; **~s** npl (flight of ~s) scale fpl, scala; **~case** n scale fpl, scala; **~way** n = **~case**

stake [steɪk] n palo, picchetto; (COMM) interesse m; (BETTING) puntata, scommessa ♦ vt (bet) scommettere; (risk) rischiare; **to be at ~** essere in gioco

stale [steɪl] adj (bread) raffermo(a); (food) stantio(a); (air) viziato(a); (beer) svaporato(a); (smell) di chiuso

stalemate ['steɪlmeɪt] n stallo; (fig) punto morto

stalk [stɔ:k] n gambo, stelo ♦ vt inseguire; **~ off** vi andarsene impettito(a)

stall [stɔ:l] n bancarella; (in stable) box m inv di stalla ♦ vt (AUT) far spegnere; (fig) bloccare ♦ vi (AUT) spegnersi; fermarsi; (fig) temporeggiare; **~s** npl (BRIT: in cinema, theatre) platea

stallion ['stælɪən] n stallone m

stalwart ['stɔːlwət] *adj* fidato(a); risoluto(a)

stamina ['stæmɪnə] *n* vigore *m*, resistenza

stammer ['stæmə*] *n* balbuzie *f* ♦ *vi* balbettare

stamp [stæmp] *n* (postage ~) francobollo; (*implement*) timbro; (*mark, also fig*) marchio, impronta; (*on document*) bollo; timbro ♦ *vi* (*also*: ~ *one's foot*) battere il piede ♦ *vt* battere; (*letter*) affrancare; (*mark with a* ~) timbrare; ~ **album** *n* album *m inv* per francobolli; ~ **collecting** *n* filatelia

stampede [stæm'piːd] *n* fuggi fuggi *m inv*

stance [stæns] *n* posizione *f*

stand [stænd] (*pt, pp* **stood**) *n* (*position*) posizione *f*; (*for taxis*) posteggio; (*structure*) supporto, sostegno; (*at exhibition*) stand *m inv*; (*in shop*) banco; (*at market*) bancarella; (*booth*) chiosco; (*SPORT*) tribuna ♦ *vi* stare in piedi; (*rise*) alzarsi in piedi; (*be placed*) trovarsi ♦ *vt* (*place*) mettere, porre; (*tolerate, withstand*) resistere, sopportare; (*treat*) offrire; **to make a** ~ prendere posizione; **to ~ for parliament** (*BRIT*) presentarsi come candidato (per il parlamento); ~ **by** *vi* (*be ready*) tenersi pronto(a) ♦ *vt fus* (*opinion*) sostenere; ~ **down** *vi* (*withdraw*) ritirarsi; ~ **for** *vt fus* (*signify*) rappresentare, significare; (*tolerate*) sopportare, tollerare; ~ **in for** *vt fus* sostituire; ~ **out** *vi* (*be prominent*) spiccare; ~ **up** *vi* (*rise*) alzarsi in piedi; ~ **up for** *vt fus* difendere; ~ **up to** *vt fus* tener testa a, resistere a

standard ['stændəd] *n* modello, standard *m inv*; (*level*) livello; (*flag*) stendardo ♦ *adj* (*size etc*) normale, standard *inv*; ~s *npl* (*morals*) principi *mpl*, valori *mpl*; ~ **lamp** (*BRIT*) *n* lampada a stelo; ~ **of living** *n* livello di vita

stand-by *n* riserva, sostituto; **to be on**

~ (*gen*) tenersi pronto(a); (*doctor*) essere di guardia; ~ **ticket** *n* (*AVIAT*) biglietto senza garanzia

stand-in *n* sostituto/a

standing ['stændɪŋ] *adj* diritto(a), in piedi; (*permanent*) permanente ♦ *n* rango, condizione *f*, posizione *f*; **of many years'** ~ che esiste da molti anni; ~ **joke** *n* barzelletta; ~ **order** (*BRIT*) *n* (*at bank*) ordine *m* di pagamento (permanente); ~ **room** *n* posto all'impiedi

standpoint ['stændpɔɪnt] *n* punto di vista

standstill ['stændstɪl] *n*: **at a** ~ fermo(a); (*fig*) a un punto morto; **to come to a** ~ fermarsi; giungere a un punto morto

stank [stæŋk] *pt of* **stink**

staple ['steɪpl] *n* (*for papers*) graffetta ♦ *adj* (*food etc*) di base ♦ *vt* cucire; ~**r** *n* cucitrice *f*

star [stɑː*] *n* stella; (*celebrity*) divo/a ♦ *vi*: **to ~ (in)** essere il (*or* la) protagonista (di) ♦ *vt* (*CINEMA*) essere interpretato(a) da

starboard ['stɑːbəd] *n* dritta

starch [stɑːtʃ] *n* amido

stardom ['stɑːdəm] *n* celebrità

stare [stɛə*] *n* sguardo fisso ♦ *vi*: **to** ~ **at** fissare

starfish ['stɑːfɪʃ] *n* stella di mare

stark [stɑːk] *adj* (*bleak*) desolato(a) ♦ *adv*: ~ **naked** completamente nudo(a)

starling ['stɑːlɪŋ] *n* storno

starry ['stɑːrɪ] *adj* stellato(a); ~-**eyed** *adj* (*innocent*) ingenuo(a)

start [stɑːt] *n* inizio; (*of race*) partenza; (*sudden movement*) sobbalzo; (*advantage*) vantaggio ♦ *vt* cominciare, iniziare; (*car*) mettere in moto ♦ *vi* cominciare; (*on journey*) partire, mettersi in viaggio; (*jump*) sobbalzare; **to ~ doing** *or* **to do sth** (in)cominciare a fare qc; ~ **off** *vi* cominciare; (*leave*) partire; ~ **up** *vi* cominciare; (*car*) avviarsi ♦ *vt* iniziare; (*car*) avviare; **~er** *n* (*AUT*) motorino d'avviamento; (*SPORT: official*) starter *m inv*; (*BRIT: CULIN*) primo piatto; **~ing point** *n* punto di partenza

startle ['stɑːtl] *vt* far trasalire; **startling** *adj* sorprendente

starvation [stɑːˈveɪʃən] *n* fame f, inedia

starve [stɑːv] *vi* morire di fame; soffrire la fame ♦ *vt* far morire di fame; affamare

state [steɪt] *n* stato ♦ *vt* dichiarare, affermare; annunciare; **the S~s** (*USA*) gli Stati Uniti; **to be in a ~** essere agitato(a); **~ly** *adj* maestoso(a), imponente; **~ly home** *n* residenza nobiliare (*d'interesse storico e artistico*); **~ment** *n* dichiarazione f; **~sman** (*irreg*) *n* statista *m*

static ['stætɪk] *n* (*RADIO*) scariche *fpl* ♦ *adj* statico(a)

station ['steɪʃən] *n* stazione f ♦ *vt* collocare, disporre

stationary ['steɪʃənərɪ] *adj* fermo(a), immobile

stationer ['steɪʃənə*] *n* cartolaio/a; **~'s (shop)** *n* cartoleria; **~y** *n* articoli *mpl* di cancelleria

station master (*RAIL*) capostazione *m*

station wagon (*US*) *n* giardinetta

statistic [stəˈtɪstɪk] *n* statistica; **~s** *n* (*science*) statistica

statue ['stætjuː] *n* statua

status ['steɪtəs] *n* posizione f, condizione f sociale; prestigio; stato; **~ symbol** *n* simbolo di prestigio

statute ['stætjuːt] *n* legge f; **statutory** *adj* stabilito(a) dalla legge, statutario(a)

staunch [stɔːntʃ] *adj* fidato(a), leale

stay [steɪ] *n* (*period of time*) soggiorno, permanenza ♦ *vi* rimanere; (*reside*) alloggiare, stare; (*spend some time*) trattenersi, soggiornare; **to ~ put** non muoversi; **to ~ the night** fermarsi per la notte; **~ behind** *vi* restare indietro;

~ in *vi* (*at home*) stare in casa; **~ on** *vi* restare, rimanere; **~ out** *vi* (*of house*) rimanere fuori (di casa); **~ up** *vi* (*at night*) rimanere alzato(a); **~ing power** *n* capacità di resistenza

stead [sted] *n*: **in sb's ~** al posto di qn; **to stand sb in good ~** essere utile a qn

steadfast ['stedfɑːst] *adj* fermo(a), risoluto(a)

steadily ['stedɪlɪ] *adv* (*firmly*) saldamente; (*constantly*) continuamente; (*fixedly*) fisso; (*walk*) con passo sicuro

steady ['stedɪ] *adj* (*not wobbling*) fermo(a); (*regular*) costante; (*person, character*) serio(a); (*: calm*) calmo(a), tranquillo(a) ♦ *vt* stabilizzare; calmare

steak [steɪk] *n* (*meat*) bistecca; (*fish*) trancia

steal [stiːl] (*pt* **stole**, *pp* **stolen**) *vt* rubare ♦ *vi* rubare; (*move*) muoversi furtivamente

stealth [stelθ] *n*: **by ~** furtivamente; **~y** *adj* furtivo(a)

steam [stiːm] *n* vapore *m* ♦ *vt* (*CULIN*) cuocere a vapore ♦ *vi* fumare; **~ engine** *n* macchina a vapore; (*RAIL*) locomotiva a vapore; **~er** *n* piroscafo, vapore *m*; **~roller** *n* rullo compressore; **~ship** *n* = **~er**; **~y** *adj* (*room*) pieno(a) di vapore; (*window*) appannato(a)

steel [stiːl] *n* acciaio ♦ *adj* di acciaio; **~works** *n* acciaieria

steep [stiːp] *adj* ripido(a), scosceso(a); (*price*) eccessivo(a) ♦ *vt* inzuppare; (*washing*) mettere a mollo

steeple ['stiːpl] *n* campanile *m*

steer [stɪə*] *vt* guidare ♦ *vi* (*NAUT: person*) governare; (*car*) guidarsi; **~ing** *n* (*AUT*) sterzo; **~ing wheel** *n* volante *m*

stem [stem] *n* (*of flower, plant*) stelo; (*of tree*) fusto; (*of glass*) gambo; (*of fruit, leaf*) picciolo ♦ *vt* contenere, arginare; **~ from** *vt fus* provenire da, derivare da

stench [stɛntʃ] *n* puzzo, fetore *m*

stencil ['stɛnsl] *n* (of metal, cardboard) stampino, mascherina; (in typing) matrice *f* ♦ *vt* disegnare con stampino

stenographer [stɛ'nɔɡrəfə*] (US) *n* stenografo/a

step [stɛp] *n* passo, (stair) gradino, scalino; (action) mossa, azione *f* ♦ *vi*: to ~ forward/back fare un passo avanti/indietro; ~ *npl* (BRIT) = **stepladder**; **to be in/out of** ~ **(with)** stare/non stare al passo (con); ~ **down** *vi* (fig) ritirarsi; ~ **on** *vt fus* calpestare; ~ **up** *vt* aumentare; intensificare; **~brother** *n* fratellastro; **~daughter** *n* figliastra; **~father** *n* patrigno; **~ladder** *n* scala a libretto; **~mother** *n* matrigna; **~ping stone** *n* pietra di un guado; **~sister** *n* sorellastra; **~son** *n* figliastro

stereo ['stɛrɪəʊ] *n* (system) sistema *m* stereofonico; (record player) stereo *m inv* ♦ *adj* (also: ~phonic) stereofonico/a

sterile ['stɛraɪl] *adj* sterile; **sterilize** ['stɛrɪlaɪz] *vt* sterilizzare

sterling ['stɜːlɪŋ] *adj* (gold, silver) di buona lega ♦ *n* (ECON) (lira) sterlina; **a pound** ~ una lira sterlina

stern [stɜːn] *adj* severo(a) ♦ *n* (NAUT) poppa

stew [stjuː] *n* stufato ♦ *vt* cuocere in umido

steward ['stjuːəd] *n* (AVIAT, NAUT, RAIL) steward *m inv*; (in club etc) dispensiere *m*; **~ess** *n* assistente *f* di volo, hostess *f inv*

stick [stɪk] (pt, pp **stuck**) *n* bastone *m*; (of rhubarb, celery) gambo; (of dynamite) candelotto ♦ *vt* (glue) attaccare; (thrust): **to** ~ **sth into** conficcare o piantare o infiggere qc in; (inf: put) ficcare; (inf: tolerate) sopportare ♦ *vi* attaccarsi; (remain) restare, rimanere; ~ **out** *vi* sporgere, spuntare; ~ **up** *vi* sporgere, spuntare; ~ **up for** *vt fus* difendere; **~er** *n* cartellino adesivo; **~ing plaster** *n*

cerotto adesivo

stick-up (inf) *n* rapina a mano armata

sticky ['stɪkɪ] *adj* attaccaticcio(a), vischioso(a); (label) adesivo(a); (fig: situation) difficile

stiff [stɪf] *adj* rigido(a), duro(a); (muscle) legato(a), indolenzito(a); (difficult) difficile, arduo(a); (cold) freddo(a), formale; (strong) forte; (price) molto alto(a) ♦ *adv*: **bored** ~ annoiato(a) a morte; **~en** *vt* rinforzare ♦ *vi* irrigidirsi; indurirsi; ~ **neck** *n* torcicollo

stifle ['staɪfl] *vt* soffocare

stigma ['stɪɡmə] *n* (fig) stigma *m*

stile [staɪl] *n* cavalcasiepe *m*; cavalcasteccato

stiletto [stɪ'lɛtəʊ] (BRIT) *n* (also: ~ heel) tacco a spillo

still [stɪl] *adj* fermo(a); silenzioso(a) ♦ *adv* (up to this time, even) ancora; (nonetheless) tuttavia, ciò nonostante; **~born** *adj* nato(a) morto(a); ~ **life** *n* natura morta

stilt [stɪlt] *n* trampolo; (pile) palo

stilted ['stɪltɪd] *adj* freddo(a), formale; artificiale

stimulate ['stɪmjʊleɪt] *vt* stimolare

stimuli ['stɪmjʊlaɪ] *npl of* **stimulus**

stimulus ['stɪmjʊləs] (pl **stimuli**) *n* stimolo

sting [stɪŋ] (pt, pp **stung**) *n* puntura; (organ) pungiglione *m* ♦ *vt* pungere

stingy ['stɪndʒɪ] *adj* spilorcio(a), tirchio(a)

stink [stɪŋk] (pt **stank**, pp **stunk**) *n* fetore *m*, puzzo ♦ *vi* puzzare; **~ing** (inf) *adj* (fig): **a ~ing** ... uno schifo di ..., un(a) maledetto(a) ....

stint [stɪnt] *n* lavoro, compito ♦ *vi*: **to** ~ **on** lesinare su

stir [stɜː*] *n* agitazione *f*, clamore *m* ♦ *vt* mescolare; (fig) risvegliare ♦ *vi* muoversi; ~ **up** *vt* provocare, suscitare

stirrup ['stɪrəp] *n* staffa

stitch [stɪtʃ] *n* (SEWING) punto; (KNITTING) maglia; (MED) punto (di sutura); (pain) fitta ♦ vt cucire, attaccare; suturare

stoat [stəut] n ermellino

stock [stɔk] n riserva, provvista; (COMM) giacenza, stock m inv; (AGR) bestiame m; (CULIN) brodo; (descent) stirpe f; (FINANCE) titoli mpl, azioni fpl ♦ adj (fig: reply etc) consueto(a), classico(a) ♦ vt (have in stock) avere, vendere; **~s and shares** valori mpl di borsa; **in ~** in magazzino; **out of ~** esaurito(a); **~ up** vi: **to ~ up (with)** fare provvista (di)

stockbroker ['stɔkbrəukə*] n agente m di cambio

stock cube (BRIT) n dado

stock exchange n Borsa (valori)

stocking ['stɔkɪŋ] n calza

stock: ~ market n Borsa, mercato finanziario; **~pile** n riserva ♦ vt accumulare riserve di; **~taking** (BRIT) n (COMM) inventario

stocky ['stɔkɪ] adj tarchiato(a), tozzo(a)

stodgy ['stɔdʒɪ] adj pesante, indigesto(a)

stoke [stəuk] vt alimentare

stole [stəul] pt of **steal** ♦ n stola

stolen ['stəuln] pp of **steal**

stomach ['stʌmək] n stomaco; (belly) pancia ♦ vt sopportare, digerire; **~ ache** n mal m di stomaco

stone [stəun] n pietra; (pebble) sasso, ciottolo; (in fruit) nocciolo; (MED) calcolo; (BRIT: weight) = 6.348 kg.; 14 libbre ♦ adj di pietra ♦ vt lapidare; (fruit) togliere il nocciolo a; **~-cold** adj gelido(a); **~-deaf** adj sordo(a) come una campana; **~work** n muratura; **stony** adj sassoso(a); (fig) di pietra

stood [stud] pt, pp of **stand**

stool [stu:l] n sgabello

stoop [stu:p] vi (also: have a ~) avere una curvatura; (also: ~ down) chinarsi, curvarsi

stop [stɔp] n arresto; (stopping place) fermata; (in punctuation) punto ♦ vt arrestare, fermare; (break off)

interrompere; (also: put a ~ to) porre fine a ♦ vi fermarsi; (rain, noise etc) cessare, finire; **to ~ doing sth** cessare or finire di fare qc; **to ~ dead** fermarsi di colpo; **~ off** vi sostare brevemente; **~ up** vt (hole) chiudere, turare; **~gap** n tappabuchi m inv; **~lights** npl (AUT) stop mpl; **~over** n breve sosta; (AVIAT) scalo

stoppage ['stɔpɪdʒ] n arresto, fermata; (of pay) trattenuta; (strike) interruzione f del lavoro

stopper ['stɔpə*] n tappo

stop press n ultimissime fpl

stopwatch ['stɔpwɔtʃ] n cronometro

storage ['stɔ:rɪdʒ] n immagazzinamento; **~ heater** n radiatore m elettrico che accumula calore

store [stɔ:*] n provvista, riserva; (depot) deposito; (BRIT: department ~) grande magazzino; (US: shop) negozio ♦ vt immagazzinare; **~s** npl (provisions) rifornimenti mpl, scorte fpl; **in ~** di riserva; in serbo; **~ up** vt conservare; mettere in serbo; **~room** n dispensa

storey ['stɔ:rɪ] (US **story**) n piano

stork [stɔ:k] n cicogna

storm [stɔ:m] n tempesta, temporale m, burrasca; uragano ♦ vi (fig) infuriarsi ♦ vt prendere d'assalto; **~y** adj tempestoso(a), burrascoso(a)

story ['stɔ:rɪ] n storia; favola; racconto; (US) = **storey**; **~book** n libro di racconti

stout [staut] adj solido(a), robusto(a); (friend, supporter) tenace; (fat) corpulento(a), grasso(a) ♦ n birra scura

stove [stəuv] n (for cooking) fornello; (: small) fornelletto; (for heating) stufa

stow [stəu] vt (also: ~ away) mettere via; **~away** n passeggero(a) clandestino(a)

straddle ['strædl] vt stare a cavalcioni di; (fig) essere a cavallo di

straggle ['strægl] vi crescere (or estendersi) disordinatamente; trascinarsi; rimanere indietro; **straggly**

adj (hair) in disordine

straight [streɪt] *adj* dritto(a); (frank) onesto(a), franco(a); (simple) semplice ♦ *adv* diritto; (drink) liscio; **to put** or **get ~** mettere in ordine, mettere ordine in; **~ away**, **~ off** (at once) immediatamente; **~en** vt (also: **~en out**) raddrizzare; **~-faced** *adj* impassibile, imperturbabile; **~forward** *adj* semplice; onesto(a), franco(a)

strain [streɪn] *n* (TECH) sollecitazione *f*; (physical) sforzo; (mental) tensione *f*; (MED) strappo; distorsione *f*; (streak, trace) tendenza; elemento ♦ vt tendere; (muscle) sforzare; (ankle) storcere; (resources) pesare su; (food) colare; passare; **~s** *npl* (MUS) note *fpl*; **~ed** *adj* (muscle) stirato(a); (laugh etc) forzato(a); (relations) teso(a); **~er** *n* passino, colino

strait [streɪt] *n* (GEO) stretto; **~s** *npl*: **to be in dire ~s** (fig) essere nei guai; **~jacket** *n* camicia di forza; **~-laced** *adj* bacchettone(a)

strand [strænd] *n* (of thread) filo; **~ed** *adj* nei guai; senza mezzi di trasporto

strange [streɪndʒ] *adj* (not known) sconosciuto(a); (odd) strano(a), bizzarro(a); **~ly** *adv* stranamente; **~r** *n* sconosciuto/a; estraneo/a

strangle ['stræŋgl] vt strangolare; **~hold** *n* (fig) stretta (mortale)

strap [stræp] *n* cinghia; (of slip, dress) spallina, bretella

strategic [strə'ti:dʒɪk] *adj* strategico(a)

strategy ['strætɪdʒɪ] *n* strategia

straw [strɔ:] *n* paglia; (drinking ~) cannuccia; **that's the last ~!** è la goccia che fa traboccare il vaso!

strawberry ['strɔ:bərɪ] *n* fragola

stray [streɪ] *adj* (animal) randagio(a); (bullet) vagante; (scattered) sparso(a) ♦ vi perdersi

streak [stri:k] *n* striscia; (of hair) mèche *f inv* ♦ vt striare, screziare ♦ vi: **to ~ past** passare come un fulmine

stream [stri:m] *n* ruscello; corrente *f*;

(of people, smoke etc) fiume *m* ♦ vt (SCOL) dividere in livelli di rendimento ♦ vi scorrere; **to ~ in/out** entrare/uscire a fiotti

streamer ['stri:mə*] *n* (of paper) stella filante

streamlined ['stri:mlaɪnd] *adj* aerodinamico(a), affusolato(a)

street [stri:t] *n* strada, via; **~car** (US) *n* tram *m inv*; **~ lamp** *n* lampione *m*; **~ plan** *n* pianta (di una città); **~wise** (inf) *adj* esperto(a) dei bassifondi

strength [strɛŋθ] *n* forza; **~en** vt rinforzare; fortificare; consolidare

strenuous ['strɛnjuəs] *adj* vigoroso(a), energico(a); (tiring) duro(a), pesante

stress [strɛs] *n* (force, pressure) pressione *f*; (mental strain) tensione *f*; (accent) accento ♦ vt insistere su, sottolineare; accentare

stretch [strɛtʃ] *n* (of sand etc) distesa ♦ vi stirarsi; (extend): **to ~ to** or **as far as** estendersi fino a ♦ vt tendere, allungare; (spread) distendere; (fig) spingere (al massimo); **~ out** vi allungarsi, estendersi ♦ vt (arm etc) allungare, tendere; (to spread) distendere

stretcher ['strɛtʃə*] *n* barella, lettiga

strewn [stru:n] *adj*: **~ with** cosparso(a) di

stricken ['strɪkən] *adj* (person) provato(a); (city, industry etc) colpito(a); **~ with** (disease etc) colpito(a) da

strict [strɪkt] *adj* (severe) rigido(a), severo(a); (precise) preciso(a), stretto(a); **~ly** *adv* severamente, rigorosamente; strettamente

stridden ['strɪdn] *pp of* **stride**

stride [straɪd] (pt strode, pp stridden) *n* passo lungo ♦ vi camminare a grandi passi

strife [straɪf] *n* conflitto; litigi *mpl*

strike [straɪk] (pt, pp struck) *n* sciopero; (of oil etc) scoperta; (attack) attacco ♦ vt colpire; (oil etc) scoprire, trovare (*bargain*) fare; (*fig*): **the thought** *or* **it ~s me that** ... mi viene in mente che ... ♦ *vi* scioperare; (*attack*) attaccare; (*clock*) suonare; **on ~** (*workers*) in sciopero; **to ~ a match** accendere un fiammifero; **~ down** *vt* (*fig*) atterrare; **~ up** *vt* (*MUS, conversation*) attaccare; **to ~ up a friendship with** fare amicizia con; **~r** *n* scioperante *m/f*; (*SPORT*) attaccante *m*; **striking** *adj* che colpisce

string [strɪŋ] (*pt, pp* **strung**) *n* spago; (*row*) fila; sequenza; catena; (*MUS*) corda ♦ *vt*: **to ~ out** disporre di fianco; **to ~ together** (*words, ideas*) mettere insieme; **the ~s** *npl* (*MUS*) gli archi; **to pull ~s for sb** (*fig*) raccomandare qn; **~ bean** *n* fagiolino; **~(ed) instrument** *n* (*MUS*) strumento a corda

stringent ['strɪndʒənt] *adj* rigoroso(a)

strip [strɪp] *n* striscia ♦ *vt* spogliare; (*paint*) togliere; (*also: ~ down: machine*) smontare ♦ *vi* spogliarsi; **~ cartoon** *n* fumetto

stripe [straɪp] *n* striscia, riga; (*MIL, POLICE*) gallone *m*; **~d** *adj* a strisce *o* righe

strip lighting *n* illuminazione *f* al neon

stripper ['strɪpə*] *n* spogliarellista *m/f*

strip-search ['strɪpsɜːtʃ] *vt*: **to ~ sb** perquisire qn facendolo(a) spogliare ♦ *n* perquisizione (*facendo spogliare il perquisito*)

striptease ['strɪptiːz] *n* spogliarello

strive [straɪv] (*pt* **strove**, *pp* **striven**) *vi*: **to ~ to do** sforzarsi di fare; **striven** ['strɪvn] *pp of* **strive**

strode [strəud] *pt of* **stride**

stroke [strəuk] *n* colpo; (*SWIMMING*) bracciata; (: *style*) stile *m*; (*MED*) colpo apoplettico ♦ *vt* accarezzare; **at a ~** in un attimo

stroll [strəul] *n* giretto, passeggiatina ♦ *vi* andare a spasso; **~er** (*US*) *n* passeggino

strong [strɒŋ] *adj* (*gen*) forte; (*sturdy:*

table, fabric etc) robusto(a); **they are 50 ~** sono in 50; **~box** *n* cassaforte *f*; **~hold** *n* (*also fig*) roccaforte *f*; **~ly** *adv* fortemente, con forza; energicamente; vivamente; **~room** *n* camera di sicurezza

strove [strəuv] *pt of* **strive**

struck [strʌk] *pt, pp of* **strike**

structural ['strʌktʃərəl] *adj* strutturale

structure ['strʌktʃə*] *n* struttura; (*building*) costruzione *f*, fabbricato

struggle ['strʌgl] *n* lotta ♦ *vi* lottare

strum [strʌm] *vt* (*guitar*) strimpellare

strung [strʌŋ] *pt, pp of* **string**

strut [strʌt] *n* sostegno, supporto ♦ *vi* pavoneggiarsi

stub [stʌb] *n* mozzicone *m*; (*of ticket etc*) matrice *f*, talloncino ♦ *vt*: **to ~ one's toe** urtare *o* sbattere il dito del piede; **~ out** *vt* schiacciare

stubble ['stʌbl] *n* stoppia; (*on chin*) barba ispida

stubborn ['stʌbən] *adj* testardo(a), ostinato(a)

stuck [stʌk] *pt, pp of* **stick** ♦ *adj* (*jammed*) bloccato(a); **~-up** *adj* presuntuoso(a)

stud [stʌd] *n* bottoncino, borchia; (*also: ~ earring*) orecchino a pressione; (*also: ~ farm*) scuderia, allevamento di cavalli; (*also: ~ horse*) stallone *m* ♦ *vt* (*fig*): **~ded with** tempestato(a) di

student ['stjuːdənt] *n* studente/essa ♦ *cpd* studentesco(a); universitario(a); degli studenti; **~ driver** (*US*) *n* conducente *m/f* principiante

studio ['stjuːdɪəu] *n* studio; **~ flat** (*US ~ apartment*) *n* monolocale *m*

studious ['stjuːdɪəs] *adj* studioso(a); (*studied*) studiato(a), voluto(a); **~ly** *adv* (*carefully*) deliberatamente, di proposito

study ['stʌdɪ] *n* studio ♦ *vt* studiare; esaminare ♦ *vi* studiare

stuff [stʌf] *n* roba; (*substance*) sostanza, materiale *m* ♦ *vt* imbottire; (*CULIN*) farcire; (*dead animal*) impagliare; (*inf*:

push) ficcare; **~ing** n imbottitura;
(CULIN) ripieno; **~y** adj (room) mal
ventilato(a), senz'aria; (ideas)
antiquato(a)

stumble ['stʌmbl] vi inciampare; to
~ **across** (fig) imbattersi in;
stumbling block n ostacolo, scoglio

stump [stʌmp] n ceppo; (of limb)
moncone m ♦ vt: **to be ~ed** essere
sconcertato(a)

stun [stʌn] vt stordire; (amaze)
sbalordire

stung [stʌŋ] pt, pp of **sting**

stunk [stʌŋk] pp of **stink**

stunning ['stʌnɪŋ] adj sbalorditivo(a);
(girl etc) fantastico(a)

stunt [stʌnt] n bravata; trucco
pubblicitario; **~man** (irreg) n cascatore
m

stupefy ['stjuːpɪfaɪ] vt stordire;
intontire; (fig) stupire

stupendous [stjuːˈpɛndəs] adj
stupendo(a), meraviglioso(a)

stupid ['stjuːpɪd] adj stupido(a); **~ity**
[-ˈpɪdɪtɪ] n stupidità f inv, stupidaggine
f

stupor ['stjuːpə*] n torpore m

sturdy ['stɜːdɪ] adj robusto(a),
vigoroso(a); solido(a)

stutter ['stʌtə*] n balbuzie f ♦ vi
balbettare

sty [staɪ] n (of pigs) porcile m

stye [staɪ] n (MED) orzaiolo

style [staɪl] n stile m; (distinction)
eleganza, classe f; **stylish** adj elegante

stylus ['staɪləs] n (of record player)
puntina

suave [swɑːv] adj untuoso(a)

sub... [sʌb] prefix sub..., sotto...;
~conscious adj subcosciente ♦ n
subcosciente m; **~contract** vt
subappaltare

subdue [səbˈdjuː] vt sottomettere,
soggiogare; **~d** adj pacato(a); (light)
attenuato(a)

subject [n ˈsʌbdʒɪkt, vb səbˈdʒɛkt] n
soggetto; (citizen etc) cittadino/a;

(SCOL) materia ♦ vt: **to ~ to**
sottomettere a; esporre a; **to be ~ to**
(law) essere sottomesso(a) a; (disease)
essere soggetto(a) a; **~ive** [-ˈdʒɛktɪv]
adj soggettivo(a); **~ matter** n
argomento; contenuto

sublet [sʌbˈlɛt] vt subaffittare

submachine gun ['sʌbməˈʃiːn-] n
mitra m inv

submarine [sʌbməˈriːn] n
sommergibile m

submerge [səbˈmɜːdʒ] vt
sommergere; immergere ♦ vi
immergersi

submission [səbˈmɪʃən] n
sottomissione f; (claim) richiesta

submissive [səbˈmɪsɪv] adj
remissivo(a)

submit [səbˈmɪt] vt sottomettere ♦ vi
sottomettersi

subnormal [sʌbˈnɔːməl] adj
subnormale

subordinate [səˈbɔːdɪnət] adj, n
subordinato/a

subpoena [səbˈpiːnə] n (LAW) citazione
f, mandato di comparizione

subscribe [səbˈskraɪb] vi contribuire;
to ~ to (opinion) approvare,
condividere; (fund) sottoscrivere a;
(newspaper) abbonarsi a; essere
abbonato(a) a; **~r** n (to periodical,
telephone) abbonato/a

subscription [səbˈskrɪpʃən] n
sottoscrizione f; abbonamento

subsequent ['sʌbsɪkwənt] adj
successivo(a), seguente; conseguente;
~ly adv in seguito, successivamente

subside [səbˈsaɪd] vi cedere,
abbassarsi; (flood) decrescere; (wind)
calmarsi; **~nce** [-ˈsaɪdns] n cedimento,
abbassamento

subsidiary [səbˈsɪdɪərɪ] adj
sussidiario(a); accessorio(a) ♦ n filiale f

subsidize ['sʌbsɪdaɪz] vt sovvenzionare

subsidy ['sʌbsɪdɪ] n sovvenzione f

subsistence [səbˈsɪstəns] n esistenza;
mezzi mpl di sostentamento;

~ **allowance** n indennità f inv di trasferta

substance ['sʌbstəns] n sostanza

substantial [səb'stænʃl] adj solido(a); (amount, progress etc) notevole; (meal) sostanzioso(a)

substantiate [səb'stænʃɪeɪt] vt comprovare

substitute ['sʌbstɪtjuːt] n (person) sostituto/a; (thing) succedaneo, surrogato ♦ vt to ~ sth/sb for sostituire qc/qn a

subterfuge ['sʌbtəfjuːdʒ] n sotterfugio

subterranean [sʌbtə'reɪnɪən] adj sotterraneo(a)

subtitle ['sʌbtaɪtl] n (CINEMA) sottotitolo; ~d adj sottotitolato(a)

subtle ['sʌtl] adj sottile; ~ty n sottigliezza

subtotal [sʌb'təʊtl] n somma parziale

subtract [səb'trækt] vt sottrarre; ~ion [-'trækʃən] n sottrazione f

suburb ['sʌbəːb] n sobborgo; the ~s la periferia; ~an [sə'bəːbən] adj suburbano(a); ~ia [sə'bəːbɪə] n periferia, sobborghi mpl

subversive [səb'vəːsɪv] adj sovversivo(a)

subway ['sʌbweɪ] n (US: underground) metropolitana; (BRIT: underpass) sottopassaggio

succeed [sək'siːd] vi riuscire; avere successo ♦ vt succedere a; to ~ in doing riuscire a fare; ~ing adj (following) successivo(a)

success [sək'sɛs] n successo; ~ful (venture) coronato(a) da successo, riuscito(a); to be ~ful (in doing) riuscire (a fare); ~fully adv con successo

succession [sək'sɛʃən] n successione f

successive [sək'sɛsɪv] adj successivo(a); consecutivo(a)

succumb [sə'kʌm] vi soccombere

such [sʌtʃ] adj tale; (of that kind): ~ a book un tale libro, un libro del genere; ~ books tali libri, libri del genere; (so much): ~ courage tanto coraggio ♦ adv talmente, così; ~ a long trip un viaggio così lungo; ~ a lot of talmente o così tanto(a); ~ as (like) come; as ~ come o in quanto tale; ~-and-~ adj tale (after noun)

suck [sʌk] vt succhiare; (breast, bottle) poppare; ~er n (ZOOL, TECH) ventosa; (inf) gonzo/a, babbeo/a

suction ['sʌkʃən] n succhiamento; (TECH) aspirazione f

sudden ['sʌdn] adj improvviso(a); all of a ~ improvvisamente, all'improvviso; ~ly adv bruscamente, improvvisamente, di colpo

suds [sʌdz] npl schiuma (di sapone)

sue [suː] vt citare in giudizio

suede [sweɪd] n pelle f scamosciata

suet ['sʊɪt] n grasso di rognone

suffer ['sʌfə*] vt soffrire, patire; (bear) sopportare, tollerare ♦ vi soffrire; to ~ from soffrire di; ~er n malato/a; ~ing n sofferenza

suffice [sə'faɪs] vi essere sufficiente, bastare

sufficient [sə'fɪʃənt] adj sufficiente; ~ money abbastanza soldi; ~ly adv sufficientemente, abbastanza

suffocate ['sʌfəkeɪt] vi (have difficulty breathing) soffocare; (die through lack of air) asfissiare

sugar ['ʃʊgə*] n zucchero ♦ vt zuccherare; ~ beet n barbabietola da zucchero; ~ cane n canna da zucchero

suggest [sə'dʒɛst] vt proporre, suggerire; indicare; ~ion [-'dʒɛstʃən] n suggerimento, proposta; indicazione f; ~ive (pej) adj indecente

suicide ['sʊɪsaɪd] n (person) suicida m/f; (act) suicidio; see also **commit**

suit [suːt] n (man's) vestito; (woman's) completo, tailleur m inv; (LAW) causa; (CARDS) seme m, colore m ♦ vt andar bene a or per; essere adatto(a) a or per; (adapt): to ~ sth to adattare qc a; well ~ed ben assortito(a); ~able adj adatto(a); appropriato(a); ~ably *adv* (*dress*) in modo adatto; (*impressed*) favorevolmente

suitcase ['su:tkeɪs] *n* valigia

suite [swi:t] *n* (*of rooms*) appartamento *m*; (*MUS*) suite *f inv*; (*furniture*): **bedroom/dining room ~** arredo *or* mobilia per la camera da letto/sala da pranzo

suitor ['su:tə*] *n* corteggiatore *m*, spasimante *m*

sulfur ['sʌlfə*] (*US*) *n* = **sulphur**

sulk [sʌlk] *vi* fare il broncio; **~y** *adj* imbronciato(a)

sullen ['sʌlən] *adj* scontroso(a); cupo(a)

sulphur ['sʌlfə*] (*US* **sulfur**) *n* zolfo

sultana [sʌl'tɑ:nə] *n* (*fruit*) uva (secca) sultanina

sultry ['sʌltrɪ] *adj* afoso(a)

sum [sʌm] *n* somma; (*SCOL etc*) addizione *f*; **~ up** *vt, vi* riassumere

summarize ['sʌməraɪz] *vt* riassumere, riepilogare

summary ['sʌmərɪ] *n* riassunto

summer ['sʌmə*] *n* estate *f* ♦ *cpd* d'estate, estivo(a); **~ holidays** *npl* vacanze *fpl* estive; **~house** *n* (*in garden*) padiglione *m*; **~time** *n* (*season*) estate *f*; **~ time** *n* (*by clock*) ora legale (estiva)

summit ['sʌmɪt] *n* cima, sommità; (*POL*) vertice *m*

summon ['sʌmən] *vt* chiamare, convocare; **~ up** *vt* raccogliere, fare appello a; **~s** *n* ordine *m* di comparizione ♦ *vt* citare

sump [sʌmp] (*BRIT*) *n* (*AUT*) coppa dell'olio

sumptuous ['sʌmptjuəs] *adj* sontuoso(a)

sun [sʌn] *n* sole *m*; **~bathe** *vi* prendere un bagno di sole; **~block** *n* protezione *f* solare totale; **~burn** *n* (*painful*) scottatura; **~burnt** *adj* abbronzato(a); (*painfully*) scottato(a)

Sunday ['sʌndɪ] *n* domenica; **~ school** *n* ≈ scuola di catechismo

sundial ['sʌndaɪəl] *n* meridiana

sundown ['sʌndaun] *n* tramonto

sundry ['sʌndrɪ] *adj* vari(e), diversi(e); **all and ~** tutti quanti; **sundries** *npl* articoli diversi, cose diverse

sunflower ['sʌnflauə*] *n* girasole *m*

sung [sʌŋ] *pp of* **sing**

sunglasses ['sʌnglɑ:sɪz] *npl* occhiali *mpl* da sole

sunk [sʌŋk] *pp of* **sink**

sun: **~light** *n* (luce *f* del) sole *m*; **~lit** *adj* soleggiato(a); **~ny** *adj* assolato(a), soleggiato(a); (*fig*) allegro(a), felice; **~rise** *n* levata del sole, alba; **~ roof** *n* (*AUT*) tetto apribile; **~screen** *n* (*protective ingredient*) filtro solare; (*cream*) crema solare protettiva; **~set** *n* tramonto; **~shade** *n* parasole *m*; **~shine** *n* (luce *f* del) sole *m*; **~stroke** *n* insolazione *f*, colpo di sole; **~tan** *n* abbronzatura; **~tan lotion** *n* lozione *f* solare; **~tan oil** *n* olio solare

super ['su:pə*] (*inf*) *adj* fantastico(a)

superannuation [su:pərænju'eɪʃən] *n* contributi *mpl* pensionistici; pensione *f*

superb [su:'pə:b] *adj* magnifico(a)

supercilious [su:pə'sɪlɪəs] *adj* sprezzante, sdegnoso(a)

superficial [su:pə'fɪʃəl] *adj* superficiale

superhuman [su:pə'hju:mən] *adj* sovrumano(a)

superimpose ['su:pərɪm'pəuz] *vt* sovrapporre

superintendent [su:pərɪn'tendənt] *n* direttore/trice; (*POLICE*) ≈ commissario (capo)

superior [su:'pɪərɪə*] *adj, n* superiore *m/f*; **~ity** [-'ɔrɪtɪ] *n* superiorità

superlative [su:'pə:lətɪv] *adj* superlativo(a), supremo(a) ♦ *n* (*LING*) superlativo

superman ['su:pəmæn] (*irreg*) *n* superuomo

supermarket ['su:pəmɑ:kɪt] *n* supermercato

supernatural [su:pə'nætʃərəl] *adj* soprannaturale ♦ *n* soprannaturale *m*

superpower ['su:pəpauə*] n (POL) superpotenza f

supersede [su:pə'si:d] vt sostituire, soppiantare

superstitious [su:pə'stɪʃəs] adj superstizioso(a)

supertanker ['su:pətæŋkə*] n superpetroliera

supervise ['su:pəvaɪz] vt (person etc) sorvegliare; (organization) soprintendere a; **supervision** [-'vɪʒən] n sorveglianza f; supervisione f; **supervisor** n sorvegliante m/f, soprintendente m/f; (in shop) capocommesso f

supine ['su:paɪn] adj supino(a)

supper ['sʌpə*] n cena

supplant [sə'plɑ:nt] vt (person, thing) soppiantare

supple ['sʌpl] adj flessibile; agile

supplement [n 'sʌplɪmənt, vb sʌplɪ'ment] n supplemento ♦ vt completare, integrare; **~ary** [-'mentərɪ] adj supplementare

supplier [sə'plaɪə*] n fornitore m

supply [sə'plaɪ] vt (provide) fornire; (equip): **to ~ (with)** approvvigionare (di); attrezzare (con) ♦ n riserva, provvista; (supplying) approvvigionamento; (TECH) alimentazione f; **supplies** npl (food) viveri mpl; (MIL) sussistenza; **~ teacher** (BRIT) n supplente m/f

support [sə'pɔ:t] n (moral, financial etc) sostegno, appoggio; (TECH) supporto ♦ vt sostenere; (financially) mantenere; (uphold) sostenere, difendere; **~er** n (POL etc) sostenitore/trice, fautore/trice; (SPORT) tifoso/a

suppose [sə'pəuz] vt supporre; immaginare; **to be ~d to do** essere tenuto(a) a fare; **~dly** [sə'pəuzɪdlɪ] adv presumibilmente; **supposing** conj se, ammesso che + sub

suppository [sə'pɒzɪtərɪ] n supposte/io

suppress [sə'prɛs] vt reprimere;

sopprimere; occultare

supreme [su'pri:m] adj supremo(a)

surcharge ['sə:tʃɑ:dʒ] n supplemento

sure [ʃuə*] adj sicuro(a); (definite, convinced) sicuro(a), certo(a); **~!** (of course) senz'altro!, certo!; **~ enough** infatti; **to make ~ of sth/that** assicurarsi di qc/che; **~-footed** adj dal passo sicuro; **~ly** adv sicuramente; certamente

surf [sə:f] n (waves) cavalloni mpl; (foam) spuma

surface ['sə:fɪs] n superficie f ♦ vt (road) asfaltare ♦ vi risalire alla superficie; (fig: news, feeling) venire a galla; **~ mail** n posta ordinaria

surfboard ['sə:fbɔ:d] n tavola per surfing

surfeit ['sə:fɪt] n: **a ~ of** un eccesso di; un'indigestione di

surfing ['sə:fɪŋ] n surfing m

surge [sə:dʒ] n (strong movement) ondata; (of feeling) impeto ♦ vi gonfiarsi; (people) riversarsi

surgeon ['sə:dʒən] n chirurgo

surgery ['sə:dʒərɪ] n chirurgia; (BRIT: room) studio or gabinetto medico, ambulatorio; (: also: **~ hours**) orario delle visite or di consultazione; **to undergo ~** subire un intervento chirurgico

surgical ['sə:dʒɪkl] adj chirurgico(a); **~ spirit** (BRIT) n alcool m denaturato

surname ['sə:neɪm] n cognome m

surpass [sə:'pɑ:s] vt superare

surplus [sə:pləs] n eccedenza; (ECON) surplus m inv ♦ adj eccedente, d'avanzo

surprise [sə'praɪz] n sorpresa; (astonishment) stupore m ♦ vt sorprendere; stupire; **surprising** adj sorprendente, stupefacente; **surprisingly** adv (easy, helpful) sorprendentemente

surrender [sə'rendə*] n resa, capitolazione f ♦ vi arrendersi

surreptitious [sʌrəp'tɪʃəs] adj

furtivo(a)

surrogate ['sʌrəgɪt] n surrogato;
~ **mother** n madre f provetta

surround [sə'raund] vt circondare; (MIL
etc) accerchiare; ~**ing** adj circostante;
~**ings** npl dintorni mpl; (fig) ambiente
m

surveillance [sə'veɪləns] n
sorveglianza, controllo

survey [n 'sə:veɪ, vb sə:'veɪ] n quadro
generale; (study) esame m; (in
housebuying etc) perizia; (of land)
rilevamento, rilievo topografico ♦ vt
osservare; esaminare; valutare; rilevare;
~**or** n perito; geometra m; (of land)
agrimensore m

survival [sə'vaɪvl] n sopravvivenza;
(relic) reliquia, vestigio

survive [sə'vaɪv] vi sopravvivere ♦ vt
sopravvivere a; **survivor** n superstite
m/f, sopravvissuto/a

susceptible [sə'septəbl] adj: ~ (**to**)
sensibile a; (disease) predisposto(a)
(a)

suspect [adj, n 'sʌspekt, vb səs'pekt]
adj sospetto(a) ♦ n persona sospetta
♦ vt sospettare; (think likely) supporre;
(doubt) dubitare

suspend [səs'pend] vt sospendere;
~**ed sentence** n condanna con la
condizionale; ~**er belt** n reggicalze m
inv; ~**ers** npl (BRIT) giarrettiere fpl; (US)
bretelle fpl

suspense [səs'pens] n apprensione f;
(in film etc) suspense m; **to keep sb in**
~ tenere qn in sospeso

suspension [səs'penʃən] n (gen AUT)
sospensione f; (of driving licence) ritiro
temporaneo; ~ **bridge** n ponte m
sospeso

suspicion [səs'pɪʃən] n sospetto

suspicious [səs'pɪʃəs] adj (suspecting)
sospettoso(a); (causing suspicion)
sospetto(a)

sustain [səs'teɪn] vt sostenere;
sopportare; (LAW: charge) confermare;
(suffer) subire; ~**able** adj sostenibile;

~**ed** adj (of effort) prolungato(a)

sustenance ['sʌstɪnəns] n nutrimento;
mezzi mpl di sostentamento

swab [swɔb] n (MED) tampone m

swagger ['swægə*] vi pavoneggiarsi

swallow ['swɔləu] n (bird) rondine f
♦ vt inghiottire; (fig: story) bere; ~ **up**
vt inghiottire

swam [swæm] pt of **swim**

swamp [swɔmp] n palude f ♦ vt
sommergere

swan [swɔn] n cigno

swap [swɔp] vt: **to** ~ (**for**) scambiare
(con)

swarm [swɔ:m] n sciame m ♦ vi (bees)
sciamare; (people) brulicare; (place): **to
be** ~**ing with** brulicare di

swastika ['swɔstɪkə] n croce f
uncinata, svastica

swat [swɔt] vt schiacciare

sway [sweɪ] vi (tree) ondeggiare;
(person) barcollare ♦ vt (influence)
influenzare, dominare

swear [swɛə*] (pt **swore**, pp **sworn**)
vi (curse) bestemmiare, imprecare ♦ vt
(promise) giurare; ~**word** n parolaccia

sweat [swet] n sudore m, traspirazione
f ♦ vi sudare

sweater ['swetə*] n maglione m

sweatshirt ['swetʃə:t] n felpa

sweaty ['swetɪ] adj sudato(a);
bagnato(a) di sudore

Swede [swi:d] n svedese m/f

swede [swi:d] (BRIT) n rapa svedese

Sweden ['swi:dn] n Svezia

Swedish ['swi:dɪʃ] adj svedese ♦ n
(LING) svedese m

sweep [swi:p] (pt, pp **swept**) n
spazzata; (also: chimney ~)
spazzacamino ♦ vt spazzare, scopare;
(current) spazzare ♦ vi (hand) muoversi
con gesto ampio; (wind) infuriare;
~ **away** vt spazzare via; trascinare via;
~ **past** vi sfrecciare accanto; passare
accanto maestosamente; ~ **up** vt, vi
spazzare; ~**ing** adj (gesture) ampio(a);
circolare; **a** ~**ing statement**

un'affermazione generica

sweet |swiːt| n (BRIT: pudding) dolce m; (candy) caramella ♦ adj dolce; (fresh) fresco(a); (fig) piacevole, delicato(a), grazioso(a); gentile; **~corn** n granturco dolce; **~en** vt addolcire; zuccherare; **~heart** n innamorato/a; **~ness** n sapore m dolce; dolcezza; **~ pea** n pisello odoroso

swell |swel| (pt **~ed**, pp **swollen**, **~ed**) n (of sea) mare m lungo ♦ adj (US: inf: excellent) favoloso(a) ♦ vt gonfiare, ingrossare; aumentare ♦ vi gonfiarsi, ingrossarsi; (sound) crescere; (also: ~ up) gonfiarsi; **~ing** n (MED) tumefazione f, gonfiore m

sweltering |ˈsweltərɪŋ| adj soffocante

swept |swept| pt, pp of **sweep**

swerve |swɜːv| vi deviare; (driver) sterzare; (boxer) scartare

swift |swɪft| n (bird) rondone m ♦ adj rapido(a), veloce

swig |swɪg| n (inf) (drink) sorsata m

swill |swɪl| vt (also: ~ out, ~ down) risciacquare

swim |swɪm| (pt **swam**, pp **swum**) n: **to go for a ~** andare a fare una nuotata ♦ vi nuotare; (SPORT) fare del nuoto; (head, room) girare ♦ vt (river, channel) attraversare o percorrere a nuoto; (length) nuotare; **~mer** n nuotatore/trice; **~ming** n nuoto; **~ming cap** n cuffia; **~ming costume** (BRIT) n costume m da bagno; **~ming pool** n piscina; **~ming trunks** npl costume m da bagno (da uomo); **~suit** n costume m da bagno

swindle |ˈswɪndl| n truffa ♦ vt truffare

swine |swaɪn| (inf!) n inv porco (!)

swing |swɪŋ| (pt, pp **swung**) n altalena; (movement) oscillazione f; (MUS) ritmo; swing m ♦ vt dondolare, far oscillare; (also: ~ round) far girare ♦ vi oscillare, dondolare; (also: ~ round: object) roteare; (: person) girarsi, voltarsi; **to be in full ~** (activity) essere in piena attività; (party etc) essere nel

pieno; **~ door** (US **~ing door**) n porta battente

swingeing |ˈswɪndʒɪŋ| adj (BRIT: defeat) violento(a); (: cuts) enorme

swipe |swaɪp| vt (hit) colpire con forza; dare uno schiaffo a; (inf: steal) sgraffignare

swirl |swɜːl| vi turbinare, far mulinello

Swiss |swɪs| adj, n inv svizzero(a)

switch |swɪtʃ| n (for light, radio etc) interruttore m; (change) cambiamento ♦ vt (change) cambiare; scambiare; **~ off** vt spegnere; **~ on** vt accendere; (engine, machine) mettere in moto, avviare; **~board** n (TEL) centralino

Switzerland |ˈswɪtsələnd| n Svizzera

swivel |ˈswɪvl| vi (also: ~ round) girare

swollen |ˈswəʊlən| pp of **swell**

swoon |swuːn| vi svenire

swoop |swuːp| n incursione f ♦ vi (also: ~ down) scendere in picchiata, piombare

swop |swɒp| n, vt = **swap**

sword |sɔːd| n spada; **~fish** n pesce m spada inv

swore |swɔː*| pt of **swear**

sworn |swɔːn| pp of **swear** ♦ adj giurato(a)

swot |swɒt| vi sgobbare

swum |swʌm| pp of **swim**

swung |swʌŋ| pt, pp of **swing**

syllable |ˈsɪləbl| n sillaba

syllabus |ˈsɪləbəs| n programma m

symbol |ˈsɪmbl| n simbolo

symmetry |ˈsɪmɪtrɪ| n simmetria

sympathetic |sɪmpəˈθetɪk| adj (showing pity) compassionevole; (kind) comprensivo(a); **~ towards** ben disposto/a verso

sympathize |ˈsɪmpəθaɪz| vi: **to ~ with** (person) compatire; partecipare al dolore di; (cause) simpatizzare per; **~r** n (POL) simpatizzante m/f

sympathy |ˈsɪmpəθɪ| n compassione f; **sympathies** npl (support, tendencies) simpatie fpl; **in ~ with** (strike) per solidarietà con; **with our deepest ~**

con le nostre più sincere condoglianze

symphony ['sɪmfənɪ] *n* sinfonia

symptom ['sɪmptəm] *n* sintomo; indizio

synagogue ['sɪnəgɒg] *n* sinagoga

syndicate ['sɪndɪkɪt] *n* sindacato

synopses [sɪ'nɒpsiːz] *npl of* **synopsis**

synopsis [sɪ'nɒpsɪs] (*pl* **synopses**) *n* sommario, sinossi *f inv*

syntheses ['sɪnθəsiːz] *npl of* **synthesis**

synthesis ['sɪnθəsɪs] (*pl* **syntheses**) *n* sintesi *f inv*

synthetic [sɪn'θetɪk] *adj* sintetico(a)

syphon ['saɪfən] *n, vb* = **siphon**

Syria ['sɪrɪə] *n* Siria

syringe [sɪ'rɪndʒ] *n* siringa

syrup ['sɪrəp] *n* sciroppo; (*also: golden ~*) melassa raffinata

system ['sɪstəm] *n* sistema *m*; (*order*) metodo; (*ANAT*) organismo; **~atic** [-'mætɪk] *adj* sistematico(a); metodico(a); **~ disk** *n* (*COMPUT*) disco del sistema; **~s analyst** *n* analista *m* di sistemi

T, t

ta [tɑː] (*BRIT: inf*) *excl* grazie!

tab [tæb] *n* (*loop on coat etc*) laccetto; (*label*) etichetta; **to keep ~s on** (*fig*) tenere d'occhio

tabby ['tæbɪ] *n* (*also: ~ cat*) (gatto) soriano, gatto tigrato

table ['teɪbl] *n* tavolo, tavola; (*MATH, CHEM etc*) tavola ♦ *vt* (*BRIT: motion etc*) presentare; **to lay** *or* **set the ~** apparecchiare *or* preparare la tavola; **~cloth** *n* tovaglia; **~ of contents** *n* indice *m*; **~ d'hôte** [tɑːbl'dəut] *adj* (*meal*) a prezzo fisso; **~ lamp** *n* lampada da tavolo; **~mat** *n* sottopiatto; **~spoon** *n* cucchiaio da tavola; (*also: ~spoonful: as measurement*) cucchiaiata

tablet ['tæblɪt] *n* (*MED*) compressa; (*of stone*) targa

table: **~ tennis** *n* tennis *m* da tavolo, ping-pong ® *m*; **~ wine** *n* vino da tavola

---
tabloid press

Il termine **tabloid press** *si riferisce ai giornali popolari, che hanno un formato ridotto e pubblicano le notizie in modo sensazionalistico; vedi anche* **quality press.**

---

tacit ['tæsɪt] *adj* tacito(a)

tack [tæk] *n* (*nail*) bulletta; (*fig*) approccio ♦ *vt* imbullettare; imbastire ♦ *vi* bordeggiare

tackle ['tækl] *n* attrezzatura, equipaggiamento; (*for lifting*) paranco; (*FOOTBALL*) contrasto; (*RUGBY*) placcaggio ♦ *vt* (*difficulty*) affrontare; (*FOOTBALL*) contrastare; (*RUGBY*) placcare

tacky ['tækɪ] *adj* appiccicaticcio(a); (*pej*) scadente

tact [tækt] *n* tatto; **~ful** *adj* delicato(a), discreto(a)

tactical ['tæktɪkl] *adj* tattico(a)

tactics ['tæktɪks] *n, npl* tattica

tactless ['tæktlɪs] *adj* che manca di tatto

tadpole ['tædpəul] *n* girino

tag [tæg] *n* etichetta; **~ along** *vi* seguire

tail [teɪl] *n* coda; (*of shirt*) falda ♦ *vt* (*follow*) seguire, pedinare; **~ away** *vi* = **~ off**; **~ off** *vi* (*in size, quality etc*) diminuire gradatamente; **~back** (*BRIT*) *n* (*AUT*) ingorgo; **~ end** *n* (*of train, procession etc*) coda; (*of meeting etc*) fine *f*; **~gate** *n* (*AUT*) portellone *m* posteriore

tailor ['teɪlə*] *n* sarto; **~ing** *n* (*cut*) stile *m*; (*craft*) sartoria; **~-made** *adj* (*also fig*) fatto(a) su misura

tailwind ['teɪlwɪnd] *n* vento di coda

tainted ['teɪntɪd] *adj* (*food*) guasto(a); (*water, air*) infetto(a); (*fig*) corrotto(a)

take [teɪk] (pt **took**, pp **taken**) vt prendere; (gain: prize) ottenere, vincere; (require: effort, courage) occorrere, volerci; (tolerate) accettare, sopportare; (hold: passengers etc) contenere; (accompany) accompagnare; (bring, carry) portare; (exam) sostenere, presentarsi a; **to ~ a photo/a shower** fare una fotografia/ una doccia; **I ~ it that** suppongo che; **~ after** vt fus assomigliare a; **~ apart** vt smontare; **~ away** vt portare via; togliere; **~ back** vt (return) restituire; riportare; (one's words) ritirare; **~ down** vt (building) demolire; (letter etc) scrivere; **~ in** vt (deceive) imbrogliare, abbindolare; (understand) capire; (include) comprendere, includere; (lodger) prendere, ospitare; **~ off** vi (AVIAT) decollare; (go away) andarsene ♦ vt (remove) togliere; **~ on** vt (work) accettare, intraprendere; (employee) assumere; (opponent) sfidare, affrontare; **~ out** vt portare fuori; (remove) togliere; (licence) prendere, ottenere; **to ~ sth out of sth** (drawer, pocket etc) tirare qc fuori da qc; estrarre qc da qc; **~ over** vt (business) rilevare ♦ vi: **to ~ over from sb** prendere le consegne or il controllo da qn; **~ to** vt fus (person) prendere in simpatia; (activity) prendere gusto a; **~ up** vt (dress) accorciare; (occupy: time, space) occupare; (engage in: hobby etc) mettersi a; **to ~ sb up on sth** accettare qc da qn; **~ings** ['teɪkɪŋz] npl (COMM) incasso

takings ['teɪkɪŋz] npl (COMM) incasso
talc [tælk] n (also: **~um powder**) talco
tale [teɪl] n racconto, storia; **to tell ~s** (fig: to teacher, parent etc) fare la spia
talent ['tælnt] n talento; **~ed** adj di talento
talk [tɔ:k] n discorso; (gossip)

chiacchiere fpl; (conversation) conversazione f; (interview) discussione f ♦ vi parlare; **~s** npl (POL etc) colloqui mpl; **to ~ about** parlare di; **to ~ sb out of/into doing** dissuadere qn da/ convincere qn a fare; **to ~ shop** parlare di lavoro or di affari; **~ over** vt discutere; **~ative** adj loquace, ciarliero(a); **~ show** n conversazione f televisiva, talk show m inv
tall [tɔ:l] adj alto(a); **to be 6 feet ~** ≈ essere alto 1 metro e 80; **~ story** n panzana, frottola
tally ['tælɪ] n conto, conteggio ♦ vi: **to ~ (with)** corrispondere (a)
talon ['tælən] n artiglio
tambourine [tæmbə'ri:n] n tamburello
tame [teɪm] adj addomesticato(a); (fig: story, style) insipido(a), scialbo(a)
tamper ['tæmpə*] vi: **to ~ with** manomettere
tampon ['tæmpon] n tampone m
tan [tæn] n (also: **sun~**) abbronzatura ♦ vi abbronzarsi ♦ adj (colour) marrone rossiccio inv
tang [tæŋ] n odore m penetrante; sapore m piccante
tangent ['tændʒənt] n: **to go off at a ~** (fig) partire per la tangente
tangerine [tændʒə'ri:n] n mandarino
tangle ['tæŋgl] n groviglio; **to get into a ~** aggroviglarsi; (fig) combinare un pasticcio
tank [tæŋk] n serbatoio; (for fish) acquario; (MIL) carro armato
tanker ['tæŋkə*] n (ship) nave f cisterna inv; (truck) autobotte f, autocisterna
tanned [tænd] adj abbronzato(a)
tantalizing ['tæntəlaɪzɪŋ] adj allettante
tantamount ['tæntəmaunt] adj: **~ to** equivalente a
tantrum ['tæntrəm] n accesso di collera
tap [tæp] n (on sink etc) rubinetto; (gentle blow) colpetto ♦ vt dare un

colpetto a; (resources) sfruttare, utilizzare; (telephone) mettere sotto controllo; **on** ~ (fig: resources) a disposizione; ~ **dancing** n tip tap m

tape [teɪp] n nastro; (also: magnetic ~) nastro (magnetico); (sticky ~) nastro adesivo ♦ vt (record) registrare (su nastro); (stick) attaccare con nastro adesivo; ~ **deck** n piastra; ~ **measure** n metro a nastro

taper ['teɪpə*] n candelina ♦ vi assottigliarsi

tape recorder n registratore m (a nastro)

tapestry ['tæpɪstrɪ] n arazzo; tappezzeria

tar [tɑ:*] n catrame m

target ['tɑ:gɪt] n bersaglio; (fig: objective) obiettivo

tariff ['tærɪf] n tariffa

tarmac ['tɑ:mæk] n (BRIT: on road) macadam m al catrame; (AVIAT) pista di decollo

tarnish ['tɑ:nɪʃ] vt offuscare, annerire; (fig) macchiare

tarpaulin [tɑ:'pɔːlɪn] n tela incatramata

tarragon ['tærəgən] n dragoncello

tart [tɑ:t] n (CULIN) crostata; (BRIT: inf: pej: woman) sgualdrina ♦ adj (flavour) aspro(a), agro(a); ~ **up** (inf) vt agghindare

tartan ['tɑ:tn] n tartan m inv

tartar ['tɑ:tə*] n (on teeth) tartaro; ~(**e**) **sauce** n salsa tartara

task [tɑ:sk] n compito; **to take to** ~ rimproverare; ~ **force** n (MIL, POLICE) unità operativa

taste [teɪst] n gusto; (flavour) sapore m, gusto; (sample) assaggio; (fig: glimpse, idea) idea ♦ vt (get flavour of) sentire il sapore di; (sample) assaggiare ♦ vi: **to** ~ **of** (or **like**) (fish etc) sapere or avere sapore di; **you can** ~ **the garlic (in it)** (ci) si sente il sapore dell'aglio; **in good/bad** ~ di buon/cattivo gusto; ~**ful** adj di buon gusto; ~**less** adj (food) insipido(a);

(remark) di cattivo gusto; **tasty** adj saporito(a), gustoso(a)

tatters ['tætəz] npl: **in** ~ a brandelli

tattoo [tə'tu:] n tatuaggio; (spectacle) parata militare ♦ vt tatuare

tatty ['tætɪ] adj (BRIT: inf) malridotto(a)

taught [tɔːt] pt, pp of **teach**

taunt [tɔːnt] n scherno ♦ vt schernire

Taurus ['tɔːrəs] n Toro

taut [tɔːt] adj teso(a)

tax [tæks] n (on goods) imposta; (on services) tassa; (on income) imposte fpl, tasse fpl ♦ vt tassare; (fig: strain: patience etc) mettere alla prova; ~**able** adj (income) imponibile; ~**ation** [-'seɪʃən] n tassazione f; tasse fpl, imposte fpl; ~ **avoidance** n elusione f fiscale; ~ **disc** (BRIT) n (AUT) ≈ bollo; ~ **evasion** n evasione f fiscale; ~**-free** adj esente da imposte

tax: ~ **payer** n contribuente m/f; ~ **relief** n agevolazioni fpl fiscali; ~ **return** n dichiarazione f dei redditi

TB n abbr = **tuberculosis**

tea [ti:] n tè m inv; (BRIT: snack: for children) merenda; **high** ~ (BRIT) cena leggera (presa nel tardo pomeriggio); ~ **bag** n bustina di tè; ~ **break** (BRIT) n intervallo per il tè

teach [ti:tʃ] (pt, pp **taught**) vt: **to** ~ **sb sth**, ~ **sth to sb** insegnare qc a qn ♦ vi insegnare; ~**er** n insegnante m/f; (in secondary school) professore/essa; (in primary school) maestro/a; ~**ing** n insegnamento

tea cosy n copriteiera m inv

teacup ['ti:kʌp] n tazza da tè

teak [ti:k] n teak m

tea leaves npl foglie fpl di tè

team [ti:m] n squadra; (of animals) tiro; ~**work** n lavoro di squadra

teapot ['ti:pɒt] n teiera

tear¹ [tɛə*] (pt **tore**, pp **torn**) n

strappo ♦ vt strappare ♦ vi strapparsi; ~ **along** (rush) correre all'impazzata; ~ **up** vt (sheet of paper etc) strappare

tear² [tɪə*] n lacrima; **in ~s** in lacrime; ~**ful** adj piangente, lacrimoso(a); ~ **gas** n gas m lacrimogeno

tearoom ['tiːruːm] n sala da tè

tease [tiːz] vt canzonare; (unkindly) tormentare

tea set n servizio da tè

teaspoon ['tiːspuːn] n cucchiaino da tè; (also: ~**ful**: as measurement) cucchiaino

teat [tiːt] n capezzolo

teatime ['tiːtaɪm] n ora del tè

tea towel n strofinaccio (per i piatti)

technical ['tɛknɪkl] adj tecnico(a); ~ **college** (BRIT) n ≈ istituto tecnico; ~**ity** [-'kælɪtɪ] n tecnicità; (detail) dettaglio tecnico; (legal) cavillo

technician [tɛk'nɪʃən] n tecnico/a

technique [tɛk'niːk] n tecnica

technological [tɛknə'lɔdʒɪkl] adj tecnologico(a)

technology [tɛk'nɔlədʒɪ] n tecnologia

teddy (bear) ['tɛdɪ-] n orsacchiotto

tedious ['tiːdɪəs] adj noioso(a), tedioso(a)

tee [tiː] n (GOLF) tee m inv

teem [tiːm] vi: **to ~ with** brulicare di; **it is ~ing** (with rain) piove a dirotto

teenage [tiːneɪdʒ] adj (fashions etc) per giovani, per adolescenti; ~**r** n adolescente m/f

teens [tiːnz] npl: **to be in one's ~** essere adolescente

tee-shirt ['tiːʃəːt] n = **T-shirt**

teeter ['tiːtə*] vi barcollare, vacillare

teeth [tiːθ] npl of **tooth**

teethe [tiːð] vi mettere i denti

teething ring ['tiːðɪŋ-] n dentaruolo

teething troubles ['tiːðɪŋ-] npl (fig) difficoltà fpl iniziali

teetotal ['tiː'təutl] adj astemio(a)

tele: ~**conferencing** n teleconferenza; ~**gram** n telegramma m; ~**graph** n telegrafo; ~**pathy** [tə'lɛpəθɪ] n telepatia

telephone ['tɛlɪfəun] n telefono ♦ vt (person) telefonare a; (message) comunicare per telefono; ~ **booth** (BRIT ~ **box**) n cabina telefonica; ~ **call** n telefonata; ~ **directory** n elenco telefonico; ~ **number** n numero di telefono; **telephonist** [tə'lɛfənɪst] (BRIT) n telefonista m/f

telesales ['tɛlɪseɪlz] n vendita per telefono

telescope ['tɛlɪskəup] n telescopio

television ['tɛlɪvɪʒən] n televisione f; **on ~** alla televisione; ~ **set** n televisore m

teleworking ['tɛlɪwəːkɪŋ] n telelavoro

telex ['tɛlɛks] n telex m inv ♦ vt trasmettere per telex

tell [tɛl] (pt, pp told) vt dire; (relate: story) raccontare; (distinguish): **to ~ sth from** distinguere qc da ♦ vi (talk): **to ~ (of)** parlare (di); (have effect) farsi sentire, avere effetto; **to ~ sb to do** dire a qn di fare; ~ **off** vt rimproverare, sgridare; ~**er** n (in bank) cassiere/a; ~**ing** adj (remark, detail) rivelatore(trice); ~**tale** adj (sign) rivelatore(trice)

telly ['tɛlɪ] (BRIT: inf) n abbr (= television) tivù f inv

temerity [tə'mɛrɪtɪ] n temerarietà

temp [tɛmp] n abbr (= temporary) segretaria temporanea

temper ['tɛmpə*] n (nature) carattere m; (mood) umore m; (fit of anger) collera ♦ vt (moderate) moderare; **to be in a ~** essere in collera; **to lose one's ~** andare in collera

temperament ['tɛmprəmənt] n (nature) temperamento; ~**al** [-'mɛntl] adj capriccioso(a)

temperate ['tɛmprət] adj temperato(a)

temperature ['tɛmprətʃə*] n temperatura; **to have** o **run a ~** avere la febbre

tempest ['tɛmpɪst] n tempesta

template ['tɛmplɪt] n sagoma

temple ['templ] n (building) tempio; (ANAT) tempia

temporary ['tempərərɪ] adj temporaneo(a); (job, worker) avventizio(a), temporaneo(a)

tempt [tempt] vt tentare; **to ~ sb into doing** indurre qn a fare; **~ation** [-'teɪʃən] n tentazione f; **~ing** adj allettante

ten [ten] num dieci

tenacity [tə'næsɪtɪ] n tenacia

tenancy ['tenənsɪ] n affitto; condizione f di inquilino

tenant ['tenənt] n inquilino/a

tend [tend] vt badare a, occuparsi di ♦ vi: **to ~ to** tendere a fare

tendency ['tendənsɪ] n tendenza

tender ['tendə*] adj tenero(a); (sore) dolorante ♦ n (COMM: offer) offerta; (money): **legal ~** moneta in corso legale ♦ vt offrire

tendon ['tendən] n tendine m

tenement ['tenəmənt] n casamento

tennis ['tenɪs] n tennis m; **~ ball** n palla da tennis; **~ court** n campo da tennis; **~ player** n tennista m/f; **~ racket** n racchetta da tennis; **~ shoes** npl scarpe fpl da tennis

tenor ['tenə*] n (MUS) tenore m

tenpin bowling ['tenpɪn-] n bowling m

tense [tens] adj teso(a) ♦ n (LING) tempo

tension ['tenʃən] n tensione f

tent [tent] n tenda

tentative ['tentətɪv] adj esitante, incerto(a); (conclusion) provvisorio(a)

tenterhooks ['tentəhuks] npl: **on ~** sulle spine

tenth [tenθ] num decimo(a)

tent: **~ peg** n picchetto da tenda; **~ pole** n palo da tenda, montante m

tenuous ['tenjuəs] adj tenue

tenure ['tenjuə*] n (of property) possesso; (of job) permanenza; titolarità

tepid ['tepɪd] adj tiepido(a)

term [tə:m] n termine m; (SCOL)

trimestre m; (LAW) sessione f ♦ vt chiamare, definire; **~s** npl (conditions) condizioni fpl; (COMM) prezzi mpl, tariffe fpl; **in the short/long ~** a breve/ lunga scadenza; **to be on good ~s with sb** essere in buoni rapporti con qn; **to come to ~s with** (problem) affrontare

terminal ['tə:mɪnl] adj finale, terminale; (disease) terminale ♦ n (ELEC) morsetto; (COMPUT) terminale m; (AVIAT, for oil, ore etc) terminal m inv; (BRIT: also: coach ~) capolinea m

terminate ['tə:mɪneɪt] vt mettere fine a

termini ['tə:mɪnaɪ] npl of **terminus**

terminus ['tə:mɪnəs] (pl **termini**) n (for buses) capolinea m; (for trains) stazione f terminale

terrace ['terəs] n terrazza; (BRIT: row of houses) fila di case a schiera; **the ~s** npl (BRIT: SPORT) le gradinate; **~d** adj (garden) a terrazze

terracotta ['terə'kɒtə] n terracotta

terrain [te'reɪn] n terreno

terrible ['terɪbl] adj terribile; **terribly** adv terribilmente; (very badly) malissimo

terrier ['terɪə*] n terrier m inv

terrific [tə'rɪfɪk] adj incredibile, fantastico(a); (wonderful) formidabile, eccezionale

terrify ['terɪfaɪ] vt terrorizzare

territory ['terɪtərɪ] n territorio

terror ['terə*] n terrore m; **~ism** n terrorismo; **~ist** n terrorista m/f

Terylene ® ['terɪli:n] n terital ® m, terilene ® m

test [test] n (trial, check, of courage etc) prova; (MED) esame m; (CHEM) analisi f inv; (exam: of intelligence etc) test m inv; (: in school) compito in classe; (also: driving ~) esame m di guida ♦ vt provare; esaminare; analizzare; sottoporre ad esame; **to ~ sb in history** esaminare qn in storia

testament ['testəmənt] n testamento;

the Old/New T~ il Vecchio/Nuovo
testamento

testicle ['testɪkl] n testicolo

testify ['testɪfaɪ] vi (LAW) testimoniare,
deporre; **to ~ to sth** (LAW)
testimoniare qc; (gen) comprovare or
dimostrare qc

testimony ['testɪmənɪ] n (LAW)
testimonianza, deposizione f

test match n (CRICKET, RUGBY) partita
internazionale

test tube n provetta

tetanus ['tetənəs] n tetano

tether ['teðə*] vt legare ♦ n: **at the end
of one's ~** al limite (della pazienza)

text [tekst] n testo; **~book** n libro di
testo

textiles ['tekstaɪlz] npl tessuti mpl;
(industry) industria tessile

texture ['tekstʃə*] n tessitura; (of skin,
paper etc) struttura

Thames [temz] n: **the ~** il Tamigi

than [ðæn, ðən] conj (in comparisons)
che; (with numerals, pronouns, proper
names) di; **more ~ 10/once** più di
10/una volta; **I have more/less
~** ne ho più/meno di te; **I have
more pens ~ pencils** ho più penne
che matite; **she is older ~ you think**
è più vecchia di quanto tu (non) pensi

thank [θæŋk] vt ringraziare; **~ you
(very much)** grazie (tante); **~s** npl
ringraziamenti mpl, grazie fpl ♦ excl
grazie!; **~s to** grazie a; **~ful** adj: **~ful
(for)** riconoscente (per); **~less** adj
ingrato(a); **T~sgiving (Day)** n giorno
del ringraziamento

Thanksgiving (Day)

*Negli Stati Uniti ogni quarto giovedì
di novembre ricorre il Thanksgiving
(Day), festa in ricordo della
celebrazione con cui i Padri Pellegrini,
fondatori della colonia di Plymouth in
Massachussets, ringraziarono Dio del
buon raccolto del 1621.*

┌─────────── KEYWORD ───────────┐

that [ðæt] (pl **those**) adj
(demonstrative) quel(quell', quello) m;
quella(quell') f; **~ man/woman/book**
quell'uomo/quella donna/quel libro;
(not "this") quell' uomo/quella
donna/quel libro là; **~ one** quello(a)
là

♦ pron 1 (demonstrative) ciò; (not "this
one") quello(a); who's ~? chi è?;
what's ~? cos'è quello?; **is ~ you?** sei
tu?; **I prefer this to ~** preferisco
questo a quello; **~'s what he said**
questo è ciò che ha detto; **what
happened after ~?** che è successo
dopo?; **~ is (to say)** cioè

2 (relative: direct) che; (: indirect) cui;
the book (~) I read il libro che ho
letto; **the box (~) I put it in** la scatola
in cui l'ho messo; **the people (~) I
spoke to** le persone con cui or con le
quali ho parlato

3 (relative: of time) in cui; **the day (~)
he came** il giorno in cui è venuto
♦ conj che; **he thought ~ I was ill**
pensava che io fossi malato

♦ adv (demonstrative) così; **I can't
work ~ much** non posso lavorare
(così) tanto; **~ high** così alto; **the
wall's about ~ high and ~ thick** il
muro è alto circa così e spesso circa
così

└───────────────────────────────┘

thatched [θætʃt] adj (roof) di paglia;
~ cottage n cottage m inv col tetto di
paglia

thaw [θɔː] n disgelo ♦ vi (ice)
sciogliersi; (food) scongelarsi ♦ vt (food:
also: **~ out**) (fare) scongelare

┌─────────── KEYWORD ───────────┐

the [ðiː; ðə] def art 1 (gen) il(lo, l') m;
la(l') f; i(gli) mpl; le fpl; **~ boy/girl/ink**
il ragazzo/la ragazza/l'inchiostro;
~ books/pencils i libri/le matite;
~ history of ~ world la storia del

mondo; **give it to ~ postman** dallo al postino; **I haven't ~ time/money** non ho tempo/soldi; **~ rich and ~ poor** i ricchi e i poveri

2 (*in titles*): **Elizabeth ~ First** Elisabetta prima; **Peter ~ Great** Pietro il grande

3 (*in comparisons*): **~ more he works, ~ more he earns** più lavora più guadagna

theatre ['θɪətə*] (*us* **theater**) *n* teatro; (*also*: **lecture ~**) aula magna; (*also*: **operating ~**) sala operatoria; **~-goer** *n* frequentatore/trice di teatri

theatrical [θɪ'ætrɪkl] *adj* teatrale

theft [θeft] *n* furto

their [ðɛə*] *adj* il(la) loro, *pl* i(le) loro; **~s** *pron* il(la) loro, *pl* i(le) loro; *see also* **my**; **mine**

them [ðɛm, ðəm] *pron* (*direct*) li(le); (*indirect*) gli, loro (*after vb*); (*stressed, after prep: people*) loro; (*: people, things*) essi(e); *see also* **me**

theme [θi:m] *n* tema *m*; **~ park** *n* parco di divertimenti (*intorno a un tema centrale*); **~ song** *n* tema musicale

themselves [ðəm'sɛlvz] *pl pron* (*reflexive*) si; (*emphatic*) loro stessi(e); (*after prep*) se stessi(e)

then [ðɛn] *adv* (*at that time*) allora; (*next*) poi, dopo; (*and also*) e poi ♦ *conj* (*therefore*) perciò, dunque, quindi ♦ *adj*: **the ~ president** il presidente di allora; **by ~** allora; **from ~ on** da allora in poi

theology [θɪ'ɒlədʒɪ] *n* teologia

theorem ['θɪərəm] *n* teorema *m*

theoretical [θɪə'rɛtɪkl] *adj* teorico(a)

theory ['θɪərɪ] *n* teoria

therapy ['θɛrəpɪ] *n* terapia

KEYWORD

there [ðɛə*] *adv* **1**: **~ is**, **~ are** c'è, ci sono; **~ are 3 of them** (*people*) sono in 3; (*things*) ce ne sono 3; **~ is no-**

one here non c'è nessuno qui; **~ has been an accident** c'è stato un incidente

2 (*referring to place*) là, lì; **up/in/down ~** lassù/là dentro/laggiù; **he went ~ on Friday** ci è andato venerdì; **I want that book ~** voglio quel libro là or lì; **~ he is!** eccolo!

3: **~, ~** (*esp to child*) su, su

thereabouts [ðɛərə'bauts] *adv* (*place*) nei pressi, da quelle parti; (*amount*) giù di lì, all'incirca

thereafter [ðɛər'ɑːftə*] *adv* da allora in poi

thereby [ðɛə'baɪ] *adv* con ciò

therefore ['ðɛəfɔː*] *adv* perciò, quindi

there's [ðɛəz] = **there is**; **there has**

thermal ['θəːml] *adj* termico(a)

thermometer [θə'mɒmɪtə*] *n* termometro

Thermos ® ['θəːməs] *n* (*also*: **~ flask**) thermos ® *m inv*

thesaurus [θɪ'sɔːrəs] *n* dizionario dei sinonimi

these [ðiːz] *pl pron, adj* questi(e)

theses ['θiːsiːz] *npl of* **thesis**

thesis ['θiːsɪs] (*pl* **theses**) *n* tesi *f inv*

they [ðeɪ] *pl pron* loro; essi(esse); (*people only*) loro; **~ say that ...** (*it is said that*) si dice che ...; **~'d = they had**; **they would**; **~'ll = they shall**; **they will**; **~'re = they are**; **~'ve = they have**

thick [θɪk] *adj* spesso(a); (*crowd*) compatto(a); (*stupid*) ottuso(a), lento(a) ♦ *n*: **in the ~ of** nel folto di; **it's 20 cm ~** ha uno spessore di 20 cm; **~en** *vi* ispessire ♦ *vt* (*sauce etc*) ispessire, rendere più denso(a); **~ly** *adv* (*spread*) a strati spessi; (*cut*) a fette grosse; (*populated*) densamente; **~ness** *n* spessore *m*; **~set** *adj* tarchiato(a), tozzo(a)

thief [θiːf] (*pl* **thieves**) *n* ladro/a

thieves [θiːvz] *npl of* **thief**

thigh [θaɪ] *n* coscia

thimble ['θɪmbl] n ditale m

thin [θɪn] adj sottile; (person) magro(a); (soup) poco denso(a) ♦ vt: to ~ (down) (sauce, paint) diluire

thing [θɪŋ] n cosa; (object) oggetto; (mania): **to have a ~ about** essere fissato(a) con; **~s** npl (belongings) cose fpl; **poor ~** poverino(a); **the best ~ would be to** la cosa migliore sarebbe di; **how are ~s?** come va?

think [θɪŋk] (pt, pp thought) vi pensare, riflettere ♦ vt pensare, credere; (imagine) immaginare; **to ~** pensare a; **what did you ~ of them?** cosa ne ha pensato?; **to ~ about sth/sb** pensare a qc/qn; **I'll ~ about it** ci penserò; **to ~ of doing** pensare di fare; **I ~ so/no!** penso di sì/no; **to ~ well of** avere una buona opinione di; **~ out** vt (plan) elaborare; (solution) trovare; **~ over** vt riflettere su; **~ through** vt riflettere a fondo su; **~ up** vt ideare; **~ tank** n commissione f di esperti

third [θəːd] num terzo(a) ♦ n terzo/a; (fraction) terzo, terza parte f; (AUT) terza; (BRIT: SCOL: degree) laurea col minimo dei voti; **~ly** adv in terzo luogo; **~ party insurance** n (BRIT) assicurazione f contro terzi; **~-rate** adj di qualità scadente; **the T~ World** n il Terzo Mondo

thirst [θəːst] n sete f; **~y** adj (person) assetato(a), che ha sete

thirteen [θəːˈtiːn] num tredici

thirty [ˈθəːtɪ] num trenta

this [ðɪs] (pl these) adj (demonstrative) questo(a); **~ man/woman/book** quest'uomo/questa donna/questo libro; (not "that") quest'uomo/questa donna/questo libro qui; **~ one** questo(a) qui
♦ pron (demonstrative) questo(a); (not "that one") questo(a) qui; **who/what is ~?** chi è/che cos'è questo?; **I prefer**

~ to that preferisco questo a quello; **~ is where I live** è dove abito qui; **~ is what he said** questo è ciò che ha detto; **~ is Mr Brown** (in introductions, photo) questo è il signor Brown; (on telephone) sono il signor Brown
♦ adv (demonstrative): **~ high/long etc** alto/lungo etc così; **I didn't know things were ~ bad** non sapevo andasse così male

thistle [ˈθɪsl] n cardo

thong [θɒŋ] n cinghia

thorn [θɔːn] n spina; **~y** adj spinoso(a)

thorough [ˈθʌrə] adj (search) minuzioso(a); (knowledge, research) approfondito(a), profondo(a); (person) coscienzioso(a); (cleaning) a fondo; **~bred** n (horse) purosangue m/f inv; **~fare** n strada transitabile; **"no ~fare"** "divieto di transito"; **~ly** adv minuziosamente; (wash, study) a fondo; (very) assolutamente

those [ðəuz] pl pron quelli(e) ♦ pl a quei(quegli) mpl; quelle fpl

though [ðəu] conj benché, sebbene ♦ adv comunque

thought [θɔːt] pt, pp of **think** ♦ n pensiero; (opinion) opinione f; **~ful** adj pensieroso(a), pensoso(a); (considerate) premuroso(a); **~less** adj sconsiderato(a); (behaviour) scortese

thousand [ˈθauzənd] num mille; **one ~** mille; **~s of** migliaia (fpl); **~th** num millesimo(a)

thrash [θræʃ] vt picchiare; bastonare; (defeat) battere; **~ about** vi dibattersi; **~ out** vt dibattere

thread [θred] n filo; (of screw) filetto ♦ vt (needle) infilare; **~bare** adj consumato(a), logoro(a)

threat [θret] n minaccia; **~en** vi (storm) minacciare ♦ vt: **to ~en sb with/to do** minacciare qn con/di fare

three [θriː] num tre; **~-dimensional** adj tridimensionale; (film) stereoscopico(a); **~-piece suit** n completo (con gilè); **~-piece suite** n salotto comprendente un divano e due poltrone; **~-ply** adj (wool) a tre fili

threshold ['θreʃhəuld] n soglia

threw [θru:] pt of throw

thrifty ['θrɪftɪ] adj economico(a)

thrill [θrɪl] n brivido ♦ vt (audience) elettrizzare; **to be ~ed** (with gift etc) essere elettrizzato(a); **~er** n thriller m inv; **~ing** adj (book) pieno(a) di suspense; (news, discovery) elettrizzante

thrive [θraɪv] (pt **thrived**, pp **thrived**) vi crescere or svilupparsi bene; (business) prosperare; **he ~s on it** gli fa bene, ha bisogno di questo; **thriving** adj fiorente

throat [θrəut] n gola; **to have a sore ~** avere (un or il) mal di gola

throb [θrɒb] vi palpitare; pulsare; vibrare

throes [θrəuz] npl: **in the ~ of** alle prese con; in preda a

thrombosis [θrɒm'bəusɪs] n trombosi f

throne [θrəun] n trono

throng [θrɒŋ] n moltitudine f ♦ vt affollare

throttle ['θrɒtl] n (AUT) valvola a farfalla ♦ vt strangolare

through [θru:] prep attraverso; (time) per, durante; (by means of) per mezzo di; (owing to) a causa di ♦ adj (ticket, train, passage) diretto(a) ♦ adv attraverso; **to put sb ~ to sb** (TEL) passare qn a qn; **to be ~** (TEL) ottenere la comunicazione; (have finished) essere finito(a); **"no ~ road"** (BRIT) "strada senza sbocco"; **~out** prep (place) dappertutto in; (time) per or durante tutto(a) ♦ adv dappertutto; sempre

throw [θrəu] (pt **threw**, pp **thrown**) n (SPORT) lancio, tiro ♦ vt tirare, gettare; (SPORT) lanciare, tirare; (rider) disarcionare; (fig) confondere; **to ~ a party** dare una festa; **~ away** vt gettare o buttare via; **~ off** vt sbarazzarsi di; **~ out** vt buttare fuori;

(reject) respingere; **~ up** vi vomitare; **~away** adj da buttare; (remark) rimessa in gioco; **thrown** pp of throw

thru [θru:] (US) prep, adj, adv = **through**

thrush [θrʌʃ] n tordo

thrust [θrʌst] (pt, pp **thrust**) vt spingere con forza; (push in) conficcare

thud [θʌd] n tonfo

thug [θʌɡ] n delinquente m

thumb [θʌm] n (ANAT) pollice m; **to ~ a lift** fare l'autostop; **~ through** vt fus (book) sfogliare; **~tack** (US) n puntina da disegno

thump [θʌmp] n colpo forte; (sound) tonfo ♦ vt (person) picchiare; (object) battere su ♦ vi picchiare; battere

thunder ['θʌndə*] n tuono ♦ vi tuonare; (train etc) **to ~ past** passare con un rombo; **~bolt** n fulmine m; **~clap** n rombo di tuono; **~storm** n temporale m; **~y** adj temporalesco(a)

Thursday ['θə:zdɪ] n giovedì m inv

thus [ðʌs] adv così

thwart [θwɔ:t] vt contrastare

thyme [taɪm] n timo

thyroid ['θaɪrɔɪd] n (also: ~ gland) tiroide f

tiara [tɪ'ɑ:rə] n (woman's) diadema m

Tiber ['taɪbə*] n: **the ~** il Tevere

tick [tɪk] n (sound: of clock) tic tac m inv; (mark) segno; spunta; (ZOOL) zecca; (BRIT: inf): **in a ~** in un attimo ♦ vi fare tic tac ♦ vt spuntare; **~ off** vt spuntare; (person) sgridare; **~ over** vi (engine) andare al minimo; (fig) andare avanti come al solito

ticket ['tɪkɪt] n biglietto; (in shop: on goods) etichetta; (parking ~) multa; (for library) scheda; **~ collector** n bigliettaio; **~ office** n biglietteria

tickle ['tɪkl] vt fare il solletico a; (fig) solleticare ♦ vi: **it ~s mi** (or gli etc) fa il solletico; **ticklish** [-lɪʃ] adj che soffre il solletico; (problem) delicato(a)

tidal ['taɪdl] adj di marea; (estuary) soggetto(a) alla marea; **~ wave** n onda anomala

tidbit ['tɪdbɪt] (US) n (food) leccornia; (news) notizia ghiotta

tiddlywinks ['tɪdlɪwɪŋks] n gioco delle pulce

tide [taɪd] n marea; (fig: of events) corso; **high/low ~** alta/bassa marea; **~ over** vt dare una mano a

tidy ['taɪdɪ] adj (room) ordinato(a), lindo(a); (dress, work) curato(a), in ordine; (person) ordinato(a) ♦ vt (also: **~ up**) riordinare, mettere in ordine

tie [taɪ] n (string etc) legaccio; (BRIT: also: neck~) cravatta; (fig: link) legame m; (SPORT: draw) pareggio ♦ vt (parcel) legare; (ribbon) annodare ♦ vi (SPORT) pareggiare; **to ~ sth in a bow** annodare qc; **to ~ a knot in sth** fare un nodo a qc; **~ down** vt legare; (to price etc) costringere ad accettare; **~ up** vt (parcel, dog) legare; (boat) ormeggiare; (arrangements) concludere; **to be ~d up** (busy) essere occupato(a) or preso(a)

tier [tɪə*] n fila; (of cake) piano, strato

tiger ['taɪgə*] n tigre f

tight [taɪt] adj (rope) teso(a), tirato(a); (money) poco(a); (clothes, budget, bend etc) stretto(a); (control) severo(a), fermo(a); (inf: drunk) sbronzo(a) ♦ adv (squeeze) fortemente; (shut) ermeticamente; **~s** (BRIT) npl collant m inv; **~en** vt (rope) tendere; (screw) stringere; (control) rinforzare ♦ vi tendersi; stringersi; **~-fisted** adj avaro(a); **~ly** adv (grasp) bene, saldamente; **~rope** n corda (da acrobata)

tile [taɪl] n (on roof) tegola; (on wall or floor) piastrella, mattonella; **~d** adj di tegole; a piastrelle, a mattonelle

till [tɪl] n registratore m di cassa ♦ vt (land) coltivare ♦ prep, conj = **until**

tiller ['tɪlə*] n (NAUT) barra del timone

tilt [tɪlt] vt inclinare, far pendere ♦ vi inclinarsi, pendere

timber ['tɪmbə*] n (material) legname m

time [taɪm] n tempo; (epoch: often pl) epoca, tempo; (by clock) ora; (moment) momento; (occasion) volta; (MUS) tempo ♦ vt (race) cronometrare; (programme) calcolare la durata di; (fix moment for) programmare; (remark etc) dire (or fare) al momento giusto; **a long ~** molto tempo; **for the ~ being** per il momento; **4 at a ~** 4 per or alla volta; **from ~ to ~** ogni tanto; **at ~s** a volte; **in ~** (soon enough) in tempo; (after some ~) col tempo; (MUS) a tempo; **in a week's ~** fra una settimana; **in no ~** in un attimo; **any ~** in qualsiasi momento; **on ~** puntualmente; **5 ~s 5** 5 volte 5, 5 per 5; **what ~ is it?** che ora è?, che ore sono?; **to have a good ~** divertirsi; **~ bomb** n bomba a orologeria; **~less** adj eterno(a); **~ly** adj opportuno(a); **~ off** n tempo libero; **~r** n (~ switch) temporizzatore m; (in kitchen) contaminuti m inv; **~ scale** n periodo; **~-share** adj: **~-share apartment/villa** appartamento/villa in multiproprietà; **~ switch** (BRIT) n temporizzatore m; **~table** n orario; **~ zone** n fuso orario

timid ['tɪmɪd] adj timido(a); (easily scared) pauroso(a)

timing ['taɪmɪŋ] n (SPORT) cronometraggio; (fig) scelta del momento opportuno

timpani ['tɪmpənɪ] npl timpani mpl

tin [tɪn] n stagno; (also: ~ plate) latta; (container) scatola; (BRIT: can) barattolo (di latta), lattina; **~foil** n stagnola

tinge [tɪndʒ] n sfumatura ♦ vt: **~d with** tinto(a) di

tingle ['tɪŋgl] vi pizzicare

tinker ['tɪŋkə*]: **~ with** vt fus armeggiare intorno a; cercare di riparare

tinned [tɪnd] (BRIT) adj (food) in scatola

tin opener ['-əʊpnə*] (BRIT) n apriscatole m inv

tinsel ['tɪnsl] n decorazioni fpl natalizie (argentate)

tint [tɪnt] n tinta; **~ed** adj (hair) tinto(a); (spectacles, glass) colorato(a)

tiny ['taɪnɪ] adj minuscolo(a)

tip [tɪp] n (end) punta; (gratuity) mancia; (BRIT: for rubbish) immondezzaio; (advice) suggerimento ♦ vt (waiter) dare la mancia a; (tilt) inclinare; (overturn: also: ~ over) capovolgere; (empty: also: ~ out) scaricare; **~-off** n (hint) soffiata; **~ped** (BRIT) adj (cigarette) col filtro

Tipp-Ex ® ['tɪpɛks] n correttore m

tipsy ['tɪpsɪ] adj brillo(a)

tiptoe ['tɪptəu] n: **on ~** in punta di piedi

tiptop ['tɪp'tɔp] adj: **in ~ condition** in ottime condizioni

tire ['taɪə*] n (US) = **tyre** ♦ vt stancare ♦ vi stancarsi; **~d** adj stanco(a); **to be ~d of** essere stanco or stufo di; **~less** adj instancabile; **~some** adj noioso(a); **tiring** adj faticoso(a)

tissue ['tɪʃu:] n tessuto; (paper handkerchief) fazzoletto di carta; **~ paper** n carta velina

tit [tɪt] n (bird) cinciallegra; **to give ~ for tat** rendere pan per focaccia

titbit ['tɪtbɪt] (BRIT) n (food) leccornia; (news) notizia ghiotta

title ['taɪtl] n titolo; **~ deed** n (LAW) titolo di proprietà; **~ role** n ruolo or parte f principale

TM abbr = **trademark**

─────────────────
KEYWORD
─────────────────

to [tu:, tə] prep **1** (direction) a; **to go ~ France/London/school** andare in Francia/a Londra/a scuola; **to go ~ Paul's/the doctor's** andare da Paul/dal dottore; **the road ~ Edinburgh** la strada per Edimburgo; **~ the left/right** a sinistra/destra

2 (as far as) (fino) a; **from here ~ London** da qui a Londra; **to count ~ 10** contare fino a 10; **from 40 ~ 50**

people da 40 a 50 persone

3 (with expressions of time): **a quarter ~ 5** le 5 meno un quarto; **it's twenty ~ 3** sono le 3 meno venti

4 (for, of): **the key ~ the front door** la chiave della porta d'ingresso; **a letter ~ his wife** una lettera per la moglie

5 (expressing indirect object) a; **to give sth ~ sb** dare qc a qn; **to talk ~ sb** parlare a qn; **to be a danger ~ sb/sth** rappresentare un pericolo per qn/qc

6 (in relation to) a; **3 goals ~ 2** 3 goal a 2; **30 miles ~ the gallon** ≈ 11 chilometri con un litro

7 (purpose, result): **to come ~ sb's aid** venire in aiuto a qn; **to sentence sb ~ death** condannare a morte qn; **~ my surprise** con mia sorpresa

♦ with vb **1** (simple infinitive): **~ go/eat** etc andare/mangiare etc

2 (following another vb): **to want/ try/start ~ do** volere/cercare di/cominciare a fare

3 (with vb omitted): **I don't want ~** non voglio (farlo); **you ought ~** devi (farlo)

4 (purpose, result): **he did it ~ help you** l'ho fatto per aiutarti

5 (equivalent to relative clause): **I have things ~ do** ho da fare; **the main thing is ~ try** la cosa più importante è provare

6 (after adjective etc): **ready ~ go** pronto a partire; **too old/young ~ ...** troppo vecchio/giovane per ...

♦ adv: **to push the door ~** accostare la porta

toad [təud] n rospo; **~stool** n fungo (velenoso)

toast [təust] n (CULIN) pane m tostato; (drink, speech) brindisi m inv ♦ vt (CULIN) tostare; (drink to) brindare a; **a piece or slice of ~** una fetta di pane tostato; **~er** n tostapane m inv

tobacco [təˈbækəu] n tabacco; **~nist** n tabaccaio/a; **~nist's (shop)** n tabaccheria

toboggan [təˈbɒgən] n toboga m inv

today [təˈdeɪ] adv oggi ♦ n (also fig) oggi m

toddler [ˈtɒdlə*] n bambino/a che impara a camminare

toe [təu] n dito del piede; (of shoe) punta; **to ~ the line** (fig) stare in riga, conformarsi; **~nail** n unghia del piede

toffee [ˈtɒfɪ] n caramella; **~ apple** n mela caramellata

toga [ˈtəugə] n toga

together [təˈgeðə*] adv insieme; (at same time) allo stesso tempo; **~ with** insieme a

toil [tɔɪl] n travaglio, fatica ♦ vi affannarsi; sgobbare

toilet [ˈtɔɪlət] n (BRIT: lavatory) gabinetto ♦ cpd (bag, soap etc) da toletta; **~ paper** n carta igienica; **~ries** npl articoli mpl da toletta; **~ roll** n rotolo di carta igienica; **~ water** n acqua di colonia

token [ˈtəukən] n (sign) segno; (substitute coin) gettone m; **book/record/gift ~** (BRIT) buono-libro/-disco/-regalo

told [təuld] pt, pp of **tell**

tolerable [ˈtɒlərəbl] adj (bearable) tollerabile; (fairly good) passabile

tolerant [ˈtɒlrnt] adj: **~ (of)** tollerante (nei confronti di)

tolerate [ˈtɒləreɪt] vt sopportare; (MED, TECH) tollerare

toll [təul] n (tax, charge) pedaggio ♦ vi (bell) suonare; **the accident ~ on the roads** il numero delle vittime della strada

tomato [təˈmɑːtəu] n (pl **~es**) pomodoro

tomb [tuːm] n tomba

tomboy [ˈtɒmbɔɪ] n maschiaccio

tombstone [ˈtuːmstəun] n pietra tombale

tomcat [ˈtɒmkæt] n gatto

tomorrow [təˈmɔrəu] adv domani ♦ n (also fig) domani m inv; **the day after ~** dopodomani; **~ morning** domani mattina

ton [tʌn] n tonnellata (BRIT = 1016 kg; US = 907 kg; metric = 1000 kg); **~s of** (inf) un mucchio or sacco di

tone [təun] n tono ♦ vi (also: ~ in) intonarsi; **~ down** vt (colour, criticism, sound) attenuare; **~ up** vt (muscles) tonificare; **~-deaf** adj che non ha orecchio (musicale)

tongs [tɔŋz] npl tenaglie fpl; (for coal) molle fpl; (for hair) arricciacapelli m inv

tongue [tʌŋ] n lingua; **~ in cheek** (say, speak) ironicamente; **~-tied** adj (fig) muto(a); **~-twister** n scioglilingua m inv

tonic [ˈtɒnɪk] n (MED) tonico; (also: ~ water) acqua tonica

tonight [təˈnaɪt] adv stanotte; (this evening) stasera ♦ n questa notte; questa sera

tonnage [ˈtʌnɪdʒ] n (NAUT) tonnellaggio, stazza

tonsil [ˈtɒnsl] n tonsilla; **~litis** [-ˈlaɪtɪs] n tonsillite f

too [tuː] adv (excessively) troppo; (also) anche; **~ much** adv troppo ♦ adj troppo(a); **~ many** troppi(e)

took [tuk] pt of **take**

tool [tuːl] n utensile m, attrezzo; **~ box** n cassetta f portautensili

toot [tuːt] n (of horn) colpo di clacson; (of whistle) fischio ♦ vi suonare; (with car horn) suonare il clacson

tooth [tuːθ] n (pl **teeth**) (ANAT, TECH) dente m; **~ache** n mal m di denti; **~brush** n spazzolino da denti; **~paste** n dentifricio; **~pick** n stuzzicadenti m inv

top [tɔp] n (of mountain, page, ladder) cima; (of box, cupboard, table) sopra m inv, parte f superiore; (lid: of box, jar) coperchio; (: of bottle) tappo; (blouse etc) sopra m inv; (toy) trottola ♦ adj più alto(a); (in rank) primo(a); (best) migliore ♦ vt (exceed) superare; (be first in) essere in testa a; **on ~ of** sopra, in cima a; (in addition to) oltre a; **from ~ to bottom** da cima a fondo; **~ up** (us ~ **off**) vt riempire; (salary) integrare; **~ floor** n ultimo piano; **~ hat** n cilindro; **~-heavy** adj (object) con la parte superiore troppo pesante

topic ['tɔpɪk] n argomento; **~al** adj d'attualità

top: **~less** adj (bather etc) col seno scoperto; **~-level** adj (talks) ad alto livello; **~most** adj il(la) più alto(a)

topple ['tɔpl] vt rovesciare, far cadere ♦ vi cadere; traballare

top-secret adj segretissimo(a)

topsy-turvy ['tɔpsɪ'təːvɪ] adj, adv sottosopra inv

torch [tɔːtʃ] n torcia; (BRIT: electric) lampadina tascabile

tore [tɔː*] pt of tear¹

torment [n 'tɔːment, vb tɔː'ment] n tormento ♦ vt tormentare

torn [tɔːn] pp of tear¹

torpedo [tɔː'piːdəu] (pl ~es) n siluro

torrent ['tɔrnt] n torrente m

torrid ['tɔrɪd] adj torrido(a); (love affair) infuocato(a)

tortoise ['tɔːtəs] n tartaruga; **~shell** ['tɔːtəʃɛl] adj di tartaruga

torture ['tɔːtʃə*] n tortura ♦ vt torturare

Tory ['tɔːrɪ] (BRIT: POL) adj dei tories, conservatore(trice) ♦ n tory m/f inv, conservatore/trice

toss [tɔs] vt gettare, lanciare; (one's head) scuotere; **to ~ a coin** fare a testa o croce; **to ~ up for** sth fare a testa o croce per qc; **to ~ and turn** (in bed) girarsi e rigirarsi

tot [tɔt] n (BRIT: drink) bicchierino; (child) bimbo/a

total ['təutl] adj totale ♦ n totale m ♦ vt (add up) sommare; (amount to) ammontare a

totally ['təutəlɪ] adv completamente

touch [tʌtʃ] n tocco; (sense) tatto;

(contact) contatto ♦ vt toccare; **a ~ of** (fig) un tocco di; un pizzico di; **to get in ~ with** mettersi in contatto con; **to lose ~** (friends) perdersi di vista; **~ on** vt fus (topic) sfiorare, accennare a; **~ up** vt (paint) ritoccare; **~-and-go** adj incerto(a); **~down** n atterraggio; (on sea) ammaraggio; (us: FOOTBALL) meta; **~ed** adj commosso(a); **~ing** adj commovente; **~line** n (SPORT) linea laterale; **~y** adj (person) suscettibile

tough [tʌf] adj duro(a); (resistant) resistente; **~en** vt rinforzare

toupee ['tuːpeɪ] n parrucchino

tour [tuə*] n viaggio; (also: package ~) viaggio organizzato o tutto compreso; (of town, museum) visita; (by artist) tournée f inv ♦ vt visitare; **~ guide** n guida turistica; **~ing** n turismo

tourism ['tuərɪzəm] n turismo

tourist ['tuərɪst] n turista m/f ♦ adv (travel) in classe turistica ♦ cpd turistico(a); **~ office** n pro loco f inv

tournament ['tuənəmənt] n torneo

tousled ['tauzld] adj (hair) arruffato(a)

tout [taut] vi: **to ~ for** procacciare, raccogliere; cercare clienti per ♦ n (also: ticket ~) bagarino

tow [təu] vt rimorchiare; **"on ~"** (BRIT), **"in ~"** (us) "veicolo rimorchiato"

towards [tə'wɔːdz] prep verso; (of attitude) nei confronti di; (of purpose) per

towel ['tauəl] n asciugamano; (also: tea ~) strofinaccio; **~ling** n (fabric) spugna; **~ rail** (us **~ rack**) n portasciugamano

tower ['tauə*] n torre f; **~ block** n (BRIT) palazzone m; **~ing** adj altissimo(a), imponente

town [taun] n città f inv; **to go to ~** andare in città; (fig) mettercela tutta; **~ centre** n centro (città); **~ council** n consiglio comunale; **~ hall** n ≈ municipio; **~ plan** n pianta della città; **~ planning** n urbanistica

towrope ['təurəup] n (cavo da)

rimorchio

tow truck (US) n carro m attrezzi inv

toxic ['tɔksɪk] adj tossico(a)

toy [tɔɪ] n giocattolo; ~ **with** vt fus giocare con; (idea) accarezzare, trastullarsi con; ~ **shop** n negozio di giocattoli

trace [treɪs] n traccia ♦ vt (draw) tracciare; (follow) seguire; (locate) rintracciare; **tracing paper** n carta da ricalco

track [træk] n (of person, animal) traccia; (on tape, SPORT, path: gen) pista; (: of bullet etc) traiettoria; (: of suspect, animal) pista, tracce fpl; (RAIL) binario, rotaie fpl ♦ vt seguire le tracce di; **to keep ~ of** seguire; ~ **down** vt (prey) scovare; snidare; (sth lost) rintracciare; **~suit** n tuta sportiva

tract [trækt] n (GEO) tratto, estensione f

tractor ['træktə*] n trattore m

trade [treɪd] n commercio; (skill, job) mestiere m ♦ vi commerciare ♦ vt: to ~ **sth (for sth)** barattare qc (con qc); **to ~ with/in** commerciare con/in; ~ **in** vt (old car etc) dare come pagamento parziale; ~ **fair** n fiera commerciale; **~mark** n marchio di fabbrica; ~ **name** n marca, nome m depositato; **~r** n commerciante m/f; **~sman** (irreg) n fornitore m; (shopkeeper) negoziante m; ~ **union** n sindacato; **~ unionist** n sindacalista m/f

tradition [trə'dɪʃən] n tradizione f; **~al** adj tradizionale

traffic ['træfɪk] n traffico ♦ vi: to ~ **in** (pej: liquor, drugs) trafficare in; ~ **circle** (US) n isola rotatoria; ~ **jam** n ingorgo (del traffico); ~ **lights** npl semaforo; ~ **warden** n addetto/a al controllo del traffico e del parcheggio

tragedy ['trædʒədɪ] n tragedia

tragic ['trædʒɪk] adj tragico(a)

trail [treɪl] n (tracks) tracce fpl, pista; (path) sentiero; (of smoke etc) scia ♦ vt trascinare, strascicare; (follow) seguire ♦ vi essere al traino; (dress etc)

struisciare; (plant) arrampicarsi; strisciare; (in game) essere in svantaggio; ~ **behind** vi essere al traino; **~er** n (AUT) rimorchio; (US) roulotte f inv; (CINEMA) prossimamente m inv; **~er truck** (US) n (articulated lorry) autoarticolato

train [treɪn] n treno; (of dress) coda, strascico ♦ vt (apprentice, doctor etc) formare; (sportsman) allenare; (dog) addestrare; (memory) esercitare; (point: gun etc): **to ~ sth on** puntare qc contro ♦ vi formarsi; allenarsi; **one's ~ of thought** il filo dei propri pensieri; **~ed** adj qualificato(a); allenato(a); addestrato(a); **~ee** [treɪ'niː] n (in trade) apprendista m/f; **~er** n (SPORT) allenatore/trice; (: shoe) scarpa da ginnastica; (of dogs etc) addestratore/trice; **~ing** n formazione f; allenamento; addestramento; **in ~ing** (SPORT) in allenamento; **~ing college** n istituto professionale; (for teachers) ≈ istituto magistrale; **~ing shoes** npl scarpe fpl da ginnastica

trait [treɪt] n tratto

traitor ['treɪtə*] n traditore m

tram [træm] (BRIT) n (also: ~car) tram m inv

tramp [træmp] n (person) vagabondo/ a; (inf. pej: woman) sgualdrina

trample ['træmpl] vt: **to ~ (underfoot)** calpestare

trampoline ['træmpəliːn] n trampolino

tranquil ['træŋkwɪl] adj tranquillo(a); **~lizer** n (MED) tranquillante m

transact [træn'zækt] vt (business) trattare; **~ion** [-'zækʃən] n transazione f

transatlantic ['trænzət'læntɪk] adj transatlantico(a)

transfer [n 'trænsfə*, vb træns'fə*] n (gen, also SPORT) trasferimento; (POL: of power) passaggio; (picture, design) decalcomania; (: stick-on) autoadesivo ♦ vt trasferire; passare; **to ~ the**

charges (BRIT: TEL) fare una chiamata a carico del destinatario; **~ desk** n (AVIAT) banco m transiti inv

transform [træns'fɔ:m] vt trasformare

transfusion [træns'fju:ʒən] n trasfusione f

transient ['trænzɪənt] adj transitorio(a), fugace

transistor [træn'zɪstə*] n (ELEC) transistor m inv; (also: ~ radio) radio f inv a transistor

transit ['trænzɪt] n: **in ~** in transito

transitive ['trænzɪtɪv] adj (LING) transitivo(a)

translate [trænz'leɪt] vt tradurre; **translation** [-'leɪʃən] n traduzione f; **translator** n traduttore/trice

transmission [trænz'mɪʃən] n trasmissione f

transmit [trænz'mɪt] vt trasmettere; **~ter** n trasmettitore m

transparency [træns'pɛərənsɪ] n trasparenza; (BRIT: PHOT) diapositiva

transparent [træns'pærnt] adj trasparente

transpire [træn'spaɪə*] vi (happen) succedere; (turn out): **it ~d that** si venne a sapere che

transplant [vb træns'plɑ:nt, n 'trænsplɑ:nt] vt trapiantare ♦ n (MED) trapianto

transport [n 'trænspɔ:t, vb træns'pɔ:t] n trasporto ♦ vt trasportare; **~ation** [-'teɪʃən] n (mezzo di) trasporto; **~ café** (BRIT) n trattoria per camionisti

trap [træp] n (snare, trick) trappola; (carriage) calesse m ♦ vt prendere in trappola, intrappolare; **~ door** n botola

trapeze [trə'pi:z] n trapezio

trappings ['træpɪŋz] npl ornamenti mpl; indoratura, sfarzo

trash [træʃ] (pej) n (goods) ciarpame m; (nonsense) sciocchezze fpl; **~ can** (US) n secchio della spazzatura

trauma ['trɔ:mə] n trauma m; **~tic** [-'mætɪk] adj traumatico(a)

travel ['trævl] n viaggio; viaggi mpl ♦ vi viaggiare ♦ vt (distance) percorrere; **~ agency** n agenzia (di) viaggi; **~ agent** n agente m di viaggio; **~ler** (US **~er**) n viaggiatore/trice; **~ler's cheque** (US **~er's check**) n assegno turistico; **~ling** (US **~ing**) n viaggi mpl; **~ sickness** n mal m d'auto (or di mare or d'aria)

travesty ['trævəstɪ] n parodia

trawler ['trɔ:lə*] n peschereccio (a strascico)

tray [treɪ] n (for carrying) vassoio; (on desk) vaschetta

treacherous ['trɛtʃərəs] adj infido(a)

treachery ['trɛtʃərɪ] n tradimento

treacle ['tri:kl] n melassa

tread [trɛd] (pt trod, pp trodden) n passo; (sound) rumore m di passi; (of stairs) pedata; (of tyre) battistrada m inv ♦ vi camminare; **~ on** vt fus calpestare

treason ['tri:zn] n tradimento

treasure ['trɛʒə*] n tesoro ♦ vt (value) tenere in gran conto, apprezzare molto; (store) custodire gelosamente

treasurer ['trɛʒərə*] n tesoriere/a

treasury ['trɛʒərɪ] n: **the T~** (BRIT), **the T~ Department** (US) il ministero del Tesoro

treat [tri:t] n regalo ♦ vt trattare; (MED) curare; **to ~ sb to sth** offrire qc a qn

treatment ['tri:tmənt] n trattamento

treaty ['tri:tɪ] n patto, trattato

treble ['trɛbl] adj triplo(a), triplice ♦ vt triplicare ♦ vi triplicarsi; **~ clef** n chiave f di violino

tree [tri:] n albero; **~ trunk** n tronco d'albero

trek [trɛk] n escursione f a piedi; escursione f in macchina; (tiring walk) camminata sfiancante ♦ vi (as holiday) fare dell'escursionismo

trellis ['trɛlɪs] n graticcio

tremble ['trɛmbl] vi tremare

tremendous [trɪ'mɛndəs] adj (enormous) enorme; (excellent) meraviglioso(a), formidabile

tremor ['tremǝ*] n tremore m, tremito; (also: earth ~) scossa sismica

trench [trentʃ] n trincea

trend [trend] n (tendency) tendenza; (of events) corso; (fashion) moda; **~y** adj (idea) di moda; (clothes) all'ultima moda

trespass ['trespǝs] vi: **to ~ on** entrare abusivamente in; **"no ~ing"** "proprietà privata", "vietato l'accesso"

trestle ['tresl] n cavalletto

trial ['traɪǝl] n (LAW) processo; (test: of machine etc) collaudo; **~s** npl (unpleasant experiences) dure prove fpl; **on ~** (LAW) sotto processo; **by ~ and error** a tentoni; **~ period** periodo di prova

triangle ['traɪæŋgl] n (MATH, MUS) triangolo

tribe [traɪb] n tribù f inv; **~sman** (irreg) n membro di tribù

tribunal [traɪ'bjuːnl] n tribunale m

tributary ['trɪbjutǝrɪ] n (river) tributario, affluente m

tribute ['trɪbjuːt] n tributo, omaggio; **to pay ~** to rendere omaggio a

trick [trɪk] n trucco; (joke) tiro; (CARDS) presa ♦ vt imbrogliare, ingannare; **to play a ~ on sb** giocare un tiro a qn; **that should do the ~** vedrai che funziona; **~ery** n inganno

trickle ['trɪkl] n (of water etc) rivolo; gocciolio ♦ vi gocciolare

tricky ['trɪkɪ] adj difficile, delicato(a)

tricycle ['traɪsɪkl] n triciclo

trifle ['traɪfl] n sciocchezza; (BRIT: CULIN) ≈ zuppa inglese ♦ adv: **a ~ long** un po' lungo; **trifling** adj insignificante

trigger ['trɪgǝ*] n (of gun) grilletto; **~ off** vt dare l'avvio a

trim [trɪm] adj (house, garden) ben tenuto(a); (figure) snello(a) ♦ n (haircut etc) spuntata, regolata; (embellishment) finiture fpl; (on car) guarnizioni fpl ♦ vt spuntare; (decorate): **to ~ (with)** decorare (con); (NAUT: a sail) orientare;

~mings npl decorazioni fpl; (extras: gen CULIN) guarnizione f

trinket ['trɪŋkɪt] n gingillo; (piece of jewellery) ciondolo

trip [trɪp] n viaggio; (excursion) gita, escursione f; (stumble) passo falso ♦ vi inciampare; (go lightly) camminare con passo leggero; **on a ~** in viaggio; **~ up** vi inciampare ♦ vt fare lo sgambetto a

tripe [traɪp] n (CULIN) trippa; (pej: rubbish) sciocchezze fpl, fesserie fpl

triple ['trɪpl] adj triplo(a)

triplets ['trɪplɪts] npl bambini(e) trigemini(e)

triplicate ['trɪplɪkǝt] n: **in ~** in triplice copia

tripod ['traɪpɔd] n treppiede m

trite [traɪt] adj banale, trito(a)

triumph ['traɪʌmf] n trionfo ♦ vi: **to ~ (over)** trionfare (su)

trivia ['trɪvɪǝ] npl banalità fpl

trivial ['trɪvɪǝl] adj insignificante; (commonplace) banale

trod [trɔd] pt of **tread**; **~den** pp of **tread**

trolley ['trɔlɪ] n carrello; **~ bus** n filobus m inv

trombone [trɔm'bǝun] n trombone m

troop [truːp] n gruppo; (MIL) squadrone m; **~s** npl (MIL) truppe fpl; **~ in/out** vi entrare/uscire a frotte; **~ing the colour** n (ceremony) sfilata della bandiera

trophy ['trǝufɪ] n trofeo

tropic ['trɔpɪk] n tropico; **~al** adj tropicale

trot [trɔt] n trotto ♦ vi trottare; **on the ~** (BRIT: fig) di fila, uno(a) dopo l'altro(a)

trouble ['trʌbl] n difficoltà f inv, problema m; difficoltà fpl, problemi; (worry) preoccupazione f; (bother, effort) sforzo; (POL) conflitti mpl, disordine m; (MED): **stomach etc ~** disturbi mpl gastrici etc ♦ vt disturbare; (worry) preoccupare ♦ vi: **to ~ to do** disturbarsi a fare; **~s** npl (POL etc) disordini *mpl*; **to be in ~** avere dei problemi; **it's no ~!** di niente!; **what's the ~?** cosa c'è che non va?; **~d** *adj* (*person*) preoccupato(a), inquieto(a); (*epoch, life*) agitato(a), difficile; **~maker** *n* elemento disturbatore, agitatore/trice; (*child*) discolo/a; **~shooter** *n* (*in conflict*) conciliatore *m*; **~some** *adj* fastidioso(a), seccante

trough [trɒf] *n* (*also: drinking ~*) abbeveratoio; (*also: feeding ~*) trogolo, mangiatoia; (*channel*) canale *m*

trousers ['trauzəz] *npl* pantaloni *mpl*, calzoni *mpl*; **short ~** calzoncini *mpl*

trousseau ['tru:səu] (*pl ~x or ~s*) *n* corredo da sposa

trousseaux ['tru:səuz] *npl of* **trousseau**

trout [traut] *n inv* trota

trowel ['trauəl] *n* cazzuola

truant ['truənt] (*BRIT*) *n*: **to play ~** marinare la scuola

truce [tru:s] *n* tregua

truck [trʌk] *n* autocarro, camion *m inv*; (*RAIL*) carro merci aperto; (*for luggage*) carrello *m portabagagli inv*; **~ driver** *n* camionista *m/f*; **~ farm** (*US*) *n* orto industriale

true [tru:] *adj* vero(a); (*accurate*) accurato(a), esatto(a); (*genuine*) reale; (*faithful*) fedele; **to come ~** avverarsi

truffle ['trʌfl] *n* tartufo

truly ['tru:lɪ] *adv* veramente; (*truthfully*) sinceramente; (*faithfully*): **yours ~** (*in letter*) distinti saluti

trump [trʌmp] *n* (*also: ~ card*) atout *m inv*

trumpet ['trʌmpɪt] *n* tromba

truncheon ['trʌntʃən] *n* sfollagente *m inv*

trundle ['trʌndl] *vt* far rotolare rumorosamente ♦ *vi*: **to ~ along** rotolare rumorosamente

trunk [trʌŋk] *n* (*of tree, person*) tronco; (*of elephant*) proboscide *f*; (*case*) baule *m*; (*US: AUT*) bagagliaio; **~s** *npl* (*also:*

swimming ~s) calzoncini *mpl* da bagno

truss [trʌs] *n* (*MED*) ♦ **~ (up)** (*CULIN*) legare

trust [trʌst] *n* fiducia; (*LAW*) amministrazione *f* fiduciaria; (*COMM*) trust *m inv* ♦ *vt* (*rely on*) contare su; (*hope*) sperare; (*entrust*): **to ~ sth to sb** affidare qc a qn; **~ed** *adj* fidato(a); **~ee** [trʌs'ti:] *n* (*LAW*) amministratore(trice) fiduciario(a); (*of school etc*) amministratore/trice; **~ful** *adj* fiducioso(a); **~ing** *adj* = **~ful**; **~worthy** *adj* fidato(a), degno(a) di fiducia

truth [tru:θ, *pl* tru:ðz] *n* verità *f inv*; **~ful** *adj* (*person*) sincero(a); (*description*) veritiero(a), esatto(a)

try [traɪ] *n* prova, tentativo; (*RUGBY*) meta *f* ♦ *vt* (*LAW*) giudicare; (*test: also: ~ out*) provare; (*strain*) mettere alla prova ♦ *vi* provare; **to have a ~** fare un tentativo; **to ~ to do** (*seek*) cercare di fare; **~ on** *vt* (*clothes*) provare; **~ing** *adj* (*day, experience*) logorante, pesante; (*child*) difficile, insopportabile

tsar [za:*] *n* zar *m inv*

T-shirt ['ti:-] *n* maglietta

T-square ['ti:-] *n* riga a T

tub [tʌb] *n* tinozza; mastello; (*bath*) bagno

tuba ['tju:bə] *n* tuba

tubby ['tʌbɪ] *adj* grassoccio(a)

tube [tju:b] *n* tubo; (*BRIT: underground*) metropolitana, metrò *m inv*; (*for tyre*) camera d'aria; **~ station** (*BRIT*) *n* stazione *f* della metropolitana

tubular ['tju:bjulə*] *adj* tubolare

TUC (*BRIT*) *n abbr* (= *Trades Union Congress*) confederazione *f* dei sindacati britannici

tuck [tʌk] *vt* (*put*) mettere; **~ away** *vt* riporre; (*building*): **to be ~ed away** essere in un luogo isolato; **~ in** *vt* mettere dentro; (*child*) rimboccare ♦ *vi* (*eat*) mangiare di buon appetito; abbuffarsi; **~ up** *vt* (*child*) rimboccare le coperte a; **~ shop** *n* negozio di pasticceria (*in una scuola*)

Tuesday ['tju:zdɪ] n martedì m inv

tuft [tʌft] n ciuffo

tug [tʌg] n (ship) rimorchiatore m ♦ vt tirare con forza; **~-of-war** n tiro alla fune

tuition [tjuː'ɪʃən] n (BRIT) lezioni fpl; (: private ~) lezioni fpl private; (US: school fees) tasse fpl scolastiche

tulip ['tju:lɪp] n tulipano

tumble ['tʌmbl] n (fall) capitombolo ♦ vi capitombolare, ruzzolare; **to ~ to sth** (inf) realizzare qc; **~down** adj cadente, diroccato(a); **~ dryer** (BRIT) n asciugatrice f

tumbler ['tʌmblə*] n bicchiere m (senza stelo)

tummy ['tʌmɪ] (inf) n pancia; **~ upset** n mal m di pancia

tumour ['tju:mə*] (US tumor) n tumore m

tuna ['tju:nə] n inv (also: ~ fish) tonno

tune [tju:n] n (melody) melodia, aria ♦ vt (MUS) accordare; (RADIO, TV, AUT) regolare, mettere a punto; **to be in/ out of ~** (instrument) essere accordato(a)/scordato(a); (singer) essere intonato(a)/stonato(a); **~ in** vi: **to ~ in (to)** (RADIO, TV) sintonizzarsi (su); **~ up** vi (musician) accordare lo strumento; **~ful** adj melodioso(a); **~r** n: **piano ~r** accordatore m

tunic ['tju:nɪk] n tunica

Tunisia [tju:'nɪzɪə] n Tunisia

tunnel ['tʌnl] n galleria ♦ vi scavare una galleria

turban ['tə:bən] n turbante m

turbulence ['tə:bjuləns] n (AVIAT) turbolenza

tureen [tə'ri:n] n zuppiera

turf [tə:f] n terreno erboso; (clod) zolla ♦ vt coprire di zolle erbose; **~ out** (inf) vt buttar fuori

Turin [tjuə'rɪn] n Torino f

Turk [tə:k] n turco/a

Turkey ['tə:kɪ] n Turchia

turkey ['tə:kɪ] n tacchino

Turkish ['tə:kɪʃ] adj turco(a) ♦ n (LING)

turco

turmoil ['tə:mɔɪl] n confusione f, tumulto

turn [tə:n] n giro; (change) cambiamento, (in road) curva; (tendency: of mind, events) tendenza; (performance) numero; (chance) turno; (MED) crisi f inv, attacco ♦ vt girare, voltare; (change): **to ~ sth into** trasformare qc in ♦ vi girare; (person: look back) girarsi, voltarsi; (reverse direction) girare; (change) cambiare; (milk) andare a male; (become) diventare; **a good ~** un buon servizio; **it gave me quite a ~** mi ha fatto prendere un bello spavento; **"no left ~"** (AUT) "divieto di svolta a sinistra"; **it's your ~** tocca a lei; **in ~** a sua volta; **a turno**; **to take ~s (at sth)** fare (qc) a turno; **~ away** vi girarsi (dall'altra parte) ♦ vt mandare via; **~ back** vi ritornare, tornare indietro ♦ vt far tornare indietro; (clock) spostare indietro; **~ down** vt (refuse) rifiutare; (reduce) abbassare; (fold) ripiegare; **~ in** vi (inf: go to bed) andare a letto ♦ vt (fold) voltare in dentro; **~ off** vi (from road) girare, voltare ♦ vt (light, radio, engine etc) spegnere; **~ on** vt (light, radio, engine etc) accendere; **~ out** vt (light, gas) chiudere; spegnere ♦ vi (voters) presentarsi; **to ~ out to be ...** rivelarsi ..., risultare ...; **~ over** vi (person) girarsi ♦ vt girare; (person) girarsi; **~ round** vi girare; (person) girarsi; **~ up** vi (person) arrivare, presentarsi; (lost object) saltar fuori ♦ vt (collar, sound) alzare; **~ing** n (in road) curva; **~ing point** n (fig) svolta decisiva

turnip ['tə:nɪp] n rapa

turnout ['tə:naut] n presenza, affluenza

turnover ['tə:nəuvə*] n (COMM) turnover m inv; (CULIN): **apple** etc **~** sfogliatella alle mele ecc

turnpike ['tə:npaɪk] (US) n autostrada a pedaggio

turnstile ['tɜːnstaɪl] n tornella

turntable ['tɜːnteɪbl] n (on record player) piatto

turn-up (BRIT) n (on trousers) risvolto

turpentine ['tɜːpəntaɪn] n (also: turps) acqua ragia

turquoise ['tɜːkwɔɪz] n turchese m ♦ adj turchese .

turret ['tʌrɪt] n torretta

turtle ['tɜːtl] n testuggine f; **~neck (sweater)** n maglione m con il collo alto

Tuscany ['tʌskənɪ] n Toscana

tusk [tʌsk] n zanna

tutor ['tjuːtə*] n (in college) docente m/f (responsabile di un gruppo di studenti); (private teacher) precettore m; **~ial** [-'tɔːrɪəl] n (SCOL) lezione f con discussione (a un gruppo limitato)

tuxedo [tʌk'siːdəu] (US) n smoking m inv

TV [tiː'viː] n abbr (= television) tivù f inv

twang [twæŋ] n (of instrument) suono vibrante; (of voice) accento nasale

tweed [twiːd] n tweed m inv

tweezers ['twiːzəz] npl pinzette fpl

twelfth [twelfθ] num dodicesimo/a

twelve [twelv] num dodici; **at ~ (o'clock)** alle dodici, a mezzogiorno; (midnight) a mezzanotte

twentieth ['twentɪθ] num ventesimo/a

twenty ['twentɪ] num venti

twice [twaɪs] adv due volte; **~ as much** due volte tanto; **~ a week** due volte alla settimana

twiddle ['twɪdl] vt, vi: **to ~ (with) sth** giocherellare con qc; **to ~ one's thumbs** (fig) girarsi i pollici

twig [twɪg] n ramoscello ♦ vt, vi (inf) capire

twilight ['twaɪlaɪt] n crepuscolo

twin [twɪn] adj, n gemello/a ♦ vt: **to ~ one town with another** fare il gemellaggio di una città con un'altra; **~-bedded room** n stanza con letti

gemelli; **~ beds** npl letti mpl gemelli

twine [twaɪn] n spago, cordicella ♦ vi attorcigliarsi

twinge [twɪndʒ] n (of pain) fitta; **a ~ of conscience/regret** un rimorso/rimpianto

twinkle ['twɪŋkl] vi scintillare; (eyes) brillare

twirl [twɜːl] vt far roteare ♦ vi roteare

twist [twɪst] n torsione f; (in wire, flex) piega; (in road) curva; (in story) colpo di scena ♦ vt attorcigliare; (ankle) slogare; (weave) intrecciare; (roll around) arrotolare; (fig) distorcere ♦ vi (road) serpeggiare

twit [twɪt] (inf) n cretino(a)

twitch [twɪtʃ] n tiratina; (nervous) tic m inv ♦ vi contrarsi

two [tuː] num due; **to put ~ and ~ together** (fig) fare uno più uno; **~-door** adj (AUT) a due porte; **~-faced** (pej) adj (person) falso(a); **~fold** adv: **to increase ~fold** aumentare del doppio; **~-piece (suit)** n due pezzi m inv; **~-piece (swimsuit)** n (costume m da bagno a) due pezzi m inv; **~some** n (people) coppia; **~-way** adj (traffic) a due sensi

tycoon [taɪ'kuːn] n: **(business) ~** magnate m

type [taɪp] n (category) genere m; (model) modello; (example) tipo; (TYP) tipo, carattere m ♦ vt (letter etc) battere (a macchina), dattilografare; **~-cast** adj (actor) a ruolo fisso; **~face** n carattere m tipografico; **~script** n dattiloscritto; **~writer** n macchina da scrivere; **~written** adj dattiloscritto(a), battuto(a) a macchina

typhoid ['taɪfɔɪd] n tifoidea

typhoon [taɪ'fuːn] n tifone m

typical ['tɪpɪkl] adj tipico(a)

typify ['tɪpɪfaɪ] vt caratterizzare; (person) impersonare

typing ['taɪpɪŋ] n dattilografia

typist ['taɪpɪst] n dattilografo/a

tyrant ['taɪərnt] n tiranno

tyre ['taɪə*] (us **tire**) n pneumatico,
gomma; **~ pressure** n pressione f
(delle gomme)

tzar [zɑ:*] n = **tsar**

U, u

U-bend ['ju:'-] n (in pipe) sifone m

ubiquitous [ju:'bɪkwɪtəs] adj
onnipresente

udder ['ʌdə*] n mammella

UFO ['ju:fəu] n abbr (= unidentified
flying object) UFO m inv

ugh [ə:h] excl puah!

ugly ['ʌglɪ] adj brutto(a)

UHT abbr (= ultra heat treated) UHT
inv, a lunga conservazione

UK n abbr = **United Kingdom**

ulcer ['ʌlsə*] n ulcera; (also: mouth ~)
afta

Ulster ['ʌlstə*] n Ulster m

ulterior [ʌl'tɪərɪə*] adj ulteriore;
~ motive n secondo fine m

ultimate ['ʌltɪmət] adj ultimo(a),
finale; (authority) massimo(a),
supremo(a); **~ly** adv alla fine; in
definitiva, in fin dei conti

ultrasound [ʌltrə'saund] n (MED)
ultrasuono

umbilical cord [ʌmbɪ'laɪkl-] n
cordone m ombelicale

umbrella [ʌm'brelə] n ombrello

umpire ['ʌmpaɪə*] n arbitro

umpteen [ʌmp'ti:n] adj non so
quanti(e); **for the ~th time** per
l'ennesima volta

UN n abbr (= United Nations) ONU f

unable [ʌn'eɪbl] adj: **to be ~ to** non
potere, essere nell'impossibilità di;
essere incapace di

unaccompanied [ʌnə'kʌmpənɪd] adj
(child, lady) non accompagnato(a)

unaccustomed [ʌnə'kʌstəmd] adj: **to
be ~ to sth** non essere abituato a qc

unanimous [ju:'nænɪməs] adj

unanime; **~ly** adv all'unanimità

unarmed [ʌn'ɑ:md] adj (without a
weapon) disarmato(a); (combat)
senz'armi

unattached [ʌnə'tætʃt] adj senza
legami, libero(a)

unattended [ʌnə'tendɪd] adj (car,
child, luggage) incustodito(a)

unattractive [ʌnə'træktɪv] adj poco
attraente

unauthorized [ʌn'ɔ:θəraɪzd] adj non
autorizzato(a)

unavoidable [ʌnə'vɔɪdəbl] adj
inevitabile

unaware [ʌnə'wɛə*] adj: **to be ~ of**
non sapere, ignorare; **~s** adv di
sorpresa, alla sprovvista

unbalanced [ʌn'bælənst] adj
squilibrato(a)

unbearable [ʌn'bɛərəbl] adj
insopportabile

unbeknown(st) [ʌnbɪ'nəun(st)] adv:
~ to all all'insaputa di

unbelievable [ʌnbɪ'li:vəbl] adj
incredibile

unbend [ʌn'bend] (irreg: like bend) vi
distendersi ♦ vt (wire) raddrizzare

unbias(s)ed [ʌn'baɪəst] adj (person,
report) obiettivo(a), imparziale

unborn [ʌn'bɔ:n] adj non ancora
nato(a)

unbreakable [ʌn'breɪkəbl] adj
infrangibile

unbroken [ʌn'brəukən] adj intero(a);
(series) continuo(a); (record)
imbattuto(a)

unbutton [ʌn'bʌtn] vt sbottonare

uncalled-for [ʌn'kɔ:ld-] adj (remark)
fuori luogo inv; (action) ingiustificato(a)

uncanny [ʌn'kænɪ] adj misterioso(a),
strano(a)

unceasing [ʌn'si:sɪŋ] adj incessante

unceremonious [ʌnserɪ'məunɪəs] adj
(abrupt, rude) senza tante cerimonie

uncertain [ʌn'sə:tn] adj incerto(a);
dubbio(a); **~ty** n incertezza

unchanged [ʌn'tʃeɪndʒd] adj

invariato(a)

uncivilized [ʌnˈsɪvɪlaɪzd] adj (gen) selvaggio(a); (fig) incivile, barbaro(a)

uncle [ˈʌŋkl] n zio

uncomfortable [ʌnˈkʌmfətəbl] adj scomodo(a); (uneasy) a disagio, agitato(a); (unpleasant) fastidioso(a)

uncommon [ʌnˈkɔmən] adj raro(a), insolito(a), non comune

uncompromising [ʌnˈkɔmprəmaɪzɪŋ] adj intransigente, inflessibile

unconcerned [ʌnkənˈsəːnd] adj: **to be ~ (about)** non preoccuparsi (di or per)

unconditional [ʌnkənˈdɪʃənl] adj incondizionato(a), senza condizioni

unconscious [ʌnˈkɔnʃəs] adj privo(a) di sensi, svenuto(a); (unaware) inconsapevole, inconscio(a) ♦ n: **the ~** l'inconscio; **~ly** adv inconsciamente

uncontrollable [ʌnkənˈtrəuləbl] adj incontrollabile, indisciplinato(a)

unconventional [ʌnkənˈvɛnʃənl] adj poco convenzionale

uncouth [ʌnˈkuːθ] adj maleducato(a), grossolano(a)

uncover [ʌnˈkʌvə*] vt scoprire

undecided [ʌndɪˈsaɪdɪd] adj indeciso(a)

under [ˈʌndə*] prep sotto; (less than) meno di; (according to) secondo, in conformità a ♦ adv (al) disotto; **~ there** là sotto; **~ repair** in riparazione

under... [ˈʌndə*] prefix sotto..., sub...; **~-age** adj minorenne; **~carriage** (BRIT) n carrello (d'atterraggio); **~charge** vt far pagare di meno a; **~clothes** npl biancheria (intima); **~coat** n (paint) mano f di fondo; **~cover** adj segreto(a), clandestino(a); **~current** n corrente f sottomarina; **~cut** vt irreg vendere a prezzo minore di; **~developed** adj sottosviluppato(a); **~dog** n oppresso/a; **~done** adj (CULIN) al sangue; (pej) poco cotto(a); **~estimate** vt sottovalutare; **~fed** adj

denutrito(a); **~foot** adv sotto i piedi; **~go** vt irreg subire; (treatment) sottoporsi a; **~graduate** n studente(essa) universitario(a); **~ground** n (BRIT: railway) metropolitana f; (POL) movimento clandestino ♦ adj sotterraneo(a); (fig) clandestino ♦ adv sottoterra; **to go ~ground** (fig) darsi alla macchia; **~growth** n sottobosco; **~hand(ed)** adj (fig) furtivo(a), subdolo(a); **~lie** vt irreg essere alla base di; **~line** vt sottolineare; **~mine** vt minare; **~neath** [ʌndəˈniːθ] adv sotto, disotto ♦ prep sotto, al di sotto di; **~paid** adj sottopagato(a); **~pants** npl mutande fpl, slip m inv; **~pass** (BRIT) n sottopassaggio; **~privileged** adj non abbiente; meno favorito(a); **~rate** vt sottovalutare; **~shirt** (us) n maglietta; **~shorts** (us) npl mutande fpl, slip m inv; **~side** n disotto; **~skirt** (BRIT) n sottoveste f

understand [ʌndəˈstænd] vt, vi capire, comprendere; **I ~ that ...** sento che ...; credo di capire che ...; **~able** adj comprensibile; **~ing** adj comprensivo(a) ♦ n comprensione f; (agreement) accordo

understatement [ʌndəˈsteɪtmənt] n: **that's an ~!** a dire poco!

understood [ʌndəˈstud] pt, pp of **understand** ♦ adj inteso(a); (implied) sottinteso(a)

understudy [ˈʌndəstʌdɪ] n sostituto/a, attore/trice supplente

undertake [ʌndəˈteɪk] (irreg: like **take**) vt intraprendere; **to ~ to do sth** impegnarsi a fare qc

undertaker [ˈʌndəteɪkə*] n impresario di pompe funebri

undertaking [ʌndəˈteɪkɪŋ] n impresa; (promise) promessa

undertone [ˈʌndətəun] n: **in an ~** a mezza voce, a voce bassa

underwater [ʌndəˈwɔːtə*] adv sott'acqua ♦ adj subacqueo(a)

underwear [ˈʌndəwɛəˌ] n biancheria (intima)

underworld [ˈʌndəwəːld] n (of crime) malavita

underwriter [ˈʌndəraɪtəˌ] n (INSURANCE) sottoscrittore/trice

undesirable [ʌndɪˈzaɪərəbl] adj sgradevole

undies [ˈʌndɪz] (inf) npl biancheria intima da donna

undo [ʌnˈduː] vt irreg disfare; **~ing** n rovina, perdita

undoubted [ʌnˈdautɪd] adj sicuro(a), certo(a); **~ly** adv senza alcun dubbio

undress [ʌnˈdrɛs] vi spogliarsi

undue [ʌnˈdjuː] adj eccessivo(a)

undulating [ˈʌndjuleɪtɪŋ] adj ondeggiante; ondulato(a)

unduly [ʌnˈdjuːlɪ] adv eccessivamente

unearth [ʌnˈəːθ] vt dissotterrare; (fig) scoprire

unearthly [ʌnˈəːθlɪ] adj (hour) impossibile

uneasy [ʌnˈiːzɪ] adj a disagio; (worried) preoccupato(a); (peace) precario(a)

uneconomic(al) [ˈʌniːkəˈnɒmɪk(l)] adj antieconomico(a)

unemployed [ʌnɪmˈplɔɪd] adj disoccupato(a) ♦ npl: **the ~** i disoccupati

unemployment [ʌnɪmˈplɔɪmənt] n disoccupazione f

unending [ʌnˈɛndɪŋ] adj senza fine

unerring [ʌnˈəːrɪŋ] adj infallibile

uneven [ʌnˈiːvn] adj ineguale; irregolare

unexpected [ʌnɪkˈspɛktɪd] adj inatteso(a), imprevisto(a); **~ly** adv inaspettatamente

unfailing [ʌnˈfeɪlɪŋ] adj (supply, energy) inesauribile; (remedy) infallibile

unfair [ʌnˈfɛəˌ] adj: **~ (to)** ingiusto(a) (nei confronti di)

unfaithful [ʌnˈfeɪθful] adj infedele

unfamiliar [ʌnfəˈmɪlɪəˌ] adj sconosciuto(a), strano(a); **to be ~ with** non avere familiarità con

unfashionable [ʌnˈfæʃnəbl] adj (clothes) fuori moda; (district) non alla moda

unfasten [ʌnˈfɑːsn] vt slacciare; sciogliere

unfavourable [ʌnˈfeɪvərəbl] (US **unfavorable**) adj sfavorevole

unfeeling [ʌnˈfiːlɪŋ] adj insensibile, duro(a)

unfinished [ʌnˈfɪnɪʃt] adj incompleto(a)

unfit [ʌnˈfɪt] adj (ill) malato(a), in cattiva salute; (incompetent): **~ (for)** incompetente (in); (: work, MIL) inabile (a)

unfold [ʌnˈfəuld] vt spiegare ♦ vi (story, plot) svelarsi

unforeseen [ʌnfɔːˈsiːn] adj imprevisto(a)

unforgettable [ʌnfəˈgɛtəbl] adj indimenticabile

unfortunate [ʌnˈfɔːtʃnət] adj sfortunato(a); (event, remark) infelice; **~ly** adv sfortunatamente, purtroppo

unfounded [ʌnˈfaundɪd] adj infondato(a)

unfriendly [ʌnˈfrɛndlɪ] adj poco amichevole, freddo(a)

ungainly [ʌnˈgeɪnlɪ] adj goffo(a), impacciato(a)

ungodly [ʌnˈgɒdlɪ] adj: **at an ~ hour** a un'ora impossibile

ungrateful [ʌnˈgreɪtful] adj ingrato(a)

unhappiness [ʌnˈhæpɪnɪs] n infelicità

unhappy [ʌnˈhæpɪ] adj infelice; **~ about/with** (arrangements etc) insoddisfatto(a) di

unharmed [ʌnˈhɑːmd] adj incolume, sano(a) e salvo(a)

unhealthy [ʌnˈhɛlθɪ] adj (gen) malsano(a); (person) malaticcio(a)

unheard-of [ʌnˈhəːdɒv] adj inaudito(a), senza precedenti

unhurt [ʌnˈhəːt] adj illeso(a)

uniform [ˈjuːnɪfɔːm] n uniforme f, divisa ♦ adj uniforme

uninhabited [ʌnɪnˈhæbɪtɪd] adj

disabitato(a)

unintentional [ʌnɪn'tenʃənəl] *adj* involontario(a)

union ['juːnjən] *n* unione *f*; (*also*: trade ~) sindacato ♦ *cpd* sindacale, dei sindacati; **U~ Jack** *n* bandiera nazionale britannica

unique [juː'niːk] *adj* unico(a)

unit ['juːnɪt] *n* unità *f inv*; (*section*: *of furniture etc*) elemento; (*team*, *squad*) reparto, squadra

unite [juː'naɪt] *vt* unire ♦ *vi* unirsi; **~d** *adj* unito(a); unificato(a); (*efforts*) congiunto(a); **U~d Kingdom** *n* Regno Unito; **U~d Nations (Organization)** *n* (Organizzazione *f* delle) Nazioni Unite; **U~d States (of America)** *n* Stati *mpl* Uniti (d'America)

unit trust (*BRIT*) *n* fondo d'investimento

unity ['juːnɪtɪ] *n* unità

universal [juːnɪ'vɜːsl] *adj* universale

universe ['juːnɪvɜːs] *n* universo

university [juːnɪ'vɜːsɪtɪ] *n* università *f inv*

unjust [ʌn'dʒʌst] *adj* ingiusto(a)

unkempt [ʌn'kempt] *adj* trasandato(a); spettinato(a)

unkind [ʌn'kaɪnd] *adj* scortese; crudele

unknown [ʌn'nəʊn] *adj* sconosciuto(a)

unlawful [ʌn'lɔːful] *adj* illecito(a), illegale

unleaded [ʌn'ledɪd] *adj* (*petrol*, *fuel*) verde, senza piombo

unleash [ʌn'liːʃ] *vt* (*fig*) scatenare

unless [ʌn'les] *conj* a meno che (non) + *sub*

unlike [ʌn'laɪk] *adj* diverso(a) ♦ *prep* a differenza di, contrariamente a

unlikely [ʌn'laɪklɪ] *adj* improbabile

unlisted [ʌn'lɪstɪd] (*us*) *adj* (*TEL*): **to be ~** non essere sull'elenco

unload [ʌn'ləʊd] *vt* scaricare

unlock [ʌn'lɔk] *vt* aprire

unlucky [ʌn'lʌkɪ] *adj* sfortunato(a); (*object*, *number*) che porta sfortuna

unmarried [ʌn'mærɪd] *adj* non sposato(a); (*man only*) scapolo, celibe; (*woman only*) nubile

unmistak(e)able [ʌnmɪs'teɪkəbl] *adj* inconfondibile

unmitigated [ʌn'mɪtɪgeɪtɪd] *adj* non mitigato(a), assoluto(a), vero(a) e proprio(a)

unnatural [ʌn'nætʃrəl] *adj* innaturale; contro natura

unnecessary [ʌn'nesəsərɪ] *adj* inutile, superfluo(a)

unnoticed [ʌn'nəʊtɪst] *adj*: **(to go) ~** (passare) inosservato(a)

UNO ['juːnəʊ] *n abbr* (= *United Nations Organization*) ONU *f*

unobtainable [ʌnəb'teɪnəbl] *adj* (*TEL*) non ottenibile

unobtrusive [ʌnəb'truːsɪv] *adj* discreto(a)

unofficial [ʌnə'fɪʃl] *adj* non ufficiale; (*strike*) non autorizzato(a) dal sindacato

unpack [ʌn'pæk] *vi* disfare la valigia (or le valigie) ♦ *vt* disfare

unpalatable [ʌn'pælətəbl] *adj* sgradevole

unparalleled [ʌn'pærəleld] *adj* incomparabile, impareggiabile

unpleasant [ʌn'pleznt] *adj* spiacevole

unplug [ʌn'plʌg] *vt* staccare

unpopular [ʌn'pɔpjulə*] *adj* impopolare

unprecedented [ʌn'presɪdəntɪd] *adj* senza precedenti

unpredictable [ʌnprɪ'dɪktəbl] *adj* imprevedibile

unprofessional [ʌnprə'feʃənl] *adj* poco professionale

unqualified [ʌn'kwɔlɪfaɪd] *adj* (*teacher*) non abilitato(a); (*success*) assoluto(a), senza riserve

unquestionably [ʌn'kwestʃənəblɪ] *adv* indiscutibilmente

unravel [ʌn'rævl] *vt* dipanare, districare

unreal [ʌn'rɪəl] *adj* irreale

unrealistic [ʌnrɪə'lɪstɪk] *adj* non

realistico(a)

unreasonable [ʌnˈriːznəbl] adj irragionevole

unrelated [ʌnrɪˈleɪtɪd] adj: ~ (to) senza rapporto (con); non imparentato(a) (con)

unreliable [ʌnrɪˈlaɪəbl] adj (person, machine) che non dà affidamento; (news, source of information) inattendibile

unremitting [ʌnrɪˈmɪtɪŋ] adj incessante

unreservedly [ʌnrɪˈzɜːvɪdlɪ] adv senza riserve

unrest [ʌnˈrest] n agitazione f

unroll [ʌnˈrəul] vt srotolare

unruly [ʌnˈruːlɪ] adj indisciplinato(a)

unsafe [ʌnˈseɪf] adj pericoloso(a), rischioso(a)

unsaid [ʌnˈsed] adj: **to leave sth ~** passare qc sotto silenzio

unsatisfactory [ˈʌnsætɪsˈfæktərɪ] adj che lascia a desiderare, insufficiente

unsavoury, (US **unsavory**) [ʌnˈseɪvərɪ] adj (fig: person, place) losco(a)

unscathed [ʌnˈskeɪðd] adj incolume

unscrew [ʌnˈskruː] vt svitare

unscrupulous [ʌnˈskruːpjuləs] adj senza scrupoli

unsettled [ʌnˈsetld] adj (person) turbato(a); indeciso(a); (weather) instabile

unshaven [ʌnˈʃeɪvn] adj non rasato(a)

unsightly [ʌnˈsaɪtlɪ] adj brutto(a), sgradevole a vedersi

unskilled [ʌnˈskɪld] adj non specializzato(a)

unspeakable [ʌnˈspiːkəbl] adj (indescribable) indicibile; (awful) abominevole

unstable [ʌnˈsteɪbl] adj (gen) instabile; (mentally) squilibrato(a)

unsteady [ʌnˈstedɪ] adj instabile, malsicuro(a)

unstuck [ʌnˈstʌk] adj: **to come ~** scollarsi; (fig) fare fiasco

unsuccessful [ʌnsəkˈsesful] adj

(writer, proposal) che non ha successo; (marriage, attempt) mal riuscito(a), fallito(a); **to be ~** (in attempting sth) non avere successo

unsuitable [ʌnˈsuːtəbl] adj inadatto(a); inopportuno(a); sconveniente

unsure [ʌnˈʃuə*] adj incerto(a); **to be ~ of o.s.** essere insicuro(a)

unsuspecting [ʌnsəˈspektɪŋ] adj che non sospetta nulla

unsympathetic [ˈʌnsɪmpəˈθetɪk] adj (person) antipatico(a); (attitude) poco incoraggiante

untapped [ʌnˈtæpt] adj (resources) non sfruttato(a)

unthinkable [ʌnˈθɪŋkəbl] adj impensabile, inconcepibile

untidy [ʌnˈtaɪdɪ] adj (room) in disordine; (appearance) trascurato(a); (person) disordinato(a)

untie [ʌnˈtaɪ] vt (knot, parcel) disfare; (prisoner, dog) slegare

until [ʌnˈtɪl] prep fino a; (after negative) prima di ♦ conj finché, fino a quando; (in past, after negative) prima che + sub, prima di + infinitive; **~ he comes** finché or fino a quando non arriva; **~ now** finora; **~ then** fino ad allora

untimely [ʌnˈtaɪmlɪ] adj intempestivo(a), inopportuno(a); (death) prematuro(a)

untold [ʌnˈtəuld] adj (story) mai rivelato(a); (wealth) incalcolabile; (joy, suffering) indescrivibile

untoward [ʌntəˈwɔːd] adj sfortunato(a), sconveniente

unused [ʌnˈjuːzd] adj nuovo(a)

unusual [ʌnˈjuːʒuəl] adj insolito(a), eccezionale, raro(a)

unveil [ʌnˈveɪl] vt scoprire; svelare

unwanted [ʌnˈwɒntɪd] adj (clothing) smesso(a); (child) non desiderato(a)

unwavering [ʌnˈweɪvərɪŋ] adj fermo(a), incrollabile

unwelcome [ʌnˈwelkəm] adj non

gradito(a)

unwell [ʌn'wɛl] adj indisposto(a); **to feel ~** non sentirsi bene

unwieldy [ʌn'wiːldɪ] adj poco maneggevole

unwilling [ʌn'wɪlɪŋ] adj: **to be ~ to do** non voler fare; **~ly** adv malvolentieri

unwind [ʌn'waɪnd] (irreg: like **wind**[1]) vt svolgere, srotolare ♦ vi (relax) rilassarsi

unwise [ʌn'waɪz] adj poco saggio(a)

unwitting [ʌn'wɪtɪŋ] adj involontario(a)

unworkable [ʌn'wəːkəbl] adj (plan) inattuabile

unworthy [ʌn'wəːðɪ] adj indegno(a)

unwrap [ʌn'ræp] vt disfare; aprire

unwritten [ʌn'rɪtn] adj (agreement) tacito(a); (law) non scritto(a)

KEYWORD

---

up [ʌp] prep: **he went ~ the stairs/ the hill** è salito su per le scale/sulla collina; **the cat was ~ a tree** il gatto era su un albero; **they live further ~ the street** vivono un po' più su nella stessa strada
♦ adv 1 (upwards, higher) su, in alto; **~ in the sky/the mountains** su nel cielo/in montagna; **~ there** lassù; **~ above** su in alto

2: **to be ~** (out of bed) essere alzato(a); (prices, level) essere salito(a)

3: **~ to** (as far as) fino a; **~ to now** finora

4: **to be ~ to** (depending on): **it's ~ to you** sta a lei, dipende da lei; (equal to): **he's not ~ to it** (job, task etc) non ne è all'altezza; (inf: be doing): **what is he ~ to?** cosa sta combinando?
♦ n: **~s and downs** alti e bassi mpl

upbringing ['ʌpbrɪŋɪŋ] n educazione f

update [ʌp'deɪt] vt aggiornare

upgrade [ʌp'greɪd] vt (house, job) migliorare; (employee) avanzare di

grado

upheaval [ʌp'hiːvl] n sconvolgimento; tumulto

uphill [ʌp'hɪl] adj in salita; (fig: task) difficile ♦ adv: **to go ~** andare in salita, salire

uphold [ʌp'həuld] (irreg: like **hold**) vt approvare; sostenere

upholstery [ʌp'həulstərɪ] n tappezzeria

upkeep ['ʌpkiːp] n manutenzione f

upon [ə'pɔn] prep su

upper ['ʌpə*] adj superiore ♦ n (of shoe) tomaia; **~-class** adj dell'alta borghesia; **~ hand** n: **to have the ~ hand** avere il coltello dalla parte del manico; **~most** adj il(la) più alto(a); predominante

upright ['ʌpraɪt] adj diritto(a); verticale; (fig) diritto(a), onesto(a)

uprising ['ʌpraɪzɪŋ] n insurrezione f, rivolta

uproar ['ʌprɔː*] n tumulto, clamore m

uproot [ʌp'ruːt] vt sradicare

upset [n 'ʌpset, vb, adj ʌp'set] (irreg: like **set**) n (to plan etc) contrattempo; (stomach) disturbo ♦ vt (glass etc) rovesciare; (plan, stomach) scombussolare; (person: offend) contrariare; (: grieve) addolorare; sconvolgere ♦ adj contrariato(a); addolorato(a); (stomach) scombussolato(a)

upshot ['ʌpʃɔt] n risultato

upside down ['ʌpsaɪd-] adv sottosopra

upstairs [ʌp'stɛəz] adv, adj di sopra, al piano superiore ♦ n piano di sopra

upstart ['ʌpstɑːt] n parvenu m inv

upstream [ʌp'striːm] adv a monte

uptake ['ʌpteɪk] n: **he is quick/slow on the ~** è pronto/lento di comprendere

uptight [ʌp'taɪt] (inf) adj teso(a)

up-to-date adj moderno(a); aggiornato(a)

upturn ['ʌptəːn] n (in luck) svolta

favorevole; (COMM: in market) rialzo

upward ['ʌpwəd] adj ascendente; verso l'alto; **~(s)** adv in su, verso l'alto

urban ['ə:bən] adj urbano(a);
~ clearway n strada di scorrimento (in cui è vietata la sosta)

urbane [ə:'beɪn] adj civile, urbano(a), educato(a)

urchin ['ə:tʃɪn] n monello

urge [ə:dʒ] n impulso; stimolo; forte desiderio ♦ vt: **to ~ sb to do** esortare qn a fare, spingere qn a fare; raccomandare a qn di fare

urgency ['ə:dʒənsɪ] n urgenza; (of tone) insistenza

urgent ['ə:dʒənt] adj urgente; (voice) insistente

urinate ['juərɪneɪt] vi orinare

urine ['juərɪn] n orina

urn [ə:n] n urna; (also: tea ~) bollitore m per il tè

us [ʌs] pron ci; (stressed, after prep) noi; see also **me**

US(A) n abbr (= United States (of America)) USA mpl

usage ['ju:zɪdʒ] n uso

use [n ju:s, vb ju:z] n uso; impiego, utilizzazione f ♦ vt usare, utilizzare, servirsi di; **in ~** in uso; **out of ~** fuori uso; **to be of ~** essere utile, servire; **it's no ~** non serve, è inutile; **she ~d to do it** lo faceva (una volta), era solita farlo; **to be ~d to** avere l'abitudine di; **~ up** vt consumare, esaurire; **~d** adj (object, car) usato(a); **~ful** adj utile; **~fulness** n utilità; **~less** adj inutile; (person) inetto(a); **~r** n utente m/f; **~r-friendly** adj (computer) di facile uso

usher ['ʌʃə*] n usciere m; **~ette** [-'ret] n (in cinema) maschera

USSR n (HIST): **the ~** l'URSS f

usual ['ju:ʒuəl] adj solito(a); **as ~** come al solito, come d'abitudine; **~ly** adv di solito

utensil [ju:'tensl] n utensile m; **kitchen ~s** utensili da cucina

uterus ['ju:tərəs] n utero

utility [ju:'tɪlɪtɪ] n utilità; (also: public ~) servizio pubblico; **~ room** n locale adibito alla stiratura dei panni etc

utmost ['ʌtməust] adj estremo(a) ♦ n: **to do one's ~** fare il possibile o di tutto

utter ['ʌtə*] adj assoluto(a), totale ♦ vt pronunciare, proferire; emettere; **~ance** n espressione f; parole fpl; **~ly** adv completamente, del tutto

U-turn ['ju:'tə:n] n inversione f a U

V, v

v. abbr = **verse**; **versus**; **volt**; (= vide) vedi, vedere

vacancy ['veɪkənsɪ] n (BRIT: job) posto libero; (room) stanza libera; **"no vacancies"** "completo"

vacant ['veɪkənt] adj (job, seat etc) libero(a); (expression) assente

vacate [və'keɪt] vt lasciare libero(a)

vacation [və'keɪʃən] (esp US) n vacanze fpl

vaccinate ['væksɪneɪt] vt vaccinare

vaccination [væksɪ'neɪʃən] n vaccinazione f

vacuum ['vækjum] n vuoto; **~ cleaner** n aspirapolvere m inv; **~ flask** (BRIT) n thermos ® m inv; **~-packed** adj confezionato(a) sottovuoto

vagina [və'dʒaɪnə] n vagina

vagrant ['veɪgrnt] n vagabondo/a

vague [veɪg] adj vago(a); (blurred: photo, memory) sfocato(a); **~ly** adv vagamente

vain [veɪn] adj (useless) inutile, vano(a); (conceited) vanitoso(a); **in ~** inutilmente, invano

valentine ['væləntaɪn] n (also: ~ card) cartolina or biglietto di San Valentino; (person) innamorato/a

valet ['væleɪ] n cameriere m personale

valiant ['vælɪənt] adj valoroso(a), coraggioso(a)

valid ['vælɪd] *adj* valido(a), valevole; *(excuse)* valido(a)

valley ['vælɪ] *n* valle *f*

valour ['vælə*] (*US* **valor**) *n* valore *m*

valuable ['væljuəbl] *adj* (*jewel*) di (grande) valore; *(time, help)* prezioso(a) ♦ **~s** *npl* oggetti *mpl* di valore

valuation [vælju'eɪʃn] *n* valutazione *f*, stima

value ['væljuː] *n* valore *m* ♦ *vt (fix price)* valutare, dare un prezzo a; *(cherish)* apprezzare, tenere a; **~ added tax** (*BRIT*) *n* imposta sul valore aggiunto; **~d** *adj (appreciated)* stimato(a), apprezzato(a)

valve [vælv] *n* valvola

van [væn] *n* (*AUT*) furgone *m*; (*BRIT: RAIL*) vagone *m*

vandal ['vændl] *n* vandalo/a; **~ism** *n* vandalismo

vanilla [və'nɪlə] *n* vaniglia ♦ *cpd (ice cream)* alla vaniglia

vanish ['vænɪʃ] *vi* svanire, scomparire

vanity ['vænɪtɪ] *n* vanità

vantage ['vɑːntɪdʒ] *n*: **~ point** posizione *f* or punto di osservazione; *(fig)* posizione vantaggiosa

vapour ['veɪpə*] (*US* **vapor**) *n* vapore *m*

variable ['vɛərɪəbl] *adj* variabile; *(mood)* mutevole

variance ['vɛərɪəns] *n*: **to be at ~ (with)** essere in disaccordo (con); *(facts)* essere in contraddizione (con)

varicose ['værɪkəus] *adj*: **~ veins** vene *fpl* varicose

varied ['vɛərɪd] *adj* vario(a), diverso(a)

variety [və'raɪətɪ] *n* varietà *f inv*; *(quantity)* quantità, numero; **~ show** *n* varietà *m inv*

various ['vɛərɪəs] *adj* vario(a), diverso(a); *(several)* parecchi(e), molti(e)

varnish ['vɑːnɪʃ] *n* vernice *f*; *(nail ~)* smalto ♦ *vt* verniciare; mettere lo smalto su

vary ['vɛərɪ] *vt, vi* variare, mutare

vase [vɑːz] *n* vaso

Vaseline ® ['væsɪliːn] *n* vaselina

vast [vɑːst] *adj* vasto(a); *(amount, success)* enorme

VAT [væt] *n abbr* (= *value added tax*) I.V.A. *f*

vat [væt] *n* tino

Vatican ['vætɪkən] *n*: **the ~** il Vaticano

vault [vɔːlt] *n (of roof)* volta; *(tomb)* tomba; *(in bank)* camera blindata ♦ *vt (also: ~ over)* saltare (d'un balzo)

vaunted ['vɔːntɪd] *adj*: **much-~** tanto celebrato(a)

VCR *n abbr* = **video cassette recorder**

VD *n abbr* = **venereal disease**

VDU *n abbr* = **visual display unit**

veal [viːl] *n* vitello

veer [vɪə*] *vi* girare; virare

vegan ['viːɡən] *n* vegetaliano(a)

vegeburger ['vedʒɪbɜːɡ*] *n* hamburger *m inv* vegetariano

vegetable ['vedʒtəbl] *n* verdura, ortaggio ♦ *adj* vegetale

vegetarian [vedʒɪ'tɛərɪən] *adj, n* vegetariano(a)

vehement ['viːɪmənt] *adj* veemente, violento(a)

vehicle ['viːɪkl] *n* veicolo

veil [veɪl] *n* velo; **~ed** *adj (fig: threat)* velato(a)

vein [veɪn] *n* vena; *(on leaf)* nervatura

velvet ['velvɪt] *n* velluto ♦ *adj* di velluto

vending machine ['vendɪŋ-] *n* distributore *m* automatico

vendor ['vendə*] *n* venditore/trice

veneer [və'nɪə*] *n* impiallacciatura; *(fig)* vernice *f*

venereal [vɪ'nɪərɪəl] *adj*: **~ disease** malattia venerea

Venetian [vɪ'niːʃən] *adj* veneziano(a); **~ blind** *n* (tenda alla) veneziana

vengeance ['vendʒəns] *n* vendetta; **with a ~** *(fig)* davvero; furiosamente

Venice ['venɪs] *n* Venezia

venison ['vɛnɪsn] n carne f di cervo

venom ['vɛnəm] n veleno

vent [vɛnt] n foro, apertura; (in dress, jacket) spacco ♦ vt (fig: one's feelings) sfogare, dare sfogo a

ventilate ['vɛntɪleɪt] vt (room) dare aria a, arieggiare; **ventilator** n ventilatore m

ventriloquist [vɛn'trɪləkwɪst] n ventriloquo/a

venture ['vɛntʃə*] n impresa (rischiosa) ♦ vt rischiare, azzardare ♦ vi avventurarsi; **business ~** iniziativa commerciale

venue ['vɛnjuː] n luogo (designato) per l'incontro

verb [vəːb] n verbo; **~al** adj verbale; (translation) orale

verbatim [vəː'beɪtɪm] adj, adv parola per parola

verdict ['vəːdɪkt] n verdetto

verge [vəːdʒ] (BRIT) n bordo, orlo; "**soft ~s**" (BRIT: AUT) banchine fpl cedevoli; **on the ~ of doing** sul punto di fare; **~ on** vt fus rasentare

veritable ['vɛrɪtəbl] adj vero(a)

vermin ['vəːmɪn] npl animali mpl nocivi; (insects) insetti mpl parassiti

vermouth ['vəːməθ] n vermut m inv

versatile ['vəːsətaɪl] adj (person) versatile; (machine, tool etc) (che si presta) a molti usi

verse [vəːs] n versi mpl; (stanza) stanza, strofa; (in bible) versetto

version ['vəːʃən] n versione f

versus ['vəːsəs] prep contro

vertical ['vəːtɪkl] adj verticale ♦ n verticale m; **~ly** adv verticalmente

vertigo ['vəːtɪgəu] n vertigine f

verve [vəːv] n brio; entusiasmo

very ['vɛrɪ] adv molto ♦ adj: the **~ book which** proprio il libro che; **the ~ last** proprio l'ultimo; **at the ~ least** almeno; **~ much** moltissimo

vessel ['vɛsl] n (ANAT) vaso; (NAUT) nave f; (container) recipiente m

vest [vɛst] n (BRIT) maglia; (: sleeveless)

canottiera; (US: waistcoat) gilè m inv

vested interests ['vɛstɪd-] npl (COMM) diritti mpl acquisiti

vet [vɛt] n abbr (BRIT: = veterinary surgeon) veterinario ♦ vt esaminare minuziosamente

veteran ['vɛtərn] n (also: war ~) veterano

veterinary ['vɛtrɪnərɪ] adj veterinario(a); **~ surgeon** (US **veterinarian**) n veterinario/a

veto ['viːtəu] (pl **~es**) n veto ♦ vt opporre il veto a

vex [vɛks] vt irritare, contrariare; **~ed** adj (question) controverso(a), dibattuto(a)

via ['vaɪə] prep (by way of) via; (by means of) tramite

viable ['vaɪəbl] adj attuabile; vitale

viaduct ['vaɪədʌkt] n viadotto

vibrant ['vaɪbrənt] adj (lively, bright) vivace; (voice) vibrante

vibrate [vaɪ'breɪt] vi: **to ~ (with)** vibrare (di); (resound) risonare (di)

vicar ['vɪkə*] n pastore m; **~age** n presbiterio

vicarious [vɪ'kɛərɪəs] adj indiretto(a)

vice [vaɪs] n (evil) vizio; (TECH) morsa

vice- [vaɪs] prefix vice...

vice squad n (squadra del) buon costume f

vice versa ['vaɪsɪ'vəːsə] adv viceversa

vicinity [vɪ'sɪnɪtɪ] n vicinanze fpl

vicious ['vɪʃəs] adj (remark, dog) cattivo(a); (blow) violento(a); **~ circle** n circolo vizioso

victim ['vɪktɪm] n vittima

victor ['vɪktə*] n vincitore m

Victorian [vɪk'tɔːrɪən] adj vittoriano(a)

victory ['vɪktərɪ] n vittoria

video ['vɪdɪəu] cpd video... ♦ n (~ film) video m inv; (also: ~ cassette) videocassetta; (also: ~ cassette recorder) videoregistratore m; **~ tape** n videotape m inv; **~ wall** n schermo m multivideo inv

vie [vaɪ] vi: **to ~ with** competere con,

rivaleggiare con

Vienna [vɪ'enə] n Vienna

Vietnam [vjɛt'næm] n Vietnam m; **~ese** adj, n inv vietnamita m/f

view [vju:] n vista, veduta; (opinion) opinione f ♦ vt (look at: also fig) considerare; (house) visitare; **on ~** (in museum etc) esposto(a); **in full ~ of** sotto gli occhi di; **in my ~** a mio parere; **~er** n spettatore/trice; **~finder** n mirino; **~point** n punto di vista; (place) posizione f

vigil ['vɪdʒɪl] n veglia

vigorous ['vɪɡərəs] adj vigoroso(a)

vile [vaɪl] adj (action) vile; (smell) disgustoso(a), nauseante; (temper) pessimo(a)

villa ['vɪlə] n villa

village ['vɪlɪdʒ] n villaggio; **~r** n abitante m/f di villaggio

villain ['vɪlən] n (scoundrel) canaglia; (BRIT: criminal) criminale m; (in novel etc) cattivo

vindicate ['vɪndɪkeɪt] vt comprovare; giustificare

vindictive [vɪn'dɪktɪv] adj vendicativo(a)

vine [vaɪn] n vite f; (climbing plant) rampicante m

vinegar ['vɪnɪɡə*] n aceto

vineyard ['vɪnjɑːd] n vigna, vigneto

vintage ['vɪntɪdʒ] n (year) annata, produzione f ♦ cpd d'annata; **~ car** n auto f inv d'epoca; **~ wine** n vino d'annata

vinyl ['vaɪnl] n vinile m

violate ['vaɪəleɪt] vt violare

violence ['vaɪələns] n violenza

violent ['vaɪələnt] adj violento(a)

violet ['vaɪələt] adj (colour) viola inv, violetto(a) ♦ n (plant) violetta; (colour) violetto

violin ['vaɪəlɪn] n violino; **~ist** n violinista m/f

VIP n abbr (= very important person)

V.I.P. m/f inv

virgin ['vɜːdʒɪn] n vergine f ♦ adj vergine inv

Virgo ['vɜːɡəʊ] n (sign) Vergine f

virile ['vɪraɪl] adj virile

virtually ['vɜːtjuəlɪ] adv (almost) praticamente

virtual reality ['vɜːtʃuəl -] n (COMPUT) realtà virtuale

virtue ['vɜːtjuː] n virtù f inv; (advantage) pregio, vantaggio; **by ~ of** grazie a

virtuous ['vɜːtjuəs] adj virtuoso(a)

virus ['vaɪərəs] n (also COMPUT) virus m inv

visa ['viːzə] n visto

vis-à-vis [viːzə'viː] prep rispetto a, nei riguardi di

visibility [vɪzɪ'bɪlɪtɪ] n visibilità

visible ['vɪzəbl] adj visibile

vision ['vɪʒən] n (sight) vista; (foresight, in dream) visione f

visit ['vɪzɪt] n visita; (stay) soggiorno ♦ vt (person: use also: ~ with) andare a trovare; (place) visitare; **~ing hours** npl (in hospital etc) orario delle visite; **~or** n visitatore/trice; (guest) ospite m/f; **~or centre** n centro informazioni per visitatori di museo, zoo, parco ecc

visor ['vaɪzə*] n visiera

visual ['vɪzjuəl] adj visivo(a); visuale; ottico(a); **~ aid** n sussidio visivo; **~ display unit** n visualizzatore m

visualize ['vɪzjuəlaɪz] vt immaginare, figurarsi; (foresee) prevedere

visually-impaired ['vɪzjuəlɪ-] adj videoleso(a)

vital ['vaɪtl] adj vitale; **~ly** adv estremamente; **~ statistics** npl (fig) misure fpl

vitamin ['vɪtəmɪn] n vitamina

vivacious [vɪ'veɪʃəs] adj vivace

vivid ['vɪvɪd] adj vivido(a); **~ly** adv (describe) vividamente; (remember) con precisione

V-neck ['viːnɛk] n maglione m con lo scollo a V

vocabulary [vəʊˈkæbjʊlərɪ] n vocabolario

vocal [ˈvəʊkl] adj (MUS) vocale; (communication) verbale; ~ **cords** npl corde fpl vocali

vocation [vəʊˈkeɪʃən] n vocazione f; ~**al** adj professionale

vociferous [vəˈsɪfərəs] adj rumoroso/a

vodka [ˈvɒdkə] n vodka f inv

vogue [vəʊg] n moda; (popularity) popolarità, voga

voice [vɔɪs] n voce f ♦ vt (opinion) esprimere; ~ **mail** n servizio di segreteria telefonica

void [vɔɪd] n vuoto ♦ adj (invalid) nullo(a); (empty): ~ **of** privo(a) di

volatile [ˈvɒlətaɪl] adj volatile; (fig) volubile

volcano [vɒlˈkeɪnəʊ] (pl ~**es**) n vulcano

volition [vəˈlɪʃən] n: **of one's own ~** di sua volontà

volley [ˈvɒlɪ] n (of gunfire) salva; (of stones, questions etc) raffica; (TENNIS etc) volata; ~**ball** n pallavolo f

volt [vəʊlt] n volt m inv; ~**age** n tensione f, voltaggio

voluble [ˈvɒljʊbl] adj loquace

volume [ˈvɒljuːm] n volume m

voluntarily [ˈvɒləntrɪlɪ] adv volontariamente; gratuitamente

voluntary [ˈvɒləntərɪ] adj volontario(a); (unpaid) gratuito(a), non retribuito(a)

volunteer [vɒlənˈtɪə*] n volontario/a ♦ vt offrire volontariamente ♦ vi (MIL) arruolarsi volontario; **to ~ to do** offrire (volontariamente) di fare

voluptuous [vəˈlʌptjʊəs] adj voluttuoso(a)

vomit [ˈvɒmɪt] n vomito ♦ vt, vi vomitare

vote [vəʊt] n voto, suffragio; (cast) voto; (franchise) diritto di voto ♦ vt: **to be ~d chairman** etc venir eletto presidente etc; (propose): **to ~ that** approvare la proposta che ♦ vi votare;

~ **of thanks** discorso di ringraziamento; ~**r** n elettore/trice; **voting** n scrutinio

vouch [vaʊtʃ]: **to ~ for** vt fus farsi garante di

voucher [ˈvaʊtʃə*] n (for meal, petrol etc) buono

vow [vaʊ] n voto, promessa solenne ♦ vt: **to ~ to do/that** giurare di fare/ che

vowel [ˈvaʊəl] n vocale f

voyage [ˈvɔɪdʒ] n viaggio per mare, traversata

V-sign [ˈviː-] n (BRIT) gesto volgare con le dita

vulgar [ˈvʌlgə*] adj volgare

vulnerable [ˈvʌlnərəbl] adj vulnerabile

vulture [ˈvʌltʃə*] n avvoltoio

W, w

wad [wɒd] n (of cotton wool, paper) tampone m; (of banknotes etc) fascio

waddle [ˈwɒdl] vi camminare come una papera

wade [weɪd] vi: **to ~ through** camminare a stento in; (fig: book) leggere con fatica

wafer [ˈweɪfə*] n (CULIN) cialda

waffle [ˈwɒfl] n (CULIN) cialda; (inf) ciance fpl ♦ vi cianciare

waft [wɒft] vt portare ♦ vi diffondersi

wag [wæg] vt agitare, muovere ♦ vi agitarsi

wage [weɪdʒ] n (also: ~s) salario, paga ♦ vt: **to ~ war** fare la guerra; ~ **earner** n salariato/a; ~ **packet** n busta f paga inv

wager [ˈweɪdʒə*] n scommessa

wag(g)on [ˈwægən] n (horse-drawn) carro; (BRIT: RAIL) vagone m (merci)

wail [weɪl] n gemito; (of siren) urlo ♦ vi gemere; urlare

waist [weɪst] n vita, cintola; ~**coat** (BRIT) n panciotto, gilè m inv; ~**line** n (giro di) vita

wait [weɪt] *n* attesa ♦ *vi* aspettare, attendere; **to lie in ~ for** stare in agguato a; **to ~ for** aspettare; **I can't ~ to** (*fig*) non vedo l'ora di; **~ behind** *vi* rimanere (ad aspettare); **~ on** *vt fus* servire; **~er** *n* cameriere *m*; **~ing** *n*: **"no ~ing"** (*BRIT: AUT*) "divieto di sosta"; **~ing list** *n* lista di attesa; **~ing room** *n* sala d'aspetto or d'attesa; **~ress** *n* cameriera

waive [weɪv] *vt* rinunciare a, abbandonare

wake [weɪk] (*pt* **woke**, **~d**, *pp* **woken**, **~d**) *vt* (*also*: **~ up**) svegliare ♦ *vi* (*also*: **~ up**) svegliarsi ♦ *n* (*for dead person*) veglia funebre; (*NAUT*) scia; **waken** *vt*, *vi* = **wake**

Wales [weɪlz] *n* Galles *m*

walk [wɔːk] *n* passeggiata; (*short*) giretto; (*gait*) passo, andatura; (*path*) sentiero; (*in park etc*) sentiero, vialetto ♦ *vi* camminare; (*for pleasure, exercise*) passeggiare ♦ *vt* (*distance*) fare or percorrere a piedi; (*dog*) accompagnare, portare a passeggiare; **10 minutes' ~ from** 10 minuti di cammino or a piedi da; **from all ~s of life** di tutte le condizioni sociali; **~ out** *vi* (*audience*) andarsene; (*workers*) scendere in sciopero; **~ out on** (*inf*) *vt fus* piantare in asso; **~er** *n* (*person*) camminatore/trice; **~ie-talkie** ['wɔːkɪ'tɔːkɪ] *n* walkie-talkie *m inv*; **~ing** *n* camminare *m*; **~ing shoes** *npl* pedule *fpl*; **~ing stick** *n* bastone *m* da passeggio; **W~man** ® ['wɔːkmən] *n* Walkman ® *m inv*; **~out** *n* (*of workers*) sciopero senza preavviso or a sorpresa; **~over** (*inf*) *n* vittoria facile, gioco da ragazzi; **~way** *n* passaggio pedonale

wall [wɔːl] *n* muro; (*internal, of tunnel, cave*) parete *f*; **~ed** *adj* (*city*) fortificato(a); (*garden*) cintato(a)

wallet ['wɔlɪt] *n* portafoglio

wallflower ['wɔːlflauə*] *n* violacciocca; **to be a ~** (*fig*) fare da

tappezzeria

wallow ['wɔləu] *vi* sguazzare

wallpaper ['wɔːlpeɪpə*] *n* carta da parati ♦ *vt* (*room*) mettere la carta da parati in

wally ['wɔlɪ] (*inf*) *n* imbecille *m/f*

walnut ['wɔːlnʌt] *n* noce *f*; (*tree*, *wood*) noce *m*

walrus ['wɔːlrəs] (*pl* ~ *or* ~**es**) *n* tricheco

waltz [wɔːlts] *n* valzer *m inv* ♦ *vi* ballare il valzer

wand [wɔnd] *n* (*also*: **magic** ~) bacchetta (magica)

wander ['wɔndə*] *vi* (*person*) girare senza meta, girovagare; (*thoughts*) vagare ♦ *vt* girovagare per

wane [weɪn] *vi* calare

wangle ['wæŋgl] (*BRIT: inf*) *vt* procurare con l'astuzia

want [wɔnt] *vt* volere; (*need*) aver bisogno di ♦ *n*: **for ~ of** per mancanza di; **~s** *npl* (*needs*) bisogni *mpl*; **to ~ to do** volere fare; **to ~ sb to do** volere che qn faccia; **~ed** *adj* (*criminal*) ricercato(a); **"~ed"** (*in adverts*) "cercasi"; **~ing** *adj*: **to be found ~ing** non risultare all'altezza

war [wɔː*] *n* guerra; **to make ~ (on)** far guerra (a)

ward [wɔːd] *n* (*in hospital: room*) corsia; (*: section*) reparto; (*POL*) circoscrizione *f*; (*LAW: child: also*: **~ of court**) pupillo/a; **~ off** *vt* parare, schivare

warden ['wɔːdn] *n* (*of park, game reserve, youth hostel*) guardiano/a, (*BRIT: of institution*) direttore/trice; (*BRIT: also*: **traffic ~**) addetto/a al controllo del traffico e del parcheggio

warder ['wɔːdə*] (*BRIT*) *n* guardia carceraria

wardrobe ['wɔːdrəub] *n* (*cupboard*) guardaroba *m inv*, armadio; (*clothes*) guardaroba; (*CINEMA, THEATRE*) costumi *mpl*

warehouse ['weəhaus] *n* magazzino

wares [weəz] *npl* merci *fpl*

warfare ['wɔːfɛə*] n guerra

warhead ['wɔːhɛd] n (MIL) testata

warily ['wɛərɪlɪ] adv cautamente, con prudenza

warlike ['wɔːlaɪk] adj bellicoso(a)

warm [wɔːm] adj caldo(a); (thanks, welcome, applause) caloroso(a); (person) cordiale; **it's ~** fa caldo; **I'm ~** ho caldo; **~ up** vi scaldarsi, riscaldarsi ♦ vt scaldare, riscaldare; (engine) far scaldare; **~-hearted** adj affettuoso(a); **~ly** adv (applaud, welcome) calorosamente; (dress) con abiti pesanti; **~th** n calore m

warn [wɔːn] vt: **to ~ sb that/(not) to do/of** avvertire or avvisare qn che/di (non) fare/di; **~ing** n avvertimento; (notice) avviso; (signal) segnalazione f; **~ing light** n spia luminosa; **~ing triangle** n (AUT) triangolo

warp [wɔːp] vi deformarsi ♦ vt (fig) corrompere

warrant ['wɔrnt] n (voucher) buono; (LAW: to arrest) mandato di cattura; (: to search) mandato di perquisizione

warranty ['wɔrntɪ] n garanzia

warren ['wɔrən] n (of rabbits) tana; (fig: of streets etc) dedalo

warrior ['wɔrɪə*] n guerriero/a

Warsaw ['wɔːsɔː] n Varsavia

warship ['wɔːʃɪp] n nave f da guerra

wart [wɔːt] n verruca

wartime ['wɔːtaɪm] n: **in ~** in tempo di guerra

wary ['wɛərɪ] adj prudente

was [wɔz] pt of **be**

wash [wɔʃ] vt lavare ♦ vi lavarsi; (sea): **to ~ over/against sth** infrangersi su/contro qc ♦ n lavaggio; (of ship) scia; **to give sth a ~** lavare qc, dare una lavata a qc; **to have a ~** lavarsi; **~ away** vt (stain) togliere lavando; (subj: river) trascinare via; **~ off** vi andare via con il lavaggio; **~ up** vi (BRIT) lavare i piatti; (US) darsi una lavata; **~able** adj lavabile; **~basin** (US **~bowl**) n lavabo; **~cloth** (US) n

pezzuola (per lavarsi); **~er** n (TECH) rondella; **~ing** n (linen etc) bucato; **~ing machine** n lavatrice f; **~ing powder** (BRIT) n detersivo (in polvere)

Washington ['wɔʃɪŋtən] n Washington f

wash: ~ing up n rigovernatura, lavatura dei piatti; **~ing-up liquid** n detersivo liquido (per stoviglie); **~-out** (inf) n disastro; **~room** n gabinetto

wasn't ['wɔznt] = **was not**

wasp [wɔsp] n vespa

wastage ['weɪstɪdʒ] n spreco; (in manufacturing) scarti mpl; **natural ~** diminuzione f di manodopera (per pensionamento, decesso etc)

waste [weɪst] n spreco; (of time) perdita; (rubbish) rifiuti mpl; (also: household ~) immondizie fpl ♦ adj (material) di scarto; (food) avanzato(a); (land) incolto(a) ♦ vt sprecare; **~s** npl (area of land) distesa desolata; **~ away** vi deperire; **~ disposal unit** (BRIT) n eliminatore m di rifiuti; **~ful** adj sprecone(a); (process) dispendioso(a); **~ ground** (BRIT) n terreno incolto or abbandonato; **~paper basket** n cestino per la carta straccia; **~pipe** n tubo di scarico

watch [wɔtʃ] n (also: wrist ~) orologio (da polso); (act of watching, vigilance) sorveglianza; (guard: MIL, NAUT) guardia; (NAUT: spell of duty) quarto ♦ vt (look at) osservare; (: match, programme) guardare; (spy on, guard) sorvegliare, tenere d'occhio; (be careful of) fare attenzione a ♦ vi osservare, guardare; (keep guard) fare or montare la guardia; **~ out** vi fare attenzione; **~dog** n (also fig) cane m da guardia; **~ful** adj attento(a), vigile; **~maker** n orologiaio/a; **~man** (irreg) n see **night**; **~ strap** n cinturino da orologio

water ['wɔːtə*] n acqua ♦ vt (plant) annaffiare ♦ vi (eyes) lacrimare; (mouth): **to make sb's mouth ~** far venire l'acquolina in bocca a qn; **in**

British ~s nelle acque territoriali
britanniche; ~ **down** vt (milk) diluire;
(fig: story) edulcorare; ~ **cannon** n
idrante m; ~ **closet** n water m
inv; ~**colour** n acquerello; ~**cress** n
crescione m; ~**fall** n cascata; ~ **heater**
n scaldabagno; ~**ing can** n
annaffiatoio; ~ **lily** n ninfea; ~**line** n
(NAUT) linea di galleggiamento;
~**logged** adj saturo(a) d'acqua;
imbevuto(a) d'acqua; (football pitch
etc) allagato(a); ~ **main** n conduttura
dell'acqua; ~**melon** n anguria,
cocomero; ~**proof** adj impermeabile;
~**shed** n (GEO, fig) spartiacque m; ~-
skiing n sci m acquatico; ~**tight** adj
stagno(a); ~**way** n corso d'acqua
navigabile; ~**works** npl impianto
idrico; ~**y** adj (colour) slavato(a);
(coffee) acquoso(a); (eyes) umido(a)

watt [wɔt] n watt m inv

wave [weɪv] n onda; (of hand) gesto,
segno; (in hair) ondulazione f; (fig:
surge) ondata ♦ vi fare un cenno con la
mano; (branches, grass) ondeggiare;
(flag) sventolare ♦ vt (hand) fare un
gesto con; (handkerchief) sventolare;
(stick) brandire; ~**length** n lunghezza
d'onda

waver ['weɪvə*] vi esitare; (voice)
tremolare

wavy ['weɪvɪ] adj ondulato(a);
ondeggiante

wax [wæks] n cera ♦ vt dare la cera a;
(car) lucidare ♦ vi (moon) crescere;
~**works** npl cere fpl ♦ n museo delle
cere

way [weɪ] n via, strada; (path, access)
passaggio; (distance) distanza f;
(direction) parte f, direzione f; (manner)
modo, stile m; (habit) abitudine f;
which ~? – **this** ~ da che parte or in
quale direzione? – da questa parte or
per di qua; **on the** ~ (en route) per
strada; **to be on one's** ~ essere in
cammino or sulla strada; **to be in the**
~ bloccare il passaggio; (fig) essere tra i

piedi or d'impiccio; **to go out of**
one's ~ (**to do**) (fig) mettercela tutta or
fare di tutto per fare; **under** ~ (project)
in corso; **to lose one's** ~ perdere la
strada; **in a** ~ in un certo senso; **in**
some ~s sotto certi aspetti; **no** ~!
(inf) neanche per idea!; **by the** ~ ... a
proposito ...; **"~ in"** (BRIT) "entrata",
"ingresso"; **"~ out"** (BRIT) "uscita";
the ~ back la strada del ritorno;
"give ~" (BRIT: AUT) "dare la
precedenza"

waylay [weɪ'leɪ] (irreg: like **lay**) vt
tendere un agguato a; attendere al
passaggio

wayward ['weɪwəd] adj capriccioso(a);
testardo(a)

W.C. ['dʌblju'si:] (BRIT) n W.C. m inv,
gabinetto

we [wi:] pl pron noi

weak [wi:k] adj debole; (health)
precario(a); (beam etc) fragile; (tea)
leggero(a); ~**en** vi indebolirsi ♦ vt
indebolire; ~**ling** ['wi:klɪŋ] n
smidollato/a; debole m/f; ~**ness** n
debolezza f; (fault) punto debole,
difetto; **to have a ~ness for** avere un
debole per

wealth [welθ] n (money, resources)
ricchezza, ricchezze fpl; (of details)
abbondanza, profusione f; ~**y** adj
ricco(a)

wean [wi:n] vt svezzare

weapon ['wepən] n arma

wear [wɛə*] (pt **wore**, pp **worn**) n
(use) uso; (damage through use)
logorio, usura; (clothing): **sports/baby**
~ abbigliamento sportivo/per neonati
♦ vt (clothes) portare; (put on) mettersi;
(damage: through use) consumare ♦ vi
(last) durare; (rub etc through)
consumarsi; **evening** ~ abiti mpl or
tenuta da sera; ~ **away** vt consumare;
erodere ♦ vi consumarsi; essere
eroso(a); ~ **down** vt consumare;
(strength) esaurire; ~ **off** vi sparire
lentamente; ~ **out** vt consumare;

(person, strength) esaurire; **~ and tear**
n usura, consumo

weary ['wɪərɪ] *adj* stanco(a) ♦ *vi:* **to
~ of** stancarsi di

weasel ['wi:zl] *n* (ZOOL) donnola

weather ['weðə*] *n* tempo ♦ *vt* (*storm,
crisis*) superare; **under the ~** (*fig: ill*)
poco bene; **~-beaten** *adj* (*face, skin*)
segnato(a) dalle intemperie; (*building*)
logorato(a) dalle intemperie; **~cock** *n*
banderuola; **~ forecast** *n* previsioni *fpl*
del tempo, bollettino meteorologico;
~man (*irreg inf*) *n* meteorologo;
~ vane *n* **= ~cock**

weave [wi:v] (*pt* **wove**, *pp* **woven**) *vt*
(*cloth*) tessere; (*basket*) intrecciare; **~r** *n*
tessitore/trice; **weaving** *n* tessitura

web [web] *n* (*of spider*) ragnatela; (*on
foot*) palma; (*fabric, also fig*) tessuto;
the (World Wide) W~ la Rete; **~site**
n (COMPUT) sito (Internet)

wed [wed] (*pt, pp* **wedded**) *vt* sposare
♦ *vi* sposarsi

we'd [wi:d] **= we had; we would**

wedding ['wedɪŋ] *n* matrimonio;
silver/golden ~ (*anniversary*) *n*
nozze *fpl* d'argento/d'oro; **~ day** *n*
giorno delle nozze *or* del matrimonio;
~ dress *n* abito nuziale; **~ ring** *n* fede *f*

wedge [wedʒ] *n* (*of wood etc*) zeppa;
(*of cake*) fetta ♦ *vt* (*fix*) fissare con
zeppe; (*pack tightly*) incastrare

Wednesday ['wednzdɪ] *n* mercoledì *m
inv*

wee [wi:] (SCOTTISH) *adj* piccolo(a)

weed [wi:d] *n* erbaccia ♦ *vt* diserbare;
~killer *n* diserbante *m*; **~y** *adj* (*person*)
allampanato(a)

week [wi:k] *n* settimana; **a ~ today/
on Friday** oggi/venerdì a otto; **~day**
n giorno feriale; (COMM) giornata
lavorativa; **~end** *n* fine settimana *m or
f inv*, weekend *m inv*; **~ly** *adv* ogni
settimana, settimanalmente ♦ *adj*
settimanale ♦ *n* settimanale *m*

weep [wi:p] (*pt, pp* **wept**) *vi* (*person*)
piangere; **~ing willow** *n* salice *m*

piangente

weigh [weɪ] *vt, vi* pesare; **to ~ anchor**
salpare l'ancora; **~ down** *vt* (*branch*)
piegare; (*fig: with worry*) opprimere,
caricare; **~ up** *vt* valutare

weight [weɪt] *n* peso; **to lose/put on
~** dimagrire/ingrassare; **~ing** *n* (*allowance*) indennità; **~ lifter** *n* pesista *m*;
~y *adj* pesante; (*fig*) importante, grave

weir [wɪə*] *n* diga

weird [wɪəd] *adj* strano(a), bizzarro(a);
(*eerie*) soprannaturale

welcome ['welkəm] *adj* benvenuto(a)
♦ *n* accoglienza, benvenuto ♦ *vt* dare il
benvenuto a; (*be glad of*) rallegrarsi di;
thank you – you're ~! grazie –
prego!

weld [weld] *n* saldatura ♦ *vt* saldare

welfare ['welfeə*] *n* benessere *m*;
~ state *n* stato assistenziale

well [wel] *n* pozzo ♦ *adv* bene ♦ *adj*:
to be ~ (*person*) stare bene ♦ *excl*
allora!; **I'm ~** ebbene!; **as ~** anche; **as
~ as** così come; oltre a; **~ done!**
bravo(a)!; **get ~ soon!** guarisci presto!;
to do ~ andare bene; **~ up** *vi*
sgorgare

we'll [wi:l] **= we will; we shall**

well: **~-behaved** *adj* ubbidiente; **~-
being** *n* benessere *m*; **~-built** *adj*
(*person*) ben fatto(a); **~-deserved** *adj*
meritato(a); **~-dressed** *adj* ben
vestito(a), vestito(a) bene; **~-heeled**
(*inf*) *adj* agiato(a), facoltoso(a)

wellingtons ['welɪŋtənz] *npl* (*also:
wellington boots*) stivali *mpl* di gomma

well: **~-known** *adj* noto(a), famoso(a);
~-mannered *adj* ben educato(a); **~-
meaning** *adj* ben intenzionato(a); **~-
off** *adj* benestante, danaroso(a); **~-
read** *adj* colto(a); **~-to-do** *adj*
abbiente, benestante; **~-wisher** *n*
ammiratore/trice

Welsh [welʃ] *adj* gallese ♦ *n* (LING)
gallese *m*; **the ~** *npl* i Gallesi;
~ Assembly *n* Parlamento gallese;
~man/woman (*irreg*) *n* gallese *m/f*;

~ rarebit n crostino al formaggio

went [wɛnt] pt of **go**

wept [wɛpt] pt, pp of **weep**

were [wəː*] pt of **be**

we're [wɪə*] = **we are**

weren't [wəːnt] = **were not**

west [wɛst] n ovest m, occidente m, ponente m ♦ adj (a) ovest inv, occidentale ♦ adv verso ovest; **the W~** l'Occidente m; **the W~ Country** (BRIT) n il sud-ovest dell'Inghilterra; **~erly** adj (wind) occidentale, da ovest; (point) a ovest; (wind) occidentale, da ovest; **~ern** adj occidentale, dell'ovest ♦ n (CINEMA) western m inv; **W~ Germany** n Germania Occidentale; **W~ Indian** adj delle Indie Occidentali ♦ n abitante m/f delle Indie Occidentali; **W~ Indies** npl Indie fpl Occidentali; **~ward(s)** adv verso ovest

wet [wɛt] adj umido(a), bagnato(a); (soaked) fradicio(a); (rainy) piovoso(a) ♦ n (BRIT: POL) politico moderato; **to get ~** bagnarsi; **"~ paint"** "vernice fresca"; **~ suit** n tuta da sub

we've [wiːv] = **we have**

whack [wæk] vt picchiare, battere

whale [weɪl] n (ZOOL) balena

wharf [wɔːf] (pl **wharves**) n banchina

wharves [wɔːvz] npl of **wharf**

KEYWORD

what [wɔt] adj 1 (in direct/indirect questions) quale; quale; **~ size is it?** che taglia è?; **~ colour is it?** di che colore è?; **~ books do you want?** quali or che libri vuole?

2 (in exclamations) che; **~ a mess!** che disordine!

♦ pron 1 (interrogative) che cosa, cosa, che; **~ are you doing?** che or (che) cosa fai?; **~ are you talking about?** di che cosa parli?; **~ is it called?** come si chiama?; **~ about me?** e io?; **~ about doing ...?** e se facessimo ...?

2 (relative) ciò che, quello che; **I saw ~ you did/was on the table** ho visto

quello che hai fatto/quello che era sul tavolo

3 (indirect use) (che) cosa; **he asked me ~ she had said** mi ha chiesto che cosa avesse detto; **tell me ~ you're thinking about** dimmi a cosa stai pensando

♦ excl (disbelieving) cosa!, come!

whatever [wɔt'ɛvə*] adj: **~ book** qualunque or qualsiasi libro + sub ♦ pron: **do ~ is necessary/you want** faccia qualunque or qualsiasi cosa sia necessaria/lei voglia; **~ happens** qualunque cosa accada; **no reason ~** or **whatsoever** nessuna ragione affatto or al mondo; **nothing ~** proprio niente

whatsoever [wɔtsəʊ'ɛvə*] adj = **whatever**

wheat [wiːt] n grano, frumento

wheedle [ˈwiːdl] vt: **to ~ sb into doing sth** convincere qn a fare qc (con lusinghe); **to ~ sth out of sb** ottenere qc da qn (con lusinghe)

wheel [wiːl] n ruota; (AUT: also: steering **~**) volante m; (NAUT) (ruota del) timone m ♦ vt spingere ♦ vi (birds) roteare; (also: ~ round) girare; **~barrow** n carriola; **~chair** n sedia a rotelle; **~ clamp** n (AUT) morsa che blocca la ruota di una vettura in sosta vietata

wheeze [wiːz] vi ansimare

KEYWORD

when [wɛn] adv quando; **~ did it happen?** quando è successo?

♦ conj 1 (at, during, after the time that) quando; **she was reading ~ I came in** quando sono entrato lei leggeva; **that was ~ I needed you** era allora che avevo bisogno di te

2 (on, at which): **on the day ~ I met him** il giorno in cui l'ho incontrato; **one day ~ it was raining** un giorno che pioveva

3 (whereas) quando, mentre; **you said**

I was wrong ~ in fact I was right mi hai detto che avevo torto, quando in realtà avevo ragione

whenever |wen'evə*| adv quando mai ♦ conj quando; (every time that) ogni volta che

where |wɛə*| adv, conj dove; **this is ~** è qui che; **~abouts** adv dove ♦ n: **sb's ~abouts** luogo dove qn si trova; **~as** conj mentre; **~by** pron per cui; **wherever** |-'evə*| conj dovunque + sub; (interrogative) dove mai; **~withal** n mezzi mpl

whet |wet| vt (appetite etc) stimolare

whether |'weðə*| conj se; **I don't know ~ to accept or not** non so se accettare o no; **it's doubtful ~** è poco probabile che; **~ you go or not** che lei vada o no

---
KEYWORD
---

which |wɪtʃ| adj 1 (interrogative: direct, indirect) quale; **~ picture do you want?** quale quadro vuole?; **~ one?** quale?; **~ one of you did it?** chi di voi lo ha fatto?
2: **in ~ case** nel qual caso
♦ pron 1 (interrogative) quale; **~ (of these) are yours?** quali di questi sono suoi?; **~ of you are coming?** chi di voi viene?
2 (relative) che; (: indirect) cui, il (la) quale; **the apple ~ you ate/~ is on the table** la mela che hai mangiato/ che è sul tavolo; **the chair on ~ you are sitting** la sedia sulla quale or su cui sei seduto; **he said he knew, ~ is true** ha detto che lo sapeva, il che è vero; **after ~** dopo di che

whichever |wɪtʃ'evə*| adj: **take ~ book you prefer** prenda qualsiasi libro che preferisce; **~ book you take** qualsiasi libro prenda

whiff |wɪf| n soffio; sbuffo; odore

while |waɪl| n momento ♦ conj mentre;

(as long as) finché; (although) sebbene per quanto + sub; **for a ~** per un po'; **~ away** vt (time) far passare

whim |wɪm| n capriccio

whimper |'wɪmpə*| n piagnucolio ♦ vi piagnucolare

whimsical |'wɪmzɪkl| adj (person) capriccioso(a); (look) strano(a)

whine |waɪn| n gemito ♦ vi gemere; uggiolare; piagnucolare

whip |wɪp| n frusta; (for riding) frustino; (POL: person) capogruppo (che sovrintende alla disciplina dei colleghi di partito) ♦ vt frustare; (cream, eggs) sbattere; **~ped cream** n panna montata; **~-round** (BRIT) n colletta

whirl |wə:l| vt (far) girare rapidamente; (far) turbinare ♦ vi (dancers) volteggiare; (leaves, water) sollevarsi in vortice; **~pool** n mulinello; **~wind** n turbine m

whirr |wə:*| vi ronzare; rombare; frullare

whisk |wɪsk| n (CULIN) frusta; frullino ♦ vt sbattere, frullare; **to ~ sb away** or **off** portar via qn a tutta velocità

whiskers |'wɪskəz| npl (of animal) baffi mpl; (of man) favoriti mpl

whisky |'wɪskɪ| (US, IRELAND **whiskey**) n whisky m inv

whisper |'wɪspə*| n sussurro ♦ vt, vi sussurrare

whist |wɪst| n whist m

whistle |'wɪsl| n (sound) fischio; (object) fischietto ♦ vi fischiare

white |waɪt| adj bianco(a); (with fear) pallido(a) ♦ n bianco; (person) bianco/a; **~ coffee** (BRIT) n caffellatte m inv; **~-collar worker** n impiegato; **~ elephant** n (fig) oggetto (or progetto) costoso ma inutile; **W~ House** n Casa Bianca; **~ lie** n bugia pietosa; **~ness** n bianchezza; **~ paper** n (POL) libro bianco; **~wash** n (paint) bianco di calce ♦ vt imbiancare; (fig) coprire

whiting |'waɪtɪŋ| n inv (fish) merlango

Whitsun ['wɪtsn] n Pentecoste f

whittle ['wɪtl] vt: to ~ away, ~ down ridurre, tagliare

whizz [wɪz] vi: to ~ past or by passare sfrecciando; ~ **kid** (inf) n prodigio

KEYWORD

who [huː] pron 1 (interrogative) chi; ~ **is it?**, ~ **'s there?** chi è?
2 (relative) che; **the man ~ spoke to me** l'uomo che ha parlato con me; **those ~ can swim** quelli che sanno nuotare

whodunit [huːˈdʌnɪt] (inf) n giallo

whoever [huːˈɛvəʳ] pron: ~ **finds it** chiunque lo trovi; **ask ~ you like** lo chieda a chiunque vuole; ~ **she marries** chiunque sposerà, non importa chi sposerà; ~ **told you that?** chi mai gliel'ha detto?

whole [həʊl] adj (complete) tutto(a), completo(a); (not broken) intero(a), intatto(a) ♦ n (all): **the ~ of** tutto il(la); (entire unit) tutto; (not broken) tutto; **the ~ of the town** tutta la città, la città intera; **on the ~, as a ~** nel complesso, nell'insieme; ~ **food(s)** n(pl) cibo integrale; ~**hearted** adj sincero(a); ~**meal** adj (bread, flour) integrale; ~**sale** n commercio e vendita all'ingrosso ♦ adj all'ingrosso; (destruction) totale; ~**saler** n grossista m/f; ~**some** adj sano(a), salutare; ~**wheat** adj = ~**meal**; **wholly** adv completamente, del tutto

KEYWORD

whom [huːm] pron 1 (interrogative) chi; ~ **did you see?** chi hai visto?; **to ~ did you give it?** a chi lo hai dato?
2 (relative) che, prep +il (la) quale (check syntax of Italian verb used): **the man ~ I saw/to ~ I spoke** l'uomo che ho visto/al quale ho parlato

whooping cough ['huːpɪŋ] n

pertosse f

whore [hɔːʳ] (inf: pej) n puttana

KEYWORD

whose [huːz] adj 1 (possessive: interrogative) di chi; ~ **book is this?**, ~ **is this book?** di chi è questo libro?; ~ **daughter are you?** di chi sei figlia?
2 (possessive: relative): **the man ~ son you rescued** l'uomo il cui figlio hai salvato; **the girl ~ sister you were speaking to** la ragazza alla cui sorella stavi parlando
♦ pron di chi; ~ **is this?** di chi è questo?; **I know ~ it is** so di chi è

why [waɪ] adv, conj perché ♦ excl (surprise) ma guarda un po'!; (remonstrating) ma (via)!; (explaining) ebbene!; ~ **not?** perché no?; ~ **not do it now?** perché non farlo adesso?; **that's not ~ I'm here** non è questo il motivo per cui sono qui; **the reason ~** il motivo per cui; ~**ever** adv perché mai

wicked ['wɪkɪd] adj cattivo(a), malvagio(a); maligno(a); perfido(a)

wickerwork ['wɪkəwɜːk] adj di vimini ♦ n articoli mpl di vimini

wicket ['wɪkɪt] n (CRICKET) porta; area tra le due porte

wide [waɪd] adj largo(a); (area, knowledge) vasto(a); (choice) ampio(a) ♦ adv: **to open** ~ spalancare; **to shoot** ~ tirare a vuoto or fuori bersaglio; ~**angle lens** n grandangolare m; ~**awake** adj completamente sveglio(a); ~**ly** adv (differing) molto, completamente; (travelled, spaced) molto; (believed) generalmente; ~**n** vt allargare, ampliare; ~ **open** adj spalancato(a); ~**spread** adj (belief etc) molto or assai diffuso(a)

widow ['wɪdəʊ] n vedova; ~**ed** adj: **to be** ~**ed** restare vedovo(a); ~**er** n vedovo

width [wɪdθ] n larghezza

wield [wi:ld] vt (*sword*) maneggiare; (*power*) esercitare

wife [waɪf] (pl **wives**) n moglie f

wig [wɪg] n parrucca

wiggle ['wɪgl] vt dimenare, agitare

wild [waɪld] adj selvatico(a); selvaggio(a); (*sea, weather*) tempestoso(a); (*idea, life*) folle; stravagante; (*applause*) frenetico(a); ◆ ~**s** npl regione f selvaggia; ~**erness** ['wɪldənɪs] n deserto; ~**life** n natura; ~**ly** adv selvaggiamente; (*applaud*) freneticamente; (*hit, guess*) a casaccio; (*happy*) follemente

wilful ['wɪlful] (US **willful**) adj (*person*) testardo(a), ostinato(a); (*action*) intenzionale; (*crime*) premeditato(a)

KEYWORD

---

will [wɪl] (pt, pp ~**ed**) aux vb **1** (*forming future tense*): **I** ~ **finish it tomorrow** lo finirò domani; **I** ~ **have finished it by tomorrow** lo finirò entro domani; ~ **you do it?** – **yes I ~/no I won't** lo farai? – sì (lo farò)/no (non lo farò)
2 (*in conjectures, predictions*): **he** ~ or **he'll be there by now** dovrebbe essere arrivato ora; **that** ~ **be the postman** sarà il postino
3 (*in commands, requests, offers*): ~ **you be quiet!** vuoi stare zitto?; ~ **you come?** vieni anche tu?; ~ **you help me?** mi aiuti?, mi puoi aiutare?; ~ **you have a cup of tea?** vorrebbe una tazza di tè?; **I won't put up with it!** non lo accetterò!
◆ vt: **to** ~ **sb to do** volere che qn faccia; **he** ~**ed himself to go on** continuò grazie a un grande sforzo di volontà ◆ n volontà; testamento

willful ['wɪlful] (US) adj = **wilful**

willing ['wɪlɪŋ] adj volenteroso(a); ~ **to do** disposto a fare; ~**ly** adv volentieri; ~**ness** n buona volontà

willow ['wɪləu] n salice m

will power n forza di volontà

willy-nilly [wɪlɪ'nɪlɪ] adv volente o nolente

wilt [wɪlt] vi appassire

win [wɪn] (pt, pp **won**) n (*in sports etc*) vittoria ◆ vt (*battle, prize, money*) vincere; (*popularity*) conquistare ◆ vi vincere; ~ **over** vt convincere; ~ **round** (BRIT) vt convincere

wince [wɪns] vi trasalire

winch [wɪntʃ] n verricello, argano

wind¹ [waɪnd] (pt, pp **wound**) vt attorcigliare; (*wrap*) avvolgere; (*clock, toy*) caricare ◆ vi (*road, river*) serpeggiare; ~ **up** vt (*clock*) caricare; (*debate*) concludere

wind² [wɪnd] n vento; (*breath*) respiro, fiato ◆ vt (*take breath away*) far restare senza fiato; ~ **power** energia eolica; ~**fall** n (*money*) guadagno insperato

winding ['waɪndɪŋ] adj (*road*) serpeggiante; (*staircase*) a chiocciola

wind instrument n (MUS) strumento a fiato

windmill ['wɪndmɪl] n mulino a vento

window ['wɪndəu] n finestra; (*in car, train*) finestrino; (*in shop etc*) vetrina; (*also: ~ pane*) vetro; ~ **box** n cassetta da fiori; ~ **cleaner** n (*person*) pulitore m di finestre; ~ **envelope** n busta a finestra; ~ **ledge** n davanzale m; ~ **pane** n vetro; ~**shopping** n: **to go** ~**shopping** andare a vedere le vetrine; ~**sill** n davanzale m

windpipe ['wɪndpaɪp] n trachea

windscreen ['wɪndskri:n] n parabrezza m inv; ~ **washer** n lavacristallo; ~ **wiper** n tergicristallo

windshield ['wɪndʃi:ld] (US) n = **windscreen**

windswept ['wɪndswept] adj spazzato(a) dal vento

windy ['wɪndɪ] adj ventoso(a); **it's** ~ c'è vento

wine [waɪn] n vino; ~ **bar** n enoteca (*per degustazione*); ~ **cellar** n cantina; ~ **glass** n bicchiere m da vino; ~ **list** n

lista dei vini; **~ merchant** n
commerciante m di vini; **~ tasting** n
degustazione f dei vini; **~ waiter** n
sommelier m inv

wing [wɪŋ] n ala; (AUT) fiancata; **~s** npl
(THEATRE) quinte fpl; **~er** n (SPORT) ala

wink [wɪŋk] n ammiccamento ♦ vi
ammiccare, fare l'occhiolino; (light)
baluginare

winner ['wɪnə*] n vincitore/trice

winning ['wɪnɪŋ] adj (team, goal)
vincente; (smile) affascinante; **~s** npl
vincite fpl

winter ['wɪntə*] n inverno; **~ sports**
npl sport mpl invernali

wintry ['wɪntrɪ] adj invernale

wipe [waɪp] n pulita, passata ♦ vt
pulire (strofinando); (erase: tape)
cancellare; **~ off** vt cancellare; (stains)
togliere strofinando; **~ out** vt (debt)
pagare, liquidare; (memory) cancellare;
(destroy) annientare; **~ up** vt asciugare

wire ['waɪə*] n filo; (ELEC) filo elettrico;
(TEL) telegramma m ♦ vt (house) fare
l'impianto elettrico di; (also: **~ up**)
collegare, allacciare; (person)
telegrafare a

wireless ['waɪəlɪs] (BRIT) n (set)
(apparecchio m) radio f inv

wiring ['waɪərɪŋ] n impianto elettrico

wiry ['waɪərɪ] adj magro(a) e
nerboruto(a); (hair) ispido(a)

wisdom ['wɪzdəm] n saggezza; (of
action) prudenza; **~ tooth** n dente m
del giudizio

wise [waɪz] adj saggio(a); prudente;
giudizioso(a)

...wise [waɪz] suffix: **time~** per quanto
riguarda il tempo, in termini di tempo

wish [wɪʃ] n (desire) desiderio; (specific
desire) richiesta ♦ vt desiderare, volere;
best ~es (on birthday etc) i migliori
auguri; **with best ~es** (in letter)
cordiali saluti, con i migliori saluti; **to
~ sb goodbye** dire arrivederci a qn;
he ~ed me well mi augurò di
riuscire; **to ~ to do/sb to do**

desiderare or volere fare/che qn faccia;
to ~ for desiderare; **~ful** adj: **it's ~ful
thinking** è prendere i desideri per
realtà

wishy-washy ['wɪʃɪ'wɔʃɪ] (inf) adj
(colour) slavato(a); (ideas, argument)
insulso(a)

wisp [wɪsp] n ciuffo, ciocca; (of smoke)
filo

wistful ['wɪstful] adj malinconico(a)

wit [wɪt] n (also: **~s**) intelligenza;
presenza di spirito; (wittiness) spirito,
arguzia; (person) bello spirito

witch [wɪtʃ] n strega

KEYWORD
---

with [wɪð, wɪθ] prep **1** (in the company
of) con; **I was ~ him** ero con lui; **we
stayed ~ friends** siamo stati da amici;
I'll be ~ you in a minute vengo
subito

2 (descriptive) con; **a room ~ a view**
una stanza con vista sul mare (or sulle
montagne etc); **the man ~ the grey
hat/blue eyes** l'uomo con il cappello
grigio/gli occhi blu

3 (indicating manner, means, cause):
~ tears in her eyes con le lacrime
agli occhi; **red ~ anger** rosso dalla
rabbia; **to shake ~ fear** tremare di
paura

4: **I'm ~ you** (I understand) la seguo;
to be ~ it (inf: up-to-date) essere alla
moda; (: alert) essere sveglio(a)

withdraw [wɪθ'drɔː] (irreg: like draw)
vt ritirare; (money from bank) ritirare;
prelevare ♦ vi ritirarsi; **~al** n ritiro;
prelievo; (of army) ritirata; **~al
symptoms** (MED) crisi f di astinenza;
~n adj (person) distaccato(a)

wither ['wɪðə*] vi appassire

withhold [wɪθ'həuld] (irreg: like hold)
vt (money) trattenere; (permission): **to
~ (from)** rifiutare (a); (information): **to
~ (from)** nascondere (a)

within [wɪð'ɪn] prep all'interno, (in

time, distances) entro ♦ adv all'interno, dentro; ~ **reach (of)** alla portata (di); ~ **sight (of)** in vista (di); ~ **a mile of** entro un miglio da; ~ **the week** prima della fine della settimana

without [wɪð'aut] prep senza; **to go** ~ **sth** fare a meno di qc

withstand [wɪθ'stænd] (irreg: like **stand**) vt resistere a

witness ['wɪtnɪs] n (person, also LAW) testimone m/f ♦ vt (event) essere testimone di; (document) attestare l'autenticità di; ~ **box** (US ~ **stand**) n banco dei testimoni

witticism ['wɪtɪsɪzm] n spiritosaggine f

witty ['wɪtɪ] adj spiritoso(a)

wives [waɪvz] npl of **wife**

wizard ['wɪzəd] n mago

wk abbr = **week**

wobble ['wɔbl] vi tremare; (chair) traballare

woe [wəu] n dolore m; disgrazia

woke [wəuk] pt of **wake**; **woken** pp of **wake**

wolf [wulf] (pl **wolves**) n lupo

wolves [wulvz] npl of **wolf**

woman ['wumən] (pl **women**) n donna; ~ **doctor** n dottoressa; **women's lib** (inf) n movimento femminista

womb [wu:m] n (ANAT) utero

women ['wɪmɪn] npl of **woman**

won [wʌn] pt, pp of **win**

wonder ['wʌndə*] n meraviglia ♦ vi: **to** ~ **whether/why** domandarsi se/ perché; **to** ~ **at** essere sorpreso(a) di; meravigliarsi di; **to** ~ **about** domandarsi di; pensare a; **it's no** ~ **that** c'è poco or non c'è da meravigliarsi che + sub; ~**ful** adj meraviglioso(a)

won't [wəunt] = **will not**

wood [wud] n legno; (timber) legname m; (forest) bosco; ~ **carving** n scultura in legno, intaglio; ~**ed** adj boschivo(a); boscoso(a); ~**en** adj di legno; (fig) rigido(a); inespressivo(a); ~**pecker** n

picchio; ~**wind** npl (MUS): **the** ~**wind** i legni; ~**work** n (craft, subject) falegnameria; ~**worm** n tarlo del legno

wool [wul] n lana; **to pull the** ~ **over sb's eyes** (fig) imbrogliare qn; ~**len** (US ~**en**) adj di lana; (industry) laniero(a); ~**lens** npl indumenti mpl di lana; ~**ly** (US ~**y**) adj di lana; (fig: ideas) confuso(a)

word [wə:d] n parola; (news) notizie fpl ♦ vt esprimere, formulare; **in other** ~**s** in altre parole; **to break/keep one's** ~ non mantenere/mantenere la propria parola; **to have** ~**s with sb** avere un diverbio con qn; ~**ing** n formulazione f; ~ **processing** n elaborazione f di testi, word processing m; ~ **processor** n word processor m inv

wore [wɔ:*] pt of **wear**

work [wə:k] n lavoro; (ART, LITERATURE) opera ♦ vi lavorare; (mechanism, plan etc) funzionare; (medicine) essere efficace ♦ vt (clay, wood etc) lavorare; (mine etc) sfruttare; (machine) far funzionare; (cause: effect, miracle) fare; **to be out of** ~ essere disoccupato(a); ~**s** n (BRIT: factory) fabbrica ♦ npl (of clock, machine) meccanismo; **to** ~ **loose** allentarsi; ~ **on** vt fus lavorare a; (person) lavorarsi; (principle) basarsi su; ~ **out** vi (plans etc) riuscire, andare bene ♦ vt (problem) risolvere; (plan) elaborare; **it** ~**s out at £100** fa 100 sterline; ~ **up** vt: **to** ~**s out at £100** ~ **ed up** andare su tutte le furie; eccitarsi; ~**able** adj (solution) realizzabile; ~**aholic** n maniaco/a del lavoro; ~**er** n lavoratore/trice, operaio/a; ~**force** n forza lavoro; ~**ing class** n classe f operaia; ~**ing-class** adj operaio(a); ~**ing order** n: **in** ~**ing order** funzionante; ~**man** (irreg) n operaio; ~**manship** n abilità; ~**sheet** n foglio col programma di lavoro; ~**shop** n officina; (practical session) gruppo di lavoro; ~ **station** n stazione f di lavoro; ~-**to-rule** (BRIT) n sciopero bianco

world [wəːld] n mondo ♦ cpd (champion) del mondo; (power, war) mondiale; **to think the ~ of sb** (fig) pensare un gran bene di qn; ~**ly** adj di questo mondo; (knowledgeable) di mondo; ~**wide** adj universale; **W~ Wide Web** n World Wide Web m

worm [wəːm] n (also: earth-) verme m

worn [wɔːn] pp of **wear** ♦ adj usato(a); ~-**out** adj (object) consumato(a), logoro(a); (person) sfinito(a)

worried ['wʌrɪd] adj preoccupato(a)

worry ['wʌrɪ] n preoccupazione f ♦ vt preoccupare ♦ vi preoccuparsi

worse [wəːs] adj peggiore ♦ adv, n peggio; **a change for the ~** un peggioramento; ~**n** vt, vi peggiorare; ~ **off** adj in condizioni (economiche) peggiori

worship ['wəːʃɪp] n culto ♦ vt (God) adorare, venerare; (person) adorare; **Your W~** (BRIT: to mayor) signor sindaco; (: to judge) signor giudice

worst [wəːst] adj il(la) peggiore ♦ adv, n peggio; **at ~** al peggio, per male che vada

worth [wəːθ] n valore m ♦ adj: **to be ~** valere; **it's ~ it** ne vale la pena; **it is ~ one's while (to do)** vale la pena (fare); ~**less** adj di nessun valore; ~**while** adj (activity) utile; (cause) lodevole

worthy ['wəːðɪ] adj (person) degno(a); (motive) lodevole; ~ **of** degno di

KEYWORD

would [wʊd] aux vb 1 (conditional tense): **if you asked him he ~ do it** se glielo chiedessi lo farebbe; **if you had asked him he ~ have done it** se glielo avesse chiesto lo avrebbe fatto
2 (in offers, invitations, requests): ~ **you like a biscuit?** vorrebbe or vuole un biscotto?; ~ **you ask him to come in?** lo faccia entrare, per cortesia;

~ **you open the window please?** apra la finestra, per favore
3 (in indirect speech): **I said I ~ do it** ho detto che l'avrei fatto
4 (emphatic): **it WOULD have to snow today!** doveva proprio nevicare oggi!
5 (insistence): **she ~n't do it** non ha voluto farlo
6 (conjecture): **it ~ have been midnight** sarà stato mezzanotte; **it ~ seem so** sembrerebbe proprio di sì
7 (indicating habit): **he ~ go there on Mondays** andava lì ogni lunedì

would-be (pej) adj sedicente

wouldn't ['wʊdnt] = **would not**

wound[1] [waʊnd] pt, pp of **wind**[1]

wound[2] [wuːnd] n ferita ♦ vt ferire

wove [wəʊv] pt of **weave**; **woven** pp of **weave**

wrangle ['ræŋgl] n litigio

wrap [ræp] vt avvolgere; (pack: also: ~ **up**) incartare; ~**per** n (on chocolate) carta; (BRIT: of book) copertina; ~**ping paper** n carta da pacchi; (for gift) carta da regali

wreak [riːk] vt (havoc) portare, causare; **to ~ vengeance on** vendicarsi su

wreath [riːθ, pl riːðz] n corona

wreck [rek] n (sea disaster) naufragio; (ship) relitto m; (pej: person) rottame m ♦ vt demolire; (ship) far naufragare; (fig) rovinare; ~**age** n rottami mpl; (of building) macerie fpl; (of ship) relitti mpl

wren [ren] n (ZOOL) scricciolo

wrench [rentʃ] n (TECH) chiave f; (tug) torsione f brusca; (fig) strazio ♦ vt strappare; storcere; **to ~ sth from** strappare qc a or da

wrestle ['resl] vi: **to ~ (with sb)** lottare (con qn); ~**r** n lottatore/trice; **wrestling** n lotta

wretched ['retʃɪd] adj disgraziato(a); (inf: weather, holiday) orrendo(a), orribile; (: child, dog) pestifero(a)

wriggle ['rɪɡl] vi (also: ~ **about**)

dimenarsi; (: *snake, worm*) serpeggiare, muoversi serpeggiando

wring [rɪŋ] (*pt, pp* **wrung**) *vt* torcere; (*wet clothes*) strizzare; (*fig*): **to ~ sth out of** strappare qc a

wrinkle ['rɪŋkl] *n* (*on skin*) ruga; (*on paper etc*) grinza ♦ *vt* (*nose*) torcere; (*forehead*) corrugare ♦ *vi* (*skin, paint*) raggrinzirsi

wrist [rɪst] *n* polso; **~watch** *n* orologio da polso

writ [rɪt] *n* ordine *m*; mandato

write [raɪt] (*pt* **wrote**, *pp* **written**) *vt, vi* scrivere; **~ down** *vt* annotare; (*put in writing*) mettere per iscritto; **~ off** *vt* (*debt, plan*) cancellare; **~ out** *vt* mettere per iscritto; (*cheque, receipt*) scrivere; **~ up** *vt* redigere; **~off** *n* perdita completa; **~r** *n* autore/trice, scrittore/trice

writhe [raɪð] *vi* contorcersi

writing ['raɪtɪŋ] *n* scrittura; (*of author*) scritto, opera; **in ~** per iscritto; **~ paper** *n* carta da lettere

written ['rɪtn] *pp of* **write**

wrong [rɒŋ] *adj* sbagliato(a); (*not suitable*) inadatto(a); (*wicked*) cattivo(a); (*unfair*) ingiusto(a) ♦ *adv* in modo sbagliato, erroneamente ♦ *n* (*injustice*) torto ♦ *vt* fare torto a; **you are ~ to do it** ha torto a farlo; **you are ~ about that, you've got it ~** si sbaglia; **to be in the ~** avere torto; **what's ~?** cosa c'è che non va?; **to go ~** (*person*) sbagliarsi; (*plan*) fallire, non riuscire; (*machine*) guastarsi; **~ful** *adj* illegittimo(a); ingiusto(a); **~ly** *adv* (*incorrectly, by mistake*) in modo sbagliato; **~ number** *n* (*TEL*): **you've got the ~ number** ha sbagliato numero

wrote [raʊt] *pt of* **write**

wrought iron [rɔːt-] *n* ferro battuto

wrung [rʌŋ] *pt, pp of* **wring**

WWW *n abbr* (= World Wide Web): **the ~** la Rete

X, x

Xmas ['eksməs] *n abbr* = **Christmas**

X-ray ['eksreɪ] *n* raggio X; (*photograph*) radiografia ♦ *vt* radiografare

xylophone ['zaɪləfəun] *n* xilofono

Y, y

yacht [jɔt] *n* panfilo, yacht *m inv*; **~ing** *n* yachting *m*, sport *m* della vela

Yank [jæŋk] (*pej*) *n* yankee *m/f inv*

Yankee ['jæŋkɪ] (*pej*) *n* = **Yank**

yap [jæp] *vi* (*dog*) guaire

yard [jɑːd] *n* (*of house etc*) cortile *m*; (*measure*) iarda (= 914 mm; 3 feet); **~stick** *n* (*fig*) misura, criterio

yarn [jɑːn] *n* filato; (*tale*) lunga storia

yawn [jɔːn] *n* sbadiglio ♦ *vi* sbadigliare; **~ing** *adj* (*gap*) spalancato(a)

yd. *abbr* = **yard(s)**

yeah [jeə] (*inf*) *adv* sì

year [jɪə] *n* anno; (*referring to harvest, wine etc*) annata; **he is 8 ~s old** ha 8 anni; **an eight-~-old child** un(a) bambino/a di otto anni; **~ly** *adj* annuale ♦ *adv* annualmente

yearn [jɜːn] *vi*: **to ~ for sth/to do** desiderare ardentemente qc/di fare

yeast [jiːst] *n* lievito

yell [jel] *n* urlo ♦ *vi* urlare

yellow ['jeləu] *adj* giallo(a)

yelp [jelp] *vi* guaire, uggiolare

yeoman ['jəumən] *n*: **~ of the guard** guardiano della Torre di Londra

yes [jes] *adv* sì ♦ *n* sì *m inv*; **to say/answer ~** dire/rispondere di sì

yesterday ['jestədɪ] *adv* ieri ♦ *n* ieri *m inv*; **~ morning/evening** ieri mattina/sera; **all day ~** ieri per tutta la giornata

yet [jet] *adv* ancora; già ♦ *conj* ma, tuttavia; **it is not finished** ~ non è ancora finito; **the best ~** finora il migliore; **as ~** finora

yew [juː] n tasso (albero)

yield [jiːld] n produzione f, resa;
reddito m ♦ vt produrre, rendere;
(surrender) cedere ♦ vi cedere; (US: AUT)
dare la precedenza

YMCA n abbr (= Young Men's Christian
Association) Y.M.C.A. m

yoga ['jəʊgə] n yoga m

yog(h)ourt ['jəʊgət] n = **yog(h)urt**

yog(h)urt ['jəʊgət] n iogurt m inv

yoke [jəʊk] n (also fig) giogo

yolk [jəʊk] n tuorlo, rosso d'uovo

KEYWORD

you [juː] pron **1** (subject) tu; (: polite
form) lei; (: pl) voi; (: very formal) loro;
~ Italians enjoy your food a voi
Italiani piace mangiare bene; **~ and I
will go** tu ed io or lei ed io andiamo
2 (object: direct) ti; la; vi; loro (after vb);
(: indirect) ti; le; vi; loro (after vb); **I
know ~** ti or la or vi conosco; **I gave
it to ~** te l'ho dato; gliel'ho dato; ve
l'ho dato; l'ho dato loro
3 (stressed, after prep, in comparisons)
te; lei; voi; loro; **I told you to do it** ho
detto a te (or a lei etc) di farlo; **she's
younger than ~** è più giovane di te
(or lei etc)
4 (impers: one) si; **fresh air does
~ good** l'aria fresca fa bene; **~ never
know** non si sa mai

---

you'd [juːd] = **you had**; **you would**

you'll [juːl] = **you will**; **you shall**

young [jʌŋ] adj giovane ♦ npl (of
animal) piccoli mpl; (people): **the ~** i
giovani, la gioventù; **~er** adj più
giovane; (brother) minore, più giovane;
~ster n giovanotto, ragazzo; (child)
bambino/a

your [jɔː*] adj il(la) tuo(a), pl i(le)
tuoi(tue); il(la) suo(a), pl i(le) suoi(sue);
il(la) vostro(a), pl i(le) vostri(e); il(la)
loro, pl i(le) loro; see also **my**

you're [juə*] = **you are**

yours [jɔːz] pron il(la) tuo(a), pl i(le)
tuoi(tue); (polite form) il(la) suo(a), pl
i(le) suoi(sue); (pl) il(la) vostro(a), pl
i(le) vostri(e); (: very formal) il(la) loro,
pl i(le) loro; see also **mine**; **faithfully**;
sincerely

yourself [jɔː'self] pron (reflexive) ti; si;
(after prep) te; sé; (emphatic) tu
stesso(a); lei stesso(a); **yourselves** pl
pron (reflexive) vi; si; (after prep) voi;
loro; (emphatic) voi stessi(e); loro
stessi(e); see also **oneself**

youth [juːθ, pl juːðz] n gioventù f;
(young man) giovane m, ragazzo;
~ club n centro giovanile; **~ful** adj
giovane; da giovane; giovanile;
~ hostel n ostello della gioventù

you've [juːv] = **you have**

Yugoslav ['juːgəʊ'slɑːv] adj, n
jugoslavo(a)

Yugoslavia ['juːgəʊ'slɑːvɪə] n
Jugoslavia

yuppie ['jʌpɪ] (inf) n, adj yuppie m/f
inv

YWCA n abbr (= Young Women's
Christian Association) Y.W.C.A. m

Z, z

zany ['zeɪnɪ] adj un po' pazzo(a)

zap [zæp] vt (COMPUT) cancellare

zeal [ziːl] n zelo; entusiasmo

zebra ['ziːbrə] n zebra; **~ crossing**
(BRIT) n (passaggio pedonale a) strisce
fpl, zebre fpl

zero ['zɪərəʊ] n zero

zest [zest] n gusto; (CULIN) buccia

zigzag ['zɪgzæg] n zigzag m inv ♦ vi
zigzagare

Zimbabwe [zɪm'bɑːbwɪ] n Zimbabwe
m

zinc [zɪŋk] n zinco

zip [zɪp] n (also: ~ fastener, (US) ~per)
chiusura f or cerniera f lampo inv ♦ vt
(also: ~ up) chiudere con una cerniera
lampo; **~ code** (US) n codice m di

avviamento postale

zodiac ['zəʊdɪæk] *n* zodiaco

zombie ['zɒmbɪ] *n* (*fig*): **like a ~** come un morto che cammina

zone [zəʊn] *n* (*also* MIL) zona

zoo [zu:] *n* zoo *m inv*

zoology [zu:'ɒlədʒɪ] *n* zoologia

zoom [zu:m] *vi*: **to ~ past** sfrecciare; **~ lens** *n* zoom *m inv*, obiettivo a focale variabile

zucchini [zu:'ki:nɪ] (*US*) *npl* (*courgettes*) zucchine *fpl*

ITALIAN VERBS

1 Gerundio 2 Participio passato 3 Presente 4 Imperfetto 5 Passato remoto 6 Futuro 7 Condizionale 8 Congiuntivo presente 9 Congiuntivo passato 10 Imperativo

andare 3 vado, vai, va, andiamo, andate, vanno 6 andrò *etc* 8 vada 10 va'!, vada!, andate!, vadano!

apparire 2 apparso 3 appaio, appari o apparisci, appare o apparisce, appaiono o appariscono 5 apparvi o apparsi, apparisti, apparve o apparì o apparse, apparvero o apparirono o apparsero 8 appaia o apparisca

aprire 2 aperto 3 apro 5 aprii o apersi, apristi 8 apra

AVERE 3 ho, hai, ha, abbiamo, avete, hanno 5 ebbi, avesti, ebbe, avemmo, aveste, ebbero 6 avrò *etc* 8 abbia *etc* 10 abbi!, abbia!, abbiate!, abbiano!

bere 1 bevendo 2 bevuto 3 bevo *etc* 4 bevevo *etc* 8 beva *etc* 9 bevessi *etc*

cadere 5 caddi, cadesti 6 cadrò *etc*

cogliere 2 colto 3 colgo, colgono 5 colsi, cogliesti 8 colga

correre 2 corso 5 corsi, corresti

cuocere 2 cotto 3 cuocio, cociamo, cuociono 5 cossi, cocesti

dare 3 do, dai, dà, diamo, date, danno 5 diedi o detti, desti 6 darò *etc* 8 dia *etc* 9 dessi *etc* 10 da'!, dia!, diano!

dire 1 dicendo 2 detto 3 dico, dici, dice, diciamo, dite, dicono 4 dicevo *etc* 5 dissi, dicesti 6 dirò *etc* 8 diciamo, diciate, dicano 9 dicessi *etc* 10 di'!, dica!, dite!, dicano!

dolere 3 dolgo, duoli, duole, dolgono 5 dolsi, dolesti 6 dorrò *etc* 8 dolga

dovere 3 devo o debbo, devi, deve,

dobbiamo, dovete, devono o debbono 6 dovrò *etc* 8 debba, dobbiamo, dobbiate, devano o debbano

ESSERE 2 stato 3 sono, sei, è, siamo, siete, sono 4 ero, eri, era, eravamo, eravate, erano 5 fui, fosti, fu, fummo, foste, furono 6 sarò *etc* 8 sia *etc* 9 fossi, fossi, fosse, fossimo, foste, fossero 10 sii!, sia!, siate!, siano!

fare 1 facendo 2 fatto 3 faccio, fai, fa, facciamo, fate, fanno 4 facevo *etc* 5 feci, facesti 6 farò *etc* 8 faccia *etc* 9 facessi *etc* 10 fa'!, faccia!, fate!, facciano!

FINIRE 1 finendo 2 finito 3 finisco, finisci, finisce, finiamo, finite, finiscono 4 finivo, finivi, finiva, finivamo, finivate, finivano 5 finii, finisti, finì, finimmo, finiste, finirono 6 finirò, finirai, finirà, finiremo, finirete, finiranno 7 finirei, finiresti, finirebbe, finiremmo, finireste, finirebbero 8 finisca, finisca, finisca, finiamo, finiate, finiscano 9 finissi, finissi, finisse, finis simo, finiste, finissero 10 finisci!, finisca!, finite!, finiscano!

giungere 2 giunto 5 giunsi, giungesti

leggere 2 letto 5 lessi, leggesti

mettere 2 messo 5 misi, mettesti

morire 2 morto 3 muoio, muori, muore, moriamo, morite, muoiono 6 morirò o morrò *etc* 8 muoia

muovere 2 mosso 5 mossi, movesti

nascere 2 nato 5 nacqui, nascesti

nuocere 2 nuociuto 3 nuoccio, nuoci, nuoce, nociamo o nuociamo, nuocete, nuocciono **4** nuocevo *etc* **5** nocqui, nuocesti **6** nuocerò *etc* **7** nuoccia

offrire 2 offerto **3** offro **5** offersi *o* offrii, offristi **8** offra

parere 2 parso **3** paio, paiamo, paiono **5** parvi *o* parsi, paresti **6** parrò *etc* **8** paia, paiamo, paiate, paiano

PARLARE 1 parlando **2** parlato **3** parlo, parli, parla, parliamo, parlate, parlano **4** parlavo, parlavi, parlava, parlavamo, parlavate, parlavano **5** parlai, parlasti, parlò, parlammo, parlaste, parlarono **6** parlerò, parlerai, parlerà, parleremo, parlerete, parleranno **7** parlerei, parleresti, parlerebbe, parleremmo, parlereste, parlerebbero **8** parli, parli, parli, parliamo, parliate, parlino **9** parlassi, parlassi, parlasse, parlassimo, parlaste, parlassero **10** parla!, parli!, parlate!, parlino!

piacere 2 piaciuto **3** piaccio, piacciamo, piacciono **5** piac qui, piacesti **8** piaccia *etc*

porre 1 ponendo **2** posto **3** pongo, poni, pone, poniamo, ponete, pongono **4** ponevo *etc* **5** posi, ponesti **6** porrò *etc* **8** ponga, poniamo, poniate, pongano **9** ponessi *etc*

potere 3 posso, puoi, può, possiamo, potete, possono **6** potrò *etc* **8** possa, possiamo, possiate, possano

prendere 2 preso **5** presi, prendesti

ridurre 1 riducendo **2** ridotto **3** riduco *etc* **4** riducevo *etc* **5** ridussi, riducesti **6** ridurrò *etc* **8** riduca **9** riducessi *etc*

riempire 1 riempiendo **3** riempio, riempi, riempie, riempiono

rimanere 2 rimasto **3** rimango, rimangono **5** rimasi, rimanesti **6** rimarrò *etc* **8** rimanga

rispondere 2 risposto **5** risposi, rispondesti

salire 3 salgo, sali, salgono **8** salga

sapere 3 so, sai, sa, sappiamo, sapete, sanno **5** seppi, sapesti **6** saprò *etc* **8** sappia *etc* **10** sappi!, sappia!, sappiate!, sappiano!

scrivere 2 scritto **5** scrissi, scrivesti

sedere 3 siedo, siedi, siede, siedono **8** sieda

spegnere 2 spento **3** spengo, spengono **5** spensi, spegnesti **8** spenga

stare 2 stato **3** sto, stai, sta, stiamo, state, stanno **5** stetti, stesti **6** starò *etc* **8** stia *etc* **9** stessi *etc* **10** sta'!, stia!, state!, stiano!

tacere 2 taciuto **3** taccio, tacciono **5** tacqui, tacesti **8** taccia

tenere 3 tengo, tieni, tiene, tengono **5** tenni, tenesti **6** terrò *etc* **8** tenga

trarre 1 traendo **2** tratto **3** traggo, trai, trae, traiamo, traete, traggono **4** traevo *etc* **5** trassi, traesti **6** trarrò *etc* **8** tragga **9** traessi *etc*

udire 3 odo, odi, ode, odono **8** oda

uscire 3 esco, esci, esce, escono **8** esca

valere 2 valso **3** valgo, valgono **5** valsi, valesti **6** varrò *etc* **8** valga

vedere 2 visto *o* veduto **5** vidi, vedesti **6** vedrò *etc*

VENDERE 1 vendendo **2** venduto **3** vendo, vendi, vende, vendiamo, vendete, vendono **4** vendevo, vendevi, vendeva, vendevamo, vendevate, vendevano **5** vendei *o* vendetti, vendesti, vendé *o* vendette, vendemmo, vendeste, venderono *o* vendettero **6** venderò, venderai, venderà, venderemo, venderete, venderanno **7** venderei, venderesti, venderebbe, venderemmo, vendereste, venderebbero **8** venda, venda, venda, vendiamo, vendiate, vendano **9** vendessi, vendessi, vendesse, vendessimo, vendeste, vendessero **10** vendi!, venda!, vende-

618

te!, vendano!

venire 2 venuto **3** vengo, vieni, viene, vengono **5** venni, venisti **6** verrò *etc* **8** venga

vivere 2 vissuto **5** vissi, vivesti

volere 3 voglio, vuoi, vuole, vogliamo, volete, vogliono **5** volli, volesti **6** vorrò *etc* **8** voglia *etc* **10** vogli!, voglia!, vogliate!, vogliano!

VERBI INGLESI

present	pt	pp	present	pt	pp
arise	arose	arisen	do (3rd	did	done
awake	awoke	awaked	person;		
be (am,	was,	been	he/		
is, are;	were		she/it/		
being)			does)		
bear	bore	born(e)	draw	drew	drawn
beat	beat	beaten	dream	dreamed,	dreamed,
become	became	become		dreamt	dreamt
begin	began	begun	drink	drank	drunk
behold	beheld	beheld	drive	drove	driven
bend	bent	bent	dwell	dwelt	dwelt
beset	beset	beset	eat	ate	eaten
bet	bet,	bet,	fall	fell	fallen
	betted	betted	feed	fed	fed
bid	bid, bade	bid,	feel	felt	felt
		bidden	fight	fought	fought
bind	bound	bound	find	found	found
bite	bit	bitten	flee	fled	fled
bleed	bled	bled	fling	flung	flung
blow	blew	blown	fly (flies)	flew	flown
break	broke	broken	forbid	forbade	forbidden
breed	bred	bred	forecast	forecast	forecast
bring	brought	brought	forget	forgot	forgotten
build	built	built	forgive	forgave	forgiven
burn	burnt,	burnt,	forsake	forsook	forsaken
	burned	burned	freeze	froze	frozen
burst	burst	burst	get	got	got, (US)
buy	bought	bought			gotten
can	could	(been	give	gave	given
		able)	go	went	gone
			(goes)		
cast	cast	cast	grind	ground	ground
catch	caught	caught	grow	grew	grown
choose	chose	chosen	hang	hung,	hung,
cling	clung	clung		hanged	hanged
come	came	come	have	had	had
cost	cost	cost	(has;		
creep	crept	crept	having)		
cut	cut	cut	hear	heard	heard
deal	dealt	dealt	hide	hid	hidden
dig	dug	dug			

620

present	pt	pp	present	pt	pp
hit	hit	hit	see	saw	seen
hold	held	held	seek	sought	sought
hurt	hurt	hurt	sell	sold	sold
keep	kept	kept	send	sent	sent
kneel	knelt,	knelt,	set	set	set
	kneeled	kneeled	shake	shook	shaken
know	knew	known	shall	should	—
lay	laid	laid	shear	sheared	shorn,
lead	led	led			sheared
lean	leant,	leant,	shed	shed	shed
	leaned	leaned	shine	shone	shone
leap	leapt,	leapt,	shoot	shot	shot
	leaped	leaped	show	showed	shown
learn	learnt,	learnt,	shrink	shrank	shrunk
	learned	learned	shut	shut	shut
leave	left	left	sing	sang	sung
lend	lent	lent	sink	sank	sunk
let	let	let	sit	sat	sat
lie	lay	lain	slay	slew	slain
(lying)			sleep	slept	slept
light	lit,	lit,	slide	slid	slid
	lighted	lighted	sling	slung	slung
lose	lost	lost	slit	slit	slit
make	made	made	smell	smelt,	smelt,
may	might	—		smelled	smelled
mean	meant	meant	sow	sowed	sown,
meet	met	met			sowed
mistake	mistook	mistaken	speak	spoke	spoken
mow	mowed	mown,	speed	sped,	sped,
		mowed		speeded	speeded
must	(had to)	(had to)	spell	spelt,	spelt,
pay	paid	paid		spelled	spelled
put	put	put	spend	spent	spent
quit	quit,	quit,	spill	spilt,	spilt,
	quitted	quitted		spilled	spilled
read	read	read	spin	spun	spun
rid	rid	rid	spit	spat	spat
ride	rode	ridden	split	split	split
ring	rang	rung	spoil	spoiled,	spoiled,
rise	rose	risen		spoilt	spoilt
run	ran	run	spread	spread	spread
saw	sawed	sawn	spring	sprang	sprung
say	said	said	stand	stood	stood

present	pt	pp	present	pt	pp
steal	stole	stolen	**tell**	told	told
stick	stuck	stuck	**think**	thought	thought
sting	stung	stung	**throw**	threw	thrown
stink	stank	stunk	**thrust**	thrust	thrust
stride	strode	stridden	**tread**	trod	trodden
strike	struck	struck, stricken	**wake**	woke, waked	woken, waked
strive	strove	striven	**wear**	wore	worn
swear	swore	sworn	**weave**	wove, weaved	woven, weaved
sweep	swept	swept			
swell	swelled	swollen, swelled	**wed**	wedded, wed	wedded, wed
swim	swam	swum	**weep**	wept	wept
swing	swung	swung	**win**	won	won
take	took	taken	**wind**	wound	wound
teach	taught	taught	**wring**	wrung	wrung
tear	tore	torn	**write**	wrote	written

I NUMERI

NUMBERS

uno(a)	1	one
due	2	two
tre	3	three
quattro	4	four
cinque	5	five
sei	6	six
sette	7	seven
otto	8	eight
nove	9	nine
dieci	10	ten
undici	11	eleven
dodici	12	twelve
tredici	13	thirteen
quattordici	14	fourteen
quindici	15	fifteen
sedici	16	sixteen
diciassette	17	seventeen
diciotto	18	eighteen
diciannove	19	nineteen
venti	20	twenty
ventuno	21	twenty-one
ventidue	22	twenty-two
ventitré	23	twenty-three
ventotto	28	twenty-eight
trenta	30	thirty
quaranta	40	forty
cinquanta	50	fifty
sessanta	60	sixty
settanta	70	seventy
ottanta	80	eighty
novanta	90	ninety
cento	100	a hundred, one hundred
cento uno	101	a hundred and one
duecento	200	two hundred
mille	1 000	a thousand, one thousand
milleduecentodue	1 202	one thousand two hundred and two
cinquemila	5 000	five thousand
un milione	1 000 000	a million, one million
primo(a)		first, 1st
secondo(a)		second, 2nd
terzo(a)		third, 3rd
quarto(a)		fourth, 4th
quinto(a)		fifth, 5th
sesto(a)		sixth, 6th

I NUMERI

settimo(a)
ottavo(a)
nono(a)
decimo(a)
undicesimo(a)
dodicesimo(a)
tredicesimo(a)
quattordicesimo(a)
quindicesimo(a)
sedicesimo(a)
diciassettesimo(a)
diciottesimo(a)
diciannovesimo(a)
ventesimo(a)
ventunesimo(a)
ventiduesimo(a)
ventitreesimo(a)
ventottesimo(a)
trentesimo(a)
centesimo(a)
centunesimo(a)
millesimo(a)
milionesimo(a)

NUMBERS

seventh
eighth
ninth
tenth
eleventh
twelfth
thirteenth
fourteenth
fifteenth
sixteenth
seventeenth
eighteenth
nineteenth
twentieth
twenty-first
twenty-second
twenty-third
twenty-eighth
thirtieth
hundredth
hundred-and-first
thousandth
millionth

Frazioni etc

mezzo
terzo
due terzi
quarto
quinto
zero virgola cinque, 0,5
tre virgola quattro, 3,4
dieci per cento
cento per cento

Fractions etc

half
third
two thirds
quarter
fifth
(nought) point five, 0.5
three point four, 3.4
ten per cent
a hundred per cent

Esempi

abita al numero dieci
si trova nel capitolo sette, a pagina sette
abita al terzo piano
arrivò quarto
scala uno a venticinquemila

Examples

he lives at number 10
it's in chapter 7, on page 7
he lives on the 3rd floor
he came in 4th
scale 1:25,000

L'ORA

THE TIME

che ora è?, che ore sono?

what time is it?

è ..., sono ...	**it is ...**
mezzanotte	midnight, twelve p.m.
l'una (della mattina)	one o'clock (in the morning), one (a.m.)
l'una e cinque	five past one
l'una e dieci	ten past one
l'una e un quarto, l'una e quindici	a quarter past one, one fifteen
l'una e venticinque	twenty-five past one, one twenty-five
l'una e mezzo *or* mezza, l'una e trenta	half-past one, one thirty
le due meno venticinque, l'una e trentacinque	twenty-five to two, one thirty-five
le due meno venti, l'una e quaranta	twenty to two, one forty
le due meno un quarto, l'una e quarantacinque	a quarter to two, one forty-five
le due meno dieci, l'una e cinquanta	ten to two, one fifty
mezzogiorno	twelve o'clock, midday, noon
l'una, le tredici	one o'clock (in the afternoon), one (p.m.)
le sette (di sera), le diciannove	seven o'clock (in the evening), seven (p.m.)

a che ora?

at what time?

a mezzanotte	at midnight
all'una, alle tredici	at one o'clock
fra venti minuti	in twenty minutes
venti minuti fa	twenty minutes ago

LA DATA

DATES

oggi	today
ogni giorno, tutti i giorni	every day
ieri	yesterday
stamattina	this morning
domani notte; domani sera	tomorrow night
l'altro ieri notte; l'altro ieri sera	the night before last
l'altro ieri	the day before yesterday
ieri notte; ieri ser	last night
due giorni/sei anni fa	two days/six years ago
domani pomeriggio	tomorrow afternoon
dopodomani	the day after tomorrow
tutti i giovedì, di *or* il giovedì	every Thursday, on Thursday
ci va di *or* il venerdì	he goes on Fridays
"chiuso il mercoledì"	"closed on Wednesdays"
dal lunedì al venerdì	from Monday to Friday
per giovedì, entro giovedì	by Thursday
un sabato a marzo	one Saturday in March
tra una settimana	in a week's time
martedì a otto	a week next/on Tuesday/Tuesday week
una settimana a domenica scorsa	a week last Sunday
questa/la prossima/la scorsa settimana	this/next/last week
tra due settimane, tra quindici giorni	in two weeks *or* a fortnight
lunedì a quindici	two weeks on Monday
il primo/l'ultimo venerdì del mese	the first/last Friday of the month
il mese prossimo	next month
l'anno scorso	last year
il primo giugno	the 1st of June, June first
il due ottobre	the 2nd of October, October 2nd
sono nato nel 1987	I was born in 1987
il suo compleanno è il 5 giugno	his birthday is on June 5th (*BRIT*) *or* 5th June (*US*)
il 18 agosto	on 18th August (*BRIT*) *or* August 18 (*US*)
nel '96	in '96
nella primavera del '94	in the Spring of '94
dal 19 al 3	from the 19th to the 3rd
quanti ne abbiamo oggi?	what's the date?, what date is it today?
oggi è il 15	today's date is the 15th, today is the 15th

LA DATA

1988 - millenovecentottantotto

10 anni esatti
alla fine del mese
a fine mese
la settimana del 30/7
giornalmente, al giorno/
  settimanalmente, alla settimana/
  mensilmente, al mese
all'anno, annualmente
due volte alla settimana/al mese/
  all'anno
adj bimestrale; *adv* bimestralmente
nel 2006
4 a.C.
79 d.C.
nel tredicesimo secolo
negli anni '80
nel 1990 e rotti

LA DATA NELLE LETTERE

9th October 1995 *or* 9 October
  1995

DATES

1988 - nineteen (hundred) and
  eighty-eight
10 years to the day
at the end of the month
at the month end (*ACCOUNTS*)
week ending 30/7
daily/weekly/monthly

annually
twice a week/month/year

bi-monthly
in the year 2006
4 B.C., B.C. 4
79 A.D., A.D. 79
in the 13th century
in *or* during the 1980s
in 1990 something

HEADINGS OF LETTERS

9 ottobre 1995

PESI E MISURE
CONVERSION CHARTS

In the weight and length charts the middle figure can be either metric
or imperial. Thus 3.3 feet = 1 metre, 1 foot = 0.3 metres, and so on.

feet		metres	inches		cm	lbs		kg
3.3	1	0.3	0.39	1	2.54	2.2	1	0.4
6.6	2	0.61	0.79	2	5.08	4.4	2	0.9
9.9	3	0.91	1.18	3	7.62	6.6	3	1.
13.1	4	1.22	1.57	4	10.6	8.8	4	1.
16.4	5	1.52	1.97	5	12.7	11.0	5	2.
19.7	6	1.83	2.36	6	15.2	13.2	6	2.
23.0	7	2.13	2.76	7	17.8	15.4	7	3.
26.2	8	2.44	3.15	8	20.3	17.6	8	3.
29.5	9	2.74	3.54	9	22.9	19.8	9	4.
32.9	10	3.05	3.9	10	25.4	22.0	10	4.
			4.3	11	27.9			
			4.7	12	30.1			

°C	0	5	10	15	17	20	22	24	26	28	30	35	37		38	40	50	10
°F	32	41	50	59	63	68	72	75	79	82	86	95	98.4		100	104	122	21

Km	10	20	30	40	50	60	70	80	90	100	110	120
Miles	6.2	12.4	18.6	24.9	31.0	37.3	43.5	49.7	56.0	62.0	68.3	74.

Liquids

gallons	1.1	2.2	3.3	4.4	5.5	pints	0.44	0.88	1.7
litres	5	10	15	20	25	litres	0.25	0.5	1